Psychology

The Science of Behavior

SEVENTH EDITION

Psychology
The Science of Behavior

NEIL R. CARLSON
The University of Massachusetts

HAROLD MILLER
Brigham Young University

C. DONALD HETH
The University of Alberta

JOHN W. DONAHOE
The University of Massachusetts

G. NEIL MARTIN
Middlesex University, UK

Allyn & Bacon

Boston   New York   San Francisco
Mexico City   Montreal   Toronto   London   Madrid   Munich   Paris
Hong Kong   Singapore   Tokyo   Cape Town   Sydney

Senior Acquisitions Editor: Stephen Frail
Editorial Assistant: Kerri Hart-Morris
Marketing Manager: Jeanette Koskinas
Production Supervisor: Patty Bergin
Editorial Production Service: Nesbitt Graphics, Inc.
Manufacturing Buyer: JoAnne Sweeney
Electronic Composition: Nesbitt Graphics, Inc.
Interior Design: Cia Boynton
Photo Researcher: Katharine S. Cebik
Cover Designer: Joel Gendron
Illustrator: Jay Alexander

Library of Congress Cataloging-in-Publication Data

Psychology : science of behavior / Neil R. Carlson ... [et al.]. -- 7th ed.
   p. cm.
 Includes bibliographical references and index.
 ISBN-13: 978-0-205-54786-9
 ISBN-10: 0-205-54786-9
 1. Psychology--Textbooks. I. Carlson, Neil R., 1942-

 BF121.C35 2010
 150--dc22

2008047663

10 9 8 7 6 5 4 3 2 1 WEB 12 11 10 09 08

Allyn & Bacon
is an imprint of

www.pearsonhighered.com

ISBN-13: 978-0-205-54786-9
ISBN-10: 0-205-54786-9

Dedications

From Neil R. Carlson

For Alexander, Gilbert, and Cedric.

From Harold Miller

To JeNeal Nicholl Miller and to Harold and Rilla Miller—steady founts of encouragement, affirmation, and love.

From C. Donald Heth

Dedicated to Shannon and to Glenn, for the joy of our travels together.

From John W. Donahoe

Dedicated to my wife, Millie, and to our children, Kirk, Lisa, and Grant.

Neil R. Carlson, *The University of Massachusetts*

Neil Carlson is Professor Emeritus at the University of Massachusetts, Amherst. His research focused on the role of the limbic system in learning and species-typical behavior. He received his undergraduate degree and Ph.D. from the University of Illinois, Urbana. In addition to writing *Psychology: The Science of Behavior*, Dr. Carlson is also the author of two best-selling behavioral neuroscience textbooks—*Physiology of Behavior* (currently in its tenth edition) and *Foundations of Physiological Psychology* (currently in its seventh edition). His books have been translated into eight languages.

Harold Miller, *Brigham Young University*

Hal Miller has been a professor of psychology at BYU since 1985. He served as Dean of General and Honors Education from 1988 to 1993 and is Karl G. Maeser General Education Professor. Dr. Miller's research interests include behavioral economics, evolutionary psychology, and educational reform. He has been associate editor of the *Journal of the Experimental Analysis of Behavior*. Dr. Miller received his Bachelor of Science degree from Arizona State University, where he studied with Peter Killeen, and his Ph.D. from Harvard University, where his dissertation adviser was R. J. Herrnstein.

C. Donald Heth, *The University of Alberta*

Don Heth received his undergraduate degree at New College in Sarasota, Florida and his Ph.D. degree at Yale University. At the University of Alberta, Dr. Heth teaches introductory psychology courses and a fourth-year seminar to students in the honors program. He is an active researcher in the areas of human wayfinding and navigation, comparative spatial cognition, and models of eating disorders. Recently he has been involved with projects to describe lost person behavior and to develop computerized tools to manage this information in operational settings.

John W. Donahoe, *The University of Massachusetts*

John Donahoe is an Emeritus Professor in the Department of Psychology and the Interdisciplinary Program in Behavioral Neuroscience at the University of Massachusetts at Amherst. Dr. Donahoe is an active researcher in the area of learning and cognition and a long-time teacher of the introductory psychology course. He is an author of *Learning and Complex Behavior* (www.lcb-online.org) and *Neural-Network Models of Cognition: Biobehavioral Foundations*. Dr. Donahoe received a Ph.D. in experimental psychology with a subspecialty in neurophysiology from the Thomas Hunt Morgan School of Biological Sciences at the University of Kentucky.

G. Neil Martin, *Middlesex University, UK*

Dr. G. Neil Martin is Reader in Psychology, a Fellow of the Royal Society of Arts, a Chartered Scientist, and Director of the Human Olfaction Laboratory at Middlesex University, London. Dr. Martin is the author of the first general European textbook on *Human Neuropsychology* (Pearson Education, 2008), now in its second edition. He also writes the best-selling European adaptation of *Psychology* with Neil Carlson, now about to go into its fourth edition. His research interests include the human senses of smell and taste, the psychology of humor, perceptions and misunderstanding of psychology, and the interactions between personality and learning style.

Brief Contents

Contents

7 PERCEPTION 187

8 MEMORY 214

11 INTELLIGENCE AND THINKING 303

12 LIFE-SPAN DEVELOPMENT 336

17 THE TREATMENT OF PSYCHOLOGICAL DISORDERS 523

Preface

In this seventh edition of *Psychology: The Science of Behavior,* we have combined our talents, experience, and psychological perspectives to provide a more global perspective on the field of psychology than most introductory textbooks. We believe that this unique view offers students a more contemporary, balanced, and exciting overview of psychology than ever before.

As authors we all share a basic philosophy about the goals of psychology as an experimental and natural science, and we have challenged one another to sharpen and refine our thinking as well as our writing. In this text we have attempted to convey our own fascination with the pursuit of knowledge. We have tried to explain how psychologists go about discovering the causes of behavior and to point out the connections between behavior and its biological underpinnings. We have provided integrated findings across different subdisciplines to show students that all of what we do as psychologists is related, even though different psychologists concern themselves with different phenomena or with different levels of analysis of these phenomena. We have continued to explore how behavior can best be understood in the context of its adaptive significance, leading students through the discovery process and enabling them to think critically about contemporary issues and their own experiences. The seventh edition again combines a scholarly survey of research with real-world applications of research results to problems that confront us today. Using the discovery method to take students inside the research process, we foster a critical understanding of the logic and significance of empirical findings.

Originally published over two decades ago, *Psychology: The Science of Behavior* has continued to evolve and improve. The foundations of the text's strength and the reasons for the text's longevity, we believe, are the clarity of writing; the quality of coverage; and the distinctive behavioral, biological, and evolutionary approaches we take in introducing and explaining topics to the student.

A Word from Author Neil Carlson

"I have long believed that one of the most important approaches to the study of behavior is biological psychology. After all, the brain is the organ responsible for all the phenomena that psychologists study—for example, perception, learning and memory, thinking and cognition, language, and emotion. And mental disorders are more than ever being understood as malfunctions of systems in the brain, caused by interactions between hereditary and environmental factors. Our knowledge of human brain functions has been expanding enormously as a result of studies using functional imaging, which permit us to see moment-to-moment activation of brain structures as volunteers perform various tasks. Advances in molecular genetics make it possible to investigate the role that genes play in the normal and abnormal development of the brain.

My coauthors and I made it our goal to show psychology as a lively and developing science. Basing the text on biology and behavior, we sought not only to describe the basic principles, but also to depict the process of research discovery in a way that is both scholarly and personally engaging.

Brain imaging, large-scale computer modeling, artificial resequencing of genetic material, and the other tools developed since the early 1980s have all extended the frontiers of psychology. But these developments only serve to remind us that we must understand the deeper implications of our discipline's discoveries. What does it mean to decode the brain's signals underlying intention and movement? Will genetic sequencing provide a catalog of psychological traits with the same detail it is providing for physical characteristics? Questions like these face us with much more immediacy than they did when this text first appeared. We hope we have provided a foundation for students to tackle these and other issues that they will face in their lives and in their study of psychology."

Pedagogical Aids

After seven editions, we believe that we have evolved a practical and efficient set of pedagogical features for an introductory text. In this edition we have revised the pedagogy to better meet the needs of a diverse group of students, with increased attention to critical thinking and learning pedagogy and a more streamlined narrative. Each chapter begins with a **chapter outline** that gives students a survey of what the chapter discusses. The chapter outline is followed by a **Prologue,** a lively narrative that illustrates phenomena covered in the chapter. **Questions to consider,** designed so students can apply what they have learned to everyday issues, follow each major section in the chapter. **Key terms** and their definitions are listed in the margins on the pages where they are introduced for ease of studying. New **case studies** provide ample opportunity for students to read about the applicable examples of psychological concepts. A new **Epilogue,** found at the close of each chapter, sheds light on the opening Prologue and brings the content of the chapter full-circle. Study aids at the end of each chapter include a **chapter summary,** divided by major chapter sections, for students to review what they have just read; **Suggestions for Further Reading,** which highlight the newest research and most interesting concepts in the chapter; and a list of applicable video, activities, and features for students to explore on **MyPsychLab.**

In addition, each chapter contains a special issues feature box called **Focus On,** which highlights a controversial issue, important cross-cultural research, or an unanswered question in the field of psychology. Encouraging students to hone their critical thinking skills, this feature includes engaging and relevant topics such as the cultural differences in the definition of intelligence, how the brain is like a computer, cultural contexts for remembering, cognitive development and television viewing, the evolution of love, and assessing therapeutic efficacy. In addition, where applicable, each chapter places emphasis on **international perspectives,** offering students a unique global view of the field of psychological research. International research is emphasized on topics such as crashing memories, response bias, social attachment, eye movement, and behavior therapy, among others.

The **visual program** continues to highlight our biological and anatomical emphasis. We have again tapped the talents of Jay Alexander, the medical illustrator responsible for the successful art program in Carlson's **Physiology of Behavior** textbook. Jay has reviewed and updated the art program throughout this edition, creating a more vibrant, diverse, and contemporary presentation.

We hope readers will find these study and review aids as well as the special features helpful as they study psychology.

New Coverage in the Seventh Edition

Psychology remains a rapidly evolving field, and the seventh edition reflects these many exciting changes. In addition to consolidation efforts, key section reorganization, and reference updates, the following is a list of some of the major revisions to this edition, organized by chapter.

CHAPTER 1

- New Prologue on developing a conception of human psychology
- New section on the scientific character of psychology relative to other disciplines
- Additional information on the influences of education and therapy on the development of psychology
- New case study on the role of education and therapy as seen in the "Wild Boy of Aveyron"
- New "Focus On" box develops a contrast between themes of Western psychology with Eastern approaches to behavior
- New Epilogue invites readers to explore the student solution developed at the beginning of the chapter

CHAPTER 2

- Additional examples for research methodology
- Additional information on cross-cultural psychology

- New case study on ethical decision making in research designs
- Additional information on qualitative research
- Additional information on single-subject research designs
- New Epilogue

CHAPTER 3

- Updated information on the relation between evolution and genetics
- Updated information on the relation between natural selection and behavior
- Updated information on selection processes as explanations of complex phenomena
- New section on the role of culture in the acceptance of evolution through natural selection
- New case study on HIV
- Updated information on the evolution of humans, especially genetic regulatory processes
- New "Focus On" section on the origins of life
- Updated and simplified presentation of genetics
- New information on the relation of genetics and language
- Updated discussion of sociology, especially altruism
- New Prologue and Epilogue on both the power and the limitations of natural selection

CHAPTER 4

- Updated information on the actions of drugs
- New case study: Poisoning with botulinum toxin
- New section on experience, learning, and neural plasticity
- New section on neurogenesis
- New case study: Effects of damage to the cerebellum
- New Epilogue on the neural basis of unilateral neglect and perception of body ownership

CHAPTER 5

- New Prologue and Epilogue showing that evolution alone cannot account for altruistic behavior in humans
- Additional information stressing the critical differences as well as the similarities between classical (Pavlovian) and operant conditioning
- New examples relating schedules of reinforcement to everyday instances of human behavior
- New case study on the tendency to give motivational interpretations to behavior that is actually due to the schedule of reinforcement
- Additional information on the contribution of both learning and genetics to drug addiction
- New "Focus On" section discussing self-control and conditioned reinforcement

- Additional information on the role of automatic reinforcement in language acquisition
- Additional information on equivalence classes and human learning
- New section on choice behavior
- New section on perceptual learning
- Additional information on learning and its neural mechanisms, including long-term potentiation

CHAPTER 6

- New Prologue on analgesia caused by a placebo
- Additional information on cochlear implants and their implication for auditory perception
- Additional information on functional imaging of responses to environmental sounds
- Additional information on neural mechanisms of amusia: loss of musical perception
- Additional information on human odor tracking
- Updated information on odor receptors
- New section on sensory-specific satiety
- Additional information on the discovery of a sensory system that responds to caresses to the skin
- Updated information on the three types of pain receptors
- New Epilogue on natural analgesia, functional imaging studies of the placebo effect, hypnotic analgesia, and shared emotional components of pain

CHAPTER 7

- Extensively updated and revised material on the visual association cortex, with emphasis on the ventral and dorsal streams in visual perception, including new case studies and new organization on:
  - Ventral Stream: Perception of Form
  - Ventral Stream: Perception of Color
  - Dorsal Stream: Perception of Spatial Location
  - Dorsal Stream: Perception of Movement
- Updated information on disorders of visual perception associated with damage to specific brain areas—fusiform face area, extrastriate body area, and parahippocampal place area
- Updated information on the perception of form from motion, including a new case study
- New Epilogue on the fundamental conundrum of perceiving what is "out there"

CHAPTER 8

- New Prologue on the Salem Witchcraft Trials and the reconstructive character of memory
- Expanded discussion of consolidation hypothesis
- New material on hippocampal place cells
- New discussion of source monitoring framework

- New material on the brain regions involved in declarative and nondeclarative memory
- Rewritten case studies of anterograde amnesia
- Additional information on Schacter's "Seven Sins" of memory
- New Epilogue

CHAPTER 9

- New Prologue on the persistent loss of consciousness, including the cases of Terry Schiavo and Jan Grzebski
- New case study on how consciousness is not a general property of all parts of the brain
- Additional information on consciousness as a language-dependent phenomenon
- New material on the conscious control of behavior
- New material on inattention blindness and brain mechanisms of attention
- New "Focus On" section devoted to recent experimental demonstrations of the out-of-body experience
- New section on sleep and learning
- New section on sleep disorders, including a new case study
- New case study on REM sleep behavior disorder
- Updated section on the neural control of sleep
- Epilogue on the use of deep brain stimulation with coma patients and the implications for theories of the origins of human consciousness

CHAPTER 10

- New case study of Sir John Hale's recovery from cerebral stroke
- Updated section on dyslexia and related brain research
- Updated section on the language acquisition device (LAD), including cross-cultural research findings and the concept of the Language Acquisition Support System (LASS)
- New section on alternative theories of language acquisition
- Updated section on the acquisition of adult rules of grammar
- Updated "Focus On" section on communication with other species, including Alex the Parrot
- Epilogue on new findings with bonobos and the implications of this research

CHAPTER 11

- Extended critique of the theory of multiple intelligences
- New case study on the loss of practical intelligence
- Updated "Focus On" section on cultural definitions of intelligence
- New section on the Flynn Effect
- New section on brain activity correlates of intelligence

- Updated "Focus On" section on race and intelligence
- Updated section on algorithms and heuristics, including Gigerenzer's concept of the adaptive toolbox and its application
- New Epilogue on Daniel Tammet, an autistic savant

CHAPTER 12

- New Prologue on the role of early experience using the example of Romanian orphans
- New material on epigenetic factors in development
- Additional information on teratogens
- New Case study elaborates on the opening Prologue with an individual family's story
- Additional information on the cultural differences in social attachment
- Updated information on the development of gender roles
- New case study of David Reimer, used to illustrate the complexity of gender identity
- Updated information on marriage and family
- New Epilogue contrasts the Romanian orphanage story with that of David Reimer

CHAPTER 13

- Entire chapter has been substantially reorganized and expanded to consolidate material on motivation with related information on health and lifestyle
- New Prologue on the Malay latah state
- New section on androgen insensitivity syndrome and transsexualism
- Updated evaluation of the James-Lange theory
- New case study on aggression
- Rewritten case study of Phineas Gage
- Integrated material on stress, stress management, and health

CHAPTER 14

- Additional information on personality traits, including speculation of "Dark Triad" traits
- New section on traits across different cultures
- New section on gender differences in personality
- New section on positive psychology
- New epilogue provides contrasting view of personality differences between identical twins and discusses possible connection to epigenetics

CHAPTER 15

- Additional information on the self, including a case study from Gilbert's research on people's prediction of their future behavior

- Additional information on the fundamental attribution error, including Wegner's research on the illusion of conscious will
- Additional information on the actor-observer effect, including cross-cultural research findings
- New material on self-handicapping
- New material on cognitive dissonance, including findings from evolutionary psychology and brain-damaged patients
- New material on attitudes toward racial equality from research in South Africa and from fMRI research
- New material on the self-fulfilling prophecy
- New case study on Kitty Genovese
- New section on the Stanford Prison Experiment and its relevance to the Abu Ghraib Prison
- Additional information in the "Focus On" section on the evolution of love
- New Epilogue on the growing intersection between social psychology and cognitive neuroscience

CHAPTER 16

- Addition of the biopsychsocial perspective to the study of psychological disorders
- New reference to the ISD in addition to the DSM
- New material on critiques of the DSM-IV and possible directions for the DSM-V
- Updated "Focus On" section on clinical versus actuarial diagnosis
- New section on disorders usually diagnosed in childhood that focuses on attention-deficit/hyperactivity disorder and autistic disorder
- New case study on autistic disorder
- New case study on obsessive-compulsive disorder
- New case study on post-traumatic stress disorder
- New case studies on culture-bound syndromes
- New case study on borderline personality disorder
- Reorganization of sections to reflect the DSM-IV ordering
- New material on dopamine pathways in substance-related disorders
- New material on the heritability of schizophrenia
- New material on the neurophysiological causes of mood disorders
- New section on post-traumatic stress disorder
- New section on borderline personality disorder
- New Epilogue on Elyn Sak's life with schizophrenia

CHAPTER 17

- New case study illustrating brief psychodynamic therapy
- New case study illustrating Gestalt therapy
- Revised section on the evaluation of insight therapies
- New material on the treatment of autistic disorder using applied behavior analysis
- Additional information on community psychology
- Additional information on the evaluation of family and couples therapy and community psychology
- New case study on antidepressant medications
- New section on drug therapy for ADHD, including a case study
- Revised "Focus On" section on the evaluation of therapeutic efficacy, with emphasis on evidence-based approaches
- New Epilogue on concerns about the extended use of drug therapy

Teaching and Learning Supplements

New Expanded Instructor's Manual (ISBN: 0-205-59734-3) Written and compiled by Ken Koenigshofer, PhD, Chaffey College and University of Maryland, University College, with dozens of new resources pulled together by a team of master teachers, the expanded Instructor's Manual is an invaluable tool for new and experienced instructors alike. First-time instructors will appreciate the detailed introduction to teaching the introductory psychology course, with suggestions for preparing for the course, sample syllabi, and current trends and strategies for successful teaching. Each chapter offers integrated teaching outlines to help instructors seamlessly incorporate all of the ancillary materials for this book into their lectures, and all Key Questions, Core Concepts, and Key Terms for each chapter are listed for quick reference. For the Seventh Edition, the Instructor's Manual offers a substantially enhanced bank of lecture launchers, handouts, and activities, and new categories of materials have been added, including new crossword puzzles, suggestions for integrating third-party videos and web resources, and cross-references to transparencies and hundreds of multimedia and video assets found in the *Psychology: Core Concepts* MyPsychLab course.

Print Test Bank and MyTest Computerized Test Bank (Print ISBN: 0-205-59735-1) Randy H. Simonson, PhD, College of Southern Idaho, has provided an extensively updated test bank containing over 2000 accuracy-checked questions, including multiple choice, completion (fill-in-the-blank and short answer), conceptual matching sequences, and critical essays. Test item questions also have been written to test student comprehension of select multimedia assets found with MyPsychLab, for instructors who wish to make MyPsychLab a more central component of their course. All questions in-

clude the correct answer, page reference, difficulty ranking, and question type designation. This product is also available in the MyTest computerized version for use in creating tests in the classroom.

PowerPoint™ Presentation (ISBN: 0-205-59732-7) An exciting interactive tool for use in the classroom, created by Linda Fayard, Mississippi Gulf Coast Community College, Jackson County Campus, the PowerPoint™ Presentation for *Psychology: The Science of Behavior* includes both images from and key topics covered in the textbook. The PowerPoint™ Presentation can be downloaded from our Instructor Resource Center at www.pearsonhighered.com. A separate Art and Figure version of these presentations contains all art from the textbook for which Pearson has been granted electronic permissions.

MyPsychLab (www.mypsychlab.com) The APA strongly recommends student self-assessment tools and the use of embedded questions and assignments. In response to these demands, Pearson's MyPsychLab offers students useful and engaging self-assessment tools, and instructors flexibility in assessing and tracking student progress. For instructors, MyPsychLab is a powerful tool for assessing student performance and adapting course content to students' changing needs—without investing additional time or resources. Students benefit from an easy-to-use site on which they can test themselves on key content, track their progress, and utilize individually tailored study plans. MyPsychLab includes an eBook plus multimedia tutorials, audio, video, simulations, animations, and controlled assessments to completely engage students and reinforce learning.

MyPsychLab is designed with instructor flexibility in mind—you decide the extent of integration into your course—from independent self-assessment for students tracked in a gradebook to total instructor-driven course management. By transferring faculty members' most time-consuming tasks—content delivery, student assessment, and grading—to automated tools, MyPsychLab enables faculty to spend more quality time with students. Instructors are provided with the results of student diagnostic tests in a gradebook and can view performance of individual students or an aggregate report of their class. Instructors can access the remediation activities students receive within their customized study plans, and can also link to extra lecture notes, video clips, and activities that reflect the content areas their class is struggling with. Instructors can bring these resources into class, or easily post them online for students to access.

For sample syllabi with ideas on incorporating MyPsychLab, see www.mypsychlab.com.

With the seventh edition of *Psychology: The Science of Behavior* comes a new generation of MyPsychLab, with dozens of improvements and new features that make MyPsychLab both more powerful and easier to use. Some highlights of the new MyPsychLab course include:

- New peerScholar On-Line Peer Grading (available only in the course management version of MyPsychLab): Class-tested for five years at the Psychology Department of the University of Toronto, with over 8000 students participating so far, peerScholar is an elegant peer-grading tool that enables instructors to implement writing assignments into even large classroom settings and encourages the students to re-assess and think critically about their own work.

- A new, more flexible, powerful, and intuitive platform for the course management version of MyPsychLab.

- A redesigned eBook that gives students the option to highlight passages and access media content directly from the eBook page.

- A new interactive Timeline tool that vividly illustrates key dates in the history of psychology through text, audio, and video.

- A new Survey tool that allows instructors to anonymously poll students.

- Redesigned Flash Cards for reviewing key terms, with audio to help students with pronunciation of difficult terminology.

- A new Podcasting tool that allows instructors to quickly and easily create their own Podcasts.

- Dozens of new video clips, animations, and podcasts, including footage of classic experiments in psychology from Pennsylvania State Media, edited by Dennis Thompson, Georgia State University.

- Continued improvements to design, course content, and grading systems based on direct customer feedback.

Please contact your local Pearson representative for more information on MyPsychLab. For technical support for any of your Pearson products, you and your students can contact http://247.pearsoned.com.

The Allyn & Bacon Introduction to Psychology Transparency Set (ISBN: 0-205-39862-6) This set of approximately 200 full-color transparencies is available upon adoption of the text from your local Allyn & Bacon sales representative.

Allyn & Bacon Digital Media Archive for Introduction to Psychology, (ISBN: 0-205-39537-6) This comprehensive source includes still images from all of our Introduction to Psychology textbooks, Web links, and animations.

Pearson Teaching Films Introductory Psychology Video Library with Annual Updates (Five DVD Set ISBN: 0-13-175432-7 / Update DVD for 2008 ISBN: 0-205-65280-8) This multi-DVD set of videos offers qualified adopters over 100 short video clips of 5 to 15 minutes in length, organized by course topic for easy lecture integration. Videos come from many of the most popular video sources for psychology content, such as ABCNews,

the Films for the Humanities series, ScienCentral, as well as videos from the Pearson video library. Additional videos will be added to the Library on an annual basis.

New! Interactive Lecture Questions for Clickers (ISBN: 0-205-68803-9) These lecture questions will jump-start exciting classroom discussions.

Acknowledgments

We are delighted to present *Psychology: The Science of Behavior* and to have had the opportunity to collaborate with one another on this seventh edition. We hope that this textbook will spark further interest in the discipline of psychology and pave the way to greater understanding of human behavior.

This book has been the product of teamwork from its very beginning. Writing this edition has been an immensely pleasurable experience because of the help we have received from others.

We are especially pleased to acknowledge the remarkable team at Allyn & Bacon, which has consistently and strongly supported the concept of a seventh edition of the Carlson text. We thank Stephen Frail for his encouragement and guidance. Erin K.L. Grelak, Development Editor, supported us throughout the entire project with patience and humor. We would also like to thank Production Supervisor, Patty Bergin, who skillfully ensured the quality, accuracy, and unique look of the text, and Kathy Smith, who guided us through the myriad requirements of production. And we thank Jeannette Koskinas for her marketing expertise in launching this edition.

Professors who write do so with an invisible audience listening to their words—the audience of previous classes and former students. We've had the good fortune to teach many fine students who, through their questions and observations, have shaped our teaching.

We've also had generous colleagues who reviewed our chapters and offered their advice. They are listed on the next page. We offer great thanks to these dedicated instructors, who took time to review the text, provided helpful feedback, and allowed us to share in their classroom experiences and those of their students. Their contributions have improved the text, and we are indebted to each of them.

We end these comments by expressing the deepest appreciation to our spouses and our families. To our loved ones, who have tolerated the disruptions produced by our work and who have supported us during this project, goes our fondest acknowledgment.

Neil R. Carlson
Harold Miller
C. Donald Heth
John W. Donahoe
G. Neil Martin

Reviewers of the Seventh Edition

Kyle Baumbauer
Texas A&M University

Jill Carlivati
George Washington University

Brian Carpenter
Washington University

Verne Cox
University of Texas at Arlington

Amy Drayton
Eastern Michigan University

Steve Dworkin
University of North Carolina at Wilmington

Mitch Earleywine
State University of New York at Albany

Preston Garraghty
Indiana University

Alexandria Guzman
University of New Haven

Christy Harnett
College of Notre Dame

Charles Kaiser
College of Charleston

Don Kates
College of Dupage

Edythe Kirk
Lamar University

Ken Koenigshofer
Chaffey College

Alan Lambert
Washington University

Joshua Landau
York College of Pennsylvania

Juliana Leding
University of North Florida

Stephen Madigan
University of Southern California

Amoria Yee Mikami
University of Virginia

Jesper Mogensen
University of Copenhagen, Denmark

Rachel Nitzberg
University of California at Davis

Fabian Novello
Clark State University

Bill Overman
University of North Carolina at Wilmington

Al Porterfield
Oberlin College

Matt Reysen
University of Mississippi

Alan Roberts
Indiana University

Michael Sakuma
Dowling College

Juan Antonio Salinas
University of Texas at Austin

Jim Schirillo
Wake Forest University

Alycia Silman
Wake Forest University

Carol Slater
Alma College

Carla Strassle
York College of Pennsylvania

George Taylor
University of Missouri, St. Louis

David Uttal
Northwestern University

Jeffrey Weatherly
University of North Dakota

John Wright
Washington State University

Erin Young
Texas A&M University

Otto Zinser
East Tennessee State University

To the Reader

This is a book about something that belongs to you. That's true in an obvious sense, given that this textbook describes the mechanisms of behavior that we, as humans, all share. You have inherited, through the intricate machinery of your ancestors' genes, a brain that once contemplated the African savannah and that now can comprehend the information age. You have also acquired, through your life's experiences, a tremendous store of knowledge and memories that affect your thoughts and emotions in ways distinctive just to you. Your psychology, in that sense, belongs to you.

But there is something else about this book that also belongs to you. Psychology is an international discipline, built by scholars around the world. It is part of the scientific knowledge of our civilization that you inherit.

There are some things you should know about the book before you start reading. Each chapter begins with a chapter outline that will tell you what to expect when you read the chapter and helps you keep track of your progress.

Because every discipline has its own vocabulary—and psychology is no exception—important terms are specially marked in the text. Each one is highlighted where its definition or description is given. These key terms are also listed and succinct definitions are provided in the margins.

The book contains tables, figures (graphs, diagrams, and drawings), and photographs. They are there to illustrate important points, and in some cases to say something that cannot be said with words alone. To help you quickly find your place again once you've looked at them, figure and table references are highlighted like this: (See FIGURE 5•10).

The end of each chapter includes a chapter summary, divided by major chapter section, for you to review what you've just read; *Suggestions for Further Reading,* which highlight the newest research and most interesting concepts in the chapter; and a list of applicable video, activities, and features for you to explore on MyPsychLab (www. mypsychlab.com).

We have not met you, but we feel as if we have been talking to you while working on this book. Writing is an "unsocial" activity in the sense that it is done alone. It can even be an antisocial activity when the writer must say, "No, I'm too busy writing to talk with you now." So as we wrote the book, we consoled ourselves by imagining that you were listening to us. You will get to meet us, at least vicariously, through our words as you read this book. If you then want to make the conversation two-way, please write or e-mail us: Neil Carlson, Department of Psychology, Tobin Hall, University of Massachusetts, Amherst, MA 01003, nrc@psych.umass.edu; Hal Miller, Department of Psychology, Brigham Young University, Provo, UT 84602, harold_miller@byu.edu; Don Heth, Department of Psychology, University of Alberta, Edmonton, Alberta T6G 2E9, dheth@ualberta.ca; or John Donahoe, Psychology Department, Behavioral Neuroscience, University of Massachusetts, Amherst, MA 01003, jdonahoe@psych.umass.edu. We hope to hear from you.

The Science of Psychology

Prologue

The Brain's Future

The moment she entered the classroom, I (Don Heth) knew Laura had something she wanted to say. She sat down, looked at me, and said: "This book is freaking us out!"

I had to stifle a smile. "Oh?" I said, with as much innocence as I could muster.

"It isn't so much the part in the book that talks about replacing some of our nervous system with electronics . . . we realize that might be possible. But this guy says that we'll soon be able to replace all of it. And get this: He talks about actually having sex with a computer! Is this guy for real?"

"Well, that's your job to decide," was my rather unhelpful response. You see, Laura and three of her classmates had been assigned to read a book by one of America's foremost authorities on technology, Raymond Kurzweil. He had entitled it *The Age of Spiritual Machines: When Computers Exceed Human Intelligence,* and in it he had engaged in some heady speculation about the future of technology. We're all familiar with devices that amplify our senses, such as hearing aids and night vi-

sion goggles. As computers get more sophisticated, Karzweil wrote, they will be capable of performing all the functions of our natural nervous system and humans will be able to "enhance" their brains with sophisticated implants. As our knowledge of the brain increases, we will, says Kurzweil in his most shocking prediction, be able to download our consciousness into a computer.

Laura's four years of studying psychology had given her a pretty good grounding in the biology of the brain. Now, she had to consider what it would mean to simulate this biology inside a computer program. She and her team had to review Kurzweil's book in a special way: As part of my class assignment, they were to work with our campus radio station and produce a thirty-minute radio documentary that would examine the plausibility of Kurzweil's predictions. And, it would be broadcasted.

In the weeks after our classroom exchange, I noticed that Laura's team was getting more and more involved in the project. I learned later that they had been spending long nights at each other's homes, working out a script and considering the interviews they had conducted with philosophers, psychologists, and computer scientists. One professor even complained to me that these students were spending too much time on *my* assignment and not enough on *hers.* Then, halfway through the term, the team asked me if they could produce a sixty-minute program.

"This assignment has forced us to think about the meaning of everything we've learned about psychology," they said. "We can do something really special if we have the additional time." Thinking I had created some kind of monster, I said yes.

On the day the assignment was due, I stopped by the station and picked up the CD with the team's program. The station manager had reviewed it and had written a note on the CD. "Yikes!" was all it said. ■

Here are two facts about the world you live in:

- There is a man whose otherwise normal life is disturbed at night, when he suddenly leaps from his bed and prowls around his bedroom growling like a lion, his fingers curled into claws. In the morning he remembers nothing of these episodes.
- When atoms are placed in a strong magnetic field, the axes around which their electrons spin become aligned with that magnetic field. If a radio pulse is directed at the atoms, they will wobble like spinning tops and then return to their alignment. It takes different amounts of time for atoms of different elements to realign.

When you started college, you undoubtedly expected to learn facts like these and to understand how they relate to other facts. As you'll soon learn, both of these facts are of interest to psychologists.

Or consider this: If you asked your fellow students the question "What does it mean to study psychology?" you likely would receive several different answers. In fact, if you asked this question of several psychologists, you would still receive more than one answer. Psychologists are probably the most diverse group of people in our society to share the same title. Psychologists engage in research, teaching, counseling, and psychotherapy; they advise industry and governmental agencies about personnel matters, the design of products, advertising and marketing, and legislation; they devise and administer tests of personality, achievement, and ability. Psychologists study a wide variety of phenomena, including physiological processes within the nervous system, genetics, environmental events, personality characteristics, mental abilities, and social interactions. And yet psychology is a new discipline; the first person who ever called himself a "psychologist" was still alive in 1920, and professors he trained lived into the 1960s and 1970s.

Psychology is exciting partly because it is so diverse and many areas are changing so rapidly. But these aspects of the field may sometimes be confusing to you, a student faced with understanding this large and complex discipline. So this first chapter will give you an overview of what it means to be a psychologist. The sections that follow will describe the nature of psychology, its goals, and its history.

The research interests of psychologists vary widely. One researcher might be interested in the origins of aggression; another might be interested in childhood memory. Psychologists seek answers to innumerable research questions through the study of behavior.

What Is Psychology?

In this book we will study the science of **psychology**—a science with a specific focus on behavior. The primary emphasis is on discovering and explaining the causes of behavior. Of course, the book will describe the applications of these discoveries to such subjects as the treatment of mental disorders and the improvement of society—but the focus will be on the way psychologists discover the facts that make these applications possible. This is an important guide to understanding psychology as a science. As you read this book, you should concentrate on how this process of discovery works.

To help you, we should make a key distinction. The word *psychology* comes from two Greek words, *psukhe*, meaning "breath" or "soul," and *logos*, meaning "word" or "reason." The modern meaning of *psycho-* is "mind" and the modern meaning of *-logy* is "science"; thus, the word *psychology* literally means "the science of the mind." But this is a little bit misleading. As the title of this book indicates, psychology is

---

psychology The scientific study of the causes of behavior; also, the application of the findings of psychological research to the solution of problems.

not the science of the mind, but the science of *behavior.* The distinction can be traced to the way psychologists have thought about the mind. Early in the development of psychology, people conceived of the mind as an independent, free-floating spirit. Later, they described it as a characteristic of a functioning brain whose ultimate role was to control behavior. Thus, the focus turned from the mind, which cannot be directly observed, to behavior, which can. And because the brain is the organ that controls behavior, psychology very soon incorporated the study of the brain. (It is this recognition, by the way, that relates the two facts cited at the start of this chapter. You will see how this is so in later chapters.)

Why Behavior Is Studied

The ultimate goal of research in psychology is to understand human behavior: to explain why people do what they do. But how do we, as psychologists, provide an "explanation" of behavior? First, we must describe it. We must become familiar with the things that people (or other animals) do. We must learn how to categorize and measure behavior so that we can be sure that other psychologists in different places are observing the same phenomena. Next, we must discover the causes of the behavior we observe—the events responsible for a behavior's occurrence. If we can discover the events that caused the behavior, we have "explained" it. Events that cause other events (including behavior) to occur are called **causal events.**

As you will see through this book, different kinds of psychologists are interested in different kinds of behavior and in different levels of explanation. For example, one psychologist might be interested in how vision is coordinated with movement; another might be interested in courtship. But even when they are interested in the same behavior, psychologists may study different categories of causal events— what has been referred to as different "levels of explanation." Some look inside the organism in a literal sense, seeking physiological causes such as the activity of nerve cells or the secretions of glands. Others look inside the organism in a metaphorical sense, explaining behavior in terms of hypothetical mental states such as anger, fear, curiosity, or love. Still others look only for events in the environment (including things that other people do) that cause behavior to occur. The word *levels* does not mean that one approach is superior or is more fundamental than another. Rather, a level of analysis refers to a common choice of causes to study and methods of research to use. The use of different levels of explanation is one reason why psychology is such a diverse discipline.

What is the purpose of this quest for explanations? Intellectual curiosity is one answer. An essential part of human nature seems to be a need to understand what makes things

work—and what could be more interesting than trying to understand our fellow human beings? But psychological research is more than an idle endeavor of curious scientists; it holds the promise of showing us how to solve our most important and pressing problems.

One reason for studying behavior is that it is one of the roots of many of the world's problems: poverty, crime, overpopulation, drug addiction, bigotry, pollution, oppression, terrorism, and war. If global warming adversely affects our planet, or if forests and lakes die because of acid rain, it will be because of our behavior. Many health-related problems—such as cardiovascular disease, some forms of cancer, and a large number of stress-related illnesses—are caused (or at least aggravated) by individuals' behavior. For example, heavy smoking, obesity, lack of exercise, poor diet, unsanitary personal habits, and stressful lifestyles are responsible for illnesses found around the world. But there are more positive reasons for studying behavior, too. There are strong relationships between behavior and health, and knowing what these are can improve your well-being. Knowing how people remember, make decisions, and evaluate outcomes can help in your business and commerce dealings. Knowing that your personal relationships with friends, relatives, and partners depend on behaviors and the way you each perceive them can help you understand yourself and others better. Knowing how learning occurs can help you study for that big test. We hope that while reading this book and learning what psychologists have discovered about human behavior, you will think about the contribution psychology could make to you and your society.

Fields of Psychology

Psychologists sometimes identify themselves in terms of their activities. Some of us are scientists, trying to discover the causes of behavior. Some of us are practitioners of *applied psychology,* applying what our scientific colleagues have learned to the solution of problems in the world outside the laboratory. And, of course, some psychologists perform both roles. The Bureau of Labor Statistics estimated that psychologists held about 106,000 jobs in 2006, with about 30,000 more employed as professors at colleges and universities across the United States (Bureau of Labor Statistics, 2006).

Areas of Psychological Research Most research psychologists work in colleges or universities or are employed by private or governmental research laboratories. Research psychologists differ from one another in two principal ways: in the *types of behavior* they investigate and in the *causal events* they analyze. That is, they describe different types of behavior, and they explain them in terms of different types of causes. For example, two psychologists might both be interested in memory, but they might attempt to explain memory in terms of different causal events—one may focus on physiological events, whereas the other may focus on environmental events.

---

causal event An event that causes another event to occur.

Physiological psychology examines the physiological basis of behavior. The organism's physiology, especially its nervous system, is considered to be the appropriate level of explanation. Physiological psychologists study almost all behavioral phenomena that can be observed in nonhuman animals, including learning, memory, sensory processes, emotional behavior, motivation, sexual behavior, and sleep. The phenomenon in nonhuman animals is considered a model that can help us understand the causal events in human behavior.

Comparative psychology is the study of the behavior of members of a variety of species in an attempt to explain behavior in terms of evolutionary adaptation to the environment. Comparative psychologists study behavioral phenomena similar to those studied by physiological psychologists. They are likely to study inherited behavioral patterns, such as courting and mating, predation and aggression, defensive behavior, and parental behavior.

Behavior genetics is the branch of psychology that studies the role of genetics in behavior. The genes we inherit from our parents include a blueprint for the construction of a human brain (see Chapter 3). Each blueprint is a little different, which means that no two brains are exactly alike. Therefore, no two people will act exactly alike, even in identical situations. Behavior geneticists study the role of genetics in behavior by examining similarities in physical and behavioral characteristics of blood relatives, whose genes are more similar than those of unrelated individuals. They also perform breeding experiments with laboratory animals to see what aspects of behavior can be transmitted to an animal's offspring. Using new techniques of molecular genetics, behavior geneticists can even alter parts of the gene during these experiments to determine how differences in the genetic code relate to behavioral differences among animals.

Cognitive psychology is the study of mental processes and complex behaviors such as perception, attention, learning and memory, verbal behavior, concept formation, and problem solving. To cognitive psychologists, the events that cause behavior consist of functions of the human brain that occur in response to environmental events. Cognitive researchers' explanations involve characteristics of inferred mental processes, such as imagery, attention, and mechanisms of language. Most cognitive psychologists do not study physiological mechanisms, but recently some have begun collaborating with neurologists and other professionals involved in brain scanning. The study of the biology of cognition has been greatly aided by the development of brain-scanning methods that permit us to measure the activity and structure of various parts of the human brain.

Cognitive neuroscience is closely allied with both cognitive psychology and physiological psychology. Researchers in this branch of psychology are generally interested in the same phenomena studied by cognitive psychologists, but they attempt to discover the particular brain mechanisms responsible for cognitive processes. One of the principal research techniques in cognitive neuroscience is to study the behavior

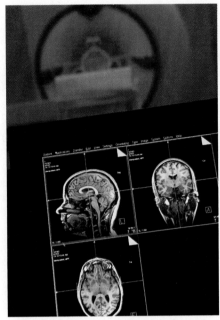

Methods that allow psychologists to scan the brain to show its structure and activity have greatly improved our understanding of the biology of cognition.

of people whose brains have been damaged by natural causes such as diseases, strokes, or tumors.

Developmental psychology is the study of the changes in behavioral, perceptual, cognitive, social, and emotional capacities of organisms as a function of age and experience. Some developmental psychologists study phenomena of adolescence or adulthood—in particular, the effects of aging. The causal events they study are as comprehensive as all of psychology: physiological processes, cognitive processes, and social influences.

Social psychology is the study of the effects people have on one another's behavior. Social psychologists explore phenomena such as perception (of oneself as well as of others); cause-and-effect relations in human interactions; attitudes

physiological psychology The branch of psychology that studies the physiological basis of behavior.

comparative psychology The branch of psychology that studies the behavior of members of a variety of species in an attempt to explain behavior in terms of evolutionary adaptation to the environment.

behavior genetics The branch of psychology that studies the role of genetics in behavior.

cognitive psychology The branch of psychology that studies mental processes and complex behaviors such as perception, attention, learning and memory, verbal behavior, concept formation, and problem solving.

cognitive neuroscience The branch of psychology that attempts to understand cognitive psychological functions by studying the brain mechanisms that are responsible for them.

developmental psychology The branch of psychology that studies the changes in behavioral, perceptual, cognitive, social, and emotional capacities of organisms as a function of age and experience.

social psychology The branch of psychology devoted to the study of the effects people have on one another's behavior.

[TABLE 1·1] Some Applied Areas of Psychology

Type of Psychologist	Area of Application	Typical Employment Setting
Clinical neuropsychologists	Identification and treatment of the behavioral consequences of nervous system disorders and injuries	Hospitals, in association with specialists who treat diseases of the nervous system
Clinical psychologists	Identification, assessment, and treatment of mental disorders	Private practice and hospitals
Community psychologists	Welfare of individuals in the social system, especially those who are disadvantaged	Community organizations
Consumer psychologists	Motivation, perception, learning, and purchasing behavior of individuals in the marketplace	Corporations and advertising agencies
Engineering psychologists and ergonomists	Perceptual and cognitive factors in the use of machinery	Corporations and engineering agencies
Forensic psychologists	Behavior as it relates to the legal and justice system	Private law firms and public agencies in the justice system
Health psychologists	Behavior that affects health and lifestyle	Hospitals, government agencies, and corporations
Organizational psychologists	Behavior in industrial work processes	Corporations and government agencies
School psychologists	Behavioral issues of students in the school setting	Educational agencies and institutions

and opinions; interpersonal relationships; group dynamics; and emotional behavior, including aggression and sexual behavior.

Personality psychology is the study of individual differences in temperament and patterns of behavior. Personality psychologists look for causal events in a person's history, both genetic and environmental. Some personality psychologists are closely allied with social psychologists; others work on problems related to adjustment to society and hence study problems of interest to applied psychologists.

Evolutionary psychology seeks to explain cognitive, social, and personality aspects of psychology by looking at their adaptive significance during the evolution of modern species. Clearly, the discoveries of comparative psychologists and behavioral geneticists are of interest to evolutionary psychologists. However, evolutionary psychologists use the theory of evolution by means of natural selection (described in Chapter 3) as a guiding principle. The task of the

evolutionary psychologist is to trace the development of such differences and to explore how their adaptive advantages might explain the behavior of modern humans.

Cross-cultural psychology is the study of the impact of culture on behavior. Because the ancestors of people of different racial and ethnic groups lived in different environments that presented different problems and opportunities, different cultures developed different strategies for adapting to their environments. Today, these strategies show themselves in laws, customs, myths, religious beliefs, and ethical principles. The importance of cross-cultural research and the interaction between biological and cultural factors on people's behavior are explored throughout this book.

Clinical psychology is the study and treatment of mental disorders and problems of adjustment. Most clinical psychologists are practitioners who try to help people solve their problems, whatever the causes. The rest are scientists who look for a wide variety of causal events, including genetic and physiological factors as well as environmental factors such as parental upbringing, interactions with siblings, and other social stimuli. They also do research to evaluate and improve methods of psychotherapy.

Although discovering the causes of behavior is important, not all psychologists are involved in research. In fact, most psychologists work outside the laboratory, applying the findings of research psychologists to problems related to people's behavior. Their fields of application are still closely related to the research specialties we've just described, but

personality psychology The branch of psychology that attempts to categorize and understand the causes of individual differences in temperament and patterns of behavior.

evolutionary psychology The branch of psychology that explains behavior in terms of adaptive advantages that specific behaviors provided during the evolution of a species. Evolutionary psychologists use natural selection as a guiding principle.

cross-cultural psychology The branch of psychology that studies the impact of culture on behavior.

clinical psychology The branch of psychology devoted to the investigation and treatment of abnormal behavior and mental disorders.

their employment situations may be quite different. TABLE 1•1 lists some of these applied areas.

How Is Psychology Used?

Sometimes applications of psychology arise because other disciplines require the special knowledge about behavior that psychologists may provide. Here are two recent examples: one in the field of law enforcement and the other in rehabilitative medicine.

Law Enforcement. If you're familiar with any of the currently popular television shows on criminal investigation agencies, you know that technology plays a large role in police detective work. Eyewitnesses who have seen a crime perpetrator can be very helpful if they can produce a useful description of the person. In the past, police officers relied on sketch artists to help an eyewitness develop a picture that could be circulated to the wider public. However, since artists vary in their skills, it is more common nowadays to use computerized systems that compose a face from a set of isolated features. An eyewitness is given a menu of different depictions of noses, eyebrows, hairlines, and so on, and from the examples selected, a composite face is constructed (see FIGURE 1•1).

Are these constructions accurate? Gary Wells and Lisa Hasel (2007) from Iowa State University argue that they are not. Although it is difficult to come up with any single estimate of accuracy, Wells and Hasel point to many cases both in the laboratory and in real life where composite drawings have led to mistaken identifications. Why would this be? It's not just a case of poor memory on the part of eyewitnesses,

because the errors occur even when well-known faces are constructed. Wells and Hasel argue that it is a consequence of the way the brain perceives and remembers faces. A number of research studies show that we remember faces as complete units rather than as isolated features. The use of composite drawing technology, then, works against the way we naturally remember a face we've seen. Wells and Hasel suggest that identification technology might become more accurate by taking into account the psychology of facial memory.

Rehabilitative Medicine. Although modern medicine has increased the survival rate of soldiers wounded in battlefields like those of Iraq and Afghanistan, it is often at the cost of the amputation of an arm or a leg. Technology can produce natural-looking prostheses, but these artificial limbs are capable of, at best, only gross and hard-to-control movement. The main impediment is that modern prostheses do not provide the sensory feedback that comes with moving a natural arm or leg.

Prompted by concern for these returning amputees, the United States Department of Defense has initiated a large project that brings together specialists in engineering with scientists who understand how the brain controls movement (Krause, 2007). The goal is to produce an artificial arm with the full function of a natural one by the year 2009. Using the knowledge of physiological psychology concerning how sensory and motor nerves work, the researchers of this project have begun efforts to "rewire" nerves from other parts of the body (such as the chest) to feel the position of an artificial arm and to control it. If this project succeeds, the knowledge of physiological psychologists and neuroscientists will have

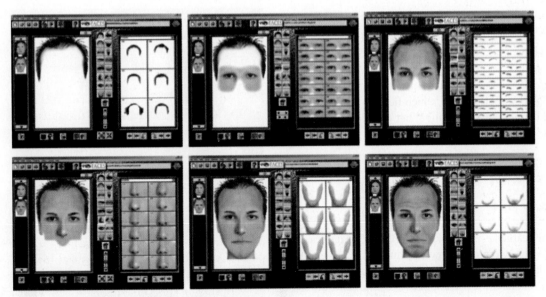

[FIGURE 1•1] An example of reconstructing the memory for a face using a computerized composite system (Faces 3.0 by IQBiometrics). In this case, the eyewitness chooses a hairline at the start and then fills in the rest of the face by choosing individual features.

(From Wells, G. L. & Hasel, L. E. [2007]. Facial composite production by eyewitnesses. *Current directions in psychological science, 16,* 6–10.)

A participant tests an artificial arm controlled by direct neural impulses.

been put to use to replace, through technology, a part of a person's nervous system. (It was, by the way, this possibility that was discussed in Ray Kurzweil's book that led to my student Laura's reaction. Perhaps his future scenario is a lot closer than we might think.)

QUESTIONS TO CONSIDER

1. Before you read this section, how would you have answered the questions "What is psychology?" and "What do psychologists do?" Would your answer be different now?
2. What problems would you like psychologists to work on?
3. If you were a psychologist, which field do you think you would be most interested in? What questions might you want to answer?

The Growth of Psychology as a Science

As mentioned earlier, psychology is a young science; it started in the late 1800s in Germany. However, humans have certainly been curious about psychological issues for much longer than that. To understand how psychology as a science came into being, we can trace its roots back through philosophy and the natural sciences, because these disciplines provided the methods

we now use to study human behavior; through the needs of society at the time, psychology became an independent science. These roots took many centuries to develop. Let's examine them and see how they set the stage in the late nineteenth century for the emergence of psychology as a science.

Philosophical Roots of Psychology

Perhaps the most notable part of our mental experience is that each of us is conscious of our own existence. Furthermore, we are aware of this consciousness and tend to relate it to our own behavior. That is, although we may sometimes find ourselves engaged in things we had not planned to do, we generally have the impression that our conscious mind controls our behavior. We consider alternatives, make plans, and then act. We get our bodies moving; we engage in behavior.

It is ironic that, although consciousness is a private experience, we give it such importance in our public lives. Even though we can experience only our own consciousness directly, we assume that our fellow human beings also are conscious; and, to at least some extent, we attribute consciousness to other animals as well. To the degree that our behavior is similar to that of others, we tend to assume that our mental states, too, resemble one another. Much earlier in the history of our species, it was common to attribute a life-giving *animus,* or spirit, to anything that seemed to move or grow independently. Because our ancestors believed that the movements of their own bodies were controlled by their minds or spirits, they inferred that the sun, moon, wind, and tides were similarly animated. This primitive philosophy is called **animism** (from the Latin *animare,* "to

Animism attempts to explain natural phenomena by supernatural means. This painting, from the tomb of Ramses VI, depicts the ancient Egyptian belief that the sun was a god, borne across the heavens on a special boat, to be swallowed each evening by Nut, the goddess of the sky.

---

animism   The belief that all animals and all moving objects possess spirits controlling their movements and thoughts.

René Descartes (1596–1650)

philosophy but also of a biological tradition that led to modern physiological psychology. He advocated a rationalistic approach—the sober, impersonal investigation of natural phenomena by means of sensory experience and human reasoning. He assumed that the world was a purely mechanical entity that, having once been set in motion by God, ran its course without divine interference. To understand the world, people had only to understand how it was constructed. This stance challenged the established authority of the Roman Catholic Church, which believed that the purpose of philosophy was to reconcile human experiences with the truth of God's revelations.

To Descartes, animals were creatures of the natural world only; accordingly, their behavior was controlled by natural causes and could be understood by the methods of science. His view of the human body was much the same: It was a machine affected by natural causes that produced natural effects. For example, the application of a hot object to a finger would cause an almost immediate withdrawal of the arm from the source of stimulation. Reactions like this did not require participation of the mind; they occurred automatically. Descartes called these actions **reflexes** (from the Latin *reflectere*, "to bend back upon itself"). Energy coming from the outside source would be reflected back through the nervous system to the muscles, which would contract (see FIGURE 1•2). The term *reflex* is still in use today, though of course we now explain the phenomenon differently.

quicken, enliven, endow with breath or soul"). Even gravity was explained in animistic terms: Rocks fell to the ground because the spirits within them wanted to be reunited with the earth.

Obviously, our interest in animism is historical. Scientific understanding of our natural world requires that we reject such notions as the idea that rocks fall because they "want to." Rather, we refer to the existence of natural forces inherent in physical matter, even if these forces are not completely understood.

Psychology as a science must be based on the assumption that behavior is strictly subject to physical laws, just like any other natural phenomenon. This assumption allows us to discover these laws objectively, using the scientific method (described in Chapter 2). The rules of scientific research impose discipline on humans, whose natural inclinations might lead them to incorrect conclusions. It seemed natural for our ancestors to believe that rocks had spirits. In contrast, the idea that feelings, emotions, imagination, and other private experiences are the products of physical laws of nature did not come easily; it was developed by thinkers and scholars through many centuries.

The ancient Greeks were the first to develop rational speculation about nature and to systematize this speculation using laws of logic and mathematics. But although the history of Western philosophy properly begins with them, we will begin here with René Descartes (1596–1650), a seventeenth-century French philosopher and mathematician. Descartes has been called the father not only of modern

[**FIGURE 1•2**] Descartes's diagram of a withdrawal reflex. The energy from the fire would be transmitted physically to the brain, where it would release a type of fluid that would inflate the muscles and cause movement

(Stock Montage, Inc.)

---

reflex An automatic response to a stimulus, such as the blink reflex to the sudden unexpected approach of an object toward the eyes.

What set humans apart from the rest of the world, according to Descartes, was their possession of a mind. The mind was not part of the natural world, and therefore it obeyed different laws. Thus, Descartes was a proponent of **dualism,** the belief that all reality can be divided into two distinct entities: mind and matter. He distinguished between "extended things," or physical bodies, and "thinking things," or minds. Physical bodies, he believed, do not think; so minds could not be made of ordinary matter. Although Descartes was not the first to propose dualism, his thinking differed from that of his predecessors in one important way: He suggested that a causal link existed between the mind and its physical housing.

Although later philosophers pointed out that this theoretical link actually contradicted the belief in dualism, the proposal of causal interaction between mind and matter was absolutely vital to the development of a psychological science. Descartes reasoned that the mind controlled the movements of the body and that the body, through its sense organs, supplied the mind with information about what was happening in the environment. He hypothesized that this interaction between mind and body took place in the pineal body, a small organ situated on top of the brain stem, buried beneath the large cerebral hemispheres of the brain. When the mind decided to perform an action, it tilted the pineal body in a particular direction, causing fluid to flow from the brain into the proper set of nerves. This flow of fluid caused the appropriate muscles to inflate and move.

How did Descartes come up with this mechanical concept of the body's movements? Western Europe in the seventeenth century was the scene of great advances in the sciences. It was not just the practical application of science that impressed Europeans; it was the beauty, imagination, and fun of it as well. Craftsmen constructed many elaborate mechanical toys and devices during this period. The young René Descartes was greatly impressed by the moving statues in the French royal gardens at Saint-Germain-en-Laye (Jaynes, 1970). These devices served as models for Descartes as he theorized about how the body worked. He conceived of the muscles as balloons. They became inflated when a fluid passed through the nerves that connected them to the brain and spinal cord, just as water flowed through pipes to activate the statues. This inflation was the basis of the muscular contraction that causes us to move.

Descartes's explanation was one of the first to use a technological device as a model of the nervous system. In science, a **model** is a relatively simple system that works on known principles and is able to do at least some of the things that a more complex system can do. For example, after scientists discovered that elements of the nervous system communicate by means of electrical impulses, researchers developed models of the brain initially based on telephone switchboards and later on computers. Abstract models, which are completely mathematical in their properties, also have been developed.

It was an English philosopher, John Locke (1632–1704), who took Descartes's analysis one step farther. Locke did not exempt the mind from the laws of the material universe. In place of Descartes's **rationalism** (pursuit of truth through reason), Locke advocated **empiricism**—the pursuit of truth through observation and experience. Locke rejected the belief, prevalent in the seventeenth century, that ideas were innately present in an infant's mind. Instead, he proposed that all knowledge must come through experience; it is empirically derived. (In Greek, *empeiria* means "experience.") His model of the mind was the *tabula rasa* or "cleaned slate"—the ancient method of writing on waxed tablets that were scraped clean before use. Locke proposed that at birth infants' minds were empty and ready to accept the writings of experience.

Locke believed that knowledge developed through linkages of primary sensations: simple ideas combined to form complex ones. Amending this notion somewhat, the Irish bishop, philosopher, and mathematician George Berkeley (1685–1753) suggested that our knowledge of events in the world also required inferences based on the accumulation of past experiences. For example, our visual perception of depth involves several elementary sensations, such as observing the relative movements of objects as we move our heads and the convergence of our eyes (turning inward toward each other or away) as we focus on near or distant objects. Although our knowledge of visual depth seems to be immediate and direct, it is actually a secondary, complex response constructed from a number of simple elements. Our perceptions of the world can also involve integrating the activity of different sense organs, such as when we see, hear, feel, and smell the same object.

As philosophers, Locke and Berkeley were speculating on the origins of knowledge and dealing with the concept of learning. (In fact, modern psychologists are still concerned with the issues that Berkeley raised.) But although they rejected Descartes's version of the mind, they still were trying to fit a nonquantifiable variable—reason—into the equation.

With the work of the Scottish philosopher James Mill (1773–1836), speculation about the mind completed an intellectual swing from animism (physical matter animated by spirits) to *materialism*—mind composed entirely of matter. **Materialism** is the belief that reality can be known only through an understanding of the physical world, of which the mind is a part. Mill did not invent materialism, but he developed it into a complete system for looking at human nature. He worked on the assumption that humans were fundamentally the same as other animals. Like other species, humans were thoroughly physical in their makeup and were completely subject to the physical laws of the universe. Essentially, Mill agreed with Descartes's approach to understanding the human body, but rejected the concept of an immaterial mind. Mind, to Mill, was as passive as the body. It responded to the environment in precisely the same way. The mind, no less than the body, was a machine.

---

dualism The philosophical belief that reality consists of mind and matter.

model In science, a relatively simple system that works on known principles and is able to do at least some of the things that a more complex system can do.

rationalism The philosophical view that all knowledge is obtained through reason.

empiricism The philosophical view that all knowledge is obtained through observation and experience.

materialism A philosophical belief that reality can be known only through an understanding of the physical world, of which the mind is a part.

$f$ocus On

How Scientific Is Psychology, Really?

Researchers who study psychology have tried hard to earn and demonstrate its scientific reputation. There are no such problems with chemistry, physics, and biology: Their history is testament to their status as a science. A new study, however, suggests that psychology is gaining on its scientific elders.

Simonton (2004) compared the scientific status of psychology with that of physics, chemistry, sociology and biology. He identified a number of characteristics that typified a general science:

- the number of theories and laws mentioned in introductory textbooks (the higher the ratio of theory to law, the "softer"—i.e., less scientific—the discipline)

- publication rate (the more frequent, the more scientific the discipline)

- the appearance of graphs in journal papers (the "harder" the discipline, the greater the number of graphs)

- the impact made by young researchers (the more scientific the discipline, the greater the agreement that a researcher's contribution is significant)

- how peers evaluated 60 of their colleagues in their own disciplines, and how often single papers are cited (referred to in research papers).

Simonton also looked at secondary measures of scientific standing: "lecture disfluency" (the number of pause words such as "uh," "er" and "um": these are more common in less formal, structured, and factual disciplines); the extent to which references in journal articles were recent; age at receipt of the Nobel prize; and perceived difficulty of the discipline. Simonton combined these measures to provide a composite measure of scientific status.

Based on the first set of indicators, Simonton found that the natural sciences were judged to be more "scientific" than the social sciences. Psychology fell right on the mean—at the junction between natural and social sciences (see **FIGURE 1·3**). However, psychology's score was much closer to biology than to sociology—the biggest gap in scores was found between psychology and sociology, suggesting that the discipline is closer to its natural science cousins than its social science acquaintances. A gap also separated chemistry and biology, suggesting that the sciences might be grouped according to three clusters: the physical sciences (chemistry and physics), life sciences (biology and psychology) and social science (sociology).

Simonton concludes with an interesting observation. He argues that psychology's position in this hierarchy does not really reflect its scientific approach but its subject matter: Because the subject matter of psychology can be viewed as not directly controllable or manipulable, it can be perceived, despite its adoption of the scientific method, erroneously as neither scientific fish nor fowl.

[**FIGURE 1·3**] According to Simonton's study, psychology's scientific status was more similar to that of biology than another discipline traditionally associated with it, such as sociology.

(From D. K. Simonton (2004). Psychology's status as a scientific discipline: Its empirical placement within an implicit hierarchy of the sciences. *Review of General Psychology, 8*, p. 65 [Fig. 2].)

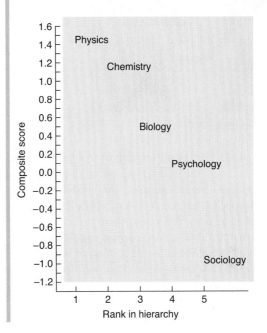

Biological Roots of Psychology

René Descartes and his model of muscular physiology were the beginning of the biological roots of psychology. Descartes's concept was based on an actual working model (the moving statue) whose movements seemed similar to those of human beings. However, Descartes relied on simple similarity as "proof" of his theory; he did not have the means to offer a scientific proof. But technological development soon made experimentation and manipulation possible in the biological realm as well. For example, Descartes's hydraulic model of muscular movement was shown to be incorrect by Luigi Galvani (1737–1798), an Italian physiologist who discovered that he could make muscles contract by applying an electrical current either directly to them or to the nerves attached to them. The muscles themselves contained the energy needed to contract; they did not have to be inflated by pressurized fluid. Indeed, an English physician, Francis Glisson (1597–1677), made the same assertion even more pointedly when he demonstrated, by having a man flex his arm in a barrel of water, that his muscles did not increase in volume as Descartes's theory would have predicted.

The work of the German physiologist Johannes Müller (1801–1858) clearly shows the way emerging biological knowledge shaped the evolution of psychology. Müller was a forceful advocate of applying experimental procedures to the study of physiology. He recommended that biologists should do more than observe and classify; they should remove or isolate animals' organs, test their responses to chemicals, and manipulate other conditions to see how the

Johannes Müller (1801–1858)

organism worked. His most important contribution to what would become the science of psychology was his **doctrine of specific nerve energies,** that different nerve fibers convey specific information from one part of the body to the brain or from the brain to one part of the body. Müller noted that the basic message sent along all nerves was the same—an electrical impulse—regardless of whether the message concerned, for example, a visual perception or an auditory sensation. What, then, accounts for the brain's ability to distinguish different kinds of sensory information? Why do we see what our eyes perceive, hear what our ears detect, and so on? After all, the optic nerves and the auditory nerves both send the same kind of message to the brain.

Müller's answer was that the messages are sent over different channels. Because the optic nerves are attached to the eyes, the brain interprets impulses received from these nerves as visual sensations. You have probably noticed that rubbing your eyes causes sensations of flashes of light. When you rub your eyes, the pressure against them stimulates visual receptors located inside them. As a result of this stimulation, messages are sent through the optic nerves to the brain. The brain interprets these messages as sensations of light.

Müller's doctrine had important implications. If the brain recognizes the nature of a particular sensory input by means of the particular nerve that brings the message, then perhaps the brain is similarly specialized, with different parts having different functions. In other words, if different nerves convey messages about different kinds of information, then those regions of the brain that receive these messages must have different functions.

Pierre Flourens (1774–1867), a French physiologist, provided experimental evidence for the implications of Müller's doctrine of specific nerve energies. Flourens operated on animals, removing various parts of the nervous system. He found that the resulting effects depended on which parts were removed. He observed what the animal could no longer do and concluded that the missing capacity must have been the function of the part removed. For example, if an animal could not move its leg after part of its brain was removed, then that region must normally control leg movements. This method of removal of part of the brain, called **experimental ablation** (from the Latin *ablatus,* "carried away"), was soon adopted by neurologists, and it is still used by scientists on animals today. Through experimental ablation, Flourens claimed to have discovered the regions of the brain that control heart rate and breathing, purposeful movements, and visual and auditory reflexes.

Paul Broca (1824–1880) applied Müller's logic, although not his method, to humans. In 1861 Broca, a French surgeon, performed an autopsy on the brain of a man who had had a stroke several years previously. The stroke (damage to the brain caused in this case by a blood clot) had robbed the man of the ability to speak. Broca discovered that the stroke had damaged part of the cerebral cortex on the left side of the man's brain. He suggested that this region of the brain is a center for speech.

Although subsequent research has found that speech is not controlled by a single "center" in the brain, the area that Broca identified (now known as *Broca's area,* see Chapter 10) is indeed necessary for speech production. The comparison of postmortem anatomical findings with patients' behavioral and intellectual deficits has become an important means of studying the functions of the brain.

In 1870 the German physiologists Gustav Fritsch and Eduard Hitzig introduced the use of electrical stimulation as a tool for mapping the functions of the brain. The results of this method complemented those produced by the experimental destruction of nervous tissue and provided some answers that experimental ablation could not. For example, Fritsch and Hitzig discovered that applying a small electrical shock to different parts of the cerebral cortex caused movements of different parts of the body. In fact, the body appeared to be "mapped" on the surface of the brain (see FIGURE 1•4). Decades later, when

[**FIGURE 1•4**] Cortical motor map. Stimulation of various parts of the motor cortex causes contraction of muscles in various parts of the body.

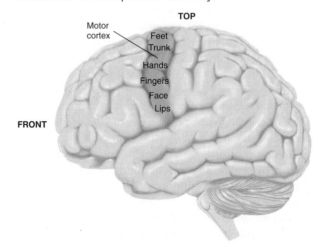

---

doctrine of specific nerve energies Johannes Müller's observation that different nerve fibers convey specific information from one part of the body to the brain or from the brain to one part of the body.

experimental ablation The removal or destruction of a portion of the brain of an experimental animal for the purpose of studying the functions of that region.

techniques of human brain surgery had advanced to the point where painless surgery could be performed on conscious patients, the Canadian neurosurgeon Wilder Penfield would be able to show that highly specific sensory experiences and even memories could be mapped in a similar way.

The work of the German physicist and physiologist Hermann von Helmholtz (1821–1894) did much to demonstrate that mental phenomena could be explained by physiological means. This extremely productive scientist made contributions to both physics and physiology. He actively disassociated himself from natural philosophy, from which many assumptions about the nature of the mind had been derived. Müller, under whom Helmholtz had conducted his first research, believed that human organs were endowed with a vital immaterial force that coordinated physiological behavior, a force that was not subject to experimental investigation. Helmholtz would allow no such assumptions about unproved (and unprovable) phenomena. He advocated a purely scientific approach that would base conclusions on objective investigation and precise measurement.

Before Helmholtz's work, the transmission of impulses through nerves was thought to be as fast as the speed of electricity in wires; under this assumption, transmission would be virtually instantaneous, considering the small distances that impulses have to travel within the human body. Helmholtz successfully measured the speed of the nerve impulse and found that it was only about 90 feet per second, which is considerably slower than the speed of electricity in wires. This finding suggested to later researchers that the nerve impulse is more complex than a simple electrical current passing through a wire, which is indeed true.

Helmholtz next sought to measure the speed of a person's reaction to a physical stimulus. Here, however, he encountered a difficulty that no amount of careful measurement could solve: He discovered that there was too much variability from person to person to formulate the kind of scientific laws that were common in physics. This variability interested scientists who followed him and who tried to explain individual differences in behavior. Because both the velocity of nerve impulses and individuals' reactions to stimuli could be measured, researchers theorized that mental events themselves could be the subject of scientific investigation. Perhaps, if the proper techniques could be developed, it would be possible to investigate what went on within the human brain. Thus, Helmholtz's research was very important in setting the stage for the science of psychology.

In Germany, a contemporary of Helmholtz's, Ernst Weber (1795–1878), began work that led to the development of a method for measuring the magnitude of human sensations. Weber, an anatomist and physiologist, found that people's ability to distinguish between two similar stimuli—such as the brightness of two lights, the heaviness of two objects, or the loudness of two tones—followed orderly laws. This regularity suggested to Weber and his followers that perceptual phenomena could be studied as scientifically as physics or biology. In Chapter 6 we will consider the study of the relation between the physical characteristics of a stimulus and the perceptions produced, a field called **psychophysics.**

Hermann von Helmholtz (1821–1894)

Applications in Education and Therapy

Descartes believed that the mind had *free will*—the ability to make decisions for which it was morally responsible. This viewpoint fit very well with Descartes's Catholic faith, which taught that the individual's soul had to choose between good and evil. But it stood in opposition to a very different, even older, conception—that individual decisions were determined by outside forces, such as the Greek concept of *fate*, the Buddhist concept of *karma*, and the human desires mentioned in the poetic musings of the Persian mathematician Omar Khayyám.

As scientific knowledge expanded, scientists studying the physical world became increasingly precise in predicting phenomena from their antecedent causes. Philosophers began to recognize that a commitment to empiricism and materialism might also imply a commitment to **determinism**—the doctrine that behavior is the result of prior events. Most psychologists assume some form of determinism, in part because of the philosophical and biological developments we've discussed. A third source of this assumption can be found in the political efforts that took place in the nineteenth century to reform society and improve individual well-being. These reformers believed that societal ills could be traced to root causes. They sought to strengthen the factors that caused beneficial effects and eliminate the ones that caused illnesses, ignorance, or unhappiness. This program makes sense only if such cause-and-effect relationships exist in human society.

Producing Change through Education. The period from Descartes's life to that of Helmholtz saw immense changes in Western politics and culture. The American and French revolutions (partly inspired by Locke's writings) ushered in a

---

psychophysics A branch of psychology that measures the quantitative relation between physical stimuli and perceptual experience.

determinism In psychology, the doctrine that behavior is the result of prior events.

new conception of government as an institution to improve the life of its citizens. Education was recognized as an important means of improvement, suggesting a role for the public in an area where such issues had previously been addressed by individuals, churches, or charities. At the same time, medical advances arising from the knowledge of biology promised cures for many diseases, including diseases of the mind.

The notion of change, of betterment, was to become an important topic of study in the 1800s. Educators and physicians began to consider the factors that cause change—whether it be in either a young pupil or a patient. Much of this speculation began with the following incident that, had it occurred in our own times, would have made the headlines of many a supermarket tabloid.

[CASE STUDY] In January of 1800, a boy about 12 years old was found living alone in the forests around Aveyron, France. Captured by the authorities, the boy seemed completely divorced from human contact and unable to speak or understand language. His description seemed to match reports from a neighboring district of a boy living alone in the fields; if so, he had been living without human support for two or three years, getting what food he could by raiding village vegetable patches. He was wearing a tattered shirt when found, but refused all attempts by the villagers to clothe him. He seemed mainly interested in food and a place to sleep. He seemed not to care about human company or any kind of social interaction. One of his caretakers showed him a mirror; the boy tried several times to reach through the mirror to grab the object he saw reflected there (Shattuck, 1980).

The village commissioner, who had been active in the French Revolution, must have found something unique about him, for he arranged to house the boy in an orphanage and recommended that the authorities in Paris be contacted. Eventually, the boy was brought to Paris, where he quickly became the object of observation and debate among French scholars. Some assumed that he had grown up in the wild and saw him as an untainted example of the natural state of humanity. Others claimed that he suffered from a mental disorder. When the argument died down, the poor boy was confined to a Parisian institute for the deaf. He was to live there, or in the company of one of its caretakers, until his death in 1828.

The "Wild Boy of Aveyron" is one of the most famous case studies in the history of psychology. Although it was clear that he was not deaf, the Parisian institute seemed to be the only place where he could be housed. There, his case was taken up by a young physician, Jean-Marc Gaspard Itard (1774–1838), who had just been hired by the institute a few months before. Itard worked with the boy (whom he named

"Victor") for about five years. Those who had studied Victor before merely observed his reactions and recorded his deficiencies of language and habits. Itard sought to discover what Victor could learn. He devised a number of procedures to teach the boy words and recorded his progress. His reports charted the successes and failures of different methods. Itard proceeded, in other words, on the assumption "that what the boy *was* hinged on what he could *become*" (Benzaquén, 2006, p. 167). His description was couched in terms of Victor's development in response to this intervention.

Unfortunately, Victor's deficits in language improved only slightly under Itard's teaching. But Itard's efforts had profound consequences beyond his single pupil. Itard had approached the problem of educating Victor much as a doctor would approach a patient: by identifying the problem and devising a procedure to cure it. Itard stressed the identification of factors that could bring about change and inspired a new approach in Europe in the education of individuals with cognitive disabilities. More broadly, educators began to discuss whether *all* children should be educated by methods suited to their individual needs.

Child education had become an important issue in the United States at about this time. Most states had adopted a system known as the "American Common School" by the late-1800s. Reformers centralized school administration, organized classes according to age, and sought the best curriculum for a given age. Educators, such as Booker T. Washington (1856–1915), and philosophers, such as John Dewey (1859–1952), advocated reforms based on the needs and faculties of children. Dewey, in particular, argued that education must match the way children's abilities developed. He argued that children learned activities that were organized around goals; instruction should match this natural way of learning. A staunch empiricist and a passionate defender of the American idea of democracy, Dewey felt that one aim of education should be to establish habits that integrate the child into the community. His views helped shape the movement in the United States known as Progressive Education.

The Law of Effect. It fell to one of Dewey's professional colleagues to suggest how such habits might be learned. Edward Thorndike (1874–1949) originally studied the behavior of animals, looking at responses that might indicate intelligence. Thorndike noticed that some events, usually those that one would expect to be pleasant, seemed to "stamp in" a response that had just occurred, thereby making it more likely to occur again. Noxious events seemed to "stamp out" the response, or make it less likely to occur. (Nowadays, we call these processes *reinforcement* and *punishment;* they are described in more detail in Chapter 5.) Thorndike defined the **law of effect** as follows:

> Any act which in a given situation produces satisfaction becomes associated with that situation, so that when the situation recurs the act is more likely than before to recur also. Conversely, any act which in a given situation produces discomfort becomes disassociated from that situation, so that when the situation recurs the act is less likely than before to recur. (Thorndike, 1905, p. 203)

---

law of effect   Edward Thorndike's statement that stimuli that occur as a consequence of a response can increase or decrease the likelihood of an organism's making that response again.

The law of effect seemed to provide a universal principle by which habits might be learned: Goals produced satisfaction and caused the action to recur more frequently. Larger activities could be built up from these activities; therefore, an ideal curriculum would be based on identifying the discrete units that make up the task to be learned. Extensive tests—some of which Thorndike himself developed and sold to school boards across the nation—would measure how well these units had been acquired (Kremer, 1976).

If this sounds to you like a step backward from Itard's progressive ideas of individual diagnosis and treatment, you're probably correct. Thorndike's emphasis on "stamping in" responses implied that learning was automatic and inevitable. To be sure, Thorndike did acknowledge the role of instinct and individual differences in behavior. But, he was so fond of his Law of Effect that he had the words *stimulus* and *response* carved above the door of his laboratory, so that students would be reminded of how he connected them.

An alternative view of children's learning was, meanwhile, being developed in Italy by Maria Montessori (1870–1952). At a time when teaching was virtually the only profession open to women, Montessori decided to enter medical school and become a doctor, an accomplishment that must have taken extraordinary perseverance. For example, it was considered improper for a woman student to see a naked body in the presence of males, so Montessori was banished from the classroom during dissections; she had to do them herself, alone, at night, surrounded by cadavers. Despite such hardships and harassments, Montessori became the first woman in Italy to earn a medical degree (Kremer, 1976).

Ironically, it is as a teacher that she is best known today. Appointed to administer an institution for children with de-velopmental disabilities, Montessori discovered Itard's work with Victor. She applied Itard's approach to individualized instruction with considerable success. Reflecting on these results, Montessori wondered whether children without such disabilities would also benefit from this approach. She received a chance to test these theories when she was asked to organize a school for poor preschool children near Rome. Montessori added some innovations of her own and developed a system now known as the *Montessori Method*. This method was based on her belief that children matured through stages: They were sensitive to different kinds of instruction at specific age ranges. Education was best when it provided exercises that matched the competency of the child at that stage. And, in contrast to Thorndike's emphasis on rewards as the basis for learning, Montessori felt that extrinsic rewards actually interfered with a child's natural incentive to learn. Montessori also believed that movement was closely related to thought, and encouraged her pupils to move around in the classroom.

Montessori attracted considerable attention in Europe, but her work had little effect on American educational practices. Montessori herself may have been part of the problem: She was a bit of an autocrat and insisted that only she could train teachers in her methods. But it's also the case that Thorndike's philosophy of learning fit better with developing trends in psychology. We'll examine these in the next section. As a consequence, it's likely that the school system you experienced from elementary grade to high school was shaped more by Thorndike than by Montessori (Lillard, 2005).

Regardless of her lack of success in North America, Montessori may have had an influence on a very important figure in psychology, Jean Piaget (1896–1980). Piaget was born in the French-speaking region of Switzerland and studied biology as a young man. In the early years of his life in Switzerland, he taught children at a school that used a modified Montessori approach. Like Montessori, he was struck by the way a child's competency to understand depended on his or her age. It wasn't just that a younger child made errors that an older child would not; what impressed Piaget was that younger children made the same *kinds* of errors. Piaget's immense influence on developmental psychology resulted from his ability to explain these systematic errors by a theory of cognitive development. Piaget's work will be described in Chapter 12.

Producing Change through Psychotherapy Before Itard took responsibility for the care of Victor, the boy had been examined by Phillippe Pinel (1745–1826). Also a physician, Pinel influenced how psychology thought about change, but in a different direction: He is now widely regarded as the father of psychiatry, the medical specialty that treats mental disorders.

Prior to Pinel's time, the care of people with mental illness was largely considered a responsibility of their family. Their treatment, typically by family members who feared or loathed their illness, could be abominable. Visitors to such households often told of how relatives would lock "the insane" in filthy cages, or chain them in pigsties. These reports eventually prompted activist governments to look for solutions,

Maria Montessori (1870–1952)

and to build asylums where persons with mental illness could be centrally cared for. Pinel was hired by the Revolutionary government of France to administer one such facility, the Salpêtrière hospital in Paris.

Pinel introduced some limited humanitarian reforms to the Salpêtrière, but his main influence was to propose that an asylum could, with proper practices, become a therapeutic institution. He and his followers tried new approaches to restore the cognitive abilities of an inmate. Mostly, these approaches were social interventions, such as long conversations with a therapist or poetry readings. They were based on the belief that mental illness had a social cause and could be cured by similar factors.

For a number of reasons, the number of asylums grew rapidly during the 1800s, along with the number of people committed to them (Shorter, 1997). It could be argued that many of these people did not truly have a mental illness, but were placed there for other reasons. Among this suspect category were the women of one ward of the Salpêtrière who were admitted with a collection of symptoms such as memory loss, intermittent paralysis, and insensitivity to painful stimuli. These women were considered to be suffering from a nervous disorder which had been given the label *hysteria*. Beginning in 1862, a neurologist by the name of Jean-Martin Charcot (1825–1893) developed a clinical practice based on observations from the ward. Neurology as a medical specialty deals with the treatment of diseases of the nervous system and is closely allied with psychiatry. Charcot proposed that hysteria was closely related to the condition produced by hypnosis and treated his patients by hypnotizing them. Although "hysteria" is no longer recognized as a disorder (its symptoms are now ascribed to other mental illnesses), Charcot's linking of hypnosis to the treatment of a mental illness was to have important consequences. We'll explore hypnosis in Chapter 9 and its place in psychotherapy in Chapter 17.

QUESTIONS TO CONSIDER

1. Explaining things, whether scientifically or through myths and legends, seems to be a human need. Can you think of an occasion in your recent experience where either you or someone talking to you used an animistic explanation? Do you think these are more common in everyday speech than the scientific explanations we have discussed?

2. Which of the philosophers, scientists, educators, or therapists described in this section appeal to you the most? Would you like to know more about any of them and their times? What questions would you like to ask these people if it were possible to meet them?

3. Thorndike exerted immense influence on the development of schools in America during the early 1900s. Do you see any vestiges of his beliefs about habits and the law of effect in your own schooling experience?

focus On

What Are the Roots of Psychology Within Chinese Culture?

Even though much of psychology's historical milestones took place in the western hemisphere, scholars of the eastern hemisphere have also reflected on human behavior, its causes, and its normal development.

China possesses one of the oldest civilizations on earth, so it is not surprising that there is much speculation on psychological matters in its history. Like Western psychology, many aspects of Chinese understanding of human nature derived from philosophical systems; however, in the case of China, these were primarily concerned with moral philosophy rather than the philosophy of knowledge.

One of the earliest classical texts in Chinese philosophy, the *I Ching,* is traditionally ascribed to teachings and practices from about 2800 BCE. Although it is usually regarded by Westerners as a system for telling the future, the Swiss psychologist Carl Jung (1875–1961) argued that it reflects a profoundly different world view than that of Western science. In contrast to the Western preoccupation with causal factors, the *I Ching* seeks to link the individual to the random, chance factors present at the time the prediction was made (Jung, 1967). If so, then much of Chinese philosophical speculation on human nature can be seen as a way of reconciling humans to the potential conflict and chaos around them. There have been three distinct systems that have influenced Chinese intellectual development, each associated with an Asian philosophy: Confucianism, Taoism, and Buddhism.

Confucius (551–479 BCE) developed guidelines for human relationships according to a hierarchical social structure: the authoritarian patriarchal family. The key to order and harmony in the midst of conflict and change, said Confucius, was in learning, throughout a lifetime, the habits by which one adapted oneself to the family. He believed that all people were born naturally identical, but that, through education, they reached their proper station in life. The habits they learned adjusted both individuals and societies to a utopian ideal. Confucius's psychology, therefore, identified certain traits as characteristics of the fully developed human being: "As a philosophy of life, we have generally associated with Confucianism the quiet virtues of patience, pacifism, compromise, the golden mean, reverence for ancestors, the aged, and the learned" (Jing & Fu, 2001, p. 408).

Taoism can be traced to the writings of two philosophers, Lao Tzu (298–212 BCE) and Chuang Tzu (369–286 BCE). Similar to the way many Greek philosophers described the world, Taoism taught that underneath the natural world of chaos there was a unifying principle of reconciliation: the *Tao.* Through the practice of meditation and suppression of violent emotions one could order one's life according to the Tao.

The third system originated with the Nepali teacher Siddhartha Gautama (ca. 566–486 BCE). As his followers believe, while meditating on the nature of suffering,

The Buddha's teaching emphasized proper living and respect for sentient beings as the desired conduct of human behavior.

Gautama achieved enlightenment, becoming a being known as the Buddha. The Buddha described his achievement as a recognition of four "noble truths": (1) that suffering is universal; (2) that it arises from desire; (3) that eliminating desire can eliminate suffering; and (4) that meditation and wisdom can eliminate desire. The Buddha's teachings reached China in several distinctive forms (e.g., Tibetan Buddhism can be markedly different from Zen Buddhism), but like Confucianism and Taoism, it stressed a particular mode of conduct, called the Eightfold Path: right understanding, thought, speech, action, livelihood, effort, mindfulness, and concentration (Lawson, Graham, & Baker, 2007). The Buddha taught that proper living and the respect for all sentient beings would achieve a permanent state of emptiness and a release from the cycle of suffering present in the world.

These three systems were moral philosophies. Unlike most Western philosophies that influenced psychology, Confucianism, Taoism, and Buddhism were based on an ideal goal to be achieved: For Confucianism, it was a harmonious society; for Taoism, reconciliation of contradiction; and for Buddhism, emptiness. Conduct, whether it was in action or in thought, was considered in terms of its purpose—to achieve those goals. Western psychology, by and large, considered questions of morality to be secondary to questions of origin and causation. Purpose was a result of other factors, such as the Law of Effect. Nevertheless, it is interesting to note that, by the late 1800s and early 1900s, Western psychology, through the work of Montessori and Thorndike, had begun to recognize the significance of education and habit formation in the development of the individual. When it became known in China, John Dewey's work was quite popular. Higgins and Zheng (2002) have also suggested that the Confucian system of examinations to determine one's place in the Chinese civil service sector may have been the origin of the mass testing movement in the United States.

Major Trends in the Development of Psychology

Psychology as a science, as distinct from philosophy and biology, began in Germany in the late nineteenth century with Wilhelm Wundt (1832–1920). Wundt was the first person to call himself a psychologist. He shared the conviction of other German scientists that all aspects of nature, including the human mind, could be studied scientifically. His book *Principles of Physiological Psychology* was the first textbook of psychology; and Wundt is generally considered to have started, in 1879, the first laboratory devoted to the study of psychological phenomena.

You may have already noted the high preponderance of German scholars in our survey of early influences on psychology. The fact that Germany was the birthplace of psychology had as much to do with social, political, and economic influences as with the abilities of the nation's scientists and scholars. The German university system was well established, and professors were highly respected members of society. The academic tradition in Germany emphasized a scientific approach to a large number of subject areas, such as history, phonetics, archaeology, aesthetics, and literature. Thus, in contrast to French and British scholars, who adopted the more traditional, philosophical approach to the study of the human mind, German scholars were open to the possibility that the human mind could be studied scientifically. German science also emphasized the importance of classification. We will see the significance of this to psychology shortly. Experimental physiology, one of the most important roots of experimental psychology, was well established in Germany. It was in this climate that Müller, Helmholtz, and Wundt conducted their research.

Wilhelm Wundt (1832–1920)

Structuralism

Wundt defined psychology as the "science of immediate experience." This approach was labeled **structuralism** by one of his students. Its subject matter was the *structure* of the mind, a structure built from the elements of consciousness, such as ideas and sensations. The raw material of structuralism was supplied by trained observers who described their own experiences. The observers were taught to engage in **introspection** (literally, "looking within"); they observed stimuli and described their experiences. Wundt and his associates made inferences about the nature of mental processes by seeing how changes in the stimuli caused changes in trained observers' verbal reports.

Like George Berkeley, Wundt was particularly interested in the way basic sensory information gave rise to complex perceptions. His trained observers attempted to ignore complex perceptions and to report only the elementary data. For example, the sensation of seeing a patch of red is immediate and elementary, whereas the perception of an apple is complex.

Wundt was an ambitious and prolific scientist who wrote many books and trained many other scientists in his laboratory. Many of these brought the new conception of psychology to North America, where it created quite a sensation. For example, in 1889, one of Wundt's protégés, James Mark Baldwin (1861–1934), was appointed professor of psychology at the University of Toronto. His employment was quite controversial: Students and prominent faculty members petitioned against his appointment, a newspaper denounced his psychological training in an editorial, and the matter almost caused a political scandal (Hoff, 1992). Baldwin survived this controversy, however, and later joined the faculty of Princeton University. There he helped start a journal, *Psychological Review,* that today is one of the premier journals in psychology. Other psychologists trained by Wundt, such as Edward Bradford Titchener, also became leaders of American psychology. However, Wundt's method did not survive the test of time; structuralism died out in the early twentieth century. The major problem with his approach was the difficulty of reporting the raw data of sensation, unmodified by experience. Also, the emphasis of psychological investigation shifted from the study of the mind to the study of behavior. More recently, psychologists have resumed the study of the human mind, but better methods are now available for studying it. Although structuralism has

been supplanted, Wundt's contribution must be acknowledged. He established psychology as an experimental science, independent of philosophy. He trained many psychologists, a number of whom established their own laboratories and continued to advance the new discipline.

Functionalism

The next major trend in psychology was known as **functionalism.** This approach was in large part a reaction against the structuralism of Wundt. Structuralists were interested in what they called the *components* of consciousness (ideas and sensations); functionalists focused on the *processes* of conscious activity (perceiving and learning). Functionalism grew from the new perspective on nature supplied by Charles Darwin (1809–1882) and his followers. Proponents stressed the biological significance (the purpose, or *function*) of natural processes, including behavior. The emphasis was on overt, observable behavior, not on private mental events.

Darwin's theory, which said that evolution occurred in response to the natural selection of inheritable traits, was important to psychology because it suggested that scientists could best explain behavior, like other biological characteristics, by understanding its role in the adaptation of an organism to its environment. Thus, behavior has a biological context. Darwin assembled evidence that behavior could be inherited. In *The Expression of the Emotions in Man and Animals,* published in 1872, he proposed that the facial gestures animals make in expressing emotions were descended from movements that previously had other functions. New areas of exploration were opened for psychologists by the ideas that an evolutionary continuity existed among various animal species and that behaviors, like parts of the body, had evolutionary histories. Darwin's cousin, Francis Galton, was one of these pioneers. He was one of the first to measure human traits objectively. The public's interest in measuring human abilities was so strong that Galton was able to set up a booth at an international exhibition in the 1880s and charge people for the privilege of being tested. (See FIGURE 1•5.)

The most important psychologist to embrace functionalism was the American scholar William James (1842–1910). As James said, "My thinking is first, last, and always for the sake of my doing." That is, thinking was not an end in itself; its function was to produce useful behavior. Although James did not produce any important experimental research during his tenure as professor of philosophy (later, professor of psychology) at Harvard University, his teaching and writing influenced those who followed him. His theory of emotion is one of the most famous and durable psychological theories. It is still quoted in modern textbooks (you will read about it later in Chapter 13 of this book). Psychologists still find it worthwhile to read James's writings; he supplied ideas for experiments that continue to sound fresh and new today.

---

structuralism   The system of experimental psychology that began with Wilhelm Wundt; it emphasized introspective analysis of sensation and perception.

introspection   Literally, "looking within" in an attempt to describe memories, perceptions, cognitive processes, or motivations.

functionalism   An approach to understanding species' behaviors and other processes in terms of their biological significance; this approach stresses the usefulness of such processes with respect to survival and reproductive success.

[FIGURE 1·5] Galton advertised his project to collect data on human abilities. Interest was so keen that he even charged people for their participation.

ANTHROPOMETRIC LABORATORY

For the measurement in various ways of Human Form and Faculty.

Entered from the Science Collection of the S. Kensington Museum.

This laboratory is established by Mr. Francis Galton for the following purposes:—

1. For the use of those who desire to be accurately measured in many ways, either to obtain timely warning of remediable faults in development, or to learn their powers.

2. For keeping a methodical register of the principal measurements of each person, of which he may at any future time obtain a copy under reasonable restrictions. His initials and date of birth will be entered in the register, but not his name. The names are indexed in a separate book.

3. For supplying information on the methods, practice, and uses of human measurement.

4. For anthropometric experiment and research, and for obtaining data for statistical discussion.

Charges for making the principal measurements:
THREEPENCE each, to those who are already on the Register.
FOURPENCE each, to those who are not:— one page of the Register will thenceforward be assigned to them, and a few extra measurements will be made, chiefly for future identification.

The Superintendent is charged with the control of the laboratory and with determining in each case, which, if any, of the extra measurements may be made, and under what conditions.

H. & W. Brown, Printers, 20 Fulham Road, S.W.

Unlike structuralism, functionalism was not supplanted. Functionalist textbooks were widely used in departments of psychology during their early years, and the tenets of functionalism strongly influenced the development of psychological explanations. One functionalist, James Angell (1869–1949), described its basic principles:

1. Functional psychology is the study of mental operations, not of mental structures. (For example, the mind remembers; it does not contain a memory.) It is not enough to compile a catalogue of what the mind does; we must try to understand what the mind accomplishes by this doing.

2. Mental processes must be studied not as isolated and independent events but as part of the biological activity of the organism. These processes are aspects of the organism's adaptation to the environment and are a product of its evolutionary history. For example, the fact that we are conscious implies that consciousness has adaptive value for our species.

3. Functional psychology studies the relation between the environment and the response of the organism to the environment. There is no meaningful distinction between mind and body; they are part of the same entity.

Consider these points when you read the section on behaviorism.

Freud's Psychodynamic Theory

While psychology was developing as a fledgling science, Sigmund Freud (1856–1939) was formulating a theory of human behavior that would greatly affect psychology and radically influence intellectuals of all kinds. Freud began his career as a neurologist, so his work was firmly rooted in biology. He soon became interested in behavioral and emotional problems and even attended one of Charcot's demonstrations on hypnosis at the Salpêtrière hospital. Freud was impressed with Charcot's demonstration of how a psychological event like hypnosis could cause a presumably neurological disorder like hysteria.

Freud's theory will be detailed in Chapter 14; we discuss him here only to mark his place in the history of psychology. His theory of the mind included structures, but his structuralism was quite different from Wundt's. Freud devised his concepts of ego, superego, id, and other mental structures through talking with his patients, not through laboratory experiments. His hypothetical mental operations included many that were unconscious and hence not available to introspection. And unlike Wundt, Freud emphasized function; his mental structures served biological drives and instincts and reflected our animal nature.

Psychology in Transition

Psychology as a science was to take a radical turn in the early decades of the twentieth century. Before we consider this change, it might help you to see how the different intellectual contributions of the structuralists and the functionalists had shaped the way psychology was practiced at universities in North America.

The controversy over James Mark Baldwin's appointment at Toronto quickly died down, helped in part when Baldwin's rival for the job was appointed to a similar position. Baldwin was given a rather handsome budget of $1,550 for equipment, which he promptly used to create one of the first psychological laboratories in North America

James Mark Baldwin (1861–1934)

Mary Whiton Calkins (1867–1930)

(Baldwin, 1892). Like the laboratories of Wundt in Germany and James at Harvard University, the Toronto facility was designed for the experimental investigation of the mind, with attention to the control of noise and light. Baldwin went immediately to work in his new environment, even publishing a paper on handedness based on observations of his infant daughter.

The new emphasis on experimentation and observation was becoming prominent in the classroom as well. Mary Whiton Calkins (1867–1930), for example, wrote a lengthy description of the psychology course she taught to seniors at Wellesley College (Calkins, 1892). Her students studied the anatomy of the brain and received laboratory exercises in the dissection of lamb brains, the measurement of sensation, and the comparison of associations to simple words. Calkins reported that the experiments on taste "were so unpopular that I should never repeat them in a general class of students who are not specializing in the subject." This leads the modern reader to wonder just what it was that she asked her students to taste.

Through the efforts of both researchers and instructors, psychology became part of university curricula throughout the United States. Professors of psychology joined academic societies and became recognized as members of an emerging scientific discipline. Wundt had founded the science of psy-

behaviorism   A movement in psychology that asserts that the only proper subject matter for scientific study in psychology is observable behavior.

chology on the assumption that it should describe the contents of the mind. By the beginning of the twentieth century, however, psychologists like James and Baldwin had returned to the problem that vexed Descartes: How do we understand the actions that the mind supposedly determines?

Behaviorism

The next major trend that we will consider, behaviorism, likewise reflected this concern with action. Behaviorists went farther than James or Baldwin, however, by rejecting the special nature of mental events and by denying that unobservable and unverifiable mental events were properly the subject matter of psychology. Behaviorists believe that because psychology is the study of observable behavior, mental events, which cannot be observed, are outside the realm of psychology. **Behaviorism** is thus the study of the relation between people's environments and their behavior, without appeal to hypothetical events occurring within their heads.

We have already examined one of the first behaviorists—Edward Thorndike, who formulated the law of effect. The law of effect is certainly in the functionalist tradition. It asserts that the consequences of a behavior act back upon the organism, affecting the likelihood that the behavior will occur again. This process is very similar to the principle of natural selection that is the basis of Darwin's theory of evolution. Just as organisms that successfully adapt to their environments are more likely to survive and breed, so behaviors that cause useful outcomes become more likely to recur.

Thorndike insisted that the subject matter of psychology was behavior. But his explanations contained mentalistic terms. For example, in his law of effect he spoke of "satisfaction," which is certainly not a phenomenon that can be directly observed. Later behaviorists recognized this contradiction and replaced terms such as *satisfaction* and *discomfort* with more objective concepts that reflected only the behavior.

Another major figure in the development of the behavioristic trend was not a psychologist at all but a physiologist: Ivan Pavlov (1849–1936), a Russian who studied the physiology of digestion (for which he later received a Nobel Prize). In

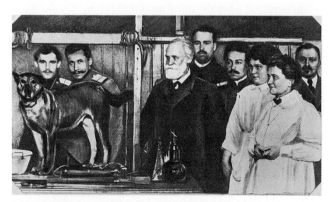

Ivan Pavlov (1849–1936) in his laboratory with some of his collaborators. His research revealed valuable information about the principles of learning.

John B. Watson (1878–1958)

the course of studying the stimuli that produce salivation, Pavlov discovered that hungry dogs would salivate at the sight of the attendant who brought in their dishes of food. Although first labeling this phenomenon a "psychic reflex," Pavlov soon traced it to the experience the dog had received. Pavlov found that a dog would salivate at a completely arbitrary stimulus, such as the sound of a bell, if the stimulus was quickly followed by the delivery of a bit of food into the animal's mouth.

Pavlov's discovery had profound significance for psychology. He showed that through experience, an animal could learn to make a response to a stimulus that had never caused this response before. This ability might explain how organisms learn cause-and-effect relations in the environment. In contrast, Thorndike's law of effect suggested an explanation for the adaptability of an individual's behavior to its particular environment. So, from Thorndike's and Pavlov's studies, two important behavioral principles had been discovered.

Behaviorism as a formal school of psychology began with the publication of a book by John B. Watson (1878–1958), *Psychology from the Standpoint of a Behaviorist.* Watson, a professor of psychology at Johns Hopkins University, was a popular teacher and writer and a very convincing advocate of the behavioral perspective. Even after leaving Johns Hopkins for a highly successful career in advertising, he continued to lecture and write magazine articles about psychology.

According to Watson, psychology was a natural science whose domain was restricted to observable events: the behavior of organisms. Watson believed that the elements of consciousness studied by the structuralists were too subjective to lend themselves to scientific investigation. He defined psychology as the objective study of stimuli and the behavior they produced. He reduced even thinking to a form of behavior—"talking to ourselves":

> Now what can we observe? We can observe behavior— *what the organism does or says.* And let us point out at once: that saying is doing—that is, behaving. Speaking overtly or to ourselves (thinking) is just as objective a type of behavior as baseball. (Watson, 1930, p. 6)

Behaviorism is still very much in evidence today in psychology. Its renowned advocates have included B. F. Skinner (1904–1990), one of the most influential psychologists of the twentieth century. But psychologists, including modern behaviorists, have moved away from the strict behaviorism of Watson; mental processes such as imagery and attention are again considered to be proper subject matter for scientific investigation.

In this sense, modern psychologists have moved more toward a view expressed by Margaret Floy Washburn (1871–1939) early in the debate over behavior. Although Washburn (1922) advocated her own version of structuralism, she suggested to behaviorists that they regard introspection itself as a form of behavior that could help them understand the inaccessible processes of mental life. Today, as Washburn would have wished, Watson's emphasis on objectivity in psychological research remains. Even those modern psychologists who most vehemently protest against what they see as the narrowness of behaviorism use the same principles of objectivity to guide their research. As research scientists, they must uphold the principles of objectivity that evolved from empiricism to functionalism to behaviorism. A psychologist who studies private mental events realizes that these events can be studied only indirectly, by means of behavior—verbal reports of inner experiences. Unlike Wundt, present-day psychologists realize that these reports are not pure reflections of these mental events; like other behaviors, these responses can be affected by many factors. Consequently, they strive to maintain an objective stance to ensure that their research findings will be valid and capable of being verified.

Margaret Floy Washburn (1871–1939)

Humanistic Psychology

For many years philosophers and other intellectuals have been concerned with what they see as the special attributes of humanity—free will, spontaneity, creativity, and consciousness. As the science of psychology developed, these phenomena received less attention than others, because researchers could not agree on objective ways to study them. Humanistic psychology developed during the 1950s and 1960s as a reaction against both behaviorism and the psychodynamic approach of Freud. Although psychodynamic theory certainly dealt with mental phenomena that could not be objectively measured, it viewed people as products of their environment and of innate, unconscious forces. Humanistic psychologists insist that human nature goes beyond environmental influences, and they argue that psychologists should study conscious processes, not unconscious drives. In addition, they note that psychoanalytical theory seems preoccupied with disturbed people, ignoring positive phenomena such as happiness, satisfaction, love, and kindness.

Humanistic psychology is an approach to the study of human behavior that emphasizes human experience, choice and creativity, self-realization, and positive growth. Humanistic psychologists emphasize the positive sides of human nature and the potential we all share for personal growth. In general, humanistic psychologists do not believe that we will understand human consciousness and behavior through scientific research. Thus, the humanistic approach has not had a significant influence on psychology as a science. Its greatest impact has been on the development of methods of psychotherapy that are based on a positive and optimistic view of human potential.

Reaction against Behaviorism: The Emphasis on Cognition

Proponents of behaviorism restricted the subject matter of psychology to observable behavior. And, despite their differences from the structuralists, they also tended to analyze behavior by dividing it into smaller elements. Even as behaviorism became the dominant trend in psychology, a contrasting school of thought began to emphasize how unobservable factors influence larger patterns of human consciousness.

This movement began when a German psychologist, Max Wertheimer (1880–1943), bought a toy that presented a series of pictures in rapid succession. Each picture was slightly different from the preceding one, resulting in the impression of continuous motion—like a movie. Wertheimer and his colleagues suggested that psychological processes provided the continuity. They therefore attempted to discover the *organization* of cognitive processes, not their elements. They called their approach **Gestalt psychology.** *Gestalt* is a German word that roughly translates into "unified form." Gestalt psychologists insisted that perceptions resulted from patterns of interactions among many elements, in the same way we recognize a song by the relations between the notes rather than by the individual notes themselves.

Although the Gestalt school of psychology no longer exists, its insistence that the elements of an experience are organized into larger units was very influential. These organizational processes are not directly observable, yet they still determine behavior. Since the 1960s, many psychologists likewise have begun to reject the restrictions of behaviorism and have turned to the study of consciousness, feelings, imagery, and other private events.

Much of *cognitive psychology* (described in the first section of this chapter) analyzes mental activities in terms of **information processing.** According to this approach information received through the senses is "processed" by various systems of neurons in the brain. Some systems store the information in the form of memory; other systems control behavior. Some systems operate automatically and unconsciously, whereas others are conscious and require effort. Because the information processing approach was first devised to describe the operations of complex physical systems such as computers, the modern model of the human brain is, for most cognitive psychologists, the computer. As you will learn in Chapter 7, however, another model—the artificial neural network—is beginning to replace the computer.

Although cognitive psychologists now study mental structures and operations, they have not gone back to the introspective methods that structuralists such as Wundt employed. They use objective research methods, just as behaviorists do. For example, several modern psychologists have studied the phenomenon of imagery. If you close your eyes and imagine what the open pages of this book look like, you are viewing a mental image of what you have previously seen. This image exists only within your brain, and it can be experienced by you and no one else. We have no way of knowing whether your images are like ours any more than we know whether the color red looks the same to you as it does to us. The experience of imagery cannot be shared in a scientific sense.

But behaviors that are based on images can indeed be measured. For example, one researcher (Kosslyn, 1973, 1975) asked a group of people to memorize several drawings. Then he asked the participants to imagine one of the drawings, focusing their attention on a particular feature of the image. Next, he asked a question about a detail of the image that was either "near" the point they were focusing on or "far" from it. For example, if they were picturing a boat, he might ask them to imagine that they were looking at its stern (back). Then he might ask whether the boat had a rudder at the stern, or whether a rope was fastened to its bow (front).

humanistic psychology An approach to the study of human behavior that emphasizes human experience, choice and creativity, self-realization, and positive growth.

Gestalt psychology A movement in psychology that emphasized that cognitive processes could be understood by studying their organization, not their elements.

information processing A model used by cognitive psychologists to explain the workings of the brain; according to this model, information received through the senses is processed by systems of neurons in the brain.

[FIGURE 1•6] A drawing used in the imagery study by Kosslyn.

(From Kosslyn, S. M. [1973]. *Perception and Psychophysics, 14,* 90–94. Reprinted with permission.of Psychonomic Society.)

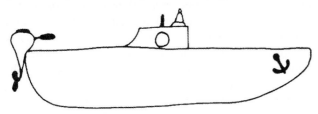

Kosslyn found that people could very quickly answer a question about a feature of the boat that was near the place they were focusing on, but that they took longer to answer a question about a part that was farther away. It was as if they had to scan their mental image to get from one place to the other. (See FIGURE 1•6.)

Because we cannot observe what is happening within a person's head, the concept of imagery remains hypothetical. However, this hypothetical concept very nicely explains and organizes some concrete results—namely, the time it takes for a person to give an answer. Although the explanation for the results of this experiment is phrased in terms of private events (mental images), the behavioral data (how long it takes to answer the questions) are empirical and objective.

Reaction against Behaviorism: The Emphasis on Neurobiology

Although the first scientific roots of psychology were in biology and physiology, the biological approach to behavior has become so prevalent since the early 1990s that it can properly be called a revolution. During the early and mid-twentieth century, the dominance of behaviorism led to a de-emphasis of biological factors in the study of behavior. At the time scientists had no way of studying what went on in the brain, but that did not prevent people from spinning elaborate theories of how the brain controlled behavior. Behaviorists rejected such speculation. They acknowledged that the brain controlled behavior but argued that because we could not see what was happening inside the brain, we should refrain from inventing physiological explanations that could not be verified.

One of the few dissenters from the prevailing behaviorist view of the time was a Canadian psychologist, Donald Hebb (1904–1985). Hebb had graduated from Dalhousie University with aspirations of being a novelist. After a brief stint teaching in Quebec, he was admitted as a part-time student at McGill University. Hebb was inspired by the physiological approach to psychology then taught at McGill by a professor who had worked with Pavlov. Challenging the behaviorists, Hebb argued that behavioral and mental phenomena could be related directly to brain activity. In his most

Donald Hebb (1904–1985)

influential work, he suggested several simple principles by which the nervous system organized itself into special "circuits" that could represent mental activity (Hebb, 1949).

Cognitive psychologists had inherited from early behaviorists a suspicion of the value of biology in explaining behavior. Thus, the cognitive revolution did not lead to a renewed interest in biology. But the extraordinary advances in neurobiology in the late twentieth century revolutionized psychology and vindicated Hebb's viewpoint (Klein, 1999). And many of Hebb's students and associates were at the forefront of subsequent developments in psychology (Adair, Paivio, & Ritchie, 1996).

Neurobiologists (biologists who study the nervous system) and scientists and engineers in allied fields have developed ways to study the brain that were unthinkable just a few decades ago. We can study fine details of nerve cells, discover their interconnections, analyze the chemicals they use to communicate with one another, produce drugs that block the action of these chemicals or mimic their effects, see the internal structure of a living human brain, and measure the activity of different parts of the brain—regions as small as a few cubic millimeters—while people are watching visual displays, listening to words, or performing various kinds of cognitive tasks. In addition, it seems as though every day we learn of new genes that play roles in particular behaviors, and drugs that are designed to duplicate or block the effects of these genes.

QUESTIONS TO CONSIDER

1. Although the science of psychology began in Germany, it soon migrated to the United States, where it flourished. Can you think of any characteristics of American society that might explain why psychology developed faster here than elsewhere in the world?

2. As you have learned, psychologists study a wide variety of behaviors. Do you think that there are any behaviors that psychologists cannot explain (or should not try to explain)?

Epilogue

The Brain's Future

For Laura and her group, reading Kurzweil's book accomplished what I had hoped. Kurzweil attempted to construct a utopian vision of the future based on the scientific assumptions that have shaped contemporary psychology: historical themes such as materialism, empiricism, and determinism. It's a challenging notion to push the working assumptions of a science into a prescription for the future. Laura and her partners in this project had to consider whether our current knowledge from the science of behavior is up to the task.

Ironically, fifty years before Kurzweil, the behaviorist B.F. Skinner had likewise written a utopian book (a novel, in this case) in which he proposed that psychology could revolutionize human society (Skinner, 1948). Kurzweil's work extends Skinner's by introducing the concept of replicating our nervous system with machinery, but the issue is the same and goes all the way back to Descartes: How far can we generalize our knowledge? If you want to hear the answer that Laura's group reached, you can hear their program at http//www.cjsr.ualberta.ca/news/news.php?s=p400 ▪

CHAPTER SUMMARY

What Is Psychology?

Psychology is the science of behavior, and psychologists study a large variety of behaviors in humans and other animals. They attempt to explain these behaviors by studying the events that cause them. Different psychologists are interested in different behaviors and in different categories of causes.

This section identified 11 different approaches to understanding the causes of behavior. Physiological psychologists study the role of the brain in behavior. Comparative psychologists study the evolution of behavior by comparing the behavioral capacities of various species of animals. Behavior geneticists study the role of genetics in behavior. Cognitive psychologists study complex human behaviors such as perception, memory, and attention. Cognitive neuroscientists study the brain mechanisms responsible for cognition. Developmental psychologists study the development of behavior throughout the life span. Social psychologists study the effects people have on one another's

behavior. Personality psychologists study individual differences in temperament and patterns of behavior. Evolutionary psychologists study the influence of natural selection on behavior. Cross-cultural psychologists study the impact of culture on behavior. Clinical psychologists study the causes and treatment of mental disorders and problems of adjustment.

In addition to thinking of psychology as a scientific discipline, we can also consider it as a profession, in which psychologists apply their knowledge of behavior to the solution of certain kinds of problems. Two recent applications discussed here were the problem of constructing facial drawings from eyewitness reports and the design of artificial limbs for amputees.

The Growth of Psychology as a Science

By the mid-nineteenth century, philosophy had embraced two concepts that would lead to the objective investigation of the human mind: the principles of materialism and empiricism. Materialism maintained that the mind was made of matter. Thus, all natural phenomena, including human behavior, could be explained in terms of physical entities: the interaction of matter and energy. Empiricism emphasized that all knowledge was acquired by means of sensory experience; no knowledge was innate. By directing attention to the tangible, sensory components of human activity, these concepts laid the foundation for a scientific approach in psychology. At this time, the divisions between science and philosophy were still blurred. Subsequent developments in the natural sciences, especially in biology and physiology, provided the necessary ingredients that, united with the critical, analytical components of philosophy, formed the scientific discipline of psychology. These ingredients were experimentation and verification.

Materialism implies the doctrine of determinism, which is opposed to the concept of free will. Determinism makes possible the prediction that an outcome will follow some cause.

Education and psychiatry became matters of public concern during the early 1800s. Both fields emphasized the causal factors that can produce change. Progressive education stressed the natural development of the child and sought methods of teaching that would match the way children normally learned. Thorndike proposed the law of effect as a principle of this learning, while Montessori argued that different methods were appropriate to different ages of a child. Psychiatry saw mental illness as possibly having social causes and explored therapies that relied either relied on either normal human discourse or specialized techniques such as hypnosis.

Major Trends in the Development of Psychology

Psychology has come a long way in a relatively short time. The first laboratory of experimental psychology was established in 1879, less than one and a half centuries ago. Wilhelm

Wundt established psychology as a discipline that was independent of philosophy. Wundt's approach was based on the premise that, through introspection, the mind's contents could be described. Even though Wundt's structuralism did not last, interest in psychology continued to grow. The discipline took on added breadth and scope with the emergence of functionalism, which stressed the adaptive value of biological phenomena. Functionalism gave rise to the objectivity of behaviorism, and scientific objectivity still dominates the way we do research.

The cognitive revolution began because some psychologists believed that a strict emphasis on observable behavior missed the complexity of human cognition and behavior—an opinion that modern behaviorists contest. The biological revolution in psychology is manifested in the increased interest of psychologists in all fields—not just physiological psychology—in the role of biological factors in behavior.

succeed with PEARSON mypsychlab

Visit MyPsychLab for practice quizzes, flashcards, and dozens of videos and animated tutorials, including the following items you can find in the "Multimedia Library":

Even the Rat was White: Robert Guthrie
Women and the Field of Psychology:
    Florence Denmark

Psychologists at Work
The Pseudoscience of Astrology

KEY TERMS

animism, *p. 8*

behavior genetics, *p. 5*

behaviorism, *p. 20*

causal event, *p. 4*

clinical psychology, *p. 6*

cognitive neuroscience, *p. 5*

cognitive psychology, *p. 5*

comparative psychology, *p. 5*

cross-cultural psychology, *p. 6*

determinism, *p. 13*

developmental
    psychology, *p. 5*

doctrine of specific
    nerve energies, *p. 12*

dualism, *p. 10*

empiricism, *p. 10*

evolutionary psychology, *p. 6*

experimental ablation, *p. 12*

functionalism, *p. 18*

Gestalt psychology, *p. 22*

humanistic psychology, *p. 22*

information processing, *p. 22*

introspection, *p. 18*

law of effect, *p. 14*

materialism, *p. 10*

model, *p. 10*

personality psychology, *p. 6*

physiological psychology, *p. 5*

psychology, *p. 3*

psychophysics, *p. 13*

rationalism, *p. 10*

reflex, *p. 9*

social psychology, *p. 5*

structuralism, *p. 18*

SUGGESTIONS FOR FURTHER READING

Kurzweil, R. (1999). *The age of spiritual machines: When computers exceed human intelligence.* New York: Viking Penguin.

Lawson, R.B., Graham, J.E., & Baker, K.M. (2007). *A history of psychology: Globalization, ideas, and applications.* Upper Saddle River: NJ: Pearson Prentice Hall.

Reese, R.J. (2005). *America's public schools: From the common school to "No Child Left Behind."* Baltimore, MD: Johns Hopkins University Press.

Shorter, E. (1997). *A history of psychiatry.* New York: John Wiley & Sons.

The book by Lawson, Graham, and Baker is an excellent history of psychology. Particularly notable is its inclusiveness: There are special chapters on the role of women in the history of psychology, the contribution of black Americans, and the development of psychology outside Europe and America. Reese's book is not centrally concerned with psychology, but you may find it of interest to know why your elementary, junior high, and high schools were organized the way they were. Shorter's work is a history of the medical profession of psychiatry. It skips around, but provides some interesting anecdotes on major figures.

The Ways a Means of Psychology

Prologue

Justine's Experiment

Justine's parents operate a small company that employs five people. The employees assemble custom equipment for oil exploration companies. The summer after her first year of college, Justine decided to put her skills to work by trying to increase the company's productivity. She reasoned that if the employees could complete more pieces of equipment per day, the company would be more profitable for her parents and the workers themselves would benefit through their profit-sharing plan.

One evening Justine stayed at the assembly laboratory to work on one of the devices herself. After a couple of hours, her neck was strained and her arms and hands tingled from maintaining a bent position over the bench at which she was working. Justine convinced her parents to invest in height-adjustable chairs to replace the existing stationary seats. When the new chairs arrived, she adjusted them so that each employee seemed to be at a comfortable position. Justine held a meeting with the employees and told them that she thought the new chairs would reduce discomfort and therefore permit them to be more productive. She said that she would keep track of how many units they finished over the next several days and would let them know if the chairs had helped. At the end of the week, the employees eagerly asked Justine how they had done. Justine proudly announced that they had completed 20% more of the testing units than they had during the same amount of time before the chairs arrived. The workers congratulated her for her insight and help.

Over the next week Justine continued to check in with the employees and to collect data. She then got together with her friend Lawrence, who had recently taken a statistics course. Lawrence helped her conduct a formal statistical test to compare the production figures for the seven workdays before Justine introduced the new chairs and the seven workdays afterward. They found that productivity had increased significantly more than would be expected by chance. Her intervention had worked, or so it appeared. Justine stopped her daily visits with the employees.

A few weeks later, though, Justine happened to look at the employees' production figures and was

Is it a change in the type of chair that can improve productivity, or the prospect of any change?

disappointed to find that productivity had fallen to the same level as before the new chairs arrived. Justine decided to start over with the old chairs, monitor the employees' output, and then reintroduce the adjustable chairs to see what would happen. After a week with the old chairs, productivity inexplicably increased 20% again. Justine was understandably perplexed. Increased productivity with the old chairs? Justine gave up on her project. What had happened? Justine was sure that she had diligently applied the scientific method and that her intervention should have had clear-cut results. ■

The goal of psychology as a science is the explanation of behavior. As scientists, the vast majority of psychologists believe that behavior, like other natural phenomena, can be studied objectively. The scientific method permits us to discover the nature and causes of behavior. This chapter will show you how the scientific method is used in psychological research. What you learn here will help you understand the research described in the rest of the book. But even more than that, what you learn here can be applied to everyday life. Knowing how a psychologist can be misled by the results of improperly conducted research can help us all avoid being misled by more casual observations. We'll see, for example, that Justine made a common, but fundamental, mistake by failing to take into account that her actions as an experimenter could be a causal factor in the behavior of her parents' employees. Understanding the scientific method can also help us, as consumers of information, distinguish worthwhile from flawed research reported in the mass media.

The Scientific Method in Psychology

To explain behavior we must use a method that is both precise enough to be clearly understood by others and general enough to apply to a wide variety of situations. We hope to be able to make general statements about the events that cause phenomena to occur.

Scientists use an agreed-upon approach to discovery and explanation—the scientific method. The **scientific method** consists of a set of rules that dictate the general procedure for

---

scientific method   A set of rules that governs the collection and analysis of data gained through observational studies or experiments.

experiment   A study in which the researcher changes the value of an independent variable and observes whether this manipulation affects the value of a dependent variable. Only experiments can confirm the existence of cause-and-effect relations among variables.

---

collecting and analyzing data that a scientist must follow in his or her research. These rules are not arbitrary; as we will see, they are based on logic and common sense. The rules were originally devised by philosophers who were attempting to determine how we could understand reality. By nature, we are all intuitive psychologists, trying to understand why others do what they do—so it is important to realize how easily we can be fooled about the actual causes of behavior. Thus, everyone, not just professional psychologists, should know the basic steps of the scientific method.

The scientific method employs a set of rules that apply to a form of research that identifies cause-and-effect relations; this form is called an **experiment,** and it consists of five steps. Some new terms introduced here without definition will be described in detail later in this chapter.

1. *Identify the problem and formulate hypothetical cause-and-effect relations among variables.* This step involves identifying variables (particular behaviors and particular environmental and physiological events) and describing the relations among them in general terms. For example, your own history of late-night studying might have convinced you of the helpful effects of caffeine on fatigue. But does caffeine help when you're about to take a test? You form the hypothesis: *Coffee consumption improves recall of learned information.* The hypothesis states that something about the first affects the second.

2. *Design the experiment.* Experiments involve the manipulation of independent variables and the observation of dependent variables. For example, if we wanted to test the hypothesis about the relation between caffeine and test performance, we might arrange an experiment in which volunteers agreed to consume a controlled amount of caffeine before being tested on some previously learned material. Each variable must be *operationally defined;* and the independent variable (caffeine consumption) must be controlled so that only it, and no other variable, is responsible for any changes in the dependent variable (recall of learned information).

3. *Perform the experiment.* The researcher must organize the material needed to perform the experiment, train the people who will perform the research, recruit volunteers whose behavior will be observed, and randomly assign each of these volunteers to an experimental group or a control group. The experiment is performed and the observations are recorded.

4. *Evaluate the hypothesis by examining the data from the study.* Do the results support the hypothesis, or do they suggest that it is wrong? This step often involves special mathematical procedures used to determine whether an observed effect is *statistically significant.* These procedures will be discussed in the Understanding Research Results section later in this chapter.

5. *Communicate the results.* Once the experimenters have learned something about the causes of a behavior, they must tell others about their findings. In most cases psychologists write an article that includes a description of the experiment's procedure and results and a discussion of their significance. They send the article to one of the many journals that publish results of psychological research. Journal editors and expert reviewers determine which research is methodologically sound and important enough to publish. In addition, researchers often present their findings at conferences or professional conventions. As a result, other psychologists can incorporate the findings into their own thinking and hypothesizing.

Following these steps decreases the chances that we will be misled by our observations or form incorrect conclusions in our research. As we shall see in Chapter 11, we as humans have a tendency to accept some types of evidence even though the rules of logic indicate that we should not. This tendency sometimes serves us well in our daily lives, but it can lead us to make the wrong conclusions when we try to understand the true causes of natural phenomena, including our own behavior.

Types of Research

Psychologists conduct three major types of scientific research. These classes of research are common across many of the sciences. The first type includes **naturalistic observation** (observation of people or animals in their natural environment) and **clinical observation**—(observation of people or animals while they are undergoing treatment or diagnosis for a psychological condition). These methods are the least formal and are constrained by the fewest rules. Naturalistic observations provide the foundations of the biological and social sciences. For example, Charles Darwin's observation and classification of animals, plants, and fossils during his voyage around the world provided him with the raw material for his theory of evolution. Maria Montessori formed many of her ideas about child development by watching children in a classroom. And Paul Broca suggested that language was located in a specific region of the brain after treating a man who had lost his ability to speak. As these examples illustrate, a researcher might perceive new facts following careful observation.

The second type, **correlational studies,** are observational in nature, but they involve more formal measurement—of environmental events, of individuals' physical and social characteristics, and of their behavior. Researchers examine the relations of these measurements in an attempt to explain the observed behaviors. At the conclusion of a correlational study, a researcher might conclude that some of the phenomena measured are related in a particular way.

Finally, experiments go beyond mere measurement. A psychologist performing an experiment makes things happen and observes the results. As you will see, following a properly designed experiment, a researcher can positively identify the causal relations among events.

Researchers communicate their results to other scientists through professional journals or conferences.

Identifying the Problem: Getting an Idea for Research

Like most professions, science is a very competitive enterprise. Most scientists want to be recognized for their work. They want to discover and explain interesting phenomena and to have other scientists acknowledge their importance. They may hope that the fruits of their research will affect the public at large. They certainly need to be hardworking and dedicated—perhaps even obstinate and relentless.

naturalistic observation Observation of the behavior of people or other animals in their natural environments.

clinical observation Observation of the behavior of people or animals while they are undergoing diagnosis or treatment.

correlational study The examination of relations between two or more measurements of behavior or other characteristics of people or other animals.

Often, science that achieves some breakthrough result is the cumulative work of many scientists who are part of a larger collective (and often international) endeavor. It often occurs in institutional settings such as universities, where scientists, students, and technicians all are involved in the effort. Such projects require financial support. Psychological research in the United States has historically been supported by major federal agencies such as the National Science Foundation and the National Institute of Mental Health. Before providing funding, these agencies rigorously review the merits of a proposed research program and its potential for long-term scientific value. They provide an independent evaluation of the worth of a scientific idea.

In this environment of competition and rigorous evaluation, a research program must be based on *good ideas*. Where do the ideas come from?

Hypotheses   A hypothesis is the starting point of any study. It is an idea, phrased as a general statement, that a scientist wishes to test through research. In the original Greek, *hypothesis* means "suggestion," and the word still conveys the same meaning. When scientists form a hypothesis, they are suggesting that a relation exists among various phenomena. Thus, a **hypothesis** is a tentative statement about a cause-and-effect relation between two or more events.

Theories   A **theory** is a set of statements that describes and explains known facts, proposes relations among variables, and makes new predictions. For example, a public safety advocate might notice an increase in traffic accidents and propose the theory that this is the result of increased cell phone use by drivers. In a sense, then, a theory is an elaborate form of hypothesis. A scientific theory operates within the scientific method to organize a system of facts and related hypotheses to explain some larger aspect of nature. A good theory fuels the creation of new hypotheses. A good theory is one that generates *testable hypotheses*—hypotheses that can potentially be supported or proved wrong by scientific research. Some theories are so general or so abstract that they do not produce testable hypotheses and hence cannot be subjected to scientific rigor. For example, if someone tells you they have a theory that UFO sightings have increased in America because people are disenchanted with organized religions, you could justifiably object that her proposed cause was not useful: She hasn't told you what *disenchantment* is or how you could tell if someone had it. Because she hasn't told you what it is, you cannot change "disenchantment" or perform an experiment involving it. So, the theory doesn't provide a hypothesis that is testable.

A theory connecting cell phone use with increased chance of a traffic accident would need to identify the causal factors responsible.

volving it. So, the theory doesn't provide a hypothesis that is testable.

The ability to test a hypothesis is one of the most important aspects of science. Natural phenomena can have many potential causes. If there is no way to choose among them, then we cannot build a consistent explanation of why the phenomenon occurs. So, a theory that does not generate testable hypotheses—either because it uses factors that cannot be observed or manipulated or because it is hopelessly vague as to what those factors are—cannot be a part of science.

Testability is particularly important to psychology, because it is often the case that psychological explanations rely on causal factors that are not directly observable. In the pages of this book that follow, there will be many instances where psychologists have found it useful to refer to such things as "memory," "attention," and "personality trait." We can't observe these directly, but we can, through a good theory, make predictions about how these factors will influence behavior.

Theories can generate testable hypotheses and still be difficult to work with. The earlier example of cell phone use and traffic accidents is a case in point, since the proposed cause—using a cell phone—contains many possible factors: Using a phone takes one of your hands off the wheel; it makes you think of situations other than driving; it blocks out other sounds, and so on. A theory that is vague is usually a poor one. In the next section, we'll see how to approach this problem.

Many, but not all, research endeavors in psychology are directed toward making some particular theory stronger. They try show that the evidence is consistent with the hypothesis, or they explore the relationship between concepts within the theory. Sometimes research stimulates us to think about old problems in new ways by showing how findings that did not appear to be related to each other can be explained by a single concept. There is even a scientific journal, *Psychological Review,* devoted to articles of this type.

---

hypothesis   A statement, usually designed to be tested by an experiment, that tentatively expresses a cause-and-effect relationship between two or more events.

theory   A set of statements designed to explain a set of phenomena; more encompassing than a hypothesis.

An important feature of naturalistic observation is that the observer remains in the background.

Naturalistic and Clinical Observations as Sources of Hypotheses and Theories

Psychology is about behavior. To understand human behavior, or the behavior of other animals, we first have to know something about that behavior. Much of what we know about behavior comes from ordinary experience: from observing other people, listening to their stories, watching films, reading novels. In effect, we perform observations throughout our lives. But systematic observations permit trained observers to discover subtly different categories of behavior and to develop hypotheses about their causes.

Psychologists who are also naturalists apply observational procedures to questions of behavior. The important feature of naturalistic observations is that the observer remains in the background, trying not to interfere with the people (or animals) being observed. For example, suppose we are interested in studying the social behavior of preschoolers. We want to know under what conditions children share their toys or fight over them, how children react to newcomers to the group, and so on. The best way to begin to get some ideas is to watch groups of children. We would unobtrusively start taking notes, classifying behaviors into categories and seeing what events provoked them—and what the effects of these behaviors might be. These naturalistic observations would teach us how to categorize and measure the children's behavior and would help us develop hypotheses that could be tested in experiments or in correlational studies.

Clinical observations are different. In the course of diagnosis or treatment, clinical psychologists can often observe important patterns of behavior. They can then report the results of their observations in detailed descriptions known as **case studies.** As with naturalistic observations, these clinical observations could form the basis of hypotheses about the causes of behavior. Unlike a naturalist, however, a clinical psychologist most likely does *not* remain in the background, because the object of therapy is to change the patient's behavior and to solve problems. Indeed, the psychologist is ethically constrained to engage in activities designed to benefit the patient; he or she cannot arbitrarily withhold some treatment or apply another just for the sake of new observations. So, like the naturalist, a clinician is bound by certain rules that limit the kinds of observations that can be made: The clinician cannot interfere with the treatment regime prescribed for the patient.

In some cases, psychologists *do* interfere with a situation in a natural or clinical setting. They may, for example, ask questions at job sites or on the street—places that we might regard as naturalistic settings. In one common procedure, a **survey study,** researchers may ask people specially designed and controlled questions, perhaps about their beliefs, opinions, or attitudes. Survey studies are designed to elicit a special kind of behavior—answers to the questions. The observations, then, are usually descriptions of the classes of responses to these questions. Many people may participate in a survey study, but they all are given the same, *standardized,* questions. As these questions become more specific and precise, they allow the same formal measurement of relations that underlies correlational studies.

A clinical psychologist, too, may manipulate the treatment given to a patient, with the desire of producing a more beneficial response. The psychologist may report the result in the manner of a case study, but such manipulation would make the process an experiment, not an observational study.

Much can be learned through careful observation of animals in their natural environment. The results of such observations often suggest hypotheses to be tested by subsequent studies.

---

case study   A detailed description of an individual's behavior during the course of clinical treatment or diagnosis.

survey study   A study of people's responses to standardized questions.

[**FIGURE 2·1**] Basic design of the driving and cell phone distraction experiment

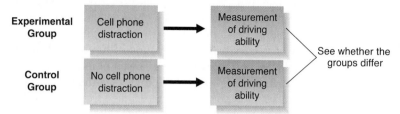

Designing an Experiment

Although naturalistic observations enable a psychologist to classify behaviors into categories and to offer hypothetical explanations for these behaviors, only an experiment can determine whether these explanations are correct. Let us see how to design an experiment. We will examine experimental variables and their operational definition and control.

Variables The hypothesis proposed earlier—"Cell phone distraction while driving increases the likelihood of a traffic accident"—describes a relation between distraction and the likelihood of a driving mistake. Scientists refer to these two components as **variables:** things that can vary in value. Thus, temperature is a variable, and so is happiness. Virtually anything that can differ in amount, degree, or presence versus absence is a variable.

Scientists either *manipulate* or *measure* the values of variables. **Manipulation** literally means "handling" (from *manus,* "hand"). Because of abuses in the history of human research (described later), the term *manipulation* is sometimes incorrectly understood to mean something that researchers do to participants. Psychologists use the word, however, to describe setting the values of a variable in order to examine that variable's effect on another variable. In the cell phone experiment, one value of the distraction variable might be "a cell phone call every minute" and another might be "complete absence of cell phone calls." Measuring variables means exactly what you think it does. Just as we measure the variable of temperature with a thermometer, so psychologists devise instruments to measure psychological variables. The results of experimental manipulations and measurements of variables help us evaluate hypotheses.

To test the cell phone distraction hypothesis with an experiment, we would assemble two groups of volunteers to serve as participants. We would ask them to perform some activity that measures driving ability. We could, for example, have them use a video game that simulates driving. We would present participants in the **experimental group** with a certain level of distraction, such as a high rate of cell phone calls. We would not give participants in the **control group** such an experience, and they therefore would have no distraction. We would then measure the ability of participants in both groups to avoid driving errors; from these results, we could then determine whether the outcomes in the two groups differed. Provided that we had randomly assigned the volunteers to make sure that our two groups were alike at the start of the experiment, we could attribute any differences in driving ability to the experimental manipulation of distraction. (See FIGURE 2·1.)

Our imaginary experiment examines the effect of one variable on another. The variable that we manipulate (distraction from a cell phone) is called the **independent variable.** The variable that we measure (likelihood of driver error) is the **dependent variable.** An easy way to keep the names of these variables straight is to remember that a hypothesis describes how the value of a dependent variable *depends* on the value of an independent variable. Our hypothesis proposes that a high frequency of cell phone distraction causes a high likelihood of driving errors. (See FIGURE 2·2.)

Scientists want to understand the causes of behavior in more than one specific situation. Thus, the variables that hypotheses deal with are expressed in general terms. Independent and dependent variables are *categories* into which various behaviors are classified. For example, we would probably classify hitting, kicking, and throwing objects at someone within the category of "interpersonal aggression." Pre-

---

variable Anything capable of assuming any of several values.

manipulation Setting the values of an independent variable in an experiment to see whether the value of another variable is affected.

experimental group The group of participants in an experiment that is exposed to a particular value of the independent variable, which has been manipulated by the researcher.

control group A comparison group used in an experiment, the members of which are exposed to the naturally occurring or zero value of the independent variable.

independent variable The variable that is manipulated in an experiment as a means of determining cause-and-effect relations.

dependent variable The variable measured in an experiment and hypothesized to be affected by the independent variable.

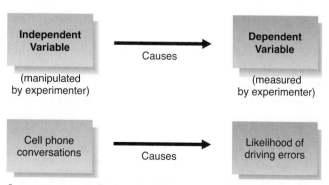

[**FIGURE 2·2**] Independent and dependent variables

sumably, these forms of aggression would have very similar causes. A psychologist must know enough about a particular type of behavior to be able to classify it correctly.

Even though one of the first steps in psychological research involves naming and classifying behaviors, however, we must be careful to avoid committing the nominal fallacy. The **nominal fallacy** is the erroneous belief that we have explained an event merely by naming it. (*Nomen* means "name.") Classifying a behavior does not explain it; classifying only prepares us to examine and discover events that cause a behavior.

For example, suppose that we see a man frown and shout at other people without provocation, criticize their work when it is really acceptable, and generally act unpleasantly toward everyone around him. Someone says, "Wow, he's really angry today!" Does this statement explain his behavior? No; it only *describes* the behavior. Instead of saying he is angry, we might better say that his behavior is hostile and aggressive. This statement does not claim to explain why he is acting the way he is. To say that he is angry suggests that an internal state is responsible for his behavior—that anger is causing his behavior. But all we have observed is his behavior, not his internal state. Even if he is experiencing feelings of anger, these feelings are not a full account of his behavior. What we really need to know is *what events made him act the way he did*. Perhaps he has a painful toothache. Perhaps he just learned that he failed to get a job he wanted. Perhaps he just read a book that promoted assertiveness. Events like these are causes of both behavior and feelings. Unless the underlying events are discovered and examined, we have not explained the behavior in a scientifically meaningful way.

Yet identifying causes is not as simple as merely identifying preceding events. Many internal and external events may precede any behavior. Some of these events are causal, but some almost certainly will be completely unrelated to the observed behavior. For example, you get off your commuter train because your stop is announced, not because someone coughs or someone else turns the page of a newspaper, even though all of these events may happen just before you stand up and leave the train. The task of a psychologist is to determine which of the many events that occurred before a particular behavior caused that behavior to happen.

The cell phone example, up to now, has this problem. There are many things that happen when you answer a call. Similarly, driving ability is a complex behavior with many components. A good theory would provide more detail about both independent and dependent variables. Let's look at a possible candidate.

Driving is clearly dependent on our ability to recognize the changing conditions ahead of us on the road. Later in this book, in Chapter 9, we'll examine a psychological condition

[**FIGURE 2·3**] An example of our ability to detect a change in a traffic scene. Study this picture for about 3 seconds. Then turn to Figure 2.4.

called *change blindness* which, as the name implies, is an insensitivity to a changed scene. For example, look at FIGURE 2·3, which depicts a traffic scene. Now look at FIGURE 2·4, which depicts the same scene—but with one detail missing. Can you tell what it is?

Most likely, you would have had trouble spotting the difference. Because the two figures were on separate pages, there's a visual interruption as you looked from one to the other. Psychologists who study change blindness feel that this interruption interferes with our ability to compare two scenes (Rensink, 2002). We could possibly generalize this to any interruption, including an auditory one. So, perhaps cell phone conversations cause accidents because they increase change blindness.

Notice that we've expanded our theory about traffic accidents considerably. Our explanation for the distracting effects of a call says that they are similar to a more general phenomenon. We can therefore understand a practical problem like preventing accidents by studying a psychological process that occurs in other situations too. Our theory about cell phones and traffic accidents suggests that factors that increase our resistance to distractions will decrease change blindness.

Operational Definitions Hypotheses are phrased in general terms, but when we design an experiment (step 2 of the scientific method) we need to decide what *particular* variables we will manipulate and measure. For example, remember our hypothesis about caffeine and test-taking? Caffeine seems to improve alertness and reaction time (e.g., Smith, 2005). Perhaps it can improve our resistance to distractions and thereby increase our ability to detect changes like those between Figures 2.3 and 2.4. Our hypothesis, then, is that caffeine consumption will decrease change blindness. To test this particular hypothesis, we must carefully describe how much caffeine we will administer to participants in our experiment and under what conditions. Similarly, we must also describe how we will measure change blindness.

[FIGURE 2·4] How does this photograph differ from the previous one?

This translation of generalities into specific operations is called an **operational definition:** the definition of independent variables and dependent variables in terms of the operations a researcher performs in order to set their values or to measure them. In our proposed experiment, a rudimentary operational definition of the independent and dependent variables and the setting in which they were studied might be the following:

Setting: Participants in the experiment are comfortably seated in front of a computer screen. Participants receive 20 change detection tests. Each test consists of a sequence in which an image like Figure 2.3 is shown for three seconds, followed by a blank white screen for a half-second, and then followed by a changed version of the first figure for three seconds. Changed versions are computer-modified versions of the first image, with one randomly selected component erased, as in Figure 2.4. The original and the changed versions alternate back and forth in this way until the participant presses a button to indicate that he or she has detected the change.

Independent variable: Two hours before the test, each participant is given a standard-sized coffee cup containing a hot decaffeinated coffee drink. For participants in the experimental group, this drink contains 0.2 grams of caffeine; for participants in the control group, the drink is not altered.

Dependent variable: On each test, change detection is measured by the time elapsed between the first appearance of the original image and the participant's pressing the response button. All participants were asked to be reasonably confident they had detected the object before pressing the button.

---

operational definition   Definition of a variable in terms of the operations the researcher performs to measure or manipulate it.

validity   The degree to which the operational definition of a variable accurately reflects the variable it is designed to measure or manipulate.

confounding of variables   Inadvertent simultaneous manipulation of more than one variable. The results of an experiment in which variables are confounded permit no valid conclusions about cause and effect.

Any general concept can be operationalized in many different ways. By selecting one particular operational definition, the researcher may or may not succeed in manipulating the independent variable or in measuring the dependent variable. For example, there are many sources of caffeine (coffee, soft drinks, condiments, and so on) and several ways of administering it (e.g., through a fluid, an injection, taken after a meal, taken four hours after a meal, and so on). Which operational definition is correct? Which set of results should we believe? To answer these questions, we need to address the issue of *validity.*

The **validity** of operational definitions has to do with how appropriate they are for testing the researcher's hypothesis—how accurately they represent the variables whose values have been manipulated or measured. Obviously, only experiments that use valid operational definitions of their variables can yield meaningful results. Let's consider this operational definition of detection: the length of the time interval between initial presentation of the original image and the pressing of the response button. How can we know that the participant has actually seen the change? Even with the best of intentions, a person in an experiment like this might be reacting to his or her own imagination rather than actual visual perception. As one possible check, we could ask each participant to point to the location of the change and to describe it. Using only those times that were associated with correct points would increase the validity of our measure.

Control of Independent Variables   We have seen that a scientist performs an experiment by manipulating the value of the independent variable and then observing whether this change affects the dependent variable. If an effect is seen, the scientist can conclude that there is a cause-and-effect relation between the variables. That is, changes in the value of the independent variable cause changes in the value of the dependent variable.

When conducting an experiment, the researcher must manipulate the value of the independent variable—and *only* the independent variable. For example, if we want to determine whether background environmental noise has an effect on people's reading speed, we must choose our source of noise carefully. If we used the sound track from a television show to supply the noise and found that it slowed people's reading speed, we could not conclude that the effect was caused purely by "noise." We might have selected an interesting show, thus distracting the participants' attention from the material they were reading because of the content of the TV program rather than because of "noise." If we want to do this experiment properly, we should use noise that is neutral and not a source of interest by itself—for instance, noise like the *sssh* sound that is heard when a radio is tuned between stations.

If we used a TV program sound track as our manipulation of noise, we would inadvertently cause **confounding of variables**—we would introduce the effects of another variable besides noise on reading speed. One of the meanings of the word *confound* is "to fail to distinguish." If a researcher inadvertently introduces one or more extra, unwanted, independent variables that vary along with the intended independent variable, he or she will not be able to distinguish the effects of any one of them on the dependent variable. That is, the effects of the variables will be confounded. In our example, the noise of the TV program would be mixed with the content of the program in the experimental condition, whereas in the control condition there would be neither noise nor content. You can see that any effect of the manipulation on reading could be due to either noise or content or even to their combination. It would be impossible to reach any conclusion about the experimental hypothesis.

It is often difficult to be sure that independent variables are not confounded. Sometimes even experienced researchers overlook a possible problem, as is illustrated in the following case.

[**CASE STUDY**] A visitor to a zoology department of a well-known university described research he had conducted in a remote area of South America. He was interested in determining whether a particular species of bird could recognize a large bird that normally preys on it. He had constructed a set of cardboard models that bore varying degrees of resemblance to the predator: They ranged from a perfect representation, to two models of noncarnivorous birds, to a neutral stimulus (such as a triangle). The researcher restrained each bird he was testing and suddenly presented it with each of the test stimuli, in decreasing order of similarity to the predator—that is, from predator to harmless birds to triangle. He observed a relation between the amount of alarm that the birds showed and the similarity that the model bore to the predator. The most predator-like model produced the greatest response. (See FIGURE 2·5.)

It was pointed out—to the embarrassment of the speaker—that the study contained a fatal flaw that made it impossible to conclude whether a relation existed between the independent variable (similarity of the model to the predator) and the dependent variable (amount of alarm).

Stimuli arranged in order of similarity to predator

[**FIGURE 2·5**] A schematic representation of the flawed predator experiment.

It's a fairly subtle but important problem. Can you figure it out? Reread the previous paragraph, consult Figure 2.5, and think about the problem before you read on.

Now, the answer: When testing the birds' responses to the models, the investigator presented each model at a different time *but always in the same order.* Very likely, even if the birds had been shown the *same* model again and again, they would have exhibited less and less of a response. We very commonly observe this phenomenon, called *habituation,* when a stimulus is presented repeatedly. The last presentation produces a much smaller response than the first. Consequently, we do not know whether the decrease in signs of alarm occurred because the stimuli looked less and less like the predator or simply because the birds became habituated to the stimuli.

Could the zoologist have carried out his experiment in a way that would have permitted him to infer a causal relation? Yes, and perhaps the solution has occurred to you already: The researcher should have presented the stimuli in different orders to different birds. Some birds would see the predator first, others would see the triangle first, and so on. Then he could have calculated the average amount of alarm that the birds showed to each of the stimuli, without contaminating the results by habituation. This type of procedure is called **counterbalancing.** To *counterbalance* means to "weigh evenly," and counterbalancing would have been accomplished if the investigator had made sure that each of the models was presented equally often (to different participant birds, of course) as the first, second, third, or fourth stimulus. The effects of habituation would thus be spread equally among all the stimuli. (See FIGURE 2·6.)

Trials	1	2	3	4

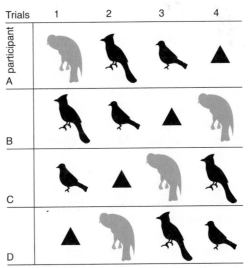

[**FIGURE 2·6**] Counterbalancing in the predator experiment. The predator experiment could be improved by changing the order of presentation of the models.

counterbalancing Systematic variation of conditions in an experiment, such as the order of presentation of stimuli, so that different participants encounter the conditions in different orders; prevents confounding of independent variables with time-dependent processes such as habituation or fatigue.

Response Bias in Different Cultures

Response bias—responding to a questionnaire in a way that is not genuine or honest but in some other irrelevant way—is an important concept in research methods because it can skew results and tell researchers something that is not very meaningful. A Dutch study of six European countries has found examples of response bias that is specific to certain cultures.

Van Herk, Poortinga, & Verhallen (2005) from The Netherlands used existing data from a multinational marketing questionnaire survey to examine response bias in participants from Greece, Italy, Spain, France, Germany, and the United Kingdom. They found that contrary to participants from northwestern European countries, those from Mediterranean countries showed an abnormally high tendency to agree with answers (acquiescence), and a greater likelihood to choose extreme response categories (e.g., selecting 1 or 5 on a five-point scale). Greek participants, in particular, significantly exhibited these response biases. Participants from Spain and Italy scored higher on these two biases than did participants from the United Kingdom, France, and Germany. The British were the least acquiescent.

The authors suggest that such differences might reflect the different types of cultures in these countries: collectivistic vs. individualistic—whether they value the skills necessary to work together or the effort of people working as individuals. The more individualistic the societies were, the less acquiescent they seemed.

Performing an Experiment

After designing a study with due regard for the dangers of confounds, we must decide how best to conduct it. We are now at step 3 of the scientific method: Perform the experiment. We must decide who will participate, what instructions to give, and what equipment and materials to use. We must ensure that the data collected will be accurate; otherwise, all effort will be in vain.

Reliability of Measurements A procedure described by an operational definition that produces consistent results under consistent conditions is said to have high **reliability.** For example, measurements of people's height and weight are extremely reliable. Measurements of their academic aptitude (by means of standard commercial tests) also are reliable, but somewhat less so.

---

response bias Responding to a questionnaire in a way that is not genuine or honest but in some other irrelevant way.

reliability The repeatability of a measurement; the likelihood that if the measurement were made again, it would yield the same value.

interrater reliability The degree to which two or more independent observers agree in their ratings of an organism's behavior.

Suppose that we operationally define detection of changed image as the time it takes before the participant blinks. Eye-blink measurements can be made reliably and accurately, but it is problematic to consider this as a valid or true measure of image detection, because there are many reasons for a participant to blink other than having detected the hidden image. Achieving reliability is usually much easier than achieving validity. Reliability is mostly a result of care and diligence on the part of researchers in the planning and execution of their studies.

Let's look at an example of a factor that can decrease the reliability of an operationally defined variable. Suppose that in our study on the effects of change detection, we select the images to be presented to each participant by randomly drawing 20 images from a large collection of digital photographs. However, some of the images were poorly scanned, so they are out of focus when projected. You can easily appreciate how this extraneous factor would affect our measurement of detection and would add to the differences we observe among the participants.

Careful researchers can identify and control most of the extraneous factors that might affect the reliability of their measurements. Conditions throughout the experiment should always be as consistent as possible. For example, the same instructions should be given to each person who participates in the experiment, all equipment should be in good working order, and all assistants hired by the researcher should be well trained in performing their tasks. Noise and other sources of distraction should be kept to a minimum.

The subjectivity of the experimenters who are taking a measurement is another factor that affects reliability. Our definition of inducing an expectation is *objective;* that is, even a non-expert could follow our procedure and obtain the same results. But researchers often attempt to study variables whose measurement is *subjective;* that is, it requires judgment and expertise. For example, suppose that a psychologist wants to count the number of friendly interactions that a child has with other children in a group. This measurement requires that someone watch the child and note each time a friendly interaction occurs. But it is difficult to be absolutely specific about what constitutes a friendly interaction and what does not. What if the child looks at another child and their gazes meet? One observer may say that the look conveyed interest in what the other child was doing and so should be scored as a friendly interaction. Another observer may disagree.

The solution in this case: First, to make the measurement as objective as possible, try to specify as precisely as possible the criteria to be used for defining an interaction as "friendly." Next, two or more people should watch the child's behavior and score it independently; that is, neither person should be aware of the other person's ratings. If the two observers' ratings agree, we can say that the scoring system has high **interrater reliability.** If they disagree, interrater reliability is low, and there is no point in continuing the study. Instead, the rating system should be refined, and the raters should be trained to apply it consistently. Any investigator who performs a study in which measuring the dependent variables requires some degree of skill and judgment must do what is necessary to produce high interrater reliability.

Selecting the Participants

Suppose a professor wants to determine which of two teaching methods works best. She teaches two courses in introductory psychology, one that meets at 8:00 A.M. and another that meets at 4:00 P.M. She considers using one teaching method for the morning class and the other for the afternoon class. She speculates that at the end of the term, the final examination scores will be higher for her morning class. If her surmise proves correct, will she be able to conclude that the morning teaching method is superior to the method used in the afternoon? No; a good researcher would understand that the method considered here would produce a significant interpretation problem. There likely would be differences between the two groups of participants other than the teaching method they experienced. People who sign up for a class that meets at 8:00 A.M. are likely, for many reasons, to differ in some ways from those who sign up for a 4:00 P.M. class. Some people prefer to get up early; others prefer to sleep late. Perhaps the school schedules athletic practices in the late afternoon, which means that athletes will not be able to enroll in the 4:00 P.M. class. Therefore, the professor would not be able to conclude that any observed differences in final examination scores were caused solely by the differences in the teaching methods. Personal characteristics of the participant groups would be confounded with the two teaching methods.

The most common way to avoid confounding participant characteristics with the manipulated values of an independent variable is **random assignment**. Random assignment means that each participant has an equal chance of being assigned to any of the conditions or groups of the experiment. Typically, random assignment is made by computer or by consulting a list of random numbers. We can expect people to have different abilities, personality traits, and other characteristics that may affect the outcome of the experiment. But if people are randomly assigned to the experimental conditions, these differences should be equally distributed across the groups. Randomly assigning students to two sections of a course meeting at the same time of day would help solve the problem faced by the professor who wants to study different teaching methods.

Even after researchers have designed an experiment and randomly assigned participants to the groups, they must remain alert to the problem of confounding participant characteristics with their independent variable manipulations. Some problems will not emerge until the investigation is actually performed. Suppose that we wish to learn whether anger decreases a person's ability to concentrate. As we'll see in the next part of this chapter, any experiment to test this would require careful consideration of the ethics of making someone angry and would be approved only

if the benefits of the results were clear. Assuming that the experiment was approved, one of the researchers might begin by acting very rudely toward the participants in the experimental group, which presumably makes them angry, but treating the participants in the control group politely. After the rude or polite treatment, the participants watch a video that shows a constantly changing display of patterns of letters. Participants are instructed to press a button whenever a particular letter appears. This vigilance test is designed to reveal how carefully participants are paying attention to the letters.

The design of this experiment seems sound. Assuming that the participants in the experimental group are really angry and that our letter identification test is a good dependent measure of concentration, we should be able to draw conclusions about the effects of anger on concentration. However, the experiment, as performed under real conditions, may not work out the way we expect. Suppose that some of our "angry" participants simply walk away. All researchers must assure participants that their participation is voluntary and that they are free to leave at any time; some angry participants may well exercise this right and withdraw from the experiment. If they do, we will now be comparing the behavior of two groups of participants that have a different mix of personal characteristics—one group composed of people who are willing to submit to the researcher's rude behavior (because the objectors have withdrawn) and another group of randomly selected people, some of whom would have left had they been subjected to the rude treatment. Now the experimental group and the control group are no longer equivalent. (See FIGURE 2·7.)

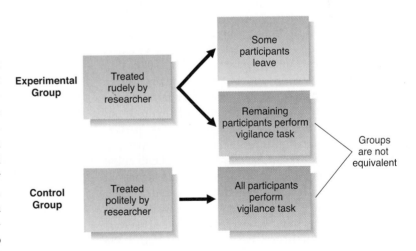

[**FIGURE 2·7**] A possible problem with the anger and concentration experiment: unequal loss of participants with specific characteristics from the comparison group.

---

random assignment   Procedure in which each participant has an equally likely chance of being assigned to any of the conditions or groups of an experiment.

Expectancy Effects Research participants are not passive beings whose behavior is controlled solely by the independent variables manipulated by the researcher. This is a basic concept in the sciences: Observation can change that which you observe. This is what is known as the *Hawthorne effect*. Back in the 1930s, the managers of the Hawthorne plant of the Western Electric company wondered whether increasing the level of lighting in the plant would increase productivity. It did, but the managers found that the increase in productivity was short-lived. They went on to do some more investigating and found that productivity actually went up when they subsequently lowered the level of lighting. The commonly accepted explanation of these findings is based on the fact that the workers knew that an experiment was being conducted and that they were being monitored. That knowledge may have made them work harder regardless of whether lighting levels were increased or decreased. The workers may even have been pleased—and motivated—by the fact that management was obviously trying to improve their work environment, and may have tried to return the favor. Of course, the effect did not last indefinitely, and eventually production returned to normal. Adair (1984) provides a detailed analysis of these original studies and the methods that have evolved in field experiments to counter the Hawthorne effect.

One way to think about the Hawthorne effect is that the participants were trying to help the researchers confirm their expectation that changes in lighting would improve productivity. There is compelling evidence that this type of cooperation with researchers can occur even in very sophisticated laboratory research: If research participants figure out the researcher's hypothesis, they will sometimes behave as if the hypothesis is true, even if it is not. For example, one issue in the design of virtual reality displays is that they can sometimes make people seasick. Many designers now test their equipment for this possibility. But, if people are given a motion-sickness questionnaire before they test the display, they report more motion sickness (Young, Adelstein, & Ellis, 2007).

The possibility that a researcher's expectations can be guessed by a participant is a dangerous state of affairs for good science. For this reason, researchers routinely keep the details of their hypotheses to themselves when dealing with participants, at least until after the independent variable is manipulated and the dependent variable measured. But the situation is more troublesome when participants manage to figure out not only the researcher's hypothesis but also the independent variable manipulations on their own. You may have heard that deception is sometimes used in psychological research. Overall, deception is relatively rare. When it is used, however, the sole reason is to disguise the nature of an independent variable manipulation (and perhaps the dependent measure). If researchers mislead participants about the reason for the ex-

perimental events, the intention is to prevent the participants from acting as if the hypothesis were true when it might in fact not be. When deception is used, researchers take great pains to disclose the truth to participants at the earliest possible moment and to reestablish a trusting relationship. Interestingly, people who actually have participated in deception experiments are generally quite accepting of the rationale for the use of this technique (Sharpe, Adair, & Roese, 1992). Let's turn now to other techniques that have been developed to reduce the likelihood that research participants will become aware of the investigator's expectations.

Single-Blind Experiments. Suppose that we want to study the effects of a stimulant drug on a person's ability to perform a task that requires good motor control. We will administer the drug to one group of participants and leave another group untreated. (Of course, the experiment will have to be supervised by a physician, who will prescribe the drug.) We will count how many times each participant can thread a needle in a 10-minute period (our operational definition of fine manual dexterity). We will then see whether taking the drug had any effect on the number of needle threadings.

But there is a problem in our design. Can you see what it is? For us to conclude that a cause-and-effect relation exists, the treatment of the two groups must be identical except for the single variable that is being manipulated. In this case the mere administration of a drug may have effects on behavior, independent of its pharmacological effects. The behavior of participants who know that they have just taken a stimulant drug is very likely to be affected by this knowledge as well as by the drug circulating in their bloodstreams.

To solve this problem we would give pills to the members of both groups. People in one group would receive the stimulant; those in the other group would receive an identical-looking pill that contained no active drug—a **placebo** pill. Participants would not be told which type of pill they were taking, but they would know that they had a 50–50 chance of receiving either the stimulant or the inactive substance. By using this improved experimental procedure, called a **single-blind study,** where the participants are kept unaware of their assignment to a particular experimental group, we could infer that any observed differences in needle-threading ability of the two groups were produced solely by the pharmacological effects of the stimulant drug.

Double-Blind Experiments. Now let us look at an example in which it is important to keep both the researchers and the participants in the dark. Suppose we believe that if patients with mental disorders take a particular drug, they will be more willing to engage in conversation. This would be an important outcome, because enhanced communicativeness could facilitate their therapy. So we give the real drug to some patients and administer a placebo to others. We talk with all the patients afterwards and rate the quality of the conversation. But "quality of conversation" is a difficult dependent variable to measure, and the rating is therefore likely to be

---

placebo   An ineffectual treatment used as the control substance in a single-blind or double-blind experiment.

single-blind study   An experiment in which the researcher knows the value of the independent variable but participants do not.

subjective. The fact that we, the researchers, know who received the drug and who received the placebo leaves open the possibility that we may, unintentionally, give higher conversation quality ratings to those who took the drug.

The solution to this problem is simple. Just as the participants should not know whether they are receiving a drug or a placebo, neither should the researchers. That is, we should use a **double-blind study.** Either another person should administer the pills, or the researchers should be given a set of identical-looking pills in coded containers so that both researchers and participants are unaware of the nature of the contents. Now the researchers' ratings of conversation quality cannot be affected by any preconceived ideas they may have. Keep in mind that someone who has no direct contact with the participants is keeping track of who gets which pills so that the effect of the independent variable manipulation can be tested.

The double-blind procedure can be used in other experiments also. Suppose that the experiment just described attempted to evaluate the effects of a new form of psychotherapy, not a drug, on the willingness of a participant to talk. If the same person does both the psychotherapy and the rating, that person might tend to see the results in the light most favorable to his or her own expectations. In this case, then, one person should perform the psychotherapy and another person should evaluate the quality of conversation with the participants. The evaluator will not know whether a particular participant has just received the new psychotherapy or is a member of the control group that received the old standard therapy.

Performing a Correlational Study

To be sure that a cause-and-effect relation exists between variables, we must perform an experiment in which we manipulate an independent variable and measure its effects on a dependent variable. But there are some variables—especially variables intrinsic to an individual—that a psychologist cannot manipulate. For example, a person's gender, genetic history, income, social class, family environment, and personality are obviously not under the researcher's control. Because these variables cannot be manipulated, they cannot be investigated by means of an experiment. Nevertheless, such variables are important and interesting, because they often affect people's behavior. A different method must therefore be used to study them: a correlational study.

The design and conduct of a correlational study is relatively simple: For each member of a group of people we measure two or more variables as they are found to exist, and we determine whether the variables are related by using a statistical procedure called *correlation.* Correlational studies often investigate the effects of personality variables on behavior. For example, we may ask whether shyness is related to daydreaming. Our hypothesis is that shy people tend to daydream more than less shy people. We decide how to assess a person's shyness and the amount of daydreaming he or she engages in each day, and we then measure these two variables for a random group of people. Some people will be very shy and some not shy at all. Some people will daydream a lot and others will hardly daydream at all. If we find that relatively shy people tend to daydream more (or less) than relatively less shy people, we can conclude that the variables are related.

Suppose that we do, in fact, find that shy people spend more time daydreaming. Such a finding tells us that the variables are related—we say they are *correlated*—but it does not permit us to make any conclusions about cause and effect. Shyness may have caused the daydreaming, or daydreaming may have caused the shyness, or perhaps some other variable that we did not measure caused both shyness and an increase in daydreaming. In other words, *correlations do not necessarily indicate cause-and-effect relations.* (See FIGURE 2•8.) An experiment is necessary to prove a cause-and-effect relation.

A good illustration of this principle is provided by a correlational study that attempted to determine whether membership in the Boy Scouts would affect a man's subsequent participation in community affairs (Chapin, 1938). The investigator compared a group of men who had once been Boy Scouts with a group of men who had not. He found that the men who had been Boy Scouts tended to join more community affairs groups later in life.

The investigator concluded that the experience of being a Boy Scout increased a person's tendency to join community organizations. However, this conclusion was not warranted. All we can say is that people who join the Boy Scouts in their youth tend to join community organizations later in life. It could be that people who, for one reason or another, are "joiners" tend to join the Boy Scouts when they are young and community organizations when they are older. To determine cause and effect, we would have to perform an experiment. For example, we would make some boys join the Boy Scouts and prevent others from doing so, and then see how many organizations they voluntarily joined later in life. But because we cannot interfere in people's lives in such a way, we can never be certain that being a Boy Scout increases a person's tendency to join community organizations later.

The news media often report the results of correlational studies as if they implied causal relations. For example, one newspaper routinely points out the high incomes earned by its subscribers, implying that by subscribing you can cause your own income to rise. But correlation does not prove causation. It could be that having a high income causes you to buy the newspaper (perhaps for the specific news of your profession). You might think of this logic when you receive that seductive recruiting brochure from some business school showing that its graduates earn 40% more than those of other schools.

---

double-blind study   An experiment in which neither the participants nor the researchers know the value of the independent variable.

[**FIGURE 2·8**] An example of a correlation. Correlations do not necessarily indicate cause-and-effect relations: Daydreaming could cause shyness, or shyness could cause daydreaming.

Daydreaming keeps a person from making many contacts with other people; experiences in fantasies are more successful and gratifying than those in real life.

He does not know how to respond in the company of other people.

Person has poor social skills; finds contacts with other people uncomfortable.

He turns to daydreaming because he receives no gratification from social contacts.

Can anything be done to reduce some of the uncertainty inherent in correlational studies? The answer is yes. When attempting to study the effects of a variable that cannot be altered (such as gender, age, socioeconomic status, or personality characteristics), we can use a procedure called **matching.** Rather than selecting participants randomly, we *match* the participants in each of the groups on all of the relevant variables except the one being studied. For instance, if we want to study the effects of shyness on daydreaming, we might select two groups of participants: one group composed of people who score very high on the shyness test and another group composed of people who score very low. We could then place further restrictions so that the effects of other variables are minimized. We could make sure that average age, intelligence, income, and personality characteristics (other than shyness) of people in the two groups are the same. If we find that the shy group is, on average, younger than the non-shy group, we will replace some of the people in the shy group with older shy people until the average age is the same.

If, after following this matching procedure, we find that shyness is still related to daydreaming, we can be more confident that the differences between the two variables are not caused by a third variable. The limitation of the matching procedure is that we may not know all the variables that should be held constant. If, unbeknownst to us, the two groups are not matched on an important variable, the results will be misleading. In any case, even the matching procedure does not permit us to decide which variable is the cause and which is the effect; we still do not know whether shyness causes daydreaming or daydreaming causes shyness.

The strengths and limitations of correlational studies will become evident in subsequent chapters in this book. For example, almost all studies that attempt to discover the environmental factors that influence personality character-

matching Systematically selecting participants in groups in an experiment or (more often) a correlational study to ensure that the mean values of important participant variables of the groups are similar.

To study possible causes of daydreaming when we cannot manipulate variables, we could use a matching procedure.

istics or the relation between these characteristics and people's behavior are correlational.

Reporting and Generalizing a Study

Scientists in all disciplines report the details of their research methods in professional publications known as *journals,* using sufficient detail that other investigators can repeat, or *replicate,* the research. The **replication** process is one of the great strengths of science; it ensures that erroneous results and incorrect conclusions are weeded out. When scientists publish a study, they know that if the findings are important enough, others will try to replicate their work to be sure that the results were not just a statistical fluke—or the result of errors in the design or execution of the original study. Statistical anomalies and incompetently conducted research usually will be uncovered through unsuccessful attempts to replicate. The insistence on replicability of research results also helps inhibit fraud in science, because the unreliability of falsified findings is likely to be discovered.

When we carry out an experiment or a correlational study, we probably assume that our participants are representative of the larger population. In fact, a representative group of participants is usually referred to as a **sample** of the larger population. For example, if we study the behavior of a group of five-year-old children, we want to make conclusions about five-year-olds in general. We want to be able to **generalize,** or extend, our specific results to the population as a whole—to conclude that the results tell us something about human nature in general, not simply about our particular participants.

Many researchers recruit their participants from introductory courses in psychology. The results of studies that use these students as participants can be best generalized to other groups of students who are similarly recruited. But in the strictest sense, the results cannot be generalized to students in other courses, to adults in general, or even to all students enrolled in introductory psychology—after all, students who volunteer to serve as participants may be different from those who do not. Even if we used truly random samples of all age groups of adults in our area, we could not generalize the results to people who live in other geographical regions. If our ability to generalize is really so limited, is it worthwhile to do psychological research?

The answer is that we are not so strictly limited. Most psychologists assume that a relation among variables that is observed in one group of humans also will be found in other groups, as long as the sample of participants is not especially unusual. For example, we may expect data obtained from prisoners to have less generality than data obtained from university students. One feature of the scientific method we have discussed before helps achieve generalizability: replication. When results are replicated with different samples of people, we gain confidence in their generalizability.

focus On

Cross-Cultural Research

Cross-cultural psychologists (see Chapter 1) are interested in studying the similarities and differences in behavior between cultures. (As an aside, *comparative psychologists,* also discussed in Chapter 1, study the similarities and differences across species.) The term *culture* traditionally referred to a group of people who live together in a common environment, who share customs and religious beliefs and practices, and who often resemble one another genetically. However, definitions of culture now vary widely. For example, "American culture" includes people of diverse ethnic and religious backgrounds, political beliefs, sexual orientation, and economic statuses, while "Fore people" includes a small, fairly homogeneous group of people living in the highlands of Papua New Guinea. Within a broadly defined culture, we can identify subcultures based on ethnicity, age, political beliefs, and other characteristics by which people define themselves. Keep in mind that "culture" is not synonymous with country or continent. Many cultures can exist within a single geographic zone.

Cross-cultural research lets psychologists test the generality of the results of a study performed with members of a particular culture. If similar studies performed with members of different cultures produce similar results, we can be more confident that we have discovered a general principle that applies broadly to members of our species. On the other hand, if the studies yield different results in different cultures, we need to carry out further research. The cross-cultural approach also lends itself to questions of immense political and economic importance. For example, think of the many issues that arise when people migrate from one culture to another (Berry, 2001).

Cultures differ with respect to two major classes of variables: biological and ecological. Biological variables include such factors as diet, genetics, and endemic diseases. Ecological variables include such factors as geography, climate, political systems, population density, religion, cultural myths, and education.

Identifying the cultural variables responsible for behavioral differences is a difficult process, for culture can be viewed as affecting behavior in different ways (Lonner & Adamopoulos, 1997). In cross-cultural research, culture is considered to be a *treatment variable*—analyzed as if it were an independent variable (Berry et al., 2002). But cultures,

---

replication Repetition of an experiment or observational study in an effort to see whether previous results will be obtained; ensures that incorrect conclusions are weeded out.

sample A selection of elements representative of a larger population—for example, a group of participants selected to participate in an experiment.

generalize To extend the results obtained from a sample to the population from which the sample was taken.

The term *culture* can refer to a large and diverse population, or to a small homogeneous group, such as the Fore people living Papua New Guinea.

like people, differ in many ways, and people are born into their cultures, not assigned to them by psychologists performing experiments. Thus, cross-cultural comparisons are subject to the same limitations we discussed when we examined correlational studies—we cannot attribute causality to a cultural factor until we have ruled these other variables out. For example, a hunting and gathering culture living in a marginal environment may show a higher level of altruism than a technological culture like ours. Does the poverty of their environment make them more attentive to each other? Or is it that the scarcity of resources brings people physically closer than in other cultures, making sharing easier to do?

Psychologists who do cross-cultural research have investigated social behaviors, personality differences, approaches to problem solving, intellectual abilities, perceptual abilities, and aesthetics. (Segall et al., 1999, provide an engaging overview.) Behind research endeavors in psychology is a guiding aim: to discover a psychological universal. According to Norenzayan & Heine (2005), psychological universals are "core mental attributes shared by humans everywhere." That is, they are conclusions from psychological research that can be generalized across groups—ways of reasoning, thinking, making decisions, interpreting why people behave in the way that they do, recognizing emotions and so on. All of these are examples of core mental attributes. A strong case for a psychological universal can be made if a phenomenon exists in a large variety of different cultures.

Cross-cultural psychologists have argued that some behaviors may be universal. They cite the recognition of basic emotions as one example (although this has been challenged, a point taken up in Chapter 13; such is the argumentativeness of psychologists). A variety of behaviors, however, is not seen, or is seen to a lesser extent, across cultures and nations. TABLE 2•1 summarizes those that have been found to vary across cultures.

One way of demonstrating a psychological universal is to examine a behavior in three or more cultures, two of which are very different, with a third falling between them. A better way, however, may be to examine a vari-

ety of cultures. This is what Daly and Wilson (1988) did, for example, when they examined sex differences in the international rates of homicide (they found that men were more likely to kill men than women were to kill women). Debate then ensues as to why this universal should exist (and that debate is often heated, as most in psychology are). A related approach is to examine the degree to which a psychological phenomenon is present—personality type is a good example of this. As Chapter 14 on Personality shows, the dominant approach in personality views us as differing along five major personality dimensions. Cross-cultural research has highlighted not only the universality of these five dimensions but also the differences or "variation" that exist between cultures within each dimension—some cultures may express more or less of a personality type such as extraversion or conscientiousness, for example.

[**TABLE 2·1**]   Behaviors That Have Been Reported to Vary across Cultures, or That May Be Less Evident in Certain Cultures. (Unfamiliar terms are defined in the chapters referred to in parentheses.)

Memory for and categorization of focal colors
Spatial reasoning (see Chapter 8)
Some types of category-based inductive reasoning (see Chapter 11)
Some perceptual illusions
Some ways of approaching reasoning
Aspects of numerical reasoning
Risk preferences in decision-making (see Chapter 11)
Self-concept (see Chapters 15 and 16)
Similarity-attraction effect (see Chapters 15)
Approach-avoidance motivation (see Chapter 13)
The fundamental attribution error (see Chapters 15)
Predilection for aggression
Feelings of control
High subjective well-being and positive affect
Communication style
Prevalence of major depression
Prevalence of eating disorders (see Chapter 13)
Mental illness
Noun bias in language learning (see Chapter 10)
Moral reasoning
Prevalence of different attachment style
Disruptive behavior in adolescence
Personality types
Response bias (see Chapter 2)
Recognition of emotion

Source: Adapted from Norenzayan & Heine (2005).

QUESTIONS TO CONSIDER

1. Global warming is an obvious problem, with the key issue being the contribution of human activity to the problem. But is the evidence for this correlational or experimental? To the extent that some evidence is correlational, at what point do you think world leaders would be willing to accept correlational evidence as conclusive?

2. How might you apply the five steps of the scientific method to a question of your own—for example, the question of whether occasionally taking time out from studying for stretching and a little exercise affects your grades?

3. What is the relation between theories and hypotheses?

4. Suppose that you were interested in studying the effects of sleep deprivation on learning ability. Which of these two variables would be the independent variable and which would be the dependent variable? How might you operationally define these variables?

5. What is the difference between description and explanation in psychology?

6. In what ways might an operational definition be reliable yet not valid? Valid yet not reliable?

Ethics

The objective study of behavior means that people and animals are the focus of psychological research. Psychologists must therefore apply the methods of science while retaining the sensitivity that is necessary to study living beings. Now that we have examined the details of the scientific method, it is important to understand how psychologists maintain this balance.

Most psychological research takes place in universities or within institutions that receive support from government agencies. Consequently, researchers do not work in the isolated environment of their own laboratory or research group. They receive the advice of their peers on how to conduct their research ethically and they are accountable for their actions. This is true of research for both human and animal behavior. In this section we'll look at the principles that guide ethical research practices.

Research with Human Participants

Great care is needed in the treatment of human participants, because we can hurt people in very subtle ways. Title 42 of the United States Code requires that every institution receiving research support funds have an institutional review board (IRB) that will review the ethics of human research and ensure that researchers comply with ethical principles and guidelines. But in addition to this regulatory requirement, psychological researchers also subscribe to the Ethical Principles of Psychologists and Code of Conduct (American Psychological Association, 2002) or follow it as a matter of

state legislation. As a code of conduct, these principles focus the attention of researchers on fundamental values and issues, because they and similar codes (e.g., Canadian Psychological Association, 2000) have developed from common social and cultural roots (see Adair, 2001; Hadjistavropoulos et al., 2002). Codes of research ethics make these shared values explicit.

Codes of human research ethics echo our widely accepted values about everyday interpersonal relations. In their everyday lives, most people believe that (1) it is wrong to hurt others needlessly; (2) it is good to help others; (3) it is usually wrong to make others do things contrary to their wishes and best interests; (4) it is usually wrong to lie to others; (5) we should respect others' privacy; (6) under most circumstances we should not break our promises to keep others' secrets; and (7) we should afford special protection to those who are relatively powerless or especially vulnerable to harm.

How are these interpersonal values translated to research relationships between researchers and participants? Codes of research ethics tell us that (1) we should minimize harm to participants, whether physical or mental; (2) we should maximize the benefits of research to participants in particular and society in general; (3) participants should be fully informed about the nature of the research in which they are invited to participate, including risks and benefits, and their **informed consent** to participate must be voluntary; (4) deception in research is generally unacceptable, although it may be tolerated under limited circumstances; (5) we should not intrude into the private lives of participants without their permission; (6) with certain exceptions, we should promise **confidentiality**—we should guarantee participants that information they provide will be kept anonymous or confidential unless they agree to make it public; and (7) vulnerable populations (e.g., children, prisoners, seriously ill patients, persons with compromised cognitive abilities) should be treated with special care. A university's IRB will have very strict guidelines about how these values must be translated into research procedures. For example, because children are members of a vulnerable population, a parent or guardian must also consent to participation in research.

[CASE STUDY] In the late 1930s, a young psychologist at the University of Iowa, Wendell Johnson, was beginning to develop a new explanation for the speech problem known as stuttering. In contrast to the prevailing theory, which held it to be a result of brain physiology, Johnson felt that stuttering originated when children were overcorrected for minor lapses of correct speech.

---

informed consent A person's agreement to participate in an experiment after he or she has received information about the nature of the research and any possible risks and benefits.

confidentiality Privacy of participants and nondisclosure of their participation in a research project.

To test this theory, Johnson and his graduate student devised a study in which children residing at a nearby orphanage were divided into different groups and given different types of feedback regarding their speech. Six children, judged to not be stutterers, were assigned to a group in which each hesitancy in speaking was pointed out to them by the experimenter over a four- to five-month period. The objective was to see if speech fluency could be adversely affected by this type of feedback (Reynolds, 2003).

Decades later, this study contrasts sharply with the research ethics we use today. The children and their caretakers (the teachers at the orphanage) were given false information to conceal the purpose of the study, and it's unclear how much the administrators knew about the intent of the project. Notice that the hypothesis envisioned that the treatment would produce speech impairments. Yet Johnson and his student apparently did not develop a pre-planned debriefing or a prearranged means to ameliorate the possible harm that might ensue (Schwartz, 2006).

When contacted sixty years later and informed of the details, the people who had been subjected to this treatment reacted with dismay and outrage (Dyer, 2001). Some reported an adult life of shyness, speech deficits, and social difficulties and, when they heard the news, attributed these problems to the consequences of the study. They sued. In August, 2007, the state of Iowa agreed to pay $925,000 to three of the surviving subjects and the estates of three others for the distress the study had caused them.

It's clearly difficult to compare an ethical decision made seventy years ago to one we would make today. However, it's helpful to consider why the former participants of this study felt so betrayed. Basically, their complaints were related to many of the principles we've just discussed: They were subjected to procedures that they, at least, felt were harmful (Principle 1); they had not given informed consent (Principle 3); they were deceived (Principle 4); and they felt that their status as wards of the state had made them vulnerable (Principle 7) (Luna, 2007). Their distress underlines the need for a code of ethics that addresses these possible results of research.

Johnson's colleagues considered him a kindly, altruistic man who would not knowingly subject children to a harmful procedure (Yairi, 2006). The lesson we can take from this episode is that such good intentions are not enough. Difficulties sometimes arise when researchers try to translate everyday values to research. Research procedures that represent good science are sometimes in conflict with respect for participants' dignity. In Chapter 15, you will read about an experiment conducted by the psychologist Philip Zimbardo, in which he attempted to study the way prison guards treated inmates under their supervision. He asked participants to play the role of either a guard or a prisoner. Although this project had considerable scientific merit and important implications for real situations (such as the incidents of abuse at Abu Ghraib prison in Iraq), Zimbardo decided to stop the project in its early stage after he realized that the role of a "prisoner" resulted in increased risk to a participant's self-esteem and dignity. The interesting problem that researchers set for themselves is how to resolve these conflicts—to accomplish the best possible research while simultaneously ensuring that participants are treated properly. Sometimes researchers speak as though the values of scientific inquiry themselves are contrary to the value of respecting people. This is not the case. Effective research procedures, not the values of scientific inquiry, are sometimes in conflict with good treatment of participants. The goal is to identify and use research procedures that are both as ethical and as scientifically valid as possible.

You may have noticed that the list of research ethics values derived from interpersonal values includes exceptions to the general rules (as is the case for the interpersonal values themselves). For example, sometimes telling participants the full truth about the nature of the research will invalidate the research results (see Principle 4). In this type of situation, the researcher may decide that concealing the hypothesis from participants, or actively deceiving them about the nature of the hypothesis, would be good science.

Yet there is a conflict with the interpersonal value of not telling lies. The result of ethical decision making and ethics review by IRBs is sometimes to identify an acceptable balance. The researcher may be permitted to use concealment or minor deception, but only if there is no foreseeable harm to participants and if the researcher can re-establish trust with participants by immediately disclosing the truth to them on completion of the experiment, a process called **debriefing.**

Research with Animals

Although most psychologists study the behavior of humans, some study the behavior of other animals. Any time another species of animal is used for research purposes, the research itself should be humane and worthwhile. Humane treatment is a matter of procedure. We know how to maintain laboratory animals in good health and in comfortable, sanitary conditions. For experiments that involve surgery, we know how to administer anesthetics and analgesics so that animals do not suffer. Most industrially developed societies have very strict regulations about the care of animals and require approval of the procedures that will be used in animal experiments. American psychologists who use animals in their research adhere to ethical guidelines developed by the American Psychological Association (2007) and regulations of various federal agencies such as the National Institutes of Health and the U.S. Department of Agriculture. Under these guidelines projects involving animals, including teaching and research projects but excepting some purely observational studies, are reviewed by a committee that must include a veterinarian and a member of the public community not affiliated with the institution where the research is carried out (Public Health Service, 2002). These committee members

---

debriefing   Full disclosure to research participants of the nature and purpose of a research project after its completion.

Should animals be used in psychological research? Most psychologists and other researchers strongly believe that animal research, conducted humanely, is necessary and ethically justified.

rigorously review the experimental procedures and have the authority to prevent or halt a project that does not adhere to ethical principles. The guidelines provide very specific instructions about how animals are to be housed, how they are to be fed, and how sources of stress are to be minimized.

Whether the use of animals in research is justified is a question that must be asked every time a study is proposed. One factor to consider is the nature of the controls placed on research activity as compared to the controls on some other uses of animals. For example, we know that, sadly, some pet owners cause much more suffering among animals than scientific research does. As Miller (1983) notes, pet owners are not required to receive permission from boards of experts that include veterinarians; nor are they subject to periodic inspections to ensure that their homes are clean and sanitary, that their pets have enough space to exercise properly, and that their diets are appropriate.

The core reality is that virtually all animals on this planet, especially our own species, are beset by medical, mental, and behavioral problems, many of which can be solved only through research involving nonhuman animals. Research with laboratory animals has produced important discoveries about the possible causes or potential treatments of neurological and mental disorders, including Parkinson's disease, schizophrenia, bipolar disorder, anxiety disorders, obsessive-compulsive disorders, anorexia nervosa, obesity, and drug addictions. Although much progress has been made, these problems are still with us and cause much human suffering.

But, as a result of discoveries you will read about in Chapter 4, we now have the ability to describe the inner workings of the human brain in healthy and alert people and to even produce motion pictures of the brain at work. This research has the promise of providing answers to the problems that have been mentioned, but only if we can understand the basic principles of neurology and behavior. Often, this understanding can only be gained by research that involves animals. Some people (e.g., the Alternatives Research and Development Foundation of Jenkinton, Pennsylvania)

have suggested that instead of using laboratory animals in our research, we could use tissue cultures or computer simulations. Unfortunately, tissue cultures or computer simulations are not necessarily interchangeable substitutes for living organisms. We have no way to study behavioral problems such as addictions in tissue cultures, nor can we program a computer to simulate the workings of an animal's nervous system. If we could, we would already have all the answers.

QUESTIONS TO CONSIDER

1. In your opinion, should principles of ethical research be absolute, or should they be flexible? Suppose that a researcher proposed to perform an experiment whose results could have important and beneficial consequences for society, perhaps a real reduction in violent crime. However, the proposed study would violate ethical guidelines, because it would involve deception and a significant degree of psychological pain for the participants. Should the researcher be given permission to perform the experiment? Should an exception be made because of the potential benefits to society?

2. Is there a difference between using animals for research and exploiting animals for other purposes? Why might people differ in the way they answer this?

3. Think of an experiment you would like to conduct. What ethical issues do you think would arise from it and how would you address these?

Understanding Research Results

Our study is finished. We have a collection of data—numbers representing the measurements of behavior we have made. Now what do we do? How do we know what we found? Was our hypothesis supported? To answer these questions, we must analyze the data we have collected. We will use some statistical methods to do so.

Descriptive Statistics: What Are the Results?

In the examples of experimental research that we have considered so far, the behavior of participants assigned to groups (conditions) was observed and measured. Once a study is finished, we need some way to compare these measurements. We use **descriptive statistics,** mathematical procedures that permit us to summarize sets of numbers. Using these procedures, we will calculate measures that summarize the performance of the participants in each group. Then we can compare these measures to see whether the groups of participants behaved differently (step 4 of the scientific method). We can also use these measures to describe the results of the experiment to others (step 5 of the scientific method). You are already familiar with

---

descriptive statistics   Mathematical procedures for organizing collections of data.

some descriptive statistics. For example, you know how to calculate the average of a set of numbers; an average is a common *measure of central tendency*. You may be less familiar with *measures of variability*, which tell us how groups of numbers differ from one another, and with measures of *relations*, which tell us how closely related two sets of numbers are.

Measures of Central Tendency When we say that the average weight of an adult male in North America is 173 pounds or that the average salary of a female university graduate was $40,750 in 2004, we are using a **measure of central tendency**, a statistic that represents many observations. There are several different measures of central tendency, but the most common is the average, also called the **mean.** We calculate the mean of a set of observations by adding the individual values and dividing by the number of observations. The mean is the most frequently used measure of central tendency in reports of psychological experiments.

Although the mean is usually selected to measure central tendency, it is not the most precise measure, especially if a set of numbers contains a few extremely high or low values. Under these conditions, the most representative measure of central tendency is the **median,** the midpoint of values. Using the median avoids the distortion produced by exceptionally large number values.

Measures of Variability Many experiments produce two sets of numbers, one consisting of the experimental group's scores and one consisting of the control group's scores. If the mean scores of these two groups differ, the researcher can conclude that the independent variable had an effect. However, the researcher must decide whether the difference between the two groups is large. To make this decision, the researcher calculates a **measure of variability**—a statistic that describes the degree to which scores in a set of numbers differ from one another. The psychologist then uses this measure as a basis for comparing the means of the two groups.

Two sets of numbers can have the same mean or median and still be very different in their overall character. For example, the mean and the median of both sets of numbers listed in TABLE 2·2 are the same, but the sets of numbers are clearly different. The variability of the scores in Sample B is greater.

One way of stating the difference between the two sets of numbers in Table 2.2 is to say that the numbers in Sample A

---

measure of central tendency A statistical measure used to characterize the value of items in a sample of numbers.

mean A measure of central tendency; the sum of a group of values divided by their number; the arithmetical average.

median A measure of central tendency; the midpoint of a group of values arranged numerically.

measure of variability A statistic that describes the degree to which scores in a set of numbers differ from one another.

range The difference between the highest score and the lowest score of a sample.

standard deviation A statistic that expresses the variability of a measurement; square root of the average of the squared deviations from the mean.

[**TABLE 2·2**] Two Sets of Numbers Having the Same Mean and Median but Different Ranges

Sample A		Sample B	
8		0	
9		5	
10	Median	10	Median
11		15	
12		20	
Total:	50	Total:	50
Mean:	50/5 =10	Mean:	50/5 = 10
Range:	12 – 8 = 4	Range:	20 – 0 = 20

range from 8 to 12 and the numbers in Sample B range from 0 to 20. The **range** of a set of numbers is simply the largest number minus the smallest. Thus, the range of Sample A is 4 and the range of Sample B is 20.

The range is not used very often to describe the results of psychological experiments, however, because another measure of variability, the **standard deviation,** has more useful mathematical properties. As TABLE 2·3 shows, to calculate the standard deviation of a set of numbers, you first calculate the mean

[**TABLE 2·3**] Calculation of the Variance and Standard Deviation of Two Sets of Numbers Having the Same Mean

SAMPLE A		
Score	**Difference between Score and Mean**	**Difference Squared**
8	10 – 8 = 2	4
9	10 – 9 = 1	1
10	10 – 10 = 0	0
11	11 – 10 = 1	1
12	12 – 10 = 2	4
Total: 50	Total:	10
Mean: 50/5 = 10	Mean (variance):	10/5 = 2
	Square root (standard deviation):	$\sqrt{2}$ = 1.41

SAMPLE B		
Score	**Difference between Score and Mean**	**Difference Squared**
0	10 – 0 = 10	100
5	10 – 5 = 5	25
10	10 – 10 = 0	0
15	15 – 10 = 5	25
20	20 – 10 = 10	100
Total: 50	Total:	250
Mean: 50/5 = 10	Mean (variance):	250/5 = 50
	Square root (standard deviation):	$\sqrt{50}$ = 7.07

and then find the difference between each number and the mean. These different scores are squared (that is, multiplied by themselves) and then summed. The mean calculated from this total is called the *variance;* the standard deviation is the square root of the variance. The more different the numbers are from one another, the larger the standard deviation will be.

Measurement of Relations In correlational studies, the investigator measures the degree to which two variables are related. For example, suppose that we have developed a new aptitude test and hope to persuade a college administrator to use the test when evaluating applicants. We need to show a relation between scores on our test and measures of success (such as grades) in the college's program. Assume that the college uses a letter grading system in which A designates the top grade and F designates a failure. To analyze our test quantitatively, we need to convert these labels into numerical scores; we use the convention that an A is 4, an F is 0, and the letters in between have corresponding values.

We give the test to 10 students entering the college and later obtain their average grades. We will have two scores for each person, as shown in TABLE 2•4. We can examine the relation between these variables by plotting the scores on a graph. For example, student R. J. received a test score of 14 and earned an average grade of 3.0. We can represent this student's score as a point on the graph shown in FIGURE 2•9. The horizontal axis represents the test score, and the vertical axis represents the average grade. We put a point on the graph that corresponds to R. J.'s score on both of these measures.

We do this for each of the remaining students and then look at the graph, called a **scatterplot,** to determine whether the two variables are related. When we examine the scatterplot (refer to Figure 2.9), we see that the points tend to be located along a diagonal line that runs from the lower left to the upper right, indicating that a rather strong relation exists between students' test scores and their average grades. High scores are associated with good grades, low scores with poor grades.

Although scatterplots are useful, we need a more convenient way to communicate the results to others, so we calculate the **correlation coefficient,** a number that expresses the strength

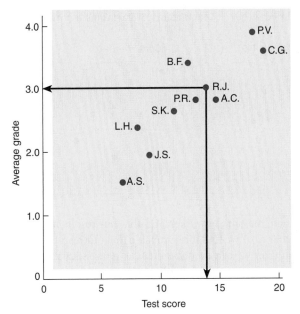

[FIGURE 2•9] A scatterplot of the test scores and average grades of 10 students. An example of graphing one data point (student R. J.) is shown by the colored lines.

of a relation. Calculating this statistic for the two sets of scores gives a correlation of +0.9 between the two variables.

The size of a correlation coefficient can vary from 0 (no relation) to plus or minus 1.0 (a perfect relation). A perfect relation means that if we know the value of a person's score on one measure, then we can predict exactly what his or her score will be on the other. Thus, a correlation of +0.9 is very close to perfect; our hypothetical aptitude test is an excellent predictor of how well a student will do at the college. A *positive correlation* indicates that high values on one measure are associated with high values on the other and that low values on one are associated with low values on the other.

Correlations can be negative as well as positive. A *negative correlation* indicates that high values on one measure are associated with low values on the other, and vice versa. An example of a negative correlation is the relation between people's mathematical ability and the amount of time it takes them to solve a series of math problems. People with the highest level of ability will take the least time to solve the problems. For purposes of prediction, a negative correlation is just as good as a positive one. Examples of scatterplots illustrating high and low correlations, both positive and negative, are shown in FIGURE 2•10.

Inferential Statistics: Distinguishing Chance from Significance

When we perform an experiment, we'd like to say that our results are not due to some rare fluke or chance accident. We

[TABLE 2•4] Test Score and Average Grades of Ten Students

Student	Test Score	Average Grade[a]
A. C.	15	2.8
B. F.	12	3.2
C. G.	19	3.5
L. H.	8	2.2
R. J.	14	3.0
S. K.	11	2.6
P. R.	13	2.8
A. S.	7	1.5
J. S.	9	1.9
P. V.	18	3.8

[a]0 = F; 4 = A

scatterplot A graph of items that have two values; one value is plotted against the horizontal axis and the other against the vertical axis.

correlation coefficient A measurement of the degree to which two variables are related.

[FIGURE 2·10] Scatterplots of variables having several different levels of correlation.

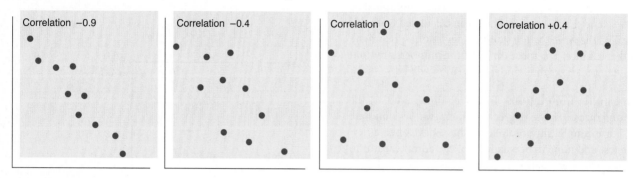

must, then, measure how likely it is that our results might be due to chance. If we find it improbable that our results are accidental, then we can describe them as possessing **statistical significance**—as being probably not due to chance. As we saw, descriptive statistics enable us to summarize our data. **Inferential statistics** enable us to calculate the probability that our results are due to chance and thereby tell us whether the results are statistically significant.

The concept of statistical significance is not easy to grasp, so I want to make sure you understand the purpose of this discussion. Recall our experiment designed to test the hypothesis that caffeine increases the rate of detection of a change in the image of a traffic scene. We give some of the participants in our experiment a measured dose of caffeine. Next, we show presentations of the original image and its changed version to participants in both groups and record how long it takes them to detect the changed image. To see whether caffeine has improved detection of the change, we calculate the mean response time for both groups. If the means are different, we can conclude that visual expectation *does* affect people's ability to recognize a change.

But how different is different? Suppose that we tested two groups of people, both treated exactly the same way. Would the mean scores of the two groups be precisely the same? Of course not. *By chance,* they would be at least slightly different. Suppose that we find that the mean score for the group that was given caffeine is lower than the mean score for the control group. How much lower would it have to be before we could rightfully conclude that the difference between the groups was significant?

Assessment of Differences between Samples The obvious way to determine whether two group means differ significantly is to look at the size of the difference. If it is large, then we can be fairly confident that the independent variable had a significant effect. If it is small, then the difference may well

be due to chance. What we need are guidelines to help us determine when a difference is large enough to be statistically significant.

The following example, based on a real classroom demonstration and results, will explain how these guidelines are constructed. A few years ago, a simple correlational study was performed to test the following hypothesis: In North America people whose first names end in vowels will, on average, be shorter than people whose first names end in consonants. (The rationale for this hypothesis will be revealed later.)

First, each student in a psychology class received a blank card and was asked to print his or her first name on the card together with his or her height. There were 76 students in the class, and the mean height for all students was 67.2 inches. Next, the participants were divided into two groups: those whose first names ended in vowels and those whose first names ended in consonants. TABLE 2·5 contains a listing of these two groups. You can see that the means for the two groups differed by 4.1 inches.

A difference of 4.1 inches seems large, but how can we be sure that it is not due to chance? What we really need to know is how large a difference there would be if the means had been calculated from two groups that were randomly selected. For comparison, the class was divided into two random groups by shuffling the cards with the students' names on them and dealing them out into two piles, "A" and "B." Then, the mean height of the people whose names were in each of the piles was calculated. Subtracting the "B" group mean from the "A" group showed that the difference between the means was −0.7 inch. (See TABLE 2·6.)

The cards were then divided into two random piles five more times, and each time the means were calculated and the "B" mean was subtracted from the "A" mean. The differences for these five random divisions ranged from −0.3 to 0.7 inch. (See TABLE 2·7.) It began to look as if a mean difference of 4.1 inches was bigger than would be expected to occur by chance.

Next, the cards were divided into two random piles 1000 times. (A computer performed this chore.) *Not once* in 1000 times was the difference between the means greater than 3.0 inches. The researcher concluded that if the class was divided randomly into two groups, the chance that the means of their heights would differ by 4.1 inches was much

---

statistical significance   The likelihood that an observed relation or difference between two variables really exists rather than being due to chance factors.

inferential statistics   Mathematical and logical procedures for determining whether relations or differences between samples are statistically significant.

[TABLE 2·5] Height (in Inches) of Selected Samples of Students

Name Ends in Consonant		Name Ends in Vowel
65	61	67
67	68	68
71	70	62
72	65	63
73	73	62
65	60	64
74	70	60
74	72	63
67	63	61
69	67	69
68	73	63
75	66	65
72	71	69
71	72	71
65	64	69
66	69	65
70	73	70
72	75	63
72	72	63
71	66	64
62	71	65
62	68	63
80	70	66
	75	62
Total:	3257	72
Mean:	3257/47 = 69.3	65
		66
		65
		65
		Total: 1890
		Mean: 1890/29 = 65.2
		Difference between means: 69.3 − 65.2 = 4.1

[TABLE 2·6] Height (in Inches) of Students Assigned Randomly to Two Groups

Group A		Group B	
65	71	63	62
72	63	62	63
72	74	70	65
70	72	70	75
61	71	65	71
69	65	64	80
66	71	75	71
70	67	63	68
66	72	70	71
65	66	75	73
66	72	67	62
65	73	65	72
64	63	68	65
72	69	63	72
63	62	69	66
65	60	67	73
62	70	68	65
67	68	60	73
	69		61
	64		74
Total: 2561		Total: 2586	
Mean: 67.4		Mean: 68.1	
	Difference: −0.7		

that the difference between the means fell between −0.2 and +0.2 inch.

The method used to determine the statistical significance of these findings involves the same principles that researchers use to determine whether the results observed in an experiment represent a real difference or are merely due to chance. In this example two possibilities were considered: (1) that the difference between the means was due to chance, and (2) that the difference between the means occurred because the last letter of a person's first name is related to his or her height. Because a difference of 4.1 inches would be expected less than one time in a thousand, the researcher rejected alternative 1

[TABLE 2·7] Mean Heights (in Inches) of Five Random Divisions of Students into Two Groups

Group A	Group B	Difference
67.6	67.9	−0.3
68.1	67.4	0.7
67.8	67.6	0.2
67.9	67.5	0.4
68.0	67.4	0.6

less than one time in a thousand, or 0.1%. Thus, it is safe to say that when the students were divided into two groups according to the last letters of their first names, they were being divided in a way that was somehow related to their height. The division was *not* equivalent to random selection; a person's height *really is* related to the last letter of his or her first name.

FIGURE 2·11 presents a frequency distribution of the differences between the means of the two groups for 1000 random divisions of the class. The height of a point on the graph represents the number of times (the frequency) that the difference between the means fell into that particular range. Notice that the most frequent case includes a difference of 0—according to the graph, there were 170 times

and concluded that alternative 2 was correct. The results supported the original hypothesis.

Ordinarily, psychologists who conduct experiments or correlational studies like this one do not use their computers to divide their participants' scores randomly 1000 times. Instead, they calculate the mean and standard deviation for each group and consult a table that statisticians have already prepared for them. The table is based on special mathematical properties of the mean and standard deviation, and describes what is called a *normal distribution;* the shape of a normal distribution is similar to the frequency distribution depicted in Figure 2.11. Using a normal distribution as a guide, psychologists can tell how likely it is that their results could have been obtained by chance. For example, the table would tell us how likely it is that the last letter of a person's first name is *not really* related to his or her height. If the likelihood of a chance result is low enough, psychologists will conclude that their research results are statistically significant. Most psychologists consider a 5% probability of chance to be statistically significant but are much more comfortable with 1% or less. Please note that statistical tests help us decide whether results are representative of the larger population, but not whether they are *important.* In general usage the word *significant* does mean "important," but *statistical* significance simply means that the results appear not to be caused by chance.

Oh yes, why would anyone ever guess (hypothesize) that the last letter of a person's first name would be related to his or her height? The answer is that in English, feminine names are more likely than masculine names to end in a vowel (Paula, Tara, Marie, etc.). Because women tend to be shorter than men, one could expect that among a group of English-speaking students, a group of students whose first names ended in vowels would be shorter, on average, than those whose first names ended in consonants.

Alternative Methods

You might be asking: Are there other ways of using the scientific method? **Qualitative research** is an alternative research method that does not use numerically measured variables. Although this sounds like a classification defined by an absence, in reality qualitative researchers add a number of new dimensions to applications of the scientific method. We'll examine a few of them here.

Qualitative psychologists examine diaries, poems, people's conversations and interactions with others, and other forms of personal expression. Their research settings can be naturalistic observation, clinical case studies, structured interviews, or even cultural ceremonies in which the researcher participates. Often, the emphasis is on gaining insight into the subjective meaning of experiences and behaviors. The data used in qualitative research can be quite varied. In a study of how people remember and reason about the spatial aspects of their neighborhoods, Hart (1979) accompanied children to their favorite haunts and asked them to draw maps or build models in a sandbox of how they would get there. Studying the same general problem of spatial knowledge, Hutchins (1995) copied the organizational charts of the U.S. Navy and transcribed the dialog between different members of the bridge staff. Gladwin (1970) studied the navigational knowledge of indigenous peoples by accompanying Oceanic sailors in their canoes across the South Pacific and describing their traditional star constellations. Clearly, a single research area (spatial cognition) can be studied in quite varied (and exotic) ways. (See FIGURE 2•12.)

qualitative research An alternative research strategy stressing the observation of variables that are not numerically measurable.

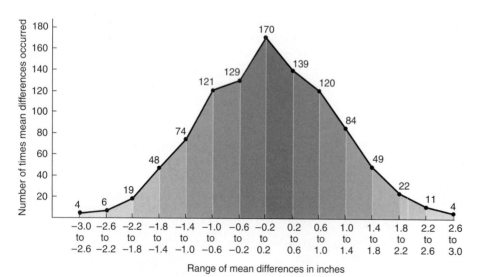

[**FIGURE 2•11**] A frequency distribution. This distribution illustrates the number of occurrences of various ranges of mean differences in height. The group of 76 people was divided randomly into two sets of numbers 1000 times.

[**FIGURE 2·12**] Some examples of qualitative data. *Upper panel:* A sketch map drawn by a nine-year-old girl of her play area, including imaginary features. From Hart, R. (1979). *Children's experience of place.* New York: Irvington. *Middle panel:* A schematic diagram of the star sightings on a typical course navigated by a Puluwat Atoll islander. From Gladwin, T. (1970). *East is a bird bird: Navigation and logic on Puluwat Atoll.* Cambridge, MA: Harvard University Press. *Lower panel:* A transcript of three bridge personnel organizing the steps of navigating a large naval ship. From Hutchins, E. (1995). *Cognition in the wild.* Cambridge, MA: MIT Press.

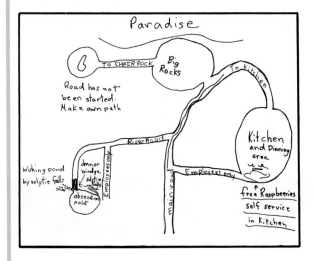

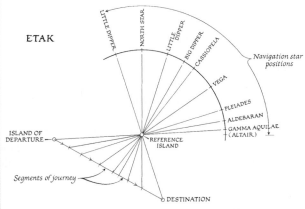

SW: John?

Recorder: Yo!

SW: Is the Dive Tower right on our beam?

Recorder: Say again?

SW: Dive Tower. Isn't it just about on our beam?

Recorder: Yeah, just about. (2 seconds) Ok, Shades?

PW: What?

Recorder: Steve's gonna be shooting the Dive Tower first, so let him say, uh, let him say the bearing first.

PW: You want Point Loma last, then?

Recorder: Yeah, that's fine.

However, you shouldn't form the impression that qualitative research is somehow exempt from the rigor that the scientific method demands. Qualitative research can, and often does, follow the five-step progression outlined earlier (although the notion of an "experiment" is usually quite different). It is also the case that qualitative data can be translated into numerical forms and analyzed with statistical techniques (Trochim, 2005). Guba and Lincoln (1981) have suggested that qualitative research results should be credible, transferable, dependable, and confirmable. *Credible* means that the data are believable from the standpoint of the participant. *Transferability* means that another person has sufficient information to generalize the results to another setting. *Dependable* means that the researcher has described all the conditions under which the results will be consistently obtained. Finally, *confirmability* means that persons other than the researcher can check the accuracy of the results. Meeting these criteria can be a considerable challenge for the qualitative researcher.

Single-subject designs are alternatives to the use of conventional statistical techniques. In a single-subject design, the researcher observes the effect of some manipulation on an individual participant or subject. The method is most often employed by behavior analysts, who are interested in the way behavior changes because of its consequences. Usually, single-subject designs employ a sequence: Behavior is measured as it occurs in some original state; this is known as the *behavioral baseline*. Then, some change is introduced, such as modifying the consequences of the behavior being observed; the researcher looks to see if the behavior has changed as well. Finally, the change is reversed in some manner, so that the baseline state is presumably reestablished. If the behavior returns to its baseline level, the researcher can be confident that a cause-and-effect relationship exists between the manipulation and the behavior.

Single-subject researchers concentrate on investigations that have one, or at most a few, participants. They believe that if the evidence of a cause-and-effect relationship in one case is strong enough, it will generalize to other cases. Furthermore, they believe that proper scientific procedures will eliminate chance factors and hence make statistical procedures superfluous. When a clinical psychologist is treating someone with a psychological problem, this is often enough: After all, the goal of therapy is to heal. A pioneer of the single-subject approach, the behaviorist B. F. Skinner, once observed: "When you have the responsibility of making absolutely sure that a given organism will engage in a given sort of behavior at a given time, you quickly grow impatient with principles, hypotheses, theorems, and statistical proof at the .05 level of significance. No one goes to the circus to see the average dog jump through a hoop significantly oftener than untrained dogs raised under the same circumstances . . ." (Skinner, 1956, p. 228).

single-subject design An alternative research strategy that examines the effects of a manipulation on an individual participant or subject.

QUESTIONS TO CONSIDER

1. Can you think of some real-life variables that you would expect to be positively and negatively correlated?
2. What does it mean to say that a study produced statistically significant results? Why might the results of a study be statistically significant but nevertheless unimportant?
3. What behaviors do you think could be studied cross-culturally and what do you predict you would find?

Epilogue

Bias and Sensitivity in Justine's Experiment

Our discussion of the ways and means of psychology gives us some insight into Justine's project described in the opening vignette. Though it cost her a sore neck and back, Justine's naturalistic observation generated her hypothesis about a possible cause. With Lawrence's help, her introduction of new chairs was a test of that hypothesis.

Justine was facing two issues common to any test of a hypothesis: Was her procedure *sensitive* and was it free of *bias*? Now that you understand the concepts of psychological research, we can explore these two issues further.

A procedure that tests a hypothesis is sensitive to the extent that it can detect whether the hypothesis is true. The fact that a hypothesis is correct could be obscured by the many chance factors that operate during an experiment. As we've seen, single-subject methods of research try to increase sensitivity by strict controls that eliminate random factors. Statistical approaches accomplish this by increasing the number of participants in a study so that random factors cancel each other out. Justine's experiment was clearly sensitive, since she was able to obtain a significant result.

Bias is a more subtle matter. Bias is the combination of factors that tend to produce positive research findings when they are not, in fact, true (Ioannidis, 2005). Irrespective of the sensitivity of a test, bias can make a non-effect look real or, in the case of reverse bias, make a real effect look false.

We have discussed several possible sources of bias. Assignment of participants to an experimental condition could be a source of bias: If Justine had given new employees the new chairs and compared their productivity to older employees, her experiment clearly would be susceptible to bias. As it was, Justine would have to be careful that the week in which she introduced the chairs didn't overlap with some other factor that could increase productivity (such as a week with a payday in it). Justine's eagerness to report a solution to her parents (akin to "publishing" an article) could also be a source of bias. The competitive nature of science similarly tends to induce a bias to prematurely publish research findings.

The lesson from Justine's story, of course, is that her very attempt to test her hypothesis was a source of bias—her own expectations and the desire of her parents' employees to match those expectations. By now, you understand this as the Hawthorne effect—a special case of expectancy effects. But there's a general point to be made here as well. Aside from naturalistic studies and some kinds of correlational research, psychological investigation is itself a form of intervention. When we, as psychologists, study behavior, we conceivably alter it. Questions of ethics have been an important part of our discussion of the ways and means of psychology. We must always consider that our procedures have consequences. Doing so makes us better psychologists and better neighbors to our fellow humans.

CHAPTER SUMMARY

The Scientific Method in Psychology

The scientific method allows us to determine the causes of phenomena. There are three basic forms of scientific research: naturalistic or clinical observations, correlational studies, and experiments. Only experiments permit us to be certain that a cause-and-effect relation exists. An experiment tests the truth of a hypothesis—a tentative statement about a relation between an independent variable and a dependent variable.

To perform an experiment, a scientist manipulates the values of the independent variable and measures changes in the dependent variable. Because a hypothesis is stated in general terms, the scientist must specify the particular operations that he or she will perform to manipulate the independent variable and to measure the dependent variable. That is, the researcher must provide operational definitions, which may require some ingenuity and hard work. Operational definitions are a necessary part of the procedure of testing a hypothesis; they also can eliminate confusion by giving concrete form to the hypothesis, making its meaning absolutely clear to other scientists.

Validity is the degree to which an operational definition succeeds in producing a particular value of an independent variable or in measuring the value of a dependent variable. Reliability has to do with the consistency and precision of an operational definition. Researchers achieve high reliability by carefully controlling the conditions of their studies and by ensuring that procedures are followed correctly.

When designing an experiment, researchers must be sure to control extraneous variables that may confound their results. Confounding of participant variables can be caused by improper assignment of participants to groups or by treatments that cause some participants to leave the experiment. Another problem involves participants' expectations. If knowledge of the experimental condition could alter the participants' behavior, one solution is to conduct the experiment with a single-blind procedure. Concealment or deception is sometimes a solution as well. If knowledge about the participants' condition might also alter the researcher's assessment of the participants' behavior, a double-blind procedure can be used.

Correlational studies involve assessing relations among variables that the researcher cannot readily manipulate. The investigator attempts to hold these variables constant by matching members in each of the groups on all relevant variables except for the one being studied. But even a well-designed correlational study cannot determine which variable is the cause and which is the effect.

Researchers are almost never interested only in the particular participants they study; they want to be able to generalize their results to a larger population. The confidence that researchers can have in their generalizations depends on both the nature of the variables being studied and the composition of the sample group of participants. Replicability also supports generalization.

Ethics

Because psychologists study living organisms, they must follow ethical principles in the treatment of these organisms. Federal law requires review by an institutional review board before any human research is undertaken in institutions receiving funding from agencies of the United States. Ethical principles for research are similar to those that guide people in their everyday lives and include minimizing harm to participants, ensuring informed consent, respecting confidentiality, and avoiding deception in most circumstances.

Research that involves the use of laboratory animals also is guided by ethical principles. It is incumbent on all scientists using these animals to see that they are housed comfortably and treated humanely, and laws have been enacted to ensure that they are. Research with animals has produced many benefits to humankind and promises to continue to do so.

Understanding Research Results

Psychologists need ways to communicate their results to others accurately and concisely. They typically employ three kinds of descriptive statistics: measures of central tendency, variability, and relations. The most common examples of these measures are the mean, the median, the standard deviation, and the correlation coefficient.

Psychologists perform experiments by observing the performance of two or more groups of participants who have been exposed to different conditions, each representing different values of the independent variable. Next, they calculate the group means and standard deviations of the values of the dependent variable that were measured. Finally, they determine the statistical significance of the results. If the probability of obtaining these results by chance is sufficiently low, the psychologists will reject the possibility that the independent variable had *no effect* and will decide in favor of the alternative—that the independent variable really did have an effect on the dependent variable.

succeed with mypsychlab

Visit MyPsychLab for practice quizzes, flashcards, and dozens of videos and animated tutorials, including the following items you can find in the "Multimedia Library":

Before Informed Consent: Robert Guthrie
Research Methods

Correlations Do Not Show Causation
Diversity in Psychological Inquiry

Distinguishing Independent and
Dependent Variables
Doing Simple Statistics

KEY TERMS

case study *p. 31*
clinical observation *p. 29*
confidentiality *p. 43*
confounding of variables *p. 34*
control group *p. 32*
correlation coefficient *p. 47*
correlational study *p. 29*
counterbalancing *p. 35*
debriefing *p. 44*
dependent variable *p. 32*
descriptive statistics *p. 45*
double-blind study *p. 39*
experiment *p. 28*
experimental group *p. 32*
generalize *p. 41*
hypothesis *p. 30*
independent variable *p. 32*
inferential statistics *p. 48*
informed consent *p. 43*
interrater reliability *p. 36*
manipulation *p. 32*
matching *p. 40*
mean *p. 46*
measure of central tendency *p. 46*

measure of variability *p. 46*
median *p. 46*
naturalistic observation *p. 29*
nominal fallacy *p. 33*
operational definition *p. 34*
placebo *p. 38*
qualitative research *p. 50*
random assignment *p. 37*
range *p. 46*
reliability *p. 36*
replication *p. 41*
response bias *p. 36*
sample *p. 41*
scatterplot *p. 47*
scientific method *p. 28*
single-blind study *p. 38*
single-subject design *p. 51*
standard deviation *p. 46*
statistical significance *p. 48*
survey study *p. 31*
theory *p. 30*
validity *p. 34*
variable *p. 32*

SUGGESTIONS FOR FURTHER READING

Ethical Issues in Psychological Testing

Blum, D. (1994). *The monkey wars.* Oxford: Oxford University Press.

Gale, A. (1995). Ethical issues in psychological research. In A. M. Coleman (Ed.), *Psychological research methods and statistics.* London: Longman.

Wilhelm, K. (2006). Do animals have feelings? *Scientific American Mind, 17*(1), 24–29.

Blum's book is a well-written, generally well-balanced account of the use of animals (primarily primates) in science research. Gale's succinct chapter is a good introduction to ethics and psychological research. Wilhelm gives a provocative look at the question of emotions in other animals.

Research Methods: General Reading

Abelson, R. P. (1995). *Statistics as principled argument.* Hillsdale, NJ: Lawrence Erlbaum Associates.

Christensen, L. B. (2003). *Experimental methodology* (9th ed.). Boston: Allyn and Bacon.

Sternberg, R. J. (2006). *Reviewing scientific works in psychology.* Washington, D.C.: American Psychological Association.

Several standard textbooks discuss the scientific method in psychological research. The Christensen book covers ethical and practical issues as well as theoretical ones. Abelson's book explores the logic behind statistical tests. Sternberg's book is actually a manual written for researchers who review other researchers' work. It's a good look at how research reports are evaluated for publication.

Alternative Research Methods

Haworth, J. (1996). *Psychological research: Innovative methods and statistics.* London: Routledge.

Hayes, N. (1997). *Doing qualitative analysis in psychology.* Hove, UK: Psychology Press.

Haworth's text covers unusual (or "innovative") approaches to studying psychology; there is not much on quantitative analysis but a great deal on surveys and the approaches taken by sub-areas of psychology (such as the single-case study in psychology and hypnotic techniques in clinical/consciousness research). The chapters in Hayes's book, written by experts in the field, introduce qualitative psychology in a readable and sometimes critical way.

Evolution, Heredity, and Behavior

Prologue

A Favored Son?

John Harold Johnson died at the young age of 25. He died from a disease called sickle-cell anemia. Sickle-cell anemia is a disorder in which the red-blood cells that carry oxygen to the body become curved and sticky. Normally, red-blood cells are flat and smooth and pass readily through even small blood vessels. However, because of the change in shape caused by sickle-cell anemia some of the red-blood cells become stuck in the smaller blood vessels. This produces a painful condition with widespread damage to the body's organs. The disease is known to run in families. But John's parents and his sister did not have the disease. How could John have sickle-cell anemia? In addition, his entire family is long-lived. John's father, for whom he was named, died recently at the age of 87 and—at this writing—his mother and sister are still alive. Moreover, John Jr.'s family was not only long-lived but highly accomplished. His father rose from a poor background to found *Ebony* magazine and several other companies. In fact, he was the first African American listed among Forbes' 400 wealthiest Americans. His mother and his sister were also achievers. His mother suggested the name for the magazine and his sister now runs the publishing company that her father founded. John Jr. seems truly a favored son by virtue of both the environments of his ancestors and his personal environment. How could John Jr. not be among the "fittest"?

More generally, how could such a potentially devastating disease remain in the human family if its effects were so terrible? Would not "survival of the fittest" eliminate the disease from the human population? The answers

John Harold Johnson Sr., founder of *Ebony* magazine.

to these puzzling questions, and many others, are provided by Darwin's principle of natural selection when coupled with the biological mechanisms that implement it—genetics. ■

The Development of Evolutionary Science

When we come upon a story like that of John Harold Johnson, Jr., we are puzzled. He seems to have had every advantage of birth and fortune and, yet, he died at a young age from a disease that runs in families. Charles Darwin was also struck by similarly puzzling observations and he searched for some way to make sense of them. Later in life, he reflected upon his achievements as follows: "My mind seems to have become a kind of machine for grinding general laws out of large collections of facts" (1888, p. 139). How did Darwin come upon his "large collection of facts"?

The Voyage of the *Beagle*

As a young man, Darwin had few scholarly interests. He spent much of his time hiking around the English countryside, examining rock formations, and shooting small game. Uncertain about what to do with his life, he began to study religion at Christ's College, Cambridge. He considered becoming a country parson—a fairly common occupation for upper-class Englishmen with undefined interests. However, in 1831, Darwin was introduced by a mutual acquaintance to Captain Robert Fitz Roy, an officer in the royal navy. Fitz Roy was looking for someone to serve as an unpaid naturalist and traveling companion during a five-year voyage on the *HMS Beagle*. The *Beagle*'s mission was to explore and survey the coast of South America and to make worldwide nautical observations that would benefit the British navy. After overcoming his father's objections, Darwin volunteered for the voyage.

During the voyage, Darwin observed the animals and plants of South America, Australia, South Africa, and the islands of the Pacific, South Atlantic, and Indian oceans. These included most notably the Galapagos Islands off the west coast of South America. Darwin spent most of his time collecting specimens of plants, objects of various sorts, and animals (most of which he shot, continuing his boyhood habit). He did not form his theory of evolution through natural selection while at sea, although he was struck by the tremendous diversity among seemingly related animals. He interpreted this diversity as being consistent with the doctrine of *essentialism*. Essentialism, which can be traced to the Greek philosopher Plato, views all living things as belonging to fixed classes or "kinds." Each class is thought to have unchanging characteristics that reflect the essential quality of each species and separate each species from others (Mayr, 2001).

The Origin of Species

Darwin returned to England in 1836 and began to sift through his collections, comparing the similarities and differences of the creatures he had found. He carefully reviewed the work of earlier naturalists. His own grandfather, Erasmus Darwin, had speculated about evolution but was unable to

Charles Darwin (1809–1882)

account for how the changes came about. Darwin also became interested in the process of **artificial selection,** a practice in which animal breeders selectively mated animals, with the goal of producing offspring that possessed desirable characteristics. Using artificial selection, breeders selectively mated sheep that grew heavier wool coats, cows that produced more abundant milk, and birds that had more beautiful plumage. For example, a pigeon fancier who wanted to produce a pigeon with beautiful plumage would examine the available variation in his colony and permit only the most beautiful birds to mate with one another. When this process was repeated over generations, the plumage of the population of birds in the colony became more pleasing. The factors that produced beautiful plumage were, in some unknown way, passed from one generation to the next. Darwin was intrigued with artificial selection and, in fact, had bred pigeons himself. (See FIGURE 3•1.) He speculated that if artificial selection could produce different varieties, perhaps some naturally occurring process would have a similar effect.

Another year and a half passed before Darwin's naturalistic observations and knowledge of artificial selection bore fruit. Darwin recalled the event in his autobiography:

> I happened to read for amusement Malthus on *Population,* and being well prepared to appreciate the struggle for existence which everywhere goes on from long continued observation of plants and animals, it at once struck me that under these circumstances favorable variations would tend to be preserved, and unfavorable ones to be destroyed. The result would be the formation of a new species. (Darwin, 1888/1950, p. 54)

---

artificial selection Procedure that differentially mates organisms to produce offspring with specific characteristics.

[FIGURE 3·1] Varieties of pigeons that have been produced through artificial selection. (a) Wild rock pigeon. This type is believed to be the ancestor of each of the other breeds of pigeons shown here. (b) Blue grizzle frillback. (c) English pouter. (d) Indian fantail.

(a)

(b)

(c)

(d)

What struck Darwin was the idea of **natural selection.** Malthus had proposed that populations increase in size faster than the resources required to sustain them and that, as a consequence, competition for resources occurs. Darwin recognized that differences among individuals competing for the same resources would inevitably favor some over others. An individual that possessed characteristics that benefited its survival would be more likely to live longer and thereby produce more offspring. If the characteristics of the more frequently reproducing individuals were heritable (that is, could be passed from one generation to the next), then natural selection would have the same effect as artificial selection but without anyone doing the selecting.

Darwin came to this realization in September 1838, but he did not publish his ideas until 20 years later. Why did he wait so long? Among other things, he devoted considerable time to gathering supportive evidence. He took great pains to develop a clear and coherent case for his account. He examined his specimens from the voyage of the Beagle, studied current research and theory in the natural sciences, conducted his own research on artificial selection, and tested out his ideas with close scientific colleagues whom he often met at a pub in London.

Darwin might have been even slower to publish his theory if another naturalist, Alfred Wallace, had not independently come up with the same idea. In 1858, Alfred Wallace—while suffering from a bout of fever in the Spice Islands—read the same book by Malthus that had inspired Darwin. Wallace also recognized that the natural environment, through its effect on differential reproduction, could be the source of evolutionary change. Unlike Darwin, however, Wallace quickly wrote up the idea and sent the paper to—of all people—Charles Darwin! Darwin was already known from his published work on related subjects. Wallace had also discovered the principle by which the natural environment could accomplish the same result as artificial selection.

Darwin and Wallace each presented their separate works before a scientific society—the Linnean Society in London. A few months thereafter, Darwin published the massive book on which he had been working for over 20 years. He described the book as an "abstract" of his ideas. Darwin's "abstract," which we know today as *On the Origin of Species* (1859), ran to 500 pages. It established both his priority in developing the principle of natural selection and his careful accumulation of evidence to support the principle.

Discovering the Mechanisms of Heredity

With natural selection, Darwin and Wallace had identified a process by which the environment selected from among varying individuals those characteristics that most benefited survival (*positive selection*), eliminated those that most harmed survival (*negative selection*), and maintained those that permitted survival (*stabilizing selection*). But what exactly was passed on from one generation to the next? Male and female pigeons with beautiful plumage passed on their fertilized eggs, not their plumage. Something in the fertilized egg had to contain the potential for developing beautiful plumage in the offspring. Moreover, this "something" must be passed on from one generation to the next if the final state of plumage is to be realized. What was this "something"?

Darwin did not know what the "something" was. He made a guess that the various organs of the body each

---

natural selection   Process whereby the environment differentially favors organisms with characteristics that affect survival and production of offspring.

contributed to the egg certain substances, which he called *gemmules*. A blending of these gemmules was then proposed to determine the characteristics of the offspring. Soon after he made his guess, however, the Scottish engineer Fleeming Jenkin demonstrated mathematically that a favorable gemmule from a parent would be so "diluted" by the presence of other gemmules that a blending theory of heredity could never support evolution. In a population of interbreeding organisms, a rare favorable gemmule would be overwhelmed by the presence of the more numerous other gemmules. In short, Darwin had a persuasive account of the contribution of variation and selection to evolution, but he had no explanation for the accumulation of these changes. And, the accumulation of changes was necessary to produce the diversity and complexity of life. Darwin betrayed the fact that he was a human being as well as a scientist when he disparaged Jenkin's analysis in a letter to a friend: "Be cautious in trusting mathematicians." Darwin had rejected the messenger and tried to ignore the message. Because Darwin did not know what was transmitted from one generation to the next, most scientists did not accept his account of evolution through natural selection until over 70 years later. What changed their minds?

The belated recognition of Gregor Mendel's work on heredity was the key. Mendel was a monk who had conducted breeding experiments using peas in his monastery garden. Pea plants vary in their characteristics—the color of the seed (yellow or green), the shape of the seed (wrinkled or smooth), and so on. He found that the characteristics of plants in successive generations were not blends of the characteristics from prior generations, as Darwin's gemmule theory supposed. Instead, the frequency with which a given characteristic appeared in the next generation of peas revealed that (a) the "factors" were passed to descendents *unchanged* (b) each parent contributed one such factor to each offspring, and (c) a factor was passed on even when it was sometimes not expressed in the offspring. Thus Mendel's experiments indicated that what was passed from one generation to the next was not a blend of gemmules but an unchanged set of factors. Mendel's factors are now called **genes** (to be discussed in more detail later in this chapter). Darwin's blending account of how characteristics were passed from one generation to the next was replaced by Mendel's *particulate* account. Mendel published the results of his experiments in a scientific journal in 1866—only seven years after Darwin's *On the Origin of Species*. However, Mendel's results did not become generally known until the early 1900s, well after Darwin's death in 1882. Darwin had died unaware of findings that were crucial to the acceptance of evolution through natural selection. Given Mendel's findings, most biologists began to accept Darwin's account of evolution when the principle of natural selection was integrated with the burgeoning science of genetics in the 1930s. This integration of natural selection with genetics is known as the *Modern Synthesis* in biology (e.g., Dobzhansky, 1937).

The Three Components of Evolution through Natural Selection

Darwin's account of **biological evolution** describes how changes take place in the characteristics of a population of organisms over time. This account stands as the primary explanatory principle of the origin, diversity, and complexity of life. It is the unifying theme of all biology. Evolution through natural selection is now understood as the result of repeated cycles of a three-component process that acts across the generations: variation, selection, and retention.

Variation The term *variation* reflects Darwin's observation that each living organism is unique—each differs somewhat from every other, even others within the same species. Before Darwin, scientists focused on the ways that members of the same species were alike—the essential features that all individuals presumably shared with the group. Individual differences were merely a nuisance that obscured the essential features of the group. After Darwin, individual differences moved to center stage. Similarities among individuals were seen as abstractions that might be useful for some purposes (for example, classification), but not fundamental to the evolutionary process. Variation between individuals provides the raw material upon which natural selection acts. Variation is the source of whatever new arises from repeated cycles of the evolutionary process because natural selection can act only on characteristics that already exist. Variation is undirected in the sense that the conditions that affect variation are different from those that affect selection (Campbell, 1974).

Selection The second component of the evolutionary process is *natural selection*. **Selection** by the environment favors (or disfavors) some variants over others. By the environment, we include not only the physical environment but also the organic environment—members of the same and different species that are competing for resources. Selection confers to the evolutionary process whatever direction it appears to have. The direction is toward an ever closer adaptation to the demands of the environment in which the individual organism finds itself. The more constant the environment, the more specialized are the various species that are competing for the resources of that environment (Mittelbach et al., 2007). But the environment is rarely constant, so the direction of evolution is not constant. Because there are many different environments, evolution is not directed toward any particular end. The

---

gene Unit of heredity, inferred from Mendel's experiments.

biological evolution Changes in characteristics over successive generations due to natural selection and mutation.

variation First component of evolution: individual members of a species differ from one another.

selection Second component of evolution, provides direction to the process.

diversity of life arises from the diversity of environments. These environments range from the extremes of the hot sulphur springs of Yellowstone Park (Ward et al.,1998) to the arctic cold of sea ice (Mock & Thomas, 2005), both of which contain life. Only to the extent that future environments share features in common with past environments does evolution through natural selection make us adapted to future environments.

Retention   The third component, **retention,** is necessary if the evolution of complex organisms is to occur. Selected variations must accumulate to produce complexity. Mendel's research demonstrated the particulate nature of heredity and allowed even rare genes to endure and have the possibility of affecting distant generations. Variation provides the raw material on which selection operates. But, unless the selected variations are retained and contribute to the pool of variations on which later selections operate, evolution cannot take place. FIGURE 3•2

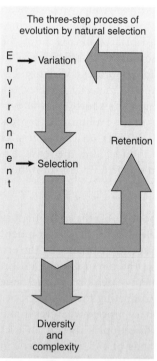

[**FIGURE 3•2**] The three-step process of evolution by natural selection. Initial differences in characteristics provide the variation on which natural selection operates within a given environment. Individuals whose characteristics favor reproductive fitness in that environment are more likely to survive. The individual's genes are retained when they are passed to the next generation and contribute to the variation on which subsequent selections operate. Over repeated cycles of this process, diverse and complex species can emerge.

---

retention   Third component of evolution: the favored variations are retained through heredity.

selectionism   Explanation of complex outcomes as the cumulative effect of the three-component process identified by Darwin.

summarizes the three-component process of evolution through natural selection. Henceforth, we refer to Darwin's approach to the explanation of complexity as **selectionism.**

Natural Selection and Behavior

Natural selection affects function (behavior) as well as structure. In fact, the effects of natural selection on structure and function are closely related: Unless a structure is used in a way that benefits survival of the population, the genes affecting that structure cannot be naturally selected. Consider the complex structure of the eye. Light-sensitive structures have independently evolved at least ten different times in the history of life, all selected by the same physical properties of light. In fact, the light-sensitive compounds in the retina may be traced to compounds that permit photosynthesis in plants. (*Photosynthesis* is the process whereby plants use energy from light to make sugars and starch.) Thus, the beginnings of vision are found in the quest for food. If the eye did not provide information that guided behavior, such as food-seeking, the various components of the eye would never have been selected. Natural selection has also favored the formation of neural circuits that govern the function of the eye as well as its structure. When an object enters the periphery of vision, the eye rapidly moves to focus on that object. (These movements are among the visual reflexes discussed in Chapter 6.) In the history of the human population, individuals who immediately attended to moving objects were more likely to behave adaptively—to avoid predators, to dodge projectiles, to greet approaching members of the group, and so on. Individuals who behaved in these ways were more likely to survive to the age of reproduction and to pass on their genes to their offspring. Among those genes are those that benefit both the structure and function of the eye.

Acceptance of Evolution through Natural Selection

Today, natural selection is the central unifying principle of biology from molecules to man. Moreover, Darwin's account of how selection processes produce the richness of life provides a natural-science-based account of how diverse and complex phenomena arise in other fields. The repeated action of the process—whether acting through physical, chemical, or biological means—can yield complex outcomes. The evolution of a solar system of planets from an initial swirling mass of randomly moving particles is but one example. Selection is provided by gravity and retention by physical processes such as friction and adhesion. As a cumulative result of these processes, the swirling particles coalesce into one or more central stars with planets possibly orbiting about them. (For more general treatments of selectionism, see Sober, 1984 and Donahoe, 2003.) Darwin gave us a way by which complex phenomena may emerge as the product of the repeated action of relatively simple processes.

[**FIGURE 3·3**] The response of people in different countries to the statement "Human beings, as we know them, developed from earlier species of animals." Responses of "True" are shown in green, "Not sure" in tan, and "False" in orange.

(From Miller, Scott, & Okamoto, 2006. *Science*, 313, 765.)

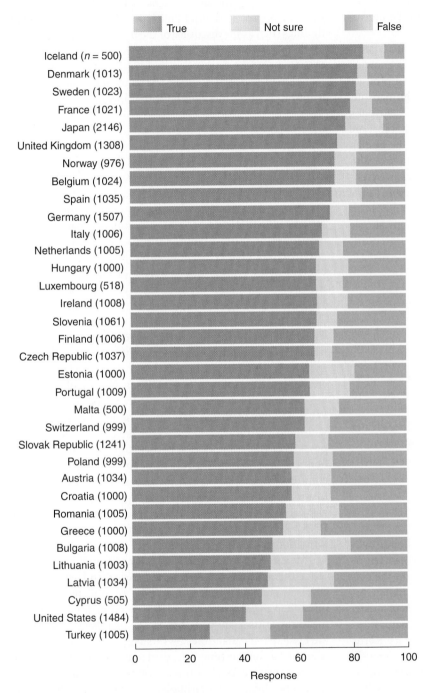

Although evolution through natural selection is very generally accepted within science, it remains controversial in some segments of society. This is particularly true in the United States. A recent survey was taken in which people were asked to respond to the following statement: "Human beings, as we know them, developed from earlier species of animals." Approximately 80% of respondents in Europe and Japan regarded this statement as true, but only 40% of

respondents in the United States—5% less than a survey conducted 20 years earlier (see FIGURE 3·3). When given the statement "Evolution is absolutely false," only 10% of Europeans agreed whereas 33% of U.S. respondents did. As Figure 3.3 shows, only respondents in Turkey were less receptive to evolution. What accounts for this difference between respondents in the United States and many industrialized nations? The analysis of other survey data indicates that the difference is primarily due to the greater prevalence of persons who believe that the founding documents of their religion have implications for science as well as for morality—whether Christianity in the United States or Islam in Turkey (Miller, Scott, & Okamoto, 2006). Recent rulings of the federal court in the United States have upheld the need to maintain the mutual independence of science and religion (Jones, 2005).

There is no necessary conflict between religion and evolution, however. For many religious scientists, an all-knowing deity would appreciate that natural selection could produce the diversity and complexity of life, including human life, without the need to "oversee" the process (Miller, 1999; Couzin, 2008). As an example, two popes—Pius XII in 1950 and John Paul II in 1996—accepted the idea that the human body may result from natural selection. However, they also believed that at some point in the process humans were endowed with a nonphysical spirit by the deity. Darwin, at the conclusion of *On the Origin of Species,* said something similar: "There is grandeur in this view of life. From simple beginnings breathed by the Creator endless forms most beautiful and most wonderful have been, and are being evolved."

QUESTIONS TO CONSIDER

1. Darwin was obviously intelligent and thought long and hard about how retention through heredity might occur. Why did Mendel succeed where Darwin failed? What general conclusion might be drawn from this example?
2. Could evolution occur with only variation and selection? Explain your answer.
3. Do natural selection and genetics always produce greater complexity over successive generations? If not, why not?
4. Can a person be a scientist and still hold religious beliefs?

Evolution of Humans

Although science is interested in all aspects of biological evolution, our greatest interest is in what evolution can tell us about ourselves. What light does evolution shed on the origins of modern humans (*Homo sapiens*, or thinking humans)? When Darwin first published *On the Origin of Species* he was reluctant to consider the implications of natural selection for humans. He was hesitant because of concerns about its reception by society in general and by his religiously devout wife Emma in particular. Also, there were scientific issues about possible limitations on the power of natural selection. The age of the Earth was mistakenly believed to be only 40–50 million years old, not enough time for the evolution of

---

fossil Remains of an animal or plant found in the Earth.

DNA Deoxyribonucleic acid. Molecule resembling a twisted ladder whose sides are connected by rungs of pairs of nucleotides (adenine, thymine, guanine, and cytosine).

bipedalism Habitually walking upright on two legs.

---

humans to have occurred. This mistake was made because radioactivity had not yet been discovered and heat from radioactive decay had slowed the cooling of Earth, making it appear younger than it was. Also, remember that Mendel's work identifying the mechanisms of heredity—the genes—was not appreciated until much later. Nevertheless, other findings such as the discovery of the first ancient human skull in 1856 (much later identified as a Neanderthal skull) encouraged Darwin to publish in 1872 *The Expression of the Emotions in Man and Animals*. The study of human evolution had begun and is now a lively field of investigation.

Human Origins

Because chimpanzees are our closest *living* relatives, some uncritical observers mistakenly believe that evolution holds that chimpanzees turned into humans. However, evolutionary change does not take place in this manner. Instead, evolution holds that chimpanzees and humans shared a common ancestor at some point in the distant past, and that this ancestor was neither a chimpanzee nor a human. Chimpanzees *never* evolved into humans. Evolution proceeds as the branching of a tree or bush, not in a straight-line fashion. What is sought are related species that can be ordered in time.

Methods for Studying Human Evolution The study of human evolution focuses on whatever remains of those species that lie along the branches that ultimately led to modern humans. These lingering remains include **fossils** as well as any signs of the culture of our predecessors, such as tools. What endures from the past are those few things that can withstand the ravages of time—the effects of chemical and physical degradation. Bones, particularly teeth and the large bones of the skull and legs, are most apt to endure. What also endures, when we are particularly fortunate, is the genetic material (**DNA,** an acronym for deoxyribonucleic acid) that has been protected within those bones. Bones, occasional DNA, and stone implements are the primary sources of information about our ancestors.

When these relics from the past are found, how can we order them in time? Which came earlier and which came later? Several independent methods are available to determine the time at which fossils were deposited. First, *relative* measures of time are provided by the *morphology* (form) of the fossil. Fossils that differ by small amounts were probably deposited at similar times because large evolutionary changes did not have enough time to occur. Most importantly, *systematic* changes in morphology are noted. In the case of human-related fossils, the skull shows progressively smaller brow ridges and less protrusion of the lower face. The leg and ankle bones show progressively better adaptation for walking on two legs (**bipedalism**). And, the fingers, thumbs, and the bones of the wrist are progressively better adapted for grasping. Second, several *absolute* measures of time help determine when a fossil was deposited. Animals breathe in small amounts of a naturally occurring radioactive form of

Stone hand-axe tools of hominids: Africa-only hominids: A. Slightly modified stone core; **Out-of-Africa Hominids:** B. *Homo erectus:* Modified stone core; C. *Homo neanderthalis* and *sapiens:* Highly modified stone core with sharpened edges.

carbon (C^{14}) while they are living, Once death has occurred and breathing stops, C^{14} is no longer inspired and begins to decay at a known and constant rate. The amount of C^{14} that remains in the fossil can help determine its age. **Carbon dating** thus provides an estimate of the time when the fossil was deposited. Counting the changes in the DNA between two fossils provides another measure. A small change is taken as evidence that a small amount of time has elapsed. The interpretation of both C^{14} and DNA is complicated, however (for example, Friderun & Cummins, 1996). Carbon dating can be influenced by changes in the amount of C^{14} in the atmosphere when the organism was alive and changes in the DNA molecule may not occur at a constant rate. That is, the so-called *molecular clock* may not "tick" at the same rate for all time and for all species. Although uncertainties remain, the course of evolution that is revealed by morphology, carbon dating, and changes in DNA has generally converged on a common order of events in human evolution and a common estimate of the time at which these events occurred.

Course of Human Evolution The two branches of the tree of life that ultimately led to humans and chimps diverged over 7 million years ago. In spite of the vast time that separates our two species, numerous resemblances remain. FIGURE 3•4 shows a side view of the brains of a chimp and a human. The similarities in their gross appearances are apparent in spite of the large differences in size. The chimp brain has an average volume of only about 370 cm³ whereas the comparable figure for humans is 1,500 cm³. This differ-

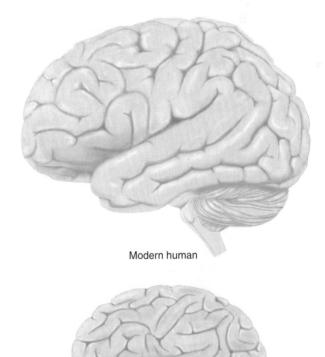

Modern human

Chimpanzee

[FIGURE 3•4] Side views of the brains of a chimpanzee and a modern human. The average chimpanzee brain weighs about 300 grams, while the average human brain weighs about 1,500 grams.

(Adapted from Balter, 2007, *Science*, 315, 1209.)

---

carbon dating   Method to determine the age at which an organism lived by measuring the amount of radioactive carbon (C^{14}).

ence in volume of the brain amounts to many millions in the total number of neurons. The behavior of chimps and humans also shows similarities. Chimps and humans both live in social groups and use tools to aid their survival. (A *tool* is any fabricated object that facilitates the behavior of the user.) In fact, chimpanzees have recently been observed to break off a slender straight branch from a tree, strip it of bark, sharpen its end, and then use the sharpened stick to spear small prey animals that sleep in the hollows of trees (Pruetz & Bertolani, 2007).

Genetic tests that compare the DNA of chimps and humans also reflect their common ancestry. About 99% of the DNA involved in the production of proteins is identical in chimps and humans (King & Wilson, 1975)! However, about 98% of the total human genome is not involved in protein production. The rest of the DNA molecule determines when and how much of the protein is produced. These genes are known as **regulatory genes.** It is with respect to regulatory genes that humans and chimps most differ (Demuth et al., 2006; Cohen, 2007a). As an example, in a region of the DNA molecule that regulates neural development there are over 60 times more differences between humans and chimpanzees than would be expected on the basis of chance alone (Pollard et al., 2007). The importance of these regions is indicated by the finding that over 110,000 of the human-specific regions of DNA have remained unchanged over evolutionary time (Prabhakar et al., 2006; Balter, 2007). If these regions were not important, chance factors in heredity would have produced many more changes. Also, there are more multiple copies of genes in humans than in chimps (Pennisi, 2006). The proteins of which chimps and humans are made are much alike, but they are assembled differently. A shack and a mansion can be built of the same materials, but the amount of material and how it is put together make all the difference.

The branching line that leads to modern humans began in East Africa over 4 million years ago according to the fossil record and, perhaps, as long as 6 million years ago according to the molecular clock. The primates that fall along the human line are called **hominids.** Their main distinguishing feature is that they habitually walk on two legs, that is, they are *bipedal.* Among the factors that likely led to the natural selection of upright walking were standing on branches to reach other branches in our more distant tree-dwelling ancestors (Thorpe, Holder, & Crompton, 2007) and carrying slowly maturing offspring who were unable to walk during the first months of life. Whatever the selecting factors, the most important benefit of bipedal walking was to free the forelimbs from the responsibility of locomotion. Now the forelimbs, and in particular the hands, could come into contact with different selecting environments that favored manual dexterity. When the forelimbs are de-

voted to locomotion, the ability to manipulate objects is of little use.

These early hominids had brains whose size increased over the next 2 million years from 350 to almost 500 cm³ (a volume of about 2 cups). This produced a brain that was larger than that of chimpanzees, but still much smaller than that of modern humans. (Because the soft tissue of the brain does not fossilize, brain size is estimated by determining the volume of the interior of the skull.) The height of these ancestors also tended to increase over evolutionary time. Early hominids were less than 5 feet tall. Other changes took place as well. The finger bones became less curved and the thumbs increased in length, which increased manual dexterity. From examining the materials surrounding these fossils, early hominids lived primarily in woodlands and later in grasslands. From examining their teeth, the diet consisted of fruits, seeds, and roots obtained through foraging. There is no evidence from the fossil record that these early hominids ever migrated out of Africa. Technically, these early hominids generally fall in the genus *Australopithecus* (ape from the south). (For a comprehensive overview of the course of human evolution, go to http://www.becominghuman.org/.)

Beginning some 2 million years ago, hominids were sufficiently changed by natural selection to be classified in a new genus, *Homo* (human). This is the genus that ultimately includes modern humans. At the beginning of this period, the brain volume is estimated at 650 cm³ and the height at just above 5 feet. With time, both measures progressively increased to the present values of 1,500 cm³ and 175 cm (5 feet, 9 inches). Members of the genus *Homo* ate a varied diet that included for the first time meat, a rich source of protein. These species also became progressively better adapted for bipedal locomotion, as judged by changes in the form of their hips, knees, and ankles as well as the placement of the head on the neck. Other changes occurred in the general proportions of the body (the relative lengths of the arm and leg) and in the form of the face (less sloping of the forehead and less protrusion of the lower face). The first members of the genus *Homo* remained in Africa, but later species migrated out of Africa to the Middle East, Asia, Europe, Oceania, and lastly the Americas (Spoor et al., 2007). The three widely migrating species of *Homo* were *H. erectus* (standing man), *H. neanderthalis* (Neanderthal man, named for the valley in Germany where their fossils were first found), and *H. sapiens* (thinking man). Only *H. sapiens*—our species—remains. (See FIGURE 3•5 for reconstructions of the skulls of a hominid that remained in Africa and three species of hominids that migrated out of Africa.) *H. erectus* became extinct after 1.5 million years, surviving for some 400,000 years. *H. neanderthalis* became extinct only 25,000 years ago, with its last outpost in southern Spain near Gibraltar (Finlayson et al., 2006). *H. sapiens* has thus far endured 200,000 years. Our species overlapped with *H. neanderthalis* in southern Europe for about 10,000 years (Grine

---

regulatory genes Genes that govern genes that code for proteins.
hominids The genus of bipedal apes ancestral to humans.

[**FIGURE 3·5**] Drawings of the partially reconstructed skulls of three hominids of the genus *Homo* that migrated out of Africa—*H. erectus, H. neanderthalis,* and *H. sapiens.*

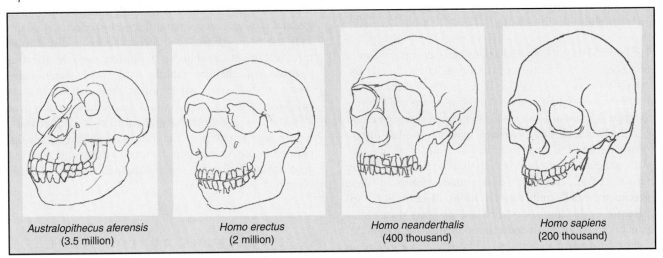

Australopithecus aferensis (3.5 million)	*Homo erectus* (2 million)	*Homo neanderthalis* (400 thousand)	*Homo sapiens* (200 thousand)

et al., 2007). (See FIGURE 3·6 for the extent of dispersion of *H. neanderthalis* and possible migratory routes of *H. sapiens* out of Africa as reflected by the fossil record; see also Li et al., 2008.) Whether interbreeding occurred between *H. sapiens* and *H. neandethalis* is a matter of current debate (Noonan et al., 2006; Pennisi, 2007). *H. sapiens* is now more widely distributed than any other animal species in the history of Earth. Reminders of our evolutionary origins remain, however. Modern-day astronauts in the frigid shadows of the mountains of the moon preserve in their

space suits the warm and moist microenvironment of our African beginnings.

We should not regard ancestral hominid species as entirely alien to ourselves. They made tools of progressively greater complexity by carving wooden implements and shaping stones into hammers and cutters. They tamed fire and made clothing. By 50,000 years ago, they crafted representational art and jewelry and they buried their dead. Moreover, our species has continued to evolve. In addition to genetic changes that counter diseases such as malaria and HIV, a

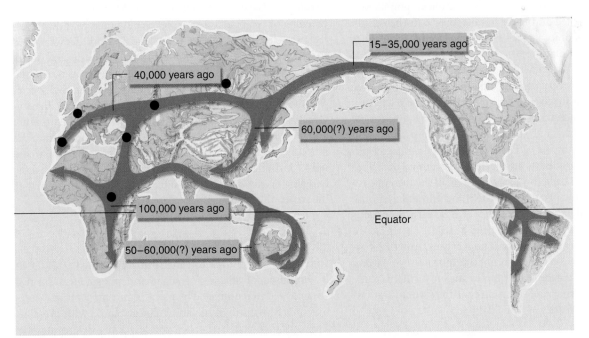

[**FIGURE 3·6**] Migrations of two species of humans (*Homo*) out of Africa. The black dots show the locations where Neanderthal (*H. neanderthalis*) fossils have been found. The green lines show some of the migratory paths taken by modern humans (*H. sapiens*) based on dated fossil remains. The dates are the approximate times of arrival of *H. sapiens* in each region.

tolerance to milk sugar (lactose) was selected in cattle-herding humans of northern Europe. Lactose was previously digestible only by nursing infants (Voight et al., 2006; Gibson, 2007). The following case illustrates the evolution of a gene and its implications for disease.

[CASE STUDY] Past selections can have unanticipated effects on survival in the present. Consider the *human immunodeficiency virus (HIV)*. HIV gradually weakens the immune systems of humans, often resulting in the collection of symptoms known as *acquired immunodeficiency syndrome (AIDS)*. Research has discovered that our not-too-distant cousins—monkeys and chimpanzees—are often infected with genetically similar viruses, *simian immune-deficient viruses (SIVs)*. However, the immune systems of these species are usually quite resistant to the effects of SIVs. Apparently, in the approximately 7 million years since chimpanzees and humans shared a common ancestor, natural selection has favored the survival of chimpanzees whose genes resisted the effects of the virus. It is believed that SIV, in either its original or a slightly altered form, was introduced into the human population through eating monkey and chimpanzee meat (so-called "bushmeat"). HIV infection first arose in Africa, perhaps as long as 50 years ago, but became recognized in the United States only in the 1980s. In southern Africa, 20% of the human population is now infected by the virus. The availability of modern forms of transportation has spread HIV rapidly and widely (Cohen, 2007b).

A recent discovery has revealed that some populations of humans are relatively resistant to the virus. These are humans who trace their ancestry to Northern European populations that were devastated during the Middle Ages by the bacterium that caused bubonic plague (the Black Death) (Galvani & Slatkin, 2003; cf. Kolata, 1998). During the 14th century, and at regular intervals thereafter, roughly one-third of the human population of Europe was killed by the Black Death. Those individuals who survived selection by the plague bacterium had immune reactions that combated the infection. It now appears that these same immune reactions resist infection and progression of the AIDS virus. The plague bacterium and the HIV virus both attack the same group of white-blood cells. As a result, the genes that benefit the immune response to bubonic plague also benefit the immune response to HIV. Over 10% of the ancestors of Northern Europeans have at least one copy of this gene, but only about 5% of Southern Europeans and almost no Africans, American Indians, or Asians. Clearly, it was not the "purpose" of natural selection by the plague bacterium to make Northern Europeans resistant to a viral infection that they would not encounter for 600 years!

Natural selection is locked in a perpetual dance with the environment, but the environment is always in the lead. The course of selection depends utterly on the environment. If the selecting environment is relatively constant or changes gradually, the process of natural selection effectively adapts us to the environment. The process appears to display purpose, but this is shown to be an illusion when the selecting environment changes rapidly with slowly reproducing species such as our own (Skinner, 1966; Sober, 1984). In sub-Saharan Africa, over 2 million people have already been killed by the HIV virus. Natural selection is again at work: A gene has been detected that is becoming increasingly duplicated in the African population and the products of this gene appear to confer some resistance to HIV (Bahcall, 2005; Julg & Goebel, 2005).

QUESTIONS TO CONSIDER

1. From what you know about how evolution works, do you think that *H. erectus* evolved into *H. neanderthalis*, and then *H. neanderthalis* evolved into *H. sapiens*?
2. If humans evolved in the way that evolutionary science indicates, does that in any way diminish the accomplishments of our species?

Heredity, Genetics, and Evolution

Recall that Darwin was not aware of Mendel's work on the breeding of pea plants. Therefore, he did not know how the effects of selection were retained. Mendel's work demonstrated that the units of heredity were transmitted in discrete form, now known as *genes*. A deeper knowledge of genetics is required if we are to better understand the evolution of our own species and the implications of natural selection for human behavior. **Genetics** is the scientific discipline that investigates the structure and functions of genes and their role in the transmission of the selecting effects of the environment from one generation to the next (Suzuki et al., 1989). Genetics is concerned with how **heredity**—genetic make-up—affects the behavioral as well as the structural characteristics of organisms.

Basic Principles of Genetics

Heredity is transmitted by genetic material called *DNA*. DNA is composed of strands of sugar and phosphate. The two strands are interconnected by pairs of four nucleotides—adenine paired with thymine and guanine paired with cytosine. The order in which the nucleotides occur determines the function of the gene. The structure of DNA was discovered by James Watson and Francis Crick in 1953. How they made their discovery is described in a fascinating (and controversial) book by Watson, *The Double Helix* (1968).

---

genetics   Study of the hereditary structures of organisms (genes).
heredity   Sum of the traits inherited from one's parents.

[FIGURE 3·7] The structure and composition of DNA. DNA resembles a twisted ladder whose sides are composed of molecules of sugar and phosphate and whose rungs are made up of combinations of four nucleotide bases: adenine, thymine, guanine, and cytosine. Genes are segments of DNA that direct the synthesis of proteins and enzymes according to the particular sequences of nucleotide bases they contain. In essence, genes serve as "recipes" for the synthesis of these proteins and enzymes, which regulate the cellular and other physiological processes of the body, including those responsible for behavior.

(Based on Watson, J. D. (1976). *Molecular biology of the gene.* Menlo Park: Benjamin.)

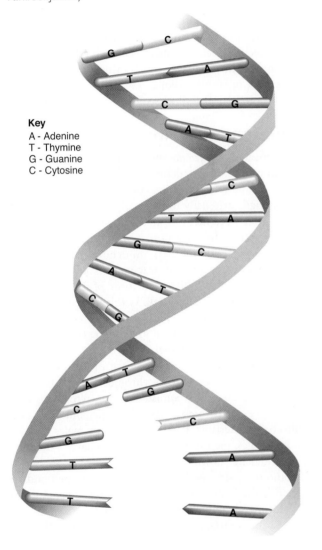

Key
A - Adenine
T - Thymine
G - Guanine
C - Cytosine

The DNA molecule is shaped like a twisted ladder. Sugar and phosphate form the sides of the ladder; the nucleotides form the rungs. (See FIGURE 3·7.) A gene is a specific sequence of nucleotides at a particular location along the DNA molecule. Some genes are composed of a short sequence of nucleotides, whereas others contain longer sequences. Regardless of their length, the sequence of nucleotides directs the synthesis of a protein molecule. Protein synthesis is guided by single-stranded molecules called **RNA** (ribonucleic acid). Through the mediation of RNA, different genes *code* the production of different proteins. The proteins, in turn, make up the structure of the body and its organs. The total set of genetic material in a species is known as the **genome**. In 1990, geneticists began an effort to determine the entire genome for our species. This work—known as The Human Genome Project—was essentially completed in 2003. It was discovered that the number of different protein-coding genes in humans was approximately 25,000. Many geneticists were surprised because this is only about twice as many genes as the common housefly (The Genome Sequencing Consortium, 2001).

Genes

Genes may be viewed as "recipes" for protein synthesis. Genes influence our physical and behavioral development in only one way—through the proteins they enable. Proteins are strings of amino acids, arranged in a chain. The order of amino acids within the string is specified by the sequence of nucleotides in the DNA molecule. A sequence of three nucleotides specifies a particular amino acid.

Strictly speaking, *there are no genes for behavior,* only for the protein-based physical structures and physiological processes that affect behavior. For example, if we were interested in the genetic basis of learning, we would look for genes that affect the synthesis of proteins that influence learning. Evidence from behavioral and pharmacological studies indicates that one of the substances in the brain that affects learning is dopamine (Schultz, 2001). We might be tempted to call the gene that affected dopamine a "learning" gene. However, this gene affects dopamine, not learning, and dopamine has other effects as well. For example, dopamine affects the contractions of smooth muscle in the stomach and intestines.

Genes also specify proteins that affect the synthesis of other proteins. These proteins are called **enzymes.** A faulty enzyme-specifying gene may produce serious physiological and behavioral problems. In addition to genes within the six-foot-long DNA molecule, large stretches consist of replications of genes and so-called "junk" DNA. Junk DNA does not provide a template for protein synthesis and for that reason is known as a *noncoding DNA.* Evidence increasingly indicates that noncoding sequences play a critical role. They contain regulatory genes that govern protein synthesis by protein-coding genes and thereby affect evolution, including human evolution (Greally, 2007).

RNA   Single-stranded nucleic acid that is involved in several functions within the cell.

genome   Total set of genetic material of an organism.

enzymes   Proteins that regulate processes that occur within cells—organic catalysts.

∫ocus ⊕n

Frontiers in Evolutionary Research

A critical challenge for natural selection is to explain not merely how the evolution of species occurred through genetic mechanisms but how the genetic mechanisms themselves were selected in the first place. How did purely physiochemical processes produce a molecule that was capable of replicating itself, albeit imperfectly? Imperfect replication is required to produce the variation upon which selection processes could operate. Science has yet to meet this challenge, but it remains an active area of research. What is known is that the process began quite early in the history of earth. Evidence of life has been found only one billion years after the formation of the Earth 4.5 billion years ago (Eiler, 2007).

Scientists are studying several nonmutually exclusive possibilities for the origin of self-replicating molecules. Perhaps energy from lightning, volcanism, or sunlight acted on chemicals present in the atmosphere or surface of the early earth. These various compounds might through chance interactions, produce a self-replicating molecule (Lorsch & Szostak, 1996). Another possibility is that pre-existing compounds interacted with undersea volcanism or with the clays of the early Earth to produce a self-replicating molecule (Gallori, Biondi, & Branciamore, 2006). Still another possibility is that various organic molecules were brought to the Earth by extraterrestrial objects such as comets and that these contained compounds from which molecular evolution began. In 2006, NASA's Project Stardust successfully returned a capsule to Earth that collected particles from the tail of a comet. These particles gave indirect evidence of organic materials. Francis Crick, the co-discoverer with James Watson of the DNA molecule, once conjectured that Earth may have been seeded with DNA molecules by an alien species (Crick at al., 1976). Whatever the origins of the compounds from which molecular evolution began, single-stranded RNA appears to have been selected before double-stranded DNA. Life began with an "RNA world" (Ma & Yu, 2006).

For an evolutionary account of complexity to prevail Darwin (1859) said, "If it could be demonstrated that any complex organ existed which could not possibly have been formed by numerous, successive, slight modifications, my theory would absolutely break down." The same requirement applies at the molecular level. For molecular evolution to occur, each change in nucleotides that produces a different protein must be beneficial, or at least neutral. A recent experiment nicely illustrates that natural selection applies equally well at the molecular level.

A population of bacteria was exposed to penicillin, an antibiotic that kills many bacteria. From prior work, it was known that changes in five pairs of nucleotides in a particular gene were necessary for a bacterium to have resistance to penicillin. Mathematically, there are 120 possible combinations of sequences by which these five pairs could be changed to reach the resistant state. However, when successive generations of bacteria were exposed to penicillin, resistance developed along only a very few of the mathematically possible sequences. This was because only a very few of the sequences produced intermediate states that benefited or permitted the survival of the bacteria. Natural selection occurs at the molecular level, but it is constrained by the same Darwinian principles that operate at the level of organisms. (For a description of a long-term study of molecular evolution, see Elena & Lenski, 2003.)

Chromosomes and Meiosis

Genes are located on *chromosomes*. (A few genes are also located in an intracellular structure called *mitochondria*. Mitochondria are important for energy production within the cell and are thought originally to have come from independent organisms that were incorporated into cells in a mutually beneficial relation. Because mitochondrial DNA is passed along from only the mother, mitochondrial DNA has played in important role in tracing human evolution.) **Chromosomes** are threadlike structures of DNA that are found in the nucleus of every cell. Within the cell, chromosomes come in pairs. We inherit 23 individual chromosomes from each parent, making a total of 23 pairs. For 22 pairs of chromosomes, the DNA molecules are of corresponding types. Thus, we have two genes for each protein, one from each pair of chromosomes. The chromosomes with corresponding genes are called **autosomes.** The remaining pair consists of the **sex chromosomes.** This pair contains genes that affect characteristics that differ between males and females. In females, the two sex chromosomes have corresponding genes and are known as *X* chromosomes. In males, one of the chromosomes does not provide completely corresponding genes and is the *Y* chromosome. Thus the sex chromosomes for females are *XX* and for males *XY*. The Y chromosome has also played an important role in tracing human evolution because only males possess and pass on its DNA.

Sexual Reproduction   **Sexual reproduction** occurs with the union of a *sperm*, which carries genes from the male, and an *ovum* (egg), which carries genes from the female. The sperm and ovum are collectively known as **germ cells.** Germ cells differ from all other cells in the body (*somatic cells*) in two ways. First, they contain only one chromosome from each of the 23 pairs of chromosomes. All somatic cells contain 23

---

chromosomes   Paired rod-like structures in the nucleus of a cell; contain genes.

autosomes   The 22 pairs of chromosomes that are not sex chromosomes.

sex chromosomes   X or Y chromosomes that contain genes affecting sexual development.

sexual reproduction   Production of offspring by combining the germ cells of a male and female.

germ cells   Reproductive cells, a collective term for the sperm and ovum taken together; have only one member of each pair of chromosome.

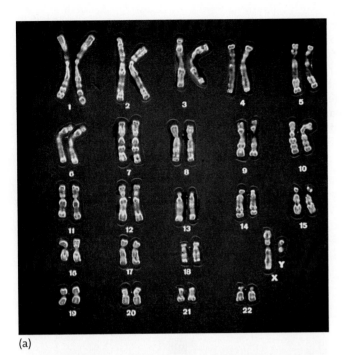

(a)

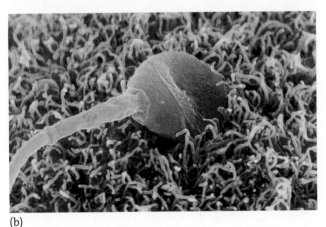

(b)

(a) Human chromosomes. The presence of a Y chromosome indicates that the sample came from a male. (b) Fertilization—a human sperm cell penetrating an egg.

[**FIGURE 3·8**] Determination of sex. The sex of human offspring depends on whether the sperm that fertilizes the ovum carries an X or a Y chromosome.

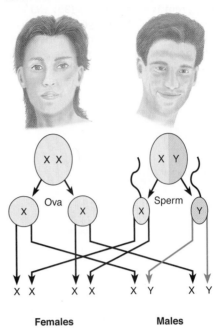

Females   **Males**

Only identical twins are genetically identical. Identical twins occur when a single ovum divides into two independent cells *after* it has been fertilized by a single sperm. This gives rise to two identical fertilized eggs. Fraternal twins occur when a female produces two ova, each of which is fertilized by a different sperm. Fraternal twins are no more alike genetically than any two siblings, but they do share a common uterine environment.

The sex of the offspring is affected by the sex chromosomes. Females produce only ova with *X* chromosomes. Each ovum contains an *X* chromosome in addition to 22 autosomes. Males produce sperm cells with either an *X* or a *Y* chromosome. Each sperm cell contains either an X or a Y chromosome in addition to 22 autosomes. Thus, the sex of offspring is determined by the presence of a Y chromosome in the sperm. Changes in the sexual development of the fetus and adult are affected by the Y chromosome. (See **FIGURE 3·8**.)

Dominant and Recessive Traits

Although each of the 22 pairs of autosomes contains corresponding pairs of genes, the members of the pair need not be identical. A given gene comes in different forms called **alleles.** (*Allele* comes from the Greek *allo* "other," as does the word "alias.") Consider eye color. The pigment found in the iris of the eye is produced by a particular pair of genes. If corresponding genes from each parent are the same allele, then the gene combination is called *homozygous* (from the Greek

pairs of chromosomes. Sperm and ova are produced by a process called **meiosis** in which the 23 pairs of chromosomes from each parent separate into two groups, with only one member of each pair joining each group. The cell then divides into two cells, each containing 23 *individual* chromosomes. The assignment of a chromosome to a group is a random process. A single individual can produce 2^{23} (8,388,608) different germ cells. Second, during meiosis corresponding portions of paired chromosomes may be interchanged. This produces a recombination of genes and adds still greater variation to the reproduction process. Because the union of a particular sperm with an ovum is also variable, the fertilized egg can produce 8,388, 608 × 8,388, 608 (70,368, 774,177,664) different possible offspring! Parenthood is a gamble, but one that all sexually reproducing species must accept if the species is to continue.

---

meiosis Process of cell division by which germ cells are produced.

allele Alternative forms of the same gene for a trait.

[FIGURE 3·9] Patterns of inheritance for eye color. (a) If one parent is homozygous for the dominant eye-color gene (BB) and the other parent is homozygous for the recessive eye-color gene (bb), then all of their children will be heterozygous for eye color (Bb) and will have brown eyes. (b) If one parent is heterozygous (Bb) and the other parent is homozygous recessive (bb), then each child will have a 50 percent chance of being heterozygous (brown eyes) and a 50 percent chance of being homozygous recessive (eye colors other than brown). (c) If one parent is homozygous dominant (BB) and the other parent is heterozygous (Bb), then each child will have a 50 percent chance of being homozygous for the dominant eye color (BB) and a 50 percent chance of being heterozygous (Bb)—and in either case will have brown eyes.

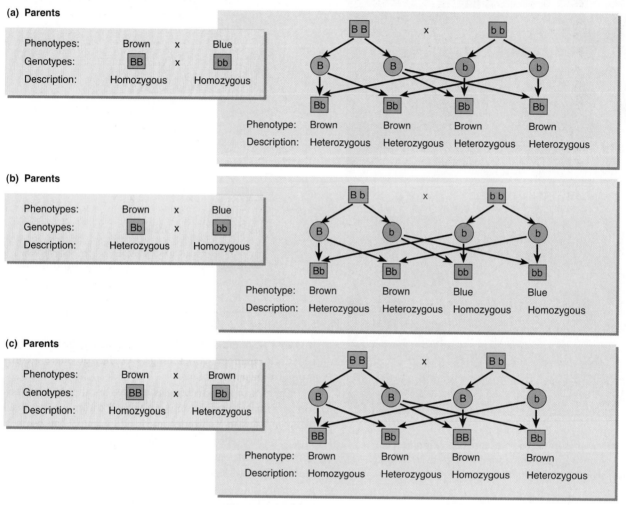

homo, "same," and *zygon,* "yolk"). However, if the parents contribute different alleles, the gene combination is said to be *heterozygous* (from the Greek *hetero,* "different"). The character or trait produced by the pair of genes depends on the particular gene combination. Some alleles are **dominant.** For dominant alleles, the character that is expressed requires the presence of only that allele. Thus the character is expressed

whether the gene is present on one or both chromosomes. When characters are expressed, the relevant genes are said to affect the organism's **phenotype,** or appearance. Other alleles are **recessive.** For recessive alleles, *both* chromosomes must contain the same allele for the character to be expressed. When a character is not expressed but the genes for that character are present, those genes are said to affect only the **genotype.** Recall the case of John Harold Johnson, Jr. The sickle-cell gene is a recessive gene. It was not expressed in the phenotype of either parent because each had only one copy of the recessive allele. The fertilized egg that produced John Jr. unfortunately had two sickle-cell alleles. (For another example of dominant and recessive genes, see FIGURE 3·9.) The sickle-cell gene affected John Jr.'s phenotype whereas it affected only the genotypes of his parents and sister.

---

dominant allele A trait that is exhibited when only one allele is present, a trait expressed in heterozygous cells.

phenotype The appearance or behavior of an organism; outward expression of the genotype.

recessive allele A trait that is expressed only when both alleles of a gene are the same, a trait expressed homozygous cells.

genotype The genetic makeup of an organism.

The genetic contributions to behavior are usually more complex than the simple dominant-recessive relation of sickle-cell anemia. Characteristics—especially behavioral characteristics—are usually affected by many genes, not just a single pair. Such characteristics are said to be under **polygenic control.** Examples of polygenic characteristics include human intelligence (see Chapter 11) and personality (see Chapter 14). In this chapter, we generally use examples of structural rather than behavioral characteristics because they provide simpler examples of the effects of genes. Mendel was fortunate in his choice of the characteristics of peas to study. Had he picked polygenic characteristics, he would not have discovered the particulate nature of heredity. Traits that are discretely expressed by single pairs of genes are called **Mendelian traits** and display the patterns of inheritance shown in FIGURE 3•9.

A second complication in assessing the genetic contributions to behavior is that traits are also affected by the environments in which the genes are expressed. For example, genetic factors are known to contribute to high-blood pressure (hypertension), but whether the characteristic is expressed depends on environmental events such as the presence of salt in the diet (Barlassina & Taglietti, 2003) or the presence of stress (Rosmand, 2005).

Importance of Genetic Diversity

As we have seen, no two individuals, except identical twins, are genetically identical. One benefit of sexual reproduction, in contrast to asexual reproduction as in fungi, is that sexual reproduction increases genetic diversity (see West-Eberhard, 2005). Offspring acquire genes from each parent and, in so doing, receive different *combinations* of genes from those of either parent. Genetically diverse species have a better chance of surviving in a changing environment because when the environment changes, some offspring may have combinations of genes that allow them to prosper in the new environment. Of course, some new combinations of genes may be unhelpful for a given individual even though the population as a whole benefits.

Sexual reproduction also benefits the repair of genetic errors because there are two copies of each gene.

Many insects have survived environmental changes because of the advantages of diversity combined with their great number of offspring. The lifespan of an insect species such as the peppered moth is very short and many generations are born and die in a relatively short time span. The most common wing color of these moths is light. However, with the advent of the Industrial Revolution in the early 1900s, tree bark became dark from soot on many of the light-colored trees where these moths rested. Because a light-colored moth on a dark background is more visible to predating birds, the lighter colored variety was eaten more frequently than their darker cousins. Over time, the darker variety became more numerous. The latent capacity of the peppered-moth genome to produce a darker wing color ensured that the species survived this change in environment (Dawkins, 1996). Rapidly reproducing species can change their nature when nature changes. In the case of the peppered moth, we may take some comfort that the lighter variety is again becoming more numerous as pollution lessens (Grant & Wiseman, 2002).

Sex-Linked Traits

If an allele on the X chromosome is not paired with a corresponding allele on the Y chromosome, a trait affected by a recessive allele on the X chromosome can be expressed. Thus, males are more likely than females to express the traits of recessive genes because males have only XY, whereas females have XX sex chromosomes. Females have two chances of getting the dominant allele, whereas males have only one. Genes that are found on the sex chromosomes give rise to **sex-linked traits.**

---

polygenic control   Characteristic affected by more than one gene, as with most behavior.

Mendelian traits   Traits showing a dominant, recessive, or sex-linked pattern of inheritance. Mendelian traits are not polygenic.

sex-linked traits   Traits affected by genes located on the sex chromosomes.

The light and dark varieties of peppered moth are shown on trees with light-colored bark (left) and with dark-colored bark. Note the differences in the visibility of the two varieties on the different backgrounds.

Hemophilia is a deleterious recessive allele. In hemophilia, clotting of the blood is delayed after an injury. Even a minor cut or a bruise may take a long time to clot. Because females have two X chromosomes, they may carry one allele for hemophilia but still have normal blood clotting because the dominant allele is present on the other X chromosome. A female fetus in which both X chromosomes have the allele for hemophilia does not survive. Males, however, have only a single X chromosome. If they have the recessive gene on the X chromosome that they received from their mother, they have the hemophilic phenotype. Hemophilia is an example of a sex-linked trait.

Some sex-related genes express themselves in both sexes and are called *sex-influenced genes*. For example, male pattern baldness develops when men inherit one or both alleles for baldness, but is seldom seen in women in either case. This is because the expression of male pattern baldness is affected by male sex hormones, which occur at much lower levels in women.

Mutations and Chromosomal Aberrations

Changes in the genome can be produced by processes other than recombination of segments of chromosomes during meiosis. Two other sources of genetic diversity are mutations or chromosomal aberrations. **Mutations** are chance alterations in the sequence of nucleotides within a single gene. Although most mutations are harmful, they may produce genes that are beneficial in some environments. Mutations occur either spontaneously during normal biological processes or as the result of external factors such as high-energy radiation. That is why dentists and physicians cover the reproductive organs with a lead apron when taking X-rays.

Hemophilia provides one of the most famous examples of mutation. Although hemophilia has appeared many times in human history, it had particularly far-reaching effects when a spontaneous mutation was passed among the royal families of nineteenth-century Europe. Through genealogical analysis, researchers have discovered that this particular mutation arose with Queen Victoria (1819–1901) of England. She was the first in her family line to bear affected children—two daughters who were carriers of the gene and one afflicted son. The tradition that nobility married only other nobility allowed the mutant gene to spread rapidly throughout the royal families of Europe, most notably to the royal family of Russia. The son of Nicholas II, the last Tsar of Russia, had

hemophilia. He and his entire family were killed at the outset of the Russian Revolution.

The second type of genetic change, **chromosomal aberration,** refers to changes in part of a chromosome (for example, deletion of a gene) or in the total number of chromosomes (for example, failure of paired chromosomes to separate during meiosis). A disorder caused by a chromosomal aberration—in this case, a partial deletion of genetic material in chromosome 5—is the *cri-du-chat syndrome*. Infants who have this syndrome have gastrointestinal, cardiac, and intellectual problems and make crying sounds that resemble a cat's mewing (hence the syndrome's name, "cry of the cat"). The severity of the syndrome is determined by the amount of genetic material that is missing. Early special education can reduce, although not eliminate, difficulties in self-care and communication. Even severe behavioral deficits with a known genetic basis, such as cri-du-chat syndrome, can be modified by experience. A much more common and less severe example is the impairment of visually guided behavior caused by myopia (near-sightedness). This is readily overcome by wearing prescription eyeglasses.

Genetic Disorders

Some genes decrease an organism's viability—its ability to survive. These "killer genes" are more common than one might think, but they are almost always recessive. When a child inherits a healthy allele from one parent and a lethal allele from the other, the lethal gene is not expressed. A few lethal genetic disorders are dominant, however, and usually express themselves in spontaneous abortions.

There are a number of human genetic disorders. Several of the more common ones with intellectual and other behavioral effects are described below.

Down's syndrome Down's syndrome (named after the British physician John Langdon Down) is caused by a chromosomal aberration in which there is an extra 21st chromosome. When an ovum is formed during meiosis, the 21st pair of chromosomes fails to separate, and then, when the ovum is fertilized, the sperm provides a third 21st chromosome. People with Down's syndrome have various degrees of impaired physical, psychomotor, and cognitive development. The frequency of Down's syndrome increases with the age of the mother, especially when the father is older as well (Rischer & Easton, 1992; Fisch et al., 2003). About 40% of all Down's syndrome children are born to women over 40. Because Down's syndrome is caused by a chromosomal aberration, it is not heritable.

Huntington's disease Huntington's disease (previously known as *Huntington's chorea;* named after the American physician George Huntington) is caused by a dominant lethal gene. However, the lethal gene is not expressed until the afflicted person is between 30 and 40 years of age. Before that time, functioning appears essentially normal. With the onset of the disease, certain

---

mutation Alterations in the nucleotides within a single gene. Can occur spontaneously or from experimental manipulation.

chromosomal aberration Displacement or deletion of genes within chromosomes, or a change in the number of chromosomes.

Down's syndrome Chromosomal aberration consisting of an extra 21st chromosome. Produces varying physical and behavioral impairment.

Huntington's disease Genetic disorder caused by a dominant lethal gene that produces progressive mental and physical deterioration after adulthood (also known as Huntington's chorea).

portions of the brain degenerate. This produces progressive mental and physical deterioration. Because the onset of Huntington's disease occurs after sexual maturity, this lethal gene can pass unrecognized from parent to child. Perhaps the best known case of Huntington's disease is that of Woody Guthrie, the author of the folk song "This land is your land, this land is my land." There is now a test to determine if a person will be afflicted with the disease, but Woody Guthrie's son, the folk singer Arlo Guthrie, decided not to take the test. Fortunately, Arlo did not inherit the lethal gene from his father.

Phenylketonuria (PKU) Phenylketonoria (PKU) is a recessive trait. Infants who are homozygous for the gene cannot break down phenylalanine, an amino acid found in many high-protein foods. As a result, blood levels of phenylalanine increase, which cause brain damage and impairment of intellectual functioning. There is now a test for the disease that is routinely given to newborns. Newborns who test homozygous for this recessive gene are placed on a low-phenylalanine diet shortly after birth. When the diet is carefully followed, brain development is normal. Again, environment and genes interact to produce the expressed characteristics of the organism (that is, the *phenotype*).

QUESTIONS TO CONSIDER

1. Eye color is inherited. How could you account for the fact that you and a sibling have different eye colors since you have the same parents?
2. Given what you now know about genetics, is it likely that there could be a single gene for such complex characteristics as intelligence or personality?
3. Does the fact that a characteristic is heritable mean that the behavior it affects cannot be changed?

Heredity and Human Behavior

Even casual observation reveals that people differ from one another. However, it may be surprising to learn that humans are genetically much less diverse than other primates. For example, we show less genetic diversity than our closest living relative, the chimpanzee (Strachan & Read, 1999). Nevertheless, each of us possesses unique combinations of genes and lives in uniquely different environments. We vary in size and shape, in personality and intelligence, and in artistic and athletic abilities to name but a few. To what extent are these differences due to genetic differences?

Answering this question is difficult. First, as described in Chapter 2, if we want to determine experimentally whether a difference is due to one variable, we must change only that variable while holding all others constant. But, we cannot vary the heredity of humans while holding their environments constant. Nor can we vary their environments while holding their heredity constant. Thus, for humans, the experimental procedures normally used to determine the effect of

a variable can only be approximated, and not fully implemented. And, even if experiments of this sort were possible with humans, we would not conduct them for ethical reasons. Another difficulty is that the effects of heredity and environment interact: If we manipulate the value of one variable and hold the other variables constant, the effect of the manipulated variable may depend on the specific values of the variables we hold constant. If the other variables are held constant at a different value, the manipulated variable might have a different effect. For example, manipulating a gene known to affect high blood pressure might have little effect when the environment was held constant with little salt. We might then incorrectly conclude that the gene had no effect on blood pressure. Keeping such complications in mind, what has research revealed about the role of genetic and environmental differences in human behavior?

Heritability

The degree to which genes affect a characteristic in a given environment is called **heritability.** Heritability is a statistical measure based on correlations. It measures the amount of variation in a trait that is due to naturally occurring genetic differences among individuals in that population. Heritability varies from 0.0 (no effect of genetic differences) to 1.0 (complete genetic determination). The measure reflects the variation of a trait in a *population* of individuals; it does not indicate the contribution of genetic factors to the characteristics of any one individual. Statistical procedures can be applied to humans because these procedures are observational and do not involve direct manipulation of variables. Darwin's cousin Francis Galton (1869) began the use of correlations to study heritability in humans. A second, and complementary, approach to assessing heritability is **behavior genetics.** Behavior genetics uses experimental methods in which genetic variables are manipulated by the researcher and the effects of these manipulations on behavior are measured. Clearly, behavior genetics is largely restricted to the study of the nonhuman animals, but the results of such studies can be used to interpret the behavior of humans.

Experimental Procedures for Studying Genetic Influences

Animal breeders have used artificial selection for many years, but laboratory methods have been employed to study the relation between heredity and behavior for only about 100 years. Most behavioral traits are continuously varying characteristics that are polygenic and the various genes may well

---

phenylketonuria (PKU) Genetic disorder caused by recessive genes that impair ability to break down phenylalanine; can cause mental retardation if untreated.

heritability Variation in a trait due to genetic factors, varies from 0.0 to 1.0.

behavior genetics The study of how genes affect behavior.

be located on different chromosomes. These polygenic traits are **nonmendelian traits.** Polygenic traits play an important role in human evolution (Carroll, 2003) and methods for their study are described shortly.

Artificial Selection Artificial selection involves selective breeding within a population of organisms. Using these procedures, the heritability of many characteristics, or traits, has been demonstrated in nonhuman animals. These traits include such things as aggression, docility, alcohol preference, running speed, and mating behavior.

Perhaps the best known example of artificial selection is a study of maze learning in rats conducted by Robert Tryon (1940). Tryon began with an unselected population of rats and had them learn to run a maze for food. As you might imagine, some rats learned the correct path with few errors and some with many errors. Tryon interbred those rats that learned with the fewest errors with their kind and interbred the rats that learned with the most errors with their kind. The offspring of this artificial-selection procedure then learned the maze. Successive generations of offspring were, in turn, interbred in the same manner.

After a number of generations of artificial selection, the maze performance of the two groups did not overlap. (See FIGURE 3·10.) It is important to note that the two groups did not differ on their first attempt at the maze, but that the difference emerged during learning. The artificial-selection procedure had produced two groups of rats that learned the correct path at different rates.

You should not conclude that the differences in maze performance indicated that their behavior could be affected only by genetic factors. For example, Cooper and Zubek (1958) showed that differences in maze performance were virtually eliminated when "maze-bright" and "maze-dull" groups of rats were both stimulated by rearing them in enriched environments (cages containing geometric objects such as tunnels,

---

nonmendelian trait   Characteristic when alleles do not have a dominant-recessive relation.

molecular genetics   The study of genetics at the level of the DNA molecule.

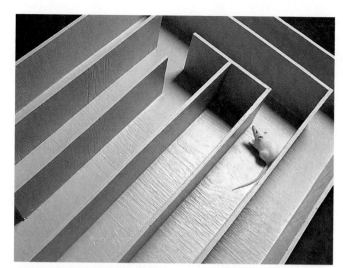

Tryon's selective breeding study showed that a rat's ability to learn how to navigate a maze was affected by genetic factors.

ramps, and blocks). Differences were also eliminated when Tryon's maze-bright rats were raised in impoverished environments (cages containing only food and water). Thus, the effects of the genetic differences depended on the environments in which the genes were expressed. It would also be a mistake to conclude that Tryon's two groups differed in some more general respect such as "intelligence" or "ability to learn." Tryon's "dull" rats learned a task that required escape from water faster than the "bright" rats (Searles, 1949, see McClearn, 1963 for a review). General effects of selection can be expected only if the selecting environments are very diverse, such as the widely differing challenges that humans and many other species have faced over evolutionary time.

Molecular Genetics **Molecular genetics** uses powerful techniques to directly manipulate genes and their expression. Molecular genetics studies genes at the level of DNA and then relates differences in genes to the structure and behavior of the organism. Perhaps its greatest accomplishment to date has been to determine essentially the entire sequence of nucleotides in the human genome.

[FIGURE 3·10] Results from Tryon's 1940 artificial breeding research of rats' ability to learn a maze. Within a few generations, differences in the rats' ability to negotiate the maze became distinct.

(Adapted from Tryon, R. C. (1940). Genetic differences in maze-learning ability in rats. *Yearbook of the National Society for the Study of Education, 39*, 111–119.)

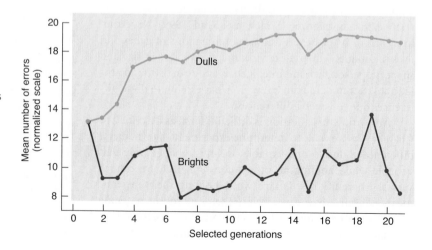

One of the techniques for studying the effects of genes at the molecular level is **knockout mutations.** Molecular biologists have developed methods that directly affect the gene by damaging genes with radiation or by inserting nucleotides that prevent the expression of a gene. This produces what is called a *knockout mutation.* In one such study with rats, the gene that was knocked out is normally expressed in a part of the brain known to be important for spatial learning in humans. When this gene was knocked out in rats, they were impaired in their ability to learn to swim to the location of a slightly submerged platform on which they could rest (Nakazawa et al., 2003). By examining the changes in performance after a gene has been knocked out, clues are obtained about the function of the gene.

The methods of molecular biology can also be combined with artificial selection to study the effects of genes on behavior. For example, a biochemically detectable change can be produced in a genetically inactive portion of a chromosome. This change then becomes a **genetic marker** for those genes that are nearby on the chromosome. When artificial selection produces a change in behavior, as in maze performance in Tryon's experiment, the genetic markers can be examined to see if different artificially selected groups vary in the frequency or placement of the genetic marker. If the groups differ, then the genes that are responsible for the difference must lie nearby on the chromosome. By using multiple markers on different chromosomes, the chance of finding the locations of relevant genes is increased. As an example, this technique has been used to isolate the location of a gene that affects exploratory behavior in fruit-fly larvae (Osborne et al., 1997).

Correlation Methods for Studying the Effects of Genes

Human behavior cannot be subjected to the experimental procedures of artificial selection and molecular genetics, such as knockouts and gene-marking. Nevertheless, much has been learned about the effects of genes on human behavior through correlation methods. In correlation methods, individuals with naturally occurring differences in behavior are examined to determine if differences in genetic variables are related to (correlated with) the behavior. With humans, we cannot manipulate the genetic make-up (the genotype), but we can observe their behavior (the phenotype). In addition, we can analyze the sequences of nucleotides to see if they are correlated with the phenotype. Such research with humans requires their informed consent.

Concordance research Concordance research takes advantage of the fact that identical twins have identical genes. Recall that identical twins, technically *monozygotic (MZ) twins,* arise from a single fertilized ovum, or zygote. The zygote divides into two genetically identical cells that develop independently thereafter. Fraternal twins, technically *dizygotic (DZ) twins,* arise from the fertilization of two different ova by two different sperm. If genes affect behavior, then MZ twins

Research with identical twins has provided psychology with information about the role of heredity in behavior traits.

should be more alike than DZ twins, or than other siblings raised in similar environments.

Two individuals are said to be *concordant* for a trait if both express that same trait. If only one of the two individuals expresses the trait, then they are said to be *discordant* for the trait. In these terms, MZ twins should be more often concordant than other pairs of individuals because they are more genetically similar. As shown in TABLE 3•1, MZ twins are indeed concordant for many traits. For example, the physical characteristic of blood type has a heritability of 1.0 and is highly concordant in MZ twins but less so in DZ twins.

[**TABLE 3•1**] Comparison of Concordance Rates between Monozygotic (MZ) and Dizygotic (DZ) Twins for Various Traits

CONCORDANCE		
Trait	**MZ**	**DZ**
Blood type	100%	66%
Eye color	99	28
Mental retardation	97	37
Measles	95	87
Idiopathic epilepsy	72	15
Schizophrenia	69	10
Diabetes	65	18
Identical allergy	59	5
Tuberculosis	57	23

Source: Table 7.4, p. 161 from *Concepts of Genetics,* 2nd ed. by William S. Klug and Michael R. Cummings. Copyright © 1986 by Scott, Foresman and Company. Reprinted by permission of Pearson Education, Inc.

---

knockout mutations   Experimentally induced genetic sequence preventing gene expression.

genetic marker   A known nucleotide sequence that occurs at a particular location on a chromosome.

concordance research   Studies the similarity of traits between twins, especially identical twins. Twins are concordant if they exhibit the same phenotype.

Environmental similarity as well as genetic similarity also affects concordance. Note the lower concordance of MZ twins for schizophrenia, which is a behavioral characteristic, than for blood type. The lower concordance reflects the contribution of environmental as well as genetic factors to schizophrenia. The concordance rate of DZ twins for schizophrenia is 10%, which is above what would be expected from a disease that occurs in only about 1% of the general population. This indicates the contribution of genetic as well as environmental facts to schizophrenia.

In research described in later chapters, studies compare the performance of MZ and DZ twins on other behavior. These studies show that genetic factors can also affect cognitive skills such as the scores on intelligence tests (Bouchard & McGue, 1981), personality traits such as extroversion (the tendency to be outgoing), language ability, and certain psychological disorders such as schizophrenia and mental retardation (Bouchard & Propping, 1993).

Segregation Analysis **Segregation analysis** is another correlation method that is used to assess genetic contributions to human behavior. Although behavioral geneticists cannot insert a genetic marker in humans, they can identify specific regions of chromosomes and correlate the presence or absence of these regions with behavioral phenotypes. These identified regions are made up of nucleotide sequences that are relatively constant. Behavior geneticists use the information from concordances and kin relations to search for traits that show strong genetic influences. The chromosomes are then examined to see if any of the various markers is differentially associated—*segregated*—with the behavioral trait. If some markers are segregated between the behavioral phenotypes, then the critical genes lie on or near the marker. Additional work in molecular biology can then be directed toward those regions of the chromosome to identify the precise gene.

The potential power of segregation analysis is illustrated in a study of a particular language deficit. The deficit is a widespread difficulty in the articulation of words, especially in the formation of grammatical word endings—for instance, forming the past tense of regular verbs by adding -*ed* as in "walk" and "walk*ed*" (Enard et al., 2002). Three generations of a family were known to have this particular language disorder. One gene on the seventh chromosome, designated by the letters FOXP2, showed a mutation that was unique to those members of the family who had the language disorder. The mutation was not seen in a large sample of unrelated individuals who did not show the language-disorder pheno-

type. This finding strongly suggests that a normally functioning FOXP2 gene affects the fine articulatory movements that make refined speech possible (Pinker, 2001). An especially intriguing result arose as a byproduct of this work. When the map of the human genome was compared to analogous genetic sequences in other primates, it was found that the FOXP2 gene had changed quite rapidly after humans diverged from the great apes (Enard et al., 2002). Based on the rate at which mutations are thought to occur, the estimated date at which the modern human form of FOXP2 emerged was within the last 200,000 years of human evolution. However, for reasons noted earlier in the study of heritability of maze learning in rats, it is simplistic to think that the FOXP2 gene is a "language gene" because the gene also affects other behavior.

QUESTIONS TO CONSIDER

1. Given what you know about how heritability is determined, would the heritability of skin color be different in the United States, Scandinavia, and Africa?
2. What problems would be faced in determining the genetic basis (if any) of human characteristics such as aggression?

Evolution and Human Behavior

Evolution through natural selection has affected not only the structure of humans but their behavior as well. In this final major section of the chapter, we consider some of the implications of natural selection for human behavior. The field of psychology that studies the effect of natural selection on behavior is called **evolutionary psychology** (Buller, 2005). Work in this field began with research on animals in biology, which focused on the implications of evolution for social behavior. Sexual and parenting behavior were of greatest interest because both directly affect reproductive fitness.

Sociobiology

Sociobiology is the study of genetic influences on social behavior (Wilson, 1975). Typically, sociobiologists observe and perform experiments on the social behavior of nonhuman animals and then explore the implications of those findings for the social behavior of humans. Thus sociobiology involves experimentation to determine the adaptiveness of a given social behavior and then uses those findings to interpret behavior in the natural environment.

Reproductive and parenting behavior have been the primary focus of sociobiological research. Much of this work has been concerned with **reproductive strategies**—the various systems of mating and rearing offspring.

---

segregation analysis Correlational method to identify sections of chromosomes that are the same for individuals expressing a common trait.

evolutionary psychology Branch of psychology studying how human behavior is affected by evolution.

sociobiology The study of genetic influences on social behavior, especially in animals.

reproductive strategies Evolutionary effects on systems of mating and rearing offspring; these need not be conscious strategies.

Reproductive Strategies Of the various reproductive strategies, our culture sanctions only **monogamy,** the mating of one female and one male. If offspring result from mating, the culture endorses sharing responsibility for raising the child. However, different reproductive strategies occur in different species and cultures—including our own (Barash, 1982). Three additional classes of reproductive strategy are possible. (See FIGURE 3•11.) **Polygyny** involves one male mating with more than one female; *polyandry* involves one female mating with more than one male; and *polygynandry* involves several females mating with several males. (*Poly* refers to many, *and* to male, and *gyn* to female.) We consider only monogamy and polygyny because they are the predominant reproductive strategies in humans.

Different reproductive strategies arise from important sex differences in the resources that each parent invests in conceiving and rearing offspring (Trivers, 1972). **Parental investment** refers to the time, physical effort, and risks to life involved in procreating, nurturing, and protecting offspring. From an evolutionary perspective, individuals who make a greater investment in parenting should be more discriminating when choosing a mate and, in turn, should be more sought after as mates.

Among humans, polygyny is a common reproductive strategy, especially in cultures in which some men have much greater resources available to them than others do—as in Africa and portions of the Middle East and Asia (Kanazawa & Still, 2001). Monogamy is the most common reproductive strategy in Western culture (Badcock, 1991). In fact, even though it is not sanctioned by Western culture, men especially engage in polygynous mating practices. In the United States, for example, 25% of men but only 15% of women are estimated to engage in extramarital sexual relations (Laumann et al., 1994). Polygynous practices are especially common with humans who have reproductively beneficial traits such as wealth or power. Think of the multiple alliances of "captains of industry" and "movie stars."

Sexual Selection Competition for mates can lead to **sexual selection,** that is, natural selection for traits that are

Large male elephant seals are more successful in competing for females than are smaller males. But is there a point at which larger size could become maladaptive?

characteristic of a particular sex, such as appearance, body size, or behavioral patterns. Elaborate displays of the peacock's tail feathers are preferred by peahens because such displays are correlated with the general health and vigor of the male. These characteristics—if heritable—favor the survival of the peahen's chicks. In the developed world, physically attractive women are generally those with a low *waist-to-hip ratio (WHR),* reflecting a greater deposition of fat on the buttocks and hips than the waist. A preference for women with low WHR is consistent with the evolutionary argument that mates are selected for their health and fitness to reproduce. However, such preferences are not universal. A study by Yu and Shepard (1998) compared the preferences for women of American men and men of the Matsigenka people in southeast Peru. These Peruvian men live in an isolated village and have not been exposed to the mass media of Western civilization. Whereas Western men prefer women with low WHR, the Matsigenka men preferred women with high WHR. Perhaps being overweight in this isolated Peruvian society was associated with coming from a relatively prosperous family that was—in turn—correlated with a favorable genetic endowment. Researchers who study the sexual preferences of men in other agricultural societies have found a similar pattern. They speculate that "the more subsistence-oriented a society is, and the more energetically expansive women's work, the more men will find fatter women attractive" (Marlowe & Wetzman, 2001). Indeed, an article posted on BBC News (July 19, 2007) quotes a husband from the Efik tribe in Africa who said that he sends his wife to a special fattening room where "I add rice and beans and more meat and fish to make her more huge and big to maintain the stature you want

	Male partner	
	One	Multiple
One	Monogamy	Polyandry
Multiple	Polygyny	Polygynandry

Female partner

[**FIGURE 3•11**] Reproductive strategies. Different numbers of males mating with different numbers of females yield the four reproductive strategies of monogamy, polygyny, polyandry, and polygynandry.

monogamy Mating strategy of one female with one male.

polygyny Mating strategy of one male with more than one female.

parental investment Resources that parents expend in procreating and nurturing offspring.

sexual selection Preference for traits that are differentially expressed in the two sexes, for example, body size.

your woman to be." His wife added, "When you are fat, it makes you look healthy. People respect you. People honor you. Wherever you go, they say, 'Your husband feed you fine.'" It is clear that sexual preferences are not influenced by natural selection alone.

Polygyny is a common reproductive strategy among mammals (including humans). The costs associated with reproduction are generally much less for males than females. Females have fewer opportunities than males to reproduce because they produce only one ovum or a few ova periodically, whereas males can produce numerous sperm at relatively frequent intervals. Thus, females can bear only a limited number of offspring in a lifetime, regardless of the number of males with whom they mate. In contrast, males are limited in their reproductive success only by the number of females that they can impregnate. Perhaps the most dramatic example of this difference is illustrated by King Ismail of Morocco, who reportedly fathered 1,056 children (Young, 1998)! Females also carry the fertilized ovum in their bodies during a long gestation period. This requires diverting a major portion of their own metabolic resources to nourishing the fetus. Because they carry the fertilized ovum, females also assume the risks that accompany pregnancy and childbirth. The contributions of males to reproduction can be quite minimal—sperm and the time for mating. Once offspring are born, females often continue to devote some of their metabolic resources to the infant by nursing it.

Females in polygynous species invest especially heavily in their offspring because the male is shared with other females. As a result, females are usually quite selective in their mates. They mate with males who possess such traits as physical size, strength, and aggressiveness. This selectivity often benefits the adaptation of both the female and her progeny. The offspring of such males will tend to possess the same adaptively significant attributes as the father and thus will be more likely to eventually win their own quests for mating privileges. Also, her female offspring will more likely be attracted to the same male attributes. To the extent that such preferences are heritable, the net effect is that the genes of the mother will have greater representation in future generations than will genes of females who mate with males having less adaptive traits. Of course, which traits are adaptive depend on the environment. For example, for humans in developed countries the intelligence of men would likely be more adaptive than their strength.

Monogamy is also common among humans. In general, monogamy occurs in species whose environments favor the contributions of both parents to the survival of offspring. In these environments, reproductive fitness benefits more from sharing parental duties than from exclusive care by

one parent. For example, a fox must provide food, milk, and protection for its offspring. A single female attempting to fulfill all of these responsibilities would put the pups at risk. Hunting would be difficult with the pups straggling along, but leaving the pups behind would risk predation. The reproductive strategy exhibited by foxes is that both parents hunt and protect the cubs. By jointly caring for the pups, both male and female foxes enhance the chance that their offspring will survive and reproduce. Thus, the parental genes will more likely be represented in the next generation.

Although both males and females in monogamous species share parenting responsibilities, females generally continue to have greater parental investment in the offspring. Many of the reasons for greater female investment endure—the limited opportunity for mating, the cost of pregnancy, and so on. As a result, very few monogamous species, including our own, are exclusively monogamous. In fact, there is a strong tendency in most monogamous species toward patterns of reproductive behavior and parental investment that approximate polygynous species (Tavris & Sadd, 1977; Badcock, 1991; Hyde & Oliver, 2000; Shackelford & Weekes-Shackelford, 2004). Of course, learning and culture, as well as the genetic legacy of the ancestral environment, affect reproductive and mating behavior in humans. The advent of effective contraception has reduced the relation between mating and child-bearing; in addition, increased opportunities for education and employment for women undoubtedly increasingly affect human reproductive strategies. Contemporary culture does not measure reproductive success only by the number of children, but also by the quality of the children's lives as well as those of their parents. Most people have the biological capacity to produce a larger number of children, but many choose not to do so.

Altruism   **Altruistic behavior** involves self-sacrifice, as when parents risk their own survival by defending their young against predators or by feeding their young in times of scarcity. If individuals behave in a manner that is a cost to themselves but a benefit to others, then that behavior is said to be *altruistic*. Altruistic behavior is of particular interest because it seems to conflict with the layman's conception of "survival of the fittest." If natural selection favors traits that benefit survival, then how could behavior that reduces survival of the individual ever be selected? And yet, abundant examples of altruism exist even among nonhuman animals.

Consider the honeybee that sacrifices its life on behalf of its hive mates when it stings an intruder, or the prairie dog that gives alarm calls that warn other prairie dogs of a predator but increases its own chances of being preyed upon. Examples of altruistic behavior abound in humans. In its most extreme form, human altruism is demonstrated when persons risk their lives to save the lives of others. How can such self-sacrifice be understood? More important for present purposes, how can evolution interpret such behavior?

---

altruistic behavior   Behavior benefiting another organism at an apparent cost to the individual who executes the action.

The evolutionary explanation of altruistic behavior is based on the following insight: It is the survival of the *genes,* not the individual who carries those genes, that is of central concern to natural selection. An individual's genes are held partially in common with all those with whom that individual is genetically related. For example, each parent shares 50% of his or her genes with each offspring—on the average half of the offspring's genes come from the mother and half from the father. Thus parents who disadvantage themselves to the benefit of their children are, in fact, benefiting their own genes! The geneticist William D. Hamilton (1964, 1970) realized that, strictly speaking, natural selection does not favor reproductive success but **inclusive fitness**—the reproductive success of individuals with whom we share genes as well as ourselves. Note that the evolutionary account of altruism does not assume that there is any conscious appreciation of the genetic consequences of altruism.

In confirmation of inclusive fitness, experiments have determined that altruistic behavior is more apt to occur when the organism that benefits is genetically related to organism that pays the cost. Bees and other social insects, such as termites, are among the most altruistic species because their special genetic relationship causes them to share a particularly high number of genes in common. Birds make alarm calls upon sighting a hawk, but only if their *relatives* are near, not otherwise (Wilson, 1975). In general, altruistic behavior most benefits close relatives such as parents, siblings, grandparents, and grandchildren. The closer the family relation, the greater the genetic overlap among the individuals involved. Such biologic favoritism toward relatives is called **kin selection** (Mayr, 2001).

Not all instances of altruistic behavior can be understood in terms of kin selection. What about altruism between unrelated individuals? Could this also be affected by genetic variables? The evolutionary biologist Trivers (1971) identified an additional genetic source of altruism. This type of altruism is known as **reciprocal altruism.** Reciprocal altruism occurs when genetically unrelated persons engage in behavior that reduces their fitness at the moment but may increase their fitness in the longer term. For example, one individual may share his food with another now and the other may, in turn, share his food later. Thus each individual has increased his own fitness by an altruistic act because the likelihood is increased that each will pass his genes to the next generation.

Reciprocal altruism is the biological version of the Golden Rule—"Do unto others as you would have them do unto you." However, the biological version is not as generous as the Golden Rule. To increase reproductive fitness, altruistic behavior must carry a low risk to the altruist and a high benefit to the recipient. The lower the cost to the altruist, the more likely the altruistic act will benefit the altruist's fitness. If the altruist is not likely ever to benefit by a reciprocal action from the recipient, the fitness of the altruist is decreased. Finally, the altruist and the recipient must

be able to recognize each other; otherwise, the behavior cannot be reciprocated. Does this genetic analysis of the conditions required for reciprocal altruism help explain why people are more likely to follow the Golden Rule in small communities than in big cities? Does this analysis help explain why people are especially good at facial recognition? Again, cultural factors and individual experience both play a role in reciprocal altruism, but genetic factors are a part of the story.

Evolutionary Psychology

Evolutionary psychology applies evolutionary thinking to the full range of human behavior (Buss, 2007; Buss et al., 1998). However, it is much more difficult to experimentally assess the effects of a given behavior on reproductive fitness in humans. As a result, efforts to understand human behavior in terms of evolutionary considerations must often be indirect and sometimes border on reasoning by analogy (Cornell, 1997; Roney, 1999). What is clear is that although natural selection undoubtedly affects human behavior—especially reproductive and parenting behavior—cultural factors also play an important role. Consider the effects of differences in parental investment on the sexual behavior of men and women. We have already seen that the preference for monogamous as contrasted with polygynous mating strategies depends on the equality of distribution of resources among men in the society. Other factors, such as the availability of effective methods of contraception, also undoubtedly affect mating strategies. In addition, it is often difficult to distinguish behavior that is a byproduct of selection for some other characteristic from behavior that has actually been an object of selection (Roney, 1999).

Evaluating Evolutionary Psychology Evolutionary psychology has been controversial among psychologists, social scientists, and the general public. Several objections have been raised by its critics, often based on an incomplete understanding of the field. One objection has been that human behavior is too complex to be understood by natural selection alone. However, no evolutionary psychologist would ever make this claim. Social behavior—indeed all behavior—is the concerted effect of both the ancestral environment, as reflected in our genes, and our individual experience, as reflected in our nervous systems. To claim that evolution has *something* to say about human behavior is not

---

inclusive fitness   Total reproductive success of those with whom the individual has genes in common, e.g., siblings.

kin selection   Selection that favors altruistic acts toward individuals with whom one has genes in common.

reciprocal altruism   Altruism in which one individual benefits another when it is likely that the other will return the benefit at a later time.

to claim that evolution has *everything* to say. Another objection has been that evolutionary psychology is based on simplistic analogies between the behavior of nonhuman animals and humans. It is true that experimental work has been largely restricted to nonhumans, but experimental work is necessarily limited in any science that deals with human behavior. Care must always be taken when applying findings from other animals to humans—or, for that matter, from any one species to another.

We are encouraged to seek commonalities in the behavior of humans and other species by the fact of evolution—that all species are related to each other through branching descent—and the fact of selection—that all species have been subjected to selection by a partially common environment. The words of Edward O. Wilson, the "father" of sociobiology are to the point.

> The purpose of sociobiology is not to make crude comparisons between animal species or between animals and men. . . . Its purpose is to develop general laws of the evolution and biology of social behavior, which might then be extended in a disinterested manner to the study of human beings. . . . To devise a naturalistic description of human social behavior is to note a set of facts for further investigation, not to pass a value judgment or to deny that a great deal of the behavior can be deliberately changed if individual societies wish. . . . Human behavior is dominated by culture in the sense that the greater part, perhaps all, of the variation between societies is based on differences in cultural experiences . . . To understand the evolutionary history . . . is to understand in a deeper manner the construction of human nature, to learn what we really are and not just what we hope we are, as viewed through the various prisms of our mythologies. (Wilson, in Barash, 1982, pp. xiv–xv)

The criticisms of evolutionary accounts of human behavior are specific examples of general reservations that have been raised about natural selection as a basis for understanding the diversity and complexity of life. Before Darwin, these phenomena seemed beyond the reach of a natural-science explanation. After Darwin, the *possibility* of a natural-science explanation of life appeared. Repeated cycles of variation, selection, and retention promised an account that appealed only to processes that could be known through the methods of science.

Today, natural selection is the central unifying principle of biology and is playing an increasing role in psychology in the form of evolutionary psychology (Caporael, 2001; see also Lickliter & Honeycutt, 2003). Darwin's account of how selection processes produced the diversity and complexity of life is seen as a general approach to the

explanation of the emergence of order and complexity in many fields. The repeated action of physical, chemical, biological, and behavioral processes—each of which could be subjected to independent scrutiny in the laboratory—may yield complex outcomes as their emergent product. (For more general treatments of selectionism, see Dennett, 1995; Mayr, 2000; and Donahoe, 2003.) Darwin has identified a means whereby complex phenomena in many fields can be understood as products of the repeated action of variation, selection, and retention. Through the selecting effect of the environment, order emerges naturally.

One general criticism of selectionism is that the complete sequence of events in the evolutionary process is not known. When complex electronic circuits are developed through a selection process, we can examine each step in the sequence and assure ourselves that the circuits came about through the cumulative effects of selection (Mead, 1989). However, when naturally occurring processes are studied, only glimpses of the entire sequence are usually visible. In the evolution of our species, for example, we see only a tooth here, a leg bone there. Darwin recognized the incompleteness of our knowledge of all of the steps in any natural process. Commenting on the meagerness of the fossil record, he remarked, ". . . we are confessedly ignorant; nor do we know how ignorant we are" (Darwin, 1859). The fossil record is now much more complete than when Darwin made his comments, but our knowledge remains imperfect. Faced with imperfect knowledge, science seeks to fill in the gaps rather than abandoning the effort. All the gaps in the course of evolution may never be filled, but none will be filled unless we seek them. Recent fossil discoveries have identified transitional forms between birds and the dinosaurs that were their ancestors (Prum, 2003) and between land-dwelling creatures and their aquatic ancestors (Daeschler, Shubin, & Jenkins, Jr., 2006). We now know much more about the evolutionary process from the fossil and molecular records.

A second general criticism of selectionism is that it undermines our uniqueness, and even our worth, as a species. Consider the sociobiological account of altruism. We prefer to think of ourselves as selfless individuals who help others out of the goodness of our hearts. Sociobiology suggests that altruism is, at least in part, a selfish act that is undertaken because it benefits the survival of our genes. But is this not a kind of selflessness? It is our genes that benefit and not us as individuals. And, most importantly, knowledge of evolution through natural selection opens the possibility of undoing the effects of those prior selections that once benefited the population as a whole but are now a burden for the individual. Through **genetic engineering** and other applications of our increasing knowledge of natural selection, we can implement *counter-selections*. Counter-selections seek to change our present environment so that we minimize the otherwise untoward effects of selection by the ancestral environment. Consider adult-onset diabetes,

---

genetic engineering   Procedures intended to alter an organism's genes to produce a more favorable phenotype.

in which the effectiveness of insulin to store excess glucose as fat is diminished. Evolutionary research indicates that this was an adaptive response in the history of our species: It increased survival in environments with intermittent food shortages. Knowing the origin of diabetes, more effective treatment regimens can now be formulated (Watve & Yajnik, 2007). Again, knowledge of evolution helps us understand and counter an effect of natural selection. If counter-selections are done wisely, is this not testimony to the uniqueness and worth of our species (Campbell, 1976)?

Culture Culture is the sum of socially transmitted knowledge, customs, and behavior patterns that is common to a particular group of people. Culture is a means—in addition to natural selection—by which the environment of one generation can affect the behavior of the next generation. Culture insures that the skills acquired by one generation are transmitted to the next generation. The changes wrought by culture occur much more rapidly than those produced by natural selection. No account of human behavior is complete without considering the effects of both evolution (the genetic legacy of the ancient past) and culture (the learned legacy of the more recent past). Although cultural influences are much more pronounced in humans than other species, some evidence of cultural transmission can be found in other social species. For example, if a chimpanzee acquires a skill, such as operating a device to secure food while separated from its group, when the trained chimp returns to the group, other individuals in the group rapidly acquire that same skill through observing the first chimp (White, Horner, & de Waal, 2005). Without cultural transmission, the group might never have acquired the skill.

By understanding how behavior developed through evolution by natural selection and through acculturation by learning, we can understand how our behavior has become adapted to the environments of the past and present. More importantly, by understanding natural selection and learning, we can better design environments that permit us not only to survive in the present but also to attain our goals in the future.

QUESTIONS TO CONSIDER

1. Does the fact that social behavior is affected by natural selection through genetic mechanisms have any implications for the concept of personal responsibility or for our legal system?

2. Suppose a child is in a dangerous situation. From an evolutionary perspective alone, should a parent risk his or her own life to rescue the child? Would your answer depend on the number of children the parent already had? Would it depend on the age of the parent?

Epilogue

A Favored Gene, Not a Favored Individual

As we have seen, natural selection operates on the level of *populations*, not of individuals. On the average, those members of the population having characteristics that favor the survival of their offspring are more likely to have their genes survive into the next generation. However, there is no guarantee that any one individual with favorable characteristics will survive and reproduce. George Washington was an individual with clearly admirable characteristics—he was a physical specimen possessed of both courage and intelligence. However, he left no offspring. To better understand the implications of the selection process for the individual, let us return to the case of that seemingly favored son John Harold Johnson, Jr. Sickle-cell anemia is now known to be caused by a gene that does not produce the disease when present in a single copy. However, as Mendel's work demonstrated, each offspring receives *two* copies of most genes—one from each parent. By chance, John Jr. received one sickle-cell gene from his father and one from his mother. But, because each parent had only one copy of the gene, they did not express the disease. Thus, knowledge of genetics lets us understand how John Jr. could have sickle-cell anemia even though his parents and sibling did not.

That leaves the question of how to account for the persistence of the sickle-cell gene in the human population. Why has such a potentially lethal genetic disease continued to plague humanity? Here, natural selection, not genetics, provides the answer. The sickle-cell gene is found primarily in people who trace their ancestry to populations that previously lived around the Mediterranean. In that region, humans have long co-existed with an insect called the *Anopheles mosquito*. This mosquito obtains the proteins needed to produce its eggs from human blood and, in the process of biting humans to get the blood, injects them with the parasite that causes malaria. The parasite then reproduces inside red-blood cells and, from time-to-time, releases more parasites from the infected cells. In so doing, the infected blood cells are destroyed. The destruction of these cells produces the symptoms of malaria—chills, anemia (due to

---

culture Socially transmitted knowledge, customs, and behavior of a group of people.

insufficient oxygen), and, not uncommonly, death. When blood vessels in the brain and other organs become clogged with the debris of the destroyed cells, those organs are damaged. Even today, almost two out of every 100 children under four years of age die of malarial infection in countries such as Angola and Sierra Leone.

What does the prevalence of malaria in John Jr.'s ancestors have to do with the persistence of the sickle-cell gene? The sickle-cell gene was selected in this ancestral population of humans because one copy of the gene causes only those few red-blood cells that were initially infected by the parasite to sickle. These few misshapen cells are then removed by the spleen and the parasite dies. Parents with only one copy of the gene are thus more likely to live long enough to have children and only one out of every four of their children will be unlucky enough to receive two copies of the gene. Thus the *population* of humans in this region benefits from the persistence of the sickle-cell gene. On the average, two out of every four children receive immunity from malaria because they have only a single copy of the gene, one child remains susceptible to malaria because he has no copy of the gene, and one child suffers sickle-cell anemia because he receives two copies. Thus, on the average, the sickle-cell gene benefits the survival of the population as a whole: Twice as many offspring benefit as lose from the continued existence of the gene. Individuals such as John Harold Johnson, Jr. pay a heavy price as the legacy of that long-ago benefit. In the environment of the United States, infection by the malarial parasite is almost nonexistent. The introduction of insecticides into the environment has eliminated the prior benefit of the sickle-cell gene, but its cost remains.

The unfortunate case of John Harold Johnson, Jr. teaches us two general and important lessons about evolution through natural selection. First, the adaptations arising from natural selection are understandable on the level of *populations* of individuals, not on the level of the individual. Although it is individuals who live or die, who reproduce or not, it is the effect of their fate on the *population* that determines the course of natural selection. John Jr. died because the genes that he carried benefited the population of which his ancestors were members. The second lesson that John Jr. teaches us is that *past* environments determine the effects of natural selection on the individual. To the extent that the present is like the past, we are well adapted. However, when the present differs from the past—as in John Jr.'s case—the illusion is shattered. Strictly speaking, natural selection "prepares" us to live in the past. It is only to the extent that past environments resemble later environments that we are adapted to the present and the future.

At first glance, evolution through natural selection seems a simple idea: If the environment favors the survival of organisms having some characteristic, then that characteristic—if heritable—becomes more common over successive generations. The complex implications of natural selection emerge only upon closer examination. As the philosopher of biology David Hull commented, "Evolution is so simple, anyone can misunderstand it." Natural selection occurs in one environment, but its effects are felt in later environments. If the later environments are similar to the environment in which the characteristic was selected, then the population is adapted to the later environments. If the later environments differ from the ancestral environment, then the illusion of adaptation is shattered. Natural selection is only as far-sighted as the environment is constant. As observed in Ecclesiastes of the Old Testament, "the race is … [not necessarily] … to the swift, the battle to the strong, or favor to men of skill. Time and chance happeneth to them all."

CHAPTER SUMMARY

The Development of Evolutionary Science

Charles Darwin observed the diversity of life during his voyage around the world in the naval ship *HMS Beagle*. On his return to England, he carried out additional observations and experiments on artificial selection. On the basis of this work, Darwin proposed that the diversity of life came about because the environment favored the survival of some organisms over others. Organisms with favored characteristics had a greater chance of surviving and producing offspring. The result of this natural-selection process was that the favored characteristics became more numerous over successive generations with different organisms becoming adapted to the different environments in which they lived.

For life to become more complex, the characteristics that were favored by natural selection had to be passed from one generation to the next. Only in that way could favored characteristics accumulate and lead to complex organisms. Darwin did not know how this happened, After his death Mendel's work on the breeding of peas was discovered and provided the answer. Mendel's work began the science of *genetics*. His work showed that the factors we now call genes were passed unchanged from one generation to the next. Thus favored characteristics could add up over time and life could become more complex under the guidance of the selecting environment.

Evolution through natural selection requires three components—*variation*, *selection*, and *retention*. Variation is required for evolutionary change. It provides the differences in characteristics that selection can favor or disfavor. Selection is the result of differential reproduction of those organisms whose characteristics benefit the survival of themselves and, ultimately, their offspring. Retention allows the favored characteristics to be passed to the next generation by genetic mechanisms, thus permitting the effects of selection to accumulate.

For religious reasons, some people in the United States and elsewhere do not accept evolution through natural selection, especially with regard to the origin of humans. Natural selection is most clearly seen at the level of *populations* of individuals, not at the level of each individual. Natural selection affects the behavior of *organisms* as well as their structures: The effect of a structure on reproductive fitness depends on how that structure is used. As an example, the beautiful feathers of a peacock's tail do not affect his reproductive fitness unless he displays the feathers when he sights a peahen and the display is favored by the peahen. Natural selection increases adaptation in the present environment only to the extent that the selecting environments of the past are like those of present.

Evolution of Humans

Human evolution can be traced through changes in *fossils*, by methods such as *carbon dating* and DNA analysis, and by the *molecular clock* through counting *nucleotide exchanges*. Using these techniques *hominids* (*bipedal* apes) first came on the scene some 4 to 6 million years ago in southeastern Africa. For about 2 million years, our hominid ancestors remained in Africa, becoming larger and progressively more proficient bipedal walkers and more skillful users of their hands. These hominids are classified in a new genus, *Homo*, when the size of their brains increased to about twice that of present-day chimpanzees and tool-making became more proficient. Species of this genus began to move out of Africa about 2 million years ago in three major, successive partially overlapping waves, first *H. erectus*, then *H. neanderthalis*, and finally *H. sapiens*. They spread across much of Europe, Africa, Asia, and Oceania and, finally, *H. sapiens* came to the Americas. Only the last of these species remains—our own.

Heredity, Genetics, and Evolution

The sequence of *nucleotides* within a *gene* controls the synthesis of proteins, which in turn make up the structure of the body. Genes are found on *chromosomes*, each of which usually contains thousands of genes. We inherit 23 individual chromosomes from each parent. The genetic endowment of individuals is a *recombination* of the genes of their parents. The recombination of genes produces tremendous genetic diversity. Genetic diversity provides the variation upon which natural selection operates and increases the possibility of adapting to changing environmental conditions.

The expression of a gene depends on several factors, whether it is a *dominant* or a *recessive* gene, how it interacts with other genes (*polygenic* traits), whether the sex of the individual is male or female, and how the environment under which that individual lives interacts with the gene. *Mutations* and *chromosomal aberrations* can change genes and alter their expression. For example, *hemophilia*, which decreases the ability of blood to clot, is the result of a mutation. *Down's syndrome*, which impairs mental development, is the result of a chromosomal aberration.

Behavior genetics is the study of how genes influence behavior. Psychologists and other scientists use both experimental methods, such as *artificial selection*, and *correlation methods*, such as *concordance* rates in *identical-twin* studies, to investigate the relation between genes and behavior.

Heredity and Human Behavior

The contributions of heredity and environment to human behavior are difficult to study because we cannot use experimental procedures to manipulate one variable while holding all others constant. However, experimental procedures such as *artificial selection* and *molecular knockouts* can be used with nonhuman animals and it clear from this work that genetic variables affect behavior. With humans, correlation procedures can be used to determine the *heritability* of a characteristic, that is, the proportion of the total variation in a characteristic that can be attributed to genetic influences. *Concordance research* and *segregation analysis* can also be used with humans because these methods do not manipulate either the environment or genes, but merely observe the relation between the presence of a gene and the occurrence of a behavior.

Evolution and Human Behavior

Evolutionary psychology is concerned with the contribution of natural selection to human behavior and seeks to identify the adaptiveness of behavior. *Sociobiology* is the part of the field that studies those aspects of social behavior in animals and humans that are related to *reproductive* and *parental behavior* because this behavior is most directly affected by natural selection. Different *reproductive strategies* have evolved because of sex differences in the *parental investment* in procreation and child-rearing. Because of greater female parental investment, *polygynous* and *monogamous* reproductive strategies are most common in humans.

Altruism is an important topic of study because it presents an intriguing scientific puzzle. Why should natural selection favor a characteristic that could lower one's own reproductive success while increasing the reproductive success of others? Sociobiology provides two principal answers to this question—*inclusive fitness* and *reciprocal altruism*.

Evolutionary psychology has been criticized on several grounds, principally that environmental factors play a greater role than genetic factors in human behavior. It attempts to understand human behavior in an evolutionary context, not to justify that behavior. By appreciating the effect of the ancestral environment on current behavior, culture can devise *counter-selections* that change those aspects of behavior that are regarded as unhelpful.

succeed with PEARSON mypsych lab

Visit MyPsychLab for practice quizzes, flashcards, and dozens of videos and animated tutorials, including the following items you can find in the "Multimedia Library":

Genetic Time Clock
Depression Among the Amish
Junk DNA

Building Blocks of Genetics
Dominant and Recessive Traits

KEY TERMS

SUGGESTIONS FOR FURTHER READING

Wilson, D. S. (2007). *Evolution for everyone: How Darwin's theory can change the way we think about our lives.* New York: Delacorte Press.

A reader-friendly introduction to Darwin's ideas and their implications for our lives.

Dawkins, R. (1986). *The blind watchmaker.* New York: W. W. Norton and Company.

A very well-written discussion of the far-reaching implications of Darwinian thinking. One reviewer of the book commented: "Readers who are not outraged will be delighted."

Darwin, C. (1859). *On the origin of species by means of natural selection.* London: Murray.

Darwin's original presentation of evolution through natural selection. A must-read for any serious student of evolution that will disabuse many of their erroneous preconceptions of his ideas.

Plomin, R., DeFries, J. C., McClearn, G. E., & McGuffin, P. (2001). *Behavioral genetics* (4th ed.). New York: Worth Publishers.

A comprehensive and technical presentation of current research in behavioral genetics.

Wilson, E. O. (1975). *Sociobiology: The new synthesis.* Cambridge, MA: Harvard University Press.

The seminal work in the field of sociobiology—a well-written, graduate-level text.

Buss, D. M. (2007). *Evolutionary psychology: The new science of the mind.* Boston: Allyn & Bacon.

A comprehensive presentation of the field.

CHAPTER

4

Biology of Behavior

85

Prologue

The Left Is Gone

Miss S. was a 60-year-old woman who had a history of high blood pressure, which was not responding well to the medication she was taking. One evening she was sitting in her reclining chair reading the newspaper when the phone rang. She got out of her chair and walked to the phone. As she did, she began to feel giddy and stopped to hold on to the kitchen table. She had no memory of what happened after that.

The next morning a neighbor, who usually stopped by to have coffee with Miss S., found her lying on the floor, mumbling incoherently. The neighbor called an ambulance, which took Miss S. to a hospital.

Two days after her admission, the neurological resident in charge of her case told a group of us that she had had a stroke in the back part of the right side of the brain. He attached a CT scan to an illuminated viewer mounted on the wall and showed us a white spot caused by the accumulation of blood in a particular region of her brain. (You can look at the scan yourself; it is shown in Figure 4.15.)

We then went to see Miss S. in her hospital room. Miss S. was awake but seemed a little confused. The resident greeted her and asked how she was feeling. "Fine, I guess," she said. "I still don't know why I'm here."

"Can you see the other people in the room?"

"Why, sure."

"How many are there?"

She turned her head to the right and began counting. She stopped when she had counted the people at the foot of her bed. "Seven," she reported. "What about us?" asked a voice from the left of her bed. "What?" she said, looking at the people she had already counted. "Here, to your left. No, toward your left!" the voice repeated. Slowly, rather reluctantly, she began turning her head to the left. The voice kept insisting, and finally, she saw who was talking. "Oh," she said, "I guess there are more of you."

The resident approached the left side of her bed and touched her left arm. "What is this?" he asked. "Where?" she said. "Here," he answered, holding up her arm and moving it gently in front of her face.

"Oh, that's an arm."

"An arm? Whose arm?"

"I don't know." She paused. "I guess it must be yours."

"No, it's yours. Look, it's a part of you." He traced with his fingers from her arm to her shoulder.

"Well, if you say so," she said, sounding unconvinced.

When we returned to the residents' lounge, the chief of neurology said that we had seen a classic example of unilateral (one-sided) neglect, caused by damage to a particular part of the brain. "I've seen many cases like this," he explained. "People can still perceive sensations from the left side of their bodies, but they just don't pay attention to them. A woman will put makeup on only the right side of her face, and a man will shave only half of his beard. When these patients put on a shirt or a coat, they will use their left hand to slip it over their right arm and shoulder, but then they'll just forget about their left arm and let the garment hang from one shoulder. They also don't look at things located toward the left—or even at the left halves of things. Once I saw a man who had just finished eating breakfast. He was sitting in his bed, with a tray in front of him. There was half a pancake on his plate. 'Are you all done?' I asked. 'Sure,' he said. I turned the plate around so that the uneaten part was on his right. He gave a startled look and said, 'Where the hell did that come from?'" ■

The human brain is the most complex object that we know. As far as our species is concerned, it is the most important piece of living tissue in the world. It is also the only object capable of studying itself. Our perceptions, our thoughts, our memories, and our emotions are all products of our brains. If a surgeon transplants a heart, a liver, or a kidney—or even all three organs—we do not ask ourselves whether the identity of the recipient has been changed. But if a brain transplant were feasible (it isn't), we would undoubtedly say that the donor of the brain was getting a new body rather than the reverse.

The Brain and Its Components

The brain is the largest part of the nervous system. It contains approximately 100 billion neural cells and about as many helper cells, which take care of important support and housekeeping functions. For many decades, neuroscientists have known that the brain contains many different types of neural cells. These cells differ in shape, size, and the kinds of chemicals they produce, and they perform different functions.

To understand how the brain works, we need to understand how individual neural cells work and how they communicate with one another. Let's look first at the basic structure of the nervous system and at the nature and functions of the cells that compose it.

Basic Structure of the Nervous System

The brain has three major functions: controlling behavior, processing and retaining the information we receive from the environment, and regulating the body's physiological processes. How does it accomplish these tasks?

[**TABLE 4·1**] The Major Divisions of the Nervous System

Central Nervous System (CNS)	Peripheral Nervous System (PNS)
Brain	Nerves
Spinal cord	

The brain cannot act alone. It needs to receive information from the body's sense organs, and it must be connected with the muscles and glands of the body if it is to affect behavior and physiological processes. The nervous system consists of two divisions. The brain and the spinal cord make up the **central nervous system.** The **spinal cord** is a long, thin structure attached to the base of the brain and running the length of the spinal column. The central nervous system communicates with the rest of the body through the **peripheral nervous system,** which consists of **nerves**—bundles of fibers that transmit information to and from the central nervous system. Sensory information (information about what is happening in the environment or within the body) is conveyed from sensory organs to the brain and spinal cord. Information from the head and neck region (for example, from the eyes, ears, nose, and tongue) reaches the brain through the **cranial nerves.** Sensory information from the rest of the body reaches the spinal cord (and ultimately the brain) through the **spinal nerves.** The cranial nerves and spinal nerves also carry information away from the central nervous system. The brain controls muscles, glands, and internal organs by sending messages to these structures through these nerves. (See TABLE 4·1.)

FIGURE 4·1 shows an overview of the nervous system. The man's back has been opened, and the back part of the vertebral column has been removed so that we can see the spinal cord and the nerves attached to it. The skull has been opened, and a large opening has been cut in the meninges, the membranes that cover the central nervous system, so that we can see the surface of the brain.

The human brain consists of three major parts: the *brain stem,* the *cerebellum,* and the *cerebral hemispheres.* FIGURE 4·2 shows a view of the left side of the brain. The lower portions of the cerebellum and brain stem extend beneath the left cerebral hemisphere; the upper portions are normally hidden.

---

central nervous system (CNS) The brain and the spinal cord.

spinal cord A long, thin collection of neural cells attached to the base of the brain and running the length of the spinal column.

peripheral nervous system (PNS) The cranial and spinal nerves; that part of the nervous system peripheral to the brain and spinal cord.

nerve A bundle of nerve fibers that transmit information between the central nervous system and the body's sense organs, muscles, and glands.

cranial nerve A bundle of nerve fibers attached to the base of the brain; conveys sensory information from the face and head and carries messages to muscles and glands.

spinal nerve A bundle of nerve fibers attached to the spinal cord; conveys sensory information from the body and carries messages to muscles and glands.

[FIGURE 4·1] The central nervous system (brain and spinal cord) and the peripheral nervous system (cranial nerves and spinal nerves).

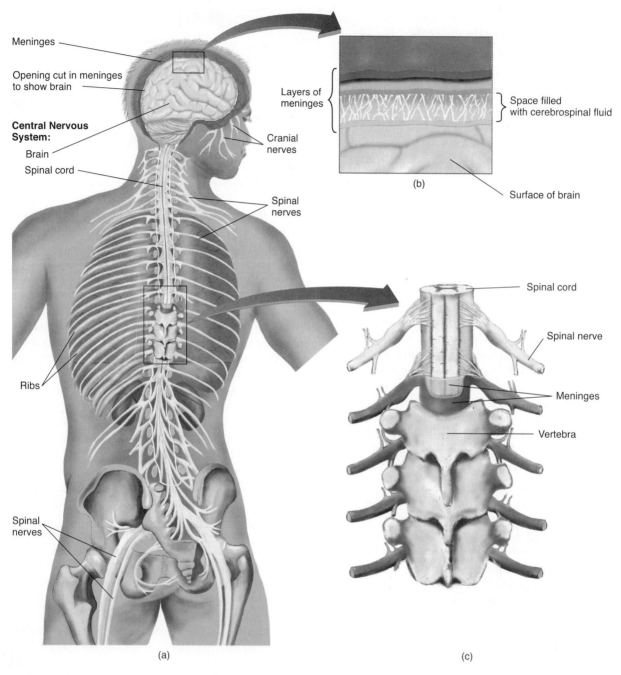

(a)

(b)

(c)

We also see the *thalamus,* a part of the brain described later in this chapter.

If the human brain is cut away from the spinal cord and removed from the skull, it looks as if it has a handle or stem.

---

brain stem The "stem" of the brain, including the medulla, pons, and midbrain.

cerebellum (*sair a bell um*) A pair of hemispheres resembling the cerebral hemispheres but much smaller and lying beneath and in back of them; controls posture and movements, especially rapid ones.

cerebral hemisphere The largest part of the brain; covered by the cerebral cortex and containing parts of the brain that evolved most recently.

The **brain stem** is one of the most primitive regions of the brain, and its functions are correspondingly basic—primarily control of physiological functions and automatic behaviors. The brains of some animals, such as amphibians, consist primarily of a brain stem and a simple cerebellum.

The **cerebellum,** attached to the back of the brain stem, looks like a miniature version of the cerebral hemispheres. The primary function of the cerebellum is to control and coordinate movements; especially rapid, skilled movements. The pair of **cerebral hemispheres** (the two halves of the *cerebrum*) form the largest part of the human brain. The cerebral hemispheres

[**FIGURE 4·2**] A view of the left side of the brain, showing its three major parts: brain stem, cerebellum, and cerebral hemisphere. The thalamus is attached to the anterior end of the brain stem.

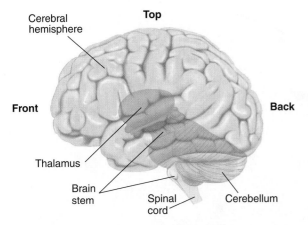

[**FIGURE 4·3**] A photograph of a slice of a human brain showing fissures and gyri and the layer of cerebral cortex that follows these convolutions.

(Harvard Medical School/Betty G. Martindale.)

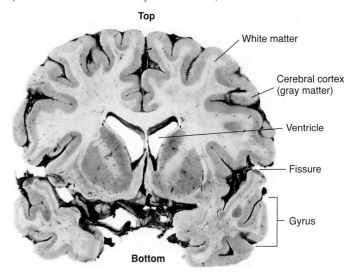

contain the parts of the brain that evolved most recently—and thus are involved in perceptions, memories, and behaviors of particular interest to psychologists. (See Figure 4.2.)

Because the central nervous system is vital to survival, it is exceptionally well protected. The brain is encased in the skull, and the spinal cord runs through the middle of the spinal column—through a stack of hollow bones known as **vertebrae.** [See Figure 4.1(c).] Both the brain and the spinal cord are enclosed by a three-layered set of membranes called the **meninges.** (*Meninges* is the plural of *meninx,* the Greek word for "membrane." You have probably heard of a disease called *meningitis,* which is an inflammation of the meninges.) The brain and spinal cord do not come into direct contact with the bones of the skull and vertebrae. Instead, they float in a clear liquid called **cerebrospinal fluid (CSF).** This fluid fills the space between two of the meninges and provides a cushion surrounding the brain and spinal cord, protecting them from being bruised by the bones that encase them. CSF is produced in the **cerebral ventricles,** hollow, fluid-filled chambers located within the brain. [See Figure 4.1(b).]

The brain is protected from chemical assault as well as physical shock. The cells of the body receive water and nutrients from the capillaries, the smallest of the blood vessels. In most of the body, the walls of the capillaries have small openings that let chemicals freely pass from the blood into the surrounding tissue. The brain is an exception: Its capillaries do not have these openings, so fewer substances can pass from the blood to the brain. This impediment to the exchange of chemicals is called the **blood–brain barrier.** Its major function is to make it less likely that toxic chemicals found in what we eat or drink can find their way into the brain, where they might do damage to neurons. Of course, many poisons can affect the brain, so this barrier is not foolproof.

The surface of the cerebral hemispheres is covered by the **cerebral cortex.** (The word *cortex* means "bark" or "rind.") The cerebral cortex consists of a thin layer of tissue approximately 3 millimeters thick. It is often referred to as **gray matter** because of its appearance. It contains billions of neural cells. (The

structure and functions of neural cells are described in the next section.) It is in the cerebral cortex that perceptions take place, memories are stored, and plans are formulated and executed. The neural cells in the cerebral cortex are connected to other parts of the brain by bundles of nerve fibers called **white matter,** so named because of the shiny white appearance of the substance that coats and insulates these fibers. FIGURE 4·3 shows a slice of the brain. As you can see, the gray matter and white matter look distinctly different.

The human cerebral cortex is very wrinkled; it is full of bulges separated by grooves. The bulges are called *gyri* (singular: gyrus), and the large grooves are called *fissures.* Fissures and gyri expand the amount of surface area of the cortex and greatly increase the number of neural cells it can contain. Animals with the largest and most complex brains, including

---

vertebra (plural, vertebrae) One of the bones that encases the spinal cord and constitutes the vertebral column.

meninges (*men in jees*) The three-layered set of membranes that enclose the brain and spinal cord.

cerebrospinal fluid (CSF) The liquid in which the brain and spinal cord float; provides a shock-absorbing cushion.

cerebral ventricle One of the hollow spaces within the brain, filled with cerebrospinal fluid.

blood–brain barrier A barrier between the blood and the brain produced by the cells in the walls of the brain's capillaries; prevents some substances from passing from the blood into the brain.

cerebral cortex The outer layer of the cerebral hemispheres of the brain, approximately 3 mm thick.

gray matter The portions of the central nervous system that are abundant in cell bodies of neurons rather than axons. The color appears gray relative to white matter.

white matter The portions of the central nervous system that are abundant in axons rather than cell bodies of neurons. The color derives from the presence of the axons' myelin sheaths.

humans and the larger primates, have the most wrinkled brains and thus the largest cerebral cortexes.

As we saw, the peripheral nervous system consists of the cranial and spinal nerves that connect the central nervous system with sense organs, muscles, internal organs, and glands. Nerves are bundles of many thousands of individual fibers, all wrapped in a tough, protective membrane. Under a microscope, nerves look something like telephone cables, with their bundles of wires. Like the individual wires in a telephone cable, nerve fibers transmit messages through the nerve, from a sense organ to the brain or from the brain to a muscle or gland. (See FIGURE 4·4.)

Cells of the Nervous System

Neurons, or neural cells, are the elements of the nervous system that bring sensory information to the brain, store memories, reach decisions, and control the activity of the muscles. Neurons can receive information from other neurons (or from cells in sense organs), process this information, and communicate the processed information to other neurons (or to cells in muscles, glands, or internal organs). Thus, neurons contain structures specialized for receiving, processing, and transmitting information. These structures are shown in FIGURE 4·5.

Neurons are assisted in their tasks by another kind of cell: the **glia.** Glia (or *glial cells*) get their name from the Greek word for *glue.* At one time, scientists thought that glia simply

---

neuron A neural cell; consists of a cell body with dendrites and an axon whose branches end in terminal buttons that synapse with muscle fibers, gland cells, or other neurons.

glia (*glee ah*) Cells of the central nervous system that provide support for neurons and supply them with some essential chemicals.

[**FIGURE 4·4**] A scanning-electron micrograph of the cut end of a nerve, showing bundles of nerve fibers (also known as axons) and sheaths of connective tissue that encase them. BV, blood vessel; A, individual axons.

(From *Tissues and Organs: A Text-Atlas of Scanning Electron Microscopy,* by Richard G. Kessel and Randy H. Kardon. Copyright © 1979 by W. H. Freeman and Co. Reprinted by permission.)

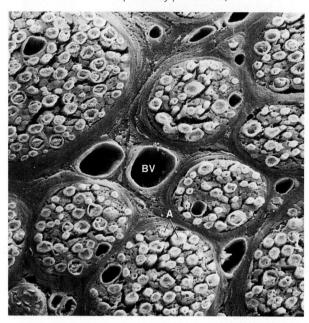

held neurons in place. They do that, but they also do much more. During development of the brain, some types of glial cells form long fibers that guide developing neurons from their place of origin to their final resting place. Other types of glia manufacture chemicals that neurons need to perform

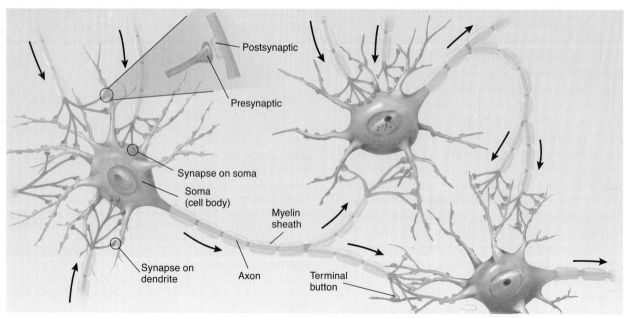

[**FIGURE 4·5**] The basic parts of a neuron and its connections with other neurons (synapses). The inset depicts the structure of a synapse.

their tasks and absorb chemicals that might impair neurons' functioning. Others form protective insulating sheaths around nerve fibers. Still others serve as the brain's immune system, protecting it from invading microorganisms.

Dendrites, treelike growths attached to the body of a neural cell, function principally to receive messages from other neurons. (*Dendron* means "tree.") They transmit the information they receive down their "trunks" to the cell body. The **soma,** or cell body, is the largest part of the neuron and contains the mechanisms that control the metabolism and maintenance of the cell. In most neurons, the soma also receives messages from other neurons. The nerve fiber, or **axon,** carries messages away from the soma toward the cells with which the neuron communicates. These messages, called *action potentials,* consist of brief changes in the electrical charge of the axon.

Axons end in **terminal buttons,** which are located at the ends of the "twigs" that branch off their ends. Terminal buttons secrete a chemical called a **neurotransmitter** whenever an action potential is sent down the axon (that is, whenever the axon *fires*). The neurotransmitter affects the activity of the other cells with which the neuron communicates. Thus, the message is *chemically* conveyed from one neuron to another. Most drugs that affect the nervous system and hence alter a person's behavior do so by affecting the chemical transmission of messages between cells.

Many axons, especially long ones, are insulated with a substance called *myelin.* The white matter located beneath the cerebral cortex gets its color from the **myelin sheaths** around the axons that travel through these areas. Myelin, part protein and part fat, is produced by glial cells that wrap parts of themselves around segments of the axon, leaving small bare patches of the axon between them. (Refer to Figure 4.5.) The principal function of myelin is to insulate axons from one another and thus to prevent the scrambling of messages. Myelin also increases the speed of the action potential.

To appreciate how important the myelin sheath is, consider the symptoms of a neurological disease: *multiple sclerosis* (MS). In this disorder, a person's immune system begins to attack parts of his or her central nervous system. Multiple sclerosis is so named because an autopsy of the brain and spinal cord will show numerous patches of hardened, damaged tissue. (*Skleros* is Greek for "hard.") The immune system of a person with multiple sclerosis attacks a protein in the myelin sheath of axons in the central nervous system, stripping it away. Although most of the axons survive this assault, they can no longer function normally, and so—depending on where the damage occurs—people who have multiple sclerosis experience a variety of neurological symptoms.

FIGURE 4•6 is a photograph made with a scanning electron microscope. It shows the actual appearance of a neuron and some terminal buttons that form synapses with it. The terminal buttons were broken off from their axons when the tissue was being prepared, but by comparing this photograph with Figure 4.5, you can begin to imagine some of the complexity of the nervous system.

[**FIGURE 4•6**] A scanning-electron micrograph of a neuron.

(*From Tissues and Organs: A Text-Atlas of Scanning Electron Microscopy,* by Richard G. Kessel and Randy H. Kardon. Copyright © 1979 by W. H. Freeman and Co. Reprinted by permission.)

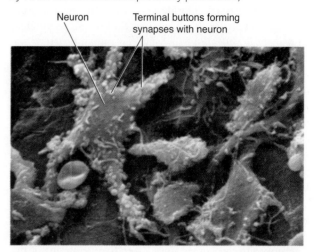

Neuron — Terminal buttons forming synapses with neuron

The Excitable Axon: The Action Potential

The message carried by the axon—the **action potential**—an electrical current, but it does not travel down the axon the way electricity travels through a wire. Electricity travels through a wire at hundreds of millions of feet per second. As you learned in Chapter 1, Hermann von Helmholtz discovered that the axon transmits information at a much slower rate—about 90 feet per second.

The membrane of an axon is electrically charged. When the axon is resting (that is, when no action potential is occurring), the inside is charged at –70 millivolts (thousandths of a volt) with respect to the outside. An action potential is an abrupt, short-lived reversal in the electrical charge of an axon. This temporary reversal begins at the end of the axon that attaches to the soma and is transmitted to the end that divides into small branches capped with terminal buttons. For convenience, an action potential is usually referred to as the *firing* of an axon.

The electrical charge of an axon at rest—the **resting potential**—occurs because of an unequal distribution of

---

dendrite   A treelike part of a neuron on which other neurons form synapses.

soma   A cell body; the largest part of a neuron

axon   A long, thin part of a neuron attached to the soma; divides into a few or many branches, ending in terminal buttons.

terminal button   The rounded swelling at the end of the axon of a neuron; releases a neurotransmitter.

neurotransmitter   A chemical released by the terminal buttons that causes the postsynaptic neuron to be excited or inhibited.

myelin sheath   The insulating material that encases most large axons.

action potential   A brief electrochemical event that is carried by an axon from the soma of the neuron to its terminal buttons; causes the release of a neurotransmitter.

resting potential   The membrane potential of a neuron when it is not producing an action potential.

positively and negatively charged particles inside the axon and in the fluid that surrounds it. These particles, called **ions,** are produced when various substances—including ordinary table salt—are dissolved in water. Molecules of table salt (sodium chloride) break down into positively charged sodium ions (Na^+) and negatively charged chloride ions (Cl^-). (In case you were wondering, sodium is abbreviated as Na because its original Latin name was *natrium*.) Normally, ions cannot penetrate the membrane that surrounds all cells. However, the membrane of axons contains special submicroscopic proteins that serve as **ion channels** or **ion transporters.** Ion channels can open or close; when they are open, a particular ion can enter or leave the axon. As we will see, the membrane of the axon contains two types of ion channels: sodium channels and potassium channels. Ion transporters work like pumps. They use the energy resources of the cell to transport particular ions into or out of the axon. (See **FIGURE 4•7.**)

When the axon is resting, the outside of the membrane is positively charged, and the inside is negatively charged, because the fluid inside the axon contains more negatively charged ions and fewer positively charged ions. When the membrane of the axon is resting, its ion channels are closed, so ions cannot move in or out of the axon. An action potential is caused when the end of the axon attached to the soma becomes excited, which opens sodium ion channels located there (you will learn about excitation later). The opening of these ion channels permits positively charged sodium ions (Na^+) to enter; this reverses the membrane potential at that location. This reversal causes nearby ion channels to open, which produces another reversal at *that* point. The process continues all the way to the terminal buttons at the ends of the branches at the other end of the axon.

Note that an action potential is a *brief* reversal of the membrane's electrical charge. As soon as the charge reverses, the sodium ion channels close, and potassium ion channels open for a short time, letting positively charged potassium ions (K^+) flow out of the axon. This outflow of positive ions restores the normal electrical charge. Thus, an action potential resembles the "wave" that sports fans often make in a stadium during a game. People in one part of the stadium stand up, raise their arms over their heads, and sit down again. People seated next to them see that a wave is starting, so they do the same—and the wave travels around the stadium. Everyone remains at the same place, but

ion A positively or negatively charged particle; produced when many substances dissolve in water.

ion channel A special protein molecule located in the membrane of a cell; controls the entry or exit of particular ions.

ion transporter A special protein molecule located in the membrane of a cell; actively transports ions into or out of the cell.

all-or-none law The principle that once an action potential is triggered in an axon, it is propagated, without becoming smaller, to the end of the axon.

sensory neuron A neuron that detects changes in the external or internal environment and sends information about these changes to the central nervous system.

motor neuron A neuron whose terminal buttons form synapses with muscle fibers. When an action potential travels down its axon, the associated muscle fibers will twitch.

[FIGURE 4•7] Ion channels and ion transporters. These structures regulate the numbers of ions found inside and outside the axon. An unequal distribution of positively and negatively charged ions is responsible for the axon's electrical charge.

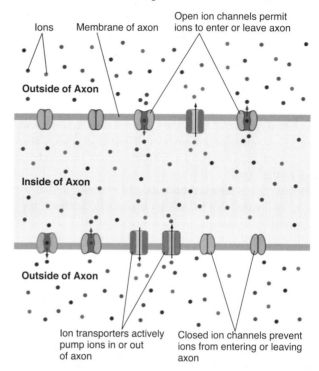

the effect is that of something circling in the stands around the playing field. Similarly, electricity does not really travel down the length of an axon. Instead, the entry of positive ions in one location reverses the charge at that point and causes ion channels in the adjacent region to open, and so on. (See **FIGURE 4•8.**)

You may be wondering what happens to the sodium ions that enter the axon and the potassium ions that leave it. This is where the ion transporters come in. As diagrammed in Figure 4.8, after an action potential has moved along the axon, the ion transporters pump sodium ions out of the axon and pump potassium ions back in, restoring the normal balance.

An action potential is an all-or-none event—either it happens or it does not. Action potentials in a given axon are all the same size; there are no large or small action potentials. This fact has been stated as the **all-or-none law.** But if action potentials cannot vary in size, how can axons convey quantitative information? For example, how can **sensory neurons**—neurons that receive information from sensory organs such as the eyes—tell other neurons in the brain about the strength of a stimulus? And how can **motor neurons**—neurons whose axons form synapses with a muscle—tell the muscle how forcefully to contract? The answer is simple: A single action potential is not the basic element of information; rather, quantitative information is represented by an axon's rate of firing. Strong stimuli (such as bright lights) trigger a high rate of firing in axons of sensory neurons that receive visual information. Similarly, a high rate of firing in the axons of motor neurons causes strong muscular contractions.

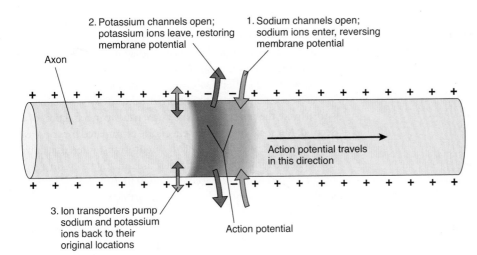

2. Potassium channels open; potassium ions leave, restoring membrane potential

1. Sodium channels open; sodium ions enter, reversing membrane potential

Axon

Action potential travels in this direction

3. Ion transporters pump sodium and potassium ions back to their original locations

Action potential

[**FIGURE 4·8**] Movement of sodium and potassium ions during the action potential. Sodium ions (Na⁺) are represented by red arrows; potassium ions (K⁺), by green arrows.

Communication with Other Cells: Synapses

Neurons communicate with other cells through **synapses,** by means of a process known as *synaptic transmission.* A synapse is the junction of a terminal button of one neuron and the membrane of another cell—another neuron or a cell in a muscle, a gland, or an internal organ. Let us first consider synapses between one neuron and another. The terminal button belongs to the **presynaptic neuron**—the neuron "before the synapse" that sends the message. As we saw, when terminal buttons become active, they release a chemical called a neurotransmitter. The neuron that receives the message (that detects the neurotransmitter) is called the **postsynaptic neuron**—the neuron "after the synapse." (Refer to detail, Figure 4.5.) A neuron receives messages from many terminal buttons, and in turn, its terminal buttons form synapses with many other neurons. The drawing in Figure 4.5 is much simplified; thousands of terminal buttons can form synapses with a single neuron.

Two major types of synapses exist: *excitatory synapses* and *inhibitory synapses.* Excitatory synapses do just what their name implies—when the axon fires, the terminal buttons release a neurotransmitter that excites the postsynaptic neurons with which they form synapses. The effect of this excitation is to increase the rate of firing of the axons of the postsynaptic neurons. Inhibitory synapses do just the opposite—when they are activated, they lower the rate at which these axons fire.

The rate at which a particular axon fires is determined by the activity of all the synapses on the dendrites and soma of the cell. If the excitatory synapses are more active, the axon will fire at a high rate. If the inhibitory synapses are more active, it will fire at a low rate or perhaps not at all. (See **FIGURE 4·9.**)

How do molecules of a neurotransmitter exert their excitatory or inhibitory effect on the postsynaptic neuron? Terminal buttons contain large numbers of **synaptic vesicles**—little bubbles of membrane that are filled with molecules of the neurotransmitter. (*Vesicle* is Latin for "little bladder.") When an action potential reaches a terminal button, it causes several of the vesicles to fuse with the inside of the presynaptic membrane, burst open, and spill their contents into the **synaptic cleft,** the fluid-filled space between the terminal button and the membrane of the postsynaptic neuron. (Note that the terminal button and the presynaptic membrane do not touch each other.) The molecules of the neurotransmitter then cause reactions in the postsynaptic neuron that either excite or inhibit it. These reactions are triggered by special submicroscopic protein molecules embedded in the postsynaptic membrane called **neurotransmitter receptors.** (See **FIGURE 4·10.**)

A molecule of a neurotransmitter binds with its receptor in the same way that a particular key fits in a particular lock. After their release from a terminal button, molecules of a neurotransmitter diffuse across the synaptic cleft, bind with the receptors, and activate them. Once they are activated, the receptors produce excitatory or inhibitory effects on the postsynaptic neuron. They do so by opening ion channels. Most ion channels found at excitatory synapses permit sodium ions to enter the postsynaptic membrane; most of those found at inhibitory synapses permit potassium ions to leave. [See **FIGURE 4·10(a).**]

As mentioned earlier, multiple sclerosis is caused by an autoimmune disorder that attacks a protein in the myelin

---

synapse The junction between the terminal button of one neuron and the membrane of a muscle fiber, a gland, or another neuron.

presynaptic neuron A neuron whose terminal buttons form synapses with and excite or inhibit another neuron.

postsynaptic neuron A neuron with which the terminal buttons of another neuron form synapses and that is excited or inhibited by that neuron.

synaptic vesicle (*vess i kul*) A small, hollow, beadlike structure found in terminal buttons; contains molecules of a neurotransmitter.

synaptic cleft A fluid-filled gap between the presynaptic and postsynaptic membranes; the terminal button releases a neurotransmitter into this space.

neurotransmitter receptor A special protein molecule located in the membrane of the postsynaptic neuron that responds to molecules of the neurotransmitter.

[FIGURE 4·9] Interaction between the effects of excitatory and inhibitory synapses. Excitatory and inhibitory effects combine to determine the rate of firing of the neuron.

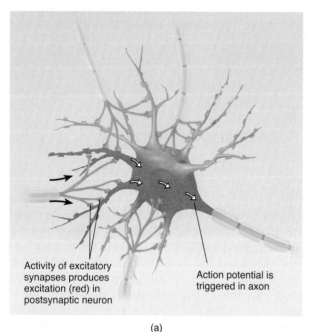

Activity of excitatory synapses produces excitation (red) in postsynaptic neuron

Action potential is triggered in axon

(a)

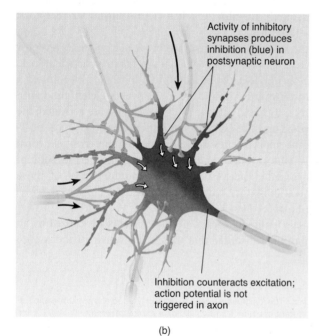

Activity of inhibitory synapses produces inhibition (blue) in postsynaptic neuron

Inhibition counteracts excitation; action potential is not triggered in axon

(b)

sheaths of axons in the central nervous system. Another autoimmune disorder attacks a different protein—the neurotransmitter receptor that is found in the membrane of muscle fibers. Almost as fast as new receptors are produced, the immune system destroys them. The result of this attack is pro-

---

reuptake   The process by which a terminal button retrieves the molecules of a neurotransmitter that it has just released; terminates the effect of the neurotransmitter on the receptors of the postsynaptic neuron.

gressive *myasthenia gravis,* or "grave muscle weakness." Myasthenia gravis is not a very common disorder, but most experts believe that many mild cases go undiagnosed. We will have more to say about this disorder later in this chapter, in a section that describes the effects of drugs on synaptic transmission.

The excitation or inhibition produced by a synapse is short-lived; the effects soon pass away, usually in a fraction of a second. At most synapses, the effects are terminated by a process called **reuptake.** Molecules of the neurotransmitter that have been released into the synaptic cleft are quickly taken up again by special transporter molecules located in the terminal button, so the neurotransmitter has only a short time to stimulate the postsynaptic receptors. [See FIGURE 4·10(b).] The rate at which the terminal button takes back the neurotransmitter determines how prolonged the effects of the chemical on the postsynaptic neuron will be. The faster the neurotransmitter is taken back, the shorter its effects will be on the postsynaptic neuron.

QUESTIONS TO CONSIDER

1. The brain is the seat of our perceptions, thoughts, memories, and feelings. Why, then, do we so often refer to our hearts as the location of our feelings and emotions? For example, why do you think we say, "He acted with his heart, not with his head"?
2. The blood–brain barrier keeps many chemicals in the blood out of the brain. In a few places in the brain, this barrier does not exist, including the part of the brain stem that contains the neural circuits that trigger vomiting. Can you think of an explanation for the lack of a blood–brain barrier in this region?

Drugs and Behavior

Long ago, people discovered that the sap, fruit, leaves, bark, or roots of various plants could alter their perceptions and behavior, could be used to relieve pain or treat diseases, or could be used as poisons to kill animals for food. They also discovered that some substances affected people's moods in ways that they wanted to experience again and again.

Why do plants produce chemicals that have specific effects on the cells of our nervous system? They do so because the chemicals are toxic to animals—primarily insects—that eat them. Of course, some chemicals produced by plants have beneficial effects in humans and have consequently been extracted or synthesized in the laboratory for use as therapeutic drugs. The therapeutic use of drugs is of obvious benefit to society, and the abuse of addictive drugs is responsible for much misery and unhappiness. But drugs are also important tools to help scientists discover how the brain works. For example, we know that certain drugs relieve anxiety, and others reduce the symptoms of schizophrenia. Discovering how these drugs affect the brain can help our understanding of the causes of these disorders and can provide information we need to develop even better forms of treatments.

[FIGURE 4·10] The release and reuptake of a neurotransmitter from a terminal button. The drawing depicts the inset portion of Figure 4.5. The arrival of an action potential at the terminal button causes several synaptic vesicles to fuse with the membrane and spill their cargo of neurotransmitter molecules into the synaptic cleft. (a) Details of the attachment of a molecule of the neurotransmitter to a postsynaptic receptor. An ion channel opens, permitting the movement of ions through the membrane that either excites or inhibits the postsynaptic neuron. For purposes of clarity, the drawing is schematic; molecules of neurotransmitter are actually much larger than individual ions. (b) Details of reuptake. Neurotransmitter transporters pump molecules of the neurotransmitter from the synaptic cleft back into the terminal button, thus ending the excitatory or inhibitory effects.

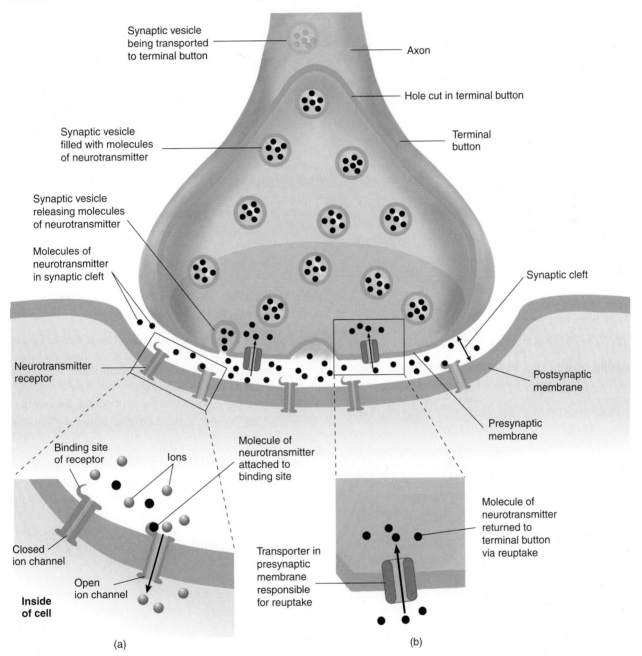

Effects of Drugs on Synaptic Transmission

Drugs that affect our thoughts, perceptions, emotions, and behavior do so by affecting the activity of neurons in the brain. As we saw, communication between neurons involves the release of neurotransmitters, which bind with receptors and either excite or inhibit the activity of the postsynaptic cell. Drugs can affect this process in many ways. They can stimulate or inhibit the release of neurotransmitters, mimic the effects of neurotransmitters on postsynaptic receptors, block these effects, or interfere with the reuptake of a neurotransmitter once it is released.

[**FIGURE 4·11**] A summary of the ways in which drugs can affect the synaptic transmission.

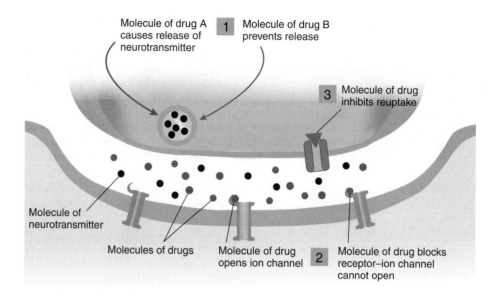

Molecule of drug A causes release of neurotransmitter

1 Molecule of drug B prevents release

3 Molecule of drug inhibits reuptake

Molecule of neurotransmitter

Molecules of drugs

Molecule of drug opens ion channel

2 Molecule of drug blocks receptor–ion channel cannot open

Through these mechanisms (and others too complicated to describe here), a drug can alter the perceptions, thoughts, and behaviors controlled by particular neurotransmitters. Let's briefly examine some of these mechanisms.

Stimulating or Inhibiting the Release of Neurotransmitters

Some drugs stimulate certain terminal buttons to release their neurotransmitter continuously, even when the axon is not firing. Other drugs prevent certain terminal buttons from releasing their neurotransmitter when the axon fires. The effects of a particular drug are usually specific to one neurotransmitter. (See step 1 in FIGURE 4·11.)

Stimulating or Blocking Postsynaptic Receptors

Neurotransmitters produce their effects by stimulating postsynaptic receptors; this excites or inhibits postsynaptic neurons by opening ion channels and permitting ions to enter or leave the neurons. Some drugs mimic the effects of particular neurotransmitters by directly stimulating particular kinds of receptors. If we use the lock-and-key analogy to describe the effects of a neurotransmitter on a receptor, then a drug that stimulates receptors works like a master key, turning the receptors on even when the neurotransmitter is not present. (See step 2 in Figure 4.11.)

Some drugs bind with receptors and do not stimulate them. This action blocks receptors, making them inaccessible to the neurotransmitter and thus inhibiting synaptic transmission. To continue the lock-and-key analogy, a drug that blocks receptors plugs up the lock so that the key will no longer fit into it.

Inhibiting Reuptake

As we saw, the effects of most neurotransmitters are kept brief by the process of reuptake. Molecules of the neurotransmitter are released by a terminal button,

stimulate the receptors in the postsynaptic membrane for a fraction of a second, and are then taken back into the terminal button. Some drugs inhibit the process of reuptake so that molecules of the neurotransmitter continue to stimulate the postsynaptic receptors for a long time. Therefore, inhibition of reuptake increases the effect of the neurotransmitter. (See step 3 in Figure 4.11.)

Neurotransmitters, Their Actions, and Drugs That Affect Them

Now that we've seen the most important ways that drugs can affect synaptic transmission, let's look at the most important neurotransmitters and consider some examples of drugs that interact with them. Because neurotransmitters have two general effects on postsynaptic membranes—excitatory or inhibitory—you might expect that two kinds of neurotransmitters would exist, but in reality, many different kinds are found—several dozen, at least.

In the brain, most synaptic communication is accomplished by two neurotransmitters: **glutamate,** which has excitatory effects, and **GABA,** which has inhibitory effects. (GABA stands for *gamma-amino butyric acid.*) Almost every neuron in the brain receives excitatory input from terminal buttons that secrete glutamate and inhibitory input from terminal buttons that secrete GABA. (Another inhibitory neurotransmitter, *glycine,* is found in the lower brain stem and the spinal cord.)

What do all the other neurotransmitters do? In general, they have modulating effects rather than information-transmitting effects. That is, the release of neurotransmitters other than glutamate and GABA tends to activate or inhibit entire circuits of neurons that are involved in particular brain functions. These effects include facilitation of learning, control of wakefulness and vigilance, suppression of impulsive behaviors, and suppression or enhancement of anxiety. Thus, because particular drugs can selectively affect neurons that secrete particular neurotransmitters, these drugs can have specific effects on behavior.

---

glutamate The most important excitatory neurotransmitter in the brain and spinal cord.

GABA The most important inhibitory neurotransmitter in the brain.

Given the importance of glutamate and GABA, let's look at these two neurotransmitters first.

Glutamate As previously mentioned, glutamate is the most important excitatory neurotransmitter in the brain. It is also the major excitatory neurotransmitter in the spinal cord. With the exception of neurons that detect painful stimuli, all sensory organs transmit information to the brain through axons whose terminals release glutamate.

One type of glutamate receptor (the *NMDA receptor*) plays a critical role in the effects of environmental stimulation on the developing brain and is also responsible for many of the changes in synaptic connections that are responsible for learning. This receptor is partially deactivated by alcohol, which accounts for the fact that binge drinkers often have no memory of what happened while they were drunk.

GABA Some drugs depress behavior, causing relaxation, sedation, or even loss of consciousness. Most of these drugs act on a particular type of GABA receptor (the GABA$_A$ receptor), increasing its sensitivity to the neurotransmitter. **Barbiturates** act this way. In low doses, barbiturates have a calming effect. In progressively higher doses, they produce difficulty in walking and talking, unconsciousness, coma, and death. A dose of a barbiturate sufficient to cause relaxation is not much lower than a fatal dose; thus, these drugs do not have much of a safety factor. Physicians rarely prescribe barbiturates.

By far the most commonly used depressant drug is ethyl alcohol, the active ingredient in alcoholic beverages. This drug also acts on the GABA$_A$ receptor. The effects of alcohol and barbiturates are additive: A moderate dose of alcohol plus a moderate dose of barbiturates can be fatal.

Many **antianxiety drugs** are members of a family known as the **benzodiazepines,** which include the well-known tranquilizer Valium (diazepam). These drugs, too, act on GABA$_A$ receptors on neurons in various parts of the brain, including a region that is involved in fear and anxiety. Benzodiazepines are much safer than barbiturates—a lethal dose is more than a hundred times higher than a therapeutic dose. They are sometimes used to treat people who are afflicted by periodic attacks of severe anxiety. In addition, some benzodiazepines serve as sleep medications.

Acetylcholine Acetylcholine (ACh) is the primary neurotransmitter secreted by the axons of motor neurons, and it is also released by several groups of neurons in the brain. Because all muscular movement is accomplished by the release of acetylcholine, you will not be surprised to learn that the immune systems of people with myasthenia gravis (described in the previous section) attack acetylcholine receptors.

The axons and terminal buttons of acetylcholinergic neurons are distributed widely throughout the brain. Three systems have received the most attention from neuroscientists. One system activates the brain mechanisms responsible for rapid eye movement (REM) sleep—the phase of sleep during which most dreaming occurs. Another system is involved in activating neurons in the cerebral cortex and facilitating learning, especially

The venom of the black widow spider causes the release of acetylcholine, which can cause numbness, muscle pain and cramps, sweating, salivation, and difficulty breathing. Fortunately, a single bite is very rarely fatal for a healthy adult.

perceptual learning. A third system controls the functions of another part of the brain involved in learning: the hippocampus. (You will see this structure later in this chapter.)

Two drugs, botulinum toxin and the venom of the black widow spider, affect the release of acetylcholine. **Botulinum toxin,** produced by a bacterium that can grow in improperly canned food, prevents the release of ACh. The drug is an extremely potent poison. Very dilute solutions (they had better be!) of this drug, usually referred to as botox, can be injected into people's facial muscles to stop muscular contractions that are causing wrinkles. **Black widow spider venom** has the opposite effect: It stimulates the release of ACh. Although the effects of black widow spider venom can also be fatal to infants or frail, elderly people, the venom is much less toxic than botulinum toxin. The following case describes the effects of the botulinum toxin in humans.

[**CASE STUDY**] One day, just before dinner, Mr. F. opened a jar of asparagus that his family had canned. He noted right away that it smelled funny. Because his family had grown the asparagus in their own garden, he was reluctant to throw it away. However, he decided that he wouldn't take any chances. He dipped a spoon into the liquid in the jar and touched it to his tongue. It didn't taste right, so he didn't swallow it. Instead, he stuck his tongue out and rinsed it

---

barbiturate A drug that causes sedation; one of several derivatives of barbituric acid.

antianxiety drug A "tranquilizer," which reduces anxiety.

benzodiazepine (*ben zoe dy azz a peen*) A class of drug having anxiolytic ("tranquilizing") effects, such as diazepam (Valium).

acetylcholine (ACh) (*a see tul koh leen*) A neurotransmitter found in the brain, spinal cord, and parts of the peripheral nervous system; responsible for muscular contraction.

botulinum toxin (*bot you lin um*) A drug that prevents the release of acetylcholine by terminal buttons.

black widow spider venom A drug that stimulates the release of acetylcholine by terminal buttons.

under a stream of water from the faucet at the kitchen sink. He dumped the asparagus into the garbage disposal.

About an hour later, as the family was finishing dinner, Mr. F. discovered that he was seeing double. Alarmed, he asked his wife to drive him to the hospital. When he arrived at the emergency room, he was seen by one of the neurological residents, who asked him, "Mr. F., you haven't eaten some home-canned foods recently, have you?"

Learning that he had indeed let some liquid from a suspect jar of asparagus touch his tongue, the resident ordered a vial of botulinum antitoxin from the pharmacy. Meanwhile, he took a blood sample from Mr. F.'s vein and sent it to the lab for some testing in mice. He then administered the antitoxin, but already he could see that it was too late: Mr. F. was showing obvious signs of muscular weakness and was having difficulty breathing. He was immediately sent to the intensive care unit, where he was put on a respirator. Although he became completely paralyzed, the life-support system did what its name indicates, and eventually his acetylcholinergic terminal buttons repaired themselves, and he regained control of his muscles. (By the way, the first symptom of his poisoning was double vision because the delicate balance among the muscles that move the eyes is upset by any interference with acetylcholinergic transmission.)

The results of the testing procedure for the presence of botulinum toxin in Mr. F.'s blood were fascinating. Plasma extracted from the blood was injected into several mice, half of which had been pretreated with botulinum antitoxin. The pretreated mice survived; the others all died. Just think: Mr. F. had touched a few drops of the contaminated liquid on his tongue and then rinsed it off immediately, but enough of the toxin entered his bloodstream so that a small amount of his blood plasma could kill a mouse.

Although the effects of most neurotransmitters on the postsynaptic membrane are terminated by reuptake, acetylcholine is an exception. After being released by the terminal button, ACh is deactivated by an enzyme that is present in the postsynaptic membrane. This enzyme, AChE (acetylcholinesterase), can be inactivated by various drugs. One of them, **neostigmine,** can help people with myasthenia gravis. The drug lets the patients regain some strength, because the acetylcholine that is released in their muscles has a more prolonged effect on the few acetylcholine receptors that remain. (Fortunately, neostigmine cannot cross the blood–brain barrier, so it does not affect the AChE found in the central nervous system.)

neostigmine (*nee o **stig** meen*) A drug that enhances the effects of acetylcholine by blocking the enzyme that destroys it.

nicotine A drug that binds with and stimulates acetylcholine receptors, mimicking the effects of this neurotransmitter.

curare (*kew **rahr** ee*) A drug that binds with and blocks acetylcholine receptors, preventing the neurotransmitter to exert its effects.

monoamine (***mahn** o a meen*) A category of neurotransmitters that includes dopamine, norepinephrine, and serotonin.

The best-known drug that affects acetylcholine receptors is **nicotine,** found in the leaves of the tobacco plant, *Nicotiniana tabacum.* Nicotine is a highly addictive drug; as evidence, consider the fact that after undergoing surgery for lung cancer, approximately 50 percent of patients continue to smoke (Hyman & Malenka, 2001). The addictive nature of nicotine indicates that acetylcholine plays a role in the reinforcement (reward) mechanisms of the brain. You'll learn more about the nature of reinforcement later in this chapter and in Chapters 5 and 13.

Another drug, **curare,** blocks acetylcholine receptors. Because these are the receptors on muscles, curare, like botulinum toxin, causes paralysis. However, the effects of curare are much faster. The drug is extracted from several species of plants found in South America, where it was discovered long ago by people who used it to coat the tips of arrows and darts. Within minutes of being struck by one of these points, an animal collapses, ceases breathing, and dies. Nowadays, curare (or any of various drugs with the same site of action) is used to paralyze patients who are to undergo surgery so that their muscles will relax completely and not contract when they are cut with a scalpel. An anesthetic also must be used, because a person who receives only curare will remain perfectly conscious and sensitive to pain, even though paralyzed. And, of course, a respirator must supply air to the lungs during the procedure.

Monoamines Dopamine, norepinephrine, and serotonin are three chemicals that belong to a family of compounds called **monoamines.** Because the molecular structures of these substances are similar, some drugs affect the activity of all of them to some degree. The monoamines are produced by several systems of neurons in the brain. Most of these systems consist of a relatively small number of cell bodies located in the brain stem, whose axons branch repeatedly and give rise to an enormous number of terminal buttons distributed throughout many regions of the brain. Monoaminergic neurons thus serve to modulate the function of widespread regions of the brain, increasing or decreasing the activities of particular brain functions.

This native of Peru is inserting a curare-tipped dart into his blowgun. Curare kills animals by blocking acetylcholine receptors, which paralyzes muscles and causes suffocation.

Dopamine (DA) has been implicated in several important functions, including movement, attention, learning, and the reinforcing effects of drugs that people tend to abuse. A progressive degenerative disease that destroys one set of DA neurons causes **Parkinson's disease,** a movement disorder characterized by tremors, rigidity of the limbs, poor balance, and difficulty in initiating movements. People with Parkinson's disease are given a drug called L-DOPA. Once this chemical reaches the brain, it is taken up by the DA neurons that still survive and is converted to dopamine. As a result, these neurons release more dopamine, which alleviates the patients' symptoms.

Dopamine has also been implicated as a neurotransmitter that might be involved in schizophrenia, a serious mental disorder, whose symptoms include hallucinations, delusions, and disruption of normal, logical thought processes. Drugs such as Thorazine (chlorpromazine) and Clozaril (clozapine) relieve the symptoms of this disorder, apparently by blocking particular types of dopamine receptors. The physiology of schizophrenia is discussed in Chapter 16.

Several drugs inhibit the reuptake of dopamine, thus serving to prolong and strengthen its effects. The best known of these drugs are amphetamine and cocaine. The fact that people abuse these drugs indicates that dopamine plays an important role in reinforcement. (Nicotine exerts its reinforcing effect by indirectly increasing the activity of terminal buttons that release dopamine.)

Almost every region of the brain receives input from neurons that secrete the second monoamine, **norepinephrine (NE).** Release of NE (also known as *noradrenaline*) appears to cause an increase in vigilance—attentiveness to events in the environment.

The third monoamine neurotransmitter, **serotonin,** has complex behavioral effects. Serotonin plays a role in the regulation of mood; in the control of eating, sleep, and arousal; and in the regulation of pain. A deficiency in the release of serotonin in the cerebral cortex is associated with alcoholism and antisocial behavior. Like NE neurons, serotonin-secreting neurons are involved in the control of REM sleep. Drugs such as Prozac (fluoxetine), which inhibit the reuptake of serotonin and thus strengthen and prolong its effects, are used to treat depression, anxiety disorder, and obsessive–compulsive disorder. A drug that causes the release of serotonin (fenfluramine) was used as an appetite suppressant in the 1990s, but adverse side effects took this drug off the market.

Several hallucinogenic drugs appear to produce their effects by interacting with serotonergic transmission. For example, **LSD** (lysergic acid diethylamide) produces distortions of visual perceptions that some people find awesome and fascinating but that simply frighten other people. This drug, which is effective in extremely small doses, stimulates one category of serotonin receptor.

Peptides As we saw earlier, terminal buttons excite or inhibit postsynaptic neurons by releasing neurotransmitters. These chemicals travel a very short distance and affect receptors located on a small patch of the postsynaptic membrane. Some neurons release chemicals that get into the general circulation of the brain and stimulate receptors on many thousands of neurons, some located a considerable distance away. These chemicals are called **neuromodulators,** because they modulate the activity of the neurons they affect. We can think of neuromodulators as the brain's own drugs. As these chemicals diffuse through the brain, they can activate or inhibit circuits of neurons that control a variety of functions; thus, they can modulate particular categories of behavior.

Most neuromodulators are peptides. (The most important exception to this rule is described in the next subsection.) **Peptides** are molecules that consist of two or more amino acids attached together by special chemical links called peptide bonds. One of the best-known families of peptides is the **endogenous opioids.** Endogenous means "produced from within"; *opioid* means "like opium." Several years ago, it became clear that opiates—drugs such as opium, morphine, and heroin—reduce pain because they have direct effects on the brain. (Please note that the term *opioid* refers to endogenous chemicals, and *opiate* refers to drugs.) The endogenous opioids stimulate special opioid receptors located on neurons in several parts of the brain. Their behavioral effects include decreased sensitivity to pain and a tendency to persist in ongoing behavior. Opioids are released while an animal is engaging in important species-typical behaviors, such as mating or fighting. The behavioral effects of opioids ensure that a mating animal or an animal fighting to defend itself is less likely to be deterred by pain; thus, conception is more likely to occur, and a defense is more likely to be successful.

People abuse opiates not because opiates reduce pain, but because they cause the release of dopamine in the brain, which has a reinforcing effect on behavior. It is this reinforcing effect that normally encourages an animal performing a useful and important behavior to continue in that behavior. Unfortunately, the reinforcing effect is not specific to useful and important behaviors and can lead to addiction.

---

dopamine (DA) A monoamine neurotransmitter involved in control of brain mechanisms of movement and reinforcement.

Parkinson's disease A neurological disorder characterized by tremors, rigidity of the limbs, poor balance, and difficulty in initiating movements; caused by degeneration of a system of dopamine-secreting neurons.

norepinephrine (NE) (*nor epp i neff rin*) A monoamine neurotransmitter involved in alertness and vigilance and control of REM sleep.

serotonin (*sair a toe nin*) A monoamine neurotransmitter involved in the regulation of mood; in the control of eating, sleep, and arousal; and in the regulation of pain.

LSD Lysergic acid diethylamide; a hallucinogenic drug that blocks a category of serotonin receptors.

neuromodulator A substance secreted in the brain that modulates the activity of neurons that contain the appropriate receptors.

peptide A category of neurotransmitters and neuromodulators that consist of two or more amino acids, linked by peptide bonds.

endogenous opioid (*ope ee oyd*) A neuromodulator whose action is mimicked by a natural or synthetic opiate, such as opium, morphine, or heroin.

To help drug addicts, pharmacologists have developed drugs that block opioid receptors. One of them, **naloxone,** is used clinically to reverse opiate intoxication. This drug has saved the lives of many drug abusers brought to the emergency room in heroin-induced comas. An injection of naloxone blocks the effects of the heroin, and the person quickly revives.

Various peptide neuromodulators other than the opioids play important roles in behaviors important to survival, such as control of eating and metabolism, drinking, mineral balance, mating, parental care, and social bonding. Some reduce anxiety; others increase it. Some promote eating; others curb the appetite. Research on the effects of these chemicals is discussed in later chapters.

Cannabinoids You have undoubtedly heard of Cannabis sativa, the plant that produces hemp and marijuana. You probably also know that the plant produces a resin that has physiological effects on the brain. The principal active ingredient in this resin is THC (tetrahydrocannibinol), which affects perception and behavior by activating receptors located on neurons in the brain. THC mimics the effects of **endogenous cannabinoids**—chemicals produced and released by neurons in the brain.

THC produces analgesia and sedation, stimulates appetite, reduces nausea caused by drugs used to treat cancer, relieves asthma attacks, decreases pressure within the eyes in patients with glaucoma, and reduces the symptoms of certain motor disorders. Conversely, THC interferes with concentration and memory, alters visual and auditory perception, and distorts perception of the passage of time (Iversen, 2003). Devane and colleagues (1992) discovered the first—and most important—endogenous cannabinoid, a lipid-like (fatlike) substance, which they named **anandamide,** from the Sanskrit word *ananda,* or "bliss."

Cannabinoid receptors are found on terminal buttons of neurons that secrete glutamate, GABA, acetylcholine, dopamine, norepinephrine, and serotonin. (That is, almost all of the neurotransmitters mentioned in this chapter.) Thus, the secretion of anandamide—or the smoking of marijuana—alters the release of these neurotransmitters, and this has widespread effects in the brain. Recent research indicates that the endogenous cannabinoids modulate the synaptic changes that appear to be responsible for learning, which accounts for the fact that THC disrupts short-term memory (Fegley et al., 2004).

---

naloxone (*na lox own*) A drug that binds with and blocks opioid receptors, preventing opiate drugs or endogenous opioids from exerting their effects.

endogenous cannabinoid (*can ob in oid*) A neuromodulator whose action is mimicked by THC and other drugs present in marijuana.

anandamide (*a nan da mide*) The most important endogenous cannabinoid.

The effects of the endogenous cannabinoids, produced and released in the brain, are mimicked by THC, the active ingredient of Cannabis sativa, the marijuana plant.

TABLE 4•2 lists the neurotransmitters discussed in this section, summarizes their effects, and lists some drugs that interact with them.

QUESTIONS TO CONSIDER

1. As we saw, opioids are useful neuromodulators because they encourage an animal to continue fighting or mating. Can you think of other behaviors that might be influenced by neuromodulators? Can you think of mental or behavioral problems that might be caused if too much or too little of these neuromodulators were secreted?

2. Suppose that a woman is taking a drug for anxiety. Suppose further that she is planning to go out for drinks with friends. Her husband advises her to enjoy an evening with her friends but not to have any drinks. Why is this a good suggestion?

3. If you were in charge of the research department of a pharmaceutical company, what new behaviorally active drugs would you seek? Analgesics? Antianxiety drugs? Antiaggression drugs? Memory-improving drugs? Should behaviorally active drugs be taken only by people who clearly have afflictions such as schizophrenia, depression, or obsessive–compulsive disorder? Or should we try to find drugs that help people who want to improve their intellectual performance or social adjustment or simply to feel happier?

[TABLE 4·2] The Major Neurotransmitters, Their Primary Effects, and Drugs That Interact with Them

Neurotransmitter	Primary Effects	Drugs That Interact with Neurotransmitter	Effects of Drugs
Glutamate	Primary excitatory neurotransmitter in brain	Alcohol	Desensitization of NMDA receptor
GABA	Primary inhibitory neurotransmitter in brain	Barbiturates Benzodiazepines ("tranquilizers") Alcohol	Desensitization of GABAA receptor
Acetylcholine (ACh)	Excites muscular contraction, activates cerebral cortex, controls REM sleep, controls hippocampus	Botulinum toxin Black widow spider venom Neostigmine Nicotine	Blocks release of ACh Stimulates release of ACh Blocks AChE, enhances effects of ACh Stimulates ACh receptors
Monoamines			
Dopamine (DA)	Facilitates movement, attention, learning, reinforcement	L-DOPA Amphetamine, cocaine Antipsychotic drugs	Increase synthesis of dopamine Inhibit reuptake of dopamine Block dopamine receptors
Norepinephrine (NE)	Increases vigilance, controls REM sleep		
Serotonin	Regulates mood, controls eating, sleep, arousal, regulation of pain, suppresses risky behaviors	Fluoxetine (Prozac) LSD	Inhibits reuptake of serotonin Stimulates certain serotonin receptors
Endogenous opioids	Reduce pain, reinforce ongoing behavior	Opiates (heroin, morphine, etc.) Naloxone	Stimulate opioid receptors Block opioid receptors
Anandamide	Analgesia, nausea reduction, decreased pressure in eyes, interference with short-term memory	THC	Stimulates cannabinoid receptors

Study of the Brain

Recent advances in science and technology have given us the means to study—and perhaps some day understand—the brain. We now have at our disposal a range of research methods that would have been impossible to imagine just a few decades ago. We have ways to identify neurons that contain particular chemicals. We have ways to use special microscopes to observe particular ions entering living neurons when the appropriate ion channels open. We have ways to inactivate individual genes or to insert new genes into laboratory animals to see what happens to the animals' physiology and behavior. We have ways to view details of the structure of a living human brain and to study the activity of various brain regions while the person is performing various perceptual or behavioral tasks. Just listing and briefly describing these methods would take up an entire chapter. This section describes only the most important research methods, which will introduce you to the research performed by physiological psychologists.

Experimental Ablation

The earliest research method of physiological psychology involved the study of brain damage. As Chapter 1 described, Pierre Flourens developed the method of experimental ablation in studies with laboratory animals, and Paul Broca applied this method when he studied a man whose brain damage had destroyed his language abilities.

To study the effect of experimental brain disruption on animal behavior, the investigator produces a **brain lesion,** an injury to a particular part of the brain, and then studies the effects of the lesion on the animal's behavior. Of course, researchers do not deliberately damage the brains of humans to study their functions. Instead, like Paul Broca, we study the behavior of people whose brains have been damaged by a stroke, by disease, or by head injury. If particular behaviors are disrupted, we can conclude that the damaged part of the brain must somehow be involved in those behaviors.

brain lesion   Damage to a particular region of the brain.

To produce a brain lesion in laboratory animals, the researcher must follow the ethical rules described in Chapter 2. The researcher first anaesthetizes an animal, prepares it for surgery, and drills a hole in its skull. In most cases, the region under investigation is located deep within the brain. To reach this region, the investigator uses a special device called a **stereotaxic apparatus** to insert a fine wire (called an electrode) or a thin metal tube (called a cannula) into a particular location in the brain. The term "stereotaxic" refers to the ability to manipulate an object in three-dimensional space. (See FIGURE 4·12.)

Once the correct region is located, its function can be altered. Experimenters can produce *electrolytic lesions* by passing an electrical current through the electrode, which produces heat that destroys a small portion of the brain around the tip of the electrode. Alternatively, they may establish *excitotoxic lesions* by injecting a chemical through the cannula that overstimulates neurons in the region around the tip of the cannula, which kills the neurons. After a few days, the animal recovers from the operation, and the researcher can assess its behavior. Later, the investigator can remove the animal's brain from the skull, slice it, and examine it under a microscope to determine the true extent of the lesion. (See FIGURE 4·13.)

Obviously, researchers studying the behavior of a person with brain damage cannot remove the brain and examine it

---

stereotaxic apparatus A device used to insert an electrode into a particular part of the brain for the purpose of recording electrical activity, stimulating the brain electrically, or producing localized damage.

CT scanner A device that uses a special x-ray machine and a computer to produce images of the brain that appear as slices taken parallel to the top of the skull.

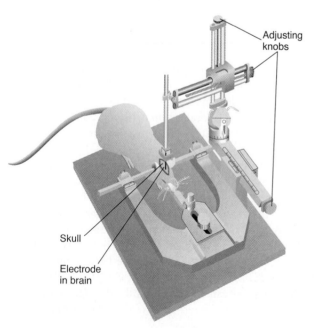

[FIGURE 4·12] A stereotaxic apparatus, used to insert a wire or a cannula into a specific portion of an animal's brain.

Skull

Electrode in brain

Adjusting knobs

[FIGURE 4·13] A brain lesion made with the aid of a stereotaxic apparatus. The photograph shows a thin slice of a mouse brain, stained with a dye that shows the location of cell bodies.

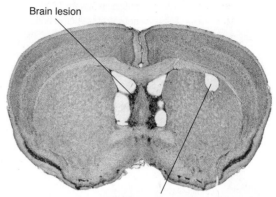

Brain lesion

Hole made in tissue to identify left and right sides of brain

(unless the person happens to die and the family consents to an autopsy for this purpose). This means that researchers seldom have the opportunity to examine the brains of patients they have studied. Fortunately, the development of brain scanners permits us to determine the location and extent of damage to a living brain.

Visualizing the Structure of the Brain

Brain-scanning techniques were originally developed to permit physicians to determine the causes of patients' neurological symptoms by locating regions of brain damage, visualizing brain tumors, or revealing abnormalities in brain structure caused by faulty development. Once researchers gained the ability to see the three-dimensional structure of the brain, they could correlate brain damage or abnormalities in brain development with the observations they had made of the behavior and abilities of patients they had studied.

The first machine to reveal the three-dimensional structure of the brain was the **CT scanner** (see FIGURE 4·14). (CT stands for *computed tomography*. *Tomos,* meaning "cut," describes the CT scanner's ability to produce a picture that looks like a slice of the brain. The device is often called a CAT *scanner*—the A is for *axial*—but the neurologists we've talked with use the term "CT." They probably think that CAT sounds a little too cute.) The scanner sends a narrow beam of x-rays through a person's head. The beam is moved around the head, and a computer calculates the amount of radiation that passes through it at various points along each angle. The result is a two-dimensional image of a "slice" of the person's head, parallel to the top of the skull.

FIGURE 4·15 shows three CT scans of the brain of a patient with an injury—Miss S., whose case is described in this chapter's Prologue. The scans are arranged from the bottom of the brain (scan 1) to the top (scan 3). You can easily see the damaged area, a white spot, in the lower left corner of scan 2.

[**FIGURE 4·14**] A patient whose brain is being scanned by a computed tomography (CT) scanner.

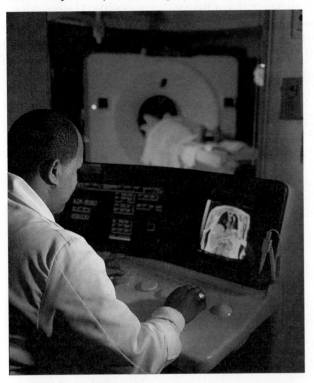

A more recent brain-imaging technique is known as **magnetic resonance imaging (MRI)**. MRI scans are produced by placing a person's head within a strong magnetic field. This field causes the molecules within its influence to become oriented with the lines of magnetic force. A radio signal is then generated around the person, which has the effect of tilting these aligned atoms, just as you might nudge a spinning top and cause it to wobble. The scanner measures the time it takes the molecules to stop wobbling and recover to their aligned state. Because different molecules take different times to recover, an image can be constructed that distinguishes between different materials within the head, such as gray matter, white matter, and cerebrospinal fluid. MRI scanners can

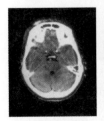
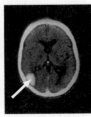
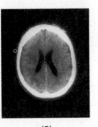

(1)   (2)   (3)

[**FIGURE 4·15**] CT scans from a patient with a brain lesion caused by a damaged area (the white spot in the lower left corner of scan 2). Because left and right are traditionally reversed on CT scans, the damaged area is actually in the right hemisphere.

(Courtesy of Dr. J. McA. Jones, Good Samaritan Hospital, Portland, Oregon. Photos provided by Neil Carlson.)

[**FIGURE 4·16**] An MRI scan of a human brain.

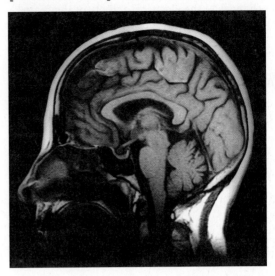

produce images of the brain with higher resolution than those produced by CT scanners (see FIGURE 4·16). However, CT scanners are still in use because they are less expensive and do not contain magnets; the magnetism exerted by an MRI scanner can interact with objects such as pacemakers or metal clips that have been placed in a patient's body.

Measuring the Brain's Activity

Because the brain's physiology involves both electrical and chemical processes, measuring techniques have been developed for each. **Microelectrodes** are extremely thin wires able to detect the electrical currents of individual neurons. With suitable amplification, microelectrodes can be used to measure the minute electrical changes of individual action potentials. Arrays of dozens of ultrathin wires can even enable a researcher to record simultaneously the activity of dozens of neurons. Other electrical recording techniques involve larger electrodes placed outside the skull. These electrodes can measure the electrical activity of large groups of neurons. For example, the **electroencephalogram (EEG)** is a recording of the brain's activity, recorded through metal disks and traced on a long sheet of paper or stored in a computer. (See FIGURE 4·17.) The EEG can be used to diagnose seizure disorders (epilepsy) and to monitor the various stages of sleep (described in Chapter 9).

In another method, known as **magnetoencephalography (MEG)**, a recording device detects the minute magnetic fields

magnetic resonance imaging (MRI) A technique with a device that uses the interaction between radio waves and a strong magnetic field to produce images of slices of the interior of the body.

microelectrode A thin electrode made of wire or glass that can measure the electrical activity of a single neuron.

electroencephalogram (EEG) An electrical brain potential recorded by placing electrodes on the scalp.

magnetoencephalography (MEG) A method of brain study that measures the changes in magnetic fields that accompany action potentials in the cerebral cortex.

[**FIGURE 4·17**] A record from an EEG machine. The pens trace changes in the electrical activity of the brain, recorded by electrodes placed on a person's scalp.

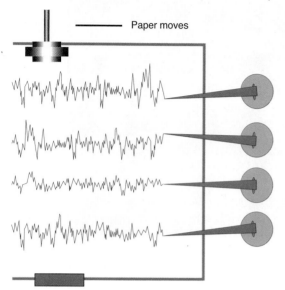

Paper moves

[**FIGURE 4·18**] Magnetoencephalography. The apparatus measures magnetic fields produced by the electrical activity of neurons on the cerebral cortex. A region of increased activity is shown in the inset in the lower right, superimposed on an image of the brain derived from an MRI scan.

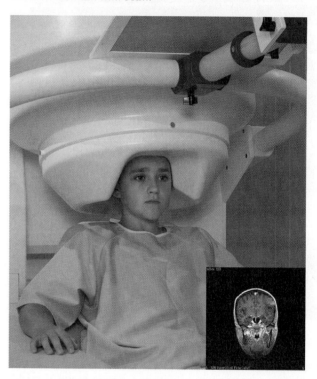

that are produced by the electrical activity of neurons in the cerebral cortex. These devices can be used clinically—for example, to find brain abnormalities that produce seizures so that they can be removed surgically. MEG can also be used in experiments to measure regional brain activity that accompanies the performance of various behaviors or cognitive tasks. (See FIGURE 4·18.)

The activity of specific brain regions can be measured by two special scanning methods: *PET scanning* and *functional MRI scanning*. **Positron emission tomography (PET)** takes advantage of the fact that when radioactive molecules decay, they emit subatomic particles called positrons. The first step in PET is to give a person an injection of a radioactive chemical that accumulates in the brain. (The chemical eventually breaks down and leaves the cells. The dose given to humans is harmless.) The person's head is placed in the PET scanner, which detects the positrons. The computer determines which regions of the brain have taken up the radioactive chemical, and it produces a picture of a slice of the brain, showing which regions contain the highest concentrations of the chemical. Researchers can use a wide variety of chemicals. For example, they can use a chemical that accumulates in metabolically active cells, in which case, the PET scan reveals the brain regions that are most active. They can also use chemicals that bind with particular receptors (for example, serotonin receptors) and determine which brain regions contain these receptors.

FIGURE 4·19 shows yet another use of PET. The scans were taken before and after dopamine-secreting neurons were surgically implanted into the brain of a person with Parkinson's disease. The scan shows an increase in the amount of dopamine in a region of the brain that controls movements, revealed by the presence of a radioactive chemical that becomes incorporated into molecules of dopamine.

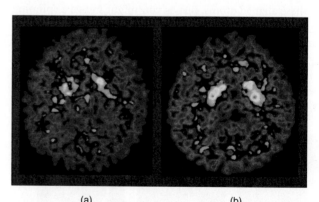

(a)   (b)

[**FIGURE 4·19**] PET scans of a patient with Parkinson's disease showing accumulation of radioactive l-DOPA in a brain region involved in movement that receives input from terminal buttons that secrete dopamine. (a) Preoperative scan. (b) Scan taken 13 months after receiving a transplant of dopamine-secreting cells. The increased uptake of l-DOPA indicates that the transplant was secreting dopamine.

(Adapted from Widner, H., et al. (1992). Bilateral fetal mesencephalic grafting in two patients with parkinsonism induced by 1-methyl-4-phenyl-1,2,3,6-tetrahydropyridine (MPTP). *New England Journal of Medicine, 327*, 1556–1563. Scans reprinted with permission.)

positron emission tomography (PET) The use of a device that reveals the localization of a radioactive tracer in a living brain.

[**FIGURE 4·20**] Functional MRI scans of human brains. Localized increases in neural activity of males (left) and females (right) while they were judging whether pairs of written words rhymed.

(From Shaywitz, B. A., et al. (1995). Sex differences in the functional organization of the brain for language. *Nature, 373*, 607–609. By permission.)

Anterior

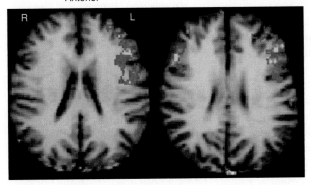

Posterior

The most recent development in brain imaging is **functional MRI (fMRI).** Biomedical engineers have devised modifications to existing MRI scanners that measure the rate of metabolism in regions of the brain by detecting levels of oxygen in the brain's blood vessels. Functional MRI scans have a higher resolution than PET scans, they can be acquired much more rapidly, and they do not require the production of radioactive chemicals with very short half-lives, which is expensive. Thus, *f*MRI has become the preferred method of measuring the activity of the human brain. (See FIGURE 4·20.)

Stimulating the Brain's Activity

So far, this section has discussed studying the brain by observing the effects of damage to parts of it, visualizing the brain's structure, and measuring the brain's activity. Another research method artificially activates neurons in particular parts of the brain to see what effects this stimulation has on behavior. For example, weak electrical stimulation of one part of a laboratory animal's brain, just sufficient to trigger action potentials in axons in that region, has a reinforcing (rewarding) effect on the animal's behavior. If the animal has the opportunity to press a lever that delivers a brief pulse of electricity through electrodes that have been surgically implanted in its brain, it will do so— up to thousands of times an hour. (See FIGURE 4·21.) The implication is that the brain has a system of neurons involved in reinforcement; this hypothesis is confirmed by recording studies in both humans and laboratory animals, which indicate that the neurons activated by this stimulation also are activated by events that reinforce behavior, such as the administration of food, water, or addictive drugs. One fMRI study of heterosexual male college students even found that the sight of a photograph of a beautiful woman activates this region (Aharon et al., 2001).

As we saw in the previous subsection, neural activity induces magnetic fields that can be detected by means of magnetoencephalography. Similarly, magnetic fields can be used to stimulate neurons by inducing electrical currents in brain tissue. **Transcranial magnetic stimulation (TMS)** uses a coil of wires, usually arranged in the shape of the numeral 8, to stimulate neurons in the human cerebral cortex. The stimulating coil is placed on top of the skull so that the crossing point in the middle of the 8 is located immediately above the region to be stimulated. Pulses of electricity send magnetic fields that activate neurons in the cortex. Because the processing of information in the cerebral cortex involves intricate patterns of activity in particular circuits of neurons, the stimulation disrupts normal activity in that region of the brain. For example, stimulation of a particular region of the cerebral cortex will disrupt a person's ability to detect movements in visual stimuli. These findings confirm the results of recording and lesion studies with laboratory animals and studies of people with brain damage, which indicate that this region is involved in perception of visual

functional MRI (fMRI)   A modification of the MRI procedure that permits the measurement of regional metabolism in the brain.

transcranial magnetic stimulation (TMS)   Direct stimulation of the cerebral cortex induced by magnetic fields generated outside the skull.

[**FIGURE 4·21**] An example of an electrical stimulation experiment. When the rat presses the switch, it receives a brief pulse of electricity to its brain through electrodes.

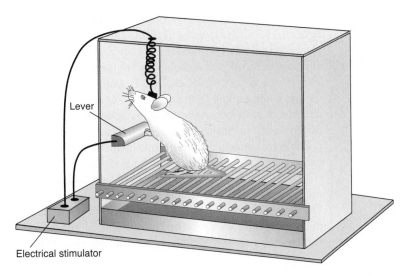

Lever

Electrical stimulator

[**FIGURE 4·22**] Transcranial magnetic stimulation. The coil applies electromagnetic stimulation to the brain, which interferes with the region of the cerebral cortex below the crossing point of the figure 8 of the coil.

(Photo by George Ruhe/*The New York Times*.)

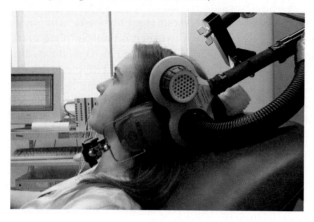

movement. In addition, TMS has been used to treat the symptoms of mental disorders such as depression.

FIGURE 4·22 shows an electromagnetic coil used in transcranial magnetic stimulation and its placement on a person's head.

Altering Genetics

Thanks to the advances in genetics discussed in Chapter 3, neuroscientists can now manipulate genetic mechanisms that control the development of the nervous system. For example, a **targeted mutation** (a genetic "knockout") can be produced in mice. This procedure inactivates a gene—for example, the gene responsible for producing a particular neurotransmitter or a particular receptor. The effects of the knockout on the animals' behavior suggest what the normal role of the neurotransmitter might be. For example, a targeted mutation that prevents production of a particular peptide causes a hereditary sleep disorder known as narcolepsy, which, we now know, is caused by degeneration of the neurons that secrete this peptide (Chemelli et al., 1999).

Researchers also can insert genes into animals' DNA, which can alter the development of the brain or the functioning of particular types of neurons after the animals are born. For example, Tang and colleagues (1999) found that a genetic modification that increased the production of a particular type of receptor increased the animals' learning ability in a particular task. Along with the findings of other experiments, these results suggest that these receptors are involved in producing changes in synapses that are responsible for memory formation.

---

targeted mutation A mutated gene (also called a "knockout gene") produced in the laboratory and inserted into the chromosomes of mice; abolishes the normal effects of the gene.

neural plasticity The production of changes in the structure and functions of the nervous system, induced by environmental events.

*f*ocus On

The Ever-Changing Brain: Neural Plasticity and Neurogenesis

Once people achieve adulthood, the organs of their bodies change very little. Muscles can grow larger or smaller, the amount of fat tissue can increase or (less often) decrease, and, of course, aging can cause pathological changes—but the structure and functions of the organs remain basically the same. The brain is the exception to this rule. The human brain reaches 95 percent its adult weight by the age of five, but significant changes in brain development continue for many years. For example, the volume of the cerebral cortex—especially that of the frontal and parietal lobes—decreases during adolescence (Gogtay et al., 2004; Toga et al., 2006). Most investigators believe that during this period, excess numbers of synapses are pruned, enhancing the efficiency of the functions of these regions of the brain. A *decrease* in tissue volume produces an *increase* in function. In any event, behavioral studies clearly indicate that people show a gain in self-control and a decreased tendency to engage in risky behavior after adolescence, which may be at least partly caused by increased effectiveness of inhibitory functions of the prefrontal cortex (Kelley, Schochet, & Landry, 2004).

Even after adolescence, experience can induce significant changes in the structure and functions of the brain. Some of the developmental changes in the brain are programmed in the genes, but the environment plays an important role in shaping our brains—not just during childhood and adolescence, but throughout our lives.

Experience, Learning, and Neural Plasticity

Research clearly indicates that experience can affect the structure and functions of the brain—a phenomenon known as **neural plasticity.** *Plasticity* (from the Greek *plastikos*) refers to the ability to be shaped or molded, and, indeed, the environment can shape the development of the brain or mold its structure and the connections of its neurons. In the 1960s, Rosenzweig and his colleagues began a research program designed to determine whether the environment could shape brain development (Rosenzweig & Bennett, 1996). The researchers divided litters of rats and placed the animals into two kinds of environments: enriched and impoverished. The enriched environment contained such things as running wheels, ladders, slides, and toys that the rats could explore and manipulate. The researchers changed these objects every day to maximize the animals' experiences and to ensure that they would learn as much as possible. In contrast, the impoverished environments were plain cages in a dimly illuminated, quiet room.

Rosenzweig and his colleagues found many differences in the brains of the animals raised in the two environments. The brains of rats raised in the enriched environment had a thicker cerebral cortex, a better blood supply, more protein content, and more acetylcholine (a neurotransmitter that plays an important role in learning, as you'll remember from earlier in this chapter). Subsequent studies have found changes on a microscopic level as well. Greenough and Volkmar (1973) found that the neurons of rats raised in the enriched environment had larger and more complex dendritic trees. Turner and Greenough (1985) found that synapses in their cerebral cortexes were larger and that more synapses were found on each of their neurons.

Evidence indicates that neural rewiring can even be accomplished in the adult brain. For example, after a person's arm is amputated, the region of the cerebral cortex that previously analyzed sensory information from the missing limb soon begins analyzing information from adjacent regions of the body, such as the stump of the arm, the trunk, or the face. The person becomes more sensitive to touch in these regions after the changes in the cortex take place (Elbert et al., 1994; Kew et al., 1994; Yang et al., 1994). London taxi drivers provide another example of brain plasticity. They spend years learning the maze-like layout of the city streets, and only after passing a demanding exam are they licensed to operate. The drivers' navigational ability must be a result of changes in the neural circuitry of their brain that occurred during their years of training. With MRI technology, Maguire and colleagues (2000) found that these taxi drivers' brains were physically different from those of other Londoners: A portion of the hippocampus, a part of the brain known to be involved in learning, was enlarged. Furthermore, the longer an individual taxi driver had spent in this occupation, the larger was the volume of this region.

The most common form of neural plasticity occurs almost every moment of every day. As we will see in Chapters 5 and 8, learning involves changes in the brain. (That shouldn't come as a surprise—where else could learning take place?) For example, learning to recognize the face of a person we just met induces changes in synaptic connections in a specialized region of the cerebral cortex. In recent years, researchers have learned much about the nature of these changes and the biochemical events responsible for them.

Neurogenesis: Birth of New Neurons in an Adult Brain

Most cells of the body turn over. That is, they live for a limited amount of time, die, and are replaced by new cells that are produced by stem cells residing nearby. Thus, our organs continuously rebuild themselves. For example, our skin cells live for about three weeks, die, and slough off the surface of our body. They are replaced by new skin cells that are produced by the division of stem cells located deep within the skin. For many years, neurobiologists have regarded the brain as the most important exception to this general rule. Their conclusion was this: The developing brain produces massive numbers of neurons before birth, continues to produce them at a slower rate postnatally, and eventually (within a few years of birth), the development of new neurons totally stops. After that point, the brain has as many neurons as it will ever have. Because neurons

can never be replaced, their number declines throughout life. As we will see, recent evidence contradicts this conclusion. In fact, the adult brain *can* produce new neurons.

Before examining this evidence, let's take a brief look at the basics of human brain development. Early in development, the brain consists of a hollow tube (the *neural tube*) that later develops into the ventricles. This tube is surrounded by the **ventricular zone,** which consists of a layer of *founder cells*—a special type of **stem cell.** During the first phase of development, founder cells divide, making new ones and increasing the size of the ventricular zone. This phase is referred to as *symmetrical division,* because the division of each founder cell produces two identical cells. Then, seven weeks after conception, founder cells receive a chemical signal to begin a period of *asymmetrical division.* During this phase, founder cells divide asymmetrically, producing another founder cell, which remains in place, and a neuron, which travels outward into the developing brain.

The period of asymmetrical division lasts about three months. The end of this stage of development occurs when the founder cells receive a chemical signal that causes them to die—a phenomenon known as **apoptosis** (literally, a "falling away"). All cells contain killer genes, but only certain cells—including the brain's founder cells—contain receptors that detect the chemical death signal and activate these genes.

But that is not the end of the matter. For many years, researchers have believed that **neurogenesis** (production of new neurons) ceases early in life and cannot take place in the fully developed brain. However, more-recent studies have shown this belief to be incorrect: The adult brain contains some stem cells that can divide asymmetrically and produce neurons. Researchers detect the presence of newly produced cells in the brains of laboratory animals by administering a small amount of a radioactive form of one of the molecules that cells use to produce the DNA, which is needed for neurogenesis. The next day, the animals' brains are removed and examined with methods described in earlier in this chapter.

Neurogenesis takes place in at least two regions of the ventricular zone in the mammalian brain (Doetsch and Hen, 2005). Stem cells in the *subventricular zone* produce neurons that migrate into the olfactory bulbs, stalklike protrusions of the brain that receive information from the odor receptors in the nose. Stem cells in the *subgranular*

---

ventricular zone A layer of cells that line the inside of the neural tube; contains founder cells that divide and give rise to cells of the central nervous system.

stem cell An undifferentiated cell that can divide and produce any one of a variety of differentiated cells.

apoptosis (*ay po toe sis*) Death of a cell caused by a chemical signal that activates a genetic mechanism inside the cell.

neurogenesis The process responsible for the production of a new neuron.

[FIGURE 4·23] Effects of learning on neurogenesis. Sections through a part of the hippocampus of rats that received training on a learning task or were exposed to a control condition that did not lead to learning. Arrows indicate newly formed cells.

(From Leuner, B., et al. (2004) Learning enhances the survival of new neurons beyond the time when the hippocampus is required for memory. *Journal of Neuroscience, 24,* 7477–7481. Copyright © 2004 by the Society of Neuroscience.)

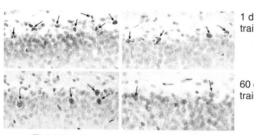

1 day after training

60 days after training

Training task   Control condition

zone produce neurons that migrate into the hippocampus, a brain region that plays a critical role in the formation of new memories. Some preliminary but inconclusive evidence suggests that neurogenesis may take place in other parts of the brain, including the cerebral cortex (Gould, 2007). Evidence from functional imaging studies suggests that neurogenesis takes place not only in the brains of laboratory animals but also in the human brain (Pereira et al., 2007).

New neurons quickly grow dendrites and axons, and establish functional synaptic connections with existing neurons that surround them (Ramirez-Amaya et al., 2006; Toni et al., 2007). Furthermore, environmental events can influence this process: Exposure to new odors increases the numbers of new neurons in the olfactory bulbs of rats, and training on a learning task enhances neurogenesis in the hippocampus. (See FIGURE 4·23.)

As you will see in Chapter 13, recent evidence suggests a link among stress, depression, and neurogenesis. Depression or exposure to stress suppresses neurogenesis in the hippocampus, and drugs or other treatments (even exercise) that reduce stress and depression reinstate neurogenesis Paizanis, Hamon, and Lanfumey, 2007). Unfortunately, no evidence exists that neurogenesis can repair the effects of brain damage, such as that caused by head injury or strokes.

QUESTIONS TO CONSIDER

1. Suppose you had an *f*MRI scanner and many volunteers. You could present various types of stimuli while scans were being taken, and you could have the volunteers perform various types of mental tasks and behaviors that did not involve their moving around. What kinds of experiments would you perform?

2. Although the basic program that controls brain development is contained in our genes, environmental factors also can influence this process. Why do you think the process of development is not completely automatic and programmed? What is the evolutionary benefit of letting the environment influence it? Would humans be better off if development were simply automatic, or does such flexibility have some potential benefits?

Control of Behavior and the Body's Physiological Functions

As you read earlier, the brain has three major functions: controlling behavior, processing and retaining information about the environment, and regulating the physiological functions of the body. The first two roles look outward toward the environment, and the third looks inward. The outward-looking roles include several functions: perceiving events in the environment, learning about them, making plans, and acting. The inward-looking role requires the brain to measure and regulate internal characteristics such as body temperature, blood pressure, and nutrient levels. The outward-looking roles are, of course, of particular interest to psychology. This section examines how the brain performs all three kinds of functions, beginning with the portions of the brain that control behavior and process information.

The cells of the brain are organized in modules—clusters of neurons that communicate with one another. Modules are connected to other modules, receiving information from some of them, processing this information, and sending the results to others. Particular modules have particular functions, just as the transistors, resistors, and capacitors in a computer chip do. The task of psychologists interested in understanding the brain is to identify the modules, discover their functions, trace their interconnections, and understand the ways in which the activities of these complex assemblies give rise to our perceptions, memories, feelings, and actions. Despite the progress we have made so far, the end of this task is not even remotely in sight.

Organization of the Cerebral Cortex

If we want to understand the brain functions most important to the study of behavior—perceiving, learning, planning, and moving—we should start with the cerebral cortex. Because we will be discussing the various regions of the cerebral cortex, it will be good to start with the names used for them. The cerebral cortex contains a large groove, or fissure, called the **central fissure.** The central fissure provides an important dividing line between the anterior (front) part of the cerebral cortex and the posterior (back) regions. (See FIGURE 4·24.)

As Figure 4.24 shows, the cerebral cortex is divided into four areas, or *lobes,* named for the bones of the skull that

---

central fissure   The fissure that separates the frontal lobe from the parietal lobe.

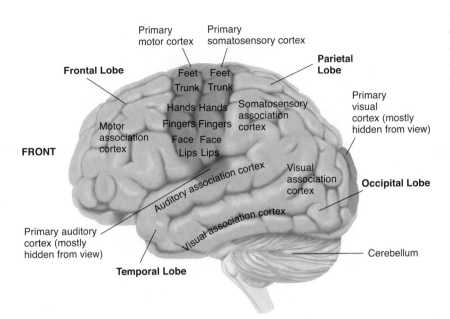

cover them: the **frontal lobe** ("front"), the **parietal lobe** ("wall"), the **temporal lobe** ("temple"), and the **occipital lobe** (*ob*, "against," *caput*, "head"). Of course, the brain contains two of each lobe, one in each hemisphere, on each side of the brain. The discussions that follow look in detail at the functions of each of these lobes.

Regions of Primary Sensory and Motor Cortex
We become aware of events in our environment by means of the five major senses: vision, audition, olfaction (smell), gustation (taste), and the somatosenses (the "body" senses: touch, pain, and temperature). Three areas of the cerebral cortex receive information from the sensory organs: the **primary visual cortex,** the **primary auditory cortex,** and the **primary somatosensory cortex.** In addition, the base of the somatosensory cortex receives gustatory information, and a portion of the frontal lobe, not visible from the side, receives olfactory information.

The three regions of primary sensory cortex in each hemisphere receive information from the opposite side of the body. Thus, the primary somatosensory cortex of the left hemisphere learns what the right hand is holding, the left primary visual cortex learns what is happening to the person's right, and so on. The connections between the sensory organs and the cerebral cortex are said to be **contralateral** (*contra*, "opposite"; *lateral*, "side"). However, the two most primitive forms of sensory information, smell and taste, are transmitted to the **ipsilateral** hemisphere. That is, the right side of the tongue and the right nostril send information to the right side of the brain.

The region of the cerebral cortex most directly involved in the control of movement is the **primary motor cortex** within the frontal lobe, located just in front of the primary somatosensory cortex. Neurons in different parts of the primary motor cortex are connected to muscles in different parts of the body. The connections, like those of the sensory regions of the cerebral cortex, are contralateral; the left

primary motor cortex controls the right side of the body and vice versa. Thus, for example, if a neurosurgeon electrically stimulates the "hand" region of the left primary motor cortex, the patient's right hand will move. (Refer to Figure 4.24.) I like to think of the strip of primary motor cortex as the keyboard of a piano, with each key controlling a different movement. We will see shortly who the "player" of this piano is.

Association Cortex
The regions of primary sensory and motor cortex occupy only a small part of the cerebral cortex. The rest of the cerebral cortex accomplishes what is done between sensation and action: perceiving, learning and remembering, planning, and moving. These processes take place in the association areas of the cerebral cortex.

---

frontal lobe   The front portion of the cerebral cortex, including the prefrontal cortex and the motor cortex; damage impairs movement, planning, and flexibility in behavioral strategies.

parietal lobe (*pa rye i tul*)   The region of the cerebral cortex behind the frontal lobe and above the temporal lobe; contains the somatosensory cortex; is involved in spatial perception and memory.

temporal lobe (*tem por ul*)   The portion of the cerebral cortex below the frontal and parietal lobes; contains the auditory cortex.

occipital lobe (*ok sip i tul*)   The rearmost portion of the cerebral cortex; contains the primary visual cortex.

primary visual cortex   The region of the cerebral cortex that receives information directly from the visual system; located in the occipital lobes.

primary auditory cortex   The region of the cerebral cortex that receives information directly from the auditory system; located in the temporal lobes.

primary somatosensory cortex   The region of the cerebral cortex that receives information directly from the somatosensory system (touch, pressure, vibration, pain, and temperature); located in the front part of the parietal lobes.

contralateral   Residing in the side of the body opposite the reference point.

ipsilateral   Residing in the same side of the body as the reference point.

primary motor cortex   The region of the cerebral cortex that directly controls the movements of the body; located in the posterior part of the frontal lobes.

[**FIGURE 4·25**] The relation between the association cortex and the regions of primary sensory and motor cortex. Arrows refer to the flow of information.

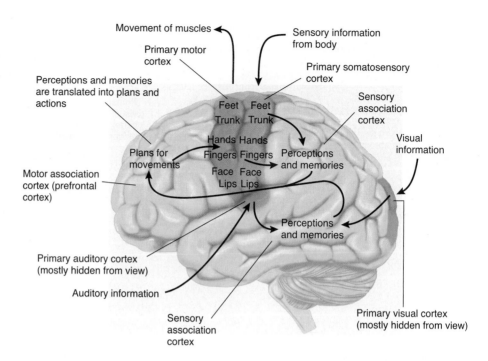

The anterior region is involved in movement-related activities, such as planning and executing behaviors. The posterior part is involved in perceiving and learning.

Each primary sensory area of the cerebral cortex sends information to adjacent regions, called the **sensory association cortex.** Circuits of neurons in the sensory association cortex analyze the information received from the primary sensory cortex; perception takes place there, and memories are stored there. Most regions of the sensory association cortex receive information from more than one sensory system, which makes it possible to integrate information from more than one sensory system. For example, we can learn the connection between the sight of a particular face and the sound of a particular voice. (Refer again to Figure 4.24.)

Just as regions of the sensory association cortex of the posterior part of the brain are involved in perceiving and remembering, so the frontal association cortex is involved in the planning and execution of movements. The anterior part of the frontal lobe—known as the **prefrontal cortex**—contains the **motor association cortex.** The motor association cortex controls the primary motor cortex; thus, it directly controls behavior. If the primary motor cortex is the keyboard of the piano, then the motor association cortex is the piano player.

Obviously, we behave in response to events happening in the world around us. Therefore, the sensory association cortex of the posterior part of the brain sends information about the environment—and information about what we have learned from past experience—to the motor association cortex (prefrontal cortex), which translates the information into plans and actions. (See **FIGURE 4·25**.)

The Thalamus If you stripped away the cerebral cortex and the white matter that lies under it, you would find the **thalamus,** located in the heart of the cerebral hemispheres. (*Thalamos* is Greek for "inner chamber.") The thalamus is divided into two parts, one in each cerebral hemisphere. Each part looks rather like a football, with the long axis oriented from front to back. **FIGURE 4·26** shows the two halves of the thalamus, along with several other brain structures that are described later in this chapter.

The thalamus performs two basic functions. The first—and most primitive—is similar to that of the cerebral cortex. Parts of the thalamus receive sensory information, integrate this information, and assist other brain regions in the control of movements. However, the second role of the thalamus—that of a relay station for the cortex—is even more important. As the cerebral hemispheres evolved, the cerebral cortex grew in size, and its significance for behavioral functions increased. The thalamus has taken on the function of receiving sensory information from the sensory organs, performing some simple analyses and passing the results on to the primary sensory cortex. Thus, all sensory information (except for olfaction, which is the most primitive of all sensory systems) is sent to the thalamus before it reaches the cerebral cortex.

Lateralization of Function

Although the two cerebral hemispheres cooperate with each other, they do not perform identical functions. Some functions are *lateralized*—performed by neural circuits located

---

sensory association cortex Those regions of cerebral cortex that receive information from the primary sensory areas.

prefrontal cortex The anterior part of the frontal lobe; contains the motor association cortex.

motor association cortex Those regions of the cerebral cortex that control the primary motor cortex; involved in planning and executing behaviors.

thalamus A region of the brain near the center of the cerebral hemispheres. All sensory information except that of olfaction is sent to the thalamus and then relayed to the cerebral cortex.

[**FIGURE 4·26**] The location of the basal ganglia, thalamus, and hypothalamus, ghosted into a semi-transparent brain.

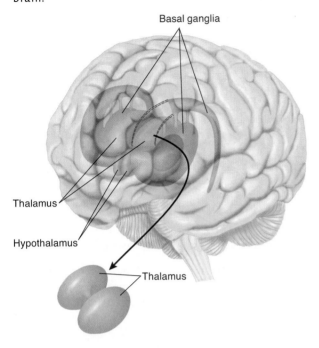

Basal ganglia

Thalamus

Hypothalamus

Thalamus

primarily on one side of the brain. In general, the left hemisphere participates in the analysis of information—the extraction of the elements that make up the whole of an experience. This ability makes the left hemisphere particularly good at recognizing serial events—events whose elements occur one after another. The left hemisphere also is involved in controlling serial behaviors. The serial functions performed by the left hemisphere include verbal activities, such as talking, understanding the speech of other people, reading, and writing. In general, damage to the various regions of the left hemisphere disrupts these abilities. (In a few people, the functions of the left and right hemispheres are reversed.) We'll look at language and the brain in more detail in Chapters 9 and 10.

In contrast, the right hemisphere is specialized for synthesis; it is particularly good at putting isolated elements together to perceive things as a whole. For example, our ability to draw sketches (especially of three-dimensional objects), read maps, and construct complex objects out of smaller elements depends heavily on circuits of neurons located in the right hemisphere. The right hemisphere is also especially involved in understanding the meaning of metaphorical statements such as "People who live in glass houses shouldn't throw stones" or the moral of stories such as the one about the race between the tortoise and the hare. Damage to the right hemisphere disrupts these abilities.

We are not aware of the fact that each hemisphere perceives the world differently. Although the two cerebral hemispheres perform somewhat different functions, our perceptions and our memories are unified. This unity is accomplished by the **corpus callosum**, a large band of axons that connects the two

cerebral hemispheres. The corpus callosum connects corresponding parts of the left and right hemispheres: the left and right temporal lobes, the left and right parietal lobes, and so on. Because of the corpus callosum, each region of the association cortex knows what is happening in the corresponding region of the opposite side of the brain. FIGURE 4·27 shows a photograph of a brain, viewed from above, that has been partially dissected. We see bundles of axons that pass through the corpus callosum, connecting groups of neurons in corresponding regions of the left and right hemispheres.

If the corpus callosum connects the two hemispheres and permits them to interchange information, what happens if the corpus callosum is cut? Neurosurgeons sometimes deliberately cut the corpus callosum (in a procedure called the *split-brain operation*) to treat a particular form of epilepsy. As a result, the two hemispheres process information independently and sometimes even attempt to engage in competing behaviors. You'll learn more about the interesting effects of this operation on perceptions and consciousness in Chapter 9.

---

corpus callosum (*core pus ka low sum*) A large bundle of axons ("white matter") that connects the cortex of the two cerebral hemispheres.

Bundles of axons in corpus callosum

Membrane that covers middle part of corpus callosum

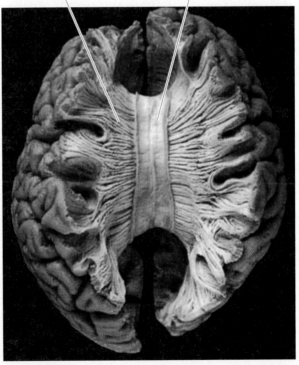

[**FIGURE 4·27**] A photograph of a brain, viewed from above, that has been partially dissected, showing bundles of axons that pass through the corpus callosum.

(Photo from Williams, T.H., Gluhbegovic, N., and Jew, J. Y. *The Human Brain: Dissections of the Real Brain*, 1980. New York: Harper & Row.)

Vision

The primary business of the occipital lobe—and of the lower part of the temporal lobe—is seeing. Total damage to the primary visual cortex, located in the inner surface of the posterior occipital lobe, produces blindness. Because the visual field is "mapped" onto the surface of the primary visual cortex, a small lesion in the primary visual cortex produces a "hole" in a specific part of the field of vision.

The visual association cortex is located in the rest of the occipital lobe and in the lower portion of the temporal lobe. (Refer to Figure 4.24.) Damage to the visual association cortex will not cause blindness, but visual acuity may be very good; people with such damage may be able to see small objects and may even be able to read. However, they will not be able to *recognize* objects by sight. For example, when looking at a drawing of a clock, these individuals may say that they see a circle, two short lines forming an angle in the center of the circle, and some dots spaced along the inside of the circle; but they will not be able to recognize what the picture shows. We'll deal with this phenomenon further in Chapter 7.

Audition

The temporal lobe contains both the primary auditory cortex and the auditory association cortex. The primary auditory cortex is hidden from view on the inner surface of the upper temporal lobe. The auditory association cortex is located on the lateral surface of the upper temporal lobe. (Refer to Figure 4.24.) Damage to the primary auditory cortex leads to hearing losses, whereas damage to the auditory association cortex produces more-complex deficits. Damage to the left auditory association cortex causes language deficits. People with such damage are no longer able to comprehend speech, presumably because they have lost the circuits of neurons that decode speech sounds. However, the deficit is more severe than that. They also lose the ability to produce meaningful speech; their speech becomes a jumble of words. We'll look again at language deficits produced by brain damage in Chapter 10.

Damage to the right auditory association cortex does not seriously affect speech perception or production, but it does affect people's ability to recognize nonspeech sounds, including patterns of tones and rhythms. The damage also can impair the ability to perceive the location of sounds in the environment. The right hemisphere is very important in the perception of space, and the contribution of the right temporal lobe to this function is to participate in perceiving the placement of sounds.

Somatosensation and Spatial Perception

The primary functions of the parietal lobe are perception of our own body and the location of objects in the world around us. (Refer to Figure 4.24.) Damage to parts of the parietal lobe that receive information from the visual system disrupts people's ability to perceive and remember the location of items in

[FIGURE 4.28] Attempts to copy a drawing of a house by patients with damage to the right parietal lobes.

(Reproduced From Gainotti, G., & Tiacci, C. (1970). *Neuropsychologia, 8,* 289–303 with permission from Elsevier.)

Model for patients to copy

Drawings by patients with right-hemisphere damage

their environment. Damage to parts of the left parietal lobe can disrupt the ability to read or write without causing serious impairment in the ability to talk and understand the speech of other people. Damage to part of the right parietal lobe can interfere with people's ability to perceive designs and three-dimensional shapes. A person with such damage can analyze a picture into its parts but has trouble integrating these parts into a consistent whole. Thus, he or she has difficulty drawing a coherent picture. (See **FIGURE 4.28**.)

The right parietal lobe also plays a role in people's ability to pay attention to stimuli located toward the opposite (left) side of the body. As we saw in the Prologue to this chapter, Miss S. displayed a symptom called unilateral neglect. A CT scan of her brain (shown in Figure 4.15) reveals that her stroke damaged part of the association cortex of the right parietal lobe. You will learn more about this phenomenon in the Epilogue of this chapter.

Most neuropsychologists believe that the left parietal lobe plays an important role in our ability to keep track of the location of the moving parts of our own body, whereas the right parietal lobe helps us keep track of the space around us. People with right parietal lobe damage usually have difficulty with spatial tasks such as reading maps. People with left parietal lobe damage usually have difficulty identifying parts of their own bodies by name. For example, when asked to point to their elbows, they may actually point to their shoulders.

Planning and Moving

As we have seen, a considerable amount of the brain is devoted to gathering and storing sensory information. Similarly, much of the brain is involved in the control of movement.

The Frontal Lobes The frontal lobes occupy the largest portion of the cerebral cortex. Although the principal function of the frontal lobes is control of movement, they also are involved in planning strategies for action, evaluating them, and changing them if necessary. They also contain a region involved in the control of speech. (Refer to Figure 4.24.)

Damage to the primary motor cortex produces a very specific effect: paralysis of the side of the body opposite to the brain damage. If a portion of the region is damaged, then only the corresponding parts of the body will be paralyzed. However, damage to the prefrontal cortex (refer to Figure 4.25) produces more-complex behavioral deficits.

People with damage to the prefrontal cortex show perseveration—they have difficulty adopting new strategies. One of the reasons for this tendency appears to be that these people have difficulty in evaluating the success of what they are doing. If given a task to solve, they may solve it readily; but if the problem is changed, they will fail to abandon the strategy and learn a new one. They have little insight into their own problems and are uncritical of their performance on various tasks.

In terms of daily living, the most important consequences of damage to the prefrontal cortex are probably lack of foresight and difficulty making plans. A person with damage to the prefrontal cortex might perform fairly well on a test of intelligence but be unable to hold a job. Presumably, planning is related to the general motor functions of the frontal lobes. Just as we can use the posterior regions of the brain to imagine something we have perceived, so we can use the frontal region to imagine something we might do. Perhaps we test various possible actions by imagining ourselves doing them and guessing what the consequences of these actions might be. When people's prefrontal cortex is damaged, they often do or say things that have unfavorable consequences because they have lost the ability to plan their actions.

The Cerebellum

The cerebellum ("little cerebrum") plays an important role in the control of movement. (Refer to Figure 4.24.) The cerebellum receives sensory information, especially about the position of body parts, so it knows what the parts of the body are doing. It also receives information from the cortex of the frontal lobes, so it knows what movements the frontal lobes intend to accomplish. The cerebellum is basically a computer that compares the location of body parts with the intended movements and assists the frontal lobes in executing these movements—especially rapid, skilled ones. Without the cerebellum, the frontal lobes would produce jerky, uncoordinated, inaccurate movements—which is exactly what happens when a person's cerebellum is damaged. Besides helping the frontal lobes accomplish their tasks, the cerebellum monitors information regarding posture and balance; it keeps us from falling down when we stand or walk, and it produces eye movements that compensate for changes in the position of the head. The following case describes the effects of damage to the cerebellum.

[CASE STUDY] Dr. S., a professor of neurology at the medical school, stood on the stage of the auditorium. A set of MRI scans appeared on the screen. "As you can see, Mr. P.'s cerebellum shows substantial degeneration."

Dr. S. left the stage and returned, pushing Mr. P. onstage in a wheelchair.

"Mr. P., how are you feeling today?"

"I'm fine," he replied. "Well, I'd feel better if I could have walked out of here myself."

"Of course."

Dr. S. talked with Mr. P. for a few minutes. We could see that his mental condition was lucid and that he had no obvious speech or memory problems.

"Okay, Mr. P., I'd like you to make some movements." He faced Mr. P. and said, "Please stretch your hands out and hold them like this." Dr. S. suddenly raised his arms from his sides and held them out straight in front of him, palms down, fingers pointing forward.

Mr. P. looked as if he were considering what to do. Suddenly, his arms straightened out and lifted from the armrests of the wheelchair. Instead of stopping when they were pointed straight ahead of him, they continued upward. Mr. P. grunted and his arms began flailing around—up, down, left, and right—until he finally managed to hold them outstretched in front of him. He was panting with the effort to hold them there.

"Thank you, Mr. P. Please put your arms down again. Now try this." Dr. S. very slowly raised his arms from his side until they were straight out in front of them. Mr. P. did the same, and this time there was no overshoot.

After a few more demonstrations Dr. S. thanked Mr. P. and wheeled him offstage. When he returned, he reviewed what we had seen.

"When Mr. P. tried to raise his arms quickly in front of him, his primary motor cortex sent messages to the appropriate muscles, and his arms straightened out and began to rise. Normally, the cerebellum is informed about the movement and, through its connections back to the motor cortex, brings the arms to rest in the intended position. Mr. P. could get the movement started just fine, but the damage to his cerebellum eliminated the help this structure gives to rapid movements, and he couldn't stop his arms in time. When he tried to move slowly, he could see and feel his arms moving, and used this feedback to control their movement. Your cerebellum isn't nearly as important in the control of simple, slow movements. For that you need your basal ganglia, but that's another story."

Recently researchers have discovered that the cerebellum may also play a role in people's cognitive abilities. For a long time neurologists have known that cerebellar damage can interfere with people's ability to speak, but the deficit seemed to involve control of the speech muscles rather than the cognitive abilities involved in language. In the 1990s, however, researchers making PET scans of the brains of people working on various types of cognitive tasks discovered that parts of their cerebellums became active—even when the people were not moving. Many neuroscientists now believe that as we learn more about the cerebellum, we will discover that its functions are not limited to motor tasks (Fordon, 2007; Olivieri et al., 2007). By the way, the cerebellum contains about as many neurons as the cerebrum does.

The Basal Ganglia The **basal ganglia** are a collection of groups of neurons located in the depths of the cerebral hemispheres, adjacent to the thalamus. (Refer to Figure 4.26.) The basal ganglia are involved in the control of slow movements and movements that involve the large muscles of the body. For example, Parkinson's disease is caused by degeneration of dopamine-secreting neurons in the midbrain whose axons travel to parts of the basal ganglia. The release of dopamine in the basal ganglia helps facilitate movements. The symptoms of Parkinson's disease are weakness, tremors, rigidity of the limbs, poor balance, and difficulty in initiating movements.

The basal ganglia also play an important role in learning—especially in learning how to perform particular actions. As we will see in the next subsection, the hippocampus is involved in learning things we can talk about, such as episodes in our lives, and in learning to get from place to place in our environment. In contrast, the basal ganglia are necessary for us to learn skilled behaviors, many of which we do not have to think about when we perform them. For example, learning the skills we need to ride a bicycle requires the participation of the basal ganglia, but being able to remember when we learned to ride and who taught us requires the participation of the hippocampus.

Episodic and Spatial Memory: Role of the Hippocampus

The **limbic system,** a set of structures located in the cerebral hemispheres, plays an important role in learning and memory and in the expression of emotion. The limbic system consists of several regions of the **limbic cortex**—the cerebral cortex located around the edge of the cerebral hemispheres where they join with the brain stem. (*Limbus* means "border"; hence the term "limbic system.") Besides the limbic cortex, the most important components of the limbic system are the *hippocampus* and the *amygdala*. The hippocampus and the amygdala get their names from their shapes; *hippocampus* means "sea horse" and *amygdala* means "almond."

FIGURE 4•29 shows a view of the right hemisphere of the brain, rotated slightly and seen from the left. We can see the limbic cortex, located on the inner surface of the right cerebral hemisphere. The left hippocampus and amygdala, located in the

[**FIGURE 4•29**] The principal structures of the limbic system.

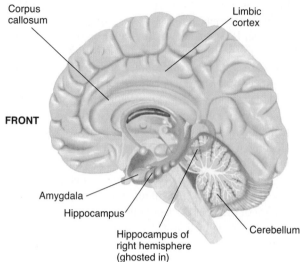

middle of the temporal lobe, are shown projecting out into the place where the missing left hemisphere would be. We can also see the right hippocampus and amygdala, "ghosted in." We also see a structure that does not belong to the limbic system—the corpus callosum. As mentioned earlier, the corpus callosum consists of a band of nerve fibers that enables the left and right cerebral hemispheres to communicate with each other.

We already encountered the **hippocampus** earlier in this chapter, where we saw evidence that when London taxi drivers successfully learn to navigate around the city, part of their hippocampus increases in size. The hippocampus is also involved in episodic memory—that is, in our ability to learn and remember experiences from our daily lives. As we will see in Chapter 8, when the hippocampus is destroyed, people can still remember events that occurred before their brains were damaged, but they lose the ability to learn anything new. For them, "yesterday" is always the time before their brain damage occurred. Everything after that slips away, just as the memory of a dream often slips away soon after a person awakens. In addition, although these people can find their way around places that were familiar to them before the damage occurred, they are unable to learn to navigate new neighborhoods—or even the interiors of buildings that are new to them.

Emotions: Role of the Amygdala

Damage to the **amygdala,** located in the middle of the temporal lobe, just in front of the hippocampus, affects emotional behavior—especially negative emotions, such as those caused by painful, threatening, or stressful events. In addition, the amygdala controls physiological reactions that help provide energy for short-term activities such as fighting or fleeing. If an animal's amygdala is destroyed, it no longer reacts to prevent events that normally produce stress and anxiety. We might think that an animal would be better off if it did not become "stressed out" by unpleasant or threatening situations, but research has shown

---

basal ganglia A group of nuclei in the brain interconnected with the cerebral cortex, thalamus, and brain stem; involved in control of slow movements and movements of large muscles.

limbic system A set of interconnected structures of the brain important in emotional and species-typical behavior; includes the amygdala, hippocampus, and limbic cortex.

limbic cortex The cerebral cortex located around the edges of the cerebral hemispheres where they join with the brain stem; part of the limbic system.

hippocampus A part of the limbic system of the brain, located in the temporal lobe; plays important roles in episodic memory and spatial memory.

amygdala (*a mig* da la) A part of the limbic system of the brain located deep in the temporal lobe; damage causes changes in emotional and aggressive behavior.

that animals with damaged amygdalas do not survive in the wild. These animals fail to compete successfully for food and other resources, and they often act in ways that provoke attacks by other animals. Similarly, people with damage to the amygdala must live in institutions where they can be cared for so that they will not harm themselves or others. We'll look at the role of the amygdala in emotion and stress in Chapters 13 and 17.

Control of Internal Functions and Automatic Behavior

The brain stem and the hypothalamus are involved in homeostasis and control of species-typical behaviors. **Homeostasis** (from the root words *homoios,* "similar," and *stasis,* "standstill") refers to maintenance of a proper balance of physiological variables such as temperature, concentration of fluids, and the amount of nutrients stored within the body. **Species-typical behaviors** are the more or less automatic behaviors exhibited by most members of a species that are important to survival, such as eating, drinking, fighting, courting, mating, and caring for offspring.

The Brain Stem   The *brain stem* contains three structures: the medulla, the pons, and the midbrain. FIGURE 4·30 shows a view of the left side of the brain. The cerebral hemispheres are semitransparent so that the details of the brain stem can be seen. We also see the hypothalamus and the pituitary gland (discussed later), which are attached to the front of the brain stem.

The brain stem contains circuits of neurons that control functions vital to the survival of the individual in particular and the species in general. For example, circuits of neurons in the **medulla**—the part of the brain stem adjacent to the spinal cord—control heart rate, blood pressure, rate of respiration, and—especially in simpler animals—crawling or swimming motions. Circuits of neurons in the **pons,** the part of the brain stem just above the medulla, are involved in control of sleep and wakefulness. Circuits of neurons in the **midbrain,** the part of the brain stem just above the pons, control movements used in fighting and sexual behavior and decrease sensitivity to pain while a person is engaged in these activities.

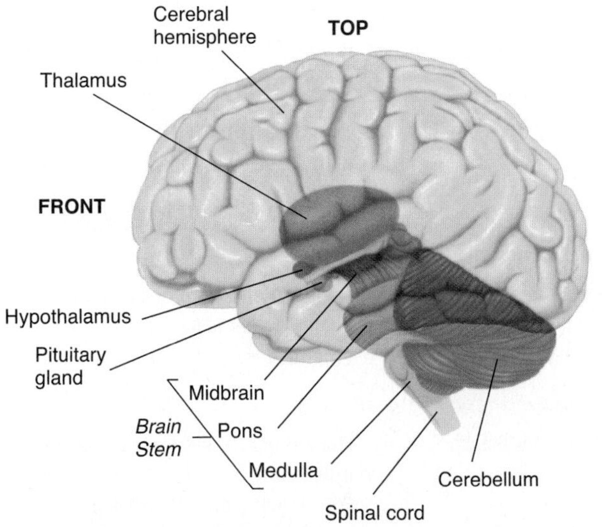

The Hypothalamus   *Hypo-* means "less than" or "beneath"; as its name suggests, the **hypothalamus** is located below the thalamus, at the base of the brain. (Refer to Figure 4.29.) The hypothalamus is a small region, consisting of less than 1 cubic centimeter of tissue (smaller than a grape), but its relative importance far exceeds its size.

The hypothalamus, like the brain stem, participates in homeostasis and species-typical behaviors. It receives sensory information, including information from receptors inside the organs of the body; thus, it is informed about changes in the body's physiological status. It also contains specialized sensors that monitor various characteristics of the blood that flows through the brain, such as temperature, nutrient content, and amount of dissolved salts. As we will see in Chapter 13, neural circuits within the hypothalamus control both eating and drinking.

The hypothalamus controls the **pituitary gland,** an endocrine gland attached by a stalk to the base of the hypothalamus. (Refer to Figure 4.30.) Hormones are chemicals produced by endocrine glands (from the Greek *endo-,* "within," and *krinein,* "to secrete"). (As we will see in the discussion of eating behavior in Chapter 13, hormones also are secreted by fat tissue and by special cells in the walls of the stomach and intestines.) **Endocrine glands** secrete hormones into the blood, which carries them to all parts of the body. **Hormones** are chemicals similar to neurotransmitters or neuromodulators,

[**FIGURE 4·30**] The divisions of the brain stem: the medulla, the pons, and the midbrain. The thalamus, hypothalamus, and pituitary gland are attached to the anterior end of the brain stem.

Labels: Cerebral hemisphere, TOP, Thalamus, FRONT, Hypothalamus, Pituitary gland, Midbrain, Brain Stem, Pons, Medulla, Cerebellum, Spinal cord

---

homeostasis (*home ee oh stay sis*)   The process by which important physiological characteristics (such as body temperature and blood pressure) are regulated so that they remain at their optimal levels.

species-typical behavior   A behavior seen in all or most members of a species, such as nest building, special food-getting behaviors, or reproductive behaviors.

medulla (*me doo la*)   The part of the brain stem closest to the spinal cord; controls vital functions such as heart rate and blood pressure.

pons   The part of the brain stem just anterior to the medulla; involved in control of sleep.

midbrain   The part of the brain stem just anterior to the pons; involved in control of fighting and sexual behavior and in decreased sensitivity to pain during these behaviors.

hypothalamus   A region of the brain located just above the pituitary gland; controls the autonomic nervous system and many behaviors related to regulation and survival, such as eating, drinking, fighting, shivering, and sweating.

pituitary gland   An endocrine gland attached to the hypothalamus at the base of the brain.

endocrine gland   A gland that secretes a hormone.

hormone   A chemical substance secreted by an endocrine gland that has physiological effects on target cells in other organs.

[**FIGURE 4·31**] The location and primary functions of the principal endocrine glands.

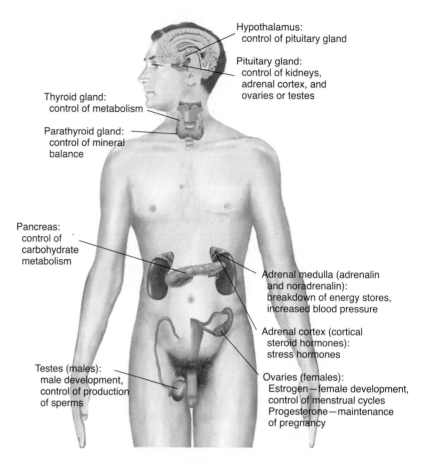

Hypothalamus:
control of pituitary gland

Pituitary gland:
control of kidneys,
adrenal cortex, and
ovaries or testes

Thyroid gland:
control of metabolism

Parathyroid gland:
control of mineral
balance

Pancreas:
control of
carbohydrate
metabolism

Adrenal medulla (adrenalin
and noradrenalin):
breakdown of energy stores,
increased blood pressure

Adrenal cortex (cortical
steroid hormones):
stress hormones

Testes (males):
male development,
control of production
of sperms

Ovaries (females):
Estrogen—female development,
control of menstrual cycles
Progesterone—maintenance
of pregnancy

except that they act over much longer distances. Like neurotransmitters and neuromodulators, hormones produce their effects by stimulating receptors. These receptors are located on (or in) particular cells, which are known as **target cells.** When hormones bind with their receptors, they produce physiological reactions in these cells. Almost every cell of the body contains hormone receptors of one kind or another. This includes neurons, which means that hormones can affect behavior by altering the activity of particular groups of neurons in the brain. For example, sex hormones have important effects on behavior, which is discussed in later chapters.

The pituitary gland has been called the "master gland," because the hormones it secretes act on target cells located in other endocrine glands; thus, the pituitary gland controls the activity of other endocrine glands. Because the hypothalamus controls the pituitary gland, the hypothalamus controls the endocrine system. The more important endocrine glands and the functions they regulate are shown in FIGURE 4·31.

The hypothalamus also controls much of the activity of the **autonomic nervous system (ANS),** a division of the pe-

ripheral nervous system that consists of nerves that control the functions of the glands and internal organs. The other division of the peripheral nervous system—the one that transmits information from sense organs to the central nervous system and from the central nervous system to the muscles, is called the **somatic nervous system.** Through the nerves of the autonomic ("self-governing") nervous system, the hypothalamus controls activities such as sweating, shedding tears, salivating, secreting digestive juices, changing the size of blood

---

target cell   A cell whose physiological processes are affected by a particular hormone; contains special receptors that respond to the presence of the hormone.

autonomic nervous system (ANS)   The portion of the peripheral nervous system that controls the functions of the glands and internal organs.

somatic nervous system   The portion of the peripheral nervous system that transmits information from sense organs to the central nervous system and from the central nervous system to the muscles.

[**TABLE 4·3**]   The Major Divisions of the Peripheral Nervous System

Division	Function
Somatic nervous system	
Sensory nerves	Transmission of information from sense organs to central nervous system
Motor nerves	Control of skeletal muscles
Autonomic nervous system	
Sympathetic branch	Support of activities that require the expenditure of energy (increased blood flow to muscles, increased supply of nutrients of muscles)
Parasympathetic branch	Support of quiet activities that help restore energy supplies (increased blood flow to digestive system, secretion of digestive enzymes)

vessels (which alters blood pressure), and the secretions of some endocrine glands. The autonomic nervous system has two branches. The **sympathetic branch** directs activities that involve the expenditure of energy. For example, activity of the sympathetic branch can increase the flow of blood to the muscles when we are about to fight someone or run away from a dangerous situation. In contrast, the **parasympathetic branch** controls quiet activities such as digestion of food. For example, activity of the parasympathetic branch stimulates the secretion of digestive enzymes and increases the flow of blood to the digestive system. (See TABLE 4·3 and FIGURE 4·32.)

Researchers can monitor the activity of the autonomic nervous system and its relation to psychological phenomena such as emotion. For example, when people become angry, their heart rate and blood pressure increase. The lie detector, described in Chapter 13, works (or, more accurately, is said to work) by recording emotional responses controlled by the autonomic nervous system.

The homeostatic functions of the hypothalamus can involve either internal physiological changes or behavior. For example, the hypothalamus is involved in the control of body temperature. It can directly lower a person's body temperature by causing sweating to occur, or it can raise it by causing shivering to occur. If these measures are inadequate, the hypothalamus can send messages to the cerebral cortex that will cause the person to engage in a learned behavior, such as turning on an air conditioner or turning up the thermostat. Damage to the hypothalamus can cause impaired regulation of body temperature, changes in food or water intake, sterility, and stunting of growth.

---

sympathetic branch   The portion of the autonomic nervous system that activates functions that accompany arousal and expenditure of energy.

parasympathetic branch   The portion of the autonomic nervous system that activates functions that occur during a relaxed state.

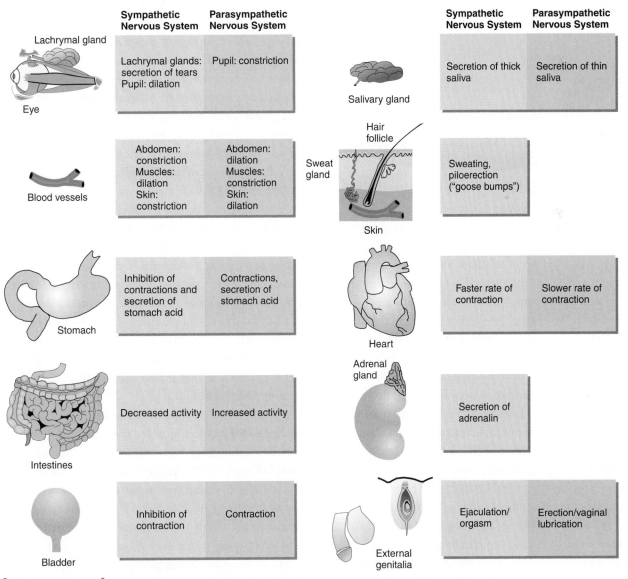

[**FIGURE 4·32**] The organs controlled by the autonomic nervous system. The reciprocal actions of the sympathetic and parasympathetic branches are noted next to each organ.

QUESTIONS TO CONSIDER

1. If you were to have a stroke (and let's hope you don't), in which region of the cerebral cortex and in which hemisphere would you prefer the brain damage to be located? Why?

2. Damage to the corpus callosum produces different behavioral deficits depending on whether the anterior or the posterior corpus callosum is affected. Why do you think this is so?

3. Explain why a brain lesion that impairs a person's ability to speak often also affects movements of the right side of the body.

4. The cerebellum is one of the largest parts of the brain and contains billions of neurons. What does this fact suggest about the complexity of the task of coordinating movements of the body?

5. Tranquilizers reduce negative emotional reactions. In what part (or parts) of the brain do you think these drugs might act? Why?

Epilogue

Unilateral Neglect

When we see people like Miss S., the woman with unilateral neglect described in the Prologue, we realize that perception and attention are somewhat independent. The perceptual mechanisms of our brain provide the information, and the mechanisms involved in attention determine whether we become conscious of this information.

Unilateral ("one-sided") neglect occurs when the right parietal lobe is damaged. As we saw, the parietal lobe is concerned with the body and its position. But that is not all. The association cortex of the parietal lobe also receives auditory and visual information from the association cortex of the occipital and temporal lobes. Its most important function seems to be to put together information about the movements and location of the parts of the body with the locations of objects in space around us.

If unilateral neglect simply consisted of blindness in the left side of the visual field and anesthesia of the left side of the body, it would not be nearly so interesting. But individuals with unilateral neglect are neither half blind nor half numb. Under the proper circumstances, they *can* see things located to their left, and they *can* tell when someone touches the left side of their bodies. But normally, they ignore such stimuli and act as if the left side of the world and of their bodies did not exist.

Volpe, LeDoux, and Gazzaniga (1979) presented pairs of visual stimuli to people with unilateral neglect—one stimulus in the left visual field and one stimulus in the right. Invariably, the people reported seeing only the right-hand stimulus. But when the investigators asked the people to say whether the two stimuli were identical, they answered correctly *even though they said that they were unaware of the left-hand stimulus.*

If you think about the story that the chief of neurology told about the man who ate only the right half of a pancake, you will realize that people with unilateral neglect *must* be able to perceive more than the right visual field. Remember that people with unilateral neglect fail to notice not only things to their left but also the *left halves* of things. But to distinguish between the left and right halves of an object, you first have to perceive the entire object—otherwise, how would you know where the middle was?

Although neglect of the left side of one's own body can be studied only in people with brain abnormalities, an interesting phenomenon seen in people with undamaged brains confirms the importance of the parietal lobe (and another region of the brain) in feelings of body ownership. Ehrsson, Spence, and Passingham (2004) studied the *rubber-hand illusion.* Normal subjects were positioned with their left hand hidden out of sight. They saw a lifelike rubber left hand in front of them. The experimenters stroked both the subject's hidden left hand and the visible rubber hand with a small paintbrush. If the two hands were stroked synchronously and in the same direction, the subjects began to experience the rubber hand as their own. If they were then asked to use their right hand to point to their left hand, they tended to point toward the rubber hand. However, if the real and artificial hands were stroked in different directions or at different times, the subjects did *not* experience the rubber hand as their own. (See FIGURE 4·33.)

While the subjects were participating in the experiment, the experimenters recorded the activity of their brains with a functional MRI scanner. (Brain scanning is described in Chapter 5.) The scans showed increased activity in the parietal lobe, and then, as the subjects began to experience the rubber hand as belonging to their body, in the *premotor cortex*, a region of the motor association cortex involved in planning movements. When the stroking of the real and artificial hands was uncoordinated and the subjects did not experience the rubber hand as their own, the

[**FIGURE 4·33**] The rubber-hand illusion. If the subject's hidden left hand and the visible rubber hand are stroked synchronously in the same direction, the subject will come to experience the artificial hand as his or her own. If the hands are stroked asynchronously or in different directions, this illusion will not occur.

(Adapted from Botwinick, M. (2004). Probing the Neural Basis of Body Ownership. *Science, 305*, 782–783.)

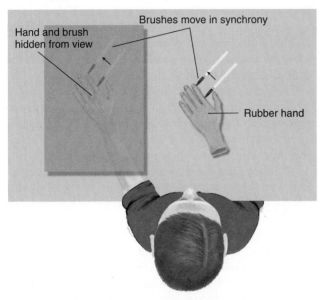

premotor cortex did not become activated. The experimenters concluded that the parietal cortex analyzed the sight and the feeling of brush strokes. When the parietal cortex detected that they were congruent, this information was transmitted to the premotor cortex, which gave rise to the feeling of ownership of the rubber hand.

CHAPTER SUMMARY

The Brain and Its Components

The brain has three major functions: controlling behavior, processing and storing information about the environment, and regulating the body's physiological processes.

The central nervous system consists of the spinal cord and the three major divisions of the brain: the brain stem, the cerebellum, and the cerebral hemispheres. The central nervous system floats in a pool of cerebrospinal fluid, contained by the meninges, which protects it from physical shock. The blood–brain barrier protects the brain from toxic substances in the blood. The cerebral cortex, which covers the cerebral hemispheres, is wrinkled by fissures and gyri. The brain communicates with the rest of the body through the peripheral nervous system, which includes the spinal nerves and cranial nerves.

The basic element of the nervous system is the neuron, with its dendrites, soma, axon, and terminal buttons. Neurons are assisted in their tasks by glia, which provide physical support, aid in the development of the nervous system, provide neurons with chemicals they need, remove unwanted chemicals, provide myelin sheaths for axons, and protect neurons from infections.

One neuron communicates with another (or with cells of muscles, glands, or internal organs) through synapses. A synapse is the junction of the terminal button of the presynaptic neuron with the membrane of the postsynaptic cell. Synaptic communication is chemical; when an action potential travels down an axon (when the axon "fires"), it causes a neurotransmitter to be released by the terminal buttons. An action potential consists of a brief change in the electrical charge of the axon, produced by the brief entry of positively charged sodium ions into the axon followed by a brief exit of positively charged potassium ions. Ions enter the axon through ion channels, and ion transporters eventually restore the proper concentrations of ions inside and outside the cell.

Molecules of the neurotransmitter released by terminal buttons bind with neurotransmitter receptors in the postsynaptic membrane and either excite or inhibit the firing of the postsynaptic cell. The combined effects of excitatory and inhibitory synapses acting on a particular neuron determine the rate of firing of that neuron.

Drugs and Behavior

Drugs can facilitate or interfere with synaptic activity. Facilitating drugs include those that cause the release of a neurotransmitter (such as the venom of the black widow spider); drugs that directly stimulate postsynaptic receptors, thus duplicating the effects of the neurotransmitter itself (such as nicotine); and drugs that inhibit the reuptake of a neurotransmitter (such as amphetamine and cocaine). Drugs that interfere with synaptic activity include those that inhibit the release of a neurotransmitter (such as botulinum toxin) and those that block receptors (such as curare).

In the brain, most synaptic communication is accomplished by two neurotransmitters: glutamate, which has excitatory effects, and GABA, which has inhibitory effects. Acetylcholine (ACh) controls muscular movements and is involved in control of REM sleep, activation of the cerebral cortex, and modulation of a brain structure involved in memory. Nicotine stimulates ACh receptors, and curare blocks them (and causes paralysis). Neostigmine, which is used to treat myasthenia gravis, suppresses the destruction of ACh by an enzyme. The monoamines also modulate important brain functions. Dopamine (DA) facilitates movements and plays a role in reinforcing behaviors. L-DOPA, which stimulates production of DA, is used to treat Parkinson's disease; and cocaine produces reinforcing effects on behavior by blocking the reuptake of dopamine. Drugs that block dopamine receptors are used to treat the symptoms of schizophrenia. The release of norepinephrine (NE) increases vigilance. The release of serotonin helps suppress aggressive behavior and risk-taking behavior, and drugs that inhibit the reuptake of serotonin are used to treat anxiety disorders, depression, and obsessive–compulsive disorder.

Most peptides serve as neuromodulators, which resemble neurotransmitters but travel farther and are dispersed more widely within the brain, where they can modulate the activity of many neurons. The best-known neuromodulators are the endogenous opioids, which are released when an animal is engaged in important behavior. Anandamide, the most important of the endogenous cannabinoids, helps regulate the release of many neurotransmitters. THC, the active ingredient in marijuana, acts on cannabinoid receptors and mimics the effects of anandamide. Cannabinoids have some beneficial effects but also impair short-term memory.

Study of the Brain

The study of the brain, with all its complexity, requires a variety of research methods. Some methods alter the brains of laboratory animals. These methods may include selective destruction of parts of the brain, recording of the brain's electrical or chemical activity, electrical or chemical stimulation of specific brain regions, or modification of the parts of the genetic code that affect neural processes. Electroencephalography and magnetoencephalography reveal the electrical events in the human brain. Other methods, including CT scans, PET imaging, and structural and functional MRI scans, provide images of the structure and activity of the human brain.

The brain changes most rapidly during fetal, childhood, and adolescent development, but neural plasticity—changes in the wiring of the brain induced by environmental events—occurs even in adulthood. Furthermore, new neurons are produced throughout life in the olfactory bulb and the hippocampus, and possibly in the cerebral cortex as well. Neurogenesis is increased by environmental stimulation and decreased by stress.

Control of Behavior and the Body's Physiological Functions

Anatomically, the cerebral cortex is divided into four lobes: frontal, parietal, occipital, and temporal. Functionally, the cerebral cortex is organized into the primary sensory cortex (with its visual, auditory, and somatosensory regions); the primary motor cortex; and the association cortex. The association cortex consists of sensory regions that are responsible for perceiving and learning and the motor regions that are responsible for planning and acting. Within the cerebral hemispheres, the thalamus relays sensory information to the cerebral cortex.

Some brain functions are lateralized; that is, the right and left hemispheres are involved with somewhat different functions. The left hemisphere is mostly concerned with the details of perception, such as the series of sounds that constitute speech or the symbols that constitute writing. The right hemisphere is mostly concerned with global events. The two hemispheres share information through the corpus callosum, a large bundle of axons.

The three lobes behind the central fissure are generally concerned with perceiving, learning, and remembering: visual information in the occipital and lower temporal lobes, auditory information in the upper temporal lobe, and somatosensory information in the parietal lobe. The parietal lobes are also concerned with perception of space and knowledge about the body, and the frontal lobes are also concerned with motor functions and planning strategies for action. The cerebellum and basal ganglia assist the frontal lobes with the details of executing movements.

The limbic system includes the limbic cortex as well as the hippocampus and the amygdala, both located within the temporal lobe. The hippocampus is involved in learning and memory, and the amygdala is involved in emotions and emotional behaviors.

The brain stem, which consists of the medulla, the pons, and the midbrain, contains neural circuits that control vital physiological functions and produce species-typical automatic movements such as those used in locomotion, fighting, and sexual behavior. The hypothalamus receives sensory information from sense receptors elsewhere in the body and also contains its own specialized receptors, such as those used to monitor body temperature. It controls the pituitary gland, which in turn controls most of the endocrine glands of the body; it also controls the internal organs through the autonomic nervous system. Hormones, secreted by endocrine glands, are chemicals that act on hormone receptors in target cells and produce physiological reactions in these cells. The hypothalamus can control homeostatic processes directly and automatically through its control of the pituitary gland and the autonomic nervous system, or it can cause neural circuits in the cerebral cortex to execute more complex, learned behavior.

succeed with ^{PEARSON} mypsychlab

Visit MyPsychLab for practice quizzes, flashcards, and dozens of videos and animated tutorials, including the following items you can find in the "Multimedia Library":

MKM and Brain Scans

Structure of Neuron
The Action Potential
Healthy vs. Unhealthy Behaviors
   and Brain Functioning

Split-Brain Experiments
Hemispheric Experiment

KEY TERMS

acetylcholine *p. 97*

action potential *p. 91*

all-or-none law *p. 92*

amygdala *p. 104*

anandamide *p. 100*

antianxiety drug *p. 97*

apoptosis *p. 107*

autonomic nervous system (ANS) *p. 116*

axon *p. 91*

barbiturate *p. 97*

basal ganglia *p. 114*

benzodiazepine *p. 97*

black widow spider venom *p. 97*

blood–brain barrier *p. 89*

botulinum toxin *p. 97*

brain lesion *p. 101*

brain stem *p. 88*

central fissure *p. 108*

central nervous system (CNS) *p. 87*

cerebellum *p. 88*

cerebral cortex *p. 89*

cerebral hemisphere *p. 88*

cerebral ventricle *p. 89*

cerebrospinal fluid (CSF) *p. 89*

contralateral *p. 109*

corpus callosum *p. 111*

cranial nerve *p. 87*

CT scanner *p. 102*

curare *p. 98*

dendrite *p. 91*

dopamine (DA) *p. 99*

electroencephalogram (EEG) *p. 103*

endocrine gland *p. 115*

endogenous cannabinoid *p. 100*

endogenous opioid *p. 99*

frontal lobe *p. 109*

functional MRI (*f*MRI) *p. 105*

GABA *p. 96*

glia *p. 90*

glutamate *p. 96*

gray matter *p.89*

hippocampus *p. 114*

homeostasis *p. 115*

hormone *p. 115*

hypothalamus *p. 115*

ion channel *p. 92*

ion *p. 92*

ipsilateral *p. 109*

limbic cortex *p. 114*

limbic system *p. 114*

LSD *p. 99*

magnetic resonance imaging (MRI) *p. 103*

magnetoencephalography (MEG) *p. 103*

medulla *p. 115*

meninges *p. 89*

microelectrode *p. 103*

midbrain *p. 115*

monoamine *p. 98*

motor association cortex *p. 110*

motor neuron *p. 92*

myelin sheath *p. 91*

naloxone *p. 100*

neostigmine *p. 98*

nerve *p. 87*

neural plasticity *p. 106*

neurogenesis *p. 107*

neuromodulator *p. 99*

neuron *p. 90*

neurotransmitter *p. 91*

neurotransmitter receptor *p. 93*

nicotine *p. 98*

norepinephrine (NE) *p. 99*

occipital lobe *p. 109*

parasympathetic branch *p. 117*

parietal lobe *p. 109*

Parkinson's disease *p. 99*

peptide *p. 99*

peripheral nervous system (PNS) *p. 87*

pituitary gland *p. 115*

pons *p. 115*

positron emission tomography (PET) *p. 104*

postsynaptic neuron *p. 93*

prefrontal cortex *p. 110*

presynaptic neuron *p. 93*

primary auditory cortex *p. 109*

primary motor cortex *p. 109*

primary somatosensory cortex *p. 109*

primary visual cortex *p. 109*

resting potential *p. 91*

reuptake *p. 94*

sensory association cortex *p. 110*

sensory neuron *p. 92*

serotonin *p. 99*

soma *p. 91*

somatic nervous system *p. 116*

species-typical behavior *p. 115*

spinal cord *p. 87*

spinal nerve *p. 87*

stem cell *p. 107*

stereotaxic apparatus *p. 102*

sympathetic branch *p. 117*

synapse *p. 93*

synaptic cleft *p. 93*

synaptic vesicle *p. 93*

target cell *p. 116*

targeted mutation *p. 106*

temporal lobe *p. 109*

terminal button *p. 91*

thalamus *p. 110*

transcranial magnetic stimulation (TMS) *p. 105*

ventricular zone *p. 107*

vertebra *p. 89*

white matter *p. 89*

SUGGESTIONS FOR FURTHER READING

Grilly, D. M. (2006). *Drugs and Human Behavior* (5th ed.). Boston: Allyn and Bacon.

Meyer, J. S., and Quenzer, L. F. (2005). *Psychopharmacology: Drugs, the Brain, and Behavior.* Sunderland, MA: Sinauer Associates.

If you are interested in learning more about the effects of drugs that are often abused, you may want to read these books, both of which contain much helpful information about the effects of popular drugs and their use and abuse in society.

Carlson, N. R. (2008). *Foundations of Physiological Psychology* (7th ed.). Boston: Allyn and Bacon.

My introductory textbook of physiological psychology discusses the topics presented in this chapter in more detail.

5

Learning and Behavior

Prologue

Learning Confronts "Survival of the Fittest"

In a New York subway station, Wesley Autrey—a 50-year-old construction worker and a veteran of the U.S. Navy—was waiting for the
arrival of his train. He was bringing his two young daughters home
from school before going to work that afternoon. As they were waiting on the subway platform, Mr. Autrey saw a man suddenly stagger
and fall onto the tracks. At just that moment, he also saw a train begin to enter the station. Mr. Autrey leaped onto the tracks and held
the man down beneath his body. The other people on the subway
platform gasped in horror because the train could not stop in time.
Five cars passed over the two men before the train came to a stop
over their bodies. Then, to the onlookers' surprise and delight, a voice
came from beneath the train, "We're O.K. down here, but I've got two
daughters up there. Let

them know their father's
O.K." When the police and
emergency medical tech-
nicians arrived, it was determined that the man
who had fallen had suf-
fered a seizure. He was
taken to a hospital, where
he was released shortly
thereafter without ill effects. As for Mr. Autrey, he
had only a grease stain on
the side of his cap to mark
the close passage of the
subway cars. He told the
authorities, "I had to make
a split-second decision."

A second challenge to
the doctrine of "survival of
the fittest" also comes
from New York, that sup-
posedly unfriendly city. Vinod Mago, a man of modest means, had
emigrated from India and earned his living as a cab driver. He
picked up a man at a hotel and drove him to the airport at JFK, a
common trip for a cab driver. As Mr. Mago was returning to the
city, his dispatcher called to say that a man had been frantically
calling all the cab companies. The man claimed to have left his
wallet in a cab, but he couldn't remember the name of the cab
company. Mr. Mago stopped his cab and looked in the back seat.
He discovered a wallet containing $5,950! Mr. Mago immediately
rushed to the airport, found the man, and returned the wallet
with the money inside. ■

How can we understand such cases? Most people's notion of "survival of the fittest" holds that we should always act selfishly and not consider the effects of our actions on others. (This is not the correct view of fitness in evolutionary science, of course, as we saw in Chapter 3.) Nevertheless, understanding the behavior of Mr. Autry and Mago challenges even the evolutionary account. Why did Mr. Autrey make his split-second decision when it threatened not only his own life but also the quality of the future lives of his wife and children? From the perspective of natural selection, his action imperiled not only his own genes but also the genes he shared with his children. And how are we to understand Mr. Mago's behavior? He could have kept the money and almost certainly have gone undetected. Would not Mr. Mago's "fitness" have been better served by keeping the money for himself and his family? Purely genetic explanations of altruism cannot account for such cases. Mr. Autry and Mr. Mago were genetically unrelated to the people whom they helped and were unlikely ever to meet them again in a city as large as New York. Thus, inclusive fitness and reciprocal altruism cannot help us understand these cases.

The explanation of such behavior requires us to understand how behavior is shaped by the *individual* environment as well as by the species environment. We have seen how the environments of our ancestors, acting though natural selection, have produced a nervous system of great complexity, but humans and other species are also products of their individual environments—their individual experiences. These experiences produce **learning.** Learning is an enduring change in the way the environment guides behavior. Science began its search for how the individual environment changes behavior at the turn of the last century in the laboratories of Ivan Pavlov in Russia and Edward Thorndike in the United States (see Chapter 1). They worked independently, and their methods differed in important respects. Nevertheless, the research programs they began have led us to a common understanding of how experience changes behavior—how learning occurs. Let us see how Pavlov and Thorndike approached their common goal.

How Learning Is Studied

To study basic learning processes, we momentarily retreat from the complicated environment of the natural world and enter the more controlled world of the laboratory. Individual differences are reduced by studying organisms whose genetic variation is known and whose prior experience is controlled. In this way, any changes in behavior that occur during the experiment can be attributed to variables manipulated within the experiment, not to preexisting differences. Pavlov and Thorndike both began searching for the conditions that promote learning by using nonhuman animals whose genetic and experiential histories

could be restricted. The principles of learning that are described in this chapter are consistent with later work with humans, including infants whose prior experience is less extensive.

Pavlov and Thorndike saw themselves as following in Darwin's footsteps (Thorndike, 1903; Pavlov, 1927; see also Donahoe, 1999). They were trying to understand how the *individual* environment changed behavior through its underlying neural mechanisms just as Darwin had previously tried to understand how the *ancestral* environment affected behavior through its underlying genetic mechanisms. In short, Pavlov and Thorndike sought a principle of selection by the individual environment that complemented natural selection by the ancestral environment.

Pavlov's Procedure

Pavlov and Thorndike began their work by using nonhuman animals—dogs for Pavlov and chicks and cats for Thorndike. Both also began by introducing into their experiments a stimulus that already evoked behavior as a result of natural selection. Such a stimulus is called an **eliciting stimulus.** The eliciting stimulus and the behavior it evokes provide reference points from which to detect changes in behavior. In Pavlov's case, a dog was lightly restrained in a harness, and food was presented after an environmental stimulus, such as the ticking sound of a metronome. (See FIGURE 5•1.) Food, the eliciting stimulus, evoked salivation.

Pavlov found that after the ticking sound had appeared before the food several times, the animal began to salivate and look toward the food bowl whenever it heard the sound. Pairing the sound with food and its elicited salivary response

[**FIGURE 5•1**] Pavlov's original classical conditioning procedure. A stimulus is presented (for example, the sound of a metronome ticking), and then the experimenter provides access to a small amount of food in a bowl. Saliva flows into a tube.

---

learning Long-lasting changes in the environmental guidance of behavior as a result of experience.

eliciting stimulus Stimulus that evokes behavior, commonly as a result of natural selection.

produced a change in the environmental guidance of behavior (i.e., learning occurred). The sound–salivation relation had been selected by the food. Before the procedure, the tone didn't evoke salivation; afterward, it did. Changes resulting from the relation of an environmental event to an eliciting stimulus frequently occur in everyday experience. We salivate when seeing an ice-cream cone and cringe when seeing an overinflated balloon about to burst. In our pasts, seeing ice cream was often followed by eating ice cream, which evoked salivation. Later, seeing ice cream is enough to evoke salivation. Similarly, seeing an overinflated balloon was previously followed by a loud popping noise, which elicited a startle response. Thereafter, seeing a balloon being over-inflated is enough to evoke cringing. (See FIGURE 5•2.)

As a more-complex everyday example of Pavlov's procedure, a psychologist told me the following story: At age 19, his wife rode in an ambulance with her father, who had had a stroke. Her father was in a stable condition, so the ambulance drove at an ordinary speed and did not use the siren. However, like most people, she had previously acquired an association between the sound of a siren and the sight of an ambulance. For a year or two thereafter, whenever she heard a siren, it elicited the emotional state that she had experienced while riding in the ambulance with her stricken father.

Thorndike's Procedure

Thorndike (1898) also introduced an *eliciting stimulus*—food—into the learner's environment. However, unlike Pavlov, Thorndike introduced the food after a r*esponse*, not after a stimulus. When a chick wandered down a maze whose walls were formed from stacks of books, the chick received food if it reached the end of the maze. Food was an eliciting stimulus that evoked salivation as well as other responses, such as approach and ingestion. Thorndike measured how long it took the chick to move through the maze and found that the time decreased over successive attempts. As

Thorndike's second example, when a cat operated a latch that allowed it to exit a chamber where it was confined, the cat received food. (See FIGURE 5•3.) The time to operate the latch grew shorter over successive trials. When the chick was placed in the alleyway, it ran instead of meandering about. When the cat was placed in the chamber (which Thorndike called a *puzzle box*), it operated the latch instead of trying to squeeze between the bars of the chamber. As with Pavlov's procedure, the introduction of a stimulus that already elicits behavior (food evokes salivation) changed how the environment guided behavior. Thorndike measured the behavior that produced the eliciting stimulus, not the elicited response itself. The critical events in Thorndike's procedure, like Pavlov's, also occur in the world outside the laboratory: Children who receive praise or treats for picking up their toys are more likely to pick them up in the future. The likelihood of engaging in a given behavior is affected by the eliciting stimuli that follow the behavior.

Comparisons between Pavlov's and Thorndike's Procedures

The fundamental similarities and differences between the Pavlov's and Thorndike's procedures are shown in FIGURE 5•4. In both procedures, the environment may be regarded as a sequence of stimuli (S) that continuously changes as the learner orients toward different stimuli. Behavior consists of a continuously changing sequence of responses (R). Into that stream of environmental and behavioral events, the experimenter introduces a stimulus that elicits a response (cf. Schoenfeld & Farmer, 1970). In Pavlov's procedure, the eliciting stimulus is introduced after another stimulus—the ticking sound of the metronome. In Thorndike's procedure, the eliciting stimulus is introduced after a response—the operation of the latch.

Pavlov's procedure controls the relation of an environmental stimulus to an eliciting stimulus. Thorndike's procedure

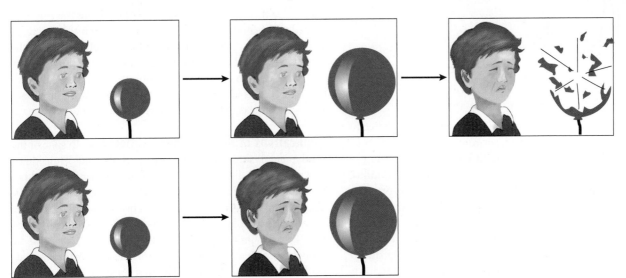

[**FIGURE 5•2**] A classical conditioning procedure outside the laboratory. A boy watches a balloon expand until it bursts, causing the boy to grimace. Thereafter, when the boy sees a balloon being overinflated, he grimaces even before the balloon bursts.

[FIGURE 5•3] Thorndike's original operant conditioning procedure. A cat placed in the puzzle box had to pull the ring of wire inside the box to operate the latch. The door would then open, and the cat could escape from the puzzle box and gain access to food. The graph shows the reduction in the time one cat needed to operate the latch over repeated trails.

(Adapted from Thorndike, E. L. (1898). Animal intelligence. *Psychological Review Monograph Supplement, 2* [whole No. 8].)

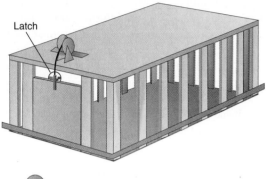

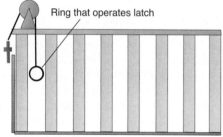

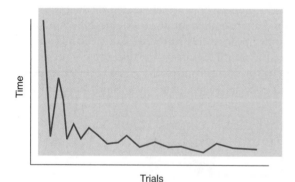

[FIGURE 5•4] The similarities and differences between Pavlov's and Thorndike's procedures. In both procedures the environment may be viewed as a continuously changing sequence of stimuli (S) and behavior as a continuously changing sequence of responses (R). Into that stream of environmental and behavioral events, a stimulus is introduced that elicits a response. In Pavlov's procedure the eliciting stimulus is introduced after another stimulus—the ticking sound of a metronome. In Thorndike's procedure the eliciting stimulus is introduced after a response—operation of the latch. Note that some response inevitably occurs before the eliciting stimulus in Pavlov's procedure and some stimulus inevitably occurs before the response in Thorndike's procedure.

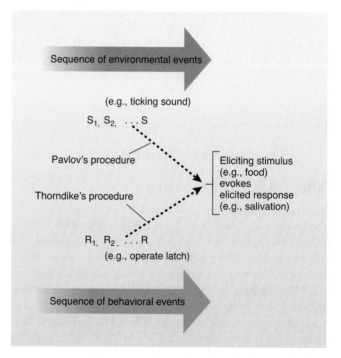

controls the relation of a response to the eliciting stimulus. In Pavlov's procedure, a specified environmental stimulus must occur before the eliciting stimulus. In Thorndike's procedure, a specified response must occur before the eliciting stimulus. However, as shown in Figure 5.4, *some* stimulus always precedes the eliciting stimulus in Thorndike's procedure, and *some* behavior always precedes the eliciting stimulus in Pavlov's procedure. Thus, the two procedures do not differ with respect to whether a stimulus or a response precedes the eliciting stimulus, but as to whether their relation to the eliciting stimulus is *reliable*. At the moment when the eliciting stimulus is first presented, learners cannot tell whether they are in Pavlov's procedure or Thorndike's. Pavlov's dog likely pricked up its ears

on hearing the ticking of the metronome, and thus this response preceded the food. Thorndike's cat saw the loop that operated the latch before pulling it, and thus this stimulus preceded the food. Given that the two procedures differ only in the reliability with which environmental or behavioral events precede the eliciting stimulus, it is not surprising that the two procedures have led to the same conclusions about the learning process.

Implications of the procedural difference In spite of the fundamental similarities between Pavlov's and Thorndike's procedures, the different relations of the environment and behavior to the eliciting stimulus have important implications. These implications were most keenly appreciated by the American psychologist B. F. Skinner (1937). Skinner realized that Pavlov's procedure limited the behavior that could be brought under environmental control to responses that were already elicited by a stimulus. The dog learns to salivate to the ticking sound, but this is a response that was previously made to food. Skinner recognized that Thorndike's procedure opened the possibility of changing the environmental guidance of *any* behavior of which the organism was capable: Simply select a response, and follow it by an eliciting stimulus. Thus, the full behavioral capabilities of the learner could be changed with Thorndike's procedure. The research stimulated by this insight ultimately led Skinner to be ranked in 1991 as the most important contemporary psychologist (Korn, Davis, & Davis, 1991).

In Pavlov's procedure, the environment acquires control of a response that typically resembles the elicited response. The elicited response is the only response that reliably occurs close in time to the eliciting stimulus. In Thorndike's procedure, another response also reliably occurs close in time to the eliciting stimulus—the response that produced the eliciting stimulus. This response, in addition to the elicited response, reliably precedes the eliciting stimulus. Thus, with Thorndike's procedure, two types of responses are simultaneously acquired. In the example of the puzzle box, the cat acquired both a latch-operating response and (presumably) a salivary response to the sight of the loop. In short, the environment of the puzzle box came to guide both the response that produced the eliciting stimulus (pulling the loop) and the elicited response (salivation evoked by food).

Note also that Thorndike's procedure did not specify the stimuli that initially permitted the loop-pulling response, if such stimuli were specifiable at all. For that reason, Skinner described this response as **emitted** instead of elicited. Because a wider range of behavior could be affected by Thorndike's procedure, "real-world" applications of learning principles more often use Thorndike's procedure. Later in life, Thorndike largely left laboratory research to apply his methods to education, becoming the most extensively published psychologist in history (Jonçich, 1968). Pavlov—as a "pure" scientist—lamented Thorndike's departure from the laboratory. However, Pavlov himself turned toward the application of his ideas to the treatment of mental illness during his later years (Pavlov, 1961/1994). Skinner and his colleagues consistently applied their research and ideas to many fields outside the laboratory, including education through programmed instruction (Skinner, 1984a), treatment of dysfunctional behavior through applied behavior analysis (see Chapters 16 and 17), and language (see Chapter 10).

Students' raising of their hands in response to their teacher's questions is reinforced by the opportunity to speak and receive attention from their teacher.

QUESTIONS TO CONSIDER

1. Can you think of an experience in your own life that meets the conditions studied by Pavlov or by Thorndike?
2. Do you think that the learning process uncovered through research with animals is likely to be the same as with humans? If you think that they might be different, in what specific ways might they differ? Why would natural selection lead you to think that they might be similar?

Conditions Required for Learning

Before we discuss the conditions required for learning, we first introduce some technical terms used in describing the procedures. Pavlov's procedure is now called a *classical* or *respondent* procedure. It is called "classical" because it was the first laboratory procedure that was systematically used to study learning. It is called "respondent" to emphasize that the behavior that is acquired is an *elicited response* to the eliciting stimulus. Henceforth, we refer to Pavlov's procedure as the **classical procedure.** Thorndike's procedure is called an *operant* or *instrumental* procedure. Thorndike's procedure is called "operant" to emphasize that the response *operates* on the environment to produce the eliciting stimulus. It is called "instrumental" to indicate that the response is instrumental in producing the eliciting stimulus. Henceforth, we refer to Thorndike's procedure as the **operant procedure.**

In the classical procedure, the stimulus that reliably precedes the eliciting stimulus is called the **conditioned stimulus.** It is so called because its ability to evoke the elicited response is *conditional* on (that is, dependent on) its preceding the eliciting stimulus. The eliciting stimulus is called the **unconditioned stimulus** because its ability to evoke the elicited response is *not* conditional on what happens *within* the experiment. The organism comes into the experiment already able to respond to the unconditioned stimulus. Conditioned and unconditioned stimuli are most commonly denoted by the acronyms *CS* and *US*, respectively. The response that is elicited by the US is called the **unconditioned response,** or *UR*. After several pairings of the CS with the US, the CS comes to evoke a response that typically

---

emitted response   Response permitted by the environment with no specific controlling stimulus.

classical procedure   Conditioning procedure in which a neutral stimulus precedes an eliciting stimulus with the result that the neutral stimulus evokes a learned response resembling the elicited response.

operant procedure   Conditioning procedure in which a response (the operant) precedes an eliciting stimulus.

conditioned stimulus (CS)   Neutral stimulus that evokes a conditional response (CR) through pairing with a US in a classical procedure.

unconditioned stimulus (US)   Stimulus, such as food, that elicits a reflexive response, such as salivation, in a classical procedure.

unconditioned response (UR)   Response that is elicited by the US in a classical procedure.

resembles the UR. Because the response that is evoked by the CS is *conditional* on the CS preceding the US/UR, it is called the **conditioned response,** or *CR*. As applied to Pavlov's original experiment, the ticking sound was the CS, the food was the US, the salivation elicited by food was the UR, and the salivation that came to occur after the CS was the CR. The learning that takes place under the controlled conditions of the classical and operant procedures is called **conditioning** in both cases. It is called conditioning to indicate that learning is *conditional* on the particular sequence of events in the two procedures. Because the conditioning that we are now discussing *increases* the strength of responding, the eliciting stimulus is also commonly referred to as a **reinforcing stimulus,** or simply a **reinforcer.**

Temporal Contiguity

Using classical and operant procedures, laboratory research has identified two factors that are necessary for learning to occur. The technical names for these factors are *temporal contiguity* and *behavioral discrepancy*. We now describe experimental evidence for each.

Temporal contiguity refers to events that occur close in time to one another. Pavlov's procedure permits the experimenter to manipulate the *temporal* (time) interval between the CS (ticking sound) and the US/UR (food/salivation). In contrast, Thorndike's procedure permits the experimenter to manipulate the temporal interval between the response (operating the latch) and the eliciting stimulus. In short, the experimenter can study the temporal relation of a stimulus to an eliciting stimulus with Pavlov's procedure and of a response to an eliciting stimulus with Thorndike's procedure. What effect does the time interval between these pairs of events have on changes in the strength of the measured response—salivation in Pavlov's case and latch-operating in Thorndike's?

Contiguity in the classical procedure
As shown in FIGURE 5•5, the CS may be presented before the US/UR, in which case the procedure is called a *forward* conditioning procedure, or after the US/UR, in which case, it is called a *backward* procedure. By using the classical procedure, the CS and the reinforcing stimulus (the US) can be presented with different time intervals between them for different learners. If the level of CR responding changes when the CS–US time interval changes, then conditioning is affected by *temporal contiguity*.

The effect of varying the time interval between the CS and the US/UR for different groups of subjects is shown in FIGURE 5•6. When the CS came *after* the US/UR—a back-

ward procedure of –50 milliseconds (ms)—or occurred *simultaneously* with the US/UR—a simultaneous procedure of 0 ms—no change occurred in the strength of the response. When the CS came *before* the US/UR (a forward procedure), the tone acquired control of the response. As Figure 5.6 shows, the strength of the CR increased as the time interval lengthened to 225 ms and then decreased as the interval lengthened further (Smith, Coleman, & Gormezano, 1969).The strength of the CR was measured by occasionally presenting the CS by itself and observing whether a CR occurred. Although the exact time interval at which conditioning is optimal varies somewhat for different CSs, USs, and learners, the general finding is that conditioning in the classical procedure occurs best when the CS precedes the US/UR by a *brief* time interval. The critical temporal relation appears to be between the CS and the UR because conditioning occurs even with a backward CS–US relation when the UR has a substantial latency and duration. A longer–latency, longer–duration UR allows even a backward CS to precede or overlap the UR (Donahoe & Vegas, 2004). Such responses are common for responses mediated by the autonomic nervous system (for example, the emotional responses elicited by noxious stimuli) (Brandon, Betts, & Wagner, 1994; McNish et al., 1997).

Contiguity in the operant procedure
Temporal relations can also be investigated with the operant procedure. In the operant procedure, the experimenter manipulates the time interval between the operant response and the reinforcing stimulus. For example, different rats can press a lever and then receive food at various time intervals after the press, or different pigeons can peck a disk on the wall of a test chamber and receive food after various time intervals. The findings from operant experiments

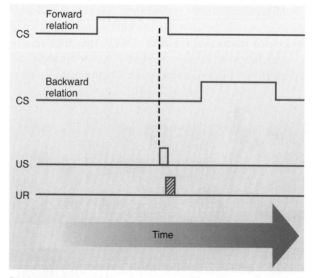

[**FIGURE 5•5**] In classical conditioning procedures, two possible temporal relations may exist between the conditioned stimulus (CS) and the unconditioned stimulus (US) and the response it elicits (UR). A forward procedure exists when the CS occurs before the US/UR. A backward procedure exists when the CS follows the US/UR.

---

conditioned response (CR) Response that is acquired by the CS in a classical procedure after the CS has been paired with the US.

conditioning Process that produces learning (change in the environmental guidance of behavior) in classical and operant procedures.

reinforcing stimulus (reinforcer) Stimulus that strengthens responding in either the classical or operant procedures, often called simply a *reinforcer*.

temporal contiguity Relation between two events that occur close together in time.

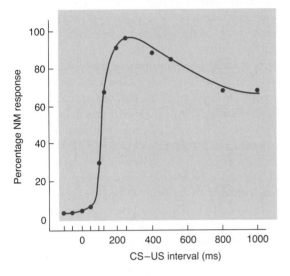

are also clear: As the delay interval increases between the operant response and eliciting stimulus, the strength of the operant response declines (Grice, 1948; Catania, 1971). The strength of the operant response increases when the eliciting stimulus follows the response by no more than a few seconds.

Studying temporal effects with the operant procedure is complicated by the fact that other behavior may occur in the interval between the operant and the reinforcer when the reinforcer is delayed. These other responses then occur closer in time to the reinforcer. As a result, they can be strengthened and interfere with the operant. For example, if pressing a lever is followed by food after five seconds have elapsed, then intervening responses—such as approaching the location where the food occurs—can be strengthened and interfere with lever pressing. The longer the time interval between the operant and the reinforcer, the greater the opportunity for interfering behavior to be conditioned. As a result, the response that actually produced the reinforcer is less strengthened (Lattal & Crawford-Godbey, 1985).

Schedules of reinforcement To investigate the effects of the precise circumstances that occur before a reinforcer, Charles Ferster and B. F. Skinner devised a number of procedures to manipulate these events (Ferster & Skinner, 1957). The procedures are collectively known as **schedules of reinforcement.** The nature of the events that can potentially occur before a reinforcer in an operant procedure is endlessly variable. We focus here on two types of manipulations—*response* requirements

and *temporal* requirements. When response requirements are manipulated, the procedures are known as **ratio schedules.** The experimenter varies the number of responses required for a reinforcer. For example, if ten responses are required to produce a reinforcer, the ratio is 10:1. As an example, a farm worker might be paid on the basis of how many pieces of fruit he picked during the day. When time requirements are manipulated, the procedures are known as **interval schedules.** For instance, if 20 seconds since the previous reinforcer must elapse before a response produces the next reinforcer, the interval is 20 seconds. Ratio and interval schedules can be either *fixed* or *variable.* If fixed, a reinforced response might occur after 10 responses on a ratio schedule or after 20 seconds on an interval schedule. If variable, an *average* of 10 responses might be required on a ratio schedule or an average of 20 seconds on an interval schedule before the response produced a reinforcer. In variable schedules, the particular value changes from one reinforcer to the next. As an example of a variable-ratio schedule, pulling the lever on a slot machine may be reinforced with money after a variable number of pulls. As an example of a variable-interval schedule, catching a fish while fly-fishing depends on the occasional presence of a fish and not the number of casts. Typical effects of these schedules are shown in FIGURE 5•7. Ratio schedules produce higher rates of responding per reinforcer than do interval schedules. (The slopes of the lines in Figure 5.7 indicate the rate of responding, with steeper slopes indicating higher rates.) Fixed-interval schedules produce low rates of responding immediately after the reinforcer but an increased rate as the schedule requirement comes closer to being met. Note that the rate of responding is more affected by the schedule on which reinforcers occur than by the mere number of reinforcers. The schedules on which responses are reinforced in the "real world" are more complex than the relatively simple cases studied in the laboratory, but the general characteristics of the behavior generated by these schedules can often be seen.

Because the rate of responding is often taken as evidence of the "motivation" of the learner, many so-called motivational effects reflect the schedule of reinforcement under which the behavior was acquired. Consider a child who asks for candy while a parent is shopping. At first, the parent says "No," but after several appeals, the parent gives in and buys the candy. The parent has reinforced asking for candy on a ratio schedule—many appeals have ultimately led to candy. On future shopping trips, the parent should expect the child to ask for candy at a high rate and for a very long time. If the parents resists as long as they can and then again relents, the child's behavior has been reinforced on an even larger ratio schedule. On the next shopping trip, the child's behavior will occur at an even higher rate and persist for an even longer

schedules of reinforcement Procedures that manipulate the temporal relation between stimuli, responses, and reinforcers.

ratio schedules Procedures in which a reinforcer is dependent on the occurrence of a number of responses; may be either fixed or variable.

interval schedules Procedures in which a reinforcer is dependent on the passage of time before the response is effective; may be either fixed or variable.

[FIGURE 5•7] Cumulative records of the effect of different reinforcement schedules on operant responding. Interval schedules are shown in the top row, ratio schedules in the bottom row. Fixed schedules are shown in the left column, variables schedules in the right column. When a curve reached its maximum, it returned to the baseline level and then increased again as responding continued. In cumulative records, each response causes the curve to move upward a small amount.

(From Donahoe, J. W., and Palmer, D. C. (1994). *Learning and Complex Behavior*, Boston, MA: Allyn and Bacon. Reprinted with permission from J. W. Donahoe.)

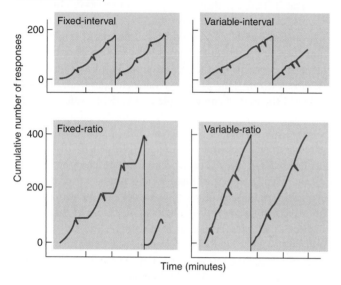

time. Unintentionally, the parent has reinforced behavior on a schedule that might cause others to describe the child as a "spoiled brat," when it is the schedule implemented by the parent and not the child that is responsible. The following case is a classroom demonstration in an advanced psychology course that provides an example of the tendency to give motivational interpretations to behavior that is actually due to the schedule of reinforcement.

[CASE STUDY] I asked students in a class to view the behavior of two pigeons and to comment on each. The first pigeon was brought into the classroom and placed in an operant chamber. The chamber had clear plastic sides so that the bird's behavior could be observed. As soon as the pigeon was placed in the chamber, it began to rapidly peck a disk located on the wall. Occasionally, a peck would be followed by the delivery of a small amount of food into a cup located beneath the disk. After several minutes, the pigeon was removed from the chamber and taken outside the classroom. The students described the first pigeon as "extremely hungry," "highly motivated," "well trained," and "very eager."

I then returned to the hallway and retrieved a "second" pigeon to be placed in the chamber. (The reason for putting quotation marks around *second* will become clear.) In contrast to the behavior of the first bird, this bird did not peck the disk rapidly. Instead, the second bird spent most of its

time wandering around the chamber with only an occasional peck to the disk. These pecks were followed by food from time to time with about the same frequency as for the first bird. After the second pigeon had been removed from the chamber, the students described its behavior very differently. The second bird was said to be "not as hungry," "lazy," "not as highly motivated as the first bird," and so on.

What was responsible for the difference in the behavior of the "two" birds? To begin with, only one bird had been used, not two, as the students had been told. After the bird had first performed, I simply went into the hallway for a minute and then returned with the same bird. (One pigeon looks pretty much like another unless you are a pigeon.) What differed between the two tests was the color of a light behind the disk—a color that the students could not see, but that the bird could. During prior training, when the disk was green, pecking occasionally produced food if *less than 2 seconds* had elapsed since the prior peck. However, when the disk was red, pecking occasionally produced food if *more than 10 seconds* had elapsed since the prior peck. Thus, the schedules reinforced fast pecking when the disk was green and slow pecking when it was red.

This example teaches us several lessons (besides that some professors are not to be trusted). First, attempting to infer motivation—whether in humans or nonhumans—is risky business when we don't know their history of reinforcement. Because we are usually ignorant of their history, we should treat our inferences about the motivations of others with caution. Second, because we are often unaware of the history of others, we have a tendency to attribute their behavior—which we can see—to internal causes—which we cannot—and not to the different schedules that actually produced the behavior.

Laboratory findings show that a reinforcer changes the environmental guidance of behavior only when it occurs very soon after the CS in the classical procedure or the response in the operant procedure. Thus, the reinforcement process acts only over a short time interval. This conclusion has been confirmed with human learners by using techniques such as air-puff–elicited eye blinks as the US and UR and with both infants and adults (Spence, 1956; Rovee-Collier & Gekoski, 1979). The conclusion that learning occurs only within a short time period surrounding the occurrence of the reinforcer is known as the *temporal contiguity* requirement.

Effects of Temporal Contiguity on Human Behavior

The relation of reinforcers to behavior in the natural environment is typically more complex than occurs in highly controlled laboratory procedures. As noted, these simpler procedures are necessary to reveal the operation of basic learning processes. Nevertheless, these same processes can be observed in human behavior. Here we consider some aspects of human behavior that show the effect of temporal contiguity.

Consider *phobias* (described in detail in Chapter 16), which are unreasonable fears of certain stimuli—for example, harmless spiders, birds, or various situations such as crowds. When the life histories of persons with phobias are closely examined, they often include experiences in which the object of the phobia has been paired with an aversive stimulus (Merckelbach & Muris, 1997). Pairing an object with a stimulus that evokes pain or fear causes the object itself to become feared, even when the fear is irrational. The stimuli that become objects of phobias are influenced by natural selection as well as by experience. Studies show that objects that are often involved in phobias, such as spiders, become CSs more rapidly when paired with a US such as an electric shock than do neutral stimuli (Ohman, et al., 1976). *Panic disorders* are also affected by the stimulus–reinforcer pairings of the classical procedure (e.g., Bouton, Mineka, & Barlow, 2001). Again, the life histories of those afflicted with panic disorders often include pairings of the feared situation with aversive USs (Acierno, Hersen, & Van Hasselt, 1993).

A particularly unfortunate effect of pairing a stimulus with a reinforcer occurs in drug addiction. When an addicting drug is taken by injection or other means, the stimuli that precede the drug are paired with the effects of the drug. These stimuli include the sight of drug paraphernalia or the prick of a needle as well as stimuli from the general environment in which the drug was taken. Drug-related stimuli then become CSs for the responses elicited by the drug. Drugs of addiction have complex effects that mimic the action of naturally occurring neurotransmitters. When neurons detect these effects, the production or action of the neurotransmitter is reduced—a kind of *homeostatic* reaction (see Chapter 4). These reactions are the URs to the US of drug ingestion. When the person experiences stimuli characteristic of the environment in which the drug was taken, conditioned reactions occur, such as decreases in production of the neurotransmitter. The decreased production becomes the CR to the CS. This decrease leads to both tolerance and withdrawal. Tolerance occurs because more of the drug must be taken to compensate for the decreased production or effect of the neurotransmitter. If the environment occurs in which the drug was previously taken but the drug does not occur, then withdrawal symptoms appear because the environment evokes a conditioned decrease in production or effect of the transmitter (Eickelboom & Stewart, 1982). Experiments with animals have confirmed these learned effects: If a rat is addicted to a drug by injection and is then injected with a placebo (a compound that has no effect, such as a weak salt solution), then the rat promptly shows withdrawal symptoms (Higgins, Budney, & Bickel, 1994; Stewart, 2004). Withdrawal due to conditioned responses is a major reason that drug treatments often fail. Addicts become drug free during a rehabilitation program, but when they return to the environment in which they were previously addicted, conditioned withdrawal responses are evoked by that environment, and relapse is likely.

Natural selection has produced a learning mechanism that is sensitive to temporal contiguity—whether the stimulus–reinforcer relation of the classical procedure or the response–reinforcer relation of the operant procedure. Usually, it takes several co-occurrences of these events before the environmental control of behavior is changed, but phobias illustrate that only a single pairing may sometimes be sufficient (see also Staddon &

Simmelhag, 1971; Timberlake & Lucas, 1985). The contiguity requirement is reasonable, given the neural mechanisms that must underlie behavioral change. The underlying processes must occur at about the same time in interconnected neurons if the connectivity between them is to change. However, the contiguity requirement also begs the question: How can we understand those instances in which we appear to be sensitive to events that occur long after the response? For example, work done in the office on Monday is not compensated by a paycheck until the end of the week. How can behavior be maintained by a paycheck if the fundamental learning process requires temporal contiguity? We address this question later in the chapter.

Behavioral Discrepancy

For many years, temporal contiguity was thought to be the only requirement for learning: If the reinforcer occurred immediately after the CS in the classical procedure or immediately after the response in the operant procedure, then the environment became able to guide the response. However, in the late 1960s and the early 1970s, it became apparent that something in addition to contiguity was required.

The clearest demonstration that learning required a second factor was provided by the **blocking design** (Kamin, 1969). The blocking design is a two-stage experimental procedure that can be implemented with either the classical or the operant procedure. In its basic form, during the first stage, a stimulus is paired with a reinforcer until a response is conditioned to that stimulus. Then, in the second stage, the stimulus continues to be presented, but a second stimulus is introduced that comes on and goes off at the same time as the original stimulus, and the reinforcer continues to occur. Thus, the reinforcer now follows *both* stimuli. As a specific example, a tone might be paired with food, which conditions salivation to the tone. Then a light is presented at the same time as the tone, and food is given as before. If temporal contiguity were all that is required for learning, then the light should also become an effective CS because the light stands in the same temporal relation to the food as the tone did during the first stage. At the conclusion of the blocking design, when the tone was presented by itself, the CR occurred. However, when the light was presented by itself, the CR usually failed to occur. What the blocking design had discovered was that the light did *not* become an effective CS even though it had a favorable temporal relation to the reinforcer. Conditioning of the CR to the light was *blocked* by prior conditioning to the tone. (See FIGURE 5•8 for a summary of the blocking design.) Blocking of conditioning was first demonstrated with the classical procedure but was soon replicated with the operant procedure (vom Saal & Jenkins, 1970).

---

blocking design Two-phase procedure in which behavior is first conditioned to one stimulus, and then a second stimulus is introduced, and conditioning continues. Behavior does not become conditioned to the second stimulus even though it is temporally contiguous with the reinforcing stimulus.

[FIGURE 5•8] A blocking design. In the experimental (blocking) group, subjects are first conditioned to respond to CS1 by following CS1 with a US. During the second phase, CS2 is introduced and accompanies CS1, and both are followed by the US. In the test phase, when CS1 and CS2 each is presented alone, only CS1 evokes a CR. In the Control group, subjects receive the same procedure as in the second phase of the experimental group, except that CS1 has not been previously conditioned and does not evoke a CR. In the Test phase, both CS1 and CS2 evoke the CR for subjects in the control group.

	Experimental (blocking) group	Control group
Conditioning phase 1	CS1 (tone) ⟶ US (food)	CS3 (click) ⟶ US (food)
Conditioning phase 2	CS1 (tone) plus CS2 (light) ⟶ US (food)	CS1 (tone) plus CS2 (light) ⟶ US (food)
Test phase	CS1 (tone) presented alone — CR CS2 (light) presented alone — **no CR**	CS1 (tone) presented alone — CR CS2 (light) presented alone — CR

The simplest interpretation of the results of the blocking design, and many related findings, was provided by Robert Rescorla and Alan Wagner (1972). In behavioral terms, an eliciting stimulus functions as a reinforcer only if it evokes a response that is not already occurring (Donahoe et al., 1982). In the blocking design, the CS that was paired with an eliciting stimulus during the first stage evoked a *change* in behavior. When the second stimulus was introduced during the next stage of the experiment, the CS already evoked salivation because it had been previously paired with food. As a result, the presentation of food did not produce a sufficient change in ongoing behavior to permit the second stimulus to acquire the CR. Only a stimulus that evokes a behavioral change—a *behavioral discrepancy*—can function as a reinforcer. In short, if the learner is already behaving in a way that is evoked by an eliciting stimulus, then the eliciting stimulus does not function as a reinforcer in that environment. Note the great economy of the learning mechanism: Conditioning occurs only when the learner is not already behaving in a way that is appropriate for that environment.

It is difficult to test the behavioral-discrepancy requirement directly with humans—humans have such a rich history of experience before entering any experiment that almost every stimulus already controls some behavior. In addition, important human behavior is not easily measurable (for example, what a person thinks when a stimulus occurs). Nevertheless, evidence from studies of human behavior supports the conclusion from nonhuman experiments (Gluck & Bower, 1988; Arcediano, Matute, & Miller, 1997). Learning occurs only when the would-be reinforcer produces a change in behavior. Gordon Bower, a prominent contributor to the literature on human learning, put it this way: "The learning mechanism seems to be 'switched on' mainly when environmental events do not confirm expectations" (Bower, 1970, p. 70). Perhaps this is why parents who lavish praise on their children's behavior with little regard to its quality may find that that their praise is ineffective as a reinforcer. Frequent praise is not surprising. Conversely, parents who dole out praise more sparingly may find the same words quite effective as reinforcers. The more deprived the learner is of contact with an eliciting stimulus, the stronger the behavior that is evoked by that stimulus when it does appear.

The stronger the behavior evoked by a stimulus, the more effectively that stimulus functions as a reinforcer (cf. Premack, 1959; Timberlake & Allison, 1974).

focus On

Insight—Can Basic Learning Processes Help Understand Complex Behavior?

Many problems that we solve in our daily lives appear to require us to behave in new ways. We may think about a problem, look at its elements, and try to imagine various solutions. We explore various options in our heads. Suddenly, we think of a new approach. We try it, and it works! In such cases, we say that we solved the problem through insight.

What Is Insight?

But what is insight? Most people regard insight as a uniquely human ability. Here, we find that at least some instances of behavior from which we infer *insight* can emerge as the cumulative product of basic learning processes.

During the early 1900s, the German psychologist Wolfgang Köhler was working at a primate research facility on one of the Canary Islands off the western coast of Africa. While in the Canary Islands, he studied problem solving in chimpanzees. In a famous example, he suspended bananas from the ceiling of the cage out of the animal's reach (Köhler, 1927/1973). The cage also contained a large box. One of the chimps, Sultan, first tried to jump up to reach the bananas. When that failed, he paced around the cage for a while and then pushed the box toward the bananas, climbed onto the box, and reached the bananas! (See **FIGURE 5•9**.) Later, when the bananas were suspended even higher, he stacked up several boxes, and on one occasion when no boxes were present, he grabbed Köhler by the hand, led him over to the bananas, and climbed on top of him.

Köhler believed that Sultan's behavior demonstrated a type of behavior—insightful problem solving—that could not be understood in terms of basic learning processes. Because Köhler saw no evidence of trial-and-error behavior, he proposed that a new process—*insight*—was required to explain the behavior.

[**FIGURE 5•9**] Insight in the chimpanzee. On observing the behavior of the chimpanzee Sultan, Köhler inferred the mental process he called "insight." Confronted with bananas suspended out of reach from the ceiling, Sultan moved a box under the bananas and climbed onto the box (or, in another instance, onto Köhler himself) to reach the bananas. (Photos © SuperStock)

A Behavioral Interpretation of Insight

What Köhler called insightful behavior may actually arise from combinations of behavior previously learned through basic conditioning processes. In one study (Epstein et al., 1984), the researchers used operant procedures with pigeons to condition two behaviors: (1) pushing a box toward a target (a green spot placed at various locations on the floor of the test chamber), and (2) climbing onto a box and pecking a miniature plastic banana that was suspended from the ceiling. Each response was separately followed by food as a reinforcer. (Flying up to peck the banana never produced food and no longer occurred.) Once pushing, climbing and pecking had been separately learned, the researchers presented the pigeon with a new situation—the box was in one location in the chamber without a spot on the floor, and the suspended banana was in a different location. The pigeon now faced a situation much like that encountered by Köhler's chimpanzee Sultan. The experimenter observed the following behavior.

> At first, the bird appeared to be confused: It stretched toward the banana, turned back and forth from the banana to the box, and so on. Then, rather suddenly, it began to push the box toward the banana, sighting the banana and readjusting the path of the box as it pushed. Finally, it stopped pushing when the box was near the banana, climbed onto the box, and pecked the banana. (Epstein, 1985, p. 132)

The pigeon had behaved in much the same way as the chimpanzee. (See **FIGURE 5•10**.) An observer who did not know the learning history of the pigeon would be tempted to attribute the pigeon's behavior to insight or some other mental process.

Epstein (1987) went on to reinforce an even great number of responses in pigeons. Pigeons received food for (1) pecking a plastic banana, (2) climbing onto a box, (3) opening a door in the transparent chamber wall, and (4) pushing a box toward a spot on the floor. The pigeon was then confronted with a banana hanging from the ceiling, but the box was behind the door. The pigeon now combined all four behaviors: The pigeon opened the door, pushed the box into the chamber, moved the box under the banana, climbed the box, and pecked the banana.

What Should We Conclude?

The demonstrations with pigeons indicate that so-called insightful behavior may emerge from combinations of previously conditioned responses. Only after the pigeon had acquired the individual responses were the problems solved. Presumably, Sultan's prior experience, too, had included moving objects around, climbing on objects to reach other objects, and so on. Sultan had lived in the wild before Köhler's research, and his learning history was unknown. Therefore, we cannot interpret Sultan's behavior with the confidence that we interpret the behavior of the pigeon

[**FIGURE 5•10**] Insight in the pigeon. The pigeon was confronted with a small plastic banana suspended out of reach from the ceiling of the test chamber. During the pigeon's training, both pushing a box and pecking a reachable banana had been reinforced with food. (Flying to the banana had been extinguished.) After its training the pigeon pushed the box under the banana, climbed onto the box, and pecked the banana, even though the bird had never been trained to make this sequence of responses.

(Photos © Norman Baxley/Baxley Media Group.)

whose history is known. However, other work with chimpanzees has shown that they solve such problems only if they have prior experience with the objects (Birch, 1945).

In Chapter 2, you learned about the *nominal fallacy*, the mistaken belief that we have explained a phenomenon simply by naming it. Simply labeling behavior as insightful does not help to understand it. If we do not know the behavior that an animal has already learned, a novel and complex sequence of responses may seem to come from nowhere. Our ignorance of the learner's history leads us to attribute the complex behavior to something inside of the learner—insight—instead of to the learner's history. To understand the conditions that are necessary for insight, we need to know more than the current situation; we need to know the learner's history.

The scientist's challenge is to dissect even the most complex behavior so that its true origins can be identified. Perhaps chimpanzees, like humans, can solve problems through some sort of mental imagery, testing possible solutions in their heads before trying them. But if such constructs as "mental imagery" and "testing solutions in one's head" are to be used, they too must be subjected to experimental analysis (Donahoe & Palmer, 1994/2005). Whatever the case, neither humans nor chimpanzees can imagine or think about objects they have never seen or actions they have never taken.

QUESTIONS TO CONSIDER

1. How would you show the roles of contiguity and discrepancy in a real-life situation?
2. In a classical procedure, the experimenter can study backward conditioning in which the reinforcer (US) comes before the CS. In an operant procedure, why can't the experimenter present the reinforcing stimulus first and then vary the time until the operant response occurs?

The Process of Learning

Psychologists who study basic learning processes believe that they will help us understand even the most complex human behavior. Just as natural selection now helps us understand the origins of complex structure (including the brain and human evolution), so basic learning processes will eventually help us understand complex function (including such behavior as problem solving and language). We learn to perceive the world, to remember what we perceive, to speak about what we remember, and so on. We now examine some important features of learning.

Acquisition

When a response is followed by a reinforcer, the response becomes stronger—more frequent, more vigorous. That is,

[**FIGURE 5•11**] An operant chamber used for the conditioning of lever pressing in rats. When the rat presses the lever, a small pellet of food can be delivered.

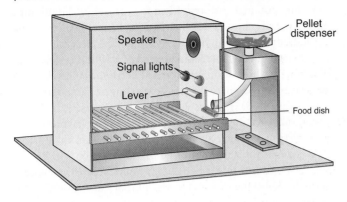

Speaker

Signal lights

Lever

Pellet dispenser

Food dish

acquisition occurs. Reinforcers change the way the environment guides behavior. Even simple laboratory procedures, such as training a rat to press a lever for food, require several stages. First, the animal is placed in a test chamber and allowed to explore the environment. (See **FIGURE 5•11**.) Exploration permits responses to weaken to various extraneous stimuli in the environment. This weakening is called **habituation** and is a simple form of learning. Habituation occurs when environmental stimuli enable responses, but the responses have no important consequences. For example, a rat might look toward the ceiling of the chamber and then rear up on its hind legs. However, if rearing has no effect (such as allowing the rat to escape the chamber), rearing declines in strength. The decline in rearing is an example of habituation. Rearing was an orienting response to stimuli from the ceiling. Responses that aid the detection of stimuli are called **orienting responses.** In Pavlov's procedure, an orienting response occurred when the dog turned toward the sound of the metronome. Habituation ensures that responses that might compete with lever pressing have a low strength. Second, the animal receives a few presentations of food from a feeder before beginning the operant procedure. Feeder training ensures that food is an effective elicitor of behavior— here, approach and eating. Last, the experimenter arranges an operant procedure in which lever pressing is followed immediately by food. Once habituation and feeder training have taken place, even a single lever press followed by food is often enough to produce increases in the strength of lever pressing, as shown in **FIGURE 5•12** (Skinner, 1938).

Shaping Most learning does not take place in a highly controlled environment, such as a test chamber. Also, the behavior that is acquired is not as simple as lever pressing. Most behavior is learned under more variable stimulus conditions and involves more complex responses. Because of this, acquisition often requires **shaping.** In shaping, a target response is acquired by reinforcing successively closer approximations to its final form. Suppose that other responses have not been habituated and that these responses compete with approaching

and touching the lever. To reduce competition, the experimenter would first deliver food when the animal merely looks at the lever, then walks toward the lever, and finally touches the lever. Given this shaping procedure, the first press would measurably increase in strength after the first food delivery. Shaping is not restricted to interventions by experimenters. The natural environment often shapes behavior. For example, some ways of pressing the lever are more efficient than others—pressing with a paw rather than the nose. Over time, the more efficient response is usually shaped by natural contingencies without the intervention of an experimenter.

Most applications of learning involve shaping (McIlvane & Dube, 2003). For example, a teacher first praises even poorly formed letters by a child just learning to write. Over time, only more accurately drawn letters are followed by approval. Shaping is also used to condition the behavior of children with behavioral problems or developmental disabilities (Sulzer-Azaroff & Mayer, 1991; Kazdin, 2005). Consider what seems to be a simple skill such as brushing one's teeth. This skill actually consists of a series of responses, each under the guidance of somewhat different stimuli. Teaching developmentally disabled children to brush their teeth is not accomplished

---

acquisition Increase in the environmental guidance of behavior as the result of either a classical- or operant-conditioning procedure.

habituation Decrease in responding to a stimulus after that stimulus is repeatedly presented without an important consequence.

orienting response Response that facilitates detecting a stimulus (for example, turning toward the source of a sound).

shaping Procedure in which successively closer approximations to a target behavior are reinforced; commonly used when acquiring complex behavior.

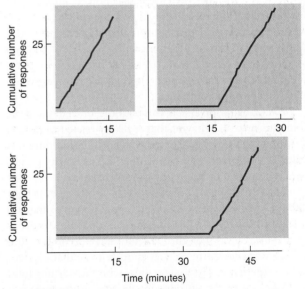

[**FIGURE 5•12**] Lever pressing after the first press was followed by a food pellet for three different animals. Note that responding was immediately strengthened and continued as further presses were also followed by food.

(Adapted from Skinner, B. F. (1938). *Behavior of Organisms.* New York: Appleton-Century.)

Parents use shaping to help their children acquire complex behavior.

by simply reinforcing proficient tooth brushing (the target response) but by reinforcing each member of the chain of responses that ultimately leads to the target behavior.

Natural Selection and Learning

Reinforcement is the process by which individual experience changes the environmental guidance of behavior. The potential for behavior to be reinforced is a product of natural selection. Reinforcement must contribute to reproductive fitness for natural selection to favor the biological mechanisms that implement it. The adaptive value of learning is obvious: Organisms that learn to interact effectively with other members of their species, to avoid predators, to gather and hunt food, and so on are more likely to survive and reproduce.

Learned behavior affects competition for mates and reproductive success, behavior that is clearly related to fitness. To document this in the laboratory, a classical procedure was instituted for a male Siamese fighting fish. A warning light came on immediately before the male was allowed to see (but not contact) another male (Hollis; 1982). As a result, the light became a CS for the behavioral and neural responses that are elicited by the sight of a possible competitor. After this experience, the light was then turned on for a few seconds before the male was allowed to contact another male that had not had this experience. The male trained with the warning light won its fight with the untrained male. Similarly, a male fish

---

reinforcement Process by which a reinforcer increases the environmental guidance of behavior.

taste aversion Conditioning in which a distinctive taste (or smell) is paired with an ingested food that produces nausea, effective even with long intervals between the taste and nausea.

that previously received a light paired with the sight of a female mated sooner and produced more offspring than a male that did not have the training (Hollis, 1997). In the natural environment, male fish that learn to respond to stimuli indicating the presence of another male or female would have a reproductive advantage over males that did not learn.

A particularly interesting example of the interplay between natural selection and learned behavior is provided by **taste aversions** (Garcia, Erwin, & Koelling, 1966; LoLordo & Droungas, 1989). In a taste-aversion experiment, an animal ingests a food with a novel taste, such as lemon flavoring. The animal is then injected with a substance that produces sickness, such as the nausea induced by lithium chloride. Even if the distinctive-tasting food is eaten hours before the nausea-inducing substance is injected, the animal learns to avoid that taste in the future. From an evolutionary perspective, the relation of taste and odor stimuli to alimentary responses is a special one: The only way for substances to enter the stomach is through the mouth, which necessarily stimulates gustatory and olfactory receptors. Because of the invariant relation over evolutionary time of taste and smell with ingestion, neural pathways that facilitate taste-aversion learning were naturally selected. An animal in the wild often takes a small bite of a novel substance and waits before ingesting more. If the animal becomes ill, it does not eat the substance again. The ability of gustatory and olfactory stimuli to acquire control of ingestive behavior, even though nausea does not occur for an appreciable time thereafter, is clearly adaptive.

Conditioned taste aversions complicate the treatment of cancer with chemotherapy. The nausea induced by chemotherapy becomes conditioned to the taste of the food that was most recently consumed. The patient then avoids that food later. This causes weight loss, which further harms the patient. To ward off chemotherapy-induced taste aversions, the patient is asked to consume a distinctively flavored, but nonpreferred, food before chemotherapy. Any conditioned taste aversion then involves only the nonpreferred food.

Conditioned Reinforcement

In laboratory studies of learning, experimenters typically use reinforcers that elicit responses that can be easily measured. Such responses can provide an objective measure of the progress of learning. Stimuli that evoke easily measured responses do so because of natural selection. For instance, a sweet substance on the tongue elicits sucking responses in infants. If organisms learn to respond to environmental stimuli that reliably precede eliciting stimuli, then the appropriate behavior begins to occur just as the reinforcer appears. For example, the sweet substance becomes more rapidly ingested. Natural selection has produced a nervous system that strengthens new environment–behavior relations because of their benefit to survival. Once evolved, the capacity for learning is exploited by other stimuli that may not evoke such easily measured behavior. For example, saying "good" after a child cleans her room strengthens that behavior, but hearing "good" does not evoke easily detectable behavior. Nevertheless, if overt behavior were not initially evoked by reinforcing stimuli, the biological mechanisms of reinforcement could never have been naturally selected. Natural selection by the environment can act only on behavior that actually occurs (the *behavioral phenotype*).

Human behavior is often reinforced by stimuli that do not evoke readily detectable responses. A child's letter writing improves with praise from a teacher, but praise itself does not evoke an obvious response. Perhaps praise evokes a subtle smile from the child, but nothing as clear-cut as a reflexive elicited response. And yet, praise from a teacher clearly serves as a reinforcer—letter writing improves. How can stimuli that do not evoke obvious responses serve as reinforcers when laboratory studies have determined that reinforcers are stimuli that evoke changes in behavior?

Pavlov and Skinner realized very early in their work that many reinforcing stimuli do not elicit easily identifiable behavior. However, they soon discovered that a stimulus would become a reinforcer if it were followed by an eliciting stimulus that did evoke behavior. By being paired with an eliciting stimulus, these formerly neutral stimuli became reinforcers themselves. Stimuli that acquire the ability to serve as reinforcers are called **conditioned,** or secondary, **reinforcers.** They are called conditioned reinforcers because their reinforcing ability is *conditional* on an individual's experience, not on natural selection. (Such stimuli are also called *secondary reinforcers,* but we prefer conditioned reinforcers because they are by no means secondary in importance for behavior outside the laboratory.) In Skinner's demonstrations of conditioning with food as a reinforcer (refer to Figure 5.12), food was accompanied by a "clicking" sound when the apparatus delivered food. Before lever-press training began, the "click" was established as a conditioned reinforcer by pairing the click with food. Once conditioning began, the "click" sounded *immediately* after a lever press. If the immediate "click" had not been given, then other responses that intervened between lever pressing and food might be strengthened more than lever pressing.

Automatic Conditioned Reinforcement Conditioned reinforcement for approximations to a target behavior is not dependent on the intervention of another person. In nontechnical terms, realizing that you are "on the right track" reinforces approximations to the target behavior. As behavior ever more closely approximates the target behavior, the stimuli produced by this behavior provide further conditioned reinforcers. The process is analogous to changing the criteria for reinforcers when training the behavior of an animal, except that no trainer is required. The automatic feedback from stimuli produced by behaving shapes the behavior automatically. Skills such as learning to draw a picture benefit from shaping with automatic conditioned reinforcement. The more similar the picture is to the appearance of the object, the greater the reinforcement for drawing.

Automatic conditioned reinforcement plays an especially important role in the acquisition of language. Consider a child first learning the meaning of a speech sound. The child might be asked to point to a dog in a picture book when a parent says, "Where's the *dog*?" Correct pointing behavior is then reinforced by the parent saying "That's right," a phrase that has already

For most people, handshakes, smiles, awards, and other forms of social approval serve as important forms of conditioned reinforcement.

been established as a conditioned reinforcer through the child's prior experience. The speech sound "dog" is thereby itself established as a stimulus that can function as a conditioned reinforcer because it has been paired with another conditioned reinforcer, "That's right." Later, as the child speaks, the more closely its own vocal responses produce sounds that are similar to the sound "dog," the greater the immediate automatic conditioned reinforcement for those vocal responses (Jusczyk, 2000). Correct pronunciation is automatically reinforced.

Extinction

Thus far, we have considered the implications of reinforcement for the *acquisition* of behavior—for increases in the strength with which the environment guides behavior. But we know that experience can also weaken behavior. Previously learned behavior can apparently be lost, such as the French vocabulary that you learned in middle school or the methods for solving quadratic equations that you learned only last year. One experience by which behavior is weakened is called

---

conditioned (secondary) reinforcer Stimulus that can function as a reinforcer after it has been paired with another stimulus that can already function as a reinforcer.

automatic reinforcement Process in which a behavior inherently produces stimuli that function as reinforcers for that same behavior; especially important in language acquisition.

[**FIGURE 5•13**] Conditioned responding during acquisition with CS–US pairings (left panel), during maintenance of conditioning with different percentages of CS–US pairings (middle panel), and during extinction when the US was not presented (right panel).

(Adapted from Gibbs, C. M., Latham, S. B., & Gormezano, I. (1978). Classical schedule and resistance to extinction. *Animal Learning and Behavior, 6,* 209–215.)

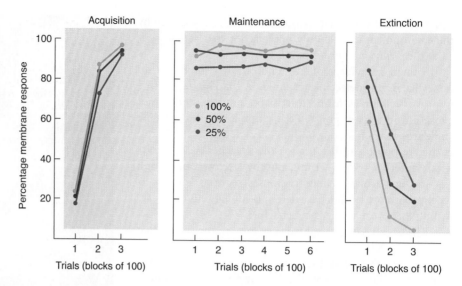

extinction. In **extinction,** a previously reinforced response is no longer reinforced, with the result that the response weakens. Just as changes in the ancestral environment may lead to extinction of a species, so changes in the individual environment may lead to extinction of behavior.

Consider a classical procedure in which a CS is presented to a rabbit followed by an aversive US applied in the region of the eye. The US elicits a nictitating-membrane response as the UR (Gibbs, Latham, & Gormezano, 1978). As shown in the left panel of FIGURE 5•13, when rabbits in three different groups were conditioned according to this procedure, responding during the CS increased to a high level. This illustrates acquisition. The training procedure was then changed so that the percentages of CS presentations followed by the US were gradually decreased. One group of animals continued to receive the US after 100% of the CSs, the second group was reduced to 50%, and the third group to only 25%. As the middle panel of Figure 5.13 shows, slowly reducing the number of reinforcers had relatively little effect on the level of responding. This illustrates a general finding: Frequent reinforcers are required for efficient acquisition of behavior, but behavior may often be maintained by less frequent reinforcers (for other effects of decreases in reinforcement, see Nevin & Grace, 2005).

The third panel of Figure 5.13 shows the effects of an extinction procedure. When the CS was no longer followed by a reinforcer, responding decreased until it reached the level seen before conditioning. The extinction findings illustrate a further point: Responding decreases less rapidly if behavior was previously maintained by *less* frequent reinforcers. This surprising finding is a general result: Responding that has been maintained by less-frequent reinforcers is often more

resistant to the effects of extinction. Technically, procedures in which not all instances of behavior are followed by a reinforcer are called **intermittent**, or **partial, reinforcement procedures.** In these terms, the finding illustrates that intermittent reinforcement increases resistance to extinction (Azrin, Hutchison, & Hake, 1966; Amsel, 1992; Capaldi et al., 2005).

Extinction does not completely eliminate the effects of prior reinforcement. If reinforcers again occur after the behavior has undergone extinction, it rapidly recovers its former strength. Reacquisition after extinction is generally much more rapid than original acquisition. Also, if an appreciable time elapses between the extinction procedure and the test for retention of conditioning, the learned response usually recovers some of its strength. The increase in responding on return to the training environment after extinction is called **spontaneous recovery.** Both rapid reacquisition and spontaneous recovery demonstrate that extinction does not completely eliminate the effects of prior learning (Estes, 1955; Kehoe, 1988).

Gambling behavior is resistant to extinction because it is intermittently reinforced.

---

extinction Decrease in a learned behavior when the behavior is no longer followed by a reinforcer.

intermittent (partial) reinforcement Procedure in which not every occurrence of a behavior is followed by a reinforcer; increases resistance to the effects of extinction.

spontaneous recovery Increase in a previously extinguished response after the passage of time.

Stimulus Generalization

We have so far focused on the behavioral changes that occur in the specific environment in which the behavior was reinforced, but the effects of experience must affect behavior in other circumstances for learning to be efficient. Children who learn to catch a red ball should also improve their ability to catch a green ball. Children who learn to read with one type font should also be able to read other type fonts. Experimental work has shown that the effects of reinforcement are not restricted to the specific environment in which learning took place. The process by which learning in one environment affects behavior in similar environments is called **stimulus generalization.**

The animal laboratory provides a clear example of stimulus generalization. Pigeons were trained to peck a yellow–green disk (wavelength of 550 nm) located on the wall of a test chamber with food as a reinforcer (Hanson, 1959). Intermittent reinforcement was used so that the operant response was resistant to the effects of extinction. Once responding became stable, the color on the disk was occasionally changed during brief periods in which reinforcers were not given. If the test stimuli had also acquired control of pecking, then stimulus generalization occurred. The results of the experiment are shown in FIGURE 5•14. Even though operant responding had been reinforced only during the yellow–green stimulus, responses now occurred to other colors. Moreover, the strength of responding varied with the similarity of the test stimuli to the training stimulus. When the disk was green or yellow, the pigeon pecked more frequently than when it was blue or orange.

Behavior that has been reinforced in one environment occurs in other environments if the other environments contain stimuli in common with the environment in which the behavior was reinforced. As a result of stimulus generalization, behavior increasingly consists of a rich mixture of responses that are available for modification by subsequent reinforcers.

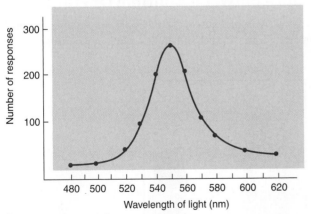

[**FIGURE 5•14**] Generalized responding to various colors (wavelengths) after training to respond to a yellow-green color (550 nm).

(Adapted from Hanson, H. M. (1959). Effects of discrimination training on stimulus generalization. *Journal of Experimental Psychology, 38*, 1–16.)

Stimulus Discrimination

Similar behavior is often similarly reinforced in similar environments. As a result, natural selection has produced a nervous system that supports stimulus generalization. Animals that learn to approach one area where water is found are also likely to approach other similar-appearing areas. However, similar environments do not always provide reinforcers for similar behavior. Some waterholes have lurking predators. When the consequences of behavior change as the environment changes, **stimulus discrimination** occurs.

Again, the animal laboratory provides the clearest examples of the formation of stimulus discriminations. As one example, pigeons whose pecking was reinforced when the disk was yellow–green received additional training in which the yellow–green color (550 nm) on the disk alternated with a yellow color (555 nm). Responding during yellow was never followed by food (Hanson, 1959). That is, an extinction procedure was instituted during yellow. Responding to the 555-nm yellow stimulus now decreased to fewer than 25 responses from about 200 responses during the test of stimulus generalization (refer to Figure 5.14). For more dissimilar stimuli—such as orange—responding fell to essentially zero. A procedure in which a response has different consequences in different environments is called a **differential conditioning procedure.** Differential conditioning produces stimulus discrimination. Stimuli that guide behavior after differential conditioning are called **discriminative stimuli.**

A differential conditioning procedure is an example of a *three-term* contingency (Donahoe, 2006a). A simple classical procedure is a *two-term* stimulus-reinforcer contingency. A simple operant procedure is a *two-term* response-reinforcer contingency. The three terms in differential conditioning are stimulus-response-reinforcer. In the preceding experiment with pigeons, differential conditioning was given in which responding was reinforced when the color was yellow–green, but not when it was yellow. What happens when a differential conditioning procedure institutes still higher-order contingencies? As an example of a four-term contingency, suppose that during a green stimulus, responding to a triangular form is reinforced, but responses to the green stimulus are not reinforced if the form is circular. On other trials in which a red stimulus is present, the three-term contingency is reversed: When red, responding to the circle is reinforced, but not to the triangle. In this procedure, the consequence of a response depends on *both* color and shape, a *four-term* contingency—

stimulus generalization Process by which behavior occurs in an environment in which it has not been reinforced, but which is similar to that environment.

stimulus discrimination Process by which the environmental guidance of behavior is restricted to the environment in which the behavior was reinforced; can be produced by extinguishing the response in other environments.

differential conditioning procedure Procedure in which behavior has different consequences as the environment changes.

discriminative stimulus Stimulus that controls behavior as the result of a differential conditioning procedure.

[**FIGURE 5•15**] A contextual discrimination. In the context of a color (green or red), responses to the shapes (triangle or circle) are reinforced differently.

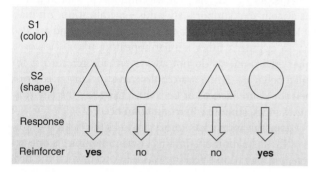

color-shape-response-reinforcer. (See FIGURE 5•15.) As the color context changes, reinforcement for responding to the different shapes changes. Procedures that implement four-term contingencies are often called **contextual discriminations.**

Equivalence Classes Both animal and human learners can learn four-term stimulus discriminations. Of greatest interest, Murray Sidman (1994) discovered that after human learners have acquired a number of different four-term discriminations, something new happens. To describe the procedure, it is useful to introduce some notation: The first stimulus in the notation indicates the contextual stimulus; the second stimulus indicates the discriminative stimuli to which the responses are differentially reinforced in that context. (See Figure 5.15.) For example, learners first acquire two separate *contextual discriminations*—an S1-S2-response-reinforcer discrimination and an S2-S3-response-reinforcer discrimination. Afterward, subjects can respond differentially to *new* stimulus combinations such as S1-S1, S2-S1, or S3-S1 *without further training*.

---

contextual discrimination Discrimination procedure in which the stimulus in whose presence the behavior is reinforced varies with the value of another stimulus, the stimulus context.

equivalence class A set of physically unrelated stimuli that all control the appropriate behavior without direct training after the stimuli have appeared in multiple contextual discriminations.

Consider the stimulus combination S3-S1. In stimulus context S3, the learner responds to S1 when given a choice between responding to S1 and other stimuli. This occurs even though responding to S1 was never reinforced in the context of S3. Human learners with a history of multiple, contextual discriminations respond to new combinations of these stimuli as if they were equivalent to one another. The stimuli are said to become members of an **equivalence class.** Despite substantial experimental effort, these emergent contextual discriminations have not been unequivocally observed in nonhumans (Sidman et al., 1982). The origin of the difference between our species and all others is not yet known. Is it due to differences in prior experience, and if so, what specific experiences are critical? Or is it due to differences in brain anatomy? (See Donahoe & Palmer, 1994/2005; Hayes, Fox, & Gifford, 2001; Hayes & Barnes-Holmes, 2001; Lowe, Horne, & Harris, 2002; Palmer, 2004; Schlund, Hoelin-Sarie, & Cataldo, 2007.)

Equivalence classes have important practical uses. Intellectually impaired children have been taught to read without explicit training. In one case, a mentally retarded boy could speak the name of an object when he saw its picture and could point to the picture when given its name. He was then trained to point to the correct printed word among several choices when he heard that word spoken by the experimenter. Note that the child had not been trained to respond to printed words with spoken words, that is, to read orally. Nevertheless, after acquiring these contextual discriminations, the child was able to speak the correct word the first time he was presented with the printed word. (See FIGURE 5•16.) That is, without explicit training, the child could read aloud! Moreover, the child also picked out the correct picture when presented with the printed word (a measure of reading comprehension). This also occurred without additional training. The study of multiple contextual discriminations is an active area of research because of both its theoretical and practical significance.

Choice between Multiple Operants

In many environments, any of a number of responses can produce reinforcers. In such situations, we are said to *choose* among

Learned relation
picture = spoken word
S1 = S2

Learned relation
printed word = picture
S3 = S1

Emergent relation
printed word = spoken word
S3 = S2 (oral reading)

[**FIGURE 5•16**] After a child with mental disabilities had learned to speak the name of an object when seeing its picture (left panel) and to point to an object when seeing the printed word (middle panel), the child was able to speak the name of the object when seeing the printed word (right panel). That is, the child was capable of oral reading without explicit training.

the responses. Consider this example: You are sitting in your dormitory room or apartment. Should you watch television, listen to music on your MP3 player, talk to your roommate, call a friend to work-out at the gym, go to the cafeteria, or—even— read the next assignment in your introductory psychology course? What do we know about learning that helps us understand choice?

Charles Ferster and B. F. Skinner (1957) began systematic work on choice and it has been most extensively studied by Richard Herrnstein and his colleagues (de Villieurs, 1977; Baum, 1979; Williams, 1988). In these studies, the learner is confronted with two or more possible responses, each with its own reinforcement schedule. For example, a pigeon might be simultaneously presented with two disks on the wall of the chamber; pecking the left disk produces food an average of once per minute, and pecking the right disk, twice per minute.

Experiments conducted with a variety of species, including humans, have yielded results of the type shown in FIGURE 5•17 (a). In a choice procedure, the proportion of responses to an alternative matches the proportion of reinforcers received for responding to that alternative. If twice as many reinforcers are received for pecking one disk, then twice as many responses are made to that disk. These findings illustrate the **matching principle.**

Subsequent research revealed that the matching relation between responding and reinforcers develops over time as the learner gains experience with the various alternatives. FIGURE 5•17 (b) shows that if the alternatives have been experienced only separately and never after switching between the alternatives, then the learner exclusively chooses the alternative that has been most frequently reinforced. However, after gaining reinforcers by switching between the alternatives, responding conforms to the matching principle. The findings shown in Figure 5.17B are from the same animal shown in panel A, but before switching had been reinforced (Crowley & Donahoe, 2004). Thus, oper-

ants of switching between the alternatives must be acquired before the matching relation emerges (see also Pliskoff, 1971; Silberberg, Hamilton, & Ziriax, 1978; Boelens et al., 1986). The matching principle has informed research on the foraging of animals in the wild as they search for food in different areas (Houston, 1987; Bell & Baum, 2002). It has also been applied to consumer choice in microeconomics, leading to the interdisciplinary field of behavioral economics (Hursh, 1984; Rachlin, 1995; Herrnstein, Rachlin, & Laibson, 1997).

focus On

Self-Control—How Does Conditioned Reinforcement Affect Self-Control?

Impulsive behavior is behavior that produces an immediate reinforcer when another available behavior would produce a larger—but delayed—reinforcer. Students who choose to go out with friends on the night before an important examination are displaying impulsive behavior in this sense. Doing well on the exam leads to a better grade at the end of the semester and, perhaps, ultimately to a better job. *Self-control* occurs when the learner chooses a delayed larger reinforcer over an immediate smaller reinforcer. A person who foregoes dessert after dinner to look better in a bathing suit next summer is displaying self-control. But how can self-control occur if behavior is strengthened by temporal contiguity between a response and a reinforcer? Would not the immediate small reinforcer always make the impulsive response stronger than the self-control response?

Psychologists have studied the emergence of self-control with both nonhuman and human learners. Learners that do not have certain kinds of experience almost always chose the immediate smaller reinforcer whether they are young children, rats, or pigeons (Green, Price, & Hamburger, 1995; Logue, 2002; Ainslie, 2003; Hackenburg, 2003). As an example, pigeons may be presented with one disk, to which pecking produces immediate access to a small amount of food, and a second disk, to which pecking produces a larger amount of food after a delay of 10 seconds. Or children may be presented with two pushbuttons, one produces a toy immediately, whereas the other produces a more-favored toy but after a delay of 10 seconds. Under these conditions, pigeons and children each choose the immediate smaller reinforcer. A change from impulsive behavior to self-control occurs when the response that produces the larger but delayed reinforcer is *immediately* followed by a conditioned reinforcer. For instance, a peck to the disk that produces a larger but delayed reinforcer could immediately cause the disk to turn green, with green persisting until food appeared 10 seconds later.

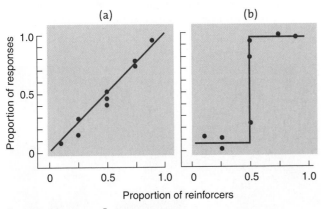

(a)   (b)

[FIGURE 5•17] Relation between the proportion of responses to one alternative and the proportion of the total reinforcers received for responding to that alternative. (a) The matching relation *after* the subject learns to switch responding between the two alternatives. (b) The almost exclusive preference for the alternative, with the higher proportion of reinforcers *before* learning to switch. (Adapted from Crowley, M. A., & Donahoe, J. W. (2004). Matching: Its acquisition and generalization. *Journal of the Experimental Analysis of Behavior, 82,* 143–159.)

matching principle In a choice situation, the proportion of responses occurring during a stimulus is the same as the proportion of reinforcers received during that stimulus.

With the immediate green conditioned reinforcer, choice shifts from impulsivity to self-control.

A second way to exploit conditioned reinforcement uses shaping. First, both responses are immediately reinforced with their respective unequal reinforcers. When no delay of reinforcement occurs, the response that produces the larger reinforcer predominates. Then the delay after the response that produces the larger reinforcer is gradually increased, while the immediate smaller reinforcer continues as before. This procedure allows stimuli characteristic of the delay period to become conditioned reinforcers because they immediately precede the larger reinforcer. Under such circumstances, the learner often persists with the self-control response (Logue et al., 1984; cf. Kehoe, Horne & Macrae, 1993).

Both of these laboratory-based, conditioned-reinforcement procedures have been used to treat impulsive responses in children with dysfunctional behavior (Stromer, McComas, & Rehfeldt, 2000). As an example, preschool children who were described by their teachers as "impulsive" consistently chose a small, immediate reinforcer and not a larger delayed reinforcer. When the procedure was changed so that the larger reinforcer now occurred immediately after its response and the delay to the reinforcer was *gradually* increased, the children shifted to the self-control response. Moreover, this behavior continued in a follow-up test several weeks later (Schweitzer & Sulzer-Azaroff, 1988).

Recent work in a natural setting confirms the adaptive value of self-control over impulsive behavior. Children who made predominantly self-control responses in laboratory tests when they were 4 years old had higher SAT scores later in life and were judged more interpersonally skillful by their peers (Mischel, Shoda, & Rodriguez, 1989). Children who behaved impulsively in the laboratory were also more apt to engage in drug use as adults, a relation between impulsivity and addiction that has been found with nonhuman animals as well (Ayduk et al., 2000; Dalley et al., 2007).

A study conducted in a very different society came to a similar conclusion. People living in a village in the Bolivian rainforest were given a choice between a relatively immediate reinforcer and a larger delayed reinforcer (Reyes-García et al., 2007). The more formal education the villagers had, the more likely they chose the delayed, but larger reinforcer. Apparently, education facilitated the generation of conditioned reinforcers that filled the temporal gap between the

choice response and the larger reinforcer. For example, a villager might write down how much was owed him and consult this record from time to time. When the investigators returned to the village five years later, they found that those who previously chose the larger delayed reinforcer had accumulated more wealth through their daily activities than those who had acted impulsively. Over a twenty-year period, the villagers who had displayed self-control in the original study were predicted to accumulate twice as much wealth! The anthropologists entitled their research "The origins of monetary income inequality." The ability to tolerate delay in reinforcement through the use of conditioned reinforcers is clearly adaptive.

Punishment

Thus far we have considered cases in which eliciting stimuli act as reinforcers; that is, they strengthen the behavior that precedes them. However, other eliciting stimuli can *weaken* the behavior that precedes them. Such stimuli act as **punishing stimuli** or **punishers.** In the animal laboratory, a punishment procedure is commonly studied by occasionally following a food-reinforced response with a moderate electric shock. Lever pressing decreases from its food-reinforced level. The shock functions as a punisher. In daily life, punishment occurs when a child reaches for candy in the grocery store, and the mother slaps the child's hand. Reaching for candy decreases, and the slap has functioned as a punisher. Stimuli act as punishers if they elicit responses that interfere with the operant that precedes them. Punishers elicit **escape** or **withdrawal behavior** and a variety of emotional responses mediated by the autonomic nervous system.

A laboratory procedure called the **conditioned emotional-response (CER),** or **conditioned-suppression procedure** uses interference between operants and shock-elicited responses to provide an indirect measure of emotional responses (Estes & Skinner, 1941). In the CER procedure, a stimulus (such as a tone) is paired with electric shock, and the tone is occasionally

Punishment occurs when an aversive stimulus immediately follows a response. Punishment need not involve a physically aversive event; social disapproval also can be punishing. Punishers elicit withdrawal, escape, and emotional behavior, so they must be used with caution.

---

punishing stimulus (punisher) Stimulus that evokes escape and withdrawal responses that interfere with the behavior that produced it.

punishment Process by which a stimulus decreases the strength of behavior by conditioning responses that interfere with the operant.

escape or withdrawal response Response that terminates or reduces contact with an aversive stimulus; the aversive stimulus may be either conditioned or unconditioned.

conditioned emotional response (CER), or conditioned suppression Procedure in which an operant response is decreased by a stimulus that has been paired with an aversive stimulus.

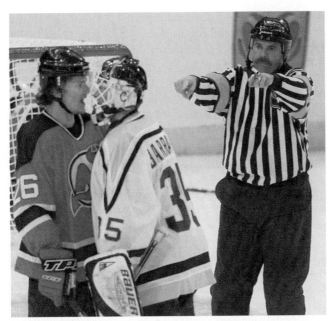

Punishment takes many forms. The aversive consequences of a penalty reduce the likelihood of an infraction.

1. We have covered a number of the effects of learning—acquisition, shaping, extinction, conditioned reinforcement, extinction, stimulus generalization, and stimulus discrimination. Can you think of real-life examples that illustrate each?
2. How can punishment strengthen the behavior of the punisher but weaken the behavior of the punished?

Biological Basis of Reinforcement

Behavioral research has revealed a great deal about the conditions necessary for learning and the process of learning itself. However, are basic learning processes rich enough to produce complex behavior as their cumulative effect—especially complex human behavior? A somewhat similar question was raised about natural selection in the earlier history of evolutionary science. That is, could the cumulative effect of a relatively simple process such as natural selection produce the tremendous complexity and diversity of life? A major factor that convinced science that natural selection could have such wide-reaching effects was the discovery of its biological basis—genetics. Skinner has encouraged the effort to find the biological basis of selection by reinforcement for, perhaps, similar reasons: "The physiologist of the future will tell us all that can be known about what is happening inside the behaving organism. His account will be an important advance over a behavioral analysis, because the latter is necessarily "historical"—that is to say, it is confined to functional relations showing temporal gaps. . . . What he discovers cannot invalidate the laws of a science of behavior, but it will make the picture of human action more nearly complete" (Skinner, 1974, pp. 236–237).

In this section, we describe some of what has been uncovered about the biological basis of learning. The search for the biological basis of learning is a very active area of current research, although it has not yet advanced as far as genetics. Nevertheless, enough is known to encourage the belief that a principle of reinforcement may have as far-reaching implications for complex function as natural selection has for complex structure (Donahoe, 2003). Here, we describe some of the neural systems and cellular processes of reinforcement.

presented while an animal is engaged in operant behavior (such as lever pressing for food). After several tone–shock pairings, operant responding decreases during the tone even before the shock appears. This decrease occurs because escape and emotional responses have become conditioned to the tone, and they interfere with lever pressing. The rat cannot simultaneously press the lever and escape from the region where the shock is given (that is, where the lever is located). Because of interference between lever pressing and shock-elicited conditioned responses, lever pressing decreases.

The Effects of Punishment The relation between operant responses and elicited responses must be considered with punishment procedures. As a particularly troubling example, spanking a child for crying uses an aversive stimulus (pain from spanking) that elicits the very behavior that the parent is trying to punish. This is not an effective procedure, in addition to its other drawbacks.

Punishment can very effectively decrease responding, but often with undesirable consequences. Consider the case in which one person punishes the behavior of another. For example, a parent whose television viewing is interrupted by children talking may stop the talking by yelling, "Shut up!" ("Shut up!" has presumably been paired with aversive stimuli in the past, for example, spanking. Thus "Shut up!" has become a conditioned punisher.) The offending behavior ceases, which immediately reinforces the behavior of the one who administered the punishment. The parent can return to the television viewing that was interrupted. However, the emotional responses elicited when the child hears "Shut up!" become conditioned to the parent. The child not only stops talking but also may stay away from the parent in the future. Punishers can be effective in the short run, but their longer-term consequences may not be.

Neural Systems of Reinforcement

Both unconditioned reinforcers, such as food, and conditioned reinforcers, such as stimuli paired with food, activate a partially common reinforcing system in the brain. Food stimulates taste and smell receptors whose axons eventually activate neurons located in nuclei in the ventral-tegmental area (VTA) of the midbrain. VTA neurons, in turn, send their axons to widespread regions of the frontal lobes and various midbrain structures,

[**FIGURE 5•18**] The frequency of firing of a single neuron in the ventral tegmental areas (VTA) of the midbrain. The upper tracing shows firing when the US was first presented. The lower tracing shows firing when a CS was presented after being paired with US.

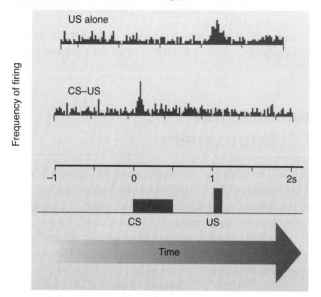

where they release the neuromodulator **dopamine.** Dopamine is intimately involved in the cellular processes that change the strength of connections (*synaptic efficacies*) between neurons. Because of the widespread projections of dopamine-releasing axons, dopamine can simultaneously affect synaptic efficacies between many neurons (Frey, 1997; cf. Donahoe & Palmer, 1994/2005).

The effect of both unconditioned and conditioned reinforcers on dopamine-releasing neurons in the VTA has been studied. In an experiment with monkeys, a visual CS was presented to a monkey followed by a squirt of orange juice into the mouth (the US). During training, the activity of VTA neurons was monitored. The upper panel of FIGURE 5•18 shows an increase in the firing of VTA neurons when the US was presented for the first time. When orange juice was squirted into the mouth, the frequency of firing of VTA neurons increased. The lower panel of Figure 5.18 shows the rate of firing to the *CS* after a number of CS–US pairings. Note that VTA neurons now fired to the onset of the CS. Thus, the CS could function as a conditioned reinforcer because it evoked the release of dopamine. If the CS were to follow an operant response, such as lever pressing, the operant

response would be reinforced by the CS. Note also in the lower panel that, after conditioning, VTA neurons no longer fired when the US was presented. This is a major contributor to blocking (Donahoe & Palmer, 1994/2005; Waelti, Dickinson, & Schultz, 2001).

The neural pathways by which conditioned reinforcers initiate activity in VTA neurons are different from those of unconditioned reinforcers. The neural pathways mediating conditioned reinforcement arise from neurons in the frontal lobes that are activated by environmental stimuli. With experienced learners for whom many stimuli have acquired the ability to guide behavior, the opportunity for conditioned reinforcement via these pathways is enormous (Goldman-Rakic, 1996). Stimuli that have been previously paired with reinforcers acquire the ability to function as conditioned reinforcers for the behavior that precedes them. We saw an example in the earlier discussion of the role of automatic conditioned reinforcement in language learning. The contribution of the frontal lobes to conditioned reinforcement may have been a major factor affecting the evolution of an especially large increase in the size of the frontal lobes in humans.

Cellular Mechanisms of Reinforcement

Knowledge of the cellular basis of reinforcement is now emerging, instigated by the pioneering work of Eric Kandel (Pittenger & Kandel, 2003), an Austrian-American neuroscientist. Kandel began his work by using a marine mollusk whose nervous system is relatively simple and whose neurons are uniquely identifiable. A simple nervous system provided the controlled conditions necessary to isolate basic cellular processes. Kandel's work on learning began some 40 years ago (Kandel & Spencer, 1968) and was recognized with a Nobel Prize in 2000. (He has written a charming autobiography; Kandel, 2006.) With the development of new and more refined experimental techniques, much current work on the cellular mechanisms of reinforcement is focused on the nervous systems of mammals. That is the work described here.

Neurons affect one another though the release of compounds called *neurotransmitters*. The primary excitatory neurotransmitter in the brain is *glutamate*. An excitatory transmitter is a molecule that facilitates the initiation of an action potential in a neuron. Glutamate is released by a presynaptic neuron and acts on two main types of glutamate receptors located in the cell membrane of a postsynaptic neuron. One glutamate receptor—the **AMPA receptor**—rapidly facilitates the initiation of action potentials in the postsynaptic neuron. A second glutamate receptor—the **NMDA receptor**—plays a critical role in learning. (AMPA and NMDA are acronyms for chemical compounds that selectively stimulate these receptors—alpha-amino-3-hydroxy-5-methyl-4-isoxazolepropionic acid and *N*-methyl-D-aspartate, respectively.) The NMDA receptor increases the ability of glutamate from the presynaptic neuron to fire

---

dopamine   Neuromodulator that increases synaptic efficacy between interconnected neurons that are active at the same time; important in reinforcement.

AMPA receptor   Type of receptor for the excitatory neurotransmitter glutamate, rapidly facilitates firing of the neuron.

NMDA receptor   Type of glutamate receptor that plays an important role in learning through changing synaptic efficacies.

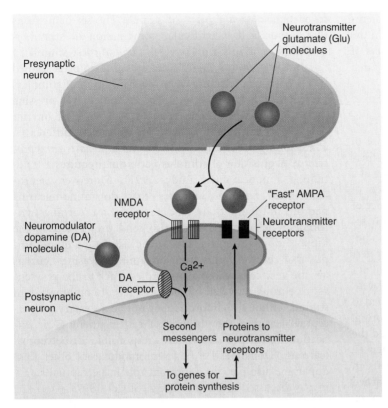

[**FIGURE 5•19**] Some of the cellular events that take place during learning. As a result of the process diagrammed here, the presynaptic neuron becomes more able to activate the postsynaptic neuron. This process occurs during long-term potentiation.

the postsynaptic neuron via AMPA receptors. When the postsynaptic neuron is sufficiently stimulated via AMPA receptors, the membrane of the postsynaptic neuron depolarizes, causing ion channels in NMDA receptors to open. The open NMDA channel permits calcium ions (Ca^{2+}) to enter the cell. When calcium enters the postsynaptic neuron, a number of intracellular events are triggered. A key event is the placement of a molecular "tag" on the AMPA receptors that have just been stimulated by glutamate. This tag lasts for several hours and marks those receptors as being recently stimulated (Frey & Morris, 1998; Bailey, Kandel, & Si, 2004). FIGURE 5•19 depicts some of the cellular events that occur when learning increases the ability of presynaptic neurons to activate postsynaptic neurons.

If the neural pathways that have recently been activated are followed by a reinforcer, then dopaminergic neurons in midbrain nuclei are stimulated. When dopamine receptors on the postsynaptic neuron are stimulated in conjunction with AMPA and NMDA receptors, a series of intracellular events (chemicals called *second messengers*) is initiated. The second messengers activate genes that lead to the synthesis of new proteins. These new proteins produce long-lasting structural changes in tagged AMPA receptors and cause new AMPA receptors to be inserted into the membrane of the postsynaptic cell. At the conclusion of this process,

glutamate released by the presynaptic neuron has an increased chance of initiating an action potential in the postsynaptic neuron. Glutamate activates more postsynaptic AMPA receptors for a longer time. The result is that synaptic transmission is facilitated along pathways by which environmental stimuli initiated neural activity that led to the reinforced response. In the laboratory, facilitation of neural transmission (increases in synaptic efficacy) can be produced by high-frequency electrical stimulation of presynaptic neurons. This is known as **long-term potentiation (LTP)** (Bliss & Lomø, 1973). LTP refers to a long-lasting increase in the excitability of the postsynaptic neuron to stimulation at particular synapses. LTP is the best candidate for the cellular basis of learning (Whitlock et al., 2006). The cellular mechanisms of reinforcement are more complex than those described here. They involve changes in both presynaptic and postsynaptic neurons, and neuromodulators in addition to dopamine (Carlson, 2007). Nevertheless, a coherent picture is emerging of the neural systems of reinforcement and of their cellular mechanisms (e.g., Pastalkova, Serrano, & Pinkhasova, 2006).

QUESTIONS TO CONSIDER

1. Why might a neuromodulator with widespread projections in the brain be particularly well suited to strengthen the neural connections important in learning?

2. Substances that are commonly abused—such as cocaine, amphetamine, and alcohol—are all known to affect the levels of dopamine in synapses. From what you know about the biological basis of learning, what effect should these substances have on drug-seeking behavior?

Learning with Experience

Behavioral science takes as a working hypothesis that even the most complex human behavior is the cumulative product of basic evolutionary and learning processes. As experience accumulates, the learner acquires an ever richer repertoire of environment–behavior relations, and an ever larger number of environmental events can function as conditioned reinforcers. As a result, present learning increasingly benefits from past learning (e.g., Tse et al., 2007). Much current work explores the implications of basic behavioral and neural processes for complex human behavior. For example, the effect of a strengthening process on connections between networks of neuron-like elements has provided

---

long-term potentiation (LTP)   Increase in the ease of firing a postsynaptic neuron by electrical stimulation of a presynaptic neuron; thought to be the neural basis of learning.

surprising insights into perceiving (see Chapter 7), remembering (see Chapter 9), and language (Elman, 1995). In the final section of the chapter, we consider three products of an extensive history of reinforcement—perceptual learning, instructional control, and observational learning.

Perceptual Learning

Behavior is guided by increasingly complex combinations of stimuli. Take, for example, learning to drive to a new destination. Every correct turn requires the combined knowledge of a number of landmarks at intersections—the presence of traffic lights, the placement of street signs, the appearance of neighboring houses, and so on. We must learn about the relation between sensory events in addition to the relation between sensory events and behavior. **Perceptual learning** refers to the process whereby specific combinations of stimuli, not merely single stimuli, come to guide behavior. In a well-known example of perceptual learning, a rat was permitted to wander about a maze without receiving food for exploring. When food was later placed in the maze, the rat learned the path to food faster than if it had not previously experienced the various stimuli in the maze (Tolman & Honzik, 1930). In the process of exploring, the rat had apparently learned something about the relation between stimuli in the maze. This perceptual learning facilitated navigating the maze when locomotion was reinforced with food. Learning about the relation between stimuli was not expressed in behavior until running was reinforced. For that reason, the experiment demonstrated what is called **latent learning.**

How is perceptual learning acquired? In Chapter 8, a brain structure called the hippocampus is shown to play an important role in memory for events. The hippocampus is located within each temporal lobe. Neurons in the hippocampus receive inputs from *polysensory neurons* in sensory-association cortex. The hippocampus then sends multisynaptic outputs back to these same regions (Amaral, 1987). Polysensory neurons are neurons that are stimulated by combinations of stimuli, that is, by inputs from more than one sensory channel. For example, a polysensory neuron might be stimulated by both visual and auditory neurons or by both color and location neurons within the visual system. The stimulation of a polysensory neuron by its sensory inputs in conjunction with the near-simultaneous stimulation by outputs from the hippocampus increases the strength of connections to the polysensory neuron. In this way, polysensory neurons become cells that respond reliably

to particular *combinations* of stimuli. The set of neurons that responds to a particular combination of stimuli is sometimes said to form a *representation* of these stimuli.

In the laboratory, simple perceptual learning is studied by reinforcing a response when a combination of stimuli is presented, but not otherwise. For example, lever pressing produces food when a tone and light occur together, but not when either the tone or light occurs alone. This differential conditioning procedure is called a *stimulus-patterning procedure*. Acquisition of stimulus patterning requires a functioning hippocampus (Rudy, 1991). Moreover, neuroanatomical research indicates that dopamine-releasing neurons in the midbrain that are crucial for learning environment–behavior relations also send projections to the hippocampus (Swanson, 1982). The cells in the hippocampus that receive inputs from dopamine-releasing neurons are the very cells whose axons project back to the polysensory neurons activated by the most recent combination of stimuli. Although reinforcers may not be necessary for perceptual learning, they facilitate the strengthening of connections to the polysensory cells responsible for perceptual learning (Donahoe, 1997). (Neuromodulators other than dopamine also play an important role in perceptual learning, as discussed in Chapter 7; e.g., Singer, 1997).

Instructional Control

Complex behavior cannot wait for the random emission of the "correct" response to produce a reinforcer. The likelihood of the complex behavior occurring by chance alone is too remote. A thousand monkeys typing on a thousand keyboards will never produce a Shakespearean sonnet, let alone a play, no matter how long they type. To acquire complex human behavior, stimuli—instructions—are often provided by others that make the to-be-reinforced response more likely (**instructional control**). Skinner (1984b) found it useful to distinguish between behavior that is best understood as the result of its consequences—*contingency-shaped behavior*—and behavior that is best understood as the result of its antecedents—*rule-governed behavior*. Instructed behavior is rule-governed behavior. If discriminative stimuli such as instructions are to guide behavior, then behavior must have a long history of reinforcement for responding to instructions. Thus rule-governed behavior is itself the result of the same basic learning processes.

The interaction between instructions and reinforcers can be studied in the laboratory. In one study, college students were told that they would receive a reinforcer (a small amount of money) when a response occurred at least 15 seconds after the previous response had produced a reinforcer (Buskist & Miller, 1986). (This will be recognized as a 15-second fixed-interval schedule.) In fact, at least 30 seconds had to elapse before the response became effective. Faced with a conflict between the instructions and the actual contingencies of reinforcement, what did the students do? At first, the behavior of misinformed students was guided by

---

perceptual learning Process by which *combinations* of environmental stimuli acquire control of behavior.

latent learning Facilitation of learning after the stimuli that guide behavior have been experienced but without the behavior being reinforced in their presence.

instructional control Guidance of behavior by discriminative stimuli, especially verbal stimuli such as directions; also known as *rule-governed behavior.*

the instructions, with a response occurring about every 15 seconds. However, because these "early" responses were not reinforced, responding began to extinguish until it slowed down to more than 30 seconds since the previous reinforcer. At that time, another reinforcer was received, and responding gained strength at the new—and correct—interval. Behavior was no longer guided by the instructions but by the events imposed by the schedule of reinforcement.

Incorrect instructions, or rules, do not always lose their ability to guide behavior. For other students in the study, responding also produced a reinforcer after 30 seconds, but the instructions falsely informed them that 60 seconds had to elapse. Guided by the false instructions, responding now occurred only after about 60 seconds had elapsed. However, because 60 seconds was greater than the correct time of 30 seconds, almost *every* response was reinforced. More-rapid responses never occurred and, as a result, could never be reinforced. Incorrect rules can continue to guide human behavior when they prevent behavior from encountering the true contingencies. For example, students who are told that they will never succeed may stop trying and, as a result, never encounter the reinforcers that would otherwise become available. In general, the guidance of behavior by instructions depends—as with all other stimuli—on the specific contingencies of reinforcement actually encountered by the learner's behavior (Catania, Mathews, & Shimoff, 1982). Behavior is shaped by realized contingencies, not possible contingencies (LeFrancois, Chase, & Joyce, 1988).

Observational Learning

Human learners benefit from the experience of others through instructions and also through observation of the behavior of others. **Observational learning** occurs when changes in the observer's behavior take place after seeing others behave in that situation. The observer can see the stimuli present when the behavior occurs, as well as the consequences of the behavior. A subset of observational learning is imitation. **Imitation** occurs when the behavior of the observer corresponds to the form of the behavior of the person being observed, and would not have occurred otherwise. How can we understand observational learning in terms of fundamental learning processes?

Observational learning in experienced learners usually occurs without special training. However, children with severe disabilities sometimes do not imitate. This is a great impediment to their learning, especially language learning in which imitation plays an important role. Three children who did not imitate the actions of the experimenter and who had never been seen to imitate others were exposed to an operant-conditioning procedure. In the procedure, the verbal stimulus "Do this" was followed by a reinforcer if the child emitted a response that was similar in form to the experimenter's behavior (Baer, Peterson, & Sherman, 1967). The required responses were relatively simple, such as hand clapping or raising one arm. If the child failed to imitate, as was always the case at the

[**FIGURE 5•20**] Training in imitation. Two children with severe disabilities, who did not imitate on their own, received explicit reinforcement for doing so. Gradually, after many different imitative responses were reinforced, the children began to imitate new actions on their first appearance.

(From Baer, D. M., Peterson, R. F., & Sherman, J. A. (1967). Development of imitation by reinforcing behavioral similarity to a model. *Journal of the Experimental Analysis of Behavior, 10,* 405–418.)

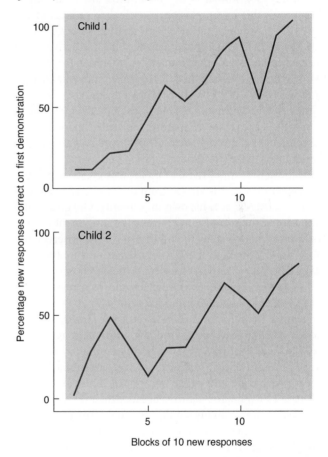

beginning of the study, the experimenter shaped the response. Shaping occurred by guiding the correct movement and following it with a reinforcer, such as a bit of food, and saying "good." Shaping was gradually eliminated for that response until the child made the response without guidance. After more than 100 different responses had been reinforced in this manner, the children began to imitate new responses, such as pulling a window shade, when they simply heard "Do this." (See FIGURE 5•20.) In short, the cumulative effect of acquiring many different imitative responses produced *generalized imitation.* (See also Horne & Erjavec, 2007.)

How can we understand the acquisition of imitation and other observational learning using basic learning processes?

---

observational learning   Changes in the behavior of an observer after seeing another learner behave in that same situation.

imitation   Observational learning in which the behavior of an observer is similar to the behavior of the one being observed.

For any generalized response to occur, a similar response must have been reinforced under similar circumstances in the past. What are the similar circumstances and reinforcers in the case of imitation?

When we see other people behave, some of the stimuli produced by their behavior are similar to the stimuli that we see when we make the same response ourselves. The motion is in a given direction, toward a particular object, other people's limbs look similar to our own limbs, and so on. Consistent with this interpretation, electrical recordings of the activity of neurons in the motor-association cortex of monkeys reveal that some of the neurons that are active when the movement of another monkey is observed are also active when the observer makes the same movement. (See Brass & Heyes, 2005 for a review of such studies.) Furthermore, research with humans using less-invasive procedures such as PET scans (see Chapter 4) shows that these areas of the brain are active only when the observed response is one that humans make (for example, biting but not barking). Finally, the activation of these brain areas is greater when the movement of others is viewed from the same perspective as when an observer sees his own movements. The greater the similarity of the stimuli produced by the movement of others to those produced by the movement of the observer, the more similar the neural activity initiated in the observer's brain. The neural activity induced in the observer occurs at the same time as the reinforcer for the responses of the other, which acts as a conditioned reinforcer to strengthen the similar neural activity of the observer (Bates, Patel, & Liddle, 2005). Thus, observing the movement of others leads to neural activity that meets the contiguity requirement of conditioning. The neurons that are similarly activated by behaving and observing are called *mirror neurons*. They are called mirror neurons because their activity in the observer's brain is highly similar to—that is, it "mirrors"—the activity when the observer makes the same response. Although the interpretation of observational learning is incomplete, these and other complex behaviors do not appear to be beyond the reach of basic learning processes (Donahoe & Palmer, 1994/2005; Hurley & Chater, 2005).

QUESTIONS TO CONSIDER

1. Why might the driver of a car be more likely to recall landmarks along the route than the passenger?
2. We often receive advice (instructions) from others about how we should behave. What factors might affect whether you would heed the advice?
3. When we see some notable activity—a baseball player hitting a home run or a person grimacing in pain—we often behave similarly. We might swing an imaginary bat or screw up our faces. Why?
4. If behavior is shaped by selection processes, does this mean that the environment controls our behavior and that we have no control over ourselves?

Epilogue

Learning Modulates "Survival of the Fittest"

Behavior is shaped by the contingencies of reinforcement encountered in a person's life. The learning process parallels the evolutionary process in that reinforcers select responses from the variation in behavior. The neural mechanisms that mediate behavior are retained by changes in synaptic efficacies. Among the many different contingencies of reinforcement are those implemented by the culture. *Culture* refers to the cumulative effect of the contingencies that are widely encountered within a given society (Horner et al., 2006). The self-sacrificing behavior of Wesley Autrey and Vinod Mago, with which we began this chapter, cannot be understood without taking into account their histories of reinforcement—histories that overrode the genetic legacy of their histories of natural selection.

We can never know with certainty what caused Wesley Autrey and Vinod Mago to behave as they did because we can never know all of the contingencies that their behavior encountered. Mr. Autrey protected a stranger who had fallen onto the tracks at great risk to his own life. When asked why he had done it, he said," I just saw someone who needed help. I did what I felt was right." What had he experienced in his past that made this action feel "right?" Was he explicitly trained to act in this way during his service in the Navy—to aid a fellow human being who was in trouble, even a stranger? Was it a result of how he was raised as a child? We cannot know for certain. However, in technical terms, Mr. Autrey's behavior was prompted by the discriminative stimulus of seeing someone in peril and strengthened by the conditioned reinforcer of knowing that he was doing the "right" thing. How can we understand the behavior of Mr. Mago, who returned a great deal of money that was clearly needed by him and his family? Here, we perhaps have a better idea of the contingencies of reinforcement that shaped his behavior. When asked why he had returned the money, Mr. Mago replied, "If money doesn't belong to me, I don't keep it. I know God is watching everybody, every second." In technical terms, returning the money was a behavior that received the immediate conditioned reinforcer of the deity's approval and avoided the conditioned aversive stimulus of the deity's displeasure.

Society clearly arranges reinforcement contingencies that strengthen altruistic behavior. Mr. Autrey received a standing ovation at the next presidential State-of-the-Union address, a Bronze Medallion from the City of New York, a check for $10,000 from Donald Trump, and a lifetime pass on the subway. Mr. Mago was given $100 by the owner of the wallet, and his behavior was described in glowing terms in a newspaper headline "The Toast of NYC." Perhaps they had heard of similar consequences for similar behavior on the part of others, which made their own behavior more likely through observational learning. Whatever the case, it is clear that their histories of reinforcement encouraged such behavior. The contingencies of reinforcement arranged by society can conflict with the contingencies of survival implemented by natural selection (Campbell, 1975). Unfortunately, our society implements less-benign contingencies as well. Two lawyers encouraged Mr. Autrey to sign a contract that entitled them to half of any income that he received from books or movies telling his story. Wesley Autrey is now suing the lawyers to nullify the contract.

CHAPTER SUMMARY

How Learning Is Studied

Ivan Pavlov studied learning by varying the relation between an environmental event and an eliciting stimulus [for example, between a tone and food (which elicits salivation)]. Pavlov's procedure is called *classical* conditioning. Edward Thorndike studied learning by varying the relation between behavior and an eliciting stimulus (for example, between lever pressing and food). Thorndike's procedure is called *operant* conditioning. However, because the learner is always in the presence of *some* environmental stimulus and is always emitting *some* behavior, the eliciting stimulus necessarily occurs after some behavior in Pavlov's procedure and after some stimuli in Thorndike's procedure. Thus, the basic nature of the conditioning process may be the same. The two procedures differ only with respect to which type of event *reliably* precedes the eliciting stimulus. Our daily lives consist of instances of both conditioning procedures.

Conditions Required for Learning

The operant relation is generally more important for understanding behavioral changes outside the laboratory. This is because *any* behavior can potentially be strengthened by a reinforcing stimulus with the operant procedure, whereas only responses that are elicited by some stimulus can be strengthened with a classical procedure. Because responses can be strengthened without specifying the stimuli that permit them, operant behavior is said to be emitted instead of elicited.

Two conditions are necessary for learning—*temporal contiguity* and *behavioral discrepancy*. Temporal contiguity means that the stimuli and responses that are affected by the reinforcer must occur close in time to the reinforcer. Behavioral discrepancy means that a stimulus functions as a reinforcer only when it evokes behavior that was not already occurring immediately before the reinforcing stimulus. The importance of behavioral discrepancy is shown by the *blocking design,* in which a stimulus that is temporally contiguous with a reinforcer does not acquire control of behavior when the stimulus is accompanied by another stimulus that already evokes the CR. Nontechnically speaking, learning occurs only when the learner is "surprised" to begin behaving in the way elicited by the reinforcer.

Although real-life situations are more complex than the highly controlled laboratory situations used to study basic conditioning processes, the learning process revealed by these procedures plays a central role in life outside the laboratory. This is illustrated by the formation of phobias, tolerance and withdrawal in drug addiction, and insightful behavior.

The Process of Learning

The occurrence of a *reinforcer* after a stimulus in the classical procedure or after a response in the operant procedure leads to *acquisition*—a change in the environmental guidance of behavior. Acquisition of complex behavior often requires *shaping*. When stimuli elicit behavior because of natural selection, as with reflexes, they are called *unconditioned reinforcers*. When stimuli serve as reinforcers because they have previously been paired with other reinforcers, they are called *conditioned reinforcers*. For example, a tone that has been paired with food can serve as a conditioned reinforcer. Stimuli need not evoke conspicuous behavior to serve as conditioned reinforcers. Conditioned reinforcers play an increasingly important role as the learner gains experience. Conditioned reinforcers are provided by stimuli in the environment and by stimuli produced by the learner's own behavior, as in *automatic reinforcement* of verbal behavior.

After a reinforcer has changed the way the environment guides behavior, the acquired response decreases in strength if the reinforcer is eliminated. That is, *extinction* occurs. Responding resists the effects of extinction if acquisition uses *intermittent reinforcement*. Extinction does not completely eliminate the effects of reinforcement, however. Responding is rapidly reacquired if the response is again reinforced and may also recover some of its strength after the mere passage of time (*spontaneous recovery*).

Reinforcers change the strength of behavior in the environment in which the behavior was reinforced. When other environments share stimuli in common with the environment in which the behavior was reinforced, these environments come to guide behavior as well. This is called *stimulus generalization.* For behavior to be closely confined to the environment in which it was reinforced, *stimulus discrimination* must occur. Stimulus discrimination occurs when behavior has different consequences as the environment varies. This is called *differential conditioning.* A particularly important effect of stimulus discrimination is found when human learners acquire multiple *contextual discriminations.* A contextual discrimination is one in which the stimulus in whose presence the response is reinforced varies with the context in which the stimulus appears. After multiple contextual discriminations, responding occurs to *new combinations* of the stimuli that were present during training. The emergence of these untrained discriminations indicates that stimuli from the various contextual discriminations have become members of an *equivalence class.*

Basic conditioning processes can interpret *choice,* that is, situations in which more than one reinforced response is possible. With experienced learners, responding in choice situations is well described by the *matching principle.* Self-control occurs when a learner in a choice situation chooses the alternative that produces a larger, but delayed, reinforcer in preference to one that produces an immediate, but smaller reinforcer. Self-control occurs when immediate conditioned reinforcers are present during the delay period. Some eliciting stimuli act as *punishers,* not reinforcers. Punishment occurs when the responses elicited by an aversive stimulus interfere with the operant behavior that immediately precedes the punisher.

Biological Basis of Reinforcement

Unconditioned and conditioned reinforcers engage much the same neural system of reinforcement—a widely projecting *neuromodulatory system* that can change the strength of synaptic connections in large regions of the brain. *Long-term potentiation* (LTP) is thought to involve the same cellular processes that occur during normal learning. During LTP, changes in receptors on the postsynaptic membrane allow the release of the neurotransmitter glutamate by the presynaptic neuron, to more effectively initiate action potentials in the postsynaptic neuron. Reinforcers stimulate release of the neuromodulator dopamine, which produces long-lasting changes in synaptic efficacies between neurons that are firing at about the same time.

Learning with Experience

Through prior experience, combinations of stimuli acquire the ability to guide behavior; that is, *perceptual learning* occurs. The hippocampus plays a critical role in perceptual learning through its effect on polysensory neurons in the sensory-association cortex. Although reinforcers may not be necessary for perceptual learning, they facilitate it. Behavior can also come to be guided by instructions (*instructional control*) and by observing the behavior of others (*observational learning*). Basic learning processes help understand even such complex behavior.

KEY TERMS

acquisition *p. 135*

AMPA receptor *p. 144*

automatic reinforcement *p. 137*

blocking design *p. 131*

classical procedure *p. 127*

conditioned (secondary) reinforcer *p. 137*

conditioned emotional response (CER), or conditioned suppression *p. 142*

conditioned response (CR) *p. 128*

conditioned stimulus (CS) *p. 127*

conditioning *p. 128*

contextual discrimination *p. 140*

differential conditioning procedure *p. 139*

discriminative stimulus *p. 139*

dopamine *p. 144*

eliciting stimulus *p. 124*

emitted response *p. 127*

equivalence class *p. 140*

escape or withdrawal response *p. 142*

extinction *p. 138*

habituation *p. 135*

imitation *p. 147*

instructional control *p. 146*

intermittent (partial) reinforcement *p. 138*

interval schedules *p. 129*

latent learning *p. 146*

learning *p. 124*

long-term potentiation (LTP) *p. 145*

matching principle *p. 141*

NMDA receptor *p. 144*

observational learning *p. 147*

operant procedure *p. 127*

orienting response *p. 135*

perceptual learning *p. 146*

punishing stimulus (punisher) *p. 142*

punishment *p. 142*

ratio schedules *p. 129*

reinforcement *p. 136*

reinforcing stimulus (reinforcer) *p. 128*

schedules of reinforcement *p. 129*

shaping *p. 135*

spontaneous recovery *p. 138*

stimulus discrimination *p. 139*

stimulus generalization *p. 139*

taste aversion *p. 136*

temporal contiguity *p. 128*

unconditioned response (UR) *p. 127*

unconditioned stimulus (US) *p. 127*

SUGGESTIONS FOR FURTHER READING

Catania, A. C. (2006). *Learning* (Interim 4th ed.). Cornwall-on-Hudson, NY: Sloan.

An introduction to the field of learning from a behavioral perspective. Integrates the literatures on animal learning with research on language, cognition, and memory.

Donahoe, J. W., & Palmer, D. C. (2005). *Learning and complex behavior*. Richmond, MA: Ledgetop Publishing. (Reprinting of Donahoe, J. W., & Palmer, D. C. (1994). *Learning and complex behavior*. Boston: Allyn & Bacon.) Supplementary material at http://www.LCB-online.org

A text that describes behavioral and biological learning processes and their implications for complex human behavior. The complex behavior includes concept formation, attention, perception, memory, imagining, problem solving, and verbal behavior with related findings from neuroscience and neuropsychology.

Donjan, M.P. (2006). *The Principles of Learning and Behavior* (5th ed.). Monterey, CA: Brooks/Cole.

A text that provides a comprehensive account of animal learning, behavior, and cognition from an associationist perspective.

Skinner, B. F. (1953). *Science and human behavior*. New York: The Free Press.

This book, although originally published more than 50 years ago, remains a valuable general statement of the relation between basic conditioning process and human behavior. The basic principles of operant conditioning and their application to a wide range of real-world phenomena are described interestingly and clearly. This book is a good choice if you want to know more about Skinner's views.

CHAPTER

6

Sensation

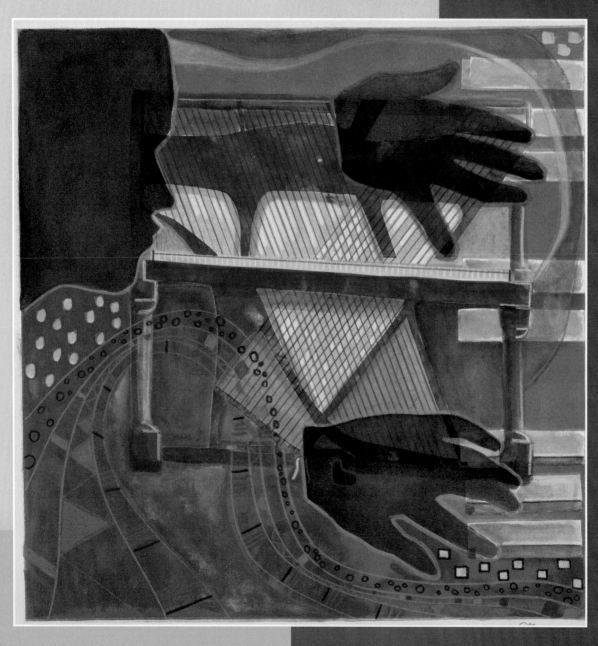

Prologue

All in Her Head?

Melissa, a junior at the state university, had volunteered to be a subject in an experiment at the dental school. She had been told that she might feel a little pain but that everything was under medical supervision, and no harm would come to her. She didn't particularly like the idea of pain, but she would be well paid; she saw in the experience an opportunity to live up to her own self-image as being as brave as anyone.

She entered the reception room, where she signed consent forms saying that she agreed to participate in the experiment and knew that a physician would be giving her a drug and that her reaction to pain would be measured. The experimenter greeted her, led her to a room, and asked her to be seated in a dental chair. He inserted a needle attached to a plastic tube into a vein in her right arm so that he could inject drugs.

"First," he said, "we want to find out how sensitive you are to pain." He showed her a device that looked something like an electric toothbrush with a metal probe on the end. "This device will stimulate nerves in the pulp of your tooth. Do you have some fillings?" She nodded. "Have you ever bitten on some aluminum foil?" She winced and nodded again. "Good, then you will know what to expect." He adjusted a dial on the stimulator, touched the tip of it to a tooth, and pressed the button. No response. He turned the dial and stimulated the tooth again. Still no response. He turned the dial again, and this time, the stimulation made her gasp and wince. He recorded the voltage setting in his notebook.

"Okay, now we know how sensitive this tooth is to pain. Now I'm going to give you a drug we are testing. It should decrease the pain quite a bit." He injected the drug and, after a short while, said, "Let's try the tooth again." The drug apparently worked; he had to increase the voltage considerably before she felt any pain.

"Now," he said, "I want to give you some more of the drug to see if we can make you feel even less pain." He gave another injection and, after a little wait, tested her again. But the drug had not further decreased her pain sensitivity; instead, it had *increased* it; she was now as sensitive as she had been before the first injection.

After the experiment was over, the experimenter walked with Melissa into a lounge. "I want to tell you about the experiment you were in, but I'd like to ask you not to talk about it with other people who might also serve as subjects." She nodded her head in agreement.

"Actually, you did not receive a painkiller. The first injection was pure salt water."

"It was? But I thought it made me less sensitive to pain."

"It did. When an innocuous substance such as an injection of salt water or a sugar pill has an effect like that, we call it a placebo effect."

"You mean that it was all in my mind? That I only *thought* that the shock hurt less?"

"No. Well, that is, it was necessary for you to think that you had received a painkiller. But the effect was a physiological one. We know that, because the second injection contained a drug that counteracts the effects of opiates."

"Opiates? You mean like morphine or heroin?"

"Yes." He saw her start to protest, shook his head, and said, "No, I'm sure you don't take drugs. But your brain makes them. For reasons we still do not understand, your believing that you had received a painkiller caused some cells in your brain to release a chemical that acts the way opiates do. The chemical acts on other neurons in your brain and decreases your sensitivity to pain. When I gave you the second injection—the drug that counteracts opiates—your sensitivity to pain came back."

"But then, did my mind or my brain make the placebo effect happen?"

"Well, think about it. Your mind and your brain are not really separate. Experiences can change the way your brain functions, and these changes can alter your experiences. Mind and brain have to be studied together, not separately." ■

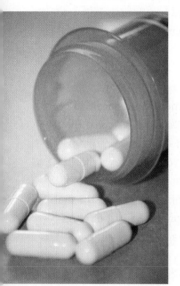

Behavior does not exist in a vacuum, nor do our thoughts and emotions. Our actions are provoked, informed, and guided by events that occur in our environment, and we think about—and have feelings about—what is happening there. Our senses are the means by which we experience the world; everything we learn about the world comes from information detected by sense organs and transmitted to our brains by sensory nerves. Without sensory input, a human brain would be utterly useless; it would learn nothing, think no thoughts, have no experiences, and control no behaviors.

Vision, to most people, is the most important sense modality. Through it we recognize family and friends, see their facial expressions and gestures, learn to read, perceive objects that are beyond our reach, and find our way around our environment. It provides us with information about the size, shape, color, and

movement of objects nearby and at a distance. Through vision, we receive some of our most powerful aesthetic experiences, in the form of art and other beautiful images—experiences rivaled only by the hearing of music that we appreciate.

The other senses also contribute to the richness of experience. Because of the role that speech plays in human culture, audition is extremely important for social behavior. With vision, it provides information about distant events, as does the sense of smell, which can tell us about sources of aromatic molecules far upwind. The other senses deal with events occurring immediately nearby, for instance, the taste of our favorite foods or the touch of a loved one. The body senses are closely tied to our own movements. When we feel an object, the experience is active, not passive; we move our hands over it to determine its shape, texture, and temperature. And information from specialized organs in the inner ear and from receptors in the muscles and joints is actually produced by our own movements. This information helps us to maintain our balance as we engage in our everyday activities.

Sensory Processing

Experience is traditionally divided into two classes: sensation and perception. Most psychologists define **sensation** as the detection of simple properties of stimuli, such as brightness, color, warmth, and sweetness. **Perception** is the recognition of objects (both animate and inanimate), their locations, their movements, and their backgrounds. According to these definitions, seeing the color red is a *sensation,* but recognizing a red apple is a *perception.* Similarly, seeing a movement is a sensation, but recognizing the trajectory of a baseball coming toward us—which informs us where we should go to catch it—is a perception. This classification is a convenient way of organizing a set of complex topics, but neither behavioral nor physiological research has established a clear boundary between sensations and perceptions.

Chapter 7 explores research on visual perception. This chapter describes our sensory mechanisms: the visual, auditory, gustatory, olfactory, and somatosensory systems. According to tradition, we have five senses, but we have several more. For example, the somatosensory system includes separate components that are able to detect touch, warmth, coolness, vibration, physical damage (pain), head tilt, head movement, limb movement, muscular contraction, and various events occurring within our bodies. Whether we choose to call each of these components "senses" depends on whether we want to overturn a tradition.

Transduction

Your brain, floating in cerebrospinal fluid, swaddled in its protective sheath of meninges, and sheltered in a thick skull, is isolated from the world around you. The only sense receptors that the brain possesses detect local conditions, such as the temperature and salt concentration of its blood supply.

---

sensation   The detection of the elementary properties of a stimulus.

perception   The detection of the more-complex properties of a stimulus, including its location and nature; involves learning.

These receptors cannot inform the brain about what is going on elsewhere. That information must be gathered by the sense organs that lie outside the brain.

Sense organs detect stimuli such as light, sound, taste, odor, or touch. Information about these stimuli is transmitted to the brain through neural impulses—action potentials carried by the axons in sensory nerves. The task of the sense organs is to transmit signals to the brain that are coded in such a way as to represent certain features of events that have occurred in the environment. The task of the brain is to analyze this information and decide what has occurred.

Transduction (literally, "leading across") is the process by which the sense organs convert energy from environmental events into neural activity. Each sense organ responds to a particular form of energy given off by an environmental stimulus and translates that energy into neural firing to which the brain can respond. The means of transduction are as diverse as the kinds of stimuli we can detect. For example, electromagnetic energy in the form of light is detected by special chemicals found in cells in our retinas, and mechanical energy in the form of pressure waves is detected by hair cells in our inner ears. In most senses, specialized sensory neurons called **receptor cells** release chemical neurotransmitters that stimulate other neurons, thus altering the rate of firing of their axons. In the somatosenses ("body senses"), dendrites of neurons respond directly to physical stimuli without the intervention of specialized receptor cells. However, some of these neurons do have specialized endings that enable them to respond to particular kinds of sensory information. TABLE 6•1 summarizes the types of transduction accomplished by our sense organs.

Sensory Coding

As we saw in Chapter 4, nerves are bundles of axons, each of which can do no more than transmit action potentials. These action potentials are fixed in size and duration; they cannot be altered. Thus, different stimuli cannot be translated into different types of action potentials, yet we can detect an enormous number of different stimuli with each of our sense organs. For example, we are capable of discriminating among tens of thousands of different colors. We can recognize up to

10,000 odors. We can also identify touches to different parts of the body; and we can further distinguish the degree of pressure involved and the sharpness or bluntness, softness or hardness, and temperature of the object touching us. But how, then, if action potentials cannot be altered, do the sense organs tell the brain that, for instance, a red apple or a yellow lemon is present—or that the right hand is holding a small, cold object or a large, warm one? The information from the sense organs must somehow be coded in the activity of axons carrying information from the sense organs to the brain.

A code is a system of signals representing information. Spoken English, written Spanish, traffic lights, key presses on a cell phone, and the electrical zeros and ones in the memory of a computer are all examples of codes. As long as we know the rules of a code, we can convert a message from one medium to another without losing any information, as when we convert from the sound of spoken English to a meaningful message. Although we do not know the precise rules by which the sensory systems transmit information to the brain, we do know that the rules take two general forms: *anatomical coding* and *temporal coding*.

Anatomical Coding Since the early 1800s, when Johannes Müller formulated his doctrine of specific nerve energies (discussed in Chapter 1), we have known that the brain learns what is happening through the activity of specific sets of neurons. Sensory organs located in different places in the body send their information to the brain through different nerves. Because the brain has no direct information about the physical energy impinging on a given sense organ, it uses **anatomical coding** to interpret the location and type of sensory stimulus according to which incoming nerve fibers are active. For example, if you rub your eyes, you will mechanically stimulate the light-sensitive receptors they contain. This stimulation produces action

---

transduction The conversion of physical stimuli into changes in the activity of receptor cells of sensory organs.

receptor cell A neuron that directly responds to a physical stimulus, such a light, vibrations, or aromatic molecules.

anatomical coding A means by which the nervous system represents information; different features are coded by the activity of different neurons.

[**TABLE 6•1**] The Types of Transduction Accomplished by the Sense Organs

Location of Sense Organ	Environmental Stimuli	Energy Transduced
Eye	Light	Radiant energy
Ear	Sound	Mechanical energy
Tongue	Taste	Recognition of molecular shape
Nose	Odor	Recognition of molecular shape
Skin	Touch	Mechanical energy
	Temperature	Thermal energy
	Vibration	Mechanical energy
	Pain	Chemical reaction
Internal organs; muscle	Stretch	Mechanical energy
Vestibular system	Tilt and rotation of head	Mechanical energy

potentials in the axons of the nerves that connect the eyes with the brain (the optic nerves). The visual system of the brain has no way of knowing that the light-sensitive receptors of the eyes have been activated by a nonvisual stimulus. As a result, the brain acts as if the neural activity in the optic nerves were produced by light—so you "see" stars and other flashes. Experiments performed during surgery have shown that artificial stimulation of the nerves that convey taste produces the perception of taste, electrical stimulation of the auditory nerve produces the perception of a buzzing noise, and so forth.

Anatomical coding enables the brain to distinguish not only among the sensory modalities, but also among stimuli of the same sensory modality. Sensory coding for the body surface is anatomical. The primary somatosensory cortex contains a neural "map" of the skin. Receptors in the skin in different parts of the body send information to different parts of the primary somatosensory cortex; thus, we can easily discriminate between a touch on the arm and a touch on the knee. Similarly, the primary visual cortex maintains a map of the visual field.

Temporal Coding **Temporal coding** is the coding of sensory information in terms of time. The simplest form of temporal code is rate. By firing at a faster or slower rate according to the intensity of a stimulus, an axon can communicate quantitative information to the brain. For example, a soft touch to the skin can be encoded by a low rate of firing, and a more-forceful touch, by a high rate. Thus, signals produced by a particular set of neurons (an anatomical code) tell where the body is being touched; the rate at which these neurons fire (a temporal code) tells how intense that touch is. It is commonly assumed that all sensory systems use rate of firing to encode the intensity of stimulation.

Psychophysics

As you learned in Chapter 1, nineteenth-century Europe was the birthplace of **psychophysics**, the systematic study of the relation between the physical characteristics of stimuli and the psychological responses (or perceptions) they produce (thus the "physics of the mind"). To study perceptual phenomena, scientists had to find reliable ways to measure people's responses to stimuli. We will examine two of these methods—the just-noticeable difference and the procedures of signal detection.

The Principle of the Just-Noticeable Difference Ernst Weber (1795–1878), a German anatomist and physiologist,

---

temporal coding A means by which the nervous system represents information; different features are coded by the pattern of activity of neurons.

psychophysics A branch of psychology that measures the quantitative relation between physical stimuli and perceptual experience.

just-noticeable difference (jnd) The smallest difference between two similar stimuli that can be distinguished. Also called *difference threshold.*

Weber fraction The ratio between a just-noticeable difference and the magnitude of a stimulus; reasonably constant over the middle range of most stimulus intensities.

investigated the ability of humans to discriminate between various stimuli. He measured the **just-noticeable difference (jnd)**—the smallest change in the magnitude of a stimulus that a person can detect. He discovered a principle that held true for many sensory systems: The jnd is directly related to the magnitude of the existing stimulus. For example, when he presented participants with two metal objects and asked them to say whether the objects differed in weight, the participants reported that the two weights felt the same unless they differed by a ratio of at least 1 in 40. That is, a person could just barely distinguish a 40-gram weight from a 41-gram weight, an 80-gram weight from an 82-gram weight, or a 400-gram weight from a 410-gram weight. Psychologically, the difference between a 40-gram weight and a 41-gram weight is equivalent to the difference between an 80-gram weight and an 82-gram weight: one jnd. Different sensory systems had different ratios. For example, the ratio for detecting differences in the brightness of white light is approximately 1 in 60. These ratios are called **Weber fractions.**

Gustav Fechner (1801–1887), another German physiologist, used Weber's concept of the just-noticeable difference to measure people's perceptual experience. That is, he measured the absolute magnitude of perceptual experience in jnds.

For example, suppose we want to measure the strength of a person's experience of light of a particular intensity. We seat the participant in a darkened room facing two disks of frosted glass, each having a light bulb behind it; the brightness of the light bulbs is adjustable. One of the disks serves as the sample stimulus; the other, as the comparison stimulus. We start with the sample and comparison stimuli turned off completely and increase the brightness of the comparison stimulus until our participant can just detect a difference. (See FIGURE 6•1.) That level of brightness is one jnd. Then we set the sample stimulus to the same intensity (one jnd) and again increase the brightness of the comparison stimulus until our participant can just tell them apart. The new level of the comparison stimulus is two

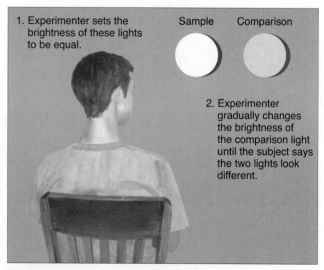

1. Experimenter sets the brightness of these lights to be equal.

Sample   Comparison

2. Experimenter gradually changes the brightness of the comparison light until the subject says the two lights look different.

[**FIGURE 6•1**] The method for determining a just-noticeable difference (jnd).

[FIGURE 6•2] A hypothetical range of perceived brightness (in jnds) as a function of intensity.

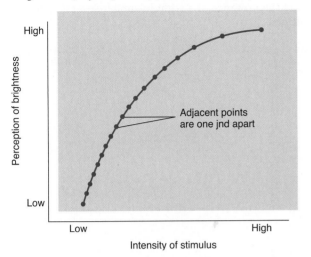

jnds. We continue making these measurements until the comparison stimulus is as bright as we can make it or until it becomes uncomfortably bright for the participant. Finally, we construct a graph indicating the perceived brightness (in jnds) in relation to the physical intensity of the stimulus. The graph, which relates the strength of a perceptual experience to physical intensity, might look something like FIGURE 6•2.

How should you interpret a graph such as Figure 6.2? First, note the two scales. The values along the X axis are measures of physical intensity—something measured with respect to the objective world. The values along the Y axis are very different. Each one is a jnd—a measure of the extent that the subjective experience is increasing. So, in other words, Figure 6.2 provides a mapping between the physical and the psychological worlds—it depicts a psychophysical function.

Second, notice that if you trace the distance between dots on the X axis, the distances become larger as you move to the right on the graph. This is a consequence of what Weber found; namely, that the amount of physical energy necessary to produce a jnd increases with the magnitude of the stimulus.

Finally, note the shape of the curve. It rises steeply at first, but then it begins to level off. This kind of curve is characteristic of the mathematical function known as a logarithm. Fechner's great contribution to psychology was to show that the ratio between the physical intensity of a stimulus and its perceived intensity followed a logarithmic function.

Signal-detection Theory Psychophysical methods rely heavily on the concept of a **threshold,** the thin line between not perceiving and perceiving. The just-noticeable difference can also be called a **difference threshold,** the *minimum* detectable difference between two stimuli. An **absolute threshold** is the *minimum* intensity of a stimulus that can be detected—that is, discriminated from no stimulus at all. Thus, the first comparison in the experiment described above—that used two frosted disks and two lamps—measured an absolute threshold. The subsequent comparisons measured difference thresholds.

Even early psychophysicists realized that a threshold is not an absolutely fixed value. When a researcher flashes a very dim light, a participant may report seeing it on some trials but not on others. By convention, the absolute threshold is the point at which a participant detects the stimulus 50 percent of the time; the difference threshold, the point at which the difference is detected 50 percent of the time. This conventional definition is necessary because of the inherent variability of activity in the nervous system. Even when neurons are not being stimulated, they are never absolutely inactive; they continue to fire even when at rest. If a very weak stimulus occurs when neurons in the visual system happen to be less active, the brain is likely to detect it. But if the neurons are already quite active, the effects of the stimulus are likely to be lost in the "noise."

An alternative method of measuring a person's sensitivity to changes in physical stimuli takes account of random changes in the nervous system. According to **signal-detection theory** (Green & Swets, 1974), every stimulus event requires discrimination between a signal (the stimulus) and noise (the combination of background stimuli and the random activity of the nervous system).

Signal-detection theory takes into account our willingness to report detecting a signal. For example, suppose you are participating in an experiment. You are seated in a quiet room, facing a small warning light. The researcher tells you that when the light flashes, you may hear a faint tone one second later. Your task is to say yes or no after each flash of the warning light, according to whether you hear the tone. At first the task is easy: Some flashes are followed by an easily heard tone; others are followed by silence. You are confident about your yes and no decisions. But as the experiment progresses, the tone gets fainter and fainter, until it is so soft that you have doubts about how you should respond. The light flashes. What should you say? Did you really hear a tone, or were you only imagining it?

At this point, your *response bias*—your tendency to say yes or no when you are not sure whether you detected the stimulus—can have an effect. According to the terminology of signal-detection theory, *hits* are saying "yes" when the stimulus is presented; *misses* are saying "no" when it is presented; *correct negatives* are saying "no" when the stimulus is not presented; and *false alarms* are saying "yes" when the stimulus is not presented. Hits and correct negatives are correct responses; misses and false alarms are incorrect responses. (See FIGURE 6•3.) Suppose you want to be very sure that you are correct when you say yes, because you would feel foolish saying you heard something that is not there. Your response bias will be to err in favor of avoiding false alarms, even at the risk of making misses. Someone else's

---

threshold The point at which a stimulus, or a change in the value of a stimulus, can just be detected.

difference threshold An alternate name for *just-noticeable difference (jnd)*.

absolute threshold The minimum value of a stimulus that can be detected.

signal-detection theory A mathematical theory of the detection of stimuli, which involves discriminating a signal from the noise in which it is embedded and which takes into account subjects' willingness to report detecting the signal.

[**FIGURE 6·3**] Four possibilities in judging the presence or absence of a stimulus.

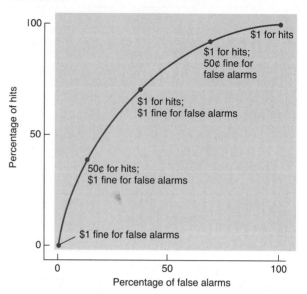

response bias might be to err in favor of detecting all the stimuli, even at the risk of making false alarms.

A person's response bias can seriously affect the threshold of detection. A person with a response bias to avoid false alarms will appear to have a higher threshold than will someone who does not want to let a tone go by without saying yes. To avoid this problem, signal-detection researchers have developed a method of assessing people's sensitivity, regardless of their initial response bias. They deliberately manipulate the response biases and observe the results of these manipulations on participants' judgments.

Suppose you were a participant and the researcher promised you a dollar every time you made a hit, with no penalty for false alarms. You would undoubtedly tend to say yes on every trial, even if you were not sure you had heard the tone; after all, you'd have nothing to lose and everything to gain. In contrast, suppose the researcher announced that she would fine you a dollar every time you made a false alarm and would give you nothing for making hits. You would undoubtedly say no every time, because you would have everything to lose and nothing to gain: You would be extremely conservative in your judgments.

Now consider your response bias under intermediate conditions. If you receive a dollar for every hit but also are fined 50 cents for every miss, you will say yes whenever you are reasonably sure you hear the tone. If you receive 50 cents for every hit but are fined a dollar for each false alarm, you will be more conservative. But if you are sure you heard the tone, you will say yes to earn 50 cents. (Note, however, that there are other, less expensive ways to change people's response biases, which is fortunate for researchers on limited budgets.) FIGURE 6·4 graphs your performance over this range of payoff conditions.

The graph in Figure 6.4 is a **receiver-operating-characteristic curve (ROC curve)**, named for its original use in research at the Bell Laboratories to measure the intelligibility of speech

receiver-operating-characteristic curve (ROC curve) A graph of hits and false alarms of subjects under different motivational conditions; indicates people's ability to detect a particular stimulus.

[**FIGURE 6·4**] A receiver-operating-characteristic (ROC) curve. The percentage of hits and false alarms in judging the presence of a stimulus under several payoff conditions.

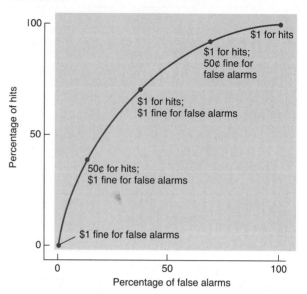

transmitted through a telephone system. The curve shows performance when the sound is difficult to detect. If the sound were louder, so that you rarely doubted you heard it, you would make almost every possible hit and very few false alarms. The few misses you made would be under the low-payoff condition, when you wanted to be absolutely certain you heard the tone. The few false alarms would occur when guessing did not matter because the penalty for being wrong was low or nonexistent. In FIGURE 6·5, the ROC curve (the magenta line) reflecting this new condition is shown together with the original curve (the

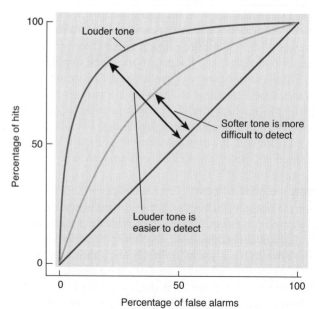

[**FIGURE 6·5**] Two ROC curves, obtained by presenting a more-discriminable stimulus (black curve) and a less-discriminable stimulus (blue curve).

blue line). The difference between the two curves demonstrates that the louder tone is easier to detect. Detectability is measured by the relative distances of the curves from a 45-degree line.

The signal-detection method is the best way to determine a person's sensitivity to the occurrence of a particular stimulus. Note that the concept of threshold is not used. Instead, a stimulus is considered more or less detectable. The person decides whether a stimulus occurred, and the consequences of making hits or false alarms can bias this decision. Signal-detection theory emphasizes that perceptual experience involves factors other than the activity of the sensory systems, factors such as motivation and prior experience.

QUESTIONS TO CONSIDER

1. Which sensory modalities would you least want to lose? Why?
2. If you could design a new sensory modality, what kind of information would it detect? What advantages would this new ability provide? Or do you think that our sense organs already detect all the useful information that is available? Why or why not?

Vision

The visual system performs a remarkable job. We take for granted the fact that in a quick glance, we can recognize what there is to see: people, objects, and landscapes, in depth and in full color. Researchers who have tried to program computers to recognize visual scenes realize just how complex this task is. This section begins our tour of the visual system. We will consider the eye and its functions in this chapter, and we'll explore visual perception in Chapter 7. But first, let's start with the stimulus: light.

Light

The eye is sensitive to light. But what is light? Light consists of radiant energy similar to radio waves. Radiant energy oscillates as it is transmitted from its source. For example, the antenna that broadcasts the programs of your favorite FM station transmits radio waves that oscillate at 88.5 MHz (megahertz, or a million times per second). Because electromagnetic energy travels at 186,000 miles per second, the waves transmitted by the FM radio antenna are approximately 11 feet apart. (One 88.5 millionth of 186,000 miles equals 11.09 feet.) Thus, the **wavelength** of the signal from the station—the distance between the waves of radiant energy—is 11 feet.

The wavelength of visible light is much shorter, ranging from 380 through 760 nanometers (a nanometer, nm, is one billionth of a meter). When viewed by the human eye, different wavelengths of visible light have different colors: for instance, 380-nm light looks violet and 760-nm light looks red.

All other radiant energy is invisible to our eyes. Ultraviolet radiation, x-rays, and gamma rays have shorter wavelengths than visible light has, whereas infrared radiation, radar, radio and television waves, and AC circuits have longer wavelengths. The entire range of wavelengths is known as the electromagnetic spectrum. The part our eyes can detect—the part we see as light—is referred to as the visible spectrum. (See FIGURE 6•6.)

The definition of the visible spectrum is based on the human visual system. Other species of animals would undoubtedly define the visible spectrum differently. For example, bees can see ultraviolet radiation that is invisible to us. Some plants have taken advantage of this fact and produce flowers that contain pigments that reflect ultraviolet radiation, presenting patterns that attract bees to them. Some snakes (notably, pit vipers such as the rattlesnake) have special organs that detect infrared radiation. This ability enables them to find their prey in the dark by detecting the heat emitted by small mammals in the form of infrared radiation.

The Eye and Its Functions

The eyes are important and delicate sense organs—and they are well protected. Each eye is housed in a bony socket and can be covered by the eyelid to keep out dust and dirt. The eyelids are edged by eyelashes, which help keep foreign matter from falling into the open eye. The eyebrows prevent sweat on the forehead from dripping into the eyes. Reflex mechanisms provide additional protection: The sudden approach of an

---

wavelength   The distance between adjacent waves of radiant energy; in vision most closely associated with the perceptual dimension of hue.

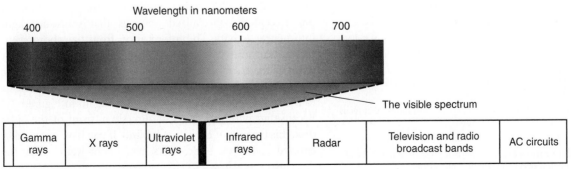

[**FIGURE 6•6**] The electromagnetic spectrum.

[**FIGURE 6•7**] A cross section of the human eye.

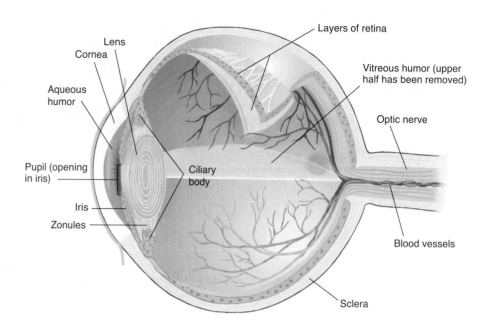

object toward the face or a touch on the surface of the eye causes automatic eyelid closure and withdrawal of the head.

FIGURE 6•7 shows a cross section of a human eye. The transparent **cornea** forms a bulge at the front of the eye and admits light. A tough white membrane called the **sclera** (from the Greek skleros, "hard") coats the rest of the eye. The **iris** consists of two bands of muscles that control the amount of light admitted into the eye. The brain controls these muscles and thus regulates the size of the pupil, which is the circular opening formed by the iris. The pupil constricts in bright light and dilates in dim light. The space immediately behind the cornea is filled with aqueous humor, which simply means "watery fluid." This fluid is constantly produced by tissue behind the cornea that filters the fluid from the blood. In place of blood vessels, the aqueous humor nourishes the cornea and other portions of the front of the eye; this fluid must circulate and be renewed. (If aqueous humor is produced too quickly or if the passage that returns it to the blood becomes blocked, the pressure within the eye can increase and cause damage to vision—a disorder known as glaucoma.) Because of its transparency, the cornea must be nourished in this unusual manner. Our vision would be less clear if the cornea had blood vessels within it.

The curvature of the cornea and of the **lens,** which lies immediately behind the iris, causes images to be focused on the **retina,** located on inner surface of the back of the eye. Although this image is upside down and reversed from left to right, the brain compensates for this alteration and appropriately interprets the information. A special set of muscles, the *ciliary muscles,* can alter its shape so that images of either nearby or distant objects can be focused on the retina. This change in the shape of the lens to adjust for distance is called **accommodation.**

Normally, the length of the eye from front to back is such that the image of the visual scene is sharply focused on the retina. However, for some people, the eye is too long or too short, so the image on the retina is out of focus. These people may need extra lenses (in the form of eyeglasses or contact lenses) to bring the image into focus. In some cases, people elect to undergo surgical reshaping of the cornea by means of a laser. People whose eyes are too long are said to be *nearsighted;* they need a concave lens to correct the focus. People whose eyes are too short are said to be *farsighted;* they need a convex lens. As people get older, the lenses of their eyes become less flexible, and it becomes difficult for them to focus on objects close to them. They may need to wear reading glasses with convex lenses or, if they already wear glasses, switch to bifocals. (See FIGURE 6•8.)

The retina performs the sensory functions of the eye. Embedded in the retina are more than 130 million **photoreceptors**—specialized neurons that transduce light into neural activity. The information from the photoreceptors is transmitted to neurons that send axons toward one point at the back of the eye—the **optic disk.** All axons leave the eye at this point and join the optic nerve, which connects to the brain. (See FIGURE 6•9, and refer again to Figure 6.7.) Because no photoreceptors lie directly in front of the optic disk, this portion of the retina is blind. If you have not yet discovered your own blind spots, you might want to try the demonstration shown in FIGURE 6•10.

---

cornea The transparent tissue covering the front of the eye.

sclera The tough outer layer of the eye; the "white" of the eye.

iris The pigmented muscle of the eye that controls the size of the pupil.

lens The transparent organ situated behind the iris of the eye; helps focus an image on the retina.

retina The tissue at the back inside surface of the eye that contains the photoreceptors and associated neurons.

accommodation Changes in the thickness of the lens of the eye that focus images of near or distant objects on the retina.

photoreceptor A receptive cell for vision in the retina; a rod or a cone.

optic disk A circular structure located at the exit point from the retina of the axons of the ganglion cells that form the optic nerve.

[**FIGURE 6•8**] Lenses used to correct nearsightedness and farsightedness.

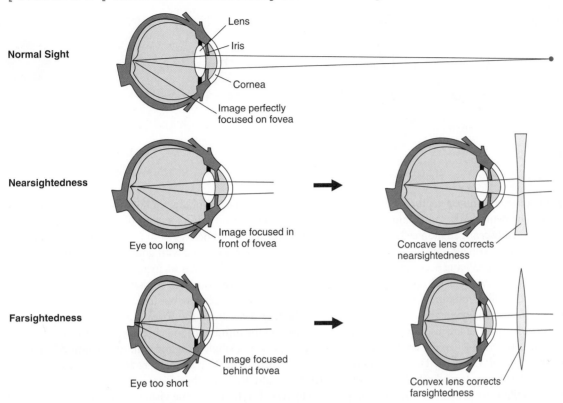

Before the seventeenth century, scientists thought that the lens sensed the presence of light. Johannes Kepler (1571–1630), the astronomer who discovered the elliptical shape of the planets' orbits around the sun, is credited with suggesting that the retina, not the lens, contained the receptive tissue of the eye. It remained for Christoph Scheiner (another German astronomer) to demonstrate in 1625 that the lens is simply a focusing device. (Perhaps astronomers had a special interest in vision and gave some thought to it during the long nights spent watching the sky.) Scheiner obtained an

ox's eye from a slaughterhouse. After carefully peeling the sclera away from the back of the eye, he was able to see an upside-down image of the world through the thin, translucent membrane that remained. As an astronomer, he was familiar with the fact that convex glass lenses could cast images, so he recognized the function of the lens of the eye.

FIGURE 6•11 shows a schematic cross-section of the retina. The retina has three principal layers. Light passes successively through the *ganglion cell layer* (front), the *bipolar cell layer* (middle), and the *photoreceptor layer* (back). Early anatomists were surprised to find the photoreceptors in the deepest layer of the retina. As you might expect, the cells that are located above the photoreceptors are transparent.

Photoreceptors respond to light and pass signals by means of a neurotransmitter to the **bipolar cells,** the neurons with which they form synapses. Bipolar cells transmit this information to the **ganglion cells,** neurons whose axons travel across the retina to form the optic nerve. Thus, visual information passes through a three-cell chain to the brain: photoreceptor → bipolar cell → ganglion cell → brain.

A single photoreceptor responds only to light that reaches its immediate vicinity, but a ganglion cell can receive

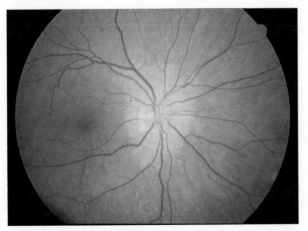

[**FIGURE 6•9**] A view of the back of the eye. The photograph shows the retina, the optic disk, and blood vessels. (Courtesy of Douglas G. Mollerstuen, New England Medical Center.)

bipolar cell   A neuron in the retina that receives information from photoreceptors and passes it on to the ganglion cells, from which axons proceed through the optic nerves to the brain.

ganglion cell   A neuron in the retina that receives information from photoreceptors by means of bipolar cells, and from which axons proceed through the optic nerves to the brain.

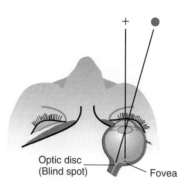

[**FIGURE 6•10**] A test for the blind spot. With the left eye closed, look at the + with your right eye, and move the page back and forth, toward and away from yourself. At about 20 centimeters, the colored circle disappears from your vision because its image falls on your blind spot.

information from many different photoreceptors. The retina also contains other types of neurons that interconnect both adjacent photoreceptors and adjacent ganglion cells. (Refer to Figure 6.11.) The existence of this neural circuitry indicates that some kinds of information processing occur in the retina.

The human retina contains two general types of photoreceptors: approximately 125 million rods and 6 million cones, so called because of their shapes. **Rods** function mainly in dim light; they are very sensitive to light but are insensitive to differences between colors. **Cones** function when the level of illumination is bright enough to see things clearly. They are also responsible for color vision. The **fovea**, a small pit in the back of the retina approximately 1 millimeter in diameter, contains only cones. (Refer to Figure 6.8.) In most cases, a cone sends signals to only one ganglion cell via the bipolar cell to which it is connected. As a consequence, the fovea is responsible for our highest acuity. (*Acuity* refers to the ability of the eye to detect fine details. The word derives from the Latin *acus*, "needle." We sometimes say of someone with good visual acuity that he or she has "sharp eyes.") When we focus on a specific point in our visual field, we move our eyes so that the image of that point falls directly on the cone-packed fovea.

Farther away from the fovea, the number of cones decreases and the number of rods increases. Up to 100 rods may send signals to a single ganglion cell. A ganglion cell that receives information from so many rods is sensitive to very low levels of light. Rods are therefore responsible for our sensitivity to very dim light, but the visual information they convey lacks the same sharpness produced by cones.

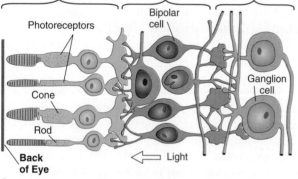

Photoreceptor Layer   Bipolar Cell Layer   Ganglion Cell Layer

Photoreceptors
Bipolar cell
Cone
Ganglion cell
Rod
Back of Eye
⟵ Light

[**FIGURE 6•11**] The cells of the retina.

(Redrawn by permission of the Royal Society and the authors from Dowling, J. E., & Boycott, B. B. (1966). *Proceedings of the Royal Society (London), Series B, 166,* 80–111.)

rod A photoreceptor that is very sensitive to light but cannot detect changes in hue.

cone A photoreceptor that is responsible for acute daytime vision and for color perception.

fovea A small pit near the center of the retina containing densely packed cones; responsible for the most acute and detailed vision.

photopigment A complex molecule found in photoreceptors; when struck by light, it splits apart and stimulates the membrane of the photoreceptor in which it resides.

rhodopsin The photopigment contained by rods.

Transduction of Light by Photoreceptors

Although light-sensitive sense organs have evolved independently in a wide variety of animals—from insects to fish to mammals—the chemistry is essentially the same in all species: A molecule derived from vitamin A is the central ingredient in the transduction of the energy of light into neural activity. (Carrots are said to be good for vision because they contain a substance that the body easily converts to vitamin A.) In the absence of light, this molecule is attached to another molecule, a protein. The two molecules together form a **photopigment.** The photoreceptors of the human eye contain four kinds of photopigments (one for rods and three for cones), but their basic mechanism is the same. When a photon (a particle of light) strikes a photopigment, the photopigment splits apart into its two constituent molecules. This event starts the process of transduction. The splitting of the photopigment causes a series of chemical reactions that stimulate the photoreceptor and cause it to send a signal to the bipolar cell with which it forms a synapse. The bipolar cell sends a signal to the ganglion cell, which then sends a signal to the brain. (See FIGURE 6•12.)

An intact photopigment has a characteristic color. **Rhodopsin,** the photopigment of rods, is pink (rhodon means "rose" in Greek). However, once photopigments are split apart by the action of light, they lose their color—they become bleached. Franz Boll discovered this phenomenon in 1876 when he removed an eye from an animal and pointed it toward

[**FIGURE 6•12**] Transduction of light into neural activity. A photon strikes a photoreceptor and causes the photopigment to split apart. This event initiates the transmission of information to the brain.

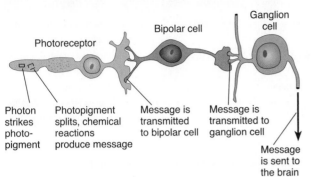

a window that opened onto a brightly lit scene. He then examined the retina under dim light and found that the image of the scene was still there. The retina was pink where little light had fallen and pale where the image had been bright. Boll's discovery led others to suspect that a chemical reaction was responsible for the transduction of light into neural activity.

After light has caused a molecule of photopigment to split and become bleached, energy from the photoreceptor's metabolism causes the two molecules to recombine. The photopigment is then ready to be bleached by light again. Each photoreceptor contains many thousands of molecules of photopigment. The number of intact, unbleached molecules of photopigment in a given cell depends on the relative rates at which they are being split by light and being put back together by the cell's energy. The brighter the light, the more bleached photopigment there is, causing decreased sensitivity to light.

Adaptation to Light and Dark

Think for a moment about how difficult it can be to find a seat in a darkened movie theater. If you have just come in from bright sunlight, your eyes do not respond well to the low level of illumination. However, after a few minutes you can see rather well—your eyes have adapted to the dark. This phenomenon is called **dark adaptation.**

As already stated, the detection of light requires that photons split molecules of rhodopsin or one of the other photopigments. When high levels of illumination strike the retina, the rate of regeneration of rhodopsin falls behind the rate of the bleaching process. With only a small percentage of the rhodopsin molecules intact, the rods are not very sensitive to light. If you enter a dark room after being in a brightly lit room or in sunlight, there are too few intact rhodopsin molecules for your eyes to respond immediately to dim light. The probability that a photon will strike an intact molecule of rhodopsin is very low. However, after a while the regeneration of rhodopsin overcomes the bleaching effects of the light energy. The rods become full of unbleached rhodopsin, and a photon passing through a rod is likely to find a target. The eye has become dark adapted.

Eye Movements

Although our field of vision is rather wide, visual acuity falls off rapidly just a small distance away from the fixation point. For example, if you focus on the first word in a line of this book, you will not be able to read the last word on that line. When we want to see what is to be found in the scene in front of us, we simply move our eyes and scan the scene, examining the important parts of it with our foveal vision.

The eyes make three types of movements: saccadic movements, vergence movements, and pursuit movements. When you scan the scene in front of you, your gaze travels from point to point as you examine important or interesting features. As you do so, your eyes make jerky **saccadic movements**—you shift your gaze abruptly from one point to another. (See FIGURE 6•13.) For example, when you read a line in this book, your eyes stop several times, moving very quickly

[**FIGURE 6•13**] Saccadic eye movements. The gaze shifts from point to point as we examine a scene. The white line traces a series of saccadic movements that might be made by someone looking at the scene shown in the photo.

(From Nature Publishing Group. (2004). *Nature Neuroscience, 7,* cover image. Reprinted with permission.)

dark adaptation   The process by which the eye becomes capable of distinguishing dimly illuminated objects after going from a bright region to a dark one.

saccadic movement   The rapid movement of the eyes that is used in scanning a visual scene, as opposed to the smooth pursuit movements used to follow a moving object.

between each stop. You cannot consciously control the speed of movement between stops; during each saccade, or jump, the eyes move as fast as they can.

When making **vergence movements,** both eyes remain fixed on the same target—or, more precisely, such movements keep the image of the target object focused on corresponding parts of the two retinas. If you hold up a finger in front of your face, look at it, and then bring your finger closer to your face, your eyes will make vergence movements toward your nose. If you then look at an object on the other side of the room, your eyes will rotate outward, and you will see two separate blurry images of your finger. As you will learn in Chapter 7, vergence eye movements assist the perception of distance.

Much of the time, the visual scene in front of us contains moving objects: other people, objects blown by the wind, automobiles, airplanes, animals. When we concentrate on one of these objects, we fix our gaze on it and smoothly track its movements with our eyes. These tracking movements, which follow the object and project its image onto the fovea, are called **pursuit movements.**

Color Vision

Among mammals, only primates have full color vision. A bull does not charge a red cape; he charges what he sees as an annoying gray object being waved at him. Many birds and fishes have excellent color vision; a brightly colored lure may really appeal to fish as much as to the angler who buys it.

Light (as we humans define it) consists of radiant energy having wavelengths between 380 and 760 nm. Light of different wavelengths gives rise to the perception of different colors. How are we able to tell the differences? Experiments have shown that three types of cones are found in the human eye, each containing a different type of photopigment. Each type of photopigment is most sensitive to light of a particular wavelength. That is, light of a particular wavelength most readily causes a particular photopigment to split. Thus, different types of cones are stimulated by different wavelengths of light. This information is what enables us to perceive colors.

Wavelength is related to color, but the terms are not synonymous. For example, the spectral colors (the colors we see in a rainbow, which contains the entire spectrum of visible radiant energy) do not include all the colors that we can see, such as brown, pink, and the metallic colors silver and gold. The fact that not all colors are found in the spectrum means

---

vergence movement The cooperative movement of the eyes, which ensures that the image of an object falls on identical portions of both retinas.

pursuit movement The movement that the eyes make to maintain an image upon the fovea.

hue A perceptual dimension of color, most closely related to the wavelength of a pure light. The effect of a particular hue is caused by the mixture of lights of various wavelengths.

brightness A perceptual dimension of color, most closely related to the intensity or degree of radiant energy emitted by a visual stimulus.

saturation A perceptual dimension of color, most closely associated with purity of a color.

[**TABLE 6·2**] Physical and Perceptual Dimensions of Color

Perceptual Dimension	Physical Dimension	Physical Characteristics
Hue	Wavelength	Length of oscillation of light radiation
Brightness	Intensity	Amount of energy of light radiation
Saturation	Purity	Intensity of dominant wavelength relative to total light energy

that differences in wavelength alone do not account for the differences in the colors we can perceive.

The Dimensions of Color Most colors can be described in terms of three physical dimensions: wavelength, intensity, and purity. Three perceptual dimensions corresponding to these physical dimensions—hue, brightness, and saturation—describe what we see. (See **TABLE 6·2.**) The **hue** of most colors is determined by wavelength; for example, light having a wavelength of 540 nm is perceived as green. A color's **brightness** is determined by the intensity, or amount of energy, of the light that is present, all other factors being equal. A color of *maximum* brightness dazzles us; a color of *minimum* brightness is simply black. The third perceptual dimension of color, **saturation,** is roughly equivalent to purity. A fully saturated color consists of light of only one wavelength—for example, pure red or pure blue. Desaturated colors look pastel or washed out. FIGURE 6·14 illustrates how a color with a particular dominant wavelength (hue) can vary in brightness and saturation.

Additive Color Mixing Vision can be considered a synthetic sensory modality. That is, vision synthesizes (puts together) rather than analyzes (takes apart). When two wavelengths of light are present, we see an intermediate color rather than the two components. (In contrast, the auditory system can be considered analytical. If a high note and a low

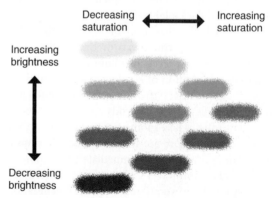

[**FIGURE 6·14**] Hue, brightness, and saturation. The colors shown have the same dominant wavelength (hue) but different saturation and brightness.

[**FIGURE 6•15**] Additive color mixing. White light can be split into a spectrum of colors with a prism and recombined through another prism.

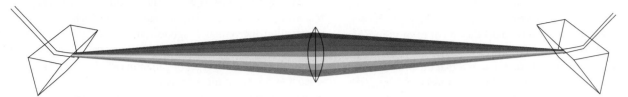

note are played together on a piano, we hear both notes instead of a single, intermediate tone.) The addition of two or more lights of different wavelengths is called **additive color mixing.** If we pass a beam of white light through a prism, we break it into the spectrum of the different wavelengths it contains. If we recombine these colors by passing them through another prism (as Sir Isaac Newton did in 1666), we obtain white light again. (See FIGURE 6•15.)

Do not confuse additive color mixing with pigment mixing—what we do when we mix paints. An object has a particular color because it contains pigments that absorb some wavelengths of light (converting them into heat) and reflect other wavelengths. For example, the chlorophyll found in the leaves of plants absorbs less green light than light of other wavelengths. When a leaf is illuminated by white light, it reflects a high proportion of green light and appears green to us.

When we mix paints, we are subtracting colors, not adding them. Mixing two paints yields a darker result. (See FIGURE 6•16.) For example, adding blue paint to yellow paint yields green paint, which certainly looks darker than yellow. But mixing two beams of light of different wavelengths always yields a lighter color. For example, when red and green light are shone together on a piece of white paper, we see yellow. In fact, we cannot tell a pure yellow light from a synthesized one made of the proper intensities of red and green light. To our eyes, both yellows appear identical.

To reconstitute white light, we do not even have to recombine all the wavelengths in the spectrum. If we shine a blue light, a green light, and a red light together on a sheet of white paper and properly adjust their intensities, the place where all three beams overlap will look perfectly white (refer to Figure 6.16). A color television or a computer screen uses this principle. When white appears on the screen, it actually consists of tiny dots of red, blue, and green light.

The spectral colors, contained in a rainbow, do not include all the colors we can see. Thus, differences in wavelength do not account for all the differences in the colors we can perceive.

additive color mixing The perception of two or more lights of different wavelengths seen together as light of an intermediate wavelength.

[**FIGURE 6•16**] Additive color mixing and paint mixing. When blue, red, and green light of the proper intensity are all shone together, the result is white light. When red, blue, and yellow paints are mixed together, the result is a dark gray.

Color Coding in the Retina In 1802 Thomas Young (1773–1829), a British physicist and physician, noted that any color that the human eye can see can be synthesized by mixing almost any set of three colors of different wavelengths. Young proposed a **trichromatic theory** ("three-color" theory) of color vision. He hypothesized that the eye contains three types of color receptors, each sensitive to a different hue, and that the brain synthesizes colors by combining the information received from each type of receptor. He suggested that these receptors were sensitive to three of the colors that people perceive as "pure": blue, green, and red. (His theory ignored the fact that people also perceive yellow as a pure color; more about this fact later.) Young's suggestion was incorporated later in the nineteenth century into a more elaborate theory of color vision developed by Hermann von Helmholtz.

Experiments in recent years have shown that the cones in the human eye do contain three types of photopigments, each of which preferentially absorbs light of a particular wavelength: 420, 530, and 560 nm. Although these wavelengths actually correspond to blue-violet, green, and yellow-green, most investigators refer to these receptors as blue, green, and red cones. To simplify the discussion here, let's pretend that the three cones respond to these three pure hues. The retina contains about twice as many red cones as green cones. There are far fewer blue cones.

The eye uses the principle of the color television screen, but in reverse: Instead of displaying colors, it senses them. If a spot of white light shines on the retina, it stimulates all three types of cones equally, and we perceive white light. If a spot of pure blue, green, or red light shines on the retina, it stimulates only one of the three classes of cones, and a pure color is perceived. If a spot of yellow light shines on the retina, it stimulates red and green cones equally well but has little effect on blue cones. (You can look back at Figure 6.6 and see that yellow is located between red and green.) Stimulation of red and green cones, then, is the signal that yellow light has been received.

Other investigators after Young and Helmholtz devised theories that took into account the fact that people also perceive yellow as a pure hue. Late in the nineteenth century, Ewald Hering (1834–1918), a German physiologist, noted that the four primary hues appeared to belong to pairs of opposing colors: red/green and yellow/blue. We can imagine a bluish green or a yellowish green, or a bluish red or a yellowish red. However, it is more difficult to imagine a greenish red or a yellowish blue. Hering originally suggested that we cannot imagine these blends because there are two types of photoreceptors, one kind responding to green and red and the other kind responding to yellow and blue. (We'll look at the reasoning behind his statement shortly.)

Hering's hypothesis about the nature of photoreceptors was wrong, but he accurately described the characteristics of the information the retinal ganglion cells send to the brain. Two types of ganglion cells encode color vision: red/green cells and yellow/blue cells. Both types of ganglion cells fire at a steady rate when they are not stimulated. If a spot of red light shines on the retina, excitation of the red cones causes the red/green ganglion cells to begin to fire at a high rate. Conversely, if a spot of green light shines on the retina, excitation of the green cones causes the red/green ganglion cells to begin to fire at a slow rate. Thus, the brain learns about the presence of red or green light by the increased or decreased rate of firing of axons attached to red/green ganglion cells. Similarly, yellow/blue ganglion cells are excited by yellow light and inhibited by blue light. Because red and green light, and yellow and blue light, have opposite effects on the rate of axon firing, this temporal coding scheme is called an **opponent process.**

The retina contains red/green and yellow/blue ganglion cells because of the nature of the connections between the cones, bipolar cells, and ganglion cells. The brain detects various colors by comparing the rates of firing of the axons in the optic nerve that signal red or green and yellow or blue. Now you can see why we cannot perceive (and therefore cannot imagine) a reddish green or a bluish yellow: An axon that signals red or green (or yellow or blue) can either increase or decrease its rate of firing. It cannot do both at the same time. A reddish green would have to be signaled by a ganglion cell firing slowly and rapidly at the same time, which is obviously impossible.

Negative Afterimages FIGURE 6•17 demonstrates an interesting property of the visual system: the formation of a **negative afterimage.** Stare at the cross in the center of the colorful but odd-looking image on the left for approximately 30 seconds. (Doing so will focus the image on the same retinal location in each eye.) Then quickly look at the cross in the center of the white rectangle on the right. You will have a fleeting experience of seeing the more familiar red and green colors of a radish—colors that are complementary, or opposite, to the ones on the left. Items that are complementary go together to make up a whole. In color vision, complementary colors are those that make white (or shades of gray) when added together.

The most important cause of negative afterimages is the adaptation in the rate of firing of retinal ganglion cells that occurs during prolonged exposure to the original stimulus. When ganglion cells are excited or inhibited for a prolonged period of time, they later show a rebound effect, firing faster or slower than normal. For example, the green of the radish in Figure 6.17 inhibits some red/green ganglion cells. When this region of the retina is then stimulated by the neutral-colored light reflected off the white rectangle, the red/green ganglion cells—no longer inhibited by the green light—fire faster than normal. Thus, we see a red afterimage of the radish.

---

trichromatic theory The theory that color vision is accomplished by three types of photodetectors, each of which is maximally sensitive to a different wavelength of light.

opponent process The representation of colors by the rate of firing of two types of neurons: red/green and yellow/blue.

negative afterimage The image seen after a portion of the retina is exposed to an intense visual stimulus; a negative afterimage consists of colors complementary to those of the physical stimulus.

Defects in Color Vision Approximately one in twenty males has some form of defective or anomalous color vision. These defects are sometimes called color blindness, but this term should probably be reserved for the very few people who cannot see any color at all. Males are affected more than females because many of the genes for producing photopigments are located on the X chromosome. Females have two X chromosomes, but males have only one; so in males, a defective gene on that chromosome will always be expressed.

There are many different types of defective color vision. Two of the three we'll consider involve the red/green system. People with these defects confuse red and green. Their primary color sensations are yellow and blue; red and green both appear yellowish. FIGURE 6•18 shows one of the figures from a commonly used test for defective color vision. A person who confuses red and green will not be able to see the number 5 in this image.

The most common defect in color vision, called **protanopia** (literally, "first-color defect"), appears to result from a lack of the photopigment for red cones. The fact that people with protanopia have relatively normal sharpness of vision suggests that they have red cones but that these cones are filled with green photopigment (Boynton, 1979). If red cones were missing, almost half of the cones would be gone from the retina, and vision would be less acute. To a person with protanopia, red

looks much darker than green. The second form of red/green defect, called **deuteranopia** ("second-color defect"), appears to result from the opposite kind of substitution: Green cones are filled with red photopigment.

This third form of color defect, called **tritanopia** ("third-color defect"), involves the yellow/blue system and is much rarer: It affects fewer than 1 in 10,000 people. People with tritanopia see the world in greens and reds; to them, a clear blue sky is a bright green, and yellow appears pink. The faulty gene that causes tritanopia is not carried on a sex chromosome; therefore, it is equally common in males and females. This defect appears to involve the loss of blue cones. There are far fewer of these than of red and green cones to begin with, and investigators have not yet determined whether the blue cones of people with tritanopia are missing or are filled with one of the other photopigments. And yes, in case you were wondering, a person with both protanopia or deuteranopia along with tritanopia will have no color vision at all, and will see the world in shades of gray.

QUESTION TO CONSIDER

Birds, certain species of fish, and some primate species have full, three-cone color vision. Why is color vision useful? What are its specific benefits for humans?

Audition

Vision involves the perception of objects in three dimensions, at various distances, and with a multitude of colors and textures. These complex stimuli may occur at a single point in time or over an extended period. They also may involve either an unchanging or a rapidly changing scene. In contrast to vision, the other senses either analyze much simpler stimuli (such as an

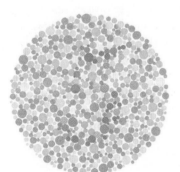

[FIGURE 6•18] A figure commonly used to test for defective color vision. People with red/green color blindness will fail to see the 5. (Courtesy of American Optical Corporation.)

protanopia A form of hereditary anomalous color vision; caused by defective "red" cones in the retina.

deuteranopia A form of hereditary anomalous color vision; caused by defective "green" cones in the retina.

tritanopia A form of hereditary anomalous color vision; caused by a lack of "blue" cones in the retina.

[FIGURE 6•19] Sound waves. Changes in air pressure from sound waves move the eardrum in and out. Air molecules are closer together in regions of higher pressure and farther apart in regions of lower pressure.

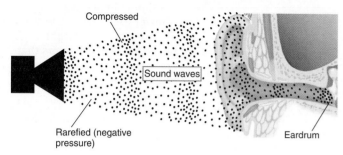

odor or a taste) or require time and stimulus change for the development of a complex perception. For example, to perceive a solid object in three dimensions by means of touch, we must manipulate it—turn it over in our hands or move our hands over its surface. The stimulus must change over time for a full-fledged perception of form to emerge. The same is true for audition: We hear nothing meaningful in an instant.

Sound

Sound consists of rhythmical pressure changes in air. As an object vibrates, it causes the air around it to move. The vibration creates waves of pressure, positive and negative, as molecules of air alternately undergo compression and rarefaction (thinning out). As a positive-pressure wave arrives at your ear, it bends your eardrum in. The following wave of negative pressure causes your eardrum to bend out. (See FIGURE 6•19.)

Sound waves are measured in frequency units of cycles per second or **hertz (Hz).** The human ear perceives vibrations

---

hertz (Hz) The primary measure of the frequency of vibration of sound waves; cycles per second.

timbre (*tamm ber*) A perceptual dimension of sound that corresponds to its complexity.

ossicle (*ahss i kul*) One of the three bones of the middle ear (the *hammer, anvil,* and *stirrup*) that transmit acoustical vibrations from the eardrum to the membrane behind the oval window of the cochlea.

cochlea (*cock lee uh* or *coke lee uh*) A snail-shaped chamber set in bone in the inner ear, where audition takes place.

oval window An opening in the bone surrounding the cochlea. The stirrup presses against a membrane behind the oval window and transmits sound vibrations into the fluid within the cochlea.

---

between approximately 30 and 20,000 Hz. Sound waves can vary in intensity (amplitude) and frequency. These variations produce corresponding changes in our perception of a sound's loudness and of its pitch (highness or lowness). Consider a loudspeaker, a device that contains a paper cone moved back and forth by a coil of wire located in a magnetic field. Alternations in the electrical current transmitted from an amplifier to this coil cause the coil (and the paper cone) to move back and forth. If the vibrations become more intense (that is, if the cone moves in and out over a greater distance), the loudness of the sound increases. (See FIGURE 6•20.) If the cone begins vibrating more rapidly, the pitch of the sound rises. A third perceptual dimension, **timbre,** corresponds to the complexity of the sound. We'll examine all three dimensions of sound waves in more detail later in the chapter.

The Ear and Its Functions

When people refer to the ear, they usually mean what anatomists call the *pinna*—the flesh-covered cartilage attached to the side of the head. (*Pinna* means "wing" in Latin.) But the pinna performs only a small role in audition. It helps funnel sound waves through the ear canal toward the middle and inner ear, where the business of hearing gets done. (See FIGURE 6•21.)

The eardrum (or, more properly, the tympanic membrane) is a thin, flexible membrane that vibrates back and forth in response to sound waves and passes these vibrations on to the receptor cells in the inner ear. The eardrum is attached to the first of a set of three middle-ear bones called the **ossicles** (literally, "little bones"). The three ossicles are known informally as the hammer, the anvil, and the stirrup, because of their shapes. The technical terms are malleus, incus, and stapes, respectively. These bones act together, in lever fashion, to transmit the vibrations of the eardrum to the fluid-filled structure of the inner ear.

The bony structure that contains the auditory receptor cells is called the **cochlea.** *Kokhlos* is the Greek word for "snail," which accurately describes its shape; refer to Figure 6.21. The cochlea is filled with a liquid. A bony chamber (the vestibule) is attached to the cochlea and contains two openings, the oval window and the round window. The last of the three ossicles (the stirrup) presses against a membrane behind the **oval window,** thus

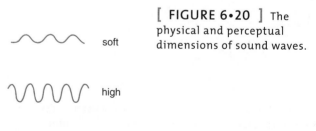

[FIGURE 6•20] The physical and perceptual dimensions of sound waves.

Physical Dimension	Perceptual Dimension				
Amplitude (intensity)	Loudness		loud		soft
Frequency	Pitch		low		high
Complexity	Timbre		simple		complex

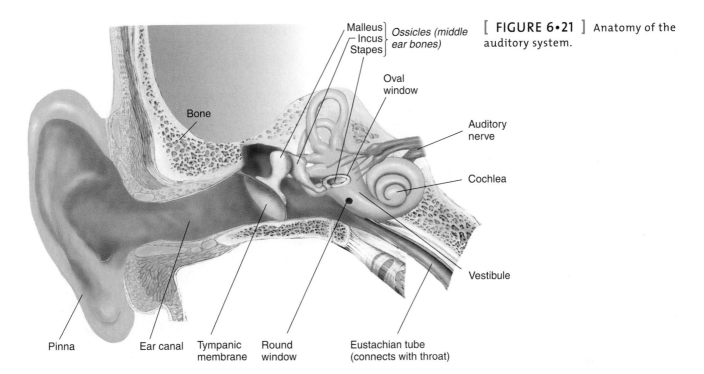

[**FIGURE 6·21**] Anatomy of the auditory system.

Malleus ⎫
Incus ⎬ Ossicles (middle ear bones)
Stapes ⎭

Oval window

Bone

Auditory nerve

Cochlea

Vestibule

Pinna   Ear canal   Tympanic membrane   Round window   Eustachian tube (connects with throat)

transmitting sound waves into the liquid inside the cochlea. The cochlea is divided into three chambers by two membranes. One of them, the **basilar membrane,** contains the auditory receptor cells. As the footplate of the stirrup presses back and forth against the membrane behind the oval window, pressure changes in the fluid above the basilar membrane cause the basilar membrane to vibrate. Because the basilar membrane varies in its width and flexibility along its length, different frequencies of sound cause different parts of the basilar membrane to vibrate.

High-frequency sounds cause the end near the oval window to vibrate, medium-frequency sounds cause the middle to vibrate, and low-frequency sounds cause the tip to vibrate. (See FIGURE 6·22.)

For the basilar membrane to vibrate freely, the fluid in the lower chamber of the cochlea must have somewhere to

---

basilar membrane (*bazz i ler*)   A membrane that divides the cochlea of the inner ear into two compartments. The receptive organ for audition resides here.

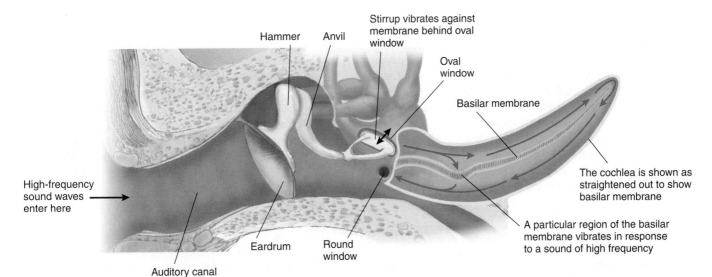

Hammer   Anvil   Stirrup vibrates against membrane behind oval window

Oval window

Basilar membrane

High-frequency sound waves enter here

The cochlea is shown as straightened out to show basilar membrane

A particular region of the basilar membrane vibrates in response to a sound of high frequency

Eardrum   Round window

Auditory canal

[**FIGURE 6·22**] Responses to sound waves. When the stirrup pushes against the membrane behind the oval window, the membrane behind the round window bulges outward. Different high-frequency and medium-frequency sound vibrations cause flexing of different portions of the basilar membrane. In contrast, low-frequency sound vibrations cause the tip of the basilar membrane to flex in synchrony with the vibrations.

[FIGURE 6•23] The transduction of sound vibrations in the auditory system.

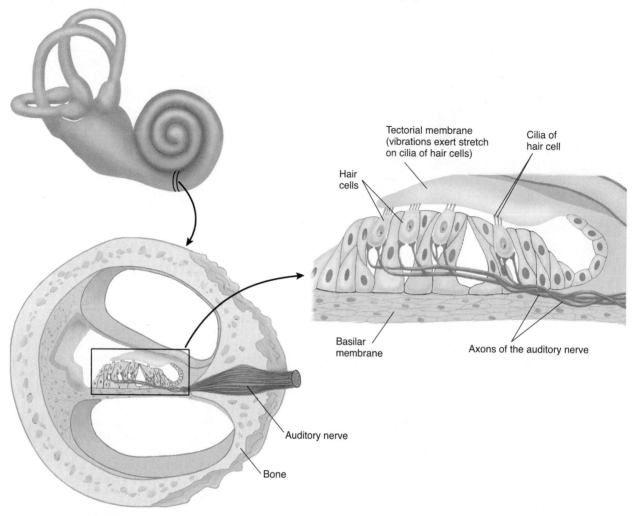

Tectorial membrane (vibrations exert stretch on cilia of hair cells)

Cilia of hair cell

Hair cells

Basilar membrane

Axons of the auditory nerve

Auditory nerve

Bone

Slice through the Cochlea

go—because unlike gases, liquids cannot be compressed. Free space is provided by the **round window.** When the basilar membrane flexes down, the displacement of the fluid causes the membrane behind the round window to bulge out. In turn, when the basilar membrane flexes up, the membrane behind the round window bulges in.

Some people have a middle-ear disease that causes bone to grow over the round window. Because their basilar membrane cannot easily move back and forth, these people have a severe hearing loss. However, their hearing can be restored by

round window An opening in the bone surrounding the cochlea. Movements of the membrane behind this opening permit vibrations to be transmitted through the oval window into the cochlea.

auditory hair cell The sensory neuron of the auditory system; located on the basilar membrane.

cilium (plural: cilia) A hairlike appendage of a cell; involved in movement or in transducing sensory information. Cilia are found on the receptors in the auditory and vestibular system.

tectorial membrane A membrane located above the basilar membrane; serves as a shelf against which the cilia of the auditory hair cells move.

a surgical procedure called *fenestration* ("window making"), in which the surgeon drills a tiny hole in the bone where the round window should be.

Sounds are detected by special neurons known as auditory hair cells, located on the basilar membrane. **Auditory hair cells** transduce mechanical energy caused by the movement of the basilar membrane into neural activity. These cells possess hairlike protrusions called **cilia** ("eyelashes"). The ends of the cilia are embedded in the **tectorial membrane,** a fairly rigid shelf that hangs over the basilar membrane like a balcony. When sound waves cause the basilar membrane to vibrate, the cilia are stretched. This pull on the cilia of the auditory hair cells is translated into neural activity. (See **FIGURE 6•23.**)

When a mechanical force is exerted on the cilia of a cell, ion channels in the membrane of the cilia open, permitting positive ions to enter. The resulting change in the membrane potential of the cilia causes the hair cell to release a neurotransmitter that causes a message to be sent through the auditory nerve to the brain.

Detecting and Localizing Sounds in the Environment

Sounds can differ in pitch, loudness, and timbre. They also come from particular locations in the auditory environment. How does the ear distinguish these characteristics? The ear's ability to distinguish sounds by their timbre depends on its ability to distinguish pitch and loudness. So let's examine these two characteristics first.

Pitch and Loudness Scientists originally thought that the sensory neurons of the auditory system represented pitch (frequency) by firing in synchrony with the vibrations of the basilar membrane. However, they subsequently learned that axons cannot fire rapidly enough to represent the high frequencies that we can hear by means of a simple temporal code (or, as auditory scientists put it, a rate code. A good, young ear can hear frequencies of more than 20,000 Hz, but axons cannot fire more than 1,000 times per second. Therefore, high-frequency sounds, at least, must be encoded in some other way.

As we saw, high-frequency and medium-frequency sounds cause different parts of the basilar membrane to vibrate. Thus, sounds of different frequencies stimulate different groups of auditory hair cells located along the basilar membrane. At least for high-frequency and medium-frequency sounds, therefore, the brain is informed of the pitch by the activity of different sets of axons in the auditory nerve that represent different groups of hair cells. (You will recognize this as an anatomical code—which auditory scientists refer to as a *place code*.) When medium-frequency sound waves reach the ear, auditory hair cells located in the middle of the basilar membrane are activated. In contrast, high-frequency sounds activate auditory hair cells located at the base of the basilar membrane near the oval window. (Refer to Figure 6.23.)

Experiments have found that damage to specific sets of hair cells along the basilar membrane causes loss of the ability to perceive specific frequencies. Perhaps the most convincing evidence that the basilar membrane uses a place code to detect pitch comes from the effectiveness of cochlear implants. **Cochlear implants** are devices that are used to restore hearing in people with deafness caused by damage to the hair cells. The external part of a cochlear implant consists of a microphone and a miniaturized electronic signal processor. The internal part contains a very thin, flexible array of electrodes, which the surgeon carefully inserts into the cochlea in such a way that it follows the snaillike curl and ends up resting along the entire length of the basilar membrane. Each electrode in the array stimulates a different part of the basilar membrane. Information from the signal processor is passed to the electrodes by means of flat coils of wire, implanted under the skin. (See FIGURE 6·24.)

The primary purpose of a cochlear implant is to restore a person's ability to understand speech. Because most of the important acoustical information in speech is contained in frequencies that are too high to be accurately represented by a rate code, the multichannel electrode was developed in an attempt to duplicate the place coding of pitch on the basilar

[**FIGURE 6·24**] A child with a cochlear implant. The microphone and processor are worn over the ear, and the headpiece contains a coil that transmits signals to the implant.

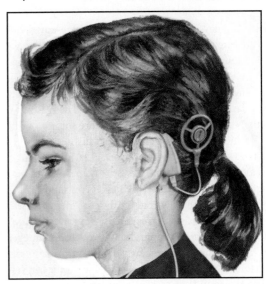

membrane (Copeland & Pillsbury, 2004). When different regions of the basilar membrane are stimulated, the person perceives sounds with different pitches. The signal processor in the external device analyzes the sounds detected by the microphone and sends separate signals to the appropriate portions of the basilar membrane. This device can work well; many people with cochlear implants can understand speech well enough to use a telephone.

Although high-frequency and medium-frequency sounds are detected because they cause different sets of hair cells to respond, low-frequency sounds are detected by a different method. Kiang (1965) recorded the electrical activity of single axons in the auditory nerve and found many that responded best to sounds of particular frequencies. Presumably, these axons originated in neurons stimulated by hair cells located on different regions of the basilar membrane. However, Kiang did not find any axons that responded uniquely to particular frequencies below 200 Hz—and yet tones lower than 200 Hz are easily perceived. How, then, are the lower frequencies encoded?

The answer is this: Frequencies lower than 200 Hz cause the tip of the basilar membrane to vibrate in synchrony with the sound waves. Neurons that are stimulated by hair cells located there are able to fire in synchrony with these vibrations, thus firing at the same frequency as the sound. The brain "counts" these vibrations (so to speak) and thus detects low-frequency sounds. This process is obviously an example of temporal (rate) coding.

What about loudness (intensity, or amplitude)? The axons of the auditory nerve appear to inform the brain of the loudness of a stimulus by altering their rate of firing—another example

---

cochlear implant An electronic device surgically implanted in the inner ear that can enable a deaf person to hear.

of temporal coding. More-intense vibrations stimulate the auditory hair cells more intensely. This stimulation causes them to release more transmitter substance, which results in a higher rate of firing by the axons in the auditory nerve.

Timbre So far we have been considering pure sine waves, but such sounds are rarely heard outside the laboratory. Instead, we usually hear sounds with a rich mixture of frequencies—sounds of complex timbre. For example, consider the sound of a clarinet playing a particular note. If we hear it, we can easily say that it is a clarinet and not a flute or a violin. The reason we can do so is that these three instruments produce sounds of different timbre, which our auditory system can distinguish.

FIGURE 6•25 shows the waveform from a clarinet playing a steady note (*top*). The shape of the waveform repeats itself regularly at the **fundamental frequency,** which corresponds to the perceived pitch of the note. A Fourier analysis of the waveform shows that it actually consists of a series of sine waves that includes the fundamental frequency and many **overtones,** integer multiples of the fundamental frequency. Different instruments produce overtones with different intensities. Electronic synthesizers simulate the sounds of real instruments by producing a series of overtones of the proper intensities, mixing them, and passing them through a loudspeaker.

When the basilar membrane is stimulated by the sound of a clarinet, different portions respond to each of the overtones. This response produces a unique anatomically coded pattern of activity in the auditory nerve, which is subsequently identified by circuits in the auditory association cortex.

Perception of Environmental Sounds Actually, the recognition of complex sounds is not quite as simple as I implied in the previous subsection. Figure 6.25 shows the analysis of a sustained sound of a clarinet. But most sounds (including those produced by a clarinet) are dynamic; that is, their beginnings, middles, and ends are different from each other. The beginning of a note played on a clarinet (the attack) contains frequencies that appear and disappear in a few milliseconds. At the end of the note (the decay), some harmonics disappear before others. If we are to recognize different sounds, the auditory cortex must analyze a complex sequence of multiple frequencies that appear, change in amplitude, and disappear. And when you consider the fact that we can listen to an orchestra and identify several instruments that are playing simultaneously, you can appreciate the complexity of the analysis performed by the auditory system. We will revisit this process later in this chapter.

The task of the auditory system in identifying particular sound sources is one of *pattern recognition*. The auditory system must recognize that particular patterns of constantly changing activity received from the hair cells on the basilar membrane belong to different sound sources, and few patterns

---

fundamental frequency The lowest, and usually most intense, frequency of a complex sound; most often perceived as the sound's basic pitch.

overtone A component of a complex tone; one of a series of tones whose frequency is a multiple of the fundamental frequency.

[**FIGURE 6•25**] Analysis of timbre. The shape of a sound wave from a clarinet is shown at the top. The waveforms under it show the frequencies into which it can be analyzed.

(Copyright © 1977 by CBS Magazines. Reprinted from *Stereo Review,* June 1977, by permission.)

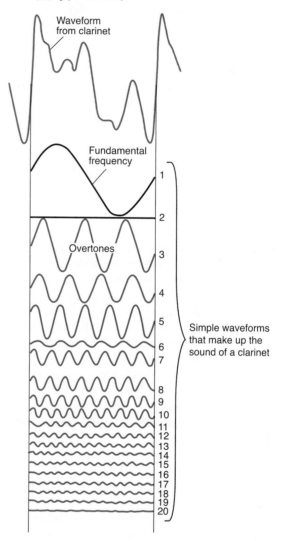

are simple mixtures of fixed frequencies. Consider the complexity of sounds that occur in the environment: cars honking, birds chirping, people coughing, doors slamming, and so on. (An even more complicated task—speech recognition—is discussed in Chapter 10.)

A functional imaging study by Lewis et al. (2004) presented subjects with recordings of environmental sounds—sounds made by various tools, animals, dropped objects, and poured or dripping liquids. They also presented these sounds recorded backward, which preserved their complexity but made it impossible for them to be recognized. All sounds activated the auditory cortex, but only recognized sounds activated a region of the left hemisphere centered on the posterior temporal lobe—a region also activated by the recognition of objects by seeing them or hearing verbal descriptions of them.

[CASE STUDY] Patient I. R., a right-handed woman in her early forties, sustained damage to regions of the cortex of her left hemisphere, including portions of the auditory association cortex. Ten years later, Peretz and her colleagues studied the effects of her brain damage on her musical ability (Peretz, Gagnon, and Bouchard, 1998; Peretz et al., 2001). Although Patient I. R. had normal hearing, could understand speech and converse normally, and could recognize environmental sounds, she showed a nearly complete *amusia*—loss of the ability to perceive or produce melodic or rhythmic aspects of music. She had been raised in a musical environment: Both her grandmother and brother were professional musicians. After her surgery, she lost the ability to recognize melodies that she had been familiar with previously, including simple pieces such as "Happy Birthday." She was no longer able to sing.

Remarkably, despite her inability to recognize melodic and rhythmic aspects of music, she insisted that she still enjoyed listening to music. Peretz and her colleagues discovered that I. R. was still able to recognize emotional aspects of music. Although she could not recognize pieces that the experimenters played for her, she recognized whether the music sounded happy or sad. She could also recognize happiness, sadness, fear, anger, surprise, and disgust in a person's tone of voice. However, she was totally insensitive to dissonant music, the sound of which irritates normal listeners. Even four-month-old babies prefer consonant music to dissonant music, which shows that recognition of dissonance develops very early in life (Zentner and Kagan, 1998). This case tells us that the brain mechanisms that recognize emotion in music or people's voices are different from those that recognize the melodic and rhythmic aspects of music.

Locating the Source of a Sound

When we hear an unexpected sound, we usually turn our heads quickly to face its source. Even newborn infants can make this response with reasonably good accuracy. Once our faces are oriented toward the source of the sound, we can detect changes in its location by as little as 1 degree. To locate the source, we make use of two qualities of sound: relative loudness and difference in arrival time.

Relative loudness is the most effective means of perceiving the location of high-frequency sounds. Acoustic energy, in the form of vibrations, does not actually pass through solid objects. Low-frequency sounds can easily make a large solid object, such as a wall, vibrate, setting the air on the other side in motion and producing a new sound across the barrier. But large solid objects cannot vibrate rapidly, so they effectively damp out high-frequency sounds. They cast a "sound shadow," just as opaque objects cast a shadow in the sunlight. The human head is one such object, and it damps out high-frequency sounds so that they appear much louder to the ear nearer the source of the sound. Thus, if a source on your right produces a high-frequency sound, your right ear will receive more-intense stimulation than your left ear will. The brain uses this difference to calculate the location of the source of the sound. (See FIGURE 6•26.)

[**FIGURE 6•26**] Localizing the source of high-frequency sounds. The head casts a "sound shadow" for high-frequency sound vibrations. The brain uses the difference in loudness to detect the location of the source of the sound.

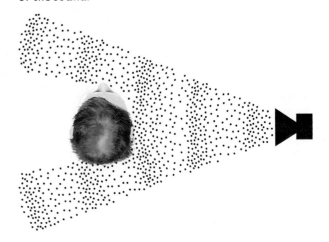

The second method involves detecting differences in the arrival time of sound pressure waves at each eardrum. This method works best for frequencies below approximately 3000 Hz. A 1000-Hz tone produces pressure waves approximately 1 foot apart. Because the distance between a person's eardrums is somewhat less than half that, a source of 1000-Hz sound located to one side of the head will cause one eardrum to be pushed in while the other eardrum is pulled out. In contrast, if the source of the sound is directly in front of the listener, both eardrums will move in synchrony. (See FIGURE 6•27.)

Researchers have found that when the source of a sound is located to the side of the head, as in Figure 6.27(a), axons in the right and left auditory nerves will fire at different times. The brain detects this disparity and so perceives the location of the sound at one side or the other. The brain can detect differences in firing times of a fraction of a millisecond. The easiest auditory stimuli to locate are those that produce brief clicks, which cause brief bursts of neural activity. Apparently, it is easiest for the brain to compare the arrival times of single bursts of sound.

The Deaf Community

From 0.1 to 0.2 percent of children in the Western world are born deaf. Deafness profoundly affects a person's ability to communicate with others. Imagine trying to join a group of people whose voices you cannot hear. But now imagine that the other people are also deaf. It is only in the company of people who have normal hearing that deafness hinders a person's ability to communicate (Erting et al., 1989; Sachs, 1989; Schein, 1989).

Deaf people aren't just people who have a particular sensory loss. They share a common culture. What unites

[**FIGURE 6·27**] Localizing the source of medium-frequency and high-frequency sounds through differences in arrival time. (a) Source of a 1000-Hz tone to the right. The pressure waves on each eardrum are out of phase; one eardrum is pushed in, whereas the other is pushed out. (b) Source of a sound directly in front. The vibrations of the eardrums are synchronized.

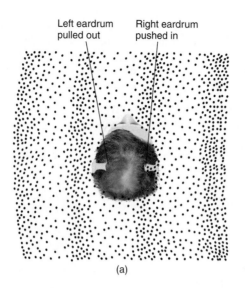

Left eardrum pulled out   Right eardrum pushed in

(a)

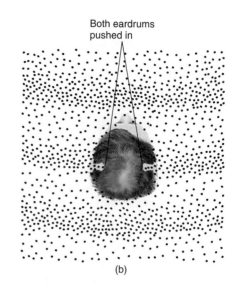

Both eardrums pushed in

(b)

the Deaf community is the ability of its members to communicate with one another visually through sign language. In this way the Deaf community provides a remedy for what would seem the disadvantage of deafness: the inability to communicate readily with others.

Not all deaf people are members of the Deaf community. People who are postlingually deaf—people who become deaf later in life after they have learned oral and written language—are unlikely to learn sign language and join the Deaf community. (In this context, *lingual,* from the word for "tongue," refers to the acquisition of spoken language.) In addition, some prelingually deaf people—people who are born deaf or who become deaf during infancy—never learn sign language, primarily because they are "mainstreamed" in community schools or attend a school for the deaf that teaches oral communication.

There is no single, universal sign language. Deaf people from North America cannot communicate with deaf people from Great Britain. (They can write to each other, of course, but written English bears no relation to the sign language used in North America or Great Britain.) However, deaf people in France and North America can understand each other reasonably well, because American Sign Language (ASL) is partly based on the sign language that was used in France in the early nineteenth century.

Several attempts have been made (invariably by people who are not deaf) to "improve" sign languages. Deaf people resent such attempts, just as you might resent it if a foreigner tried to improve the English language by cleaning up its inconsistencies. Most people cherish their native languages, and deaf people are particularly proud of theirs.

The education of deaf persons poses special problems. Deafness follows the so-called 90 percent rule. That is, 90 percent of deaf children have parents who can hear, 90 percent of deaf people marry other deaf people, and 90 percent of deaf parents have children who can hear. Most parents of deaf children, not being themselves deaf, know nothing about the Deaf community. Thus, they are unable to

transmit to their children the most important characteristic of this community: a sign language. The current practice of "mainstreaming" children who have disabilities—that is, placing them in neighborhood schools with the rest of the population—means that most deaf children's teachers have no experience educating deaf students. Most of their teachers have never even met a deaf child before. Thus, deaf youngsters may not learn a sign language until late childhood or adolescence, when they finally meet other deaf people. Some never learn it.

Some schools for deaf students use the oralist approach to education. Children are taught to communicate orally with the rest of the population by reading lips and speaking. Both tasks are extremely difficult. Try watching a news broadcast with the sound turned off to see how much you can understand. Ask a friend to mouth, "bear, bar, pear," and see if you can detect the difference. Of course, you could get better with years of practice, but even a very skilled lip-reader must do a lot of guessing and anticipating. And you would be starting out knowing English as a

Communication by means of American Sign Language is as rapid, efficient, and rich in nuance and detail as communication by means of any spoken language.

native language, so you would know what words to look out for and anticipate. A congenitally deaf child taught with the oralist approach starts out with no knowledge of language at all, which makes the process doubly difficult. Also, learning to lipread and to speak (without the opportunity to hear yourself) takes so much time that not much of the school day is left for other academic subjects.

Most people in the Deaf community who communicate with one another by means of signing have negative reactions to oral communication. The difficult task of deciphering lip movements makes them feel tense. They also realize that their pronunciation is imperfect and that their voices sound strange to others. They feel at a disadvantage with respect to hearing people in a spoken conversation. In contrast, they feel relaxed and at ease when communicating with other deaf people by signing. A young man wrote about his experience when he entered Gallaudet University, an institution for deaf students in Washington, D.C., that uses sign language:

> As I made my way through many educational and enjoyable semesters, learning a "new" way of communicating, I was enthralled. I was able to understand a person 100 percent of the time without having to lipread or depend on notes. It is a special feeling to relax and listen when in the past you have had to pay so much attention to the person you were speaking with that you could never really relax. (Mentkowski, 1983, p. 1)

Like other people who closely identify with their cultures, members of the Deaf community feel pride in their common heritage and become defensive when they perceive threats to it. Some deaf people say that if they were given the opportunity to hear, they would refuse it. Some deaf parents have expressed happiness when they learned that their children were born deaf: They no longer needed to fear that their children would not be included in their own Deaf culture.

The cochlear implant, a technological development described earlier in this chapter, is perceived by many members of the Deaf community as a serious threat to their culture. Cochlear implants are most useful for two groups: people who became deaf in adulthood and very young children. Cochlear implants in postlingually deaf adults pose no threat to the Deaf community, because postlingually deaf persons never were members of Deaf culture. Putting a cochlear implant in a young child, however, means that the child's early education will take the oralist approach. In addition, many deaf people resent the implication that deafness is something that needs to be repaired. They see themselves as different but not at all defective.

QUESTIONS TO CONSIDER

1. A naturalist once noted that when a male bird stakes out his territory, he sings with a very sharp, staccato song that says, in effect, "Here I am, and stay away!" In contrast, if a predator appears in the vicinity, many birds will emit alarm calls that consist of steady whistles that start and end slowly. Knowing what you do about the two means of localizing sounds, why do you think these two types of calls have different characteristics?

2. If you had a child who was born deaf, would you send him or her to a school that taught sign language or to a school that emphasized speaking and lip-reading? Why? Now imagine that you are deaf (or, if you are deaf, that you are hearing). Does your answer change? Why or why not?

The Chemical Senses

We have two senses specialized for detecting chemicals in our environment: taste and smell. Together, they are referred to as the **chemosenses.**

Gustation

Taste, or **gustation,** is the simplest of the sensory modalities. Taste is not the same as flavor; the flavor of a food includes its odor and texture as well as its taste. You have probably noticed that the flavors of foods are diminished when you have a head cold. This loss of flavor occurs not because your taste buds are inoperative but because mucus congestion makes it difficult for odor-laden air to reach your receptors for the sense of smell. Without their characteristic odors to serve as cues, onions taste much like apples (although apples do not make your eyes water).

Taste Receptors and the Sensory Pathway Taste reception begins with the tongue. The tongue has a corrugated appearance marked by creases and bumps. The bumps are called **papillae** (from the Latin, meaning "nipple"). Each

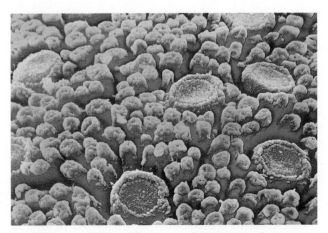

A photograph of taste buds taken with a scanning electron microscope.

---

chemosense One of the two sense modalities (gustation and olfaction) that detect the presence of particular molecules present in the environment.

gustation The sense of taste.

papilla A small bump on the tongue that contains a group of taste buds.

[**FIGURE 6•28**] The tongue. (a) Papillae on the
surface of the tongue. (b) A taste bud.

Cross-section of a papilla

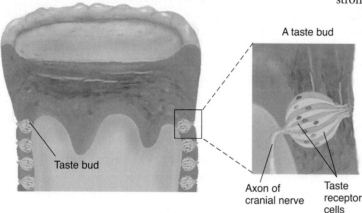

A taste bud

Taste bud

Axon of
cranial nerve

Taste
receptor
cells

(a)   (b)

[**FIGURE 6•28**] The tongue. (a) Papillae on the
surface of the tongue. (b) A taste bud.

papilla contains numerous taste buds (in some cases as many
as 200). A **taste bud** is a small organ containing receptor cells
shaped like the segments of an orange. The cells have hairlike
projections called microvilli that protrude through the pore
of the taste bud into the saliva that coats the tongue and fills
the trenches of the papillae. (See **FIGURE 6•28.**) Molecules of
chemicals dissolved in the saliva stimulate the receptor cells
by interacting with specialized receptor molecules on the microvilli. The receptor cells form synapses with dendrites of
neurons that send axons to the brain through three different
cranial nerves. Taste receptor cells have a life span of only ten
days. They quickly wear out, being directly exposed to a
rather hostile environment. As they degenerate, they are replaced by newly developed cells; the dendrite of the bipolar
neuron is passed on to the new cell (Beidler, 1970).

The Five Qualities of Taste   Gustation is clearly related to
eating; this sense modality helps us to determine the nature of
things we put in our mouths. The five qualities of taste are bitterness, sourness, sweetness, saltiness, and umami. You are familiar with the first four qualities, and we will consider the fifth
one shortly. The gustatory system of most vertebrates responds
to all five taste qualities. (An exception is the cat family; lions,
tigers, leopards, and house cats do not detect sweetness—but
then, none of the food they normally eat is sweet.) Clearly,
sweetness receptors are food detectors. Most sweet-tasting
foods, such as fruits and some vegetables, are safe to eat
(Ramirez, 1990). Saltiness receptors detect the presence of
sodium chloride. In some environments, inadequate amounts
of this mineral are obtained from the usual source of food, so
sodium chloride detectors help the animal to detect its

presence. If the body's store of sodium falls too low, the body
cannot retain water. Blood volume will decrease, which can
cause heart failure. Not surprisingly, loss of sodium stimulates a
strong craving for the salty taste of sodium chloride.

Researchers now recognize the existence of a fifth
taste quality: *umami.* **Umami,** a Japanese word that
means "good taste," refers to the taste of monosodium
glutamate (MSG), a substance that is often used as a
flavor enhancer in Asian cuisine (Kurihara, 1987; Scott
& Plata-Salaman, 1991). The umami receptor detects
the presence of glutamate, an amino acid found in proteins. Presumably, the umami receptor provides the
ability to taste proteins, an important nutrient.

Most species of animals will readily ingest substances that taste sweet or somewhat salty. Similarly,
they are attracted to foods that are rich in amino acids,
which explains the use of MSG as a flavor enhancer.
However, they will tend to avoid substances that taste
sour or bitter. Because of bacterial activity, many foods become
acidic when they spoil. The acidity tastes sour and causes an
avoidance reaction. (Of course, we have learned to make highly
preferred mixtures of sweet and sour, such as lemonade.) Bitterness is almost universally avoided and cannot easily be
improved by adding some sweetness. Many plants produce poisonous alkaloids, which protect them from being eaten by
animals. Alkaloids taste bitter; thus, the bitterness receptor undoubtedly serves to warn animals away from these chemicals.

Olfaction

The sense of smell—**olfaction**—is one of the most puzzling
sensory modalities and is unlike the other sensory modalities
in two important ways. First, people have difficulty using
words to describe odors. Second, odors have a powerful ability to evoke memories and feelings, even many years after an
event (Chu & Downes, 2000). At some time in their lives,
most people encounter an odor that they recognize as belonging to their childhood, even though they cannot identify
it specifically. The phenomenon may occur because the olfactory system sends information to the limbic system, a part of
the brain that plays a role in both emotions and memories.

Olfaction, like audition, seems to be an analytical sensory modality. That is, when we sniff air that contains a mixture of familiar odors, we usually can identify the individual
components. The molecules do not blend together and produce a single odor the way lights of different wavelengths
produce a single color. For example, when visiting a carnival,
we can distinguish the odors of popcorn, cotton candy,
crushed grass, and diesel oil in a single sniff.

Although many other mammals, such as dogs, have more
sensitive olfactory systems than humans do, we should not un-
derrate our own. The olfactory system is second only to the
visual system in the number of sensory receptor cells, with an
estimated 10 million cells. We can smell some substances at
lower concentrations than the most-sensitive laboratory instruments can detect. For years we have written that one reason

---

taste bud   A small organ on the tongue that contains a group of gustatory
receptor cells.

umami (*oo mah mee*)   The taste sensation produced by glutamate;
identifies the presence of amino acids in foods.

olfaction   The sense of smell.

for the difference in sensitivity between our olfactory system and those of other mammals is that other mammals put their noses where odors are the strongest—just above the ground. For example, a dog following an odor trail sniffs along the ground, where the odors of a passing animal may have clung. Even a bloodhound's nose would not be very useful if it were located five or six feet above the ground, as ours is. It was gratifying to learn that a scientific study established the fact that when people sniff the ground like dogs do, their olfactory systems work much better. Porter et al. (2006) prepared a scent trail—a string moistened with essential oil of chocolate and laid down in a grassy field. The subjects were blindfolded and wore earmuffs, kneepads, and gloves, which prevented them from using anything other than their noses to follow the scent trail. They did quite well, and adopted the same zigzag strategy used by dogs. (See FIGURE 6•29.) As the authors wrote, these findings ". . . suggest that the poor reputation of human olfaction may reflect, in part, behavioral demands rather than ultimate abilities" (Porter et al., 2006, p. 27).

Anatomy of the Olfactory System

FIGURE 6•30 shows the anatomy of the olfactory system. The receptor cells lie in the **olfactory mucosa,** patches of mucous membrane on the roof of the nasal sinuses, just under the base of the brain. The receptor cells have cilia that are embedded in the olfactory mucosa. They also have axons that pass through small holes in the bone above the olfactory mucosa and form synapses with neurons in the olfactory bulbs. The **olfactory bulbs** are stalklike structures located at the base of the brain. They contain neural circuits that perform the first analysis of olfactory information.

The interaction between odor molecule and receptor cell is similar to the interaction between neurotransmitter and postsynaptic receptor on a neuron. That is, when a molecule of an odorous substance fits a receptor molecule located on the cilia of a receptor cell, the cell becomes excited. This excitation is passed on to the brain by the axon of the receptor cell.

[**FIGURE 6•29**] Scent-tracking behavior by a dog and a human. The path followed during the scent tracking is shown in red.

(From Porter, J., Craven, B., Khan, R. M., Chang, S.-J., Kang, I Judkewitz, B., Volpe, J., Settles, G., & Sobel, N. (2007). Mechanisms of scent-tracking in humans. *Nature Neuroscience, 10,* 27–29.)

Unlike information from all other sensory modalities, olfactory information is not sent to the thalamus and then relayed to a specialized region of the cerebral cortex. Instead, olfactory information is sent directly to several regions of the limbic system—in particular, to the amygdala and to the limbic cortex of the frontal lobe.

---

olfactory mucosa (*mew koh za*) The mucous membrane lining the top of the nasal sinuses; contains the cilia of the olfactory receptors.

olfactory bulb One of the stalklike structures located at the base of the brain that contain neural circuits that perform the first analysis of olfactory information.

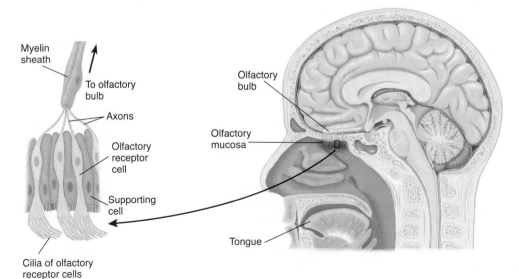

[**FIGURE 6•30**] The olfactory system.

The Dimensions of Odor We know that there are five qualities of taste, and a color can be specified in terms of hue, brightness, and saturation. Research in molecular biology has found that the olfactory system contains several hundred different receptor molecules, located in the membrane of the cilia of the receptor cells (Buck & Axel, 1991). These receptor molecules detect different categories of odors. Humans have 339 different types of olfactory receptors, and mice have 913 (Malnic, Godfrey, & Buck, 2004; Godfrey, Malnic, & Buck, 2004).

Humans can recognize up to 10,000 different odorants, and other animals can probably recognize even more of them (Shepherd, 1994). Even with 339 different olfactory receptors, that leaves many odors unaccounted for. And every year, chemists synthesize new chemicals, many with odors unlike those that anyone has previously detected. How can we use a relatively small number of receptors to detect so many different odorants?

The answer is that a particular odorant binds to more than one receptor. Thus, because a given glomerulus receives information from only one type of receptor, different odorants produce different *patterns* of activity in different glomeruli. Recognizing a particular odor, then, is a matter of recognizing a particular pattern of activity in the glomeruli. The task of chemical recognition is transformed into a task of spatial recognition.

FIGURE 6•31 illustrates this process (Malnic et al., 1999). The left side of the figure shows the shapes of eight hypothetical odorants. The right side shows four hypothetical odorant-receptor molecules. If a portion of the odorant molecule fits the binding site of the receptor molecule, it will activate it and stimulate the olfactory neuron. As you can see, each odorant molecule fits the binding site of at least one of the receptors and in most cases fits more than one of them. Notice also that the *pattern* of receptors activated by each of the eight odorants is different, which means that if we know which pattern of receptors is activated, we know which odorant is present. Of course, even though a particular odorant might bind with several different types of receptor molecules, it might not bind equally well with each of them. For example, it might bind very well with one receptor molecule, moderately well with another, weakly with another, and so on. (See Figure 6.31.) Presumably, the brain recognizes particular odors by recognizing different patterns of activation that it receives from the olfactory bulbs.

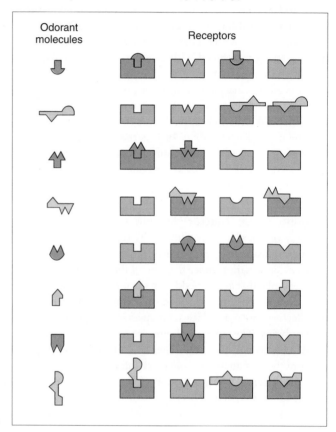

[**FIGURE 6•31**] A hypothetical explanation of coding of olfactory information. Different odorant molecules attach to different combinations of receptor molecules. (Activated receptor molecules are shown in blue.) Unique patterns of activation represent particular odorants.

(Adapted from Malnic, B., Hirono, J, Sato, T., & Buck, L. B. (1999). Combinatorial receptor codes for odors. *Cell, 96,* 713–723.)

Odorant molecules   Receptors

focus On

Sensory-Specific Satiety

Have you ever found that after eating all you wanted of a really good meal you found that you could still manage to eat some dessert? (Who hasn't?) This phenomenon is an example of sensory-specific satiety (SSS), the decrease in the pleasantness and consumption of a specific food—but not a food with a different taste or texture—after eating it to satiety. This phenomenon explains why we tend to eat more of a meal if it is composed of a variety of different foods than just a single dish. SSS has survival value; if we become bored with eating one food, we are more likely to be motivated to taste some other foods, thus eating a greater variety of nutrients.

Rolls et al. (1981) found that if people eat a food to satiety, they will eat much more of an unexpected second course if it consists of a different food than if it consists of the same food. The subjects' ratings of the pleasantness of the food correlated well with the amount they ate. In another study, participants ate either a four-course meal of sausages, bread and butter, chocolate dessert, and bananas or ate only one of these foods to satiety. The subjects ate 60 percent more when foods were presented together than when they were presented separately (Rolls et al., 1981b). Even shape influences the amount of food eaten. If subjects are given three courses of pasta of different shapes, they eat more than when they are given three courses of the same pasta (Rolls et al., 1982).

SSS is also seen in the sense of smell. In an experiment in which participants were asked to rate the pleasantness of the odors of banana, tangerines, fish paste, chicken, and rose water before and after consuming bananas and chicken to satiety. Ratings of the pleasantness of chicken and banana odors (but not odors of other foods) significantly declined after satiety (Rolls & Rolls, 1997).

A functional imaging study by O'Doherty et al. (2000) suggests that a brain region, the orbitofrontal cortex (OFC), is involved in sensory-specific satiety. The investigators measured the response of the OFC to the odor of bananas before and after people had eaten all the bananas they wanted. The investigators found that the activation in the OFC was smaller when people sniffed the odor after they were satiated. No such decrease was observed when people sniffed the odor of vanilla, which indicates that the change was specific to the odor of the food eaten to satiety.

In another functional-imaging study, volunteers ate chocolate to satiety while their brains were scanned (Small et al., 2001). The subjects first ate a chunk of chocolate, rated it for pleasantness, and were then asked if they would like another. If they said yes, they were given another piece and again asked to rate its pleasantness. This continued until the participants indicated that they had eaten enough chocolate. The researchers found that when participants ate chocolate that they found pleasant, there was increased activity in several brain regions, including the *insula* (a region of the cerebral cortex hidden deep in the fissure that separates the frontal and parietal lobes) and a part of the OFC called the caudomedial OFC. When participants were sated, activity blood flow increased in several different brain regions, including a different part of the OFC (the caudolateral OFC) but *not* the insula.

Small and her colleagues suggest that the brain activity elicited by chocolate before and after satiation reflects two different systems, which mediate two aspects of behavior: approach and avoidance. That is, activation of the insula and caudomedial OFC reflect motivation to approach a desirable stimulus, and activation of the caudolateral OFC reflects motivation to avoid an undesirable stimulus. Activation of the insula is correlated with self-reports of cocaine craving among people who abuse this drug (Wang et al., 1999), and damage to the insula decreases the smoker's craving for cigarettes and makes it easy for them to quit smoking (Naqvi et al., 2007).

QUESTIONS TO CONSIDER

1. Bees and birds can taste sweet substances, but cats and alligators cannot. Obviously, the ability to taste particular substances is related to the range of foods a species eats. If, through the process of evolution, a species develops a greater range of foods, what do you think comes first, the food or the receptor? Would a species start eating something having a new taste (say, something sweet) and later develop new taste receptors by which to detect the taste, or would the taste receptors evolve first and then provide the animal with a new taste when it came across the food? Why?

2. As we saw, odors have a peculiar ability to evoke memories—a phenomenon vividly described by Marcel Proust in his novel *Remembrance of Things Past* and named the *Proust effect* in his honor. Have you ever encountered an odor that you knew was familiar, but you couldn't say exactly why? What explanations can you think of? Might this phenomenon have something to do with the fact that the sense of olfaction appeared very early during the evolutionary development of the human brain?

The Somatosenses

The body senses, or **somatosenses,** include our abilities to respond to touch, vibration, pain, warmth, coolness, limb position, muscle length and stretch, tilt of the head, and changes in the speed of head rotation. As we will see, each of these stimuli is detected by a different type of receptor.

Many experiences require simultaneous stimulation of several different sensory modalities. For example, taste and odor alone do not determine the flavor of spicy food; mild (or sometimes not-so-mild) stimulation of pain detectors in the mouth and throat gives hot food its special characteristic. Sensations such as tickle and itch are apparently mixtures of varying amounts of touch and pain. Similarly, our perception of the texture and three-dimensional shape of an object that we touch involves our senses of pressure, muscle and joint sensitivity, and motor control simultaneously (to manipulate the object). If we handle an object and find that it moves smoothly in our hands, we may conclude that it is slippery. If, after handling this object, our fingers subsequently slide across each other without much resistance, we perceive a feeling of oiliness. In contrast, if we perceive vibrations when we move our fingers over an object, we may consider it rough. And so on. If you close your eyes as you manipulate soft and hard, warm and cold, and smooth and rough objects, you can make yourself aware that the separate sensations interact and give rise to a complex perception.

The following discussion of the somatosenses groups them into three major categories: the skin senses, the internal senses, and the vestibular senses.

The Skin Senses

The entire surface of the human body is *innervated* (supplied with nerves) by the dendrites of neurons that transmit somatosensory information to the brain. Cranial nerves convey information from the face and the rest of the front portion of the head (including the teeth and the inside of the mouth and

---

somatosense Bodily sensations; sensitivity to such stimuli as touch, pain, and temperature.

[FIGURE 6•32] Sensory receptors. (a) In hairy skin. (b) In hairless skin.

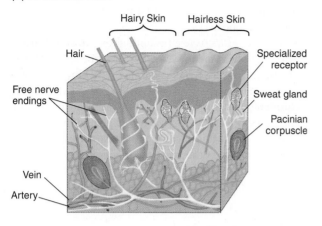

throat); spinal nerves convey information from the rest of the body's surface. All somatosensory information is detected by the dendrites of neurons; the system uses no separate receptor cells. However, some of these dendrites have specialized endings that modify the way they transduce energy into neural activity.

FIGURE 6•32 shows the sensory receptors found in hairy skin and in smooth, hairless skin (such as the skin on the palms of the hands or soles of the feet). The most common type of skin sensory receptor is the **free nerve ending,** which resembles the fine roots of a plant. Free nerve endings infiltrate the middle layers of both smooth and hairy skin and surround the hair follicles in hairy skin. If you bend a single hair on your forearm, you will see how sensitive the free nerve endings are.

The largest of the specialized skin receptors, called the **Pacinian corpuscle,** is actually visible to the naked eye. Pacinian corpuscles are very sensitive to touch. When they are moved, their axons fire a brief burst of impulses. Among the possible functions of Pacinian corpuscles is providing information about vibration.

Other specialized receptors detect different sensory qualities, including pressure, warmth, coolness, and pain.

Touch and Pressure Psychologists speak of touch and pressure as two separate sensations. They define touch as the sensation of very light contact of an object with the skin, and pressure as the sensation produced by more forceful contact. Sensations of pressure occur only when the skin is actually moving (being pushed in), which means that the pressure detectors respond only while they are being bent. If you rest your forearm on a table and place a small weight on your skin, you will feel the pressure at first, but eventually you will feel nothing

at all, if you keep your arm still. You fail to feel the pressure not because your brain "ignores" incoming stimulation but because the sensory endings no longer send impulses to your brain. Studies that have measured very slow, very minute movements of a weight sinking down into the skin have shown that sensory transmission ceases when the movements stop. With the addition of another weight on top of the first one, movement and sensory transmission begin again (Nafe & Wagoner, 1941). Of course, a person will feel a very heavy weight indefinitely, but the sensation of pain rather than pressure.

The ability to localize precisely the part of the body being touched varies widely across the surface of the body. The most sensitive regions are the lips and the fingertips. The most common measure of tactile discrimination (the ability to tell touches apart) is the **two-point discrimination threshold.** To determine this measure, a researcher touches a person with one or both legs of a caliper and asks the person to say whether the sensation is coming from one or two points. (See FIGURE 6•33.) The farther apart the legs of the caliper are before the person reports feeling two separate sensations, the lower the sensitivity of that region of skin. For example, we can detect two very closely spaced points on our lips, but the spacing must be much larger for us to detect them on our forearm, and very much larger on our back.

[CASE STUDY] In the past, neuroscientists believed that in humans tactile information was transmitted to the central nervous system only by large-diameter, rapidly conducting myelinated axons. However, Olausson et al. (2002) discovered a new category of tactile sensation that is transmitted by small-diameter unmyelinated axons. At age 31, patient G. L., a 54-year-old woman, "suffered a permanent and specific loss of large myelinated [sensory axons] after episodes of acute [nerve diseases] that affected her whole body below the nose. A . . . nerve biopsy indicated a complete loss of large-diameter myelinated fibers. . . . Before the present study, she denied having any touch sensibility below the nose, and she lost the ability to perceive tickle [after her nerves were damaged]. She states that her perceptions of temperature, pain and itch are intact" (Olausson et al., 2002, pp. 902–903).

G. L. could detect the stimuli that are normally attributed to small-diameter unmyelinated axons—temperature, pain, and itch—but she could not feel when her skin was

[FIGURE 6•33] The method for determining the two-point discrimination threshold.

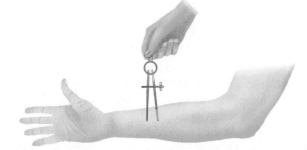

---

free nerve ending   An unencapsulated (naked) dendrite of somatosensory neurons.

Pacinian corpuscle (*pa chin ee un*)   A specialized, encapsulated somatosensory nerve ending, which detects mechanical stimuli, especially vibrations.

two-point discrimination threshold   The minimum distance between two small points that can be detected as separate stimuli when pressed against a particular region of the skin.

being touched with a stationary or vibrating object. However, when the hairy skin on her forearm or the back of her hand was stroked with a soft brush, she reported a faint, pleasant sensation. The investigators concluded that besides conveying information about pain and temperature, small-diameter unmyelinated axons constitute a "system for . . . touch that may underlie emotional, hormonal and affiliative responses to caresslike, skin-to-skin contact between individuals" (Olausson et al., 2002, p. 900). That sounds like a nice system to have, doesn't it?

Temperature We can detect thermal stimuli over a very wide range of temperatures, from less than 8° C (noxious cold) to more than 52° C. (noxious heat). Investigators have long believed that no single receptor could detect such a range of temperatures, and recent research indicates that this belief was correct. At present, we know of six mammalian thermoreceptors (Voets et al., 2004). One of these receptors, which is sensitive to ranges of temperatures close to body temperature, is found in the anterior hypothalamus (Güler et al., 2002), the region of the brain that is responsible for measuring and maintaining body temperature.

Some of the thermal receptors respond to particular chemicals as well as to changes in temperature. For example, one of them is stimulated by menthol, a compound found in the leaves of many members of the mint family. As you undoubtedly know, peppermint tastes cool in the mouth, and menthol is added to some cigarettes to make the smoke feel cooler (and perhaps to try to delude smokers into thinking that the smoke is less harsh and damaging to the lungs). Menthol provides a cooling sensation because it binds with and stimulates this receptor and produces neural activity that the brain interprets as coolness. As we will see in the next subsection, chemicals can produce the sensation of heat also.

Pain Pain reception, like temperature reception, is accomplished by the networks of free nerve endings in the skin. There appear to be at least three types of pain receptors (usually referred to as nociceptors, or "detectors of noxious stimuli"). High-threshold mechanoreceptors are free nerve endings that respond to intense pressure, which might be caused by something striking, stretching, or pinching the skin. A second type of free nerve ending appears to respond to extremes of heat, to acids, and to the presence of capsaicin, the active ingredient in chile peppers (Kress & Zeilhofer, 1999). (Note that we say that chile peppers make food taste "hot.") Caterina et al. (2000) found that mice with a targeted mutation against this receptor showed less sensitivity to painful high-temperature stimuli and would drink water to which capsaicin had been added. Ghilardi et al. (2005) found that a drug that blocks this type of receptor reduced pain in patients with bone cancer, which is apparently caused by the production of acid by the tumors.

Another type of nociceptor contains receptors that are sensitive to *ATP*, a chemical that serves as an energy source in all cells of the body (Burnstock & Wood, 1996). ATP is released when the blood supply to a region of the body is disrupted or when a muscle is damaged. It is also released by rapidly growing tumors. Thus, these nociceptors may be at least partly responsible for the pain caused by angina, migraine, damage to muscles, and some kinds of cancer.

Pain is a complex perception involving not only intense sensory stimulation but also emotion. That is, a given sensory input to the brain might be interpreted as pain in one situation and as pleasure in another. For example, when people are sexually aroused, they become less sensitive to many forms of pain and may even find such intense stimulation pleasurable. Opiates such as morphine produce *analgesia* (a reduction in pain) by stimulating opioid receptors on neurons in the brain; these neurons block the transmission of pain information. In contrast, some tranquilizers (e.g., diazepam [Valium]) depress neural systems that are responsible for the emotional reaction to pain but do not diminish the intensity of the pain. Thus, people who have received a drug such as Valium will report that they feel the pain but that it does not bother them as much.

Pain—or the fear of pain—is one of the most effective motivators of human behavior. It also serves us well in the normal course of living. As unpleasant as pain is, we would have difficulty surviving without it. People without any sensitivity to pain, caused by a genetic deficit that prevents them from detecting noxious stimuli, have failed to recognize that they have sprained an ankle or broken a bone, and have died of an undetected inflamed appendix.

A particularly interesting form of pain sensation occurs after a limb has been amputated: Up to 70 percent of amputees report that they feel as though their missing limbs still exist and that they often hurt. This phenomenon is referred to as the **phantom limb** (Melzack, 1992; Ramachandran & Hirstein, 1998). People who have phantom limbs report that the limbs feel very real; that if they try to reach something with their missing limb, it feels as though the limb responds. Sometimes they perceive the limb as protruding, and they may feel compelled to avoid knocking the limb against a door frame or sleeping with the limb between them and the mattress. People have reported all sorts of sensations in phantom limbs, including pain, pressure, warmth, cold, wetness, itching, sweatiness, and prickliness.

Melzack suggests that the phantom-limb perception is inherent in the organization of the parietal cortex. As we saw in Chapter 4, the parietal cortex is involved in our perception of our own bodies. Indeed, people who have sensory neglect, caused by lesions of the right parietal lobe, have been seen to push their own legs out of bed, believing that they actually belong to someone else. Melzack reports that some people who were born with limbs missing nevertheless experience the phantom limb. This suggests that our brains are genetically programmed to provide sensations from all four limbs—even if one or more limbs are absent.

---

phantom limb   Sensations that appear to originate in a limb that has been amputated.

The Internal Senses

Sensory receptors located in our internal organs, bones and joints, and muscles convey painful, neutral, and, in some cases, pleasurable sensory information. For example, the internal senses convey the pain of arthritis, the physical location of our limbs in three dimensions, the pangs of hunger, and the pleasure of a warm drink descending to our stomach.

Muscles contain special sensory receptors. One class of receptors, located at the junction between muscles and the tendons that connect them to the bones, provides information about the amount of force the muscle is exerting. These receptors protect the body by inhibiting muscular contractions when they become too forceful. During competition, weight lifters may receive injections of a local anesthetic near the tendons of some muscles to eliminate this protective mechanism. This enables the athletes to lift even heavier weights. Unfortunately, tendons may snap or bones may break under the increased force.

Another stretch-detection system consists of spindle-shaped receptors distributed throughout the muscle. These receptors, appropriately called **muscle spindles**, inform the brain about changes in muscle length. Although we are not conscious of the specific information provided by the muscle spindles, the brain uses the information, together with information from joint receptors, to keep track of the locations of parts of our body and to control muscular contractions.

The Vestibular Senses

What we call our "sense of balance" involves several senses, not merely one. For example, if you stand on one foot and then close your eyes, you immediately realize how important vision is to balance. The **vestibular apparatus** of the inner ear provides additional sensory input that helps us remain upright.

The three liquid-filled **semicircular canals**—located in the inner ear and oriented at right angles to one another—detect changes in the rotation of the head. (See FIGURE 6·34.) Rotation of the head causes motion of the liquid, which stimulates the receptor cells located in the canals.

Another set of inner ear organs, the **vestibular sacs**, contains crystals of calcium carbonate that are embedded in a gelatin-like substance attached to receptive hair cells. In one sac, the receptive tissue is on the wall; in the other, it is on the floor. When the head tilts, the weight of the calcium carbonate crystals shifts, producing different forces on the cilia of the hair cells. These forces change the activity of the hair cells, and the information is transmitted to the brain.

---

muscle spindle   A muscle fiber that functions as a stretch receptor; arranged parallel to the muscle fibers responsible for contraction of the muscle, it detects muscle length.

vestibular apparatus   The receptive organs of the inner ear that contribute to balance and perception of head movement.

semicircular canal   One of a set of organs in the inner ear that responds to rotational movements of the head.

vestibular sac   One of two sets of receptor organs in each inner ear that detect changes in the tilt of the head.

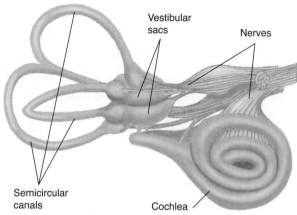

[**FIGURE 6·34**] The three semicircular canals and two vestibular sacs located in the inner ear.

The vestibular sacs help us maintain an upright head position. They also participate in a reflex that enables us to see clearly even when the head is being jarred. When we walk, our eyes are jostled back and forth. The jarring of the head stimulates the vestibular sacs to cause reflex movements of the eyes that partially compensate for the head movement. People who lack this reflex because of localized brain damage must stop walking to see things clearly—for example, to read a street sign.

QUESTION TO CONSIDER

Why does repetitive vestibular stimulation (like that provided by a boat ride on rough water) sometimes cause nausea and vomiting? What useful functions might this response serve?

Epilogue

Natural Analgesia

The brain contains neural circuitry through which certain types of stimuli can produce analgesia, primarily through the release of the endogenous opioids (the opiate-like chemicals produced in the brain). What functions does this system perform? Most researchers believe that it prevents pain from disrupting behavior in situations in which pain is unavoidable and in which the damaging effects of the painful stimuli are less important than the goals of the behavior. For example, males fighting for access to females during mating season will fail to pass on their genes if pain elicits withdrawal responses that interfere with fighting. Indeed, these conditions (fighting or mating) *do* diminish pain.

Komisaruk and Larsson (1971) found that genital stimulation produced analgesia. They gently probed the cervix of female rats with a glass rod and found that the procedure diminished the animals' sensitivity to pain. It also increased the activity of neurons in the periaqueductal gray matter and decreased the pain response in the thalamus (Komisaruk & Steinman, 1987). The phenomenon also occurs in humans; Whipple and Komisaruk (1988) found that self-administered vaginal stimulation reduces women's sensitivity to painful stimuli but not to neutral tactile stimuli. Presumably, copulation also triggers analgesic mechanisms. The adaptive significance of this phenomenon is clear: Painful stimuli that are encountered during sexual intercourse are less likely to cause the behavior to be interrupted; thus, the chances of pregnancy are increased. (As you will recall, passing on one's genes is the ultimate criterion of the adaptive significance of a trait.)

Pain can also be reduced, at least in some people, by administering a pharmacologically inert placebo. When some people take a medication that they believe will reduce pain, it triggers the release of endogenous opioids and actually does reduce pain sensations. This effect is eliminated if the people are given an injection of naloxone, a drug that blocks opiate receptors (Benedetti, Arduino, & Amanzio, 1999). Thus, for some people, a placebo is not pharmacologically inert—it has a physiological effect. The experimenter in the chapter prologue used this drug when he blocked the analgesic effect of Melissa's own endogenous opiates. The placebo effect may be mediated through connections of the frontal cortex with a region of the midbrain that controls the transmission of pain information to the brain. A PET imaging study by Zubieta et al. (2005) confirmed that analgesia produced by a placebo caused the release of endogenous opiates in the brain.

A functional imaging study by Wager et al. (2004) supports this suggestion. They administered painful stimuli (heat or electrical shocks) to people's skin with or without the application of an "analgesic" skin cream that was actually an unmedicated placebo. They observed a placebo effect—reports of less-intense pain and decreased activity in the primary pain-reactive regions of the brain. They also observed increased activity of the prefrontal cortex and the midbrain. Presumably, the expectation of decreased sensitivity to pain activated the prefrontal cortex, and connections of this region with the midbrain activated endogenous mechanisms of analgesia.

Another procedure, hypnosis, can also reduce pain—or at least, people's reaction to pain. Rainville et al. (1997) produced pain sensations in human subjects by having them put their arms in ice water. Under one condition, the researchers used hypnosis to diminish the unpleasantness of the pain. The hypnosis worked; the subjects said that the pain was less unpleasant, even though it was still as intense. Functional imaging showed that the painful stimulus activated both the primary somatosensory cortex and the *anterior cingulate cortex,* a region of the limbic cortex in the frontal lobe. When the subjects were hypnotized and found the pain less unpleasant, the activity of the anterior cingulate cortex decreased—but the activity of the primary somatosensory cortex remained high. It appeared that the pain signal was still strong, but that it produced less of an unpleasant emotional reaction. Several functional imaging studies have shown that under certain conditions, stimuli associated with pain can activate the anterior cingulate cortex even when no actual painful stimulus is applied.

In a functional imaging study of romantically involved couples, Singer et al. (2004) found a painful electrical shock delivered to the back of women's hands activated both the somatosensory cortex and the anterior cingulate cortex. When the women saw their partners receive a painful shock but did not receive one themselves, the anterior cingulate cortex became active, but the somatosensory cortex did not. Thus, the emotional component of pain—in this case, a vicarious experience of pain, provoked by empathy with the feelings of a loved one—caused responses in the brain similar to the ones caused by actual pain. Just as we saw in the study by Rainville et al. (1997), the somatosensory cortex is activated only by an actual noxious stimulus. These studies indicate that different brain mechanisms are involved in perception of pain and the unpleasant feeling that pain normally provokes.

CHAPTER SUMMARY

Sensory Processing

We experience the world through our senses. Our knowledge of the world stems from the accumulation of sensory experience and subsequent learning. All sensory experiences are the result of energy from events that is transduced into activity of receptor cells, which are specialized neurons. Transduction causes changes in the activity of axons of sensory nerves, and these changes in activity inform the sensory mechanisms of the brain about the environmental event. The information received from the receptor cells is transmitted to the brain by means of two coding schemes: anatomical coding and temporal coding.

To study the nature of subjective experience scientifically, we must be able to measure it. In nineteenth-century Germany, Weber devised the concept of the just-noticeable difference (jnd), and Fechner used the jnd to measure perceived intensity of stimuli. Signal-detection theory gave rise to methods that enabled psychologists to assess people's sensitivity to stimuli despite individual differences in response bias. The methods of psychophysics apply to all sensory modalities, including sight, hearing, taste, smell, and touch.

Vision

Imagine yourself watching an ice-skating competition on television with a friend. The cornea and lens of each eye cast an image of the screens on your retinas, which contain photoreceptors: rods and cones. In bright illumination, only your cones gather visual information; your rods work only when the light is very dim. The energy from the light that reaches the cones in your retinas is transduced into neural activity when photons strike molecules of photopigment, splitting them into their two constituents. This event causes the cones to send information through the bipolar cells to the ganglion cells. The axons of the ganglion cells form the optic nerves and have synapses with neurons in the brain.

Vision requires the behavior of looking, which consists of moving our eyes and head. The eyes have a repertoire of movements that function for visual perception. Experiments using stabilized images show that small, involuntary movements keep an image moving across the photoreceptors, thus preventing them from adapting to a constant stimulus. (As you will see later in this chapter, other sensory systems also respond better to changing stimuli than to constant ones.) As the skaters glide across the ice, your eyes follow them with pursuit movements. Now your friend says something, so you turn your head toward him. Your eyes make rapid saccadic movements so that you can look directly at your friend's face. These vergence movements orient the eyes so that each eye is fixed on the same point. Because your friend is closer to you than the television screen, you must also accommodate for the change in distance, adjusting the focus of the lenses of your eyes.

When an image of the visual scene is cast on the retina, each part of the image has a different color, which can be specified in terms of its hue (corresponding to the dominant wavelength), brightness (intensity), and saturation (purity). Information about color is encoded trichromatically by your cones; the red, green, and blue cones respond in proportion to the amount of the appropriate wavelength contained in the light striking them. This information is transformed into an opponent-process coding, signaled by the firing rates of red/green and yellow/blue ganglion cells, and is transmitted to the brain. If you stare for a while at a colored image and then look at a light-colored blank wall, you will see a negative afterimage. If you are a male, the chances are about 1 in

20 that you will have some defect in red/green color vision. If this is the case, your red or green cones contain the wrong photopigment. Male or female, chances are very slim that you will have a blue/yellow defect caused by the absence of functioning blue cones.

Audition

The human auditory system is sophisticated enough to differentiate among a vast array of sounds. Audition translates the physical dimensions of sound—amplitude, frequency, and complexity—into the perceptual dimensions of loudness, pitch, and timbre for sounds ranging from 30 to 20,000 Hz. Sound-pressure waves put the process in motion by setting up vibrations in the eardrum, which are passed on to the ossicles. Vibrations of the stirrup against the membrane behind the oval window create pressure changes in the fluid within the cochlea that cause the basilar membrane to vibrate. This causes the auditory hair cells on the basilar membrane to move relative to the tectorial membrane. The resulting pull on the cilia of the hair cells stimulates them to secrete a neurotransmitter that excites auditory neurons and stimulates axons in the auditory nerve, which brings this information to the brain.

Two different methods of detection enable the brain to recognize the pitch of a sound. Different high-frequency and medium-frequency sounds are perceived when different parts of the basilar membrane vibrate in response to these frequencies. Low-frequency vibrations are detected when the tip of the basilar membrane vibrates in synchrony with the sound, which causes some axons in the auditory nerve to fire at that frequency.

Locating the source of a sound depends on two systems. The ear locates low-frequency sounds by differences in the arrival time of the sound waves in each ear. It locates high-frequency sounds by differences in intensity that result from the "sound shadow" cast by your head.

The auditory system analyzes sounds with complex timbre into their constituent frequencies, each of which causes a particular part of the basilar membrane to vibrate. All of these functions proceed automatically, so the brain can hear the sound of a clarinet or any other combination of fundamental frequency and harmonics. The sources of complex sounds are recognized by a region in the posterior temporal lobe that is also involved in recognizing objects by sight.

The Deaf community consists of deaf people who communicate visually by means of a sign language. The social isolation that a deaf person may feel among oral communicators disappears in the company of other people who can sign. Communication by sign languages can be as accurate and efficient as spoken communication.

The Chemical Senses

Both gustation and olfaction are accomplished by cells whose receptors respond selectively to various kinds of molecules. Taste buds have at least five kinds of receptors, which respond to molecules that we perceive as sweet, salty, sour, bitter, or umami. To most organisms, sweet, umami, and moderately salty substances taste pleasant, whereas sour or bitter substances taste unpleasant. Sweet, umami, and salty receptors permit us to detect nutritious foods and sodium chloride. Sour and bitter receptors help us avoid substances that might be poisonous.

Olfaction is a remarkable sense modality. Olfactory information combines with information about taste to provide us with the flavor of a food present in our mouths. We can distinguish countless different odors and can recognize smells from childhood, even if we cannot remember when or where we first encountered them. Although we recognize similarities between different odors, most seem unique. Unlike visual stimuli such as colors, odors do not easily blend. The detection of different odors appears to be accomplished by a little more than 300 different receptor molecules located in the membrane of the cilia of the olfactory receptor cells. The brain recognizes particular odors by analyzing the pattern of neural activity produced by activation of these receptors.

The Somatosenses

The somatosenses gather several different kinds of information from different parts of the body. The skin senses of temperature, touch and pressure, vibration, and pain inform us about the nature of objects that come in contact with our skin. The sensitive Pacinian corpuscles in the skin detect vibration. A special set of receptors detects the pleasurable feeling of a caress. The skin's temperature receptors convey the sense of warmth or coolness, responding chiefly to changes in temperature but also, in some cases, to chemicals such as menthol or capsaicin. Also in the skin, free nerve endings give rise to sensations of pain. The internal senses convey sensations such as hunger pangs or the pain of a kidney stone. Sensory receptors in our muscles and joints inform the brain of the movement and location of our arms and legs. The vestibular senses help us keep our balance and produce eye movements that compensate for head movements.

succeed with mypsychlab

Visit MyPsychLab for practice quizzes, flashcards, and dozens of videos and animated tutorials, including the following items you can find in the "Multimedia Library":

Ear Ringing
Noise and the Brain
Brain Pain

Normal Vision, Nearsightedness
Light and the Optic Nerve

Weber's Law

KEY TERMS

absolute threshold *p. 157*
accommodation *p. 160*
anatomical coding *p. 155*
auditory hair cell *p. 170*
basilar membrane *p. 169*
bipolar cell *p. 161*
brightness *p. 164*
chemosense *p. 175*
cilium *p. 170*
cochlea *p. 168*
cochlear implant *p. 171*
color mixing *p. 165*
cone *p. 162*
cornea *p. 160*
dark adaptation *p. 163*
deuteranopia *p. 167*
difference threshold *p. 157*
fovea *p. 162*
free nerve ending *p. 180*
fundamental frequency *p. 172*
ganglion cell *p. 161*
gustation *p. 175*
hertz (Hz) *p. 168*
hue *p. 164*
iris *p. 160*
just-noticeable difference (jnd) *p. 156*
lens *p. 160*
muscle spindle *p. 182*
negative afterimage *p. 166*
olfaction *p. 176*
olfactory bulb *p. 177*
olfactory mucosa *p. 177*
opponent process *p. 166*
optic disk *p. 160*
ossicle *p. 168*
oval window *p. 168*
overtone *p. 172*
Pacinian corpuscle *p. 180*

papilla *p. 175*
perception *p. 154*
phantom limb *p. 181*
photopigment *p. 162*
photoreceptor *p. 160*
protanopia *p. 167*
psychophysics *p. 156*
pursuit movement *p. 164*
receiver-operating-characteristic curve (ROC curve) *p. 158*
receptor cell *p. 155*
retina *p. 160*
rhodopsin *p. 162*
rod *p. 162*
round window *p. 170*
saccadic movement *p. 163*
saturation *p. 164*
sclera *p. 160*
semicircular canal *p. 182*
sensation *p. 154*
signal-detection theory *p. 157*
somatosense *p. 179*
taste bud *p. 176*
tectorial membrane *p. 170*
temporal coding *p. 156*
threshold *p. 157*
timbre *p. 168*
transduction *p. 155*
trichromatic theory *p. 166*
tritanopia *p. 167*
two-point discrimination threshold *p. 180*
umami *p. 176*
vergence movement *p. 164*
vestibular apparatus *p. 182*
vestibular sac *p. 182*
wavelength *p. 159*
Weber fraction *p. 156*

SUGGESTIONS FOR FURTHER READING

General

Coren, S., Ward, L. M., & Enns, J. T. (2003). *Sensation and perception* (6th ed.). New York: Wiley.

Vision

Bruce, V., Green, P. R., & Georgeson, M. A. (2003). *Visual perception: Physiology, psychology and ecology* (4th ed.). New York: Psychology Press.

Gregory, R. L. (1997). *Eye and brain: The psychology of seeing* (5th ed.). Princeton, N.J.: Princeton University Press.

Audition

Yost, W. A. (2000). *Fundamentals of hearing: An introduction* (4th ed.). San Diego, CA: Academic Press.

Chemical Senses

Doty, R. L. (2003). *Handbook of olfaction and gustation* (2nd ed.). New York: Dekker.

Martin, G. N. (2004). A neuroanatomy of flavour. *Petits Propos Culinaires, 76,* 58–79.

Smith, D. V., & Margolskee, R. F. (2001). Making sense of taste. *Scientific American, 284(3),* 26–33.

Sensory-Specific Satiety

Naqvi, N. H., Rudrauf, D., Damasio, H., & Bechara, A. (2007). Damage to the insula disrupts addiction to cigarette smoking. *Science, 315,* 531–534.

O'Doherty, J., Rolls, E. T., Francis, S., Bowtell, R., McGlone, E., Kobal, G., Renner, B., & Ahne, G. (2000). Sensory-specific satiety-related olfactory activation of the human orbitofrontal cortex. *Neuroreport, 11,* 399–403.

Rolls, B. J., Rolls, E. T., Rowe, E. A., & Sweeney, K. (1981a). Sensory specific satiety in man. *Physiology and Behavior, 27,* 137–142.

Rolls, B. J., Rowe, E. A., & Rolls, E. T. (1982). How flavour and appearance affect human feeding. *Proceedings on the Nutrition Society, 41,* 109–117.

Rolls, B. J., Rowe, E. A., Rolls, E. T., Kingston, B., Megson, A., & Gunary, R. (1981b). Variety in a meal enhances food intake in man. *Physiology and Behavior, 26,* 215–221.

Rolls, E. T., & Rolls, J. H. (1997). Olfactory sensory-specific satiety in humans. *Physiology and Behavior, 61,* 461–473.

Small, D. M., Zatorre, R. J., Dagher, A., Evans, A. C., & Jones-Gotman, M. (2001). Changes in brain activity related to eating chocolate: From pleasure to aversion. *Brain, 124,* 1720–1733.

Wang, G. J., Volkow, N. D., Fowler, J. S., Cervany, P., Hitzemann, R. J., Pappas, N. R., Wong, C. T., & Felder, C. (1999). Regional brain metabolic activation during craving elicited by recall of previous drug experiences. *Life Sciences, 64,* 775–784.

Perception

Prologue

The Case of Mrs. R.

Mrs. R.'s recent stroke had not impaired her ability to talk or to move about, but it had affected her vision. Mrs. R. went to see Dr. L., a young neuropsychologist.

"How are you, Mrs. R.?" asked Dr. L.

"I'm fine. I can do just about everything that I did before I had my stroke."

"Good. How is your vision?"

"Well, I'm afraid that's still a problem."

"What seems to give you the most trouble?"

"I just don't seem to be able to recognize things. When I'm working in my kitchen, I know what everything is as long as no one moves anything. A few times my husband tried to help me by putting things away, and I couldn't see them any more." She laughed. "Well, I could see them, but I just couldn't say what they were."

Dr. L. took some objects out of a paper bag and placed them on the table in front of Mrs. R.

"Can you tell me what these are?" he asked. "And," he added, "please don't touch them."

Mrs. R. stared intently at the objects. "No, I can't rightly say what they are."

Dr. L. pointed to one of them, a wristwatch. "Tell me what you see here," he said.

Mrs. R. looked thoughtful, turning her head one way and then the other. "Well, I see something round, and it has two things attached to it, one on the top and one on the bottom." She continued to stare at it. "There are some things inside the circle, I think, but I can't make out what they are."

"Pick it up."

She did so, made a wry face, and said, "Oh. It's a wristwatch." At Dr. L.'s request, she picked up the rest of the objects, one by one, and identified each of them correctly.

"Do you have trouble recognizing people, too?" asked Dr. L.

"Oh, yes!" she sighed. "While I was still in the hospital, my husband and my son both came in to see me, and I couldn't tell who was who until my husband said something—then I could tell which direction his voice was coming from. Now I've trained myself to recognize my husband. I can usually see his glasses and his bald head, but I have to work at it. And I've been fooled a few times."

"What does a face look like to you?" asked Dr. L.

"Well, I know that it's a face, because I can usually see the eyes, and it's on top of a body. I can see a body pretty well, by how it moves." She paused a moment. "Oh, yes, I forgot, sometimes I can recognize a person by how he moves. You know, you can often recognize friends by the way they walk, even when they're far away.

I can still do that. That's funny, isn't it? I can't see people's faces very well, but I can recognize the way they walk."

Dr. L. made some movements with his hands. "Can you tell what I'm doing?" he asked.

"Yes, you're mixing something—like some cake batter."

He mimed the gestures of turning a key, writing, and dealing out playing cards, and Mrs. R. recognized them without any difficulty.

"Do you have any trouble reading?" he asked.

"Well, a little, but I don't do too badly."

Dr. L. handed her a magazine, and she began to read the article aloud—somewhat hesitantly, but accurately. "Why is it," she asked, "that I can see the words all right but have so much trouble with things and with people's faces?" ■

The primary function of the sense organs, as we saw in Chapter 6, is to provide information to guide behavior. But the sensory mechanisms cannot achieve this function by themselves. Consider vision, for example, in light of the opening case. The brain receives fragments of information from approximately 1 million axons in each of the optic nerves. It combines and organizes these fragments into the perception of a scene—objects having different forms, colors, and textures, residing at different locations in three-dimensional space. Even when our bodies or our eyes move, exposing the photoreceptors to entirely new patterns of visual information, our perception of the scene before us does not change. The brain keeps track of the body's movements and those of the eyes and compensates for the constantly changing patterns of neural firing that these movements cause. **Perception,** as indicated in Chapter 6, is the process of responding to the information that the sense organs provide and gives unity and coherence to sensory input. Perception implies meaningfulness—that we understand what the sensory systems are conveying and respond in a knowing way to it.

Perception is a rapid, automatic, largely unconscious process; it is not a deliberate, effortful activity in which we puzzle out the meaning of what we see. We do not first see an object and then perceive it; we simply perceive the object. Although occasionally what we see is ambiguous, requiring us to reflect on what it might be or gather further evidence to decide what it is, doing so is more problem solving than perceiving. If we look at a scene carefully, we can describe the elements of the objects that are present, but we do so because we perceive the objects and the background of which they are a part. For example, if you look at a tall, cylindrical object

on a countertop, you immediately perceive a glass and subsequently perceive the smudges near its top, the lettering on its side, and the few sips of beverage remaining at its bottom. Also note that our awareness of the process of visual perception comes only after it is complete; we are presented with a finished product, not the details of the process.

The distinction between sensation and perception is not easy to make; in some respects, the distinction is arbitrary. Probably because of the importance we give to vision and because of the richness of the information provided by our visual system, psychologists make a more-explicit distinction between visual sensation and perception than they do for the other sensory systems. Hence, this chapter on perception will focus primarily on the visual system, while recognizing that the other perceptual systems could be analyzed similarly. We will examine the most important task of auditory perception—recognizing spoken words—in Chapter 10. You will recall that, in its consideration of vision, Chapter 6 focused largely on the eye. Accordingly, in this chapter, we turn first to the brain's processing of information transmitted from the eyes.

Brain Mechanisms of Visual Perception

Although the eyes contain the photoreceptors that detect areas of different brightness and color in the visual field, perception takes place hierarchically in the brain. The optic nerves send visual information to the thalamus, which relays the information to the primary visual cortex, located in the occipital lobe at the back of the brain. In turn, neurons in the primary visual cortex send visual information to the visual association cortex—the brain regions where visual perception takes place. (See FIGURE 7•1.)

The Primary Visual Cortex

Our knowledge of the earliest stages of visual analysis has come from investigations of the activity of individual neurons in the thalamus and the primary visual cortex. For example, in their pioneering studies, Nobel Prize laureates David Hubel and Torsten Wiesel inserted microelectrodes—extremely small wires with microscopically sharp points—into various regions of the visual systems of cats and monkeys to detect the action potentials produced by individual neurons (Hubel & Wiesel, 1977, 1979, 2004). The signals picked up by the microelectrodes are electronically amplified and sent to a recording device for later analysis.

After positioning a microelectrode close to a neuron, Hubel and Wiesel presented various stimuli on a large screen in front of the open-eyed but anesthetized animal. The anesthesia makes the animal unconscious but does not prevent neurons in the visual system from responding. The researchers moved a

---

perception The brain's use of information provided by sensory systems to produce a response.

[FIGURE 7·1] The visual system of the brain. Arrows represent the flow of visual information. Sensory information from the eye is transmitted through the optic nerve to the thalamus, and from there it is relayed to the primary visual cortex. The results of the analysis performed there are sent to the visual association cortex of the occipital lobe (first level) and then on to that of the temporal lobe and parietal lobe (second level). At each stage, additional analysis takes place.

(From Carlson, N. R. (2004). *Physiology of Behavior*, 8/e. Published by Allyn and Bacon, Boston, MA. Copyright © 2004 by Pearson Education. Reprinted by permission of the publisher.)

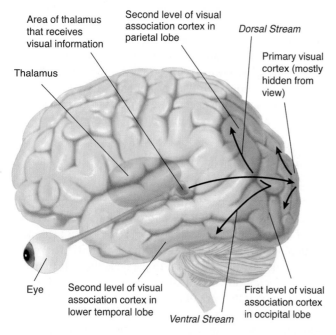

stimulus around on the screen until they located the point where it had the largest effect on the electrical activity of the neuron. Next, they presented stimuli of various shapes to learn which ones produced the greatest response from the neuron.

From their experiments, Hubel and Wiesel concluded that the geography of the visual field is retained in the primary visual cortex. That is, the surface of the retina is "mapped" on the surface of the primary visual cortex. However, this map on the brain is distorted, with the largest amount of area given to the center of the visual field, where our vision is most precise. The map is actually like a mosaic—a picture made of individual tiles or pieces of glass. Each "tile" or, in neural terms, **module,** consists of a block of tissue approximately 0.5 × 0.7 millimeters in size and containing approximately 150,000 neurons. All of the neurons within a module receive information from the same small region of the retina. The primary visual cortex contains approximately 2,500 of these modules.

---

module An area of tissue in the primary visual cortex whose neurons receive their input from the same small region in the retina.

receptive field That portion of the visual field in which the presentation of visual stimuli will produce an alteration in the firing rate of a particular neuron.

Because each module in the primary visual cortex receives information from a small region of one retina, that means it receives information from a small region of the visual field—the scene that is currently projected onto the retina. Hubel and Wiesel found that neural circuits within each module analyzed various characteristics of their own particular part of the visual field—that is, of their **receptive field.** For example, some circuits detected the presence of lines passing through the field and signaled the orientation of these lines (that is, the angle they made with respect to the horizon). Other circuits detected the width of these lines. Others detected the movement of the lines and the direction of these movements. Still others detected the lines' colors.

FIGURE 7·2 shows a recording of the responses of an orientation-sensitive neuron in the primary visual cortex. This neuron is located in a cluster of neurons that receives information from a small portion of the visual field. (That is, the neuron has a small receptive field.) The neuron responds maximally when a line oriented at 50 degrees to the vertical is placed in this location—especially when the line is moving through the receptive field. This response is highly specific to orientation; the neuron responds very little when a line having a 70-degree or 30-degree orientation is passed through the receptive field. Other neurons in this cluster share the same receptive field but respond to lines of different orientations. Thus, the orientation of lines that pass through this receptive field is signaled by an increased rate of firing of particular neurons in the cluster.

The Visual Association Cortex

Although the primary visual cortex is necessary for visual perception, the perception of objects and of the totality of the visual scene does not take place there. If you closed one eye and looked at the scene in front of you through a drinking straw, you would see about the amount of information received by an individual module of the primary visual cortex. Thus, for us to perceive objects and entire visual scenes, the information from these individual modules must be combined. That combination takes place in the visual association cortex.

Two Streams of Visual Analysis Visual information analyzed by the primary visual cortex is further analyzed in the visual association cortex. So far, investigators have identified more than two dozen distinct regions and subregions of the visual cortex of the rhesus monkey. These regions are arranged hierarchically, beginning with the primary visual cortex (Grill-Spector & Malach, 2004). Circuits of neurons analyze particular aspects of visual information and send the results of their analysis to other circuits, which perform further analysis. At each step in the process, successively more-complex features are analyzed. Remarkably, within a matter of milliseconds, the process leads to the perception of the scene and the objects in it. The higher levels of the perceptual process also interact with memories. The viewer recognizes familiar objects and learns to recognize new, unfamiliar ones.

[**FIGURE 7·2**] Responses of a single cortical neuron to lines of particular orientations that are passed through its receptive field.

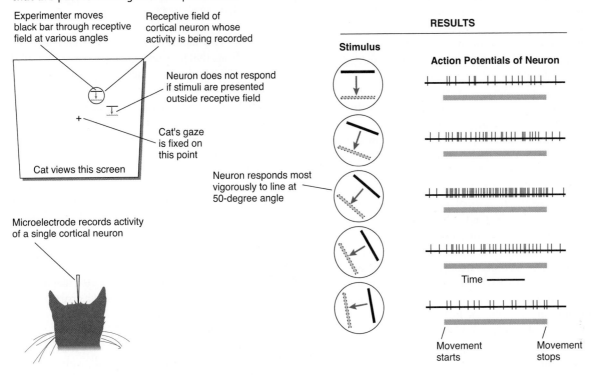

Experimenter moves black bar through receptive field at various angles

Receptive field of cortical neuron whose activity is being recorded

Neuron does not respond if stimuli are presented outside receptive field

Cat's gaze is fixed on this point

Cat views this screen

Neuron responds most vigorously to line at 50-degree angle

Microelectrode records activity of a single cortical neuron

RESULTS

Stimulus

Action Potentials of Neuron

Time ———

Movement starts

Movement stops

Neurons in the primary visual cortex send axons to the region of the visual association cortex that surrounds the striate cortex. At this point, the visual association cortex divides into two pathways: the **ventral stream** and the **dorsal stream** (Ungerleider & Mishkin, 1982; Tong & Pearson, 2007). Figure 7.1 shows that the ventral stream continues forward and ends in the inferior temporal cortex. The dorsal stream ascends into the posterior parietal cortex. The ventral stream functions in the recognition of *what* an object is, that is, what *form* it has, as well as what *color* it has. For the dorsal stream, it is *where* an object is located and whether it is *moving*. (See FIGURE 7·3.)

ventral stream The flow of information from the primary visual cortex to the visual association area in the lower temporal lobe; used to form the perception of an object's shape, color, and orientation (the "what" system).

dorsal stream The flow of information from the primary visual cortex to the visual association area in the parietal lobe; used to form the perception of an object's location in three-dimensional space (the "where" system).

[**FIGURE 7·3**] A schematic diagram of the types of analyses performed on visual information in the primary visual cortex and the various regions of the visual association cortex.

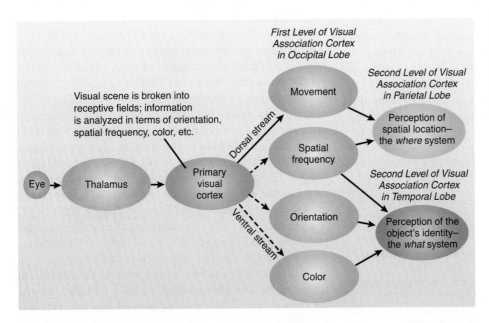

First Level of Visual Association Cortex in Occipital Lobe

Visual scene is broken into receptive fields; information is analyzed in terms of orientation, spatial frequency, color, etc.

Movement

Spatial frequency

Orientation

Color

Dorsal stream

Ventral stream

Eye

Thalamus

Primary visual cortex

Second Level of Visual Association Cortex in Parietal Lobe

Perception of spatial location— the *where* system

Second Level of Visual Association Cortex in Temporal Lobe

Perception of the object's identity— the *what* system

The Ventral Stream: Perception of Form Studies with laboratory animals have found that the recognition of visual patterns and identification of particular objects takes place in the inferior temporal cortex, located at the end of the ventral stream. It is here that analyses of form and color are put together, and perceptions of three-dimensional objects emerge (Riesenhuber & Poggio, 2002).

Functional-imaging studies and the study of people with damage to the visual association cortex confirm the conclusions of animal studies. Brain damage can cause a category of deficits known as **visual agnosia.** *Agnosia* ("failure to know") refers to an inability to perceive or identify a stimulus that exists within a specific sensory modality. The inability occurs even though the person can perceive the details of the stimulus and otherwise retain relatively normal intellectual capacity. Mrs. R., whose case was described in the Prologue, had visual agnosia. She could not identify common objects by sight, even though she had relatively normal visual acuity. When she was permitted to hold an object that she could not recognize visually, she could immediately recognize it by touch and say what it was. Clearly she had not lost her memory of the object or simply forgotten how to say its name.

Prosopagnosia (prah-suh-pagg-NOSE-yuh) is the inability to recognize familiar faces (*prosopon* is Greek for "face"). That is, patients with this disorder can recognize that they are looking at a face and can recognize its gender, approximate age, and ethnicity, but they cannot say whose face it is—even if it belongs to a relative or close friend. They see eyes, ears, a nose, a mouth, but they cannot recognize the particular configuration of these features that identifies a specific individual's face. They still remember who these people are and will usually recognize them when they hear their voice. Perhaps the best-known case of prosopagnosia was reported by the neurologist Oliver Sacks (2006).

[CASE STUDY] The patient, Dr P., was a renowned music teacher, who attended a neurological examination with his wife. On rising to leave, Dr P. looked around for his hat. He put out his hand and placed it on his wife's head, then attempted to lift it to his head, as if it were a hat! Had she spoken he would have instantly recognized her. As another patient said, "I have trouble recognizing people from just faces alone. I look at their hair color, listen to their voices . . . I use clothing, voice, and hair. I try to associate something with a person one way or another . . . what they wear, how their hair is worn" (Buxhaum, Glosser, & Coslett, 1999, p. 43).

Studies with brain-damaged people and functional imaging studies indicate that face-recognizing circuits are found in the **fusiform** (FYOO-zih-form) **face area (FFA),** a region of the ventral stream located at the base of the brain.

Several kinds of evidence suggest that face-recognition circuits develop as a result of experience in seeing people's faces. For example, brain lesions that produce prosopagnosia can also impair the ability of a farmer to recognize his cows or the ability of a driver to recognize her own car except by reading its license plate (Bornstein, Stroka, & Munitz, 1969; Damasio, Damasio, & Van Hoesen, 1982). In other words, the failure of recognition is not confined to faces. Two recent functional imaging studies (Gauthier et al., 2000; Xu, 2005) found that when bird or car experts viewed pictures of birds or cars, the FFA was activated. This did not occur when nonexperts viewed the same pictures. Thus, Tarr and Gauthier (2000) suggested that the FFA be relabeled as the *flexible* fusiform area, given its participation in the visual recognition of diverse objects.

To test whether activation of the FFA is specific to face recognition and not to the recognition of familiar objects in general, Rhodes et al. (2004) showed faces and pictures of Lepidoptera (moths and butterflies) to experts in the latter. By using *f*MRI, they found greater activation in the FFA in response to faces than to Lepidoptera, supporting the claim that the FFA is differentially involved in face perception. As we will see in Chapter 16, people with autistic disorder fail to develop normal social relations. In severe cases, they give no indication even that other people exist. Grelotti, Gauthier, and Schultz (2002) found that people with autistic disorder showed a deficit in the ability to recognize faces and that looking at faces failed to activate the FFA. The authors speculated that other brain abnormalities associated with autistic disorder may result in a lack of interest in other people and consequently in the failure to acquire face recognition during childhood, as normally would occur.

Functional-imaging studies have revealed several additional regions of the ventral stream that are differentially responsive to particular categories of visual stimuli. For example, the **extrastriate body area (EBA)** is specifically activated by photographs, silhouettes, or stick figures of human bodies or body parts and not by control stimuli such as photographs or drawings of tools, scrambled silhouettes, or scrambled stick drawings of bodies (Downing et al., 2001). Urgesi, Berlucchi, and Aglioti (2004) found that when the EBA was temporarily inactivated by transcranial magnetic stimulation (see Chapter 4), people lost the ability to recognize photographs of body parts but not parts of faces or motorcycles. A separate region of the ventral stream, the **parahippocampal place area (PPA),** is activated by visual scenes (that is, collections of several objects) and backgrounds. Steeves et al. (2004) reported the case of a woman with bilateral damage to the ventral stream that resulted in profound visual agnosia for objects. Functional imaging showed that her PPA was undamaged. She was still able to recognize both natural and

---

visual agnosia   The inability of a person who is not blind to recognize the identity or use of an object by means of vision; usually caused by damage to the brain.

prosopagnosia   A form of visual agnosia characterized by difficulty in the recognition of people's faces; may be accompanied by difficulty in recognizing other complex objects; caused by damage to the visual association cortex.

fusiform face area (FFA)   A region of the ventral stream in the human brain containing face-recognizing circuits.

extrastriate body area (EBA) A region of the ventral stream in the human brain that is activated by images of bodies or body parts but not faces.

parahippocampal place area   A region of the ventral stream in the human brain that is activated by visual scenes and backgrounds.

human-made scenes, such as beaches, forests, deserts, cities, markets, and rooms. However, she was unable to recognize the specific objects that belonged to these scenes.

Ventral Stream: Perception of Color

Laboratory research has shown that individual neurons in a region of the ventral stream respond to particular colors, which suggests that this region is involved in combining the information from red/green and yellow/blue signals that originate in retinal ganglion cells (see Chapter 6). Heywood, Gaffan, and Cowey (1995) found that damage to this region disrupted the ability of monkeys to distinguish different colors. The animals could still distinguish between different shades of gray, so the deficit was not caused by a more general impairment of visual perception.

Lesions of a particular region of the human ventral stream can also cause loss of color vision without disrupting visual acuity. The patients describe their vision as resembling a black-and-white film (Damasio et al. 1980; Heywood & Kentridge, 2003). The condition is known as **cerebral achromatopsia** (ey-krow-muh-TOP-see-uh; the word means "vision without color"). If the brain damage occurs on only one side of the brain, people will lose their color vision in only half of the visual field (see FIGURE 7•4). If the damage is bilateral, they lose all color vision and cannot even imagine colors or remember the colors of objects they saw before their brain damage occurred.

A functional MRI study by Hadjikhani et al. (1998) found a color-sensitive region in the human ventral stream. Indeed lesions that cause achromatopsia must damage either this region or other brain regions that provide input to it.

The Dorsal Stream: Perception of Spatial Location

The parietal lobe (see Chapter 4) receives visual, auditory, somatosensory, and vestibular information and is involved in spatial and somatosensory perception. Damage to the parietal lobe disrupts performance on a variety of tasks that require (a) perceiving and remembering the location of objects, and (b) controlling the movement of the eyes and the limbs. As Figure 7.1 shows, the end of the dorsal stream is located in the posterior parietal cortex.

Studies with monkeys and functional-imaging studies with humans indicate that neurons in the dorsal stream are involved in visual attention and control of eye movements, the visual control of reaching and pointing, as well as the visual control of grasping and other hand movements, and the perception of depth (Snyder, Batista, & Anderson, 2000; Culham & Kanwisher, 2001; Astafiev et al., 2003; Tsao et al., 2003; Frey et al., 2005).

Goodale and his colleagues (Goodale & Milner, 1992; Goodale et al., 1994; Goodale & Westwood, 2004) suggested that the primary function of the dorsal stream of the visual cortex is to guide actions rather than simply to perceive spatial locations. As Ungerleider and Mishkin (1982) originally put it, the ventral and dorsal streams of the visual association cortex tell us "what" the object is and "where" it is located, respectively. Instead, Goodale and his colleagues recommend the combination of "what" and "how," that is, how to perform the action. For example, a woman with bilateral lesions of the posterior parietal cortex had no difficulty recognizing line drawings (indicating that her ventral stream was intact), but picking up objects was difficult for her (Jakobson et al., 1991). She could easily perceive differences in the size of wooden blocks placed in front of her. But she could not adjust the distance between her thumb and forefinger to the size of a block in order to pick it up. In contrast, a patient with profound visual agnosia caused by damage to the ventral stream *could not* distinguish between wooden blocks of different sizes but *could* adjust the distance between her thumb and forefinger when she picked them up. Moreover, she made this adjustment before she actually touched the blocks (Milner et al., 1991; Goodale et al., 1994). This suggests that visual information in the dorsal stream was sufficient to enable the adjustment. Functional imaging of the same patient (James et al., 2003) showed normal activity in the dorsal stream while she was picking up objects.

The suggestion by Goodale and his colleagues that the function of the dorsal stream is captured better by the notion of *how* rather than *where* should not imply an absence of the capacity to recognize spatial location. After all, if the primary role of the dorsal stream is to direct movements toward objects, it *must* be involved in locating them. In addition, it must possess information about their size and shape, or it could not control the distance between thumb and forefinger when objects are grasped and picked up.

Dorsal Stream: Perception of Movement

We need to know not only what things are but also where they are and where they are going. Without the ability to perceive the velocity (that is, the direction and speed) of objects, we could

[**FIGURE 7•4**] A photograph illustrating the way the world would look to a person who had achromatopsia in the right visual field, caused by damage on the left side of the brain to the region of the visual association cortex shown in Figure 7.1.

(Photo courtesy of Neil Carlson.)

cerebral achromatopsia The inability to discriminate colors; caused by damage to the visual association cortex.

not predict where they will be. We would be unable to catch them or avoid letting them catch us.

Brain research with laboratory animals has identified a region of the visual association cortex that contains neurons that respond differentially to movement. The region is located in the extrastriate cortex. Damage to this region severely disrupts a monkey's ability to perceive moving stimuli (Siegel & Andersen, 1986). Bilateral damage to a similar region in humans produces a similar loss, known as **akinetopsia** (ay-kinn-eh-TOP-see-yuh). For example, Zihl et al. (1991) reported the case of a woman with such damage.

[**CASE STUDY**] Patient L. M. had an almost total loss of movement perception. She was unable to cross a street without traffic lights, because she could not judge the speed at which cars were moving. Although she could perceive movements, she found moving objects very unpleasant to look at. For example, while talking with another person, she avoided looking at the person's mouth because she found its movements very disturbing. When the investigators asked her to try to detect movements of a visual target in the laboratory, she said, "First, the target is completely at rest. Then it suddenly jumps upwards and downwards" (Zihl et al., 1991, p. 2244). She was able to see that the target was changing its position, but she did not perceive it in motion between those positions. (Carlson, 2007, p. 201)

Walsh et al. (1998) used transcranial magnetic stimulation temporarily to inactivate the same region in normal human participants. The investigators found that, during the stimulation, participants were able to recognize different-shaped objects displayed on a computer screen but were unable to detect which of the objects was moving. When the stimulation was absent, they had no trouble detecting the motion.

Form from Motion Perception of movement can even help us to perceive three-dimensional forms—a phenomenon known as *form from motion* (as well as *biological motion*). Johansson (1973) demonstrated just how much information we can derive from movement. He dressed actors in black and attached small lights to several points on their bodies, such as their wrists, elbows, shoulders, hips, knees, and feet. He made movies of the actors in the darkened room while they were performing various behaviors, such as walking, running, jumping, limping, doing pushups, and dancing with a partner who was also equipped with lights. Even though observers who watched the films could see only a pattern of moving lights against a dark background, they could readily perceive the pattern as belonging to a moving human and could identify the behavior the actor was performing. Subsequent studies (for example, Kozlowksi & Cutting, 1977) showed that people could even tell, with reasonable accuracy, the sex of the actor wearing the lights. The cues appeared to

be supplied by the relative amounts of movement of the shoulders and hips as the actor walked.

A functional imaging study by Grossman et al. (2000) found that when people viewed a video that showed form from motion, a bilateral brain region [specifically, the ventral bank of the posterior end of the superior temporal sulcus (SULL-kuss)] became active. However, more activity was observed in the right hemisphere, whether the video images were presented to the left or the right visual field. Grossman and Blake (2001) found that this same region was activated even when people just *imagined* that they were watching points of light representing form from motion.

Perception of form might seem like something that only shows up in a laboratory, but it does occur under natural circumstances. For example, people with visual agnosia often can still perceive *actions* (such as someone pretending to stir food items in a bowl or to deal out some playing cards from a deck), even though they are unable to recognize the objects by sight. Thus, they may be able to recognize friends by the way they walk, even though they cannot recognize their faces. The following case study is illustrative.

[**CASE STUDY**] Lê et al. (2002) reported the case of patient S. B., a 30-year-old man whose ventral stream was extensively damaged bilaterally by encephalitis (inflammation of the brain) when he was three years old. As a result, he was unable to recognize objects, faces, textures, or colors. However, he could perceive movement and could even catch a ball that was thrown to him. Furthermore, he could recognize other people's arm and hand movements that mimed common activities such as cutting something with a knife or brushing one's teeth, and he could recognize people he knew by their gait. (Carlson, 2007, p. 202)

Such clinical findings suggest that form from motion involves brain mechanisms different from those involved in the perception of objects. Recall that Mrs. R. in the Prologue could recognize forms from motion (those of Dr. L. when he mimed turning a key, writing, and dealing playing cards) and had no difficulty perceiving spatial location and movement. On this basis, it seems reasonable to conclude that her profound visual agnosia, including prosopagnosia, was attributable to ventral stream deficits.

QUESTIONS TO CONSIDER

1. If you partially damaged your primary visual cortex, what would your symptoms be? Your visual association cortex partially? How would this affect your normal functioning?
2. If you had one of the perceptual deficits described in this section, what coping strategies might you adopt? Suppose that you could not identify people by sight, or recognize your automobile. Or suppose that you could not recognize common objects but could read. How could you arrange things so that you would function at a high level of independence?

---

akinetopsia   Loss of the ability to perceive movement due to damage in
   the visual association cortex.

3. Suppose that you had complete achromatopsia. What would you miss seeing? What practical difficulties would you face, and how would you cope with them?

Visual Perception of Objects

At this point we turn from a consideration of brain mechanisms in visual perception to consider the relation between visual perception and the physical characteristics of the environments in which perception takes place. As previously mentioned, when we look at the world, we do not first see patches of colors, the frequency of vertical lines, or shades of brightness per se. We see things—cars, streets, people, desks, books, trees, dogs, chairs, walls, flowers, clouds, cell phones—with immediacy. We see where each thing is located, how large it is, and whether it is moving. We recognize familiar things; we also recognize when we see something we have never seen before. This section considers factors that contribute to the immediacy of perception, to knowing right away what something is and where it is located.

Figure and Ground

We classify most of what we see as either object or background. Objects are things having particular shapes and particular locations in space. (In this context, people can be considered as objects.) Backgrounds are perceived as less well formed and serve mostly to help us judge the location of objects we see in front of them. Psychologists use the terms **figure** and **ground** to label an object and its background, respectively. Whether you perceive an item as a figure or as a part of the ground is not an intrinsic property of the item. Rather, it depends on your behavior as observer. If you are watching some birds fly overhead, they are figures, and the

[**FIGURE 7·5**] "The Slave Market with Disappearing Bust of Voltaire." A painting by Salvadore Dali in which figure and ground can be reversed. You can see either two housewomen in their characteristic dress or a bust of the 18th-century abolitionist philosopher.

[**FIGURE 7·6**] The object on the left is defined by its boundaries. When the boundaries disappear, as in the camouflage on the right, it is not readily perceived.

blue sky and clouds behind the birds are the ground. If, instead, you are watching the clouds move, then the birds become the ground. If you are looking at a picture hanging on a wall, it is a figure. If you are looking at a person standing between you and the wall, the picture is part of the ground. Sometimes we receive ambiguous cues and have difficulty telling what is figure and what is ground. For example, do you see the bust of Voltaire in FIGURE 7·5?

In a study of Chinese and American participants, Chua, Boland, and Nisbett (2005) asked them to look at scenes containing objects that appeared against complex backgrounds. The researchers monitored the participants' eye movements and found that Americans tended to focus more quickly on the objects, whereas the Chinese participants' eye movements were concentrated on the background. It was the authors' conclusion that the difference may reflect Americans' relatively greater cultural emphasis on individuality and that of the Chinese on collectivity and thus the context.

One of the most important aspects of the perception of an object's form is the existence of a boundary. If a sharp and distinct change in brightness, color, or texture is seen, we may perceive an edge. If this edge forms a continuous boundary, we probably will perceive the space enclosed by the boundary as a figure rather than a ground. Otherwise, we may be slower to detect the figure. (See FIGURE 7·6.)

---

figure A visual stimulus that is perceived as an object.

ground A visual stimulus that is perceived as a background against which objects are seen.

[FIGURE 7·7] Object perception and boundaries. We immediately perceive even an unfamiliar figure when it is closed.

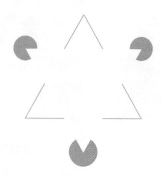

Gestalt Laws of Perceptual Organization

Although most figures are defined by a boundary, the presence of a boundary is not necessary for the perception of an object. FIGURE 7·7 demonstrates illusory contours—lines that do not exist on the page. In this figure, the three pie-shaped objects (resembling Pacman) and the three pairs of line segments intersecting at 45-degree angles produce the visual illusion of two triangles, one on top of the other. Note that the illusory triangle that looks as if it is superimposed on three green circles even appears to be brighter than the background.

Early in the twentieth century, a group of German psychologists developed a theory of perception based on our readiness to perceive whole scenes and not their elements per se (see Hothersall, 2004). As Chapter 1 discussed, they called their movement *Gestalt psychology,* and they maintained that in perception, the whole is more than the sum of its parts. That is, because of the innate characteristics of the visual system of the brain, we are prepared to see a scene and not just its elements. What we perceive is a holistic pattern, a form, a Gestalt that reflects more the arrangement or organization of the elements.

Gestalt psychologists proposed several principles or laws that describe our ability to distinguish a figure from its ground and also tell why we are more likely to perceive certain figures than others. In this way, the laws may be thought of as describing common perceptual biases or preferences. They include:

1. The Gestalt **law of proximity** states that elements that are closest together will be perceived as belonging together (see FIGURE 7·8(a)).

2. The Gestalt **law of symmetry** refers to our tendency to perceive symmetrical elements as belonging together in a pattern, regardless of their distance from each other. For example, gazing at a tiled floor or tiled wall containing tiles of different color arranged in an alternating pattern may prompt the perception of a particular color zigzagging across the floor or wall.

3. The Gestalt **law of similarity** states that elements that have a similar appearance will be perceived as part of the same object (see FIGURE 7·8(b)).

4. The Gestalt **law of continuity** or good continuation refers to the relative simplicity of prediction. Which of the two sets of gray dots best describes the continuation of the line of black dots in FIGURE 7·8(c)? Most people choose the gray dots that continue the curve down and to the right. It seems simpler to perceive the line as following a smooth course than as suddenly making a sharp bend.

5. The Gestalt **law of closure** states that our visual system often "closes" the outline of an incomplete figure. For example, FIGURE 7·8(d) looks as if it might be a triangle, but if you place a pencil on the page so that it covers both of the gaps, the figure is undeniably a triangle.

6. The Gestalt **law of common fate** states that elements that move in the same direction will be perceived as belonging together and forming a figure. In the forest, an animal is camouflaged if its surface is covered with the same elements found in the background—spots of brown, tan, and green; its boundary is obscured. As long as the animal remains stationary, no perceptual basis appears for organizing the elements that belong to it alone, and it remains well hidden. However, once it moves, the elements on its surface will move together, and the animal's size and shape will quickly be visible. (Note the similarity between this example and the phenomenon of form from motion.)

law of proximity A Gestalt law of perceptual organization; elements located closest to one another are perceived as belonging to the same figure.

law of symmetry A Gestalt law of perceptual organization; symmetrical objects are perceived as belonging together even if a distance separates them.

law of similarity A Gestalt law of perceptual organization; similar elements are perceived as belonging to the same figure.

law of continuity A Gestalt law of perceptual organization; given two or more possible interpretations of the elements that form the outline of a figure, the brain will adopt the simplest interpretation.

law of closure A Gestalt law of perceptual organization; elements missing from the outline of a figure are "filled in" by the visual system.

law of common fate A Gestalt law of perceptual organization; elements that move together give rise to the perception of a particular figure.

Models of Pattern Perception

Stimulus objects, large and small, can come together simultaneously or in a sequence and be perceived as a pattern. Cognitive psychologists interested in the cognitive processes responsible for perception attempt to identify and analyze the steps that take place between the time a person's eye is exposed to objects and the time when a pattern is perceived (Peterson, 2005). They collect behavioral data and try to make inferences about the nature of these intervening processes. Let's look at some of the models cognitive psychologists have proposed.

(a)

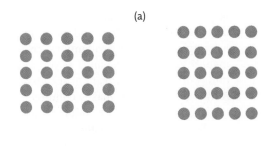

(b)

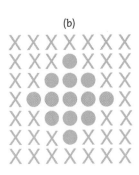

(c)

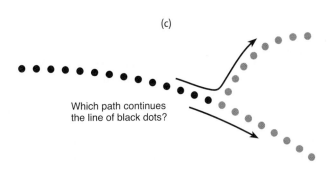

Which path continues
the line of black dots?

(d)

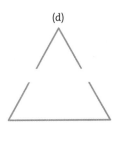

[**FIGURE 7·8**] (a) *The Gestalt law of proximity.* Different spacing of the dots produces five vertical or five horizontal lines. (b) *The Gestalt law of similarity.* Similar elements are perceived as belonging to the same form. (c) *The Gestalt law of good continuation.* It is easier to perceive a smooth continuation than an abrupt shift. (d) *The Gestalt law of closure.* We tend to supply missing information in order to close a figure and separate it from its background. Lay a pencil across the two gaps and see how much stronger the perception of a complete triangle becomes.

Templates and Prototypes Our ability to recognize the shape of an object might be explained by special memories known as templates. A **template** is a device used to produce a series of objects that resemble each other. For example, a cookie cutter is a template used to cut out identical shapes from a flat sheet of dough. According to the template model, visual perception reverses the process. When a particular pattern of visual stimuli is encountered, the visual system searches its store of templates and compares each of them with the pattern. If it finds a match, the pattern is recognized as familiar. Templates stored in memory could be used to identify patterns of stimuli as letters or numbers, or as more sophisticated objects such as cats or dogs.

The template model of pattern recognition has the virtue of simplicity. However, most cognitive psychologists dismiss it as infeasible—the visual system would have to store an impossibly large number of templates. A more feasible model of pattern perception suggests that the visual system compares patterns of stimuli with prototypes rather than templates. A **prototype** (Greek for "original model") is an idealized pattern; it resembles a template but is used in a much more flexible way. The visual system does not require an exact match between the present pattern and a specific template but instead accepts a degree of disparity. Think of how many different people you can recognize by sight, how

We can recognize particular objects as well as general categories of objects.

template A hypothetical pattern that is stored in the nervous system and is used to perceive objects or shapes by a process of comparison.

prototype A hypothetical idealized pattern that resides in the nervous system and is used to perceive objects or shapes by a process of comparison; recognition can occur even when an exact match cannot be found.

[**FIGURE 7·9**] Distinctive features. We easily recognize all of these items as the letter *N*.

many different buildings in your town or city you can identify, how many of the pieces of furniture in your house and in your friends' houses you are familiar with—the list will be very long indeed. Evidence from studies of nonhuman primates suggests that increased familiarity with categories of objects may lead to the development of more specific prototypes (Humphrey, 2003).

Distinctive Features   How complete does the information in a template or prototype have to be for pattern recognition to occur? Does it have to exist as an image, or can it exist in some shorthand way? Some cognitive psychologists have suggested another approach to object perception in terms of **distinctive features**—the essential physical features that specify a particular category of objects. For example, FIGURE 7·9 contains several examples of the capital letter N. Although the examples vary in size and style, you have no trouble recognizing them.

A classic experiment by Neisser supports the hypothesis that object perception involves distinctive features. FIGURE 7·10 shows one of the tasks Neisser used that involved two vertical arrays of letters. Scan through them until you find the letter Z, which occurs once in each array.

Chances are good that you found the Z much faster in the left column than in the right column, just as the participants in Neisser's study did. Perhaps you guessed why: The letters in the left column have few distinctive features in common with those found in the letter Z, so the Z stands out from the others. In contrast, the letters in the right column have many features in common with the target letter, and thus the Z is camouflaged, so to speak.

An ambitious theory of feature-based object perception was proposed by Biederman (1987, 1995). Critical to the theory is a fixed set of "primitives," or feature detectors for specific three-dimensional geometrical shapes—called *geons*—that reside in the brain. A sample of geons appears in FIGURE 7·11, together with familiar objects that represent combinations of geons. The perception of an object occurs as the brain analyzes its visual image using geons. Biederman argued that it is possible to decode all visual information, even the most complex—for example, a face—in terms

of geons. The theory also specifies brain areas where geon detection may take place, and recent research with monkeys has implicated the inferotemporal cortex (Kayeart, Biederman, & Vogels, 2005), which as you might recall, is the terminus of the lateral stream of the visual association cortex. Although the theory makes comprehensive claims, as you might expect, it is not without detractors (see Pinker, 1997).

Some phenomena cannot easily be explained by the distinctive-features model. According to the model, perception consists of analysis and synthesis: The visual system first identifies the features of a pattern and then combines them to determine what the pattern is. We might expect, then, that more complex patterns have more distinctive features and would take longer to perceive. In reality, the addition of more features, especially in the form of contextual cues, often speeds the process of perception. The tendency for certain stimuli to "pop out" during visual search of a display provides evidence that perception does not necessarily involve a strict search for features. For example, Enns and Rensink (1991) found that the orientation (downward to the right or upward to the left) of wire-frame objects like those in panel (a) in FIGURE 7·12 was quickly detected in a visual search. If the vertices of the object were not connected, however, as in panel (b), orientation was much more difficult to detect. In another study. Pilon and Friedman (1998) found that misaligned vertices, as at the bottom right of panel (c), were difficult to detect when vertices were

GDOROC	IVEMXW
COQUCD	XVIWME
DUCOQG	VEMIXW
GRUDQO	WEXMVI
OCDURQ	XIMVWE
DUCGRO	IVMWEX
ODUCQG	VWEMXI
CQOGRD	IMEWXV
DUZORQ	EXMZWI
UCGROD	IEMWVX
QCUDOG	EIVXWM
RQGUDO	WXEMIV
DRGOQC	MIWVXE
OQGDRU	IMEVXW
UGCODQ	IEMWVX
ODRUCQ	IMWVEX
UDQRGC	XWMVEI
ORGCUD	IWEVXM
QOGRUC	VMIWEX

[**FIGURE 7·10**] A letter-search task. Look for the letter *Z* hidden in each vertical array.

(Adapted from Neisser, U., *Scientific American*, 1964, *210*, 94–102. Copyright © 1964 by *Scientific American*. All rights reserved.)

---

distinctive features   Physical characteristics of an object that help distinguish it from other objects.

[**FIGURE 7·11**] Geons for perception. (a) Several different geons. (b) The combination of two or three geons (indicated by the numbers) into common three-dimensional objects.

(Adapted from Biederman, I. In *An Invitation to Cognitive Science. Vol 2: Visual Cognition and Action*, edited by D. N. Osherson, S. M. Kosslyn, and J. Hollerbach. Copyright © 1990 by the Massachusetts Institute of Technology; published by MIT Press, Cambridge, MA.)

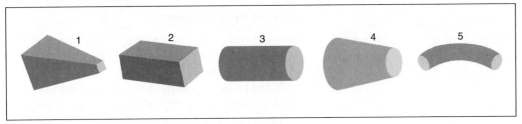

(a) Geons

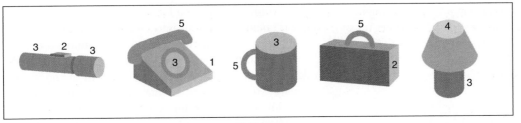

(b) Objects

not connected. Presumably, only by connecting the vertices with solid lines, and thus providing additional features, was "pop-out" perception achieved.

It also may be the case that prolonged exposure to particular features simplifies object perception. For example, try to read the paragraph that appears in FIGURE 7·13. Most of the words in the paragraph have been scrambled—except for the first and last letters—yet you probably are able to make your way through the paragraph with only a slight slowing of your normal reading speed. Demonstrations such as this suggest that your ability to perceive the meaning of visual

stimuli—in this case strings of letters—may eventually rely on only some of the features that are present; for example, the "outer boundaries" of words. Dehaene (2003) has speculated that such ability derives from the exploitative reuse of brain modules that originally served other functions, such as object recognition in the natural world. He used the term "neural recycling" to refer to this possibility.

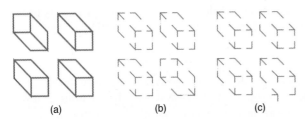

[**FIGURE 7·12**] Wire-frame figures similar to those used by Enns and Rensink (1991) and Pilon and Friedman (1998). Panel (a) depicts the wire-frame figures with connected vertices; panel (b) depicts figures with unconnected vertices. Pilon and Friedman used figures like those depicted in panel (c), in which the individual vertices in a figure were individually rotated and could be misaligned with the rest of the figure.

(Redrawn from Enns and Rensink (1991) and Pilon and Friedman (1998). Copyright © 1998. Canadian Psychological Association. Reprinted with permission.)

Aoccdrnig to rseerach at Cmabrigde Uinervtisy, it deosn't mttaer in waht oredr the ltteers in a wrod are, the olny iprmoatnt thing is taht the frist and lsat ltteer be at the rghit pclae. The rset can be a tatol mses and you can sitll raed it wouthit a porbelm. This is bcuseae the huamn mnid deos not raed ervey lteter by istlef, but the wrod as a wlohe. Amzanig huh?

PS: Hwo'd you lkie to run tihs by yuor sepll ckehcer?

[**FIGURE 7·13**] A paragraph in which the letters in each word have been scrambled except for the first and last letters.

("Are Reading and Writing Innate Skills?" www.brainconnection.com/content/198_1. Reprinted by permission of Scientific Learning Corporation.)

focus On

Does the Brain Work Like a Computer?

When we try to understand something extremely complicated (such as the functioning of the human brain), we tend to think in terms of things that are familiar to us. Although cognitive psychology as a discipline dates back to the early twentieth century, most of its philosophy and methodology have developed since the mid-1960s (Gardner, 1987). During this time, the best-known physical device that performs functions similar to those of the human brain has been the computer. The computer continues to provide much of the inspiration for the models of human brain function proposed by cognitive psychologists. As you look back over the chapter thus far, note the frequent use of terms compatible with the computer: information, pathway, connection, system, process, pattern, storage, etc. Just how similar is a computer to the human brain?

Using Computers to Model Cognitive Processes

Computers can be programmed to store any kind of information that can be coded in numbers or words, can solve any logical problems that can be explicitly described, and can compute any mathematical equations that can be written. Therefore—in principle, at least—they can be programmed to do the things we do: perceive, remember, make logical deductions, solve problems. Consequently, psychologists, linguists, and computer scientists have constructed computer-inspired models of memory, visual pattern perception, speech comprehension, reading, and the control of movement, for example (see Baars & Gage, 2007).

The creation of computer programs that simulate human cognitive processes belongs to a branch of cognitive science known as **artificial intelligence (AI).** For instance, to construct a program that simulates human perception and classification of certain types of patterns, AI researchers begin with a computational model. In addition to specifying what the task of pattern perception requires, the model generates a computer program. If the program fails to recognize the patterns when they are presented, then the researchers know that something is wrong with the model or with the way it has been implemented in the program. They may revise the model until the program finally works, or they decide to try a new model.

Critics of artificial intelligence have pointed out that although it is entirely possible to write a program that performs a task the human brain performs—and to show that the brain produces exactly the same results—the brain may perform the task in an entirely different way. Given the way computers work and what we know about the structure of the human brain, some critics argue that the computer program is guaranteed to work differently (see, e.g., Dreyfus & Dreyfus, 2000).

Serial and Parallel Processing

A computer works one step at a time. In other words, a computer is a *serial processor*. Each step takes time, even if it is measured in thousandths or millionths of a second. A complicated program will contain more steps and will take more time to execute. For example, for visual processing, a computer must first analyze the scene that is transmitted through an input device, such as a digital camera. The program must then convert information about the brightness of each point in the scene into a number and store the numbers in a memory location. Then it examines each memory location, one at a time, and does calculations that determine the locations of lines, edges, textures, and shapes. Finally, it tries to determine what these details represent.

Humans do some things extremely quickly that it takes computers much longer to do. If the brain were to operate in serial fashion like a computer, it could never keep up with a computer, because neurons cannot fire more than a thousand times per second (Rumelhart, McClelland, & the PDP Research Group, 1986). Obviously, when we perceive visual images, our brain is not processing information step by step. Instead, the brain appears to be a *parallel processor,* in which many different neural modules (collections of circuits of neurons) work simultaneously at different tasks. The brain breaks a complex task into many smaller ones, and separate modules work on each of them. Because the brain consists of many billions of neurons, it can afford to devote different modules to different tasks. That is, it can use *parallel distributed processing* with many things happening at the same time, thus finishing the task in an instant. Parallel distributed processing has contributed to the success of computer programs that have defeated world chess champions (Saletan, 2007) and checker-playing programs guaranteed not to lose (Chang, 2007).

Artificial Neural Network Models

In recent decades, psychologists have begun to devise models of cognitive processes that are based, more or less, on the way the brain seems basically to be constructed. These models are called **artificial neural networks.** Donald Hebb (1949) developed the concept of a neural network long before the age of modern computers. Now cognitive psychologists and neuroscientists have pursued the implications of Hebb's ideas to considerable lengths.

Investigators developing artificial neural networks construct a network of simple units that have properties like those of neurons (see Faucett, 1994). The units are connected to one another through junctions similar to synapses. Like synapses, these junctions can have either excitatory or inhibitory effects. When a unit is activated, it

---

artificial intelligence (AI)   A field of cognitive science in which researchers design computer programs to simulate human cognitive abilities; this endeavor may help cognitive psychologists understand the mechanisms that underlie these abilities.

artificial neural networks   A model of the nervous system based on interconnected networks of units that have some of the properties of neurons.

[**FIGURE 7·14**] A simple neural network used as a model of brain function. The circles are units having properties similar to those of neurons. The connections (arrows) can be excitatory or inhibitory, depending on the particular network.

Inputs

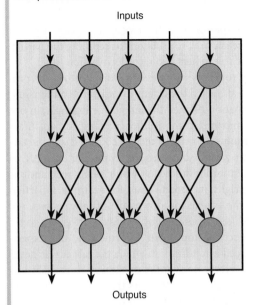

Outputs

sends a message to the units with which it communicates, and so on. Some of the units of a network have input lines that can receive signals from the "outside," which could represent a sensory organ or the information received from another network. Other units have output lines, which could communicate with other networks or produce actions. (See **FIGURE 7·14**.) The specific connections between units can be either strengthened or weakened by the extent to which the response matches the desired outcome in some way. In this sense, artificial neural networks not only mimic the structural connections between neurons in the brain but also simulate brain plasticity.

Artificial neural networks can be taught to "recognize" particular stimuli. A stimulus is presented, and the network's output is monitored. If the response is incorrect, the network receives a signal indicating the correct response. This signal causes the strength of some of the connections to be changed (a process known as "backward propagation"), just as learning is thought to alter the strength of synapses in the brain. After several repetitions, the network learns to make correct responses. Artificial neural networks can learn to recognize not only particular patterns but also variations on that pattern. Some networks also appear to learn general rules about the occurrence of features within a pattern (Berkeley et al., 1995). In a specific application to the acquisition of reading, selectively disabling some of the network's connections produced errors similar to dyslexia (Hinton & Shallice, 1991). Other applications to developmental disorders have been reported (see, e.g., Munakata, Casey, & Diamond, 2004; Elman, J. L., 2005).

So what is the answer to the question posed at the beginning of this section: Does the brain work like a computer? The answer seems to be that it does, but not like the most familiar kind of computer—the serial processor—that cognitive psychologists first used as a basis for constructing models of brain function. Instead, the brain seems to be organized as a parallel processor using a massive array of neural networks.

[**FIGURE 7·15**] Simple elements that are difficult to recognize without a context.

[**FIGURE 7·16**] An example of top-down processing. The context facilitates our recognition of the items shown in Figure 7.20.

(Adapted from Palmer, S. E. in *Explorations in Cognition*, edited by Donald A. Norman and David E. Rumelhart. Copyright © 1975 by W. H. Freeman and Company. Used with permission.)

Bottom-Up and Top-Down Processing: The Roles of Features and Context

We often perceive objects under conditions that are less than optimal; the object is in a shadow, camouflaged against a similar background, or obscured by fog. Nevertheless, we usually manage to recognize it correctly. We are often helped by the context in which we see the object. For example, look at the four objects in **FIGURE 7·15**. Can you tell what larger object they belong to? Now look at **FIGURE 7·16**, where, with the aid of a context, they are easily recognized.

An early study by Palmer (1975) made the same point by using more general forms of context. He first showed his participants familiar scenes, such as a kitchen. (See **FIGURE 7·17**.) Next, he showed drawings of individual objects and asked participants to identify them. The drawings were shown very rapidly, making them difficult to identify. Sometimes the participants were shown an object that was appropriate to the kitchen scene, such as a loaf of bread. Other times, they were shown a similarly shaped but non-kitchen object, such as a mailbox. Palmer found that when the objects fit the context provided by the scene, the participants correctly identified about 84 percent of them. When they did not, performance decreased to about 50 percent. In the no-context control condition, under which participants did not first see a scene, performance was intermediate. Thus, compared with the no-context control condition, an appropriate context facilitated recognition, and an inappropriate context interfered with it.

The Palmer study suggests the parallel operation of two processes—one that uses information directly available from the stimulus (the drawing of a loaf of bread) and the other that

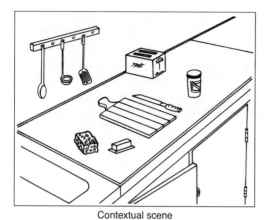

Contextual scene

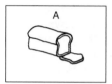

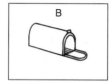

Target object (presented very briefly)

[**FIGURE 7·17**] Stimuli from the experiment by Palmer (1975). After looking at the contextual scene, the participants were shown one of the stimuli below it very briefly.

(From Palmer, S. E. (1975). *Memory and cognition, 3*, 519–526. Reprinted by permission of the Psychonomic Society, Inc.)

uses information from memory (objects that a typical kitchen would contain). Cognitive psychologists often refer to first process as *bottom-up processing* and the second as *top-down processing*. In **bottom-up processing** (also called *data-driven* or *stimulus-driven processing*), the process starts with the features—the bits and pieces—of the stimulus, beginning with the image that falls on the retina. This information is processed hierarchically by successively higher levels of the visual system until the highest levels (the "top" of the system) are reached, and the object is perceived. **Top-down processing** (also called *knowledge-driven processing*), involves the use of contextual information supplied from memory—the "big picture." The application of this model to Palmer's study, for example, suggests that information from memory about kitchen-specific features was sent from the "top" of the system down through lower levels. Then, when the participant saw a drawing of a loaf of bread, information about its features came up more readily through the successive levels of the bottom-up system, and recognition was faster and more accurate. In other words, information from the top (typical kitchen contents) primed the processing of information from the bottom (the loaf of bread).

The relative contribution of top-down and bottom-up processing to visual search was the focus of a series of experiments reported by Wolfe et al. (2003). In the design of their studies, the

researchers sought to minimize top-down information to isolate the bottom-up process. In one study designed to vary the extent of top-down information available to participants, the researchers presented stimuli containing red or green lines that were arranged either vertically or horizontally. On each trial, the participant judged whether the stimulus met the description provided by the experimenter (the target). Feedback (right or wrong) followed each trial. In addition to recording the participant's answer, the researchers also recorded reaction time.

To separate top-down processing from bottom-up processing, Wolfe et al. varied the extent to which the dimensions of color or orientation defined the target. For example, in one condition that maximized the influence of top-down information, any stimulus that contained the color red was the target; the orientation of the bars was irrelevant. For example, in FIGURE 7·18, the stimulus on the left would be correct, and the stimulus on the right, incorrect. Thus, for example, a participant could use the simple top-down rule of "always pick red when it appears" and be assured of success. Conversely, to reduce the influence of top-down information, the experimenters introduced a condition in which the target was never consistently red, green, horizontal, or vertical. Instead it was any stimulus in which one of the bars that appeared was discrepant from all the other bars in color or orientation. Thus in Figure 7.18 both of the stimuli would be correct. Now no simple top-down rule in terms of color or orientation applied. The researchers argued that this allowed bottom-up influences a larger role in the participants' judgments. Consequently, average reaction time was slowest in that condition. It was fastest in the condition with full top-down information.

Perceptual ("What") and Action ("Where") Systems: A Possible Synthesis

Our examination of the visual perception of objects has brought us to a puzzle. It is clear that the features of objects play some role in our ability to recognize them, but it is less

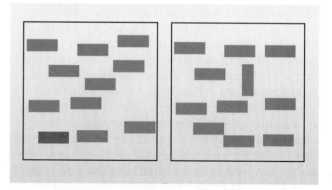

[**FIGURE 7·18**] Two sample stimuli from the Wolfe et al. study (2003) that varied the relative influence of bottom-up and top-down information.

(Adapted from Wolfe, J. M., Butcher, S. J., Lee, C., & Hyle, M. (2003). Changing your mind: On the contributions of top-down and bottom-up guidance in visual search for feature singletons. *Journal of Experimental Psychology: Human Perception and Performance, 29*, 483–502.)

bottom-up processing Perception based on successive analyses of the details of the stimuli that are present.

top-down processing Perception based on information provided by the context in which a particular stimulus is encountered.

TAE CAT
RED
SPOT
FISH

clear that feature-analysis theories can fully explain that ability. Top-down factors such as context exert powerful influences, but we still must ask how that influence is exerted.

In most cases, visual perception seems to consist of a combination of top-down and bottom-up processing. FIGURE 7·19 shows several examples of objects that can be recognized only by a combination of both forms of processing. Our knowledge of the configurations of letters in words (top-down processing) provides us with the contexts that permit us to organize (and expedite) the flow of featural information from the bottom up. Concluding that the perception of objects requires the interaction of both types of processing still leaves unanswered the question of what that interaction is composed of. How do bottom-up and top-down processing come together to produce object recognition?

This puzzle is likely to remain unsolved for some time, but findings from cognitive neuroscience are providing some provocative clues. For example, Goodale and Milner (2005) described extensive observations of a Scottish woman named "Dee."

[**CASE STUDY**] While living in Italy, Dee had carbon monoxide poisoning that left her unable to identify objects visually. Once she returned to Scotland and was examined there, it became clear that her visual deficits were not global but specific in a peculiar way. She had normal acuity and could readily discriminate colors and surface textures. For example, she could tell that a kitchen bowl was made of red plastic. However, she would not be able to identify the object as a bowl. She was unable to identify the boundaries of objects—the edges, curves, and corners by which the object was differentiated from another object or from its background. Nonetheless, she was still able to reach for specific objects appropriately. For example, Dee would be unable to tell whether the slot on a mailbox was oriented horizontally or vertically, but if you gave her an envelope and asked her to deposit it in the slot, her movements would be just right. Moreover, if asked to draw an object she was familiar with, she could do so reasonably well but not if drawing with her eyes closed, because she could not recognize the object she had drawn.

Goodale and Milner (2005) suggest a strong dissociation between what they describe as "vision for perception" (the "what" system) and "vision for action" (the "where" system). These two categories of vision are consistent with the ventral and dorsal streams in the visual association cortex that were introduced earlier in the chapter. The what system provides us with information about objects and their meanings and involves pathways that lead to the temporal lobe—the ventral stream. The where system provides us with information necessary for acting on objects with guided movement and involves pathways that lead to the parietal lobe—the dorsal stream.

Dee's brain damage apparently affected her perception of objects—her what system—but left intact her ability to respond to the location and orientation of objects—her where system. The dorsal stream provides information necessary for guiding our actions toward objects but does not provide us with the ability to recognize or name them. Dee's condition is reminiscent of that of Mrs. R., who, in the Prologue, could not identify an object as a watch. When asked to pick it up, she did so readily, and having done so, could now say what it was. Goodale and Milner argue that visual perception involves the interplay between these two systems. The dorsal stream responds to the location and orientation of objects and coordinates the actions we take with respect to them. The ventral stream gives us information about what the objects are so that we know, for example, that it will take less effort to turn this page than it will to turn the cover of this book.

QUESTIONS TO CONSIDER

1. Find examples of figure and ground in your immediate visual environment. Try changing your focus of attention to make items previously seen as figures become part of the ground and vice versa. Provide examples from your own experience of each of the Gestalt laws of perceptual organization.

2. Approximately how many unique objects do you think you can recognize at this point in your life? How many more do you think you will learn to recognize during the years ahead of you? What problem(s) does this potential for unlimited acquisition pose for a theory of object perception?

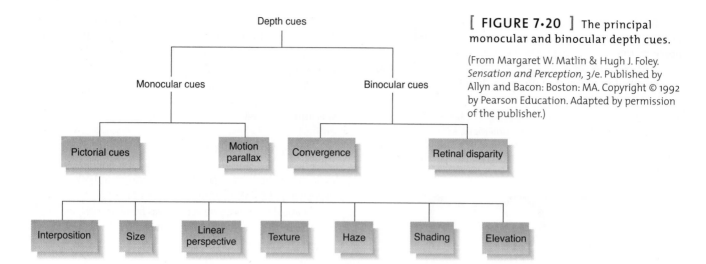

[FIGURE 7·20] The principal monocular and binocular depth cues.

(From Margaret W. Matlin & Hugh J. Foley. *Sensation and Perception*, 3/e. Published by Allyn and Bacon: Boston: MA. Copyright © 1992 by Pearson Education. Adapted by permission of the publisher.)

3. What do you do when you try to assemble the pieces of a complex picture puzzle? Relate this experience to the concepts of templates, prototypes, and distinctive features.

4. Suppose that Goodale and Milner are correct about a visual system that is specialized for movements such as reaching. Are you aware of orienting your hand when you reach for, say, a computer mouse that is at an odd angle on a tabletop? What might this say about the role of consciousness in guided movement?

Visual Perception of Space and Motion

We not only are able to perceive the objects in our environment (what) but also can judge quite accurately their relative location in space and their movements, as well as our movements relative to them (where). In this section, we take up the perception of depth and movement.

Depth Perception

Depth perception requires that we perceive the distance between us and objects in the environment as well as their distance from one another. This is an impressive feat, given that the three-dimensional quality of depth perception must be derived from the two-dimensional images that fall on the retina in each eye. We accomplish this feat by means of two kinds of visual cues: binocular ("two-eye") and monocular ("one-eye"). Binocular cues arise from the fact that the visual

---

binocular cue   A cue for the perception of depth that requires the use of both eyes.

monocular cue   A cue for the perception of depth that requires the use of only one eye.

convergence   In depth perception, the result of conjugate eye movements whereby the fixation point for each eye is identical; feedback from these movements provides information about the distance of visual objects from the viewer.

retinal disparity   The fact that objects located at different distances from the observer will fall on different locations on the two retinas; provides a binocular cue for depth perception.

---

fields of the two eyes overlap. Only animals that have eyes on the front of the head (such as primates, cats, and some avian species) have **binocular cues** as well as **monocular cues** available to them. Animals that have eyes on the sides of their heads (such as rabbits and fish) are strictly dependent on monocular cues. In a comparative study of animal taxa, Heesey (2008) concluded that binocularity may have evolved in mammals as a means of detecting camouflaged prey at night, particularly in arboreal environments.

Among the monocular cues, one involves movement and thus must be experienced in the natural environment or in a motion picture. The others are available in a drawing or a photograph and were originally identified by visual artists and only later studied by psychologists. FIGURE 7·20 provides a classification of the principal distance cues. Let's look more closely at each.

Binocular Cues   An important cue for distance is supplied by **convergence.** Recall from Chapter 6 that the eyes make conjugate movements so that both look at (converge on) the same point of the visual scene. If an object is very close to your face, your eyes are turned inward. If it is farther away, they turn straight ahead. Thus, the eyes can be used like range finders. The brain controls the extraocular muscles that move each eye and presumably can compute the angle between them and, from that, the distance between the object and the eyes. Convergence is most important for perceiving the distance of objects located close to us—especially those we can reach with our hands. (See FIGURE 7·21.)

Another important cue for the perception of distance is provided by **retinal disparity.** (Disparity means "unlikeness" or "dissimilarity.") Hold up a finger of one hand at arm's length, and then hold up a finger of the other hand midway between your nose and the distant finger. If you look at one of the fingers, you will see a double image of the other one. (Try it; you may be surprised.) Because of the physical distance between the eyes, whenever they are pointed in a particular direction, the images of objects at different distances will fall on different portions of the retina in each eye. The disparity between the images of an object on the two retinas

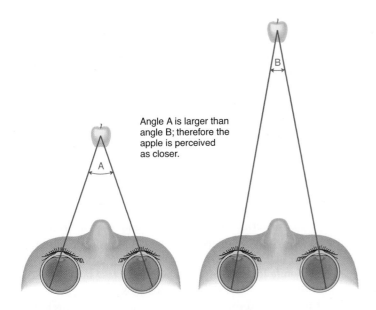

Angle A is larger than angle B; therefore the apple is perceived as closer.

[**FIGURE 7·21**] Convergence. When the eyes converge on a nearby object, the angle between them is greater than when they converge on a distant object. The brain uses this information in perceiving the distance of an object.

is an important source of information about their distance from you. Hubel (1995) described a class of cells in the primary visual cortex of monkeys—*binocular cells*—that fire in response to the slightly disparate images from each eye.

Research on retinal disparity has sometimes used a *stereoscope,* a device that shows two slightly different pictures, one to each eye. The pictures are taken by a camera equipped with two lenses, located a few inches apart, just as our eyes are. When you look through a stereoscope, you see a three-dimensional image. In an ingenious experiment, Julesz (1965, 2006) demonstrated that retinal disparity is essential for the perception of depth. With a computer, he produced two displays of randomly positioned dots. If some of the dots in one of the displays were displaced slightly to the right or the left of where they were found in the other display, the two displays produced the perception of a three-dimensional scene when viewed together through a stereoscope.

FIGURE 7·22 shows a pair of these random-dot stereograms. If you look at them very carefully, you will see that some of the dots near the center in the right stereogram have been moved slightly to the left in the left stereogram. Some people can look at these figures without using a stereoscope and see depth. If you want to try this, hold the book at arm's length and stare at

the space between the figures, at the same time pretending you are looking "through" the book at something behind it. If you keep looking, you may be able to make the two images fuse into one, located right in the middle. Eventually, you may see a small square in the center of the image, raised above the background. The process can be eased by using special viewers that separate the images. The growing popularity of 3-D movies testifies to the entertainment potential of retinal disparity.

Monocular Cues Among the most important monocular cues is **interposition** ("placed between"). If one object is placed between you and another object so that the closer object partially obscures your view of the more distant one, you can immediately perceive which object is closer to you. Obviously, interposition works best when you are familiar with the objects and know what their shapes should look like. In FIGURE 7·23, panel (a) can be seen either as two rectangles located one in front of the other—panel (b)—or as a rectangle nestled against an L-shaped object—panel (c). Because we tend to perceive an ambiguous drawing on the basis of shapes that are already familiar, we are more likely to perceive Figure 7.23 (a) as two rectangles, one partly hiding the other.

Another important monocular cue is provided by the **relative size** of an object. For example, if an automobile casts a very small image on our retinas, we will perceive it as being far away. We already know how large cars are, so our visual system automatically computes the approximate distance based on the size of the retinal image.

FIGURE 7·24 shows two columns, one closer than the other. The scene demonstrates **linear perspective:** the tendency

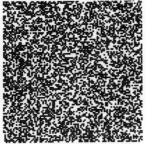

[**FIGURE 7·22**] A pair of random-dot stereograms.

(From Julesz, B. (1965). Texture and visual perception. *Scientific American, 12,* 38–48.)

interposition   A monocular cue for depth perception; an object that partially blocks another object is perceived as closer.

relative size   A monocular cue for depth perception based on the retinal size of an object.

linear perspective   A monocular cue for depth perception; the arrangement of lines drawn in two dimensions such that parallel lines receding from the viewer are seen to converge at a point on the horizon.

[FIGURE 7•23] Interposition. The two objects shown in panel (a) could be two identical rectangles, one in front of the other, as shown in (b), or a rectangle and an L-shaped object, as shown in (c). When the objects are familiar. We tend to see them in their simplest form—in this case, a rectangle. As a result, the shape slightly to the right is perceived as being partly hidden and thus farther away from us.

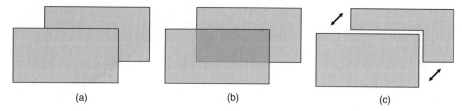

(a)   (b)   (c)

for parallel lines that recede from us eventually to converge at a single point. Thus, objects accompanied by greater convergence are perceived as farther away.

A **texture gradient** provides another cue for the distance of objects. A coarser texture appears to be closer, and a finer texture looks more distant. (See FIGURE 7•25.) The earth's atmosphere, which always contains a certain amount of **haze,** also can supply cues about the relative distance of objects or parts of the landscape. Parts of the landscape that are farther away become less distinct because of haze in the air. (See FIGURE 7•26.)

The patterns of light and shadow in a scene—its **shading**—can provide us with cues about distance, although the cues that shading provides may not tell us much about the absolute distances of objects. FIGURE 7•27 illustrates this phenomenon. Some of the circles look convex, as if they bulge out toward you (bumps); others look concave, as if they are hollowed out (dimples). You may perceive this figure as a collection of dimples surrounded by bumps. Try turning the page upside down. The only difference is the direction of the shading, but your perception of the bumps and dimples changes. The visual system appears to interpret the scene as if it were illuminated from above. Thus, the top of a convex object will be in light and the bottom will be in shadow and vice versa for a concave object. Using a "pop-out" image comparable to Figure 7.27, Sun and Perona (1998) found that dimples tended to pop out faster when the perceived direction of lighting was slightly more from the top left. The next

[FIGURE 7•24] Linear perspective. The use of straight lines that converge to a single point gives the appearance of distance and makes the two inset columns look similar in size.

[FIGURE 7•25] Textures. Variations in texture can produce the perception of distance. The stones diminish in size toward the top of the photo; we therefore perceive the top of the photo as being farther away from us.

(Photo © Bohdan Hrynewych/Stock, Boston)

texture gradient   A monocular cue for depth perception; the relative fineness of detail present in the surfaces of objects or the ground or floor.

haze   A monocular cue for depth perception; objects that are less distinct in their outlines and texture are perceived as farther from the viewer.

shading   A monocular cue for depth perception; the apparent light source determines whether the surface of an object is perceived as concave or convex.

[FIGURE 7·26] Cues from atmospheric haze. Variation in detail, owing to haze, produces the perception of distance.

(Photo © Mark Keller/SuperStock)

[FIGURE 7·28] Depth cues supplied by elevation. The objects nearest the horizontal line appear farthest away from us.

(From Margaret W. Matlin & Hugh J. Foley. *Sensation and Perception,* 3/e. Published by Allyn and Bacon, Boston, MA. Copyright © 1992 by Pearson Education. Adapted by permission of the publisher.)

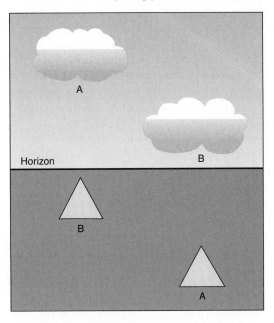

time you visit an art gallery, check the shadows in portraits and see if the artists have followed this convention.

Horizon proximity provides another cue for distance. When we are able to see the horizon, we perceive objects near it as being distant and those above or below it as being nearer to us. For example, cloud B and triangle B in FIGURE 7·28 appear farther away than cloud A and triangle A even though the triangles are the same size, as are the clouds.

Another important source of distance information is **motion parallax** (*parallax* comes from a Greek word meaning "change"). Try the following demonstration: Focus on an object a few feet in front of you. Then move your head from side

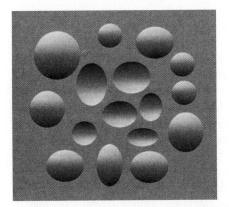

[FIGURE 7·27] Depth cues supplied by shading. A viewer tends to interpret this configuration as a group of bumps surrounding a group of dimples.

(From Sun, J. & Perona, P. (1998). *Nature Neuroscience, 1.* Reprinted by permission from Macmillan Publishers, Ltd.)

to side while continuing to focus. The rest of the scene will move back and forth with the motion of your head. However, the part of the scene that is closer to you than the object you are focusing on will move faster across the field of vision than the part of the scene that is farther away from the object. This perceived difference in objects' relative rate of motion is the cue for distance. In the natural world, it may be particularly useful for predators' perception of the distance to their prey.

*f*ocus On

How Does Culture Affect Visual Perception?

As we saw in Chapter 4, the development of the nervous system is shaped by interplay between heredity and environment. The development of visual perception certainly involves learning. From birth onward, we explore our environment with our eyes. The patterns of light and dark, color, and movement produce changes in the visual system of the brain.

Consider geographical variables. If our physical environment lacks certain features, we may fail to recognize them if we encounter them later in life. For example, we might expect that people living in a treeless environment without pronounced vertical features would perceive the world differently

horizon proximity A monocular cue for depth perception; objects closer to the horizon appear farther away that objects more distant from the horizon.

motion parallax A monocular cue for depth perception; as we pass by a scene, objects closer to us appear to move farther than those more distant.

from inhabitants of dense forests who are surrounded by vertical features but very seldom encounter vast, open fields.

The variance in cultural codes found in pictorial representations may also affect perceptual development. For example, visual artists have learned to use the monocular depth cues (except motion parallax) in paintings, but not all these cues are represented in the traditional art of all cultures. For example, in many cultures, visual art lacks linear perspective. Will the absence of particular monocular cues in the art of a particular culture mean that people from this culture will not recognize those cues when they view art from another culture? Although it is quite rare for members of one culture to fail to recognize another culture's pictures as pictures (Russell et al., 1997), consider what occurred when Deregowski et al. (1972) presented members of the Me'en tribe of Ethiopia, a culture unfamiliar with pictures, with a series of pictures from a children's coloring book. They responded by smelling the pictures, listening to the pages while flexing them, and giving close attention to the texture of the pages. According to Berry et al. (1992), Asians who are unfamiliar with art that uses linear perspective are more likely to judge the shapes that appear in Figure 7.24 as other than rectangles.)

Segall, Campbell, and Herskovits (1966) presented the Müller-Lyer illusion (and several others) to groups of participants from Western and non-Western cultures. (See **FIGURE 7·29**.) Most investigators believe that the Müller-Lyer illusion is a result of experience with the angles formed by the intersection of walls, ceilings, and floors (Redding and Hawley, 1993). The angled lines can be seen as examples of linear perspective. (See **FIGURE 7·30**.) Segall and his colleagues did find that people from "carpentered" cultures were more susceptible to this illusion.

The effects on visual perception of a culture's language have received close attention in psychological research. In

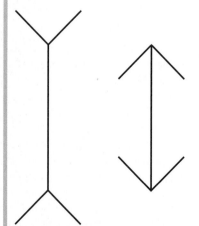

[**FIGURE 7·29**] The Müller-Lyer illusion. The two vertical lines are actually equal in length, but the one on the left appears to be longer.

---

linguistic relativity hypothesis   The hypothesis that the language a person speaks influences his or her thoughts and perceptions.

[**FIGURE 7·30**] The impact of culture on the Müller-Lyer illusion. People from "non-carpentered" cultures that lack rectangular corners are less likely to be susceptible to this illusion. Although the two vertical lines are actually the same height, the line on the right looks shorter.

(Photos courtesy of Neil Carlson)

the mid-nineteenth century, the British statesman William Gladstone noted that the writings of the ancient Greeks did not contain words for brown or blue. Is it possible the ancient Greeks did not perceive these colors? At about the same time, a German ophthalmologist, H. Magnus (1880) investigated this hypothesis by gathering both linguistic and perceptual data. He sent questionnaires and color chips to colleagues living in the Americas and asked them to test the abilities of the native people to distinguish among various colors. Magnus was surprised to discover very few cultural differences in people's ability to perceive the colors. Linguistic differences did not appear to reflect perceptual differences.

The issue emerged again in the mid-twentieth century as the **linguistic relativity hypothesis,** sometimes called the Whorfian hypothesis. Briefly stated, the hypothesis asserts that the language used by the members of a particular culture strongly influences the thoughts and perceptions that characterize the culture. Supporters of linguistic relativity suggested that color names are cultural conventions—that members of a given culture could have divided the countless combinations of hue, saturation, and brightness that we call colors into any number of different categories. Each category was assigned a name, and when members of that culture looked out at the world, they perceived each of the colors they saw as belonging to one of these categories.

Two anthropologists, Berlin and Kay, tested this hypothesis (Berlin & Kay, 1969; Kay, 1975). They studied a wide range of languages and found 11 primary color terms: in English, they are black, white, red, yellow, green, blue, brown, purple, pink, orange, and gray. The authors referred to these as focal colors. Not all languages used all 11 terms (as English does). Some languages used only two terms: black and white. If a language contained words for three primary colors, they were for black, white, and red. If it contained words for six primary colors, they were for black, white, red, yellow, green, and blue. The fact that all cultures had words for focal colors suggests that the physiology of the visual system—and not arbitrary cultural conventions—is responsible for the selection of color names.

Other evidence supports this conclusion. In their study of infants' color perception, Bornstein (1975) and Bornstein, Kessen, and Weiskopf (1976) found evidence for color categories identical to those of adults, and Zemack and Teller (2007) reported that infants' color preferences remain stable. Eleanor Heider (1971) reported that both children and adults found it easier to remember a color chip of a focal color (such as red or blue) than one of a nonfocal color (such as turquoise or peach). In her study of a specific culture—the Dani culture of New Guinea—Rosch (formerly Heider) found that the language of the Dani people has only two basic color terms: *mili* ("black") and *mola* ("white"). Rosch assembled two sets of color chips, one containing focal colors and the other containing nonfocal colors. She taught her participants arbitrary names that she made up for the colors. Even though the participants had no words in their language for any of the colors, the group learning names for focal colors learned the names faster and remembered them better (Heider, 1972; Rosch, 1973).

Although Rosch's experiments have been interpreted as evidence against linguistic relativity. Roberson et al. (2000) claimed evidence supporting it. They compared British adults with adult speakers of Berinmo, a language spoken by a stone-age cultural group that lives in Papua, New Guinea. Berinmo speakers have five basic color terms, including *nol,* which describes shades of green, blue, and purple, and *wor,* which covers yellow, orange, brown, and khaki. Unlike British adults, then, Berinmo speakers do not distinguish green and blue as colors with separate names, nor do they discriminate among the different colors denoted by the word "wor."

Roberson and her colleagues showed participants from both linguistic groups three cards, each with a color on it, and asked them to pick the color that was different from the other two. For English speakers, when shown two shades of green and a shade of blue, the choice was obvious: the shade of blue was different. For the Berinmo speakers, however, the distinction between two greens and a blue was arbitrary; all three were nol colors. They chose the blue only about half the time. However, when shown cards with a yellow, a khaki, and a green shade, the tables were turned. For the Berinmo speakers, the choice was between two wor cards and a nol. For the English speakers, the distinction looked arbitrary. Roberson and her colleagues found that each group of speakers could distinguish colors across its own linguistic category boundaries, but was only at a chance level when making decisions relevant in the other group's language.

What may we conclude from the research summarized here? Obviously perceptual "primitives" exist; that is, perceptual universals that cross cultural boundaries—color, brightness, form, and quantity, for example. But within these universal categories, cultural differences may very well shape diverse subcategories, as the work of Roberson et al. suggests. Among the elements of culture, language may be a particularly powerful producer of perceptual diversity. Chapter 10 examines the way in which a culture's language maps onto perceptual experience and ultimately allows social agreement about what was perceived.

Constancies of Visual Perception

Although Gestalt psychologists argued that similarities in human brains assure perceptual regularities—the Gestalt laws of perception—learning also plays a role in perception. Repeated exposure to a particular set of objects may allow us eventually to classify them accurately despite dramatic differences in the sensory information they produce. If you close the book you are reading and turn it around in front of you, the light reflected from the book will create quite different retinal images. Now imagine that another person is holding the same book while standing several feet from you and turns it around in much the same way. The retinal images will be much smaller. In both cases, however, you will recognize the size and shape of the book easily. Such experience-based invariance in our recognition of objects is referred to as **perceptual constancy** and comes in several types—*form* (or shape) *constancy, size constancy, color constancy,* and *brightness constancy.* Even though the viewing conditions may vary considerably, we learn that certain characteristics of objects remain the same.

Motion Perception

Detection of movement is one of the most primitive perceptual abilities. It is exhibited even by animals whose visual systems do not obtain detailed images of the environment. In animals that must avoid obstacles and elude predators, accurate estimation of motion is essential. Pigeons are a good example, as they are prey to fast-moving predators able to catch them in flight. Sun and Frost (1998) found that the pigeon's visual system contains three distinct classes of neurons that

---

perceptual constancy The experience-based ability to recognize an object and certain of its characteristics—its form, size, color, and brightness—as invariant despite the shifting retinal images it produces.

separately carry information about looming objects. The information provided by these neurons provides a sort of "early warning" system of an impending collision, as well as an accurate estimate of the time to collision. Of course, the human visual system can detect more than the mere presence of movement. We can detect what is moving in our environment and the direction in which it is moving.

Chapter 6 made the point that all sensory systems show adaptation and aftereffects. Motion is no exception. Perhaps you have stood on a foot bridge and stared at the water in the stream below you as it ran under the bridge. If you shifted your gaze and looked down at the bridge instead, it may have appeared to move in the direction opposite that of the water. Tootell et al. (1995) presented research participants with a display showing a series of concentric rings moving outward like the ripples in a pond. When the rings suddenly stopped moving, the participants had the impression of the opposite movement—that the rings were moving inward. During this time, the researchers produced *f*MRI images of the participants' brains. The scans showed increased activity in the dorsal stream of the visual association cortex, which lasted as long as the illusion of movement did. Thus, the neural circuits that give rise to this illusion appear to be located in the same region that responds to actual moving stimuli.

Compensation for Eye Movements Objects in the visual field move, but if a person moves his or her eyes, head, or whole body, the image on the retina will move, even if everything within the person's visual field remains stable. (Recall the demonstration of motion parallax, see page 207.) Often, of course, both kinds of movements will occur at the same time. This presents a problem for the visual system: to determine which images of motion are produced by movements of objects in the environment and which are produced by movements of the person's own eyes, head, and body.

To illustrate this problem, think about how this page of the book is projected onto your retinas as you read it. If we could make a digital recording of one of your retinas, we would see that the image of the page projected there is in constant movement as your eyes make several saccades along a line and then snap back to the beginning of the next line. Conversely, if you look at a single point on the page (say, a period at the end of sentence) and then move the page around while following the same point with your eyes, you perceive the book as moving, even though the image on your retina remains fairly stable. (Try it.) Then think about the images on your retinas while you are driving in busy traffic, constantly moving your eyes around to keep track of your own location and that of other cars moving in different directions at different speeds. At every instant, the visual system is distinguishing movements that originate with you (eyes and head) from those of objects external to you.

Haarmeier et al. (1997) reported the case of a German patient with bilateral damage to the visual association cortex who could not compensate for image movement caused by head and eye movements. When the patient moved his eyes, it looked to him as if the world were moving in the opposite direction. Without the ability to compensate for head and eye movements, any movement of the image on the retina was perceived as movement of objects in the environment.

Perception of Movement When It Is Absent If you sit in a darkened room and watch two small lights that are alternately turned on and off at a certain rate, your perception will be of a single light moving back and forth. You will not see the light turn off at one position and then turn on at the second position. If the distance and timing are just right, the light will appear to stay on at all times, quickly moving between the positions. This demonstration is known as the **phi phenomenon** and was originally studied by the Gestalt psychologists referred to earlier in the chapter. Theater marquees, "moving" neon signs, and computer animations make use of it. This characteristic of the visual system accounts for the fact that we perceive the images in motion pictures and on television as continuous rather than discrete. The images actually jump from place to place, but we perceive smooth movement.

QUESTIONS TO CONSIDER

1. Why do you suppose that artists sometime hold their thumbs up in front of them while looking at the scenes they are painting?
2. Why does the full moon appear to be larger when it appears just above the horizon than when it appears overhead?

A Fundamental Conundrum

As in previous chapters, the case studies cited in Chapter 7 give us pause: What is going on in the patient's perception? What is missing, specifically? And what has happened to the brain to produce such unusual symptoms? The case of Mrs. R is illustrative. Somehow a cerebral stroke had altered her brain so that she, who was a perfectly intelligent woman otherwise, could no longer perform what children could easily perform and what she had long

---

phi phenomenon The perception of movement caused by the turning on and off of two or more lights, one at a time, in sequence; often used on theater marquees; responsible for the apparent movement of images in movies and television.

performed almost automatically—naming familiar objects. She often could name their characteristic features, but somehow she couldn't tie those features together sufficiently to produce the right name. Only when additional information was provided—through gesture or movement or by direct contact, for example—did things finally click.

The case of Mrs. R. and the related case of Dee remind us that, even though once-familiar stimuli are present, the appropriate, knowledgeable response to them may not be forthcoming. Something about the disruption of cerebrovascular functioning in Mrs. R. and the too-long exposure to carbon monoxide in Dee had changed their brains sufficiently to render them visually agnostic.

In analyzing perception, psychologists sometimes make a distinction between *distal* and *proximal* stimuli (see Gibson, 1960). A distal stimulus is, as the term implies, at a distance—out there. It is the source of the energy, emitted or reflected, that strikes the sensory receptors. A proximal stimulus is close by, immediate—the image on the retina for example. In the case of Mrs. R and Dee, the distal stimuli used by the cognitive neuroscientists who examined them—the items used in formal or informal testing—were similar to those the two women had encountered many times before their brain injury. The new strangeness of their responses to those items—their inability to name them accurately—was due not to the changes in the distal stimuli but to changes in the processing of the proximal stimuli.

The differences in the brains of Mrs. R. and Dee before and after brain injury may account for the dramatic change in their ability to name familiar objects accurately. Their cases bring to light a larger issue: that all of us are dependent on the proximal stimuli that are available to us. None of us has direct access to the distal stimuli. We are, as Plato famously put it, captives of our senses. We only perceive what is proximal.

What this implies is that the "world out there"—the world of other people and of nonhuman objects, the world that includes the parts of our own bodies that perceive— are constructions. Theirs is a provisional reality. We could never perceive them directly, but only the proximal stimuli they are presumed to induce.

A fundamental conundrum exists here: what it means to perceive reality. Our study of perception may make us more humble about offering such claims. It may also allow us to better appreciate the delicious insights of the American poet, Wallace Stevens, who, on gazing out at the ocean in the dusk at Key West, saw a woman walking along the beach, singing. He wondered about the origin of her song—was she singing what she heard from the waves, or was it something else? With formidable insight into the constructedness of human perception, Wallace went on:

> It was her voice that made
> The sky acutest at its vanishing.
> She measured to the hour its solitude.
> She was the single artificer of the world
> In which she sang, And when she sang, the sea,
> Whatever self it had, became the self
> That was her song, for she was the maker. Then we,
> As we beheld her striding there alone,
> Knew that there never was a world for her
> Except the one she sang, and singing, made.

> —[From "The Idea of Order at Key
> West" (Stevens, 1972)]

CHAPTER SUMMARY

Brain Mechanisms of Visual Perception

Visual information proceeds from the retina to the thalamus and then to the primary visual cortex. This brain area is organized into modules, each of which receives information from a small region of the retina. Neural circuits within each module analyze specific information from their part of the visual field, including the orientation and thickness of lines, movements, and color.

The visual cortex consists of the primary visual cortex and the visual association cortex. Studies with laboratory animals, functional-imaging studies with humans, and the study of patients with damage to specific regions of the visual association cortex indicate that the visual association cortex consists of two streams. The ventral stream, which ends in the inferior temporal cortex, is involved with the visual perception of objects and color. Damage to this region can cause cerebral achromatopsia (inability to perceive colors) or various forms of visual agnosia, including prosopagnosia (inability to recognize faces). The development of neural circuits in the fusiform face area may be a result of extensive experience in looking at faces. Specific regions of the ventral stream are also devoted to the perception of bodies or body parts or of scenes and backgrounds. The dorsal stream, which ends in the parietal cortex, is involved in perception of space and in visually guided control of reaching, grasping, and manipulating. Regions of the dorsal stream are also involved in the perception of motion.

Visual Perception of Objects

Perception of objects requires, first, recognition of figure and ground. The Gestalt laws of proximity, symmetry, continuity, closure, and common fate describe some of the ways we distinguish figure from ground, even when the outlines of the figures are not explicitly bounded by lines.

Psychologists have advanced hypotheses about the mechanism of pattern perception, or the visual recognition of particular shapes. The first hypothesis suggests that our brain contains templates of all the shapes we can perceive. We compare a particular pattern of visual input with these templates until we find a fit. But can the brain hold infinitely many shapes? Another hypothesis suggests that our brain contains prototypes, which are more flexible than simple templates. According to a different hypothesis, prototypes are collections of distinctive features (such as the two parallel lines and the connecting diagonal of the letter N). One such view posits the brain's possession of a set of feature detectors known as geons. Further hypotheses are based on the artificial neural network model and assert that the ability of neural networks to learn to recognize patterns of input is the best explanation of pattern perception.

Cognitive psychologists originally based their information-processing models of the human brain on the computer as a serial processor. However, the fact that a computer program can simulate a brain function does not mean that the brain and the computer perform the function in the same way; they do not. The brain consists of billions of interconnected neurons that operate comparatively slowly. However, by doing many things simultaneously, the brain can perform complex operations quickly. It acts as a parallel processor. Thus, more recent attempts to devise models of mental functions—especially pattern perception—have used artificial neural networks that operate in parallel fashion. This approach uses assemblies of units having properties similar to those of neurons.

Perception involves both bottom-up and top-down processing. Our perceptions are influenced not only by the details of the particular stimuli we see (bottom-up), but also by prior knowledge of their relations to each other and by our expectations (top-down). Evidence from cognitive neuroscience suggests that our perceptions arise from a system that is specialized for object identification—the "what" system—that involves the ventral stream. A second system—the "where" system—involves the dorsal stream and may function independently to guide our actions in three-dimensional space.

Visual Perception of Space and Motion

Our visual system accomplishes a remarkable feat: It manages to accurately perceive objects, even in the face of movement and changes in levels of illumination. Because the size and shape of a retinal image—a two-dimensional image—vary with the location of an object relative to the eye, accurate form perception requires depth perception—perception of the locations of objects in three-dimensional space. Depth perception comes from binocular cues (from convergence and retinal disparity) and monocular cues (from interposition, size, linear perspective, texture, haze, shading, visual horizon, and head and body movements).

A person's culture may affect his or her perceptions, but probably not in a fundamental way. The linguistic relativity hypothesis, which suggested that language could strongly affect the way we perceive the world, has received limited empirical support. It is also possible that experience with some environmental features, such as particular geographical features or buildings composed of straight lines and right angles, may influence the way people perceive the visual world.

As a consequence of repeated exposure to the same classes of objects under what may be very different conditions, we learn to recognize them as unchanged, despite the diverse retinal images they produce. These perceptual constancies may be specific to the form, size, color, and brightness of objects.

Because our bodies may well be moving while we are visually following some activity in the outside world, the visual system has to make further compensations. It keeps track of the commands to the eye muscles and compensates for the direction in which the eyes are pointing. Movement is perceived when objects move relative to one another. In particular, a smaller object is likely to be perceived as moving across a larger one. Movement is also perceived when our eyes follow a moving object, even though its image remains on the same part of the retina.

The phi phenomenon is our tendency to see a sequence of discrete images as a continuously moving object. Because of the phi phenomenon, we perceive television shows and movies as real motion, not as a series of disconnected images.

succeed with mypsychlab

Visit MyPsychLab for practice quizzes, flashcards, and dozens of videos and animated tutorials, including the following items you can find in the "Multimedia Library":

Receptive Fields
Top-Down Processing
Five Well-Known Illusions

Distinguishing Figure-Ground Relationships
Gestalt Laws of Perception
Perceptual Set

KEY TERMS

akinetopsia *p. 194*

artificial intelligence *p. 200*

artificial neural
  networks *p. 200*

binocular cue *p. 204*

bottom-up processing *p. 202*

cerebral achromatopsia
  p. 193

convergence *p. 204*

distinctive features *p. 198*

dorsal stream *p. 191*

extrastriate body area *p. 192*

figure *p. 195*

fusiform face area *p. 192*

ground *p. 195*

haze *p. 205*

horizon proximity *p. 206*

interposition *p. 205*

law of closure *p. 196*

law of common fate *p. 196*

law of continuity *p. 196*

law of proximity *p. 196*

law of similarity *p. 196*

law of symmetry *p. 196*

linear perspective *p. 205*

linguistic relativity
  hypothesis *p. 208*

Module *p. 190*

monocular cue *p. 204*

motion parallax *p. 207*

parahippocampal place
  area *p. 192*

Perception *p. 189*

perceptual constancy
  p. 209

phi phenomenon *p. 210*

prosopagnosia *p. 192*

prototype *p. 197*

receptive field *p. 190*

relative size *p. 205*

retinal disparity *p. 204*

shading *p. 206*

template *p. 197*

texture gradient *p. 205*

top-down processing
  p. 202

ventral stream *p. 191*

visual agnosia *p. 192*

SUGGESTIONS FOR FURTHER READING

Bruce, V., & Young, A. W. (1998). *In the eye of the beholder: The science of face perception.* Oxford: Oxford University Press.

A comprehensive look at the psychology and physiology of face perception, with reference to works of art featured in an exhibit at the Scottish National Portrait Gallery.

Dowling, J. E. (2004). *The great brain debate: Nature or nurture?* Washington, DC: Joseph Henry Press.

A foremost expert on the visual system examines the development of visual perception in the context of the larger issue of gene–environment interaction.

Goldstein, E. B. (2004). *Blackwell handbook of sensation and perception.* Oxford: Blackwell.

A collection of authoritative overviews of sensory systems and perceptual processes in vision, audition, olfaction, gustation, and the cutaneous senses.

Goodale, M., & Milner, D. (2004). *Sight unseen: An exploration of conscious and unconscious vision.* Oxford, UK: Oxford University Press.

Drawing from clinical observations of a patient with visual agnosia, this provocative book introduces the concept of two visual systems: one for the perception of objects and the other for the control of movement.

Hoffman, D. D. (1998). *Visual intelligence: How we create what we see.* New York: Norton.

This is an authoritative work on visual perception as representation, that is, on how the visual system creates models of the visual world.

Hubel, D. H., & Wiesel, T. (2004). *Brain and visual perception: The story of a 25-year collaboration.* New York: Oxford University Press.

One half of the Nobel-prize–winning team provides a marvelous summary of their work and its implications.

Pinker, S. (1997). *How the mind works.* New York: Norton.

If you only read one book about cognitive neuroscience, you'll do no better than this comprehensive, well-told introduction.

Sacks, O. (1998). *The island of the colorblind.* New York: Vintage.

The noted neurologist and superb storyteller weaves a fascinating tale of research findings in Micronesia and their larger, darwinian implications. Part of the book is devoted to his observations of an isolated population of individuals with achromatopsia.

CHAPTER

8

Memory

Prologue

The Salem Witch Trials

In 1680, Juan, a slave to a New England farmer, testified in a court deposition that, about a month before, he had seen two black cats while eating dinner. Juan thought this strange because the farm housed only one cat. What made it stranger was that, only the week before, his horses had startled and had run away from him. But also—and here Juan's testimony was to take a turn down a deadly path—he remembered seeing his neighbor, Bridget Oliver, sitting in his barn that same afternoon with an egg in her hand. Juan remembered seeing her clearly, but unaccountably, she was nowhere to be found a few seconds later.

Juan's testimony about events a month old must have been threatening for Bridget to hear. For this was the town of Salem, Massachusetts, and Bridget was on trial for witchcraft. Manifestations of a sinister invisible world were considered plausibly real, and testimony like Juan's was regarded as hard evidence of a capital crime. Fortunately for Bridget, her jurors weren't persuaded this time, and she was acquitted of witchcraft, but the suspicions of witchcraft lingered. A few years later, they would lead to her death.

In 1692, in a nearby village, a group of young girls began showing mysterious ailments while remembering strange visitations. For reasons that are debated to this day, their stories touched off an unprecedented level of community hysteria and fear. Gossip about Bridget's earlier brush with charges of witchcraft must have reached these girls, for they soon began to name her as one of the apparitions that afflicted them. Bridget by this time had remarried after the death of her husband and was known as Bridget Bishop. Her remarriage (it was her third) and a penchant for clothing that was a bit too colorful by Puritan standards probably accelerated the gossip around her. Whatever the cause, her neighbors began to remember other odd instances and to relate them to the grand jury. One recalled that, fourteen years ago, he had encountered Bridget on the way to his father's mill, and, shortly thereafter, the wheel of his cart had fallen off. Another, relying on an eight-year-old memory, said that he had exchanged words with Bridget, and right thereafter, had seen a black pig that had vanished when he approached it. Two

Bridget Bishops's tombstone. Bridget was accused of witchcraft and subsequently killed.

215

workmen claimed that, seven years ago, they had seen some unusual dolls in a house that Bridget had lived in.

Bridget was hauled once again into court to defend herself against charges of witchcraft. This time she had no hope. To her plea that she didn't even know what a witch was, her interrogator snarled, "How do you know then that you are not a witch?" One has to admire the cool contempt in her answer to this verbal trap: "I do not know what you say." But such courage was no match for the hysteria around her.

Bridget Bishop was put on trial for witchcraft on June 2, 1692. Within eight days, she would be tried, convicted, and executed. ■

Bridget Bishop was the first of the so-called "Salem witches" to be tried and executed. Although the legal charge against her related to a supposed spectral assault on the young girls of Salem Village, the issue turned on whether evidence existed that Bridget had practiced witchcraft before (Norton, 2003). Much of the testimony that convicted her concerned supposedly supernatural occurrences recollected many years later (remarkably, records of this testimony still exist; see Boyer & Nissenbaum, 1972). Bridget was condemned, in part, because the people of her time believed that a narrative recollection was a reliable mirror of the experience. To be sure, people could lie, and they could forget; but a memory that was honestly real to the recaller was considered plausibly real itself. (The only substantive debate about the veracity of the evidence was whether Satan was manipulating real events to make the innocent look guilty.) Yet notice the small twists of coincidences in the stories told against Bridget: If that argument had occurred after the pig sighting, would it have been so damning? If another cat had strayed into Juan's farm without his remembering it, would his dinnertime vision have seemed so mysterious? Notions of devilment aside, Bridget's life rested on the assumption that her accusers could accurately reconstruct a sequence of events months or years in the past. This is a remarkable belief, yet, in everyday matters, it's an assumption we make all the time.

Overview of Memory

Recall from Chapter 5 that learning is the tendency for behavior to change as a result of experience; learning reflects the brain's plasticity. Our ability to learn allows us to engage in an enormous variety of behaviors in response to different situations. But a lapse of time may occur between the act of learning and a change in behavior caused by that learning. For example, you may observe that a new restaurant has opened, and then, some days later, decide you want to eat out. Choosing the new restaurant is possible because you have retained information about it.

This chapter concerns **memory**—the cognitive processes of encoding, storing, and retrieving information. **Encoding** is the active process of putting stimulus information into a form that can be used by our memory system. **Storage** is the process of maintaining information in memory. **Retrieval** includes the active processes of locating and using information stored in memory. Our choosing the restaurant, then, is a joint result of encoding the location, type of food, and other attributes of the restaurant, storing this information, and retrieving it when you are later looking for a place to eat.

One of the first things to note about memory is that you are aware of these processes in different ways. Noticing the restaurant, judging its compatibility to your tastes, marking its location—all are activities that can be described; we are highly conscious of them. (Consciousness will be the topic of Chapter 9.) In contrast, most of the time, the storage of the information is not so directly available. You don't actively think of every restaurant you've seen every moment of the day; neither do we consciously think about every person we've met, every song we've heard, and every place we've been in such a continuous way. The information is latent and unactivated. Retrieval is a bit of a blend. Quickly now, what is the last line to the carol "Silent Night"? Normally, you have to start thinking about earlier parts of the song before you can retrieve its ending. Retrieving the information is a progressive reactivation.

In 1949, Donald Hebb used this active/latent distinction to suggest that the brain remembered information in two different ways—a view known as *dual trace theory* (Hebb, 1949). Information that was active was in this state because neurons were firing continuously. Hebb thought this activity was due to feedback circuits of neurons. Repeated firing, in turn, strengthened the synaptic efficiency of the circuit, leading to structural changes in the neurons involved. This structural change would persist after the activity had ceased. The brain therefore retained traces of an experience either in an active state or in the latent structural state. The gist of Hebb's theory has been strikingly supported by the finding of long-term potentiation, discussed in Chapter 5.

Back in the 1960s, Richard Atkinson and Richard Shiffrin suggested a way of thinking about memory that psychologists have found useful. They proposed that memory takes at least three forms: sensory memory, short-term memory, and long-term memory (Atkinson & Shiffrin, 1968). The first two roughly correspond to memory systems that retain active traces, whereas the last retains latent traces. **Sensory memory** is memory in which representations of the physical features of a stimulus are stored for a very brief time—perhaps for a second or less. This form of memory is difficult to dis-

---

memory   The cognitive processes of encoding, storing, and retrieving information.

encoding   The process by which sensory information is converted into a form that can be used by the brain's memory system.

storage   The process of maintaining information in memory.

retrieval   The active processes of locating and using stored information.

sensory memory   Memory in which representations of the physical features of a stimulus are stored for very brief durations.

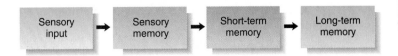

[**FIGURE 8·1**] A simplified model of information flow in human memory.

tinguish from the act of perception. The information contained in sensory memory represents the original stimulus fairly accurately and contains all or most of the information that has just been perceived. For example, sensory memory contains a brief image of a sight we have just seen or a fleeting echo of a sound we have just heard. The function of sensory memory appears to be to hold information long enough for it to become part of the next form of memory, short-term memory.

Short-term memory is an immediate memory for stimuli that have just been perceived. As we will soon see, its capacity is limited in terms of the number of items it can store and its duration. If you go to the movies and the cashier tells you "Your movie is playing in theater six," you obviously need to remember it long enough to find the entrance. We can remember information like this by keeping it active, such as repeating it once or twice. However, if you let the information become inactive (say, you stop to talk with friends and buy some popcorn), you may not be able to remember it later. Information soon leaves short-term memory, and unless it is stored in long-term memory, it will be lost forever.

To demonstrate the fact that short-term memory can hold only a limited amount of information for a limited time, read the following numbers to yourself just once, and then close your eyes and recite them back.

1 4 9 2 3 0 7

You probably had no trouble remembering them. Now, try the following set of numbers, and go through them only once before you close your eyes.

7 2 5 2 3 9 1 6 5 8 4

Very few people can repeat 11 numbers; in fact, you may not have even bothered to try once you saw how many numbers there were. Even if you practice, you will probably not be able to recite more than seven to nine independent pieces of information that you have seen only once. Thus, short-term memory has definite limits (Marois & Ivanoff, 2005).

If you wanted to, you could recite the 11 numbers again and again until you had memorized them. You could rehearse the information in short-term memory until it was eventually part of **long-term memory**—memory in which information is represented on a permanent or near-permanent basis. Unlike short-term memory, long-term memory has no known limits; and, as its name suggests, it is relatively durable. For example, Standing (1973) showed people 10,000 color slides and found that they could recognize most of them weeks later, even though they had seen them just once. Presumably, long-term memory involves physical changes

that take place in the brain. If we stop thinking about something we have just perceived (that is, something contained in short-term memory), we may not remember the information later. However, information in long-term memory need not be continuously rehearsed. We can stop thinking about it until we need the information at a future time.

The implication that information flows from one type of memory to another has been termed the "modal model" of memory because it seems so widely assumed. (See FIGURE 8·1.) However, some cognitive psychologists argue that it is unnecessary to assume that distinctive types of memory exist (Crowder, 1993). Instead, they suggest that there is really only one memory, but several phases in the way information is continuously processed. A loose analogy might be in the way cars could be manufactured in the global economy. One car-maker might manufacture the frame in Japan, ship it to a factory in Canada to add the engine, and then finish the assembly at a factory in the United States. The different factories would have their own methods of operation, and the transfer of cars from one to another is a significant part of the story. The alternative method is to assemble the entire car in different stages within the same factory. The emphasis in the second method is on the way the car body changes as it moves through the process. The next few sections will follow the general outline of Figure 8.1, but you will see that psychologists have discovered that memory is more complex than this model would have us believe (Healy & McNamara, 1996).

Sensory Memory

Information we have just perceived remains in sensory memory just long enough to be transferred to short-term memory. We become aware of sensory memory only when information is presented so briefly that we can perceive its aftereffects. For example, a thunderstorm at night provides us with an opportunity to become aware of visual sensory memory. When a bright flash of lightning reveals a scene, we see things before we recognize them. That is, we see something first, then study the image it leaves behind. Although we probably have a sensory memory for each sense modality, research efforts so far have focused on the two most important forms: *iconic* (visual) and *echoic* (auditory) memory.

---

short-term memory An immediate memory for stimuli that have just been perceived. It is limited in terms of both capacity (72 chunks of information) and duration (less than 20 seconds).

long-term memory Memory in which information is represented on a permanent or near-permanent basis.

Images to which we are briefly exposed, such as a bolt of lightning, linger momentarily in iconic memory.

Iconic Memory

Visual sensory memory, called **iconic memory** (*icon* means "image"), is a form of sensory memory that briefly holds a visual representation of a scene that has just been perceived. Because the representation is so closely tied to the perception, this form of memory is sometimes called "visible persistence." To study this form of memory, Sperling (1960) presented visual stimuli to people on a screen for extremely brief durations. Sperling flashed a set of letters (three rows of letters) on the screen for 50 milliseconds. (See FIGURE 8·2.) He then asked the participants to recall as many letters as they could, a method known as the *whole-report procedure*. On average, participants could remember only four or five letters. They insisted that for a brief time they could see more; however, the image of the letters faded too fast for people to identify them all.

To determine whether the capacity of iconic memory accounted for this limitation, Sperling used a partial-report procedure. He sounded tones when presenting the stimuli, and he asked people to name the letters in only one of the three horizontal rows: Depending on whether a high, middle, or low tone was sounded, they were to report the letters in the top, middle,

---

iconic memory   A form of sensory memory that holds a brief visual image of a scene that has just been perceived; also known as visible persistence.

echoic memory   A form of sensory memory for sounds that have just been perceived.

[**FIGURE 8·2**] The critical features of Sperling's iconic memory study.

(Adapted from Sperling, G. (1960). The information available in brief visual presentations. *Psychological Monographs, 74*, 1–29.)

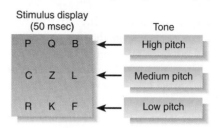

or bottom line. When the participants were warned beforehand to which line they should attend, they had no difficulty naming all three letters correctly. But then Sperling sounded the tone *after* he flashed the letters on the screen. The participants had to select the line from the mental image they still had: *They could use only information from memory*. With brief delays, they recalled the requested line of letters with high accuracy. For example, after seeing all nine letters flashed on the screen, they would hear the high tone, direct their attention to the top line of letters in their iconic memory, and "read them off" much as one might read the headlines in a newspaper. The participants' high level of performance indicated that there was little difference between having the letters physically present in front of them and having them present as a memory. However, Sperling also varied the delay between flashing the nine letters on the screen and sounding the high, medium, or low tone. If the delay was longer than one second, people could report only around 50 % of the letters. Apparently, during the delay, the information had faded before all of it could be transferred to longer lasting memory. This result indicated that the image of the visual stimulus fades quickly from iconic memory. It also explains why participants who were asked to report all nine letters failed to report more than four or five. They had to scan their iconic memory, identify each letter, and name it verbally. This process took time, and during this time the image of the letters was fading and the information becoming unreliable (Dixon, et al., 1997). Although their iconic memory originally contained all nine letters, participants had time to recognize and report only four or five before the mental image disappeared.

Echoic Memory

Auditory sensory memory, called **echoic memory,** is a form of sensory memory for sounds that have just been perceived. It is necessary for comprehending many sounds, particularly those that constitute speech. When we hear a word pronounced, we hear individual sounds, one at a time. We cannot identify the word until we have heard all the sounds, so acoustical information must be stored temporarily until all the sounds have been received. For example, if someone says "harbor," we may think of an anchorage for ships; but if someone says "harvest," we will think of something entirely different. The first syllable we hear—*har*—has no meaning by itself in English, so we do not identify it as a word. However, once the last syllable is uttered, we can put the two syllables together and recognize the word. At this point, the word enters short-term memory. Echoic memory holds a representation of the initial sounds until the entire word has been heard. Although early use of partial-report procedures suggested that echoic memory lasts less than 4 seconds (Darwin, Turvey, & Crowder, 1972), more recent evidence employing repeated patterns of random, or "white," noise indicates that echoic memory can last up to 20 seconds (Kaernbach, 2004). Indeed, if you consider your ability to recognize a friend's voice over the telephone, there's a sense in which we retain sound patterns for much longer (Winkler & Cowan, 2005). This everyday phenomenon presents a problem for the simplified model that we've been discussing. To understand why, we need to consider the next stages in that model: short-term and long-term memory.

QUESTIONS TO CONSIDER

1. It is easy to understand how we can rehearse verbal information in short-term memory—we simply say the information to ourselves again and again. But much of the information we learn is not verbal. Can we rehearse nonverbal information in short-term memory? How do we do so?

2. Suppose that your iconic memory malfunctioned—that instead of holding information only briefly, your iconic memory retained information for longer periods of time. What complications or problems might follow from such a malfunction? Would there be any advantages to this sort of malfunction?

Short-Term or Working Memory

Short-term memory has a limited capacity, and most of the information that enters it is subsequently forgotten. What, then, is its function? Before we try to answer this question, let us examine its nature a little more closely.

Encoding of Information in the Short-Term: Interaction with Long-Term Memory

So far, the story I have been telling about memory has been simple: Information in sensory memory enters short-term memory, where it may be rehearsed for a while. The rehearsal process keeps the information in short-term memory long enough for it to be transferred into long-term memory. After that, a person can stop thinking about the information; it can be recalled later, when it is needed (refer to Figure 8.1).

However, this simple story is incomplete. First of all, information does not simply "enter short-term memory." For example, read the letters below. Put them into your short-term memory, and keep them there for a few seconds while you look away from the book.

P X L M R

How did you keep the information in short-term memory? You would probably say that you repeated the letters to yourself. You may even have whispered or moved your lips. You are able to say the names of these letters because many years ago you learned them. But that knowledge is stored in long-term memory. Thus, when you see some letters, you retrieve information about their names from long-term memory, and then you hear yourself rehearse those names (out loud or silently, "within your head"). The five letters you looked at contain only visual information; their names came from your long-term memory, which means that the information put into short-term memory actually came from long-term memory.

To convince yourself that you used information stored in long-term memory to remember the five letters, study the symbols below, look away from the book, and try to keep them in short-term memory for a while.

ζ ∩ ∂ ∋ ℘

Could you do it? You have never learned the names of these symbols, so you have no way of rehearsing them in short-term memory. Perhaps, then, FIGURE 8·3 more accurately

[**FIGURE 8·3**] Relations between iconic memory, short-term memory, and long-term memory. Letters are read, transformed into their acoustic equivalents, and rehearsed as "sounds" in the head. Information can enter short-term memory from both iconic memory and long-term memory. Visual information enters short-term memory from iconic memory, but what is already known about that information (such as names of letters) is moved from long-term memory to short-term memory.

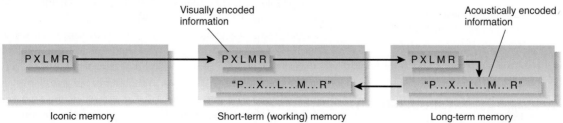

represents the successive stages of the memory process than does the diagram you saw in Figure 8.1.

You can see now that short-term memory is more than a simple way station between perception and long-term memory. Information can enter short-term memory from two directions: from sensory memory or from long-term memory. In Figure 8.3 this feature is represented by arrows pointing to short-term memory from both iconic memory and long-term memory. Perhaps another example will clarify the process further. When we are asked to multiply 7 by 19, information about the request enters our short-term memory from our sensory memory. Actually performing the task, though, requires that we retrieve some information from long-term memory. What does *multiply* mean? What is *7*, and what is *19*? At the moment of the request, such information is not being furnished through our senses; it is available only from long-term memory. Note, however, most versions of the model of Figure 8.1 assume that information is not recalled directly from long-term memory. Instead, it is first moved into short-term memory and then recalled. So, short-term memory contains information when we are trying to encode that information and when we are trying to retrieve it.

The fact that short-term memory contains both new information and information retrieved from long-term memory, and also seems more than a passive recording of information, has led some psychologists, such as Alan Baddeley, to prefer the decidedly more active term **working memory** (Baddeley, 1993). Working memory does seem to work on what we have just perceived. In fact, working memory represents a sort of behavior that takes place within our heads. It represents our ability to remember what we have just perceived and to think about it in terms of what we already know (Haberlandt, 1994). We use this form of memory to remember what a person says at the beginning of a sentence until we finally hear the end. We use it to remember whether any cars are coming up the street after we look left and then right. We use it to think about what we already know and to come to conclusions on the basis of this knowledge. These behaviors are similar to what were described as short-term memory, and from now on this chapter will use the terms *short-term memory* and *working memory* interchangeably. Some psychologists, however, prefer to distinguish the two forms of memory on the basis of the functions they serve (Kail & Hall, 2001).

---

working memory   Memory for new information and information retrieved from long-term memory; used in this text as another name for short-term memory.

primacy effect   The tendency to remember initial information. In the memorization of a list of words, the primacy effect is evidenced by better recall of the words early in the list.

recency effect   The tendency to recall later information. In the memorization of a list of words, the recency effect is evidenced by better recall of the last words in the list.

Primacy and Recency Effects

Imagine yourself as a participant in a memory study. You are asked to listen to the researcher as she slowly reads words, one at a time, off a long list. As soon as she finishes reading the list, she asks you to write down each word that you can remember. (This task is called a free-recall task.) Which words in the list do you think you are most likely to remember? If you are like most people in free-recall tasks of this type, you will tend to remember the words at the beginning and the end of the list and forget the words in between. The tendency to remember the words at the beginning of the list is called the **primacy effect;** the tendency to remember words at the end of the list is called the **recency effect.**

What causes these effects? Research that has addressed this question points to two factors (Atkinson & Shiffrin, 1968). The primacy effect appears to be due to the fact that words earlier in a list have the opportunity to be rehearsed more than do words in the other parts of a list. This makes good sense—the first words are rehearsed more because, at the experiment's outset, these are the only words available to rehearse. The rehearsal permits them to be stored in long-term memory. As more and more words on the list are presented, short-term memory becomes more and more full, so words that come later have more competition for rehearsal time. Because the first words on the list are rehearsed the most, they are remembered better.

What about the recency effect? Atkinson and Shiffrin (1968) point out one possible explanation: Because the words at the end of the list were the last to be heard, they are still available in short-term memory. Thus, when you are asked to write the words on the list, the last several words are still available in short-term memory, even though they did not undergo as much rehearsal as words at the beginning of the list.

The Limits of Working Memory

How long does information remain in working memory? The answer to this question was provided in classic studies conducted by John Brown (1958) and Lloyd and Margaret Peterson (1959). The Petersons presented participants with a stimulus composed of three consonants, such as *JRG*. Not surprisingly, with rehearsal, people easily recalled the consonants 30 seconds later. The Petersons then made the task a bit more challenging: They prevented the participants in their study from rehearsing by assigning a distracter task. After they presented the participants with *JRG*, they asked them to count backward by 3s from a three-digit number they gave them immediately after they had presented the set of consonants. For example, they might present people with *JRG*, then say, "397." The participants would count out loud, "397 . . . 394 . . . 391 . . . 388 . . . 385," and so on until the researchers signaled them to recall the consonants. The accuracy of participants' recall was determined by the length of the interval between presentation of the consonants and the signal for recall. (See FIGURE 8•4.) When rehearsal was disrupted by backward counting—which prevented participants from rehearsing information in short-term memory—the consonants

[FIGURE 8·4] Limits of recall from working memory. Shown here is the percentage correct in the recall of the stimulus as a function of the duration of the distracter task used in the study by Peterson and Peterson.

(Adapted from Peterson, L. M., & Peterson, M. J. (1959). Short-term retention of individual verbal items. *Journal of Experimental Psychology, 58*, 193–198.)

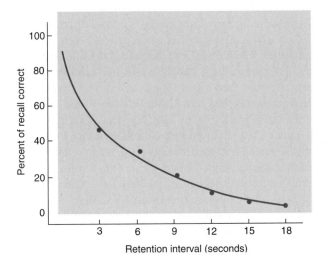

remained accessible in memory for only a few seconds. After a 15- to 18-second delay between the presentation of the consonants and the recall signal, recall dropped to near zero. So, for now at least, we can conclude that stimuli remain in working memory for less than 20 seconds *unless they are rehearsed.*

As a matter of fact, working memory may be even more limited. Muter (1980) pointed out that in the procedure used by Brown and the Petersons, the counting task always appeared after the letters. Consequently, participants in their experiments would be expecting a distraction. What would happen if a distraction were *unexpected*? This would be like hearing a phone number you wanted to remember and then having the doorbell ring right afterward. Muter examined this question by using the Peterson procedure, but with the counting task appearing only on a small proportion of trials, making it unexpected. He found that an unexpected distractor seriously disrupted working memory: most people found it hard to recall three letters after only 2 seconds.

And what is the capacity of working memory? A while ago, you were asked to try to repeat 11 numbers, which you were almost certainly unable to do. Miller (1956), in an article entitled "The Magical Number Seven, Plus or Minus Two," demonstrated that people could retain, on average, about seven pieces of information in their short-term memories: seven numbers, seven letters, seven unrelated words, or seven tones of a particular pitch. But if we can remember and think about only seven pieces of information at a time, how can we manage to write novels, design buildings, or even carry on simple conversations? The answer comes in a particular form of encoding of information that Miller called **chunking.** In chunking, information is simplified by rules, which make the information easily remembered once the rules are learned.

A simple demonstration illustrates this phenomenon. Read the 10 numbers printed below and see whether you have any trouble remembering them.

1 3 5 7 9 2 4 6 8 0

These numbers are easy to retain in short-term memory because we can remember a rule to chunk the numbers instead of 10 independent numbers. In this case, the rule concerns odd (1, 3, 5, 7, and 9) and even (2, 4, 6, 8, and 0) numbers. The actual limit of short-term memory, then, is seven chunks, not necessarily seven individual items. Thus, the total amount of information we can store in short-term memory depends on the particular rules we use to organize it.

In life outside the laboratory (and away from the textbook), we are seldom required to remember a series of numbers. The rules that organize our short term memories are much more complex than those that describe odd and even numbers, but the principles of chunking apply to more realistic learning situations. For example, say the group of words below, look away from the page, and try to recite the words from memory.

along got the was door crept locked slowly he until passage the he to which

No doubt you found the task hopeless; there was just too much information to store in short-term memory. Now try the following group of words:

He slowly crept along the passage until he got to the door, which was locked.

This time you were probably much more successful. Once the same 15 words are arranged in a sequence that makes sense, they are not difficult to store in short-term memory.

Unless we actively rehearse the material we are studying, we are unlikely to remember it for very long: It is relegated to short-term memory, in which information is stored for relatively short periods of time.

---

chunking A process by which information is simplified by rules, which make it easily remembered once the rules are learned. For example, the string of letters NBCCBSNPR is easier to remember if a person learns the rule that organizes them into smaller "chunks": NBC, CBS, and NPR.

The capacity of short-term memory for verbal material is not measured in letters, syllables, or words. Instead, the limit depends on how much *meaning* the information has. The first set of words above merely contains 15 different words. Because few people can immediately recite back more than five to nine independent items, we are not surprised to find that we cannot store 15 jumbled words in short-term memory. However, when the items are related, we can store many more of them. We do not have to string 15 words together in a meaningless fashion. Instead, we can let the image of a man creeping down a passage toward a locked door organize the new information. Thus, we can read or hear a sentence, understand what it means, and remember that meaning.

This aspect of short-term memory suggests a way of making working memory more efficient in everyday use. If information can be organized into a more meaningful sequence, there is less to be remembered. McNamara and Scott (2001) taught people to chain unrelated words together as they listened to them. The chaining technique was simple: People were to imagine a story involving these words. This technique sharply improved short-term memory. Later in this chapter, we discuss similar strategies to improve long-term memory.

Varieties of Working Memory

So far, you have seen short-term or working memory referred to in the singular, but evidence suggests that working memory can contain a variety of sensory information: visual, auditory, somatosensory, gustatory, and olfactory. It also can contain information about movements that we have just made (motor memories), and it may provide the means by which we rehearse movements that we are thinking about making. Is all this information contained in a single system, or do we have several independent working memories?

Baddeley (1993, 2000) has suggested that working memory consists of several components, all coordinated by a "central executive" function. One component maintains verbal information; another retains memories of visual stimuli. A third component might serve to store more general information, including memory for nonspeech sounds (such as the sound of your friend's voice over the telephone), touch, odors, or other types of information.

Phonological Working Memory Although we receive information from different senses, much of it can be encoded verbally. For example, we can see or smell a rose and think the word *rose;* we can feel the prick of a thorn and think the word *sharp;* and so on. Thus, seeing a rose, smelling a rose, and feeling a thorn can all result in words running through our working memory. How is verbal information stored in working memory?

Evidence suggests that the short-term storage of words, whether originally presented visually or acoustically, occurs in **phonological short-term memory**—short-term or working memory for verbal information. The Greek word *phōne* means both "sound" and "voice"; as the name implies, phonological coding could involve either the auditory system of the brain or the system that controls speech. As we shall see, it involves both.

In an experiment Conrad (1964) showed how quickly visually presented information becomes encoded acoustically. He briefly showed people lists of six letters (each list was shown within 4.5 seconds) and then asked them to write the letters. The errors these people made were almost always acoustical rather than visual. For instance, they sometimes wrote *B* when they had seen *V* (these letters sound similar), but they rarely wrote *F* when they had seen *T* (these letters look similar). Keep in mind that Conrad presented the letters visually. The results suggested that people read the letters, encoded them acoustically ("heard them in their minds"), and remembered them by rehearsing the letters as sounds. During this process, they might easily mistake a *V* for a *B*.

The fact that the errors seem to be acoustical may reflect a form of acoustical coding in working memory. That is, phonological memory may be produced by activity in the auditory system—say, circuits of neurons in the auditory association cortex. People often talk to themselves. Sometimes, it's aloud; sometimes, they whisper or simply move their lips. At other times, no movements can be detected, but people still report that they are thinking about saying something. They are engaging in **subvocal articulation,** an unvoiced speech utterance. Even though no actual speech movement may occur, it is still possible that activity occurs in the neural circuits in the brain that normally control speech. When we close our eyes and imagine seeing something, the mental image is undoubtedly caused by the activity of neurons in the visual association cortex. Similarly, when we imagine saying something, the "voice in our head" is probably controlled by the activity of neurons in the motor association cortex. Research suggests that even deaf children perform acoustical encoding in terms of the movements they would make to pronounce letters (Conrad, 1970). People may therefore use both acoustic and articulatory codes: They may simultaneously hear a word and feel themselves saying it in their heads. Phonological codes stored in long-term memory also may help to strengthen the rehearsed information (Roodenrys et al., 2002).

The best neurological evidence for the existence of phonological short-term memory comes from a disorder called **conduction aphasia,** which is usually caused by damage to a region of the left parietal lobe. Conduction aphasia appears as a profound deficit in phonological working memory. People who have conduction aphasia can talk and can comprehend what others are saying, but they are very poor at repeating precisely what they hear. When they attempt to repeat words that other people say, they often get the meaning correct but use different words. For example, if asked to repeat the sentence, "The cement truck ran over the bicycle," a person who has conduction aphasia may reply, "The concrete mixer got into an accident with a bike."

---

phonological short-term memory Short-term memory for verbal information.

subvocal articulation An unvoiced speech utterance.

conduction aphasia An inability to remember words that are heard, although they usually can be understood and responded to appropriately. This disability is caused by damage to Wernicke's and Broca's areas.

[**FIGURE 8·5**] A diagram showing how conduction aphasia is caused.

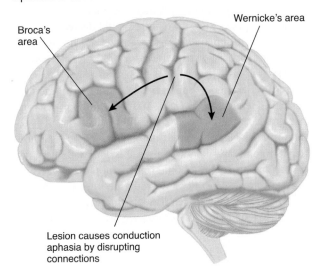

Broca's area

Wernicke's area

Lesion causes conduction aphasia by disrupting connections

Most investigators believe that conduction aphasia is caused by brain damage that disrupts the connections between two regions of the cerebral cortex that play important roles in people's language ability. These two regions are *Wernicke's area,* which is concerned with the perception of speech, and *Broca's area,* which is concerned with the production of speech. (We'll look at these areas in more detail in Chapter 10.) As we've seen, phonological working memory appears to involve both articulatory and acoustical coding. Because the brain damage that produces conduction aphasia disconnects regions of the brain involved in speech perception and production, perhaps the damage disrupts acoustical short-term memory by making such subvocal verbal rehearsal difficult or impossible. (See FIGURE 8·5.)

Visual Working Memory Verbal information can be received by means of the auditory system or the visual system—that is, we can hear words or read them. As we saw in the previous section, both forms of input produce acoustic and articulatory codes in phonological working memory, but much of the information we receive from the visual system is nonverbal. We recognize objects, perceive their locations, and find our way around the environment. We can look at objects, close our eyes, and then sketch or describe them. We can do the same with things we saw in the past. Thus, we apparently possess a working memory that contains visual information, either obtained from the immediate environment by means of the sense organs or retrieved from long-term memory.

Much of what we see is familiar; we have seen the particular items—or similar items—before. Thus, our visual working memory does not have to encode all the details, the way a photograph copies all the details in the scene gathered by the lens of a camera. For example, our short-term memory of the sight of a dog does not have to store every visual feature we saw, such as four legs, whiskers, ears, a tail. Instead, we already have mental images of dogs in our long-term memory. When we see a dog, we can

select a prototype that fits the bill, filling in a few features to represent the particular dog we just saw.

DeGroot (1965) performed an experiment that provides a nice example of the power of encoding visual information in working memory. He showed chessboards to expert players and to novices. If the positions of the pieces represented an actual game in progress, with legal moves, the experts could glance at the board for a few seconds and then look away and report the position of each piece; the novices could not. However, if the same number of pieces had been placed haphazardly on the board, the experts recognized immediately that their positions made no sense, and they could not remember their positions any better than a nonexpert could. Thus, the experts' short-term memories for the positions of a large number of chess pieces depended on organizational rules stored in long-term memory as a result of years of playing chess. Novices could not remember the location of the pieces in either situation, because they lacked long-term memories for patterns of chess pieces on a board and could not acquire the information as efficiently (Reingold, et al., 2001).

Humans have a remarkable ability to manipulate visual information in working memory. Shepard and Metzler (1971) presented people with pairs of drawings that could be perceived as three-dimensional constructions made of cubes. The participants' task was to see whether the shape on the right was identical to the shape on the left; some were and some were not. Even when the shapes were identical, the one on the right was sometimes drawn as if it had been rotated. For example, in FIGURE 8·6, the shape on the right in panel

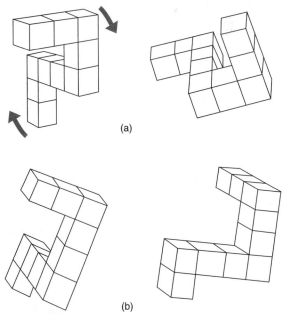

(a)

(b)

[**FIGURE 8·6**] The mental rotation task. (a) The shape on the right is identical to the one on the left but rotated 80 degrees clockwise. (b) The two shapes are different.

(Adapted from Shepard, R. N., & Metzler, J. Mental rotation of three-dimensional objects. *Science,* 1971, 171, 701–703. Reprinted with permission from AAAS. Copyright © 1971 by the AAAS.)

Expert chess players can remember the position of many pieces during a game because their experience allows efficient encoding.

(a) is identical but has been rotated clockwise 80 degrees; but in panel (b), the two shapes are different.

Shepard and Metzler found that people were very accurate in judging whether the pairs of shapes were the same or different. However, they took longer to decide when the right-hand shape was rotated. They reported that they formed an image of one of the drawings in their heads and rotated it until it was aligned the same way as the other one. (Mental manipulation of shapes is an important component of the ability to design and construct tools, buildings, bridges, and other useful objects.) If the participants' rotated images coincided with the other drawings, they recognized them as having the same shape. If they did not, they recognized them as being different (Shepard & Metzler, 1971).

Loss of Information from Short-Term Memory

The essence of short-term memory is its transience; hence, its name. Information enters from sensory memory and from long-term memory; is rehearsed, thought about, and modified; and then leaves. Some of the information controls ongoing behavior, and some of it causes changes in long-term memory, but ultimately it is lost from short-term memory. What causes it to leave?

As mentioned earlier, psychologists have described working memory as a kind of behavior that we use to maintain information over the short term. This way of thinking about working memory provides a useful framework to explain how we lose information, if we assume that information has a tendency to be degraded or to decay with time. Rehearsal activity of phonological short-term memory, such as subvocal articulation, prevents decay. Nairne (2002) has suggested a metaphor of how this might work. Working memory, Nairne says, is like a juggler trying to maintain several plates or balls in the air. As long as the juggler works actively at catching and throwing the plates, they don't fall and hit the ground (decay). With increased skill or more effort, the juggler can keep even more plates in the

air, but any distraction or other competing behavior will reduce the number of plates that can be juggled.

If you accept this metaphor, then consider this: Anything that makes the plates easier to handle should decrease the risk that they will be dropped. With respect to words, shorter words are easier to articulate and therefore should be easier to rehearse. Psychologists have shown that shorter words are remembered better under conditions of short-term memory (e.g., Tehan, Hendry, & Kocinski, 2001)—a finding that supports the rehearsal-and-decay explanation.

However, as Nairne himself points out, "decay" is a nonspecific term and risks falling prey to the nominal fallacy discussed in Chapter 2. Why should information decay? Perhaps more active processes work to degrade the information or to make it more difficult to recall. Later in this chapter, after we have surveyed long-term memory, we discuss one such possibility.

QUESTIONS TO CONSIDER

1. Suppose that someone has sustained a brain injury that prohibits her from putting information into, and getting information out of, long-term memory. Would this injury affect only her long-term memory, or would her short-term memory be affected, too? Can you think of an experiment that you could perform that would answer this question? What would this person's life be like?
2. Take a few moments to imagine the shortest route you can take to get from your home to your favorite restaurant. In terms of how your short-term memory operates, explain how you are able to accomplish this bit of mental imagery.

Learning and Encoding in Long-Term Memory

As we have seen, information that enters short-term memory may or may not be available later. It depends on the number of "chunks" of information and how much time has elapsed. But once information has successfully made its way into long-term memory, it remains relatively stable (Burt, Kemp, & Conway, 2001). Of course, we do forget things, but nevertheless, our brains have the remarkable ability to store vast amounts of information and numerous experiences from our past.

What kinds of information can be stored in long-term memory? To answer this question, let us consider the kinds of things we can learn. We can learn to recognize things: objects, sounds, odors, textures, and tastes. Thus, we can remember perceptions received by all of our sensory systems, which means that we have visual memories, auditory memories, olfactory memories, somatosensory memories, and gustatory memories. Perceptual memories also can contain information about the order in which events occurred, so we can remember the plot of a movie we saw or hear the melody of a song in our heads.

We can also learn from experience. We can learn to make new responses—as when we learn to operate a new machine,

The performance of complex behaviors likely involves connections between sensory and motor association areas of the cortex.

ride a bicycle, or say a new word—or we can learn to make old responses in new situations. Perceptual memories presumably involve alterations in circuits of neurons in the sensory association cortex of the brain—visual memories in the visual cortex, auditory memories in the auditory cortex, and so on. Memories that involve combinations of perceptual information presumably involve the establishment of connections between different regions of the association cortex. Motor memories (memories for particular behaviors) presumably involve alterations in circuits of neurons in the motor association cortex of the frontal lobes. Thus, learning to perform particular behaviors in particular situations likely involves the establishment of connections between the appropriate regions of the sensory and motor cortexes.

Memory involves both active and passive processes. Sometimes we use deliberate strategies to remember something (to encode the information into long-term memory), as when we rehearse the lines of a poem or memorize famous dates for a history course. At other times, we simply observe and remember without any apparent effort, as when we tell a friend about an interesting experience we had. Memories can be formed even without our being aware of having learned something. What factors determine whether we can eventually remember information and experiences? Let's look at some hypotheses that have been proposed.

The Consolidation Hypothesis

Hebb's dual-trace theory was based on the distinction between active processing of information and latent retention due to structural changes in the brain. One way to think about the traditional view of memory is that sensory memory and short-term memory represent information in its active state. That is, these two memory systems do not represent places in the brain *per se,* but instead are the result of brain processes that keep the information active (Crowder, 1993). Once this activity subsides, the information can be retained only through longer-lasting structural changes.

The change of information from a state of short-term activation into structural changes in the brain has been called

consolidation. These structural changes make the information stronger, easier to recall, and more resistant to forgetting. Consolidated information is long-term memory. Rehearsal itself is not consolidation; it is viewed as one of the mechanisms that allow consolidation to occur. In addition, consolidation may occur without awareness and could be a lengthy process.

Some of the best evidence in favor of the consolidation hypothesis comes from events that disrupt brain functioning. From the earliest times, people have observed that a blow to the head can affect memory. A blow to the head disrupts the balance in ions surrounding brain cells. The neurons' ion pumps increase as a result, causing large metabolic changes (Iverson, 2005). In such "closed-head injury" incidents, individuals' working memory seems to be strongly impaired (McAllister, et al., 2004). For example, Dutch amateur boxers were given standard tests for memory ability before and after a boxing match and compared with nonboxers who simply exercised; the memory scores for the boxers showed significant impairments (Matser, et al., 2000). In very severe cases, the injury produces a prolonged lack of memory for events, a condition called **retrograde amnesia** (*retro-* means "backward": in this case, backward in time). Consolidation theorists assume that this occurs because the brain centers for consolidation have been damaged. Significantly, retrograde amnesia shows a distinctive pattern: recent memories are affected more strongly than older ones (Brown, 2002). This is the pattern that consolidation theory would predict: recent memories have had less time to be consolidated and therefore are weaker, more difficult to retrieve, and more prone to forgetting.

The Levels-of-Processing Approach

The modal model discussed at the start of this chapter makes several assertions about the learning process. For one, the model asserts that all information gets into long-term memory only after passing through short-term memory. Also, it asserts that the most important factor determining whether a particular piece of information reaches long-term memory is the amount of time it spends in short-term memory.

Craik and Lockhart (1972) developed a different approach. They pointed out that the act of rehearsal may effectively keep information in short-term memory but does not necessarily result in the establishment of long-term memories. They suggested that people engage in two different types of rehearsal: maintenance rehearsal and elaborative rehearsal. **Maintenance rehearsal** is the rote repetition of verbal information—simply repeating an item over and over. This behavior serves to maintain the information in short-term

---

consolidation   The change of information from a state of short-term activation into structural changes in the brain. These changes are considered permanent and are hence part of long-term memory.

retrograde amnesia   Loss of the ability to retrieve memories of the past, particularly memories of episodic or autobiographical events.

maintenance rehearsal   Rote repetition of information; repeating a given item over and over again.

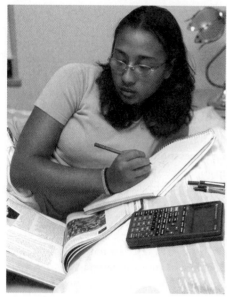

Taking notes while studying from a text (left) is a more active method of processing information than merely highlighting important passages in the text (right). Note taking involves deep processing, and highlighting involves shallow processing.

In contrast with the traditional model of rehearsal, Craik and Lockhart (1972) proposed a levels-of-processing framework for understanding the way information enters long-term memory. They suggested that memory is a by-product of perceptual analysis. A central processor, analogous to the central processing unit of a computer, can analyze sensory information on several different levels. Craik and Lockhart conceived of the levels as being hierarchically arranged, from shallow (superficial) to deep (complex), providing the kind of information as the earlier sentence did about the old man and the watch. A person can control the level of analysis by *paying attention* to different features of the stimulus. If a person focuses on the superficial sensory characteristics of a stimulus, then these features will be stored in memory. If the person focuses on the meaning of a stimulus and the ways in which it relates to other things the person already knows, then these features will be stored in memory. For example, consider the word written below.

tree

You can see that the word is written in black type, that the letters are lowercase, that the bottom of the stem of the letter *t* curves upward to the right, and so on. Craik and Lockhart referred to these characteristics as *surface features* and to the analysis of these features as **shallow processing.** Maintenance rehearsal is an example of processing that is relatively shallow. In contrast, consider the meaning of the word *tree*. You can think about how trees differ from other plants, what varieties of trees you have seen, what kinds of foods and what kinds of wood they provide, and so on. These features refer to a word's meaning and are called *semantic features*. Their analysis is called deep processing. Elaborative rehearsal is an example of deep processing. According to Craik and Lockhart, **deep processing** generally leads to better retention than surface processing does.

memory but does not necessarily result in lasting changes. In contrast, when people engage in elaborative rehearsal, they think about the information and relate it to what they already know. **Elaborative rehearsal** involves more than new information. It involves deeper processing: forming associations, attending to the meaning of the information, thinking about that information, and so on. Thus, we *elaborate* on new information by recollecting related information already in long-term memory. Here's a practical example: You are more likely to remember information for a test by processing it deeply or meaningfully; simply rehearsing, or "cramming," the material to be tested will not do.

This example suggests that a memory is more effectively established if the item is presented in a rich context—a context that is likely to make us think about the item and imagine an action taking place. Consider the different images conjured up by these two sentences (Craik & Tulving, 1975):

He dropped the watch.

The old man hobbled across the room and picked up the valuable watch.

The second sentence provides much more information. The image that is evoked by the more-complex sentence provides the material for a more complex memory. This complexity makes the memory more distinctive and thus helps us pick it out from all the other memories we have.

Knowledge, Encoding, and Learning
You might think that memory would be related to knowledge: As we gain more knowledge over time, our recall of that knowledge ought to improve. However, merely possessing knowledge does not always facilitate recall; even the brightest people have problems with remembering things. What seems to be more important is what happens during the encoding of information. Remember, encoding involves getting material into memory. More than that, how we encode information is likely to affect our ability to remember it later. We have already seen that, to some degree, encoding information involves paying attention to it. We have also seen that if we can

---

elaborative rehearsal Processing information on a meaningful level, such as forming associations, attending to the meaning of the material, thinking about it, and so on.

shallow processing Analysis of the superficial characteristics of a stimulus, such as its size or shape.

deep processing Analysis of the complex characteristics of a stimulus, such as its meaning or its relation to other stimuli.

make material more meaningful during encoding, we may decrease the likelihood of forgetting that information later.

Automatic Versus Effortful Processing. Psychologists and educators have long known that practicing or rehearsing information enhances retrieval. Practicing or rehearsing information, through either shallow or deep processing, is called **effortful processing.** As a student, you know that the more you concentrate on your studies, the more likely it becomes that you will do well on an exam. But your experience also tells you that you have stored information in memory that you never rehearsed in the first place. Somehow, without any effort, information is encoded into your memory. This formation of memories of events and experiences with little or no attention or effort is called **automatic processing.**

Encoding Specificity. When encoding is not automatic, it is effortful, and the most useful effort we can expend is to attempt to make the new material meaningful. We can think of making new or difficult material meaningful as *elaborative encoding;* you encountered this idea earlier as elaborative rehearsal. Two conclusions concern elaborative encoding. First, it seems clear that more rehearsal is better than less.

The second conclusion concerns **encoding specificity,** the principle that *how* we encode information determines our ability to retrieve it later. For example, suppose that someone reads you a list of words that you are to recall later. The list contains the word *beet* along with several terms related to music, such as *melody, tune,* and *jazz.* When asked if the list contained the names of any vegetables, you may report that it did not. Because of the musical context, you may have encoded *beet* as *beat* and never thought of the root vegetable while you were rehearsing the list (Flexser & Tulving, 1978).

Many experiments have made the point that meaningful elaboration during encoding is helpful and probably necessary for the formation of useful memories. Imagine, for example, trying to remember the following passage:

> With hocked gems financing him, our hero bravely defied all scornful laughter that tried to prevent his scheme. "Your eyes deceive," he had said. "An egg, not a table, correctly typifies this unexplored planet." Now three sturdy sisters sought proof, forging along, sometimes through calm vastness, yet more often over turbulent peaks and valleys. Days became weeks as many doubters spread fearful rumors about the edge. At last, from nowhere, welcome winged creatures appeared, signifying momentous success.

How do you think you would have done on this task? Could you have remembered this passage very well? Probably not, for it is phrased rather oddly. However, what if, *before* you read the paragraph, you were told that it had a title: "Columbus Discovers America"? Do you think you might have encoded the story differently and so improved your recall? Dooling and Lachman (1971) found that people who were told the title of a story such as this remembered the information much better, but if they were given

the title *after* they had read and processed the story, their recall was not improved (Bransford & Johnson, 1972). Apparently, the time to make information meaningful is during encoding.

Criticisms of the Levels-of-Processing Approach The concept of processing depth has been useful in guiding research efforts to understand how we learn and remember. However, many psychologists have noted that the distinction between shallow and deep processing has never been rigorously defined. The difference between looking at the shape of the letters of a word and thinking about its meaning is clear, but most instances of encoding cannot be so neatly categorized. The term *depth* seems to be metaphorical. It roughly describes the fact that information is more readily remembered when we think about it in relation to what we already know, but it is not exact and specific enough to satisfy most memory theorists.

Another problem with trying to understand exactly what is meant by a term such as *depth of processing* is that no matter what we may ask a person to do when we present a stimulus (for example, "Count the letters"), we have no way of knowing what else he or she may be doing that may aid recall of that item. In other words, researchers may not be able to control the depth to which a person processes information because they have no way of peering into his or her head and knowing exactly how the information is being manipulated. For each of us, our memory, its processes, and its contents are private. Memory, like all cognitive processes, is not an observable phenomenon.

Some psychologists have criticized the assertion that tasks that encourage people to focus on superficial features of stimuli inevitably lead to poorer memory than do tasks that encourage them to focus on deeper features. For example, after reading something new, people often can remember exactly where the information appeared on a page (Rothkopf, 1971). Despite such exceptions, however, the levels-of-processing approach has succeeded in showing that we deal with information in different ways depending on what we need to use it for. These ways provide a context for the way we later remember it.

Improving Long-Term Memory through Mnemonics

When we can imagine information vividly and concretely, and when it fits into the context of what we already know, it is easy to remember later. Earlier, I described how chaining words together in a meaningful pattern can improve working memory. Vividness and context can improve remembering;

---

effortful processing Practicing or rehearsing information through either shallow or deep processing.

automatic processing Forming memories of events and experiences with little or no attention or effort.

encoding specificity The principle that how we encode information determines our ability to retrieve it later.

[**FIGURE 8·7**] The method of loci. Items to be remembered are visualized in specific, well-known places.

Cheese | Milk | Eggs | Taco sauce | Lettuce

 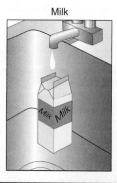   

mnemonic systems (from the Greek *mnemon,* meaning "mindful") that take advantage of this fact. **Mnemonic systems**—special techniques or strategies consciously used to improve memory—use information already stored in long-term memory to make memorization an easier task.

Mnemonic systems do not simplify information; they make it more elaborate. More information is stored, not less. However, the additional information makes the material easier to recall. Furthermore, mnemonic systems organize new information into a cohesive whole so that retrieval of part of the information ensures retrieval of the rest of it. These facts suggest that the ease or difficulty with which we learn new information depends not on *how much* we must learn but on *how well it fits with what we already know.* The better it fits, the easier it is to retrieve.

Method of Loci In Greece before the sixth century BCE, few people knew how to write, and those who did had to use cumbersome clay tablets. Consequently, oratory skills and memory for long epic poems (running for several hours) were highly prized, and some people earned their livings by cultivating these abilities. Because people could not carry around several hundred kilograms of clay tablets, they had to

keep important information in their heads. To do so, the Greeks devised the **method of loci,** a mnemonic system in which items to be remembered are mentally associated with specific physical locations. (The word *locus* means "place"; the plural is *loci,* pronounced "low sigh.")

Suppose that you wish to remember a short shopping list without writing it down. Your list consists of five items: cheese, milk, eggs, taco sauce, and lettuce. To use the method of loci technique, you would first think of a familiar place, perhaps your house. Next, you would mentally walk through your house, visually placing different items from your list at locations—*loci*—in the house: a package of cheese hanging from a coat rack, milk dripping from the kitchen faucet, eggs lying in the hallway, a bottle of taco sauce on the kitchen chair, and a head of lettuce on the sofa. (See FIGURE 8·7.) Then, in the grocery store, you would mentally retrace your path through the house and note what you had stored at the different loci. Any familiar location will do the trick as long as you can visually and vividly imagine the items to be remembered in the various landmarks.

Peg-Word Method A similar technique is the **peg-word method** (Miller, Galanter, & Pribram, 1960). As with the method of loci, the goal involves visually associating the new with the familiar. In the peg-word method, the familiar material is a set of "mental pegs" that you already have in memory. One way to create pegs is to take the numbers from 1 to 10 and rhyme each number with a peg word; for example, one is a bun, two is a shoe, three is a tree, four is a door, five is a hive, and so on. So for your grocery list you might imagine the package of cheese in a hamburger *bun,* a *shoe* full

---

mnemonic system A special technique or strategy consciously used in an attempt to improve memory.

method of loci (low-sigh) A mnemonic system in which items to be remembered are mentally associated with specific physical locations or landmarks.

peg-word method A mnemonic system in which items to be remembered are associated with a set of mental pegs already in memory, such as key words of a rhyme.

of milk, eggs dangling from a *tree,* taco sauce on a *door,* and the lettuce on top of a bee*hive*. In the grocery store you would review each peg word in order and recall the item associated with it. At first this technique may seem silly, but ample research suggests that it actually works (Marshark, et al., 1987).

Narrative Stories and Songs Another useful aid to memory is to place information into a **narrative** to link items to be remembered together by a story. Bower and Clark (1969) showed that even inexperienced people can use this method. The investigators asked people to try to learn 12 lists of 10 concrete nouns each. They gave some of the people the following advice:

> A good way to learn the list of items is to make up a story relating the items to one another. Specifically, start with the first item and put it in a setting which will allow other items to be added to it. Then, add the other items to the story in the same order as the items appear. Make each story meaningful to yourself. Then, when you are asked to recall the items, you can simply go through your story and pull out the proper items in their correct order. (Bower & Clark, 1969, p. 181)

Here is a typical narrative, described by one of the participants (list words are italicized): "A *lumberjack darted* out of the forest, *skated* around a *hedge* past a *colony* of *ducks*. He tripped on some *furniture,* tearing his *stocking* while hastening to the *pillow* where his *mistress* lay."

People in the control group were merely asked to learn the lists and were given the same amount of time as the people in the "narrative" group to study them. Both groups could remember any given 10-word list equally well immediately afterward. However, when all of the lists had been learned, recall of all 120 words was far superior in the group that had constructed narrative stories.

Music, like narrative, provides a structure for information. Songs that link melody to a sequence of words could serve the same role as the narrative elements of a story. Many advertisers

Long-term memory has no known limits. Shakespearean actors, like these actors performing a scene from *The Taming of the Shrew,* may remember their parts long after their performances are over.

use music with their messages, apparently believing that placing their slogan in a song will improve its memorability (Yalch, 1991). Some evidence supports this notion. Wallace (1994) asked people to learn the words to a ballad by listening to either a spoken or a sung version. She found that, provided people had a chance to learn the melody of the song, they learned the sung ballad more quickly than the spoken version. Changing the melody after each verse, in contrast, failed to improve learning. Melodies also slow the rate at which you hear information, which can allow you to encode the information better (Kilgour, Jakobson, & Cuddy, 2000).

Obviously, mnemonic systems have their limitations. They are useful for memorizing information that can be reduced to a list of words, but not all information can easily be converted to such a form. For example, if you were preparing to take an examination on the information in this chapter, figuring out how to encode it into lists would probably take you more time than studying and learning it by the more-traditional methods suggested in the study guide.

QUESTION TO CONSIDER

Suppose that a friend comes to you for advice about studying for an upcoming English test. He explains to you that half of the test involves multiple-choice questions over key terms, and the other half involves essay questions about the narrative of several short stories. Based on what you now know about encoding and memory, what suggestions might you offer him regarding how to prepare for the test? (Hints: Is there a difference between how rote information is best encoded and how more elaborate, complex information is best encoded? What role might the idea of levels of processing play in preparation for a test?)

The Organization of Long-Term Memory

As we just saw, memorization is not a simple, passive process. Many investigators believe that long-term memory consists of more than a simple pool of information. Instead, different kinds of information are encoded differently and stored in different ways (Sherry & Schacter, 1987).

Episodic and Semantic Memory

Endel Tulving suggested that there are two kinds of long-term memory: episodic memory and semantic memory (Tulving, 1972). **Episodic memory** provides us with a record of our life experiences. Events stored there are autobiographical; episodic memory consists of memory about specific things

---

narrative A mnemonic system in which items to be remembered are linked together by a story.

episodic memory A type of long-term memory that serves as a record of life experiences.

(a)

(b)

Remembering the correct spelling of a word involves semantic memory—memory for academic-type information (a). Remembering important life events, such as an important social event, involves episodic memory—memory for specific events that occurred at a specific time (b).

we have done, seen, heard, felt, tasted, and so on. The memories are tied to particular contexts: this morning's breakfast, your fifteenth birthday party, the first time you went skiing, and so forth. **Semantic memory** consists of conceptual information; it is a long-term store of data, facts, and information, including words and their meanings. Your knowledge of what psychology is, how human sensory systems operate, and how behavior is affected by its consequences is now part of your semantic memory. (If not, you need to review some of the material presented earlier in this book!) In other words, information of the "academic" type is stored as semantic memory. Semantic memories appear to interact with episodic ones. For example, when you go shopping, you undoubtedly remember the kinds of items you usually buy. Suppose you like yogurt for breakfast. Your preference is a fact about yourself that you recall from semantic memory. However, when you're trying to decide whether it's time to buy some more yogurt on this shopping trip, you'd probably try to think of the last time you looked in the refrigerator. Remembering whether you had eaten the last of the yogurt is a decision you would have to make from episodic memory.

The distinction between episodic and semantic memory reflects the fact that we make different uses of things we have learned: We describe things that happened to us (or that we witnessed) or talk about facts we have learned. The following case provides evidence that different brain regions are involved in episodic memory and semantic memory.

[CASE STUDY] K. C. was born in 1951. At the age of 30, he had a serious closed head injury in a motorcycle accident [that caused extensive brain damage]. . . . His intelligence

and language are normal; he has no problems with reading or writing; his ability to concentrate and to maintain focused attention are normal; his thought processes are clear; he can play the organ, chess, and various card games; his ability to visually imagine things is intact; and his performance on primary (short-term) memory tasks is normal. He knows many objective facts concerning his own life, such as his date of birth, the address of his home for the first 9 years of his life, the names of the some of the schools he attended, [and] the make and color of the car he once owned. . . . [However], he cannot recollect any personally experienced events. . ., whereas his semantic knowledge acquired before the critical accident is still reasonably intact. His knowledge of mathematics, history, geography, and other "school subjects," as well as his general knowledge of the world is not greatly different from others' at his educational level. (Tulving, 2002, pp. 13–14)

As you can see, K. C.'s episodic memories were destroyed by the brain damage that he sustained, but his semantic memories are relatively intact.

Explicit and Implicit Memory

For many years, most cognitive psychologists studied memory as a conscious operation. Experimenters presented people with lists of words, facts, episodes, or other kinds of stimuli and asked them to recognize or recollect the items later. In many cases, a verbal response was required. In recent decades, however, psychologists have come to appreciate the fact that people also possess an unconscious memory system, which is capable of controlling complex behaviors (Squire, 1992). Psychologists use the terms *explicit memory* and *implicit memory* when making this distinction. **Explicit memory** is memory of which we are aware; we know that we have learned something, and we can talk about what we have learned with others. (For this reason, some psychologists prefer to use the term *declarative memory*.) **Implicit memory** is unconscious;

semantic memory   A type of long-term memory that contains data, facts, and other information, including vocabulary.

explicit memory   Memory that can be described verbally and of which a person is therefore aware.

implicit memory   Memory that cannot be described verbally and of which a person is therefore not aware.

we cannot talk directly about its contents. However, the contents of implicit memory can affect our behavior. Some psychologists use the term *procedural memory,* because this system is responsible for remembering "how-to" skills such as bicycle riding; still others use the term *nondeclarative memory.* (See FIGURE 8•8.)

Implicit memory appears to operate automatically. It does not require deliberate attempts on the part of the learner to memorize something. It does not seem to contain facts; instead, it controls behaviors. For example, suppose we learn to ride a bicycle. We do so quite consciously and develop episodic memories about our attempts: who helped us learn, where we rode, how we felt, how many times we fell, and so on. But we also acquire implicit memories: We learn to ride. We learn to make automatic adjustments with our hands and bodies that keep our center of gravity above the wheels. Most of us cannot describe the rules that govern our behavior. For example, what do you think you must do if you start falling to the right while riding a bicycle? Many cyclists would say that they compensate by leaning to the left. But they are wrong; what they really do is turn the handlebars to the right. Leaning to the left would actually make them fall faster, because it would force the bicycle even farther to the right. The point is that although they have learned to *make* the appropriate movements, they cannot necessarily describe in words what these movements are.

The acquisition of specific behaviors and skills (such as driving a car, turning the pages of a book, playing a musical instrument, dancing, throwing and catching a ball, etc.) is probably the most important form of implicit memory. We do not need to be able to describe these activities to perform them. We may not be aware of all the movements involved while we are performing them.

The Biological Basis of Long-Term Memory

Psychologists agree that long-term memory involves more or less permanent changes in the structure of the brain. Much of what we know about the biology of human memory has been derived from studies of people who have memory loss—amnesia—or from studies of animals in which investigators use some of the methods described in Chapter 4 to learn more about the specific brain mechanisms involved in memory. In more recent years, functional imaging studies with humans help us determine which parts of the brain become active when we learn or remember particular kinds of memories.

Human Anterograde Amnesia Damage to particular parts of the brain can permanently impair people's ability to form new long-term memories, a phenomenon known as **anterograde amnesia.** (*Anterograde* means "in a forward direction.") The brain damage can be caused by the effects of long-term alcoholism, severe malnutrition, disease, stroke, head trauma, or surgery (Parkin et al., 1991). In most cases, people with anterograde amnesia can still remember events that occurred before the damage, but they cannot remember what has happened since that time. They do not learn the names of people they subsequently meet, even if they see them daily for years. For these people, yesterday is always some time in the past, before they sustained their brain damage. (Yes, as time goes by, they are surprised to see such an old person looking back at them in the mirror.)

One of the most famous cases of anterograde amnesia is that of patient H. M. (Milner, Corkin, & Teuber, 1968; Milner, 1970; Corkin et al., 1981). H. M.'s case is interesting because his amnesia is both severe and relatively uncontaminated by other serious neuropsychological deficits.

[CASE STUDY] In 1953, when H. M. was 27, a neurosurgeon removed part of the temporal lobe on both sides of his brain. The surgery was performed to alleviate very severe epilepsy, which was not responding to drug treatment. The surgery cured the epilepsy, but it caused anterograde amnesia. (This type of operation is no longer performed.)

Since the operation, H. M. has been unable to learn anything new. He cannot identify by name people he has met since the operation. His family moved to a new house after his operation, and he never learned how to get around in the new neighborhood. (His parents have since died, and he now lives in a nursing home where he can be cared for.) He is capable of remembering a small amount of verbal information as long as he is not distracted; constant rehearsal can maintain information in his short-term memory. However, rehearsal does not appear to have any long-term effects; if he is distracted for a moment, he will completely forget whatever he had been rehearsing. Indeed, because he so quickly forgets what previously happened, he does not easily become bored. He can endlessly reread the same magazine or laugh at the same jokes, finding them fresh and new each time.

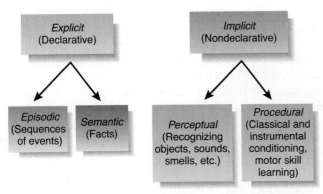

[**FIGURE 8•8**]   Major categories of long-term memory.

anterograde amnesia   A condition in which a person has difficulty forming new long-term memories of events that occur after that time.

H. M. is aware that he has a memory problem. For example, here is his response to an investigator's question.

> Every day is alone in itself, whatever enjoyment I've had, and whatever sorrow I've had. . . . Right now, I'm wondering. Have I done or said anything amiss? You see, at this moment everything looks clear to me, but what happened just before? That's what worries me. It's like waking from a dream; I just don't remember. (Milner, 1970, p. 37)

Since the case of H. M. was reported, many investigators have described similar cases of people who acquired an anterograde amnesia after sustaining damage to the temporal lobes. The critical site of damage appears to be the hippocampus, a structure located deep within the temporal lobe, and regions of the cortex of the medial temporal lobe with which the hippocampus is connected. (Look back at Figure 4.29, which illustrates the shape and location of the hippocampus.)

H. M.'s memory deficit is striking and dramatic. However, when he and other patients with anterograde amnesia are studied more carefully, it becomes apparent that the amnesia does not represent a total failure in learning ability. When the patients are appropriately trained and tested, we find that they are able to acquire new implicit (nondeclarative) memories. For example, Cavaco et al. (2004) tested amnesic patients on a variety of tasks modeled on real-world activities, such as weaving, tracing figures, operating a stick that controlled a video display, and pouring water into small jars. Both amnesic patients and normal subjects did poorly on these tasks at first, but their performance improved through practice. Thus, as you can see, patients with anterograde amnesia are capable of a variety of tasks that require perceptual learning, stimulus–response learning, and motor learning.

The most remarkable thing is that although the patients can learn to perform these tasks, *they do not remember anything about having learned them.* They do not remember the experimenters, the room in which the training took place, the apparatus that was used, or any events that occurred during the training. When we learn to ride a bicycle, we form two different kinds of memories: explicit (episodic) memories—the details of who taught us and where the training took place—and implicit (nondeclarative) memories—the skills required to ride a bicycle successfully. Clearly, the hippocampus is involved in forming new explicit memories, but is not necessary for the formation of new implicit memories.

After H. M.'s family moved, he was unable to learn how to get around in the new neighborhood. Many studies have found that one of the features of anterograde amnesia is the inability to form new spatial memories—to learn to use spatial cues to navigate in a new environment. For example, Luzzi et al. (2000) reported the case of a man with temporal lobe damage who lost his ability to find his way around a new environment. The only way he could find his room was by counting doorways from the end of the hall or by seeing a red napkin that was located on top of his bedside table.

The Roles of the Hippocampus and Basal Ganglia Just what role does the hippocampus play in the consolidation of episodic memories? Through its connections with the medial temporal cortex, the hippocampus receives information from all association areas of the cerebral cortex and sends information back to them (Gluck & Myers, 1997). Thus, the hippocampal formation is in a position to know—and to influence—what is going on elsewhere in the brain. Most investigators believe that permanent long-term memories of episodes are stored in the cerebral cortex, not in the hippocampus. However, through its connections with the cerebral cortex, the hippocampus plays an essential role in consolidating these memories. The consolidation process takes time, but once it is completed, the hippocampus is no longer needed for retrieval of the memory of these episodes. Thus, people with anterograde amnesia are able to recall episodic memories of events that occurred before their brain damage occurred (Miyashita, 2004; Squire & Bayley, 2007).

If declarative memories are consolidated through the actions of the hippocampus, what brain regions are responsible for nondeclarative memories? Evidence suggests that the basal ganglia play an essential role. Several experiments have shown that people with diseases of the basal ganglia have deficits that can be attributed to difficulty in learning automatic responses. For example, Owen et al. (1992) found that patients with Parkinson's disease were impaired on learning a visually

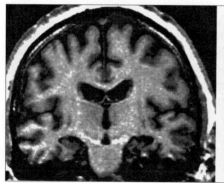
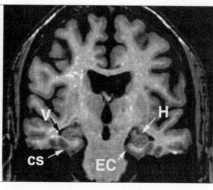

An *f*MRI photo of a brain with a larger-than-average hippocampus as compared to an fMRI of a normal brain.

cued instrumental conditioning task, and Willingham and Koroshetz (1993) found that patients with Huntington's disease failed to learn a sequence of button presses. (Parkinson's disease and Huntington's disease are both degenerative diseases of the basal ganglia.)

A series of experiments using both structural and functional brain imaging provides evidence for the role of the hippocampus in declarative learning and the role of the basal ganglia in nondeclarative learning. Hartley et al. (2003) trained subjects to find their way in a computerized virtual-reality town. Some subjects became acquainted with the town by exploring it, giving them the opportunity to learn where various landmarks (shops, cafés, etc.) were located with respect to each other. Other subjects were trained to follow a specific pathway from one landmark to the next, making a sequence of turns to get from a particular starting point to another. The investigators hypothesized that the first task, which involved spatial learning, would require the participation of the hippocampus, whereas the second task, which involved learning a set of specific responses to a set of specific stimuli, would require the participation of the basal ganglia. The results were as predicted: Functional MRI revealed that the spatial task activated the hippocampus, and the response task activated the caudate nucleus (a component of the basal ganglia).

Iaria et al. (2003) used a similar task that permitted subjects to learn a maze either through distant spatial cues or through a series of turns. About half of the subjects spontaneously used spatial cues, and the other half spontaneously learned to make a sequence of responses at specific locations. Again, fMRI showed the hippocampus was activated in people who followed the spatial strategy and the caudate nucleus was activated in those who followed the response strategy. Even more remarkably, a structural MRI study by Bohbot et al. (2007) found that people who tended to follow a spatial strategy had a larger-than-average hippocampus, and people who tended to follow a response strategy had a larger-than-average caudate nucleus. (You may recall from Chapter 4 that the right hippocampus of London taxi drivers, who have learned an extremely complex layout of streets, is larger than average.)

Explicit Memory in Animals Although the words "explicit" and "declarative" cannot apply to nonhuman animals (after all, they cannot talk), the distinction between these two categories of memory systems is also seen in species besides our own. Although we cannot ask laboratory animals to tell us about episodes that occurred earlier in their lives, we can certainly determine whether they can perform spatial tasks similar to the ones just described.

In one common spatial learning task, rats are placed in a large circular tank filled with water mixed with an opaque white powder. This apparatus is known as the "Morris water maze," after the investigator who developed it (Morris et al., 1982). The murky water hides the location of a small platform, situated just beneath the surface of the liquid. The experimenters put the rats into the water and let them swim until they encounter the hidden platform and climb onto it. They release the rats from a new position on each trial, which means that they cannot simply learn to swim in a particular direction. After a few trials, normal rats learn to swim directly to the hidden platform from wherever they were released.

The Morris water maze requires spatial learning; to navigate around the maze, the animals get their bearings from the relative locations of stimuli located outside the maze—furniture, windows, doors, and so on. But the maze can be used for stimulus–response learning, too. If the animals are always released at the same place, they learn to head in a particular direction—say, toward a particular landmark they can see above the wall of the maze (Eichenbaum, Stewart, & Morris, 1990).

If rats with hippocampal lesions are always released from the same place, they learn this nonrelational, stimulus–response task about as well as normal rats do. However, if they are released from a new position on each trial, they swim in what appears to be an aimless fashion until they finally encounter the platform. (See FIGURE 8•9.)

One of the most intriguing discoveries about the hippocampal formation was made by O'Keefe and Dostrovsky (1971), who recorded the activity of individual pyramidal cells in the hippocampus as an animal moved around the environment. The experimenters found that some neurons fired at a high rate only when the rat was in a particular location. Different neurons had different *spatial receptive fields;* that is, they responded when the animals were in different locations. A particular neuron might fire twenty times per second when the animal was in a particular location but only a few times per hour when the animal was located elsewhere. For obvious reasons, these neurons were named **place cells.**

When a rat is placed in a symmetrical chamber, where few cues exist to distinguish one part of the apparatus from another, the animal must keep track of its location from objects it sees (or hears) in the environment outside the maze. Changes in these items affect the firing of the rats' place cells as well as their navigational ability. When experimenters move the stimuli as a group, maintaining their relative positions, the animals simply reorient their responses accordingly. However, when the experimenters interchange the stimuli so that they are arranged in a new order, the animals' performance (and the firing of their place cells) is disrupted. (Imagine how disoriented you might be if you entered a familiar room and found that the windows, doors, and furniture were in new positions.)

Evidence indicates that firing of hippocampal place cells appears to reflect the location where an animal "thinks" it is. Skaggs and McNaughton (1998) constructed an apparatus that contained two nearly identical chambers

place cell A neuron that becomes active when the animal is in a particular location in the environment; most typically found in the hippocampal formation.

[**FIGURE 8·9**] The Morris water maze. (a) Environmental cues present in the room provide information that permits the animals to orient themselves in space. (b) Variable and fixed start positions. Normally, rats are released from a different position on each trial. If they are released from the same position every time, the rats can learn to find the hidden platform through stimulus-response learning. (c) Performance of normal rats and rats with hippocampal lesions using variable or fixed start positions. Hippocampal lesions impair acquisition of the relational task. (d) Representative samples of the paths followed by normal rats and rats with hippocampal lesions on the relational task (variable start positions).

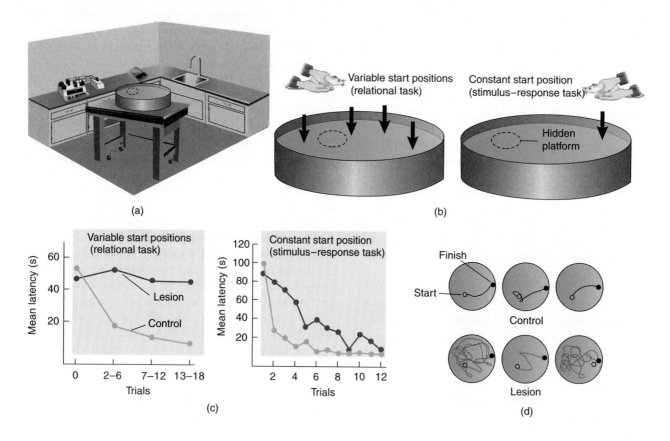

connected by a corridor. Each day, rats were placed in one of the chambers, and a cluster of electrodes in the animals' brains recorded the activity of hippocampal place cells. Each rat was always placed in the same chamber each day. Some of the place cells showed similar patterns of activity in each of the chambers, and some showed different patterns, which suggests that the hippocampus "realized" that there were two different compartments but also "recognized" the similarities between them. Then, on the last day of the experiment, the investigators placed the rats in the other chamber of the apparatus. For example, if a rat was usually placed in the north chamber, it was placed in the south chamber. The firing pattern of the place cells in at least half of the rats indicated that the hippocampus "thought" it was in the usual chamber—the one to the north. However, once the rat left the chamber and entered the corridor, it saw that it had to turn to the left to get to the other chamber and not to the right. The animal apparently realized its mistake, because for the rest of that

session the neurons fired appropriately. They displayed the "north" pattern in the north chamber and the "south" pattern in the south chamber. (See FIGURE 8·10.)

QUESTIONS TO CONSIDER

1. What is your earliest memory? How old were you? Why do you think you can't remember events that occurred before that time?

2. When getting directions to a particular location in an unfamiliar city, some people prefer step-by-step directions (turn right at the third traffic light, cross the railroad tracks, turn left at the next stop sign, etc.), whereas others prefer to have a map that they can follow. What are the advantages and disadvantages of each strategy? How would you expect these preferences to be related to the hippocampus and caudate nucleus?

[**FIGURE 8·10**] The apparatus used in the study by Skaggs and McNaughton (1998). Place cells reflect the location where the animal "thinks" it is. Because the rat was normally placed in the north chamber, its hippocampal place cells responded as if it were there when it was placed in the south chamber one day. However, once it stuck its head into the corridor, it saw that the other chamber was located to its right, so it "realized" that it had just been in the south chamber. From then on, the pattern of firing of the hippocampal place cells accurately reflected the chamber in which the animal was located.

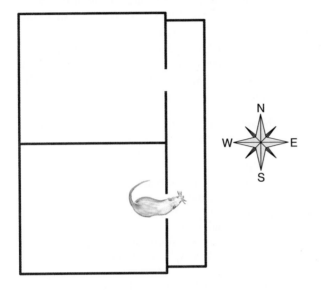

Remembering, Recollecting, and Forgetting

So far, we have looked at research and theorizing on the act of learning and the nature of long-term memory. But what do we know about remembering, the process of retrieving information from long-term memory, and forgetting, the absence of this process?

How Long Does Memory Last?

The question "How long does memory last?" has fascinated psychologists and other researchers for many years. In fact, a German psychologist, Hermann Ebbinghaus, reported the results of the first experiment to determine memory duration back in 1885. Using himself as a participant, Ebbinghaus memorized 13 nonsense syllables such as *dax, wuj, lep,* and *pib.* He then studied how long it took him to relearn the original list after intervals varying from a few minutes up to 31 days. FIGURE 8·11 shows what he found. Much of what he learned was forgotten very quickly—usually within a day or two. But even after 31 days, he could still recall some of the original information.

Ebbinghaus's research dealt with remembering nonsense syllables. What about remembering aspects of real life? For example, how long might you remember the important experiences of your youth? Schmidt et al. (2000) tried to answer this question by asking former students of an elementary school in

[**FIGURE 8·11**] Ebbinghaus's (1885) forgetting curve.

(Adapted from Ebbinghaus, H. (1885/1913). *Memory: A contribution to experimental psychology.* (Translated by H. A. Ruger & C. E. Bussenius.) New York: Teacher's College, Columbia University.)

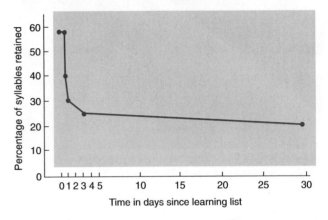

the city of Heerlen in the Netherlands to recall the street names around the school. Dutch cities have many meandering streets, so the participants of this study would have had extensive experience trying to remember the many places of their childhood neighborhood. Schmidt and colleagues found that, on average, participants who had moved away recalled about 60% of the street names that could be named by participants who still lived there. Plotted as a function of the number of years since they had last visited the neighborhood, recall of street names showed a large decrease in ability to recall for the first four years, followed by little further forgetting for the next forty years. (See FIGURE 8·12.) Interestingly, recall declined with the number of times participants had moved between different cities, showing that another city's geography could interfere with their memory. We'll return to this possibility in the next section. In general, the rate of forgetting of this kind of information, which also includes knowledge of a second language, people's names, music, and special situations, is greatest in the first few years after it is learned and decreases slowly afterwards (Bahrick, 1984; Kausler, 1994).

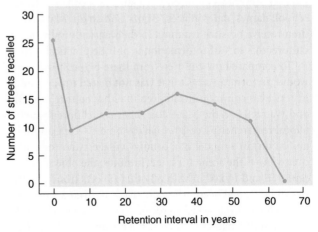

[**FIGURE 8·12**] Observed number of street names recalled by former students of a Dutch elementary school as a function of the years that they were not exposed to the neighborhood.

Researchers have found that there is little decline in recall of information such as names and faces, even after 50 years.

focus On

Cultural Contexts for Remembering

Although it is true that many people "know" the same things—the basic rules of arithmetic, the fact that the sun rises in the east, and so on—it is also true that the way we use our memory, the way we get information out of our memory, and the personal meaning of that information differ considerably from person to person. We should not be surprised to learn, then, that culture provides an important context for remembering.

Some researchers, such as Mistry and Rogoff (1994), argue that "remembering is an activity that is defined . . . in terms of its function in the social and cultural system" (p. 141). According to this view, the act of remembering cannot be separated from its cultural context. In support of this position, let's consider two studies that compared the remembering abilities of Guatemalan Maya and American children.

In the first study (Rogoff & Waddell, 1982), the children were given a test of free recall of lists of material they had learned earlier. The American children performed better—after all, American children learn such lists consistently in school: names, dates, places, events, and so on. Maya children receive no such training. In their agriculturally based culture, this sort of information is of little practical value.

To compare how children from these two cultures would perform on a task that was not biased toward the experiences common to children in either culture, Rogoff and Waddell had the Maya and American children watch a local researcher place 20 small toy objects (cars, animals, and so on) in a model of a country village. After the children viewed the scene for a few minutes, the objects were removed and mixed in with 60 other objects from which the 20 items had been originally selected. After a short delay, each child was asked to reconstruct the scene the way the researcher had constructed it. This time, the Maya children performed as well as the American children. (In fact, they did slightly better.) The cross-cultural differences

were eliminated when the American children were not permitted to use well-practiced, culturally based mnemonic strategies. The Maya children did not have defective memories; their culture simply had not prepared them for learning long lists of unrelated items.

Cultural customs also seem to affect remembering. In a second study, Rogoff and Waddell asked American and Maya children to recall a story five minutes after hearing it told in their respective native languages by a local teenager. Although the story was taken from Maya oral history, neither the Maya nor the American children had heard the story before. Interestingly, though, the American children seemed to remember the story better than the Maya children did, as evidenced by their retelling of the story to an adult. For example, consider the responses of two children, one from each culture (as cited in Mistry & Rogoff, 1994).

As retold by the Maya child:

> When the angel came, cha (so I have been told), from Heaven, well, when the angel came, he came to see the flood (The adult listener prompts: What else?) He ate the flesh of the people. . . . (and then?) He didn't return right away, cha. . . . (What else?) That's all. He threw up, cha, he threw up cha, the flesh. "I like the flesh," he said, cha. . . . (What else?) "Now you're going to become a buzzard," they told him, cha. . . . (With further prompts, the retelling continued similarly.) (p. 140)

Here is the same story as retold by an American child:

> There once was a buzzard and he was an angel in heaven and God sent him down to . . . to take all the dead animals and um, and so the buzzard went down and he ate the animals and then he was so full he couldn't get back up to heaven and so he waited another day and then he flew back up to heaven and God said, "You're not an angel anymore," and he goes, "Why?" And . . . and he said that "you ate the raw meat and now you're a buzzard and you'll have and . . . and you'll have to eat the garbage," and . . . and he goes, "I didn't eat anything," and God said, "Open your mouth and let's see," and then he opened his mouth and there was all the raw meat and he goes, "It's true I did eat, I did eat the meat," and God goes, "That's . . . that's why you're the buzzard now," and the . . . and the . . . and . . . and so the buzzard flew down and he, um, then he ate all the trash and everything. (p. 139)

If you were asked to say which of these children retold the story better, clearly you would say the American child did. You would probably express some surprise at the Maya child's *inability to remember* the story any better than he did. What you might not know, though, is that in Maya culture, children do not speak openly to adults. When they cannot avoid speaking to an adult, they must include the word *cha* (so I have been told) in their conversation to show to the adult that they are not behaving disrespectfully by having superior knowledge. Thus, the Maya child may have remembered the story, but the discomfort produced

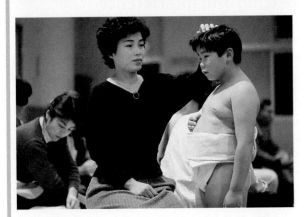

The culture in which we are raised plays an important role in providing us with learning experiences and memories of those experiences.

by having to retell it to an adult may have interfered with his ability to provide the adult with the story's details. In contrast, the American child, who undoubtedly was used to speaking freely to adults, *appeared* to have a better memory for the story.

Remembering or verbally expressing a memory is not an activity that occurs independent of cultural practices and rules. Culture influences remembering to the extent that it provides the context for what information is learned, the strategies for learning it, and social contingencies for expressing it.

Remembering and Recollecting

Remembering is a process that seems enormously variable. Thinking about examinations you may have taken should help make that point. Sometimes the information you need comes to mind immediately; at other times, it's an effort to remember information you just studied. In these latter cases, what is effortful is the attempt to come up with the thoughts (the internal stimuli) that cause the information to be retrieved.

The retrieval of implicit memories seems automatic: When the appropriate stimulus occurs, it automatically evokes the appropriate response. For example, when I open my car door, I do not have to think about how the latch works; my hand goes to the appropriate place, my fingers arrange themselves in the proper positions, and I make the necessary movements. In some cases, explicit memories, too, are retrieved automatically. Whisper your name to yourself. How did you manage to remember what your name is? How did you retrieve the information needed to move your lips in the proper sequence? Those questions simply cannot be answered by the method of introspection. The information simply pops out at us when the proper question is asked (or, more generally, when the appropriate stimulus is encountered).

Reading provides a particularly compelling example of the automatic nature of memory retrieval. When an experienced reader looks at a familiar word, the name of the word occurs immediately, and so does the meaning. It is difficult to look at a word and not think of its name. FIGURE 8•13 contains a list of words that can be used to demonstrate a phenomenon known as the Stroop effect (MacLeod, 1991; Stroop, 1935). Look at the words and, as quickly as you can, say the names of the colors in which the words are printed; do not read the words themselves.

Most people cannot completely ignore the words and simply name the colors; the tendency to think of the words and pronounce them is difficult to resist. The Stroop effect indicates that even when we try to suppress a well-practiced memory, it tends to be retrieved automatically when the appropriate stimulus occurs.

But what about the fact that some memories seem to be difficult to recall? The experience is often frustrating. We know that the information is "in there someplace," but we just cannot seem to get it out: "Oh, what is his name? I can see his face; he has a moustache, and he's skinny. It seems like his

[**FIGURE 8·13**] The Stroop effect. Name the color in which each word is printed as quickly as you can; you will find it difficult to ignore what the words say.

blue blue blue green green yellow red yellow yellow blue red green yellow yellow green yellow yellow red yellow green blue yellow red blue green green blue blue green red

name starts with a D: Don? No. Dave? Nope. Dennis? No, that's not it either—what is his name?! Now I remember, his name is Doug. Doug Hoisington, a friend of mine in New York." This phenomenon is known as the **tip-of-the-tongue phenomenon** and has fascinated psychologists since the days of William James (1893). It was first studied carefully during the 1960s (Brown & McNeill, 1966), and since then we have learned a good deal about it (A. S. Brown, 1991). It is a common, if not universal, experience; it occurs about once a week and increases with age; it often involves proper names and knowing the first letter of the word; and it is solved during the experience about 50% of the time.

The active search for stimuli that will evoke the appropriate memory, as exemplified in the tip-of-the-tongue phenomenon, has been called recollection (Baddeley, 1982). Recollection may be aided by contextual variables, including physical objects, suggestions, or other verbal stimuli. These contextual variables are called retrieval cues. For example, if you're trying to remember who gave you a particular gift at your last birthday party, you might find it helpful to look at photographs. The pictures of the people and the image of the scene provide retrieval cues for the information you're trying to recall.

Retrieval cues demonstrate that memory may be a response to internal stimuli. When we say we remember something, we are describing that response. But are we describing that response accurately?

Marcia Johnson has argued that remembering is based on our ability to discriminate different responses to retrieval cues (Johnson, 2006). Her theory is known as the source-monitoring framework and is based on the premise that remembering requires the ability to discriminate between different internal experiences. Experiences that are due to real episodes in our life must be differentiated from other experiences, based on vividness, plausibility, emotional context, and other factors.

For example, suppose you have an heated discussion with your mother. Later that day, you describe this to your brother when he comes home from work, who takes your mother's side and repeats many of her arguments, adding some of his own. If you try to recall this incident months later, you now have a problem: Which of the arguments were hers and which were your brother's? Both are vivid and both elicit the emotion you felt at the time. Because they're so similar, you might find it hard to distinguish who said what. Indeed, you might even fail to distinguish that you had two separate arguments and "remember" that you were arguing with both your mother and your brother at the same time.

The source-monitoring framework suggests that retrieval cues are supplemented by perceptual and cognitive processes that help us evaluate the accuracy of a memory. In the example we've been discussing, you might rely on logical clues to refine your memory, such as deducing that because your brother worked that day, he couldn't have been present when you argued with your mother. Johnson's approach to memory emphasizes the extent to which the subjective qualities of experience, our knowledge, and the social and motivational context of an episode are all factors that determine our ability to remember. These can be very important: in the Focus On section later in this chapter, we see how errors in source monitoring cause people to "remember" airplane crashes that they could not possibly have seen.

Forgetting and Interference

Although long-term memory appears to last for a long time, you have probably heard the notion that people often forget something they once knew because so much time has elapsed since the memory was last used that the memory has *decayed*. A similar term has been used to describe the loss of items from short-term memory when they are not rehearsed. But the notion that items are forgotten because they decay provides little explanation. Why does time have this effect? One popular alternative explanation for long-term memory failure is *interference*. (It has also been used to describe some aspects of short-term memory failure as well.)

The concept of interference is based on the well-established finding that some memories may interfere with the retrieval of others. An early study by Jenkins and Dallenbach (1924) showed that we are less likely to remember information after an interval of wakefulness than after an

---

tip-of-the-tongue phenomenon An occasional problem with retrieval of information that we are sure we know but cannot immediately remember.

retrieval cues Contextual variables, including physical objects, or verbal stimuli, that improve the ability to recall information from memory.

What do these famous lines have in common? "Beam me up, Scotty," "Me Tarzan, you Jane," "Play it again, Sam," "Elementary, my dear Watson"? Their fame, yes. But none of these lines attributable to their characters were actually said. The fact that people quote them may lead you to remember them incorrectly, as the source monitoring framework would suggest.

[**FIGURE 8·14**] Interference in memory retrieval. The graph shows the mean number of nonsense syllables people recalled after sleeping or staying awake for varying intervals of time.

(Adapted from Jenkins, J. G., & Dallenbach, K. M. (1924). Oblivescence during sleep and waking. *American Journal of Psychology, 1924, 35,* 605–612. Copyright © 1924 by the Board of Trustees of the University of Illinois. Used with permission of the University of Illinois.)

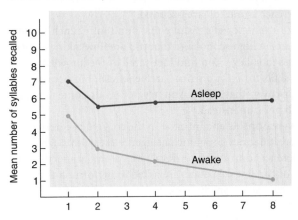

interval of sleep, presumably because of new memories that are formed when we are awake. (See FIGURE 8·14.)

Subsequent research soon showed that two types of interference exist in retrieval. Sometimes we experience **retroactive interference**—when we try to retrieve information, other information, which we have learned more recently, interferes. The top part of FIGURE 8·15 charts how researchers test for the effects of retroactive interference. The experimental group first learns a list of words (we'll call the list "A"). Next, during the retention interval, the experimental group learns a second list of words, "B." Finally, the experimental group is asked to recall the first list of words ("A"). Meanwhile, the control group learns only the words in list "A"—the group is not asked to learn the words in list "B" during the retention interval. However, the control group is asked to recall the words in list "A" immediately after the retention interval. If the experimental group recalls fewer words during the test than does the control group,

retroactive interference is said to have occurred in the people in that group.

To take a real-life example, you may have a hard time recalling the presents you received on your seventh birthday because you have had many birthdays since. If your seventh birthday had been just yesterday, you would likely show perfect recall. When memories that interfere with retrieval are formed *after* the learning that is being tested, we have retroactive interference.

At other times, retrieval is impaired by **proactive interference,** in which our ability to recall new information is reduced because of information we learned previously. The bottom

---

retroactive interference Interference in recall that occurs when recently learned information disrupts our ability to remember older information.

proactive interference Interference in recall that occurs when previously learned information disrupts our ability to remember newer information.

Retroactive Interference

Group	Initial learning	Retention interval	Retention test
Experimental	Learn A	Learn B	Recall A
Control	Learn A		Recall A

Proactive Interference

Group	Initial learning		Retention interval	Retention test
Experimental	Learn A	Learn B		Recall B
Control		Learn B		Recall B

[**FIGURE 8·15**] Retroactive and proactive interference.

part of Figure 8.15 illustrates the experimental procedure used to test for proactive interference. In this procedure, before learning a list (we'll call it list "B" in this procedure) the experimental group learns the words in another list, "A." The control group learns only the words in list "B." Both groups then experience a retention interval before they are asked to recall the words in list "B." If the experimental group recalls fewer words in list "B" during the test than does the control group, proactive interference is said to have occurred.

For example, let's assume that you took French for several years in high school and that you are now taking a Spanish class in college. You find that some of the knowledge and study skills from high school are beneficial, but occasionally you discover that when you try to recall some Spanish, French pops up instead.

As reasonable and intuitive as the concept of interference may be, it has not gone unchallenged. Researchers agree that interference can affect retrieval, but some argue that the kinds of recall tasks people are asked to perform in the laboratory are exceptionally likely to be affected by interference. In real life, such effects may not be so powerful. For example, meaningful prose, such as the kind found in novels, is resistant to interference. Laboratory studies most often use lists of nonsense syllables and unrelated words.

Reconstruction: Remembering as a Creative Process

Much of what we recall from long-term memory is not an accurate representation of what actually happened. Many errors in memory, however, are not mere inaccuracies: They tend to show systematic patterns. Often, our recollection corresponds to what makes sense to us at the time we retrieve it. It becomes, in other words, a plausible account of what *might* have happened or even of what we think *should* have happened. Psychologists have long recognized that the context of remembering is a very important determinant of memory.

The Role of Schemas From the discussion about encoding specificity earlier in the chapter, you'll recall that when a retrieval cue is understood to have a different meaning at the time of remembering than it did at the time of encoding, it loses its effectiveness. The framework that provides the meaning is called a **schema**. Schemas help us encode information in more meaningful ways, but they also can induce systematic errors. For example, thinking of living things as either animals, plants, or fungi might help you classify organisms; however, your schema of "living things" might lead you to overlook the possibility that viruses could be a form of life.

An early experiment by Bartlett (1932) called attention to the way schemas affect memory. The experimenter had people read a story or essay or look at a picture. Then he asked them on several later occasions to retell the prose passage or draw the picture. Each time, the participants "remembered" the original a little differently. If the original story had contained peculiar and unexpected sequences of events, people tended to retell it in a more coherent and sensible fashion, as if their memories had been revised to make the information accord more closely with their own schema for what the story was about. Bartlett concluded that people remember only a few striking details of an experience and that during recall, they reconstruct the missing portions in accordance with their own interpretation of what was likely.

Eyewitness Testimony Elizabeth Loftus (1979) has investigated a different set of variables that affect the recall of details from episodic memory. Her research indicates that the kinds of questions used to elicit information can have a major effect on what people remember. In courts of law, lawyers are not permitted to ask witnesses leading questions—questions phrased so as to suggest what the answer should be. Loftus's research showed that even subtle changes in a question can affect people's recollections. For example, Loftus and Palmer (1974) showed people films of car accidents and asked them to estimate vehicles' speeds when they *contacted, hit, bumped, collided,* or *smashed* each other. As FIGURE 8•16 shows, the people's estimates of the vehicles' speeds were directly related to the force of the impact suggested by the verb, such as *hit,* that appeared in the question.

In a similar experiment, when people were asked a week after viewing the film whether they saw any broken glass (there was none), people in the *smashed* group were most likely to say yes. Thus, a leading question that encouraged them to remember the vehicles going faster also encouraged them to remember that they saw nonexistent broken glass. The question appears to have modified the memory itself.

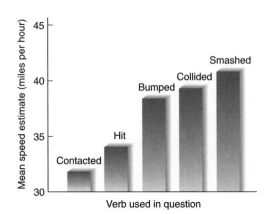

[**FIGURE 8•16**] Leading questions and recall. Shown are the mean estimated speeds of vehicles as recalled by people in the study by Loftus and Palmer (1974).

(Based on data from Loftus, E. F., & Palmer, J. C. (1974). Reconstruction of automobile destruction: An example of the interaction between language and memory. *Journal of Verbal Learning and Verbal Behavior, 13,* 585–589.)

---

schema A mental framework or body of knowledge that organizes and synthesizes information about a person, place, or thing.

The questions asked during a pretrial investigation may affect an eyewitness's later testimony.

Another experiment indicates that how events are reviewed affects this suggestibility. Lane et al. (2001) showed people a videotape of a staged crime, then asked questions that were designed to suggest things that were not part of the video. For example, the witnesses might be asked, "At the beginning of the scene, a young man dressed in jeans, a T-shirt, and gloves entered the house. Did he enter through the door?" In the video, the thief did not wear gloves; the test was to see if witnesses would incorrectly include the gloves in their recall of the scene later on. Before recalling information about the scene, however, they were asked, as witnesses might reasonably be asked to do, to review the videotape mentally. Some were asked to review as much detail as possible; others were asked to review only the highlights. Instructions to focus on details led to an increased tendency to incorporate the suggested, and false, information, such as the presence of gloves. Apparently, after being asked to review details, eyewitnesses rehearse the suggestions and come to view these as true.

Experiments such as these have important implications for eyewitness testimony in courts of law. A judge can prevent a lawyer from asking leading questions during a trial, but he or she cannot undo the effects of leading questions put to the witness during pretrial investigations. Many experiments indicate that learning new information and recalling it later are active processes—we do not simply place an item of information in a mental filing cabinet and pick it up later (Roediger & McDermott, 1995). We organize and integrate information in terms of what we already know about life and have come to expect about particular experiences. Thus, when we recall the memory later, it may contain information that was not part of the original experience. Even more disturbing, our confidence in this new information may be quite high.

At first, this phenomenon may appear to be maladaptive because it means that we cannot always trust our own recollections, no matter how hard we try to be accurate. However, our tendency to reconstruct memories probably reflects the fact that information about an episode can be more efficiently stored by means of a few unique details. The portions of an episode that are common to other experiences, and hence resemble information already stored in long-term memory, need not be retained. If every detail of every experience had to be encoded uniquely in long-term memory, perhaps we would run out of storage space. Unfortunately, this process sometimes leads to instances of faulty remembering, both in the witness stand and in life in general.

Flashbulb Memories Are some memories immune to this reconstructive process? One possibility is that some episodic memories are acquired under such powerful personal experiences of emotion and surprise that they become especially vivid and long-lasting. Consider your personal memory of when you first heard about the attack on the World Trade Center on September 11, 2001. Can you recall where you were, what you were doing, and who gave you the news? Do you remember your personal feelings? The feelings of those around you? Can you recall what you did next?

Roger Brown and James Kulik provided a name for memories activated by events of extreme surprise and great personal consequence: **flashbulb memories.** Using the assassination of President John F. Kennedy as an example, Brown and Kulik (1977) suggested that surprising, traumatic events could result in the encoding of some (but not all) of the context surrounding the individual at the time. When they asked people in 1977 to recollect their personal situation at the time they heard of Kennedy's 1963 assassination, they discovered that most accounts included the information behind the six questions asked in the last paragraph. Brown and Kulik speculated that flashbulb memories were not only especially vivid but also, possibly, especially long-lasting or even permanent.

However, other evidence suggests that flashbulb memories are not immune to the effects of distortion and modification discussed in the previous section. Schmolck, Buffalo, and Squire (2000) looked at an event that, although it was less consequential than the Kennedy assassination or 9/11, nevertheless produced flashbulb memories in students at the University of California: the 1995 acquittal of O. J. Simpson in his trial for the murder of his wife, Nicole, and her friend Ron Goldman. The investigators asked the students to record their reactions to the event three days after it happened. Then, either 15 months or 32 months later, they asked them to recall the event again. In general, recollection after 15 months was accurate. After 32 months, however, more than 40% of the recollections were seriously distorted. Schmolck, Buffalo, and Squire found that of 50 individuals who could be described as having a flashbulb memory of the verdict, 38% could not remember it as they had originally described it three days after the event. A significant source of error in the years after the event was in people's recall of the source of the news, with many people misreporting that they had heard about the verdict from the media rather than from another person. Rather than saying they couldn't remember, these individuals apparently assumed that because they get much of their news from the media, they must have heard about the Simpson verdict the same way. This assumption was then incorporated into their memory of the event.

---

flashbulb memories Memories established by events that are highly surprising and personally of consequence.

focus ⊕n

In the opening vignette of this chapter, we saw how witnesses in the Salem witchcraft trials testified to fantastic episodes of supernatural occurrences. In reading some of these accusations, you might have immediately thought that the witnesses were lying; people could not possibly recall things so counter to actual fact. Or could they?

Daniel Schacter has suggested that memory can exhibit seven deficiencies or "sins." These sins of memory are transience, absent-mindedness, blocking, misattribution, suggestibility, bias, and persistence. The first three are deficiencies of omission: Transience is the weakening of memory over time; absent-mindedness is the failure to register information that needs to be memorized; and blocking is the failure to retrieve information we know we possess. The other four are deficiencies of commission and add wrong information to our memory: Misattribution confuses different sources of memory; suggestibility embellishes memory under the influence of misleading questions or statements from others; bias creates errors because of our own beliefs; and persistence brings to mind information that we would rather forget (Schacter, 2001; Schacter & Dodson, 2002).

Schacter's "seven sins" have particular relevance to the criminal justice system. In many criminal investigations—particularly those in which little or no physical evidence is available—the memory of witnesses becomes especially important. Their ability to remember events and faces can determine the success or failure of the investigation—and of the subsequent prosecution, should a suspect be brought to trial. But memories of eyewitnesses are transient, especially when the events in question are fast-paced, confusing, and frightening. Elizabeth Loftus has explored some of the implications of memory deficiencies in her laboratory, but it is relevant to consider how many of these deficiencies could occur outside the laboratory.

In 1996, inspired in part by Loftus's work, Crombag, Wagenaar, and van Koppen (1996) pushed the notion of an eyewitness to the limit. In 1992, a Boeing 747 had crashed into an Amsterdam apartment building, creating a blazing fire but with, fortunately, fewer casualties than first feared. Crombag, Wagenaar, and van Koppen subsequently circulated a questionnaire to college students and faculty asking whether they had seen the television footage of the moment when the plane hit the building. Although no such footage existed, 55% of the respondents to the questionnaire claimed to have personally seen it. Furthermore, from among this group claiming to have seen the footage, 82% were so confident of what they had seen that they provided details about the crash. A group of law students tested later was even more prone to false memories of the crash: 66% of them claimed to have seen it.

Crashing memories have been found for other high-profile events. For example, Jelicic, et al. (2006) asked undergraduates whether they had seen video of the murder of a prominent Dutch politician, Pim Fortuyn. Again, no such footage existed; yet, 63% of respondents reported seeing it. Asked if they could describe details of what they had seen, 23% provided accounts.

What produces this tendency to confidently recall memories of things that cannot be? Jelicic et al. (2006) found evidence that it was associated with a tendency to fantasize. People reporting memories of the film were more likely to answer *yes* to questions like "In general, I spend at least half of the day fantasizing or daydreaming" and "My fantasies are so vivid that they are like a good film." In another study, Smeets et al. (2006) found that crashing memories depend in part on the way the question is asked. By using the nonexistent Pim Fortuyn assassination film as their example, Smeets et al. found that they received the highest number of false recollections when they asked about the film in an ambiguous way ("Did you see the amateur film about the Fortuyn shooting?") rather than in a highly specific manner ("Did you see the amateur film of the moment Fortuyn was shot by Volkert van der G.?"). When the question was phrased in the first way 63% answered *yes*; 30% answered positively to the second phrasing. So, as in the work by Loftus and her colleagues, language plays an important role in how we evaluate our memories, leading us to commit Schacter's "sin" of suggestibility.

Suggestibility is not the sole cause of a crashing memory, however. Smeets et al. (2006) also asked about the film in a very neutral manner: "Do you remember whether there was a film of the moment Fortuyn was shot by Volkert van der G.?" Twenty-seven percent of their participants could remember there being such a film. Crombag, Wagenaar, and van Koppen (1996) suggested that misattribution (another one of the sins) could play a strong role. Perhaps, because the event was such a prominent one to Dutch citizens, people imagined what the shooting was like and incorporated that image into memory of video that they did see.

If so, this possibility validates another legal principle. Crombag, Wagenaar, and van Koppen point out the principle of many Western legal traditions is to prohibit "hearsay" testimony—testimony about what someone else has remembered. Far from being just a legal nicety, the prohibition against hearsay testimony emphasizes that evidence must have a clear source. Our memory system may not be the best for keeping its sources straight.

QUESTIONS TO CONSIDER

1. Given what you know about memory, was Ebbinghaus right to use nonsense syllables?
2. Recall a particularly important event in your life. Think about the activities that led up to this event and how the event has affected your life since. How much of the information you recall about this event is accurate? How many of the details surrounding this event have you reconstructed? How would you go about finding the answers to these questions?

Epilogue

The Salem Testimony Reconsidered

Reading the transcripts of the Salem Witch Trials is a sobering experience. The charges sound preposterous, the evidence flimsy, and the sentences were harsh. One man, who refused to enter a plea at his trial, was placed under heavy rocks and crushed to death over a two-day period. Before the trials ended, fifteen women and six men had been executed. One quickly gains an appreciation as to what the term "witch-hunt" really means.

Many theories have been advanced to explain the accusations. It's conceivable that some of the young girls who started the witch-hunt had a mental illness; however, it seems unlikely that all were. Perhaps they became frightened at what they had started and couldn't find a way to admit it. From this distance in time, the answer will probably never be fully known.

What is startling, even now, is the credulity of the investigators, judges, and jurors for testimony that was based on fantasy. One incident brings this home: Early in the investigation, the young girls accused a four-year-old child of haunting them. The authorities promptly jailed this unfortunate girl. Undoubtedly confused and terrified, and relying on a child's imagination, she told her inquisitors that she had been given a black snake that sucked her blood. The investigators noted for the record that they then found a small wound, "the size of a flea bite," on the child's finger. Given that she had been housed in the town jail, it probably was, indeed, a flea bite. Asked who had given her the snake, she mentioned her mother. Accused with testimony like that, her mother, Sarah Good, was hanged nine days after Bridget Bishop.

Now that you've learned about the work of Elizabeth Loftus and others, you can better appreciate how much the interrogators contributed to the whole episode. The witnesses must have also received some strong coaching, implicit or not, from their neighbors in the village—each with their own agendas. The opening vignette also hinted that subtle matters of timing may have played a role. A sighting of a mysterious black pig after an argument with a presumed witch makes for a much better schema than some random encounter. Similarly, remembering that he lost some coins right after she gave them to him probably seemed like a more plausible scenario to one of Bridget's accusers than admitting his own absentmindedness. Finally, one can't help but wonder how many of the encounters with apparitions in the middle of the night were merely dreams confused as reality.

As the research with Dutch street names shows, we are capable of recalling information from our past to a surprising extent. Yet, memory is not a DVD recorder. Memory is the outcome of brain processes that evolved for special functions, and we weren't designed by natural selection to be perfect courtroom witnesses. As Schacter has put it, our memory is prone to seven deadly sins. In all likelihood, that was the real devil at work in Salem.

CHAPTER SUMMARY

Sensory Memory

Memory involves encoding, storage, and retrieval. An early view of memory suggested that it consisted of three forms: sensory, short-term, and long-term. The characteristics of each form differ, which suggests that the three forms differ physiologically as well. Sensory memory is very limited—it provides temporary storage until newly perceived information can be stored in short-term memory. Short-term memory contains a representation of information that has just been perceived, such as an item's name. Although the capacity of short-term memory is limited, we can rehearse the information as long as we choose, thus increasing the likelihood that we will remember it indefinitely (that is, that it will enter long-term memory).

Information in iconic memory is considered to last for only a very short time. The partial-report procedure shows that when a visual stimulus is presented in a brief flash, all of the information is available for about a second. If the viewer is asked to recall one line of information after one second, the information is no longer present in iconic memory. Although echoic memory was originally considered a similar type of memory for auditory stimulation, recent evidence suggests it can last longer.

Short-Term or Working Memory

Information in short-term memory is encoded according to previously learned rules. Information in long-term memory determines the nature of the encoding. Because short-term memory contains information retrieved from long-term memory as well as newly perceived information, many researchers conceive of it as working memory. Working memory is not simply a way station between sensory memory and long-term memory; it is where thinking occurs. When presented with a list of items, we tend to remember the items at the beginning of the list (the primacy effect) and at the end of the list (the recency effect) better than items in the middle of the list. The primacy effect presumably occurs because we have a greater opportunity to rehearse items early in the list and thus store them in long-term memory, and the recency effect because we can retrieve items at the end of the list that are still stored in short-term memory.

Working memory lasts for about 20 seconds and has a capacity of about seven items—give or take two. We often simplify large amounts of information by organizing it into "chunks" of information, which can then be more easily rehearsed and remembered.

Although each sensory system probably has a working memory associated with it, psychologists have devoted most of their attention to two kinds: phonological and visual working memory. The existence of acoustical errors (rather than visual ones) in the task of remembering visually presented letters suggests that information is represented phonologically in short-term memory. Because deaf people (but only those who can talk) also show this effect, the code appears to be articulatory. Phonological working memory is encoded acoustically as well. People who have conduction aphasia show a specific deficit in phonological short-term memory, apparently because their brain damage interrupts direct communication between Wernicke's area and Broca's area.

The processes of working memory act to maintain information over time. Variables that affect rehearsal ability, such as the length of the items being remembered, affect short-term memory. This account, however, raises the question as to what might cause items to decay when they are not rehearsed.

Learning and Encoding in Long-Term Memory

Long-term memory appears to consist of physical changes in the brain—probably within the sensory and motor association cortexes. Consolidation of memories is likely caused by rehearsal of information, which sustains particular neural activities and leads to permanent structural changes in the brain.

Craik and Lockhart's model of memory points out the importance of elaboration in learning. Maintenance rehearsal, or simple rote repetition, is usually less effective than elaborative rehearsal, which involves deeper, more meaningful processing. These theorists assert that long-term memory is a by-product of perceptual analysis. The level of processing can be shallow or deep and is controlled by changes in the amount of attention we pay to information. Having read a description of Craik and Tulving's experiment, you can probably remember the end of the sentence "The old man hobbled across the room and picked up the valuable _____."

Encoding of information to be stored in long-term memory may take place automatically or effortfully. The principle of encoding specificity—how we encode information into memory—determines the ease with which we can later retrieve that information. To produce the most

durable and useful memories, information should be encoded in ways that are meaningful. However, critics of the levels-of-processing model point out that shallow processing sometimes produces very durable memories, and the distinction between shallow and deep has proved impossible to define explicitly.

Mnemonic systems are strategies used to enhance memory and usually use information that is already contained in long-term memory as well as visual imagery.

The Organization of Long-Term Memory

Episodic and semantic memory involve different memories: We remember events that happen to us as episodic memories, whereas general facts are remembered as semantic memories. Another distinction—between explicit and implicit memory—has received much attention. We use explicit memory when we remember facts and events that we can consciously describe. Implicit memory, in contrast, is unconscious; it is, for example, the memory system that we use when we acquire specific behaviors and skills.

Much of what we have learned about the biological basis of memory comes from studies involving humans with brain damage and from laboratory studies in which animals undergo surgical procedures that produce amnesia. Anterograde amnesia appears to reflect a deficit of explicit memory but not a major impairment of implicit memory. The deficit in explicit memory appears to be strongly related to normal functioning of the hippocampus; it may be that the hippocampus is involved in the consolidation of long-term explicit memory. Conversely, the basal ganglia may be responsible for implicit memory. The behavior of laboratory animals also demonstrates this distinction between episodic and other kinds of memories.

Remembering, Recollecting, and Forgetting

Remembering sometimes requires the generation of thoughts that are associated with the information and the discrimination of their source. As research of childhood memories shows, the forgetting of information occurs primarily in the first few years after it is learned, and the rate of forgetting decreases slowly thereafter. Once we have learned something and retained it for a few years, chances are that we will remember it for a long time afterward. The process of remembering information is influenced by how cultures teach their members to learn about the world. In addition, a culture's customs governing social interaction may influence what people tell others about what they have learned.

Sometimes retrieval of one memory is made more difficult by the information contained in another memory, a phenomenon known as *interference*. In retroactive interference, information that we have recently learned interferes with our recollection of information learned earlier. In proactive interference, information that we learned a while ago interferes with information we have learned more recently. Although interference has been demonstrated in the laboratory, interference may not operate so obviously in real life. Prose and other forms of everyday language appear to be more resistant to interference than are the nonsense syllables often used in memory experiments.

Recalling a memory of a complex event entails a process of reconstruction that uses old information. As Loftus's research has established, our ability to recall information from episodic memory is influenced by retrieval cues, such as the questions lawyers ask people in courts of law to establish how an event occurred. Sometimes the reconstruction introduces new "facts" that we perceive as memories of what we previously perceived. Reconstructions also affect the recollection of flashbulb memories—especially vivid memories of surprising and consequential events. This reconstructive process undoubtedly makes more efficient use of the resources we have available for storage of long-term memories.

Reconstructions can be so strong that people may even claim to have witnessed impossible events. Schacter has suggested seven "sins of memory." Two of these, suggestibility and misattribution, might be responsible for memories of events that did not happen.

succeed with mypsychlab

Visit MyPsychLab for practice quizzes, flashcards, and dozens of videos and animated tutorials, including the following items you can find in the "Multimedia Library":

The Effects of Sleep and Stress on Memory:
   Jessica Payne
Memory: Elizabeth Loftus

Encoding, Storage, and Retrieval in Memory
Key Processes in Stages of Memory

Serial Position Effect
Experiencing the Stroop Effect

KEY TERMS

SUGGESTIONS FOR FURTHER READING

Luria, A. R. (1968). *The mind of a mnemonist.* New York: Basic Books.

Given the importance of learning and forgetting in almost everyone's life, it is not surprising that many popular books have been written about human memory. This book is the great Russian neurologist's account of a man with an extraordinary memory.

Loftus, E. F., & Ketcham, K. (1994). *The myth of repressed memory: False memories and allegations of sexual abuse.* New York: St. Martin's.

Elizabeth Loftus is an internationally recognized authority on remembering. She has researched and written extensively on the errors people make in recalling events. This book deals with case studies of individuals who purportedly were able to recall significant events that had been "repressed" because of their traumatic nature. As Loftus and Ketcham note, such repressed memories likely never existed in the first place. You might wish to compare what you learn in this book with the actual Salem trial documents; they can be found online at http://jefferson.village.virginia.edu/salem/home.html.

Ormrod, J. E. (2008). *Human learning* (5th ed.). Upper Saddle River, NJ: Pearson.

Schacter, D. L. (2001). *The seven sins of memory.* Boston: Houghton Mifflin.

The Ormrod book is an upper-level undergraduate text that contains a well-written and thoughtful consideration of memory and its processes. The book's discussion of memory is placed in the larger context of learning processes, such as those discussed in Chapter 5. The Schacter book is an engaging overview of memory errors.

Consciousness

"Moonlight Serenade"

Prologue

The Persistent Loss of Consciousness

It is not usual to learn of persons who have lost consciousness due to head injury, heart failure, stroke, or disease, and who continue to live but never regain consciousness. Often their condition is referred to as "living in a coma." Despite the sustained efforts of the physicians and nurses who attend them, the condition persists for years. Then one day, all of a sudden, the patient awakens and begins a return to normalcy, or at least to as much normalcy as might be recoverable after so long an absence. In other cases, no awakening and no recovery may occur, but instead, the solemn decision is made by loved ones to remove the life-sustaining devices and allow life to expire.

The cases of Jan Grzebski (gurr-ZEB-skee) and Terri Schiavo (SHY-voe) illustrate these end points. Grzebski was a railroad worker in his native Poland when, in 1988, an accident on the job rendered him comatose and, in the judgment of the physicians who treated him, unlikely to live more than a few years. In June 2007, Grzebski suddenly was no longer comatose. Now 65, recovery from the 19-year lapse in his consciousness meant repeated amazement as he came face to face with the altered circumstances—locally and nationally—in the no-longer-Communist country. He credited his wife, who had provided constant care, with his recovery. In commenting on his experience while comatose, he spoke only of dim recollections of family events to which his wife had taken him and of efforts she and their children made to communicate with him.

Terri Schiavo was an American who became an international celebrity while in a persistent vegetative state (PVS). It followed acute respiratory and cardiac arrest that occurred early in 1990 and was accompanied by extensive brain damage. She was 26. Initially she was in a comatose condition. The diagnosis of PVS came later and included the failure to display voluntary action and to interact and communicate purposefully. After persistent rehabilitative efforts, her husband made the decision, consistent with what he claimed were Terri's wishes, to withdraw life support. Her parents objected on grounds that she remained conscious. What followed was a high-profile, sometimes bitter legal contest for the right to decide Terri's fate—a contest waged in state and federal courts

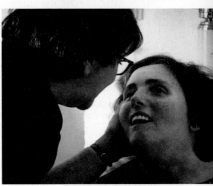

and eventually involving the U.S. Congress and Supreme Court. The contest unfolded amid highly publicized campaigns by citizens who organized on both sides of the issue. Ultimately the decision sided with the husband's right, and, in 2005, Terri's life ended through dehydration.

In the interest of his wife's recovery, Terri's husband took her to the University of California, San Francisco in late 1990 for an experimental procedure that involved the implantation of a device that produced electrical stimulation of the thalamus. Although the treatment lasted for several months, it was unsuccessful. ■

The cases cited in the Prologue made reference to a comatose state and to a persistent vegetative state. Shadlen and Kiani (2007) drew distinctions between them: "**Coma.** The patient seems to be asleep and cannot be awoken. . . . **Persistent vegetative state (PVS).** This is similar to coma in all respects except that, at times, the patient does not seem to be asleep." They also identified a third condition: "**Minimally conscious state (MCS).** In contrast to PVS, patients show occasional signs of arousal and organized behavior. Nevertheless, for the most part, there is a profound deficit of consciousness" (p. 540). These states are further differentiated from the *locked-in syndrome,* which is distinguished by near-complete paralysis of the voluntary muscles (León-Carrión et al., 2002). Clearly, there are different ways to characterize unconsciousness and, if symmetry holds, perhaps different ways to characterize consciousness as well.

What is consciousness, and why are we conscious? How do we direct our consciousness from one object or event to another, paying attention to some while ignoring others? What about the alternation of consciousness that appears to take place in hypnosis–can another person really take control of our thoughts and actions? Why do we regularly undergo the profound alternation of consciousness called sleep? This chapter first explores what it is to be conscious and to be self-conscious, that is, to have a sense of perceptions, thoughts, memories, and feelings that are one's own. Then it examines the phenomenon of selective attention before looking at the brain mechanisms that have been implicated in consciousness. Finally, the chapter turns to topics typically of interest to students—hypnosis and sleep, including dreams.

---

coma A condition in which an individual seems to be sleeping but cannot be awakened.

persistent vegetative state A condition similar to coma except that the individual intermittently appears to be awake.

minimally conscious state A condition in which the individual shows occasional arousal and organized behavior but otherwise appears to be asleep.

consciousness The awareness of complex private processes such as perception, thinking, and remembering.

Consciousness as a Language-Dependent Phenomenon

It is one thing to be aware of what is happening in the world "out there" beyond one's body as well as within one's body. Such awareness amounts to one's ability to report those happenings verbally or in other ways that people recognize. But it is something else to know why we are aware of our actions, our perceptions, our thoughts, our memories, and our feelings. Is some purpose served by such abilities? Philosophers have puzzled over this question for centuries without finding a convincing answer. Early behaviorists approached the issue by denying that there was anything to explain. For them, the only subject matter for psychological investigation was behavior. They argued that consciousness was not behavior, though aspects of consciousness, such as thinking, might turn out to be very subtle forms of behavior. More recently, investigators have begun to apply the methods of inquiry developed jointly by psychology and neuroscience, and finally we seem to be making some progress. The nature of consciousness is coming into clearer focus. This section of the chapter makes the claim that having consciousness relies on having language (see Chapter 10) and on using it to affect others' actions. Thus, consciousness may have social effects.

The Adaptive Significance of Consciousness

To discover the functions of consciousness, we must not confuse consciousness with complex cognitive processes such as perceiving, thinking, or remembering. **Consciousness** is the awareness of these processes, not the processes themselves. Thus, consciousness is its own process, a process that exists in addition to perception, thinking, remembering, and feeling.

It is difficult to see why a living organism having elaborate behavioral abilities plus consciousness would have any

When do we become aware of our own existence?

advantages over an organism that possessed the same abilities but lacked consciousness. If the behaviors of these two types of organisms were identical in all situations, they should be equally successful. For this reason, it may more fruitful to approach the question of adaptive functionality from a different angle. Consider the possibility that consciousness is a by-product of another characteristic of the human brain that does have useful functions. What might this characteristic be?

Let us reflect on what we know about consciousness. First, although the word consciousness is a noun, it does not refer to a thing. The word "life" is a noun, too, but modern biologists know better than to look for "life." Instead, they study the *characteristics* of living organisms. Similarly, rather than look for consciousness per se, we might study the characteristics of conscious organisms. So, then, what does it mean to be conscious? Consciousness refers to private experience, which therefore cannot be shared directly nor can we directly experience the consciousness of another. We experience our own consciousness and can say publicly what it is like. We conclude that other people are conscious because they are like us and because they can tell us that they, too, are conscious. (In Chapters 12 and 16, this will be referred to as having a *theory of mind*.)

Another clue to the functions of consciousness is that we are not conscious of everything about ourselves, nor are we equally conscious of the same thing all the time. That is, consciousness is not a general property of all parts of the brain. This becomes clear in the following case.

[CASE STUDY] Laverne J. had brought her grandfather to see Dr. M., a neuropsychologist. Mr. J. had had a stroke that had left him almost completely blind; all he could see was in a tiny spot at the middle of his visual field. Dr. M. had learned about the situation from Mr. J.'s neurologist and had asked Mr. J. to come to his laboratory so that he could do some tests there as part of his research project.

Dr. M. helped Mr. J. find a chair and sit down. Mr. J., who walked with the aid of a cane, gave it to his granddaughter to hold for him. "May I borrow that?" asked Dr. M. Laverne nodded and handed it to him. "The phenomenon I'm studying is called blindsight," he said. "Let me see if I can show you what it is."

"Mr. J., please look straight ahead. Keep looking that way, and don't move your eyes or turn your head. I know that you can see a little bit straight ahead of you, and I don't want you to use that piece of vision for what I'm going to ask you to do. Fine. Now, I'd like you to reach out with your right hand and point to what I'm holding."

Dr. M. moved and stood to the side of Mr. J. He held out the cane but remained silent. "But I don't see anything—I'm blind!" said Mr. J., obviously exasperated. Dr. M. continued to point the cane toward him.

Mr. J. shrugged his shoulders and pointed, extending his arm in the direction of the cane. He looked startled when his finger encountered the end of the cane.

"Gramps, how did you do that?" asked Laverne, amazed. "I thought you were blind."

"I am!" he said, emphatically. "It was just luck."

"Let's try it just a couple more times," said Dr. M. "Keep looking straight ahead." He changed his position and reversed the cane, so that now the handle was pointing toward Mr. J.

Mr. J. reached out with an open hand and grabbed hold of the cane.

"Good," said Dr. M. "Now put your hand down, please, and try it again." Dr. M. quickly rotated the cane 90 degrees, so that the handle was oriented vertically. As Mr. J.'s arm came up, he turned his wrist so that his hand matched the orientation of the handle, which he grabbed hold of again.

"Good. Thank you, you can put your hand down." Dr. M. turned to Laverne. "I think it's safe to say that there's a lot more to your grandfather's vision than just luck."

The phenomenon Dr. J. was studying was **blindsight,** an odd-seeming word that refers to a clinical condition in which a person with cortical damage is unaware of visible objects ("I'm blind") while otherwise behaving as though they are visible. Mr. J. could reach accurately for objects that he insisted he couldn't see. Someone observing the situation, who didn't know that Mr. J. was blind, naturally would assume he could see them. But Mr. J. remained adamant. All he was aware of was what appeared in the tiny spot at the middle of his visual field, but none of the objects he reached for appeared there. Blindsight is caused by damage to the visual cortex, or to pathways leading into or from it (Weiskrantz, 1986, 1999; Danckert & Rossetti, 2005). Apparently, a part of the visual system can control our ability to react to the presence of objects, directing our eye movements, our limbs, and other behaviors toward or away from them, but not at the level of awareness that would be considered conscious. Linden (2007) has referred to blindsight as evidence of an amphibian (or reptilian) core of consciousness that, despite subsequent evolutionary overlays, continues to reside in the human brain. (However, see Fendrich et al., 1992, and Weiskrantz, 1996, for alternative views that depend on retinal pathways and undamaged cortical regions, respectively.) Conscious awareness comes about with a special effort that can be referred to as concentrating or "paying" attention. Exerting such efforts allows us to report them to ourselves and other people, that is, to be conscious of them.

Consciousness and the Ability to Communicate

It is no coincidence that the principal evidence we have of consciousness in ourselves and other people comes through the use of language. That is, the most likely explanation for consciousness lies in its relation to language. Our ability to

---

blindsight The ability of a person who cannot perceive objects in a part of his or her visual field to reach for them accurately while remaining unaware of seeing them.

communicate (through words, signs, or other symbolic means) provides us with the ability to be aware (conscious) and self-aware (self-consciousness).

How does the ability to communicate symbolically give rise to consciousness? Consider what can be accomplished through verbal communication: we can express our needs, perceptions, thoughts, memories, intentions, and feelings to other people, and they, to us. All of these accomplishments require two general capacities. First, we must be able to translate private events—such as thinking, remembering, and feeling, for example—into language. This means that the brain mechanisms for communicating with others must receive input from the systems of the brain involved in perceiving, thinking, remembering, feeling, and so on (see Gazzaniga, 1987). Second, our words must have an effect on the person who is receiving them. Once the words are decoded in the receiver's brain, they must affect the listener's own perceptions, thoughts, memories, feelings, and—behavior. The last is critical. Otherwise we would be unsure of whether the communication had been received. For example, if we describe a specific event that we witnessed, our listener may be able to imagine that event and remember the description, but it is something in the listener's behavior that gives us confidence that such imagining and remembering actually have occurred. Of course, we can also be our own talkers and listeners. We can make plans in words, think about the consequences of these plans in words, and use words to produce behaviors—all without actually ever saying the words aloud. As we saw in Chapter 8, thinking in words appears to involve *subvocal articulation*. Thus, the brain mechanisms that permit us to understand words and produce speech are the same ones we use to think. Similarly, investigators have noted that when deaf people are thinking to themselves (Sacks, 2000), they often make small movements with their hands, just as those of us who can hear and speak sometimes talk to ourselves under our breath.

Are humans the only organisms with consciousness? Based on other species' communication systems, the answer is probably not. The evolutionary process is incremental: New traits and abilities—including the ability of humans to use language—build on those that that already exist. Most forms of communication among animals other than humans—for example, mating displays and alarm calls—are inborn and automatic and probably do not involve consciousness. However, other animal species may learn forms of communication, just as we learn our own language. Certainly, your dog can learn to communicate with you—to tell you when it wants to eat, go for a walk, or play. This learned ability to report may indicate consciousness, but consciousness with a particular inflection—dog consciousness. Humans' ability to communicate with language seems to surpass by far that of any other species. Thus, we assume our consciousness is much more highly developed. But the underlying brain mechanisms, such as the hippocampal mechanisms implicated in explicit memory we examined in Chapter 8, may be present in species closely related to ours (Morris, 2001). Studies looking at the behavior of animals viewing mirror images suggest that other primate species may possess something like self-awareness (see Boysen and Himes, 1999, for a review; but also see Bekoff, 2002, for a critique).

A daub of red paint on the chimpanzee's face draws a knowing response to its reflection in the mirror. The animal rubs at the paint. Is its response evidence of self-awareness?

Does Conscious Thought Control Behavior?

In the past, psychologists found fault with using consciousness to explain behavior. Many considered it pointless to explain something we could observe (behavior) in terms of something we could not (consciousness). This view has lately been reconsidered, largely because of the techniques of brain research described in Chapter 4 and experimental procedures to be described in later chapters, especially Chapter 15. Today psychologists are more willing to address some of the deeper issues that figured in the discipline's early history.

Recent research in cognitive psychology and cognitive neuroscience has addressed the issue of conscious control of behavior and been helpful in distinguishing action from conscious action. Some of the research uses the phenomenon of visual illusions discussed in Chapter 7. For example, consider the two crayons in FIGURE 9•1. Although they are both the same size, the horizontal crayon tends to look shorter—a visual illusion known as the "top-hat illusion" because it is often demonstrated by using judgments about the crown versus the brim of a top hat. Suppose, now, that I ask you to pick up each crayon by grasping the ends. Would you reach for the horizontal crayon with your fingers closer together?

It seems reasonable to suppose that the fingers would move closer together to grasp shorter objects. Goodale and his colleagues have evidence that our actions are little affected by our visual judgments, including those involving illusions. In one experiment, Ganel and Goodale (2003) compared perceptual judgments of object shape with the ability to pick up the object. They showed participants a wooden block on a table and asked them whether the block was wide or narrow. They then replaced the block with another and again asked for a judgment of width. This continued for several trials. It is easy to judge width under these conditions when the blocks all have the same length, but if the blocks vary in length, the task becomes more difficult. Shape, in other words, is holistic, in the sense meant by the Gestaltists discussed in Chapter 7. However, when Ganel and Goodale

[**FIGURE 9·1**] The "top-hat illusion" depicted with naturalistic objects. The two crayons are the same lengths; however, the vertically positioned crayon looks longer.

asked the participants to take hold of a block at its middle, their grasping action was not affected by variation in length. In other words, the distance between their fingers was the same for the blocks they had previously perceived to be of varying widths. According to Ganel and Goodale, our perceptual judgment of objects—what they are, what features they have (such as their width), and so on—may be based on a different visual system from the one we use for actions (such as picking them up).

If our perception differs from our actions, then what might this imply about consciousness and behavior? When you reach for the coffee cup on your desk, is the sequence of actions controlled by your conscious thoughts of picking it up? Certainly, the thought and the action go together, but remember the lesson from Chapter 2: Correlation does not necessarily imply causation. It could be that the conscious thought and the coordinated actions have a common cause elsewhere in the brain, or it may be that actions caused the conscious thought (Wegner, 2003).

Some of the brain-recording techniques discussed in Chapter 4 have been used to test these possibilities. In a set of experiments performed in 1983, Libet and his colleagues (Libet et al., 1983; see also Libet, 2002, 2004) instructed participants to make a simple flick of their wrist while watching a rapidly moving clock hand displayed in front of them. They were to report the location of the clock hand at the moment they became aware of an intention to flick their wrist. Their verbal reports indicated that they experienced the intention

about three-tenths of a second before the actual movement began. The researchers also measured the "readiness potential," the electrical brain activity of the motor cortex. This potential occurred about seven-tenths of a second before the wrist movement began—even earlier than the conscious intention. Remarkably, the brain seemed to be starting the movement before there was awareness of "willing" it.

Considerable controversy exists over what these observations mean. Much of the debate concerns how to interpret the readiness potential. Recall that the readiness potential precedes a person's awareness of the intention to act. Does it reflect the brain's "decision" to initiate a movement? Haggard and Eimer (1999) reasoned that if the readiness potential was the cause of movement, then it should show covariation in time with awareness. That is, the later awareness is reported, the later the readiness potential will occur. On each trial, they asked participants to move either their left or right index finger and to report when they were aware of the intention to move it. The researchers identified those trials on which the report of awareness was "late" (that is, closer in time to the actual movement) to see whether the readiness potential was also late. It was not. However, they also used another measure of brain activity, the "lateralized readiness potential." Remember from Chapter 4 that motor control of the body is contralateral, with the left motor cortex controlling the right side of the body. The lateralized readiness potential measures the difference between the activity in the two motor cortices. This potential did covary with the report of awareness. When awareness was late, the lateralized readiness potential also was late; when awareness was early, the potential appeared earlier.

So the lateralized readiness potential may reflect brain activity that leads to awareness of the initiation of action, but it involves both sides of the brain. This may imply that it results from an even earlier brain event. In other words, the lateralized readiness potential may be only a step in a sequence of brain activity leading up to conscious awareness. To explore this sequence further, Haggard and Clark (2003) contrasted awareness of both voluntary and involuntary movements. It is possible to elicit involuntary muscle twitches by delivering transcranial magnetic stimulation (TMS; another technique described in Chapter 4). The researchers used this technique to produce involuntary movements of the participants' right index finger and compared trials with stimulation with those in which a participant used the finger to press a key voluntarily. As in the Libet et al. experiment, each participant watched a clock hand spinning around a dial and reported where the clock hand was when he or she became aware of either moving the finger or the involuntary movement produced by TMS. On some trials, called "operant" trials, a tone was presented a fourth of a second after movement occurred, and the participant was asked to also report the position of the clock hand at the time the tone sounded. Often on these trials, the participant reported the perception of causing the tone to come on.

An interesting pattern emerged. On the operant trials, the participants reported being aware of moving their finger later than on the trials involving involuntary movements of the finger. They also reported the tone occurring earlier than on the involuntary trials. In other words, they perceived that, on the voluntary trials, awareness of their intentional movement and of the tone occurred closer together, which may have been critical for their perception of having turned the tone on. On involuntary trials, the perception was that the two events were farther apart. Haggard and Clark argued, therefore, that that brain must "bind together" the experience of voluntary movement with its external consequences. This binding process may be essential if we are to recognize specific external events as the consequences of our behaviors (see also Haggard, 2005).

So then, what does it mean to be conscious? As you have just read, consciousness is defined as more than merely being awake. Rather it depends crucially on being able to report on one's perceptions, thoughts, feelings—on the "what" of one's private experience—in ways that others acknowledge as appropriate. In addition, it is important to remember that consciousness is not a single condition but consists of distinguishable states, just as unconsciousness does.

QUESTIONS TO CONSIDER

1. What do you think about the possibility that members of other species may be conscious? What evidence would you look for to answer this question?

2. If our thesis about human consciousness is correct, babies acquire consciousness as they acquire language. How might this conclusion be related to the fact that we cannot remember what happened to us when we were very young?

3. Suppose a person were raised in isolation and never came in contact with (or communicated with) another person. That person would not have language. What would that person's private experience be like?

Selective Attention

We do not become conscious of all the stimuli detected by our sensory organs. For example, if an angler is watching a large trout circling underneath an artificial fly she has deftly cast on the water, she probably will not notice the chirping of birds in the trees behind her or the temperature of the water surrounding her wading gear or the floating twigs drifting by with the current. Her attention is completely devoted to the behavior of the fish, and she is poised to respond with the appropriate movements of her fly rod if the fish takes the fly. The process that controls our focus on specific categories of events in the environment, to the exclusion of others, is called **selective attention.**

---

selective attention   The process that controls our awareness of, and readiness to respond to, particular categories of stimuli or stimuli in a particular location to the exclusion of others.

divided attention   The process by which we distribute awareness among different stimuli or tasks so that we can respond to them or perform them simultaneously.

But now consider what happens if the fish strikes. The angler's task changes drastically to one of divided attention: She must monitor the tension on the line, control the rod, and watch her footsteps on the slippery rocks underneath as she maneuvers into position to reel in her catch. **Divided attention** is the process by which we allocate our attention to two or more tasks to perform them simultaneously (the term *multitasking* is similar).

Attention may be related to consciousness. Selective attention narrows our awareness to particular experiences, at the same time leaving us unaware of others. Divided attention is basically a different decision process of the brain that determines how our awareness will be allocated between different experiences. Attention may be shifted suddenly and automatically, as when an unexpectedly intense stimulus (such as a loud and novel sound) occurs [Pavlov (1927) referred to it as the *orienting reflex*]. A rapid shift of attention to a novel stimulus may allow the individual to respond to it more effectively than otherwise and may thus be considered adaptive, or the shift may be controlled by others' instructions ("Hey, pay attention to the car on your right!"). We may try to divide our attention, to multitask, as when we use a cell phone while driving—with possibly adverse consequences. For example, Strayer and Drew (2007) reported that driving while talking on a cell phone produces *inattention blindness*, which is discussed in a later section. Attention to visual events, in particular, tends to act like a spotlight, or perhaps more like a zoom lens, that highlights the events within a spatial context (McCormick, Klein, & Johnston, 1998). The brain's attentional mechanisms serve to enhance our responsiveness to certain stimuli, effectively tuning out irrelevant information. As we saw in the case of blindsight, attention may be irrelevant to certain kinds of experiences in which behavior proceeds without awareness.

Attention also plays an important role in memory. By exerting control over the information that reaches short-term memory, it determines what information ultimately becomes stored in explicit long-term memory. But, as Chapter 8 indicated, the storage of information in implicit memory does not require conscious attention. Thus, information is not necessarily lost if we fail to attend to it.

Why, then, does attention exist? Why not process all of the information that our sensory receptors capture? After all, we may miss something important if our attention is directed elsewhere. The answer, according to Broadbent (1958), is that the brain mechanisms responsible for processing sensory information have a limited capacity. Only so much information can be accommodated by these mechanisms at any instant in time. Thus, we need another mechanism that serves as a gatekeeper, controlling the flow of information over time. Broadbent suggested that attention solves this problem by serving as a filter—allowing information of one type (such as the fly on the water in my fishing example) to be processed while deflecting other information (such as the birds chirping in that example). Although the concept of selective attention as a gatekeeper is widely accepted, it remains the subject of ongoing research.

The trading-market floor swirls with visual and auditory messages that vie for the traders' attention.

Auditory Information

The first experiments to investigate selective attention systematically took advantage of the fact that we have two ears. Cherry (1953; see also Hugdahl, 1988) devised a **dichotic** (die-KAH-tick) **listening test** that requires a person to listen to one of two messages presented simultaneously, one to each ear. (Dichotic means "divided into two parts.") He placed headphones on his participants and presented recordings of different spoken messages to each ear. He asked the participants to "**shadow**" the message presented to one ear—continuously to repeat back aloud what that voice was saying. Shadowing ensured that participants would pay attention to only that message.

Cherry was interested in what happened to the information that entered the unattended ear—the unshadowed message. In general, it appeared to be lost. When questioned about

what they had heard in that ear, participants responded that they had heard something, but they could not say what it was. Even if the voice presented to the unattended ear suddenly began talking in a foreign language, the change was not reported.

These results suggest that a sensory channel that is a specific stream of sensory input (in this case, the message presented to one ear) can simply be turned off. Perhaps the neurons in the auditory system that detect sound from the unattended ear are inhibited and cannot respond to sounds presented to that ear as they would ordinarily. (See FIGURE 9·2(a) for a depiction of this possibility.)

The story is not that simple, however. Other evidence shows that selective attention is not simply a matter of turning off a sensory channel. Some information gets through regardless, as long as the ear is healthy. For example, if a person's name is suddenly included in the message presented to the unattended ear, he or she will very likely hear it and remember it later (Moray, 1959, 1970). Or, if the message presented to the unattended ear contains sexually explicit words, participants tend to notice them immediately (Nielsen & Sarason, 1981). The fact that some kinds of information presented to the unattended ear can so readily capture attention indicates that even unattended verbal information undergoes some analysis. If the unattended information is, in fact, "filtered out" at some level, this filtration must not occur until after the sounds are identified as words. (See FIGURE 9·2(b).)

---

dichotic listening test A task that requires a person to listen to one of two different messages being presented simultaneously, one to each ear, through headphones.

shadowing The act of continuously repeating verbal material aloud as soon as it is heard.

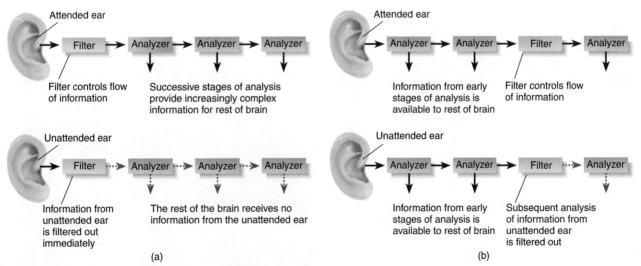

(a)

(b)

[**FIGURE 9·2**] Models of selective attention in the dichotic listening task. (a) Filtering of unattended sensory information immediately after it is received by the sensory receptors. This model cannot explain the fact that some information presented to the unattended ear enters consciousness. (b) Filtering of unattended sensory information after some preliminary analysis.

[**FIGURE 9·3**] Shadowing a message that switches ears. When the message switches, the person must retrieve from memory some words that were heard by the unattended ear.

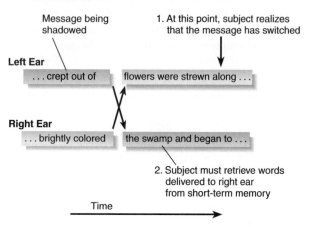

Message being shadowed

1. At this point, subject realizes that the message has switched

Left Ear
. . . crept out of   flowers were strewn along . . .

Right Ear
. . . brightly colored   the swamp and began to . . .

2. Subject must retrieve words delivered to right ear from short-term memory

Time

McKay (1973; see also Johnson & Proctor, 2003) showed that messages presented to the unattended ear can influence verbal processing even when the listener is not conscious of them. In the attended ear, participants heard sentences such as the following:

> They threw stones toward the bank yesterday.

While this sentence was being presented, the word "river" or the word "money" was presented in the unattended ear. Later, participants were asked which of the following sentences they had heard:

> They threw stones toward the side of the river yesterday.
> They threw stones toward the savings and loan association yesterday.

Of course, neither of these sentences had been presented. But as Sachs (1967) showed in a classic study (see Chapter 8), people quickly forget the particular words a sentence contains, although they remember its meaning for much longer. McKay found that the participants' choices between the two sentences were consistent with whether the word "river" or "money" had been presented to the unattended ear. They did not specifically recall hearing the words themselves, but the words had nevertheless affected their perception of the meaning of the word "bank" in the original sentence.

Besides being able to attend to and remember some of the information in the unattended sensory channel, we are able to store information temporarily as it arrives. No doubt you have had the following sort of experience. You are intently reading or thinking about something, when you suddenly become aware that someone nearby has asked you a question. You look up and say, "What?" but then proceed to answer the question before the other person has had a chance to repeat it. First you became aware that you had just been asked a question, but you did not know what it was. However,

a moment later, you remembered what the question was—you heard it again in your mind's ear, so to speak. That information, held in temporary storage, now became accessible to your language system, and you answered the question.

Treisman (1960, 1988) showed that participants can follow a message that is being shadowed even if it switches from one ear to the other. Suppose a participant is shadowing the message presented to the left ear, while the message to the right ear is unshadowed. (See FIGURE 9·3.) In the example given in Figure 9.3, the participant says "crept out of the swamp" and not "crept out of flowers." Apparently, the participant's switch from one message to the other occurs when the originally shadowed message begins to make no sense. However, by the time the participant becomes aware that "crept out of flowers" makes no sense, "the swamp" has already been presented to the right ear. Because the participant is able to continue the message without missing any words—"crept out of the swamp"—he or she must be able to retrieve the latter words from memory of the unshadowed message. Thus, even though an unshadowed message cannot be remembered later, it remains long enough to be retrieved, but only if attention is directed to it soon after the words are presented. According to Treisman (1969), the "gatekeeping" role of selective attention is not that of a nonpermeable filter. Rather, nonattended information remains available, if only partially, and can still be retrieved under the right conditions.

Selective attention to auditory messages has practical significance outside the laboratory. For example, sometimes we have to sort out one message from several others. It isn't as simple as hearing one voice in one ear and another voice in the other. For example, we may be trying to converse with one person while we are in a room in which several other people are carrying on their own conversations. Even in the situation shown in FIGURE 9·4, we can usually sort out one voice from another—an example of what Cherry (1953) originally termed

[**FIGURE 9·4**] The cocktail-party phenomenon. We can follow a particular conversation even when other conversations are going on around us.

the "**cocktail-party problem**" (also referred to as the *cocktail-party phenomenon*). In this case we are trying to listen to the person opposite us and to ignore the cross-conversation of the people to our left and right. Our ears receive a jumble of sounds, but we are able to pick out and string together those that form a meaningful message, ignoring the rest. To do this is effortful, and following one person's words in such circumstances is even more difficult when what he or she is saying is not very interesting, that is, not very attention getting. If we overhear a few words of another conversation that seems more interesting, attention likely will stray to that conversation. If it contains our name, such straying is almost unstoppable.

Visual Information

Since the pioneering work on dichotic listening, the study of selective attention has increasingly involved visual stimuli. This research has shown that people can successfully attend either to the location of the information or to the nature of the information (as revealed by its physical features, such as form or color).

Location   Sperling's classic studies on sensory memory (see Chapter 8) were probably the first to demonstrate the role of attention in selectively transferring visual information into verbal short-term memory (or, for our purposes here, into consciousness). Later psychologists studied the same phenomenon in more detail. For example, Posner, Snyder, and Davidson (1980; Posner and DiGirolamo, 2000) instructed participants to watch a computer-controlled display screen. A small mark in the center of the screen served as a fixation point for the participants' gaze. A warning stimulus then appeared near the fixation point, followed by the target stimulus—a letter displayed just slightly to the left or the right of the fixation point. The warning stimulus consisted of either a plus sign or an arrow that pointed right or left. The arrows served as cues to the participants to expect the letter to occur either to the right or to the left. The plus sign served as a neutral stimulus devoid of spatial cues. The participants' task was to press a button as soon as they detected the letter.

On 80 percent of the trials, the arrow accurately pointed toward the location in which the letter was presented. However, on the rest of the trials, the arrow pointed away from the location. The warning stimulus clearly had an effect on the participants' response times: When the arrows correctly informed them of the location of the letter, they responded faster; and when they were incorrectly informed, they responded more slowly. (See FIGURE 9·5.)

This study shows that selective attention can affect the detection of visual stimuli: If a stimulus occurs where we expect it, we perceive it more quickly; if it occurs where we do not expect it, we perceive it more slowly. Because the participants' gaze remained fixed on the center of the screen in this study, the allocation of attention to one side of the fixation point or the other occurred independent of any eye movements. The results of the study suggest that selective attention sensitizes the neural circuits for detecting a particular kind of stimulus, making it more readily located. By analogy, suppose

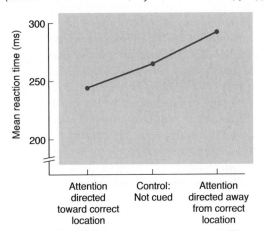

[FIGURE 9·5] Location as a cue for selective attention. Mean reaction time in response to a letter displayed on a screen after participants received a cue directing attention toward the location in which the letter appears was less than when no cue or an incorrect cue was received.

(Based on data from Posner, Snyder, and Davidson (1980).)

you misplace your car keys and search for them in several places, to no avail; a roommate notices you searching and mentions having seen them in the kitchen near the toaster. Sure enough, you locate them there right away, even though they had been in the same place during your earlier search.

A possible clue to the way these attentional circuits work comes from an interesting extension of the task used by Posner and his colleagues. Suppose the arrow is completely nonpredictive (that is, it sometimes points to where the letter will be presented but just as often does not). As we know, when the letter is presented right after the arrow is presented, people are usually faster at recognizing the letter when it appears at the location the arrow indicated. That is, even though the arrow is sometimes correct and sometimes wrong, the attentional "spotlight" is directed by the arrow. However, if the interval between the presentation of the arrow and the letter is a little longer (about 100 to 300 milliseconds), then recognition is now slower when the letter appears at the location to which the arrow pointed. Posner and his colleagues have called this surprising effect the **inhibition of return (IOR)**. Speaking loosely, once the arrow appears, the attentional spotlight sweeps momentarily over to the location signaled by the arrow. Because no letter appears there, it sweeps back, but then is inhibited from returning immediately to the same spot where it swept originally. It's as if, having shifted to the location indicated by the arrow, the attentional system is now slower to return to it (Posner & Cohen, 1984). Some have argued that IOR biases attention to novel stimuli. Recently, it has been extended to more complex phenomena, such as memory for words (Massen

---

cocktail-party problem   Trying to follow one conversation while other, potentially distracting conversations are going on around us.

inhibition of return (IOR)   A reduced tendency to perceive a target when the target's presentation is consistent with a cue, but the target is presented a few hundred milliseconds after the cue.

& Stegt, 2007) and facial cues (Stoyanova, Pratt, & Anderson, 2007). Continuing the earlier analogy, if, given your roommate's mention, you looked for your keys near the toaster but failed to find them there, you would probably be unlikely to search again in the vicinity of the toaster.

Features The second dimension of selective visual attention are the features of the object being attended to (Vecera & Farah, 1994; Desimone & Duncan, 1995). Sometimes, two events happen in close proximity, but we can separate them, watching one while ignoring the other. For example, Neisser and Becklen (1975) showed participants a videotape that presented a situation similar to that confronted by the person who is trying to listen to a specific voice at a cocktail party. The videotape contained two different action sequences presented one on top of the other: a game in which people are passing a basketball around and a hand game in which people try to slap their opponents' hands, which are resting on top of theirs. The participants could easily follow one game and remember what had happened in it; however, they could not attend simultaneously to both games. (See FIGURE 9•6.)

What happens to the information that is not attended to? As we have seen, in the auditory system, information that is of personal relevance, such as someone calling our name, can override attention to something else. Similarly, our name seems to jump out if it appears in print, even if it appears in text that we ignore (Neisser, 1969). In an evolutionary perspective, this readiness to tune rapidly to personally relevant information may have conferred a selective advantage.

Recent evidence suggests that the visual system is prone to **inattention blindness** (Most et al., 2005), a failure to perceive an event when attention is diverted elsewhere. You may have had the experience of shopping in a crowded place, looking for a particular item and, while doing so, failing to notice that a friend was shopping only a few feet away. But suppose you were watching the game mentioned earlier in which participants were asked to count the number of times a basketball was passed between them, and a woman in a gorilla suit walked right through the action, stopping in the middle to pound her chest? (See FIGURE 9•7.) You would definitely notice that, right? Remarkably, half of the research participants who observed this action in a film sequence designed by Simons and Chabris (1999) failed to notice the gorilla. This occurred despite the fact that the unusual event was in the center of the action. Interestingly, the unusual nature of the event seemed to make it more likely to be missed: When the game was interrupted by a woman carrying an umbrella, more of the participants noticed her. In related experiments using picture and words, Finnish researchers Koivisto and Revonsuo (2007) showed that unexpected stimuli (for example, a person in a gorilla suit) semantically unrelated to the current interests of the observer (counting the number of times the basketball is passed) are more likely to remain unseen.

Simons and Rensink (2005) have made the general point that, although our visual experience is rich with information,

[**FIGURE 9•6**] Drawings of the scenes from the videotapes in Neisser and Becklen's study. (a) The hand game. (b) The basketball game. (c) The two games superimposed.

(Reprinted from Neisser, U., & Becklen, R. (1975). *Cognitive Psychology*, 1975, 7, 480–494. Copyright © 1975, with permission from Elsevier.)

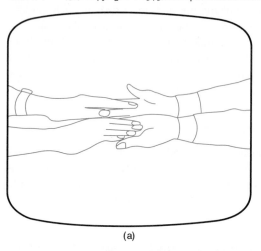

(a)

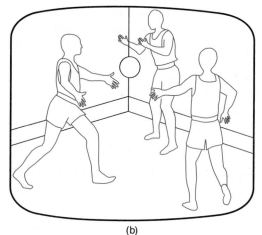

(b)

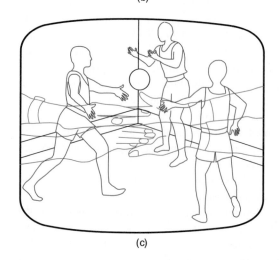

(c)

---

inattention blindness Failure to perceive an event when attention is diverted elsewhere.

[**FIGURE 9·7**] A frame from the film constructed by Simons and Chabris for their study of inattentional blindness. Observers were asked to watch a basketball passing game being played by two teams and to count the passes between members of each team. As they watched, a woman wearing a gorilla suit walked in from the right, paused in the middle of the game facing the camera, and then walked out to the left. Half of the observers failed to notice this unusual event. To learn more about the "gorilla" study or to view the original video, go to www. viscog.net

(From Simons, D. J., & Chabris, C. F. (1999). Gorillas in our midst: Sustained inattentional blindness for dynamic events. *Perception*, 28, 1059–1074, Figure 3. Reprinted with permission from Pion Limited, London. Figure provided by Daniel Simons.)

our ability to represent it in memory may be limited. We saw such limitations in Chapter 8. Perhaps when we attend selectively to the visual world, consciousness requires that the rest of it remains relatively unchanging. After all, people we're talking to don't spontaneously change hair color or the clothes they're wearing just because we briefly look away from them.

Would we notice it if they did? Surprisingly, the answer seems to be no, at least under some circumstances. If a visual display is artificially changed during an eye movement or other visual distraction, **change blindness** often results: People often fail to notice significant changes in the display (O'Regan, Rensink, & Clark, 1999). In one memorable study, people who were talking to a construction worker failed to notice when the person himself changed during a brief distraction (Simons & Levin, 1998)!

Brain Mechanisms of Selective Attention

As previously noted, a possible explanation for selective attention is that some components of the brain's sensory system are temporarily sensitized, which enhances their ability to detect particular categories of stimuli. For example, if a research participant were watching for changes in stimulus shapes, colors, or movements (that is, if the person's attention were focused on one of these attributes), we might expect to see increased activity in the portions of the visual cortex devoted to the analysis of shapes, colors, or movements.

This result is exactly what Corbetta and colleagues (1991) found. They instructed participants to look at a computerized display containing 30 colored rectangles, which could change in shape, color, or speed of movement. The stimuli were the same during each condition of the experiment. Thus, the only difference between the conditions was the type of stimulus change the participants were instructed to report.

The investigators used a PET scanner to measure brain activity as the participants watched the display. They found that paying attention to shape, color, or speed of movement caused activation of different regions of the visual association cortex. More recent work by Shulman et al. (2003) used *f*MRI to parse selective visual attention into sensory, search, and detection components according to the same brain regions Corbetta et al. had identified.

Luck and colleagues (1993) obtained similar results in a study with monkeys and the activity of single neurons in the visual association cortex. When a visual cue indicated that the monkey should watch for a stimulus to be presented in a particular location within the visual field, neurons that received input from that location began firing more rapidly, even before the stimulus was presented. These neurons thus seemed to be "primed" for detecting a stimulus.

The interrelatedness of visual memory (specifically, iconic memory—see Chapter 8) and visual selective attention was recently reported by Ruff, Kristjánsson, and Driver (2007). They instructed participants to look at a fixation point in the center of a screen, and then to report the number of specific objects that were presented in either the left or right half of a brief display. The objects were circles that were either partially or fully closed. Three circles appeared in each half of the display. Participants pressed a button to signal the number of closed circles. A tone indicated which half of the display the report should come from. The cue was presented either shortly (200 milliseconds) before or after the display appeared. The pre-cue activated selective attention, and the post-cue, iconic memory.

By using *f*MRI, the researchers found similar brain activity after pre-cues and post-cues. The activity occurred in the lateral occipital cortex that was contralateral to the side on which the cued display was presented. That is, if the tone signaled a report of the circles in the right visual field, then activity increased in the left lateral occipital cortex. (Recall from Chapter 6 that, in the visual system, the flow of information from the right visual field is to the left visual cortex, and vice versa.) This occurred regardless of whether the tone functioned as a pre-cue or post-cue. Ruff et al. concluded that similar mechanisms are involved in selective visual attention and iconic memory, respectively.

---

change blindness Failure to detect a change when vision is interrupted.

1. Have you ever had an experience in which someone asked you a question when you weren't paying attention, and then, before the question could be repeated, you realized what it was? How long do you think the unattended information lasts before it is eventually lost? Can you think of an experiment that would permit you to find out? If so, briefly describe it.

2. Let's reconsider the cocktail-party problem. Suppose that a person is carrying on a conversation and then happens to overhear a word or two from another conversation that seems much more interesting. Wanting to be polite, the person tries to ignore the other conversation but finds it difficult, hemming and hawing while trying to attend to both conversations. Should we regard this example as a failure of selective attention? Or is it actually useful that we usually don't become so absorbed in one thing that we miss out on potentially interesting information? What is your view, and why?

3. It isn't unusual for students to say they have a hard time studying because they are easily distracted. This implies that paying attention is effortful, that studying effectively can be hard work. If you were trying to make this point, which research findings cited in this section of the chapter would be most useful to you? Why?

Consciousness and the Brain

We know that brain damage can alter human consciousness. For example, Chapter 8 described the phenomenon of anterograde amnesia, caused by damage to the hippocampus. Although people with this defect cannot form new verbal memories, they can learn some kinds of tasks (Sacks, 2007). However, they remain unaware they have learned, even when their behavior indicates they have. The brain damage does not prevent all kinds of learning, but it does prevent awareness of what has been learned.

If human consciousness is related to speech, then it is probably related to the brain mechanisms that control comprehension and production of speech. This hypothesis suggests that for us to be aware of an event, information about it must be transmitted to neural circuits in the brain responsible for language ability. Several reports of cases of human brain damage support this suggestion. Let's consider some examples.

Isolation Aphasia: A Case of Global Unawareness

Geschwind, Quadfasel, and Segarra (1968) described the case of a woman who had severe brain damage as a result of inhaling

isolation aphasia   Language disorder in which a person cannot comprehend speech or produce meaningful speech but is able to repeat speech and to learn new sequences of words.

carbon monoxide from a faulty water heater. The damage spared the primary auditory cortex, the speech areas of the brain, and the connections between these areas. However, the damage destroyed large parts of the visual association cortex and isolated the speech mechanisms from other parts of the brain. The syndrome that Geschwind and colleagues reported is referred to as **isolation aphasia** (see Hegde, 2001), a language disturbance in which a person is unable to comprehend speech or to produce meaningful speech but is able to repeat speech and to learn new sequences of words. It is also classified as *mixed transcortical aphasia* (Berthier, 1999).

The woman remained in the hospital until she died nine years later. During this time, she made few movements except with her eyes, which were able to follow moving objects. She gave no evidence of recognizing objects or people in her hospital environment. She did not spontaneously say anything, answer questions, or give any signs that she understood what other people said to her. By all available criteria, she was not conscious of anything that was going on, much like Jan Gzrebski and Terri Schiavo, described in the Prologue. However, the woman could repeat words that were spoken to her. And if someone started a poem she recognized, she would finish it. For example, if someone said, "Roses are red, violets are blue," she would respond, "Sugar is sweet, and so are you." She even learned new poems and songs and sang along with the radio—but never in any knowing or conscious way. Her case suggests that consciousness is not simply a matter of the brain's speech mechanisms. It requires their connectedness to other parts of the brain, including those that serve memory and attention. Of course, it is also possible that the limitations of awareness that were observed could be attributed to more generalized loss rather than to that specific to speech mechanisms. It is important to realize the difficulties that can beset any claim of a specific deficit due to a specific site of brain damage. Alternative ways to account for the deficit will almost always exist.

Visual Agnosia: Loss of Awareness of Visual Perceptions

The case just described was of a woman who appeared to have completely lost her awareness of herself and her environment. In other instances, people with brain damage have become selectively unaware, that is, unaware of particular kinds of information. For example, in blindsight, individuals can point to and grasp objects they cannot see—or rather, that they are not aware of seeing. Margolin, Friedrich, and Carlson (1985) studied a young man with a different kind of disconnection between perception and awareness. His brain had been damaged by an inflammation of the blood vessels, and he consequently had *visual agnosia* (recall the case of Mrs. R. in Chapter 7)—the inability to recognize the identity of an object visually. The man had great difficulty identifying common objects by sight. For example, he could not say what a hammer was by looking at it, but he quickly identified it when he was permitted to pick it up and feel it. He was not blind; he could

[**FIGURE 9·8**] Hypothetical exchanges of information within the brain of a patient with visual agnosia.

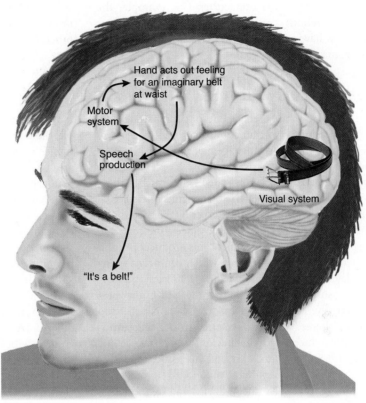

walk around without bumping into things, and he had no trouble making visually guided movements to pick up an object that he wanted to identify. The researchers' simplest conclusion was that his disease had damaged the neural circuits responsible for visual perception.

However, the simplest was not their eventual conclusion. Although the patient had great difficulty visually recognizing objects or pictures of objects, he often made hand movements that appeared to be related to the object he could not identify. For example, when shown a picture of a pistol, he stared at it with a puzzled look, then shook his head and said that he couldn't tell what it was. While continuing to study the picture, he clenched his right hand into a fist and began making movements with his index finger. When asked what he was doing, he looked at his hand, made a few tentative movements with his finger, and then raised his hand in the air and moved it forward each time he moved his finger. He was unmistakably miming the way a person holds and fires a pistol. "Oh!" he said. "It's a gun. No, a pistol." Clearly, he was not aware of what the picture was until he paid attention to what his hand was doing. On another occasion, he looked at a picture of a belt and said it was a pair of pants. Then he was asked him to point to where the legs and other parts of the pants were. When he tried to do so, he became puzzled. His hands went to the place where his belt buckle ordinarily would be (he was wearing hospital pajamas at the time) and moved his hands as if he were feeling one. "No," he said, after noticing the motions of his hand. "It's not a pair of pants—it's a belt!" FIGURE 9·8 depicts a possible neural basis for his discovery.

The patient's visual system was not normal, yet it functioned better than could be inferred from his verbal behavior alone. That is, he was aware in a way that his words failed to indicate. The fact that he could mime the use of a pistol or feel an imaginary belt buckle with his hands indicated that his visual system worked well enough to initiate appropriate nonverbal behaviors, although not the appropriate words. Once he selectively attended to what his hands were doing, he could name the object.

Although the patient had lost his ability to read, speech therapists were able to teach him to use finger spelling to read, the form of spelling used by deaf people. He could not say what a particular letter was, but he could learn to make a particular hand movement when he saw the letter. After he had learned the finger-spelling alphabet, he could read slowly and laboriously by making the hand movements for each letter and learning the sequences of movement that corresponded to words.

This case could be interpreted as supporting the conclusion that consciousness is synonymous with a person's ability to talk about his or her perceptions or memories. In this particular situation, disruption of the normal interchange between the visual perceptual system and the verbal system prevented the patient from being directly aware of his own visual perceptions. Instead, it was as if his hands talked to him, telling him what he had just seen. Conversely, it is possible that, although brain damage prevented direct visual recognition of objects, alternative forms of recognition may have been supported by undamaged areas of association cortex (for example, the kinesthetic association cortex; Fiehler et al., 2008). Thus recognition may have occurred without the need for access to speech mechanisms.

The Split-Brain Syndrome

A surgical procedure exists whose effects demonstrate dramatically how various brain functions can be disconnected from one another and from language mechanisms. It is used rarely and as something of a last resort for people who have severe epilepsy that cannot be controlled with drugs. In these people, highly erratic neural activity first engulfs one cerebral hemisphere and is transmitted to the other by the corpus callosum, the large bundle of axons that connects the cortex in one hemisphere with that in the other. This produces a grand mal or generalized epileptic seizure, which can occur many times each day, preventing the individual from leading a normal life. Neurosurgeons discovered that the **split-brain operation**—cutting the corpus callosum to disconnect the two cerebral hemispheres (sometimes referred to as a callosumotomy)—greatly reduces the frequency of the seizures.

Sperry (1966) and Gazzaniga and his associates (Gazzaniga, 1970, 2000; Gazzaniga & LeDoux, 1978) studied split-brain patients extensively. Normally, the left and right cerebral cortices exchange information through the corpus callosum. With one exception (described later), each hemisphere receives

split-brain operation A surgical procedure that severs the corpus callosum, thus abolishing the direct connections between the cortex of the two cerebral hemispheres.

sensory information from the opposite side of the body and controls muscle movements on that side. The corpus callosum permits these activities to be coordinated, so that what originates in one hemisphere may be transmitted to the other. After the two hemispheres are surgically disconnected, they are essentially independent. The sensory mechanisms, perceptions, memories, and motor systems of one hemisphere are essentially isolated from those of the other. The effects of this disconnection are not obvious to a casual observer, for the simple reason that only one hemisphere—in most people, the left—controls speech. The right hemisphere can comprehend speech reasonably well but because Broca's speech area (Chapter 10) is located in the left hemisphere; the right hemisphere cannot produce speech.

With only the left hemisphere able to talk, a casual observer will not detect the independence of the operations of the right hemisphere. Even the patient's left hemisphere has to learn about the independent existence of the right. One of the first things these patients report after the surgery is that their left hand "seems to have a mind of its own." For example, they may find themselves putting down a book held by the left hand, even though they are reading it with great interest. At other times, they may surprise themselves by making obscene gestures with the left hand. Because the right hemisphere controls the movements of the left hand, the left hemisphere is informed about them only when they occur.

An exception to the cross-hemispheric transmission of sensory information noted earlier is the olfactory system. When a person with the corpus callosum intact sniffs a flower through the left nostril, only the left hemisphere receives the sensation. Thus, if the right nostril of a split-brain patient is blocked, and the left nostril is left open, the patient will accurately identify odors verbally. Conversely, if the odor enters

[**FIGURE 9·9**] Identification of an object by a person with a split brain in response to an olfactory stimulus.

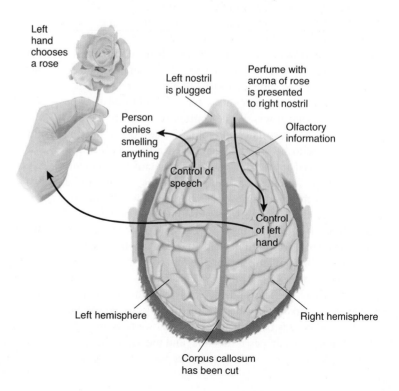

Left hand chooses a rose

Left nostril is plugged

Perfume with aroma of rose is presented to right nostril

Person denies smelling anything

Olfactory information

Control of speech

Control of left hand

Left hemisphere

Right hemisphere

Corpus callosum has been cut

only the right nostril, the patient will say that he or she doesn't smell anything, but the sensory signals were transmitted to the right hemisphere, and the odor is perceived there. This fact can be demonstrated by asking the patient to reach for some objects hidden from view by a partition. If asked to use the left hand only, and with the left nostril blocked, the patient will select the object that corresponds to the odor—a plastic flower for a floral odor, a toy fish for a fishy odor, a small plastic tree for the odor of pine, and so forth. But if the left nostril is blocked, the right hand fails this test, because it is controlled by the left hemisphere, which did not receive the odor signals. (See FIGURE 9•9; Gazzaniga, 1989.)

As we saw in Chapter 4, the left hemisphere, besides giving us the ability to read, write, and speak, is good at other tasks that require verbal abilities, such as mathematics and logic. The right hemisphere excels at visual and spatial perception and skills related to the visual arts. For example, if a split-brain patient tries to use his or her right hand to arrange blocks in a pattern to duplicate a geometrical design provided by a researcher, the hand will fumble with the blocks and fail to arrange them properly. The left hand may then brush the right hand aside and proceed to complete the task. It is as if the right hemisphere becomes impatient with the ineptitude of the left.

$f$ocus O̶n

Embodied Consciousness and the Out-of-Body Experience

Human consciousness is embodied. The ability to report one's perceptions, thoughts, and feelings to others, and to oneself, generally includes the report that such events occur within one's skin, that one is reporting on how it seems from "in here." Psychologists have an interest in understanding the necessary and sufficient conditions for the near-universal experiences of consciousness, including consciousness of self (also called "embodied consciousness").

How is embodied consciousness studied? Ehrrson (2007) attempted this by experimentally inducing out-of-body experiences (OBEs) in their participants. Participants at the Karolinska Institute in Stockholm were healthy adults who wore head-mounted viewing devices that received their input from a pair of video cameras located two meters behind them. The cameras were placed side by side so as to simulate a pair of eyes. The images from the left camera appeared in the left-eye display of the device the participant wore, and the images from the right camera in the right-eye display. The experimenter stood to the right of the seated participant and, while in the participant's view, moved a pair of plastic rods. With the rod in his right hand, the experimenter stroked the participant's chest and, simultaneously with his left hand, moved the rod just below the cameras, as if stroking an invisible chest

in approximately the same location. In their viewers, participants only saw Ehrrson's arm moving, but this occurred as they felt the rod on their own chests.

After two minutes of exposure to chest stroking, the participants completed a questionnaire designed to test the strength of the illusion they reported, namely, that they were actually sitting behind their bodies and looking at them from that altered position. According to Ehrrson, "You really feel that you are sitting in a different place in the room and you're looking at this thing in front of you that looks like yourself and you know it's yourself but it doesn't feel like yourself." (Miller, 2007, p. 1021). In a second experiment, Ehrrson measured the participants' skin-conductance response (SCR), a widely used correlate of emotional arousal. To induce the OBE, he used the plastic rods as he had previously and introduced a control condition in which, instead of applying the rods simultaneously, he alternated their application. In both conditions, he interrupted the use of the plastic rods by suddenly picking up a hammer and swinging it toward the imaginary chest. The emotional reaction was immediate in terms of the participants' movements and the SCR, and was greater in the experimental than the control condition.

Lenggenhager et al. (2007) reported a study conducted at the Swiss Federal Institute of Technology in Lausanne. Their participants stood and wore 3-D video-display devices in which the computer-controlled images originated from a video camera placed 2 meters behind them. Thus they viewed a virtual body that seemed to be located in front of them about the same distance. They subsequently viewed the back of the virtual body being stroked by a highlighter pen at the same time their own backs were stroked (the synchronous condition; see FIGURE 9.10(a)). In another condition (asynchronous), the stroking alternated as in Ehrrson's study. After exposure to stroking, participants were blindfolded, led away from their original position and asked to return to it. They tended to end up at a position ahead of where they had been originally, that is, closer to the virtual body. This finding, together with the participants' responses to a self-attribution questionnaire, suggested that they perceived themselves to be in the virtual body. This illusion was replicated in a second experiment that involved the participant's virtual body, a virtual fake body, and a virtual body-sized rectangular solid (see FIGURES 9.10(b), 9.10(c)). Both the virtual real body and fake body produced the illusion—"It felt as if the virtual condition was my body"—but the virtual object condition did not.

Although the procedures used in the two laboratories produced the illusion of spatial displacement of body consciousness, it fell short of the more widely known phenomenon in which individuals report leaving their bodies and viewing them from a distance. Still, the findings provide the strong suggestion that the feeling of being an embodied self depends on the integration of visuospatial and somatosensory information. A disjunction between the two forms of information may render us susceptible to the experience of being ourselves in other bodies.

[FIGURE 9·10] (a) The participant appears in dark blue pants and views his own virtual body (light blue pants) in front of him. Stroking of the back occurs either synchronously or asynchronously. (b) A virtual fake body (red pants) replaces the virtual own body. (c) A virtual object appears in place of the virtual own body.

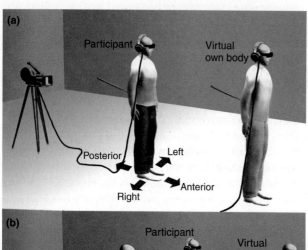

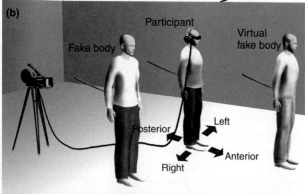

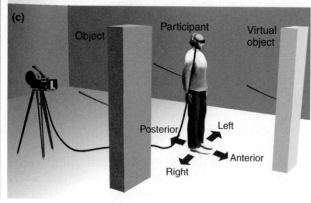

QUESTIONS TO CONSIDER

1. Some split-brain patients have reported that they can use only one hand to hold a book while reading. If they use the other hand, they find themselves putting the book down, even though they want to continue reading. Which hand puts the book down? Why does it do so?

2. When a stimulus is presented to the right hemisphere of a split-brain patient, the person (speaking with his or her left hemisphere) claims to be unaware of it. Because the right hemisphere cannot talk to us, should we conclude that it lacks conscious self-awareness? If you think it is conscious, has the surgery produced two independent consciousnesses where only one previously existed? If so, how different would they be?

Hypnosis

Hypnosis is a specific and unusual form of verbal control that apparently enables one person to control some of another person's (or one's own) behavior, including thinking and perceiving (see Kihlstrom, 2004). Under hypnosis, a person can be induced to bark like a dog, act like a baby, or tolerate being pierced with needles or exposed to icy coldness. Although these examples are sometimes the stuff of entertainment, hypnosis is important to psychology because it provides insights into the nature of consciousness. It also has effective applications in psychotherapy and medicine (Gafner & Benson, 2003; Stewart, 2005).

Although hypnosis may have been in use among religious cults in classical Greece (Spanos & Chaves, 1991), the modern phenomenon of hypnosis, or mesmerism, was introduced by Franz Anton Mesmer (1734–1815), a Viennese physician. He found that when he passed magnets back and forth over people's bodies (in an attempt to restore their "magnetic fluxes" and cure them of disease), they often would convulse and enter a trancelike state during which seemingly miraculous cures could be achieved. As Mesmer discovered later, the patients were not affected directly by the magnetism of the iron rods; they were responding to his undoubtedly persuasive and compelling personality. We now know that convulsions and trancelike states do not necessarily accompany hypnosis, and we also know that hypnosis does not reliably cure physical illnesses. Mesmer's patients' symptoms were alleviated by suggestions he provided during the trance. In some cases, the alleviation was shorter-lived than in others but adequately impressive to allow him a storied career in Vienna and later in Paris (see Wegner, 2003).

Hypnotic Induction and Suggestion

A person undergoing hypnotic induction can be alert, relaxed, tense, lying quietly, or exercising vigorously. There is no need to move an object in front of her or his face while saying, "You are getting sleepy." Numerous techniques can be used to induce hypnosis in a susceptible person (Temes, 2004). The only essential feature seems to be the person's understanding that he or she is to be hypnotized (see Killeen & Nash, 2003).

Not everyone is hypnotizable. Hypnotic susceptibility varies from person to person. Psychologists who study hypnotic phenomena use tests known as hypnotic susceptibility scales to measure individual differences (Hilgard, 1986). Once hypnotized, people are very suggestible. Their behavior will conform to what the hypnotist suggests, even to the extent of appearing to misperceive reality. Generally, hypnotic suggestions are of three types (Kirsch & Lynn, 1998):

- Ideomotor suggestions are those in which the hypnotist suggests that a particular action will occur without awareness of voluntary action, such as raising an arm.

- Challenge suggestions are those for which the hypnotized individual will be unable to perform a normally voluntary action.

- Cognitive suggestions may induce the hypnotized person to report distortions of perceptual or cognitive experiences, such as not feeling pain or not being able to remember something.

One of the most dramatic phenomena of hypnosis is **posthypnotic suggestion,** in which a person is given instructions under hypnosis and follows those instructions after returning to a nonhypnotized state. Typically this requires the use of a cue. For example, a hypnotist might tell a man that he will become unbearably thirsty when he sees the hypnotist look at her watch. She might also admonish him not to remember anything on leaving the hypnotic state, so that **posthypnotic amnesia** is also achieved. After leaving the hypnotic state, the man acts normally and professes ignorance of what he perceived and did during hypnosis, perhaps even apologizing for not having succumbed to hypnosis. The hypnotist later looks at her watch, and the man suddenly rises and leaves the room to get a drink of water.

The most common report of persons undergoing hypnosis is that the actions they perform seem to occur with much less effort than would be the case when out of hypnosis. Sometimes the lack of effort is accompanied by an absence of voluntariness—the arm that rises in response to the hypnotist's suggestion is described as having "a mind of its own" (see Nash, 2001).

Research has indicated that when changes in perception are induced through cognitive suggestions, the changes occur in explicit perception but not in implicit perception. That is, the change is not so much in what the person perceives but in what she or he reports about the perceptions. For example, Miller, Hennessy, and Leibowitz (1973) used the Ponzo illusion to test the effects of hypnotically induced blindness. Although the two parallel horizontal lines in the left portion of FIGURE 9•11 are the same length, the top one looks longer than the bottom one. This effect is produced by the presence of the slanted lines to the left and right of the horizontal ones; if these lines are removed, the horizontal lines appear to be the same length. Through hypnotic suggestion, the researchers made the slanted lines "disappear." Even though the participants reported that they could not see the slanted lines, they still perceived the upper line as longer than the lower one. This result indicates that the visual system continues to process sensory information during hypnotically induced blindness; otherwise, the participants would have perceived the lines as equal in length. The reported blindness appeared to occur not because of altered activity in the visual system but because of altered activity in the verbal system (and in consciousness).

[**FIGURE 9•11**] The Ponzo illusion and hypnotic blindness. The short horizontal lines are actually the same length. Even when a hypnotic suggestion made the slanted lines disappear, the visual system still perceived the illusion.

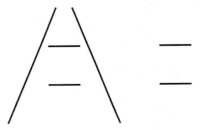

Rainville et al. (1999, 2002) reported studies of hypnotized participants instructed to relax or to reduce the perception of pain produced by the immersion of their hands in hot water. By using EEG and PET measures (see Chapter 4), the researchers found that brain activity and regional cerebral blood flow shifted between the two tasks. Specifically, hypnotically induced relaxation lowered overall cortical activity and made it less likely that activity in the cortical area associated with one sensory modality would suppress activity in an area associated with another modality. With the pain-reduction task, however, activity increased in the cortical and subcortical areas associated with selective attention.

QUESTION TO CONSIDER

Some people prefer explanations that demystify puzzling phenomena such as hypnosis. Others resist such explanations, arguing that an interesting phenomenon is spoiled by an explanation that necessarily places it in the realm of science. How do you respond to each of these viewpoints?

Sleep

Sleep is not a state of unconsciousness—it is a state of *alternate* consciousness. During sleep, we have dreams that can be just as vivid as waking experiences, and yet we forget most of them as soon as they are over. Our amnesia leads us to think that we were unconscious while we were asleep. Two distinct kinds of sleep occur—and thus, two states of consciousness during sleep.

We spend approximately one third of our lives sleeping—or trying to. You might therefore think that the reason we sleep would be clearly understood by scientists who study this phenomenon. And yet, despite the efforts of many talented researchers (see Kleitman, 1939, for an early example), we are still not completely sure why we sleep. Before we discuss proposed functions of sleep, you should understand the stages of sleep.

---

posthypnotic suggestion   A suggestion made by a hypnotist that is carried out some time after the participant has left the hypnotic state and usually according to a specific cue.

posthypnotic amnesia   Failure to remember what occurred during hypnosis; induced by suggestions made during hypnosis.

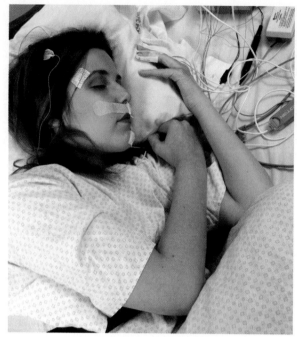

A participant prepared for a night's sleep in a sleep laboratory.

(Photo © Christian Voulgaropoulos/ISM/phtake, Inc.)

The Stages of Sleep

Sleep is not uniform. We can sleep lightly or deeply; we can be restless or still; we can have vivid dreams, or our consciousness can be relatively uninvolved. Researchers have found that sleep occurs in stages that usually follow an orderly, predictable sequence.

The best research on human sleep is conducted in a sleep laboratory, which consists of one or several small bedrooms adjacent to an observation room, where the researcher spends the night (trying to stay awake). The researcher prepares the sleeper for electrophysiological measurements by attaching electrodes to the scalp to monitor the electroencephalogram (EEG) and to the chin to monitor muscle activity, recorded as the **electromyogram (EMG).** Electrodes attached around the eyes monitor eye movements, recorded as the **electro-oculogram (EOG).** In addition, other electrodes and transducing devices can be used to monitor autonomic measures such as heart rate, respiration, and changes in the ability of the skin to conduct electricity.

During wakefulness, the EEG of a normal person shows two basic patterns of activity: *alpha activity* and *beta activity*. **Alpha activity** consists of regular, medium-frequency waves

---

electromyogram   A record of muscle activity.

electro-oculogram   A record of eye movements.

alpha activity   Rhythmical, medium-frequency electroencephalogram activity, usually indicating a state of quiet relaxation.

beta activity   Irregular, high-frequency electroencephalogram activity, usually indicating a state of alertness or arousal.

theta activity   Electroencephalogram activity of 3.5 to 7.5 Hz; occurs during the transition between sleep and wakefulness.

---

of 8 to 12 Hz. The brain produces this activity when a person is resting quietly, not particularly aroused or excited, and not engaged in strenuous mental activity (such as problem solving). The other type of waking EEG pattern, **beta activity,** consists of irregular, mostly low-amplitude waves of 13 to 30 Hz. Beta activity reflects the fact that many different neural circuits in the brain are actively processing information. This activity occurs when a person is alert and attentive to events in the environment or is thinking actively. (See **FIGURE 9·12.**)

By using Figure 9.12 as a guide, let's look at a typical night's sleep of a female college student recorded in the laboratory. (Of course, we would obtain similar results from a male, with one exception, which is noted later.) The experimenter attaches the electrodes, turns the lights off, and closes the door. The participant becomes drowsy and soon enters stage 1 sleep, marked by the presence of some **theta activity** (3.5–7.5 Hz). About 10 minutes later, she enters stage 2 sleep. The EEG during this stage is generally irregular but contains periods of theta activity and *K complexes*—sudden sharp,

Awake

Alpha activity   Beta activity

Stage 1 sleep

Theta activity

Stage 2 sleep

Seconds

0 1 2 3 4 5

Stage 3 sleep

Delta activity

Stage 4 sleep

Delta activity

REM sleep

Theta activity   Beta activity

[FIGURE 9·12] An EEG recording of the stages of sleep.

(Adapted from Horne, J. A. (1989). *Why We Sleep: The Functions of Sleep in Humans and Other Mammals.* Oxford, England: Oxford University Press, 1989. Copyright © 1988 Oxford University Press. Reprinted by permission of Oxford University Press.)

high-amplitude waveforms. It is not unusual for persons awakened from stage 1 or stage 2 sleep to deny being asleep.

About 15 minutes later, the participant enters stage 3 sleep, signaled by the occurrence of high-amplitude **delta activity** (slower than 3.5 Hz). The distinction between stage 3 and stage 4 is not clear-cut; stage 4 simply contains a greater percentage of delta activity. The sleep of stages 3 and 4 is called **slow-wave sleep.**

About 90 minutes after the beginning of sleep (and about 45 minutes after the onset of stage 4 sleep), we notice an abrupt change in a number of physiological measures recorded from the participant. The EEG suddenly becomes mostly desynchronized, with a sprinkling of theta waves, very similar to the record obtained during stage 1 sleep. We also note that her eyes are rapidly darting back and forth beneath her closed eyelids. We also see that the EMG becomes silent; a profound loss of muscle tonus is present. Physiological studies have shown that, aside from occasional twitching of the hands and feet, a person actually becomes paralyzed during REM sleep. This peculiar stage of sleep is very different from the quiet sleep we saw earlier. It is usually referred to as **REM sleep** (for the rapid eye movements that characterize it).

If we arouse the participant during REM sleep and ask her what was going on, she will almost always report that she had been dreaming. The dreams of REM sleep tend to be narrative in form; a story-like progression of events is noted. If we wake her during slow-wave sleep and ask, "Were you dreaming?" she will most likely say, "No," but she might report the presence of a thought, an image, or some emotion.

During the rest of the night, the participant's sleep alternates between periods of REM and non-REM sleep. Each cycle is approximately 90 minutes long, containing a 20- to 30-minute bout of REM sleep. Thus, an 8-hour sleep will contain four or five periods of REM sleep. FIGURE 9•13 shows a graph of a typical night's sleep. The vertical axis indicates the EEG activity that is being recorded; thus REM sleep and stage 1 sleep are placed on the same line because similar patterns of EEG activity occur at these times. Note that most slow-wave sleep (stages 3 and 4) occurs during the first half of night.

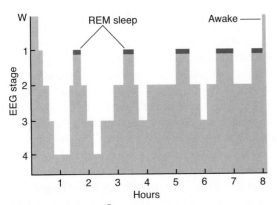

[**FIGURE 9•13**] Typical progression of stages during a night's sleep. The dark blue shading indicates REM sleep.

(From Hartmann, E. (1967). *The Biology of Dreaming*, 1967. Courtesy of Charles C. Thomas, Publisher, Ltd., Springfield, Illinois.)

[**TABLE 9•1**] Principal Characteristics of REM Sleep and Slow-Wave Sleep

REM Sleep	Slow-wave Sleep
Rapid EEG waves	Slow EEG waves
Muscular paralysis	Lack of muscular paralysis
Rapid eye movements	Slow or absent eye movements
Penile erection or vaginal secretion	Lack of genital activity
Story and narrative dreams	Static, rarely narrative dreams; night terrors; sleepwalking

Subsequent bouts of non-REM sleep contain more and more stage 2 sleep, and bouts of REM sleep (indicated by the horizontal bars) become more prolonged. (See Figure 9.13.)

As we saw, during REM sleep, we become paralyzed; most of our spinal and cranial motor neurons are strongly inhibited. (Obviously, the ones that control respiration and eye movements are spared.) At the same time, the brain is very active. Cerebral blood flow and oxygen consumption are accelerated. In addition, during most periods of REM sleep, a male's penis will become at least partially erect, and a female's vaginal secretions will increase. However, these genital changes are reflexive and usually *not* associated with sexual arousal or dreams of a sexual nature. TABLE 9•1 lists the principal characteristics of REM sleep and the deeper stages of slow-wave sleep.

Functions of Sleep

Sleep is one of the few universal behaviors. All mammals, all birds, and some cold-blooded vertebrates spend part of each day sleeping. Sleep is seen even in species that would seem to be better off without it. For example, the Indus dolphin (*Platanista indi*) lives in the muddy waters of the Indus estuary in Pakistan (Pilleri, 1979). Over the ages, it has become blind, presumably because vision is not useful in the animal's environment. (It has an excellent sonar system, which it uses to navigate and find prey.) The Indus dolphin never stops swimming; doing so would result in injury, because of the dangerous currents and the vast quantities of debris carried by the river during the monsoon season. However, despite the dangers caused by sleeping, sleep has not disappeared. Pilleri (1979) captured two Indus dolphins and studied their habits. He found that they slept a total of seven hours a day, in very brief naps of 4 to 60 seconds each. If sleep did not perform an important function, we might expect that it, like vision, would have been eliminated in this species through the process of natural selection.

delta activity   Rhythmical electroencephalogram activity with a frequency of less than 3.5 Hz, indicating deep (slow-wave) sleep.

slow-wave sleep   Sleep other than REM sleep, characterized by regular, slow waves on the electroencephalogram.

rapid-eye-movement (REM) sleep   A stage of sleep during which dreaming, rapid eye movements, and muscular paralysis occur and the EEG shows beta activity.

Sleep as Repair   The universal nature of sleep suggests that it does something important. But just what? The simplest explanation for sleep is that it serves to repair the wear and tear on our bodies caused by moving and exercising. Perhaps our bodies just get worn out by performing waking activities for 16 hours or so.

It should be easy to discover why we sleep by seeing what happens to a person who goes without sleep. However, sleep-deprivation studies with human subjects have provided little evidence that sleep is needed to keep the body functioning normally. Horne (1978) reviewed more than 50 experiments in which people had been deprived of sleep. He reported that most of them found that sleep deprivation did not interfere with people's ability to perform physical exercise. Thus, the primary role of sleep does not seem to be rest and recuperation of the body. However, people's cognitive abilities are affected, even though they may remain unaware of their deprivation-induced deficits (Van Dongen et al., 2003); some people reported perceptual distortions or even hallucinations and had trouble concentrating on mental tasks. Perhaps sleep provides the opportunity for the *brain* to rest.

During stage 4 sleep, the metabolic activity of the brain decreases to about 75 percent of the waking level (Sakai et al., 1979), which suggests that stage 4 sleep gives the brain a chance to rest. If people are awakened during slow-wave sleep, they act groggy and confused—as if their cerebral cortex has been shut down and has not yet resumed its functioning. These observations suggest that during stage 4 sleep, the brain is, indeed, resting.

An ingenious study by Horne and Minard (1985) found that mental exercise seems to increase the demand for slow-wave sleep. The investigators asked volunteers to show up for an experiment in which they were supposed to take tests designed to assess reading skills. When the people turned up, they were told that the plans had been changed. They were invited for a day out, at the expense of the researchers. (Not surprisingly, they willingly accepted.) They spent the day visiting an art exhibition, a shopping center, a museum, an amusement park, a zoo, and an interesting mansion. After a scenic drive through the countryside, they watched a movie at a local theater. They were driven from place to place and certainly did not become overheated by exercise. After the movie, they returned to the sleep laboratory. They said they were tired, and they readily fell asleep. Their sleep duration was normal, and they awoke feeling refreshed. However, their slow-wave sleep—particularly stage 4 sleep—was increased.

de Bruin, Beersma, and Daan (2002), working in the Netherlands, reported a different outcome when they assigned male participants to two groups. One engaged in what the researchers termed "light mental activity" and watched videos while relaxing for 8 hours. The other group performed complex tasks using a computer, tasks that required their sustained attention, memory, and problem-solving skills for the same length of time. Participants in the latter group could not be roused as readily shortly after falling asleep, but there were no other differences between the groups. de Bruin et al. concluded that slow-wave sleep does not increase with a more demanding workload prior to sleep.

Sleep and Learning   Research with both humans and laboratory animals indicates that sleep does more than allow the brain to rest: It also aids in the consolidation of long-term memories (Marshall and Born, 2007; Rasch & Born, 2008). Slow-wave sleep and REM sleep play different roles in memory consolidation.

As we saw in Chapter 8, two major categories of long-term memory exist: declarative memory (also called explicit memory) and nondeclarative memory (also called implicit memory). Declarative memories include those that people can talk about, such as memories of past episodes in their lives. They also include memories of the relations between stimuli or events, such as the spatial relations between landmarks that permit us to navigate around our environment. Nondeclarative memories include those gained through experience and practice that do not necessarily involve an attempt to "memorize" information, such as learning to drive a car, throw and catch a ball, or recognize a person's face. Research has found that slow-wave sleep and REM sleep play different roles in the consolidation of declarative and nondeclarative memories.

Before we tell you about the results of this research, let's compare the consciousness of a person engaged in each of these stages of sleep. During REM sleep, people normally have a high level of consciousness. If we awaken people during REM sleep, they will be alert and clear-headed and will almost always be able to describe the details of a dream that they were having. However, if we awaken people during slow-wave sleep, they will be groggy and confused, and will usually tell us that nothing was happening. So which stages of sleep do you think aid in the consolidation of declarative and nondeclarative memories?

We would have guessed that REM would be associated with declarative memories, and slow-wave sleep, with nondeclarative memories. However, just the opposite is true. Let's look at evidence from two studies that looked at the effects of a nap on memory consolidation. Mednick, Nakayama, and Stickgold (2003) asked participants to learn a nondeclarative visual discrimination task at 9:00 A.M. The participants' ability to perform the task was tested ten hours later, at 7:00 P.M. Some, but not all, of the participants took a 90-minute nap during the day between training and testing. The investigators recorded the EEGs of the sleeping participants to determine which of them engaged in REM sleep and which of them did not. (Obviously, all of them engaged in slow-wave sleep, because this stage of sleep always comes first in normal people.) The investigators found that the performance of participants who did not take a nap was worse when they were tested at 7:00 P.M. than it had been at the end of training. The participants who engaged only in slow-wave sleep did about the same during testing as they had done at the end of training. However, the participants who engaged in REM sleep performed significantly better. In other words, REM sleep, but not slow-wave sleep, facilitated the consolidation of a nondeclarative memory. (See FIGURE 9·14.)

[**FIGURE 9·14**] Role of REM sleep in learning a nondeclarative visual discrimination task. Only after a 90-min nap that included both slow-wave sleep and REM sleep did the subjects' performance improve.

(Adapted from Mednick, S., Nakayama, K., and Stickgold, R. *Nature Neuroscience*, 2003, *6*, 697–698.)

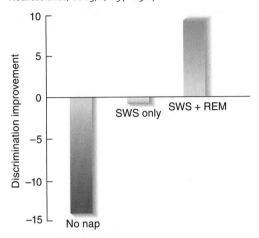

In the second study, Tucker et al. (2006) trained participants on two tasks: a declarative task (learning a list of paired words) and a nondeclarative task (learning to trace a pencil-and-paper design while looking at the paper in a mirror). Afterward, some participants were permitted to take a nap lasting for about one hour. Their EEGs were recorded, and they were awakened before they could engage in REM sleep. The participants' performance on the two tasks was then tested six hours after the original training. The investigators found that a nap consisting of slow-wave sleep increased the participants' performance on the declarative task but had no effect on performance of the nondeclarative task. (See FIGURE 9·15.) So these two experiments (and others we have not described) indicate that REM sleep facilitates consolidation of

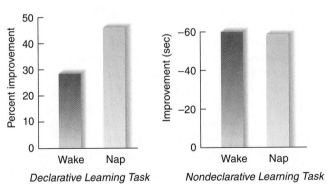

Declarative Learning Task   *Nondeclarative Learning Task*

[**FIGURE 9·15**] Role of slow-wave sleep in learning a declarative learning task (list of paired words) and a nondeclarative learning task (mirror tracing). After a nap that included just slow-wave sleep, only subjects who learned the declarative learning task showed improved performance, compared with subjects who stayed awake.

(Adapted from Tucker, M. A., Hirota, Y., Wamsley, E. J., Lau, H., Chaklader, A., and Fishbein, W. *Neurobiology of Learning and Memory*, 2006, *86*, 241–247.)

nondeclarative memories, and slow-wave sleep facilitates consolidation of declarative memories.

One last experiment on this topic: In a Belgian research lab, Peigneux et al. (2004) asked participants to learn their way around a computerized virtual-reality town. This task is very similar to what people do when they learn their way around a real town. They must learn the relative locations of landmarks and streets that connect them so that they can find particular locations when the experimenter "placed" them at various starting points. As we saw in Chapter 8, the hippocampus plays an essential role in learning of this kind. Peigneux and his colleagues used functional brain imaging to measure regional brain activity and found that the same regions of the hippocampus were activated during route learning and during slow-wave sleep the following night. These patterns were *not* seen during REM sleep. Thus, although people awakened during slow-wave sleep seldom report that they had been dreaming, the sleeping brain appears to rehearse information that was acquired during the previous day. (Many studies with laboratory animals that directly recorded the activity of individual neurons in the animals' brains have obtained the same results.)

Dreaming

One of the most fascinating aspects of sleep is the fact that we enter a fantasy world several times each night during which we perceive imaginary events and perform imaginary behaviors. Again, why do we do so?

Consciousness during Sleep
As noted earlier, a person who is awakened during REM sleep and asked whether anything is happening will almost always report a dream. The typical REM-sleep dream resembles a play or movie—it has a narrative form. Conversely, reports of narrative, story-like dreams are rare among people awakened from slow-wave sleep. In general, cognitive activity during slow-wave sleep appears to be more static. It involves situations rather than narratives, and generally the situations are unpleasant. For example, a person awakened from slow-wave sleep might report a sensation of being crushed or suffocated. It is during slow-wave sleep that young children will experience **night terrors** (a vague but anguished emotion with no clear memory of its cause) and **sleepwalking.**

Almost everyone has four or five bouts of REM sleep each night, with accompanying dreams. Yet if the dreamer does not happen to awaken while the dream is in progress, it is lost. People who claimed not to have had a dream for many years have slept in a sleep laboratory and found that, in fact, they did dream. They were able to remember their dreams when the researcher awakened them during REM sleep. Solms (2000) has argued that the connectedness of REM sleep and dreaming is only apparent. Though they coincide, they are distinct processes, controlled by different mechanisms.

---

night terrors   The experience of anguish without a clear memory of its cause; occurs during slow-wave sleep, usually in childhood.

sleepwalking   The experience of walking during sleep without a clear memory of doing so; occurs during slow-wave sleep, usually in childhood.

Functions of Dreams Two major research approaches exist to the study of dreaming: psychological analysis of the contents of dreams, and cognitive neuroscientific research on the nature and functions of REM sleep. The first approach is closely associated with Sigmund Freud's proposal that dreams symbolize unfulfilled desires of which we are unaware. The second approach considers dreams to be the product of the brain's information processing

Dreaming as Wish Fulfillment Beginning in ancient times, dreams were regarded as meaningful. For example, they were used to prophesy the future, to decide whether to go to war, and to determine the guilt or innocence of a person accused of a crime. At the beginning of the twentieth century, Sigmund Freud (1900) proposed what was to become a very influential theory of dreaming. For Freud, dreams arise out of inner conflicts between unconscious desires (primarily sexual ones) and cultural prohibitions against acting on these desires. Although all dreams represent unfulfilled wishes, their contents are disguised and expressed symbolically—the result of what Freud referred to as "dreamwork." The **latent content** of the dream (*latent* is from the Latin word for "hidden") is transformed into the **manifest content** (the actual storyline or narrative) of the dream. Taken at face value, the manifest content may seem incidental, but a knowledgeable psychoanalyst can interpret the unconscious desires that are disguised as symbols in the manifest content of the dream. For example, climbing a set of stairs or shooting a gun might symbolize the desire for sexual intercourse. One problem with Freud's theory is that it is not falsifiable, that is, disprovable. Even if the theory is wrong, a psychoanalyst can always provide a plausible interpretation of a dream that reveals hidden conflicts disguised in obscure symbols.

Dreaming as Story Construction Hobson and Pace-Schott (2002) advanced a model of brain activity during sleep that explains dreaming without relying on unconscious conflicts or wish fulfillment. As we will see later, research with laboratory animals has shown that REM sleep occurs when a circuit of acetylcholine-secreting neurons in the area of the brain stem known as the pons (see Chapter 4) becomes active. This activation in turn stimulates rapid eye movements, activation of the cerebral cortex, and muscular paralysis—all components of REM sleep. (Yes, other species exhibit REM sleep, and they appear to dream, too, which may support the claim of some form of consciousness in those species.) The activation of the visual system

produces both eye movements and images. Several experiments have found that the particular eye movements a person makes during a dream correspond, at least roughly, to the content of a dream. That is, the eye movements are those that a person would be likely to make if the imaginary events were really occurring (Dement, 1974; Dement and Vaughan, 2000). The images evoked by cortical activation often incorporate episodic memories of recent events or other contents of recent thinking. Presumably, the circuits responsible for these memories are more readily activated because of their recency.

Hobson and Pace-Schott (2002) suggest that both slow-wave sleep and REM sleep work together. Memories that are consolidated during slow-wave sleep are reactivated during REM sleep and newly consolidated with other memories. The activation of these brain mechanisms produces fragmentary images that our brains try to render meaningful by piecing them together in at least roughly plausible narratives. This theory is known as the **activation–synthesis theory,** because it proposes that activation of the cortex by the pons causes the brain to create a narrative experience quite apart from the sensory activation that occurs during waking. When we later communicate these experiences to ourselves or to others, we call them dreams. Although this view of dreaming does not attach necessary significance to the content of dreams, some theorists argue that the synthesis provided by the cortex serves an adaptive function, such as the simulation of threatening events (Revonsuo, 2000).

Dreaming as Learning As we saw earlier, sustained sleep deprivation impairs people's ability to perform tasks that require alertness and vigilance, but what happens when only REM sleep is disrupted? Research participants who are sleeping in a laboratory can be selectively deprived of REM sleep. A researcher awakens them whenever the **polygraph** record indicates they have entered REM sleep. The researcher must also awaken control participants just as often at random intervals to identify any effects produced by simply being awakened several times during the night.

If someone is deprived of REM sleep on several consecutive nights and is then allowed to sleep without interruption, the onset of REM sleep becomes more frequent during the uninterrupted sleep. It is as if there is an increased need for REM sleep. The effect is referred to as *REM rebound*: The person engages in more bouts of REM sleep than normal during the next night or two, as if catching up on what was missed.

Several investigators have suggested that REM sleep may play a role in learning, a view consistent with the activation-synthesis theory. Smith and Lapp (1991) observed increased REM sleep in college students during examination periods, which may be a time of increased learning. Walker (2005) focused on procedural (as opposed to semantic) learning and distinguished between acquisition and consolidation of learning. Within the latter, he further distinguished two stages: stabilization and enhancement. Although acquisition and stabilization occur when one is

---

latent content   The hidden message of a dream produced by the unconscious.

manifest content   The apparent storyline of a dream.

activation-synthesis theory   A theory of dreaming that explains dreams as resulting from the incidental synthesis of cortical activity produced by mechanisms in the pons.

polygraph   An instrument that records changes in physiological processes such as brain activity, heart rate, and breathing.

awake, enhancement seems to require sleep. Research participants who had acquired stable performance in skilled motor reaching and finger-tapping tasks nonetheless showed improvement after sleep.

Many studies with laboratory animals have shown that chronic deprivation of REM sleep impairs their ability to learn a complex task, although they still manage to learn it. Thus, REM sleep may be essential for learning. If it does play a role in human learning, the effect appears to be subtle—at least in adults (Maquet, 2001). In fact, neurologists (see, for example, Lavie et al., 1984; Gironell et al., 1995) have described patients who showed little or no REM sleep after sustaining damage to the brain stem, but few, if any, serious side effects. After brain injury, one patient completed high school, attended law school, and entered law practice.

Disorders of Sleep

Because we spend about one third of our lives sleeping, sleep disorders can have a significant impact on our quality of life. They can also affect the way we feel while we are awake.

Insomnia Insomnia is reported to affect approximately 25 percent of the population occasionally and 9 percent regularly (Ancoli-Israel and Roth, 1999). But we need to define *insomnia* carefully. The amount of sleep individuals require varies. A short sleeper may feel fine with 5 hours of sleep; a long sleeper may still feel unrefreshed after 10 hours of sleep. Insomnia must be defined in relation to a person's particular sleep needs.

For many years, the goal of sleep medications was to help people fall asleep. However, if a medication puts people to sleep right away but produces grogginess and difficulty concentrating the next day, it has limited value. Many drugs traditionally used to treat insomnia had just this effect. Fortunately, researchers now recognize that the evaluation of a new sleep medication must include the quality of wakefulness the following day, and "hangover-free" drugs are being developed and marketed (Hajak et al., 1995).

Narcolepsy Narcolepsy (*narke* means "numbness," and *lepsis* means "seizure") is a neurological disorder characterized by sleep (or some of its components) at inappropriate times. The primary symptom of narcolepsy is the sleep attack—an overwhelming urge to sleep that can happen at any time but occurs most often under monotonous, boring conditions. Sleep generally lasts for 2 to 5 minutes, and the person usually wakes up feeling refreshed.

The most striking symptom of narcolepsy is **cataplexy** (from *kata*, "down," and *plexis*, "stroke"). During a cataplectic attack, a person will suddenly wilt and fall, then lie there, *fully conscious*, for a few seconds to several minutes. What apparently happens is that one of the components of REM sleep—muscular paralysis—occurs at an inappropriate time.

Cataplexy is usually precipitated by strong emotional reactions or by sudden physical effort. Laughter, anger, or an effort to catch a suddenly thrown object can trigger a cataplectic attack. Common triggers include attempting to discipline one's children and making love (an awkward time to become paralyzed!). Wise (2004) notes that patients with narcolepsy often try to avoid thoughts and situations that are likely to evoke strong emotions.

Lin et al. (1999) discovered that a mutation of a specific gene causes narcolepsy in laboratory animals. The product of this gene is a receptor for a recently discovered peptide neurotransmitter called **hypocretin,** so called because the lateral *hypo*thalamus contains the cell bodies of the neurons that *secrete* this peptide. Hypocretin helps stabilize sleep/waking cycles and suppresses the inappropriate onset of components of REM sleep. In humans, narcolepsy appears to be caused by a hereditary autoimmune disorder (Nishino et al., 2000). Most humans who develop narcolepsy are born with hypocretin-secreting neurons, but during adolescence, the immune system attacks these neurons, and the symptoms of narcolepsy begin.

The symptoms can be treated with stimulant drugs. In the past, patients have been treated with drugs such as amphetamine or methylphenidate (also known as Ritalin), but most people are treated with modafinil, a drug that has a low potential for abuse (Saper, Scammell, and Lu, 2006).

REM Sleep Behavior Disorder Schenck et al. (1986) reported the existence of an intriguing disorder: REM sleep behavior disorder. As you now know, REM sleep is accompanied by paralysis. Although the neural circuits of the brain that control body movements are extremely active during REM sleep (McCarley and Hobson, 1979), people remain immobile.

That people are paralyzed during REM sleep suggests the possibility that, but for the paralysis, they would act out their dreams. Indeed, they would. The behavior of people who exhibit REM sleep behavior disorder corresponds with the contents of their dreams. Consider the following case:

[CASE STUDY] I was a halfback playing football, and after the quarterback received the ball from the center, he lateraled it sideways to me and I'm supposed to go around end and cut back over tackle and—this is very vivid—as I cut back over tackle, there is this big 280-pound tackle waiting, so I, according to football rules, was to give him my shoulder and bounce him out of the way . . . when I came to I was standing in front of our dresser and I had [gotten up out of bed and run and] knocked lamps, mirrors and everything off the dresser, hit my head against the wall and my knee against the dresser. (Schenck et al., 1986, p. 294)

---

insomnia A general category of sleep disorder related to difficulty in falling asleep and remaining asleep.

narcolepsy A sleep disorder characterized by sleep attack—irresistibly falling asleep at inappropriate times.

cataplexy A symptom of narcolepsy; although awake, the individual is temporarily paralyzed.

hypocretin A neurotransmitter secreted by cells in the hypothalamus; helps regulate sleep-wake cycles.

Like narcolepsy, REM sleep behavior disorder appears to be a neurodegenerative disorder (Schenck et al., 1993). It is often associated with better-known neurodegenerative disorders such as Parkinson's disease (Boeve et al., 2007). The symptoms of REM sleep behavior disorder are the opposite of those of cataplexy. Rather than exhibiting paralysis outside REM sleep, patients with REM sleep behavior disorder *fail* to exhibit paralysis *during* REM sleep. As you might expect, the drugs used to treat the symptoms of cataplexy will heighten the symptoms of REM sleep behavior disorder. Instead, its symptoms are usually treated with clonazepam, a tranquilizer (Schenck and Mahowald, 2002).

Problems Associated with Slow-Wave Sleep Some maladaptive behaviors occur during slow-wave sleep, especially during its deepest phase, stage 4. These behaviors include bedwetting (*nocturnal enuresis*) and sleepwalking (*somnambulism*). Both behaviors occur most frequently in children. Often bedwetting can be cured by training methods, such as an electronic circuit ring device that rings a bell when the first few drops of urine are detected in the bed sheet. Sleepwalking usually cures itself as the child gets older. This phenomena does not occur during REM sleep; a sleepwalking person is *not* acting out a dream.

Schenck et al. (1991) reported nineteen cases of people with histories of eating during the night while they were asleep, a condition the authors labeled **sleep-related eating disorder.** Almost half of the patients had become overweight from night eating. Once patients realize that they are eating in their sleep, they often use such stratagems as keeping their food under lock and key or setting alarms that will awaken them when they try to open their refrigerator. Morgenthaler and Silber (2002) reported that sleep-related eating disorder may occur together with *restless legs syndrome,* which is marked by frequent, disruptive involuntary leg movements (Hening et al., 1999) and *obstructive sleep apnea,* that is, the cessation of breathing during sleep due to constriction of the airway.

Several sleep disorders, including *delayed sleep phase syndrome* (*DSPS*), are related to malfunctions of the circadian rhythm (see below; Dagan, 2001). Individuals with DSPS tend to fall asleep very late at night and to have real difficulty rising the next morning. They may well sleep until noon. However, when allowed to sleep without externally imposed restrictions, the length of sleep was normal.

Brain Mechanisms of Sleep

If sleep is a behavior, then some parts of the brain must be responsible for its occurrence. Researchers have discovered

---

sleep-related eating disorder Occurs during sleepwalking as the individual seeks out food and consumes it, usually with no memory of having done so.

circadian rhythm A daily rhythmical change in behaviors or physiological processes.

suprachiasmatic nuclei An area of the hypothalamus that provides a biological clock for circadian rhythms.

Late-term fetuses and newborn infants spend much time in REM sleep, which has led some investigators to hypothesize that this activity plays a role in brain development.

several brain regions that have special roles in sleep and biological rhythms.

The Circadian Clock Let us first consider biological rhythms. Some rhythms are controlled by an internal "clock" located in the brain. This clock controls **circadian rhythms**—rhythms that oscillate once a day (*circa,* "about"; *dies,* "day").

The clock that controls circadian rhythms is located in a small pair of structures located at the bottom of the hypothalamus: the **suprachiasmatic nuclei (SCN).** The activity of neurons in the SCN oscillates once each day; the neurons are active during the day and inactive at night. Connections between the SCN and other brain regions permit the SCN to control daily cycles of sleep and wakefulness, hormone secretion, body temperature, and many other physiological functions. If people are placed in a windowless room with constant lighting, they will continue to show circadian rhythms, controlled by the oscillations of their SCN. However, because this biological clock is not very accurate (its cycle length is 25 hours), people's circadian rhythms will eventually get out of synchrony with the day/night cycles outside the building. But within a few days after leaving the building, their rhythms will be resynchronized with those of the sun. This resynchronization involves a direct connection between the eyes and the SCN. Each morning, when we see the light of the sun (or turn on the room lights), our biological clock resets and begins ticking off the next day.

Neural Control of Sleep When we are awake and alert, most of the neurons in our brain—especially those of the forebrain—are active, permitting us to pay attention to and process sensory information, to think about what we are perceiving, and to engage in a variety of behaviors during the day. The level of brain activity is largely controlled by several small clusters of neurons in the midbrain and hindbrain whose axons travel forward, branch repeatedly, and form synaptic connections with the billions of neurons in the forebrain. The terminal buttons of these neurons release four neurotransmitters, which were described in Chapter 4: norepinephrine (NE), serotonin (5-HT), acetylcholine (ACh), and dopamine (DA). Another group of neurons, located in the posterior hypothalamus, releases a neurotransmitter called histamine. (Yes, antihistamines can make us drowsy by inhibiting the effects of these neurons. However, today's antihistamines do not cross the blood–brain barrier, so they do not cause drowsiness.) These neurotransmitters activate forebrain neurons in different ways, controlling different aspects of alertness and behavioral arousal. For simplicity, we collectively refer to the neurons that release these neurotransmitters as arousal neurons.

For many years, researchers have known that the activity of our arousal neurons determines whether we are awake or asleep: A high level of activity of these neurons keeps us awake, and a low level puts us to sleep. The question has been: What causes the activity of the arousal neurons to decrease, thus putting us to sleep? An answer to this question was suggested in the early twentieth century by a Viennese neurologist, Constantin von Economo, who observed that patients afflicted by a new type of encephalitis that was sweeping through Europe and North America showed the severe disturbance of sleep and waking (Triarhou, 2006). Most patients slept excessively, waking only to eat and drink. According to von Economo, these patients had brain damage at the junction of the brain stem and forebrain, that is, at a location where the axons of the arousal neurons entering the forebrain would be destroyed. Some patients, however, showed just the opposite symptoms: They slept only a few hours each day. Although they were tired, they had difficulty falling asleep and usually awakened shortly thereafter. Von Economo reported that patients who displayed insomnia had damage to the region of the anterior hypothalamus. We now know that this region, usually referred to as the **preoptic area,** is the one most involved in the control of sleep. The preoptic area contains neurons whose axons form inhibitory synaptic connections with the brain's arousal neurons. When our preoptic neurons (let's call them *sleep neurons*) become active, they suppress the activity of our arousal neurons, and we fall asleep (Saper, Scammell, & Lu, 2005).

What makes us become sleepy and eventually puts us to sleep? (In other words, what activates neurons in the preoptic area?) Two factors influence the preoptic sleep neurons. The first is time of day. As we saw earlier, sleep is affected by our circadian rhythms, which are controlled by the SCN. Unless we are on an unusual schedule (or work late into the night or engage in an enjoyable activity), we get sleepy sometime after dark, go to bed, and fall asleep. The SCN is connected to the preoptic sleep neurons and thus affects our sleep/waking cycles.

The second factor reflects the reason we sleep: to provide an opportunity for the brain to rest (Basheer et al., 2004). One of the products of brain metabolism is a chemical called **adenosine.** The more active cells in our brain are, the more adenosine they produce, and some of this adenosine leaks out into the fluid that surrounds them. One of the effects of adenosine in the brain is to increase the activity of the preoptic sleep neurons. So if we have a long, busy day that keeps our neurons active, the accumulation of adenosine activates the preoptic area, which suppresses the activity of the arousal neurons, and we become sleepy. The busier the day or the longer we stay awake, the more adenosine accumulates, and the sleepier we get. Once we fall asleep, the metabolic rate of our brain decreases, and the level of adenosine decreases. If we get a good night's sleep, adenosine levels are low by the time our SCN signals that it is time to wake. The activity of the preoptic sleep neurons decreases, the activity of the arousal neurons increases, and we wake up. (See FIGURE 9•16.)

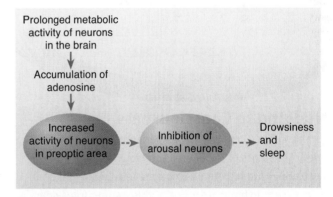

[**FIGURE 9•16**] The role of adenosine in sleep. Extended neural activity causes adenosine accumulation, which activates neurons in the preoptic areas of the anterior hypothalamus. In turn, this inhibits the arousal neurons in the midbrain and hindbrain, inducing sleep.

---

preoptic area An area of the hypothalamus that contains neurons that inhibit arousal neurons to produce sleep.

adenosine A product of brain metabolism; activates neurons in the preoptic area, inducing sleep.

QUESTIONS TO CONSIDER

1. Some people report they are "in control" of some of their dreams—that they feel as if they decide what comes next and are not simply swept along passively. Have you ever had this experience or that of a "lucid dream," in which you were aware of the fact that you were dreaming? What characteristics of a person might allow her or him to take control of dreams?

2. What does dreaming accomplish? Some researchers believe that the subject matter of a dream has little if any significance—it is the REM sleep itself that is vital. Others believe that the subject matter has consequence. Some researchers believe that if we remember a dream, the dream failed to accomplish all of its functions. Others say that remembering is useful, because it can give us some insights into our problems. What is your position on these two controversies?

3. Until recently (that is, in terms of the evolution of our species), our ancestors tended to go to sleep when the sun set and to wake up when it rose. Once our ancestors learned how to control fire, they undoubtedly stayed up somewhat later, sitting in front of a fire. But it was only with the development of cheap, effective lighting that many members of our species adopted the habit of staying up late and waking several hours after sunrise. Considering that the neural mechanisms of sleep evolved long ago, how might changes in our daily rhythms affect our physical and intellectual abilities?

Epilogue

Nudging to Consciousness

For most of us, there is a daily experience of emerging from one of the stages of the altered consciousness known as sleep and resuming our waking consciousness. Cycles of activity in certain brain areas assure this resumption. Generally it is accomplished in a way that gives us little pause: We are the same person—the same self—that fell asleep several hours earlier. Moreover, the intervening time seems to have passed in the blink of an eye, despite the evidence of the clock and the grogginess and occasional stiffness that may attend awaking. To have it otherwise is the stuff of science fiction, from Washington Irving's tale of Rip Van Winkle to Franz Kafka's Gregor Samsa in "The Metamorphosis."

The Prologue introduced cases of adult patients who spent long years in coma (Jan Grzebski) or in a persistent vegetative state (Terri Shiavo). You will recall that Michael Shiavo arranged for his wife to receive direct electrical stimulation of the thalamus in hopes of her recovery. The procedure was unsuccessful. However, a recent report of a similar procedure with a patient in a minimally conscious state (MCS) was encouraging (Schiff et al., 2007). In this case, the patient had been in MCS for six years after traumatic brain injury. The design of the experiment alternated the periods when deep-brain stimulation was applied with those when it was absent. Recovery of function accompanied stimulation, including his near-immediate resumption of fine motor movements, including speech. But this was more than waking from sleep, as he was unable to sustain his new consciousness when the stimulation was discontinued. Although the neural circuits that brought about his awakening may have been different from those described in the chapter for sleep and waking, his resumption of at least partial function can be considered analogous to the daily experience of waking and resuming one's self. We can only wonder about the extent to which the newly awakened patient recognized his self.

The nudging to altered consciousness reported in the case study was achieved by deliberately altering the patterns of electrical activity in the interior of the patient's brain. By analogy, we might ask about the alterations of brain activity that nudged the human species toward its own form of consciousness at some point during the evolutionary past. What changes instrumented by natural selection "awakened" human consciousness in the first place and ultimately led to humans having a sense of self?

Attempts to answer these questions have surged in recent years and demonstrate the growing nexus between psychology, neuroscience, computer science, and philosophy. Jaynes's (1976) masterwork on the origins of human consciousness posits an ancestral era not so long ago when the voices inside a person's head were not recognizably one's own but those of others whom one held in high esteem. According to Jaynes, a widespread cataclysm brought the necessary historical conditions for the discrimination of one's own voice among the others vying for one's private attention, and human consciousness, as we know it, emerged. Jaynes articulated his theory with rich references to human history as well as to brain structures and clinical disorders.

More recently, Damasio (1994, 1999) has introduced a neurologically inspired theory of human emotion that depends heavily on brain mechanisms for mapping the moment-to-moment state of the body and monitoring changes in that state that are induced by the arrival of sensory messages. Damasio distinguishes between what he terms core consciousness and extended consciousness and illustrates the emergence of the latter from the former with neurological case studies.

Greenfield (2000) and Koch (2004) represent a different approach to the analysis of consciousness that emphasizes neural activity distributed across multiple brain areas rather than relying on localized brain areas as the substrate of consciousness. The principal difference in their views is in what the neurons responsible for consciousness are doing. Greenfield requires the emergence of synchronous firing (that is, large numbers of neurons firing in temporal harmony). For Koch, all that is required is that the stream of consciousness be accompanied by a corresponding cascade of demonstrably different (but not synchronous) patterns of neural activity.

Perhaps it is appropriate to conclude this chapter with a humble expression of thanks—for our consciousness—and a humble acknowledgement that we are still unraveling the mystery of its origin and functions. The autobiographical words of Eiseley (1975), who, desperately ill with the flu, had just taken his last final examination as a college student, are apt:

> On that afternoon without knowing the results of my efforts, I slowly climbed the second-floor steps of my rooming house. As I fumbled for the key to my door I suddenly heard, very far away, as though in another part of the house, the small faint thump of something hitting the floor. That was the last I knew until I awoke upon the landing. Everything had grown dark and I crawled frantically about on my knees, dimly realizing that I had lost all sense of direction. Instinctively, I seemed to know that there was a stairway in back of me down which I might tumble. My location slowly came back through the sense of touch. I threw open the door and tumbled in upon my bed.
>
> . . . what if I had not recovered consciousness upon that upstairs landing? When one faints there is normally a little forthcoming awareness, a final chance to get down before one falls. I had dropped as though a bullet felled me. The thud of my head hitting the floor had sounded so remote I never had time to relate it to myself. I simply ceased to be. There was a body lying in the dusk on the stairs, but whatever motivated that body, consciously dwelt upon its problems, looked after its needs, had vanished.
>
> . . . I was gone so far into the dark that no dream whispered to me, no sound again troubled my ear. Consciously I did not exist. But something was still alert within me . . . Something, some toiling cellular entity of which I was unaware was searching me out, reconstructing me, setting failing ganglions to sputtering, reactivating all manner of wildly spinning compasses. . . . In all my remaining years I have been grateful to those unseen toilers, who, when my will had failed, had recreated what individually they neither knew nor cared about. (pp. 74–78)

CHAPTER SUMMARY

Consciousness as a Language-Dependent Phenomenon

Consciousness, as it is defined here, is related to the activity of language and motor mechanisms of the brain. The private use of language (thinking to oneself) and private nonverbal processes may be considered conscious if we can describe them to ourselves or others. In the same way, our consciousness of external events is demonstrated by our ability to verbalize about our perceptions of them. These perceptions may be different from the actions we take to interact with the external events. Even our awareness of "voluntary" movements may be a by-product of other brain activities that initiate behavior and bind perceived events in ways that produce such awareness. However, it would be misleading to suppose that language necessarily predicates consciousness. Forms of consciousness may well have existed before the emergence of language.

Selective Attention

As we saw in the first section of this chapter, consciousness can be analyzed as a social phenomenon derived through evolution of the brain mechanisms responsible for our ability to communicate with one another (and, in addition, with ourselves). However, because verbal mechanisms can contain only a limited amount of information at one time, we cannot be conscious of all that occurs in the environment. The process of selective attention determines which stimuli will be noticed and which will be ignored. Dichotic listening experiments show that what is received by the unattended ear is lost within a few seconds unless something causes the listener to take heed of it; after those few seconds, what was presented is lost. Studies using visually presented information indicate that attention can focus on location or on shape: We can locate objects in physical space and also say what they are. Possibly because visual stimulation is so complex, distractions can produce inattentional blindness in certain conditions. Brain-imaging studies have found that when people pay attention to particular features of visual stimuli, the activity of particular regions of the brain is enhanced.

Consciousness and the Brain

The suggestion that consciousness is a function of our ability to communicate with one another receives support from some cases of human brain damage. As we saw, people with certain kinds of damage can point to objects they say they cannot see; people with isolation aphasia can perceive speech and talk without apparent awareness; and a patient with a particular form of visual agnosia can make appropriate hand movements when looking at objects that cannot be consciously recognized. Thus, brain damage can disrupt a person's awareness of perceptual mechanisms without disrupting other functions performed by these mechanisms. Although a person whose corpus callosum has been severed can make perceptual judgments with the right hemisphere, he or she cannot talk about them and appears to be unaware of them.

Hypnosis

Mesmer introduced the modern form of hypnosis that features induction and suggestion, including posthypnotic amnesia. Susceptibility to hypnosis varies among individuals. A common experience while in hypnosis is that of reduced effort and the suspension of voluntary control. There are several theories of hypnosis, but research shows that it largely alters what the hypnotized individual reports rather than what that person perceives.

Sleep

Sleep consists of several stages of slow-wave sleep, characterized by increasing amounts of delta activity in the EEG, and REM sleep. REM sleep is characterized by beta activity in the EEG, rapid eye movements, general paralysis (with twitching movements of the hands and feet), and dreaming. Sleep is behavior, not simply an altered state of consciousness. Although evidence suggests that sleep is not necessary for repairing the wear and tear of daily life, sleep may play an important role in providing an opportunity for the brain to rest. Sleep also contributes to memory consolidation. Specifically, research involving memory tasks and the presence or absence of naps showed that slow-wave sleep contributes to the consolidation of declarative (explicit) memories and REM sleep to that of nondeclarative (implicit) memories.

Although narrative dreams occur only during REM sleep, people often are conscious of static situations during slow-wave sleep. Freud suggested that dreams provide the opportunity for unconscious conflicts to express themselves symbolically in dream content. An alternative suggestion—the activation-synthesis theory—is that dreams are the brain's effort to make sense of the pons-initiated activation of the cerebral cortex. The function of REM sleep in adults is uncertain, but it may be involved somehow in learning. Long bouts of REM-sleep deprivation result in the REM rebound in which sleep is dominated by the REM component.

Sleep disorders include difficulty falling asleep and remaining asleep, which is known as *insomnia,* the sudden onset of sleep at inappropriate times known as *narcolepsy* (and related cataplexy), and REM sleep behavior disorder in which REM-specific paralysis no longer occurs. The slow-wave sleep disorders include bedwetting, sleepwalking, and sleep-related eating disorder.

The suprachiasmatic nucleus of the hypothalamus controls circadian (daily) rhythms. This clock is reset when morning light strikes the retina. Clusters of activity neurons in the midbrain and hindbrain control wakefulness. Neurons in the preoptic area of the hypothalamus inhibit the activity neurons and thereby induce sleep. Time of day and the level of adenosine are two factors that control these sleep neurons.

succeed with mypsychlab

Visit MyPsychLab for practice quizzes, flashcards, and dozens of videos and animated tutorials, including the following items you can find in the "Multimedia Library":

Hypnosis
Roberta: Insomnia
Lucid Dreaming

Theories of Dreaming

Hypnosis

KEY TERMS

activation-synthesis theory *p. 268*

adenosine *p. 271*

alpha activity *p. 264*

beta activity *p. 264*

blindsight *p. 249*

cataplexy *p. 269*

change blindness *p. 257*

circadian rhythm *p. 270*

cocktail-party problem *p. 255*

coma *p. 248*

consciousness *p. 248*

delta activity *p. 265*

dichotic-listening test *p. 253*

divided attention *p. 252*

electromyogram *p. 264*

electro-oculogram *p. 264*

hypocretin *p. 269*

inattention blindness *p. 256*

inhibition of return *p. 255*

insomnia *p. 269*

isolation aphasia *p. 258*

latent content *p. 268*

manifest content *p. 268*

minimally conscious state *p. 248*

narcolepsy *p. 269*

night terrors *p. 267*

persistent vegetative state *p. 248*

polygraph *p. 268*

posthypnotic amnesia *p. 263*

posthypnotic suggestion *p. 263*

SUGGESTIONS FOR FURTHER READING

Damasio, A. (2000). *The feeling of what happens: Body and emotion in the making of consciousness*. New York: Harcourt.

A leading neuroscientist looks at the topic of consciousness and offers an unconventional suggestion regarding its origins.

Dennett, D. C. (1992). *Consciousness explained*. Boston: Little, Brown.

This book provides a provocative look at consciousness from a philosophical, psychological, and computational viewpoint.

Gazzaniga, M. S. (2008). *Human: The science behind what makes us unique*. New York: Ecco.

A major figure in cognitive neuroscience shares his view of the brain as an evolutionary product in which language uniquely inflects human sociality.

Jaynes, J. (2000). *The origin of consciousness in the breakdown of the bicameral mind*. Boston: Houghton Mifflin.

Jaynes's book presents the intriguing hypothesis that human consciousness is a recent phenomenon that emerged long after the evolution of the human brain as we know it now. You do not need to agree with Jaynes's thesis to enjoy reading this scholarly book.

Nash, M., & Barnier, A. (Eds.) (2008). *The Oxford handbook of hynosis: Theory, research, and practice*. New York: Oxford University Press.

A scholarly overview of historical and contemporary research in hypnotic phenomena and applications.

Horne, J. (2006). *Sleepfaring: A journey through the science of sleep*. Oxford: Oxford University Press.

Horne's book about sleep is wide-ranging and well-referenced.

Linden, D. (2007). *The accidental mind: How brain evolution has given us love, memory, dreams, and God*. Cambridge, MA: Belknap Press of Harvard University Press.

An entertaining overview of the evolutionary process that produced the unique patchwork that is the human brain.

Hofstadter, D. (2007). *I am a strange loop*. New York: Basic Books.

A highly evocative, autobiographical introduction to the strange-loop theory of consciousness. Alternately humorous and touching, Hofstadter develops the theory by reference to many analogies, including computer analogies and Gödel's impossibility theorem.

Language

Prologue

Prologue: Touring with Tourette's

Oliver Sacks was feeling uneasy and just a little bit scared. The celebrated neurologist from New York City had traveled the world, researching and writing about the normal and abnormal workings of the human brain. But at this moment, on a lonely highway in the Canadian province of British Columbia, he was most concerned about the moment-to-moment functioning of the brain belonging to the man in the driver's seat next to him, Carl Bennett.

Bennett lived and worked in British Columbia, and he had just taken Sacks to one of his favorite spots, a ranch in one of the spectacular mountain valleys of the interior ranges. Now they were driving back, and Bennett's behavior at the wheel would have seemed bizarre, even shocking, to any observer who didn't know him. Jerking the wheel violently right and left, Bennett erratically steered the vehicle down the mountain road. He took his hands off the wheel for a few seconds at a time to tap the windshield frenetically. And his conversation was peppered with strange expressions like "hootey-hoot" and "hideous," repeated often and rhythmically. "Don't worry," he said to Sacks. "I've never had an accident driving." Oddly enough, Sacks found this comforting.

Bennett had been diagnosed with Tourette's syndrome—a psychological disorder marked by sudden nervous tics of behavior and language. Bennett's tics included tapping, readjustments of the steering wheel, and spontaneous, nonsensical words. His speech was normally peppered with bizarre expressions such as "babaloo mandel," and "hideous." Bennett couldn't say what many of them meant or why they appeared.

Remarkably, Bennett could suppress the erratic movements when absolutely necessary, and could inhibit his odd blurting whenever he needed to communicate clearly and precisely. Sacks knew. He had just seen Bennett wield a scalpel in a delicate operation at the hospital near Bennett's home. Bennett, you see, was a surgeon. Conversations with nurses, colleagues, and patients included his regular strange utterances, along with other verbal and motor tics that characterize a person with

The noted neurologist and author, Oliver Sacks

277

Tourette's, but they ceased the moment surgery started. Bennett's motions were smooth, decisive, controlled; his speech melded into the normal flow of operating room commands and observations. "It's like a miracle," one of his surgical assistants observed. "The way the Tourette's disappears."

True to his prediction, Bennett and Sacks arrived back from the ranch without an accident. Bennett looked over at a still-shaken Sacks. "I've got an idea. Your flight to New York leaves from Calgary International. To save you the long drive, I'll fly you to Calgary tomorrow in my private plane." ■

As Oliver Sacks's experience with Carl Bennett reminds us, our use of language is behavior. The transmission and reception of signals provided by arbitrary sounds (spoken language) and marks (written language) can alter our own and others' behavior. When distorted by the influence of Tourette's syndrome, words mean no more than other erratic behaviors, such as the shoulder twitches and finger tapping that Bennett engaged in. When organized as language, however, words can communicate the complex steps of a surgical procedure. Sacks's visit with Bennett (Sacks, 1995) nicely illustrates this distinction. Language is the most complex ability we possess. With the exception of sexual behavior (without which one's genes would not survive), communication is probably the most important of all human social behaviors.

This chapter addresses three major topics in language. The first is speech—specifically, how the sounds of speech are recognized and produced and how recognition leads to meaning. The principal emphasis is on the brain mechanisms associated with speech comprehension and production and on the clinical consequences when those mechanisms are impaired. The second topic is reading, with much the same interest in how the brain recognizes written text and produces meaning from it. We'll also consider clinical disorders of reading. The chapter's final topic is the acquisition of language and, specifically, the patterns that characterize the child's emergence as a fluent speaker of language within a brief span of years. Of particular interest is the possibility that the human brain possesses a language-acquisition device. The chapter ends by exploring the question of whether other species can acquire language.

Speech Comprehension and Production

When we speak to someone, we produce a series of sounds in a continuous stream, punctuated by pauses and modulated by stresses and changes in pitch. We speak sentences as a string of

People's earliest attempts at written communication took the form of stylized pictures, such as these petroglyphs located in the Great Gallery of Horseshoe Canyon in Utah.

sounds, emphasizing (stressing) some, quickly gliding over others, raising the pitch of our voice on some, lowering it on others. We maintain a regular rhythmic pattern of stress. We pause at appropriate times—for example, between phrases—but we do not pause after pronouncing each word. Thus, speech does not come to us as a series of individual words; we must extract the words from a stream of speech (Liberman, 1996; Miller & Eimas, 1995). Like our ability to recognize faces visually, the auditory system recognizes the patterns underlying speech rather than just the sounds themselves (Sinha, 2002). But what are these patterns, and how do we do recognize them?

Speech Recognition

Any analysis of speech usually begins with its elements, or **phonemes,** the basic elements of speech. For example, the word *pin* consists of three phonemes: /p/ + /i/ + /n/. Many experiments have investigated how we discriminate among phonemes. Let us consider just one distinction that we can detect: **voice-onset time,** the delay between the initial sound of a consonant and the onset of vibration of the vocal cords. Voicing is the vibration of the vocal cords. The distinction between voiced and unvoiced consonants permits us to distinguish between /p/ and /b/, between /k/ and /g/, and between /t/ and /d/. Try to figure out the difference yourself by saying *pa* and *ba*. Pay attention to what the sounds are like, and not to how you move your lips to make them. You might place your fingers on your throat and feel the difference there while making the sounds.

The difference is very subtle. When you say *pa*, you first build up a little pressure in your mouth. When you open your lips, a puff of air comes out. The *ah* sound does not occur

---

phoneme The minimal unit of sound in a language, such as /p/.

voice-onset time The delay between the initial sound of a consonant (such as the puffing sound of the phoneme /p/) and the onset of vibration of the vocal cords.

immediately, because the air pressure in your mouth and throat keeps air from leaving your lungs for a brief time. Your vocal cords do not vibrate until air from your lungs passes through them. The delay in voicing that occurs when you say *pa* is very slight: only 0.06 second. *Pa* is therefore considered an unvoiced consonant. When you say *ba,* you do not first build up pressure. Your vocal cords start vibrating as soon as your lips open. *Ba* is a voiced consonant. Try saying *pa* and *ba* aloud a few more times, and note the difference. Your vocal cords will start vibrating just a little later when you say *pa.*

The auditory system performs a formidably complex task in enabling us to recognize these speech sounds. The functional imaging technologies described in Chapter 4 have provided new insight into how this happens. By using *f*MRI scans, Belin, Zatorre, and Ahad (2002) found that some regions of the brain responded more when people heard human vocalizations (both speech and nonspeech) than when they heard other sounds of the natural world. Regions in which there was a large difference were located in the temporal lobe, specifically, the auditory cortex. (Refer to Figure 4.30.) Analyzing detailed information of speech, also known as phonemic discrimination, begins with auditory processing of the sensory differences, and this occurs in both hemispheres (Binder et al., 2004). However, regions of the left auditory cortex seem to specialize in recognizing specific aspects of speech. Scott, Blank, Rosen, and Wise (2000) identified some of these areas using PET scans. They played recordings of either natural speech, speech that was computer-distorted and unintelligible but contained the phonemic complexity of the sounds, or speech that was intelligible but lacked the normal frequencies of human speakers. Some brain areas responded to both natural and unintelligible speech; others responded only to speech that was intelligible—even if it was highly distorted. (See FIGURE 10•1.)

As the sounds of individual phonemes likely are different from speaker to speaker in normal speech, the auditory cortex must therefore rely on information that transcends those differences. Perhaps this information is based on larger segments of speech, such as that provided by syllables. A behavioral experiment conducted by Ganong (1980) supports this suggestion. Ganong found that the perception of a phoneme is affected by the sounds that follow it. He used a computer to synthesize a novel sound that fell between those of the phonemes /g/ and /k/. When the sound was followed by *ift,* the participants heard the word *gift,* but when it was followed by *iss,* they heard *kiss.* These results suggest that we recognize speech sounds in pieces larger than individual phonemes. In addition, the results are analogous to the effects of context on visual stimuli (refer to Figure 7.22).

Recognition of Words in Continuous Speech: The Importance of Learning and Context

Phonemes combine to become **morphemes,** which are the smallest units of a language that convey meaning. *Pin* is a pair of morphemes—/p/, which is also a phoneme, and /in/. Removing /p/ from *pin* changes the meaning of the utterance. For that reason, /p/ is also a morpheme (specifically, a *bound* morpheme, as, by itself, it has no

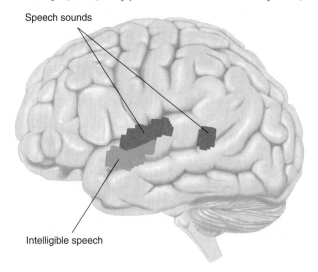

[FIGURE 10•1] Results of PET scans indicating regions of the superior temporal lobe that respond to speech sounds. Dark brown: Regions that responded to phonetic information (normal speech sounds or a computerized transformation of speech that preserved the complexity of the speech sounds but rendered it unintelligible). Light brown: Region that responded only to intelligible speech (normal speech sounds or a computerized transformation that removed most normal frequencies but preserved intelligibility).

(Adapted from Scott, S. K., Blank, E. C., Rosen, S., & Wise, R. J. S. (2000). *Brain,* 123, 2400–2406. By permission of Oxford University Press.)

meaning; by contrast /in/ is a *free* morpheme; see Katamba, 2003). Adding another morpheme—/s/—changes the meaning to the plural of *pin.* Morphemes alone and in combination form the words of a language.

These larger units of speech are established by learning and experience. Sanders, Newport, and Neville (2002) examined brain wave activity when people listened to a continuous string of sounds. The sounds were composed of short two-letter syllables spliced together, such as the sound string

Babupudutabatutibubabupubu ("bah-boo-poo-doo-tah-bah-too-tee-boo-bah-boo-poo-boo")

Sanders and her colleagues then took some three-syllable sounds from the continuous stream (such as the sequence dutaba) and designated them as "words." They asked their participants to study these nonsense words carefully. A recognizable electrical signal, called the N100 wave, appears in the electroencephalographic (EEG) record shortly after (in fact, 100 milliseconds after) the onset of a word. It serves as an electrophysiological correlate of word perception. Before participants' study of the nonsense words, no N100 wave had appeared in conjunction with them. Sanders and her co-workers found that, after participants learned the nonsense sounds as

---

morpheme The minimal unit of meaning in a language, such as /p/ + /in/ to form *pin.*

words, they showed the N100 response—despite the fact that there were no additional auditory cues by which to segment the string of sounds.

In addition to learning words, we also learn the contexts in which they are spoken. Even though speech is filled with hesitations, muffled sounds, and sloppy pronunciations, we are able to recognize what is being said because of the context in which it occurs. Context affects the perception of words through top-down processing. (Recall the discussion in Chapter 7.) Other contexts also affect word perception. For example, although we tend to think of a conversation as involving only sounds, we also use other types of cues present in the environment to help us understand what someone is saying. If we are standing at a snack shop at a beach, for example, and someone says, "I scream," we are likely to hear it as "ice cream" (Reynolds & Flagg, 1983).

Understanding the Meaning of Speech

The meaning of a sentence (or of a set of connected sentences that are telling a story) is conveyed in many ways, such as by the words used, the order in which words are combined, and the pattern of rhythm and emphasis of the speaker. Let us examine some of these features.

Syntax If we want a listener to understand our speech, we must follow the conventions or "rules" of language. We must use words with which the listener is familiar and combine them in specific ways. For example, if we say, "The two boys looked at the heavy box," we can expect to be understood; but if we say, "Boys the two looking heavy the box at," we will not be. Only the first sentence follows the rules of English grammar.

All languages have a *syntax,* or *grammar.* They all follow certain principles, which linguists call **syntactical rules,** for combining words to form phrases, clauses, or sentences. (*Syntax,* like *synthesis,* comes from the Greek *syntassein,* "to put together.") Syntax provides important information. Consider the following sentence: *A little girl picked the pretty flowers.* A linguist (or an English teacher) can analyze the sentence and identify the part of speech for each word. However, linguists and English teachers could *understand* sentences like this while they were still children—even before they learned such terms as *articles, noun phrases,* and so on. Our understanding of syntactical rules emerges automatically without their being taught to us explicitly. In Chapter 8, we saw that some memories (*implicit memories*) are not easily described, if at all, whereas others (*explicit memories*) can be. Apparently the syntactical rules of

our language are learned implicitly. We are no more conscious of them when we listen to speech than a child is conscious of the formal laws of physics when he or she learns to ride a bicycle.

In trying to understand what people say (or write) we pay attention to certain syntactical cues such as *word order, function words, content words, word meanings,* and *prosody.*

Word order is important in spoken and written English. If we say, "The A X's the B," we are indicating that the agent is A, the object is B, and the thing being done is X. For example, in the sentences *The boy hit the ball* and *The ball hit the boy,* word order tells us who does what to whom. Word order does not play this role in all languages, however.

Words can be classified as function words or content words. **Function words** include determiners, quantifiers, prepositions, and conjunctives, for example, *a, the, some, many, to, from,* and *but.* **Content words** include nouns, verbs, and most adjectives and adverbs: *apple, rug, went, caught, heavy, mysterious, thoroughly,* and *sadly.* Content words express meaning; function words express the relations between content words. As we shall see later, people with a particular type of brain damage lose the ability to comprehend syntax. Part of this deficit is the inability to understand function words or to use them correctly in speech.

Word meanings, or **semantics,** also provide important cues to the syntax of a sentence. (*Semantics* comes from the Greek *sema,* "sign.") For example, consider the following set of words: *Frank discovered a louse combing his beard.* The syntax of this sentence is ambiguous. Is Frank combing Frank's beard? Is the louse combing Frank's beard? Is the louse combing the louse's beard? According to the rules of English grammar, it's the louse doing the combing. But our knowledge of the world and of the usual meanings of words tells us that Frank was doing the combing, because people, not lice, have beards and combs.

The varying stresses, rhythms, and changes in pitch that accompany speech, called **prosody,** also helps us understand the meaning of speech. Prosody can emphasize the syntax of a word or a group of words or even can serve as the primary source of syntactic information. Prosody is extremely important in language comprehension, because so much of our communication relies on spoken forms. Consider the following two sentences used in a study by Steinhauer, Alter, and Friederici (1999):

> Since Jay always jogs 5 miles seems like a short distance to him.
> Since Jay always jogs 5 miles this seems like a short distance to him.

The first sentence probably seemed a bit harder to comprehend. That's because we lack the prosody cues conveyed by normal speech (cues approximated by the punctuation that could ordinarily occur). If you read the sentence aloud as it would normally be spoken, you will find yourself slightly elongating the word *jogs,* lowering the pitch of your voice at the end of the word, and pausing briefly before continuing. These cues signal that the words *5 miles* belong with *seems* rather than with *jogs.* Putting a comma between *jogs* and *miles* would accomplish in print what we would normally do

---

syntactical rule A grammatical rule of a particular language for combining words to form phrases, clauses, and sentences.

function word A preposition, article, or other word that conveys little of the meaning of a sentence but is important in specifying its grammatical structure.

content word A noun, verb, adjective, or adverb that conveys meaning.

semantics The meanings and the study of the meanings of words.

prosody The use of changes in intonation and emphasis to convey meaning in speech besides that specified by the particular words.

in speech. For example, question marks and periods have correspondence to speech; spoken questions generally end with a rising tone, whereas declarative sentences do not.

Although we don't normally notice these cues as we process spoken language, they are certainly part of our ability to segment the spoken stream of sounds and to understand it. Using sentences in German (their study was conducted with German participants) that approximated the two English sentences above, Steinhauer and colleagues placed a pause between *jogs* and *five* in the second sentence. In this case, the syntactic cues to meaning conflicted with the normal prosody. People who heard this hybrid sentence were virtually unanimous in detecting the mismatch. Furthermore, analysis of the electroencephalographic recordings of participants' brain activity showed the kind of activity that accompanies unexpected events.

Deep Structure, Surface Structure, and Meaning Noam Chomsky (1957, 1965), a noted linguist, suggested that newly formed sentences are represented in the brain in terms of their meaning, which he called their **deep structure.** It represents the gist or kernel of what the person intended to say. To speak or write the sentence, the brain must transform the deep structure into the appropriate **surface structure:** the particular form the sentence takes.

An example of a "slip of the tongue" recorded by the linguist Victoria Fromkin (1973) gives us some clues about the way a sentence's deep structure can be transformed into a particular surface structure.

> *Rosa always date shranks.*

The speaker actually intended to say, "Rosa always dated shrinks" (meaning psychiatrists or clinical psychologists). We can speculate that the deep structure of the sentence's verb phrase was something like this: *date* [past tense] + *shrink* [plural]. The words in brackets represent the names of the syntactical rules that are to be used in forming the surface structure of the sentence. Obviously, the past tense of *date* is *dated,* and the plural of *shrink* is *shrinks.* However, something went wrong during the transformation of the deep structure (meaning) into the surface structure (words and syntax). Apparently, the past-tense rule got applied to the word *shrink,* resulting in *shrank.* The plural rule also got applied, resulting in the nonsense word *shranks.* (See **FIGURE 10·2.**) Following Fromkin's lead, Erard (2007) compiled a long list of slips of the tongue that illustrate their root in the linearity of language. For example, there's the usher who asked politely, "May I sew you to your sheet?" Or the minister who asked God to fill the congregation with "fresh veal and new zigor." Or the politicians and commentators who switched Osama and Obama. In each case, what might be considered errors in translation from deep to surface structure are imposed by the requirement that words necessarily follow one another.

Most psycholinguists agree that the distinction between surface structure and deep structure is important. Later in this chapter, we will encounter more neuropsychological evidence

[FIGURE 10·2] Deep structure and surface structure. A possible explanation for the error in the sentence *Rosa always date shranks.*

in favor of Chomsky's distinction. However, psycholinguists generally disagree with Chomsky about the particular nature of the cognitive mechanisms through which deep structure is transformed into surface structure and vice versa (Bohannon, 1993; Hulit & Howard, 1993; Pinker, 1994; Tanenhaus, 1988).

Knowledge of the World Comprehension of speech also involves knowledge about the world and about particular situations we may encounter there (Carpenter, Miyake, & Just, 1995). Schank and Abelson (1977) first suggested that this knowledge is organized into **scripts,** which specify various kinds of events and the event-related interactions that people have witnessed or have learned about from others. Once the speaker has established which script is being referred to, the listener can fill in the details. For example, consider the following sentences (from Hunt, 1985): *I learned a lot about the bars in town yesterday. Do you have an aspirin?* To understand what the speaker means, you must be able to do more than simply understand the words and analyze the syntax. You must know something about a particular kind of bar; for example, that they serve alcoholic beverages and that "learning a lot about them" probably involved some drinking. You also must know that drinking these beverages can lead to a headache and that aspirin is a remedy for headaches.

Brain Mechanisms of Speech Production and Comprehension

Studies of people with brain damage and PET studies of people without brain damage who engaged in verbal behavior suggest that mechanisms involved in producing and comprehending speech are located in different areas of the cerebral cortex.

---

deep structure The essential meaning of a sentence, without regard to the grammatical features (surface structure) of the sentence that are needed to express it in words.

surface structure The grammatical features of a sentence; its words and syntax.

script A person's knowledge about the characteristics typical of a particular type of event or situation; assists the comprehension of speech.

[**FIGURE 10•3**] The locations of Broca's area, Wernicke's area, and associated areas involved in language deficits.

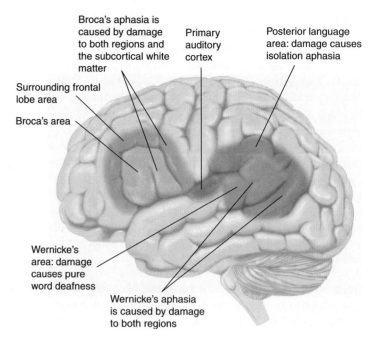

Broca's aphasia is caused by damage to both regions and the subcortical white matter

Primary auditory cortex

Posterior language area: damage causes isolation aphasia

Surrounding frontal lobe area

Broca's area

Wernicke's area: damage causes pure word deafness

Wernicke's aphasia is caused by damage to both regions

Speech Production and Comprehension: Evidence from Broca's Aphasia The neural mechanisms that control speech production appear to be located in the frontal lobes. Damage to a region of the motor association cortex in the left frontal lobe (Broca's area) disrupts the ability to speak. This condition is known as **Broca's aphasia** ("uh-FAZE-yuh"; sometimes referred to as an *expressive aphasia*), a language disorder characterized by slow, laborious, nonfluent speech (*aphasia* refers to deficits in the use or comprehension of language that generally are the result of brain damage). It is named for Paul Broca (1824–1880), an influential nineteenth-century neurologist. When trying to converse with patients who have Broca's aphasia, most people find it hard to resist supplying the words the patients are obviously groping for. Although the patients often mispronounce words, the words they do manage to speak are meaningful. They obviously have something to say, but the damage to the frontal lobe makes it difficult for them to express it in other than somewhat telegraphic fashion. (See FIGURE 10•3.)

Carl Wernicke (1848–1905) suggested that Broca's area contains motor memories—in particular, memories of the sequences of muscle movements that are needed to articulate words. Speaking involves rapid movements of the tongue, lips, and jaw, and these movements must be coordinated with one another and with those of the vocal cords; thus, talking requires sophisticated motor control mechanisms. Obviously, circuits of neurons somewhere in the brain, when properly activated, will cause these sequences of movements

to be executed. The mechanisms that control these movements also adjust to somatosensory feedback (Tremblay, Shiller, & Ostry, 2003). Because damage to the lower left frontal lobe (including Broca's area) disrupts the ability to articulate words, this region is the most likely candidate for the location of these "speech programs." The fact that this region is located just in front of the part of the primary motor cortex that controls the muscles used for speech certainly supports this conclusion.

In addition to their role in the articulation of words, neural circuits located in the lower left frontal lobe appear to perform more complex functions. Damage to Broca's area often produces **agrammatism:** impaired ability to use syntactical rules to produce or comprehend speech. For example, patients with Broca's aphasia rarely use grammatical markers such as *-ed* or auxiliaries such as *have* (as in *I have gone*). A study by Saffran, Schwartz, and Marin (1980) illustrates this difficulty. The following quotations are from agrammatic patients attempting to describe pictures:

Picture of a boy being hit in the head by a baseball
    The boy is catch . . . the boy is hitch . . . the boy is hit the ball. (p. 229)
Picture of a girl giving flowers to her teacher
    Girl . . . wants to . . . flowers . . . flowers and wants to . . . The woman . . . wants to . . . The girl wants to . . . the flowers and the woman. (p. 234)

In an ordinary conversation, Broca's aphasics (that is, patients with Broca's aphasia) seem to understand everything that is said to them. The striking disparity between their speech and their comprehension often leads people to assume that the patients' comprehension is normal, but this is an error. To test individuals diagnosed with agrammatism for their speech comprehension, Schwartz, Saffran, and Marin (1980) showed them a pair of drawings, read a sentence aloud, and then asked

---

Broca's aphasia   Severe difficulty in articulating words, especially function words, caused by brain damage that includes Broca's area, a region of the left (speech-dominated) frontal cortex.

agrammatism   A language disturbance; difficulty in the production and comprehension of grammatical features, such as proper use of function words, word endings, and word order. Often seen in cases of Broca's aphasia.

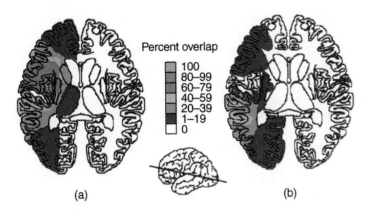

(a)   (b)

[**FIGURE 10•4**] Evidence for involvement of the insular cortex in speech articulation. Percentage overlap in the lesions of 25 patients (a) with speech articulation difficulties and (b) without speech articulation difficulties. The only region common to all lesions that produced speech articulation difficulties was the precentral gyrus of the insular cortex.

(Reprinted with permission from Dronkers, N. F. (1996). *Nature, 384,* 159–161. Copyright © 1996 Macmillan Magazines Limited.)

the patients to point to the appropriate picture. The patients heard 48 sentences such as *The clown applauds the dancer* and *The robber is shot by the cop.* For the first sentence, one picture showed a clown applauding a dancer, and the other showed a dancer applauding a clown. On average, the patients responded correctly to only 62% of the pictures (chance would be 50%). In contrast, the performance of people without brain damage on such a simple task is close to 100%.

To understand why damage to Broca's area produced a partial loss of function rather than complete loss, it may be helpful to refer to Karl Lashley's *law of mass action* (Lashley, 1930). Lashley was among the foremost neuroscientists of the 20th century. After training rats to perform visual discriminations, he selectively removed larger and larger segments of brain tissue to study the effects of that loss on performance in the discrimination task. He found that the location of the removal did not play nearly as large a role in performance decrement as the relative amount of tissue removed. That is, the brain acted as a mass, and, as more of the mass was removed, it grew less able to sustain performance. A similar principle has been shown in the case of neural networks (see Chapter 7; Grossberg, 1971).

The agrammatism that accompanies Broca's aphasia appears to disrupt patients' ability to use word order to comprehend the meaning of a sentence. Thus, these patients' comprehension deficit parallels their production deficit. If they hear a sentence such as *The mosquito was swatted by the man,* they can understand that it concerns a man and a mosquito and the action of swatting. Because of their knowledge of men and mosquitoes, they will have no trouble figuring out who is doing what to whom. But a sentence such as *The cow was kicked by the horse* does not provide any extra cues from their knowledge of the world; in the absence of those cues, the meaning of the sentence remains ambiguous (e.g., Zurif, 1990).

Broca's area seems to affect a hierarchy of language functions. That is, on one level, the damage creates difficulty in sequencing the muscles of speech, producing articulation problems. At a higher level, the problems involve appropriate syntactical cues. We might then expect brain areas critical to the articulation function to be located closer to the motor areas of the frontal cortex. Indeed, research

evidence supports this possibility. Dronkers (1996) examined MRI and CT scans of 25 patients with severe vocal articulation disorders. More than half of the cases involved the joint diagnosis of Broca's aphasia. Depicted in FIGURE 10•4(a) are the areas in which the brain damage overlapped across the different patients. You can see that all of the patients had damage in a region deep within the frontal cortex known as the *insula.* Compare this with Figure 4.30 on page 115, and you will see how close this region is to the motor areas of the lips and face. In contrast, Dronkers found no damage to this area among a group of individuals without articulation problems. (See FIGURE 10•4(b).) Other studies have produced similar findings (e.g., Caplan, Alpert, & Waters, 1999; Donnan, Darbey, & Saling, 1997). More recently Dronkers et al. (2004) used neuroimaging to show that lesions in middle-temporal regions outside Broca's area are important for the comprehension of words and other areas for the comprehension of sentences.

Broca's area and surrounding brain regions may also be responsible for linguisitic sequences other than those involving speech, including the sign language systems used by many people in the Deaf community, such as American Sign Language (see Chapter 6). Although they do not require vocal articulation, these languages depend on syntactic cues, just as spoken languages do. Petitto and colleagues (2000) studied the cerebral blood circulation (by using PET scans) of profoundly deaf sign-language users when they were asked to produce verbs in response to nouns. They found enhanced activity in the left inferior frontal cortex and speculated that brain regions involved in language processing may not be specific to a sensory modality, such as sound.

Speech Comprehension and Production: Evidence from Wernicke's Aphasia

Spoken language requires the production of utterances as well as the understanding of utterances. Whereas damage to Broca's area affects the ability to speak, the ability to comprehend speech obviously begins in the auditory system, which is needed if the brain is to analyze sequences of sounds and to recognize them as words. Recognition is the first step in comprehension. Recognizing a spoken word is a complex perceptual task that relies on memories of sequences of sounds. This task appears to be accomplished by neural circuits in the upper part of the left temporal lobe—a region that has come to be known as **Wernicke's area.**

Brain damage in the left hemisphere that invades Wernicke's area as well as the surrounding region of the temporal and parietal lobes produces a disorder known as **Wernicke's aphasia.** The symptoms of Wernicke's aphasia are poor speech recognition and the production of meaningless speech. However, unlike speech production in Broca's aphasia, the speech associated with Wernicke's aphasia is fluent and unlabored; the patient does not strain to articulate words and appear to be searching for them. The patient's voice rises and falls normally, so that when you listen to the speech of a patient with Wernicke's aphasia, it appears to be syntactical. That is, the patient uses function words such as *the* and *but* and complex verb tenses and subordinate clauses. However, the patient uses few content words, and the words are strung together nonsensically. In extreme deficits, speech deteriorates into a meaningless jumble, sometimes referred to as "word salad," as in the following example:

> *Examiner:* What kind of work did you do before you came into the hospital?
>
> *Patient:* Never, now mista oyge I wanna tell you this happened when happened when he rent. His—his kell come down here and is—he got ren something. It happened. In thesse ropiers were with him for hi—is friend—like was. And it just happened so I don't know, he did not bring around anything. And he did not pay it. And he roden all o these arranjen from the pedis on from iss pescid. In these floors now and so. He hadn't had em round here. (Kertesz, 1981, p. 73)

Given the speech deficits of patients with Wernicke's aphasia, the clinical assessment of their ability to comprehend speech must rely on their nonverbal behavior. That is, we cannot assume that they do not understand what other people say to them just because they do not give a lucid answer. In a commonly used test of comprehension, clinicians assess these patients' ability to understand questions by asking them to point to objects on a table in front of them. For example, they are asked to "point to the one with ink." If they point to an object other than the pen that is shown, they are assumed not to have understood the request. When tested this way, patients with severe Wernicke's aphasia show poor comprehension of speech.

Because Wernicke's area is a region of the auditory association cortex, and because a comprehension deficit is so prominent in Wernicke's aphasia, this disorder has been characterized as a *receptive aphasia*. Wernicke suggested that the region that now bears his name is the location of memories of the sequences of sounds that constitute words. This hypothesis is reasonable; it suggests that the auditory association cortex of Wernicke's area makes it possible to recognize the sounds of words, just as the visual association cortex in the lower part of the temporal lobe makes possible the visual recognition of objects.

But why should damage to an area responsible for the ability to recognize spoken words disrupt people's ability to speak? A possible answer is that Wernicke's aphasia, like Broca's aphasia, actually appears to consist of several deficits. The abilities that are disrupted include recognition of spoken words, comprehension of the meaning of words, and the ability to convert thoughts into words (Basso, 2003).

Comparing Broca's Aphasia and Wernicke's Aphasia with PET and fMRI Studies

The results of studies using PET scans are generally consistent with the results of studies of language-impaired patients with brain damage. First, several studies have found that patients with Broca's aphasia show abnormally low activity in the lower left frontal lobe; patients with Wernicke's aphasia show low activity in the temporal/parietal area of the brain (Karbe et al., 1989; Karbe, Szelies, Herholz, & Heiss, 1990; Metter, 1991; Metter et al., 1990). These results explain the fact that lesions in the depths of the frontal or temporal/parietal cortex can sometimes produce aphasia by disrupting normal activity there—activity that involves connections between cortical and subcortical areas.

Other PET-scan studies have investigated the neural activity of people without brain injury while they performed verbal tasks. FIGURE 10•5 shows PET scans from a study by Petersen and colleagues (1988). Listening passively to a list of nouns activated the primary auditory cortex and Wernicke's area, whereas reading the nouns activated the primary motor cortex and Broca's area. When people were asked to think of verbs that were appropriate to use with the nouns, even more intense activity was seen in Broca's area.

Brain imaging by using fMRI scans has helped supplement this picture. Binder and colleagues (1997) produced

---

Wernicke's area   A region of the auditory association cortex located in the upper part of the left temporal lobe; involved in the recognition of spoken words.

Wernicke's aphasia   A disorder caused by damage to the left temporal and parietal cortex, including Wernicke's area; characterized by deficits in the recognition of speech and by the production of fluent but essentially meaningless speech.

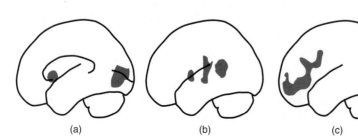

(a)   (b)   (c)

[FIGURE 10•5] PET scans of participants in a study by Petersen and colleagues (1988). (a) Listening passively to a list of nouns. (b) Silently reading a list of nouns. (c) Thinking of verbs related to a list of nouns.

whole-brain scans of individuals processing semantic characteristics of spoken words as opposed to tones that served as control stimuli. With semantic stimuli, the scans showed activation of Wernicke's area, a result that supports the standard model we have been examining. The semantic stimuli also activated large areas of the temporal and parietal areas outside Wernicke's area, as well as frontal lobe regions around Broca's area. Processing the meaning of words most likely involves other areas of the cortex as well, such as the temporal gyri (see Kreisler et al., 2000, for an MRI-based review of lesion locations in aphasia). On the basis of clinical studies of aphasia and neuroimaging, Poeppel and Hickok (2004) argue that the classical model involving Broca's and Wernicke's area and connections between them is outmoded and should be replaced by a new model that draws from several other brain areas.

[CASE STUDY] Sir John Hale was a world-renowned scholar of the Italian Renaissance who had a cerebral stroke in his late sixties. His wife Sheila cared for him until his death at age 75 and later wrote a book (Hale, 2007) about the stroke's devastating effects on her husband's language and her efforts to cope with his loss.

What was immediately clear after the stroke was that his aphasia extended to speech as well as reading and writing but not in a comprehensive way. For example, he had real difficulty reading for pleasure but could follow scholarly journals. Efforts to teach him to match words to pictures were largely unsuccessful but resulted in the emergence of new sounds, such as *da* or *whoah*. Speech therapists were skeptical of his ability to recover, but an incident at a dinner party persuaded a particular therapist, Elizabeth, that John was up to it. She lifted up her arm and asked him what is was:

"John said, '*Da whoahs.*'
   Elizabeth said, 'No, John, listen to yourself. Now listen to me: ahm.'
   John said, 'Ahhhm.'
   'No, John, you're saying ahhhm. It's not quite right, is it? What is this? This is my . . .?'
   John said, 'Ahm.'" (Hales, 2003, p. 162)

Elizabeth summarized John's situation metaphorically: "It was as though the road between Naples and Rome had been blown up. You can still travel between the two cities, but you have to make your way through the rubble to find an alternative route." Or "The British Library has been shaken by an earthquake. The books have been hurled off the shelves. They're all mixed up and the catalogs can't be found. The books are like your words: There they are, but you have no means of finding them." (p. 165–166)

After 3 years of therapy, John could only speak a few simple words. For the most part, his speech consisted of utterances that Sheila recognized as descriptive of extended sequences of actions:

"Over lunch he tells me about his morning. *Mmmmmm* means walking along minding his own business. *Arrr-up!* with his left hand describing an arc means that he has crossed a bridge. He meets a friend: broad smile, greeting gestures; they go into a pub; mime of conversation: *bah-bahbahbahbah*—and drinking. Or John gets on a bus: sounds of changing gears, starting and stopping." (p. 178)

Unlike his speech, John's writing made a strong recovery, and much that characterized him before the stroke carried over to his impoverished efforts at conversation— his charm, exuberance, intellectuality, his chuckles and smile—thereby sustaining the impression of those who knew him before the stroke as someone whose exhilaration for life was unblighted.

QUESTIONS TO CONSIDER

1. Suppose that you were asked to assess the abilities and deficits of patients with Broca's aphasia. What abilities and deficits would you focus on? What specific tasks would you include in your assessment to test for the presence of particular deficits?
2. What would the thoughts of a patient with severe Wernicke's aphasia be like? In what ways could you test these patients to see if their thinking was any more coherent than their speaking?

Reading

Although the comprehension and production of spoken language have a long history in the human past, the comprehension and production of written language are much more recent. Initially written language was pictorial. Arbitrary symbols gradually made their appearance as cues to pronunciation when a pictorial symbol was ambiguous. With the notable exception of Chinese (and other Asian writing systems based on Chinese), most modern languages use alphabetic writing systems in which a small number of symbols represent the sounds used to pronounce words.

Scanning of Text

As we saw in Chapter 6, our eyes make rapid jumps, called saccades ("suh-KAHD"), as we scan a scene. These same rapid movements occur when we read. A French ophthalmologist discovered saccadic eye movements while watching people read (Javal, 1879).

We do not receive information from the visual environment while the eyes are actually moving but only during the brief **fixations** that occur between saccades. The average fixation lasts about 250 milliseconds (ms, 1/1000 of a

---

fixation   A brief interval between saccadic eye movements during which the eye does not move; the brain accesses visual information during this time.

[**FIGURE 10•6**] The pattern of fixations made by two readers. Ovals indicate the locations of fixations in the line of text below them; the numbers within the ovals indicate durations of the fixations (in milliseconds). Arrows indicate backtracking to text already examined. (a) A good reader. (b) A poor reader.

(After Buswell (1937). From M. A. Just and P. A. Carpenter, *The Psychology of Reading and Language Comprehension*. Published by Allyn and Bacon, Boston, MA. Copyright © 1987 by Pearson Education. Reprinted by permission of the publisher.)

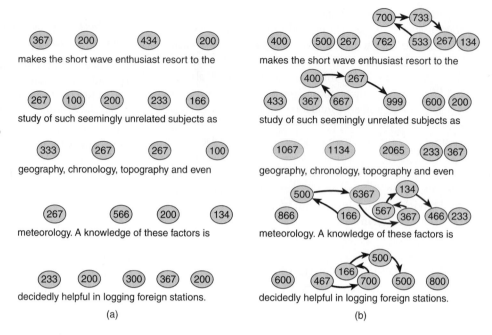

(a)   (b)

second), but duration can vary considerably. FIGURE 10•6 shows the patterns of fixations made by a good reader (a) and a poor reader (b). The ovals above the text indicate the locations of the fixations in the line of text that appears below, and the numbers indicate their duration (in ms). All of the good reader's saccades were in the forward direction, whereas the poor reader looked back and examined previously read words several times (indicated by the arrows). In addition, the good reader's fixations were, on average, considerably shorter.

What do we look at when we read? Research with eye-tracking cameras has shown that college students typically fixate on most of the words in a text when they are asked to read it carefully enough to understand its meaning. They fixate on 80% of the content words but on only 40% of the function words (Reichle et al., 1998). Of course, function words are generally shorter than content words, but the difference is not simply a matter of word size. Readers are more likely to skip over short function words such as *and* or *the* than over short content words such as *ant* or *run* (Carpenter & Just, 1983).

Eye movements provide an excellent window into the dynamics of the reading process. Apparently, as we read a sentence, we analyze it word by word (Rayner & Pollatsek, 1989). Of course, some words contribute more to our understanding than others do. Sometimes we must wait to see how a sentence turns out to understand its beginning. The less frequently a word occurs in normal usage, the greater the fixation time (e.g., Rayner, Sereno, & Raney, 1996); presumably, we take longer to recognize and understand unusual words. For example, the word *sable* has a longer fixation than the word *table*. Gaze time is longer for unpredictable than for predictable words, even when comparison words in experiments are matched for word length and frequency of usage (Reichle et al.,

1998). Besides spending a longer time fixating on unusual words, readers spend more time fixating on longer words. If word familiarity is held constant, the amount of time a word receives is proportional to its length (Carpenter & Just, 1983).

When people read Chinese, the amount of time they fixate on each character is proportional to its complexity—the number of brushstrokes used to make it.

Phonetic and Whole-Word Recognition: Evidence from Cognitive Neuroscience

Most psychologists who study the reading process believe that readers have two basic ways to recognize words: phonetic and whole-word recognition (Rayner et al., 2002; McGuinness, 2004; Snowling & Hulme, 2005). **Phonetic reading** involves the decoding of the sounds that letters or groups of letters make. For example, most readers of English would probably pronounce *praglet* in approximately the same way. Our ability to pronounce this nonsense word depends on our knowledge of the relation between letters and sounds in the English language. We use such knowledge to "sound the word out." But do we have to "sound out" familiar, reasonably short words such as *table* or *grass*? It appears that we do not; we recognize each of these words as a whole. In other words, we also engage in **whole-word reading.** Whole-word recognition not only is faster than phonetic decoding but also is absolutely necessary in a language (such as English) in which spelling is not completely phonetic.

If a reader is relatively inexperienced, he or she will have to sound out most words and, consequently, will read rather slowly. Experienced readers will have had so much practice looking at words that they will quickly recognize most of them as whole units. During reading, phonetic and whole-word reading may alternate. If the word is familiar, the whole-word method will suffice. If the word is unfamiliar, the whole-word method will fail, and the reader will turn to the phonetic method long enough to read the word. FIGURE 10·7 illustrates elements of the reading process, although in admittedly oversimplified fashion.

Inexperienced readers rely on phonetic reading when they encounter unfamiliar words.

Dyslexia The best evidence demonstrating that people can read words without sounding them out comes from studies of patients with acquired dyslexias. *Dyslexia* means "faulty reading." *Acquired* dyslexias are those caused by damage to the brains of people who already know how to read. In contrast, *developmental* dyslexias are reading difficulties that become apparent when children are learning to read. Developmental dyslexias may involve anomalies in brain circuitry and are discussed later in the chapter.

Investigators have reported several types of acquired dyslexias. We look at three of them here. All are caused by damage to the left parietal lobe or left temporal lobe, but the precise anatomy of dyslexias is not well understood. **Surface dyslexia** is a deficit in whole-word reading (Marshall & Newcombe, 1973; McCarthy & Warrington, 1990). The term "surface" reflects the fact that people with this disorder make errors related to the visual appearance of the words and to phonological rules, not to the meaning of the words, which could be considered "deeper" than their appearance. Because patients with surface dyslexia have difficulty recognizing words as wholes, they are obliged to sound them out. Thus, they can easily read words with regular spelling, such as *hand, tablet,* or *chin.* However, they have difficulty reading words with irregular spelling, such as *sew, pint,* or *yacht.* They may read these words as *sue, pinnt,* and *yatchet.* They have no difficulty reading pronounceable nonwords, such as *glab, trisk,* and *chint.* (See FIGURE 10·8.)

[CASE STUDY] Law and Or (2001) reported the case of a patient (C.M.L.), who was a salesperson in Hong Kong, where she was a native speaker and reader of the Cantonese

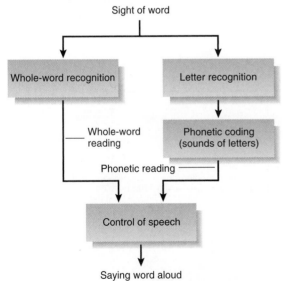

Sight of word

Whole-word recognition

Letter recognition

Whole-word reading

Phonetic coding (sounds of letters)

Phonetic reading ——————

Control of speech

Saying word aloud

[**FIGURE 10·7**] A simplified model of the reading process, showing whole-word and phonetic reading. The model considers only reading a single word aloud. Whole-word reading is used for most familiar words; phonetic reading is used for unfamiliar words and for nonwords such as *glab, trisk,* or *chint.*

---

phonetic reading Reading by decoding the phonetic structure of letter strings; reading by "sounding out."

whole-word reading Reading by recognizing a word as a whole; "sight reading."

surface dyslexia A reading disorder in which people can read words phonetically but have difficulty reading irregularly spelled words by the whole-word method.

[FIGURE 10•8] A model of surface dyslexia. Only phonetic reading remains.

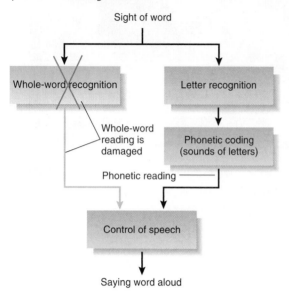

dialect of Chinese. In her early 40s, she was in an accident in which she had a head injury. The swelling on her brain was life-threatening, and she received an emergency left frontal and left temporal lobectomy. Although she manifested retrograde amnesia when she regained consciousness and could no longer recognize family members, she spoke fluently and did not exhibit sensory or motor impairments. About 18 months later, the researchers presented a series of line drawings from several semantic categories, including animals, electrical appliances, body parts, furniture, and clothing. In response to the drawings, C.M.L. was given several tasks, including naming the picture aloud, writing the name of the picture, reading the name of the picture, matching the spoken name to the picture, and matching the written name to the picture.

From their analysis of the results, the researchers concluded that the specific errors C.M.L. produced indicated her greater ability to read and write than to name objects—either orally or in writing. For example, in oral naming, she said "tomato" in response to the picture of an onion and "duckling" to the picture of a frog. In written naming, she wrote "watermelon" in response to a picture of a peach and "ballpoint pen" following a picture of a Chinese brush pen. The authors attributed this difference to C.M.L.'s retention of the ability to access the individual phonological elements when reading and writing. In contrast, such access was irrelevant for naming pictures, just as it would be when reading whole words.

---

phonological dyslexia A reading disorder in which people can read familiar words but have difficulty reading unfamiliar words or pronounceable nonwords because they cannot sound out words.

direct dyslexia A reading disorder caused by brain damage in which people can read words aloud without understanding them.

Patients with **phonological dyslexia** have the opposite problem; they can read by the whole-word method but cannot sound out words. Thus, they can read words they are already familiar with, but they have great difficulty figuring out how to read unfamiliar words or pronounceable nonwords (Beauvois & Dérouesné, 1979; Dérouesné & Beauvois, 1979). People with phonological dyslexia still may be excellent readers if they have already acquired a good reading vocabulary before their brain damage occurs. (See **FIGURE 10•9**.)

Phonological dyslexia provides evidence that whole-word reading and phonetic reading involve different brain mechanisms. Phonetic reading, which is the only way we can read nonwords or words we have not yet learned, entails letter-to-sound decoding. It also requires more than decoding of the sounds produced by single letters; for example, some sounds are transcribed as two-letter sequences (known as digraphs, such as *th* or *sh*), and the addition of the letter *e* to the end of a word can lengthen an internal vowel (*can* becomes *cane*). Further, evidence from PET scans (Fiez et al., 1999) and *f*MRI scans (Gaillard et al., 2000) suggests that phonetic reading activates the left frontal lobe in the area associated with Broca's aphasia.

We know that recognizing a spoken word is different from understanding it. **Direct dyslexia** resembles a form of aphasia considered in Chapter 9, isolation aphasia, except that the words in question are written, not spoken (Lytton & Brust, 1989; Schwartz, Marin, & Saffran, 1979). People with this disorder can read words aloud *even though they cannot understand the words they are saying*. After sustaining a stroke that damaged his left frontal and temporal lobes, Lytton and Brust's (1989) patient lost the ability to communicate verbally; his speech was meaningless, and he was unable to comprehend what other people said to him. However, he could read words that were already familiar to him. He could

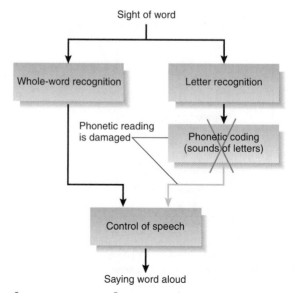

[FIGURE 10•9] A model of phonological dyslexia. Only whole-word reading remains.

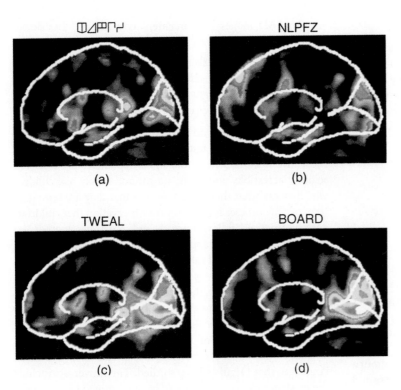

(a)   (b)

TWEAL   BOARD

(c)   (d)

[**FIGURE 10•10**] PET scans of the medial surface of the brains of people who read (a) letterlike forms, (b) strings of consonants, (c) pronounceable nonwords, and (d) real words.

(Reprinted with permission from Petersen, S. E., Fox, P. T., Snyder, A. Z., & Raichle, M. E. *Science*, 1990, *249*, 1041–1044. Copyright © 1990 AAAS.)

not read pronounceable nonwords; thus, he had lost the ability to read phonetically. His comprehension deficit seemed complete; when the investigators presented him with a word and several pictures, one of which corresponded to the word, he correctly read the word aloud but had no idea which picture went with it.

The symptoms of developmental dyslexias resemble those of acquired dyslexias (Vellutino & Fletcher, 2005). They first manifest themselves in childhood and tend to occur in families, which suggests the presence of a genetic (and hence developmental) component. Grigorenko (2001) reported studies of the prevalence of developmental dyslexias, ranging from 1% in Japan and China to 33% in Venezuela, with a 26-nation mean of 7%. Several studies have found evidence that brain abnormalities in a portion of Wernicke's area may be responsible for developmental dyslexias (Galaburda, 1993; Galaburda & Kemper, 1979; Galaburda et al., 1985). In addition, Galaburda, Menard, and Rosen (1994) found evidence that structural differences in the auditory system of the brain may play a role in this disorder. Brain-imaging data indicate that people with developmental dyslexias can use both Broca's area and Wernicke's area for language processing. However, these individuals lack the degree of synchrony of neural activity in the two areas shown by people without dyslexia (Paulesu et al., 1996). In other words, dyslexic patients may not be able to combine the activity of the two areas.

As we mentioned earlier, PET studies have shown that the auditory association cortex is activated by the sound of words but not by other sounds. Petersen et al. (1990) obtained similar results by using visual stimuli. These investigators presented people with four types of visual stimuli: unfamiliar letter-like forms, strings of consonants, pronounceable nonwords, and real words. They found that although all visual stimuli activated the primary visual cortex, one region of the visual association cortex was activated only by pronounceable nonwords or by real words; that is, by familiar combinations of letters. Presumably, damage to this region, or faulty development of the neural circuits located there, is responsible for some forms of dyslexia. (See FIGURE 10•10.)

A more recent study involving Finnish participants and the use of MEG found temporal but not anatomical differences in the responses of developmentally dyslexic and nondyslexic adults (Helenius et al., 1999). The participants viewed sentences presented one word at a time. The final word in the sentence was manipulated to be expected, unexpected but meaningful, sharing the same first letters as the expected word but nonmeaningful, and unexpected as well as nonmeaningful. Although no differences in the spatial distribution of cortical responses were observed between the two groups, cortical activation by word meaning began later in dyslexic participants, and their cortical responses were significantly weaker than those of normal readers.

Reduced cerebral activity in the left occipitotemporal area of developmentally dyslexic adults was reported by McCrory et al. (2005). PET scanning occurred as participants were asked to read words and name pictures consisting of line drawings. The lower activity appeared for both tasks, prompting the authors to conclude that deficits in reading words and naming pictures may have a common neurological basis. The failure to integrate phonology and visual information properly may characterize developmental dyslexia.

1. Suppose someone close to you received a head injury that caused phonological dyslexia. What would you do to try to help her read better? (Hint: It would probably be best to build on the abilities she retained after the injury.) Suppose she needed to learn to read some words she had never seen before. How would you help her do so?

2. Young children (and even some adults) often move their lips while they read. Why do you think they do so?

Language Acquisition by Children

How do children learn to communicate verbally with other people? How do they master the syntactical rules needed to transform a thought into a coherent sentence? How do they learn the meanings of thousands of words? And why do they do all of this? Do other people shape children's babble into words by appropriately reinforcing their verbal behavior, or do innate mechanisms ensure children's acquisition of language without a dependence on reinforcement? This section addresses these and other questions related to children's verbal development.

Language Acquisition Device

Many linguists have concluded that the ability to learn a first language is innate. A child only must live in the company of speakers of a language to acquire that language. To explain how this happens, linguists have proposed that a child's brain contains a **language acquisition device (LAD)** that embodies rules of "universal grammar." Because each language expresses these rules in slightly different ways, the child must learn the details, but the basics are already there in the brain (Chomsky, 1965; Lennenberg, 1967; McNeill, 1970; Miller, 1987).

The assertion that an innate LAD guides children's acquisition of a first language is part of a general theory about the cognitive structures responsible for language and its acquisition (Pinker, 1990, 1994, 2007). The most important components of the theory are as follows:

1. Children who are learning a language make hypotheses about the syntactical rules they need to follow. These hypotheses are confirmed or disconfirmed by the speech they hear.

2. An LAD is a part of the brain and guides children's hypothesis formation. Because they have this device, there are certain types of hypothetical rules they will never entertain and certain types of sentences they will never utter.

3. An LAD makes reinforcement unnecessary; the device provides the motivation for the child to learn a language.

4. A critical period exists for learning a language. An LAD works best during childhood; after childhood (approximately age 12), languages are difficult to learn and almost impossible to master, especially in their spoken form.

At present we have no way to evaluate the first assertion—that children make and test hypotheses about syntactical rules. Most investigators believe that these hypotheses are not consciously accessible, and, thus, we cannot simply ask children why they say what they do. To assume that they are testing alternative hypotheses is based on the observation that children's speech sometimes follows one rule and sometimes another. For example, children often apply the regular past-tense rule even to irregular verbs, saying "I catched it" or "She hitted me," as if they are testing the hypothesis that all events in the past are expressed by adding *-ed* to the word that denotes the action.

A more important—and testable—assertion is the LAD guides a child's hypothesis testing. The most important piece of evidence in favor of this assertion is the discovery of **language universals**: characteristics that can be found in all languages that linguists have studied. The universals include the existence of noun phrases (*The quick brown fox . . .*); verb phrases (*. . . ate the chicken*); grammatical categories of words such as nouns and adjectives; and syntactical rules that permit the expression of subject–verb–object relations (*Maddie hit Andy*), plurality (*two birds*), and possession (*Rachel's pen*).

The fact that all languages share certain characteristics does not mean that language acquisition is the product of innate brain mechanisms. For example, Hebb, Lambert, and Tucker (1973) observed that language universals may simply reflect universal realities of the world. Objects come in slightly different shapes, sizes, and colors, so we can expect languages to develop ways (such as adjectives) to distinguish among them. Similarly, when people deal with one another and with nature, their interactions often take the form of an agent's acting on an object. Thus, the fact that all languages have ways of expressing these interactions is not surprising. It is not unreasonable to suppose that the same kinds of linguistic practices have been independently invented at different times and in different places by different cultures.

Even if some language universals are dictated by reality, others could indeed be the result of an LAD. For example, consider the following sentences (Pinker, 1990):

A1. *Irv drove the car* into the garage.

A2. Irv drove the car.

B1. *Irv put the car* into the garage.

B2. Irv put the car.

Someone (such as a child learning a language) who heard sentences A1 and A2 could reasonably infer that sentence B1 could be transformed into sentence B2. But the inference obviously is false; sentence B2 is syntactically incorrect. The syntactical rules that say that sentence A2 is acceptable but that sentence B2 is not are complex; and their complexity is taken as evidence that they must be innate, not

---

language acquisition device (LAD) A theoretical endowment unique to humans that is postulated to account for the fact that, regardless of geographical location and often severely restricted environments, children tend to acquire a first language in highly similar fashion.

language universal A characteristic feature found in all natural languages.

learned. As Pinker (1990) concludes, "The solution to the problem [as to why children do not utter sentence B2] must be that children's learning mechanisms ultimately do not allow them to make the generalization" (p. 206).

Recent evidence for this view comes from an *f*MRI study by Musso and colleagues (2003), who examined the brain activity of native German speakers as they learned samples of one of two types of language: a real but unfamiliar language (such as Italian or Japanese) or an artificial language that used Italian or Japanese words but violated syntactical principles common to both languages. In contrast to the natural languages, Musso and colleagues constructed their artificial languages to contain arbitrary syntactical conventions based solely on linear word order. For example, to construct a question, the word order of a sentence simply would be reversed. To ask whether Paolo is eating the pizza, the artificial language would read *Pizza la mangia Paolo*? Or to construct a negative statement, the word *no* would be added after the third word of a sentence, as in *Paolo mangia la no pizza* ("Paolo eats the no pizza"). Musso and colleagues found that the natural language samples triggered activity in a specific region—Broca's area. Learning the artificial language produced only nonspecific activity across large areas of the brain.

The third assertion of the LAD theory is that language acquisition occurs without the need of reinforcement—or even of correction. Brown and Hanlon (1970) recorded dialogue between children and parents and found that adults generally did not show disapproval when the children's utterances violated syntactical rules or approval when they were within the rules. Instead, approval appeared to be contingent on the truth or accuracy of the children's statements. If there is no differential reinforcement, how can we explain the fact that children eventually learn to speak in syntactically correct ways?

It is undoubtedly true that adults seldom say, "Good, you said that right," or "No, you said that wrong." However, a study by Bohannon and Stanowicz (1988) found that adults are likely to repeat children's syntactically correct sentences verbatim but to correct those that are incorrect. For example, if a child says, "That be monkey," an adult might say, "Yes, that is a monkey." Adults were also more likely to ask for clarification in the wake of syntactically incorrect sentences. In this way, they provide the information children need to correct faulty speech. It is also the case that adults talk differently to children than they do to other adults; specifically, they speak in ways that would seem to be optimal for promoting learning. According to Newport, Gleitman, and Gleitman (1977), almost all speech directed to young children (at least, in industrialized English-speaking societies) is syntactically correct.

It is also the case that children do not acquire a language that they simply overhear. Bonvillian, Nelson, and Charrow (1976) studied children of deaf parents whose only exposure to spoken language was through television or radio. This exposure was not enough; although the children listened to and watched television and listened to the radio, they did not learn to speak English.

The final assertion—that an LAD works best during childhood—has received the most experimental support.

A young child's direct interaction with adult speakers is a critical feature of language acquisition.

For example, Newport and Supalla (cited in Johnson & Newport, 1989) studied the ability of people who were deaf from birth to use sign language. They found that the earlier the training began, the better the person was able to communicate. Also, Johnson and Newport (1989) found that native Korean and Chinese speakers who moved to North America learned English grammar better if they arrived during childhood. The advantage did not appear to be a result of differences in motivation to learn a second language. Such results are consistent with the hypothesis that something happens to the brain after childhood that makes it more difficult to learn a language.

More recently, Coppola and Newport (2005) studied the gestural systems of three deaf Nicaraguans. The independently developed systems allow the individuals to communicate with their hearing families. The authors referred to the systems as "home sign." Their analysis of the systems proceeded on the assumption that the individuals had been isolated from exposure to conventional language, spoken or signed. The deaf individuals were presented with a large number of brief video clips containing actions involving either one person or object, a pair of persons, or a person and an object. The participants were asked to describe each event to a communicative partner, who was, in turn, asked to select from a set of four pictures the event the participants had described gesturally.

The authors reported that, irrespective of the number of persons or the type of action the video clip portrayed, the participants almost always began their description in the same way. What they did was what a hearing person would do in describing the clip—begin with a noun phrase that became the subject of a sentence. Despite their isolation from linguistic conventions, the participants still structured their descriptions according to those conventions. The authors concluded that "the grammatical subject appears to be part of the bedrock on which [home sign] language forms" (p. 19253).

Although nature gives a strong nudge to a child's first-language acquisition, as suggested by the LAD theory, the linguistic environment remains a critical component of that acquisition. Bruner (1983, 1998) called attention to many ways in which the child's linguistic environment is conducive, referring to it as the **Language Acquisition Support System** (or **LASS,** in an obvious play on LAD). For Bruner, language is inherently interactive, and those who have already acquired language are in a position to behave toward the children in ways that encourage their successful acquisition as well.

Gallaway and Richards (1994) described several aspects of the LASS that are consequential for children's acquisition of language, including the following:

- The types of language directed toward the child by the primary caregivers
- The range of the child's environments in which language is used
- The differential roles of family members in the child's acquisition of language
- The immediate consequences that follow the child's early use of language

Some of these aspects are addressed in later sections of the chapter.

Alternative Theories of Language Acquisition
Tomasello (2005) has argued for a *usage-based* linguistic approach to language acquisition. In this view, young children begin to learn the regularities of language, and the exceptions thereto, a word or phrase at a time. They do so not by means of an LAD but through two sets of skills: intention-reading skills and pattern-finding skills. Both sets begin to develop during the year after birth and provide a kind of cognitive scaffolding for the acquisition of increasingly more complex language structures in the ensuring years.

Bates and Dick (2002) called attention to the parallels between developmental milestones for language during the first 2.5 years and the gestures that children develop. For example, word production and word naming emerge at roughly the same time the child begins to perform what Bates and Dick term "recognitory gestures." For example, children might put a brush to their hair at the same time they say *brush*. The authors assert that language acquisition draws from more-general abilities that it shares with other developing domains and not from a specialized LAD. In addition, they suggest, on the basis of *f*MRI and TCM studies, that language and gesture acquisition share common neural systems.

Recognition of Speech Sounds by Infants

Language development starts even before birth. Although the sounds that reach a fetus are somewhat muffled, speech sounds can still be heard. The voice that a fetus hears best and most often is obviously that of its mother. DeCasper and

Spence (1986) found that newborn infants preferred hearing their mothers reading a passage they had read aloud several times before the babies were born to hearing them read a passage they had never read before. Presumably, the infants had learned something about the rhythm and intonation of the passage they had heard in utero. Some evidence indicates that newborns can learn to discriminate speech sounds while they sleep (Cheour et al., 2002).

Developmental psychologists have devised a clever technique to determine what sounds a very young infant can perceive. A special pacifier nipple is placed in the baby's mouth. The nipple is connected by a plastic tube to a pressure-sensitive switch that converts the infant's sucking movements into electrical signals. These signals can be used to turn on auditory stimuli. Each time the baby sucks, a particular sound is presented. If the auditory stimulus is novel, the baby usually begins to suck at a high rate. If the stimulus remains the same, its novelty wears off (that is, habituation occurs), and the rate of sucking decreases. With another new stimulus, the rate of sucking may again suddenly increase, unless the baby cannot tell the difference. If the two stimuli sound the same to the infant, the rate of sucking remains low after the change.

By using this technique, Eimas, Siqueland, Jusczyk, and Vigorito (1971) found that 1-month-old infants could tell the difference between the sounds of the consonants *b* and *p*. They presented the sounds *ba* and *pa*, synthesized by a computer. The infants discriminated between speech sounds having voice-onset times that differed by only 20 ms. Even very early during postnatal development, the human auditory system is able to make very fine discriminations.

TABLE 10·1 lists some of the responses infants make to various speech sounds.

[**TABLE 10·1**] **Examples of Responses Infants Make to Various Speech Sounds**

First Age of Occurrence	Response
Newborn	Is startled by a loud noise
	Turns head to look in the direction of sound
	Is calmed by the sound of a voice
	Prefers mother's voice to a stranger's
	Discriminates among many speech sounds
1–2 months	Smiles when spoken to
3–7 months	Responds differently to different intonations (e.g., friendly, angry)
8–12 months	Responds to name
	Responds to "no"
	Recognizes phrases from games (e.g., "Peekaboo," "How big is baby?")
	Recognizes words from social routines (e.g., waves in response to "bye bye")
	Recognizes some words

Source: Berko Gleason, J. (1993). *The development of language.* New York: Macmillan. Used by permission.

---

language acquisition support system (LASS)   A cultural system that aids the child's acquisition of a first language by providing the forms of interaction conducive to acquisition.

The Prespeech Period and the First Words

Kaplan and Kaplan (1970) outlined the progression of early vocalizations in infants. The first sound that a baby makes is crying. As we shall see in Chapter 12, this aversive stimulus serves an important function: It produces useful reactions from the baby's caregivers. At about 1 month of age, infants start making other sounds, including *cooing* (so called because of the prevalence of the *oo* sound). Often during this period, infants also make a series of sounds that resemble a half-hearted attempt to mimic the sound of crying.

At around 6 months, an infant's sounds begin to resemble those that occur in speech. Even though their *babbling* does not contain words—and does not appear to involve attempts to communicate verbally—the sounds infants make, and the rhythm in which the sounds are articulated, reflect the adult speech that infants hear. Infants often engage in "serious conversations" with their caregivers, taking turns "talking" with them. Infants alter the stream of sounds they make, almost as if they are using a secret language (Menn & Stoel-Gammon, 1993). They are also able to discriminate and categorize the rhythms and tempos of sounds (Trehub & Thorpe, 1989). At this age, they also show evidence of long-term memory for the sound patterns of words read to them (Jusczyk & Hohne, 1997).

A study by Kuhl and colleagues (1992) provides further evidence of the effect of children's verbal environment on their language development. Native speakers learn not to distinguish between slight variations of sounds present in their language; they do not even hear the differences. For example, Japanese contains a sound that comes midway between /l/ and /r/. Different native speakers pronounce the sound differently, but all pronunciations are recognized as examples of the same phoneme. When native speakers of Japanese learn English, they have great difficulty distinguishing the sounds /l/ and /r/. Presumably, the speech sounds a child hears alter the brain mechanisms responsible for recognizing them so that minor variations are not even perceived.

When does this alteration occur? Most researchers suppose that it happens after children begin to learn the meanings of words at around 10 to 12 months of age. Kuhl and her colleagues found, however, that the alteration takes place much earlier. These researchers studied 6-month-old infants in the United States and Sweden. The infants were seated in their mothers' laps, where they watched a researcher sitting nearby, playing with a silent toy. Every 2 seconds, a loudspeaker located to the infant's left presented the sound of a vowel. From time to time the sound was altered. If the infant noticed the change and looked at the loudspeaker, the researcher reinforced the response by activating a toy figure that pounded on a miniature drum. Thus, the procedure provided a test of infants' ability to distinguish slight differences in vowel sounds. (See FIGURE 10•11.)

The researchers presented two different vowel sounds, one found in English but not in Swedish, and the other

[**FIGURE 10•11**] A child being tested in the experiment by Kuhl and her colleagues (1992).

(Photo © James Wilson/Woodfin Camp & Associates)

found in Swedish but not in English. From time to time, they varied the sound slightly. The reactions of the Swedish infants and the American infants were strikingly different. Swedish infants noticed when the English vowel changed but not when the Swedish vowel changed; American infants did the opposite. In other words, by the age of 6 months, the infants had learned not to pay attention to slight differences in speech sounds of their own language but were still able to distinguish slight differences in speech sounds they had never heard. Even though they were too young to understand the formal meaning of what they heard, the speech of people around them had affected the development of their auditory perception.

At about 1 year of age, a child begins to produce words. The first sounds children use to produce words appear to be similar across all languages and cultures: The first vowel is usually the soft *a* sound of *father,* and the first consonant is a stop consonant produced with the lips—*p* or *b.* Thus, the first word is often *papa* or *baba.* The next feature to be added is nasality, which converts the earlier sounds into *m.* Thus, the next word is often *mama.* Parents everywhere may interpret these combinations of sounds as their baby's attempts to address them directly.

The first sounds used in words contain the same phonemes that are found in the babbling sounds the child is already making; thus, speech emerges from prespeech sounds. Yet although young children learn words from their caregivers and from older children, they often invent their own **protowords,** unique strings of phonemes that serve word-like functions. Children use these protowords consistently in particular situations (Menn & Stoel-Gammon, 1993).

The development of speech sounds continues for many years. Some sequences are added quite late. For example, the *str* of *string* and the *bl* of *blink* are difficult for young children

---

protoword A unique string of phonemes that an infant invents and uses as a word.

to produce; they usually say *tring* and *link,* omitting the leading consonant. Most children recognize sounds in adult speech before they can produce them. Consider this conversation (Dale, 1976):

> *Adult*: Johnny, I'm going to say a word two times and you tell me which time I say it right and which time I say it wrong: *rabbit, wabbit.*
>
> *Child*: *Wabbit* is *wight* and *wabbit* is *wong.*

Although the child could not pronounce the *r* sound, he clearly could recognize it.

The Two-Word Stage

At around 18 to 20 months of age, children start putting two words together, and their linguistic development takes a leap forward. It is at this stage that linguistic creativity becomes more apparent; children begin to say things they have never heard. Consider the creativity expressed in *allgone outside,* said by a child when the door to her house was closed once she was inside.

Like first sounds, children's two-word utterances are remarkably consistent across all cultures that have been observed. Children use words in the same way, no matter what language their parents speak. Even deaf children who learn sign language from their parents put two words together in the same way as children who can hear (Bellugi & Klima, 1972). Deaf children whose parents do not know sign language invent their own signs and use them in orderly, "rule-governed" ways (Goldin-Meadow & Feldman, 1977). Thus, the grammar of children's language at the two-word stage appears to be universal (Owens, 1992).

For many years developmental **psycholinguists** described the speech of young children in terms of adult syntax, but researchers now recognize that children's speech simply follows different rules. Young children are incapable of forming complex sentences because their vocabulary is small, partly because their short-term "working" memory is limited (they cannot yet encode a long string of words), and partly because their cognitive development has not yet reached a stage at which they can learn syntactical rules (Locke, 1993). As a result, their utterances in the two-word stage are dominated by content words. The absence of function words gives their language an abbreviated but nevertheless efficient form, much like that found in telegrams, where nouns, action words, and modifiers predominate. For that reason, it is sometimes referred to as *telegraphic speech.* Examples include "Momma go" as the telegraphic version of "Momma has gone" and (pointing at a man) "Man funny" as the correspondent to "That man is funny."

---

psycholinguistics A branch of psychology devoted to the study of verbal behavior and related cognitive abilities.

child-directed speech The speech of an adult directed toward a child; differs in several ways from adult-directed speech and tends to facilitate the learning of language by children.

How Adults Talk to Children

Parents do not talk to children the way they talk to adults; they use only short, simple, well-formed, repetitive sentences and phrases (Brown & Bellugi, 1964). In fact, such speech deserves its own label: **child-directed speech,** also known as *motherese* (Snow, 1986). In a comprehensive review of the literature, deVilliers and deVilliers (1978; see also Werker et al., 1996) found that adults' speech to children is characterized by clear pronunciation, exaggerated intonations, careful distinctions between similar-sounding phonemes, relatively few abstract words and function words, and a tendency to isolate constituents that undoubtedly enables young children to recognize them as units of speech.

Another important characteristic of child-directed speech is that it tends to refer to tangible objects the child can see, to what the child is doing, and to what is happening around the child (Snow et al., 1976). Words are paired with objects the child is familiar with, which is the easiest way to learn them. For example, caregivers make statements and ask questions about what objects are called, what noises they make, what color they are, what actions they are engaging in, whom they belong to, and where they are located. Their speech contains more content words and fewer function words (Newport, 1975; Snow, 1977).

Adults often expand children's speech by imitating it while putting it into more complex forms. This undoubtedly helps the child learn about syntactical structure (Brown, 1973; Brown & Bellugi, 1964). Consider the following exchange:

> *Child*: Baby highchair.
>
> *Adult*: Baby is in the highchair.
>
> *Child*: Eve lunch.
>
> *Adult*: Eve is having lunch.
>
> *Child*: Throw daddy.
>
> *Adult*: Throw it to daddy.

Infants also exert control over what their caregivers talk about. The topic of conversation usually involves what the infant is playing with or is guided by what the infant is gazing at (Bohannon, 1993). This practice means that infants hear speech that refers to what they are already attending to, which undoubtedly facilitates language acquisition. Tomasello and Farrar (1986) found that infants of mothers who talked mostly about the objects of their infants' gazes uttered their first words earlier than other infants and also developed larger vocabularies early in life. Werker, Pegg, and McLeod (1994) found that, when infants were shown a video of a Cantonese speaker talking to either an infant or to an adult, babies from both Cantonese- and English-speaking homes preferred to look at the infant-directed communication.

In some instances, parents and early-childhood educators have taught American Sign Language to hearing children (Dennis & Azpin, 2005; Thomson & Nelson-Metlay, 2005) in an adjunct to spoken language. There are suggestions that the addition of signed images to speech may help some children acquire language by multiplying the modalities in which the message is conveyed. For the same reason, signing may be an asset to phonological awareness as a basis for literacy.

Acquisition of Adult Rules of Grammar

As children develop past the two-word stage around age 2, they begin to learn and use more and more of the syntactical rules that adults use. The first form of sentence lengthening appears to be the expansion of object nouns into noun phrases (Bloom, 1970). For example, *That ball* becomes *That a big ball*. Next, verbs get used more often, articles are added, prepositional phrases emerge, and sentences become more complex. These changes involve the use of **inflections** and *function words*. Function words, you recall, are the short words (*the, to, and,* and so on) that help shape the syntax of a sentence. Inflections are special suffixes we add to words to change their syntactical or semantic function. For example, the inflection *-ed* changes most verbs into the past tense (*change* becomes *changed*), *-ing* can turn a verb into a noun (*make* becomes *making*), and *-'s* indicates possession (*Paul's truck*). The rules that govern the use of inflections or function words are rarely made explicit. That is, a parent seldom says, "When you want to use the past tense, be sure to add *-ed* to the verb"—nor would a young child understand this instruction. Instead, children must listen to speech and figure out how to express such concepts as the past tense.

Studies of children's speech have told us something about how this informal process of learning occurs. As noted earlier, the most frequently used verbs in most languages are *irregular*. Forming the past tense of such verbs in English does not involve adding *-ed*. (Examples are *go/went, throw/ threw, buy/bought, see/saw,* and *can/could*.) Because irregular verbs get more use than regular ones do, children learn them first, producing the past tense easily in sentences such as *I ran, I fell down,* and *She hit me*. Soon afterward, they discover the regular past tense inflection and expand their vocabulary, producing sentences such as *He dropped the ball*. But they also begin to say *I runned, I falled down,* and *She hitted me*—all examples of **overgeneralization errors**. Having formed a syntactical rule from their experience, they apply it to all verbs, including the irregular ones that they were previously using correctly. It takes children several years to learn to use the irregular past tense correctly again (Pinker, 1999).

English-speaking children as young as 3 years of age know how to combine nouns to describe relations between objects. Nicoladis (2003) showed children pictures that could be described by compound nouns. (See **FIGURE 10·12**.) Then she asked them: "What is this?" Three- and four-year-old children generally gave three types of responses: Compound nouns such as *fish shoes* were the most frequent, followed by prepositional phrases (e.g., *fish on shoes*) or single words (e.g., *shoes*). Three-year-olds were just as likely as 4-year-olds to create compound words—although, somewhat surprisingly, they were less likely to comprehend compound words or to choose them from a set of alternatives.

[**FIGURE 10·12**] An object that could be described by a compound noun.

(Reprinted from Nicoladis, E., What compound nouns mean to preschoool children, *Brain and Language, 84,* 38–49, Copyright © 2003 with permission from Elsevier.)

In his book, *Crazy English*, Richard Lederer provides a whimsical sample of the puzzles that irregularities in English pose:

> If adults commit adultery, do infants commit infantry? If olive oil is made from olives, what do they make baby oil from? If a vegetarian eats vegetables, what does a a humanitarian consume? A writer is someone who writes, and a stinger is something that stings, but fingers don't fing, grocers don't groce, hammers don't ham, humdingers don't humding, ushers don't ush, and haberdashers do not haberdash . . . .
>
> . . . If the plural of *tooth* is *teeth,* so shouldn't the plural of *booth* be *beeth*? One goose, two geese—so one moose, two meese? If people ring a bell today and rang a bell yesterday, why don't we say that they flang a ball? If they wrote a letter, perhaps they also bote their tongue. (Quoted in Pinker, 2007, p. 40)

Acquisition of Meaning

How do children learn to use words and understand their meaning? The simplest explanation is that they hear a word spoken at the same time that they see (or hear, or touch) the object to which the word refers. After several such pairings, the word becomes part of their vocabulary. Children first learn the names of things with which they interact, or things that change (and thus attract their attention). For example, they are quick to learn words like *cookie* or *blanket* but slow to learn words like *wall* or *window* (Pease, Gleason, & Pan, 1993; Ross et al., 1986).

Suppose we give a young boy a small red plastic ball and say "ball." After a while, the child says "ball" when he sees it.

---

inflection A change in the form of a word (usually by addition of a suffix) to denote a grammatical feature such as tense or number.

overgeneralization The creation of grammatical errors when a child uses an inferred syntactical rule to form the past tense of verbs.

Yet we cannot conclude from this behavior that he knows the meaning of *ball*. So far, he has encountered only one referent for the word: a small ball made of red plastic. If he says "ball" when he sees an apple or an orange, or even the moon, we must conclude that he does not know the meaning of *ball*. This type of error is called **overextension**—the use of a word to denote a larger class of items than is appropriate. If the boy uses the word to refer only to the small red plastic ball, his error is called an **underextension**—the use of a word to denote a smaller class of items than is appropriate.

Both overextensions and underextensions are normal. Caregivers often correct children's overextensions. The most effective type of instruction occurs when an adult provides the correct label and points out the features that distinguish the object from the one with which the child has confused it (Chapman, Leonard, & Mervis, 1986). For example, if a child calls a yo-yo a "ball," the caregiver might say, "That's a yo-yo. See? It goes up and down" (Pease, Gleason, & Pan, 1993, p. 130).

Graham, Baker, and Poulin-Dubois (1998) looked at how children 16 to 19 months of age responded to this type of information provided by adults. They assigned artificial names to objects, and then observed whether children would gaze at another object that matched a given item. For example, a child was shown a baby stroller while the researcher said, "This is a wug." Then two pictures were presented. One was the picture of another stroller and the other a picture of a baby. At the same time, the researcher said, "Find the wug." Children gazed at the picture of the second stroller longer when the artificial label was used to describe the stroller than when no label was used. In contrast, the amount of time spent looking at the baby was not affected by the use of a label. Graham and her colleagues interpreted these results as indicative of children's tendency to assign the language labels spoken by adults to basic categories. Their sensitivity to categorical references and their ability to use them seem to underlie children's rapid acquisition of vocabulary between the ages of 2 and 6 years (Poulin-Dubois, Graham, & Sippola, 1995).

The Role of Memory in Understanding the Meanings of Written Words and Sentences

Recognizing a written word is a matter of perception. The primary task is visual. But, as described in the previous section, when we encounter an unfamiliar word, we use phonological rules to "sound it out." Either way, though, once we recognize a word, the next step in the reading process is understanding its meaning.

We learn the meanings of words through experience. The meanings of content words involve memories of objects, actions, and their characteristics—visual, auditory, somatosensory, olfactory, and gustatory. These memories of the meanings of words are distributed throughout the brain. For example, our understanding of the meaning of the word *apple* involves memories of the sight of an apple; the way it feels in our hands; the crunching sound we hear when we bite into it; and the texture, taste, and odor we experience when we chew it. But what about the understanding of abstract content words, such as the nouns *honesty* and *justice*? These words are probably first understood as adjectives: An *honest student* is someone who does not cheat on exams or plagiarize when writing papers; an *honest bank clerk* does not steal money; and so on. Our understanding of these words depends on our direct experience with such people or on our vicarious experience with them through stories we read or hear about. By itself, the word *honesty* is abstract; it does not refer to anything concrete. The understanding of most function words is also abstract. For example, the word *and* serves to link two or more things being discussed; the word *or* indicates a choice; the word *but* indicates that a contradiction will be expressed in the next phrase.

As we read (or hear) a sentence, the words and phrases we encounter activate memories that permit us to understand their meanings. Unless we have to pause to figure out an obscure allusion (which should not happen very often in the case of good writing and speaking), memory activation is an automatic, unconscious process. When we read the sentence, *She opened her mouth to let the dentist examine her aching tooth*, we very quickly picture a specific scene. Our understanding depends not only on comprehension of the specific words but also on our knowledge of dental chairs, dentists, toothaches and their treatment, and so on.

A phenomenon known as **semantic priming** gives us some hints about the nature of activation of memories triggered by the perception of words and phrases. Semantic priming is a facilitating effect: The presentation of a word facilitates the recognition of words having related meanings (Tulving & Schacter, 1990). The process involves similarities in the meanings of words. For example, if a person sees the word *bread*, he or she will be more likely to recognize successfully a fuzzy image of the word *butter*. Presumably, the brain contains circuits of neurons that serve as "word detectors" and are involved in visual recognition of particular words (McClelland & Rumelhart, 1981; Morton, 1979). Reading the word *bread* activates word detectors and other neural circuits involved in memories of the word's meaning. Apparently the activation spreads to circuits denoting related concepts, such as *butter*. Thus, our memories must be linked according to our experiences, direct or vicarious, of the relations between specific concepts.

FIGURE 10•13 suggests how neural representations of concepts may be linked together in a network. The concept "piano" has many different features, including the sounds a piano makes, its size, the shapes it can have, its parts, people who play it or tune it or move it, and so on. Depending on the context in which it is perceived, the word *piano* can activate

---

overextension The use of a word to denote a larger class of items than is appropriate; for example, referring to the moon as a *ball*.

underextension The use of a word to denote a smaller class of items than is appropriate; for example, referring only to one particular animal as a dog.

semantic priming The facilitating effect of a word on the recognition of words having related meanings that are presented subsequently

[**FIGURE 10•13**] A network of neural representations of concepts. Recognizing the word *piano* activates neural representations of features related to pianos. The blue ovals indicate the concepts activated by the sentence *The piano was lifted.*

(From Marcel Adam Just and Patricia A. Carpenter, *The Psychology of Reading and Language Comprehension.* Copyright © 1987 by Allyn and Bacon. Reproduced with permission.) (Illustration at right © Julie Delton/ Photodisc/Getty Images)

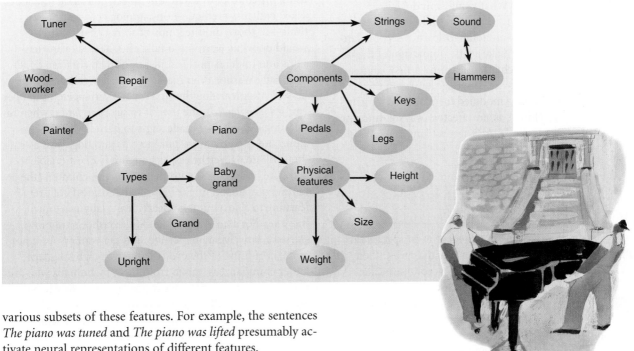

various subsets of these features. For example, the sentences *The piano was tuned* and *The piano was lifted* presumably activate neural representations of different features.

Context effects, an example of top-down processing (see Chapter 7), have been demonstrated through semantic priming. For example, Zola (1984) asked people to read either of two sentences such as the following while he recorded their eye movements with an eye-tracking camera.

1. Movie theaters must have adequate popcorn to serve their patrons.

2. Movie theaters must have buttered popcorn to serve their patrons.

Zola found that people made a significantly shorter fixation on the word *popcorn* in sentence 2. Let us consider why they did so. The word *adequate* does not normally occur with the word *popcorn,* so the people who read sentence 1 were unprepared for this word when they got to it. However, *buttered* certainly goes with *popcorn,* especially in the context of a movie theater. Thus, the context provided by the sentence may have facilitated activation of the word detector for *popcorn,* making it easier for participants to recognize.

Semantic priming studies have also shed some light on another aspect of the reading process—the development of a mental model. Many investigators believe that as a person reads text, he or she generates a mental model of what the text is describing (see Chapter 11 for a discussion of mental models). If the text contains a narrative, the reader may imagine the scenes, the people, and the actions that are described there. For example, Glenberg, Meyer, and Lindem (1987)

asked participants to read the following sentences. Some saw the words *put on;* others saw *took off:*

> John was preparing for a marathon in August. After doing a few warm-up exercises, he put on/took off his sweatshirt and went jogging. He jogged halfway around the lake without too much difficulty.

After the participants had read the last sentence, the researchers flashed the word *sweatshirt* on a screen and measured the participants' reaction times. Those who had read *put on* recognized the word faster than did those who had read *took off.* Presumably, the mental model of the first group of participants contained a man wearing a sweatshirt; thus, the word detector for *sweatshirt* was primed.

Reading may therefore involve two types of memory. As we scan text, we use memory for the words in the sentences to discern the meanings of other words, as in the *buttered popcorn* example. But we also retain a memory for the mental model we construct from the narrative. Singer and Ritchot (1996) suggest that these are two different abilities, and that each makes an independent contribution to reading efficiency. However, recent research suggests that reading involves different types of memory and different types of models, which can be characterized as memory-based processes and explanation-based processes, respectively (Gerrig & O'Brien, 2005).

QUESTIONS TO CONSIDER

1. Think of examples of child-directed speech that you may have overheard (or engaged in yourself when talking with a young child). How would you feel if you were speaking to a baby who suddenly lost interest in you? Would you be motivated to do something to regain the baby's attention? Why? What would you do?

2. Do you think it is easier for a young child to learn a first language than it is for an adult to learn a second language? How could you make a fair comparison of the interactions that young children learning a first language and adults learning a second language have with the people they talk to? Could a modified form of child-directed language be developed as an effective way of tutoring adults who attempt to learn a second language? Would this be effective? Why or why not?

Communication with Other Species

The members of most species can communicate with one another. Certainly insects communicate: A female moth ready to mate can release a chemical that will bring male moths from miles away. A dog can tell its owner that it wants to go for a walk by bringing its leash in its mouth and whining while waiting at the door. Many of the higher primates, such as gorillas, use gestures to communicate (Pika, Liebal, & Tomasello, 2003). On the basis of inventories of gestures and facial/vocal signals observed in captive bonobos and chimpanzees, Pollick and deWaal (2007) recently proposed that gestures may underlie the evolutionary emergence of language. Although facial/vocal signals were highly similar between the two species, gestures were much more variable, and more so among bonobos than chimpanzees.

In the 1960s Beatrice and Roger Gardner, of the University of Nevada, began Project Washoe (Gardner & Gardner, 1969, 1978), a remarkably successful attempt to teach sign language to a female chimpanzee named Washoe. Previous attempts to teach chimps to learn and use human language had focused on speech (Hayes, 1952). These attempts had failed, because chimps lack the control of tongue, lips, palate, and vocal cords that humans have and thus cannot produce the variety of complex sounds that characterize human speech. Gardner and Gardner realized this limitation and decided to attempt to teach Washoe a manual language—a language that makes use of hand movements. Chimps' hand and finger dexterity is excellent. The manual language the Gardners chose was based on American Sign Language, one of the sign languages used by deaf people. It contains function words and content words as well as syntactic rules.

Washoe was 1 year old when she began to learn sign language; by the time she was 4, she had a vocabulary of more than 130 signs. Like children, she used single signs at first, and then began to produce two-word sentences such as *Washoe sorry, gimme flower, more fruit,* and *Roger tickle.* Sometimes she strung three or more words together, by using the concept of agent and object: *You tickle me.* She asked and answered questions, apologized, made assertions—in short, did the kinds of things that children would do while learning to talk. She showed overextensions and underextensions, just as human children do. Occasionally Washoe even made correct generalizations by herself. After learning the sign for the verb *open* (as in *open box, open cupboard*), she used it to say *open faucet* when requesting a drink. She made signs to herself when she was alone and used them to "talk" to cats and dogs, just as children will do. Nevertheless, although it is questionable to compare her progress with that of human children (the fairest comparison might be with that of deaf children learning to sign), humans clearly learn language much more readily than Washoe did. Still, Washoe's training started relatively late in her life, and her trainers were not, at the beginning of the project, fluent in sign language. Other chimpanzees, raised from birth by humans who are native speakers of ASL, have begun to use signs when they are 3 months old (Gardner & Gardner, 1975).

Chimpanzees apparently can use symbols to represent real objects and can manipulate these symbols logically. These abilities are two of the most powerful features of language. Premack (1976) taught chimpanzees to "read" and "write" by arranging plastic tokens into "sentences." Each token represents an object, action, or attribute such as color or shape, much the way words do. His first trainee, Sarah, whom he acquired when she was 1 year old, learned to understand complex sentences such as *Sarah insert banana in pail, apple in dish.* When she saw the disks arranged in this order, she obeyed the instructions.

Even though humans are the only primates that speak words, other species can recognize them. Sue Savage-Rumbaugh (1990; Savage-Rumbaugh & Shanker, 1998) taught Kanzi, a bonobo or pygmy chimpanzee, to communicate with humans by pressing buttons that contained symbols for words (known as *lexigrams*). Kanzi's human companions talked with him, and he learned to understand them. During a 3-month period, Savage-Rumbaugh and her colleagues tested Kanzi with 310 spoken sentences, 302 of which the chimpanzee had never heard before. Only situations in which Kanzi could not have been guided by nonverbal cues from the human companions were counted; often, Kanzi's back was to the speaker. He responded correctly 298 times. TABLE 10•2 presents specific examples of these sentences and Kanzi's actions.

Savage-Rumbaugh and her colleagues took an interesting further step by comparing Kanzi's language performance with that of a 2-year-old human girl (Savage-Rumbaugh

[**TABLE 10·2**] **Semantic Relations Comprehended by Kanzi, a Bonobo**

Semantic Relations	N*	Examples (Spoken)
Action–object	107	*"Would you please carry the straw?"* Kanzi looks over a number of objects on the table, selects the straw, and takes it to the next room.
Object–action	13	*"Would you like to ball chase?"* Kanzi looks around for a ball, finds one in his swimming pool, takes it out, comes over to the keyboard, and answers "Chase."
Object–location	8	*"Would you put the grapes in the swimming pool?"* Kanzi selects some grapes from among several foods and tosses them into the swimming pool.
Action–location	23	*"Let's chase to the A-frame."* Kanzi is climbing in trees and has been ignoring things that are said to him. When he hears this he comes down rapidly and runs to the A-frame.
Action–object–location	36	*"I hid the surprise by my foot."* Kanzi has been told that a surprise is around somewhere, and he is looking for it. When he is given this clue, he immediately approaches the speaker and lifts up her foot.
Object–action	9	*"Kanzi, the pine cone goes in your shirt."* Kanzi picks up a pine cone and puts it in his shirt.
Action–location–object	8	*"Go the refrigerator and get out a tomato."* Kanzi is playing in the water in the sink. When he hears this he stops, goes to the refrigerator, and gets a tomato.
Agent–action–object	7	*"Jeannine hid the pine needles in her shirt."* Kanzi is busy making a nest of blankets, branches, and pine needles. When he hears this, he immediately walks over to Jeannine, lifts up her shirt, takes out the pine needles, and puts them in his nest.
Action–object–recipient	19	*"Kanzi, please carry the cooler to Penny."* Kanzi grabs the cooler and carries it over to Penny.
Other: object–action–recipient, action–recipient–location, etc.	68	

*N, number of sentences to which Kanzi responded correctly.

Source: From Savage-Rumbaugh, E. S. (1990). *Developmental Psychobiology, 23,* 599–620. Copyright © 1990. Reprinted with permission of John Wiley & Sons, Inc.

et al., 1993). The test was a stringent one. Both Kanzi and the child (over a period of time) were given more than 600 commands in oral English. All of the commands were novel. Care was taken to avoid methodological flaws. For example, Kanzi could not see the person who gave him his commands, removing the possibility that he would merely read subtle behavioral cues rather than understand the spoken commands. Likewise, to avoid observer bias, the person who

Researcher Sue Savage-Rumbaugh taught her chimp, Kanzi, to communicate using a special keyboard.

scored reactions to the commands could not hear the commands. Kanzi and the child performed equally well, although with time the girl progressed beyond Kanzi's abilities. Nevertheless, Kanzi made a good showing in comparison to the child.

One conclusion from the studies of language-like abilities in other species is that linguistic ability is social behavior. It builds on attempts at nonverbal communication in social situations. The most successful attempts to teach a language to other species are those in which the animal and the trainer have established a close relationship and can successfully communicate nonverbally by means of facial expressions, movements, and gestures. Alex and Kanzi and other animals involved in such studies clearly have perceived their trainers as sufficiently valuable to merit continued exchange. More generally, such success in teaching language to other species calls into question the necessity of an LAD. After all, why should others species possess a device for the acquisition of an ability that is uniquely human?

The year 2007 saw the death of two famous animals— Alex the parrot and Washoe the chimpanzee. Each was a long-time, distinguished participant in research on language acquisition by nonhuman species. Alex was an African gray parrot, whose trainer, Irene Pepperberg, of Brandeis University, worked with him for 30 years (Pepperberg, 2000;

Talbot, 2008). He acquired a vocabulary of 150 words and could use them to categorize objects. He could use single digits to count and could name shapes and colors. For example, if presented with a red paper square, he could tell his trainer what its color and shape were and, given the opportunity to touch it, that it was made of paper. His last words to Pepperberg on the night before his death were, "You be good, see you tomorrow. I love you." (Carey, 2007)

QUESTION TO CONSIDER

Would you like to talk with a chimpanzee? If so, what would you like to talk about? What would it take to convince you that the animal was using something like a simplified human language, as opposed to simply repeating words and phrases learned by rote? Some people seem to be uncomfortable with the idea that the difference in the ability of humans and other primates to communicate may be a matter of degree and not an all-or-none matter. How do you feel about this issue? Finally, does teaching a chimpanzee a human language confer special responsibilities on the teacher? If so, what are they?

Epilogue

Slips in the Linguistic Divide

Oliver Sacks's wild ride, courtesy of Dr. Bennett, as reported in the prologue, reminds us of the sometimes antic disparity between what we speak and our actions otherwise. Which of us has not caught herself or himself in such a gaffe—calling out, "Let me get the door," only to discover that you are pointing your remote-control car-door opener at the still-locked door to your apartment. Whereas Dr. Bennett's bizarre outbursts and preoccupations were of the clinical variety associated with Tourette's syndrome, they still exemplify the at least occasional difficulty of aligning one's linguistic behavior with the nonlinguistic.

Highly regarded scholars have argued that such difficulty should be uniquely human, as *Homo sapiens sapiens* is the only species endowed with language. Hauser, Chomsky, and Fitch (2002) have pointed to the property of recursion (as illustrated by the multilayered sentence *I just got back from the class taught by the professor who was at the pizza restaurant where my friend and his roommate ate last night*) as dividing language from all other forms of communication that have been observed in other species. For Pinker and Jackendorf (2005), the list of unique properties

is longer and includes phonological rules, syntactical rules, and speech perception.

Despite such weight of argument, some continue to chip away at the assertion of uniqueness, looking for evidence in the unexpected actions of other, particularly primate, species. Recently Lyn (2007) has focused the errors made by a pair of bonobos (one of them the previously mentioned Kanzi). The data were recorded over a 10-year period and consisted of vocabulary tests given to the animals by means of an extensive keyboard consisting of lexigrams. Kanzi and the female bonobo, Panbanisha, had lexigraphic vocabularies of nearly 400 symbols and could combine them in complex, language-like sequences.

What Lyn found was that the patterns of errors in tests, in which the animal was shown a photo or listened to a spoken word and had to press the correct lexigram, were not random. For example, if the photo featured a blackberry, then the errors were likely to involve lexigrams that had the same sound, belonged to the same semantic categories (edible, fruit), or had a similar appearance. Errors were especially likely to involve combinations of these categories. Thus, the lexigram for *cherry* was a perfect candidate. Lyn's analysis pointed up the similarity between the bonobos' errors and those typical of children in similar conditions. However, a notable exception was found. Children typically make errors within syntactic categories (as mistaking *tree* for *cherry*—both nouns—would be), but the bonobos did not, prompting Lyn to speculate that, unlike children, they do not discriminate between semantic and syntactic categories.

A parallel between the errors made by bonobos and by children exists in the linguistic slips made by adult speakers and adult users of sign language. German linguists Hohenberger, Happ, and Leuninger (cited by Erard, 2007) used an experimental method for inducing slips in their participants. They found that the errors produced by German speakers ("slips of the tongue") were also produced by deaf persons who used German Sign Language ("slips of the hand"), although not necessarily with the same frequencies. Also, participants using sign language were more likely to correct their errors, presumably because signing occurs more slowly than speaking and therefore may be more readily self-monitored. (See Thompson, Emmorey, & Gollan, 2005, for an analysis of the "tip of the fingers" phenomenon in deaf users of American Sign Language comparable to the "tip of the tongue" phenomenon in English speakers that was described in Chapter 8.)

These findings suggest a linguistic production system that is not necessarily a respecter of species differences nor of whether the language produced is spoken or manual. Further studies of patterns of errors in linguistic production may reveal its specific neural substrates and take us closer to understanding Dr. Bennett's remarkable performance at the wheel.

CHAPTER SUMMARY

Speech Comprehension and Production

Language provides an orderly system of communication. The recognition of sounds in continuous speech is a complex process. Phonemes are recognized even though their pronunciation is affected by neighboring sounds, by accents and speech peculiarities, and by vocal stresses. Studies have shown that we distinguish between voiced and unvoiced consonant phonemes by means of voice-onset time. Research has also shown that the primary unit of analysis is not individual phonemes but combinations of phonemes. Learning and contextual information are additional factors in recognizing what we hear.

Morphemes are the smallest units of meaning. Meaning is a joint function of syntax and semantics. All users of a particular language observe syntactical rules that establish the relations of the words in a sentence to one another. These rules are not learned explicitly. Research indicates that people can learn to apply rules of an artificial grammar without being able to state the rules.

Speech comprehension requires more than an understanding of syntax and semantics; it also requires knowledge of the world. When we are listeners, we must share knowledge about the world with the speaker if we are to understand what she or he is referring to.

The effects of brain damage suggest that memories of the sounds of words are located in Wernicke's area and that memories of the muscular movements needed to produce them are located near Broca's area. Thus, Wernicke's area is necessary for speech comprehension, and Broca's area is necessary for speech production. Function words and other syntactical features of speech related to motor operations involve mechanisms in the frontal lobes. Broca's aphasia (caused by damage that extends beyond the boundaries of Broca's area) is characterized by nonfluent but meaningful speech that is scarce in function words but rich in content words.

Reading

Recognition of written words is a complex perceptual task. The eye-tracking camera allows researchers to study people's eye movements and fixations and to learn about the reading process. For example, we analyze a sentence word by word as we read it, pausing longer on long or unusual words.

Once a word has been perceived, recognition of its pronunciation and meaning takes place. Long or unfamiliar words

are sounded out—that is, they are read phonetically. In contrast, short, familiar words are recognized as wholes. In fact, only whole-word reading will enable us to know how to pronounce words such as *cow* and *blow*, or *bone* and *one*, which have irregular spellings. Experienced readers use both whole-word and phonetic reading. If a word is recognized as a whole, readers move on; if not, they continue to decode it phonetically. The distinction between these two forms of word recognition is supported by behavioral data and by studies of people with acquired dyslexias. People with surface dyslexia have difficulty with whole-word reading, whereas people with phonological dyslexia have difficulty sounding out unfamiliar words or pronounceable nonwords. In addition, people with direct dyslexia can read words but cannot understand their meaning. Developmental dyslexias appear to be caused by abnormal development of parts of the left hemisphere and may reflect an inability to combine information from Broca's area and Wernicke's area.

The meanings of words are learned through experience. The phenomenon of semantic priming suggests that some neural circuits recognize the visual form of words, whereas other circuits encode various aspects of the meanings of words. Connections between these circuits are responsible for our ability to recognize meaningful associations. Semantic priming has been used to study the processes of word recognition and comprehension of meaning.

Language Acquisition by Children

Some researchers believe that a child learns language by means of a brain mechanism called a language acquisition device, which contains universal grammatical rules and motivates language acquisition. Although children's verbal performance can be described by complex rules, it is possible that simpler rules—which children could reasonably be expected to learn—can also be devised. Everyone agrees that deliberate reinforcement is not necessary for language learning, but a controversy exists about just how important child-directed behavior is. A critical period for language learning may exist, but the evidence is not yet conclusive. In addition to a particular interval of time being critical, the quality of one's experience during that interval will be critical as well.

Child-directed speech is very different from that directed toward adults; it is simpler and clearer, and it generally refers to items and events in the present environment. As young children gain more experience with the world and with the speech of adults and older children, their vocabulary grows, and they learn to use adult rules of grammar. Although the first verbs they learn tend to have irregular past tenses, once they learn the regular past tense rule (add -*ed*), they apply this rule even to irregular verbs they previously used correctly.

Studies of the ability of other species, including parrots, chimpanzees, and bonobos, to learn language enable us the better to understand the types of experiences necessary for the acquisition of the skills involved in producing and understanding spoken and unspoken language.

succeed with mypsychlab

Visit MyPsychLab for practice quizzes, flashcards, and dozens of videos and animated tutorials, including the following items you can find in the "Multimedia Library":

Language Learning
Stimulating Language Development
Encouraging Literacy
Birds and Language
Child-Directed Language

KEY TERMS

agrammatism *p. 282*
Broca's aphasia *p. 282*
child-directed speech *p. 294*
content word *p. 280*
deep structure *p. 281*
direct dyslexia *p. 288*
fixation *p. 285*
function word *p. 280*
inflection *p. 295*
language-acquisition device (LAD) *p. 290*
language-acquisition support system (LASS) *p. 292*
language universal *p. 290*
morpheme *p. 279*
overextension *p. 296*
overgeneralization *p. 295*
phoneme *p. 278*

phonetic reading *p. 287*
phonological dyslexia *p. 288*
prosody *p. 280*
protoword *p. 293*
psycholinguistics *p. 294*
script *p. 281*
semantic priming *p. 296*
semantics *p. 280*
surface dyslexia *p. 287*
surface structure *p. 281*
syntactical rule *p. 280*
underextension *p. 296*
voice-onset time *p. 278*
Wernicke's aphasia *p. 284*
Wernicke's area *p. 284*
whole-word reading *p. 287*

SUGGESTIONS FOR FURTHER READING

Berko Gleason, J. (2004). *The development of language.* Boston: Allyn & Bacon.

A noted developmental psycholinguist offers an excellent overview of language acquisition during infancy and childhood.

Calvin, W. H. (2004). *A brief history of the mind: From apes to intellect and beyond.* New York: Oxford University Press.

If you are intrigued by the evolutionary origins of cognition and language, this book provides a stimulating introduction.

Carter, R. (1998). *Mapping the mind.* London: Weidenfeld & Nicolson.

This book provides a beautifully illustrated introduction to brain areas and their correlated psychological functions, including language.

Just, M. A., & Carpenter, P. A. (1987). *The psychology of reading and language comprehension.* Boston: Allyn & Bacon.

Experts in eye-movement research focus on the psychology of written language, including reading disorders.

Miller, G. A. (1987). *Spontaneous apprentices: Children and language.* New York: Seabury Press.

This brief memoir by a highly regarded founder of cognitive science offers poignant reflections on his serious search for an elusive target: how children acquire a first language.

Pinker, S. (2007). *The stuff of thought: Language as a window into human nature.* New York: Viking.

A highly readable collection of essays on the language of thought and language per se, children's acquisition of language, metaphors, and profanity.

Rayner, K., & Pollatsek, A. (1994). *The psychology of reading.* Mahwah, N.J.: Lawrence Erlbaum & Associates.

A companion piece to Just and Carpenter, this book provides a richly referenced summary of research and theory on the acquisition of reading and the liabilities that accompany it.

Savage-Rumbaugh, E. S., Shanker, S., & Taylor, T. J. (1998). *Apes, language, and the human mind.* New York: Oxford University Press.

Savage-Rumbaugh is a central figure in the ape language controversy, which is the focus of this wide-ranging summary of research and theory.

Intelligence and Thinking

Prologue

Multiple Intelligences? A Case Study of Brain Damage

Mr. V. is a 72-year-old man who has had a massive stroke in his right hemisphere that has paralyzed the left side of his body. He seems intelligent, and this impression has been confirmed for his doctor by the results from a standard IQ test administered by a psychologist. Specifically, the test showed that Mr. V. could define rather obscure words, provide the meanings of proverbs, and do mental arithmetic; his verbal intelligence was in the upper 5% of the population. The fact that English is not his first language makes his performance even more remarkable. However, he did poorly on tasks that required him to deal with shapes and geometry. He could not put together colored blocks to duplicate a pattern shown in a drawing. Thus, his performance intelligence score was much lower.

Mr. V. reacted indifferently to his symptoms. When his doctor asked him some simple questions about himself and his lifestyle—for example, about his favorite pastime, Mr. V. answered, "I like to walk. I walk at least 2 hours each day around the city, but mostly I like to walk in the woods. I have maps of most of the nearby parks on the walls of my study, and I mark all the trails I've taken. I figure that in about 6 months I will have walked all of the trails that are short enough to do in a day. I'm too old to camp out in the woods."

"You're going to finish up those trails in the next 6 months?" asks his doctor.

"Yes, and then I'll start over again!" Mr. V. replies.

"Mr. V., are you having any trouble?" asks the doctor.

"Trouble? What do you mean?"

"I mean physical, medical, difficulties."

"No." Mr. V. gives him a slightly puzzled look.

"Well, what are you sitting in?"

Mr. V. gives his doctor a look that indicates he thinks the question is rather stupid—or perhaps insulting. "A wheelchair, of course," he answers.

"Why are you in a wheelchair?"

Now Mr. V. looks exasperated; he obviously does not like to answer foolish questions. "Because my left leg is paralyzed!" he snaps.

Mr. V. talks about continuing his walking schedule when he obviously knows that he can't walk. Does he think that he will recover soon?

"No, that's not it," says Mr. V.'s doctor. "He knows what his problem is, but he doesn't really understand it. The people at the rehabilitation hospital are finding it difficult because he keeps trying to go outside for a walk.

"The problem Mr. V. experiences stems from the fact that intelligence is made up of a variety of skills that must be coordinated, and the results of their use must be synthesized. The right hemisphere

is specialized in seeing many things at once: in seeing the parts of a geometric shape and grasping its overall form or in recognizing the elements of a situation and understanding what it means. That is what's wrong. He can tell you about his paralyzed leg, about the fact that he is in a wheelchair, and so on, but he does not put these facts together and realize that his days of walking are over. Mr. V. is very intelligent, but his judgment can be lacking because of the stroke damage." ∎

What is intelligence? In general if people do well academically or succeed at more complex tasks, we consider them to be intelligent. Thus, a critic who writes a witty, articulate review of an artist's exhibition of paintings may be viewed as intelligent, whereas the painter is viewed as talented. Psychologists often define **intelligence** as a person's ability to learn and remember information, to recognize concepts and their relations, and to apply the information and recognition by behaving in an adaptive way. Recently, psychologists have pointed out that any definition of intelligence depends on cultural judgments of adaptiveness (e.g., Sternberg & Grigorenko, 2008; Suzuki & Ponteretto, 2007). Analyses of the types of skills that enable people to survive and flourish in different cultures suggest that we may need to broaden the generally accepted definition to include a wider range of abilities and contexts. The case study of Mr. V suggests a similar view: The brain sustains not a single type of intelligence but a multiplicity, including verbal intelligence, visual–spatial intelligence, and intrapersonal (how well you know yourself) intelligence, as we shall see.

Intelligence: Is It Global or Componential?

People vary in many ways, such as in their abilities to learn and use words, to solve arithmetic problems, and to perceive and remember spatial information. Psychologists have assumed that we can best investigate the nature of intelligence by studying the ways in which people differ on tests of such abilities. In doing so it is critical to ask whether intelligence is a single, overarching—that is, *global*—ability that affects all types of intellectual performance? Or is it, instead, a composite of separate, independent abilities?

Psychologists have devised intelligence tests that yield a single number, usually called an *intelligence quotient* or *IQ score*. But the fact that the tests provide a single score does not itself mean that intelligence is a global ability. For example,

suppose that we wanted to devise a test of athletic ability. We could ask people to run, jump, throw and catch a ball, lift weights, balance on a narrow beam, and perform other athletic feats. We could measure their performance on each task and then combine these numbers in some way to yield a total score that we could call the *AQ*, or *athleticism quotient*.

Would this single measure—the AQ—be useful in predicting who would be the best skier, or baseball player, or swimmer, or gymnast? Because athletic ability consists of a variety of skills, and different sports require different combinations of skills, the AQ could turn out to be a useful predictor for some sports but useless for others. Similarly, psychologists debate whether intelligence should be considered singular and indivisible or whether it should be considered the composite of several abilities that may or may not be independent of one another. We examine three theories of intelligence: a general factor theory, an information-processing theory, and a neuropsychological theory, that is, a theory that draws support from studies of people with brain damage, such as Mr. V.

Different cultures have different definitions of intelligence. Members of the Aitutaki tribe from the Cook Islands have particular respect for a person's ability to obtain food from the sea.

---

intelligence A person's ability to learn and remember information, to recognize concepts and their relations, and to apply the information and recognition by behaving in an adaptive way.

Spearman's *g* Theory

The British psychologist Charles Spearman (1863–1945) proposed the ***g* factor,** which is a general factor of intelligence (Spearman, 1927). Spearman did not call the *g* factor "intelligence"; he considered the term too vague. Instead, he defined the *g* factor in terms of three "qualitative principles of cognition": apprehension of experience, eduction of relations, and eduction of correlates. (*Eduction*, not "edu*cation*," is the process of drawing or bringing out—that is, of figuring out from given facts.) A common task on tests of intellectual abilities—solving analogies—requires all three principles (Sternberg, 1997). For example, consider the following analogy:

LAWYER : CLIENT :: DOCTOR : _____

This analogy problem is read as "LAWYER is to CLIENT as DOCTOR is to _____." Spearman's term *apprehension of experience* refers to people's ability to perceive and understand what they experience and is illustrated by reading and understanding each of the words in the analogy. The *eduction of relations* is illustrated by perceiving the relation between LAWYER and CLIENT; namely, that the lawyer works for the client. The *eduction of correlates* involves applying a rule inferred from one case to a similar case. Thus, in the example, this means educing that the person whom a doctor works for is a PATIENT.

Empirical evidence for Spearman's theory comes from correlations among various tests of specific abilities. Most of these tests are at least moderately correlated, that is, the correlations are in the range from 0.3 to 0.7 (see Chapter 2). This means that a person who scores well on a vocabulary test also tends to score better than average on other tests, such as arithmetic or spatial reasoning. On the basis of this finding, Spearman concluded that a general factor (*g*) accounted for the correlations between different tests of ability.

Recent work by Gottfredson (2004, 2007) has extended Spearman's claim for the centrality of *g* in intellectual performance. Gottfredson contends that *g* predicts performance well beyond the domain of IQ testing and influences personal success in virtually all important areas of life. She identifies four areas in particular—work, daily self-maintenance, chronic illness, and accidents—in which the ability to deal with complexity provides an advantage to individuals with higher levels of *g*. In addition, she argues that *g* is a robust predictor by itself: that information about an individual's more specific mental abilities or socioeconomic status, for example, adds little to what *g* predicts alone.

Evidence from Factor Analysis Together with Karl Pearson (1852–1936), an illustrious statistician, Spearman developed a statistical procedure known as **factor analysis.** This procedure

permits researchers to identify underlying factors that contribute to performance on intelligence tests (see Carroll, 1993). Suppose that a group of people take several different tests of intellectual ability. If each person's scores on several of these tests correlate with one another, we can conclude that the tests are measuring a single factor. Factor analysis determines which tests can be grouped together. For example, Birren and Morrison (1961) administered the most widely used measure of intelligence, the Wechsler Adult Intelligence Scale (WAIS, described in the next section), to 933 people. This test at that time consisted of 11 different subtests. The researchers calculated the correlations each subtest had with every other subtest and then applied factor analysis to the correlations.

TABLE 11•1 lists the results of the factor analysis. It revealed three factors, labeled A, B, and C. The numbers in the three columns in the table are called *factor loadings;* they express the degree to which a particular test is related to a particular factor. On factor A, the largest factor loading is for Vocabulary, followed by Information, Comprehension, and Similarities. (For detailed descriptions of the subtests, see Table 11.5 on p. 314.) The intermediate loadings are for Picture Completion, Arithmetic, Picture Arrangement, and Digit Symbol. Digit Span, Object Assembly, and Block Design have the lowest loadings. Because verbal subtests have the heaviest loading on factor A, that factor might be labeled *verbal ability*. Because most of the subtests have at least a moderate loading on factor A, it may be reasonable to call it *general intelligence*. Digit Span has a heavy loading on factor B (.84), and Arithmetic and Digit Symbol have moderate loadings. Perhaps factor B contributes to *maintaining information in short-term memory* and *manipulating numbers*. Factor C appears to apply mainly to Block Design, Object Assembly, Picture Completion, and Picture Arrangement. An appropriate name for this factor might be *spatial ability*.

[**TABLE 11•1**] Three Factors Derived by Factor Analysis of Scores on WAIS Subtests

	Factors		
Subtest	A	B	C
Information	0.70	0.18	0.25
Digit span	0.16	0.84	0.13
Vocabulary	0.84	0.16	0.18
Arithmetic	0.38	0.35	0.28
Comprehension	0.63	0.12	0.24
Similarities	0.57	0.12	0.27
Picture completion	0.41	0.15	0.53
Picture arrangement	0.35	0.18	0.41
Block design	0.20	0.14	0.73
Object assembly	0.16	0.06	0.59
Digit symbol	0.24	0.22	0.29

Source: Adapted from *Multivariate Statistical Methods,* 4th ed., by D. F. Morrison. Copyright © 2005. Reprinted with permission from Brooks/Cole, a division of Thomson Learning. www.thomsonrights.com. Fax 800-730-2215.

***g* factor** According to Spearman, a factor that is common to performance on all intellectual tasks; includes apprehension of experience, eduction of relations, and eduction of correlates.

factor analysis A statistical procedure that identifies the factors that groups of data, such as test scores, have in common.

Although factor analysis generates clues about the nature of intelligence, by itself it is not a theory of intelligence, as it can never be more meaningful than the individual tests to which it is applied. To identify the relevant factors in human intelligence, it is obviously advantageous to include an extensive variety of tests in the factor analysis. Although many are available (Geisinger et al., 2007), factor analysis can never reveal abilities that are not measured by the tests it is used to investigate. For example, the WAIS does not contain a test of musical ability. If it did, factor analysis might reveal an additional factor related to that ability.

Factor analyses of intelligence testing have revealed a range of specific factors. In an early study, Louis Thurstone (1938) administered a battery of 56 tests to 218 college students. In his analysis, he extracted seven factors, which he labeled Verbal Comprehension, Verbal Fluency, Number, Spatial Visualization, Memory, Reasoning, and Perceptual Speed. At first, Thurstone thought that his results contradicted Spearman's hypothesized g factor. However, Hans Eysenck (1939) suggested that a second factor analysis could be performed on Thurstone's factors. If the further analysis found one common factor among the seven factors, then Spearman's g factor would be supported.

Raymond Cattell (1963) performed just such a second-order factor analysis and found not one but two major factors. He called them fluid intelligence (g_f) and crystallized intelligence (g_c). **Fluid intelligence** largely has to do with detecting relations in specified informational contexts, such as classifying figures or seeing patterns in a repeating series of items. **Crystallized intelligence** involves drawing on previously acquired information and skills, such as vocabulary, arithmetic, and general information—the kind of thing learned in schools. Cattell regarded fluid intelligence as closely related to a person's native capacity for intelligent performance; in other words, to the individual's potential ability to learn and to solve problems. In contrast, crystallized intelligence is what a person has already developed through the use of his or her fluid intelligence. Horn's (1994, 1998) interpretation differs somewhat. He cites evidence suggesting that both factors are learned but that g_f refers to informal learning, whereas g_c refers to culture-specific, school-centered learning.

According to both Cattell and Horn, if two people share similar experiences, the person with the greater fluid intelligence will develop the greater crystallized intelligence. However, a person with a high fluid intelligence exposed to an intellectually impoverished environment will develop a poor crystallized intelligence. TABLE 11·2 presents a summary of tests that load more heavily on g_f or g_c.

Sternberg's Triarchic Theory of Intelligence

Robert Sternberg (1988a; Sternberg et al., 2008) devised a triarchic ("ruled by three") theory of intelligence that derives from the information-processing approach used by many cognitive psychologists—the approach that focuses on the

[**TABLE 11·2**] **Summary of Tests with Large Factor Loadings on g_f or g_c**

Test	g_f	g_c
Figural relations: Deduction of a relation when this is shown among common figures	0.57	.01
Memory span: Reproduction of several numbers or letters presented briefly	0.50	0.00
Induction: Deduction of a correlate from relations shown in a series of letters, numbers, or figures, as in a letter series test	0.41	0.06
General reasoning: Solving problems of area, rate, finance, and the like, as in an arithmetic reasoning test	0.31	0.34
Semantic relations: Deduction of a relation when this is shown among words, as in an analogies test	0.37	0.43
Formal reasoning: Arriving at a conclusion in accordance with a formal reasoning process, as in a syllogistic reasoning test	0.31	0.41
Number facility: Quick and accurate use of arithmetical operations such as addition, subtraction, and multiplication	0.21	0.29
Experiential evaluation: Solving problems involving protocol and requiring diplomacy, as in a social relations test	0.08	0.43
Verbal comprehension: Advanced understanding of language, as measured in a vocabulary reading test	0.08	0.68

Source: Adapted from Horn, J. L. (1968). Organization of abilities and the development of intelligence. *Psychological Review, 75,* 242–259. Copyright ©1968 by the American Psychological Association.

ways in which people perceive, analyze, store, and apply information in their daily interactions with the environment (see Hunt, 1995). The theory identifies three major aspects of intelligence: analytic intelligence, creative intelligence, and practical intelligence. As you will see, these three components go beyond the abilities measured by most tests of intelligence. Taken together, they contribute to what Sternberg (1996, 2005) calls **successful intelligence,** which is a person's ability to

---

fluid intelligence According to Cattell, intellectual abilities that operate in relatively culture-free informational contexts and involve the detection of relationships or patterns, for example.

crystallized intelligence According to Cattell, intellectual abilities that have developed through exposure to information-rich contexts, especially schools; expressed in general knowledge and skills.

successful intelligence According to Sternberg, the ability to analyze and manage personal strengths and weaknesses effectively; in Sternberg's scheme, successful intelligence draws on analytic, creative, and practical intelligence.

[**TABLE 11·3**] An Outline of Sternberg's Triarchic Theory of Intelligence

Analytic Intelligence
Metacomponents (e.g., planning)
Performance components (e.g., word recognition)
Knowledge-acquisition components (e.g., adding new words to vocabulary)

Creative Intelligence
Novel tasks
Automated tasks

Practical Intelligence
Adaptation (fitting in to a given environment)
Selection (finding a niche in the environment)
Shaping (changing the environment)

(a) analyze his or her strengths and weaknesses, (b) use the strengths to greatest advantage, and (c) minimize the impact of weaknesses by overcoming or compensating for them. **TABLE 11·3** provides a summary of the key concepts of Sternberg's triarchic theory.

Analytic intelligence consists of the cognitive mechanisms people use to plan and execute tasks. Verbal ability and deductive reasoning, as revealed by factor analysis, are facets of analytic intelligence. Sternberg suggests that the components of analytic intelligence serve three functions. *Metacomponents* (higher-level components) are the processes by which people decide what a problem is about, select a strategy for solving it, and allocate their resources to that solution (Sternberg, 2005). For example, good readers vary the amount of time they spend on a passage according to how much information they need to extract from it; this is the metacomponent. *Performance components* are the processes actually used to perform the task—for example, word recognition or rehearsal in working memory. *Knowledge-acquisition components* are the processes that the person uses to gain new knowledge, including sifting through information, extracting what is relevant, and integrating it with what he or she already knows.

The second part of Sternberg's theory deals with **creative intelligence** (Sternberg, 2003b). This is the ability to (a) deal effectively with novel situations and (b) solve familiar problems automatically. For Sternberg, people with high creative intelligence are able to deal more effectively with novel situations than

are individuals with low creative intelligence. They can better analyze a situation and bring cognitive resources to bear on the problem, even if encountering it for the first time. After solving a particular type of problem several times, the person with good creative intelligence is also able to "automate" the procedure, so that similar problems can be solved without much thought, freeing cognitive resources for more demanding work. Another interesting dimension of creative intelligence is that people high in such intelligence are willing to tolerate criticism and the initial rejection of their new ideas (Sternberg, 2006). Because new ideas often threaten those who have the power to implement them, creative people must learn when the time is right to press their ideas.

The third part of Sternberg's theory deals with **practical intelligence**—intelligence reflecting the process of natural selection in human evolutionary history. Practical intelligence takes three forms: *adaptation, selection,* and *shaping.* Adaptation refers to developing useful skills and behaviors that allow a person to meet the demands of one's environment. In different cultural contexts, adaptation will take different forms. For example, knowing how to distinguish between poisonous, edible, and medicinal plants is an important skill for members of the Malaysian Sarawak hunter–gatherer tribe. For many people in the United States, knowing how to shop for bargains is an important skill. Sternberg argues that both sociocultural and physical contexts have a strong impact on the development of practical intelligence (e.g., Sternberg & Grigorenko, 2001). Other writers go so far as to say that context underpins intelligence—"smart contexts" make "smart people" (Barab & Plucker, 2002; Plucker & Barab, 2005).

The second form of practical intelligence, *selection,* involves a person's ability to find his or her own niche in the environment. Most of us have known students who, although seemingly brilliant, never found agreeable interests in life and fell far short of what they seemed capable of achieving. They seem like brilliant but tragic dreamers. Sternberg's theory stresses the importance of actively finding a good match between self and environment.

Knowing how to distinguish between poisonous plants, edible plants, and plants with medicinal properties is an important skill. This woman, a member of the Sarawak tribe, is collecting medicinal herbs in a Malaysian rain forest.

---

analytic intelligence   In Sternberg's triarchic theory, the cognitive mechanisms people use to plan and execute tasks; includes metacomponents, performance components, and knowledge-acquisition components.

creative intelligence   In Sternberg's triarchic theory, the ability to deal effectively with novel situations and to solve problems automatically that have been encountered previously.

practical intelligence   In Sternberg's triarchic theory, intelligence that reflects the behaviors that were subject to natural selection: adaptation (initially fitting self to environment by developing useful skills and behaviors); selection (finding an appropriate niche in the environment); and shaping (changing the environment).

Sternberg's is an optimistic approach, in that, when an adequate person–environment match is not present (adaptation is not successful) or a person cannot find a suitable alternative environment (selection is not successful), she or he may change the environment itself. This third form of practical intelligence is *shaping*. For example, a person whose talents are not appreciated by his or her employer may decide to start his or her own business. A student who pursues one major with limited success may switch to a different major and thrive there.

Observations of people with extensive frontal lobe injury support Sternberg's conceptualization of practical intelligence. Even after sustaining massive damage to the frontal lobes (for example, during a car accident), people often continue to score well on standard intelligence tests. Thus, we may be tempted to conclude that their intelligence is unimpaired, but such people may lose the ability to plan their lives or even their daily activities. That is, they may have a considerable loss of practical intelligence while maintaining their more traditionally defined intelligence, as the following case illustrates.

[CASE STUDY] A formerly successful physician had received a head injury that severely damaged his frontal lobes. Even though he still had a high IQ as measured by intelligence tests, he could no longer perform his job as a physician. He became a delivery truck driver for his brother, who owned a business. He was able to carry out this job only because his brother did all the planning for him, carefully laying out his route and instructing him to call if he encountered any trouble. The man's behavior lost its previous flexibility and insightfulness. If he found the front door locked at a store where he had gone to deliver an order, it would not occur to him to go around to the back; his brother had to suggest that by telephone. Clearly, the man's behavior lacked a crucial component of practical intelligence.

Gardner's Theory of Multiple Intelligences

Howard Gardner (1983, 1999, 2006) formulated a theory of multiple intelligences that goes beyond a single type or even a few primary types of intelligence. From Gardner's perspective the intelligences are potentials situated within cultures; that is, they may or may not be activated in the individual, depending on the extent to which the individual's culture values the expression of those potentials. Gardner believes that each of the intelligences he identifies is the result of evolution and has separate, unique neuropsychological underpinnings. One of the criteria for identifying an intelligence is distinctive evidence of a neurological substrate. Gardner argues that cases exist in which brain damage impairs one type of intelligence but leaves others intact, and vice versa—just as in the case of Mr. V, whose localized brain damage impaired specific types of abilities, such as visual–spatial orientation and awareness of his new physical constraints. In other cases, damage to various regions of the left hemisphere can impair verbal abilities. Another example of ability-specific isolation is people with damage to the frontal or temporal lobes—especially of the right hemisphere—who may have difficulty evaluating the significance of social situations but still function quite well in other nonsocial situations (see Damasio, 1994).

Findings such as this led Gardner (1999) to identify eight separate intelligences that meet his criteria. (See TABLE 11•4.) Each person possesses all eight, but, as already noted,

[**TABLE 11•4**] An Outline of Gardner's Theory of Multiple Intelligences

Type of Intelligence	Description	Relevant Activities and Professions
Logical–mathematical intelligence	Ability to reason logically and to process mathematical equations	Conduct systematic investigations; scientists, mathematicians, logicians
Verbal–linguistic intelligence	Ability to use language, sensitivity to meanings and sounds of words	Learn new languages easily, write and speak clearly; writers, teachers, lawyers
Visual–spatial intelligence	Ability to understand patterns in closed or open spaces	Organize objects and activities in three-dimensional space; sculptors, architects, pilots
Naturalist intelligence	Ability to understand patterns in nature	Identify and categorize plants and animals, notice regularities of weather conditions; taxonomists, farmers, hunters, herbal medicine practitioners, meteorologists
Bodily–kinesthetic intelligence	Ability to control the body precisely	Use of the body to solve problems and create; athletes, dancers, actors, mechanics, surgeons
Musical intelligence	Ability to understand and create musical patterns	Composition and performance of music; composers, lyricists, musicians
Intrapersonal intelligence	Ability to understand the self, including awareness of skills, emotions, thoughts, and intentions	Personal integrity, strength of character; can be manifested in many different life contexts, but may not be obvious to outsiders
Interpersonal intelligence	Ability to recognize differences among people and to understand others' emotions, intentions, and motivations	Leadership and interpersonal problem solving; politicians, clergy, mediators, psychologists

each intelligence may develop to a greater or lesser extent. Three of the intelligences—*logical–mathematical intelligence, verbal–linguistic intelligence,* and *visual–spatial intelligence*—were previously identified by other theorists and are often included to a greater or lesser extent in intelligence tests developed independent of Gardner's work (e.g., see Table 11.5 on p. 314). You may also notice the potential overlap of some of the intelligences with Sternberg's notion of practical intelligence. For example, Gardner's *naturalist intelligence* fits well with Sternberg's notion of adaptation as a part of practical intelligence, when applied to the specific example of being able to distinguish edible and poisonous plants. The difference is that Sternberg's adaptation is a quality broadly associated with practical abilities, whereas Gardner assigns naturalist intelligence independent status among the other intelligences.

Beyond the three already-familiar intelligences, psychologists generally have not recognized the remainder of Gardner's intelligences as intelligence per se. For example, they have tended not to consider skill in moving the body (Gardner's bodily–kinesthetic intelligence) as a measure of intelligence, although this ability was undoubtedly selected during the evolution of the species. Individuals who could more skillfully prepare tools, hunt animals, climb trees, descend cliffs, and perform other tasks requiring physical skills were more likely to survive and reproduce. Such skills have generally been regarded as representing something other than intelligence per se. It may be more reasonable to consider them as talents, for example. In its favor, Gardner's theory recognizes the cultural situatedness of intelligence, especially in non-Western cultures. As with the earlier example of plants, the ability of a member of the Puluwat culture of the Caroline Islands to navigate across the sea by the stars serves as an example of naturalist intelligence (Gladwin, 1970).

Although Gardner has not been involved directly in the development of formal measures that reflect elements of the intelligences, others have done so. The Emotional Quotient Inventory (EQ-i; Bar-On, 1997), for example, draws on elements of Gardner's *interpersonal* and *intrapersonal intelligences* and on complementary work by Mayer and Salovey (e.g., Mayer & Salovey, 1993; Salovey et al., 2004) to measure so-called *emotional intelligence.* This form of intelligence roughly corresponds to an individual's awareness of her or his emotional state and to the ability to control one's emotions. Dawda and Hart (2000) reported that the Bar-On EQ-i may indeed be useful for measuring differences among people on the interpersonal and intrapersonal dimensions Gardner identified. More recently, Bar-on et al. (2004) described biological substrates for emotional and social intelligence, including the ventromedial prefrontal cortex, the amygdala, and insular cortices.

Critics of Gardner's theory generally have focused on (a) his uneven use of his own criteria for defining an intelligence; (b) his neglect of the research supporting *g*; (c) his claim that the multiple intelligences are independent of each other; and (d) the confusing pattern of results from research efforts to apply the theory in educational contexts. In addition, Willingham (2004) called attention to the widespread but questionable assumption among educators who seek to apply the theory that the intelligences are interchangeable, that is, that a higher level of one intelligence may somehow compensate for the lower level of another. Whether the assumption is consistent with Gardner's theory remains unclear.

*f*ocus ⊕n

Cultural Definitions of Intelligence

Intelligence is not culture free. Most Western societies include academic skills such as verbal ability and formal reasoning in their definitions of intelligence and regard nonacademic abilities as something else, such as talents, but this Western view may not be applicable in other cultures.

Scribner (1977) visited two tribes of people in Liberia, West Africa, the Kpelle and the Vai. She found that the tribespeople gave what Westerners would consider wrong answers to **syllogisms,** a tool for measuring deductive logic (that is, reasoning from already established premises; syllogisms are discussed later in the chapter). This is not to say, however, that the people could not reason logically. They simply approached problems differently. For example, Scribner presented the following problem to a Kpelle farmer. At first glance, this appears to be a reasonable problem, even for a person without formal schooling, because it refers to the farmer's own tribe and to an occupation he is familiar with.

All Kpelle men are rice farmers. Mr. Smith is not a rice farmer. Is he a Kpelle man?

The man replied:

Subject: I don't know the man in person. I have not laid eyes on the man himself.

Experimenter: Just think about the statement.

Subject: If I know him in person, I can answer that question, but since I do not know him in person, I cannot answer that question.

Experimenter: Try and answer from your Kpelle sense.

Subject: If you know a person, if a question comes up about him, you are able to answer. But if you do not know the person, if a question comes up about him, it's hard for you to answer. (Scribner, 1977, p. 490)

The farmer's response did not show that he was unable to solve a problem in deductive logic. Instead, it indicated that, as far as he was concerned, the question was unreasonable.

---

syllogism A logical construction that contains a major premise, a minor premise, and a conclusion. The major and minor premises are assumed to be true, and the truth of the conclusion is to be evaluated by deductive reasoning.

His response contained an example of logical reasoning: "If you know a person . . . you are able to answer."

Scribner found that sometimes people without formal schooling would reject the premises of her syllogism, replace them with what they knew to be true, and then solve the new problem as they had defined it. For example, she presented the following problem to a Vai tribesperson:

> All women who live in Monrovia are married.
>
> Kemu is not married.
>
> Does she live in Monrovia?

The answer was yes. The respondent said, "Monrovia is not for any one kind of people, so Kemu came to live there." The suggestion that only married women live in Monrovia was absurd, because the tribesperson knew otherwise. Thus, if Kemu wanted to live there, she could—and did.

More recently, Nisbett (2003) characterized fundamental differences between East Asian (primarily Chinese, Korean, and Japanese) and Western (primarily American) cultures in their cultural views of intelligence. Westerners tend to *atomism,* that is, to objectification and categorization in their emphasis on analysis. By contrast, East Asians tend to holism, to attend to the whole rather than the parts, to emphasize change and contradiction, and to seek the "Middle Way" between opposing claims. For example, Japanese and American participants each viewed animated underwater scenes and were asked to describe the scenes. American participants typically began by reporting items in the foreground—"the big fish, maybe a trout, swimming past to the right." Japanese participants first referred to the context—"a lake or a pond"—and to the relatedness of the components they observed—"the big fish swimming past the gray seaweed."

With their international collaborators, Sternberg and Grigorenko have studied intelligence among tribespeople in Kenya. Grigorenko et al. (2001) identified four concepts of intelligence among the Luo: *rieko,* which corresponds to academic intelligence and specific skills; *luoro,* which refers to social characteristics such as considerateness, responsibility, and respect; *paro,* which may be considered to approximate Sternberg's notion of practical intelligence; and *winjo,* which is equivalent to comprehension. The researchers concluded that the four types of intelligence formed two principal categories—social–emotional intelligence and cognitive competence. Of the four, only *rieko,* was closely associated with Western concepts of intelligence.

In a study involving Kenyan children between the ages of 12 and 15, Sternberg et al. (2001) devised a test of the children's tacit knowledge of medicinal plants that were available in the area where their village was located. A premium was placed on such knowledge, given the widespread parasitic infections that threatened the children. Knowing which plants to take was critical to the maintenance of daily functioning. Sternberg and his colleagues found that the children's scores correlated poorly with those on more conventional tests of academic intelligence and achievement. This discrepancy may contribute to the skepticism among adults toward the value of schooling and may pit academic and practical intelligence against one another.

Clearly, it may be a serious error to measure the intellectual ability of people in other cultures against our own cultural standards. Among traditional tribal peoples, problems may be solved by the application of logical reasoning to facts gained through direct experience in specific ecologies (see Sternberg & Grigorenko, 2004, 2007). The deductive-reasoning ability of such peoples is not necessarily inferior to ours; it is simply different, as a consequence of adapting to different environmental demands (see Diamond, 1997, for a remarkable extension of this basic idea—his claim that the differences between highly technological cultures and preliterate cultures are attributable to guns, germs, and steel).

QUESTIONS TO CONSIDER

1. How do you define intelligence in your everyday life? Would your definition work as well for someone from a different culture from the one in which you live? Why or why not?
2. How would you define the deficits exhibited by Mr. V. in the Prologue, in terms of one or more of the theories of intelligence discussed in this section?
3. Gardner has considered the possibility of a "spiritual" intelligence. What do you think about the possibility that such a thing exists? What criteria would you recommend to decide whether to add spiritual intelligence as a ninth intelligence?

Intelligence Testing

Intelligence testing is a controversial topic because of its importance in contemporary society. Many employers use specialized aptitude tests (such as the Wonderlic Personnel Test), which are modifications of intelligence tests, to help them select employees. Because the scores achieved on these tests have major implications for the quality of people's adult lives, testing has become one of the most important areas of applied psychology (e.g., Hough & Oswald, 2000). Today, hundreds of tests of specific abilities are available, such as manual dexterity, spatial reasoning, vocabulary, mathematical aptitude, musical ability, creativity, and memory (Geisinger et al., 2007). General tests of scholastic aptitude exist, some of which you have probably taken yourself in school. All these tests vary widely in reliability, validity, and ease of administration, as will be evident in what follows. Taken together, their common purpose is to tell the difference between individuals. (See **FIGURE 11•1.**)

[FIGURE 11·1] The normal curve and data from intelligence testing. (a) A mathematically derived normal curve. (b) A curve showing the distribution of IQ scores of 850 children 2.5 years of age.

(From Terman, L. M., and Merrill, M. A. *Stanford–Binet Intelligence Scale.* Copyright © 1960 by The Riverside Publishing Company. "The Normal Curve and Data from Intelligence Testing" from the Stanford–Binet Intelligence Scales reproduced with permission of the publisher. All rights reserved.)

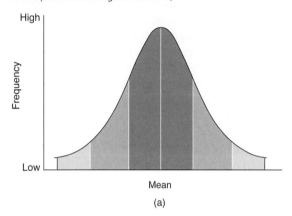

(a)

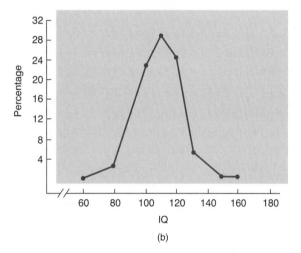

(b)

Intelligence Tests

Modern intelligence tests began in France, with the work of the psychologist Alfred Binet (1857–1911). Binet's test, later adapted by American psychologists, is still used today. Another psychologist, David Wechsler, devised two new intelligence tests, one for adults (the WAIS) and another for children (the Wechsler Intelligence Scale for Children or WISC), both of which we'll look at in more detail later in the chapter.

Binet–Simon Scale   An intelligence test developed by Binet and Simon in 1905; the precursor of the Stanford–Binet Scale.

norms   Data obtained from large numbers of individuals that permit the score of any one individual to be assessed relative to the scores of his or her peers.

mental age   A measure of a person's intellectual development; the average level of intellectual development that could be expected in a child of a particular age.

Stanford–Binet Scale   An intelligence test that consists of various tasks grouped according to mental age; provides the standard measure of the IQ.

The Binet-Simon Scale   Binet's approach included measuring a variety of psychological abilities (such as imagery, attention, comprehension, imagination, judgments of visual space, and memory for various stimuli) that appeared representative of the traits that distinguished people of high and low intelligence (see Binet & Henri, 1896).

The French government asked Binet to look into problems associated with teaching children who had learning difficulties. To identify children who were unable to profit from typical classroom instruction and who therefore needed special attention and programs, Binet and a colleague, Théodore Simon, assembled a collection of tests, many of which had been developed by other psychologists and educators, and published the **Binet-Simon Scale** in 1905. The word *scale* refers to the fact that the purpose of testing is measurement. The tests were arranged in order of difficulty, and the researchers obtained norms for each test. **Norms** are averaged data obtained from large numbers of individuals and allow the score of any one individual to be assessed relative to his or her peers. In this case, the norms are distributions of scores obtained from children of various ages. Binet and Simon also provided a detailed description of the testing procedure, which was essential for obtaining reliable scores. Without a *standardized* procedure for administering a test, different test givers may obtain different scores from the same child. Differences in the test givers' manner of engaging the child, of posing questions, and responding to the child's answers are possible sources of variance in the scores obtained.

Binet revised the 1905 test to assess the intellectual abilities of both typical children and those with learning problems. The revised versions provided a procedure for estimating a child's **mental age**—the average level of intellectual development for a child of a particular age. For example, if a child of 8 scores as well as average 10-year-old children, his or her mental age is 10 years. Binet did not develop the concept of IQ, which relies on the notion of mental age as well as the child's chronological age, nor did he believe that the mental age derived from the test scores expressed a simple trait called "intelligence." Instead, he conceived of the overall score as the average of several different abilities.

The Stanford–Binet Scale   In the United States, Lewis Terman of Stanford University translated and revised the Binet–Simon Scale. The revised group of tests, published in 1916, became known as the **Stanford–Binet Scale.** Revisions by Terman and Maud Merrill were published in 1937 and 1960. The most recent edition (SB5) was published in 2004 (Roid & Barram, 2004). The Stanford–Binet Scale, which is widely used in North America and may be used with individuals from age 2 through 85, consists of various tasks grouped according to mental age. The scale is organized according to five factors: Fluid Reasoning, Knowledge, Quantitative Reasoning, Visual–Spatial Processing, and Working Memory. Simple tests include identifying parts of the body and remembering which of three small cardboard boxes contains a marble. Intermediate tests include tracing a simple maze with a pencil and repeating five digits orally. Advanced tests include explaining the difference between two abstract words that are close in meaning (such as *fame* and *notoriety*) and completing complex sentences that are presented partially.

The 1916 Stanford–Binet Scale contained a formula for computing IQ, a measure devised by Stern (1914). The **intelligence quotient (IQ)** is based on the idea that if test scores indicate that a child's mental age is equal to his or her chronological age (that is, calendar age), the child's intelligence is average; if the child's mental age is above or below his or her chronological age, the child is more or less intelligent than average. This relation is expressed as the quotient of mental age (MA) and chronological age (CA). The result, when multiplied by 100, is called the **ratio IQ:**

$$IQ = (MA \div CA) \times 100$$

Multiplication by 100 is a convenience for eliminating fractions. For example, if a child's mental age is 10 and the child's chronological age is 8, then his or her ratio IQ is (10 ÷ 8) × 100 = 125.

The 1960 version of the Stanford-Binet Scale replaced the ratio IQ with the **deviation IQ.** The aim was to avoid various problems that had become apparent with the ratio IQ, such as the fact that mental age tends not to increase in adulthood, even though chronological age does. Instead of using the ratio of mental age to chronological age, the deviation IQ compares a test taker's score with those received by other people of the same chronological age. (The deviation IQ was created by David Wechsler, whose work is described in the next section.) For example, suppose that a child's score is one standard deviation above the mean for his or her age. The standard deviation of the ratio IQ scores is 16 points, and the score assigned to the average IQ is 100 points. (See Chapter 2 for a description of the standard deviation, a measure of variability.) If a child's score is 1 standard deviation above the mean for his or her age, the child's deviation IQ score is 100 + 16 (the standard deviation) = 116. A child who scores 1 standard deviation below the mean has a deviation IQ of 84 (100 − 16). (See FIGURE 11•2.)

Wechsler's Tests Over his long career as chief psychologist at New York City's Bellevue Psychiatric Hospital, David Wechsler (1896–1981) developed several widely used tests of intelligence. His goals were to devise tests of intelligence that were not limited to a single performance index, that were not limited to verbal content, and that avoided cultural and linguistic biases. In this way, they would be more useful for his work with his patients. The Wechsler–Bellevue Scale, published in 1939, was specifically designed to produce norms for adults and was revised in 1942 for use in the armed forces. It was superseded in 1955 by the **Wechsler Adult Intelligence Scale (WAIS).** This test was revised in 1981 (the WAIS-R) and again in 1997 (the WAIS-III). The **Wechsler Intelligence Scale for Children (WISC),** first published in 1949 and revised most recently in 2003 (the WISC-IV), closely resembles the WAIS. Wechsler also devised an intelligence test for preschool children, a memory scale, and other measures of ability.

The WAIS-III consists of several subtests, divided into the two principal categories of intelligence that Wechsler identified: *verbal* and *performance.* TABLE 11•5 lists the subtests and a typical question or problem for each. The norms obtained for the WAIS-III permit the test giver to calculate a deviation IQ score.

The WAIS has become the most popular individually administered adult intelligence test (Butcher et al., 2007). An important advantage is that it tests verbal and performance abilities separately. Neuropsychologists often use it, because people with brain damage tend to score very differently on the performance and verbal tests; thus, comparisons of performance

---

intelligence quotient (IQ) A simplified single measure of general intelligence; by definition, the ratio of a person's mental age to his or her chronological age.

ratio IQ A formula for computing the intelligence quotient: mental age divided by chronological age, multiplied by 100.

deviation IQ A procedure for computing the IQ; compares an individual's score with those received by other individuals of the same chronological age.

Wechsler Adult Intelligence Scale (WAIS) An intelligence test for adults devised by David Wechsler; contains subtests divided into verbal and performance categories.

Wechsler Intelligence Scale for Children (WISC) An intelligence test for children devised by David Wechsler; similar in form to the Wechsler Adult Intelligence Scale.

[**FIGURE 11•2**] Calculating the deviation IQ score.

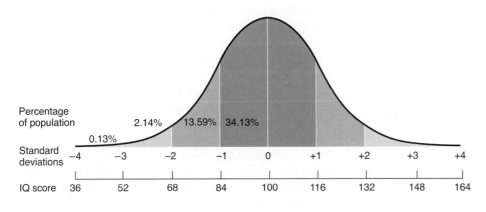

Percentage of population

0.13% 2.14% 13.59% 34.13%

Standard deviations   −4   −3   −2   −1   0   +1   +2   +3   +4

IQ score   36   52   68   84   100   116   132   148   164

[**TABLE 11·5**] WAIS-III Subtests and Typical Questions or Problems

Subtest	Typical Question or Problem
Verbal	
Information	"What is the capital of France?"
Digit span	"Repeat these numbers back to me: 46239."
Vocabulary	"What does the word *conventional* mean?"
Arithmetic	"Suppose you bought six postcards for 13 cents each and gave the clerk a dollar. How much change would you receive?" (Paper and pencil cannot be used.)
Comprehension	"Why are we tried by a jury of our peers?"
Similarities	"How are goldfish and canaries similar to each other?"
Letter/number search	The test giver reads a list of out-of-sequence letters and numbers and instructs the person to repeat the items back in sequence.
Performance	
Picture completion	The test giver shows the person a picture with a missing part (such as a mouse without its whiskers) and says, "Tell me what's missing."
Picture arrangement	The test giver shows a series of cartoon pictures (without words) and instructs the person to arrange them in the proper sequence.
Block design	The test giver shows a picture and four or nine blocks divided diagonally into red and white sections, and then instructs the person to arrange the blocks so that they match the design in the picture.
Object assembly	The test giver gives the person pieces of cardboard cut like a jigsaw puzzle and instructs him or her to assemble them. (When properly assembled, the pieces form the shape of a common object.)
Digit symbol	The test giver presents a set of 10 symbols paired with the 10 digits and instructs the person to write the corresponding symbols beneath each of a long series of numerals.
Symbol search	The test giver presents a string of symbols, then instructs the person to say whether either of two symbols shown separately also appears in the string of symbols.
Matrix reasoning	The test giver shows the person a matrix containing designs in three of the quadrants and instructs him or her to select the correct missing design from five options.

and verbal test scores may suggest the presence of undiagnosed brain damage. Conversely, because people who have had few educational and cultural opportunities often do worse on the verbal tests than on the performance tests, the comparison of scores helps indicate what these individuals' scores might have been had they been raised in more favorable environments.

Reliability and Validity of Intelligence Tests

As you will recall from Chapter 2, the adequacy of a measure is defined by its *reliability* and *validity*. In the case of intelligence testing, researchers assess reliability in terms of the correlation between the scores people receive on the same test on two different occasions; perfect reliability is 1.0. High reliability is achieved by means of standardized test administration and objective scoring: All test takers are exposed to the same conditions during testing, and all test givers score responses in the same way. The acceptable reliability of a modern test of intellectual ability should be at least .85 (on a 1.0 scale).

One way to establish the validity of an intelligence test is by the strength of the correlation between test scores and the **criterion**—an independent measure of the variable that is being assessed, such as grades in school. The importance of criterion validity can be illustrated by the research literature on self-reported intelligence. No single, agreed-on criterion measure assesses validity, not least because no single definition of intelligence is accepted. We can, however, look at Binet's original goal of intelligence testing—the prediction of scholastic aptitude; that is, the prediction of success in academic subjects. The evidence is reasonably clear. School performance, as measured by grades, has a correlation of about .50 with IQ scores (Neisser et al., 1996). Keep in mind, though, that this correlation does not mean that IQ *determines* school performance. A correlation of that size means that about 75% of the variability among students in their school performance is due to factors other than IQ scores. The proportion of the variance explained by IQ scores equals the square of the correlation coefficient: $(.50)^2 = .25$, or 25%. This leaves 75% of the variance unexplained. The list of potential influences other than IQ on scholastic success is lengthy—but probably includes quality of instruction, family emphasis on education, personal interest and motivation, effort and persistence, and peer-group attitudes toward school. Consistent with Binet's goal, a study of high school students in Italy (De Fabio and Busoni, 2007) found that scores on a measure of fluid intelligence (Advanced Progressive Matrices) were highly

---

criterion An independent measure of the variable a test is designed to measure.

correlated with scores on a national achievement examination that students took in the final year of school and also with high school GPA. An additional component of the study showed a strong positive correlation between these academic measures and the personality factor of conscientiousness (see Chapter 14).

A Puzzling Phenomenon: The Flynn Effect

Over the past few decades, one of the most curious phenomena of intelligence measurement is that test scores are increasing. The phenomenon is not confined to a particular part of the world but is worldwide. It seems that people everywhere are becoming more intelligent. The phenomenon was first identified by James Flynn (1987) and is now referred to as the Flynn Effect (Herrnstein & Murray, 1994; see also Sternberg, 2008). Flynn examined IQ test scores from several countries and found generational increments in IQ from one generation to the next across the 20th century—a finding diametrically opposed to the common wisdom that intelligence is conserved across time. A direct consequence of the phenomenon was the need to establish new norms for intelligence tests every generation or so, as mean performance on the tests kept inching up.

More recently, Dickens and Flynn (2001) offered a model by which to account for the Flynn effect. They begin by characterizing the originators of the first widely used intelligence tests as "viewing the world through scientific spectacles"—a perspective that was presumably rare at the time. With the advance of science and technology in the 20th century, an increasingly large proportion of schoolchildren in economically advanced nations began to share the scientific spectacles and thus to do increasingly well on the IQ tests. Flynn (2007) speculated that the gains in mean IQ scores have now largely played out in developed nations and that the 21st century will see a similar phenomenon taking place in developing countries. According to Flynn, "This would eliminate the IQ gap that separates those two worlds and refute those who see the lower IQs of developing nations as a largely fixed cause of lack of economic progress" (p. 175). As evidence of this second wave of the Flynn effect, Dickens and Flynn (2006) documented a recent reduction in the IQ gap between blacks and whites in the United States (see later).

Brain Activity Correlates of Intelligence

Differential patterns of brain activity may offer new criteria for the validation of IQ tests. In one experiment Haier and colleagues (Haier, White, & Alkire, 2003) recorded the brain activity of participants who were watching videos. Certain brain regions were more active for participants who performed well on the nonverbal Raven's Advanced Progressive Matrices test than for participants who performed poorly. In related work using *f*MRI scans, Haier, Jung, Yeo, Head, and Alkire (2004) found that individuals with higher IQ scores had proportionately higher volumes of gray matter in certain regions of the brain than did individuals with lower scores. Jung and Haier (2007) conducted a comprehensive review of studies involving a variety of neuroimaging techniques and proposed a parietofrontal theory of intelligence. Specifically, the differential patterns of activation in a brain network consisting of the association cortices and parietal and frontal brain regions predict a person's scores on tests of intelligence and may be considered the biological substrate for such intelligence.

The Use and Abuse of Intelligence Tests

Because test scores have such important consequences for people's opportunities, it is imperative that intelligence tests be valid and be used appropriately. As much of the variability on grades and job performance is due to factors other than IQ, the best and fairest practice is to consider IQ as one of several predictors relevant to such decisions—and to recognize both the problems and the utility of IQ testing. Let's look more closely at some problems as well as some valid uses of tests.

The Problem of Cultural Bias

Critics of intelligence testing have argued that the results of some tests are strongly affected by what people have learned (e.g., Miller-Jones, 1989), not just by the test takers' inherent abilities. Consider the effects of a person's family background and culture on his or her ability to answer questions such as "Who wrote *Romeo and Juliet*?" "What is a hieroglyph?" and "What is the meaning of *catacomb*?" (Vernon, 1979, p. 22). Obviously, a child from a family with a strong educational background is much more likely to be able to answer these questions than a child from a less educated family. The worst form of this bias occurs when entire groups of people are disadvantaged because the content of the test material is foreign to their own cultural contexts.

Critics of intelligence testing are concerned with fairness. For example, a test's cultural bias may compromise a student's performance, and the interpretation of test results may lead to a self-fulfilling prophecy.

Test makers have responded to the criticism of cultural bias, and tests are now less likely to contain questions that are obviously biased (see Helms, 1997). This is not to say that problems of cultural bias have disappeared. It is hard to make bias-free tests, because test makers (like the rest of us) are strongly socialized in their cultures to assume that what they themselves know is common knowledge. For example, Darou (1992) tells a story of presenting a standard analogy question to a tribal councilor in a remote Arctic village: "Saw is to whine, as snake is to . . ." (p. 97), for which the scored correct answer would be "hiss." The person questioned could not generate the correct answer. The reason? Most saws that people in that particular region had experience with were handsaws and chain saws, neither of which whine like a power saw. Clinching the cultural inappropriateness of the question was the fact that no snakes lived in the area. Colapinto (2007) has reported a similarly ill-fated effort involving an indigenous Amazonian tribe.

Even when questions having obvious cultural bias are excluded from tests, different experiences can lead to different test-taking strategies in subtler ways (e.g., Helms, 1992). For example, as we saw earlier, Kpelle tribespeople approach hypothetical logical problems very differently from people in literate societies. Their "failure" to solve such problems indicates cultural differences, not necessarily intellectual differences.

Other aspects of the testing context can influence performance. Considerable research has been devoted to the "stereotype threat," wherein test-takers may view themselves as representing a larger group and consequently perform more poorly (Steele, Spencer, & Aronson, 2002). Smith et al. (2008) showed that the perception of personal power may also affect performance in tests of cognitive abilities.

The Problem of Self-Fulfilling Prophecy

In some ways, intelligence testing can be potentially harmful, even if cultural bias were minimized. Good reason exists to believe that knowledge about children's intelligence scores can set in motion the *self-fulfilling prophecy* phenomenon. A self-fulfilling prophecy occurs when people's expectations about what will happen lead them to act in ways that make the expectations come true, even if the expectations were unfounded in the first place (Merton, 1948). In short, if teachers learn that a child has a low intelligence test score, they may see encouragement of and special attention to the child as a waste of time—time perhaps better spent with students who have greater ability. Likewise, parents who learn that their child has scored low on an intelligence test may try to persuade the child away from academic pursuits. The reactions of both teachers and parents would be ill advised, because we know that intelligence scores are just part of the overall picture of a child's intellectual ability.

Often the reactions of teachers and parents reflect the view that intelligence is not malleable. Thus, little point exists

in working with the child whose scores are low if such work is unlikely to make a difference. Failure to provide the child with special attention and customized teaching could seal the child's fate, and, ironically, produce the poor academic performance that was expected on the basis of the intelligence test scores. The prophecy (i.e., the expectation) of academic failure would be fulfilled, even though the child might well have been able to do well academically, given proper support (Dweck, 2004). Although ethical considerations prevent direct testing of this possibility, related research strongly suggests that these concerns are well placed (e.g., Madon et al., 2001; Rosenthal, 1985).

Children can fulfill their own prophecies. You can imagine the potential for discouragement when a child learns that the result of an intelligence test was a low score. Expecting not to perform well academically could produce actual performance that falls far short of the child's actual potential. (See Chapter 15 for further discussion of self-fulfilling prophecy.)

Identifying Specific Learning Needs

Intelligence testing can bring important benefits when it is used for Binet's original purpose: to identify students who require special instruction. Children with severe learning problems may develop a sense of inferiority if they are placed in mainstream classes without appropriate specialized teaching support. These tests also can identify exceptionally bright students who are performing poorly because they are bored with the pace of instruction or who have been labeled troublemakers by their teachers.

Intelligence tests also remain an accepted means of evaluating the extent of mental disabilities, and thus, of indicating the most appropriate remedial program for a child. The term **mental retardation** ("mental delay") was originally applied to children with severe learning problems because such children appeared to achieve intellectual skills and competencies at a significantly later age than children typically do. Because they have a demonstrable degree of intellectual disability, they may have difficulty—in

With appropriate education, most people with mild mental retardation can lead independent lives and perform well at jobs.

---

mental retardation Cognitive development that is substantially below normal; often caused by some form of brain damage or abnormal brain development. Also known as *cognitive disability or intellectual disability.*

some cases, extreme difficulty—with the usual tasks of living. They also must deal with prejudice and discrimination (see Chapter 15). Being intelligent is a highly valued quality in Western societies, and people with intellectual deficits often are the target of derision. Unfortunately, being different often translates into being "bad." Many people also believe that if a person has an intellectual disability, he or she lacks normal emotions, desires, and needs. These beliefs are, of course, false. Nevertheless, the term *mental retardation* is still the professionally accepted label and is used here for the purpose of describing the degrees of this disability. In other contexts, *cognitive disability* or *intellectual disability* may be a better term.

According to the American Psychiatric Association (2000), degrees of mental retardation are defined jointly by IQ scores and adaptive limitations in everyday living (see Jacobson & Mulick, 1996). The most severe classification, *profound mental retardation*, is applied when a person has an IQ score below 20 or 25. This is a very rare level of disability that involves problems in all domains of life and also is associated with severe motor difficulties. The person shows little cognitive development during his or her early years. People with this degree of disability typically require permanent supervision and care. The next category is severe mental retardation, which is used when a person's IQ score is between 20 to 25 and 35 to 40. This degree of disability includes difficulty with speech development during the early years. People with severe mental retardation may profit from special education programs and can contribute to their own care, although they almost always need close supervision. People with moderate mental retardation have IQ scores between 35 to 40 and 50 to 55, are able to learn most basic life skills, are able to hold well-supervised jobs, and can live semi-independently with some supervision and assistance. The vast majority of people with mental retardation (about 90%) are classified as having mild mental retardation. IQ scores for this level fall between 50 to 55 and approximately 70. Although people with mild mental retardation may need assistance and support from time to time, they generally are able to live independently and to learn the skills and responsibilities needed to maintain employment. It is important to recall again that IQ by itself does not determine a person's achievement and satisfaction with life. Families, neighbors, schools, communities, and special programs are all significant contributors to the well-being of people with intellectual disabilities.

QUESTIONS FOR FURTHER THINKING

1. Would you like to know your own IQ score? Why? What difference(s) would knowing your IQ score make in your life? How would you feel if your IQ score were "average"?

2. Suppose you wanted to devise an intelligence test of your own. What kinds of tasks would you include? What abilities would these tasks measure?

The Roles of Heredity and Environment

Abilities of various kinds—intellectual, athletic, musical, and artistic—appear to run in families. Why? Are the similarities due to heredity, or are they the result of a common environment, including similar educational opportunities and exposure to people with similar kinds of interests? We considered this problem briefly in Chapter 3; now we examine it in more detail. As you will see, both hereditary and environmental factors play a substantial role in the development of intelligence. Neither acts in isolation.

The Meaning of Heritability

When we ask how much influence heredity has on a given trait, we are usually asking about the heritability of the trait. As we saw in Chapter 3, **heritability** is a statistical measure that applies to a specific population. It is the proportion of the observed variability in the trait within that population that is directly produced by the genetic variability in the population. The value of statistic can vary from 0 to 1.0. The heritability of many physical traits in most populations is very high; for example, eye color is affected almost entirely by hereditary factors and little, if at all, by the environment. Thus, the heritability of eye color is close to 1.0.

Heritability is a concept that many people misunderstand. It does not describe the extent to which one's genes are responsible for producing a particular trait. It measures the relative contributions of differences in genes and differences in environmental factors to the overall observed variability of the trait in a particular population. An example may make this distinction clear. Consider the heritability of hair color among Inuit. Assume that all young Inuit have black hair. Because all mem-

Eye color is a heritable trait with a heritability close to 1.0.

---

heritability A statistical measure of the degree to which the variability of a particular trait in a population results from the genetic variability within the population; has a value from 0 to 1.0.

bers of the Inuit population possess the same versions of the genes that determine hair color, no genetic variability is found in the population. Therefore, the heritability of hair color among Inuit is zero. This may sound odd to you, because you know that hair color is genetically determined. How can a trait be genetically determined, indeed inherited, but have zero heritability? The key point is that genetic determination and heritability are not the same thing. The term *heritability* refers only to the genetic influence on the distribution of differences in a trait—the variability—within a specific population. If no genetic differences exist among individuals in the population, then a trait has a heritability of zero. In other words, both genes and environment contribute to the variation observed in a specific trait within a sample. For this reason, trying to estimate the extent to which one of them contributes to that trait is necessarily influenced by the extent to which the other varies in the same sample.

Heritability of IQ We measure the heritability of intelligence through observation of the trait within a population. By measuring the correlation between IQ scores and various genetic and environmental factors, it is possible to estimate the heritability of IQ in that population. Clearly, if hereditary factors do influence intelligence, its heritability necessarily will be less than 1.0, possibly considerably less, because many environmental factors (including the mother's prenatal health and nutrition, the child's nutrition, the educational level of the child's parents, the parents' income level, and the quality of the child's school) require consideration.

In other words, a person does not inherit a specific IQ score. Rather, a person inherits genes that influence the development of her or his intelligence within the environments in which the person develops. The life you experience early in the womb, your home, your schools, and your neighborhood all influence your IQ in conjunction with your genes. Most important, remember that heritability estimates do not apply to individuals (see Sternberg & Grigorenko, 1999, for an interesting discussion of this point). The estimates apply only to populations. Also keep in mind that knowing the heritability of a trait is .50 does not mean that 50% of the trait is inherited by an individual. Rather, we would say that half of the variability in the trait, as measured in the specific population of interest, can be accounted for by the genetic variability that exists there. Again, heritability refers to populations, not to individuals.

When we consider behavior genetic studies that attempt to measure the heritability of intellectual abilities, we should remember the following:

1. The heritability of a trait depends on the amount of variability of genetic factors in a given population. If there is little genetic variability, genetic factors will appear to be unimportant. Because the ancestors of people living in developed Western nations came from all over the earth, genetic variability is likely to be much higher in those nations than in an isolated community of people in a remote part of the world. Therefore, if a person's IQ score is affected by genetic

factors, the measured heritability of IQ will be higher in, say, North America than in an isolated community.

2. The relative importance of environmental factors in intelligence depends on the amount of environmental variability that occurs in the population. If environmental variability is low, then environmental factors will appear to be unimportant. In a hypothetical population with low variability in the environmental factors relevant to intellectual development—a population in which all children are raised in the same way by equally skilled and conscientious caregivers, all schools are equally good, all teachers have equally effective personalities and teaching skills, and no one is discriminated against—the effects of environmental variability will be relatively small, and those of genetic variability will be relatively large. In contrast, in a population in which only a few privileged people receive a good education, environmental factors will be responsible for much more of the variability in intelligence: In this case, the effects of environmental variability would be large relative to those of genetic variability.

3. Heritability is affected by the degree to which genetic inheritance and environment interact. Genetic factors and environmental factors often affect each other. For example, suppose that because of genetic differences, some children are mellow, and others are excitable. Suppose that the excitable children will profit most from a classroom in which distractions are kept to a minimum and teachers are themselves mellow and soothing. Further suppose that the mellow students will profit most from an exciting classroom that motivates them to work their hardest. Thus, if all students are taught in a mellow classroom, the excitable children will learn more and obtain better IQ scores. If all students are taught in an exciting classroom, the mellow children will do better and obtain the higher scores. In an ideal world, of course, a child's learning environment would be optimal for his or her genetic inheritance.

Sources of Environmental and Genetic Effects during Development

Donald Hebb (1949, 1966) set the stage for our current understanding of how genetics and environment contribute to intelligence. In his neuropsychological theory of behavior, Hebb explained that both biological and environmental factors before and after birth can affect intellectual abilities. His view was that the term "intelligence," as used by psychologists, reflects two components. The first component (*Intelligence A*) is the hereditary, biological potential for intellectual development. The second component (*Intelligence B*) reveals the effect of biological development coupled with environmental influences on intellectual functioning. Intelligence B, then, is what IQ tests measure. From this perspective, newborn infants cannot be said to possess any substantial intellectual abilities; rather, we say they are more or less capable of developing these abilities as they grow older. Therefore, prenatal influences affect a child's potential intelligence by affecting the development of the brain. Factors that impair brain development will necessarily also impair the child's potential intelligence.

The factors that control the development of a human organism are incredibly complex. Although development of a human organism is programmed genetically, environmental factors affect development well before a person is born. Harmful prenatal environmental factors include physical trauma (for instance, injury to the mother in an automobile accident) and toxins. A developing fetus can be exposed to toxins from diseases contracted by the mother during pregnancy (such as rubella) or from other sources. A pregnant woman's intake of drugs can have disastrous effects on fetal development. Genetic abnormalities can also impair development. The best-known example is Down syndrome, which was described in Chapter 3. Although it is a genetic disorder, it is not hereditary; it results from imperfect division of the 21st pair of chromosomes during the development of an ovum or (more rarely) a sperm. Chapter 3 also described phenylketonuria (PKU), an inherited metabolic disorder that disrupts brain development.

A child's brain continues to develop from birth onward. Environmental factors can promote or impede that development. Postnatal factors such as birth trauma, diseases, or toxic chemicals can prevent optimal development and thereby affect the child's intelligence. For example, encephalitis (inflammation of the brain), when contracted during childhood, can result in mental retardation. So can the ingestion of poisons such as mercury or lead, as well as malnutrition. Educational influences in the environment, including home life and schooling (to mention only two), can nurture a child's intelligence. By contrast, a less-than-optimal environment may limit the expression of a child's intellectual potential.

The interactive effects of environmental and genetic factors are complex. The effects of hereditary factors on adult intellectual ability are necessarily indirect, and many environmental factors exert their effects throughout the journey to adulthood. Because an adult's intellectual abilities are the product of a long chain of events, we cannot isolate the effects of the earliest factors. The types of genetic and environmental factors that influence potential intelligence at each stage of development are summarized here.

Conception. A basic genetic endowment sets in place the potential for the later development of intellectual abilities.

Prenatal development. Good nutrition and a normal pregnancy predict optimal fetal brain development and the achievement of optimal intellectual potential. Drugs, maternal disease, toxic substances, poor nutrition, and physical accidents can impair fetal brain development, thus lowering that potential. Genetic disorders, such as Down syndrome and phenylketonuria, also can impair brain development.

Birth. Anoxia (lack of oxygen) or head trauma can cause brain damage.

Infancy. The brain continues to develop and grow. Good nutrition continues to be important. Sensory stimulation and interaction with responsive physical and social environments are important for cognitive development. An infant's environment and brain jointly determine his or her intelligence.

Childhood and later life. A person's intelligence continues to be jointly determined by environmental factors and brain structure and chemistry. Rich environmental stimulation continues to be vital to intellectual abilities into old age.

A Sample of Results from Heritability Studies

Estimates of the degree to which heredity influences a person's intellectual ability come from several sources. As Chapter 3 indicated, the two most powerful methods are comparisons between identical and fraternal twins and comparisons between adoptive and biological relatives. As you read about studies pertaining to general intelligence and specific abilities, remember what heritability does and does not mean. If the heritability of a trait is .50, this does not mean that 50% of the trait was inherited. It means that 50% of the variance for that trait in a specific population is determined by the genetic variance in the population

General Intelligence TABLE 11•6 presents correlations for IQ scores between people with varying degrees of kinship. The data in the table were obtained from a summary by Henderson (1982) of several studies. As you can see, the correlation between two people is indeed related to their genetic similarity. For example, the correlation between identical twins is larger than that between fraternal twins. The correlation between a biological parent and a child is approximately the same regardless of whether the child is raised by the parent (.35 versus .31). The correlation, in turn, is higher than that between an adopted child and the parent who raises him or her (.16).

[**TABLE 11•6**] Correlations between IQ Scores for Members of Various Kinship Pairs

Relationship	Rearing	Percentage of Genetic Similarity	Correlation
Same individual	–	100	0.87[a]
Identical twins	Together	100	0.86
Fraternal twins	Together	50	0.62
Siblings	Together	50	0.41
Siblings	Apart	50	0.24
Parent–child	Together	50	0.35
Parent–child	Apart	50	0.31
Adoptive parent–child	Together	?	0.16

[a]The correlation is not 1.0 because a person's score may vary from one test to another due to tiredness, distraction, etc. Nevertheless, such a high correlation shows the high reliability of IQ tests.

Source: Adapted from Henderson, N. D. Human behavior genetics, pp. 403–440. Reprinted, with permission, from the *Annual Review of Psychology*, Volume 33. © 1982 by Annual Reviews, www.annualreviews.org.

Genetics clearly makes a difference, but how much? Neisser and colleagues (1996) summarized the evidence on the heritability of IQ and estimated it to be at about .45 in childhood and about .75 in late adolescence. In other words, it appears that heritability of IQ increases with age. Studies of people in their eighth and ninth decades likewise show higher IQ heritability estimates than typically seen for children (Mc-Clearn et al., 1997). How could this be? The answer suggested by Neisser and colleagues and other researchers (e.g., Sternberg & Grigorenko, 1999) is that until early adulthood, a person is subject to the authority and decisions of many other people and institutions. The environment therefore stands to play a relatively important role in the development of the individual's intelligence. When people become independent, however, they can begin to choose their own environments. To the extent that those choices reflect the heritable component of intelligence, the influence of the chosen environments becomes less distinct from the influence of their genes.

The interaction between genes and environment was highlighted in research reported by Turkheimer and his associates (Turkheimer et al., 2003). The researchers analyzed results from 7-year-old identical and fraternal twins who were part of a previous longitudinal study in the United States. Many of the children in the study were raised in families whose socioeconomic status was at or below the level defined as poverty. Other twins in the study were raised in families considered affluent. The researchers used sophisticated statistical procedures to assign the variance in scores on the WISC to three categories: genes, shared environment (that is, the environments in which both twins would have been present), and nonshared environment (those in which one twin would have been present but not the other). Their results were surprising and revealed a considerable interaction. For the population of impoverished families, heritability of IQ is nearly zero; 60% of the variance was accounted for by shared environment. For the population of affluent families, the results were essentially the opposite—heritability close to 60% and percentage of the variance accounted for by shared environment, close to zero. Clearly the environments that characterize poverty interact much more diversely with genes than do those that characterize affluence.

Specific Abilities So far, we have looked at the effects of genetic factors on tests of intelligence. Scarr and Weinberg (1978) compared specific intellectual abilities of parents and their adopted and biological children and of children and their adopted and biological siblings. To do so, they administered four of the subtests of the Wechsler Adult Intelligence Scale: Arithmetic, Vocabulary, Block Design, and Picture Arrangement. (Table 11.5 described these subtests.) TABLE 11·7 shows the results. As you can see, the correlations between biological relatives were considerably higher than those between adoptive relatives, indicating that genetic factors played a more significant role than shared environmental factors. With the exception of Vocabulary, adopted children showed little resemblance to other members of their adoptive family.

[**TABLE 11·7**] Correlations between IQ Scores in Adoptive and Biological Families

WAIS Subscale	RELATIONSHIP		
	Father–Offspring	Mother–Offspring	Sibling
Adoptive family correlations			
Arithmetic	0.07	−0.03	−0.03
Vocabulary	0.24	0.23	0.11
Block design	0.02	0.13	0.09
Picture arrangement	−0.04	−0.01	0.04
Biological family correlations			
Arithmetic	0.30	0.24	0.24
Vocabulary	0.39	0.33	0.22
Block design	0.32	0.29	0.25
Picture arrangement	0.06	0.19	0.16

Source: Adapted from Scarr, S., & Weinberg, R. A. (1978). *American Sociological Review, 43,* 674–692.

These results suggest that a person's vocabulary is more sensitive to his or her home environment than are other specific intellectual abilities. Presumably, such factors as the availability of books, parental interest in reading and conversation, and the complexity of the vocabulary used by the parents have a significant effect on the verbal skills of all members of the household, whether or not they are biologically related.

If a difference in general intelligence is found between females and males, it appears to be quite small relative to the differences between the genders in specific abilities. Women typically score higher on tests of verbal ability, and men, on tests of visual–spatial ability (Halpern, 2004). In other words, women and men are intellectual equals but achieve that parity through different patterns of intellectual performance and possibly different patterns of brain activity. Johnson and Bouchard (2007) examined a variety of possible neuroanatomical bases for the differences and described a new three-factor model of intelligence (verbal, perceptual, and image rotation) that accounts for the gender differences in specific abilities.

focus **On**

The Issue of Race and Intelligence

The fact that heredity plays an important role in the development of intelligence raises the question of whether people of some racial or ethnic groups are generally more intelligent than those of others. The harmful effects of racism on the lives of countless people make this far from an academic question. A word in advance: As we'll discuss shortly, it is actually inaccurate to refer to a "race" of people, but because discussion on this subject generally uses the word *race* rather than another term, we will use that word here.

Are There Racial Differences in Intelligence?

Many studies have established that racial differences exist in scores on various tests of intelligence. For example, people in the United States who are identified as "black" generally score an average of 85 on IQ tests, whereas people who are identified as "white" score an average of 100 (Jensen, 1985; Lynn, 1978; see Flynn, 2007, for a claim that the difference has decreased over the past 30 years). Remember from Chapter 2, however, that averages, or means, do not tell us about the variability of scores. This is an especially important point in the socially significant context of differences between races. What the means fail to tell us is that the variation of scores within each race is far greater than the variation between the two races. In other words, IQ scores of the two races overlap much more than they differ. Some whites score higher than blacks, and some blacks score higher than whites, but a seemingly reliable difference is found on average.

The issue is not the difference in average scores themselves but what those differences mean. The simplest explanation, and the one most widely accepted, has been that the historical and continued disadvantaged status of many black people in the United States suppresses the intellectual development of a large enough proportion that a mean difference in test scores is predictable and understandable.

A more-provocative stance is the thesis that the racial differences in scores on intelligence tests reflect heritable factors. *The Bell Curve*, a book written by American social scientists Richard Herrnstein and Charles Murray (1994), provoked a furor among psychologists and in the news media. The book asserted that psychologists agree that a single general factor corresponding to intelligence exists, that IQ is for all intents and purposes genetically determined, that racial differences in IQ are the result of heredity, and that IQ is almost impossible to modify through education and special programs. However, many influential psychologists (e.g., Horn, 2002; Sternberg, 1995) vehemently disagree with these conclusions.

What Is the Evidence for Racial Differences in Intelligence?

Sternberg (1995) examined *The Bell Curve's* major claims and cited research evidence against all of them. As we have already seen in this chapter, most psychologists believe that intelligence cannot be accounted for by a single factor. If you ask people what they mean by the word *intelligence*, three factors rather than one typically emerge in their responses: verbal ability, practical problem-solving ability, and social competence (Sternberg et al., 1981). Different cultures emphasize these factors differently; some weight social competence as more important, whereas others favor competence on cognitive tasks (Berry, 1984, 2001; Okagaki & Sternberg, 1993; Ruzgis & Grigorenko, 1994).

What about the assertions that IQ is almost impossible to modify? Special programs have been successful in raising children's IQ scores—on the order of 8 to 20 points (see Ramey, 1994; Wahlsten, 1997b). Herrnstein and Murray (1994) went farther by claiming that there are diminishing returns on the advanced education of black people, but there are data to show otherwise (Myerson, Rank, Raines, & Schnitzler, 1998). The gain in general cognitive ability from college education is actually greater for blacks than for whites.

What about genes? For many reasons, we cannot conclude that the observed racial differences in average test scores are the result of heredity. First, let's examine the concept of *race*. Biologists use the term to identify a population of plants or animals that has some degree of reproductive isolation from other members of the species. Any isolated group of organisms will, as a result of chance alterations in genes and differences in local environment, become genetically differentiated over time. Groups of humans whose ancestors mated only with other people who lived in a restricted geographical region tend to differ from other groups on a variety of hereditary traits, including stature, hair color, skin pigmentation, and blood type. However, subsequent migrations and invasions caused mating between many different groups of people. As a result, human racial groups have become much more similar than they are different.

Many researchers have used the trait of skin pigmentation to classify people by race. Two chemicals, melanin (a pigment) and keratin (a fibrous protein), cause skin to be black and yellow, respectively; a combination produces brown skin, and lighter-colored skin contains little of either substance. Evidence suggests that the selective value of greater skin pigmentation is related to its ability to protect against the effects of sunlight (Loomis, 1967). Such protection was important near the equator, where the sun is intense all year, but was less important in temperate zones. Because vitamin D is synthesized primarily through the action of sunlight on deep layers of the skin, lack of pigmentation was advantageous to residents of northern latitudes—except to those living in Arctic regions, where vitamin D was readily available from fish and seal meat. The selective advantage of differences in skin pigmentation is obvious, but no research shows that these differences are correlated with intellectual ability.

The second reason that we cannot conclude definitively that racial differences in test scores are caused by heredity is the existence of cultural differences. Most of the data used in the studies cited in *The Bell Curve* come from the United States; extensive data from other countries and cultures were not included in those studies.

What Should We Conclude?

Some authors have flatly stated that no racial differences exist in biologically determined intellectual potential, but this claim, like the assertion that blacks are inherently less intelligent than whites, has received mixed support at best.

Although differences in skin pigmentation offer adaptive advantages that are correlated with geography, research offers no basis for a correlation of those differences with intellectual ability.

Although we know that American blacks and whites can experience different environments, the question of whether any hereditary differences exist has not been answered. However, given that at least as much variability exists in intelligence between two people selected at random as is found between the average black person and the average white person, knowing a person's race tells us little if anything about how intelligent he or she may be.

Still, Murray (2005), after careful consideration of the major interventions designed to reduce the black–white IQ difference in the United States, points to the persistence of that difference and argues that additional research must be pursued to help us understand the difference and its implications for the larger culture. Dickens and Flynn (2006) have viewed the narrowing of black-white IQ as inevitable, given the march of factors responsible for the so-called Flynn effect described earlier.

Hunt and Carlson (2007) reflected on the continuing debate and urged several principles for conducting research on racial/ethnic differences in intelligence. Among the principles were these:

- When measurements are used to draw inferences from contrasts between the groups, the measurements must be shown to be valid in all the groups involved.
- Summaries of the literature must be done carefully and given appropriate qualifications.
- In discussing results, consider alternative frameworks. Avoid studies in which the interpretation of outcomes depends crucially on one's theoretical framework.
- Remember that the relative size of heritability and environmental effects depends on the population being considered.
- Be willing to say "We don't know."

The final principle now seems to be an apt conclusion and an open invitation to new research.

QUESTIONS FOR FURTHER THINKING

1. What types of early human environments may have favored natural selection of particular kinds of abilities—for example, mathematical ability, spatial ability, perceptual ability, or ability to memorize stories?
2. Among the continuing contested issues in education is the system of "tracking"—assigning students with different levels of intellectual ability to different classes. Take the point of view of students who have (a) high or (b) low levels of ability, and state arguments for and against this practice.

Thinking and Problem Solving

One of the most important components of intelligence is *thinking*, which includes categorizing, reasoning, solving problems, and making decisions. Thinking is an activity that takes place where no one else can see it—inside our heads. Because thinking is private, we know what we ourselves think but can only infer what others think from their observable behavior. When we think, we classify, manipulate, and combine perceptions. As a result, we may think something we did not think before (although this new thinking could be incorrect).

As with intelligence, the purpose of thinking is, in general, to solve problems adaptively. The problems may involve simple classifications (What is that, a bird or a bat?). They may involve decisions about courses of action (Should I buy a new car or pay to fix the old one?). Or they may require the construction, testing, and evaluation of complex plans of action (How am I going to manage to earn money to support my family, help raise our children, and continue my education so that I can get out of this dead-end job—and still be able to enjoy life?). Much, but not all, of our thinking involves language. We certainly think with words, but we also think with shapes and images. Thus, it's important to consider verbal as well as nonverbal processes in thinking (Holyoak & Spellman, 1993; Reber, 1992).

In this section, we consider important elements and goals of thinking: classification and concept formation, logical reasoning, and problem solving.

Classification and Concept Formation

When we categorize, we classify things according to their characteristics. When we attempt to solve a problem involving a particular object or event, we often use information that we have already learned about similar objects or events. To take a simple example, when we enter someone's house for the first time, we recognize chairs, lamps, tables, and other pieces of furniture even though we may have never seen these particular objects before. Because we can classify them according to already existing categories, we know where to sit, how to increase the level of illumination, where to place our coffee mug, and how to carry on a conversation.

A **concept** is a way of representing a category of objects, actions, events, or states of being that share certain attributes. Each of the following is a concept: cat, comet, team, destroying, playing, forgetting, happiness, truth, justice. Most thinking deals with the relations and interactions among concepts. For example, *The hawk caught the sparrow* describes an interaction between two birds; *Studying for the examination was fun* describes an attribute of a particular action related to an event (however far-fetched the statement may seem); and *Youth is a carefree time of life* describes an attribute of a state of being.

Concepts exist because the members of the categories they represent have consequences for us. For example, *mean dogs* may hurt us, whereas *friendly dogs* may bring delight. *Mean dogs* tend to growl, bare their teeth, and bite, whereas *friendly dogs* tend to wag their tails and invite affectionate contact. Once we have learned the concepts of mean and

friendly dogs, we can then respond appropriately to dogs we may encounter from then on. Another way to state this is that our experiences with particular dogs *generalize* to others (recall the concept of stimulus generalization in Chapter 5).

Types of Concepts A **formal concept** is a category defined by a list of essential characteristics, as formalized in a dictionary definition. For example, dogs have four legs, tails, fur, and wet noses; are carnivores; can bark, growl, whine, and howl; pant when they are hot; bear live young; and so on. Thus, a formal concept is a category that has rules of membership and exclusion (with all of the attendant problems of where to draw the line, as with dogs that are hairless or barkless).

Psychologists have studied the nature of formally defined concepts, such as species of animals. In a well-known study, Collins and Quillian (1969) suggested that these concepts are organized hierarchically in semantic memory (see Chapter 8 for a discussion of this category of memory). Each concept in a hierarchy is defined by a set of characteristics. Consider the hierarchy of concepts related to animals shown in FIGURE 11•3. At the top is the general concept *animal*. It is associated with the characteristics common to all animals, such as *has skin, can move around, eats, breathes,* and so on. Linked to the concept *animal* and subordinate to it are specific groups of animals, such as birds, fish, and mammals, along with their characteristics. Nested lower in the hierarchy are still more specific concepts, such as types of birds and types of fish.

---

concept A category of objects or events that share certain attributes.

formal concept A category of objects or events defined by a list of common essential characteristics, much as in a dictionary definition.

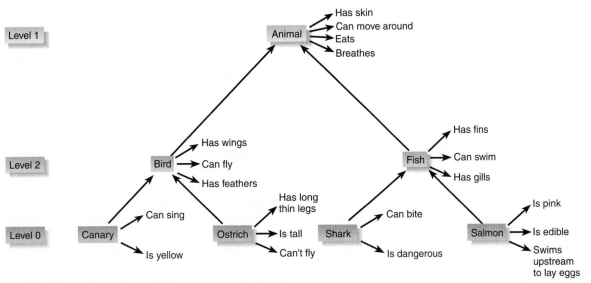

[**FIGURE 11•3**] Collins and Quillian's model of the hierarchical organization of concepts in semantic memory.

(After Collins and Quillian (1969). From Robert L. Solso, *Cognitive Psychology*, 2/e. Published by Allyn and Bacon, Boston, MA. Copyright © 1988 by Pearson Education. Reprinted by permission of the publisher.)

Collins and Quillian assumed that the characteristics common to concepts at a particular level of the hierarchy would be found *not* at that level but at the next higher level. Such an arrangement would produce an efficient and economical organization of memory. For example, all birds have wings. Thus, we need not remember that a canary, a blue jay, a robin, and an ostrich all have wings; we need only remember that each of these concepts belongs to the higher category of *bird* and that birds have wings.

Collins and Quillian tested the validity of their model by presenting questions about the characteristics of various concepts, such as the concept *canary*. They asked their participants to respond "true" or "false" to statements such as *A canary eats.* When the question dealt with characteristics that were specific to canaries (such as *can sing* or *is yellow*), the participants responded quickly. If the question dealt with a characteristic that was associated with the higher-lying concept *animal* (such as *has skin* or *breathes*), the participants took a longer time to answer. The researchers inferred that, when asked a question about a characteristic that applied to all birds or to all animals, the participants had to "travel up the tree of concepts" from the entry for canary until they found the level that provided the answer. The farther they had to go, the longer the process took.

This model of hierarchical structure has an appealing simplicity to it, but further research suggests that human brains do not follow such tidy, logical schemes in classifying concepts and their characteristics For example, Devlin et al. (2002) involved participants in semantic decision tasks involving (a) four different categories—animals, fruits, tools, and vehicles—or (b) natural kinds and human-made items. By using PET and *f*MRI measures, they identified a network of brain areas that was activated similarly by natural kinds and human-made items. They found no consistent evidence for differences in activation that were category specific.

Although categories and subcategories must somehow be linked in memory, the structure appears not to be straightforwardly logical and systematic. People may indeed conceive of objects in terms of a hierarchy, but a particular person's hierarchy of animals need not resemble that compiled by a zoologist. For example, Rips, Shoben, and Smith (1973) found that people said "yes" to *A collie is an animal* faster than they did to *A collie is a mammal.* According to Collins and Quillian's model, *animal* comes above *mammal* in the hierarchy, so the results should have been the opposite.

Eleanor Rosch (1975, 1999, 2002; Mervis & Rosch, 1981), whose work was discussed in Chapter 7, proposed that people do not look up the meanings of concepts in their heads the way they do in dictionaries. In addition, the concepts we use in everyday life are likely to be nonformal or **natural concepts,** not the formal categories known to experts who have examined characteristics most of us are not aware of. Natural concepts are categories based on personal perceptions and interactions with the real world. For example, some objects in the world have wings, beaks, and feathers, and they fly, build nests, lay eggs, and make high-pitched noises. Other objects are furry, have four legs and tails, and run around on the ground. Formal concepts consist of carefully defined sets of rules governing membership in a particular category. In contrast, natural concepts are collections of memories of particular examples with shared similarities that may not be especially well defined—theirs is a "family resemblance." Formal concepts are used primarily by experts (and by people studying to become experts), whereas natural concepts are used by ordinary people in their daily lives.

Rosch further suggests that people's natural concepts consist of collections of memories of particular instances, called **exemplars,** that share similarities. The boundaries between formal concepts are precise, whereas those between natural concepts are fuzzy—the distinction between a member and a nonmember is not always clear. For this reason, to nonexperts, not all members of a concept are equally good examples of that concept. A robin is a good exemplar of *bird;* a penguin or an ostrich seems a poor one. Although we may ultimately acknowledge that a penguin is a bird because we have been taught that it is, we often qualify that acknowledgment by making statements such as "Strictly speaking, a penguin is a bird." Exemplars provide the important characteristics of a concept—characteristics we can readily perceive when we encounter a member of the category to which the concept refers.

According to Rosch, natural concepts vary in their levels of precision and detail. As in the structure proposed by Collins and Quillian, they may be included in a hierarchy that ranges from very detailed to very general. When we think and talk about concepts, we usually deal with **basic-level concepts,** for example, *chair* and *apple.* They belong to more general concepts, such as *furniture* and *fruit,* which are called **superordinate concepts.** Other concepts that refer to more particular types of items within a basic-level category, such as *lawn chair* and *Granny Smith apple,* are called **subordinate concepts.** (See FIGURE 11•4.)

Basic-level concepts are what people spontaneously name when they see a member of the category. That is, all types of chairs tend to be called "chair," unless a special reason exists to use a more-precise label (for example, if you wanted to buy a lawn chair). People tend to use basic-level concepts for a very good reason: *cognitive economy.* The use of subordinate concepts may waste time and effort on meaningless distinctions, and the use of superordinate concepts may lack important information. In one study, Rosch and colleagues (1976) presented participants with various concepts from all three levels and gave them 90 seconds to list as many attributes as they could for each

---

natural concept A category formed from a person's perceptions of and interactions with things in the world; based on exemplars.

exemplar A memory of a particular example of an object or an event that is used as the basis for a natural concept.

basic-level concept A concept that makes essential distinctions at an everyday level.

superordinate concept A general or overarching concept that includes basic-level concepts.

subordinate concept A more-specific concept that falls within a basic-level concept.

The robin (lower photo) is a better exemplar of the concept *bird* than the penguin (upper photo) is, even though both are birds.

concept. The participants supplied few attributes for superordinate concepts but were able to think of many more for basic-level concepts. Subordinate concepts evoked no more attributes than basic-level concepts did. Thus, basic-level concepts, associated with a collection of subordinate concepts and their

Level of Concept

Superordinate	Basic	Subordinate

Examples

Fruit	Oranges	Cortland
Vegetables	Apples	McIntosh
Fish	Peaches	Granny Smith
Meat	Pears	Delicious
Cereals	Bananas	Winesap

[**FIGURE 11•4**] Examples of basic-level, subordinate, and superordinate concepts.

[**FIGURE 11•5**] Concept formation. Participants were asked which of the groups of shapes (shown in the columns) were most similar. (a) Three pairs of geometrical shapes. (b) The same shapes with the addition of squares.

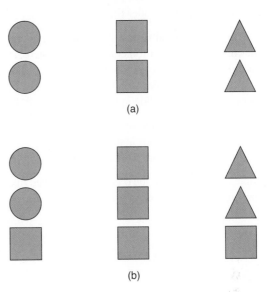

(a)

(b)

characteristics, provide us with the most information in the most efficient manner. By thinking in terms of basic-level concepts, people do not have to travel up or down a tree, as they would in the structure proposed by Collins and Quillian, to find the attributes that belong to the concept. The attributes are directly attached to the exemplars that constitute it.

It is important to recognize that concepts can represent something more complex than simple exemplars or collections of attributes. Goldstone, Medink, and Gentner (1991) showed research participants groups of figures and asked them to indicate which were most similar to each other. When they showed the participants pairs of triangles, squares, and circles, the participants said that the squares and triangles were most similar, presumably because both contained straight lines and angles. However, when they added a square to each of the pairs, the participants said that the two most similar groups were the triangles plus square and the circles plus square. (See FIGURE 11•5.) The concept was now perceived as "two things and a square." If the participants had been simply comparing the attributes of specific objects, then the addition of a square to the pairs should not have changed their decision.

Deductive Reasoning

Concepts are the raw material of thinking. Thinking that is reasoning involves the manipulation and combination of concepts. Among its most common forms are deductive reasoning and inductive reasoning.

Deductive reasoning produces specific conclusions from general principles or rules. Series problems and syllogisms

***

deductive reasoning The mental process by which people arrive at specific conclusions from general principles or rules.

are often used to study deductive reasoning. Consider the following series problem:

> John is taller than Phil.
> Sue is shorter than Phil.
> Therefore, John is taller than Sue.

Proceeding in simple logical steps will have led you to recognize that the conclusion to the problem is correct as stated.

Let's try another syllogism. As you may remember, a syllogism consists of two premises from which a conclusion can be drawn. Is the conclusion in the following syllogism correct?

> All mammals have fur.
> A bat is a mammal.
> Therefore, a bat has fur.

Most people understand that the conclusion is indeed justified by the premises. But now look at these two syllogisms:

> All Xs are Y.
> Z is an X.
> Therefore, all Xs are Z.

and

> All nemots have some hair.
> A zilgid has some hair.
> Therefore, all zilgids are nemots.

Although the conclusions are not warranted on logical grounds for the latter two syllogisms, many people consider them to be correct. For the first of these, try replacing X with "planet," Y with "round," and Z with "Jupiter." The last syllogism is just as misleading. The first premise says only that all nemots have some hair—it leaves open the possibility that no nemot is a zilgid. Still not clear? Try substituting "cat" for nemot and "dog" for zilgid. Why is it that we make such mistakes when the answers become so obvious when we make concrete substitutions? A possible answer lies in the concept of mental models.

Mental Models Psychologists used to believe that people solved deductive reasoning problems by applying formal rules of logic. If people did so, however, it should not matter whether they dealt with letters of the alphabet, planets, cats and dogs, or numbers; they would identify the underlying structure of the problem and solve it sooner or later. However, Johnson-Laird (Johnson-Laird, 1999, 2001) suggests that in reality people approach such problems by creating **mental models.**

A mental model of a situation represents a *possibility* (Johnson-Laird, 1999) of what might be true given certain premises. A mental model includes semantic information, because most problems have meaningful content, specify relations among elements of the problem, and rely more or less on knowledge about the world. Spatial arrangements also

---

mental model A cognitive representation of a possibility that a person can use to solve deductive problems.

[**FIGURE 11•6**] A mental model. People often solve logical problems by imagining a spatial representation of the facts.

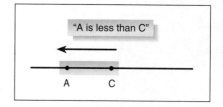

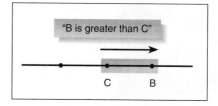

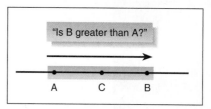

play a central role in the theory of mental models. Johnson-Laird (1985) maintained that syllogistic reasoning is much more highly correlated with spatial ability than with verbal ability. Spatial ability includes the ability to visualize shapes and to manipulate them mentally. For example, read the following problem and answer it: "A is less than C. B is greater than C. Is B greater than A?" To compare A with B, you must remember the order of the three elements. One kind of mental model is an imaginary line with *small* at one end and *large* at the other. You place each item on the line as you encounter it. When all three are in place on the line, the possibilities are plain, and you can answer the question. (See FIGURE 11•6.) Consider another problem: "The pie is sweeter than the cake. The custard is not as sweet as the cake. Is the custard sweeter than the pie?" In this case, you may have produced a mental model in which desserts were arrayed in a line and, given the possibilities, found it easier to answer the question.

A potential downside of mental models that involve the comparison of a series of items is that the use of the model may obscure some of the information it is supposed to represent. For example, read the following passage used in a study of reading comprehension:

> Although the four craftsmen were brothers, they varied enormously in height. The electrician was the very tallest, and the plumber was shorter than him. The plumber was taller than the carpenter, who, in turn, was taller than the painter. (Just & Carpenter, 1987, p. 202)

The researchers found that, after reading this passage, participants could answer questions about differences in height that could only be inferred more easily than they could

[FIGURE 11•7] A mental model of the craftsmen experiment. Although the passage describing the craftsmen explicitly compared the heights of the plumber and the carpenter, people had to infer that the electrician was taller than the painter. Nevertheless, participants could judge the relative heights of the electrician and the painter faster than those of the plumber and the carpenter.

[FIGURE 11•8] A spatial model of reasoning: "What do you call your mother's sister's son?"

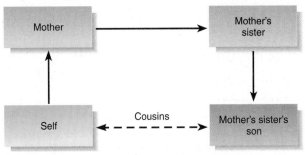

answer questions about the differences that were directly stated in the passage. For example, they were faster to answer the question "Who is taller, the electrician or the painter?" than the question "Who is taller, the plumber or the carpenter?" The passage explicitly states that the plumber is taller than the carpenter. Answering this question requires only remembering that specific bit of information. Answering the question about the electrician and painter, however, requires an inference and therefore should take more time than merely repeating what the passage stated. A plausible explanation of this discrepancy is that when participants read the passage, they constructed a mental model that represented the four brothers along a line and arranged in order of height. In the model, the painter is clearly the shortest, and the electrician is clearly the tallest. Thus, a comparison involving the two extremes can be made very quickly. (See FIGURE 11•7.)

Here is a different type of problem to illustrate the same point: "What do you call your mother's sister's son?" Most people report that they answer this question by constructing the image of a family tree, with their mother above them, their mother's sister to the side, and her son below her. Then, comparing that location with their own, they can easily see that the answer is "cousin." (See FIGURE 11•8.) Consistent with Johnson-Laird's claim that spatial representation is a significant feature of deductive reasoning, Luria (1973) found that people with damage to the parietal lobes had difficulty answering such questions. As you learned in Chapter 4, the parietal lobes are involved with somatosensory and spatial abilities. More recently, German researchers (Knauff et al., 2002) used *f*MRI to identify an occipitoparietal-frontal network whose selective activation correlated with participants' use of mental models to solve deductive-reasoning problems.

Finally, consider another complex problem, adapted from an experiment by Wason and Johnson-Laird (1972),

that is known as a *selection task*. The instructions accompany a set of four cards and read as follows:

> Your job is to determine which of the cards you need to turn over to test the following rule decisively:
> If a vowel is on one side of a card, an even number is on the other side.
> You have only one opportunity to make this decision. You are not permitted to inspect the cards one at a time. You must name the card or cards that you absolutely must see to test the rule.

The participants were shown four cards like those illustrated in FIGURE 11•9. Read the problem again, look at the cards, and decide which card or cards you would have to see.

Most people in the experiment said that they would need to see card (a) (the letter A), and they were correct: If no even number is on the back of card (a), then the rule is not correct. However, many participants failed to realize that card (a) is not enough. Card (d) (the number 7) also must be inspected. True, no even number is on this card, but what if a vowel is on the other side? If so, then the rule is again proved wrong. Many participants also wanted to see card (c) (the number 4), but no need existed to do so. The hypothesis says nothing about whether an even number can be on one side of the card without there being a vowel on the other side.

The card task is very abstract, and previous examples have shown us that concreteness can increase the ease with which people reach "logical" conclusions, even if they do not do so by using formal logic. Would relating the card–vowel problem to familiar, concrete content make it easier? The answer comes from research such as that conducted by Griggs and Cox (1982). These experimenters asked people to decide which cards should be turned over to test the following rule: "If a

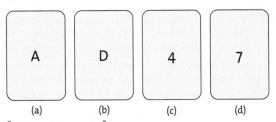

[FIGURE 11•9] Cards used in a formal test of problem solving.

[FIGURE 11•10] Cards used in a socially situated version of the problem-solving test.

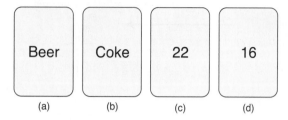

(a)   (b)   (c)   (d)

person is drinking beer, she or he must be over age 21." As shown in FIGURE 11•10, the cards represented people who were drinking; their age was on one side, and their beverage (beer or Coke), on the other. Which card(s) would you turn over?

Most participants correctly chose cards (a) and (d). They knew that if someone were drinking beer (a), they had to check that she or he was older than 21 for the rule to be true. Similarly, if someone was 16 years old (d), they knew that they needed to check the card to see that she or he was not drinking beer for the rule to be true. The participants readily recognized the fact that they did not need to know the age of someone drinking Coke, and that someone 22 years old can drink whatever beverage she or he prefers.

One possible explanation for the greater ease of solving this more concrete problem is that mental models involving Coke, beer, and teenagers are easier to construct and manipulate than those involving vowels and numbers. There are, however, possibilities. Cheng and Holyoak (1985), for example, proposed that people have sets of helpful rules (called "pragmatic reasoning schemas") by which to determine relations such as causality, permission, and obligation. According to Cheng and Holyoak, these schemas are more likely to be evoked by the meaningful beer–age task, which requires consideration of whether an action (drinking) is permitted, than by the more-abstract vowel–number task.

It is not unusual for creative scientists and technologists to report that they use mental models to reason logically and to solve practical and theoretical problems (Krueger, 1976). For example, physicist and Nobel laureate Richard Feynman said that he favored bizarre mental models when keeping track of the characteristics of complex mathematical theorems. Such models allowed him to see whether the theorems were logical and consistent. Among his many highly quotable statements was this: "What I cannot create, I cannot understand." Here is how Feynman described his reasoning:

> When I'm trying to understand . . . I keep making up examples. For instance, the mathematicians would come in with a . . . theorem. As they're telling me the conditions of the theorem, I construct something that fits all the conditions. You know, you have a set (one ball)–disjoint (two balls). Then the balls turn colors, grow hairs, or whatever, in my head as they [the mathematicians] put

---

inductive reasoning   The mental process by which people infer general principles or rules from specific information.

The noted physicist Richard Feynman was a member of the expert panel that investigated the Challenger disaster.

> more conditions on. Finally, they state the theorem, which is some . . . thing about the ball which isn't true for my hairy green ball thing, so I say "False!" (Feynman, 1985, p. 70)

Such use of mental models by a gifted theorist strengthens the conclusion that being able to convert abstract problems into tangible models is an important aspect of intelligent thinking. It was Feynman, after all, who first brought to light the cause of the tragic deaths of the Challenger astronauts (Feynman, 2001).

Inductive Reasoning

Deductive reasoning involves applying the rules of logic to produce conclusions from general principles or rules. This type of reasoning works well when general principles or rules have already been worked out, but how do we accumulate new knowledge and formulate new general principles or rules? Having read Chapter 2 of this book, you already know the answer—by following the scientific method. Relatively few people know the rules of the scientific method, and even those who do may seldom follow them in their daily lives.

Inductive reasoning is, in some ways, the opposite of deductive reasoning, which, if properly followed, results in a conclusion that is certain. Inductive reasoning consists of inferring general principles or rules from specific facts and leads to a conclusion that is, at best, only highly probable. A well-known laboratory example of inductive reasoning works like a guessing game (see Bruner, Goodnow, & Austin, 1956). The participants are shown cards that contain figures differing in several characteristics, such as shape, number, and color. On each trial, the participants are given two cards and asked to choose the one that represents a particular concept. After they choose a card, the researcher says "right" or "wrong." (See FIGURE 11•11.)

[FIGURE 11•11] Examples of the type of cards used in a test of inductive reasoning.

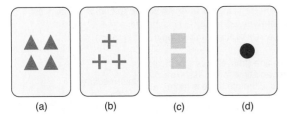

(a) (b) (c) (d)

One trial is not enough to recognize the concept. For example, if the first trial reveals that card (a) is correct, then the concept could be *red,* or *four,* or *triangle,* or some combination of these, such as *red triangle, four red shapes,* or even *four red triangles.* Information gained from the second trial may allow the participant to rule out some of these hypotheses. For example, if, on the second trial, four red squares is a correct card choice, it appears that shape does not matter, but color and number do. The participant solves the problem in steps, much the way a scientist does: Form a hypothesis on the basis of the available evidence, and test that hypothesis on subsequent trials. If it is proved false, abandon it, try to think of a hypothesis consistent with what went before, and test the new hypothesis.

Logical Errors in Inductive Reasoning

Obviously, people can be trained to follow the rules of the scientific method. However, without special training, they likely follow commonsense rules, some of which work and some of which do not. Psychologists interested in human inductive reasoning have identified several tendencies that lead us astray. It is precisely because of such tendencies that we need to learn specific rules (such as those of the scientific method) to increase confidence in our conclusions.

Two of the tendencies that interfere with our ability to reason inductively are the failure to seek information that would be provided by a comparison group and the disinclination to seek evidence that would indicate whether a hypothesis is false. (In Chapter 15, we investigate two others: the *representativeness* and *availability heuristics.*)

Failure to Consider a Comparison Group. Suppose you learn that 79% of the people with a particular disease get well within a month after taking a new experimental drug (Stich, 1990). What will you conclude? Is the drug effective? The correct answer to this question is, "We cannot conclude anything—we need more information." Specifically, we need to know what happens to people with the disease if they do not take the drug. If we find that only 22% of these people recover within a month, we can reasonably conclude that the drug is effective; 79% is much greater than 22%. Conversely, if we find that 98% recover without taking the drug, we could conclude that the drug is worse than useless—it actually interferes with recovery. In this case, we need a control group. Most people are inclined to conclude that, because 79%

seems like a high figure, the drug must work. Realizing the necessity for a control group does not come naturally. Unless people are explicitly taught the logic of control-group designs, they likely will not recognize the need for them.

Failure to seek or use information that would be provided by a control group has been called **base rate neglect.** The term *base rate* refers to the rate of occurrence of a phenomenon in the absence of a particular intervention. In the drug example, the rate of recovery in a control group would provide a base rate.

Confirmation Bias. Another tendency that interferes with inductive reasoning is the disinclination to seek evidence that would indicate whether a hypothesis is false. Instead, people tend to seek evidence that might confirm their hypothesis; that is, they exhibit the **confirmation bias.** For example, Wason (1968) presented participants with the series of numbers "two, four, six" and asked them to try to figure out the rule to which the numbers conformed. The participant was to test his or her hypothesis by making up series of numbers and stating them to the researcher, who would respond with "yes" or "no." Then, whenever the participant decided that sufficient information had been gathered, he or she stated the hypothesis. If it was correct, the problem was solved. If it was not, the participant was asked to think of a new hypothesis and test it in turn.

Several rules could explain the series "2, 4, 6." The rule could be "even numbers," or "each number is two more than the preceding one," or "the middle number is the mean of the first and third number." For example, if the hypothesis was that each number was two more than the preceding one, the participant might say, "10, 12, 14" or "61, 63, 65." Very few participants tried to test their hypotheses by choosing a series of numbers that did not conform to the hypothesized rule, such as "12, 15, 22." The series "12, 15, 22" does conform to the actual rule. The rule was so simple that few people figured it out: Each number must be larger than the number preceding it.

The confirmation bias can be potent. Unless people are taught to do so, they tend not to think of or to test possible counterexamples that might disprove their hypotheses. Again, they fail to act as scientists would. The confirmation bias in inductive reasoning has a counterpart in deductive reasoning. For example, consider the following sentences (Johnson-Laird, 1985):

> All the pilots are artists.
> All the skiers are artists.
> True or false: All the pilots are skiers.

Many people say "true." They test the truth of the conclusion by imagining a person who is a pilot and an artist and a skier—and that person complies with the rules. Therefore, they

---

base rate neglect In decision making, the failure to consider available information that bears on the issue at hand, such as the failure to consider the data from a control group.

confirmation bias A tendency to seek evidence that might confirm a hypothesis rather than evidence that might disconfirm it.

decide that the conclusion is true. But if they would try to disconfirm the conclusion—to look for an example that would fit the first two sentences but not the conclusion—they would easily find one. Could a person be a pilot but not a skier? Of course; the first two sentences say nothing to rule out that possibility. There are artist–pilots and there are artist–skiers, but nothing says that there must be artist–pilot–skiers.

Problem Solving

Thinking solves problems. An enormous variety of problems face us in our daily lives. Our ability to solve them is related to academic success, occupational success, and overall success in life. Trying to improve as a problem solver is a commendable goal across one's lifetime.

The Spatial Metaphor According to Holyoak (1990), having a goal but lacking a clear understanding of how to attain it is a problem. Recall Johnson-Laird's contention that mental models used in reasoning are often spatial. When we talk about problems, we often use spatial metaphors to describe them (Lakoff & Turner, 1989). For example, we may think of the solving of a problem as *finding a path to the solution*. We may have to *get around roadblocks* that we encounter or *backtrack when we hit a dead end*. If we *get lost*, we may try to *approach the problem from a different angle*. If we have experience with particular types of problems, we may *know some shortcuts to the solution*.

In a classic work, Newell and Simon (1972) used spatial metaphors to characterize the problem-solving process. At the beginning of a person's attempt to solve a problem, the *initial state* is different from the *goal state*—if it were not, there would be no problem. The person solving the problem has a number of *operators* available. Operators are actions that the person can take to change the current state of the problem. Metaphorically, operators move the current state from one position to another. A person's knowledge of the operators that are available depends on education and experience. In addition, various costs may be associated with different operators; some may be more difficult, expensive, or time consuming than others. The *problem space* consists of all possible states that can be achieved if all possible operators are applied. A *solution* is a sequence of operators (a "path") that moves the initial state to the goal state.

FIGURE 11·12 illustrates this process schematically. The circles represent the current or possible states that can exist while the problem is being solved. The arrows represent the operators—the actions that can be taken. Some actions are reversible (double arrows); others are not. A solution follows a path from the initial state to the goal state.

---

algorithm A procedure that consists of a series of steps that, if followed, will solve a specific type of problem.

heuristic A general rule that guides decision making.

means–ends analysis A general heuristic method of problem solving that involves looking for differences between the current state and the goal state and seeking ways to reduce the differences.

[**FIGURE 11·12**] Newell and Simon's spatial conceptualization of the problem-solving process.

(Adapted from Holyoak, K. J. in *An Invitation to Cognitive Science: Volume 3: Thinking*, edited by D. N. Osherson and E. E. Smith. Cambridge, MA: MIT Press, 1990. Copyright © 1990.)

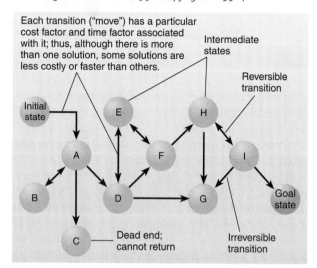

Algorithms and Heuristics Some kinds of problems can be solved by following a sequence of operators known as an **algorithm**. Using an algorithm means following a procedure consisting of series of steps that, if followed in the correct sequence, will provide a solution. For example, you are undoubtedly familiar with an algorithm known as "long division." If you properly apply the steps of this algorithm (which involves the operators of division and subtraction) to divide one number by another, you will obtain the correct answer.

Many problems are not as tidy or as easy to solve as those in long division. When no algorithm to follow exists, we may turn to a **heuristic** instead. Heuristics (hyoo-RIS-tiks; derived from the Greek *heuriskein*, "to discover") are general rules, or "rules of thumb," that are useful in guiding our search for a solution to a problem. Heuristics tell us what to pay attention to, what to ignore, and what strategy to take. As such, they may be considered shortcuts. For example, if you encounter an unfamiliar word while reading, you probably try to infer its meaning from the context provided by the words around it rather than turning directly to the dictionary. Later, if you do consult the dictionary, often as not, you may find you were pretty close.

Heuristical methods can be very specific, or they can be quite general in addressing large categories of problems. Newell and Simon (1972) suggested a general strategy that can be used to solve any problem. They referred to it as **means–ends analysis** and illustrated its use in a computer program for problem solving. The principle behind this form of analysis is that a person should look for differences between the current state and the goal state and seek ways to reduce these differences. Borrowing from Figure 11.12, one might begin with an analysis of differences between the initial and goal states, and then identify potential intermediate states that would systematically reduce those differences. The steps of this method are as follows (Holyoak, 1990, p. 121):

1. Compare the current state to the goal state and identify differences between the two. If there are none, the problem is solved; otherwise, proceed.

2. Identify possible operators and select one that would reduce one of the differences between current state and goal state.

3. If the operator can be applied, do so; if not, set a new subgoal of reaching a state at which the operator could be applied. Then apply means–ends analysis to this new subgoal until the operator can be applied or the attempt to use it is abandoned.

4. Return to step 1.

Suppose the goal is to clear 2 feet of snow off your driveway the morning after a heavy storm. Initially you reject several possible operators because they are too time consuming or too costly (*dig the snow off with my hands* or *melt the snow with a propane torch*). You decide to apply the operator *start the snowblower and run it up and down the driveway*. Unfortunately, you find that the snowblower will not start, which means that you need to establish a subgoal: Fix the snowblower.

One possible operator is *put the snowblower in the car and take it to a mechanic*, but the snow on the driveway precludes that option. Therefore, you decide to *fix the snowblower yourself*, but you're not sure what needs fixing. You consider some possible actions, including *take the engine apart to see whether something inside is broken*, but you decide to try some simpler steps, such as *see whether the wire is attached to the spark plug* or *see whether there is gasoline in the tank*. You find the wire attached but the gas tank empty. The only operator that will get you to your subgoal is *put gasoline in the tank*, but you find the gasoline can empty. Therefore, you create another subgoal: Get some gasoline.

At a gas station? No, you can't move the car. A neighbor? The snow is so deep that you do not want to fight your way through the drifts. The tank of your car? That's it: Remove *some gasoline from the car's fuel tank*. But how do you get it out? New operator: *Find rubber hose to siphon the gasoline into the tank of the snowblower*. You do so, you start the engine, and you clear the snow off the driveway. Voilà! The problem is solved. At that point, you may be ready to establish a new goal: take a nap.

In this example, the individual's activity was oriented at all times toward reducing the distance between the current state and the goal state. When problems were encountered along the way (for example, specific operators could not be applied), then subgoals were created, and other operators applied until the goal was reached. The means (that is, the operators) were always directed toward the ends (goals and subgoals).

Successful problem solving may involve more than merely applying various operators to see whether they bring

Problem solving takes many forms. When a snowblower's gas tank is empty, starting it can be a problem. The heuristic method of means–ends analysis may well provide a solution.

us closer to the goal. It also may benefit from *planning*. When we plan, we may act vicariously, "trying out" various actions in our heads before acting on one of them or not. Obviously, planning requires that we know something about the consequences of the actions we are considering. For that reason experts are usually better at planning than novices are. If we do not know the consequences of particular actions, we may be obliged to try them all to see what happens. Planning is especially important when many possible operators are available, when they are costly or time consuming, or when they are irreversible. An operator that leads to a dead end means failure to solve the problem.

Research by Gigerenzer (1999, 2007) and colleagues in Germany and elsewhere has revealed what they refer to as an *adaptive toolbox* that each of us has for use in problem solving and decision making. The toolbox consists of simple heuristics that we apply intuitively, that is, rapidly and usually without awareness, and are accompanied by "gut feelings," They are by no means fail-safe, but more often than not they serve us well, especially if we use them in decision-making environments for which they are well suited.

To illustrate, consider three psychology majors—one just beginning the major, a second who has completed all courses required for the major, and a third who is about halfway through the major requirements. Each student is asked to take a quiz consisting of pairs of terms. For each pair, the student is asked to indicate which of the terms is "more cognitive" than the other. If the pair were *short-term memory v. schedule of reinforcement*, for example, the former would be correct. The first student is unfamiliar with almost all of the terms. By contrast, the second student recognizes all of them but never considered them as being more or less cognitive. The third student recognizes only about half the terms but also never considered them along a cognitive dimension. How will each student fare on the quiz?

According to Gigerenzer (2007), the third student is likely to receive a higher score than the other two. By guessing with every pair, the first student will answer correctly about half the time. Although the second student recognizes all the terms, being unsure of how to rate them means being in the similar predicament of having to guess in each case. The partial ignorance of the third student actually becomes an asset. Sometimes the third student will have to guess like the first student did (specifically, when confronting a pair of terms when neither is familiar) and sometimes like the second student did (when both terms are familiar). In the remainder of cases, however, when one term is familiar and the other is not, the student may well use what Gigerenzer terms the *recognition heuristic*: "If you recognize one object but not the other, then infer that the recognized object has higher value" (p. 118). By choosing the term that is familiar—that is, by using gut feelings—the student is more likely to choose the term that is more cognitive and thus have a higher score overall.

Only the third student was in a position to use the recognition heuristic. Its use might well produce a higher score because, in the course of the psychology major, terms more explicitly cognitive are likely to be encountered with greater frequency than those less so. Thus, what is familiar is likely to be more cognitive and thus have a recognitional advantage. The recognition heuristic may be successful in other decision-making contexts, as Gigerenzer shows, but it is not guaranteed to be so. Thus, you are ill advised to change your study strategy to one in which you deliberately avoid studying half the material to use the recognition heuristic when it comes time to be evaluated. Instead, study on!

QUESTIONS FOR FURTHER THINKING

1. Think of a new concept you have learned recently. Describe its characteristics. Then think of an exemplar. Which was easier to do? Why?

2. Chapter 2 described the scientific method. Some of the rules and procedures you learned in that chapter were designed to prevent the errors in logical thinking that were described in this chapter. Relate the scientific method to one or more of these errors.

3. Over the next few days, try to catch yourself making one of the errors of reasoning described in this section. Describe your experience, then indicate how you will attempt to prevent the same error in the future.

Epilogue

Selective Intelligence: The Autistic Savant

The predicament of Mr. V described in the Prologue is, in some ways, the opposite of that faced by persons who have been identified as *autistic savants*. Recall that Mr. V had high scores on the verbal and quantitative subtests of the WAIS-III, even though English was not his first language. He did poorly on performance subtests and also failed to comprehend that his confinement to a wheelchair put strict limits on the kinds of activities he could participate in. We may consider him an example of a highly intelligent person whose brain injury disrupted that intelligence quite selectively. According to his doctor, it was Mr. V's judgment that suffered. He could no longer assemble certain pieces of information available to him to draw reasonable, realistic conclusions. The right-hemisphere stroke stripped his intelligence of one of its identifying features—rational judgment—while leaving the rest of it seemingly intact.

Autistic savants (Heaton & Wallace, 2004) combine the characteristics of savants (persons of remarkable but narrowly specialized intellect) with those of persons diagnosed with autistic spectrum disorder (see Chapter 17). Although some feature of their intelligence increases spectacularly, the rest of it lags far behind. Take the case of Daniel Tammet (Tammet, 2007), an Englishman, who had an epileptic seizure at the age of 3 years. After the seizure, a remarkable pattern of abilities—and disabilities–emerged. To be fair, irregularities occurred in his infancy, but only after the seizure did he began to display the curious, storied abilities that became his signature.

Tammet speaks seven languages and has developed his own as well, which he calls Mänti. He can perform prodigious calculations instantaneously—multiplying 377 by 495—and can recall the first 22,000 digits of pi effortlessly. He is obsessed with rigid order, counting the stitches in a visitor's shirt while avoiding ever looking that person in the eye. He can't drive, finds it impossible to tell left from right, and is overwhelmed by the dizzying details of a supermarket or the uncountable many pebbles at a beach. On the one hand, wondrously proficient; on the other, at a striking loss.

The link between intelligence and the brain comes to the fore in cases like those of Mr. V. and autistic savants like Daniel Tammet. For Mr. V. it was sudden damage to the left hemisphere. For autistic savants, evidence is found of damage in the left hemisphere (Snyder et al., 2003). Such findings share a resonance with Gardner's claim that different forms of intelligence be uniquely assignable to brain areas. At the same time, research interest is increasing in the differential patterns of brain activity that accompany decision making and other forms of problem solving (see, e.g., Koechlin and Hyafil, 2007; Sanfey, A. G., 2007; Volz et al., 2006). Future work promises to reveal in ever more detail the complexities of the interplay between brain, behavior, and environment in fashioning human intelligence.

CHAPTER SUMMARY

Intelligence: Is It Global or Componential?

Although intelligence often is represented by a single score, the IQ, modern investigators do not deny the existence of specific intellectual abilities. What is controversial is whether a general factor also exists. Spearman thought so; he named the factor *g* and demonstrated that people's scores on various specific tests of ability were correlated. Thurstone performed a factor analysis on 56 individual tests that revealed the existence of seven factors, not a single *g* factor. Eysenck reasoned that because these factors were themselves correlated, a factor analysis on them was justified. Cattell performed such an analysis and obtained two factors, and he confirmed this result with factor analyses of tests of his own construction. The nature of the tests that loaded heavily on these two factors suggested the factors he named fluid intelligence (g_f) and crystallized intelligence (g_c), with the former representing a person's native ability and the latter representing what a person learns.

Sternberg's triarchic theory of intelligence relies on information-processing mechanisms as they are applied in natural and cultural environments. According to Sternberg, we use analytic intelligence to plan and execute tasks. We use creative intelligence to apply past strategies to new problems. Finally, we use practical intelligence to adapt to, select, or shape our environment. Gardner's theory of multiple intelligences begins with neuropsychology and is based primarily on the types of skills that can be selectively lost because of brain damage. His definition of eight intelligences includes abilities that are commonly regarded as "skills" or "talents." Like Sternberg's theory, Gardner's theory emphasizes the significance of the cultural contexts in which behavior occurs. Research from non-Western cultures points up the differences in cultural definitions of intelligence and the role of local environments in shaping critical skills of reasoning and problem solving.

Intelligence Testing

Alfred Binet developed a test that was designed to assess students' intellectual abilities to identify children with special educational needs. Although the test that later superseded his, the Stanford–Binet Scale, provided for calculation of IQ, Binet believed that "intelligence" was actually a composite of several specific abilities. For him, the concept of mental age was a convenience, not a biological reality. David Wechsler's two intelligence tests, the WAIS-III for adults and the WISC-IV for children, are widely used today. The information provided by the verbal and performance scores helps neuropsychologists diagnose brain damage and can provide at least a rough estimate of the innate ability of poorly educated people.

The reliability of modern intelligence tests is excellent, but assessing their validity is still difficult. Because no single-criterion measure of intelligence exists, psychologists often validate intelligence tests by comparing test-takers' scores with other measures of achievement, such as scholastic success. The Flynn effect refers to intergenerational increases in IQ scores in economically advanced nations during the 20th century and may reflect increased acquisition of the scientific worldview possessed by the originators of intelligence tests.

Intelligence tests can have both good and bad effects on the people who take them. The principal benefit is identifying children with special needs (or special talents) who will profit from special programs. The principal danger is that stigmatizing those who score poorly can result in a self-fulfilling prophecy or otherwise deprive them of the opportunity for good jobs or further education. Tests are also used for the classification of individuals whose low scores indicate disabilities ranging from mild to profound mental retardation.

The Roles of Heredity and Environment

Variability in all physical traits is co-determined by genetic variability, environmental variability, and an interaction between genetic and environmental factors. A measure of the degree to which genetic variability is responsible for the observed variability of a particular trait in a particular population is called heritability. It is important to remember that heritability is not an indication of the degree to which the trait is determined by genetic factors.

Intellectual development is affected by many factors both prenatally and postnatally. A person's heredity, because of its effect on brain development, affects his or her intellectual potential. This potential can be permanently reduced during prenatal or postnatal development by injury, toxic chemicals, poor nutrition, or disease.

Twin studies and studies comparing biological and adoptive relatives indicate that both genetic and environmental factors affect intelligence. Correlations in IQ scores of pairs of individuals vary with their biological relatedness.

Some people have suggested that racial differences in intellectual ability are the result of differences in heredity. However, the available data do not support this suggestion unequivocally. First, race is almost always defined culturally, not genetically.

Second, we cannot rule out the effects of environmental differences. Because performance on IQ tests can be influenced by what people have previously learned, it reflects environmental factors as well as genetic ones. Members of some racial groups have fewer opportunities for environmental interactions that promote intellectual growth. For that reason, it is difficult to draw conclusions about whether the racial differences in IQ are hereditary. The little evidence we do have suggests that when educational opportunities are equalized, the difference in test scores narrows.

Thinking and Problem Solving

Thinking often is directed at problem solving and decision making. To think requires the use of concepts. Formal concepts are defined explicitly by the essential characteristics of objects and events. In everyday life, we use natural concepts instead—collections of memories of particular examples, called exemplars. Natural concepts exist at the basic, subordinate, and superordinate levels. Much of our thinking occurs at the level of basic concepts.

Deductive reasoning reaches conclusions on the basis of general principles. That is, we take information that is already known and determine whether particular occurrences are consistent with that information. One of the most important skills in deductive reasoning is the ability to construct mental models to represent the problems we are attempting to solve.

Inductive reasoning infers general principles from particular information and involves generating and testing hypotheses. Without special training (such as learning the rules of the scientific method), people often neglect base rates or show a confirmation bias—the tendency to look only for evidence that confirms a given hypothesis. Problem solving is often best pursued spatially: We follow a path in the problem space from the initial state to the goal state, by using operators to get to each intermediate state. Sometimes a problem fits a particular pattern and can be solved with an algorithm—an already formulated set of steps to follow. In most cases, however, we must attack a problem by following a heuristic—a general rule that helps guide our search for a path to the solution of a problem. A useful heuristic is means–ends analysis, which involves taking steps that reduce the distance from the current state to the goal. If obstacles are encountered, subgoals are created, and attempts are made to reach them. Each of us possesses an adaptive toolbox of simple heuristics for successful decision making in the right environments.

succeed with mypsych lab

Visit MyPsychLab for practice quizzes, flashcards, and dozens of videos and animated tutorials, including the following items you can find in the "Multimedia Library":

Sternberg's Triarchic Theory of Intelligence
How to Be a Critical Thinker
The Two-string Problem

Intuition and Discovery in Problem Solving
Gardner's Theory of Intelligence
Explore Your Mental Space

KEY TERMS

algorithm *p. 330*
analytic intelligence *p. 308*
base rate neglect *p. 329*
basic level concept *p. 324*
Binet–Simon Scale *p. 312*
concept *p. 323*
confirmation bias *p. 329*
creative intelligence *p. 308*
criterion *p. 314*
crystallized intelligence *p. 307*
deductive reasoning *p. 325*
deviation IQ *p. 313*
exemplar *p. 324*
factor analysis *p. 306*
fluid intelligence *p. 307*
formal concept *p. 323*
g factor *p. 306*
heritability *p. 317*
heuristic *p. 330*
inductive reasoning *p. 328*

intelligence *p. 305*
intelligence quotient (IQ) *p. 313*
means–ends analysis *p. 330*
mental age *p. 312*
mental model *p. 326*
mental retardation *p. 316*
natural concept *p. 324*
norms *p. 312*
practical intelligence *p. 308*
ratio IQ *p. 313*
Stanford–Binet Scale *p. 312*
subordinate concept *p. 324*
successful intelligence *p. 308*
superordinate concept *p. 324*
syllogism *p. 310*
Wechsler Adult Intelligence Scale (WAIS) *p. 313*
Wechsler Intelligence Scale for Children (WISC) *p. 313*

SUGGESTIONS FOR FURTHER READING

Aiken, L. (2006). *Psychological testing and assessment* (12th ed.). Boston: Allyn & Bacon.

This authoritative guide to the construction and use of psychological tests is a next step if you have a serious technical interest in psychometrics.

Diamond, J. (1997). *Guns, germs, and steel: The fates of human societies*. New York: W. W. Norton.

This best-selling essay attempts to answer the question of how certain civilizations came to dominate others without there being large differences in intelligence between them. It does so in scholarly, provocative fashion.

Flynn, J. R. (2007). *What is intelligence?* Cambridge, England: Cambridge University Press.

This somewhat quirky book introduces the so-called Flynn effect and the evidence for it before proceeding to offer a theory of the effect and of its eventual disappearance.

Gardner, H. (1999). *Intelligence reframed: Multiple intelligences for the 21st century*. New York: Basic Books.

This is the founding work for what has become a major alternative to psychometric theories of intelligence; highly readable and humane.

Gigerenzer, G. (2007). *Gut feelings: The intelligence of the unconscious*. New York: Viking Penguin.

This book is an anecdote-filled introduction to the concept of the adaptive toolkit and its contents and applications across a variety of human contexts ranging from advertising to the practice of medicine.

Kaplan, R. M., & Saccuzzo, D. P. (2005). *Psychological testing: Principles, application, and issues* (6th ed.). Pacific Grove, CA: Brooks/Cole.

Like Aiken's book, this book offers a comprehensive overview of the types of psychological tests, their construction, their interpretation, and attendant controversies.

Polya, G. (2004). *How to solve it: A new aspect of mathematical method*. Princeton, NJ: Princeton University Press.

This book is a classic, a still timely introduction to practical problem solving in mathematics; a trove of insights and clever, heuristical applications. You will sense a master teacher at work.

Sternberg, R. J. (2003). *Wisdom, intelligence, and creativity synthesized*. New York: Cambridge University Press.

An influential, information in processing–based theory of intelligence and its measurement unfolds in the pages of this book.

CHAPTER 12

Life-Span
Developme

Prologue

A Rescue Mission

On December 25, 1989, furious at the way he had ruled their country, Romanian revolutionaries executed Nicolae Ceauşescu and his wife, Elena. In the subsequent months, the outside world learned that, among the horrors of their regime, the Ceauşescus had perpetrated a terrible ordeal on the nation's young children. Anxious to increase the country's birth rate and, at the same time pay off the national debt with food exports, Ceauşescu had restricted access to birth control while confiscating farm harvests. Thousands of families had no choice but to consign their infant children to state-run orphanages.

Collectively, these orphanages were warehouses for children. Many were unheated, with poor sanitation, few trained staff, and few resources. Westerners who visited the orphanages after the coup found many children left naked and forgotten in crowded wards. By almost any comparison, the children of these orphanages had suffered extreme neglect and deprivation of adult company.

Anxious to help, many couples from other countries sought to adopt these children. Thousands of orphans found foster homes in foreign countries, with parents who had made the special effort to rescue them and to provide a nurturing environment. Although complaints about bureaucratic corruption forced the Romanian government to suspend international adoptions in 2001, for a time it seemed that, at least in the case of those adopted children, adoption had allowed some to escape the ravages of the orphanage system.

Elinor Ames, a Canadian psychologist who spearheaded an effort to rescue some of the orphans, soon found that there were troubling aftermaths (Fisher et al., 1997). When Ames and her colleagues interviewed the parents who had adopted these children, she found that even though the children were still young, they showed significant difficulties in adjusting to their new lives. The parents reported eating problems (usually voracious appetites), medical problems, and frequent bouts of repetitive and robotic movements. Compared to Canadian children, the Romanian orphans also showed more problems related to siblings and peers. They seemed unable to adapt to new social situations and to adjust their behavior to life outside an institution. At the time, these children were about 2 to 3 years of age.

To Ames and her colleagues in 1997, the future of these children looked deeply uncertain. How extensive was the psychological damage caused by the neglect these children received early in life? How broad were the effects? The children's bodies responded quickly to improvements in their environments. Could psychological damage be likewise repaired by the efforts of the foster parents who had adopted them? What does the future hold for these children? ■

In this chapter, we discuss the physical, intellectual, and social changes we go through as we age, and some problems associated with abnormal development, similar to those described in the chapter prologue. We examine each of the major developmental periods of a person's life—prenatal development, infancy and childhood, adolescence, adulthood, and old age—and look at the psychological processes that change over these periods. TABLE 12·1 shows highlights of common physical and psychological changes people experience throughout the phases of the life span.

Developmental psychologists study both the similarities and the differences among people as they develop and change. Because they study change, developmental psychologists use special strategies of research. In a **cross-sectional study,** individuals of different ages are simultaneously compared with respect to some test or observation. For example, a developmental psychologist might present mathematical problems to groups of 5-, 7-, and 9-year-olds to measure the children's grasp of the concept of negative numbers. In contrast, a **longitudinal study** compares observations for the same individuals at different times of their lives. A longitudinal study of children's grasp of negative numbers might test a

cross-sectional study A study of development in which individuals of different ages are compared at the same time.

longitudinal study A study of development in which observations of the same individuals are compared at different times of their lives.

prenatal period The approximately 9 months between conception and birth. This period is divided into three developmental stages: the zygotic, the embryonic, and the fetal.

group of children when they were 5 years of age, and then repeat the test on the same children at 7 and then at 9.

Cross-sectional studies are usually more convenient to carry out, and they avoid the problems associated with repeatedly testing or observing the same individuals. However, they contain an important problem in interpretation. We examine this problem in connection with a concrete issue later in this chapter. Meanwhile, let's begin our consideration of life-span development by exploring the prenatal period.

Prenatal Development

The **prenatal period** extends over the approximately 9 months between conception and birth. The length of a normal pregnancy is 266 days, or 38 weeks. During this time, development depends on two factors whose effects characterize themes of this chapter. First, the genetic contribution from egg and sperm determines the genotype of the new individual. We saw in Chapter 3 how this genetic material can replicate, producing descendants that are genetic copies of this single cell. A child develops from this single source of genetic "instructions."

Although all cells of an individual (with the exception of reproductive cells) have the same genetic contents, they obviously differ—blood cells are not the same as neurons. Some factor must direct the mechanisms of replication so that cells that are genetically identical will develop along different paths. The biological mechanisms that determine development do this by suppressing and enhancing the chemical basis by which cells replicate. One example of how this process has worked is apparent from just looking around you: Although men and women have obvious differences, it is the case that the sexes are otherwise pretty similar. Yet, as we saw earlier (see Figure 3.8), women have two copies of the X chromosome, whereas men have only one. Because the X chromosome is larger and has many more genes than the Y, it would be expected that women would produce more of the proteins controlled by X chromosome genes, yet, this does not occur. Through a process known as X-chromosome inactivation, one of the X chromosomes is "silenced" shortly after

[TABLE 12·1] Phases of the Life Span

Phase	Approximate Age	Highlights
1. Prenatal period	Conception through birth	Rapid physical development of both nervous system and body
2. Infancy	Birth to 2 years	Motor development; attachment to primary caregiver
3. Childhood	2 years to 12 years	Increasing ability to think logically and reason abstractly; refinement of motor skills; peer influences
4. Adolescence	13 years to about 20 years	Thinking and reasoning becomes more adultlike; identity search; continued peer influences
5. Adulthood	20 years to 65 years	Love, committed relationship; career; stability and then decrease in physical abilities
6. Old age	65 years and older to death	Reflection on life's work and accomplishments; physical health deteriorates; preparation for death; death

fertilization so that most of its genes do not produce the proteins they normally would. This means that, although a woman receives an X chromosome from her mother and another from her father, only one of these is active. (Which one is largely a matter of chance.) Furthermore, each cell passes along the inactivation to the next generation of cells, so that all cells in an adult woman reflect the silencing that occurred early in life. Interestingly, a woman's germ cells reactivate the silenced chromosome, so that a woman can pass along, say, her father's X chromosome—even if it was silenced in her.

Inactivation occurs because the proteins that surround the DNA molecule undergo complex chemical changes that condense the protein structure and make the DNA contained within it nonfunctional (Brockdorff & Turner, 2007). These changes persist through cell divisions, condensing the same part of the chromosome in later cells and passing along the inactivation. In this way, a molecular change early in the life of a woman affects all the cells that develop thereafter, although the DNA code itself has not changed.

X-chromosome inactivation is one example of an **epigenetic modification,** a modification of cell inheritance that is not due to alterations of the DNA sequence itself. Epigenetic changes include the way the DNA molecule is folded within other proteins, chemical changes in the structure of the DNA molecule itself, and complex modifications in the way DNA information is mapped into protein synthesis (Allis, Jenuwein, & Reinberg, 2007). Epigenetic modifications form a second factor of early development and illustrate the important point that the cell's chemical environment moderates the expression of its genetic code.

Stages of Prenatal Development

The union of the ovum (egg) and sperm, or conception, is the starting point for prenatal development. During the **zygotic stage,** which lasts about 2 weeks, the zygote, or the single new cell that is formed at conception, replicates many times, and the internal organs begin to form. By the end of the first week, the zygote consists of about 100 cells. Many of the cells are arranged in two layers: one layer for the skin, hair, nervous system, and sensory organs, and the other for the digestive and respiratory systems and glands. Near the end of this stage, a third layer of cells appears that will eventually develop into muscles and the circulatory and excretory systems.

The **embryonic stage** of prenatal development, the second stage, begins at about 2 weeks and ends about 8 weeks after conception. During this stage, development occurs at an incredibly rapid pace. By a month after conception, a heart has begun to beat, a brain and spinal cord have started to function, and most of the major body structures are beginning to form. By the end of this stage, the major features that define the human body—arms, hands, fingers, legs, toes, shoulders, head, and eyes—are discernible. Behaviorally, the embryo can react reflexively to stimulation. For example, if the mouth is stimulated, the embryo moves its upper body and neck. Because so many changes depend on a delicate chemical balance, the embryo at this stage

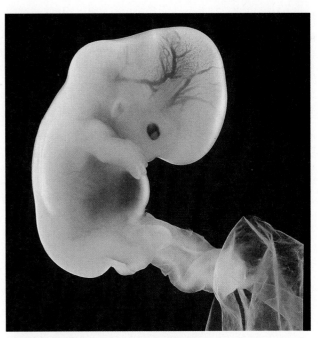

As this photograph of a six-week-old fetus illustrates, most of the major features that define the human body are present near the end of the embryonic stage of development (which starts at about two weeks and ends about eight weeks after conception).

is most susceptible to external chemical influences, including alcohol and other drugs, or toxins produced by diseases such as rubella (German measles). These substances are **teratogens** (from the Greek *teras,* meaning "monster"). The term *teratogen* refers to any substance, agent, or event that can cause mental or physical birth defects.

The beginning of sexual development occurs during the embryonic stage. Recall from Chapter 3 that the 23rd chromosome pair determines the sex of the embryo. The female partner always contributes an X chromosome to this pair at conception, whereas the male partner contributes either an X or a Y chromosome. If the male partner contributes a Y chromosome, the embryo will become a male (XY); if it is an X, the embryo will become a female (XX). Early in prenatal development, the embryo develops a pair of gonads that will become either ovaries or testes. (The word *gonad* comes from the Greek *gonos,* "procreation.") If a Y chromosome is present, a gene located on it causes the production of a chemical signal that makes the gonads develop into testes. Otherwise, the gonads become ovaries.

---

epigenetics   Mechanisms through which cells inherit modifications that are not due to DNA sequences.

zygotic stage   The first stage of prenatal development, during which the zygote divides many times and the internal organs begin to form.

embryonic stage   The second stage of prenatal development, beginning 2 weeks and ending about 8 weeks after conception, during which the heart begins to beat, the brain starts to function, and most of the major body structures begin to form.

teratogens   Substances, agents, and events that can cause birth defects.

[FIGURE 12•1] Differentiation and development of the sex organs.

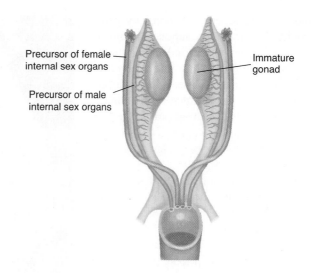

Precursor of female internal sex organs

Immature gonad

Precursor of male internal sex organs

Early in Fetal Development

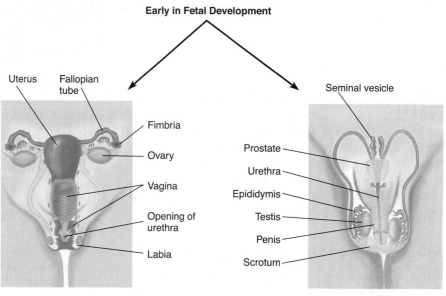

Uterus

Fallopian tube

Fimbria

Ovary

Vagina

Opening of urethra

Labia

Adult Female

Seminal vesicle

Prostate

Urethra

Epididymis

Testis

Penis

Scrotum

Adult Male

The presence or absence of testes determines the development of the other sex organs. If testes are present, they begin to secrete a class of sex hormones known as **androgens** (*andros* means "man"; *gennan* means "to produce"). The most important androgen is testosterone. Androgens bring about the development of the male internal sex organs, the penis, and the scrotum. These hormones are therefore absolutely necessary for the normal development of a male's sex organs. The development of female sex organs (uterus, vagina, and labia) occurs on its own; it does not need to be stimulated by a hormone. (See FIGURE 12•1.)

The **fetal stage** is the final period of prenatal development and lasts about 7 months. It officially begins with the appearance of bone cells and ends with birth. At the end of the second month of pregnancy, the fetus is about 1.5 inches long and weighs about 1 ounce. By the end of the third month, the development of major organs is completed, and the bones and muscles are beginning to develop. The fetus is now 3 inches long and weighs about 3 ounces. The fetus may show some movement, especially kicking.

By the end of the fourth month, the fetus is about 6 inches long and weighs about 6 ounces. It is also now sleeping and waking regularly. Fetal movements also become strong enough to be felt by the mother, and the heartbeat is loud enough to be heard through a stethoscope. Sound and light sensitivity will emerge within a few weeks. During the sixth month, the fetus grows to more than a foot long and weighs about 1.5 pounds. The seventh month is a critical month: If the fetus is born at this point, it has a fair chance of surviving. However, fetuses mature at different rates; some 7-month-old fetuses may be mature enough to survive premature birth, whereas others may not.

androgens The primary class of sex hormones in males. The most important androgen is testosterone.

fetal stage The third and final stage of prenatal development, which lasts for about 7 months, beginning with the appearance of bone tissue and ending with birth.

During the last 2 months of prenatal development, the fetus gains weight at the rate of about half a pound per week. On average the fetus is about 20 inches long and weighs about 7 pounds at the end of this period. The fetus is ready to be born.

Threats to Normal Prenatal Development

Probably the single most important factor in the fetus's development is the mother's diet: The food she eats and the vitamins and minerals she ingests are the fetus's only source of nutrition. If the mother is extremely malnourished, the fetus's nervous system develops abnormally, and intellectual deficits may result.

Not only malnutrition but also teratogens, as mentioned earlier, can cause birth defects. Psychologists who study birth defects are very interested in how drugs affect the fetus. Certain antibiotics, especially when taken in large quantities over long periods, can produce fetal defects. For example, tetracycline, a common antibiotic, can cause irregularities that develop later in the bones and in the coloration of the teeth. Cocaine use by mothers during pregnancy produces dramatic effects. If a pregnant woman uses cocaine, an increased risk of premature birth, low birth weight, and a smaller-than-normal head circumference occurs. One study showed that growth deficits attributable to prenatal cocaine exposure were still remarkable in children at age 7 (Covington et al., 2002). Research evidence also suggests that prenatal exposure to cocaine interferes with neural development, and that long-term consequences may ensue in the areas of arousal and attention (Bard, Coles, Plaatzman, & Lynch, 2000; Potter, et al., 2000; Singer et al., 2002; Mayes, et al., 2003). Further, some babies are born addicted and show withdrawal symptoms such as hyperactivity, irritability, tremors, and vomiting (Zuckerman & Brown, 1993).

A pregnant woman's cigarette smoking is another behavior that can affect the fetus. The carbon monoxide contained in cigarette smoke reduces the supply of oxygen to the fetus. Reduced oxygen levels are particularly harmful to the fetus during the last half of pregnancy, when the fetus is developing most rapidly and its need for oxygen is greatest. The main physical effects of mothers' smoking are increased rates of miscarriages, low-birth-weight babies, premature births, and births by cesarean section (Floyd et al., 1993; Kirchengast & Hartmann, 2003). Research suggests that prenatal exposure to cigarette smoking may produce lowered arousal levels in newborns (Franco et al., 2000), and there are indications of relatively uncommon but statistically related birth defects, such as cleft palate (e.g., Chung et al., 2000). Maternal smoking is associated with deficits in the ability of a newborn baby's brain to process speech sounds (Key et al., 2007) and may be related to behavior problems in adolescence (Weissman et al., 1999).

The damaging effects of alcohol use during pregnancy have been most widely studied (Steinhausen & Spohr, 1998; Kelly, Day, & Streissguth, 2000; Streissguth, 2001; Henderson, Kesmodel, & Gray, 2007). These effects can include both pre- and postnatal growth deficits, deformations of the eyes and mouth, low brain mass, other brain and central nervous system abnormalities, and heart deformation—the problems collectively known as fetal alcohol syndrome, or FAS (Niccols, 2007). Even if children with FAS are reared in healthy environments with regular, nutritious meals, their physical and intellectual development still falls short of that of normal children. The effects of alcohol on the fetus depend on its age and the amount that the mother consumes. Conflicting advice is found on this issue (Nathanson, Jayesinghe, & Roycroft, 2007; O'Brien, 2007). In the face of uncertainty, the best advice should be clear: Don't drink during pregnancy.

Tragically, some teratogens are much more difficult to avoid. Among these are the chemicals that occur in our environment because of industrial or agricultural pollution. For example, many pesticides use a class of chemicals based on phosphorus. Sánchez-Peña et al. (2004) found that Mexican agricultural workers exposed to such organophosphorus pesticides had a much larger risk of damage to the chromosome structure of their sperm cells than did those without such exposure. Of course, pesticides are just one of the many contaminants that we may be exposed to; lead, mercury, and polychlorinated biphenyls (PCBs) are other environmental teratogens. Their prevalence in our environment has led some researchers to seek "anti-teratogens" that could reduce these risks (e.g., Guna Sherlin and Verma, 2001).

QUESTIONS TO CONSIDER

1. Each of us experiences similar prenatal developmental stages and processes, so why do differences among people start to emerge from this very early period?
2. What would be the significance of showing that a fetus can learn?
3. Suppose that you are a psychologist working in a pediatric clinic. A woman, pregnant with her first child, asks you for advice on what she can do to care for her unborn child. Based on what you now know about prenatal development, what advice would you give her?

Physical and Perceptual Development in Infancy and Childhood

The terms "infant" and "toddler" apply to babies up to the age of 2 years. A newborn human infant is helpless and absolutely dependent on adult care. Recent research has shown, however, that newborns do not passively await the ministrations of their caregivers (Gartstein, Crawford, & Robertson, 2008). They quickly develop skills that shape the behavior of the adults with whom they interact. This section looks at motor

[FIGURE 12•2] Milestones in a child's motor development.

(Adapted from Shirley, M. M. (1933). *The first two years: Vol. 2. Intellectual development.* Minneapolis: University of Minnesota Press.)

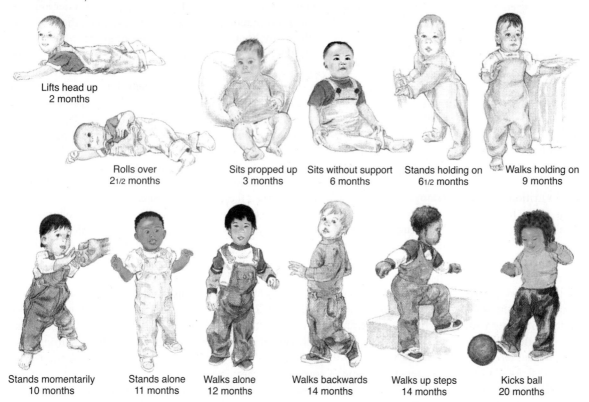

Lifts head up
2 months

Rolls over
2 1/2 months

Sits propped up
3 months

Sits without support
6 months

Stands holding on
6 1/2 months

Walks holding on
9 months

Stands momentarily
10 months

Stands alone
11 months

Walks alone
12 months

Walks backwards
14 months

Walks up steps
14 months

Kicks ball
20 months

Motor Development

Normal motor development follows a distinct pattern, which appears to be dictated by maturation of the muscles and the nervous system. The term **maturation** refers to any relatively stable change in thought, behavior, or physical growth that is due to the aging process and not to experience. Although individual children progress at different rates, their development follows the same basic maturational pattern. (See FIGURE 12•2.)

At birth, the infant's most important movements are reflexes—automatic movements in response to specific stimuli. The most important reflexes are the rooting, sucking, and swallowing responses. If a baby's cheek is lightly touched, the baby will turn its head toward the direction of the touch (the rooting response). If the object makes contact with the baby's lips, the baby will open its mouth and begin sucking. When milk or any other liquid enters the mouth, the baby will automatically make swallowing movements. Obviously, these reflexes are important for the baby's survival. As we see later

development and perceptual development in infancy and early childhood; in the next section we examine some influential theories of cognitive development.

in this chapter, these behaviors are important for an infant's social development as well.

Development of motor skills requires two ingredients: maturation of the child's nervous system and practice. Development of the nervous system is not complete at birth; considerable growth occurs during the first several months, and the amount of this growth seems to be associated with IQ in later childhood (Gale et al., 2004). Important changes in brain structure occur throughout the life span as a result of experience (Kolb & Whishaw, 1998; Kolb, Gibb, & Robinson, 2003).

Particular kinds of movements must await the development of the necessary neuromuscular systems, but motor development is not merely a matter of using these systems once they develop. Instead, physical development of the nervous system depends to a large extent on the ways the baby moves while interacting with the environment. In turn, more complex movements depend on further development of the nervous system, creating an interplay between motor and neural development. Thus, different steps in motor development are both an effect of previous development and a cause of further development (Thelen & Corbetta, 2002).

Perceptual Development

We have known for a long time that fetal experience with sensory stimuli can prepare the way for the newborn's experience.

---

maturation   Any relatively stable change in thought, behavior, or physical growth that is due to the aging process and not to experience.

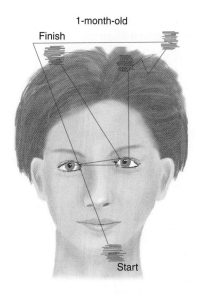

1-month-old

Finish

Start

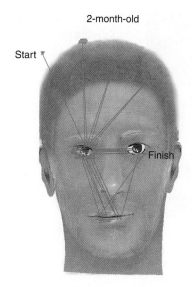

2-month-old

Start

Finish

[**FIGURE 12•3**] The scanning sequence used by infants viewing faces.

(From Salapatek, P. (1975). Pattern perception in early infancy. In *Infant Perception: From Sensation to Cognition, Vol 1: Basic Visual Processes*, edited by L. B. Cohen and P. Salapatek. New York: Academic Press. Copyright © 1975. Reprinted with permission from Elsevier.)

Kisilevsky et al. (2003) found that playing a recording of the mother's voice outside her abdomen increased the heart rate of her fetus, whereas playing a stranger's voice did not. At the time of birth, a child's senses are already functioning, at least to a certain extent (e.g., Maurer & Maurer, 1988). We know that the newborn's auditory system can detect sounds, because the baby will show a startle reaction when presented with a sudden loud noise. Similarly, a bright light will elicit eye closing and squinting. A cold object or a pinch will produce crying, so the sense of touch must be present. If held firmly and tilted backward, a baby will stiffen and flail his or her arms and legs, indicating that babies have a sense of balance. We also know that newborn infants have a sense of taste, because they indicate their taste preferences by facial expression and by choosing to swallow or not to swallow different liquids. Infants have an early-developing ability to distinguish odors, an ability that can be seen as an element of mother–infant bonding. For example, infants at 2 weeks can distinguish their own mother from other lactating women by breast odor (Porter, et al., 1992). We also know that infants very early on can recognize and prefer their mother's voice (e.g., DeCasper & Fifer, 1980; Purhonen et al., 2005). Research shows that preference and discrimination likely develop before birth as a result of the fetus's in utero exposure to the mother's voice (Kisilevsky et al., 2003).

Observations such as these establish the sensory abilities of infants, but when do infants develop the capacity to interpret sensory signals? Is perception present at birth? Developmental psychologists have looked at many perceptual systems to answer this question. We consider two systems: the perception of forms and the perception of distance.

Form Perception Researchers study the visual perceptual abilities of infants by observing their eye movements with an eye-tracking device while showing them visual stimuli. A harmless spot of infrared light, invisible to humans, is directed onto the baby's eyes. A special television camera, sensitive to infrared light, records the spot and superimposes it on an image of the display that the baby is looking at. The technique is precise enough to enable experimenters to tell which parts of a stimulus the baby is scanning. For example, Salapatek (1975) reported that a 1-month-old infant tends not to look at the inside of a figure. Instead, the baby's gaze seems to be "trapped" by the edges. Babies have low visual acuity at this age, so the results are largely a result of their looking at areas of high contrast. By the age of 2 months, the baby scans across the border to investigate the interior of a figure. FIGURE 12•3 shows a reconstruction of the paths followed by the eye scans of infants of these ages. (The babies were looking at real faces, not the drawings shown in the figure.)

The work by Salapatek and his colleagues suggests that at the age of 1 or 2 months, babies do not perceive complete shapes; their scanning strategy is limited to fixations on a few parts of the object at which they are looking. By 3 months, however, babies show clear signs of pattern recognition. For example, by this age, they prefer to look at stimuli that resemble the human face (Rosser, 1994), and by 4 or 5 months, they can discriminate between even very similar faces (Fagan & Singer, 1979; Bornstein & Arterberry, 2003).

Distance Perception The ability to perceive three-dimensional space comes at an early age. Gibson and Walk (1960) placed 6-month-old babies on what they called a visual cliff. On one side of this apparatus is a platform containing a checkerboard pattern. The platform adjoins a glass shelf mounted 3 or 4 feet over a floor that also is covered by the checkerboard pattern. Most babies who could crawl would not venture out onto the glass shelf. The infants acted as if they were afraid of falling; that is, they could perceive the distance between themselves and the floor.

Remember from Chapter 7 that several different types of cues in the environment contribute to depth perception. One cue arises from retinal disparity. As explained in Chapter 7, under normal circumstances, points on objects that are different distances from the viewer fall on slightly different points

A visual cliff. The child does not cross the glass bridge.

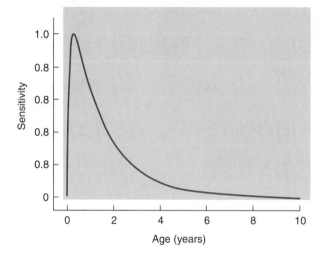

[FIGURE 12•4]   Sensitivity of stereopsis development to disruption in retinal disparity.

(Adapted from Fawcett, S. L., Wang, Y-Z., and Birch, E. E. (2005). The critical period for susceptibility of human stereopsis. *Investigative Ophthalmology & Visual Science, 46*, 521–525.)

of the two retinas. The perception of depth occurs when the two images are fused through visual processing. This form of depth perception, stereopsis ("solid vision"), depends on neurons that can respond to identical objects that stimulate different parts of the two eyes' retina (Parker, 2007). We are not born with neurons that do this. Rather, regions of the brain's visual system develop the connections that create neurons with this capacity. These connections will not develop unless animals have experience viewing objects with both eyes and consistent disparity during a period early in life.

The dependence of stereopsis on proper retinal disparity has important implications for the development of normal vision. If an infant's eyes are crossed, the same objects have inconsistent disparity, and the brain does not learn the relation between disparity and distance. Crossed vision can be corrected through surgery or through special glasses, but an infant requires disparity at a particular age to experience depth perception through stereopsis. Fawcett, Wang, & Birch (2005) examined children who had experienced crossed vision in infancy to see when loss of disparity most affects stereopsis. There are different reasons why crossed vision occurs, but overall, it has its worst influence at 3.5 months after birth, although its influence can affect stereopsis even at 4 years of age. (See FIGURE 12•4.)

Critical and Sensitive Periods in Perceptual Development

Psychologists use the term **critical period** to denote a specific time during which certain experiences must occur if an individual is to develop normally. Many perceptual, behavioral, and cognitive abilities are subject to critical periods. For example, as we saw in the opening prologue and as we shall see later in this chapter, if infants are not exposed to a stimulating environment and do not have the opportunity to interact with caregivers during the first 2 years of their lives, their cognitive development will be impaired.

critical period   A specific time in development during which certain experiences must occur for normal development to take place.

sensitive period   A period during which certain experiences have a greater effect on development than they would have if they had occurred at another time.

Other abilities may show a weaker dependence on experience: The ability in question may develop in response to experience that occurs any time within a broad range, but the effect may be stronger during some periods than during others. This weaker form of dependency is often referred to as a **sensitive period.** Acquisition of a second language seems to be such a case. A person can learn a second language throughout life; but, as we saw in Chapter 10, a second language is learned more easily in childhood than later.

Critical periods and sensitive periods demonstrate that human development is more than an unfolding of a genetically determined program. It consists of a continuous interaction between physical maturation and environmental stimulation.

QUESTIONS TO CONSIDER

1. Suppose you are expecting your first child. How might you design your child's room (or nursery) to facilitate motor and perceptual development? What kinds of toys would you include in the room? What sorts of experiences might you wish to have with your child to promote normal motor and sensory development?
2. If it could be shown that a child is genetically predisposed to prefer some visual stimuli over others, what stimuli would they be?

Cognitive Development in Infancy and Childhood

As children grow, their nervous systems mature, and they undergo new experiences. Perceptual and motor skills develop in complexity and competency. Children learn to recognize people and their voices, begin to talk and respond to the speech of others, and learn how to solve problems. Infants as young as 12 months are even able to form memories of specific events (see Bauer, 2002). In short, their cognitive capacities develop.

This section begins by highlighting the importance of a responsive environment to cognitive development; then we turn to Piaget's theory, Vygotsky's theory, the information-processing model, and the controversial question of television's impact on cognitive development.

The Importance of a Responsive Environment

Cognitive development is the process by which infants get to know things about themselves and their world. One of the first steps in a baby's cognitive development is for the baby to learn that events in the environment can be dependent on its own behavior. It appears that the type of setting that is most effective in promoting cognitive development is an environment in which the infant's behavior has tangible effects.

In an experimental test of this hypothesis, Watson and Ramey (1972) presented three groups of infants with a mobile 10 minutes per day for 14 days. A pillow containing a pressure-sensitive switch was placed under each baby's head, and the mobile was suspended above the baby's face. For one group, the mobile automatically rotated whenever the infant moved its head and activated the switch. For another group, the mobile remained stationary. For a third group, the mobile intermittently moved on its own (but not in response to infant head movements). So the first group of infants had experience controlling the mobile's movements, whereas the other two groups experienced no association between their own actions and the mobile's movement.

The babies were tested again. This time, the mobile was connected to the pillow switch for infants in all three of the experimental groups. Infants who had learned the contingency

Watson and Ramey's experiment using mobiles demonstrated the importance of a responsive environment in promoting cognitive development.

between head turning and mobile movement again turned their heads when they saw the mobile. They seemed to have learned that they could control its movements. In contrast, when the babies in the second and third groups were given the opportunity to make the mobile move by turning their heads, they did not learn to do so. It was as if they had learned from their prior experience that they could not affect whether the mobile would move. Research using similar methods found that infants were visibly pleased when they controlled the onset of a Sesame Street music video (Lewis, Alessandri, & Sullivan, 1990). Losing this type of contingent control, conversely, produces facial expressions of anger (Lewis et al., 1990; Sullivan & Lewis, 2003). The babies in the mobile study showed the importance of a responsive environment. In contrast, J.F. spent the first 3 years of her life in a Romanian orphanage and, in all that time, had only once been outside for fresh air and sunshine. The following case illustrates J.F.'s story.

[**CASE STUDY**] When J.F.'s prospective foster parents first saw her, sores and dirt covered her skin, and her fingernails were so long they curled around to the other side. One of her legs was so disfigured by injections of tranquilizing drugs that it would later need surgery to help her walk. Although 3 years of age, she looked less than half that age. The Canadian woman who was visiting felt so touched by the child's plight that she dropped her plans to adopt a younger child, and adopted J.F. instead.

J.F.'s new mother and father tried hard to provide the care that the child had been denied for the first 3 years of her life, but J.F. seemed incapable of accepting the attachment between a child and her parents. As described by Faulder (2006), J.F.'s emotional maturity was like that of an 18-month-old. Her mother described her as always in "spin cycle"—unable to focus on any behavior, even on play. The problems of adjustment that Elinor Ames had observed in her sample had, in J.F.'s case, led to a downward spiral.

By the time she was 10, J.F.'s behavior had turned her household into a "living hell." She had been diagnosed with the conditions of autism, attention deficit, and hyperactivity. Other suspected conditions included attachment disorder and Tourette's syndrome. One day, overwhelmed by the chaos of J.F.'s behavior, her mother phoned the social agency screaming for help. Up to this point, a stable home life and the love of two parents had not been enough. J.F. would spend the next 6 years living in a group home in another town.

Findings from research on infant control of stimuli in their environments are consistent with a great deal of other evidence about adults (as you will see in later chapters). For each of us, the abilities to extend ourself and to affect objects and other people are important aspects of personal and social functioning. Le Mare, Audet, & Kurytnik (2007) studied the frequency with which the foster parents of Romanian adoptees used social-support agencies and found that the parents requested help more often than those of nonadopted children. The group differences were especially pronounced when the adopted children were between 10 and 11 years of age, when the parents sought assistance for behavioral and academic problems.

Nelson (2007) suggested that at key times, the brain's development requires the stimulation that normal childhood provides; without this stimulation, regions of the brain lack directions for further development. Cognitive and social development might be characterized as a sequence. If earlier periods in the sequence are disrupted, then development is delayed. This notion of sequence, with distinct and ordered stages, was suggested by early observers of child development, such as Baldwin and Montessori (see Chapter 1). Nowadays, it is most closely associated with the theories of Jean Piaget.

The Work of Jean Piaget

Jean Piaget (1896–1980), was a Swiss researcher who viewed cognitive development as a maturational process. Piaget considered himself a philosopher concerned with the development of knowledge rather than a developmental psychologist. Piaget's work began with observations he made on his own children. He noticed that they tended to engage in behaviors that were distinctive to their age and to make related mistakes in problem solving. Other children of similar ages tended to engage in similar behaviors and to make the same kinds of mistakes. He concluded that these similarities are the result of a sequence of development that all normal children follow. Completion of each period, with its corresponding abilities, is the prerequisite for entering the next period.

An important component of Piaget's theory is the notion of an **operation.** In the field of both logic and mathematics, an operation is a transformation of an object or thing. For example, multiplication by 2 transforms 6 into 12. Similarly, saying "Rhonda is my sister" transforms your conception of "Rhonda" into another conception, that of "my sister." For Piaget, an important logical characteristic of an operation is that it is invertible; that is, it can be reversed. By inverting the operation of multiplication into division, we can transform 12 back to 6. According to Piaget, an important aspect of cognitive development is whether a child possesses the ability to use operations of different types.

As children develop, Piaget suggested, they acquire mental representations or frameworks that are used for understanding and dealing with the world and for thinking about and solving problems. As Chapter 8 explained, a mental framework that organizes and synthesizes information

According to Piaget, children develop schemas, such as schemas for grasping objects or putting them into their mouths, that become the basis for understanding current and future experiences.

about a person, place, or thing is known as a schema. Piaget proposed that schemas are first defined in terms of objects and actions but that later they become the basis of the concrete and abstract concepts that constitute adult knowledge. For example, a baby girl is said to have a "grasping schema" when she is able to grasp a rattle in her hand. Once she has learned how to grasp a rattle, she can then apply the same schema to other objects. Later, she can incorporate the "grasping schema" with others to accomplish the behavior of picking an object up. At this point, she will possess a "picking up schema."

Let's consider schemas further. Infants acquire schemas by interacting with their environment. According to Piaget, two processes help a child adapt to his or her environment: assimilation and accommodation. **Assimilation** is the process by which new information is incorporated into existing schemas. For example, suppose that a young boy has schemas for what adults are like and for what children are like. Adults are tall and drive cars. Children are short and ride bikes. When this child meets new children and adults, they will usually fit, or be assimilated, into his existing schemas and will be properly categorized. But our child will be challenged when he meets his mother's older sister Marge, who is no taller than the average 12-year-old and rides a bike. The child will need to account for the fact that Aunt Marge is nevertheless identifiably an adult. The process by which existing schemas are changed by new experiences is called **accommodation**. Our children's schemas for children and adults will have to change to include the possibility that some short people are adults rather than children. As you continue in this chapter, keep in mind that assimilation and accommodation apply not just to categorization of people and objects, but to methods of doing things and even to abstract concepts as well.

---

operation In Piaget's theory, a logical or mathematical rule that transforms an object or concept into something else.

assimilation In Piaget's theory, the process by which new information about the world is incorporated into existing schemas.

accommodation The process of altering the thickness of the lens to focus images of near or distant objects on the retina. In Piaget's theory of cognitive development, the process by which existing schemas are modified or changed by new experiences.

[**TABLE 12·2**] The Four Periods of Piaget's Theory of Cognitive Development

Period	Approximate Age	Major Features
Sensorimeter	Birth to 2 years	Grasp of object permanence; deferred imitation; rudimentary symbolic thinking
Preoperational	2 to 6 or 7 years	Increased ability to think symbolically and logically; egocentrism; cannot yet master conservation problems
Concrete operational	6 or 7 years to 11 years	Mastery of conservation problems; understanding of categorization; cannot think abstractly
Formal operational	11 years upward	Ability to think abstractly and hypothetically

Piaget's Four Periods of Cognitive Development Although development is a continuous process, Piaget argued that at key points in an individual's life, the two processes of assimilation and accommodation fail to adjust adequately to the child's knowledge of the world. At these points, by a process that Piaget labeled **equilibration,** the individual's schemas are radically reorganized. According to Piaget, these key points in a child's life divide cognitive development into four periods: sensorimotor, preoperational, concrete operational, and formal operational. (See TABLE 12·2.) What a child learns in one period enables him or her to progress to the next period. Crucially, it matters whether the schemas of an earlier period can be reorganized in a way that will permit operations to occur in the next. The periods in Piaget's theory are more than just intervals of time; they are necessary stages in a progression from primitive sensory knowledge to abstract reasoning.

The Sensorimotor Period The **sensorimotor period,** which lasts for approximately the first 2 years of life, is the first stage in Piaget's theory of cognitive development. It is marked by an orderly progression of increasingly complex cognitive development ranging from reflexes to symbolic thinking. During this period, cognition is closely tied to external stimulation, including that produced by physical objects and people (see Muller & Carpendale, 2000).

At around 3 months, infants become able to follow moving objects with their eyes. If an infant's doll disappears behind a barrier, the infant will continue to stare at the place where the doll has disappeared but will not search for it.

At around 5 months, infants can grasp and hold objects and gain experience with manipulating and observing them. They also can anticipate the future position of a moving object. If a doll is made to pass behind a screen, infants will turn their eyes toward the far side of the screen, seeming to anticipate the doll's reappearance on the other side.

An important development in the sensorimotor period is the child's grasp of **object permanence:** the realization that objects do not cease to exist when they are out of sight. Until about 6 months of age, children appear to lose all interest in an object that disappears from sight—the saying "out of sight, out of mind" seems particularly appropriate. In addition, cognition is inseparable from action or behavior: Thinking is doing.

During the last half of the first year, infants develop much more complex concepts concerning the nature of physical objects. They grasp objects, turn them over, and investigate their properties. By looking at an object from various angles, they learn that the object can change its visual shape and still be the same object. In addition, if an object is hidden, infants will actively search for it; their object concept now contains the rule of object permanence. For infants at this stage of development, a hidden object still exists. Out of sight is no longer out of mind. In the game of peekaboo, babies laugh because they know that after momentarily disappearing, you will suddenly reappear and say, "Peekaboo!"

By early in the second year, awareness of object permanence is well enough developed that infants will search for an object in the last place they saw it hidden. However, at this stage, infants can keep track of changes only in a hiding place they can see. For example, if an adult picks up an object, puts it under a cloth, drops the object while his or her hand is hidden, closes the hand again, and removes the hand from the cloth, infants will look for the object in the adult's hand. When they do not find the object there, they look puzzled or upset and do not search for the object under the cloth. (See FIGURE 12·5.)

The Preoperational Period. Piaget's second period of cognitive development, the **preoperational period,** lasts from approximately age 2 to age 7 and involves the ability to think logically as well as symbolically. This period is characterized by rapid development of language ability and of the ability to represent things symbolically. The child arranges toys in new ways to represent other objects (for example, a row of blocks can represent a train), begins to classify and categorize objects, and starts learning to count and to manipulate numbers. During the preoperational period, schemas are reorganized around words. Words are symbols that have no physical

---

equilibration A process activated when a child's abilities to assimilate and accommodate fail to adjust.

sensorimotor period The first period in Piaget's theory of cognitive development, lasting from birth to 2 years, and marked by an orderly progression of increasingly complex cognitive development from reflexes to object permanence to deferred imitation and rudimentary symbolic thinking.

object permanence In Piaget's theory, the idea that objects do not cease existing when they are out of sight.

preoperational period The second period in Piaget's theory of cognitive development, lasting from 2 years of age to 7, and representing a transitional period between symbolic and logical thought. During this stage, children become increasingly capable of speaking meaningful sentences.

[FIGURE 12•5] Object permanence. An infant will not realize that the object has been left under the cloth.

(Adapted from Bower, T. G. R. (1972). *Development in infancy* (2nd ed.). Copyright © 1982 by W. H. Freeman and Company. Used with permission.)

Object is in researcher's hand.

Researcher closes hand...

...puts hand under cloth...

...removes hand, leaving object under the cloth.

Infant looks in researcher's hand.

Obviously upset, infant quits.

resemblance to the concept they represent; Piaget referred to such abstract symbols as signs. Signs are social conventions. They are understood by all members of a culture. A child who is able to use words to think about reality has made an important step in cognitive development.

Egocentrism, a child's belief that others see the world in precisely the way he or she does, is another important characteristic of the preoperational period. A preoperational child sees the world only from his or her own point of view. For example, a preoperational child playing hide-and-seek may run to a corner, turn his back to you, and "hide" by covering his eyes. Although in plain sight of you, he believes that because he cannot see you, you must not be able to see him.

A third important characteristic of the preoperational period—and the reason for its name—is that the child's schemas do not permit invertible operations. For example, if pennies piled into a neat stack on a table are picked up and spread out all over the tabletop, they have been transformed

from a column into a different array. A child in the preoperational period cannot conceptualize that this operation can be reversed. Instead, he or she believes something about the pennies has radically changed and will describe the pennies as being different in some way.

Piaget's work demonstrated this belief quite clearly and, in doing so, showed that a child's representation of the world is strikingly different from that of an adult. For example, most adults realize that the volume of water remains constant when the water is poured from a short, wide container into a taller, narrower container, even though its level is now higher. However, early in the preoperational period, children will fail to recognize this fact; they will say that the taller container contains more water. (See FIGURE 12•6.) The ability to realize that an object retains volume, mass, length, or number when it undergoes various transformations is referred to as a grasp of **conservation;** the transformed object conserves its original properties. FIGURE 12•7 depicts three additional tests of children's understanding of conservation.

The Period of Concrete Operations. Piaget's third stage of cognitive development, the **period of concrete operations,** spans approximately ages 7 to 11 and involves children's developing understanding of the conservation principle and other concepts, such as categorization. The end of this period marks the transition from childhood to adolescence. The period of concrete operations is characterized by the emergence of the

---

egocentrism   Self-centeredness; Piaget proposed that preoperational children can see the world only from their own perspectives.

conservation   The fact that specific properties of objects (for example, volume, mass, length, or number) remain the same despite apparent changes in the shape or arrangement of those objects.

period of concrete operations   The third period in Piaget's theory of cognitive development, lasting from age 7 to 11, during which children come to understand the conservation principle and other concepts, such as categorization.

[**FIGURE 12·6**] Conservation. In the preoperational period, a child does not grasp the fact that the volume of a liquid remains the same even if the liquid is poured into a different-shaped container.

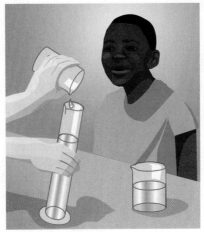

ability to perform logical analysis, by an increased ability to empathize with the feelings and attitudes of others, and by an understanding of more complex cause-and-effect relations.

The child becomes much more skilled at the use of symbolic thought. For example, even before the period of concrete operations, children can arrange a series of objects in order of size and can compare any two objects and say which is larger. However, if they are shown that stick A is larger than stick B and that stick B is larger than stick C, they cannot infer that stick A is larger than stick C. Children become capable of making such inferences during the early part of this period. At this stage, however, although they can reason with respect to concrete objects, such as sticks that they have seen, they cannot do so with hypothetical objects. For example, they cannot solve the following problem: "Judy is taller than Frank, and Frank is taller than

Carl. Who is taller, Judy or Carl?" The ability to solve such problems awaits the next period of cognitive development.

The Period of Formal Operations. During the **period of formal operations,** which begins at about age 11, children first become capable of abstract reasoning. They can now think and reason about hypothetical objects and events. They also begin to understand that under different conditions, their behavior can have different consequences. Formal operational thinking is not "culture free"; that is, it is influenced by cultural variables,

---

period of formal operations   The fourth period in Piaget's theory of cognitive development, from age 11 onward, during which individuals first become capable of more formal kinds of abstract thinking and hypothetical reasoning.

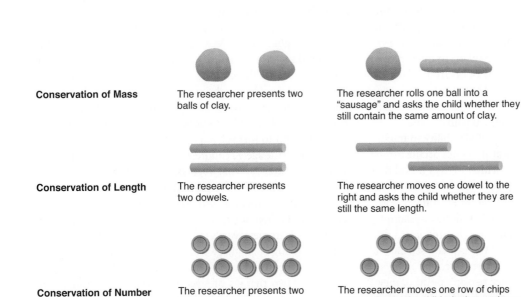

[**FIGURE 12·7**] Various tests of conservation.

(Adapted from *Of Children: An Introduction to Child Development,* 4th ed., by Guy R. Lefrancois, Belmont, CA: Wadsworth Publishing Company.)

Conservation of Mass   The researcher presents two balls of clay.   The researcher rolls one ball into a "sausage" and asks the child whether they still contain the same amount of clay.

Conservation of Length   The researcher presents two dowels.   The researcher moves one dowel to the right and asks the child whether they are still the same length.

Conservation of Number   The researcher presents two rows of poker chips.   The researcher moves one row of chips apart and asks the child whether each row still contains the same number.

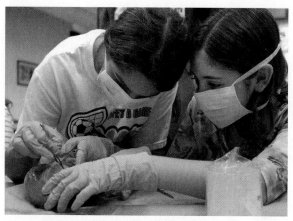

Formal operational thinking is influenced by cultural variables, especially formal schooling.

especially formal schooling (Piaget, 1972; Rogoff & Chavajay, 1995). Without exposure to the principles of scientific thinking, such as those taught in middle school and high school science classes, people do not develop formal operational thinking.

According to Piaget, not all people pass through all four stages and reach the formal operational period, even as physically mature adults. In some cases, adults show formal operational thought only in their areas of expertise. Thus, a mechanic may be able to think abstractly while repairing an engine but not while solving math or physics problems. A physicist may be able to reason abstractly when solving physics problems but not while reading poetry. However, once an individual does reach the formal operational level of thinking, he or she will always (except in the case of damage to the brain from injury or disease) perform intellectually at that level.

Evaluation of Piaget's Contribution Piaget's theory has had an enormously positive impact, stimulating interest and research in developmental psychology and educational psychology (e.g., Brainerd, 2003; Voyat, 1998). Not all of Piaget's conclusions have been universally accepted, however. One criticism leveled at Piaget is that he did not always define his terms operationally. Consequently, it is difficult for others to interpret the significance of his generalizations. Many of his studies lack the proper controls discussed in Chapter 2. Thus, much of his work was not experimental, which means that cause-and-effect relations among variables cannot be identified with certainty.

Research evidence suggests that a child's ability to understand conservation of various physical attributes occurs earlier than Piaget supposed. For example, Gelman (1972) found that when the appropriate task is used, even 3-year-old children are able to demonstrate a grasp of conservation of number. Also, some children are able to anticipate conservation (for example, by predicting what will happen if a liquid is poured into a differently shaped glass) even if they fail the actual test (Caroff, 2002). Piaget also appears to have underestimated the ability of young children to understand another person's point of view. In other words, children are less egocentric at early ages than Piaget thought (Flavell, 1992). Children as young as 2 years old make inferences about other people's knowledge that require

understanding what the others could or could not have seen happen (O'Neill, 1996).

Although Piaget's method of observation led him to underestimate some important abilities, his meticulous observations of child behavior have been extremely important in the field of child development and have had a great influence on educational practice.

Vygotsky's Sociocultural Theory of Cognitive Development

Another important contributor to our understanding of cognitive development was the Russian psychologist Lev Vygotsky (1896–1934). Although Vygotsky's work was conducted during the 1920s and early 1930s, his writings continue to influence present-day conceptualizations of cognitive development during childhood (Kozulin & Falik, 1995).

Vygotsky agreed with Piaget that experience with the physical world is an important factor, but he disagreed that this is the whole story. He argued that the culture in which a child lives also plays a significant role in the child's cognitive development (Vygotsky, 1934/1987). Vygotsky argued that children do not learn to think about the physical world in a vacuum. The cultural context—what they hear others say about the world and how they see others interact with physical aspects of the world—matters (Behrend, Rosengren, & Perlmutter, 1992; Thomas, 1996). Thus, parents, teachers, friends, and many others help children acquire ideas about how the world works. We would expect, then, that the development of children raised in nonstimulating environments devoid of interesting interactions with other people, with books, and, yes, with television would lag behind that of children raised in more stimulating environments.

Vygotsky further believed that children's use of speech also influences their cognitive development. Children up to about age 7 often talk to themselves. When drawing in a coloring book, a child may say, "I'll color her arms and face green and her pants black." Piaget would focus on such talk as reflecting egocentrism. Vygotsky's focus would be different. He would say that the child's talk reflects a cognitive developmental process—the child is developing a mental plan that will serve as a guide to subsequent behavior. According to Vygotsky, language is the basis for cognitive development, including the abilities to remember, to solve problems, to make decisions, and to formulate plans.

After about age 7, children stop vocalizing their thoughts and instead carry on what Vygotsky labeled inner speech. Inner speech represents the internalization of words and the mental manipulation of them as symbols for objects in the environment. As children interact with their parents, teachers, and peers, they learn new words to represent new objects. Given Vygotsky's linking of language with thought, this increased facility with language would imply better cognitive skill as well.

These two themes of Vygotsky's theory—the interconnection between thought and language, and the importance of society and culture—led him to propose a developmental distinction important to educational psychologists. The skills and problem-solving abilities that a child can show on his or her own indicate the level of development that the child has mastered. Vygotsky called this the **actual developmental level.** For Piaget, this level would represent the limit of the child's cognitive skill. However, Vygotsky argued that a patient parent or a skilled mentor could assist a child to achieve a potentially higher level. Perhaps you've had the experience of studying for the Scholastic Aptitude Test and being stumped by a particular kind of problem. That would, loosely, define your actual developmental level. But now suppose a teacher shows you a method for solving the problem that not only makes perfect sense to you but also helps you to solve similar problems. That increased capacity for problem solving resulting from guided help, Vygotsky called the **zone of proximal development.** And indeed, as the "expertise" of the people they interact with increases, so do the children's cognitive skills. For example, Rogoff and her colleagues (e.g., Rogoff, 1990) have shown that children become better problem solvers if they practice solving problems with their parents or with more experienced children than if they practice the problems alone or with children of similar cognitive ability.

Applying Information-Processing Models to Cognitive Development

As our knowledge about human memory has expanded since the time of Piaget and Vygotsky, developmental psychologists have examined how an information-processing perspective on human sensation, perception, and memory might fit within an account of human development. One approach is to consider how processes of memory might change during development, and what effects these changes might have. Another approach has looked not at the processes of cognition per se, but rather at the knowledge base that children have at different ages. Presumably, if we knew how a child understood the world, we would be able to know how he or she would encode, store, and retrieve the semantic information required to adjust to it.

Changes in Cognitive Processes   Can infants remember? Piaget's observations on the concept of object permanence seemed to indicate that infants younger than 6 months do not encode objects; therefore, they cannot remember them. Rovee-Collier and her colleagues, however, challenged this conclusion by using a variation of the mobile task described at the start of this section (e.g., Rovee-Collier, 1999). Infants from 2 to 6 months of age were shown a mobile that they could move by means of a ribbon attached to one of their legs. After varying amounts of time, they would be shown the mobile again, but with the ribbon disconnected. If the infant kicked at a rate higher than normal, Rovee-Collier would conclude that the infant recognized the mobile on the second presentation. Infants 6 to 18 months of age were tested in a similar way by using a mechanical switch to operate a toy train.

Rovee-Collier's results suggest not only that memory is present in infants, but also that the retention span increases

[**FIGURE 12•8**]   Retention of memory of the sight of an infant mobile or a toy train by infants 2 to 18 months of age. Blue circles depict data from infants tested with a mobile that they could move by leg motions. Orange circles depict data from infants trained with the toy train. Six-month-old infants were tested with both the mobile and the train.

(From Rovee-Collier, C. (1999). The development of infant memory. *Current Directions in Psychological Science, 8,* 80–85. Copyright © 1978 American Psychological Society.)

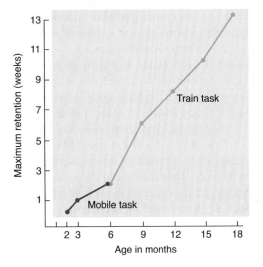

systematically over the 2- to 18-month period of life (Rovee-Collier, 1999). FIGURE 12•8 shows data from both the mobile and train test situations; the maximal delay over which the infants show retention is plotted against their age. By using a similar procedure, Rovee-Collier and her colleagues have shown that retrieval cues increase retrieval in infants—and that infants apparently demonstrate an implicit/explicit differentiation similar to that discussed in Chapter 8.

Case (1998) claimed that cognitive development is a matter of a child's becoming more efficient in using memory and other cognitive processes. The heart of Case's model is a hypothetical information-processing construct similar to short-term or working memory, whose chief function is the processing of information from the external world. According to Case, as the brain matures, so does its capacity to process greater amounts of information by using memory. The result is the acquisition of central conceptual structures—networks of schemas that allow children to understand the relations among the objects and events represented by the schemas. As increasingly complex central conceptual structures are formed, children advance to higher levels of cognitive development, as represented in Piaget's stages.

---

actual developmental level   In Vygotsky's theory, the stage of cognitive development reached by a child, as demonstrated by the child's ability to solve problems on his or her own.

zone of proximal development   In Vygotsky's theory, the increased potential for problem-solving and conceptual abilities that exists for a child if expert mentoring and guidance are available.

Changes in Cognitive Content The increased complexity of children's knowledge as they develop has figured prominently in development theories. Contemporary research based on information-processing models of memory has clarified the importance of the specific knowledge an individual can use to encode information, store it, or retrieve it. We have seen, for example, that elaborative rehearsal is more effective in maintaining information than is simple repetition. As Case suggests, increased cognitive ability is facilitated by a richer knowledge of the world surrounding the child. This simple proposition has encouraged many developmental psychologists to examine the content of infants' and children's knowledge in certain areas or domains.

One important domain is the world of physics and mechanical action. Infants show knowledge of at least some of the laws of physics at an early age. One very simple law is an optical one: When one object passes behind another, it is occluded, or blocked from view, but if a gap exists in the occluding object, the object should be visible. Luo and Baillargeon (2005) found that infants develop this knowledge piece by piece. They discovered this by using the fact that even young infants will react to unexpected events by prolonged looking. By comparing the amount of time infants spend looking at one scene as opposed to another, it's possible to infer what infants consider to be "normal" and what is "unexpected."

To understand Luo and Baillargeon's experiment, think of an old-fashioned theater stage with a main curtain across the front and side curtains on the left and right. If someone were to wave at you, walk behind the left side curtain, and later emerge at the edge of the right side curtain, you would find nothing unusual about that sequence. But if the central curtain were raised and you saw someone enter one side and exit the other without seeing that person cross the open stage, you'd be pretty surprised, right? It would appear that this person had teleported from behind the left curtain to the right curtain. When Luo and Baillargeon (2005) used a bit of stage magic to accomplish this apparent act of teleportation, infants of this age spent a lot of time looking at the scene.

This knowledge about occlusion is only partially present in infants. Luo and Baillargeon performed another test, similar to what the stage would be like if the central curtain were only half raised. Now, you would expect to see legs as someone walked across the stage. Infants 2 and a half months of age, however, are not surprised if they don't see this partial occlusion (although infants of 3 months are). Rather, the younger infants are surprised if they do see the partial occlusion. They seem to treat a partial gap as if it were no gap at all. Apparently, knowledge about optical occlusion develops incrementally, as infants acquire an understanding about the solidity and continuity of occluding objects.

Theory of Mind Another important domain, especially as the infant or child encounters social settings, is knowledge about others' beliefs or state of mind. For example, suppose you notice that your professor keeps a whiteboard marker in a drawer of the classroom podium. One day, you come to the classroom early, before your professor, and see someone from the class before yours reach into the drawer, pick up the marker, and leave with it. You would still expect your professor to look for the marker in the drawer. You recognize that your knowledge about the marker can be different from your professor's. You have developed expectations about how experiences relate to beliefs, something that developmental psychologists describe as **theory of mind.**

Four-year-olds seem capable of correctly inferring how events can shape the state of mind or beliefs of another. But 3-year-olds do not: They use their own beliefs to predict the beliefs and actions of others. Developmental psychologists have observed this difference in a procedure sometimes called the "Sally-Anne" test (e.g., Baron-Cohen, Leslie, & Frith, 1985). A child is shown two dolls—Sally and Anne. The Sally doll is shown placing a marble in a basket within a doll house and then shown leaving the house. While she is away, the Anne doll takes the marble and places it in a box. The Sally doll returns to the house, and the child is asked: "Where will Sally look for her marble?" A 3-year-old girl watching this little drama would think that, because she knows where the marble is, another, such as Sally, would know that too. She has, in other words, not differentiated her own beliefs from another's. By the following year, however, she will have developed a type of "naive psychology" by which she will recognize that other people's behaviors follow patterns based on their own beliefs (Kail, 2001; Slaughter & Repacholi, 2003).

Wellman, Cross, and Watson (2001) examined the results of 178 separate studies on theory of mind. Their analysis showed that the results of the studies were consistent and robust. Children improved on false-belief tasks from age 3 to 5. The understanding of belief and false belief was also found to be culture free (at least, not specific to the cultures included in the analysis). Whether European, North American, East Asian, Australian, or African, children acquired understanding of others' beliefs at around the same time. Some forms of tasks do improve performance when compared with others, however. Two reasons could explain this: either these forms are a more sensitive measure of theory of mind, or they are easy for unrelated reasons; unfortunately, the analysis doesn't suggest which is correct. When studies across the developmental trajectory are analyzed, a significant and discernible improvement occurs with age, for easy and difficult tasks.

The term "naive psychology" is not meant to imply anything negative. When a child develops a theory of mind, he or she acquires a sophisticated tool for predicting the actions of others. Think of your own ability to understand a friend's nuanced reaction to a forgotten birthday greeting, and you'll recognize the significance of this developmental change. It's been suggested that the lack of a theory of mind may underlie some severe developmental disorders, such as autism (Baron-Cohen, Leslie, & Frith, 1985).

---

theory of mind Expectations concerning how experience affects mental states, especially those of another.

focus On

Cognitive Development and Television Viewing

Cognitive development is influenced by many factors. These factors vary enormously, but almost all children in industrialized societies, even those in the poorest households, are exposed for several hours a day to a near-universal factor—television. Although certainly other modern media resemble television's visual experience, such as video games and the Internet, it has been argued that television is especially important to the development of children because it is present in almost every home, occupies a large part of a child's time, and is accessible to children across a wide span of their lives (Huston & Wright, 1998). It is important to understand the impact of this technological presence on a child's cognitive development.

How much of a child's time is dominated by the medium? Estimates vary according to the method used. A study of Australian 5-year-old children that asked parents to fill out diaries of what their children did reported a median of 114 minutes per day spent watching television—more than any other activity aside from sleeping (Tey et al., 2007). Boys tend to view more television than do girls; and, across all ages, children with low IQs from low-income families watch more television than do other children (Huston, Watkins, & Kunkel, 1989; Huston et al., 1990). According to Anderson and Collins (1988), while watching television, children often are engaged in other activities: They eat, play with toys, draw or color pictures, read, play games, sleep, talk with others, or do their homework. They often enter and leave the room while the television is on.

Two issues concern us here—the content of television programs and the general effects of the medium itself. Let us consider content first. One of the best examples of good television is demonstrated by Sesame Street, a program that was devised to teach school-readiness skills such as counting, letter recognition, and vocabulary. Research indicates that the program has succeeded in its goals; children who watch Sesame Street have better vocabularies, have better attitudes toward school, adapt better to the classroom, and have more positive attitudes toward children of other races (Fisch & Truglio, 2001). Rice et al. (1990), studied a large sample of 3- to 5-year-old children from a wide range of socioeconomic backgrounds and found that children of all backgrounds profited from watching Sesame Street—the advantages were not restricted to middle-class children. Conversely, many television programs are full of violence, and watching them may well promote aggressiveness and impatience with nonviolent resolution of disagreements in the children who watch such shows (Huesmann, et al., 2003; Murray, 2008). (We examine more research on this issue in Chapter 13.)

The second issue that people have raised about children and television regards the nature of the medium itself. Many people who have written about the potential effects

Does television viewing promote or retard cognitive development in children?

of television as a medium on children's cognitive development have concluded that the medium is generally harmful. Winn (2002) metaphorically described television and related computer technologies as the "plug-in drug" and others have argued that it dominates a child's attention to the exclusion of other developmental opportunities. Studies that actually observe children who are watching television find no such effects. Children are rarely "glued" to the television set. They look away from it between 100 and 200 times each hour (Anderson & Field, 1983). They rarely look at the screen for much more than 1 minute at a stretch. Their viewing behavior is related to program content: They tend to pay attention when they hear other children's voices, interesting sound effects, or peculiar voices, and when they see movement on the screen. They tend not to pay attention when they hear men's voices or see no signs of activity on the screen (Anderson & Lorch, 1983). If they hear certain kinds of sounds, children turn their attention away from the alternative activity and look at the screen to see whether something interesting is happening. The child is an active viewer, using the sights and sounds of the program to choose when to pay attention (Bickham, Wright, & Huston, 2001).

However, as a visual medium, television could be considered as a competitor to other behaviors that require visual attention, such as reading. Indeed, one criticism of television—that it retards children's reading achievement—has received some support. Measurements of children's reading skills before and after television became available suggested that television viewing decreased the reading skills of young children (Corteen & Williams, 1986). However, the effects were slight and were not seen in older children. Perhaps, then, television viewing does interfere with reading achievement in young children. As our parents told us when we were young, trying to read with the television on in the background is not conducive to comprehension and learning (Armstrong & Chung, 2000).

However, the possibility exists that television programs could do more to stimulate children's cognitive development. We have focused on the potential harm that may be done by watching television, not on the potential good that could be achieved through this medium. Educational programs and other shows that take into account children's developmental needs would seem to be especially conducive to the stimulation of children's imagination, creativity, language skills, and prosocial behavior. This, of course, is a hypothesis, and like the hypothesis of negative effects, would need to be empirically tested.

QUESTIONS TO CONSIDER

1. In a Question to Consider earlier in this chapter, we asked you to design a home environment that would facilitate your child's motor and perceptual development. How might you also construct that environment to facilitate your child's cognitive development? What types of toys would you give your child, and what kinds of personal interactions would you want to have with him or her?

2. Suppose that you want to develop a test for determining which of Piaget's periods of cognitive development a child is in. What kinds of activities would you include in such a test, and how would the child's behavior with respect to those activities indicate the child's stage of development?

Social Development in Infancy and Childhood

The first adults with whom infants interact are usually their parents. As many studies have shown, a close relationship called attachment is extremely important for infants' social development. **Attachment** is a social and emotional bond between infant and caregiver. It involves both the warm feelings that the parent and child have for each other and the comfort and support they provide for each other, which become especially important during times of fear or stress. This interaction must work both ways, with each participant fulfilling certain needs of the other. According to theorist John Bowlby (1907–1990), the innate capacity for the development of attachment is a part of the native endowment of many organisms (Bowlby, 1969, 1988). Bowlby and Mary Ainsworth have developed an approach that has succeeded in identifying many of the variables that influence attachment in humans (Ainsworth & Bowlby, 1991). We are going to look at what Bowlby, Ainsworth, and other researchers have learned about human attachment.

Be mindful that cultural variables strongly influence the development of attachment. Interactions between in-

---

attachment   A social and emotional bond between infant and caregiver that spans both time and space.

Attachment is the cornerstone of an infant's social development, and it has important implications for the parent's social behavior as well.

fant and parent produce different sorts of attachment behaviors that vary from culture to culture. For example, in an extensive comparison of cross-cultural attachment patterns, Harwood (Harwood, Miller, & Irizarry, 1995; Miller & Harwood, 2002) found that white American mothers want their children to be self-sustaining individuals and so emphasize independence, self-reliance, and self-confidence in their interactions with their children. In contrast, Puerto Rican mothers want their children to be polite and law-abiding, and thus stress the importance of respect, courtesy, interdependence, and tact in interacting with their children.

Behaviors of the Infant That Foster Attachment

What factors cause attachment to occur? Evidence suggests that human infants are innately able to produce special behaviors that shape and even control the behavior of their caregivers. As Bowlby (1969) noted, the most important of these behaviors are sucking, cuddling, looking, smiling, and crying.

Sucking   A baby must be able to suck to obtain milk, but not all sucking is related to nourishment. Piaget (1952) noted that infants often suck on objects even when they are not hungry. Nonnutritive sucking appears to be an innate behavioral tendency in infants that serves to inhibit a baby's distress. In modern societies, most mothers cover their breasts between feedings or feed with a bottle, so a baby's nonnutritive sucking must involve inanimate objects or the baby's own thumb.

Cuddling   Infants of all species of primates have special reflexes that encourage front-to-front contact with their mothers. For example, a baby monkey clings to its mother shortly after birth. This clinging leaves the mother free to use her hands

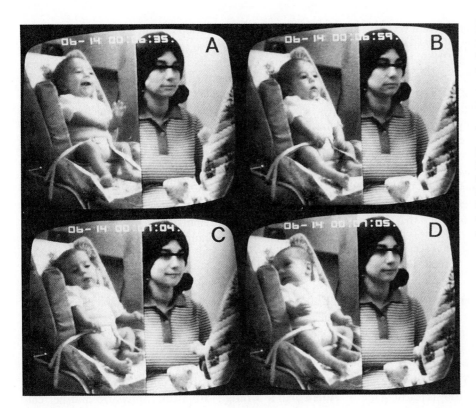

[**FIGURE 12•9**] Reaction of an infant to its mother's expressionless face. Although each panel shows mother and infant side by side, they actually faced each other. The infant greets the mother with a smile and, getting no response, eventually turns away from her.

(From Tronick, E., Als, H., Adamson, L., Wise, S., & Brazelton, T. B. The infant's response to entrapment between contradictory messages in face-to-face interaction. *Journal of the American Academy of Child Psychiatry*, 1978, 17, 1–13. Copyright © 1978 American Academy of Child Psychiatry.)

and feet. Human infants are carried by their parents and do not hold on by themselves. However, infants do adjust their posture to mold themselves to the contours of the parent's body. This cuddling response plays an important role in reinforcing the behavior of the caregiver.

Psychologist Harry Harlow (1905–1981) conducted a series of experiments on infant monkeys and showed that clinging to a soft, cuddly form appears to be an innate response (Harlow, 1974). Harlow and his colleagues isolated baby monkeys from their mothers immediately after birth and raised them alone in cages containing two mechanical surrogate mothers. One surrogate mother was made of bare wire mesh but contained a bottle that provided milk. The other surrogate was padded and covered with terry cloth but provided no nourishment.

The babies preferred to cling to the cuddly surrogate and went to the wire model only to eat. If they were frightened, they would rush to the cloth-covered model for comfort. These results suggest that close physical contact with a cuddly object is a biological need for a baby monkey, just as food and drink are. A baby monkey clings to and cuddles with its mother because the contact is innately reinforcing, not simply because she provides food.

Looking In human infants, looking serves as a signal to parents: Even very young infants seek eye-to-eye contact with their parents. If a parent does not respond when eye contact is made, the baby usually shows signs of distress. Tronick and colleagues (1978) observed face-to-face interactions between mothers and their infants. When the mothers approached their babies, they typically smiled and began talking in a gentle, high-pitched voice. In return, infants smiled and stretched their arms and legs. The mothers poked and gently jiggled their babies, making faces at them. The babies responded with facial expressions, wiggles, and noises of their own.

To determine whether the interaction was really two-sided, the researchers had each mother approach her baby while keeping her face expressionless or masklike. At first, the infant made the usual greetings, but when the mother did not respond, the infant turned away. (See FIGURE 12•9.) From time to time, the infant would look at her again, giving a brief smile, but again would turn away when the mother continued to stare without changing her expression. These interactions were recorded on videotape and were scored by raters who did not know the purpose of the experiment, so the results were not biased by the researchers' expectations.

Smiling and Imitation By the time an infant is 5 weeks old, visual stimuli begin to dominate as elicitors for smiling. A face (especially a moving one) is a more reliable elicitor of a baby's smile than a voice is; even a moving mask will cause an infant to smile. At approximately 3 months of age, specific faces—those of people to whom the infant has become attached—will elicit smiles. Furthermore, newborns and infants will often repeat the facial movements of another, suggesting the presence of an early mechanism for imitation (Lepage & Théoret, 2007). The significance of these observations should be obvious. An infant's smile is very rewarding. Almost every parent reports that parenting becomes a real joy when the baby starts to smile as the parent approaches—the infant is now a "person."

Crying   For almost any adult, the sound of an infant's crying is intensely distressing or irritating. For a baby, the event that most effectively terminates crying is being picked up and cuddled, although unless the baby is fed and made more comfortable, he or she will soon begin crying again. Because picking up the baby stops the crying, the parent learns through negative reinforcement (see Chapter 5) to pick up the infant when he or she cries. Thus, crying serves as a useful means for a cold, hungry, colicky, or wet child to obtain assistance.

Individual differences in how caregivers perceive distress in an infant's crying is an important quality that determines adult reactions and is influenced by context and expectations. Wood and Gustafson (2001), for example, found that adults responded more quickly to infant cries that they personally interpreted as communicating distress; they somewhat inhibited their response to the same cries if they believed the infant needed sleep.

Although an infant's behavioral repertoire is limited, it is apparent that a complex process is at work. At a very early age, perhaps through innate mechanisms, infants perform behaviors that their adult caregivers find reinforcing. The baby, in other words, is partially teaching the parent. From the baby's perspective, what is the object of this? Evolutionary psychologists would respond that the baby is teaching the parent to behave in ways that enhance the baby's chances to survive and eventually reproduce.

The Nature and Quality of Attachment

For an infant, the world can be a frightening place. The presence of a primary caregiver provides a baby with considerable reassurance when he or she first becomes able to explore the environment. Although the unfamiliar environment produces fear, the caregiver provides a secure base that the infant can leave from time to time to see what the world is like. Let's look at two categories of behavior that develop as infants explore their world: first, stranger anxiety and separation anxiety; and second, reactions to strange situations.

---

stranger anxiety   The wariness and fearful responses, such as crying and clinging to their caregivers, that infants exhibit in the presence of strangers.

separation anxiety   A set of fearful responses, such as crying, arousal, and clinging to the caregiver, that an infant exhibits when its caregiver attempts to leave the infant.

Strange Situation   A test of attachment in which an infant is exposed to different stimuli that may cause distress.

secure attachment   A kind of attachment in which infants use their mothers as a base for exploring a new environment. In the Strange Situation test, securely attached infants will venture out from their mothers to explore, but will return periodically.

resistant attachment   A kind of attachment in which infants show mixed reactions to their mothers. In the Strange Situation test, when mothers return after being absent, such infants may approach their mothers but at the same time may continue to cry or even push their mothers away.

avoidant attachment   As observed in the Strange Situation test, a kind of attachment in which infants avoid or ignore their mothers and often do not cuddle when held.

Stranger Anxiety and Separation Anxiety   Attachment partially reveals itself in two specific forms of infant behavior: stranger anxiety and separation anxiety. **Stranger anxiety,** which usually appears in infants between the ages of 6 and 12 months, consists of wariness and sometimes fearful responses, such as crying and clinging to their caregivers, that infants exhibit in the presence of strangers. **Separation anxiety** is a set of fearful responses, such as crying, arousal, and clinging to the caregiver, that an infant exhibits when the caregiver attempts to leave the infant. Separation anxiety first appears in infants when they are about 6 months old and generally peaks at about 15 months—a finding consistent across many cultures (Kagan, Kearsley, & Zelazo, 1978). Like stranger anxiety, separation anxiety can occur under different conditions with different degrees of intensity. For example, if an infant is used to being left in a certain environment, say a day-care center, he or she may show little or no separation anxiety (Maccoby, 1980). The same holds true for situations in which the infant is left with a sibling or other familiar person (Bowlby, 1969). However, if the same infant is left in an unfamiliar setting with unfamiliar people, he or she is likely to show separation anxiety (Bowlby, 1982). Familiarity, then, at least for infants, breeds attachment.

Ainsworth's Strange Situation   Ainsworth and her colleagues (Ainsworth, et al., 1978) developed a test of attachment based on unfamiliar situations called the **Strange Situation.** The Strange Situation consists of a series of eight episodes, during which a baby is exposed to various events that might cause some distress related to attachment and security. In different episodes of increasing stress, the researcher introduces the infant and its parent to an unfamiliar playroom and then leaves, the parent leaves and later is reunited with the infant, or a stranger enters the playroom with or without the parent present. The Strange Situation is based on the idea that if the attachment process has been successful, an infant should use his or her mother as a secure base from which to explore an unfamiliar environment. The episodes permit the observation of separation anxiety, stranger anxiety, and the baby's reactions to comforting by both the parent and the stranger.

The use of the Strange Situation led Ainsworth and her colleagues to identify three patterns of attachment; a fourth was identified later by Main and Solomon (1990).

- **Secure attachment** is the ideal pattern: The infants show a distinct preference for their caregiver over the stranger. Infants may cry when their caregiver leaves, but they stop crying and seek contact when she returns. The majority of babies form a secure attachment. Babies may also form three types of insecure attachments.

- Babies with **resistant attachment** show tension in their relations with their caregiver. Infants stay close to their caregiver before the caregiver leaves but show both approach and avoidance behaviors when the caregiver returns. Infants continue to cry for a while after their caregivers return and may even push them away.

- Infants with **avoidant attachment** generally do not cry when they are left alone, and they tend to react to strangers much as they react to their caregivers. When their caregiver returns, these infants are likely to avoid or ignore her. They tend not to cling and cuddle when they are picked up.

- Babies with **disoriented attachment** have the least quality of attachment and appear to be the most troubled. They react to their caregiver in confused and contradictory ways. They may stop crying when held, but they may show no emotion on their faces, turn their heads away from their caregiver, or become rigid. A common way of describing the emotional tone of such infants is that they appear dazed.

Although infants' personalities certainly affect the nature of their interactions with their caregivers and hence the nature of their attachment, mothers' behavior appears to be the most important factor in establishing a secure or insecure attachment (Ainsworth, et al., 1978; Pederson & Moran, 1996; Pederson, et al., 1998). Mothers of securely attached infants tend to be those who respond promptly to their crying and who are adept at handling them and responding to their needs. The babies apparently learn that their mothers can be trusted to react sensitively and appropriately. Mothers who do not modulate their responses according to their infants' own behavior—who appear insensitive to their infants' changing needs—are most likely to foster avoidant attachment. Mothers who are impatient with their infants and who seem more interested in their own activities than in interacting with their offspring tend to foster resistant attachment. Some evidence indicates that mothers who interfere with their infants' behaviors, but without sensitivity to their infants' needs, are likely to foster disoriented attachment (Carlson, 1998). Of course, mothers are not the only people who can form close attachments with infants; so do fathers (see Parke, 2000) and other adults who interact with them.

In our culture, secure attachment would seem to be more adaptive in terms of getting along with both peers and adults than would insecure attachment. It has become clear that attachment plays an influential role in social relationships, including those that we form in adolescence and adulthood, such as romantic love (Feeney & Noller, 1991). Among women, insecure attachment in infancy seems to be correlated with clinical depression and difficulties in coping with stress in adult life (Barnas, Pollina, & Cummings, 1991).

Effects of Child Day Care   This recognition of the importance of attachment inevitably leads to the question of whether child day care has deleterious effects on a child's development. In recent decades, many families have entrusted their infants to day care because both parents work. In 2004, for example, 53% of mothers of children younger than 1 year were employed outside the home (United States Department of Labor, 2005). Thus, because so many infants spend many of their waking hours away from their families, the question of the effects of day care is not simply academic.

Without question, the quality of care provided in a day-care setting is critical (Zaslow, 1991). High-quality day care

Notwithstanding the importance of attachment, high quality day care can benefit social development.

either produces no impairment of attachment or actually benefits social development (Field, 1994; Broberg, et al., 1997; National Institute of Child Health and Human Development, 1997), although it is difficult to generalize this conclusion across the full range of day-care programs available, because this latter issue is measured by correlational methods (NICHD Early Child Care Research Network, 2003). Nevertheless, high-quality day care is expensive, and not enough subsidized spaces are available for all of the families that need them. Worldwide, the day care available to low-income families is generally of lower quality than that available to middle- or upper-income families. Regrettably, the infants who receive the poorest day care tend to be members of unstable households, often headed by single mothers. Thus, they are at risk of receiving a double dose of less-than-optimal care.

Approaches to Child Rearing

Our consideration of social development has emphasized the way the child and the parents affect each other. A family, in other words, is a type of system in which the members have interacting roles. The parents provide the support for the child's attachment. However, the child also controls much of the parent's behavior through reactions that are intrinsically reinforcing. It is a developmental partnership.

As Vygotsky recognized, the child–parent partnership works best when the parent provides scaffolding for the child's development. **Scaffolding** is the matching of the mentor's efforts to the child's developmental level. For example, when teaching a child the motor skills of riding a bicycle, a mother might run alongside the child, taking her hands off the bicycle during straight segments, but helping her child do the steering. As she becomes more confident in her child's

---

disoriented attachment   As observed in the Strange Situation test, a kind of attachment in which infants behave in confused and contradictory ways toward their mothers.

scaffolding   The matching of a mentor's efforts to a child's developmental level.

ability to steer, she can reduce this help. When well practiced, scaffolding is generally the most effective form of parent–child instruction or mentoring (Meadows, 1996).

Social adjustment is a type of skill, and it is interesting to consider what types of child-rearing practices best support its development. The notion of scaffolding would imply that certain approaches to parenting will work best in the child–parent partnership. What might those approaches be?

Parents seem to adopt one of four approaches when raising their children: authoritarian, permissive, authoritative, or indifferent (Baumrind, 1983, 1991). Authoritarian parents establish firm rules and expect them to be obeyed without question. Disobedience is met with punishment. Permissive parents adopt the opposite strategy: They impose few rules and do little to influence their children's behavior. Authoritative parents also establish rules and enforce them, but not merely through punishment. Instead, they seek to explain the relation between the rules and punishment. Authoritative parents also allow exceptions to the rules. They set rules, not as absolute or inflexible laws, but rather as general behavioral guidelines. Indifferent parents exhibit a lack of interest in their children's behavior, to the point of possible neglect.

Not surprisingly, authoritarian parents tend to have children who are more unhappy and distrustful than are children of permissive or authoritative parents. You might imagine that children of permissive parents would be the most likely to be self-reliant and curious. Not so. They appear to be the least so, probably because they never received parental encouragement and guidance for developing these sorts of behaviors. Rather, they are left on their own without the benefit of learning directly from an adult's experience and without the guidance needed to learn self-control. Authoritative parents bring up their children in an environment in which individuality and personal responsibility are encouraged, and so they tend to rear children who are self-controlled, independent, and socially competent. Psychologically, then, one important element in raising happy and independent children is an open line of communication between parent and child. As you might expect, children of indifferent parents tend to be the least competent (Baumrind, 1991).

Cultural differences also seem to play a role in child rearing, as Vygotsky suggested. Children living in the United States but from Mexican families with mothers who had received limited schooling, U.S. children whose mothers' had extensive schooling, and children of Mexican families with mothers who had extensive schooling were studied to see the degree of social cooperation that would be seen when three children from each group were given a task to complete together (Mejia-Arauz et al., 2007). The task was to follow instructions for origami.

Children from Mexican families with mothers who had received limited schooling not strongly influenced by U.S. or European influences were more likely to work on the task

together than were the other groups. The U.S. children were more likely to work individually or in pairs; they were also more likely to chat more when interacting than to interact nonverbally (which was the common form of interaction in the Mexican children). The results seem to confirm studies showing that certain cultures (even children from those cultures)—such as those in Mexico—are more likely to show evidence of collaboration on a shared task.

Interactions with Peers

Although the attachment between an infant and his or her primary caregiver is the most important social interaction in early life, a child's social development also involves other people. A normal infant develops attachments with other adults, and with older siblings, if there are any. But interaction with peers—children of a similar age—is especially significant to social development. This is not attachment in the sense that we have discussed so far, because attachment depends on a caregiving relationship. At this stage, infants and children don't provide care for each other. Nevertheless, the relationships are important.

Harlow and his colleagues (e.g., Harlow, 1974) showed that social contact with peers is essential to an infant monkey's social development. An infant monkey that is raised with only a cuddly surrogate mother can still develop into a reasonably normal adult if it has peers to play with. However, an isolated monkey that does not interact with other juveniles before puberty shows severe deficits. When a previously isolated adolescent monkey is introduced to a colony of normally reared age mates, it will retreat with terror and huddle in a corner in a desperate attempt to hide.

QUESTIONS TO CONSIDER

1. We know that attachment occurs in humans and other primates. Do you think it occurs in other species, especially other mammalian species, as well? What kind of evidence would you need to collect to say that it does? Could you develop a test like Harlow's for researching attachment in other species? Develop your answer with a specific species in mind; for example, cats or dogs.

2. If there were a predisposition to certain attachment styles, when do you think it would first appear?

Development of Gender Roles

Physical development as a male or a female is only one aspect of sexual development (Bostwick & Martin, 2007). The social side of sexual development is also important. **Gender identity** is a person's private sense of being male or female and consists primarily of the person's acceptance of membership in a particular group of people: males or females. **Gender roles** are cultural expectations about the ways in which men and

---

gender identity A person's private sense of being male or female.

gender role Cultural expectations about the ways in which a male or a female should think and behave.

Many people acquire their gender identities and gender roles as a result of the gender stereotypes they learn as children.

women should think and behave. Closely related to them are **gender stereotypes**—beliefs about differences between the behaviors, abilities, and personality traits of males and females. Society's gender stereotypes have an important influence on the behavior of its members. Many people unconsciously develop their gender identity and gender roles based on gender stereotypes they learned as children. This section considers the part gender stereotypes play in influencing the nature and development of gender roles.

Berk (2005) noted that by age 3, many children perceive themselves as being a boy or a girl. At that same age, boys and girls (though girls more than boys) have a fairly good grasp

of gender roles and stereotypes (e.g., O'Brien et al., 2000). Later, in the process of learning what it means to be boys or girls, children associate some attitudes, abilities, and behaviors with one gender or the other (e.g., Jacklin & Maccoby, 1983). For example, Meelissen and Drent (2008) found that, in a sample of Dutch elementary school children, most boys felt that boys, in general, know more about computers than girls. About a third of the girls felt the same.

Where do children learn gender stereotypes? Although a child's peer group and teachers are important, parents play an especially important role in the development of gender stereotypes (Deaux, 1999). Parents tend to encourage and reward their sons for playing with "masculine" toys such as cars and trucks and objects such as baseballs and footballs (Fagot and Hagan, 1991) and encourage baby boys to generate gross motor activity, whereas they are more soothing and calming with baby girls (Smith and Lloyd, 1978). Parents also tend to encourage and reward their daughters for engaging in "feminine" activities that promote dependence, warmth and sensitivity, such as playing house or hosting a make-believe tea party (Dunn, Bretherton, & Munn, 1987; Lytton and Romney, 1991). Parents who do not encourage or reward these kinds of stereotypical activity tend to have children whose attitudes and behavior reflect fewer sex stereotypes (Weisner & Wilson-Mitchell, 1990).

In supposedly "masculine" academic subjects, girls are perceived as performing less well than boys. Many reasons have been suggested for the discrepancy, but one of the most frequently cited is socialization: that is, parents and teachers are more likely to engage boys in science and scientific explanations than they are girls.

In an ingenious experiment to test this hypothesis, Crowley et al. (2001) sought the permission of parents visiting a Californian children's museum to film and record their interactions with their children as they made their way around the exhibitions. Data were collected from 298 interactions between mothers and fathers and their daughters and sons on 26 days over a 30-month period. Conversations were rated according to whether they involved explanations, descriptions of, or directions for exhibitions.

The researchers found that parents were more likely to explain exhibits to their sons than to their daughters. If the behavior of parents helps shape the behavior of their children, the researchers suggest that this disparity could have a significant effect on the child's interest in and knowledge of science.

The Nature of Gender Differences

The origin and nature of gender differences has long been and is likely to continue to be a controversial topic in psychology (Shibley Hyde & Plant, 1995; Eagly & Wood, 1999; Wood & Eagly, 2002). Consider the following case of D.R., which illustrates how complex the issue is.

---

gender stereotypes Beliefs about differences in the behaviors, abilities, and personality traits of males and females.

[**CASE STUDY**] D.R. was born as the elder of two identical twin boys. When he was 8 months of age, he underwent what was to have been routine circumcision to correct a urinary problem. Tragically, the surgery went horribly wrong, and D.R.'s penis was physically destroyed. D.R. would not be able to live as a normal boy.

In their efforts to come to grips with this accident, D.R.'s parents sought medical and psychological advice on how best to raise their son. They accepted the rather controversial advice that D.R.'s sex should be reassigned by removing his testes and raising him as a girl. This program of surgical and psychological therapy had been performed on intersex individuals (those both with sexual characteristics that are not phenotypically male or female), but its use on a unambiguous boy was experimental.

For 14 years, D.R.'s parents tried to raise him as a girl. The physicians and therapists who had developed this protocol could compare D.R.'s development with that of his twin brother. Many of their reports during this time were interpreted to show that D.R.'s upbringing had successfully acculturated him to be, psychologically, a girl.

The reality, apparently, was quite different. As a child, D.R. was not told of what had been done to him, but he remembers never feeling comfortable as a girl. He was teased in school and reacted strongly with physical aggression. Although he would wear feminine clothing to please his mother, he never felt comfortable in it. When asked by his therapists to envision his future, he would imagine himself as an adult male. He prided himself on being able to dominate his twin brother and would adopt the role of the protector. Throughout his childhood, he preferred to urinate standing up.

D.R.'s childhood and early adolescence were marked by his steadfast resistance to acting the gender role of a girl. Faced with his obvious unhappiness with his life, his parents told him the truth when he was 14. The news actually came as a relief to D.R., because he had been dreading the demands that puberty would bring; he decided immediately that he wanted to revert to the sex of his birth. In the subsequent years, he became popular, as a young man, with peers of both sexes. Within 10 years, D.R. would marry and become a stepfather with three children.

Part of the controversy over gender differences stems from the way differences between males and females are measured and the apparent magnitude of those differences, and part of it stems from the sociopolitical implications of the differences (for example, sexism). Berk (2005) reviewed the research on gender differences and concluded that the most reliable differences are the following: On average, girls show earlier verbal development, more effective expression and interpretation of emotional cues, and a higher tendency to comply with adults and peers. Boys show stronger spatial abilities, more aggression, and greater tendency toward risk taking. Boys also are more likely to show developmental problems such as language disorders, behavior problems, or physical impairments.

These differences are unlikely to be wholly biologically determined. Socialization undoubtedly has a strong influence.

Gender differences for many psychological characteristics are small. For example, after reviewing scores obtained from the Wechsler Intelligence Scales and the California Achievement Tests between 1949 and 1985, Feingold (1993). concluded that cognitive gender differences were small or nonexistent in preadolescent children and small in adolescents. Deaux (1985) reported that, on average, only 5% of the variability in individual differences among children can be attributed to gender; the other 95% is due to individual genetic and environmental factors. Therefore, gender, by itself, is not a very good predictor of a person's talents, personality, or behavior.

Children readily learn gender stereotypes and adopt the roles that society deems appropriate for their gender. Two causes—biology and culture—may be responsible.

Biological Causes A likely site of biologically determined gender differences is the brain. Studies using laboratory animals have shown that the exposure of a developing brain to male sex hormones has long-term effects. The hormones alter the development of the brain and produce changes in the animals' behavior, even in adulthood (Carlson, 2005; Bostwick & Martin, 2007). In addition, the human brain shows some structural gender differences. These, too, are probably caused by exposure to different patterns of hormones during development (Kolb & Stewart, 1995), although the precise effects of these differences on the behavior of males and females are not well understood at present. As well, investigations using *f*MRI techniques show

a   Women minus men

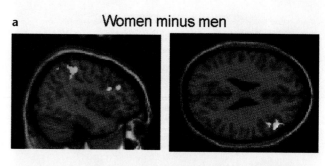

b   Men minus women

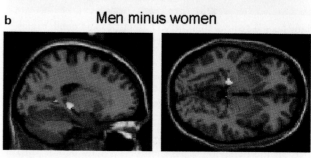

Men and women show different patterns of brain activity during navigation of a virtual maze. Women show greater activity than men in right hemispheric structures (bright areas in top photos) and men show greater activity than women in the left hippocampus (bright areas in bottom photos).

(Grön, G., Wunderlich, A. P., Spitzer, M., Tomczak, R., & Riepe, M. W. (2000). Brain activation during human navigation: Gender different neural networks as substrate of performance. *Nature Neuroscience, 3,* 404–408.)

neural activation differences between men and women during navigation in a virtual maze; men show greater activation of the left hippocampus, and women show greater involvement of right hemispheric structures (Grön et al., 2000).

Gender differences in two types of cognitive ability—verbal ability and spatial ability—may be at least partly caused by differences in the brain. Girls tend to learn to speak and to read sooner than boys, and boys tend to be better at tasks requiring spatial perception. Kimura (1999) suggested possible reasons for these sex differences. When the human brain was evolving into its present form, our ancestors were hunter–gatherers, and men and women probably had different roles. Women, because of restrictions on their movements imposed by childbearing, were more likely to work near the home, performing fine manual skills with small objects. Men were more likely to range farther from home, engaging in activities that involved coordination of body movements with respect to distant objects, such as throwing rocks or spears or launching darts toward animals. In addition, men had to be able to keep track of where they were so they could return home after following animals for long distances.

According to Ecuyer-Dab and Robert (2004), however, this dichotomy suggests that rather than showing a superior spatial advantage by men over women, it shows how context can affect the way in which each sex expresses its specific spatial skills: spatial cognition in men would be used to navigate the environment for a mate and food, whereas women's spatial cognition developed to deal with the immediate environment because they were more concerned with the survival of their offspring in the home. They, therefore, had no need to develop the navigational spatial skills that men did. In short, men developed and evolved large-scale navigation mechanisms, and women evolved small-scale ones. Ecuyer-Dab and Robert cited evidence from recent studies to support the hypothesis. Women, for example, were more likely than men to use landmarks when giving map directions. Men were more likely to provide more detail on direction and distance; although women are capable of doing this, they simply do not use these references as their primary source of information.

If the evolutionary reasoning is correct, it is possible to see why, on average, men's spatial abilities would be expressed differently from those of women. But why would females learn to speak and read sooner than males? Many researchers believe that our ancestors used hand gestures long before verbal communication developed. Kimura suggests that fine motor control and speech production are closely related—that the neural circuits that control the muscles we use for speech may be closely related to those we use to move our hands. Presumably, then, women would be better at both.

Buss (1995) argued that other differences in the adaptive challenges that men and women have faced in the course of evolution also have led to gender differences. As you learned in Chapter 3, chief among these adaptive challenges are issues tied to reproduction. For women, such challenges include identifying and attracting a mate who is willing to invest his resources (time, energy, property, food, and so on) in her and her children. For men, they include identifying and attracting a fertile mate who is willing to copulate with him. Buss argued that over the course of evolution, men and women have come to differ because the challenges posed by reproduction and child rearing require different strategies for their successful resolution.

Kimura's and Buss's accounts are based on evolutionary arguments that can be tested only indirectly. However, they provide a good example of the biological approach—in particular, the functional, evolutionary approach—to an understanding of human behavior.

Cultural Causes Although evolutionary forces may have laid the groundwork for gender differences in brain mechanisms associated with verbal ability and spatial ability, practice at and training in tasks involving these abilities can improve people's performance at them (Hoyenga & Hoyenga, 1993). Most psychologists believe that socialization plays the most significant role in the establishment of gender role differences. First adults and then peers teach, by direct instruction and by example, what is expected of boys and girls. These expectations are deeply ingrained in our culture and unconsciously affect our perceptions and our behavior.

The effect of gender on an adult's perception of infants is clear and has been confirmed in many studies. What about differences in the behaviors adults direct toward boys and girls? The strongest difference in the way parents socialize their sons and daughters appears to lie in their encouragement of gender-typed play and their choice of "gender-appropriate" toys. Many parents encourage their boys to play with trucks, blocks, and other toys that can be manipulated; they encourage their girls to play with dolls. However, a cross-cultural review of 172 studies conducted in North America, Australia, and Western Europe concluded that parents do not consistently treat their sons and daughters differently in any other important ways (Lytton & Romney, 1991).

Although parents do encourage "gender-appropriate" play, evidence suggests that biological factors may play an initial role in children's preferences. Although fathers are less likely to give dolls to 1-year-old boys than to 1-year-old girls, the boys who do receive the dolls are less likely to play with them (Snow, Jacklin, & Maccoby, 1983). Perhaps, as Lytton and Romney (1991) suggest, adults' expectations and encouragement build on children's innate tendencies, producing an amplifying effect. Then, because boys' toys provide more opportunity for developing motor skills, spatial skills, and inventiveness, and girls' toys provide more opportunity for nurturance and social exchange, some important differences in gender roles may become established.

Once children begin to play with other children outside the home, peers have a significant influence on the development of their gender roles. Stern and Karraker (1989) found that the behavior of 2- to 6-year-old children toward a baby was influenced by the children's knowledge of the baby's gender even more than was the behavior of adults. By the time children are 3 years old, they reinforce gender-typed play by praising, imitating, or joining the behavior. In contrast, they criticize gender-inappropriate behavior (Langlois & Downs, 1980).

Of course, the research cited in this section describes tendencies of parents and children to act in a particular way. Some parents make a conscious attempt to encourage their children's interest in both "masculine" and "feminine" activities, with the hope that doing so will help keep all opportunities for achievement and self-expression open to them, regardless of their gender.

QUESTIONS TO CONSIDER

1. Can you imagine an alternative course of human evolution in which gender roles would have developed along different lines? What events in the course of human evolution could have happened (but did not, of course) that would have changed the nature of gender roles as we know them today?

2. Imagine that you were born the opposite gender—that instead of being a male, you are a female, or vice versa. In what significant ways would your life be different? For example, in what important ways would your social, emotional, and intellectual experiences be different? (Be careful not to base your answer on stereotypes you have of the other gender.)

Moral Development

The word *morality* comes from a Latin word that means "custom." Moral behavior is behavior that conforms to a generally acknowledged set of rules. With very few exceptions, by the time a person reaches adulthood, the person has accepted his or her culture's rules about personal and social behavior. These rules vary in different cultures and may take the form of codified laws or of informally accepted taboos (Chasdi, 1994). Moral reasoning is the way these rules are used cognitively. Consequently, a close relation exists between moral reasoning and cognitive development. Let us begin our look at moral development by considering the way a child acquires a concept of morality. The pioneer in this field, as in cognitive development, was Jean Piaget.

Piaget's Theory of Moral Development

According to Piaget, the first stage of moral development (ages 5 to 10 years) is **moral realism,** which is characterized by egocentrism, or self-centeredness, and blind adherence to rules. Egocentric children can evaluate events only in terms of their personal consequences. The behavior of children at this stage is not guided by the effects it might have on someone

---

moral realism The first stage of Piaget's model of moral development, which includes egocentrism and blind adherence to rules.

morality of cooperation The second stage of Piaget's model of moral development, which involves the recognition of rules as social conventions.

else, because young children are not capable of imagining themselves in the other person's place. Thus, in Piaget's view, young children do not consider whether an act is right or wrong but only whether it is likely to have good or bad consequences for them personally. Punishment is a bad consequence, and the fear of punishment is the only real moral force at this age. A young child also believes that rules come from parents (or other authority figures, such as older children or God) and that rules cannot be changed.

As children mature, however, two changes occur. First, older children judge an act by the intentions of the actor as well as by the consequences of the act—unlike young children, who consider only an act's objective outcomes, not the subjective intent that lay behind the act. For example, Piaget told children two stories, one about John, who accidentally broke 15 cups, and another about Henry, who broke 1 cup while trying to do something that was forbidden to him. When young children were asked which of the two boys was the naughtiest, they said that John was, because he broke 15 cups. They did not take into account the fact that the act was entirely accidental, as more mature individuals would.

Second, as children mature cognitively, they become less egocentric. Their lack of egocentrism makes them more capable of empathy. Children who are no longer egocentric (older than age 7) can imagine how another person feels. This shift away from egocentrism means that children's behavior may be guided not merely by the effects their actions have on the children themselves but also by the effects they have on others. At around 10 years of age, children enter Piaget's second stage of moral development, **morality of cooperation.** During this stage, rules become more flexible; the child is more empathic but also understands that many rules (such as those that govern games) are social conventions that may be altered by mutual consent.

Kohlberg's Theory of Moral Development

Piaget's description of moral development was considerably elaborated on by the psychologist Lawrence Kohlberg (1927–1987). Kohlberg studied boys between 10 and 17 years of age over the course of several years. He presented the children with stories involving moral dilemmas. For example, one story described a man named Heinz whose wife was dying of a cancer that could be treated only by a medication discovered by a druggist living in the same town. The man could not afford the price demanded by the druggist, so the distraught man broke into the druggist's store and stole enough of the drug to save his wife's life. The boys were asked what Heinz should have done and why he should have done it. On the basis of his research, Kohlberg decided that moral development progressed through three levels, which he divided into seven stages. (See TABLE 12•3.)

[TABLE 12·3] Levels and Stages of Kohlberg's Theory of Moral Development

Level and Stage	Highlights
Preconventional Level	
Stage 1: Morality of punishment and obedience	Avoidance of punishment
Stage 2: Morality of naive instrumental hedonism	Egocentric perspective; weighing of potential risks and benefits
Conventional Level	
Stage 3: Morality of maintaining good relations	Morality based on approval from others
Stage 4: Morality of maintaining social order	Morality defined by rules and laws
Postconventional Level	
Stage 5: Morality of social contracts	Recognition that societal rules are for the common good, although individual rights sometimes outweigh laws
Stage 6: Morality of universal ethical principles	Perception of societal laws and rules as based on ethical values
Stage 7: Morality of cosmic orientation	Adoption of values that transcend societal norms

Although Kohlberg's theory is a stage theory like Piaget's, it is less tied to a specific age. Moral development involves a sequence, so that early stages are more characteristic of children, and later stages tend to characterize adults. However, what is important is the progression of stages rather than any particular age at which a stage might appear. Kohlberg's first two stages belong to the **preconventional level,** during which morality is externally defined. During stage 1, morality of punishment and obedience, children blindly obey authority and avoid punishment. When asked to decide what Heinz should do, children at this stage base their decisions on fears about Heinz's being punished for letting his wife die or for committing a crime. During stage 2, morality of naive instrumental hedonism, children make moral choices egocentrically, guided by the pleasantness or unpleasantness of the consequences of a behavior. Heinz's dilemma is reduced to a weighing of the probable risks and benefits of stealing the drug.

The next two stages belong to the **conventional level,** which includes an understanding that the social system has an interest in people's behavior. During stage 3, morality of maintaining good relations, children want to be regarded by people who know them as good, well-behaved children. Moral decisions are based on perceived social pressure; so either Heinz should steal the drug because people would otherwise regard him as heartless, or he should not steal it because they would regard him as a criminal. During stage 4, morality of maintaining social order, laws and moral rules are perceived as in-

struments for maintaining social order and, as such, must be obeyed. Thus, both protecting a life and respecting people's property are seen as rules that help maintain social order.

Kohlberg also described a final level of moral development—the **postconventional level,** during which people realize that moral rules reflect important underlying principles that apply to all situations and societies. During stage 5, morality of social contracts, people recognize that rules are social contracts, that not all authority figures are infallible, and that individual rights can sometimes take precedence over laws. During stage 6, morality of universal ethical principles, people perceive rules and laws as being justified by abstract ethical values, such as the value of human life and the value of dignity. In stage 7, the morality of cosmic orientation, people adopt values that transcend societal norms as they grapple with issues such as "why be moral at all?" This stage represents the zenith of moral development. As Kohlberg noted, only a very few people—perhaps the prophets of major religions—ever reach stage 7. Kohlberg believed that not all people reach the postconventional level of moral development.

Evaluation of Piaget's and Kohlberg's Theories of Moral Development

Piaget's and Kohlberg's theories have greatly influenced research on moral development, but they also have come under some criticism. For example, Piaget's research indicated that children in the first stage (moral realism) respond to the magnitude of a transgression rather than to the intent behind it; even adults respond to the magnitude of a transgression, and rightly so. The theft of a few postage stamps by an office worker is not treated in the same way as the embezzlement of hundreds of thousands of dollars.

Kohlberg's conclusions also have been challenged. For example, Carpendale (2000) points out that it is not uncommon for people to perform at less than their highest level of achieved moral reasoning, although Kohlberg believed that people would use lower levels only if extreme conditions undermined their higher moral sense. Many researchers agree with Rest (1979), who concluded that Kohlberg's "stages" are not coherent entities but do describe a progression in the ability of children to engage in more and more complex moral reasoning.

---

preconventional level Kohlberg's first level of moral development, which bases moral behavior on external sanctions such as authority and punishment.

conventional level Kohlberg's second level of moral development, in which people realize that a society has instituted moral rules to maintain order and to serve the best interests of members of the society.

postconventional level Kohlberg's third and final level of moral development, in which people come to understand that moral rules include principles that apply across all situations and societies.

Laticia's parents are going away for the weekend and ask her to go with them. Laticia, who is 15 years old, says that she can't go because she has a special soccer practice on Saturday. Disappointed, her parents accept her answer; they agree to let her stay home, because they know how important soccer is to her. Later, after they return, they learn that Laticia lied to them about the practice. When they confront her, she tells them that she knows that she lied to them but that she did it so as not to hurt their feelings—she really did not want to go away with them for the weekend. Laticia's parents say that they understand her dilemma, but that they feel they must punish her anyway for breaking an important family rule. How do you suppose that Piaget and Kohlberg would explain Laticia's level of morality? How would they explain her parents' level of morality?

Adolescence

After childhood comes adolescence, the threshold to adulthood. (In Latin, *adolescere* means "to grow up.") The transition between childhood and adulthood is as much social as it is biological. In some societies, people are considered to be adults as soon as they are sexually mature, at which time they may assume adult rights and responsibilities, including marriage. In most industrialized societies, in which formal education often continues into the late teens and early 20s, adulthood officially comes several years later. The end of adolescence is difficult to judge, because the line between adolescence and young adulthood is fuzzy: no distinct physical changes mark this transition. In this section, we explore the physical, social, and cognitive changes that mark the adolescent years.

Physical Development

Puberty (from the Latin *puber*, meaning "adult"), the period during which people's reproductive systems mature, marks the beginning of the transition from childhood to adulthood. Many physical changes occur during this stage: People reach their ultimate height, develop increased muscle size and body hair, and become capable of reproduction.

Sexual Maturation   The internal sex organs and genitalia do not change much for several years after birth, but they begin to develop again at puberty. When boys and girls reach about 11 to 14 years of age, their testes or ovaries secrete hormones that begin the process of sexual maturation. This activity of the gonads is initiated by the hypothalamus, the part of the brain to which the pituitary gland is attached. The hypothalamus instructs the pituitary gland to secrete hormones, which in turn stimulate the gonads to secrete sex hormones. These sex hormones act on various organs of the body and initiate the changes that accompany sexual maturation.

The sex hormones secreted by the gonads cause growth and maturation of the external genitalia and of the gonads themselves. In addition, these hormones cause the maturation of ova and the production of sperm. All of these structures are considered primary sex characteristics, because they are essential to the ability to reproduce. The sex hormones also stimulate the development of secondary sex characteristics, the physical changes that distinguish males from females. Before puberty, boys and girls look much the same—except, perhaps, for their hairstyles and clothing. At puberty, adolescent males' testes begin to secrete testosterone; this hormone causes their muscles to develop, their facial hair to grow, and their voices to deepen. Females' ovaries secrete estradiol, the most important estrogen, or female sex hormone. Estradiol causes women's breasts to grow and their pelvises to widen, and it produces changes in the layer of fat beneath the skin and in the texture of the skin itself.

Development of the adult secondary sex characteristics takes several years, and not all characteristics develop at the same time. The process begins in girls at around age 11. The first visible change is the accumulation of fatty tissue around the nipples, followed shortly by the growth of pubic hair. The spurt of growth in height commences, and the uterus and vagina begin to enlarge. The first menstrual period, menarche, begins at around age 12 on average—at about the time a girl's rate of growth in height begins to decline. In boys, sexual maturation begins slightly later. The first visible event is the growth of the testes and scrotum, followed by the appearance of pubic hair. A few months later, the penis begins to grow, and the spurt of growth in height starts. The larynx grows larger, which causes the voice to become lower. Sexual maturity in males occurs at around age 15. The growth of facial hair usually occurs later; often a full beard does not grow until the late teens or early 20s.

Behavioral Effects of Puberty   The changes that accompany sexual maturation have a profound effect on young people's behavior and self-concept. They become more sensitive about their appearance. Many girls worry about their weight and the size of their breasts and hips. Many boys worry about their height, the size of their genitals, their muscular development, and the growth of their beards. In addition, most adolescents display a particular form of egocentrism that develops early in the transition into the stage of formal operations: self-consciousness. Some developmental psychologists believe that self-consciousness results from teenagers' difficulty in distinguishing their own self-perceptions from the views other people have of them, although the evidence for this is not conclusive (Vartanian, 2000).

Because the onset of puberty occurs at different times in different individuals, young adolescents can find themselves more or less mature than some of their friends, and this difference can have important social consequences. An early study by Jones and Bayley (1950) found that early-maturing boys tended also to become more socially mature and were most likely to be

---

puberty   The period during which people's reproductive systems mature, marking the beginning of the transition from childhood to adulthood.

perceived as leaders by their peers. Late-maturing boys tended to become hostile and withdrawn and often engaged in negative attention-getting behavior. Later studies have generally confirmed these findings (Peterson, 1985; Brooks-Gunn, 1988). The effect of age of maturity in girls is less clear. Some studies indicate that early-maturing girls may benefit from higher status and prestige; but they also are more likely to engage in norm-breaking behaviors such as stealing, cheating on exams, staying out late, and using alcohol (Brooks-Gunn, 1989). Brooks-Gunn suggested that the primary cause of the norm-breaking behaviors is the fact that early-maturing girls are more likely to become friends with older girls.

Cognitive Development

The techniques described in Chapter 4, such as functional magnetic resonance imaging (fMRI), have enabled researchers to how the brain develops as individuals become adolescents. Giedd et al. (1999) compared the development of the brains of people as they aged from age 4 to 20 years, at 2-year intervals, by using magnetic resonance imaging. They found that white matter increased steadily over time, but the development of gray matter was slightly more irregular. Recall from Chapter 4 that gray matter is made up of blood vessels and neurons, whereas white matter is made up of nerve fibers. The development of gray matter peaked just before adolescence and occurred in specific regions of the brain. Frontal and parietal lobe development peaked at 12 and 16 years, respectively, but occipital lobe development continued to 20 years. Although the initial sample was large ($N = 145$), the number of individuals who underwent more than three scans was only 33, which suggests caution in interpreting the results; nevertheless, the results do suggest that development in some form continues past adolescence to adulthood. How is this brain development reflected in behavior? As Piaget saw it, adolescents' cognitive changes were based on the logical power of abstract reasoning. In late childhood, said Piaget, a child entered the stage of formal operations. Adolescence, then, should be characterized as a sort of Sherlock Holmesian phase in which adolescents apply deductive skills to problems. Certainly evidence exists that this period of development is marked by increased facility with the tools of formal reasoning (Morris & Sloutsky, 2002). However, as we saw in Chapter 11, formal logic does not necessarily dominate adult thinking, let alone that of adolescents. We use heuristics, biases, and mental models in place of, or as supplements to, formal logic. The prevalence of these strategies for reasoning has led some investigators (e.g., Klaczynski, 2004) to suggest that two reasoning systems exist: an analytic processing system and an experiential processing system. The **analytic processing system** is the basis of deliberate, abstract, and higher-order reasoning. It provides the capacity to remove a problem from its context and to apply logical rules to solve it. The **experiential processing system,** conversely, is rapid, mostly unconscious, and heuristic. It provides the memories for particular solutions to problems and forms the basis for the biases and stereotypes that we may apply to problems.

Adolescence may be the time at which we not only develop our analytic abilities but also become good at knowing when they must be used. The two systems give us a large number of reasoning tools, which work in some cases but not in all. Thus, cognitive development during adolescence is marked by choice: The individual shows increased capacity to select consciously the mode of reasoning appropriate to the context (Keating, 2004).

Social Development

During adolescence, a person's behavior and social roles change dramatically. As a child, a person is dependent on parents, teachers, and other adults. As an adolescent, he or she is expected to assume more responsibility. Relations with peers also suddenly change; teenagers begin to have romantic attachments. Adolescence is not simply a continuation of childhood, then; it marks a real transition from the dependency of childhood to the relative independence of adulthood. Adolescence is also a period during which many young people seek out new experiences and engage in reckless behavior—behavior that involves psychological, physical, and legal risks for them as well as for others, such as driving too fast, having unprotected sex, or using illegal drugs. These behaviors often reflect the great challenges teenagers face as they search for an identity, focus on self-perceptions, cope with their emerging sexuality, and adjust to new relationships with peers and parents.

Forming an Identity Erik Erikson, a psychoanalyst who studied with Anna Freud, Sigmund Freud's daughter, developed a theory of psychosocial development that divides human development into eight stages. Erikson proposed that people encounter a series of crises or conflicts in their social relations with other people and that the way these conflicts are resolved

The transition between childhood and adulthood is as much social as it is biological.

---

analytic processing system   The basis of deliberate, abstract, and higher-order reasoning.

experiential processing system   The basis of rapid, mostly unconscious, and heuristic reasoning.

[TABLE 12.4] Erikson's Eight Stages of Psychosocial Development

PERIOD	STAGE	OUTCOME	
		Positive Resolution	**Negative Resolution**
Childhood	1. Crisis of trust vs. mistrust 2. Crisis of autonomy vs. self-doubt 3. Crisis of initiative vs. guilt 4. Crisis of competence vs. inferiority	Trust, security, confidence, independence, curiosity, competence, industry	Insecurity, doubt, guilt, low self-esteem, sense of failure
Adolescence	5. Crisis of identity vs. role confusion	Strong sense of self-identity	Weak sense of self
Adulthood	6. Crisis of intimacy vs. isolation 7. Crisis of generativity vs. stagnation 8. Crisis of integrity vs. despair	Capacity to develop deep and meaningful relationships and care for others; consideration for future generations; personal sense of worth and satisfaction	Isolation, unhappiness, selfishness, stagnancy, sense of failure and regret

determines the nature of development. According to Erikson, the resolution of these conflicts is development. If a given conflict is resolved positively, the outcome is happy; if it is not resolved or is resolved negatively, the outcome is unhealthy and impairs development. Because the nature of people's social relations changes throughout life, their psychosocial development does not end when they become adults. TABLE 12.4 lists Erikson's eight stages of development, the nature of the crisis that defines each stage, and the possible consequences.

Erikson argued that the primary crisis faced by adolescents is identity versus role confusion. If young people are able to develop plans for accomplishing career and personal goals and to decide which social groups they belong to, they have formed a personal identity. Failure to form an identity leaves a teenager confused about his or her role in life. You have probably heard the term "identity crisis," as in "She's having an identity crisis." Erikson coined this phrase.

Erikson's concept of the identity crisis has been researched extensively by Marcia (1980, 1994; Bradley & Marcia, 1998), who asserted that developing an identity consists of two components, crisis and commitment. Marcia defines a crisis as a period during which an adolescent struggles intellectually to resolve issues related to personal values and goals. For example, a teenager who questions his or her parents' religious and moral values is experiencing a crisis. Commitment is a decision based on consideration of alternative values and goals that leads to a specific course of action. For instance, a teenager who decides to go to a different religious institution than his or her parents is said to make a commitment. In this case, the teenager also is said to identify with the beliefs of that institution.

Marcia hypothesized that adolescents experience different degrees and combinations of crisis and commitment. Some teenagers never experience crises, and others do but may never resolve them. Marcia developed four main possibilities, which he called identity statuses. (See FIGURE 12.10.) As shown in the figure, in Marcia's model, adolescents who experience a crisis, consider alternative solutions to it, and are committed to a course of action based on personal values are said to be identity achievers. Identity achievers are self-confident and have a

high level of moral development (Dellas & Jernigan, 1990). Adolescents who experience a crisis but do not resolve it and therefore cannot become committed are said to be in moratorium. Teenagers who are in moratorium will express doubts about an identity but are still seeking information regarding it. Adolescents who have not experienced a crisis but who are nonetheless committed to a course of action are said to be in foreclosure. Teenagers in foreclosure are typically adolescents who identify strongly with people such as their parents and never consider alternatives to those identities. They can be dogmatic in their views and may feel threatened by others who challenge their identities (Frank, Pirsch, & Wright, 1990). Adolescents who do not experience a crisis and who do not become committed are said to experience identity diffusion. Because they have not considered alternative courses of action and made a decision, teenagers who are identity diffused, especially over a long period, tend to be immature and impulsive and to have a sense of hopelessness about the future (Archer & Waterman, 1990). Erikson would probably have considered these people identity confused.

Marcia's research has shown that adolescents move in and out of the different statuses as they experience new situ-

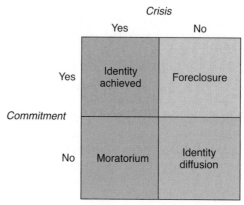

[FIGURE 12.10] Marcia's four identity statuses. Different combinations of crises and commitment yield four different identity statuses.

ations and crises. A teenager does not necessarily move progressively from one status to another. For example, after thinking about whether to major in business or engineering, a college student may decide on engineering because she thinks that she will like the work and earn good money. In terms of this decision, she is an identity achiever. However, after taking several engineering courses, she may decide that she really doesn't like engineering after all. Now she must decide whether to keep her major or to change it. She is now no longer committed; she is in moratorium.

Marcia's research is interesting for two reasons. First, it shows that most adolescents do indeed experience crises in their search for an identity—although "crisis" may be too strong a word for it, as many teens resolve its challenges without stress. Second, it shows that a teenager's psychological reaction to a crisis depends on the time at which he or she is dealing with it. That four possible avenues can be involved in achieving an identity testifies to the complexity of "finding oneself."

Identity and Self-Perception The search for a personal identity brings with it changes in self-concept and self-esteem (Berk, 2005). During childhood, children tend to perceive themselves in terms of both physical traits, such as "I am a boy and have brown hair and blue eyes," and individual personality characteristics, such as "I am honest" or "I am smart" (Damon & Hart, 1992). During adolescence, teenagers become more focused on their social relationships and tend to perceive themselves more in terms of their interactions with others. They may use phrases such as "I am outgoing" or "I am trustworthy" to describe themselves. In late adolescence, teenagers begin to perceive themselves more in terms of the values that they hold. They may now describe themselves in terms of their political, social, or philosophical views, as in "I am a conservative" or "I am an environmentalist." As a teenager strives to develop an identity, earlier self-perceptions, including those held during childhood, are incorporated into his or her emerging self-concept. Newer self-perceptions do not merely replace older ones. Instead, the newer ones augment the older ones.

Sexuality Sexuality was always a part of life (after all, our species has managed to propagate during all periods of history), but since the latter part of the 20th century, it has become much more open and evident than it was previously— and this is notably the case among adolescents. With so many examples of adult sexual behaviors given them, it is not surprising that adolescents adopt sexuality as part of their identity. According to the Centers for Disease Control and Prevention, 30% of female teens between the ages of 15 and 17 have had sexual intercourse; 31% of male teens of this age also reported having experienced sex (Abma, et al., 2004).

Of course, a possible consequence of sexuality is that adolescents may find themselves becoming parents. Statistics from a 2005 survey found that, among sexually active 9th through 12th grade students, 44% of female and 30% of male students

reported that a condom was not used during their last sexual intercourse (Centers for Disease Control and Prevention, 2006). Preliminary data for 2006 in the United States showed that the birth rate among women 15 to 19 years of age was 41.9 births per 1,000 women (Hamilton, Martin, & Ventura, 2007).

Relations with Parents As adolescents begin to define their new roles and to assert them, they almost inevitably come into conflict with their parents. However, research indicates that most of the differences between people of different generations are in style rather than in substance. Adolescents and their parents tend to have similar values and personal ideals (Zentner & Renaud, 2007). Unless serious problems occur, family conflicts tend to be provoked by relatively minor issues, such as messy rooms, loud music, clothes, curfews, and household chores. These problems tend to begin around the time of puberty; if puberty occurs particularly early or late, so does the conflict (Paikoff & Brooks-Gunn, 1991).

QUESTIONS TO CONSIDER

1. What important behavioral effects did you experience as a result of your own sexual maturation? In what ways did your social and emotional lives change? How does your experience compare with those of your friends who underwent puberty before or after you did?
2. It is often said (by adults) that adolescents act as if they are incapable of properly judging risk. Do you think this is true? Could this be related to the different types of identity resolutions discussed by Marcia?

Adulthood and Old Age

It is much easier to outline child or adolescent development than adult development; children and adolescents change faster, and the changes are closely related to age. Adult development is much more variable. Physical changes in adults are more gradual. Mental and emotional changes during adulthood are more closely related to individual experience than to age. In the social realm, some people achieve success and satisfaction with their careers; others hate their jobs. Some marry and have happy family lives; others never adjust to the roles of spouse and parent. No single description of adult development will fit everyone.

Physical Development

As we grow older, we can count on one set of changes— physical alterations. Our physical abilities peak at around age 30 and decline gradually thereafter. By maintaining a well-balanced diet, exercising regularly, and not smoking, drinking, or using drugs, we can, in large measure, help our bodies maintain some of their physical vigor even into old age. This is not to say that good diet and exercise habits can make a

Loss of physical ability during adulthood can be minimized by following a program of regular exercise.

70-year-old look and feel like a 25-year-old, but if we don't eat well and exercise regularly, we will have less physical energy and poorer muscle tone than if we do. Apparently, staying in shape as a younger adult pays off in later life. Older people who were physically fit as younger adults are generally in better health and feel better about themselves than do those who weren't (Perlmutter & Hall, 1995).

Unfortunately, though, even prudent diets and exercising cannot reverse the physical changes that accompany aging. People in their later 40s, 50s, and 60s often experience decreases in visual acuity and in depth perception, hearing, sensitivity to odors and flavors, reaction time, agility, physical mobility, and physical strength.

Muscular strength peaks during the late 20s or early 30s and then declines slowly thereafter as muscle tissue gradually deteriorates. By age 70, strength has declined by approximately 30% in both men and women (Young, Stokes, & Crowe, 1984). However, age has much less of an effect on endurance than on strength. Both laboratory tests and athletic records reveal that older people who remain physically fit show remarkably little decline in the ability to exercise for extended periods (Spirduso & MacRae, 1990).

Although it is easy to measure a decline in the sensory systems (such as vision or hearing), older people often show very little functional change in these systems. Most people learn to make adjustments for their sensory losses, using additional cues to help them decode sensory information. For example, people with hearing loss can learn to attend more carefully to other people's gestures and lip movements; they also can profitably use their experience to infer what is said.

Functional changes with age are also minimal in highly developed skills. For example, Salthouse (1984, 1988) found that experienced older typists continued to perform as well as younger ones, despite the fact that they performed less well on standard laboratory tests of sensory and motor skills,

---

Alzheimer's disease   A fatal degenerative disease in which neurons of the
  brain progressively die, causing loss of memory and deterioration of other
  cognitive processes.

including the types of skills that might be expected to be important in typing. The continuous practice these typists received enabled them to develop strategies to compensate for their physical decline.

Cognitive Development

Psychologists have studied the effects of education and experience on intellectual abilities and have questioned whether intelligence inevitably declines with age. Most of us can conceive of a future when we can no longer run as fast as we do now or perform well in a strenuous sport, but we do not like to think of being outperformed intellectually by younger people. Research indicates that people can get old without losing their intellectual skills.

Cognitive Development and Brain Disease Before we consider the normal effects of aging in a healthy individual, we should look at some changes that can be caused by disease. As people become older, they have a greater risk of developing dementia (literally "an undoing of the mind")—a class of diseases characterized by the progressive loss of cortical tissue and a corresponding loss of mental functions. The most prevalent form of dementia is **Alzheimer's disease.** About 2–3% of Americans between the age of 71 and 79 show diagnostic evidence of Alzheimer's disease; the prevalence rate increases rapidly with age, such that 30% of people 90 years of age or older show the disease (Plassman et al., 2007). Three relatively distinct subgroups of Alzheimer's patients are found (Fisher, Rourke, & Bieliauskas, 1999). The disease may manifest itself through (1) global deficits, or it may be most evident in functions identified with (2) the left hemisphere (deficits in word knowledge) or (3) the right hemisphere (deficits in the ability to copy geometric forms). In general, though, Alzheimer's disease is characterized by progressive loss of memory and other mental functions (Ashford, Schmitt, & Kumar, 1996). At first, the person may have difficulty remembering appointments and may sometimes fail to come up with words or people's names. As time passes, the individual shows increasing confusion and increasing difficulty with tasks such as balancing a checkbook. In the early stages of the disease, memory deficit involves recent events; but as the disease progresses, even old memories are affected. If the person ventures outside alone during the advanced stages of the disease, he or she is likely to become lost. Eventually the person becomes bedridden, becomes completely helpless, and finally dies (Terry & Davies, 1980; Khachaturian & Blass, 1992).

Geneticists have discovered an association between defects on chromosomes 14, 19, and 21 and at least one kind of Alzheimer's disease, which seems to involve reduced levels of the neurotransmitter acetylcholine (Gottfries, 1985; Selkoe, 1989; Cruts & Van Broeckhoven, 1996; Schellenberg, 1997; Poduslo & Yin, 2001). Alzheimer's disease produces severe degeneration of the hippocampus and cerebral cortex, especially the association cortex of the frontal and temporal lobes.

[**FIGURE 12•11**] Alzheimer's disease. A computer-enhanced photograph of a slice through the brain of a person who died of Alzheimer's disease (left) and a normal brain (right). Note that the grooves (sulci and fissures) are especially wide in the Alzheimer's brain, indicating degeneration of the brain.

(Photo © Alfred Pasieka/Photo Researchers, Inc.)

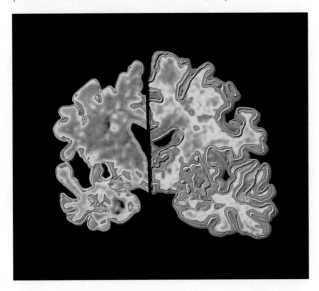

FIGURE 12•11 shows a computer-enhanced photograph of a slice through a normal brain (right) and the brain of a patient who died of Alzheimer's disease (left). You can see that much of the tissue of the Alzheimer's brain has been lost; the grooves in the brain (sulci and fissures) are much wider.

Cognitive Development and Normal Aging Aging affects different intellectual abilities to different degrees. Schaie (1990), describing the results of the Seattle Longitudinal Study of Aging, reported that on average, people's scores on five tests of intellectual abilities showed an increase until their late 30s or early 40s, then a period of stability until their mid-50s or early

60s, followed by a gradual decline. FIGURE 12•12 shows the participants who maintained stable levels of performance on each of the tests over a 7-year period. As you can see, the performance of most of the participants—even the oldest—remained stable, although some reductions appeared. Subsequent results from the Seattle Longitudinal Study of Aging (Schaie, 1996) suggest that these declines are due to the way different intellectual abilities change with age. Some abilities, such as the ability to perform rapid numerical or perceptual tasks, decline markedly as age increases. Verbal ability, as measured by vocabulary, shows little change. Other abilities, such as verbal memory, show a moderate decline at advanced age.

Related research by Kirasic (1991) has shown that, at least for performance on spatial tasks, deficits in short-term memory may coincide with aging. For example, Kirasic and Bernicki (1990) showed young and older adults 66 slides of a walk through a real neighborhood. Sometimes the slides were in the correct order; at other times, they were mixed up. All participants were then asked to make distance estimates between some of the scenes shown in the slides. Both younger and older participants performed equally well in estimating distances for the slides presented in logical order. But older participants performed less well than younger participants when the slides were scrambled. Kirasic and Bernicki concluded that information from the slides presented in normal order was encoded into short-term memory similarly for both sets of participants. However, the scrambled presentation of slides taxed available resources in the older participants' short-term memory, resulting in performance decline.

If memory shows wear with age, one might reasonably suspect that intelligence, too, would show a similar decline. This was once thought to be true, based on results from cross-sectional studies (studies that compare different age groups on the same task). However, we now know that intelligence does not decline until late adulthood, largely thanks to the work of Schaie and Strother (1968), who compared results from a cross-sectional approach with results from a longitudinal approach. For example, look at FIGURE 12•13, which

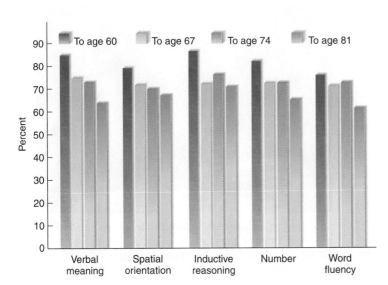

[**FIGURE 12•12**] Results from the Seattle Longitudinal Study of Aging. Percentage of participants of various age groups who maintained stable levels of performance on each of five tests of intellectual ability over a seven-year period.

(From Schaie, K. W. In *Handbook of the Psychology of Aging*, 3rd ed., edited by J. E. Birren and K. W. Schaie. San Diego: Academic Press, 1990. Reprinted with permission from Elsevier.)

[**FIGURE 12•13**] A comparison of cross-sectional and longitudinal data concerning changes in verbal ability with age. In contrast to the cross-sectional data, the longitudinal data show that verbal ability increased gradually to about age 55 and then decreased gradually.

(Based on Schaie, K. W., & Strother, C. R. (1968). A cross-sequential study of age changes in cognitive behavior. *Psychological Bulletin, 70,* 675. Reprinted with permission from K. Warner Schaie.)

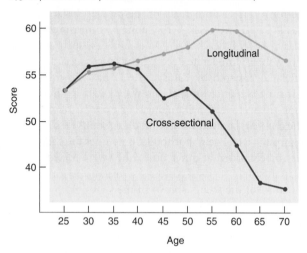

shows performance on a verbal abilities subsection of an intelligence test plotted as a function of age. (Here, verbal abilities means the ability to understand ideas represented by words.) The cross-sectional data indicate that intelligence scores decrease—and rather precipitately so—after age 50. But the longitudinal data paint a different picture: Scores increase until about age 55, then decline gradually.

Why would different methods produce these different patterns of results? Cross-sectional studies do not take into account possible cohort effects—the fact that the people being tested were reared in different time periods. Thus, one explanation for these disparate results is that the older people tested had not had the same educational and career opportunities as their younger counterparts might have had. The longitudinal method takes this possibility into consideration by testing the same people at regular intervals spanning many years. In doing so, it gives a more accurate picture of the relation between age and intelligence.

Many investigators believe that intelligence can be divided into two broad categories. In general, older people in good health do well on tests of crystallized intelligence—of the mental abilities that depend on knowledge and experience. Vocabulary, the ability to see similarities between objects and situations, and general information all are aspects of crystallized intelligence. Conversely, fluid intelligence—the capacity for abstract reasoning—appears to decline with age (Baltes & Schaie, 1974; Horn, 1982). The abilities to solve puzzles, to memorize a series of arbitrary items such as unrelated words or letters, to classify figures into categories, and to change problem-solving strategies easily and flexibly are aspects of fluid intelligence.

The facts that older people excel in crystallized intelligence and that younger people excel in fluid intelligence are reflected in the kinds of intellectual endeavors for which the two age groups seem to be best suited. For example, great mathematicians usually make their most important contributions during their 20s or early 30s; apparently the ability to break out of the traditional ways of thinking and to conceive new strategies is crucial in such achievements. In contrast, great contributions to literature and philosophy, in which success depends heavily on knowledge and experience, tend to be made by older people. Evidence exists, too, that mental activity pursued in the first two decades of life can increase cognitive functioning later. Fritsch et al. (2007) looked at a number of cognitive abilities of a sample of older adults in their mid-70s and statistically related their performance to IQ tests and school activities when these people were in their teen years. They found that participation in high school activities requiring intellectual skills was associated with higher verbal fluency as an older adult. IQ as an adolescent also was positively associated with increased episodic memory, speed of information processing, and general cognitive skill when the person had participated in intellectual activities in high school.

Social Development

Recall from Table 12.4 that Erikson believed that the adult years consist of three psychosocial stages during which the conflicts are intimacy versus isolation, in which people succeed or fail in loving others; generativity versus stagnation, in which people either withdraw inwardly and focus on their problems or reach out to help others; and integrity versus despair, in which people review their life with either a sense of satisfaction or despair.

Adult development occurs against the backdrop of what many developmental psychologists consider to be the two most important aspects of life: love and work. For most of us, falling in love is more than just a compelling feeling of wanting

Studies of aging must take into account the possibility that people of different ages were reared in different time periods and may have had different educational experiences.

to be with someone. It often brings with it major responsibilities, such as marriage and children. Work, too, is more than just a way to pass time. It involves setting and achieving goals related to income, status among peers, and accomplishments outside the family. For most adults, overall satisfaction with life reflects the degree to which they have been successful in marriage, raising a family, and achieving goals. With this in mind, let's look briefly at how love and work ebb and flow over the course of adult development.

Marriage and Family Most young people envision themselves falling in love and getting married. Fifty-one percent of women and 66% of men agreed with the statement "It is better to get married than to go through life being single" (Martinez, et al., 2006). Whether men and women actually encounter that life or not, statistics indicate that the path can take many turns. The most comprehensive description of marriage and family patterns is the National Survey of Family Growth, which completed a large survey in 2002 . Among women 15 to 44 years of age, 46% were currently married. Cohabitation with a male, however, was a common pattern reported by 43% of women—either before marriage, or as an arrangement for women who had never married. Of women in the 15- to 44-year age group surveyed, 48% had, in their lifetime, one husband or cohabiting male partner; 27% had never married or cohabited (Chandra et al., 2005). For men, 42% were in currently in a marriage; 49% had cohabited with a woman. In contrast to women, only 37% had a marriage or cohabiting relationship with a single woman during their lifetime (Martinez, et al., 2006).

Romantic relationships, whether they lead to marriage or cohabitation, need not involve a member of the opposite sex. Roisman et al. (2008) looked at the quality of the relationship between engaged, married, gay male, and lesbian couples. They found that positive views of their relationship were expressed similarly by married woman, married men, gay males, and lesbians. Relative to those in longer-term relationships, dating heterosexual couples and engaged women have more positive evaluations of their relationships. When individuals interacted with each other, committed couples—either opposite sex or same sex—were judged as having a higher quality of interaction than were heterosexual dating couples. In other words, same-sex partnerships were indistinguishable from opposite-sex relationships in terms of perceived and actual quality.

What produces a positive relationship? Of course, romantic partners wrestle with that issue all the time. One intriguing hint may be found in the early experience we might have had with the romantic partners we would have observed in our childhood—our caregivers. Earlier, we discussed how different caregiver behaviors could result in secure or insecure attachment personalities. Simpson et al. (2007) examined how attachment issues—assessed in adulthood—could affect the kind of care one would want to receive from a romantic partner. They assessed the attachment state of men and women who were dating and classified them as exhibiting either secure or insecure attachment attitudes toward

For most adults, satisfaction with life reflects the degree to which they have been successful in marriage, raising a family, and achieving goals.

their childhood caregivers. They then looked to see how, as a couple, each partner would react to different kinds of support given by the other when they were discussing relationship problems. A person with secure attachment responded best when his or her romantic partner offered emotional support; in contrast, someone with insecure attachment seemed to prefer practical advice.

Partners certainly test their relationship if it involves raising children. Both men and women in the National Survey of Family Growth said, "The rewards of being a parent are worth it, despite the cost and work it takes," with fewer than 5% disagreeing. A majority of both men and women said that they would be upset if they failed to have children, and a majority of women (but not of men) agreed that gay or lesbian adults should have the right to adopt children (Martinez, et al., 2006).

A strong majority of the National Survey of Family Growth believed "It is more important for a man to spend a lot of time with his family than to be a success at his career" (Martinez, et al., 2006). Of course, the care of young children is a difficult responsibility, but as children grow older and become more self-sufficient, the day-to-day burdens of raising a family taper off, and spouses are able to spend more time with each other. However, adolescents pose new problems for their parents: Teenage offspring may question parental authority, and their burgeoning social agendas may put a wrinkle in their parents' personal and social calendars. For many parents, rearing adolescents, particularly during the years just before young people leave home, represents the low point of marital happiness (Cavanaugh, 1990).

Generally speaking, once a family's youngest child has left home, marital happiness increases—and it continues to do so through the remainder of the couple's life together. It once was thought that the "empty nest" posed problems for the middle-aged couple, particularly for the mother, who in earlier generations was thought to define her role mainly around her children. Although parents may miss daily contact with their children, they also feel happy (not to mention relieved) that a major responsibility of life—raising self-reliant children who become responsible members of society—has been completed successfully. Just as important, the parents now have time for each other and freedom to pursue their own interests. Empty-nest couples report an increase in marital happiness. If they maintain frequent contact with their children, they also report increased satisfaction with life (White & Edwards, 1990).

Work   The task of raising a family must be balanced against the demands of work outside the home. Events that occur in the workplace often affect the quality of home life. A promotion and a raise can mean that the family can now do things that they could not before—they can now pursue a new hobby or travel together. Working long hours to get that raise can decrease the amount of time that a couple can spend together with their children.

With the dramatic increase in the number of women who work outside the home since the early 1970s, many psychologists have focused their research efforts on understanding dual-earner marriages—those in which both parents work in full- or part-time jobs. In 2006, 52% of married-couple families had two wage earners (Bureau of Labor Statistics, May 9, 2007), making this an important area of future study.

Death   Death is the final event of life. It is both a biological and a social event—family and friends are affected in many ways by the death of a loved one. Although a death may claim a life at any time, most people die when they are old. One question that developmental psychologists have asked about death and dying among the elderly is, "How do old people view the inevitability of their own deaths?"

At one time or another, most of us contemplate our own deaths. Some of us may contemplate death more than others, but the thought of death crosses everyone's mind at least occasionally. As you might expect, elderly people contemplate their deaths more often than do younger people. For the most part, they fear death less than their younger counterparts do (Kalish, 1976). Why? No one knows for sure, but a tentative explanation may be that older people have had more time to review the past and to plan for the future in the knowledge that death is close at hand. Thus, they are able to prepare themselves psychologically (and financially) for death.

Contemplating and preparing for death, though, is not like knowing that you are actually dying. The changes in attitudes that terminally ill people experience have been studied by Elisabeth Kübler-Ross (1969, 1981). After interviewing hundreds of dying people, Kübler-Ross concluded that people undergo five distinct phases in psychologically coping with death. The first stage is denial. When terminally ill people learn of their condition, they generally try to deny it. Anger comes next—people go through a period of resenting the certainty of death. In the third stage, bargaining, people attempt to negotiate their fate with God or others, pleading that their lives be spared. But even while bargaining, they actually realize that

they are going to die. This leads to depression, the fourth stage, which is characterized by a sense of hopelessness and loss. The fifth and final stage, acceptance, is marked by a more peaceful resignation to reality.

Kübler-Ross's work points up the psychological factors involved in dying and provides an interesting model of how the dying come to grips with their fate. Her conclusions, though, have not escaped criticism. Her research was not scientific—her method for interviewing people was not systematic, and her results are largely anecdotal. Moreover, of the five stages, only denial appears to be universal. Apparently, not all terminally ill people have the same psychological responses to the fact that they are dying.

Despite its flaws, however, Kübler-Ross's work is important because it has enhanced awareness, both scientific and public, of the experiences undergone by people who are terminally ill. The scientific response, as you might guess, has been to do medical research in the hope of prolonging the lives of people with cancer and other terminal illnesses. The public response has emphasized attempts to provide support for dying individuals and their families, often through hospice services (Aiken, 2001). In past centuries, hospices were places where strangers and pilgrims could find rest and shelter. Today, hospice programs provide invaluable medical and psychological support for dying persons and their families.

QUESTION TO CONSIDER

Imagine that you are the director of a new community mental health program for adults. The focus of this program is on prevention—on minimizing the negative effects of the aging process on adults who participate in the program. Your first task is to design a comprehensive plan to maximize adults' physical, social, emotional, and intellectual capacities. What activities would you include in such a plan? Why?

Epilogue

It may have occurred to you that the two case histories of this chapter, those of J. F. and D. R., provide different perspectives on the topic of development. D. R.'s biological constitution dominated his rearing conditions. As much as can be determined, his family genuinely tried to raise him as a girl. Nevertheless, D.R. did not think of himself as a girl, and, when given the choice, decided to live his life as a man. Nature seems to have trumped over nurture.

J. F.'s genetic history isn't known, and it is possible that the trouble she experienced with her foster family originated with a congenital disorder. However, her case is not that different from those of a large number of Romanian orphans, and the great common factor to all of them is the neglect they suffered during their early institutionalization. Nurture (or rather, lack of it) seems to have predominated in her case.

How can we make sense of these two disparate outcomes? The concept of critical periods may provide a clue. Charles A. Nelson of Harvard Medical School, who has studied the effect of institutional neglect on brain development (e.g., Nelson, 2007), suggests that early cognitive and social growth depends on genetic and environmental influences in two ways: experience-expectant mechanisms and experience-dependent ones. The first responds to the kind of environment that should be common to all of us as members of our species. It includes nutrition, shelter, and parental care. Our genetic mechanisms rely on these features, because they have been reliably part of our evolutionary history. When they fail to occur, as they did for the children caught in the Ceauşescu regime, then the normal sequences of development lack the necessary foundations. It would be like expecting an automobile to operate on the surface of the moon—its design is based on assumptions that don't apply in the other environment.

Experience-dependent mechanisms provide the fine tuning of development. If the expectancies of the environment are met, then these mechanisms respond to the normal variation of rearing conditions. D. R.'s basic psychological needs were met by a concerned and loving family from birth—the surgical accident notwithstanding—and he does not seem to have exhibited the attachment deficits from which many of the Romanian orphans suffer. If his past had not been disclosed to him, he might well have been able to live as an adult female. His genetic background had still prepared him for life as a male, and it seems likely that he would have not fit a conventional gender role in those circumstances. It seems clear that he would have had a much happier childhood if his nurturing had matched his nature.

Liane Faulder, the reporter who described J. F.'s story, called it "one of the most emotionally difficult stories I have witnessed in my career." Anyone who reads her account (Faulder, 2006) would have to concur. Even as an adult, J. F. exhibits an emotional detachment that she herself finds hard to comprehend. Nevertheless, it is gratifying to end this story by saying that, when she was 18 and could make the decision as an adult, J. F. returned to live with her foster parents, who never stopped giving her the love she was denied as a baby.

J.F. at age 18 with her foster parents.

CHAPTER SUMMARY

Prenatal Development

The three stages of prenatal development span the time between conception and birth. In just 9 months, the zygote grows from a single cell, void of human resemblance, into an embryo and then a fully developed fetus. Gender is determined by the sex chromosomes. Male sex organs are produced by the action of a gene on the Y chromosome that causes the gonads to develop into testes. The testes secrete androgens, which stimulate the development of male sex organs. If testes are not present, the fetus develops as a female. The most important factor in normal fetal development is the mother's nutrition. Normal fetal development can be disrupted by the presence of teratogens, which can cause intellectual deficits and physical deformities. One well-studied teratogen is alcohol, which, when consumed by a pregnant woman, may lead to fetal alcohol syndrome.

Physical and Perceptual Development in Infancy and Childhood

A newborn infant's first movements are actually reflexes that are crucial to its survival. For example, the rooting, sucking, and swallowing reflexes are important in finding and consuming food. More sophisticated motor skills develop and are refined through natural maturation and practice.

A newborn's senses appear to be at least partially functional at birth. However, normal development of perceptual abilities, like that of motor abilities, depends on experience. Genetically, an infant has the potential to develop motor and sensory abilities that coincide with the maturation of its nervous system, but for this potential to be realized, the infant's environment must give the infant opportunities to test and practice these skills. If an infant is deprived of the opportunity to practice them during a critical or sensitive period, these skills may fail to develop fully, which will affect his or her performance as an adult.

Cognitive Development in Infancy and Childhood

The first step in a child's cognitive development is learning that many events are contingent on his or her own behavior. This understanding occurs gradually and is controlled by the development of the nervous system and by increasingly complex interactions with the environment.

Piaget hypothesized that a child's cognitive development is divided into four periods. The periods are determined by the joint influences of the child's experiences with the physical and social environment and the maturation of the child's nervous system. An infant's earliest cognitive abilities are closely tied to the external stimuli in the immediate environment; objects exist for the infant only when they are present. Gradually, infants learn that objects exist even when hidden. The development of a grasp of object permanence leads to the ability to represent things symbolically, which is a prerequisite for the use of language. Next to develop is the ability to perform logical transformations on concepts. A key aspect of these transformations is that that they are reversible. Piaget designated these transformations as concrete operations and thought that their appearance was accompanied by the recognition that some properties were preserved across physical transformations. Around the age of 11, a child develops more adult-like cognitive abilities—abilities that may allow the child to solve difficult problems by means of abstract reasoning, or formal operations.

Critics point out that in some cases, Piaget's tests of cognitive development underestimated children's abilities. For example, if tested appropriately, it is evident that children understand the conservation of various properties earlier than Piaget thought, and that their egocentrism is less pronounced than his tests indicated. Nevertheless, his conclusions continue to have a profound impact on the field of child development.

Vygotsky's writings and the research they have stimulated have showed that the sociocultural context in which children grow up has a significant impact on their cognitive development. In particular, language appears to influence how children learn to think, solve problems, formulate plans, make decisions, and contemplate ideas.

Information-processing accounts of cognitive development have been developed more recently. These accounts describe how cognitive development proceeds according to the brain's information-processing capacity. Capacity expands because of three factors: brain maturation, practice using schemas, and the integration of schemas for different objects and events. Such models essentially reinterpret Piaget's theory in the language of information processing.

Social Development in Infancy and Childhood

Because babies are totally dependent on their parents, the development of attachment between parent and infant is crucial to the infant's survival. A baby has the innate ability to shape and reinforce the behavior of the parent. To a large extent, the baby is the parent's teacher. In turn, parents reinforce the baby's behavior, which facilitates the development of a durable attachment between them. Some of the behaviors that babies possess innately are sucking, cuddling, looking, smiling, and crying. These behaviors promote parental responses and are instrumental in satisfying physiological needs.

Normally, infants show both stranger anxiety and separation anxiety. They also tend to be afraid of novel stimuli, but the presence of their caregiver provides a secure base from which they can explore new environments. Ainsworth's Strange Situation allows a researcher to determine the nature of the attachment between infant and caregiver. By using this test, several investigators have identified some of the variables—some involving infants and some involving mothers—that influence secure or insecure attachment. Fathers, as well as mothers, can form close attachments with infants.

Development also involves the acquisition of social skills. Interaction with peers is probably the most important factor in social development among children and adolescents. However, a caregiver's style of parenting also can have strong effects on the social development of children and adolescents, especially when the caregiver engages in scaffolding. Authoritative parents, compared with authoritarian, permissive, and indifferent parents, tend to rear more competent, self-reliant, and independent children.

Development of Gender Roles

Children's gender roles tend to conform to their society's gender stereotypes. Very few real differences exist between the sexes, and those that do are relatively small. Female children tend to show earlier verbal development, are better at expressing emotion and interpreting emotional cues, and show more compliance with adults and peers. Male children tend to have better spatial abilities, are more aggressive, and tend to take more risks.

Some of these differences may have biological roots. Kimura suggested that the different tasks performed by our ancestors shaped brain development and favored men with better spatial skills and women with better fine motor skills. Buss argued that challenges related to reproduction and child rearing have caused gender differences in how these challenges are solved. Socialization undoubtedly plays a significant part in gender role differences.

Research has shown that both parents and peers tend to encourage children to behave in "gender-appropriate" ways—especially with regard to play activities and toys. However, scientific studies have revealed few other reliable differences in the ways parents treat young boys and girls.

Moral Development

Piaget suggested that moral development consists of two principal stages: moral realism, characterized by egocentrism and blind adherence to rules, and morality of cooperation, characterized by empathy and a realization that behavior is judged by the effects it has on others. Kohlberg suggested that moral development consists of three levels, each further divided into stages. During the preconventional level, morality is based on the personal consequences of an act. During the conventional level, morality is based on the need to be well regarded and on sharing a common interest in social order. During the postconventional level, which is achieved by only a few people, morality becomes an abstract, philosophical virtue.

Critics of Piaget and Kohlberg point out that the stages of moral development are not necessarily fixed and that individuals will often perform at a level lower than what they are capable of. However, it is recognized that as children mature, they become progressively able to reason about more complex moral situations.

Adolescence

Adolescence is the transitional stage between childhood and adulthood. Puberty is initiated by the hypothalamus, which causes the pituitary gland to secrete hormones that stimulate maturation of the reproductive system as well as secondary sex characteristics.

Puberty marks a significant transition, both physically and socially. Early maturity appears to be socially beneficial to boys, because early maturers are more likely to be perceived as leaders. The effects of early maturity in girls are mixed; although their advanced physical development may help them acquire some prestige, early-maturing girls are more likely to engage in norm-breaking behavior.

Conflict may underlie cognitive development in adolescence. Just before adolescence, children develop the tools of logical reasoning. However, adult reasoning uses a variety of reasoning strategies, of which logic is just one. Adolescence may be a period of growth in our capacity to choose among these strategies.

A focal point in adolescent development is the formation of an identity. Both Erikson and Marcia argue that adolescents face an identity crisis, the outcome of which determines the nature and level of identity that teenagers will form. Marcia argues that forming an identity has two primary components—the crisis itself and the commitment or decision that a young person makes regarding a course of action after considering possible alternatives. The extent to which a teenager experiences a crisis and the way in which he or she resolves it lead to identity achievement, moratorium, foreclosure, or identity diffusion. An adolescent's identity is bound to his or her perceptions of self which, during this time of life, will often be based on social relationships.

Sexuality becomes important in adolescence, and many people engage in sexual intercourse in their teens. Although adolescence brings conflicts between parents and children, these conflicts tend to be centered on relatively minor issues. Most adolescents hold the same values and attitudes concerning important issues as their parents do.

Adulthood and Old Age

Up to the time of young adulthood, human development can reasonably be described as a series of stages: a regular sequence of changes that occur in most members of our species. However, development in adulthood is much more variable, and few generalizations apply. Aging brings with it a gradual deterioration in people's sensory capacities as well as changes in physical appearance that many people regard as unattractive.

Older people are more likely than young people to develop dementia because of illnesses such as Alzheimer's disease. Rather than undergoing sudden intellectual deterioration, older people are more likely to exhibit gradual changes, especially in abilities that require flexibility and the learning of new behaviors. Intellectual abilities that depend heavily on crystallized intelligence—an accumulated body of knowledge—are much less likely to decline than are those based on fluid intelligence—the capacity for abstract reasoning.

Adult social development occurs within the context of love, marriage, family, and work. Marriages appear to be most unhappy just before the children leave home—possibly because of the emotional and time demands that adolescents place on their parents. Many families have parents who both work, which helps ease the financial burdens of raising a family and meeting long-term financial obligations.

Older people have less fear of death than do younger people, perhaps because they have had more time to contemplate and prepare for it. In interviews with terminally ill people, Kübler-Ross found that many people seem to go through a five-stage process in facing the reality that they are going to die. Although her research has been found to have some methodological flaws, it has drawn both scientific and public attention to the plight of terminally ill individuals and the necessity of properly caring for them.

succeed with mypsychlab

Visit MyPsychLab for practice quizzes, flashcards, and dozens of videos and animated tutorials, including the following items you can find in the "Multimedia Library":

 Fetal Development Attachment in Infants

 Cross-Sectional and Longitudinal Research Designs Key Issues in Developmental Psychology

 Attachment Classifications in the Strange Situation Teratogens and Their Effects

KEY TERMS

accommodation *p. 346*

actual developmental level *p. 361*

Alzheimer's disease *p. 368*

analytic processing system *p. 365*

androgens *p. 340*

assimilation *p. 346*

attachment *p. 354*

avoidant attachment *p. 356*

conservation *p. 348*

conventional level *p. 363*

critical period *p. 344*

cross-sectional study *p. 338*

disoriented attachment *p. 357*

egocentrism *p. 348*

embryonic stage *p. 339*

epigenetics *p. 339*

equilibration *p. 347*

experiential processing system *p. 365*

fetal stage *p. 340*

gender identity *p. 358*

gender role *p. 358*

gender stereotypes *p. 359*

longitudinal study *p. 338*

maturation *p. 342*

moral realism *p. 362*

morality of cooperation *p. 362*

object permanence *p. 347*

operation *p. 346*

period of concrete operations *p. 348*

period of formal operations *p. 349*

postconventional level *p. 363*

preconventional level *p. 363*

prenatal period *p. 338*

preoperational period *p. 347*

puberty *p. 364*

resistant attachment *p. 356*

scaffolding *p. 357*

secure attachment *p. 356*

sensitive period *p. 344*

sensorimotor period *p. 347*

separation anxiety *p. 356*

Strange Situation *p. 356*

stranger anxiety *p. 356*

teratogens *p. 339*

theory of mind *p. 352*

zone of proximal development *p. 351*

zygotic stage *p. 339*

SUGGESTIONS FOR FURTHER READING

Berk, L. E. (2005). *Infants, children, and adolescents* (5th ed.). Boston: Allyn & Bacon.

This text presents an excellent overview of research and theory in the fields of infant, childhood, and adolescent development.

Lemme, B. H. (2006). *Development in adulthood* (4th ed.). Boston: Allyn & Bacon.

A well-written and thorough introduction to the major issues involved in the study of adult development.

Hoyenga, K. B., & Hoyenga, K. T. (1993). *Gender-related differences: Origins and outcomes.* Boston: Allyn & Bacon.

This book examines gender differences from evolutionary, physiological, and cultural perspectives.

Harwood, R. L., Miller, J. G., & Irizarry, N. L. (1997). *Culture and attachment: Perceptions of the child in context.* New York: Guilford Press.

As its title implies, this book considers cultural variables that influence the development of attachment between infants and their caregivers, including socioeconomic status, perceptions of different attachment behaviors, and perceptions of children themselves.

Colapinto, J. (2000). *As nature made him: The boy who was raised as a girl.* Toronto, ON: HarperCollins.

Colapinto's book is an excellent description of the case of D.R., described in the text. D.R. did reveal his full identity for the sake of Colapinto's book in an effort to make his story known and to change medical thinking about the value of sexual reassignment after genital trauma. You can find full details about his story in this account. Sadly, D.R.'s life became increasingly unhappy; he died in 2004.

CHAPTER

13

Motivation, Emotions, and Health

Prologue

"Robotic" Behavior? Or Something Else?

Malaysians have a word, *latah*, that describes a very unusual condition. People susceptible to latah react to unexpected or startling stimuli with elaborate and fitful reactions lasting several minutes. During this time, a latah person will sometimes shout, imitate another, or blindly follow instructions. Robert Bartholomew, an anthropologist who married into an extended Malay family, describes an episode involving his wife's aunt:

> I first observed S. while attending my brother-in-law's wedding as this timid, decrepit, wizen-faced woman was intentionally startled by S.'s elderly uncle, who walked near her and slapped his hands together. She responded with a short vulgar phrase, stood up, lost all inhibition, and began following each of her teaser's commands and mimicking his every gesture. During the ensuing 10-minute episode, S. was "made to" cry like a baby, perform silat (Malay self-defense), dance vigorously, and partially disrobe, all to the obvious amusement of the entire wedding party, who crowded around her inside the bride's parents' home. She would occasionally improvise gestures, such as lifting her sarong in a sexually suggestive manner and utter the most vile words and phrases. (Bartholomew, 1984, p. 333).

This hyperreactivity to unexpected sounds and events has been a puzzle since it was first described by Western observers. The latah behaviors occur as a result of a powerful stimulus, in the same way that any of us might jump or startle when a balloon pops. But, unlike a reflexive startle, the behaviors are elaborate. Tanner and Chamberland (2001) studied a group of 15 Indonesian women with this condition, and noted that, as in the case of S., a latah state is marked by vulgar speech, imitation of sounds and gestures, and automatic obedience. Most reflexes are quick, short, and simple responses directly elicited by specific stimuli. Are the elaborate behaviors of latah similar to reflexes?

Within Malay culture, the answer is yes. A person in a latah state is considered as acting involuntarily. Behaviors that would normally be regarded as scandalous are excused or even, as in the case of S. described earlier, considered amusing. Persons in latah are not held responsible for their actions. Instead, a relative or a friend will assume responsibility to make sure a latah woman doesn't harm herself or anyone else during that state (Winzeler, 1999), and the person provoking the latah state is considered in control (Bartholomew, 1984).

Conversely, much of a latah person's behavior seems like a performance, designed to attract attention to someone who might otherwise be ignored. Bartholomew (1984) found that S.'s startle response was much more muted when nobody was present but him. Despite claiming to not like the "teasing," she never asked her relatives to desist, so, the curious collection of latah behaviors could be a deception.

Are the behaviors of a latah state unconscious and involuntary? Or are they deliberate and willful? ■

Working on homework produces results that have been reinforced in the past, and the stimuli arising from these results serve as conditioned reinforcers to maintain the behavior until the assignment is finished.

We are all capable of a wide range of behavior, a range whose breadth is ever increasing as we gain experience. However, our full behavioral repertoire is not expressed at every moment. At one moment, we behave in one way, and at another moment, in a different way—even when the environment is constant. In everyday language, we say that we were *motivated* to act differently at different times.

What Is Motivation?

Motivation is a term we all use informally, but in psychology, it refers to the major factors that affect whether and how we behave at a given time. **Motivation** has to do with the instigation, strength, and persistence of behavior and is derived from a Latin word meaning "to move." A person eats or not depending on how long it has been since the last meal or whether he or she is dieting. People talk to others depending on whether they are friends or strangers. Because *motivation* is a term from the everyday vocabulary, not the laboratory, and because the factors that affect the likelihood of a given behavior are numerous, the topic includes a diverse set of phenomena.

As we see in this chapter, some motivational phenomena are dependent primarily on the individual environment (selection by reinforcement), and others are dependent primarily on the ancestral environment (natural selection). Of course, all behavior is affected by both reinforcement and natural selection. Because so many factors influence which behavior occurs out of the many of which we are capable, some motivational phenomena are treated in later chapters—such as dissonance reduction in social behavior (Chapter 15). Among the aspects of motivation considered in the present chapter are reinforcement, aggression, and sexual behavior, as well as emotion, a frequent accompaniment of motivation that includes feelings, expressive behavior, and related physiological changes. We discuss eating and sexual behavior and their complex motivational and emotional aspects. Finally, we examine the topic of stress—how it originates, how it affects our health, and how we can learn behaviors to cope with it.

Reinforcement and Motivation

Motivation cannot be separated from reinforcement and punishment. As explained in Chapter 5, we are motivated to perform operant behavior that has been followed by attaining a reinforcer or escaping a punisher. The initiation of learned behavior depends on the presence of discriminative stimuli for the behavior. When the present environment contains these stimuli, the behavior occurs. When it does not, the behavior does not occur. Because people vary in their histories of differential conditioning (see Chapter 5), they often respond differently in the same environment. An observer, not knowing their different histories, attributes different motivations to the two individuals.

An example from the animal learning laboratory may illustrate the point. Suppose that two pigeons are placed in individual operant chambers and that each pigeon receives food after it has pecked a disk 100 times. One pigeon has had a history in which, at first, a single peck is required for food, and then 5 pecks, and then 10 pecks, and so on. That is, an increasing number of pecking responses has been shaped. It is likely that this pigeon will eventually receive the food even though 100 pecks are required. The second pigeon, however, has had a history in which only a single peck was required for food. It is likely that responding by the second pigeon will extinguish before the 100th peck has occurred. Thus, the first pigeon appears motivated, and the second, unmotivated, even though the opportunity for reinforcement is seemingly the same for both birds.

Untoward Effects of Reinforcement: Intrinsic and Extrinsic Motivation

Usually, people apply reinforcements when they are necessary to maintain behavior that would not otherwise occur or persist. Children might never keep their rooms tidy if they did not receive encouragement for this behavior. *Extrinsic* reinforcers (stimuli produced by natural environmental contingencies or by others) may initially be needed to encourage and maintain behavior if *intrinsic* reinforcers (stimuli produced by the person's own behavior) are lacking. But what happens when would-be reinforcers ever have an undesired effect on motivation?

---

motivation A group of phenomena that affect the nature, strength, or persistence of an individual's behavior.

Overjustification Effect Some psychologists have hypothesized that providing extrinsic rewards for behavior that is already maintained by intrinsic rewards may actually weaken the target behavior (e.g., Ryan & Deci, 2002; Vallerand & Ratelle, 2002; Oliver & Williams, 2006). This is called the **overjustification effect.** The general idea behind the concept of overjustification is that the superfluous application of extrinsic rewards for behavior that is intrinsically motivated creates a shift to extrinsic rewards, the net result being a loss of intrinsic motivation. As long as the extrinsic rewards are available, an observer may not notice a difference, but what happens when extrinsic rewards are no longer provided? The overjustification theory predicts that after a shift occurs from intrinsic to extrinsic motivation and extrinsic rewards disappear, the person will lose interest in the activity. That is, if the behavior has become maintained by the extrinsic rewards, the behavior will weaken when these rewards are no longer available.

A study by Lepper, Greene, and Nisbett (1973) was among the first of many to demonstrate the overjustification effect. The investigators first carefully documented the free-play activities preferred by a large number of children in a day-care setting. Among the favorite activities was drawing with large felt markers on sheets of newsprint. Drawing, therefore, showed behavioral evidence of intrinsic motivation. The children did not need to play with the art materials, but they did so without any extrinsic consequences. Two weeks after this preliminary assessment, the researchers returned and for 1 day randomly assigned the children to one of three conditions. In one condition, each child was asked to produce a drawing to win a prize. Thus, the prize was contingent on the children's performing the requested behavior. Moreover, the children expected to receive prizes for drawing. Children in a second condition also were asked to make a drawing but were not offered the extrinsic reward. However, they unexpectedly received the same prize as children in the first condition when they had completed drawing. In a third condition, the children were neither offered nor given the prize.

After a delay of 1 or 2 weeks, the researchers returned and unobtrusively observed children during their normal free-play time. Remember that during free-play periods, no one was present who might offer or give extrinsic rewards to the children—they were on their own. The results of these observations revealed a strong overjustification effect. Children who had previously received an expected prize played with the drawing materials less than did children in the other two groups. In terms of overjustification, they showed less intrinsic motivation during their free-play period. The children who received an unexpected prize in the prior session showed no evidence that their intrinsic motivation had been

undermined. They spent about the same amount of time drawing as before. When the prize was unexpected, no shift from intrinsic to extrinsic motivation occurred. This finding has been replicated with children and adults across a variety of activities and in laboratory and field settings (see Ryan & Deci, 2000).

Learned Helplessness Organisms with a history in which their behavior has been ineffective in determining its consequences become less sensitive to the consequences of their behavior. That is, they lose motivation, because they have learned that they are powerless to affect their own destinies. Maier and Seligman (1976) reported a series of animal experiments that demonstrated this effect, which is called **learned helplessness.** Learned helplessness involves learning that the consequences of behavior are independent of one's behavior—that an aversive outcome cannot be avoided or escaped or that an appetitive outcome cannot be achieved.

The basic experiment in this area was conducted by Overmeier and Seligman (1967). These researchers placed dogs in an apparatus in which unavoidable shocks were given. Next, they placed each dog in another apparatus in which the animal underwent a series of trials that provided a warning stimulus before an electrical shock. In this second situation, the animals could avoid the shocks by stepping over a small barrier to the other side of the apparatus. Dogs in a control group quickly learned to step over the barrier and avoid the shock. However, dogs that had previously received inescapable shocks in the other apparatus failed to learn. They just squatted in the corner and took the shock as if they had learned that it made no difference what they did. They had learned to be helpless. A related effect was found with appetitive stimuli: Acquisition of a learned response is impaired if animals receive food regardless of their behavior before experimenters make food contingent on the response (Engberg, et al., 1972).

Some psychologists believe that learned helplessness has important implications for human motivation (Seligman, 1975; Seligman & Nolen-Hoeksema, 1987; Job, 2002). When people have experiences in which they are powerless to control the events that happen to them, they may become depressed, and their motivational level may decrease. The change in motivation occurs because the helplessness training reduces their expectation that performing a task will bring success. Learned helplessness has also been likened to a personality trait; that is, people who have had major experiences with unsolvable dilemmas may not try to succeed in other types of tasks, including problems they could solve (Overmeier, 1998).

What Determines the Strength of Behavior?

We often make assumptions about people's level of motivation from the rate at which responding occurs. As an example, when you look around the library, you may see some students

---

overjustification effect The undermining of intrinsic motivation by the application of extrinsic rewards to intrinsically motivated behavior.

learned helplessness Reduced ability to learn a solvable avoidance task after exposure to an inescapable aversive stimulus; thought to play a role in depression.

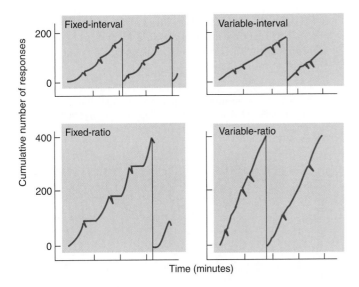

[**FIGURE 13·1**] Cumulative records of the effect of different reinforcement schedules on operant responding. Interval schedules are shown in the top row, ratio schedules in the bottom row. Fixed schedules are shown in the left column, variables schedules in the right column. When a curve reached its maximum, it returned to the baseline level and then increased again as responding continued.

(From Donahoe, J. W., and Palmer, D. C. (1994). *Learning and Complex Behavior*. Boston, MA: Allyn and Bacon. Reprinted with permission from J. W. Donahoe.)

hunched over their books, intently reading, making notes, and so on; others may be staring off into space or idly looking about. You may be tempted to conclude that the first group is motivated, and the second is not. But is this right? Remember that motivation is closely tied to reinforcement. Hence, we need to consider how reinforcement determines the strength of behavior.

Schedules of Intermittent Reinforcement

Remember from Chapter 5, a **schedule of reinforcement** specifies the conditions that must occur before a response produces a reinforcer. Schedules that manipulate response requirements are called **ratio schedules.** Schedules that manipulate temporal variables are called **interval schedules.** It turns out that many behavioral characteristics that are conventionally ascribed to differences in motivation are actually products of the schedules of reinforcement under which a response was acquired. When we do not know the schedule of reinforcement under which the response was acquired, we often attribute the strength of responding to the level of motivation.

Our concern here is primarily with the effects of schedules of *intermittent* reinforcement—schedules in which only *some* responses are followed by a reinforcer. The study of intermittent schedules is of general importance because the reinforcement contingencies encountered in the natural environment are usually intermittent, not continuous. Sometimes passing the butter at dinner is followed by a "Thank you," but often it is not. Sometimes casting a fishing line catches a fish; very often it does not. Furthermore, different types of intermittent reinforcement will produce patterns of behavior that are very different. Looking out the window might, paradoxically, be a sign that studying is reinforced—it's just that it's reinforced according to a schedule that produces such pauses in the motivated behavior.

Schedules of reinforcement are often somewhat variable. The number of saw-strokes to cut a board varies with the hardness of the wood; the time before the bus arrives varies with the amount of traffic, and so on. For that reason, laboratory studies of schedules of reinforcement have investigated the patterns of responding produced by both fixed and variable schedules. In fixed schedules, the response produces a reinforcer after a constant number of responses (*fixed-ratio schedules*) or the passage of a constant amount of time (*fixed-interval schedules*). In variable schedules, the response produces a reinforcer after a varying number of responses (*variable-ratio schedules*) or a varying amount of time since the prior reinforcer (*variable-interval schedule*). Illustrative examples of the patterns of behavior produced by these four combinations of ratio and interval, and fixed and variable schedules of reinforcement are shown in FIGURE 13·1.

Figure 13.1 plots responding on a different type of graph than we have seen previously. This graph is a **cumulative record** of responses. In a cumulative record, every response moves the curve upward as time passes. Cumulative records allow us to detect patterns readily in responding over time. Inspection of these cumulative records reveals two major trends. First, ratio schedules generally produce higher rates of responding than do interval schedules. This may be one reason that many union contracts outlaw so-called piece-work agreements in which pay is dependent on the number of goods produced. Such agreements produce more work for less pay. Management also has concerns about ratio (piece-work) schedules of pay because high rates of production can lower the quality of work unless considerable oversight occurs. Second, variable schedules produce more-uniform rates of responding than do fixed schedules. In fixed schedules, the learner comes to discriminate that responses are not reinforced

---

schedule of reinforcement Reinforcement procedure that specifies the conditions necessary for reinforcement.

ratio schedules Reinforcement schedules in which reinforcers are dependent on a designated number of responses.

interval schedules Reinforcement schedules in which reinforcers are dependent on a response after a designated period has elapsed.

cumulative record Graphic presentation of data in which every response moves the curve upward as time passes.

after a response has been recently reinforced. Research has shown that the failure to respond at the beginning of a fixed-interval or fixed-ratio schedule becomes more pronounced as the response or time requirement grows larger. Once responding has begun, however, it continues at a substantial rate, particularly with fixed-ratio schedules. (See Figure 13.1.) Something similar occurs when we have a large project to complete. Beginning the project is the most difficult part. We find every excuse not to begin—the room is too warm, the neighbors are too noisy, and so on. However, once we begin, we often consistently work for prolonged periods.

Research with schedules of reinforcement has shown that the conditions that immediately precede the reinforced response acquire the greatest control of the response. These conditions include not only the environmental events at the moment of reinforcement but any persisting effects of prior environmental and behavioral events. For example, because the times of emission of responses are always somewhat variable, the response that satisfies a ratio requirement is more likely to be part of a "burst" of responses than to be a single discrete response. Accordingly, responding in bursts (rapid responding) is more apt to be followed by a reinforcer than is a single response (Williams, 1968). Thus, high rates of responding are differentially produced by ratio schedules.

Through the introduction of computers, research on schedules began to better control the precise conditions present when a response was reinforced. A major conclusion from the work on schedules of reinforcement is that many of the differences in the strength of responding that were formerly attributed to differences in the level of motivation are due to differences in the schedule under which the behavior was acquired. Consider a child at the grocery store who repeatedly asks a parent to buy candy, even after the parent has said no many times. We might be tempted to attribute the child's persistence to a high motivation to obtain candy. It is more likely that repeated requests have, in the past, eventually led to the parent's buying the candy. Thus, the parent has unintentionally reinforced pleading for candy on a variable-ratio schedule, and the behavior now occurs at high rate and for long periods without reinforcement.

Deprivation of Reinforcers
Our level of motivation, as reflected by our rate of responding, is affected by factors other than the schedule of reinforcement. Another major factor is **deprivation** of a reinforcer—how long it has been since we contacted a particular reinforcer. The opportunity to eat a piece of cake may be an effective reinforcer, but it will be less so if you have just eaten a piece of the cake. The chance to play a video game may be an effective reinforcer, but it will be less so if you already have been playing for several hours. Absence does, in fact, make the heart grow fonder. (Although, when it comes to human relationships, it may depend on how

---

deprivation Reduction of an organism's contact with a stimulus below the level that the organism would choose; for example, reduced contact with food in food deprivation.

[**FIGURE 13·2**] Effect of hours of food deprivation on the rate of responding on a variable-interval schedule of reinforcement. The rate of responding could not affect the rate of reinforcement.

(Clark, F. C. (1958). The effect of deprivation and frequency of reinforcement on variable interval responding. *Journal of the Experimental Analysis of Behavior, 1,* 221–228. Copyright © 1958 by the Society for the Experimental Analysis of Behavior, Inc. Reprinted by permission.)

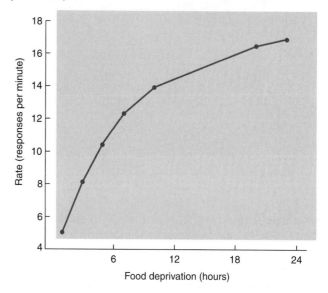

one judges the reason for the absence—see Roehling & Bultman, 2002).

Ethical considerations usually preclude the study of deprivation with humans, but the effect of deprivation of reinforcers on levels of motivation can be studied quite precisely under the controlled conditions of the animal laboratory. For example, the lever-pressing behavior of rats was studied with different levels of food deprivation (Clark, 1958). Lever pressing produced food on a 1-minute variable-interval schedule. Because an interval schedule of reinforcement was used, changes in the rate of responding had no effect on the rate at which food occurred—lever pressing could not produce food until an average of 1 minute had passed. Thus, the rate of lever pressing shows the effect of deprivation of the reinforcer unaffected by other variables. FIGURE 13·2 depicts the results of the experiment. Clearly, as the level of deprivation increased, the rate of responding increased, even though the increase did not produce more reinforcers. Deprivation of a reinforcer, whether of food or a loved one, increases the level of motivation.

Availability of Reinforcers for Other Behavior
The level of motivation for a response is affected not only by the scheduling and deprivation of reinforcers but also by the availability of competing reinforcers for other responses. A piece of vanilla cake may be an effective reinforcer, but less so if chocolate cake is also available. Playing *Pac-Man* may be reinforcing, but less so if *Quake* or *Halo 3* is also available.

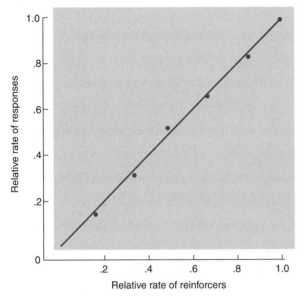

Again, animal experiments most clearly reveal the effect of this variable. Pigeons were placed in a test chamber in which either of two disks could be pecked. Pecking either disk was reinforced with food, but according to different schedules of reinforcement for each disk. Schedules of reinforcement in which more than one operant is measured are called **concurrent schedules.** The world outside the laboratory typically confronts us with complex concurrent schedules in which several alternative responses are available, each with its associated schedule of reinforcement, and we must choose between the alternatives.

In the pigeon experiment, responding was reinforced on each disk according to different variable-interval reinforcement schedules. Once again, the use of variable-interval schedules ensured that the pigeons' rate of responding had little effect on the rate at which reinforcers occurred, thus revealing the effect of the alternative source of reinforcement while controlling other variables. FIGURE 13·3 shows changes in the relative rate of responding to an alternative as a function of the relative rate of reinforcers for that response (Herrnstein, 1970). The choice of an alternative clearly depended on how the reinforcers for that response compared with the reinforcers for the other response. Choice matched the relative reinforcers for the alternative. This result, known as the

matching relation, has been found in a wide range of studies, including studies with humans (Baum, 1974).

What Determines the Persistence of Behavior?

Another common measure of motivation is the persistence of behavior when responding is challenged in various ways—by the withholding of reinforcers, by reinforcement of competing behavior, and so on (Nevin & Grace, 2000). In Chapter 5, we saw that behavior acquired with intermittent reinforcement was more resistant to extinction than was behavior acquired with continuous reinforcement. What happens during intermittent reinforcement that makes behavior more persistent?

Among the important factors is the particular *sequence* of reinforced and unreinforced responses during training (Capaldi, et al., 2005). Studies have shown that if intermittent training ensures that a reinforced response occurs only after a series of unreinforced responses, resistance to extinction is greatly enhanced. Training that consists of the same number of unreinforced responses, but in which the reinforcers do not occur after long series of unreinforced responses, does not produce behavior that is nearly as resistant to extinction. In other words, succeeding after several failures causes the learner to resist the effects of subsequent failure. As applied to human behavior outside the laboratory, these findings suggest that experiencing failure in our past facilitates persistence of later performance, but only if failure was eventually followed by success. The "school of hard-knocks" does not by itself teach us to endure in the face of adversity. On the contrary, experiencing tough times can lead us to give up, unless success sometimes occurs (recall the discussion of learned helplessness).

One meaning of motivation is persistence—working steadily on projects that take much time and effort to complete.

---

concurrent schedule Reinforcement schedule in which reinforcers are available for responding on two or more alternative operants.

matching relation In concurrent reinforcement schedules, the equal relation between the proportion of responses to a given alternative and the proportion of reinforcers received for those responses.

In studies of extinction, psychologists discovered another motivational effect: Environmental stimuli that are present during extinction become aversive. The aversive properties of these stimuli are evident in several ways. First, it has long been known that laboratory animals acquire responses if they allow them to escape environments in which extinction is scheduled. The motivational effects of extinction are called **frustration** (Amsel, 1962). Second, if another animal is present when the learner's responses undergo extinction, the other animal may be attacked—a finding that has been observed in humans (Kelly & Hake, 1970; Lerman, Iwata, & Wallace, 1999). This phenomenon is called **extinction-induced aggression.** Extinction causes other members of the species to become eliciting stimuli for aggressive behavior and thereby establishes the opportunity to aggress as a reinforcing stimulus. For obvious reasons, most studies on frustration and extinction-induced aggression have been conducted with nonhumans; however, frustration in response to extinction is widely prevalent in mammals (Papini, 2003), and the applicability to human behavior seems clear. The quiet office worker who pounds on the candy machine when it fails to dispense a purchase is probably displaying extinction-induced aggression. A similar phenomenon also may occur when groups within society who are not prospering blame other groups for their misfortune, as in scapegoating.

In the next sections, we explore several motivated behaviors, including aggression and emotion. Because many of the examples of reinforcement that we've just discussed involve food, we'll begin with the motivational factors that determine eating.

QUESTIONS TO CONSIDER

1. What are some of the ways in which you might seek to explain the following behavior, given what you know about schedules of reinforcement? A child keeps asking his parents to take him out to play, even after the parents say that they are busy and will go out to play later. So what could the parents do to make this behavior less likely in the future?
2. When people have tough times as they are growing up, they can better withstand life's later difficulties. When might this be true, and when might it not?

---

frustration   An emotional response produced when a formerly reinforced response is extinguished.

extinction-induced aggression   Aggression toward another organism when responding is extinguished.

system variable   The variable controlled in a regulatory process; for example, temperature in a heating system.

set point   Optimal value of the system variable in a regulatory process. The set point for human body temperature is 98.6°F (37°C).

detector   Mechanism that signals when the system variable deviates from its set point in a regulatory process.

correctional mechanism   Mechanism that restores the system variable to the set point in a regulatory process.

Eating

In this section, we see that the regulation and expression of eating is one of the most complex motivated behaviors. All other motivations are dependent on it. If life were not sustained by eating, other motivations would be irrelevant.

What Starts a Meal?

It is helpful to consider eating as the result of a regulatory system whose components are analogous to those found in control systems in engineering. A regulatory system has four essential features: the **system variable** (the characteristic to be regulated), a **set point** (the optimal value of the system variable), a **detector** that monitors the value of the system variable, and a **correctional mechanism** that restores the system variable to the set point. A simple example of such a regulatory system is a thermostat that controls the temperature of a room by monitoring departures from the temperature at which it is set. When the room temperature falls below the desired temperature, the heat is turned on; when the temperature rises above the desired temperature, the heat is turned off. The system variable is the temperature of the room, and the detector is the thermostat. (See FIGURE 13•4.) Although the control of eating is much more complex than the control of heating by a thermostat, the basic elements are similar. Several system variables must be controlled—body weight, caloric intake, energy output, body temperature; several detectors—receptors in the gastrointestinal tract, liver, and brain; and several correctional mechanisms—behavioral and social as well as physiological. Hunger and satiety (the state of being fed to capacity) might appear to be two sides of the same coin, but investigations have shown that the factors that cause a meal to begin are not the same as the factors that end it. Therefore, this discussion considers separately the factors that begin and end a meal.

Physiological Factors   The reasons for beginning a meal must somehow be related to the fact that the body needs nourishment: Physiological factors clearly are involved in eating, but how do physiological factors help determine *when* to eat?

Cannon and Washburn (1912) proposed that eating begins when we have an empty stomach. They suggested that the walls of an empty stomach rub against each other to produce

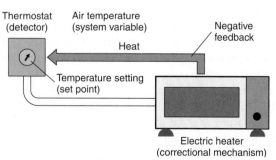

[**FIGURE 13•4**] An example of a regulatory system.

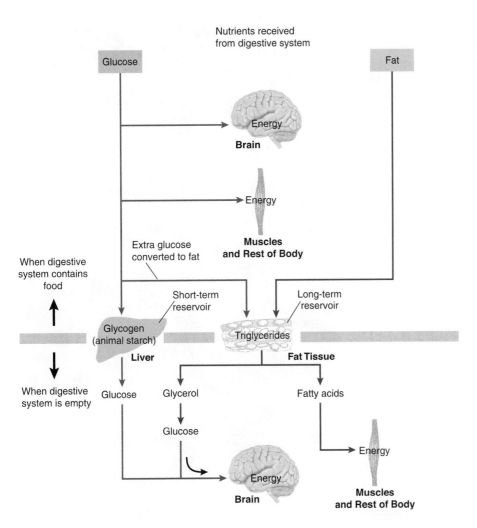

Nutrients received
from digestive system

Glucose

Fat

Energy

Brain

Energy

**Muscles
and Rest of Body**

Extra glucose
converted to fat

When digestive
system contains
food

Short-term
reservoir

Long-term
reservoir

Glycogen
(animal starch)

Triglycerides

Liver

Fat Tissue

When digestive
system is empty

Glucose

Glycerol

Fatty acids

Glucose

Energy

Brain

Energy

**Muscles
and Rest of Body**

[**FIGURE 13·5**] Overview of
food metabolism. When the
digestive system contains food,
glucose nourishes the brain and
muscles. Extra glucose is stored in
the liver and converted to fat. When
the digestive system is empty,
glucose obtained from glycogen
stored in the liver nourishes the
brain until this short-term reservoir
is used up. Fatty acids from fat
tissue nourish the muscles, and
glycerol is converted to glucose to
nourish the brain.

what are commonly called "hunger pangs." Some skeptics called Cannon's explanation of hunger "the rumble theory." Observations of surgical patients indicated that there was more to the onset of eating than hunger pangs. Removal of the stomach did not abolish hunger pangs, and these patients reported the same feelings of hunger and satiety that they had experienced before surgery (Inglefinger, 1944). (The patients had their stomachs removed because of cancer or large ulcers, and their esophagi had been attached directly to their small intestines.) Although the patients ate small, frequent meals because they had no stomachs to hold food, their reports of feelings of hunger and their total food intake were essentially normal.

Depletion of the body's store of nutrients is a more likely cause of hunger. The primary fuels for the cells of our body are glucose (a simple sugar) and fatty acids (compounds produced by the breakdown of fats). If the digestive system contains food, these nutrients are absorbed into the blood and nourish our cells. But the digestive tract is sometimes empty; it is empty when we wake up every morning. A reservoir must store nutrients to keep the cells of the body nourished when the gut is empty. Indeed, two reservoirs are present—a short-term reservoir and a longer-term reservoir. The short-term reservoir stores carbohydrates, and the long-term reservoir stores fats.

The short-term reservoir is located in the cells of the muscles and the liver, and it is filled with a carbohydrate—a

form of animal starch called **glycogen.** When glucose is present in the bloodstream after the digestion of a meal, some glucose is used for fuel, but some is converted into glycogen and stored in the liver. The longer-term reservoir is the adipose tissue (fat tissue) found beneath the skin and in various locations in the abdomen. Adipose tissue consists of cells capable of absorbing nutrients from the blood, converting them to triglycerides (fats), and storing them. Fat cells can expand enormously in size to store triglycerides. The primary difference between obese and normal-weight persons is the *size* of their fat cells, not their number.

The long-term reservoir keeps us alive during prolonged fasting. Once the level of glycogen in our short-term reservoir of carbohydrates is depleted, fat cells release fatty acids and a carbohydrate called *glycerol.* Brain cells metabolize glucose exclusively, whereas the other cells of the body can metabolize fatty acids. Because glycerol converts into glucose, the brain is nourished even after the short-term reservoir has been depleted. (See FIGURE 13·5.)

Because of the importance of glucose as a fuel, Mayer (1955) proposed the glucostatic hypothesis of hunger.

---

glycogen Insoluble carbohydrate synthesized from glucose and stored in
the liver; can be converted back to glucose.

According to the **glucostatic hypothesis,** hunger occurs when the level of glucose in the blood falls below a set point, which occurs when the glycogen in the short-term reservoir has been depleted. Mayer proposed that the decrease in blood sugar was detected by receptors on glucose-sensitive neurons in the brain called *glucostats*. (The term *glucostat* is analogous to *thermostat* but refers to the detection of glucose rather than of temperature.) Mayer suggested that these detectors activate neural circuits that make a person hungry and stimulate the correctional mechanism of eating.

Subsequent research with both rats and humans demonstrated that the glucostatic hypothesis was too simple. Eating can be instigated in a number of different ways. An empty stomach causes a hormone, *ghrelin,* to be secreted. This hormone is a potent stimulator of eating (Kojima et al., 1999; Ariyasu et al., 2001). Also, the liver contains two different types of nutrient receptors, one that detects the level of glucose and the other that detects the level of fatty acids (see Langhans, 1996). Both sets of receptors activate pathways that project to the brain; these pathways, in turn, activate neural circuits that initiate eating. For example, if a drug that blocks glucose receptors is injected into the vein that brings blood from the intestines to the liver, eating occurs immediately (Novin, VanderWeele, & Rezek, 1973). Moreover, if the nerves (vagus nerves) that carry information from these receptors to the brain are cut, eating fails to occur. Finally, the brain itself contains receptors that detect the level of glucose, and blocking these receptors also induces eating (Ritter, Dinh, & Zhang, 2000). Because the control of eating is so important to survival, natural selection has produced multiple interrelated mechanisms whereby eating is initiated.

Environmental Factors   Most people in Western society eat three times per day. As the time approaches for a meal, we become hungry and eat. This regular pattern of eating is not determined solely by biological need; it is at least partially determined by habit. For many of us, eating is initiated not by deprivation of nutrients but by environmental stimuli, such as the time shown by the clock on the wall.

If you have ever had to miss a meal, you may have noticed that your hunger did not continue to grow indefinitely. Instead, it subsided some time after the meal would normally have been eaten, only to grow again just before the scheduled time of the next one. Hunger, then, can wax and wane according to a learned schedule controlled by environmental stimuli.

Besides learning *when* to eat, we learn *what* to eat. What we accept as food depends on our culture and location. Our tastes also are shaped by habits acquired early in life. A child whose family exclusively eats a meat-and-potatoes diet will probably not become a venturesome gastronome. We are

What we eat and how we eat are determined by cultural factors.

more likely to feel hungry and to consume more food in the presence of companions who are doing the same (de Castro, 2002; Lumeng & Hillman, 2007).

What Stops a Meal?

We have seen that several factors—both behavioral and physiological—can initiate a meal, but what *ends* it? What brings a meal to a conclusion? Consider what happens when you eat. Your stomach fills with food, and the digestive process begins. However, about an hour passes before significant amounts of nutrients are absorbed into the bloodstream from the intestines. Therefore, the body's supply of fuel is not replenished until a considerable time after the meal begins. If you were to continue to eat until the nutrients actually entered the bloodstream, your stomach would burst. Other factors must be responsible for stopping the meal.

The physiological factors that stop a meal are divided into two groups—those that arise from the immediate effects of eating a meal and those that are produced by the longer-term consequences. The primary immediate cause of satiety is the stimulation of receptors by a distended stomach. In experiments with rats, eating does not occur if food is directly introduced into the stomach, even though the food was nei-

---

glucostatic hypothesis   The hypothesis that hunger is caused by a low level of glucose in the blood; glucose levels are assumed to be monitored by specialized sensory neurons called glucostats.

ther tasted nor smelled. If procedures are used to remove food from the stomach after it has been eaten, eating continues unabated (Deutsch & Gonzales, 1980). The stomach rather precisely measures the volume of its contents. Food-deprived rats were allowed to eat their fill, then some of the contents of the stomach were removed via a tube. When the rats were again allowed to eat, they ate almost exactly as much as had been taken out (Davis & Campbell, 1973).

The stomach appears to contain receptors that inform the brain about the chemical nature as well as the quantity of its contents. The ability to detect the nutritional value of food is important; eating should stop relatively soon if the food is nutritious but should continue for a longer time if it is not. In one experiment, researchers injected either milk or a dilute salt solution into the stomachs of food-deprived rats and 30 minutes later allowed them to eat (Deutsch, Young, & Kalogeris, 1978). The animals that had received milk ate less than those that had received the salt solution. Because the animals could not taste what had been put in their stomachs, the nutritional value had to be detected by receptors in the stomach. You can try an experiment of your own: Drink two glasses of water when you are hungry, and see what effect that has on your appetite.

The intestines also contain receptors that detect the presence of nutrients. The duodenum, the portion of the intestines into which the stomach empties, secretes a hormone called CCK that suppresses eating (Smith & Gibbs, 1992). Further along the sequence of events that occur after a meal, the liver also has receptors that detect nutrients. After nutrients have been absorbed from the stomach and intestines, they enter the bloodstream and stimulate the receptors in the liver. If investigators stimulate these receptors by directly injecting nutrients into the veins supplying the liver of a rat, the rat's eating is reduced, even though its stomach is empty (Tordoff & Friedman, 1988; Langhans, Grossmann, & Geary, 2001).

Longer-term signals for satiety are produced by the adipose tissue that stores fat. The discovery of this signal came after studies with a strain of genetically obese mice. The *ob mouse* (as the strain is called) has a low metabolism, overeats, and becomes extremely fat. As these mice age, they develop diabetes, as do many obese humans, both young and old. Researchers in several laboratories have discovered a genetic basis for the obesity of these animals (Campfield, et al., 1995; Halaas, et al., 1995; Pelleymounter, et al., 1997). These animals have a mutation in a gene, called OB, that normally produces a protein known as *leptin* (from the Greek word *leptos*, meaning "thin"). Leptin is secreted by fat cells that have absorbed a large amount of triglyceride and acts on receptors in the hypothalamus to inhibit hunger. Because of their mutant OB gene, ob mice are unable to synthesize leptin.

Leptin has profound effects on metabolism and eating, acting as an antiobesity hormone. If ob mice are given daily injections of leptin, their metabolic rates increase, their body temperatures rise, they become more active, and they eat less. As a result, their weight returns to normal. The treatment

[**FIGURE 13·6**] The effects of leptin on obesity in mice of the ob (obese) strain. The ob mouse on the left is untreated; the one on the right received daily injections of leptin.

(Photo courtesy of Dr. J. Sholtis, The Rockefeller University. Copyright © 1995 Amgen, Inc.)

works even when the leptin is injected directly into the brain, indicating that the chemical acts directly on the neural circuits that control eating and metabolism (see Woods, et al., 1998). FIGURE 13·6 shows an untreated ob mouse and an ob mouse that has received injections of leptin.

Maffei and colleagues (1995) found that leptin is secreted in humans and that the level of leptin in the blood is correlated with obesity. If normal levels of leptin are produced by human fat cells, why do some people nevertheless overeat and become obese? Much ongoing research continues to be devoted to the puzzle of obesity, to which we now turn.

Obesity

The physiological mechanisms that control eating are generally effective. Nevertheless, eating is not well regulated in many people, who become either too fat or too thin. Does what we have learned about the normal regulation of food intake help us understand these problems?

Studies in the United States indicate that the percentage of the population judged as obese by the *body mass index* (BMI) was more than one third in 2006 (Ogden, et al., 2007). The BMI varies with the person's age, height, and weight but is associated with risk of death from various causes. In an extensive review of these risks, Wadden, Brownell, and Foster (2002) suggested some of the benefits resulting from interventions for obesity. They reviewed studies suggesting that the risk of mortality increases by around 30% in people with a moderately high BMI; this percentage continues upward to 40% when BMI is very high (Manson et al., 1995). The causes of death in obese people include stroke, diabetes, and cancer (these correlate with obesity). Obese people also have social and physical complications. Obese girls complete fewer years in school, despite having just as good grades as those who remain, are less likely to marry, and earn less than their nonobese counterparts. Obese people also elicit negative aesthetic judgments from others.

Obesity is extremely difficult to treat. Success at weight loss depends on the goals of the person losing the weight. First, people must be motivated to lose weight. Second, they must realize that weight-reduction programs are designed for health rather than aesthetic reasons. For example, until recently, interventions were guided toward helping people achieve their ideal weight (rather than a weight that would reduce the risk of ill health). Current emphasis, however, is on reducing health complications, therefore a loss of 5–15% can be effective in producing this reduction, even though the patient/client may not be happy with having lost so little weight and expect a weight loss of 20–35% (Blackburn, 1995; O'Neil et al., 2000). One study reported that weight reduction of 7 kg/m² combined with 150 minutes of exercise per week reduced the likelihood of developing diabetes by 58% (Diabetes Prevention Program Research Group, 2002, cited in Wadden, Brownell, & Foster, 2002).

Causes of Obesity Many psychological variables have been suggested as causes of obesity, including relatively low impulse control, inability to delay gratification, and maladaptive eating styles (primarily eating too fast). However, in a review of the literature, Rodin, Schank, and Striegel-Moore (1989) found that none of these suggestions has received empirical support. Unhappiness and depression seem to be *effects* of obesity, not its causes, and dieting may make these problems worse.

As with the factors that stop eating, no single explanation exists for obesity, but many partial ones are known. Habit plays an important role in the control of food intake. Early in life, when we are most active, we form our ideas about how much food constitutes a meal. Later in life, we become less active, but we do not always reduce our food intake accordingly. We fill our plates according to what we think is a proper-sized meal (or perhaps the plate is filled for us), and we eat everything, ignoring the satiety signals that might tell us to stop before the plate is empty. These behavioral factors may also help explain why people have so much difficulty losing weight.

Metabolic factors also play an important role in obesity. (The word *metabolism* refers to the physiological processes that produce energy from nutrients.) Just as cars differ in their fuel efficiency, so do people. Rose and Williams (1961) studied pairs of individuals who were matched for weight, height, age, and activity. One member of a pair might consume twice as many calories per day as the partner but nevertheless maintain the same weight. People with an efficient metabolism deposit excess calories in the long-term nutrient reservoir, fat cells. Over time, the reservoir grows, and the individuals become obese. In contrast, people with an ineffi-

cient metabolism can eat large meals without getting fat. All of their calories are spent to maintain muscles and heat production. Whereas a fuel-efficient automobile is desirable, a fuel-efficient body runs the risk of becoming obese in many modern-day environments in which calories are plentiful.

An evolutionary basis may exist for high metabolic efficiency—whatever the factors that produce it. Food was only intermittently available during human prehistory. The ability to store extra nutrients in the form of fat when food was available would therefore have been a highly adaptive trait (e.g., Assanand, Pinel, & Lehman, 1998). In addition, the known variability in metabolism among people today may reflect the specific environments in which their ancestors lived (e.g., James & Trahurn, 1981). A relative scarcity of food would promote the evolution of efficient metabolisms that would allow people to function on a relatively small number of calories per day.

Another evolutionary consideration in the origins of obesity has been developed by Pinel, Assanand, and Lehman (2000). They observe that the evolutionary response to intermittently available food was fat storage during periods of high food availability and fat use during periods of food scarcity. Today, therefore, high rates of obesity are occurring in many countries because we regularly store energy in the form of fat but do not have the scarcities that would cause us to draw on those stores. In other words, our biological heritage promotes overeating and excess storage of fat because the environments of the present differ from the environments of the past in which natural selection took place. Research has shown that animals will eat more when they experience a taste that has been associated in the past with few calories (Pierce et al., 2007). Nowadays, with so many foods on the market that vary in their caloric content (e.g., low-fat but artificially sweetened snacks), our ability to learn the relation between the foods we need and their tastes may be hampered (Davidson & Swithers, 2004).

We saw earlier that large fat cells secrete a protein, leptin, that lowers weight by increasing the metabolic rate (that is, by making the metabolism less efficient) and decreasing food intake. Why, then, do some people become fat? Are they like ob mice, with defective OB genes? In most cases, the answer is no (Maffei et al., 1995). The fat cells of most obese people do secrete leptin; the receptors in the brain that normally detect leptin, however, may be deficient. For leptin to reduce weight, the brain must contain functioning leptin receptors. It is too soon to know whether the discovery of leptin and leptin receptors will aid in the treatment of obesity (de Luis et al., 2008).

Anorexia Nervosa and Bulimia Nervosa

Overeating is the most common eating problem in Western societies today. However, some people have the opposite problem: They have **anorexia nervosa,** a disorder characterized by a severe decrease in eating (Uyeda, et al., 2002). Both male and female humans can be afflicted with anorexia ner-

---

anorexia nervosa Eating disorder characterized by severe weight loss due to reduced food intake, sometimes to the point of starvation.

vosa, but the disorder is about 3 to 4 times more common in women. The literal meaning of the word *anorexia* is a loss of appetite, but people with this disorder generally do *not* lose their appetites. They limit their intake of food despite intense preoccupation with food and its preparation. They may enjoy thinking about food and preparing meals for others to consume; they may even hoard food that they do not eat. However, they have an intense fear of becoming obese, and this fear continues even if they become dangerously thin. Many reduce weight by cycling, running, or almost constant walking and pacing. When the weight loss becomes severe, menstruation stops. Anorexia nervosa is difficult to treat; as many as 6% of people with anorexia nervosa die of causes related to the disorder (Neumarker, 1997).

The fact that anorexia nervosa is seen primarily in young women has prompted both biological and social explanations. The disorder sometimes runs in families, and current studies estimate that more than 50% of the variation in the occurrence of anorexia nervosa is affected by genetic factors (Klein & Walsh, 2004). Many psychologists believe that the emphasis Western cultures place on slimness—especially in women—is largely responsible for this disorder (see Pinhas et al., 1999). One account states that if a young person responds to this pressure with excessive dieting and exercise, a complex biological and behavioral pattern emerges that produces self-

starvation (Pierce & Epling, 1997). Söndersten and colleagues (e.g., Zandian et al., 2007) suggested that activity and starvation activate systems of reward and attention that reinforce dieting; effective treatment depends on reestablishing reinforcement for normal eating behaviors.

Another eating disorder, **bulimia nervosa,** is characterized by a loss of control of food intake and is again more common in women. (The term *bulimia* comes from the Greek words *bous,* meaning "ox," and *limos,* meaning "hunger.") People with bulimia nervosa periodically gorge themselves with food, especially desserts and snack foods, especially in the afternoons or evenings. These binges are usually followed by self-induced vomiting or the use of laxatives accompanied by feelings of depression and guilt (Halmi, 1996; Steiger, Lehoux, & Gauvin, 1999). With this combination of bingeing and purging, the net nutrient intake of bulimics varies considerably. Weltzin et al. (1991) reported that 19% of bulimics undereat, 37% eat a normal amount, and 44% overeat. Episodes of bulimia are sometimes seen in patients with anorexia nervosa. Bulimia nervosa is seldom fatal, but it can result in poor health outcomes. Its causes are as uncertain as those of anorexia nervosa.

The Brazilian model, Ana Carolina Reston, died in 2006 of complications traced to anorexia nervosa. It was reported that she had lived on a diet of apples and tomatoes and died with a body mass index of 13.4. Her relatives said that she resisted being called anorexic.

focus On

Eating Disorders in Other Cultures

It is almost a cliché to say that eating disorders have increased significantly in the past few decades and that this increase is most obvious in young women raised in "the West." Like most clichés, however, it is underpinned by a strong element of truth and evidence. Eating disorders are still more common in Western cultures and more common in girls and women than in boys and men. (See **FIGURE 13•7.**) According to Prince (1985), the most well-known eating disorder (after obesity) is anorexia nervosa, and evidence indicates that this disorder may be culture bound, that is, limited to culture "primarily by reason of certain of their psychosocial features."

In a review of the extent to which anorexia and bulimia nervosa are culture bound, Keel and Klump (2003) showed that anorexia has been reported in every non-Western region of the world, but that bulimia nervosa appears most frequently in Western cultures. Although suggesting that the former may be culture bound, the authors caution that anorexia is a more widely studied and accepted disorder than is bulimia, and the lack of extensive evidence on the prevalence of bulimia may explain its greatest appearance in studies of Western participants.

bulimia nervosa Eating disorder characterized by gorging binges followed by self-induced vomiting or use of laxatives; often accompanied by feelings of guilt and depression.

[FIGURE 13·7] Prevalence rates of anorexia nervosa and bulimia nervosa across different ethnic and cultural groups.

(Adapted from Soh, N. L., Touyz, S. W., & Surgenor, L. J. (2006). Eating and body image disturbances across cultures: A review. *European Eating Disorders Review, 14,* 54–65.)

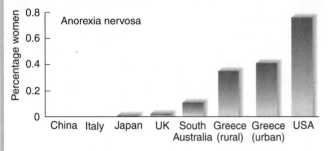

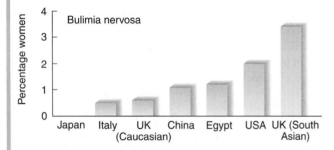

If we accept the study's conclusion, however, and try and explain why the discrepancy should arise, one factor that might be important is the availability of high-sugar, fatty, palatable foods. Binge eating involves eating these foods to excess; there must, therefore, be a ready source of them. The great prevalence of bulimia in the West may, therefore, reflect the fact that more of this food is available. It does not explain, however, why the bingeing occurs in the first place. The authors suggest a possible genetic predisposition to bulimia, citing evidence that the disorder may share genetic transmission with other "neuroses" such as phobias. This idea may be too general to be valid, however. Why should genetic predisposition to bingeing be transmitted along with genetic predisposition to being afraid?

Another, but counterintuitive, possibility is that overeating may be exacerbated by the presence of *diet* foods. Davidson and Swithers (2004) noted that diet foods are typically sweetened. This reduces the brain's ability to associate sweet tastes with high calories. Consequently, individuals who have consumed many low-calorie but sweet foods may overeat whenever they encounter a sweet meal. If you've ever seen someone order a large fast-food meal and then ask for a diet drink, you get the idea. Davidson and Swithers proposed this account as an explanation of obesity trends in the United States, where low-calorie products have become quite popular. However, it may also be a possible contributing cause to the behaviors associated with bulimia.

---

intraspecific aggression   An attack by an animal on another member of its species.

1. In some cultures and times (such as Europe in the Baroque era), it was desirable to be overweight. Why might that have been? Why might thinness be associated with desirability in our culture?
2. Do you think that the fact that most people with anorexia nervosa are female is caused entirely by social factors (such as the emphasis on thinness in our society)? Do you think that biological factors (such as hormonal differences) also play a role? Can you think of any ways to answer these questions experimentally?

Aggressive Behavior

Aggression is a serious problem in human society. Every day, we hear of incidents involving violence and cruelty. If we are to live in a safer world, we must learn about the causes of aggressive behavior. Many factors influence a person's tendency to commit acts of aggression, including frustration when our behavior is no longer reinforced, childhood experiences, exposure to violence in the media, and physiological factors. Various aspects of aggressive behavior have been studied by biological, behavioral, and social scientists. We examine some of the key variables that affect human aggression; but first, let's look at research on nonhuman animals in their natural environments.

Ethological Studies of Aggression

Violence and aggression are seen in many species other than our own. If aggression were harmful to survival of a population, we would not expect it to be so prevalent in nature. Ethologists—zoologists who study the behavior of animals in their natural environments—have analyzed the causes of aggression and have shown that in many cases, aggressive behavior does have value for the survival of species.

Intraspecific aggression is aggression by one animal against another member of its own species. Ethologists have shown that intraspecific aggression has several biological advantages. First, it tends to disperse a population of animals, forcing some into new territories. The adaptations required by these new environments increase the flexibility of the species. Second, rivalry among males for mating opportunities perpetuates the genes of the healthier, more vigorous animals. The human situation, of course, is somewhat different from that of other species because of culture. Culture, through learning, provides a means whereby the selecting effects of previous environments may be transmitted to the next generation by other than genetic means. Perhaps intraspecific aggression has outlived whatever usefulness it may have had for humans.

Ethologists studying aggression have discovered a related set of behaviors in many species: ritualized threat gestures.

Threat gestures communicate an animal's aggressive intent to other members of the species before actual violence begins. For example, if one dog intrudes on another's territory, the defender growls and bares its teeth, raises the fur on its back (presumably making it look larger to its opponent), and stares at the intruder. Almost always, the dog defending its territory drives the intruder away. Threat gestures are particularly important in species whose members are able to kill one another. For example, wolves often threaten each other with growls and bared teeth but rarely bite each other. To forestall an impending attack, one of the animals must show that it does not want to fight—that it admits defeat. The submissive animal makes an **appeasement gesture.** If a pair of wolves gets into a fight, one animal usually submits to the other by lying down and exposing its throat. The sight of a helpless and vulnerable opponent apparently terminates the victor's hostility, and the fight ceases. The aggression of the dominant animal is appeased. Because an all-out battle between two wolves would probably end in the death of one and serious injury to the other, the tendency to perform ritualized displays has an obvious advantage to the survival of each of them. These rituals also can provide information to both participants as to which is the stronger (Hurd, 1997).

Hormones and Aggression

In birds and most mammals, male sex hormones (androgens, such as testosterone) exert a strong effect on aggressiveness. In nonhuman species, testosterone exerts an **organizational effect** on the brain, altering the development of both the brain and the sex organs, and an **activational effect** on some forms of aggressive behavior during adulthood. These effects are called activational effects because the hormone activates sex organs and brain circuits that have already developed. (We look more closely at these effects later in the chapter.) As shown in FIGURE 13·8, for example, a normal adult male mouse will fiercely attack other male mice that intrude into its territory; but if a male mouse is castrated early in life, before its brain has matured, it will not attack another male later, even if given injections of testosterone (Conner & Levine, 1969). As always, natural selection and learning interact to determine behavior. As an illustration, pigeons establish literal pecking orders that determine the ranks of birds in the colony. In one study, low-ranking male pigeons increased their rank after they had been injected with testosterone *and*

their aggressive behavior (pecking another pigeon) had been reinforced with food in another situation. However, neither testosterone alone nor reinforcing aggressive behavior alone had such an effect (Lumia, 1972).

Do hormones also influence aggressive behavior in humans? It has been shown that persons of either sex with higher testosterone levels appear to be more aggressive (Starzyk & Quinsey, 2001). Some male perpetrators of sexual assault have been treated with drugs that block androgen receptors and thus prevent androgens from exerting their normal effects. The rationale is based on animal research that indicates that androgens promote both sexual behavior and aggression in males. The efficacy of such treatment of humans with antiandrogens for aggression or for the resolution of sexual problems has yet to be established (Lehne & Money, 2000; Brett, et al., 2007).

We must remember that correlation does not necessarily indicate causation. A person's environment can affect his or her testosterone level. For example, one very thorough study found that the blood testosterone levels of a group of five men confined on a boat for 14 days changed as the men established a dominance–aggression ranking among themselves: The higher the rank, the higher the testosterone level (Jeffcoate, et al., 1986). Yet in a correlational study such as this, we cannot be sure that high testosterone levels cause people to become dominant or violent; perhaps their success in establishing a position of dominance increases their testosterone levels relative to those of the people they dominate.

Some athletes have taken anabolic steroids to increase their muscle mass and strength and, supposedly, their competitiveness. Anabolic steroids include natural androgens and synthetic hormones that have androgenic effects. This would lead us to expect increases in aggressiveness among these athletes, and indeed, several studies have found exactly that effect. For example, male weight lifters who were taking anabolic

---

threat gesture Stereotyped gesture that signifies that one animal is likely to attack another.

appeasement gesture Stereotyped gesture made by a submissive animal in response to a threat gesture by a dominant animal; tends to avert an attack.

organizational effect (of hormone) The effect of a hormone on tissue differentiation and development.

activational effect (of hormone) The effect of a hormone that occurs in the fully developed organism; may depend on the organism's prior exposure to the organizational effects of hormones.

[**FIGURE 13·8**] Organizational and activational effects of testosterone on aggressive behavior of male mice that were castrated immediately after birth.

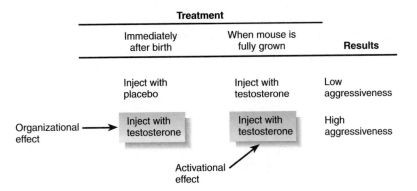

Treatment		
Immediately after birth	When mouse is fully grown	**Results**
Inject with placebo	Inject with testosterone	Low aggressiveness
Inject with testosterone	Inject with testosterone	High aggressiveness

Organizational effect

Activational effect

steroids were found to be more aggressive and hostile than those who were not (Yates, Perry, & Murray, 1992). Again, bear in mind that we cannot be certain that the steroid was responsible for the increased aggressiveness: Perhaps it was the men who were already more competitive and aggressive who chose to take the steroids. Taken together, however, the research findings strongly suggest (although they do not prove) that androgens stimulate aggression in humans, as in other animals.

Environmental Variables That Affect Human Aggression

Environmental variables, including the behavior of family members and peers, as well as the impact of the media, can play a part in human aggression.

Imitation of Aggression Many parents discipline their children through physical methods, like spanking, or verbal methods, such as scolding. The discomfort that these methods produce is used by the parent as an aversive stimulus that will either punish a behavior that the parent wants to suppress, or increase through negative reinforcement a behavior that the parent wants to encourage (see Chapter 5). However, another possibility exists: the child may learn to imitate the parent's actions and show an increase in physical or verbal aggression. Bandura, Ross, and Ross (1961) showed that this could occur even when the aggression is produced by a relative stranger. They brought children into a playroom with several toys. Some of the children were accompanied by an adult model who, after a few minutes, began to punch a large plastic doll. (The doll was a popular toy at the time, marketed under the name "Bobo"; the experiment is often referred to as the "Bobo study.") Other children either had no model or had a model who played quietly and nonaggressively with other toys. Later, all children were given a mildly frustrating experience (the experimenter took away some other toys) in the presence of the Bobo doll, and their reactions noted. Children who had seen an adult punch and kick the doll responded in the same way, even repeating some of the verbally aggressive shouts that the model had used. As a group, they were much more aggressive toward the doll than were children in the other groups.

The Bandura, Ross, and Ross study raised the disturbing possibility that physical methods of discipline may actually increase aggression through imitation learning (Widom, 1989). A large percentage of nonviolent people may have been spanked when they were children, with no obvious harm. However, when parents habitually resort to aggression, their children may learn to do the same. To take an extreme example, many (although by no means all) parents who beat their children have themselves been victims of child abuse (Proeve & Reilly, 2007). It is important to note, however, that most adults who were physically abused as children manage to avoid repeating the pattern with their own children (Salter et al., 2003).

Violent behavior in video games could be a source of aggression through imitation.

Most parents do not beat their children or even spank them frequently, but there is another opportunity for imitation in our society: violent behavior on television and in movies, comic books, and video games. Does the continued observation of violence in the mass media lead children to choose aggressive means to solve their problems? Or are the television networks and movie studios correct when they argue that children have no trouble separating fact from fantasy and that the mass media only give us what we want anyway?

Psychologists and sociologists have shown keen interest in this question. Numerous researchers have studied the possible effects of media violence by using correlational methods in both real-life environments and the laboratory. What can be concluded from the hundreds of investigations? Generally, a positive correlation exists between the amount of violent media programming that children watch and subsequent aggressive behavior, although the strength of the correlation depends on many factors, such as whether behavior is studied in the laboratory or in actual home settings (see Bushman & Huesmann, 2001; Huesmann, et al., 2003). The relation holds even when people are tracked from childhood to adulthood (Johnson et al., 2002; Huesmann, et al., 2003). The obvious conclusion would seem to be that violent media programming causes increased violence among those who watch it. Yet as suggestive as such studies are, we must be careful to observe the fundamental problem with correlational studies (see Chapter 2). Again, correlation does not prove causation. Any effort at reducing violence in society requires that we make the right decisions about where to put our resources and attention. If media violence is a major culprit, then that is where a great deal of our attention and efforts should go. However, another possibility is that causation flows in the opposite direction. We must ask whether the results of the media-violence studies might simply show that the degree to which people are predisposed to violence causally affects the amount of violent programming they choose to watch (e.g., Freedman, 2002). For example, it would not be surprising if aggressive boys chose to watch more aggressive programming than nonaggressive boys did. People watch programs that interest them. Thus, the alternative hypothesis about causal directionality is plausible. It may be that violent programming does substantially increase violence and aggression in our society, but the research carried out to date has not established this beyond a doubt.

QUESTIONS FOR FURTHER THOUGHT

1. From the point of view of evolution, aggressive behavior and a tendency to establish dominance have useful functions. In particular, they increase the likelihood that only the healthiest and most vigorous animals will reproduce. Can you think of examples of good and bad effects of these tendencies among members of our own species?
2. Given what you know about the psychology of aggression, how would you make a person less aggressive? If a person is aggressive because of more secretion of a particular hormone, does this excuse his or her behavior?

Sexual Behavior

Sexual behavior is not motivated by a physiological need, the way eating is. Because we must perform certain behaviors to reproduce, the process of natural selection has ensured that our brains are constructed in such a way as to cause enough of us to mate with each other that the species will survive.

Effects of Sex Hormones on Behavior

Sex hormones—hormones secreted by the testes and ovaries—have effects on cells throughout the body. In general, these effects promote reproduction. For example, they cause the production of sperms, build up the lining of the uterus, trigger ovulation, and stimulate the production of milk. Sex hormones also affect nerve cells in the brain, thereby affecting behavior.

Sex hormones do not *cause* behaviors. Behaviors are responses to particular situations and are affected by people's experiences in the past. What sex hormones do is affect people's *motivation* to perform particular classes of reproductive behaviors. We therefore start our exploration of sexual behavior with the motivational effects of sex hormones.

Effects of Androgens As you saw in Chapter 12, androgens such as testosterone are necessary for male sexual development. During prenatal development, the testes of male fetuses secrete testosterone, which causes the male sex organs to develop. This hormone also affects the development of the brain through organizational effects because they alter the sex organs and the brain. Studies using laboratory animals have shown that if the organizational effects of androgens on brain development are prevented, the animal later fails to exhibit male sexual behavior, but activation effects are also

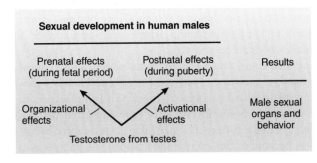

[**FIGURE 13·9**] Organizational and activational effects of testosterone on male sexual development and behavior in humans.

important. Males cannot have an erection and engage in sexual intercourse unless testosterone is present in adulthood. (See FIGURE 13·9.)

One of the effects of androgens on men is increased interest in sexual behavior. When levels of testosterone decline in adult men (which can occur because of aging, disease, or other factors), they report decreased interest in sex, along with other changes such as increased irritability and depression (Tenover, 1998). Providing artificial delivered testosterone supplements to men with this problem increases their interest in sex, the ability to have erections, and the frequency of sexual intercourse (Seftel et al., 2004). Thus, we may conclude that testosterone definitely affects male sexual performance.

This last study showed that a *placebo*—a nonactive chemical that a participant couldn't distinguish from the drug treatment—produced some of the same changes (although not so much). So, interest in sex, and even the physiological changes that accompany it, are also affected by psychological factors (see Rupp & Wallen, 2008). For example, men's interest in sexually explicit photographs will vary with their levels of testosterone, but the effect seems to be at least partially due to the hormone increasing their attention to the sexual aspects of the pictures (Rupp & Wallen, 2007).

Although testosterone affects sexual motivation, it does not determine the *object* of sexual desire. A homosexual man who receives injections of testosterone will not suddenly become interested in women. If testosterone has any effect, it will be to increase his interest in sexual contact with other men. Sexual orientation is discussed in a later section.

Effects of Progesterone and Estrogen In most species of mammals, the hormones estradiol and progesterone have strong effects on female sexual behavior. The levels of these two sex hormones fluctuate during the menstrual cycle of primates and the **estrous cycle** of other female mammals. The difference between menstrual cycles and estrous cycles is primarily that the lining of the primate uterus—but not that

---

estrous cycle Ovulatory cycle in mammals other than primates; the sequence of physical and hormonal changes that accompany the ripening and disintegration of ova.

of other mammals—builds up during the first part of the cycle and sloughs off at the end. A female mammal of a non-primate species—for example, a laboratory rat—will receive the advances of a male only when the levels of estradiol and progesterone in her blood are high. This condition occurs around the time of ovulation, when copulation is likely to make her become pregnant.

Women and other female primates are unique among mammals in their sexual activity: They are potentially willing to engage in sexual behavior at any time during their reproductive cycles. Some investigators have suggested that this difference in the pattern of sexual interest was favored by evolution because of the longer time that primate parents must care for their infants. The willingness to mate at any time during a female's menstrual cycle made monogamous relationships possible; because the male could look forward to his mate's receptivity at any time during her menstrual cycle, he would be less likely to look for other partners.

Although ovarian hormones do not *control* women's sexual activity, they may still have an influence on their sexual interest. A study by Van Goozen et al. (1997) found that the sexual activity initiated by men and women showed very different relations to the woman's menstrual cycle (and hence to her level of ovarian hormones). Men initiated sexual activity at about the same rate throughout the woman's cycle, whereas sexual activity initiated by women showed a distinct peak around the time of ovulation, when estradiol levels are highest. (See FIGURE 13•10.)

Laeng and Falkenberg (2007) obtained evidence that estradiol can affect a woman's interest in a romantic partner.

[**FIGURE 13•10**] Mean percentage of sexual activity initiated by women or their partners during the woman's menstrual cycle.

(Reproduced from Van Goozen, S. H. M., Wiegant, V. M., Endert, E., Helmond, F. A., & Van de Poll, N. E. (1997). Psychoendocrinological assessment of the menstrual cycle: The relationship between hormones, sexuality, and mood. *Archives of Sexual Behavior, 26*, 359–382.)

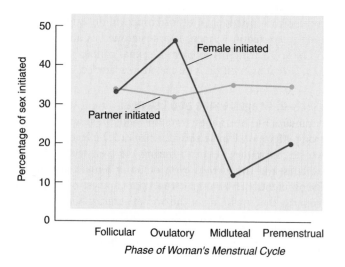

[**FIGURE 13•11**] Mean change in pupil diameter of women (either using oral contraceptives or not) when viewing photographs of their boyfriends, plotted over the phases of their hormonal cycles.

(Reproduced from Laeng, B., & Falkenberg, L. (2007). Women's pupillary response to sexually significant others during the hormonal cycle. *Hormones and Behavior, 52*, 520–530.)

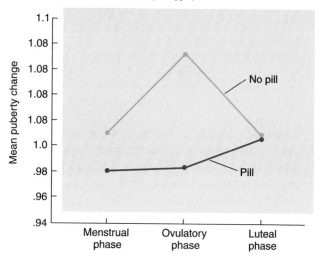

When people look at an emotionally significant stimulus, changes in their autonomic nervous system cause their pupils to dilate. This response is automatic and unintentional. Laeng and Falkenberg found that when women looked at pictures of their boyfriends around the time of ovulation, their pupils dilated more than they did at other times in their menstrual cycles. These differences were *not* seen in women taking birth-control pills, which suppress the secretion of estradiol. (See FIGURE 13•11.)

Sexual Orientation

Homosexual behavior (engaging in sexual activity with members of the same sex; from the Greek *homos*, meaning "the same") is seen in male and female animals of many different species. When humans reach puberty, the effects of sex hormones on their maturing bodies and on their brains increase their interest in sexual activity. As sexual interest increases, people develop a special interest in members of either the other sex or same sex. Why does opposite-sex attraction occur? And why does same-sex attraction sometimes occur? As we shall see, research has not yet provided definite answers to these questions, but it has provided some hints.

An ambitious project reported by Bell, Weinberg, and Hammersmith (1981) studied a large number of male and female homosexuals. The participants were asked about their relationships with their parents, siblings, and peers and about their feelings, gender identification, and sexual activity. The results provided little or no support for traditional theories of homosexuality, which stress the importance of a person's early environment. The major conclusions of the study follow:

1. Sexual orientation appears to be determined before adolescence and before homosexual or heterosexual activity. The most important single predictor of adult homosexuality was a self-report of homosexual feelings, which usually occurred 3 years before first genital homosexual activity. This finding suggests that homosexuality is a deep-seated tendency. It also tends to rule out the suggestion that seduction by an older person of the same sex plays an important role in the development of homosexuality.

2. Most homosexual men and women have engaged in some heterosexual experiences during childhood and adolescence, but in contrast to their heterosexual counterparts, they found these experiences unrewarding. This pattern is also consistent with the existence of a deep-seated predisposition before adulthood.

3. A strong relation exists between gender nonconformity in childhood and the development of homosexuality. Gender nonconformity is characterized by an aversion in boys to "masculine" behaviors and in girls to "feminine" behaviors.

The results of the study are consistent with the hypothesis that homosexuality is at least partly determined by biological factors. That is, biological variables predispose a child to behavior that is more typical of the other sex and eventually to sexual arousal by members of his or her own sex.

Is there evidence of what these biological causes of homosexuality may be? We can immediately eliminate the possibility that male homosexuals have insufficient levels of testosterone; well-adjusted male homosexuals have normal levels of testosterone (Garnets & Kimmel, 1991). Prenatal exposure to hormones and chemicals plays a large role in the development of homosexuality in both sexes (Swaab, 2007). Additional evidence comes from postmortem studies of the brains of deceased homosexual men. Compared with the brains of heterosexual males, these brains show differences in the size of two subregions of the hypothalamus and of a bundle of axons that connects the right and left temporal lobes (Swaab & Hofman, 1990; LeVay, 1991; Allen & Gorski, 1992). These findings do not prove that these brain areas are directly involved in sexual orientation. However, they do suggest that the brains of homosexuals were exposed to lower levels of androgens before birth or that their brains were relatively insensitive to these hormones (Berenbaum & Snyder, 1995).

In addition, Blanchard and Bogaert (1996) discovered that homosexual men are more likely than heterosexual men to have older brothers (but not younger brothers or older sisters). The more older brothers a man had, the more likely that he would become heterosexual. This finding was replicated in samples from a variety of countries by the original investigators and by other investigators. Bogaert (2006) found that the effect was seen only if a man had older biological brothers, born to the

same mother. The likelihood of homosexuality was not related to the presence of older adoptive brothers, or older brothers with the same father. So far, the most plausible explanation is that each time a woman carries a male fetus, her immune system becomes exposed to proteins that occur only in males. This exposure leads to development of maternal antibodies against these proteins that affect brain development of subsequent male fetuses (Blanchard & Ellis, 2001; Bogaert, 2003).

A final factor that may play a role in sexual orientation is heredity. Twin studies take advantage of the fact that identical twins have identical genes, whereas the genetic similarity between fraternal twins is, on the average, 50%. Bailey and his colleagues (Bailey & Pillard, 1991; Bailey et al., 1993) studied pairs of twins in which at least one member identified himself or herself as homosexual. If both twins are homosexual, they are said to be *concordant* for this trait. If only one is homosexual, the twins are said to be *discordant*. Thus, if homosexuality has a genetic basis, the percentage of monozygotic twins who are concordant for homosexuality should be higher than that for dizygotic twins. This is exactly what the investigators found: The concordance rate was 52% versus 22% for male twins, and 48% versus 16% for female twins.

Although less research has been done on the origins of female homosexuality, Cohen-Bendahan, van de Beek, and Berenbaum (2005) found that the incidence of homosexuality was several times higher than the national average in women who had been exposed prenatally to high levels of androgens. (The cause of the exposure was a genetic condition that causes the adrenal glands to secrete abnormally high levels of androgens—an event that begins prenatally.) Thus, sexual orientation in females may indeed be affected by biological factors, including prenatal hormones.

To summarize, evidence suggests that two major biological factors—heredity and the prenatal environment (exposure to hormones and maternal antibodies)—affect a person's sexual orientation. These research findings certainly contradict the suggestion that a person's sexual orientation is a matter of choice. It appears that homosexuals are no more responsible for their sexual orientation than heterosexuals are. Ernulf, Innala, and Whitam (1989) found that people who believed that homosexuals were "born that way" expressed more positive attitudes toward them than did people who believed that they "chose to be" or "learned to be" that way. Thus, we can hope that research on the origins of homosexuality will reduce prejudice based on a person's sexual orientation. The question "Why does someone become homosexual?" will probably be answered when we find out why someone becomes *heterosexual*.

Transsexualism and Androgen Insensitivity Syndrome

As we saw, when the organizational effects of androgens are blocked in male laboratory animals, the animals fail to develop normal male sex behavior. In humans, male sex behavior also appears to depend on prenatal androgens (Money & Ehrhardt, 1972; MacLean, Warne, & Zajac, 1995). Some people are insensitive to androgens. They have **androgen insensitivity syndrome,** caused by a genetic mutation that prevents the formation of androgen receptors. Because the cells of the body cannot respond to androgens, the person develops female external genitalia instead of a penis and scrotum. The person does not develop ovaries or a uterus.

When an individual with one X chromosome and one Y is born with androgen insensitivity syndrome, the parents face the choice of whether to raise the child as a boy or as a girl. (This situation is different from the case of D.R., described in Chapter 12, whose gender assignment resulted from genital trauma.) If the individual is to be raised as a girl, the testes (which remain in the abdomen) are removed and, at the appropriate time, the person is given estrogen pills to induce puberty. Subsequently, the individual will function sexually as a woman. However, whether the adult is comfortable with this gender identity is a complex issue, depending on the degree of androgen insensitivity and the amount of psychological support received (see Hughes et al., 2006, for a review).

Prenatal androgens also appear to have an effect on certain regions of the brain, including one region in the forebrain known as the bed nucleus of the stria terminalis (BNST). The BNST is larger in men than in women (Zhou et al., 1996). This difference is not present in childhood, but rather appears later in life, around the time of puberty (Chung, De Vries, & Swaab, 2002). The region is the same size for both heterosexual and homosexual men, suggesting that, although this region may differentiate male sexuality from female, it is not involved in male homosexuality.

The BNST, however, may be related to sexual *identification* rather than sexual *orientation*. Some individuals, typically described as **transsexual,** see themselves as belonging to a different sex than that which they were assigned at birth. A transsexual person, for example, might feel herself to be a female trapped inside a male body. Post mortem studies of people born as males but identifying as females have found that the size of the BNST in these individuals is, indeed, similar to that of females (Zhou et al., 1995). Based on when they seek medical consultation regarding it, transsexual people recognize their condition sometime after puberty (van Kesteren, Gooren, & Megens, 1996)—about the time that the BNST begins to show a size difference between males and females.

QUESTIONS FOR CONSIDERATION

1. Whatever the relative roles played by biological and environmental factors may be, most investigators believe that a person's sexual orientation is not a matter of choice. Why do you think so many people consider sexual orientation to be a moral issue?

---

androgen insensitivity syndrome A condition caused by a congenital lack of functioning androgen receptors; in a person with XY sex chromosomes, causes the development of a female with testes but no internal sex organs.

transsexual An individual who perceives himself or herself as belonging to a different sex than that which they were assigned at birth.

2. During the Summer Olympics of 1992, a heated controversy arose over the use of sex testing of female athletes. One of the effects of androgens is to increase the size and strength of skeletal muscles; thus, men generally have greater physical strength than women have. To prevent men from disguising themselves as women and unfairly competing in women's events, the officials decided to confirm women's sex by taking a sample of cells and examining their chromosomes. Thus, a woman with androgen insensitivity syndrome and an XY genotype would be disqualified from Olympic competition in women's events—and this occurred in 1992. In your opinion, is this practice fair? Why or why not?

Emotion

Until this point, we have focused on forms of behavior that are most intimately related to motivation—the operant behavior instigated by reinforcement, eating, the aggressive behavior instigated by aversive stimuli, and the reproductive behavior instigated by sexual stimuli. However, these same stimuli also elicit other important effects. These effects fall under the heading of emotion. The word **emotion** refers to the behavior, physiological reactions, and subjective feelings that accompany motivated behavior. When we are motivated, we display a wide range of emotional reactions—happiness, sadness, fear, and so forth. Different emotions are evoked by specific kinds of situations and provide distinctive stimuli that affect the subsequent behavior of the person experiencing the emotion and the behavior of others who detect the emotion. For example, we communicate emotions to others by means of postural changes, facial expressions, and nonverbal sounds (such as sighs, moans, and laughs). These expressions serve useful social functions: They tell other people how we feel and—more to the point—what we are likely to do. For example, they warn a rival that we are angry or tell friends that we are sad and would like some comfort and reassurance. They can also indicate that a danger might be present or that something interesting seems to be happening.

Emotions as Response Patterns

If you ask people to define the word "emotion," they will probably talk about feelings. But the ultimate reason for the existence of emotions is to provide patterns of behavior that are appropriate to particular situations. Evolution has selected for patterns of emotional responses that are useful to the individual making them.

Emotional reactions have three components—behavioral, autonomic, and hormonal. The behavioral component consists of muscular movements appropriate to the situation that elicits them. For example, if a father sees his toddler venture onto a busy street, he will run to prevent the child from being hurt. In addition, his autonomic nervous system and the secretion of hormones by his adrenal glands will facilitate the behavioral component by mobilizing energy for vigorous movement. The father's heart rate will increase, the arteries that supply blood to his muscles will dilate, and his rate of respiration will increase.

Conditioned Emotional Responses Like other behavior, emotional responses can be modified by experience. For example, once we have learned that a particular situation is dangerous, we become frightened when we next encounter that situation. This type of response, acquired through a classical procedure, is called a **conditioned emotional response** (see Chapter 5). A conditioned emotional response is produced when a neutral stimulus is paired with an emotion-producing stimulus. A early demonstration that emotions can be conditioned was made by Watson and Rayner in 1920. They were able to study a 9-month-old boy that they named "Albert B." Albert has a healthy child who seemed to Watson and Rayner "on the whole stolid and unemotional." However, they discovered that a loud noise, made by striking a steel bar with a hammer, could startle Albert and make him cry. A little later, when Albert was 11 months old, they showed him a live white rat—an animal that Albert has shown no fear of previously—and then, when Albert reached for it, they struck the bar. After two pairings of the white rat and the sound, Watson and Rayner observed that Albert was much more hesitant to touch the rat. After five pairings, he showed definite signs of fear, crying, and crawling away from the rat. Watson and Rayner's conditioning procedure had produced an acquired fear.

Research by physiological psychologists indicates that a particular brain region plays an important role in the expression of conditioned emotional responses. This region is the amygdala, which is located in the temporal lobe, just in front of the hippocampus (refer to Figure 4.29). The amygdala is a region of convergence between sensory systems and systems responsible for behavioral, autonomic, and hormonal components of conditioned emotional responses (Amaral et al., 1992; Pitkänen et al., 1997; Stefanacci and Amaral, 2000).

Studies with animals have found that damage to the amygdala disrupts components of conditioned emotional responses. If this region is destroyed, animals no longer show signs of fear when confronted with stimuli that have been paired with aversive events. In addition, they act tame when handled by humans, their blood levels of stress hormones are lower, and they are less likely to develop stress-induced illnesses (Coover, Murison, & Jellestad, 1992; Davis, 1992; LeDoux, 1992). These effects are also seen in people who have sustained damage to the amygdala through stroke or disease (Bechara et al., 1995). Conversely, when the amygdala is stimulated by means of electrodes or by the injection of an excitatory drug, animals show physiological and behavioral signs of fear and agitation (Davis, 1992), and humans report feelings of fear. Such findings indicate that the autonomic and hormonal components of emotional responses are under the control of the amygdala and may contribute to the harmful

effects of long-term stress. (We examine the topic of stress later in this chapter.)

Aggression, Moral Judgment, and Impulse Control

Earlier, we looked at aggression as it related to motivational stimuli, such as threats or appeasement gestures. Aggression in humans is often accompanied by emotions such as anger and fear, so it is appropriate to consider it in connection with emotions. Consider the following case history:

[CASE STUDY] By the time Joshua had reached the age of 2, . . . he would bolt out of the house and into traffic. He kicked and head-butted relatives and friends. He poked the family hamster with a pencil and tried to strangle it. He threw regular temper tantrums and would stage toy-throwing frenzies. "At one point he was hurting himself—banging his head against a wall, pinching himself, not to mention leaping off the refrigerator. . . . Showering Joshua with love . . . made little difference: By age 3, his behavior got him kicked out of his preschool. (Holden, 2000, p. 581)

The muscular movements made during aggression are programmed by neural circuits in the brain stem. The activity of the brain stem circuits appears to be controlled by the hypothalamus and the amygdala, which also influence many other species-typical behaviors. And, of course, the activity of these structures is controlled by perceptual systems that detect the status of the environment, including the presence of other animals. Aggression, and the emotions that accompany it, are therefore the result of a number of brain processes.

Role of Serotonin Several studies have found that serotonergic neurons play an inhibitory role in human aggression. For example, a depressed rate of serotonin release in the brain (indicated by low levels of the breakdown products of serotonin in the cerebrospinal fluid) are associated with aggression and other forms of antisocial behavior, including assault, arson, murder, and child beating (Lidberg et al., 1984, 1985; Virkkunen et al., 1989). Coccaro et al. (1994) studied a group of men with personality disorders (including a history of impulsive aggression). They found that the men with the lowest serotonergic activity were most likely to have close relatives with a history of similar behavior problems.

If low levels of serotonin release contribute to aggression, perhaps drugs that act as serotonin agonists might help to reduce antisocial behavior. A study by Coccaro and Kavoussi (1997) found that fluoxetine (Prozac), a serotonin agonist, decreased irritability and aggressiveness, as measured by a psychological test. Joshua, the little boy described in the

---

conditioned emotional response A classically conditioned response that occurs when a neutral stimulus is followed by an aversive stimulus; usually includes autonomic, behavioral, and endocrine components such as changes in heart rate, freezing, and secretion of stress-related hormones.

introduction to this subsection, came under the care of a psychiatrist who prescribed monoaminergic agonists and began a course of behavior therapy that managed to stem Joshua's violent outbursts and risk-taking behaviors.

Role of the Ventral Prefrontal Cortex Many investigators believe that impulsive violence is a consequence of faulty emotional regulation. For most of us, frustrations may elicit an urge to respond emotionally, but we usually manage to calm ourselves and suppress these urges. The ventral prefrontal cortex plays a special role in control of emotional behaviors—especially anger and aggression.

The **ventral prefrontal cortex** is located at the base of the anterior frontal lobes. Its inputs provide it with information about what is happening in the environment and what plans are being made by the rest of the frontal lobes, and its outputs permit it to affect a variety of behaviors and physiological responses, including emotional responses organized by the amygdala. Evidence suggests that the ventral prefrontal cortex serves as an interface between brain mechanisms involved in automatic emotional responses (both learned and unlearned) and those involved in the control of complex behaviors. This role includes using our emotional reactions to guide our behavior and in controlling the occurrence of emotional reactions in various social situations. The fact that the ventral prefrontal cortex plays an important role in control of emotional behavior is shown by the effects of damage to this region. The following case is the first—from the mid-1800s—and the most famous example of this.

[CASE STUDY] Phineas Gage, the foreman of a railway construction crew, was using a steel rod to ram a charge of blasting powder into a hole drilled in solid rock. Suddenly, the charge exploded and sent the rod into his cheek, through his brain, and out the top of his head. (See FIGURE 13.12.) He survived, but he was a different man. Before his injury he was serious, industrious, and energetic. Afterward, he became childish, irresponsible, and thoughtless of others. His outbursts of temper led some people to remark that it looked as if Dr. Jekyll had become Mr. Hyde. He was unable to make or carry out plans, and his actions appeared to be capricious and whimsical. His accident severely damaged the ventral prefrontal cortex (Damasio et al., 1994).

Moral Judgment Evidence suggests that emotional reactions guide moral judgments as well as decisions involving personal risks and rewards and that the prefrontal cortex plays a role in these judgments as well. Consider the following moral dilemma: You see a runaway trolley with five people aboard hurtling down a track leading to a cliff. Without your intervention, these people will soon die. However, you

[**FIGURE 13·12**] A reconstruction of the skull of Phineas Gage and the rod that passed through his head. The steel rod entered his left cheek and exited through the top of his head.

(From Damasio, H., Grabowski, T., Frank, R., Galaburda, A. M., and Damasio, A. R. (1994) *Science, 264,* 1102–1105. Copyright 1994 American Association for the Advancement of Science.)

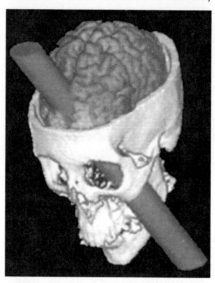

are standing near a switch that will shunt the trolley off to another track, where the vehicle will stop safely. But a worker is standing on that track, and he will be killed if you throw the switch to save the five helpless passengers. Should you stand by and watch the trolley go off the cliff, or should you save them—and kill the man on the track?

Most people conclude that the better choice would be to throw the switch; saving five people justifies the sacrifice of one man. But consider a variation of this dilemma. As before, the trolley is hurtling toward doom, but no switch is at hand to shunt it to another track. Instead, you are standing on a bridge over the track. An obese man is standing there too, and if you give him a push, his body will fall on the track and stop the trolley. (You are too small to stop the trolley, so you cannot save the five people by sacrificing yourself.) What should you do?

Most people balk at pushing the man off the bridge, even though the result would be the same as the first dilemma: one person lost, five people saved. Whether we kill someone by sending a trolley his way or by pushing him off a bridge into the path of an oncoming trolley, he dies when the trolley strikes him. But somehow pushing a person's body and causing his death seems more emotionally wrenching than throwing a switch that changes the course of a runaway trolley. Thus, moral judgments appear to be guided by emotional reactions and are not simply the products of rational, logical decision-making processes.

In a functional imaging study, Greene et al. (2001) presented people with the moral dilemmas such as the one just described and found that thinking about them activated

---

ventral prefrontal cortex The region of the prefrontal cortex at the base of the anterior frontal lobes, involved in control of emotional behavior.

several brain regions involved in emotional reactions, including the medial prefrontal cortex. Making innocuous decisions, such as whether to take a bus or train to some destination, did not activate these regions. Perhaps, then, our reluctance to push someone to his death is guided by the unpleasant emotional reaction we feel when we contemplate this action.

If the prefrontal cortex helps to mediate the role of emotions in moral judgments, then damage to this area should impair such judgments. Tendencies toward antisocial behavior are apparently associated with decreased volume of the prefrontal cortex and a lack of prefrontal activation during an aversive conditioning procedure (Raine et al., 2002; Birbaumer et al., 2005).

Raine et al. (1998) found evidence of decreased prefrontal activity and increased subcortical activity (including the amygdala) in the brains of convicted murderers. These changes were seen primarily in impulsive, emotional murderers. The prefrontal activity of cold-blooded, calculating, predatory murderers—whose crimes were not accompanied by anger and rage—was closer to normal. Presumably, increased activation of the amygdala reflected an increased tendency for display of negative emotions, and the decreased activation of the prefrontal cortex reflected a decreased ability to inhibit the activity of the amygdala and thus control the people's emotions.

Earlier in this section, we saw that decreased activity of serotonergic neurons is associated with aggression, violence, and risk taking. As we have just seen, decreased activity of the prefrontal cortex is also associated with antisocial behavior. These two facts appear to be linked. The prefrontal cortex receives a major projection of serotonergic axons. Research indicates that serotonergic input to the prefrontal cortex activates this region. In addition, several studies have found evidence for deficits in serotonergic innervation of the medial prefrontal cortex in people with a history of impulsive violence. For example, a PET study found evidence for decreased serotonergic input to the medial prefrontal cortex of such people (Frankle et al., 2005).

As we saw earlier, impulsive aggression has been successfully treated with specific serotonin reuptake inhibitors such as fluoxetine (Prozac). New et al. (2004) used a PET scanner to measure regional brain activity of people with histories of impulsive aggression before and after 12 weeks of treatment with fluoxetine. They found that the drug increased the activity of the orbitofrontal cortex and reduced aggressiveness.

QUESTIONS FOR CONSIDERATION

1. Phobias can be seen as dramatic examples of conditioned emotional responses. These responses can even be contagious; we can acquire them without direct experience with an aversive stimulus. For example, a child who sees a parent show signs of fright in the presence of a dog may also develop a fear reaction to the dog. Do you think that some prejudices might be learned in this way, too?

2. From the point of view of evolution, aggressive behavior and a tendency to establish dominance have useful functions. In particular, they increase the likelihood that only the most healthy and vigorous animals will reproduce. Can you think of examples of good and bad effects of these tendencies among members of our own species?

The Expression and Recognition of Emotions

We have considered emotions as organized response patterns (behavioral, autonomic, and hormonal) that are produced by environmental stimuli that are motivating. For example, being confronted with a threat not only motivates escape behavior but also evokes various emotional responses. At the same time, emotions exist, in part, because expressions of emotion communicate important information to other members of the species. Members of many species (including humans) convey their emotions to others by means of postural changes and facial expressions. Such responses tell other individuals how we feel and—more to the point—what we are likely to do. For example, they warn when we are angry and should be left alone or when we are sad and would welcome comfort. This section reviews research on the expression and recognition of emotions.

The Social Nature of Emotional Expressions in Humans

The expression of emotions is significantly social. For example, Lee and Wagner (2002) asked women to recount a positive and a negative emotional event that had happened to them in the past year. They were given a microphone to speak into but, unknown to them, they were also being videotaped. (This use of concealment required special justification on the basis of the ethical issues discussed in Chapter 2; Lee and Wagner provide a good account of how they resolved this dilemma.) For half of the women, a female acquaintance sat across from them as they described these experiences; for the other participants, this acquaintance left the room, and they spoke only into the microphone. Later, the videotapes were watched to see when a participant showed positive or negative facial expressions.

When participants described their experiences alone, there was a good correspondence between the emotional experience they were describing and their facial expressions: positive experiences were accompanied by positive expressions, and negative experiences, by negative expressions. However, the physical presence of another person affected facial expressions. Individuals showed significantly more positive facial expressions when they were talking about a positive experience to an acquaintance than when they were alone. So, a social setting seemed to amplify the expression of positive feelings, but negative facial expressions were fewer in the presence of another. So social context can depress the expression of negative emotions.

We tend to think that our facial expressions are closely linked to our emotional experiences. However, as we saw in the case of other emotional behaviors, facial expressions also serve as communication. We use them to manage others' impressions of our own state, which breaks down the link between our experience of emotion and our external expression of it.

The Universality of Emotional Expressions in Humans

The social content of emotional expression raises the question of culture. Different cultures and communities possess their own languages. Do they possess their own emotional expressions? Charles Darwin thought that emotions had evolved, and, based on information he received from anthropologists, suggested that emotions were expressed the same way in different cultures.

In the late 1960s, Ekman and Friesen undertook a series of cross-cultural observations that validated those of Darwin (Ekman, Friesen, & Ellsworth, 1972). They visited an isolated tribe in a remote area of New Guinea—the South Fore tribe, a group of 319 adults and children who had never been exposed to Western culture. If they were able to identify accurately the emotional expressions of westerners as well as they could identify those of members of their own tribe, and if their own facial expressions were the same as those of Westerners, then the researchers could conclude that these expressions were not culturally determined.

Because translations of single words from one language to another are not always accurate, Ekman and colleagues told little stories to describe an emotion instead of presenting a single word. They told the story to a subject, presented three photographs of Westerners depicting three different emotions, and asked the subject to choose the appropriate one. This they were able to do. In a second study, they asked Fore tribespeople to imagine how they would feel in situations that would produce various emotions, and the researchers videotaped their facial expressions. They showed photographs of the videotapes to American college students, who had no trouble identifying the emotions. Four of them are shown in FIGURE 13•13. The caption describes the story that was used to elicit each expression. TABLE 13•1 shows the degree of accuracy of various cultures at recognizing facial expressions of emotion.

However, not all psychologists have agreed with Ekman's conclusions. Although the finding that facial expressions can be identified cross-culturally is robust, little agreement exists on what these findings mean. Critics such as Fridlund (1992, 1994) argued that all facial expressions are communicative and that to single out a group of emotional facial expressions ignores the fundamental social nature of facial expression. Expressions may be not emotional signals but social tools used for communication: We can communicate happiness or

[FIGURE 13•13] Portraying emotions. Ekman and Friesen asked South Fore tribesmen to make faces (shown in the photographs) when they were told stories. (a) "Your friend has come and you are happy." (b) "Your child has died." (c) "You are angry and about to fight." (d) "You see a dead pig that has been lying there a long time."

(From Ekman, 1980, *The face of man: Expressions of universal emotions in a New Guinea village.* New York: Garland STPM Press. Photos © Paul Ekman 1972–2004. Reprinted with permission.)

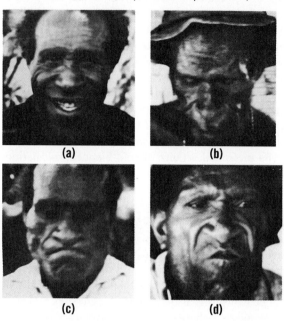

approval via a smile, but this smile may not be generated by genuine emotion but by social cues or needs. This objection is difficult, in part, to counter because expressions may sometimes be used for nonemotional purposes. Smiling may indeed be an expression of joy, but it can also be an expression of sarcasm or even, in sinister contexts, threat. What critics suggest is that facial expressions do not reflect the emotion but the social signalling of the emotion; the two are different.

[TABLE 13•1] Cross-cultural accuracy in recognizing emotion

Expression	US	Chile	Brazil	Argentina	Japan
Happiness	97	90	92	94	87
Fear	88	78	77	68	71
Disgust	84	85	86	79	82
Anger	68	76	82	72	63
Surprise	91	88	81	93	87
Sadness	87	91	82	88	80
Average	86	85	83	82	78

Adapted from: Elfenbein, H.A. and Ambady, N. (2003) Universals in cultural differences in recognizing emotions. *Current Directions in Psychological Science,* 12, *5,* 159–164.

Other critics, such as Russell (1991, 1994), even questioned whether the cross-cultural findings are robust. Russell argued in some detail that the faults in the methodology in these experiments, particularly the method of presenting each emotion sequentially and asking respondents to choose from a list of alternative descriptions the expression they have seen, make the conclusions of these studies uninterpretable.

It has been suggested that people better recognize emotions within their own cultural group. However, Beaupre and Hess (2005) have challenged this view. They measured emotional recognition in a sample of French-Canadian, sub-Saharan Africans, and Chinese participants living in Canada. All samples performed similarly when asked to recognize expressions of emotion in the in-group and out-group faces, but some groups were better at this task in general (regardless of nationality of the face). French-Canadians recognized sadness more accurately than did the other two cultures and recognized shame more accurately than did the Chinese. The researchers argue, however, that because the stimuli used in the experiment derive from North American investigations, this benefited the French-Canadians, hence their better accuracy.

Cultural Differences Perhaps members of some cultures recognize emotions more accurately because these emotions are more important to them. Researchers from the University of Illinois asked European American, Asian American, Japanese, Indian, and Hispanic students to report their emotional experiences over a 1-week period and how many pleasant and unpleasant emotions they generally experienced (Scollon et al., 2004). Individuals from Asian cultures reported less life satisfaction and fewer pleasant emotions than did North Americans, a finding that has also been reported within a nation—Asian Americans appear to show this pattern more than do European Americans (Diener et al., 1995; Okazaki, 2000).

The researchers also found that the Hispanic Americans reported the greatest levels of pride, whereas the three Asian samples reported the least, with the Indian sample reporting the least within these (suggesting that pride is not a greatly valued emotion in these cultures and that it may be perceived negatively, rather than positively). No cultural differences were found for sadness but some were found for guilt: Japanese and Asian Americans reported greater levels of guilt than did the European Americans and Hispanics. The Indian sample reported the least. The three Asian cultures reported significantly fewer pleasant emotions (and more negative emotions) than did the other cultures.

Situations That Produce Emotions: The Role of Cognition

Emotions rarely occur spontaneously; they are provoked by particular stimuli, as we saw with conditioned emotional responses, and are affected by social context, as you just read. Emotions are the products of cognitive processes as well. For humans, the emotions evoked by eliciting stimuli can recur in later situations if they engage cognitive processes such as memory. As can memory, our emotions can be affected by the circumstances of retrieval. For example, Italian students who had recently participated in a large peaceful demonstration recalled it as being more violent than it was when they saw altered photographs implying violence; they also rated it significantly more negative and said that they were unlikely to attend another (Sacchi, Agnoli, & Loftus, 2007).

Humans often experience emotions on the basis of their judgments about the significance of particular situations. For example, a pianist who is satisfied with her performance may perceive applause as praise for outstanding artistry, judging the applause to be a positive evaluation of her own worth. She will feel pride and gratification. In this case, her emotional state is produced by social reinforcement—the expression of approval and admiration by other people. However, if the pianist believes that she has performed poorly, she may judge the applause as the mindless enthusiasm of people who have no taste and for whom she feels only contempt. Furthermore, the page-turner is also present on the stage and thus also perceives the applause. However, because he does not evaluate the applause as praise for anything he did, the page-turner does not experience the emotions the pianist feels. The applause may even make him feel jealous. Clearly, a given set of stimuli does not always elicit the same emotion. Judgments about the significance of the stimuli determine the emotion the person feels. (We look at the role of appraisal in the perception of stress later in this chapter.)

Feelings of Emotions

Emotions are accompanied by physiological reactions, and these reactions can evoke feelings of emotion. We can easily understand why. Strong emotions increase the heart rate and can produce irregular breathing, queasy feelings in the internal organs, trembling, sweating, reddening of the face, or even fainting. We may ask whether these physiological reactions *constitute* the emotion or are merely symptoms of some other underlying process.

The theory developed by the physiologists Walter Cannon and Phillip Bard and an earlier theory proposed by the psychologist William James and the physiologist Carl Lange are two somewhat different approaches to feelings of emotion. The **James-Lange theory** proposed that the physiological and behavioral responses to emotion-arousing stimuli produced feelings of emotion (James, 1884; Lange, 1887). The **Cannon–Bard theory** contended that feelings of emotion were relatively independent of the physiological and behavioral responses to emotion-arousing stimuli (Cannon, 1927).

James-Lange theory Theory of emotion proposing that behavioral and physiological responses are directly elicited by situations; feelings of emotions are produced by feedback from these behavioral and physiological responses.

Cannon–Bard theory Theory of emotion proposing that feelings of emotion, as well as behavioral and physiological responses, are directly elicited by the environment.

Cannon and Bard, based on the evidence available at the time, incorrectly believed that autonomic and behavioral responses to emotion-arousing stimuli were too slow and too indistinct to affect the rapidly occurring and often subtle differences in feelings of emotion. As an illustration of the difference between the theories, Cannon and Bard took the position that the sight of an approaching bear evokes both physiological/behavioral responses and, largely independently, feelings of fear.

In contrast, James and Lange believed that the sight of the bear evokes physiological/behavioral responses and that stimuli produced by these responses, in turn, evoke feelings of fear. That is, the sight of the bear first evokes running and increases in heart rate, and then, after these changes are sensed, feelings of fear. In essence, the James–Lange theory states that emotion-producing situations elicit an appropriate set of physiological responses, such as trembling, sweating, and increased heart rate. The situations also elicit behaviors such as clenching of fists or fighting. The brain receives sensory feedback from the muscles and from the organs that produce these responses, and it is this feedback that constitutes our subjective feelings of emotion. As James put it:

> The bodily changes follow directly the perception of the exciting fact, and . . . our feelings of the same changes as they occur is the emotion. Common sense says we lose our fortune, are sorry, and weep; we meet a bear, are frightened, and run. . . . The hypothesis here to be defended says that this order of sequence is incorrect. . . . The more rational statement is that we feel sorry because we cry, angry because we strike, afraid because we tremble, and not that we cry, strike, or tremble because we are sorry, angry or fearful, as the case may be. (James, 1890, p. 449)

James's approach is closely related to a process called *attribution*, which we encounter in Chapter 15. Attribution theory in social psychology is concerned with how we draw conclusions about the causes of other people's behavior. The James–Lange theory says that we go through much the same process when we draw conclusions about our own behavior. We observe our own physiological and behavioral responses and, based on that information, attribute feelings to ourselves. Our emotional feelings are based on what we find ourselves doing and on the sensory feedback we receive from the activity of our muscles and internal organs. Where feelings of emotions are concerned, we are self-observers. Thus, patterns of emotional responses and expressions of emotions give rise to feelings of emotion. By this reasoning, emotional feelings are the products of emotional responses. (See FIGURE 13.14.)

James's description of the process by which emotional feelings are produced may seem odd. We usually believe that we directly experience feelings without physiological or behavioral intermediaries. We tend to see the outward manifestations of emotions as secondary events. But have you ever found yourself in an unpleasant confrontation with someone and discovered that you were trembling, even though you did not think that you were so upset by the encounter? Or were you ever surprised to find yourself blushing in response to

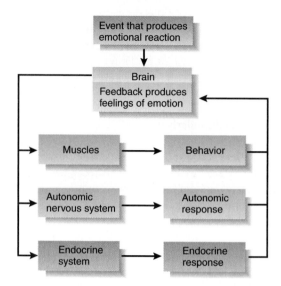

[**FIGURE 13·14**] A diagrammatic representation of the James-Lange theory of emotion. An event in the environment triggers behavioral, autonomic, and endocrine responses. Feedback from these responses produces feelings of emotions.

some remark? Or did tears ever come to your eyes while watching a film that you did not think was affecting you? What might you conclude about the causes of your emotional feelings in situations like these? Would you ignore the evidence of your own physiological and behavioral reactions?

Effects of Spinal Cord Injury and Autonomic-System Damage: Evaluation of the James-Lange Theory

A way to evaluate the James-Lange theory of feelings of emotion is to assess the feelings of individuals with diminished sensory feedback from physiological and behavioral responses. In one of the first attempts to test the theory this way, Hohmann (1966) collected data about the intensity of emotional feelings of people who had had damage to their spinal cords. If feedback from the body is important, Hohmann reasoned, then emotional feelings would be less intense if the injury were high up in the spinal cord, thereby eliminating most bodily sensations, than if it were low in the cord, thereby permitting some bodily sensations. (See FIGURE 13.15.)

Hohmann found some support for what the James-Lange theory would predict,, but later research has been less kind to the theory. For example, Cobos et al. (2002) examined how people reacted to photographs that elicit emotions. They showed the participants in their study images that evoked positive or negative feelings and measured several behavioral reactions. Some of the participants in this study were people with spinal cord injuries. In general, their reactions were very similar to the reactions of people without injuries; importantly, when asked to judge their ability to feel different kinds of emotion, no clear difference was related to the level of the spinal cord injury.

It may be that emotional feelings do not require bodily sensations, but that they are nevertheless affected by them (Tsuchiya & Adolphs, 2007). For example, one of Hohmann's

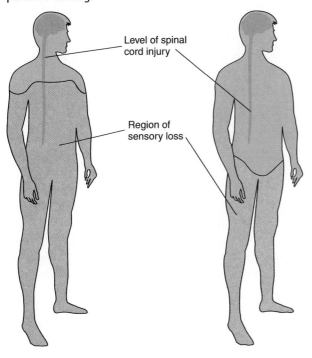

[**FIGURE 13·15**] Hohman's investigation of emotion in people with spinal cord damage. The higher the spinal cord damage, the less intense was the person's feeling.

Level of spinal cord injury

Region of sensory loss

patients with high spinal cord injuries suggested that the severely diminished feedback did change feelings, although not necessarily behavior.

> Sometimes I act angry when I see some injustice. I yell and cuss and raise hell, because if you don't . . . I've learned people will take advantage of you, but it doesn't have the heat to it that it used to. It's a mental kind of anger. (Hohmann, 1966, pp. 150–151)

QUESTIONS TO CONSIDER

1. We can move our facial muscles to simulate expressions of emotions, but these expressions are usually less convincing than spontaneous ones. Have you ever tried to suppress a smile when you wanted to seem serious or to look happy when you were really feeling sad? If you wanted to be an actor, how might you try to develop realistic expressions of emotions?

2. As you know, we tend to become accustomed to our present circumstances. If we finally achieve a goal we have been striving for—a car, a well-paying job, a romantic attachment with a wonderful person—we find that the happiness it brings us is not permanent. But if we then lose what we have gained, we are even less happy than we were in the first place. Would it make evolutionary sense for a person to be happy all the time?

3. We can control the display of our emotions, but can we control our feelings? Can you think of any ways to make yourself feel happy or stop feeling angry?

Stress and Health

At some point, we've all experienced stress, whether it was taking a difficult exam or coping with the loss of a friend. **Stress** is a pattern of physiological, behavioral, emotional, and cognitive responses to real or imagined stimuli that are perceived as blocking a goal or endangering or otherwise threatening our well-being. These stimuli are generally aversive and are called **stressors.** Stress is a product of natural selection. It is a behavioral adaptation that helped our ancestors fight or flee from wild animals and enemies. Likewise, stress often helps us confront or escape threatening situations (Linsky, Bachman, & Straus, 1995). Although stress is not a direct product of cultural evolution, the changes in the environment wrought by cultural evolution have helped make stress commonplace.

Stressors come in many forms. They may be catastrophic in nature (see Meichenbaum, 1995), or they may belong to the class of trivial everyday irritations. Stressors are not always bad. Some stressors, such as athletic competition and class exams, can affect behavior in positive ways. When stress is extended over long periods, however, it can have negative effects on both psychological and physical health (Selye, 1991).

The Biological Basis of Stress

Our physiological response to stressors is governed by the autonomic nervous system, which is controlled by the hypothalamus. When an individual senses a stressor, the hypothalamus sends signals to the autonomic nervous system and to

Stressors, such as the flooding of the homes and businesses of New Orleans residents in the aftermath of Hurricane Katrina in 2005, threaten our normal life routine and well-being.

---

stress A pattern of physiological, behavioral, emotional, and cognitive responses to stimuli (real or imagined) that are perceived as endangering our well-being.

stressors Stimuli that are perceived as endangering our well-being.

the pituitary gland, both of which respond by stimulating body organs to change their normal activities:

1. Heart rate increases, blood pressure increases, blood vessels constrict, blood sugar levels increase, and blood flow is directed away from extremities and toward major organs.

2. Breathing becomes deeper and faster, and air passages dilate, allowing more air to enter the lungs.

3. Digestion stops, and perspiration increases.

4. The adrenal glands secrete adrenaline (epinephrine), which stimulates the heart and other organs.

The physiological changes prepare us for some action. Accompanying these physiological changes can be a pattern of behaviors, emotions, or cognitive responses. We may also feel the stress response as an emotion, although the emotion may depend on the nature of the stressor; stress may make us feel frightened in some situations or exhilarated in others. Finally, our cognitive state may be altered, as when we respond to fright with anticipation of danger.

In two cases, such responses can be maladaptive. First, stress can produce anxiety, which may impair your ability to perform a task. As you may have experienced yourself, anxiety can make it more difficult to perform on an exam, deliver a public speech, compete during an athletic event, or remember lines in a play. The second case, as I've mentioned, involves the effects of prolonged and severe stress. Many people's lifestyles place them in situations in which they are confronted with stressors daily. As we will see shortly, such lifestyles place these people at increased risk of illness.

Selye's General Adaptation Syndrome

Much of what we know about the effects of dealing with prolonged and severe stressors on the body stems from the work of endocrinologist Hans Selye. Through his work with laboratory animals, Selye found that prolonged exposure to severe stressors produces a sequence of three physiological stages: *alarm, resistance,* and *exhaustion.* (See FIGURE 13.16.) Selye (1956/1976, 1993) referred to these stages collectively as the **general adaptation syndrome.**

The responses in the *alarm stage* involve arousal of the autonomic nervous system and occur when an organism is first confronted with a stressor. During this stage, the organism's resistance to the stressor temporarily decreases to below normal, and the organism may experience shock—impairment of normal physiological functioning. With continued exposure to the stressor, the organism enters the *stage of resistance,* during which its autonomic nervous system returns

---

general adaptation syndrome   The model proposed by Selye to describe the body's adaptation to prolonged exposure to severe stressors. The body passes through a sequence of three physiological stages: alarm, resistance, and exhaustion.

fight-or-flight response   Physiological reactions that help ready us to fight or to flee a dangerous situation.

[**FIGURE 13·16**] The general adaptation syndrome as proposed by Hans Selye.

(Figure 2, the three phases of the general adaptation syndrome, from *Stress without Distress* by Hans Selye, M.D. Copyright © 1974 by Hans Selye, M.D. Reprinted by permission of HarperCollins Publishers.)

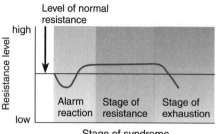

to normal functioning. Resistance to the stressor increases and eventually plateaus at above-normal levels. The stage of resistance, then, reflects the organism's adaptation to environmental stressors. However, with continued exposure to the stressor, the organism enters the *stage of exhaustion.* During this stage, the organism loses its ability to adapt, and resistance plummets to below-normal levels, leaving the organism susceptible to illness and even death. Biologically speaking, we are able to adapt to the presence of environmental stressors for only so long before we become susceptible to exhaustion and illness. The extent to which people can adapt varies across individuals and depends on how the stressor is perceived.

Earlier we considered that emotional responses evolved because they are useful and adaptive. Why, then, can they harm our health? The answer appears to be that our emotional responses are designed primarily to cope with short-term events. The physiological responses that accompany negative emotions prepare us to threaten or fight rivals or to run away from dangerous situations. Harvard physiologist Walter Cannon (1953) popularized the phrase **fight-or-flight response,** which refers to the physiological reactions that prepare us for the strenuous efforts required by fighting or running away. Normally, once we have bluffed or fought with an adversary or run away from a dangerous situation, the threat is over, and our physiological condition can return to normal. As long as the responses are brief, the physiological responses do not have adverse long-term effects. But when the threatening situations are continuous rather than episodic, they produce a more or less continuous stress response. This continued state of arousal can lead to heart disease and other physical problems.

Several studies have demonstrated the deleterious effects of stress on health. For example, survivors of concentration camps, who were obviously subjected to long-term stress, have generally poorer health later in life than do other people of the same age (Cohen et al., 1953). Holocaust survivors who were children during the Second World War are more likely to display psychosocial problems and posttraumatic symptoms today (Cohen, Brom, & Dasberg, 2001).

Physiological Mechanisms Involved in Stress Why does prolonged stress affect physical health? As we discussed earlier, emotions consist of behavioral, autonomic, and hormonal responses. The latter two components—autonomic and hormonal—are the responses that can have adverse effects on health. (Of course, the behavioral components can, too, if a person rashly gets into a fight with someone much bigger and stronger.) Because threatening situations generally call for vigorous activity, the autonomic and hormonal responses help make the body's energy resources available. The sympathetic branch of the autonomic nervous system is activated, and the adrenal glands secrete epinephrine, norepinephrine, and steroid stress hormones. Because the effects of sympathetic activity are similar to those of the adrenal hormones, we limit our discussion to the hormonal responses.

Epinephrine releases the stored form of glucose that is present in the muscles, thus providing energy for strenuous exercise. Along with norepinephrine, epinephrine also increases blood flow to the muscles by increasing the output of the heart, which also increases blood pressure. In the short term, these changes are beneficial, because they prepare the body for fight-or-flight responses. Over the long term, however, these changes contribute to heart problems. The other stress-related hormone is cortisol, a steroid secreted by the cortex of the adrenal gland. Cortisol is called a **glucocorticoid,** one of a group of steroids that have profound effects on glucose metabolism, effects similar to those of epinephrine. In addition, glucocorticoids help break down protein and convert it to glucose, help make fats available for energy, increase blood flow, and stimulate behavioral responsiveness, presumably by affecting the brain. They have other physiological effects, too, some of which are only poorly understood. Almost every cell in the body contains glucocorticoid receptors, which means that few parts of the body are unaffected by these hormones. (See **FIGURE 13.17.**)

The most harmful effects of stress are caused by the prolonged secretion of glucocorticoids (Selye, 1956/1976). Although the short-term effects of glucocorticoids are essential, the long-term effects are damaging. These effects include elevated blood pressure, damage to muscle tissue, one form of diabetes, infertility, stunted growth, inhibition of the inflammatory responses, and suppression of the immune system. High blood pressure can lead to heart attacks and stroke. Children subjected to prolonged stress may not attain their full height. Inhibition of the inflammatory response makes it more difficult for the body to heal itself after an injury, and suppression of the immune system makes an individual vulnerable to disease.

Extreme stress has even been shown to cause brain damage in young primates (Uno et al., 1989). The investigators studied a colony of vervet monkeys housed in a primate center in Kenya. They found that some monkeys died, apparently as a result of stress. Vervet monkeys have a hierarchical society, and monkeys near the bottom of the hierarchy are picked on by the others; thus, they are almost continuously subjected to stress. The deceased monkeys had enlarged adrenal

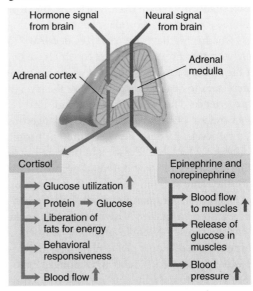

[**FIGURE 13·17**] Control and effects of the secretion of epinephrine, norepinephrine, and cortisol by the adrenal glands.

glands, a sign of chronic stress. In addition, neurons in a particular region of their hippocampal formations were completely destroyed. Stress-induced damage of this nature is especially worrying, because the hippocampus plays a vital role in learning and memory (see Chapter 8). Severe stress appears to cause brain damage in humans as well. Jensen, Genefke, and Hyldebrandt (1982) found evidence of brain degeneration in CT scans of people who had been tortured. Victims of mass violence show similar results (Weinstein, Fucetola, & Mollica, 2001).

Cognitive Appraisal and Stress

Selye's model has been useful for understanding the biological components involved in stress, but it does not explain the role of psychological components in stress. The effects of other stressors, such as situations that cause fear or anxiety, depend on people's perceptions and emotional reactivity. That is, because of individual differences in temperament or experience with a particular situation, some people may find a situation stressful, and others may not. In these cases, it is the *perception* that counts.

Richard Lazarus argues that our *perception* of the stressor determines, to a large extent, the stress we experience (Lazarus & Folkman, 1984; Lazarus, 2000). According to Lazarus, an individual's stress levels are affected by his or her **cognitive appraisal,** or perception, of the stressful situation.

---

glucocorticoid A hormone, such as cortisol, that influences the metabolism of glucose, the main energy source of the body.

cognitive appraisal Our perception of a stressful situation; occurs in two stages, primary appraisal and secondary appraisal.

According to this model, cognitive appraisal is a two-stage process. In the first stage, **primary appraisal,** we evaluate the threat: We attempt to judge the seriousness of the perceived threat posed by the stressor. If we decide that the threat is real, we pass to the second stage, **secondary appraisal,** during which we assess whether we have the resources necessary to cope adequately with the threat. The extent to which we believe both that the stressor is serious and that we do *not* have the resources necessary to deal with it determines the level of stress we will experience. The belief that we cannot deal effectively with a stressor perceived as extremely dangerous leads to the highest levels of stress. Because different people may evaluate differently both the stressor and their ability to cope with it, they are likely to show different levels of stress when faced with the same stressor. We know from common experience that this is true. For example, people vary tremendously in their reactions to snakes: A harmless garter snake will arouse intense fear in some people and none in others.

Selye's findings, then, do not apply to all people; individual differences exist in how people react to prolonged exposure to stress. Some people show little, if any, risk of becoming ill during or after chronic stress. Kobasa and her colleagues (Kobasa, 1979; Kobasa, et al., 1985; Maddi, 2002) refer to these people as *hardy* individuals. In a study of how business executives coped with long-term stress, Kobasa found that some became ill, and some did not. She wanted to determine what caused this difference. Through detailed analyses of her participants' responses to different psychological inventories, she found that the hardy executives viewed the stressors in their lives as challenges and that they met these challenges head-on—they did not avoid them or become anxious about them. They also felt that they had control over the challenges (stressors) rather than that the challenges had control over them. In other words, Kobasa's findings support Lazarus's idea of the importance of cognitive appraisal in dealing with stress: How we initially size up the stressor, how we tackle it, and the extent to which we believe that we can control the stressor seem to influence whether we become at risk for illnesses related to being chronically stressed.

QUESTIONS FOR CONSIDERATION

1. What kinds of stressors do you face in your life? When confronted with a stressor, what kinds of physiological, emotional, cognitive, and behavioral reactions do you experience? What makes some stressors more aversive to you than others?

2. Has the stress response outlived its usefulness to our species? It seems as though this response was more useful to our prehistoric ancestors in avoiding predators and finding food than it is to us in our work and play. In your opinion, would our lives be better off without this response? Explain.

Behaviors Related to Stress and Impaired Health

A healthy lifestyle, including eating right, exercising, and avoiding cigarette smoking, is a pattern of living that enhances an individual's well-being, both physical and psychological; an unhealthy lifestyle is a pattern that diminishes physical and psychological well-being. The top five causes of deaths in 2004 among persons in the United States were heart disease, cancer, stroke, lower respiratory disease, and accidental injury (Heron, 2007). The first three of these were similarly ranked 25 years ago. Yet increasing evidence from the health sciences indicates that most, if not all, of these five causes can be linked in some way to unhealthy lifestyles.

To make this connection, we need to consider specific components of a lifestyle: the behaviors that diminish well-being. We all know that on occasion a child develops brain cancer or a physically fit athlete dies of a heart attack, but these are the exceptions: Generally speaking, over the long term, our behavior can affect our physical and psychological well-being.

Stress Reactions and CHD

One of the leading causes of death in Western societies is **coronary heart disease (CHD)**—diseases of the heart and blood vessels. CHD can cause heart attacks and strokes. Heart attacks occur when the blood vessels that serve the heart become blocked, whereas strokes involve the blood vessels in the brain. The two most important risk factors in CHD are high blood pressure and a high level of cholesterol in the blood.

The likelihood that a person will have CHD may depend partly on how he or she reacts to stress. For example, Wood et al. (1984) examined the blood pressure of people who had been subjected to a cold pressor test when they were children. The cold pressor test reveals how people's blood pressure reacts to the stress caused when one of their hands is placed in a container of ice water for 1 minute. Wood and his colleagues found that 70% of their study participants who hyperreacted to the stress when they were children had high blood pressure as adults, compared with 19% of those who showed little reaction to the stress as children.

Given that certain physiological reactions to stress are associated with CHD, then other behavioral, emotional, or cognitive stress responses may be as well. In the mid-twentieth century, while trying to find the reason that some patients

---

primary appraisal The first stage of cognitive appraisal, during which we evaluate the seriousness of a threat (stressor).

secondary appraisal The second stage of cognitive appraisal, during which we evaluate the resources we have available to deal with a threat (stressor).

coronary heart disease (CHD) The narrowing of blood vessels that supply oxygen and nutrients to the heart.

developed CHD and others did not, Friedman and Rosenman (1959, 1974) identified a behavior pattern that appeared to differentiate the two groups. They characterized the relatively CHD-prone individuals with the **type A behavior pattern** as persons with excessive competitive drive, an intense disposition, impatience, hostility, fast movements, and rapid speech. People with the **type B behavior pattern** were less competitive; less hostile; and more patient, easygoing, and tolerant; they moved and talked more slowly, and they also were less likely to have CHD. Friedman and Rosenman developed a questionnaire that distinguished between these two types of people. The test is rather interesting, because the person who administers it is not a passive participant. The interviewer asks questions in an abrupt, impatient manner, interrupting the test taker if he or she takes too much time to answer a question. The point of such tactics is to try to elicit type A behavior.

The possibility of a relation between type A personality and CHD has generated a great deal of research. For example, the Western Collaborative Group Study (Rosenman et al., 1975) examined 3,154 healthy men for 8.5 years. Among many other results, the Group found that the type A behavior pattern was associated with twice the rate of CHD of non–type A behavior patterns. However, contradictory results regarding whether the type A behavior pattern is a risk factor for CHD have been obtained since, and it is important to disentangle them.

An emerging understanding of these inconsistent results focuses on how the type A personality is measured. Researchers tend to find positive links between the type A pattern and CHD when they identify type A individuals through observation and evaluation of their behaviors during interviews, but not when they rely on self-report questionnaires (e.g., Pitts & Phillips, 1998). Many plausible explanations may be made for the conflicting evidence, then. For example, direct observation of type A–related behaviors simply may be a better measure of type A style than the self-descriptive method of classification. Or perhaps the two measurement methods identify only partially overlapping components of type A style, and only the behavioral component is related strongly to CHD risk.

How can we understand these research findings? The generally agreed-on conclusion is that personality variables are involved in susceptibility to heart attack, but that we need a better definition of just what these variables are. In addition, it is possible that different personality variables are associated with different risk factors, which makes it difficult to tease out the relevant variables. Personality factors certainly play an important role in CHD, but the precise nature of this role is still emerging through ongoing research.

Psychoneuroimmunology

Stress also can impair the functions of the immune system—the system that protects us from illnesses caused by viruses, microbes, fungi, and other types of invaders. The branch of

A T lymphocyte at work destroying tumor cells.

science that studies the interactions between the immune system and behavior (mediated by the nervous system, of course) is called **psychoneuroimmunology.**

The Immune System The **immune system,** a network of organs and cells that protects the body from invading bacteria, viruses, and other foreign substances, is one of the most complex systems of the body. Its function is to protect us from infection. Because infectious organisms have developed devious tricks through the process of evolution, our immune system has evolved devious tricks of its own. The description here is abbreviated and simplified, but it presents some of the important elements of the system.

The immune system depends on special white blood cells, called lymphocytes, that develop in the bone marrow and in the thymus gland. Some of the cells, produced in bone marrow and called **B lymphocytes,** roam through the blood or lymph glands and sinuses; others, produced in the thymus and called **T lymphocytes,** reside permanently in one place. If we think of the immune system as if it were the police

---

type A behavior pattern   A behavior pattern characterized by impatience, high levels of competitiveness and hostility, and an intense disposition; supposedly associated with an increased risk of CHD.

type B behavior pattern   A behavior pattern characterized by patience, relatively low levels of competitiveness and hostility, and an easygoing disposition; supposedly associated with a decreased risk of CHD.

psychoneuroimmunology   Study of the interactions between the immune system and behavior as mediated by the nervous system.

immune system   A network of organs and cells that protects the body from invading bacteria, viruses, and other foreign substances.

B lymphocytes   White blood cells that develop in bone marrow and release immunoglobulins to defend the body against antigens.

T lymphocytes   White blood cells that develop in the thymus gland and produce antibodies that defend the body against fungi, viruses, and multicellular parasites.

department of the body, then B lymphocytes serve the function of mobile patrols, whereas T lymphocytes are like a stakeout team that stays in one place. The immune reaction occurs when the body is invaded by a foreign organism. Two types of specific immune reactions are found: chemically mediated and cell mediated. Chemically mediated immune reactions involve antibodies. All bacteria have unique proteins on their surfaces called **antigens.** These proteins serve as the invaders' calling cards, identifying them to the immune system. Through exposure to the bacteria, the immune system learns to recognize these proteins. The result of this learning is the development of special lines of cells that produce specific **antibodies**—proteins that recognize antigens and help kill the invading microorganism. One type of antibody is released into the circulation by B lymphocytes, which receive their name from the fact that they develop in bone marrow. These antibodies, called **immunoglobulins,** are chains of protein. Each of five different types of immunoglobulins is identical, except for one end, which contains a unique receptor. A particular receptor binds with a particular antigen, just as a molecule of a hormone or a transmitter substance binds with its receptor. When the appropriate line of B lymphocytes detects the presence of an invading bacterium, the cells release their antibodies, which bind with the bacterial antigens. The antibodies either kill the invaders directly or attract other white blood cells, which then destroy the invaders. (See FIGURE 13.18(a).) This type of defense is described as chemically mediated because it is accomplished by the immunoglobulins.

The other type of defenses mounted by the immune system, cell-mediated immune reactions, are produced by T

---

antigens The unique proteins found on the surface of bacteria; these proteins enable the immune system to recognize the bacteria as foreign substances.

antibodies Proteins in the immune system that recognize antigens and help kill invading microorganisms.

immunoglobulins Disease-fighting antibodies that are released by B lymphocytes.

autoimmune diseases Diseases such as rheumatoid arthritis, diabetes, lupus, and multiple sclerosis, in which the immune system attacks and destroys some of the body's own tissue.

lymphocytes. These cells also produce antibodies, but the antibodies remain attached to the outside of the cell membranes. When antigens bind with their surface antibodies, the cells either directly kill the invaders or signal other white blood cells to come and kill them. (See FIGURE 13.18(b).) T lymphocytes defend the body primarily against fungi, viruses, and multicellular parasites.

In addition to the immune reactions produced by lymphocytes, *natural killer cells* continuously prowl through tissue. When they encounter a cell that has been infected by a virus or that has become transformed into a cancer cell, they engulf and destroy it. Thus, natural killer cells constitute an important defense against viral infections and the development of malignant tumors.

Our immune system normally protects us; however, at times, it can cause us harm. Allergies provide a good example. Allergic reactions occur when an antigen from some substance causes cells of the immune system to overreact, releasing a particular immunoglobulin that produces a localized inflammatory response. The chemicals released during this reaction can enter general circulation and cause life-threatening complications. Allergic responses are harmful, and why they occur is unknown.

The immune system can do something else that harms the body—it can attack the body's own cells. **Autoimmune diseases** occur when the immune system becomes sensitized to a protein present in the body and attacks the tissue that contains this protein. Exactly what causes the protein to be so targeted is not known. What is known is that autoimmune diseases often follow viral or bacterial infections. Presumably, in learning to recognize antigens that belong to the infectious agent, the immune system develops a line of cells that treat one of the body's own proteins as foreign. Some common autoimmune diseases include rheumatoid arthritis, diabetes, lupus, and multiple sclerosis.

Neural Control of the Immune System Stress can suppress the immune system, resulting in greater vulnerability to infectious diseases, and it can also aggravate autoimmune

[**FIGURE 13·18**] Immune reactions. (a) Chemically mediated reaction. The B lymphocyte detects an antigen on a bacterium and releases a specific immunoglobulin. (b) Cell-mediated reaction. The T lymphocyte detects an antigen on a bacterium and kills it, either directly or by attracting other white blood cells.

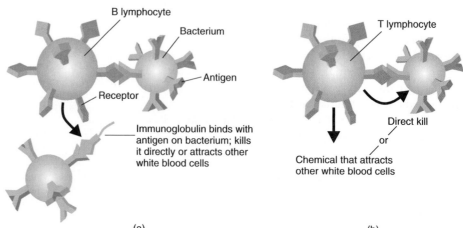

(a)   (b)

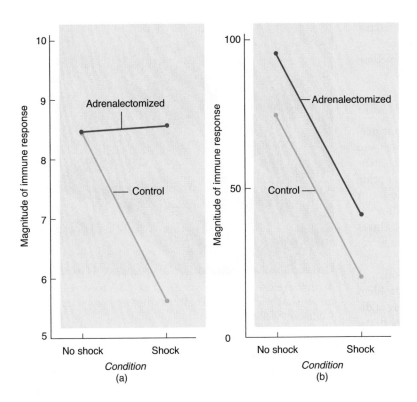

[**FIGURE 13·19**] Effects of the removal of rats' adrenal glands on immune-system suppression produced by stress (inescapable shocks). (a) Number of white blood cells (lymphocytes) found in the blood. (b) Stimulation of lymphocyte production after exposure to an antigen.

(Based on data from Keller, S. E., Weiss, J. M., Schleifer, S. J., Miller, N. E., & Stein, M. (1983). Stress-induced suppression of immunity in adrenalectomized rats. *Science*, 221, 1301–1304.)

diseases. It may even affect the growth of cancers. What is the physiological explanation for these effects? One answer, and probably the most important one, points to neural control—and indeed to the brain.

Stress increases the secretion of glucocorticoids, and these hormones directly suppress the activity of the immune system. Because the secretion of glucocorticoids is controlled by the brain, the brain is obviously responsible for the effect of these hormones on the immune system. All types of white blood cells have glucocorticoid receptors, and suppression of the immune system is presumably mediated at least in part by these receptors (Solomon, 1987). For example, in a study of rats, Keller and colleagues (1983) found that the stress of inescapable shock decreased the number of lymphocytes in the animals' blood. This effect was abolished by removal of the adrenal gland. Thus, the decrease in lymphocytes appears to have been caused by the release of glucocorticoids triggered by the stress. (See FIGURE 13.19(a).)

However, the same authors found that removal of the adrenal glands did not abolish the effects of stress on another type of immune response: stimulation of lymphocytes by an antigen. (See FIGURE 13.19(b).) Thus, not all effects of stress on the immune system are mediated by glucocorticoids; additional mechanisms must exist. These other mechanisms may involve direct neural control. The bone marrow, the thymus gland, and the lymph nodes all receive neural input. Although researchers have not yet obtained direct proof that this input modulates immune function, it would be surprising if it did not.

The immune system also appears to be sensitive to chemical compounds produced by the nervous system. The best evidence comes from studies of the opioids produced by the brain. In research with rats, Shavit and colleagues (1984) found that inescapable intermittent shock produced both analgesia (decreased sensitivity to pain) and suppression of the production of natural killer cells. These effects both seem to have been mediated by brain opioids, because both effects were abolished when the researchers administered a drug that blocks opiate receptors. Shavit and colleagues (1986) found that they could suppress natural killer cell activity by injecting morphine directly into an animal's brain; thus, the effect of the opiates appears to take place in the brain. We do not yet understand the mechanism by which the brain affects the natural killer cells. As you can see, the links between stress and the immune system are complex and involve multiple mechanisms (Moynihan, 2003).

QUESTION FOR CONSIDERATION

What kinds of unhealthy behaviors are part of your lifestyle? What psychological processes influenced how these behaviors developed? Why do you keep engaging in these behaviors?

Coping with Everyday Stress

Regardless of our lifestyle, stress is a fact of everyday life. As we've seen, how much stress we experience and the degree to which stress impairs our health depend to a large extent on our perception of the threat posed by the stressor. In this section, we look at two general categories of everyday stress, major stressors and ordinary day-to-day hassles; then we consider various coping strategies, including the method known as stress inoculation training.

Coping Styles and Strategies

Each of us can learn to control stress or to change our perception of it. We may not always be able to predict when and where we will encounter stressors or to control their intensity, but we can mitigate their damaging effects by adopting coping strategies that are consistent with our lifestyles. A **coping strategy** is simply a plan of action that we follow, either in anticipation of encountering a stressor or as a direct response to stress as it occurs, and which is effective in reducing the level of stress we experience.

According to Lazarus and Folkman (1984; Folkman & Lazarus, 1991), two types of coping responses occur: problem focused and emotion focused. **Problem-focused coping** is directed toward the source of the stress. For example, if the stress is job related, a person might try to change conditions at work or might take courses to acquire skills that will enable him or her to obtain a different job. **Emotion-focused coping** is directed toward our own personal reaction to the stressor. For example, a person might try to relax and forget about the problem or to find solace in the company of friends. Obviously, if a stress-producing problem has a potential solution, problem-focused coping is the best strategy. If it does not, then emotion-focused coping is the only option. Health psychologists have shown that several common emotion-focused coping techniques are effective in controlling stress: aerobic exercise, cognitive reappraisal, progressive relaxation training, and social support.

Aerobic Exercise Aerobic exercise has many benefits. People who engage regularly in aerobic exercise are likely to live longer than people who do not exercise regularly (Leitzmann et al., 2007). Those who consistently make time for aerobic exercise also tend to report reduced stress. Consider the results of an experiment involving mildly depressed female university students (McCann & Holmes, 1984). The students were assigned to one of three groups: a control group that received no treatment for depression, a group that received relaxation training, and a group that engaged in aerobic exercise (jogging and dancing). The students rated their depression levels at the beginning of the experiment and then again

Aerobic exercise, such as jogging, not only has positive effects on physical health but also reduces stress and promotes feelings of well-being.

10 weeks later. As expected, self-reported levels of depression in the control condition showed no change. Students given relaxation training showed a slight decrease in depression. Those who participated in aerobic exercise showed a large decrease in depression.

Although we know that aerobic exercise is effective in reducing stress, we do not yet know exactly how it reduces stress. One possibility is that increased heart and lung efficiency coupled with the lower blood pressure that results from aerobic exercise simply makes people feel better. Another possibility is that people who can adjust their schedules to make room for regular workouts have a greater sense of control than do those who cannot find the time for exercise. People who make exercise a priority in their schedules have to control other aspects of their lives to ensure that they do indeed exercise. People who have an internal locus of control ("internals") take responsibility for the course of their lives. One possibility, then, is that internals, more than externals, will attend to threats to their health and initiate steps to prevent illness (Avison & Cairney, 2003).

Cognitive Reappraisal Aerobic exercise is not the coping strategy of choice for everyone. Some people find that simply altering their perceptions of the threat posed by stressors reduces stress. This coping strategy is called **cognitive reappraisal** (or *cognitive restructuring*) and is an extension of Lazarus and Folkman's (1984) idea of cognitive appraisal. The rationale underlying this strategy is easy to grasp: If our cognitive appraisal of a stressor is a determining factor in stress, then *reappraising* that stressor as less threatening should reduce stress. Sometimes simply learning to substitute an incompatible response, such as replacing a negative statement with a positive comment, is sufficient to reduce stress (Meichenbaum, 1977). For example, students who have test

---

coping strategy A plan of action that a person follows to reduce the experience of stress, either in anticipation of encountering a stressor or in response to its occurrence.

problem-focused coping Any coping behavior that aims to reduce stress by reducing or eliminating a stressor.

emotion-focused coping Any coping behavior that aims to reduce stress by changing our own emotional reaction to a stressor.

cognitive reappraisal Any coping strategy in which we alter our perception of the threat posed by a stressor to reduce stress. Also called cognitive restructuring.

anxiety perceive tests as extremely threatening. They may say to themselves "I am going to flunk the test tomorrow" or "That test is going to be so hard." To reappraise the stressor in this case would involve replacing these statements with remarks such as "I'm going to pass that test tomorrow" or "Sure, that test will be hard, but I'm ready for it."

Cognitive reappraisal is an effective coping strategy because it is often a more realistic approach to interpreting the threat posed by stressors than is the original appraisal. We have good reason to appraise a charging bear as a real threat, but not a psychology exam. After all, we may not be able to deal well with the bear, but we can always learn how to take tests and improve our study habits. An additional benefit of cognitive reappraisal is that it teaches the individual that he or she can take control of stressful situations.

Relaxation Training A third coping strategy is simply learning to relax when confronted with a stressor. Relaxing is based on the same principle as cognitive reappraisal: Substitute an incompatible response for the stress reaction. Consider the following example. You are anxious to get home, but you are caught in rush-hour traffic. Your blood pressure increases, you begin to perspire, and you feel a knot forming in your stomach. What would happen if you were to relax? First, the chain of responses started by the hypothalamus would gradually recede; second, you would feel less stress.

One procedure for producing relaxation is the **progressive relaxation technique.** It involves three steps: (1) recognizing your body's signals informing you that you are experiencing stress; (2) using those signals as a cue to begin relaxing; and (3) relaxing by focusing your attention on different groups of muscles, beginning with those in the head and neck and proceeding to those in the arms and legs. Here is an example of how relaxation may be used to reduce feelings of stress. Suppose that when confronted by a stressor—for example, a test—you respond by tensing certain muscles: those in your hand and fingers that you use to hold your pen or pencil and those around your mouth that you use to clench your teeth. Once you become aware of these responses, you can use them as cues to relax the muscle groups involved.

Social Support Although all of us experience stress, the experience is a subjective and private matter. Nobody else can truly know what we feel inside. However, being confronted by a stressor and coping with stress are often social matters. We learn as children to seek others—parents, siblings, and friends—when we need help. This is a pattern of coping that continues over the life span.

Social support, the help that we receive from others in times of stress, is an important coping strategy for many people for two reasons. First, we can benefit from the experience of others in dealing with the same or similar stressors. We may learn how to reappraise the situation if others show us how to cope. Second, other people can provide encouragement

Seeking help from family members in times of stress is one type of coping strategy.

and incentives to overcome the stressor when we might otherwise fail to cope with the stressful situation.

Stress Inoculation Training According to psychologist Donald Meichenbaum, the best way to cope with stress is to take the offensive—to have a plan in mind for dealing with stressors before you are actually confronted by them. In other words, people should not wait until they are faced with a stressor to cope with it. Instead, they should anticipate the kinds of stressors most likely to affect them and develop the most effective possible coping plan for dealing with specific stressors. Meichenbaum (1985, 1993) devised a problem-focused coping method called **stress inoculation training,** which focuses on helping people develop coping skills that will decrease their susceptibility to the negative effects of stress. Stress inoculation training has been found to be effective in reducing stress levels among people working in a variety of settings, including nurses, teachers, police trainees (Bishop, 1994), military personnel (Armfield, 1994), bankers (Cambronne, Shih, & Harri, 1999), social workers (Keyes, 1995), and athletes (Newcomer & Perna, 2003). Stress inoculation training usually occurs in a clinical setting involving a therapist and a client. As shown in TABLE 13.2, the process takes place over three phases and aims to achieve seven goals.

Suppose that, like many people, you are uncomfortable in new social situations. You feel comfortable around friends and people you know well, but you become anxious or

---

progressive relaxation technique A stress-reduction method in which a person learns to (1) recognize body signals that indicate the presence of stress; (2) use those signals as a cue to begin relaxing; and (3) relax groups of muscles, beginning with those in the head and neck and proceeding to those in the arms and legs.

stress inoculation training The stress management program developed by Meichenbaum to help people develop coping skills that increase their resistance to the negative effects of stress.

[**TABLE 13·2**] **Summary of the Phases and Goals of Meichenbaum's Stress Inoculation Training Program**

Conceptualization Phase

Goal 1: Learning the transactional nature of stress and coping.

Goal 2: Learning to become better at realistically appraising stressful situations by cultivating self-monitoring skills with respect to negative or maladaptive thoughts, emotions, and behaviors.

Skills Acquisition and Rehearsal Phase

Goal 3: Learning problem-solving skills specific to the stressor.

Goal 4: Learning and rehearsing emotion-regulation and self-control skills.

Goal 5: Learning how to use maladaptive responses as cues to implement the new coping strategy.

Application and Follow-Through Phase

Goal 6: Learning to practice imagery rehearsal, using progressively more difficult or stressful situations.

Goal 7: Learning to apply new coping skills to other, perhaps unexpected, stressors.

Source: Adapted from Meichenbaum, D. (1985). *Stress inoculation training.* New York: Pergamon Press, pp. 21–26.

nervous when you meet people for the first time. You become so nervous that it interferes with your ability to function socially—you may even avoid social situations in which you are likely to meet new people. How might you use Meichenbaum's system to deal with this stressor?

The first phase of the system is called the *conceptualization phase* and involves two basic goals. Goal 1 involves learning about the *transactional* nature of stress and coping. Stress and coping are strongly influenced by the interaction of cognitive and environmental variables. A person experiences stress to the extent that he or she appraises the stressor—an environmental variable—as taxing or overwhelming his or her ability to cope with it—a cognitive variable. In Meichenbaum's view, coping is any behavioral–cognitive attempt to overcome, eliminate, or otherwise control the negative effects caused by the stressor (see also Lazarus & Folkman, 1984).

If, as in our example, you are uncomfortable in new social situations, you will therefore begin by understanding the transactional nature of stress. In this case, you perceive meeting new people as stressful. You may avoid going to parties and other social functions, which makes you feel better because the anxiety goes away. Although you really want to become more outgoing, you become anxious in such social situations: Your stomach tenses, your palms sweat, and you worry about what to say and how to act. In other words, specific environmental variables—social functions, meeting new people, and so on—cause cognitive and emotional discomfort, such as anxiety and nervousness. You feel inadequate in coping with these types of social situations.

Goal 2 involves becoming better at realistically appraising stressful situations by taking stock of, or self-monitoring, patterns in maladaptive thinking, feeling, and behaving. A person may keep a diary, or a "stress log," to record stressful events, the conditions under which these events occur, and his or her reactions to these events. In our example, you would approach this goal by asking yourself several questions: Which social situations make you feel the most nervous? Are there instances when meeting new people is not anxiety provoking? Do you feel less anxious when you are forced to meet people on your own or when a friend introduces you to others? By answering questions such as these, you learn more about the specific elements of the social situation that are stressful.

The second phase outlined in Table 13.2 is called the *skills acquisition and rehearsal phase* and includes Goals 3 through 5. Goal 3 involves learning specific problem-solving skills aimed at reducing stress. For example, a person may learn to identify and define a specific stressor and outline a plan for dealing with it in behavioral terms. This planning process should include developing alternative ideas for dealing with the stressor and considering the possible consequences of each alternative. At this point, a person may find relaxation training and self-instructional training, in which he or she learns to make positive self-statements when confronted by a stressor, helpful. With respect to our social anxiety example, you might identify meeting a person of the opposite sex as a specific social stressor. You might think about attending a party a friend of yours is having next Friday night. You could resolve to introduce yourself to the first person of the opposite sex that you meet there. Your specific fear might be that after introducing yourself, you'll have nothing further to say. The skill you must learn is to consider what you might say and what topics might be mutually interesting.

Goal 4 involves learning and rehearsing emotion-regulation and self-control skills. These skills help people remain calm

The first step in applying a stress inoculation program to social shyness is to understand the transactional nature of social stressors and coping behaviors.

and rational when confronted with a stressor. For example, when meeting new people, try to focus on what you must do to meet people rather than on your own anxiety. Goal 5 involves learning how to use maladaptive responses as a cue to invoke the new coping strategy. For example, when faced with a social stressor, you may feel yourself getting tense. This feeling of tension is your cue to implement specific aspects of your inoculation training, which should help reduce your level of stress.

The *application and follow-through phase* is the third and final phase of Meichenbaum's program and includes Goals 6 and 7. Goal 6 involves *imagery rehearsal*, in which a person practices coping with the stressor by imagining being confronted by that stressor in progressively more difficult situations. The purpose of rehearsing the coping skills is to build confidence in your ability to use the new coping strategy. In our social example, you would picture yourself meeting someone who you have seen before but do not know, and you would imagine how you would respond if the person asked you a particular question.

Goal 7 involves learning to apply new coping abilities to both expected and unexpected stressors. To accomplish this, you might imagine additional social situations in which you would feel anxious; imagine implementing the coping strategy in response to the anxiety; and, finally, imagine feeling relieved as a result of coping with the stressor. After such imagery rehearsal, going to a real party and meeting new people should be less stressful. You may not become the life of the party, but you should be more comfortable mingling with your fellow partygoers.

Stress is an inevitable consequence of environmental change. Both large changes, such as a natural disaster or a new job, and small changes, such as remembering that we have a quiz tomorrow, contribute to the overall level of stress that we experience at any one time. Whether stress impairs our health depends on three variables: the extent to which we appraise the stressor as threatening, the extent to which we engage in good health practices, and the extent to which we use coping strategies effectively.

QUESTIONS FOR CONSIDERATION

1. Which general approach do you take to coping with the stress in your life, a problem-focused or an emotion-focused strategy? What led you to develop this style of coping? How effective are you at coping with stress?
2. What stressors do you seem to be able to handle better than your friends? What stressors are some of your friends better at handling than you? To what extent do differences in perception of the threat posed by these stressors account for these differences in coping success?
3. Think of a stressor that is especially difficult for you to deal with. Develop an outline for coping with it based on Meichenbaum's stress inoculation training program. Explain why your program may or may not be effective.

Epilogue

What's the Reason?

The people of Malaysia excuse the actions of a person in a latah state, because they attribute her behavior to the provocation of the teaser. Although the behaviors might be deeply scandalous, the person performing them is not held accountable. It's the teaser—an external agent—who has caused the action. If a woman acted the same way without provocation, however, that would be a different matter.

Unless you are Malay yourself, latah is not part of your culture; yet, our attitudes towards motivation are not that much different. Suppose you were having a meal with an acquaintance, and someone jostled your arm, causing you to spill water on your friend. Any reasonable observer would excuse you and blame the incident on the person who jostled you. If, however, you were suddenly and by yourself to pour water on your friend, then the *motive* for your action becomes the issue, and you are blamed. That same observer might conclude that you were angry, or hostile, or, perhaps, that you harbored some deep resentments that bubbled to the surface, causing you to take them out on your friend. The irony is that, as we hold ourselves accountable for our actions, we also tend to use internal causes as explanations. When we do this, we attribute our actions or another's to causes that we cannot see and that we may not even be able to understand.

Many psychologists in the early 1900s viewed the central questions of psychology in motivational terms and used concepts such as drives, instincts, and impulses. Sigmund Freud, whose theories we discuss in the next chapter, was one such scholar. As our knowledge of psychology has increased, however, we've been able to replace these unobservable explanations with descriptions that relate either to an individual's past (such as learned coping strategies) or to our ancestral history (such as evolved homeostatic mechanisms). The result has been not only a more integrated view of motivation, but one that is also more adaptable to solving the issues people face in dealing with problems of health.

Robert Bartholomew, who can speak from person acquaintance with latah persons, suggested that the paradox of latah behavior might be understood from nonmysterious and observable factors. Simply put, he has suggested that latah is a form of deception: The behaviors are performances in which the actor knows very well what she is doing. Why are they done? Many cultural reasons may exist, but it's not hard to see how all the attention a latah performance brings could be reinforcing to a someone who is ordinarily ignored at family functions and generally overlooked. The motivation for latah behaviors is therefore in the past experiences of one of its practitioners.

Bartholomew's explanation is not without its critics, who think that deception is too strong a word for something that may be neurologically or culturally determined. However, Nature presents us with puzzles about behavior all the time and can be infinitely more deceptive about the solutions. We must resist the tendency to interpret motivated behavior in terms of amorphous causes. Our understanding of people—and our ability to help them—presupposes a clearer understanding of the causes of their actions. ■

CHAPTER SUMMARY

Reinforcement and Motivation

Motivation is a general term for a group of phenomena affecting the *nature, strength,* and *persistence* of behavior. It includes a tendency to perform responses that bring an individual into contact with an appetitive stimulus or that move it away from an aversive one. Very often we infer an organism's level of motivation from differences in the rate or vigor of responding, but these may simply reflect differences in the schedule of reinforcement under which the behavior was acquired. Behavior is initiated when the environment contains stimuli that were present when the behavior was reinforced. However, giving reinforcers when a behavior is already being adequately maintained may actually reduce performance when those reinforcers are withdrawn. Extrinsic reinforcers sometimes undermine the effect of intrinsic reinforcers, a phenomenon known as overjustification. Also, a history in which behavior does not affect the occurrence of important events may foster learned helplessness.

The strength of behavior, as reflected in the rate and timing of its occurrence, is often the result of the schedule of reinforcement under which the behavior was acquired and not the level of motivation. Common schedules of intermittent reinforcement vary the response requirements (ratio schedules) or time requirements (interval schedules) before a response produces a reinforcer.

Deprivation of contact with reinforcers—whether they be food or friends—increases the reinforcing value of those stimuli. The presence of competing reinforcers for other responses, in contrast, weakens the effectiveness of a reinforcer.

The persistence of responding when reinforcers are infrequent or absent is enhanced if the behavior was acquired with an intermittent schedule of reinforcement. The increase in persistence is greatest when the reinforcer occurs after a series of unreinforced responses.

Eating

Hunger is the emotional feeling that motivates and accompanies eating. Eating is a complex regulatory system with many variables to be controlled and many controlling factors. Eating occurs for both physiological and cultural–social reasons. Physiologically, the most important event appears to be the detection of a reduced supply of nutrients available in the blood. Detectors in the liver measure glucose and fatty acid levels, and detectors elsewhere in the body measure the level of fatty acids. Both sets of detectors inform the brain of the need for food and arouse hunger. Social factors and habit are perhaps the most important day-to-day instigators of hunger and eating in a society in which food is plentiful. We stop eating for different reasons. Detectors responsible for satiety, located in the walls of the stomach and in receptors in the liver and brain, monitor both the quality and the quantity of the food that has been eaten. Long-term control of eating appears to be regulated by a hormone known as leptin, which is released by fat cells and detected by cells in the brain. The effects of this hormone decrease meal size and increase metabolic rate, thus helping the body metabolize its supply of triglycerides.

Sometimes normal control mechanisms fail, and people gain too much weight. For any individual, genetic and environmental factors interact to cause the person's weight to deviate from the norm. People differ in the efficiency of their metabolisms, and this efficiency can lead to obesity. Experiences such as repeated bouts of weight loss and gain may promote obesity.

Anorexia nervosa is a serious, sometimes life-threatening disorder. Most anorexic patients are young women. Although they avoid eating, they remain preoccupied with food. Psychologists believe that a social emphasis on thinness may be an underlying factor that contributes to the development of the disorder. However, physiological and genetic factors are also implicated. Bulimia nervosa is another disorder, characterized by bingeing followed by self-induced purging. It, too, can result in poor health outcomes.

Aggressive Behavior

In many species, aggression serves useful purposes within limits. Ethological studies of other species reveal the presence of mechanisms to limit violence: Threat gestures warn of an impending attack, and appeasement gestures propitiate the potential aggressor. In males of most species of animals, androgens clearly have effects on aggressive behavior. The same is probably true of humans, but the evidence is primarily correlational.

Parental and media violence may affect aggression in society through the process of imitation. In the case of media, correlational data cannot establish whether watching violent programming produces aggression against others or innate aggressiveness produces watching violent programming.

Sexual Behavior

The sex hormones are secreted by the testes and ovaries and have effects on cells throughout the body. Sex hormones affect people's motivation to perform particular classes of reproductive behaviors. Much of these effects occur because sex hormones alter the organization of sex organs and the brain during development. Testosterone, an androgen, increases sexual motivation in men, but does not, in itself, determine the object of sexual desire. In women, the hormones estradiol and progesterone fluctuate during the menstrual cycle. Ovarian hormones do not control women's sexual activity, but sexual interest seems to increase in response to high levels of estradiol.

At puberty, the effects of sex hormones on a person's maturing body and brain increase interest in sexual activity. Most people develop a special interest in members of the other sex, but some develop same-sex attractions. Although homosexuality was once regarded as a disorder, no evidence exists to support this. Some evidence hints that homosexuality develops at least partly in response to biological factors. These factors are not as simple as a difference in hormonal levels but may involve the organizing effects of sex hormones on the developing embryo. Studies of homosexuality in twins show a higher concordance of homosexuality within identical twins than within pairs of nonidentical twins. Thus, both experiential effects of the prenatal environment and genetic effects influence the development of same-sex attraction. Prenatal exposure to androgens can have a significant effect on the development of the sex organs and on a region of the forebrain. Transsexuality in males may reflect the fact that, in these individuals, this region looks more female-like than male.

Emotion

Emotion refers to the behavior, the physiological reactions, and the subjective feelings that accompany motivated responses. Emotions provide patterns of behavior that help us respond appropriately to situations. Emotional reactions have three components—behavioral, autonomic, and hormonal. The behavioral component of emotion is particularly evident in conditioned emotional responses, which are learned when a neutral stimulus is paired with an emotion-producing stimulus. Research has shown that the autonomic and hormonal components of emotional responses are under the control of the amygdala.

The muscular movements that an animal makes when engaged in aggressive behaviors are programmed by neural circuits in the brain stem. Serotonergic neurons have been implicated in the inhibition of human aggression. Low levels of serotonin release may contribute to aggression, and serotonin agonists decrease irritability and aggressiveness.

The ventral prefrontal cortex plays a crucial role in the regulation of emotion, by integrating information from regions that control automatic emotional responses with other areas that control more complex behaviors. Moral decision making also seems to be controlled by the prefrontal cortex. This area of the brain receives major projections of serontonergic axons. Serontonin reuptake inhibitors increase the activity of this region, which may enhance its ability to control other regions involved in aggression, such as the amygdala.

The Expression and Recognition of Emotions

Expressive behavior communicates important information about emotions to other people. An observational study of humans indicated that smiles appear to occur most often when someone is there to see the smile. This finding supports the social nature of emotional expression.

Emotions are provoked by particular motivational stimuli, and in humans, these stimuli include those from cognitive processes as well as observable behavior. For example, emotions can be produced by memories of previous emotion-arousing situations.

Emotions are accompanied by feelings that come from inside the body. James and Lange suggested that the physiological and behavioral reactions to emotion-producing situations were perceived as feelings. Thus, feelings of emotion were not the causes but the results of these reactions. Hohman's early study of people with spinal cord damage was consistent with the James-Lange theory, but subsequent research found that people who could no longer feel reactions from most of the body reported emotional feelings similar to those of people without such deficits.

Stress and Health

Stress consists of our physiological, behavioral, emotional, and cognitive responses to stressors—stimuli that either prevent us from obtaining a goal or endanger our well-being. Selye's well-known model describes how prolonged exposure to stress can lead to illness and sometimes death. The stress response, which Cannon called the fight-or-flight response, is useful as a short-term response to threatening stimuli but is harmful in the long term. This response includes increased activity of the sympathetic branch of the autonomic nervous system and increased secretion of epinephrine, norepinephrine, and glucocorticoids by the adrenal glands.

Although increased levels of epinephrine and norepinephrine can increase blood pressure, most of the harm to health comes from glucocorticoids. Prolonged exposure to high levels of these hormones can increase blood pressure, damage muscle tissue, lead to infertility, inhibit growth, inhibit the inflammatory response, and suppress the immune system. It can also damage the hippocampus. Because the harm caused by most stressors comes from our own response to them, individual differences in psychological variables can alter the effects of stressful situations. An individual's perception of stress is especially important. Hardy individuals, who cope well with stress, view stressors as challenges over which they have control.

Behaviors Related to Stress and Impaired Health

Research on the type A behavior pattern suggests that some personality variables can predict the likelihood of CHD. However, the research findings are mixed, and some studies suggest that health-related behaviors may be more important than patterns of emotional reactions.

Psychoneuroimmunology is a field of study that investigates interactions between the immune system, as mediated by the nervous system, and behavior. The immune system includes several types of white blood cells that produce chemically mediated and cell-mediated responses. The immune system can cause harm when it triggers an allergic reaction or when, in autoimmune diseases, it attacks the body's own tissues.

Increased blood levels of glucocorticoids are the most important mechanism by which stress impairs immune functioning. Neural input to the bone marrow, lymph nodes, and thymus gland also may play a role; and naturally occurring opioids appear to suppress the activity of internal killer cells.

Coping with Everyday Stress

Stress may stem from a wide variety of sources. Even positive events such as becoming married can produce stress. Stress may lead to physical illness when a person undergoes several stressful events over a short period of time. However, the extent to which people become ill appears to depend on the extent to which they perceive a stressor as a threat to their well-being and the extent to which they believe they can cope with that threat.

Lazarus and Folkman identified two types of coping. Problem-focused coping involves trying to reduce stress by attempting to change the event or situation producing the stress. Emotion-focused coping centers on changing our personal reaction to the stressful event or situation. Emotion-focused coping may involve activities such as aerobic exercise, cognitive reappraisal, and relaxation training. Seeking social support also can help reduce stress.

Meichenbaum's stress inoculation training program is a problem-focused coping strategy that prepares people to cope with anticipated stressors. The program involves three phases and seven goals. In the first phase people learn how to conceptualize the transactional nature of stress. In the second phase, they build coping skills specific to the stressors in their lives and practice or rehearse these skills in hypothetical situations. In the third phase, people prepare to implement these coping skills in real-life situations. The seven goals of stress inoculation training focus on specific kinds of knowledge,

cognition, behavior, and coping strategies designed to help people anticipate, confront, and reduce the threat posed by stressful situations.

succeed with mypsychlab

Visit MyPsychLab for practice quizzes, flashcards, and dozens of videos and animated tutorials, including the following items you can find in the "Multimedia Library":

Food and the Brain
Eating Disorders

Evolutionary Drive, Arousal, Cognitive, and Humanistic Theories of Motivation
Physiological, Evolutionary, and Cognitive Theories of Emotion
The Effects of the Hypothalamus on Eating Behavior

Recognizing Facial Expressions of Emotions

KEY TERMS

activational effect (of hormone) *p. 391*

androgen insensitivity syndrome *p. 396*

anorexia nervosa *p. 388*

antibodies *p. 408*

antigens *p. 408*

appeasement gesture *p. 391*

autoimmune diseases *p. 408*

B lymphocytes *p. 407*

bulimia nervosa *p. 389*

Cannon–Bard theory *p. 401*

cognitive appraisal *p. 405*

cognitive reappraisal *p. 410*

concurrent schedule *p. 383*

conditioned emotional response *p. 397*

coping strategy *p. 410*

coronary heart disease (CHD) *p. 406*

correctional mechanism *p. 384*

cumulative record *p. 381*

deprivation *p. 382*

detector *p. 384*

emotion-focused coping *p. 410*

estrous cycle *p. 393*

extinction-induced aggression *p. 384*

fight-or-flight response *p. 404*

frustration *p. 384*

general adaptation syndrome *p. 404*

glucocorticoid *p. 405*

glucostatic hypothesis *p. 386*

glycogen *p. 385*

immune system *p. 407*

immunoglobulins *p. 408*

SUGGESTIONS FOR FURTHER READING

Carlson, N. R. (2006). *Physiology of Behavior* (9th ed.). Boston: Allyn & Bacon.

This is a good intermediate-level text that describes in detail the physiological bases of motivation and emotion.

Ekman, p. (2003). *Emotions revealed: Recognizing faces and feelings to improve communication and emotional life.* New York: Times Books/Henry Holt and Co.

Ekman offers a very readable account of his work on facial expressions of emotion.

Franken, R. E. (2002). *Human motivation* (5th ed.). Pacific Grove, CA: Brooks/Cole Publishing.

Examines the general principles of motivation as well as specific types of motivated behavior.

Logue, A. W. (2005). *The psychology of eating and drinking* (3rd ed.). New York: W. H. Freeman.

This book covers alcohol abuse as well as eating and eating disorders.

LeVay, S. (1993). *The sexual brain*. Cambridge, MA: MIT Press.

A well-written book on sexual behavior and the social and biological variables that affect it.

Jenkins, J. M., Catley, K., & Stein, N. L. (Eds.). (1998). *Human emotions: A reader*. Malden, MA: Blackwell Publishers.

Bauby, J.-D. (1997). *The diving bell and the butterfly*. (tran. J. Leggatt). New York: Knopf.

The book by Jenkins, Catley, and Stein contains chapters by many experts in the field of emotion. Bauby's book is probably one of the most unusual ever written. The author was the senior editor of a French fashion magazine when a stroke left him with "locked-in syndrome"—a horrifying condition that leaves a person completely paralyzed yet also normally conscious. Bauby wrote the book by using the only movement he could make: by blinking his eye to choose individual letters. It is a moving experience to read his description of emotional experience. It also provides new insight into the subjective evidence behind the James-Lange theory.

Bartholomew, R. E. (2000). *Exotic deviance: Medicalizing cultural idioms from strangeness to illness*. Boulder, CO: University Press of Colorado.

Bartholomew describes the latah experience, and many other interesting behaviors motivated by cultural factors.

Personality

Prologue

Identical Twins Raised Apart

The identical twin boys were separated at the age of 37 days and were adopted by two different working-class families. Coincidentally, both were named Jim by their adoptive families. They did not meet each other again until they were 39 years old. Both Jims liked math in school, but neither liked spelling. At 10 years of age, they both developed sinus headaches; a few years later, they both developed migraine headaches. They both used the same words to describe their head pain. The twins had identical pulse rates and blood pressures, and both put on 10 pounds of weight at the same time in their lives. Both Jims were clerical workers who enjoyed woodworking, served as volunteers for police agencies, enjoyed spending their vacations in the tropics, had married and divorced women named Linda, chewed their nails, owned dogs named Toy, and drove Chevrolets.

Bridget and Dorothy, also identical twins, were 39 years old when they were reunited. Each came to their meeting wearing seven rings on her fingers, two bracelets on one wrist, and a watch and a bracelet on the other. Although the two women were raised by families of widely different socioeconomic levels, their personalities were very similar. The most striking difference between them was that the twin raised by the family of modest means had problems with her teeth.

Oskar and Jack were born in Trinidad. Their mother, a German, took Oskar back to Germany, where he was raised as a Catholic. He became a member of a Nazi youth group. Jack was raised by his father in the Caribbean as a Jew. He spent part of his adolescence on a kibbutz in Israel. At the time of their reunion, Oskar lived in Germany, and Jack, in southern California. When the twins met at the airport, both were wearing wire-rimmed glasses and two-pocket shirts with epaulets. Both had moustaches. They both liked spicy foods and sweet liqueurs, tended to fall asleep while watching television, kept rubber bands on their wrists, thought it funny to sneeze in a crowd of people, flushed the toilet before using it, and read magazines from back to front. Although their backgrounds were

The reunion of this pair of twins, the Jims, prompted Dr. Thomas Bouchard to initiate the Minnesota Study of Twins Reared Apart.

very different, their scores on a widely used personality test were similar.

These striking cases of identical twins reunited in adulthood suggest that heredity plays an important role in shaping personality. However, like all pieces of anecdotal evidence, such case histories must be regarded as clues, subject to confirmation by careful scientific evaluation. The Minnesota Study of Twins Reared Apart is one of several research projects designed to determine the roles of heredity and environment in the development of personality. ■

Common experience tells us that no one else is just like us, but how do we describe these differences? If you were asked "How does your best friend differ from you?" you would probably use descriptions that generalize that person's behaviors, such as "He tends to see only the good in people, whereas I'm more realistic." or "She's a bit of a neat-freak compared with me." We try to convey something about our friend that covers more than just the here and now.

Everyday observations like these provide a starting point for psychology's study of personality. But psychology's approach to studying personality is more than informal generalizations. To psychologists, the concept generally has a much more specific definition: **Personality** is a particular pattern of behavior and thinking that prevails across time and situations and differentiates one person from another. The goal of psychologists who study personality is to discover the causes of individual differences in behavior.

What types of research efforts are necessary to study personality? Some psychologists devote their efforts to the development of tests that can reliably measure differences in personality. Others try to identify the events—biological and environmental—that cause people to behave as they do. Thus, research on human personality requires two kinds of effort: identifying personality characteristics and determining the variables that produce and control them (Buss, 1995). Keep in mind that in the study of personality, we must be careful to avoid the nominal fallacy. As you will recall from Chapter 2, the nominal fallacy is the false belief that the causes of an event are explained by simply naming and identifying them. Merely *identifying* and *describing* a personality characteristic is not the same as *explaining* it.

---

personality A particular pattern of behavior and thinking prevailing across time and situations that differentiates one person from another.

personality types Different categories into which personality characteristics can be assigned based on factors such as developmental experiences or physical characteristics.

personality trait An enduring personal characteristic that reveals itself in a particular pattern of behavior in a variety of situations.

Trait Theories of Personality

Among the first categorizations of personality was one based on the concept of personality traits. Personality theorists who study traits use the term much in the way we often think of personality in everyday life—to denote a set of personal characteristics that determine the different ways we act and react in a variety of situations (Sneed, McCrae, & Funder, 1998). However, as you will see, trait theorists do not all agree on exactly which characteristics to include. Let's begin by differentiating personality *types* from personality *traits*.

Personality Types and Traits

The earliest known explanation for individual differences in personality was proposed by the Greek physician Hippocrates in the fourth century BC and refined by his successor Galen in the second century AD. The theory was based on then-common medical beliefs that originated with the ancient Greeks. The body was thought to contain four humors, or fluids: yellow bile, black bile, phlegm, and blood. People were classified according to the disposition supposedly produced by the predominance of one of these humors in their systems. Choleric people, who had an excess of yellow bile, were bad-tempered and irritable. Melancholic people, who had an excess of black bile, had gloomy and pessimistic temperaments. Phlegmatic people, whose bodies contained an excessive amount of phlegm, were sluggish, calm, and unexcitable. Sanguine people had a preponderance of blood (*sanguis*), which made them cheerful and passionate. (See FIGURE 14•1.)

Later biological investigations, of course, discredited the humoral theory. However, the notion that people could be divided into different **personality types**—different categories into which personality characteristics can be assigned based on factors such as developmental experiences—persisted long afterward. After identifying and defining personality types, theorists must determine whether these types actually exist and whether knowing an individual's personality type can lead to valid predictions about his or her behavior in different situations.

Most investigators today reject the idea that people can be assigned to discrete categories. Instead, they generally conceive of individual differences in personality as being differences in degree, not kind. Rather than focusing on types, many current investigators prefer to measure the degree to which an individual expresses a particular personality trait. A **personality trait** is an enduring personal characteristic that reveals itself in a particular pattern of behavior in different situations. A simple example illustrates the difference between types and traits. We could classify people into two different *types*: tall people and short people. Note that this is an either/or categorization. We do use these categorical terms in everyday language, but we all recognize that height is best conceived of as a *trait*—a dimension on which people differ along a wide range of values. If we measure the height of a

[**FIGURE 14·1**] Characteristics of the four humors, according to a medieval artist: (a) *choleric*—violent and aggressive temperament; (b) *melancholic*—gloomy and pessimistic temperament; (c) *phlegmatic*—sluggish, relaxed, and dull temperament; and (d) *sanguine*—outgoing, passionate, and fun-loving temperament.

Illustrations © Bettmann/CORBIS.

(a) (b) (c) (d)

large sample of people, we will find instances all along the distribution, from very short to very tall, with most people falling in between the extremes. (See FIGURE 14·2.) It is not that people are only either tall or short (analogous to personality types) but that people vary in the extent to which they show tallness or shortness (analogous to personality traits).

We've all had experiences with people who behave in different characteristic ways: Some are friendly, some are mean, some are lazy, some are timid, and some are reckless. Trait theories of personality fit this commonsense view. However, personality traits are not the same as patterns of behavior: They are factors that underlie these patterns and are responsible for them; they produce physical or material states that are the causes of our behaviors. This does not mean that the acquisition of personality traits is strictly biological and that learning is not involved. However, if our personality traits are changed through learning, those changes must have a neurological basis in the brain. In other words, we carry our personality traits around with us in our heads—or, more exactly, in our brains.

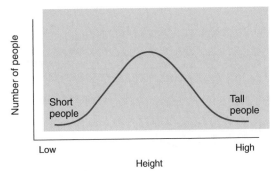

[**FIGURE 14·2**] The distribution of height. We can measure people's heights, a trait, on a continuous scale. We can also look at the extremes and divide people into the categories of short and tall types.

Identification of Personality Traits

Trait theorists are still in the process of discovering, describing, and naming the regular behavior patterns that people exhibit. In this section, we introduce several influential trait-categorization models: the theories of Gordon Allport, Raymond Cattell, and Hans Eysenck, as well as the five-factor model and related frameworks proposed by other trait psychologists.

Allport's Search for Traits Gordon Allport (1897–1967) was one of the first psychologists to search systematically for a basic core of personality traits. He began his work by identifying all words in an unabridged dictionary of the English language that described aspects of personality (Allport & Odbert, 1936); he found approximately 18,000 such entries. Allport then conducted analyses that identified those words that described only stable personality characteristics. He eliminated words that represented temporary states, such as *flustered*, or evaluations, such as *admirable*.

Why did Allport undertake this exercise? He believed that the considerable extent to which trait labels appear in human languages attests to the importance of traits in how people think about themselves and others. Indirectly, then, the wealth of trait terms in English helped confirm his belief that a well-developed trait theory would have value in understanding human functioning. Allport believed that traits are neuropsychological properties that lead to behavioral consistency over time and contexts by producing functional similarity in the way each of us interprets and experiences events. That is, people with a particular trait react similarly across situations, because they experience a unique sense of similarity across those situations that guides their feelings, thoughts, and behavior. Evidence suggests that some traits persist over time. In a 44-year longitudinal study, researchers found that creativity and some aspects of personality remained consistent over time (Feist & Barron, 2003).

According to Allport, some traits have greater influence on their possessors than others. The most powerful of all are those he termed *cardinal traits*. Cardinal traits exercise a strong unifying influence on a person's behavior. Allport believed that these traits are rare, but that people characterized by them clearly stand out from the crowd. Examples include Adolf Hitler and his relentless exercise of oppressive power, Nelson Mandela's commitment to justice, and Mother Teresa's selfless devotion. In contrast, *central traits* are less singular in their influence than cardinal traits but capture important characteristics of an individual. When we say that someone is honest and warm to distinguish that person from others, we capture Allport's meaning of central traits. Finally, Allport's category of *secondary traits* includes characteristics that have only a minor influence on the consistency of individual behavior. An example would be a person's tendency to change jobs frequently.

Allport's research stimulated other psychologists to think about personality in terms of traits or dispositions. Most modern trait theories can be traced to Allport's earlier theoretical work. Like Allport, modern trait theorists maintain that only when we know how to describe an individual's personality will we be able to explain it.

Cattell: Sixteen Personality Factors

Raymond Cattell (1905–1998) used Allport's list of 18,000 trait words as a starting point for his own theory of traits. Cattell winnowed this large word set down to 171 adjectives that he believed made up a relatively complete set of distinct *surface traits* (those that are apparent in observable behaviors). He then used the process of factor analysis (see Chapter 11) to identify clusters of these traits that he believed in turn represented underlying traits. Cattell analyzed questionnaire responses from thousands of people in this manner; eventually he identified the 16 key personality

---

extroversion The tendency to seek the company of other people, to engage in conversation and other social behaviors with them, and to be spontaneous.

introversion The tendency to avoid the company of other people, to be inhibited and cautious; shyness.

neuroticism The tendency to be anxious, worried, and full of guilt.

Surface traits, such as friendliness, are those traits that are obvious to others.

factors shown in FIGURE 14•3. He referred to these 16 traits as *source traits*, because in his view, they were the cornerstones on which personality is built. These 16 traits group the surface traits together into different independent contributions to an individual's personality. Figure 14.3 illustrates a personality profile of a hypothetical individual rated on Cattell's 16 factors. Think of someone you know well. Do you think you would be able to predict how they would score on these factors? Do you think these factors would help you predict the behavior of someone you did not know?

Eysenck: Three Factors

Hans Eysenck (1916–1997) also used factor analysis to devise a theory of personality (Eysenck, 1970; Eysenck & Eysenck, 1985). His research identified three important factors: extroversion, neuroticism, and psychoticism. These factors are bipolar dimensions. That is, extroversion is the opposite of introversion, neuroticism is the opposite of emotional stability, and psychoticism is the opposite of self-control. Individuals are rated on a continuum between the poles of these factors. People high in **extroversion** have an outgoing nature and a high level of activity. In general, extroverts like people and socializing, are spontaneous, and take risks. **Introversion** is at the opposite end of the scale: Introverts are shy, reserved, and careful. People at the high end of **neuroticism** are fraught with worry and guilt and are moody and unstable. Those who score

---

[FIGURE 14•3] A hypothetical personality profile using Cattell's 16 personality factors.

(Adapted from the 16PF® Practitioner Report. Copyright © 2005 by the Institute for Personality and Ability Testing, Inc., Champaign, Illinois, USA. Reproduced with permission. All rights reserved.)

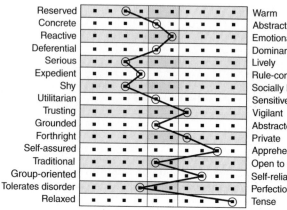

Reserved		Warm
Concrete		Abstract
Reactive		Emotionally stable
Deferential		Dominant
Serious		Lively
Expedient		Rule-conscious
Shy		Socially bold
Utilitarian		Sensitive
Trusting		Vigilant
Grounded		Abstracted
Forthright		Private
Self-assured		Apprehensive
Traditional		Open to change
Group-oriented		Self-reliant
Tolerates disorder		Perfectionistic
Relaxed		Tense

low on neuroticism are even-tempered and are characterized by **emotional stability. Psychoticism** involves an aggressive, egocentric, and antisocial nature; in contrast, a person with **self-control** has a kind and considerate nature and is obedient of rules and laws. Note that Eysenck's use of the term "psychoticism" is different from its use by most clinical psychologists; his term refers to antisocial tendencies, not to a mental illness. A person at the extreme end of the distribution of psychoticism in Eysenck's model would receive the diagnosis of antisocial personality disorder. (We look at this disorder in more detail in Chapter 16.)

TABLE 14·1 lists some questions that have high correlations or factor *loadings* (see Chapter 11 for a description of factor loadings) on Eysenck's three dimensions. The best way to understand the meaning of these traits is to read the questions and to imagine the kinds of people who would answer yes or no to each group. If a factor loading is preceded by a minus sign, it means that people who say no receive high scores on the trait; otherwise, high scores are obtained by those who answer yes.

Eysenck argued that the most important aspects of a person's personality are determined by the combination of that person's positions on the three dimensions of extroversion, neuroticism, and psychoticism—just as colors are produced by the combinations of the three dimensions of hue, saturation, and brightness. FIGURE 14·4 illustrates the effects of various combinations of the first two of these dimensions—extroversion and neuroticism—and relates them to the four dispositions described by Hippocrates and Galen.

[**TABLE 14·1**] Some Items from Eysenck's Tests of Extroversion, Neuroticism, and Psychoticism

Factor	Loading
Extroversion	
Do you like mixing with people?	.70
Do you like plenty of bustle and excitement around you?	.65
Are you rather lively?	.63
Neuroticism	
Do you often feel "fed up"?	.67
Do you often feel lonely?	.60
Does your mood often go up and down?	.59
Psychoticism	
Do good manners and cleanliness matter much to you?	−.55
Does it worry you if you know there are mistakes in your work?	−.53
Do you like taking risks for fun?	.51

Source: Adapted from Eysenck, H. J., & Eysenck, M. W. (1985). *Personality and individual differences: A natural science approach.* New York: Plenum Press. Reprinted with kind permission from Springer Science and Business Media and from the H. J. Eysenck Memorial Fund.

[**FIGURE 14·4**] Eysenck's theory illustrated for two factors. According to Eysenck, the two dimensions of neuroticism (labeled here as stable versus unstable) and introversion–extroversion combine to form a variety of personality characteristics. The four personality types based on the Greek theory of humors are shown in the center.

(From Eysenck, H. J. (1973). *The inequality of man.* London: Temple Smith. Reprinted with permission from the H. J. Eysenck Memorial Fund.)

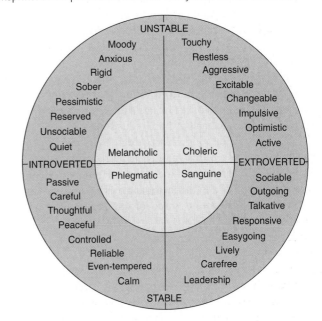

Eysenck's theory has received considerable support, especially from his own laboratory, which was highly productive. Most trait theorists accept the existence of his three factors, because they have emerged in factor analyses performed by many different researchers.

The Five-Factor Model Recall that Allport attempted to discover personality traits through an analysis of the words we use in everyday language to talk about personality. Languages reflect the observations of members of a culture; that is, people invent words to describe distinctions they notice. An analysis of such distinctions by Tupes and Christal (1961), replicated by Norman (1963), has led to the five-factor model (Costa & McCrae, 1998a; McCrae & Costa, 1997, 1999, 2004). The **five-factor model** proposes that personality is composed of five primary dimensions: neuroticism, extroversion, openness, agreeableness, and conscientiousness. These factors are

---

emotional stability The tendency to be relaxed and at peace with oneself.

psychoticism The tendency to be aggressive, egocentric, and antisocial.

self-control Behavior that produces a larger, long-term reward when people are faced with the choice between it and a smaller, short-term reward; also the tendency to be kind, considerate, and obedient of laws and rules.

five-factor model A theory stating that personality is composed of five primary dimensions: neuroticism, extroversion, openness, agreeableness, and conscientiousness. This theory was developed using factor analyses of ratings of the words people use to describe personality characteristics.

measured by the **Neuroticism, Extroversion, and Openness Personality Inventory** or **(NEO-PI-R).** (The name was chosen before the factors of agreeableness and conscientiousness were added, and the "R" stands for "revised." If you want a more useful mnemonic to remember the dimensions, think of the acronym OCEAN for openness, conscientiousness, extroversion, agreeableness, and neuroticism.)

The NEO-PI-R consists of 240 items that can potentially be used to describe the person being evaluated. The test items can be answered by the participant or by someone he or she knows well (Costa & McCrae, 1998b). The test items are brief sentences, such as "I really like most people I meet" or (for ratings by someone else) "She has a very active imagination." The person completing the test rates the accuracy of each item on a scale of 1 to 5, from *strong disagreement* to *strong agreement.* The sums of the answers to different sets of items represent scores on each of the five factors.

The five-factor model is regarded by many personality psychologists as a robust model of personality (Wiggins & Trapnell, 1997; Wiggins & Pincus, 2002; Paunonen, 2003). Although it originated in the factor analysis tradition of Cattell, it seems to incorporate some of the traits suggested by Eysenck, especially neuroticism and extroversion (Goldberg, 1993). It has considerable cross-cultural applicability (e.g., McCrae et al., 1998; Allik & McCrae, 2002, 2004). Self-ratings on the NEO-PI-R agree closely with ratings by family members (García, et al., 2007). Furthermore, it predicts other aspects that seem related to personality. DeNeve and Cooper (1998) showed that the five factors can be used to predict subjective well-being, and Vollrath (2000) found moderate predictability for responses to "daily hassles" experienced by college students. Barrick, Mount, and Judge (2001) reported a meta-analysis of studies measuring job performance relative to the five personality dimensions. Generally speaking, extroversion seems to predict success in jobs that require leadership (managerial positions) or in jobs demanding the ability to improvise to reach goals (sales positions). Not surprisingly, conscientiousness predicts success across job classifications.

Is there a biological basis for these five factors? A rapidly accumulating body of evidence points to a very strong degree of heritability (Jang, Livesley, & Vernon, 1996; Loehlin, et al., 1998; McCrae et al., 2000; Livesley, Jang, & Vernon, 2003). Correlations in traits are higher within monozygotic twins than dizygotic twins (Vernon, et al., 2008). The data suggest that environmental factors pale beside genetic influences.

Finally, five is not necessarily the final number of fundamental personality dimensions. Jackson (Jackson & Tremblay, 2002) argued that a six-factor model may be more appropriate. According to Jackson, the conscientiousness factor in the traditional five-factor model actually represents two distinct dimensions. One of these component dimensions, *methodicalness,* reflects planfulness and a need for orderliness. The other, *industriousness,* is characterized by perseverance and achievement orientation.

The Dark Triad Some personality psychologists have suggested that a special cluster of traits may underlie socially offensive personalities. For example, it has been noted that habitual criminals sometimes exhibit great skill in manipulating individuals, while exhibiting little sign of the regret that most people feel when their actions harm or offend others. The skill at manipulation has been called **Machiavellianism** after the Italian writer of the Renaissance classic on politics, *The Prince.* A pronounced lack of empathy and a high degree of impulsivity has been identified with a trait known as **psychopathy.** Paulhus and Williams (2002) suggested that these two traits, together with a trait called **narcissism,** which leads to grandiosity and feelings of superiority, formed a "Dark Triad" of overlapping negative traits. The Dark Triad is considered distinct from the Big Five, although low to moderate correlations are found between them (Jakobwitz & Egan, 2006; Egan & McDorkindale, 2007). Male subjects tend to score higher on tests that measure Dark Triad traits, although the intercorrelations between the traits are similar across the sexes. So, although women may not exhibit Dark Triad traits as much as men, women who have this personality manifest it in the same general way that men would. Vernon, et al. (2008) also measured the correlation of Dark Triad traits between twins, and find considerable genetic influence on these traits.

At their extreme, the Dark Triad personality seems to epitomize the notion of a cold, calculating, domineering, and remorseless criminal. It may be that this represents a "criminal personality type." However, it's probably a mistake to label these traits intrinsically maladaptive. Traits are collective descriptions for certain behaviors, and behaviors are adaptive or not, depending on the context. The increasing social isolation of the modern world may reward many of the milder aspects of the Dark Triad.

Traits across Cultures Any comprehensive theory of personality must be able to encompass all cultures, countries, and languages. If personality comprises a standard set of factors, which we all exhibit to a lesser or greater extent, then these factors should be exhibited or reported cross-culturally. If not, then the theory is culture specific and describes only personality within a limited number of cultures.

In personality, problems in demonstrating universality lie in taxonomy. Do the same words mean the same thing across cultures? For example, various cultures attribute different meanings to factor 5 (conscientiousness) of the Big Five model

---

Neuroticism, Extroversion, and Openness Personality Inventory (NEO-PI-R) The instrument used to measure the elements described in the five-factor model (neuroticism, extroversion, openness, agreeableness, and conscientiousness).

Machiavellianism A personality trait measuring skill at manipulating other people for one's own ends.

psychopathy A personality trait measuring impulsivity and lack of empathy or remorse for harm caused by one's actions.

narcissism A personality trait measuring grandiosity and feelings of superiority.

(Caprara and Perugini, 1994). It means something different to the Dutch, Hungarians, and Italians, and to the Americans, Germans, Czechs, and Poles. In a review of the evidence for the universality of a collection of basic personality traits, Boele de Raad, from the University of Groningen in The Netherlands, suggested that the best one can do is to find acceptable counterparts of the Big Five in all cultures; the first three factors of the model can be found in most cultures, but the cross-cultural validity of others may be questionable (DeRaad, 1998).

McCrae and Terracciano (2005) asked college students from 50 cultures, including Arabic and Black African cultures, to identify a man or woman they knew well and rate him or her by using the third-person version of the Revised NEO Personality Inventory. The Big Five structure was replicated in almost all cultures (Morocco and Nigeria were two of the half dozen or so not to show this pattern). Women were more positive than men in rating others, especially when rating other women.

In a separate study of the geography of personality traits, Allik & McRae (2004) examined whether respondents from 36 cultures differed according to the Big Five personality dimension. They found that the culture's temperature or its distance from the equator was not related to personality. However, cultures that were geographically close appeared to share similar personality traits: the greatest geographical distinction was between European and American cultures, and Asian and African cultures. Americans and Europeans were significantly more extraverted and open to experience but less agreeable than peoples from other cultures. Why?

The authors suggest that the results may be due to shared gene pools (China and Korea, for example, share genetic ancestry) or to features of those cultures. Studying the process of acculturation—the assimilation of a person's behavior with that person's culture—might help identify which is correct. For example, a study of Chinese people who emigrated to Canada found that differences between these people and European Canadians was attenuated the longer the Chinese lived in Canada (McCrae et al., 1998). Openness and agreeableness, in particular, increased in the immigrant group, but introversion remained stable and did not match levels seen in European Canadians. These data suggest that some personality traits might be adopted or enhanced by acculturation, but others may not.

Can cultures also differ according to what they believe about personality? Implicit trait theories describe whether people ascribed differences in personality to stable traits or, instead, to the immediate context or situation of an individual. In a later section of this chapter, we look at how personality theorists approach this question. Here, we consider what the layperson believes. Church et al. (2005) investigated cross-cultural beliefs about personality in what they called two individualistic cultures—America and Australia—and two collectivistic cultures—Mexico and the Philippines. They hypothesized that the more individualistic the culture, the greater or stronger the culture's beliefs in traits, rather than in situations, as determinants of behavior. Trait beliefs were stronger in Americans than in Mexicans or Philippinos, but contextual beliefs were weaker.

Individuals within cultures that are geographically close appear to share similar Big Five personality traits.

QUESTIONS TO CONSIDER

1. Think of one personality trait that you are sure you possess. How did you come to possess this trait? To what extent does possessing this trait explain the kind of person you are?

2. Consider the culture you have been raised in. Are some of the traits we've discussed more valued than others within your culture? Do you think this might have an impact on the likelihood that you would show such traits?

3. Make a list of all of the personality traits that you feel describe you. Which approach to personality—Cattell's, Eysenck's, or the five-factor model—do you think best represents the personality traits you possess? What are the reasons for your answer?

Psychobiological Approaches

The statistical evidence from factor analysis provides a description of consistent patterns of behaviors that we can identify as traits. At the beginning of the chapter, it was noted that we carry our personality traits around in our brains. That is, personality traits are the result of actions of the brain. Although we are far from understanding the psychobiology of personality, some progress has been made.

Research into the genetic basis of personality suggests that traits such as extroversion may be inherited.

Heritability of Personality Traits

Cattell and Eysenck, among other trait theorists, asserted that a person's genetic history has a strong influence on his or her personality. Many studies have shown that some personality traits are strongly heritable (e.g., Bouchard & Hur, 1998; Krueger, Markon, & Bouchard, 2003).

Psychologists assess the heritability of a trait by comparing identical and fraternal twins, comparing twins raised together and twins raised apart, and comparing twins raised by biological and adoptive relatives (see Chapter 3). Many studies have found that identical twins are more similar to each other on a variety of personality measures than are fraternal twins, which indicates that these characteristics are heritable (e.g., McCrae et al., 2000; Jang et al., 2002; Livesley, Jang, & Vernon, 2003; Vernon, et al., 2008). FIGURE 14•5 shows correlations for "big five" personality traits between members of identical and fraternal twin pairs. Identical twins' personality traits correlate much more than do those of fraternal twins. Bouchard (1997) found that identical twins' personality traits generally correlated nearly twice as much as those of fraternal twins. The similarities shown by the identical twins in the prologue—Jim and Jim, who were separated early in life and

united many years later—attest to the strength of genetic factors in influencing personality.

Zuckerman (1991) compiled the results of 11 studies using various tests of Eysenck's personality factors of extroversion, neuroticism, and psychoticism. Every study found that identical twins were more similar than fraternal twins on every measure. According to Zuckerman's calculations, the best estimates of the heritability of these three traits are, for extroversion, 70%; for psychoticism, 59%; and for neuroticism, 48%. The results of these studies suggest that heredity is responsible for 50 to 70% of the variability in these three personality traits. Thus, it might appear that the remaining 30 to 50% of the variability would be caused by differences in environment. In other words, some family environments should tend to produce extroverts, others should tend to produce introverts, and so on.

Research indicates, however, that the matter is not so simple. If family environment has a significant effect on personality characteristics, then identical twins raised together should be more similar than those raised apart. In the studies reviewed by Zuckerman (1991), they were not. Several of those studies measured the correlation in personality traits of pairs of identical twins raised together and apart. Taken as a group, these studies found no differences—indicating that differences in family environment seem to account for none of the variability of personality traits in the twins who were tested. Researchers are now developing more sensitive measures of family environment variables (e.g., Vernon, et al., 1997; Keltikangas-Järvinen & Heinonen, 2003). As these techniques evolve, we should be better able to examine the relative contributions of genetics and experience to personality.

As we saw in Chapter 3, heredity and environment do interact. The major source of the interaction seems to be the effect that people's heredity has on their family environments (Plomin & Bergeman, 1991; Plomin & Asbury, 2001). That is, a person's genetic endowment plays an important role in determining how family members interact with him or her. Two possible explanations exist for these results: The family environments could have been more similar for

[**FIGURE 14•5**] Correspondence between personality traits of identical and fraternal twins. These data show the degree to which the scores of identical and fraternal twins are correlated on each of the "big five" personality traits. The correlations for identical twins are more than double those of fraternal twins on each trait. This indicates that genes we receive from our parents do influence personality structure.

(Adapted from Bouchard, T. J. Jr. (1997). *The genetics of personality.* In K. Blum & E.P. Noble (Eds.), *The handbook of psychiatric genetics* (pp. 273–296). Boca Raton, FL: CRC Press Inc. Reproduced by permission of the Routledge/Taylor & Francis Group, LLC, and T. J. Bouchard.)

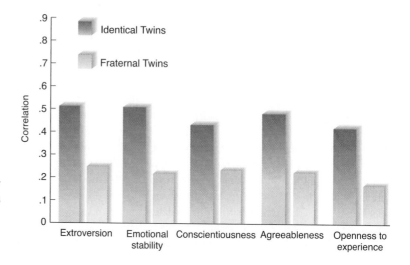

identical twins than for fraternal twins, or the family environments could have really been the same in all cases but simply have been *perceived* as different by the fraternal twins. Evidence suggests that the first possibility is correct. That is, the family environments really were more similar for identical twins (Loehlin, 1992).

How can this be? One might think that each family has a certain environment and that everyone in the household would come equally under its influence. Even within a family, each member experiences different social interactions. Although aspects of a family are shared by the entire household, the factors that play the largest role in shaping personality development appear to come from unique social interactions between an individual and other family members. Because of hereditary differences, one child may be more sociable; this child will be the recipient of more social interactions. Another child may be abrasive and disagreeable; this child will be treated more coldly. In the case of identical twins, who have no hereditary differences, the amount and style of social interaction with each twin is likely to be similar. Thus, although a child's environment plays an important part in his or her personality development, hereditary factors play a large role in determining the nature of this environment.

One caution about this interpretation is in order. Although the studies cited have been replicated in several cultures, none of them has investigated the effects of the full range of cultural differences in family lives. That is, when comparisons have been made between twins raised together and those raised apart, almost all have involved family environments *within* the same culture. It is possible that cultural differences in family environments could be even more important than the differences produced by a person's heredity. Hur (2005) found that the shared environment of Korean families affected aspects of self-perception more than it did in American families.

Should we assume that all personality traits are a product, direct or indirect, of a person's heredity? The answer is no. Some attributes and attitudes show a strong effect of shared environment but almost no effect of genetics. For example, twin studies have found a strong influence of family environment, but not of heredity, on involvement in religion, masculinity/femininity, attitudes toward racial integration, and intellectual interests (Loehlin & Nichols, 1976; Rose, 1995). Thus, people tend to *learn* from their family environments some important social attitudes associated with their personalities.

Another way of examining the question of heredity is to look at personality early in life, in infancy. The NEO-PI-R was not designed to be administered to infants, but psychologists use a related concept to describe the behaviors of infants— **temperament,** or each infant's individual pattern of behaviors and emotional reactions. Parents often will characterize their infant children in terms of temperament (as when your mother recalls you as a "fussy" or "quiet" baby), and several scales exist for measuring temperaments in infants and preschool children. For example, in one assessment questionnaire,

caregivers are asked a variety of questions, such as "When your child was being approached by an unfamiliar adult while shopping or out walking, how often did your child show distress or cry?" Unlike the case with personality, as yet no commonly agreed-on description of temperament exists; however, one measure, the Toddler Behavior Assessment Questionnaire, proposes that temperament can be measured with respect to five dimensions: activity level, pleasure, social fearfulness, anger proneness, and interest/persistence.

The environmental factors of the family that affect temperament seem to be the unique social influences we just discussed. Correlations between infant siblings who are adopted and not related are very low (Saudino, 2005). The different temperaments of children within a family seem to be based on their individual interactions with other family members. As children develop, their temperaments show some change. Generally, the changed aspects of temperament seem to be the result of environmental factors, whereas the stable aspects are controlled by genetics (Saudino, 2005).

Brain Mechanisms in Personality

Patients with damage to the front of the brain, the orbitofrontal cortex, behave differently from those with damage to other areas of brain; they are more impulsive, engage in more inappropriate behavior, and report more anger and less happiness (Berlin, Rolls, & Kischika, 2004). Traumatic brain injury to the frontal lobe in children as young as 5 or as old as 14 is associated with personality changes seen 6 and 12 months after injury (Max et al., 2006). Curiously, given the marked changes in "personality" observed in frontal lobe patients, Berlin, Rolls, & Kischika (2004) found no significant differences between the groups on a standard measure of personality (the Big Five). Where, if anywhere, do the neural correlates of personality reside?

Studies of healthy individuals have provided more-specific but complex data. Canli et al. (2001) predicted that extraversion would be correlated with greater brain activation when people watch pleasant images, whereas neuroticism would be correlated with greater brain activation when participants watch unpleasant images. Their hypothesis was based on the assumption that extroverts would be more positively disposed and would respond enthusiastically to pleasant stimuli, whereas neurotic participants would react intensely to negative stimuli. This pattern was found in an *f*MRI study of 14 women.

You saw in Chapter 13 that the amygdala is activated when participants see fearful faces, especially ones that increase in intensity. Canli et al. (2002), however, also found that personality type—specifically, extraversion—is associated with amygdala activation when participants watch happy faces. The more extrovert the individual, the greater the activation in this structure. No other interaction between emotion and personality was found.

---

temperament An individual's pattern of behaviors and emotional reactions.

Zuckerman (1991) suggests that extroversion, neuroticism, and psychoticism are determined by the neural systems responsible for reinforcement, punishment, and arousal. People who score high on extroversion are particularly sensitive to reinforcement—perhaps their neural reinforcement systems are especially active. People who score high on neuroticism are anxious and fearful. If they also score high on psychoticism, they are hostile as well. People who score high on psychoticism have difficulty learning when not to do something. As Zuckerman suggested, they have a low sensitivity to punishment. They also have a high tolerance for arousal and excitation; in other words, we could say that their optimal level of arousal is abnormally high. TABLE 14·2 summarizes Zuckerman's hypothetical explanations for the three major personality dimensions.

Few studies have directly tested the hypothesis that personality differences can be accounted for by biological differences. However, research using laboratory animals has provided support for Zuckerman's suggestions concerning neuroticism. A neurotic person avoids unfamiliar situations because he or she fears encountering aversive stimuli, whereas an emotionally stable person is likely to investigate unfamiliar situations to see whether anything interesting will happen. The same is true for other species. For example, about 15% of kittens avoid novel objects, and this tendency persists when they become adults; some adult cats are timid, whereas others are bold. When a timid cat encounters a novel stimulus (such as a rat), the neural circuits in its amygdala responsible for defensive responses become more active (Adamec & Stark-Adamec, 1986). (Yes, some cats are afraid of rats.)

Biological Basis for Shyness Kagan, Reznick, and Snidman (1988) investigated the possibility that timidity in social situations (shyness) has a biological basis in humans. They noted that about 10 to 15% of normal children between the ages of 2 and 3 become quiet, watchful, and subdued when they encounter an unfamiliar situation. In other words, like the kittens, they are shy and cautious in approaching novel stimuli. Childhood shyness seems to be related to two personality dimensions: a low level of extroversion and a high level of neuroticism (Briggs, 1988).

Kagan and his colleagues (1988) selected two groups of 21-month-old and 31-month-old children according to their reactions to unfamiliar people and situations. The shy group consisted of children who showed signs of inhibition, such as clinging to their mothers or remaining close to them, remaining silent, and failing to approach strangers or other novel stimuli. The children in the non-shy group showed no such inhibition; these children approached the strangers and explored the novel environment. The children were similarly tested for shyness several more times, up to the age of 7.5 years.

The investigators found shyness to be an enduring trait: Children who were shy at the ages of 21 or 31 months continued to be shy at the age of 7.5 years. In addition, the two groups of children showed differences in their physiological reactions to the test situation. Shy children were more likely to show increases in heart rate, their pupils tended to be more dilated, their urine contained more norepinephrine, and their saliva contained more cortisol. (Norepinephrine and cortisol are two hormones secreted during times of stress. Furthermore, their secretion in fear-provoking situations is controlled by the amygdala.) Obviously, the shy

[**FIGURE 14·6**] Two regions of the brain that are activated by viewing facial stimuli: the amygdala (Amy) and the ocipito-temporal cortex (OTC). People who, as two year olds, were inhibited in their reactions showed greater activation in the Amy region when, as adults, they saw novel faces, compared to people who were uninhibited as children. (Photograph from Schwartz, C.E., Wright, C.I., Shin, L.M., Kagan, J., & Rauch, S.L. (2003). Inhibited and uninhibited infants "grown up": Adult amygdalar response to novelty. *Science, 300,* 1952–1953.)

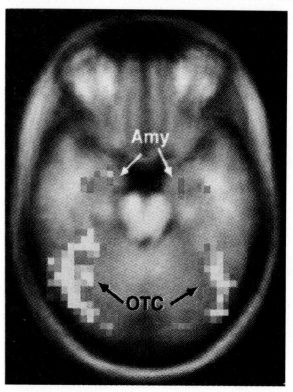

[TABLE 14·2] Zuckerman's (1991) Hypothetical Biological Characteristics That Correspond to Personality Dimensions

Personality Trait	Biological Characteristics
Extroversion	High sensitivity to reinforcement
Neuroticism	High sensitivity to punishment
Psychoticism	Low sensitivity to punishment; high optimum level of arousal

children found the situation stressful, whereas the non-shy children did not.

This study suggests that the biological basis of an important personality characteristic during childhood—shyness—may be the excitability of neural circuits that control avoidance behaviors. When Kagan and his colleagues first raised this possibility, the methods of functional brain imaging were not available, but 20 years later, they had a chance to test, as adults, some of the children who had been classified as either shy or not at the age of 2 years. People who had shown signs of inhibition and shyness as 2-year-olds showed greater activity in the amygdala when they viewed pictures of unfamiliar faces than when they saw familiar faces. (See **FIGURE 14·6**.) Adults who had not shown inhibition as infants did not exhibit this difference (Schwartz et al., 2003).

*f*ocus ⊕n

Gender Differences in Personality

From a very early age, people in all cultures learn that boys and girls and men and women are different in at least two ways—physically and psychologically. The psychological differences often are more difficult to detect than the physical differences, but nonetheless, males and females tend not only to perceive aspects of their environments differently, but also to behave differently under some circumstances. Usually these cultures hold certain beliefs, called stereotypes, about differences between males and females (see Chapter 12). In general, stereotypes about men are more flattering than are those about women: Men are stereotyped as being more competent, independent, decisive, and logical. Women are stereotyped as being less competent, competitive, ambitious, independent, and active (Broverman et al., 1972).

For example, consider how males and females in three different Papua New Guinea tribes are expected to act (Harris, 1991). Among the Arapesh, both men and women are expected to be cooperative and sympathetic, much as Western cultures expect the ideal "mom" to be. Among the Mundugumor, both men and women are expected to be fierce and aggressive, similar to what we might expect of the men in our culture whom we call "macho." Finally, among the Tchambuli, women shave their heads, are boisterous, and provide food; the men tend to focus on art, their hairstyles, and gossiping about women.

These stereotypes are social constructions based on cultural expectations of how a man or a woman should behave. Are there differences between genders with respect to the Big Five traits? General sex differences were reported in a 55-culture study by Schmitt et al. (2008). In a sample of just over 17.5 thousand participants, they found that women reported higher levels of neuroticism, extraversion, agreeableness, and conscientiousness than did men and that these differences were much more pronounced in cultures that are healthy, prosperous, and more egalitarian. Chapman et al. (2007) likewise found that women showed moderately higher measures of Neuroticism and Agreeableness. The gender difference in Agreeableness suggests a link to social behavior.

A social behavior that shows large gender differences is aggression. During play, young boys react to provocation with greater anger than do young girls (Fabes et al., 1996). In a longitudinal study of elementary and high school students, boys were shown to be more aggressive than girls, and patterns of aggression were found to be less stable for boys than for girls (Woodall & Matthews, 1993).

Even so, gender differences in aggression may vary in different cultures. In one study of preschoolers, for example, American and Israeli girls were shown to start fewer fights than did their respective male counterparts, but Israeli girls started more fights than did American boys (Lauer, cited in Bower, 1991). The higher levels of aggression among Israeli children may be due in part to their country's constant preparation for and frequent participation in military conflicts.

Several other gender differences related to personality and social behavior have been documented. Males tend to emerge as leaders when the groups to which they belong need to accomplish a specific task. Females tend to emerge

To a large extent, the specific culture in which people live influences the gender-linked behavioral tendencies and personality traits of males and females.

as leaders when the groups to which they belong stress interpersonal relationships (Eagly & Karau, 1991). Males tend to report higher thresholds for pain than do females, and females on average report a greater willingness to report pain than does the typical male (Wise et al., 2002). Females tend to be more empathetic and tend to offer assistance to others when the situation demands comforting others. Men are more likely to offer assistance when the situation demands physical aid (Eisenberg et al., 1991). Likewise, males tend to be less intimate, whereas females tend to be more empathetic and expressive in their relationships (Buss, 1995).

QUESTIONS TO CONSIDER

1. Of identical twin boys, one is much more outgoing than the other. If personality traits are heritable, how would you explain this difference—how can twins share 100% of their genes yet have different "personalities"?

2. Are you a thrill seeker? To what extent do you seek out situations that might be considered risky or at least mildly exciting? Depending on your answers to these questions, what might Zuckerman say about your personality (in terms of psychoticism)?

Social Cognitive Approaches

Some psychologists view personality as the result of a behavioral learning process in which environmental variables act on the individual to produce behaviors. We might interpret certain behaviors in terms of traits like "extroversion," but the key question is why "extrovert behaviors" are frequently demonstrated by a particular person, and why that person might use them in one situation but not in another.

Models that interpret personality as behavior stem partially from B. F. Skinner's experimental analysis of behavior (see Chapter 5). Although Skinner's work has influenced contemporary personality theory, he should not be mistaken for a personality theorist. Personality was definitely not Skinner's focus, but his ideas have relevance when we consider personality as a description for a certain set of behaviors.

Skinner believed that the consequences of behavior were important causal factors. Environmental variables are those that define the contingencies between stimuli, behaviors, and outcomes. Behavior is consistent from one situation to the next if it is maintained by similar kinds of consequences across those situations. Behavior changes only when the consequences change.

Behaviorists influenced by Skinner's approach have attempted to apply the experimental analysis of behavior to social contingencies and social behaviors. However, many choose to apply a behavioral approach by blending it with cognitive theory. The result is **social cognitive theory,** which embodies the idea that both the consequences of behavior and an individual's beliefs about those consequences determine personality. Because many of the consequences we receive for our behaviors come from others, social behaviors are important sources for the behaviors and thoughts that distinguish us as individuals. One such researcher is Albert Bandura (b. 1925) who combined elements of learning theory with cognitive concepts to explain social behavior.

Expectancies and Observational Learning

Bandura's theory is based on **observational learning,** which is learning through observation of the consequences that others (usually called *models*) experience as a result of their behaviors. Observational learning is undoubtedly important in animal species whose young must learn a behavior before they are physically able to perform it. Your own experience is no doubt filled with examples of observational learning—it is partly through observation that we learn to dance, to make a paper airplane, to write in cursive, and to engage in many other activities. The more complex the behavior, *the more times we must observe it being executed, and practice what we have observed,* before we can learn it well. Learning to tie a shoelace requires more attention to details than learning to roll a ball across the floor.

Observational learning is more than just imitation. It also depends on reinforcement, as in other forms of learning. The nature of the reinforcement differs, however, in that it is the model who is reinforced. In other words, reinforcement is *vicarious,* and not directly experienced by the observer.

At the heart of the social learning theory account of personality is the idea that personality develops as we observe and imitate the actions of others. Our observation of a model performing a behavior leads to an expectancy that our performance of the same behavior will produce a favorable result.

---

social cognitive theory   The idea that both consequences of behavior and an individual's beliefs about those consequences determine personality.

observational learning   Learning that takes place when we see the kinds of consequences others (called models) experience as a result of their behavior.

The vicarious nature of some learning experiences is obvious in children as they imitate the actions of others. A 3-year-old who applies deodorant to herself does so not because this behavior has been reinforced in the past, but rather because after watching her mother do it, she expects it would be "fun" for her to do so, too.

Vicarious reinforcement is made possible, in Bandura's theory, through cognition (Bandura, 1986, 1995, 2002; Bandura & Locke, 2003). In particular, individuals can form an expectancy based on their behaviors. An **expectancy** is an individual's belief that a specific consequence will follow a specific action. To put it another way, expectancy has to do with how someone perceives the contingencies of reinforcement for his or her own behavior. If a person does something, it may be because he or she expects to be rewarded or punished. In different situations, expectancies may vary. For example, a young boy may learn that he can get what he wants from his younger sister by hitting her. However, on one occasion, his parents may catch him hitting his sister and punish him. His expectancy may now change: He may still get what he wants by behaving aggressively, but if he is caught, he'll be punished. This new expectancy may influence how he behaves toward his sister in the future, especially when his parents are present.

Reciprocal Determinism and Self-Efficacy

Bandura, unlike many other theorists, does not believe that either personal characteristics (traits) or the environment alone determines personality (Bandura, 1978). Rather, he argued for **reciprocal determinism**—the idea that behavior, environmental variables, and cognitive variables interact to determine personality. (See FIGURE 14•7.) We know that our actions can affect the environment. We also know that the environment can affect our behavior. Likewise, our perceptions may affect the ways in which we behave to change the environment, and in turn, those changes can influence our perceptions. For example, when our acts of kindness are met with kindness in return, we perceive the environment as friendly and are apt to show kindness under other, similar circumstances. Likewise, when we are treated rudely, we perceive the environment as unfriendly (perhaps hostile) and will likely attempt to avoid or change similar environments in the future.

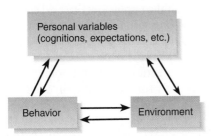

[**FIGURE 14•7**] Patterns of interaction in reciprocal determinism. According to Bandura, behavior, environment, and cognitive variables, such as expectations and perceptions, interact to determine personality.

The term **self-efficacy** refers to a person's beliefs about his or her ability to act as required in a particular situation to experience satisfying outcomes (Bandura, 1982, 1997). According to Bandura, our degree of self-efficacy is an important determinant of whether we will attempt to make changes in our environment. Each day we make many decisions based on our perceptions of the extent to which our actions will produce reinforcement. Our actions are based on our evaluation of our competency. Moreover, self-efficacy not only determines whether we will engage in a particular behavior; it also determines the extent to which we will maintain that behavior in the face of adversity. For example, if you believe that you are underqualified for a job as ski instructor at a fancy ski resort, even though you really want the job, you are not apt to apply for an interview—you expect that nothing good could come of the effort. However, if you are confident of your qualifications, you will surely attempt to get an interview. Even if you are turned down for that job, you may interview for a position at another resort, because you are sure of your abilities. Eventually your abilities will produce the outcome you want. Low self-efficacy can hamper both the frequency and the quality of behavior–environment interactions, whereas high self-efficacy can facilitate both.

Personality across Time

Earlier we saw that trait theorists seek to explain two aspects of personality: the distinctiveness of any one individual, and the aspects of personality that stay the same within that individual. Is this second objective reasonable? Does stability to personality exist? Can the introverted high school student become a social star in college?

One extreme position, consistent with the behavior approach, is to assume that the behaviors that make up our personality are specific to a given situation and are not the result of any persevering traits. This position is known as **situationism.** In Chapter 5, we examined how discriminative stimuli control behaviors; perhaps personality is likewise dependent on the stimuli that control behaviors. Would a person high in conscientiousness stop at a red light at 3:00 in the morning with no one around and no chance of being caught? If you think the answer is "no," then you probably see the point.

This question is amenable to empirical test and has been the subject of much research (see the *Focus On* feature later in this section). In response to this research, some personality psychologists have argued for theories that represent the

---

expectancy   The belief that a certain consequence will follow a certain action.

reciprocal determinism   The idea that behavior, environment, and person variables interact to determine personality.

self-efficacy   People's beliefs about how well or badly they will perform tasks.

situationism   The view that the behaviors defining a certain personality are determined solely by the current situation rather than by any persevering traits.

situation as part of the rules that govern behavior. Stability in personality, in this view, is a consequence of stability in the underlying rules. Variation results from the way the situation activates those rules. For example, social cognitive theory might say that your use of swear words in your verbal behavior would be affected by whom you were talking to. Perhaps your parents are stricter about swearing than your friends. Consequently, your speech would be more conservative when you talk to your parents than when you talk to your friends. If you're often with your friends, your personality might be seen as "tougher."

One possible scheme that makes these factors explicit is the model proposed by Walter Mischel, whose early work was strongly based on situationism, but who has modified that position since. Mischel, like Bandura, believes that much of personality is learned through interaction with the environment. Also like Bandura, Mischel emphasizes the role of cognition in determining how people learn the relationship between their behavior and its consequences. In addition, though, Mischel argues that individual differences in cognition, or **person variables,** as he calls them, account for differences in personality. Five person variables, as follows, figure prominently in this version of social cognitive theory (Mischel, 1990, 2003; Mischel, Cantor, & Feldman, 1996):

- *Competencies.* We each have different skills, abilities, and capacities. What we know and the kinds of behaviors that have been reinforced in the past influence the kinds of actions in which we will likely engage in the future.

- *Encoding strategies and personal constructs.* We also differ in our ability to process information. The way we process information determines how we perceive different situations. One person may perceive going on a date as fun, and so may look forward to it; another person may perceive going on a date as potentially boring, and so may dread it.

- *Expectancies.* On the basis of our past behavior and our knowledge of current situations, we form expectancies about the effects of our behavior on the environment. Expecting our behavior to affect the environment positively leads to one action; expecting our behavior to affect it negatively leads to another.

- *Subjective values.* The degree to which we value certain reinforcers over others influences our behavior. We seek those outcomes that we value most.

- *Self-regulatory systems and plans.* We monitor our progress toward achieving goals and subject ourselves to either self-punishment or self-reinforcement, depending on our progress. We also modify and formulate plans regarding how we think a goal can best be achieved.

---

person variables   Individual differences in cognition, which, according to Mischel, include competencies, encoding strategies and personal constructs, expectancies, subjective values, and self-regulatory systems and plans.

Mischel's is a dynamic view; it envisions people's thoughts and behaviors undergoing constant change as they interact with the environment. New plans are made, and old ones are reformulated; people adjust their actions in accordance with their competencies, subjective values, and expectancies of behavior–environment interactions. Between these periods of change, however, person variables provide stable rules for behavior akin to those described by trait theories.

focus On

Traits versus Situations as Predictors of Behavior

Social cognitive theorists stress the importance of the environment as an influence on behavior and tend to place less emphasis on the role of enduring personal traits. They argue that the situation often plays a strong role in determining behavior. In contrast, trait theorists argue that personality traits are stable characteristics of individuals and that knowing something about these traits permits us to predict an individual's behavior in a variety of situations. What evidence exists for both positions?

The Case for Situationism

Mischel (1968, 1976) suggested that stable personality traits do not exist—or that if they do, they are of little importance. Situations, not traits, best predict behavior, Mischel argued. He asks us to consider two situations: (1) a party to celebrate someone's winning a large sum of money in a lottery, and (2) a funeral. People will be much more talkative, cheerful, and outgoing at the party than at the funeral. In this case, knowing the situation has much more predictive value for behavior than knowing the test score someone might receive on a test of introversion–extroversion.

Mischel can cite a wealth of empirical research evidence for his position. One of the first of these studies was performed in the 1920s. Hartshorne and May (1928) designed a set of behavioral tests to measure the traits of honesty and self-control and administered them to more than 10,000 students in elementary and high schools. The tests gave the children the opportunity to be dishonest—for example, to cheat on a test, lie about the amount of homework they had done, or keep money with which they had been entrusted. In all cases, the researchers had access to what the children actually did. They found that a child who acted honestly (or dishonestly) in one situation did not necessarily act the same way in a different situation.

Mischel (1968) reviewed evidence from research performed after the Hartshorne and May study and found that most personal characteristics showed the same low cross-situational consistency—0.30 or lower. He concluded that the concept of personality trait was not very useful.

The Case for Personality Traits

Other psychologists disagree with Mischel. For example, Epstein (1979, 1986) claimed that personality traits are more stable than some of the studies had suggested. He noted that assessments of cross-situational consistency usually test a group of people on two occasions and correlate their behavior in one situation with their behavior in the other. Epstein showed that repeated measurements across several days yielded much higher correlations. In a study of his own, a group of 28 undergraduates kept daily records of their most pleasant and most unpleasant experiences for a month. For each experience, they recorded the emotions they felt, their impulses to action, and their actual behavior. The correlation between a given participant's emotions, impulses, or behavior on any 2 days was rather low—on the order of 0.30. However, when Epstein grouped measurements (that is, correlated the ratings obtained on odd-numbered days with those obtained on even-numbered days), the correlation rose dramatically—to around 0.80. That is, the correlation became much higher when the records of a group of days were compared with those of a different group of days than when a single day was compared with another single day.

A Reconciliation?

Mischel and Shoda (1995, 1998) proposed a move toward reconciliation of the trait and situations approaches in the form of what they call the cognitive–affective processing system approach (CAPS). The CAPS approach recognizes the multiple influences of biology, affect, cognition, and learning. An individual's personality is a network of relatively stable components, such as expectations, beliefs, memories, and feelings. However, the specific components that are active at a specific time depends on the interaction that occurs with the environment and among the components themselves. As an example, Shoda and Smith (2004) point to Shakespeare's classic play, *Hamlet*. Hamlet's uncle, Claudius, is a cold and treacherous killer who, if he had been real rather than fictitious, would probably have scored high on the Dark Triad traits. Nevertheless, he manages to hide his nature and his crime from Hamlet through most of the play. It is only when Hamlet stages a play recreating the crime that the specific feelings and memories of his past cause Claudius, through his behavior, to reveal his guilt.

Through their CAPS framework, Mischel and Shoda appear to extend an olive branch to traditional trait theory. However, this acknowledgment that both traits and situation can interact leaves unresolved the question of how each should be studied. Funder (2006) suggested that future research in personality theory will need to grapple with issues such as what makes a situation similar or different, and what is the source of behavioral variation.

Locus of Control

With the growth of the Internet, email has become a widespread means of communication. For many people, email is a convenient way to keep in touch and to conduct business, but it has no special urgency. In contrast, others view email messages as much more pressing matters; they feel compelled to respond to each message as quickly as possible. Hair, Renaud, and Ramsay (2007) found that among this latter type of user were people who viewed the rapid nature of email as a positive and helpful aspect; for others, though, it was considered a source of considerable stress.

What could account for this difference? If you think about how email affects your own life, one aspect about it is undeniable: it can be a considerable source of distraction. If you yourself find the pace of electronic communication stressful, it could be because you regard it and other external distractions as unavoidable influences on your life that you cannot control. Lack of control could be the source of your stress.

Social cognitive theorist Julian Rotter (1966, 1990) focused on the extent to which people perceive themselves to be in control of the consequences of their behavior. Theories of **locus of control** (plural: loci of control) focus on whether people believe that the consequences of their actions are controlled by internal person variables or by external environmental variables. A person who expects to control his or her own fate—or, more technically, who perceives that rewards are dependent on his or her own behavior—has an *internal locus of control*. A person who sees his or her life as being controlled by external forces unaffected by his or her own behavior has an *external locus of control*. (See **FIGURE 14•8**.)

Rotter developed the *I-E Scale,* which assesses the degree to which people perceive the consequences of their behavior to be under the control of internal or external variables. The I-E Scale contains 29 pairs of statements with which a person indicates his or her degree of agreement. A typical item on the scale might look something like this:

> The grades that I get depend on my abilities and how hard I work to get them.

> The grades that I get depend mostly on my teacher and his or her tests.

Researchers score the scale by counting the number of choices consistent with either the internal or the external locus of control orientation. Scores may range from 0 to 23, with lower scores indicative of greater internal locus of control. The highest possible score is 23, because six of the choice pairs are nonscored "filler" items. Of all the populations Rotter has assessed with the I-E Scale, a group of U.S. Peace Corps volunteers showed the highest level of internal locus of control (Rotter, 1966).

---

locus of control An individual's beliefs that the consequences of his or her actions are controlled by internal, person variables or by external, environmental variables.

[**FIGURE 14•8**] Internal and external loci of control. People having internal loci of control perceive themselves as able to determine the outcomes of the events in their lives. People having external loci of control perceive the events in their lives as determined by environmental variables.

Internal Locus of Control

Poor performance on test	Good performance on test
It's my own fault. I should have spent more time studying.	Great! I knew all that studying would pay off.

External Locus of Control

Poor performance on test	Good performance on test
These tests are just too hard. The questions are impossible.	Did I get lucky or what? The teacher must really have gone easy on the grading.

When Rotter published his work on the I-E Scale in 1966, the concept captured the imaginations of researchers; it seemed to be an antidote to what was perceived in the 1960s as an overemphasis on drive and motivational concepts (Lefcourt, 1992). The attraction has been long lived, and the scale has been used in hundreds if not thousands of studies of social behavior in a wide variety of situations. Consider some of the findings obtained from research using the I-E Scale (Lefcourt, 1966, 1992):

- People with an internal locus-of-control orientation believe that achievement of their goals depends on their personal efforts toward accomplishing those goals.

- People having an internal locus-of-control orientation will work harder to obtain a goal if they believe that they can control the outcome in a specific situation. Even when people with external orientations are told that a goal can be obtained with their own skill and effort, they tend not to try as hard as those having internal orientations.

- People having internal orientations also are more likely to be aware of and to engage in good health practices. They are more apt to take preventive medicines, to exercise regularly, to diet when appropriate, and to quit smoking than are people having external orientations.

- People having high internal locus of control tend to have strong academic achievement goals and to do well in school. They are, however, also likely to blame themselves when they fail, even when failure is not their fault. People with an external locus of control tend to blame others for their failures.

Whether theories of locus of control can explain our modern angst about email and the speed of modern communication is a bit less clear. Hair, Renaud, and Ramsay (2007) found that people with external locus of control

also reported more difficulty handling distractions and extraneous interruptions. This is consistent with the view that external locus of control is related to seeing one's life as controlled by outside influences. However, scores on the I-E scale did not correlate well with reported stress from email, suggesting that something else about the medium makes it such a modern burden.

A person's belief about his or her locus of control is fundamentally a belief about the source of controlling influences; what is the source of this belief? Is locus of control determined by experience, or is it more like a trait? Either of these two possibilities is consistent with the concept of locus of control. Johansson et al. (2001) found that individual differences between twins in their beliefs about how chance affected their health (an external belief) was attributable to shared family environment rather than genetic sources. This implies that beliefs about locus of control may be determined by one's experiences.

People having internal orientations are more likely to engage in good health practices.

Positive Psychology

As you saw in Chapter 1, psychology has for many years concerned itself with improving human welfare and with healing mental disorders. In the course of that history, psychologists have often looked to those instances in which personality factors have impeded or limited the potential of an individual. Negative factors are often stronger than positive ones (e.g., Rozin & Royzman, 2001), so in this respect, psychologists may be repeating an inherent bias for negativity.

Martin Seligman suggested that psychology should concern itself with the beneficial aspects of personality that make life rewarding and fulfilling (e.g., Seligman and Csikszentmihalyi, 2000). **Positive psychology** is a psychological program that examines optimal human functioning (Linley et al., 2006). It is an agenda that many psychologists have adopted to study the origins, processes, and mechanisms that lead to psychological well-being, satisfaction, and fulfillment. Like humanistic psychology, which is discussed later in the chapter, positive psychology concerns the valued aspects of personality. It is, however, more closely identified with the scientific methods of biological, behavioral, cognitive, and social research.

As one example of positive psychology, Fincham and Beach (2007) looked at forgiveness as a factor in the quality of a marriage. Forgiveness is an active process by which an individual voluntarily reduces the negative emotions felt toward a transgressor. Married life (or any close partnered relationship, for that matter) produces many opportunities for forgiveness. Fincham and Beach asked married individuals to consider an instance in which their partner had said or done something to hurt them. They then looked at whether a tendency to forgive that act was correlated with the quality and happiness of marriage, either at the time, or 12 months later. It turned out that, for both husbands and wives, a tendency to forgive was correlated with the quality of the marriage at the time. (Interestingly, wives' tendency to forgive their husbands did not correlate with their husbands' tendency to forgive them.)

It's worth noting that the social roles for women (see Chapter 12) place a strong emphasis on social skills, and this may encourage them to see forgiveness as an active strategy to maintain a strong marital bond. Positive psychology would seek to understand this interplay between personality variables that promote a valued relationship. The cognitive and behavioral approaches of this section would be helpful to this understanding.

QUESTIONS TO CONSIDER

1. Think of a situation in which you modeled your behavior after someone else's. What factors led you to imitate this behavior? To what extent did you form an expectancy that imitating this behavior would lead to a particular consequence?
2. Provide a personal example of reciprocal determinism. Explain the interaction of behavior, environmental variables, and cognitive variables in this example.
3. Do you believe that you have an internal or an external locus of control? Give an example of a recent decision that you made or a social interaction that you had. How would your life be different if you adopted the opposite locus-of-control orientation?

The Psychodynamic Approach

For many people, the name Sigmund Freud is synonymous with psychology. Indeed, his work has had profound and lasting effects on Western culture. Terms such as *ego, libido, repression, rationalization,* and *fixation* are as familiar to many laypeople as to clinicians. Before Freud formulated his theory, people believed that most behavior was determined by rational, conscious processes. Freud was the first to claim that what we do is often irrational and that the reasons for our behavior are seldom conscious. The mind, to Freud, was a battleground for the warring factions of instinct, reason, and conscience; the term **psychodynamic** refers to this struggle. As you will soon see, although Freud's work began with the clinical treatment of patients with psychological problems, it later provided a framework for explaining how psychodynamic factors determine personality.

The Development of Freud's Theory

Sigmund Freud (1856–1939) was a Viennese physician who acquired his early training in neurology in the laboratory of Ernst Wilhelm von Brücke, an eminent physiologist and neuroanatomist. Freud's work in the laboratory consisted mostly of careful anatomical observation rather than experimentation. Careful observation also characterized his later work with human behavior; he made detailed observations of individual patients and drew inferences about the structure of the human mind from these cases.

Freud, after studying in Paris with Jean Martin Charcot, who was investigating the usefulness of hypnosis as a treatment for hysteria, opened his own medical practice in Vienna. He began an association with the prominent physician Josef Breuer. They published a seminal book called *Studies on Hysteria,* and one of the cases cited in it, that of Anna O., provided the evidence that led to some of the most important tenets of Freud's theory. Anna O. had a staggering number of symptoms, including loss of speech, disturbances in vision, headaches, and paralysis and loss of feeling in her right arm. Under hypnosis, Anna was asked to think about the time when her symptoms had started. Each of her symptoms appeared to have begun just when she was unable to express a strongly felt emotion. While under hypnosis she experienced

---

positive psychology A program of psychology that examines the basis of optimal human functioning, with emphasis on the origins, processes, and mechanisms of human well-being.

psychodynamic Characterized by conflict among instincts, reason, and conscience; describes the mental processes envisioned in Freudian theory.

these emotions again, and the experience gave her relief from her symptoms. It was as if the emotions had been bottled up, and reliving the original experiences uncorked them. This release of energy (which Breuer and Freud called *catharsis*) presumably eliminated her symptoms.

Apparently, the woman was not cured, however. Ellenberger (1972) discovered hospital records indicating that Anna O. continued to take morphine for the distress caused by the disorders Breuer had supposedly cured. Freud appears to have eventually learned the truth, but this fact did not become generally known until recently. Breuer's failure to help Anna O. with her problems does not really undermine Freud's approach, however. The Freudian theory of personality must stand or fall on its own merits, despite the fact that one of its prime teaching examples appears to be largely fiction.

Freud concluded from his observations of patients that all human behavior is motivated by instinctual drives, which, when activated, supply "psychic energy." According to Freud, if something prevents the psychic energy caused by activation of a drive from being discharged, psychological disturbances will result.

Freud believed that instinctual drives are triggered by events in a person's life. Traumatic events may seriously threaten the desired state of psychic energy equilibrium. During a traumatic event, a person may try to deny or hide a strong emotional reaction rather than express it. Indeed, sometimes we must hide and not act on strong emotions, according to Freud. But there is a cost to hiding emotional reactions and suppressing the psychic energy that fuels them: The emotion may be expressed neurotically—that is, with excessive anxiety. The individual will not be able to recall the extreme emotional reactions, because they will be embedded in the **unconscious,** the inaccessible part of the mind. Unconscious emotions, however, still exert control over conscious thoughts and actions. As we will see later, according to Freud, the ways in which those emotions eventually find a degree of release will help define our unique personalities.

Freud also believed that the mind actively prevents unconscious memories of traumatic events from reaching conscious awareness. That is, the mind *represses* the memories of anxiety-provoking traumatic events from being consciously discovered. Freud used the metaphor of an iceberg to describe the mind. Only the tip of an iceberg is visible above

water; the much larger and more important part is submerged. Likewise, the conscious mind hides a larger and more important part of the mind—the unconscious. To understand someone's personality, we must tap into that individual's unconscious.

Structures of the Mind: Id, Ego, and Superego

Freud was struck by the fact that psychological disturbances could stem from events that a person apparently could no longer consciously recall, although the events could be revealed during hypnosis. This phenomenon led him to conclude that the mind consists of unconscious, preconscious, and conscious elements. The *unconscious* includes mental events of which we are not aware; the *conscious* entails mental events of which we are aware; and the *preconscious* involves mental events that may become conscious through effort.

Freud divided the mind into three structures: the id, the ego, and the superego. (See FIGURE 14•9.) The operations of the **id** are completely unconscious. The id contains the **libido,** which is the primary source of instinctual motivation for all psychic forces. The id obeys only one rule—to obtain immediate gratification in whatever form it may take—called the **pleasure principle.** If you are hungry, the id compels you to eat; if you are angry, the id prompts you to strike out or to seek revenge or to destroy something; if you are sexually aroused, the id presses for immediate sexual gratification. It is important to understand that for Freud, the id was a source of unrestrained, uncivilized, and ultimately harmful behavior.

The **ego** is the thinking, planning, and protective self; it controls and integrates behavior. It acts as a mediator, negotiating a

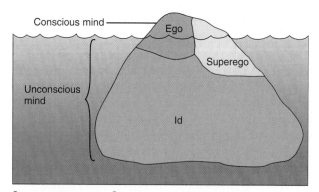

[**FIGURE 14•9**] Freud's conception of the structure of the mind. Freud compared the conscious portion of the mind to the tip of an iceberg and the unconscious portion to the larger part of the iceberg below the water's surface. The id is completely unconscious, but both the ego and the superego may be partially conscious and partially unconscious. In addition, Freud argued that part of the mind is preconscious (not shown in this figure), containing information that may be brought into consciousness through effort.

---

unconscious   The inaccessible part of the mind.

id   The unconscious reservoir of libido, the psychic energy that fuels instincts and psychic processes.

libido   An insistent, instinctual force that is unresponsive to the demands of reality; the primary source of motivation.

pleasure principle   The rule that the id obeys: Obtain immediate gratification, whatever form it may take.

ego   The general manager of personality, making decisions balancing the pleasures that will be pursued at the id's demand against the person's safety requirements and the moral dictates of the superego.

[**TABLE 14·3**] Freudian Defense Mechanisms

Defense Mechanism	Description	Example
Repression	Unconsciously barring memories of traumatic experiences from reaching conscious awareness.	Being unable to remember traumatic childhood sexual abuse or other traumatic events that occurred earlier in life.
Reaction Formation	Replacing an anxiety-provoking idea with its opposite.	Having intense feelings of dislike for a person but acting friendly and kind toward him or her.
Projection	Denying your unacceptable feelings and desires and finding them in others.	Denying your hostility toward a person but believing that that person is hostile toward you.
Sublimation	Channeling psychic energy from an unacceptable drive into a more acceptable one.	Diverting energy from the sex drive to produce a work of art.
Rationalization	Creating an acceptable reason for a behavior that is actually performed for a less acceptable reason.	Asserting that you enjoy a wrestling match as an athletic contest when in fact you enjoy the vicarious violence.
Denial	Negating or dismissing the reality of an unpleasant truth.	Asserting that a loved one is not dead but is missing in action and unable to communicate.

This table shows several of the most frequently used defense mechanisms.

compromise among the pressures of the id, the counterpressures of the superego (described next), and the demands of reality. The ego's functions of perception, cognition, and memory perform this mediation. The ego is driven by the **reality principle**—the tendency to satisfy the id's demands realistically, which almost always involves compromising the demands of the id and the superego. Adherence to the reality principle involves delaying gratification of a drive until an appropriate goal is located. To ward off the demands of the id when these demands cannot be gratified, the ego uses defense mechanisms (described later). Some of the functions of the ego are unconscious.

The **superego** is subdivided into the conscience and the ego-ideal. The **conscience** is the internalization of the rules and restrictions of society. It determines which behaviors are permissible and punishes wrongdoing with feelings of guilt. The **ego-ideal** is the internalization of what society values and what the person will strive to achieve.

Freud believed the mind to be full of conflicts. A conflict may begin when one of the two primary drives, the sexual instinctual drive or the aggressive instinctual drive, is aroused. The id demands gratification of these drives but often is held in check by the superego's internalized prohibitions against the behaviors that the drives tend to produce. *Internalized prohibitions* are rules of behavior learned in childhood that protect the person from the guilt he or she would feel if the instinctual drives were allowed to express themselves. The result of the conflict is *compromise formation,* in which a compromise is reached between the demands of the id and the suppressive effects of the superego. According to Freud, phenomena such as dreams, artistic creations, and slips of the tongue (we now call them Freudian slips) are examples of compromise formation.

Defense Mechanisms

According to Freud, the ego contains **defense mechanisms**—mental systems that become active whenever the id's unconscious instinctual drives come into conflict with the superego's internalized prohibitions. The signal for the ego to use one of its defenses is the state of anxiety produced by an intrapsychic conflict, which motivates the ego to apply a defense mechanism and thus reduce the anxiety. TABLE 14·3 presents six important defense mechanisms along with examples.

Interestingly, researchers have found that the use of defense mechanisms predicts personality changes in later adulthood (Cramer, 2003). The investigators measured participants' personality traits over a 24-year period by using the five-factor model. Although most personality traits remained reasonably stable, the use of defense mechanisms such as denial and projection correlated with an increased neuroticism, decreased extroversion, and decreased agreeableness among some study participants in later adulthood. The use of these defense mechanisms was not found to be negative in all cases, though. Among

---

reality principle   The tendency to satisfy the id's demands realistically, which almost always involves compromising the demands of the id and superego.

superego   The repository of an individual's moral values, divided into the conscience—the internalization of society's rules and regulations—and the ego-ideal—the internalization of the individual's goals.

conscience   The internalization of the rules and restrictions of society; it determines which behaviors are permissible and punishes wrongdoing with feelings of guilt.

ego-ideal   The internalization of what a person would like to be—his or her goals and ambitions.

defense mechanisms   Mental systems that become active whenever unconscious instinctual drives of the id come into conflict with internalized prohibitions of the superego.

Freud argued that creativity was often the result of sublimation—the redirection of psychic energy from unacceptable actions, such as unrestrained sexual behavior, to acceptable actions, such as the jointly sensual and creative work shown here.

participants who used defense mechanisms, low scores on IQ tests were found to correlate with positive personality traits.

Freud's Psychosexual Theory of Personality Development

Freud believed that personality development involves passing through several *psychosexual stages* of development—stages in which the individual seeks pleasure from specific parts of the body called *erogenous zones*. As we will see, each stage of personality development involves deriving physical pleasure from a different erogenous zone. (Freud used the term "sexual" to refer to physical pleasures and to the many ways an individual might seek to gratify an urge for such pleasure. When referring to children, he did not use the term to refer to adult sexual feelings or orgasmic pleasure.)

Freud's theory of personality development has been extremely influential because of its ability to explain personality disorders in terms of whole or partial **fixation**—arrested

---

fixation A brief interval between saccadic eye movements during which the eye does not move; the brain accesses visual information during this time. Also, in Freudian theory, the continued attachment of psychic energy to an erogenous zone due to incomplete passage through one of the psychosexual stages.

oral stage The first of Freud's psychosexual stages, during which the mouth is the major erogenous zone because it appeases the hunger drive.

anal stage The second of Freud's psychosexual stages, during which the primary erogenous zone is the anus because of the pleasure derived from vacating a full bowel.

phallic stage The third of Freud's psychosexual stages during which the primary erogenous zone is the genital area and pleasure derives from both direct genital stimulation and general physical contact.

---

development due to a person's failure to pass completely through a given stage of development. Freud believed that a person becomes fixated at a particular stage of development when he or she becomes strongly attached to the erogenous zone involved in that stage.

For Freud, personality development begins in infancy. Because newborn babies can do little more than suck and swallow, their sexual instinctual drive finds an outlet in these activities. We can think of infants at this stage as being dominated by the id. Over- or undergratification of the hunger drive during this **oral stage** can result in fixation. Undergratification might result from early weaning, and overgratification, from too zealous attempts by parents to feed the infant. According to Freud, too little gratification during the oral stage will set in motion the development of personality traits related to dependency—what we commonly refer to as "clinging vine" characteristics. Too much gratification, or overstimulation, will lay the groundwork for the development of aggressive personality characteristics. Other oral-stage fixation activities include habits such as smoking, hoarding, and excessive eating.

The **anal stage** of personality development begins during the second year of life. According to Freud, sensual pleasure derives from emptying the bowels. Around this time, most parents place demands on their toddlers to control their bowels, to delay their gratification, through toilet training. The stage is set for the early development of ego functions—the deliberate management of id impulses (in this case, the desire to vacate the bowels as soon as the urge arises). The way that parents toilet train their infants will again have a stage-setting effect on later personality development. Harsh toilet training characterized by punishment when a child fails to reach the toilet may lead to fixation at this stage. The personality characteristics that start to develop will center on orderliness and a need for control. In their adult form, we would refer to these characteristics as compulsiveness and, at an extreme, megalomania (a single-minded need for power and control). Mild toilet training, the preferred method, involves encouraging and praising the infant for successfully producing the bowel movement at the right place and time. The stage is set for pride in the expression of id needs coupled with appropriate ego control. Personality characteristics that should evolve include creativity and emotional expressiveness.

At around age 3 years, a child discovers that it is pleasurable to play with his penis or her clitoris (again, an immature sexuality), and enters the **phallic stage.** (*Phallus* means "penis," but Freud used the term "phallic stage" for children of both genders.) Children during this stage form strong immature sexual attachments to the parent of the opposite sex. This occurs, according to Freud, because mothers predominantly nurture male children and fathers predominantly nurture female children. In other words, opposite-sex parents become the focus of sensual pleasure for children during this stage. According to Freud, children experience jealousy of their same-sex parent's close relationship with the opposite-sex parent—the parent that children want exclusively for themselves.

The process diverges for boys and girls beyond this point. A boy's love of his mother is mixed with hostility

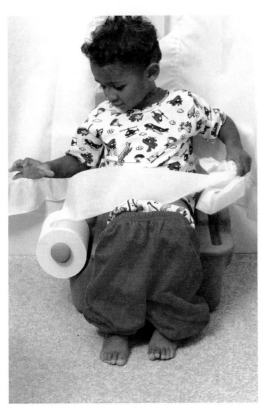

Does toilet training affect personality development? Freud thought so: He asserted that improper toilet training caused personality development to become fixated during the anal stage of psychosexual development.

toward and, importantly, fear of his rival father. Freud believed that boys unconsciously fear being punished by their fathers for their desire for their mothers, including the ultimate punishment—castration. These elements constitute the *Oedipus complex* (after the king of Greek mythology who unknowingly married his mother after killing his father). This rich mix of emotions demands resolution.

A girl's love of her father and envy of her mother, Freud said, is complicated by her discovery that she does not have a penis. This discovery, Freud theorized, leads to *penis envy* and girls' magical belief that they can acquire a penis through their attachment to their father. They then gravitate even more strongly toward their fathers, who have the organ they do not, to associate with power and compensate for their self-perceived weakness. These powerful emotions are what Freud called the *Electra complex*. (In Greek mythology, Electra, aided by her brother, killed her mother and her mother's lover to avenge her father's death.)

The conflict for both girls and boys is resolved through a process called *identification*. According to Freud, children of both sexes turn their attention to their same-sex parent—the father for boys and the mother for girls. They begin to imitate their same-sex parent in many ways and in a sense to idolize them. The effect of this imitation is to build a strong bond between the flattered and approving parent and the

attentive, hero-worshipping son or heroine-worshipping daughter. Fear and envy are resolved. Gender roles are learned, and anxiety over the genitals is resolved. This process of identification is also the initial source of *superego* development. Through their admiration and imitation of the same-sex parent, children learn society's fundamental principles of right and wrong (as interpreted by the parents, of course).

After the phallic stage comes a **latency period** of several years, during which the child's sexual instinctual drive is mostly submerged. After this period is the onset of puberty. The child, now an adolescent, begins to form adult sexual attachments to young people of the other sex. Because the sexual instinctual drive now finds its outlet in heterosexual genital contact, this stage is known as the **genital stage.**

According to Freud, the results of psychosexual development amount to the building blocks of personality and general psychological functioning. Children develop basic ego and superego functions and gender role identities. Their own special mixes of fixations will follow them through life and manifest themselves as distinctive personality traits.

Further Development of Freud's Theory: The Neo-Freudians

As you might imagine, Freud's theory created quite a controversy in the Victorian era when it was unveiled. Its emphasis on childhood sexuality and on seething internal conflicts seemed preposterous and offensive to many. Yet the theory's proposal that adults' thoughts and behavior stem from unconscious forces as well as from early childhood experiences was revolutionary and was recognized by many scholars as a genuinely original idea. Freud attracted many followers who studied his work closely but did not accept it completely. Each of these people agreed with Freud's view on the dynamic forces operating within the psyche. Each of them disagreed with Freud, though, on how much importance to place on the role of unconscious sexual and aggressive instincts in shaping personality.

Carl Jung Many scholars and physicians of the early twentieth century were influenced by Freud's psychodynamic theory and studied with him. One of these people was Carl Jung (1875–1961). Freud called Jung "his adopted eldest son, his crown prince and successor" (Hall & Nordby, 1973, p. 23). However, Jung developed his own version of psychodynamic theory, in which he deemphasized the importance of sexuality. He also disagreed with his mentor on the structure of the unconscious. Freud had little tolerance, and often much sarcasm, for those who disagreed with him. After 1913, he and Jung never saw each other again. Jung continued to develop his theory after the split, drawing ideas from mythology, anthropology,

---

latency period In Freudian theory, the period between the phallic stage and the genital stage, during which sexual urges are submerged.

genital stage The final of Freud's psychosexual stages (from puberty through adolescence). During this stage the adolescent develops adult sexual desires.

history, and religion, as well as from an active clinical practice in which he saw people with psychological disorders.

One of Jung's more important contributions to psychodynamic theory was his idea of the **collective unconscious,** which contains shared ("collective") memories and ideas inherited from our ancestors. Stored in the collective unconscious are **archetypes,** inherited and universal thought forms and patterns that allow us to notice particular aspects of our world. From the dawn of our species, all humans have had roughly similar experiences with things such as mothers, evil, masculinity, and femininity. Each one of these is represented by an archetype. For example, the *shadow* is the archetype containing basic instincts that allow us to recognize aspects of the world such as evil, sin, and carnality. Archetypes are not stored images or ideas—we are not born with a picture of evil stored somewhere in our brains—but inherited dispositions to behave, perceive, and think in certain ways.

Alfred Adler

Alfred Adler (1870–1937), like Jung, studied with Freud. Also like Jung, Adler believed that Freud had overemphasized sexuality. Adler argued that feelings of inferiority play the key role in personality development. At birth, we are dependent on others for survival. Early in our development, we encounter mostly older, more experienced people who are more capable than we are in almost every aspect of life. The inferiority we feel may be social, intellectual, physical, or athletic. These feelings create tension that motivates us to compensate for the deficiency. Emerging from this need to compensate is a **striving for superiority,** which Adler believed to be the major motivational force in life. In Adler's theory, superiority connotes a "personal best" approach rather than defining achievement merely in terms of outperforming others. Our unique experiences with inferiority, and our consequent strivings for superiority, become organizing principles in our lives and therefore define our personalities.

According to Adler (1939), an individual's striving for superiority is affected by another force, *social interest,* which is an innate desire to contribute to society. So although individuals have a need to seek personal superiority, they have a greater desire to sacrifice for causes that benefit the society as a whole. Thus, whereas Freud believed that people act in their own self-interests, motivated by the id, Adler believed that people desire to help others, directed by social interest. In asserting that positive rather than negative motives direct personality, Adler's ideas represented a sea change in psychodynamic theory.

---

collective unconscious According to Jung, the shared unconscious memories and ideas inherited from our ancestors over the course of human evolution.

archetypes Universal thought forms and patterns that Jung believed resided in the collective unconscious.

striving for superiority Our motivation to achieve our full potential. Adler argued that striving for superiority is born from our need to compensate for our inferiority.

basic orientations Horney's sets of personality characteristics that correspond to the strategies of moving toward others, moving against others, and moving away from others.

Karen Horney

Karen Horney (1885–1952), like other Freudian dissenters, did not believe that sex and aggression are the primary determinants of personality. She did agree with Freud, though, that anxiety is a basic problem that people must address and overcome.

According to Horney, individuals have basic anxiety caused by insecurities in relationships. People often feel alone, helpless, or uncomfortable in their interactions with others. For example, a person who begins a new job is often unsure of how to perform his or her duties, whom to ask for help, and how to approach his or her new co-workers. Horney theorized that to deal with basic anxiety, the individual has three options (Horney, 1950):

- *Moving toward others.* Accept the situation, and become dependent on others. This strategy may entail an exaggerated desire for approval or affection.

- *Moving against others.* Resist the situation, and become aggressive. This strategy may involve an exaggerated need for power, exploitation of others, recognition, or achievement.

- *Moving away from others.* Withdraw from others, and become isolated. This strategy may involve an exaggerated need for self-sufficiency, privacy, or independence.

Horney believed that these three strategies corresponded to three basic orientations with which people approach their lives. These **basic orientations** reflect different personality characteristics. The *self-effacing solution* corresponds to the moving-toward-others strategy and involves the desire to be loved. The *self-expansive solution* corresponds to the moving-against-others strategy and involves the desire to master oneself. The *resignation solution* corresponds to the moving-away-from-others strategy and involves striving to be independent of others. For Horney, personality is a mixture of these three strategies and basic orientations. As the source of anxiety varies from one situation to the next, so may the strategy and basic orientation used to cope with it.

Erik Erikson

Erik Erikson (1902–1994) studied with Anna Freud, Sigmund Freud's daughter. Erikson emphasized social aspects of personality development rather than biological factors. He also differed with Freud about the timing of personality development. For Freud, the most important development occurs during early childhood. Erikson emphasized the ongoing process of development throughout the life span. As we saw in Chapter 12, Erikson proposed that people's personality traits develop as a result of a series of crises they encounter in their social relations with other people. Because these crises continue throughout life, psychosocial development does not end when people become adults. Erikson's theory of lifelong development has been very influential, and his term "identity crisis" has become a familiar, although possibly overextended household term (see Table 12.4 in Chapter 12).

Melanie Klein and Object-Relations Theory Yet another dissenter from Freud's ideas was Melanie Klein (1882–1960). Klein thought that the psychodynamic battleground that Freud proposed occurs very early in life, during infancy. Furthermore, its origins are different from the basis Freud proposed. An infant begins life utterly dependent on another. That other person, of course, is the infant's mother. The interactions between infant and mother are so deep and intense that they form the focus of the infant's structure of drives. Some of these interactions provoke anger and frustration (as when the mother withdraws the feeding infant from her breast); others provoke strong emotions of dependence as the child begins to recognize that the mother is more than a breast to feed from. These reactions threaten to overwhelm the individuality of the infant. The way in which the infant resolves the conflict, Klein believed, is reflected in the adult's personality (Gomez, 1997).

Klein's work stimulated a contrasting school of psychodynamic theory called **object-relations theory.** According to object-relations theory, adult personality reflects the relationships that the individual establishes with others when the individual is an infant. The term "object" is not confined to inanimate things; rather, it includes the people, especially the mother, that the infant must relate to. For object-relations theorists, relationships are the key to personality development. An individual forms a mental representation of his or her self, of others, and of the relationships that tie them together. For many object-relations theorists, the need that drives the development of personality is not sexual gratification, as Freud believed, but rather the need for other human beings (Westen, 1998).

Some Observations on Psychodynamic Theory and Research

Sigmund Freud's theory has profoundly affected psychological theory, psychotherapy, and literature. His ideas have provided many people with food for thought. However, his theory has received little empirical support, mainly because he used concepts that are difficult to operationalize. How can anyone study the ego, the superego, or the id? How can a researcher prove (or disprove) through experimentation that an artist's creativity is the result of a displaced aggressive or sexual instinctual drive? Although the theories of Jung, Adler, Horney, Erikson, and Klein have their followers, they have not led to much in the way of scientific research. Conversely, some of Freud's fundamental concepts are alive and well today. In later chapters, you will read about evidence for unconscious processing of social information and about the impact on well-being of discussing traumatic events.

QUESTIONS TO CONSIDER

1. Have you ever found yourself using any of the Freudian defense mechanisms discussed in this chapter? If so, under what circumstances do you tend to use them, and what unconscious conflict do you suppose you might be protecting yourself from?

2. Do you possess any behaviors that might represent fixations? If so, what are they, and what fixations do they represent?

3. Which neo-Freudian view on personality development makes the most sense to you? Why do you feel this way—what is your rationale for concluding that one view is more sensible than the others? Which of the theories best explains your own personality development? Provide an example.

The Humanistic Approach

The **humanistic approach** to the study of personality emphasizes the positive, fulfilling elements of life. Humanistic psychologists are interested in nurturing personal growth, life satisfaction, and positive human values. These theorists believe that people are innately good and that each of us has an internal drive for **self-actualization**—the realization of our true intellectual and emotional potential. The two most influential humanistic theorists have been Abraham Maslow and Carl Rogers.

Maslow and Self-Actualization

For Abraham Maslow (1908–1970), human motivation is based on a hierarchy of needs. Our motivation for different activities passes through several levels, with entrance to subsequent levels dependent on our first satisfying needs in previous levels. (See FIGURE 14•10.) If an individual's needs are not met, he or she cannot scale the hierarchy and so will fail to attain his or her true potential.

In Maslow's view, understanding personality requires understanding this hierarchy. Our most basic needs are *physiological needs,* including needs for food, water, oxygen, rest, and so on. Until these needs are met, we cannot be motivated by needs found in the next level (or any other level). If our physiological needs are met, we find ourselves motivated by *safety needs,* including needs for security and comfort as well as for peace and freedom from fear. Once the basic survival and safety needs are met, we can become motivated by *attachment needs,* the need to love and to be loved, to have friends and to be a friend. Next, we seek to satisfy *esteem needs*—to be competent and recognized as such. You are probably beginning to get the picture: We are motivated to achieve needs higher in the hierarchy only after first satisfying lower needs. If we are able to lead a life

---

object-relations theory The theory that personality is the reflection of relationships that the individual establishes with others as an infant.

humanistic approach An approach to the study of personality that emphasizes the positive, fulfilling aspects of life.

self-actualization The realization of our true intellectual and emotional potential.

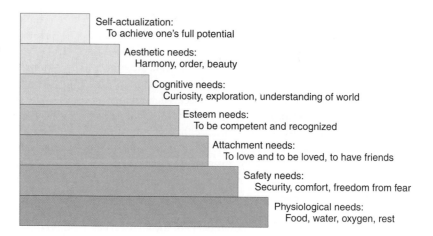

Self-actualization:
To achieve one's full potential

Aesthetic needs:
Harmony, order, beauty

Cognitive needs:
Curiosity, exploration, understanding of world

Esteem needs:
To be competent and recognized

Attachment needs:
To love and to be loved, to have friends

Safety needs:
Security, comfort, freedom from fear

Physiological needs:
Food, water, oxygen, rest

in which we possess food, shelter, love, esteem, intellectual stimulation, and beauty, then we are free to pursue self-actualization.

Maslow based his theory partially on his own assumptions about human potential and partially on his case studies of historical figures whom he believed to be self-actualized, including Albert Einstein, Eleanor Roosevelt, and Frederick Douglass. Maslow examined the lives of each of these people to assess the common qualities that led each to become self-actualized. In general, he found that these individuals were very accepting of themselves and of their life circumstances; were focused on finding solutions to pressing cultural problems rather than to personal problems; were open to others' opinions and ideas; were spontaneous in their emotional reactions to events in their lives; had strong senses of privacy, autonomy, human values, and appreciation of life; and had a few very close, intimate friendships rather than many superficial ones.

Maslow (1964) believed that the innate drive for self-actualization is not specific to any particular culture. He viewed it as a fundamental part of human nature. In his words, "Man has a higher and transcendent nature, and this is part of his essence . . . his biological nature of a species which has evolved" (p. xvi).

Rogers and Conditions of Worth

Carl Rogers (1902–1987) also believed that people are motivated to grow psychologically, aspiring to higher levels of fulfillment as they progress toward self-actualization (Rogers, 1961). Like Maslow, Rogers believed that people are inherently good and have an innate desire to become better. Rogers, though, did not view personality development in terms of satisfying a hierarchy of needs. Instead, he believed that personality development centers on our *self-concept,* or our opinion of ourself, and on the way we are treated by others.

Rogers argued that all people have a need for *positive regard,* or approval, warmth, love, respect, and affection flowing from others. Young children, in particular, show this need when they seek approval for their actions from parents and siblings. The key to developing a psychologically healthy personality is for us to develop a positive self-concept or image of ourself. How do we do this? Rogers's answer is that we are happy if we feel that others are happy with us. Likewise, we also are unhappy with ourselves when others are disappointed in or unsatisfied with us. Thus, our feelings toward ourselves depend to a large extent on what others think of us. As children, we learn that certain conditions or criteria must be met before others give us positive regard. Rogers called these criteria **conditions of worth.**

Positive regard is often conditional. For example, parents may act approvingly toward their young son when he helps in the kitchen or in the yard but not when he pinches his younger sister or tells a fib about how many cookies he has taken from the cookie jar. The boy learns that what others

Abraham Maslow considered Albert Einstein to possess qualities representative of self-actualization, including self-acceptance, a focus on finding solutions to cultural problems, open-mindedness, and spontaneity.

conditions of worth Conditions that others place on us for receiving their positive regard.

think of him depends on his actions. Soon, too, he may come to view himself as others view him and his behavior: "People like me when I do something good, and they don't like me when I do something bad."

Although conditions of worth are a necessary part of the socialization process, they can have negative effects on personality development if satisfying them becomes the individual's major ambition. In Rogers's view, children often want others to like them to the extent that gaining positive regard is a major focus of their lives. So long as any individual focuses chiefly on seeking positive regard from others, he or she may ignore other aspects of life, especially those that lead to positive personality growth. In Rogers's view, then, conditions of worth may stand in the way of self-actualization. According to Rogers, the solution to this problem is **unconditional positive regard,** or love and acceptance that has no strings attached. In a family setting, this means that parents may establish rules and expect their children to obey them, but not through methods that compromise the children's feelings of worth and self-respect. For example, if a child misbehaves, the parents should focus on the child's behavior and not on the child. The parent is free to stop destructive behavior but should not implicitly undermine the child's self-concept through negative labeling ("What a stupid thing to do;" "You're such a bad girl;" "You must want to hurt Mommy"). Implementing unconditional regard in this way permits children to explore life within reasonable bounds and thereby to realize their inherent potential. Rogers would

According to Rogers, all people have a basic need for approval, warmth, and love from others. This need is best met through unconditional positive regard: love and acceptance with no strings attached.

say that parents need to understand and believe that their children are intrinsically good. Bad behavior, in his view, results only when the child's positive potential is being undermined or constrained by the social environment.

In developing his theory, Rogers used unstructured interviews in which the client, not the therapist, directed the course of the conversation. Rogers believed that if the therapist provides an atmosphere of unconditional positive regard, clients will eventually reveal their *true selves*, the kind of people they now are, as well as their *ideal selves*, the kind of people they would like to become. We examine Rogers's approach to therapy in more detail in Chapter 17.

Some Observations on the Humanistic Approach

The humanistic approach is impressive because of its emphasis on individuals' quest for a healthy and positive life for themselves and others. Indeed, the approach has wide appeal to those who seek an alternative to the more mechanistic biologically or environmentally determined views of human nature. However, critics point out two closely related problems with the humanists' approach.

First, many of the concepts used by humanistic psychologists are defined subjectively and so are difficult to test empirically. For example, how might we empirically examine the nature of self-actualization? Few published studies have even attempted to answer this question. By now you know the hallmark of a good scientific theory—the amount of research it generates. On this count, the humanistic approach comes up short by scientific standards. Keep in mind, though, that humanistic theorists are aware that the structure of their theories hinders the use of scientific research methods. Maslow, for instance, simply did not care—he believed that the scientific method was a hindrance to the development of psychology. Many humanistic psychologists believe that a deeper understanding of human nature can be achieved without the scientific method.

A second criticism of the humanistic approach is that it cannot account for the origins of personality. It is subject to the nominal fallacy; it describes personality, but it does not explain it. Humanistic psychologists believe that the impulse toward self-actualization is an innate tendency, but no research shows this to be so. Conditions of worth are said to hamper a child's quest for self-actualization and thus to alter the course of personality development away from positive psychological growth. However, the humanistic approach provides no objective explanation of this process.

Before moving on to the next section, take a few moments to examine TABLE 14•4, which reviews each of the major theories of personality discussed.

---

unconditional positive regard   In Rogers's approach, the therapist's assertion that a client's worth as a human being is not dependent on anything that he or she thinks, does, or feels; love and acceptance of an individual with no strings attached.

[TABLE 14.4] A Summary of the Major Personality Theories

Theory	Primary Figures	Primary Emphases	Primary Strengths	Primary Limitations
Trait	Allport, Cattell, Eysenck, McCrae, Costa	An individual's traits determine personality.	Focuses on stability of behavior over long periods; attempts to measure traits objectively.	Largely descriptive; ignores situational variables that may affect behavior.
Psychobiological	Zuckerman, Plomin, Kagan	Genetics and the brain and nervous system play important roles in personality development.	Emphasizes the interaction of biology and environment in determining personality; uses rigorous empirical approach.	Relies on correlational methods in determining the role of genetics in personality.
Social Learning	Bandura, Mischel, Rotter	Personality is determined by both the consequences of behavior and our perception of those consequences.	Focuses on direct study of behavior and stresses rigorous experimentation.	Ignores biological influences on personality development; often more descriptive than explanatory.
Psychodynamic	Freud, Jung, Adler, Horney, Erikson, Klein	Personality is shaped by unconscious psychic conflicts and the repression of anxiety-provoking ideas and desires.	Argues that behavior may be influenced by forces outside conscious awareness.	Built on basic concepts that are not empirically testable.
Humanistic	Maslow, Rogers	Positive aspects of human nature and the quest to become a better person are central to personality.	Proves useful in therapeutic settings.	Contains untestable concepts; primarily descriptive.

QUESTIONS TO CONSIDER

1. Are you a self-actualized person? If not, what obstacles might be standing in the way of your reaching your true potential?
2. Describe some of the conditions of worth that others have imposed on you as you have developed into an adult. Explain how your experience confirms or disconfirms Rogers's idea that conditions of worth are impediments to personal growth and to the development of a healthy self-concept.

Assessment of Personality

One of the best ways to get to know people—what they are like and how they react in certain situations—is to spend time with them. Obviously, psychologists do not have the luxury of spending large amounts of time with people to learn about their personalities. Generally, they have only a short period to accomplish this goal. From this necessity, personality tests were first developed. The underlying assumption of any personality test is that personality charac-

teristics can be measured. This final section of the chapter describes the two primary types of personality tests—objective tests and projective tests—and discusses the three tests most frequently used by clinical psychologists (Watkins, et al., 1995).

Objective Tests of Personality

Objective personality tests are similar in structure to classroom tests. Most contain multiple-choice and true/false items, although some allow test takers to indicate the extent to which they agree or disagree with an item. The responses that participants can make on objective tests are constrained by the test design. The questions asked are unambiguous, and explicit rules for scoring the participants' responses can be specified in advance.

One of the oldest and most widely used objective tests of personality is the **Minnesota Multiphasic Personality Inventory (MMPI)**, originally devised in 1939. The purpose for developing the test was to produce an objective, reliable method for identifying various personality traits that were related to mental health. The developers believed that this test would be valuable in assessing people for a variety of purposes. For instance, it would provide a specific means of determining how effective psychotherapy was. Improvement in people's scores over the course of treatment would indicate that the treatment was successful. The test was developed by administering several hundred true/false items to several groups of people in mental institutions in Minnesota who had been diagnosed as having certain psychological disorders. Clinicians had ar-

---

objective personality tests Tests for measuring personality that can be scored objectively, such as a multiple-choice or true/false test.

Minnesota Multiphasic Personality Inventory (MMPI) An objective test originally designed to distinguish individuals with psychological problems from normal individuals. The MMPI has since become popular as a means of attempting to identify personality characteristics of people in many everyday settings.

rived at these diagnoses through psychiatric interviews with the patients. The control group consisted of relatives and friends of the patients, who were tested when they came to visit them. (Whether these people constituted the best possible group of normal participants is questionable.)

The current, revised version of this test, the MMPI-2, has norms based on a sample of people that is much more representative ethnically and geographically than the original sample was (Graham, 1990; see also Butcher, 2000). It includes 567 questions, grouped into 10 *clinical scales* and several *validity scales*. A particular item can be used on more than one scale. For example, both people who are depressed and people who are hypochondriacal tend to agree that they have gastrointestinal problems. The clinical scales include terms traditionally used to label psychiatric patients, such as hypochondriasis, depression, and paranoia.

Four validity scales were devised to provide the tester with some assurance that participants are answering questions reliably and accurately and that they can read the questions and pay attention to them. The ? scale ("cannot say") is simply the number of questions not answered. A high score on this scale indicates either that the person finds some questions irrelevant or that the person is evading issues he or she finds painful.

The L scale ("lie") contains items such as "I do not read every editorial in the newspaper every day" and "My table manners are not quite as good at home as when I am out in company." A person who disagrees with questions like these is almost certainly not telling the truth. A high score on the L scale suggests the need for caution in interpreting other scales and also reveals something about the participant's personality.

The F scale ("frequency") consists of items that are answered one way by at least 90% of the normal population. The usual responses are "false" to items such as "I can easily make other people afraid of me, and sometimes do it for the fun of it" and "true" to items such as "I am liked by most people who know me." A high score on this scale indicates carelessness, poor reading ability, or very unusual personality traits.

The K scale ("defensiveness") was devised to identify people who are trying to hide their feelings to guard against internal conflicts that might cause them emotional distress. A person receives a high value on the K scale by answering "false" to statements such as "Criticism or scolding hurts me terribly" and "At times, my mind seems to work more slowly than usual."

As well as being used in clinical assessment, the MMPI has been used extensively in personality research, and several other tests, including the California Psychological Inventory and the Taylor Manifest Anxiety Scale, are based on it. However, the MMPI was developed as a way of assessing clinical states. A clinical psychologist is faced with a very different task from that of a personality theorist describing general traits of personality. Thus, the factors that might be important to the Five Factor explanation of behavior may not be relevant to questions of therapy or the classification of mental disorders.

A recent development in personality assessment has been a movement to produce an "open source" set of personality tests that can be used by researchers around the world. One such project is the International Personality Item Pool. The items included in this set are specifically designed to be readily translated into other languages, facilitating cross-cultural comparisons. The project is still under development, but does promise to have a large impact on personality research (Goldberg, et al., 2006). You can examine the current status of this project at www.ipip.ori.org.

Projective Tests of Personality

Projective tests of personality are different in form from objective ones and are derived from psychodynamic theories of personality. Psychoanalytically oriented psychologists believe that behavior is determined more by unconscious processes than by conscious thoughts or feelings. Thus, they believe that a test that asks straightforward questions is unlikely to tap the real roots of an individual's personality characteristics. **Projective tests** are designed to be ambiguous; the hope is that test-takers' answers will be more revealing than simple agreement or disagreement with statements provided by objective tests. The assumption of projective tests is that individuals will "project" their personalities into the ambiguous situations and thus will make responses that give clues to their personalities. To someone trained in the interpretation of projective tests, these clues can provide insight into the individual's personality. In addition, the ambiguity of the tests makes it unlikely that participants will have preconceived notions about which answers are socially desirable. Thus, it will be difficult for participants to give biased answers in an attempt to look better (or worse) than they actually are.

The Rorschach Inkblot Test One of the oldest projective tests of personality is the Rorschach Inkblot Test, published in 1921 by Hermann Rorschach, a Swiss psychiatrist. The **Rorschach Inkblot Test** consists of 10 pictures of inkblots. Rorschach published these pictures from images made by spilling ink on a piece of paper and then folding the paper in half, producing blots that were symmetrical in relation to the line of the fold. Five of the inkblots in the test are black and white, and five are colored. (See FIGURE 14•11.) The participant is shown each card and asked to describe what it looks like. Then the cards are shown again, and the participant is asked to point out the features he or she used to de-

---

projective tests Unstructured personality measures in which a person is shown a series of ambiguous stimuli, such as pictures, inkblots, or incomplete drawings. The person is asked to describe what he or she "sees" in each stimulus or to create stories that reflect the theme of the drawing or picture.

Rorschach Inkblot Test A projective test in which a person is shown a series of symmetrical inkblots and asked to describe what he or she thinks they represent.

[**FIGURE 14·11**] An inkblot similar to one of the blots that appear in the Rorschach Inkblot Test.

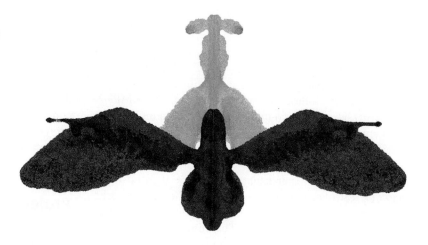

termine what was seen. The responses and the nature of the features the participant uses to make them are scored on several dimensions.

In the following example described by Pervin (1975), a person's response to a particular inkblot (not the example shown in Figure 14.11) might be "Two bears with their paws touching one another playing pattycake, or could be they are fighting, and the red is the blood from the fighting." The classification of this response, also described by Pervin, would be: Large detail of the blot was used, good form was used, movement was noted, color was used in the response about blood, an animal was seen, and a popular response (two bears) was made. A possible interpretation of the response might be:

> Subject starts off with popular response and animals expressing playful, "childish" behavior. Response is then given in terms of hostile act with accompanying inquiry. Pure color response and blood content suggest he may have difficulty controlling his response to the environment. Is a playful, childlike exterior used by him to disguise hostile, destructive feelings that threaten to break out in his dealings with the environment? (Pervin, 1975, p. 37)

Although the interpretation of people's responses to the Rorschach Inkblot Test was originally based on psychoanalytical theory, many investigators have used it in an empirical fashion. That is, a variety of different scoring methods have been devised, and the scores obtained by these methods have been correlated with clinical diagnoses, just as investigators have done with people's scores on the MMPI. When this test is used empirically, the style and content of the responses are not interpreted in terms of a theory (as Rorschach interpreted them) but are simply correlated with other measures of personality.

Thematic Apperception Test (TAT) A projective test in which a person is shown a series of ambiguous pictures that involve people. The person is asked to make up a story about what the people are doing or thinking. The person's responses are believed to reflect aspects of his or her personality.

The Thematic Apperception Test Another popular projective test, the **Thematic Apperception Test (TAT)**, was developed in 1938 by psychologists Henry Murray and C. D. Morgan to measure various psychological needs. People are shown a picture of a very ambiguous situation and asked to tell a story about what is happening in the picture—to explain the situation, what led up to it, what the characters are thinking and saying, and what the final outcome will be. The idea is that test takers will "project" themselves into the scene and that their stories will therefore reflect their own needs.

As you might imagine, scoring is difficult and requires a great deal of practice and skill. The tester attempts to infer the psychological needs expressed in the stories. Consider the responses of one woman to several TAT cards, along with a clinician's interpretation of these responses (Phares, 1979). The questions asked by the examiner are in parentheses.

> Card 3BM. Looks like a little boy crying for something he can't have. (Why is he crying?) Probably because he can't go somewhere. (How will it turn out?) Probably sit there and sob hisself to sleep. Card 3GF. Looks like her boyfriend might have let her down. She hurt his feelings. He's closed the door on her. (What did he say?) I don't know. Card 10. Looks like there's sorrow here. Grieving about something. (About what?) Looks like maybe one of the children's passed away. Interpretation: The TAT produced responses that were uniformly indicative of unhappiness, threat, misfortune, a lack of control over environmental forces. None of the test responses were indicative of satisfaction, happy endings, etc. . . . In summary, the test results point to an individual who is anxious and, at the same time, depressed. (Phares, 1979, p. 273)

The pattern of responses in this case is quite consistent; few people would disagree with the conclusion that the woman is sad and depressed. However, not all people provide such clear-cut responses, and interpreting differences in the stories of people who are relatively well adjusted is much more difficult. As a result, distinguishing among people with different but normal personality traits is hard.

Evaluation of Projective Tests

Most empirical studies have found that projective tests such as the Rorschach Inkblot Test and the TAT have poor reliability and little validity. For example, Eron (1950) found no differences between the scores of people in mental hospitals and the scores of college students. (You can supply your own joke about that.) Entwisle (1972) reported that "recent studies . . . yield few positive relationships between need achievement [measured by the TAT] and other variables" (p. 179). Lundy (1988) suggests that in many of the situations used to validate the TAT, test takers are likely to realize that they are talking about themselves when they tell a story about the cards and may be careful about what they say.

Even if people taking the TAT are not on their guard, their scores are especially sensitive to their moods (Masling, 1960, 1998). Therefore, the scores they receive on one day are often very different from those they receive on another day, but a test of personality is supposed to measure enduring traits that persist over time and in a variety of situations. The TAT also has been criticized for potential gender bias, mostly because of male-dominated themes, such as power, ambition, and status, used to score the test (Worchel, Aaron, & Yates, 1990).

The reliability and validity of the Rorschach Inkblot Test also are rather low. One study that used the most reliable scoring method found little or no correlation between participants' scores on the Rorschach and their scores on six objective tests of personality (Greenwald, 1990, 1999).

If projective tests such as the Rorschach and the TAT have been found to be of low reliability and validity, why do many clinical psychologists and psychiatrists continue to use them? The primary reason seems to be tradition. The use of these tests has a long history, and the rationale for the tests is consistent with psychodynamic explanations of personality. Many psychodynamic and clinical psychologists still argue that the tests provide them with valuable tools for discovering and evaluating inner determinants of personality (Watkins, 2000).

QUESTIONS TO CONSIDER

1. Which kind of personality inventory—objective tests or projective tests—do you suppose would be more effective in revealing important aspects of your personality? Why?

2. If your results on a personality inventory revealed that you possess a personality trait that you didn't think you had (especially if it is a negative trait), how would you react? Would you tend to disparage the test, or would you admit that in fact this trait is part of your personality?

3. What kinds of personality differences between men and women have you noticed? Are these differences genuine, or do your observations reflect the stereotypes you hold of the sexes? How do you know?

Epilogue

Identical Twins Raised Together

The similarity shown by some cases of identical twins raised apart, such as the two Jims, Bridget and Dorothy, and Oskar and Jack, is impressive. Oskar and Jack, for example, were raised in very different countries and were brought up to identify with remarkably dissimilar cultures. Yet they showed parallels in many behaviors–such as choice of shirt style and type of eyeglasses. What could explain the odd quirks like wearing rubber bands on their wrists?

Although the twins in this prologue share identical genomes, it's obviously a stretch to say that genes control behavior to this level of detail. One of the values of personality theory to psychology is that it provides a higher-level description of behaviors. The study of personality helps us understand which of the similarities and differences are important. Knowing how to group behaviors together helps us analyze the causal factors behind them.

As a concrete example, consider two women, born as identical twins, interviewed by Kaminsky and his colleagues (Kaminsky et al., 2008). When these twins were young, their parents dressed them identically, making them physically indistinguishable. As girls, they were the best of friends and, as adults, they remain emotionally close. Yet they followed very different paths in life: One twin left home when she was 17, traveled, learned languages, and eventually became a war correspondent. She covered many of the world's hotspots, saw people killed, and married, in her forties, a cameraman who also worked on war assignments. They have no children. Her twin, who had no interest in learning a language, stayed home, married while young to a lawyer, had two children, and now works in a law office. When tested on various personality measures, such as the MMPI, they showed many differences. For example, the second twin, working in the law office, showed traits reflecting anxiety, tension, and discomfort, whereas the war correspondent did not. Basically, in several measures, the war correspondent showed traits that seemed risk seeking, whereas her twin sister seemed risk averse.

The twins in this study are the other side of the twin question: They were raised together, but show strong differences in the careers they chose and the way they lived their lives. The source of these differences has been difficult to identify; Kaminsky and his colleagues found some clues in the epigenetic changes that were discussed in Chapter 12. These clues concerned a region of the twins' genome that has been linked to the ability to handle stress—an obvious link to their different tolerance for risk. If clues like these can be confirmed, it may be that the information supplied by tests such as the MMPI will be linked to specific regions on the genome.

CHAPTER SUMMARY

Trait Theories of Personality

We can conceive of personality characteristics as types or traits. The earliest theory of personality classified people into types according to their predominant humor, or body fluid. Today most psychologists conceive of personality differences as being matters of degree, not of kind.

The search for core personality traits began with Allport, who studied how everyday words are used to describe personality characteristics. Although Allport never isolated a core set of traits, his work inspired others to continue the search for such traits. Several researchers developed their trait theories through factor analysis. Cattell's analyses indicated the existence of 16 personality factors. Eysenck's research suggested that personality is determined by three dimensions: extroversion (versus introversion), neuroticism (versus emotional stability), and psychoticism (versus self-control). McCrae and Costa's five-factor model, based on an analysis of words used to describe people's behavioral traits, includes neuroticism, extroversion, openness, agreeableness, and conscientiousness. Ongoing research may identify additional fundamental personality dimensions including socially negative traits such as the "Dark Triad" of Machiavellianism, narcissism, and psychopathy. Studies of similarities in traits across different cultures have found that the first three traits of the five-factor model can be found in most cultures, and that when people describe someone known to them, they generally use traits from the five-factor model. Some differences exist between cultures, however, and people who immigrate into another culture exhibit changes in some specific traits.

Psychobiological Approaches

Studies of twins indicate that personality factors, especially extroversion, neuroticism, and psychoticism, are affected strongly by genetic factors. However, little evidence is found for an effect of common family environment, largely because each individual's family environment is strongly affected by hereditary factors, such as personality and physical attributes. Family environment does have an influence on social attitudes. Study of infants' temperaments suggests that activity level, social fearfulness, anger proneness, and interest have a genetic component; genetic similarity, however, was less predictive of similarity in expressing happiness.

Important personality traits are likely to be the products of neural systems responsible for reinforcement, punishment, and arousal. Zuckerman believes that extroversion is determined by a sensitive reinforcement system, neuroticism by a sensitive punishment system (which includes the amygdala), and psychoticism by the combination of a deficient punishment system and an abnormally high optimal level of arousal.

Research on shyness indicates that childhood shyness is a relatively stable trait that can be seen in the way children react to strangers and strange situations. The differences between shy and non-shy children manifest themselves in physiological responses controlled by the amygdala that indicate the presence of stress. This pattern of amygdala reactivity persists into adulthood.

Social Cognitive Approaches

Social cognitive theory blends Skinner's notion of reinforcement or other approaches to learning with cognitive concepts, such as expectancy, to explain social interaction and personality. According to Bandura, people learn the relation between their behavior and its consequences by observing how others' behavior is rewarded and punished. Bandura also believes that personality is the result of reciprocal determinism—the interaction of behavior, environment, and cognitive variables. The extent to which a person is likely to attempt to change his or her environment is related to self-efficacy, the expectation that the individual will be successful in producing the change. People with low self-efficacy tend not to try to alter their environments; just the opposite is true for people with high self-efficacy. Mischel has argued that personality differences are due largely to individual differences in cognition. These variables include competencies, encoding strategies and personal constructs, expectancies, subjective values, and self-regulatory systems and plans.

In the past, psychologists disagreed about the relative importance of situations and personality traits in determining a person's behavior. It now appears that personality traits are correlated with behavior, especially when multiple observations of particular behaviors are made. In addition, some situations (such as a funeral or a stoplight) are more powerful than others, exerting more control on people's behavior. Traits and situations interact: Some people may be affected more than others by a particular situation, and people tend to choose the types of situations in which they find themselves. Rotter's research has shown that locus of control—the extent to which people believe that their behavior is controlled by person variables or by environmental variables—is also an important determinant of personality. Positive psychology seeks to integrate knowledge of social and cognitive psychology to explain valued aspects of life, such as happiness and satisfaction.

The Psychodynamic Approach

Freud proposed that the mind is full of conflicts between the primitive urges of the id, the practical concerns of the ego, and the internalized prohibitions of the superego. According to Freud, these conflicts tend to be resolved through compromise formation and through ego defenses such as repression, sublimation, and rationalization. Freud's theory of psychosexual development, a progression through the oral, anal, phallic, and genital stages, provided the basis for a theory of personality and personality disorders.

Freud's followers—most notably Jung, Adler, Horney, Erikson, and Klein—embraced different aspects of Freud's theory, disagreed with other aspects of it, and embellished still other aspects. Jung disagreed with Freud about the structure of the unconscious and the role of sexuality in personality development, and he saw libido as a positive life force. Adler also disagreed with Freud on the importance of sexuality; instead, he emphasized our need to compensate for our inferiority and our innate desire to help others as the major forces in personality development. Horney argued that personality is the result of the strategies and behaviors people use to cope with anxiety, which she believed is the fundamental problem that all people must overcome in the course of normal personality development. Erikson maintained that personality development is more a matter of psychosocial processes than of psychosexual processes. He viewed personality development as involving eight stages, each of which requires resolution of a major conflict or crisis. Resolving the conflict allows the person to pass to the next stage; failing to resolve it inhibits normal personality development. Klein suggested that psychodynamic conflict occurs early in infancy and centers on the relation between the infant and the mother. Her work formed the basis for object-relations theory, which posits that relationships with others constitute the fundamental basis of personality.

The Humanistic Approach

The humanistic approach attempts to understand personality and its development by focusing on the positive side of human nature and on self-actualization, or people's attempts to reach their full potential.

Maslow argued that self-actualization is achieved only after the satisfaction of several other important but lower-level needs; for example, physiological, safety, and attachment needs. Maslow's case study analyses of people whom he believed to be self-actualized revealed several common personality characteristics, including self-acceptance, a focus on addressing cultural rather than personal problems, spontaneity, preservation of privacy, an appreciation for life, and possession of a few intimate friendships.

According to Rogers, the key to becoming self-actualized is developing a healthy self-concept. The primary roadblocks in this quest are conditions of worth—criteria that we must meet to win the positive regard of others. Rogers maintained that too often people value themselves only to the extent that they believe other people do. As a result, they spend their lives seeking the acceptance of others instead of striving to become self-actualized. Rogers proposed that only by treating others with unconditional positive regard can we help people to realize their true potentials.

Although the humanistic approach emphasizes the positive dimensions of human experience and the potential that each of us has for personal growth, it has been faulted for being unscientific. Critics argue that its concepts are vague and untestable and that it is more descriptive than explanatory.

Assessment of Personality

Objective tests contain items that can be answered and scored objectively, such as true/false or multiple-choice questions. One of the most important objective personality tests is the Minnesota Multiphasic Personality Inventory (MMPI), which was devised in 1939 to discriminate empirically among people who had been assigned various psychiatric diagnoses. The MMPI has been used widely in research on personality. More recently, researchers interested in personality have turned to tests not based on people with mental disorders, such as the NEO-PI-R.

Projective tests, such as the Rorschach Inkblot Test and the Thematic Apperception Test, contain ambiguous items that elicit answers that supposedly reveal aspects of personality. Because answers on these tests can vary widely, test administrators must receive special training to interpret them. Unfortunately, evidence suggests that the reliability and validity of projective tests are not particularly high.

succeed with mypsychlab

Visit MyPsychLab for practice quizzes, flashcards, and dozens of videos and animated tutorials, including the following items you can find in the "Multimedia Library":

EXPLORE

The Five Factor Model
The Id, Ego, and Superego
Defense Mechanisms
Personality Assessment

KEY TERMS

anal stage *p. 438*

archetypes *p. 440*

basic orientations *p. 440*

collective unconscious *p. 440*

conditions of worth *p. 442*

conscience *p. 437*

defense mechanisms *p. 437*

ego *p. 436*

ego-ideal *p. 437*

emotional stability *p. 423*

expectancy *p. 431*

extroversion *p. 422*

five-factor model *p. 423*

fixation *p. 438*

genital stage *p. 439*

humanistic approach *p. 441*

id *p. 436*

introversion *p. 422*

latency period *p. 439*

libido *p. 436*

locus of control *p. 433*

Machiavellianism *p. 424*

Minnesota Multiphasic-
Personality Inventory
(MMPI) *p. 444*

narcissism *p. 424*

neuroticism *p. 422*

Neuroticism, Extroversion,
and Openness Personality
Inventory (NEO-PI-R)
p. 424

object-relations theory *p. 441*

objective personality tests
p. 444

observational learning
p. 430

oral stage *p. 438*

person variables *p. 432*

personality *p. 420*

personality trait *p. 420*

personality types *p. 420*

phallic stage *p. 438*

pleasure principle *p. 436*

positive psychology *p. 435*

projective tests *p. 445*

psychodynamic *p. 435*

psychoticism *p. 423*

psychopathy *p. 424*

reality principle *p. 437*

reciprocal determinism
p. 431

Rorschach Inkblot Test
p. 445

self-actualization *p. 441*

self-control *p. 423*

self-efficacy *p. 431*

situationism *p. 431*

social cognitive theory
p. 430

striving for superiority
p. 440

superego *p. 437*

temperament *p. 427*

Thematic Apperception Test
(TAT) *p. 446*

unconditional positive
regard *p. 443*

unconscious *p. 436*

SUGGESTIONS FOR FURTHER READING

Carver, C. S., & Scheier, M. F. (2003). *Perspectives on personality* (5th ed.). Boston: Allyn & Bacon.

Wiggins, J. S. (Ed.). (1996). *The five-factor model of personality: Theoretical perspectives.* New York: Guilford Press.

Theories of personality, personality testing, and research on the determinants of personality receive thorough coverage in these two texts.

Bandura, A. (1986). *Social foundations of thought and action: A social cognitive theory.* Englewood Cliffs, NJ: Prentice-Hall.

In this book, Bandura presents his account of social cognition and social behavior, which is derived from the behaviorist tradition and cognitive psychology.

Freud, S. (1957). *General introduction to psychoanalysis* (J. Riviere, Trans.). New York: Permabooks.

Jones, E. (1953). *The life and work of Sigmund Freud.* New York: Basic Books.

The best resource on Freud's theories of personality is Freud himself. Jones provides an interesting discussion of Freud's life as well as of his writings.

CHAPTER

15

Social Psychology

Prologue

Caveat Emptor

[*Note*: This vignette is from the anonymous annals of new-car buyers who also happen to be psychologists.]

A few years ago, Joyce decided to buy a new family car. With her son's help, she had done extensive background research and had a good idea of what the dealer cost was for the model she wanted and what a reasonable commission for a salesperson would amount to. She went to a dealer near her home, took a test drive, and settled down with her salesman, Greg, to negotiate the deal.

Greg quoted an unbelievably low price. Joyce had to ask him to repeat it. With factory-to-dealer discounts and other incentives, she couldn't imagine how they were going to make any money. "Deal!" she exclaimed. They completed the formal offer; and she gave Greg a check for several thousand dollars as a down payment to lock in the agreement. It only was then that she heard the dreaded salesperson phrase, "I'll have to show this to my manager to get his okay. It shouldn't take long."

Joyce knew then that she was in the middle of a process called "lowballing," a technique whereby a salesperson quotes an unusually low price, only to find a reason (for example, a mistake in reading the invoice) to raise the price later. The down-payment check is meant to commit the buyer to the deal (more about this later in the chapter). Now she was supposed to sit in the salesperson's office, happily daydreaming about driving her new car. Being a psychologist, though, she knew better. She sat there becoming more and more irritated while Greg was drinking a cup of coffee or whatever he did to spend the time other than talking to the manager.

Sure enough, Greg returned and said, "Geez, I really messed this up. I usually work in used cars. I'm just not up on these prices. My manager really blew a gasket. Your car is $8,000 more than I told you. You're going to have to come close to that. I can knock off maybe $500."

"No," Joyce said, "I'm only willing to pay what we agreed on."

Greg countered with, "No, the car is worth way more than that. You have to up your offer."

"No," Joyce reiterated, "you need to stand behind your first offer to me, or I'm going home. I teach about lowballing in my psychology class at the university. I know what you're doing, and you can give it up now."

To her surprise, Greg immediately caved, and Joyce got the car for the price he originally quoted. While she was signing the final papers, two other salespeople cornered Greg about blowing the deal and teasing him about belonging on the used car lot. ■

Most human activities are social: We spend many of our waking hours interacting with other people. Our behavior affects the way others act, and their behavior in turn affects our actions. The subdiscipline within psychology that studies these effects, as you may recall from Chapter 1, is called **social psychology.** Social psychology is, in the words of Gordon Allport (1968), the examination of "how the thoughts, feelings, and behavior of individuals are influenced by the actual, imagined, or implied presence of others" (p. 3).

This chapter considers two principal concerns of social psychology. The first is social cognition and evaluation—how we think about others, how we account for what others do, and how we evaluate or form attitudes about others. The second concern focuses on how others' actions affect our own—on our relationships with people in groups both large and small, including the dyad (two people) in love. These concerns revolve around social interactions and their effects. Interactions with other people affect all aspects of human behavior from infancy through old age. The important people in our lives shape our perceptions, emotions, thinking, and personality. Social psychologists have found that even the most private and seemingly subjective aspects of our lives, such as interpersonal attraction, can be studied with an impressive degree of scientific rigor.

Social Cognition

Understanding a person's social behavior requires considerable attention to that person's environment, both physical and social. The ability of a person to size up a social situation depends on many of the cognitive processes you have already studied. Among these are memory for people, places, and events (see Chapter 8); concept formation skills (Chapter 11); and, more fundamentally, the sensory and perceptual abilities you learned about in Chapters 6, 7, and 9 (also see Fiske & Taylor, 1991; Kunda, 1999; Bodenhausen, Macrae, & Hugenberg, 2003). Social psychologists apply knowledge of these basic psychological processes to research on **social cognition**—to understanding how people perceive, think about, and respond to the social world (Moskowitz, 2005; McGovern, 2007). Important topics of study in social cognition are impression formation, self-concepts, and attribution processes.

Impression Formation

All of us form impressions of others: friends, neighbors, colleagues, and even strangers—virtually everyone we meet or learn about through the reports of others. In doing so, we assign characteristics to people. We may, for example, think of someone as friendly or hostile, helpful or selfish. A major task of social psychology is to understand how we form these impressions. In Solomon Asch's (1952) words, "How do the perceptions, thoughts, and motives of one person become known to other persons?" (p. 143). To answer this question, psychologists study **impression formation,** the way in which we integrate information about another person's characteristics into a coherent sense of who the person is. As Asch argued more than half a century ago, we form our impressions of others on the basis of rules that are more complex than mere sums of the characteristics we observe.

Schemas As you saw in Chapter 12, a central concept in the study of cognitive development is that of the *schema*, a set of rules or representations by which we organize and synthesize information about a person, place, or thing to interpret the world (Markus, 1977; Wyer & Srull, 1994; Olson, Roese, & Zanna, 1996). The first time you visited a professor in his or her office, for example, there were probably few surprises. Your "professor" schema successfully guided your interactions with the individual you encountered. However, you probably would have been surprised had your professor's office been filled with soccer trophies, autographed photos of rock stars, or paintings of Elvis on black velvet—furnishings inconsistent with your schema.

Central Traits Social schemas also aid you in making sense of other people and their actions. Information about specific traits affects your overall sense of what a person is like. If a person is described as "witty, smart, and warm," your general impression of the person probably will be quite positive. But what would your reaction be if the person were described instead as "witty, smart, and cold"? What would account for the difference? Asch (1946) proposed that certain traits, called **central traits,** organize and influence our impressions of a person to a greater extent than do other traits. Note the similarity between Asch's concept of central traits and that of Allport as defined in Chapter 14. Asch (1946) tested the concept by using the "warm-cold" dimension. In one study, for example, he provided all participants with the same basic list of adjectives describing a hypothetical person: Participants heard that the person was intelligent, skillful, industrious, determined, practical, and cautious. Some participants were told that the person was also "warm," whereas others were told that the person was also "cold." Overall, those who heard the list that included "warm" formed more positive impressions of the imaginary person than did those who heard "cold." Participants in the "warm" condition also were more likely to speculate that the person was also generous, happy, and altruistic.

---

social psychology The branch of psychology devoted to the study of the effects people have on one another's behavior.

social cognition The processes involved in perceiving, thinking about, and acting on social information.

impression formation The integration of information about another person's traits into a coherent sense of who the person is.

central traits Characteristics of the individual, which, according to Asch, have greater influence on one's impression of another person.

Forming impressions of others involves sensory and perceptual processes as well as memory and concept formation skills, including schemas.

More recent work suggests that the negative influence of the "cold" trait is stronger than the positive influence of the "warm" trait (Singh, et al., 1997; Singh & Teoh, 2000). This imbalance may occur because people tend to have a general bias toward positivity in forming impressions of others (e.g., Sears, 1983; Heyman & Giles, 2004). Thus, negative information, such as that conveyed by a negative central trait, may be more heavily weighted in the context of a generally positive impression than another piece of positive information about the person would be (Skowronski & Carlston, 1989).

The Primacy Effect   Getting to know someone usually takes time, because it requires multiple interactions. Suppose the first time you see a young man is at a party, where he is loud and boisterous and having a good time with his friends. Later you learn he is a math major with excellent grades who is actually quite reserved. What is your impression of this person: Loud and boisterous, or bright and shy? Seeking to determine whether first impressions might overpower later impressions, Asch (1946) presented one of the following lists of words to each of two groups of people:

Intelligent, industrious, impulsive, critical, stubborn, envious

Envious, stubborn, critical, impulsive, industrious, intelligent

Notice that these lists contain the same traits but in reverse order. After the participants heard the list, Asch asked them to describe the personality of a person having these characteristics. People who heard the first list imagined the person as someone who was able and productive but who

possessed some shortcomings. The person described by the second list, however, was seen as someone who had serious problems. The tendency to form an impression of a person based on the initial information we receive about him or her is called the **primacy effect** (not to be confused with the primacy effect discussed in Chapter 8, which had to do with remembering lists of words). The primacy effect reflects the greater attention we give to initial information about traits as opposed to later information (Park, 1986; Belmore, 1987). Consistent with this attentional interpretation, Webster, Richter, and Kruglanski (1996) found that the primacy effect was more pronounced for college-student participants who had completed a lengthy, tiring final examination than for those in a control group who remained relatively alert.

The Self

If you are asked who you are, how do you respond? You might state your name, that you are a student, and perhaps add that you are from a certain place or have a particular interest or hobby. Alternatively, you could say something about your family, nationality, ethnicity, or religion. You could potentially describe yourself in many ways, all of which would reflect your **self-concept**—your knowledge, feelings, and beliefs about yourself. Your self-concept is also your "self-identity"— your perception of your distinct individuality in the context of events that are relevant to defining who you are. For cognitive psychologists, the **self-schema** organizes the knowledge, feelings, and beliefs you have about your self (Markus, 1977). According to an early theory (Cooley, 1909), we possess "looking-glass selves." Others' responses to us teach us who we are; we learn to see ourselves as they see us. More recent work (see Yeung & Martin, 2003) questions this view, however, and suggests that the shaping of self is not so one-directional.

Evidence suggests that the self-concept begins to emerge at an early age. When infants aged 9 to 12 months are placed in front of a mirror, they readily respond to the image in the mirror, making faces and gesturing otherwise. If a spot of rouge is applied to the end of their nose, they may point to it in the reflection but do not reach for their own nose. However, by age 21 months, they demonstrate self-recognition by reaching for the spot directly (Leather, 2004),

The self-concept is dynamic; it can change with experience (Markus & Nurius, 1986). Depending on experience, each of us has many potential selves that we may become. Can you imagine the different twists and turns your life might take in the future and how your self-concept could be affected as a result? Can you imagine circumstances that might lead you to change your major, drop out of school, get married or divorced, win the lottery—and how your self-concept would be affected in turn? In one study, researchers asked people who had experienced a traumatic life event (for example, the death of a family member or friend) to describe their current and possible future selves (Markus & Nurius, 1986; Ruvolo & Markus, 1992). All participants reported they

---

primacy effect   The tendency to form an impression of a person based on the initial information one receives about her or him.

self-concept   One's knowledge, feelings, and beliefs about oneself.

self-schema   The cognitive representation of the self-concept.

were worried, upset, and depressed and lacked control over their lives. That is, everyone described similar current selves. Nonetheless, different participants described different sorts of possible future selves. Those who had not yet recovered from the traumatic event predicted that they would be unhappy and lonely. Those who had recovered predicted just the opposite: They saw themselves as happy, self-confident, and having many friends. Thus, thinking of ourselves only in terms of who we are at present often does not accurately reflect how we will think of ourselves in the future or the kind of person we might become.

Gilbert (2006) characterizes our inclination to estimate our future selves based on imagined images of what the future will bring in the following passage:

> . . . Yes, other people are probably right now experiencing the very things I am merely contemplating, but I can't use other people's experiences as proxies for my own because those other people are not me. Every human being is as unique as his or her fingerprints, so it won't help me much to learn about how others feel in the situations that I'm facing. Unless those other people are my clones and have had all the same experiences I've had, their reactions and my reactions are bound to differ. I am a walking, talking idiosyncrasy, and thus I am better off basing my predictions on my somewhat fickle imagination than on the reports of people whose preferences, tastes, and emotional proclivities are so radically different from my own. (p. 224).

For Gilbert, such reliance on one's imagination as the guide to future selves is flawed for three reasons. The first is illustrated by an experiment involving three different groups of participants. The first group (reporters) received a gift certificate to a local ice cream parlor before engaging in a lengthy, tedious task in which they monitored a TV screen and counted geometric shapes that appeared there. They then reported how they felt. The second group (simulators) were informed that they would receive the gift certificate and would engage in the same boring task. They were asked to predict how happy they would feel after completing the task. The third group (surrogators) were given randomly selected responses from the reporters but not told what the prize would be. This minimized their use of imagination in saying how they would feel at a later point.

After making their predictions, those in the simulator and surrogator groups were given the prize, performed the task, and reported their feelings. Simulators were not nearly as happy as they had predicted, whereas the surrogators' predictions were right on the mark. According to Gilbert, such findings make an important point about our reliance on imagination as a guide to the future—it is too selective to be trusted. Better to rely on the reports of others who have already had the experience. Gilbert listed two other shortcomings of imagination—presentism (projecting the present onto the future) and rationalization (failing to recognize that events in the future are likely to seem different once they occur).

Influences on the Self Identifying the complex interchange between biological, familial, social, cultural, and other influences on the self is a daunting challenge, but social psychologists have taken up the task with particular enthusiasm (e.g., see Berry, 2003; Matsumoto, 2003; Lehman, Chiu, & Schaller, 2004). Among the issues they addressed are the formation of the self-concept, the perceptions people form of others, and the extent to which others may influence the development of a person's self-concept (Heine, 2001; Markus & Kitayama, 2003). For example, North American parents may encourage their children to eat their dinner by admonishing them to "think about all the starving children in the world and how lucky you are not to have to go hungry," whereas in Japan, parents often urge reluctant eaters to "think of the farmer who worked so hard to produce this rice for you; if you don't eat it, he will feel bad, for his efforts will have been in vain" (Markus & Kitayama, 1991). As this example shows, Western cultures often emphasize individual uniqueness and the ways in which individuals differ (well-fed vs. starving). In contrast, Japanese and other Eastern cultures often emphasize our relatedness to others (the child to the farmer).

Markus and Kitayama (1991) have proposed categories of self-concepts that reflect such cultural differences. What they call *independent construal* emphasizes the uniqueness of the self, the self's autonomy from others, and self-reliance. Thus, although other people have undenied influence on a person's behavior, a person's self-concept is largely defined independent of others. By contrast, *interdependent construal* emphasizes human interconnectedness and the crucial role others play in developing a person's self-concept.

One study considered the implications of construal for the common experiences of success and failure. Heine and colleagues (2001) reasoned that people with an independent construal of self would view their traits as relatively stable. People with an interdependent construal, conversely, should view their traits as relatively unstable and therefore likely to shift. Indeed, the researchers found that Canadian students of European descent were more likely to persist on a task after a successful experience than after failure, whereas Japanese students from Kyoto University were more likely to persist after a failure than after a success. If people believe that personal traits are likely to persist, then success will likely breed further efforts to succeed. If, conversely, they believe that traits can change to affect outcomes, then endeavoring to change in the wake of failure may lead to success.

If you are from a Western culture, you may have interpreted the theory and research described to mean, "People from Western cultures have better self-concepts and approaches to life than do people from Eastern cultures." Such a conclusion would follow from the way your culture values and encourages independence and stability of the self. A reader from an Eastern culture, however, could well read these same paragraphs and conclude: "People from Eastern cultures have better self-concepts and approaches to life than do people from Western cultures." Eastern cultures tend to value and emphasize the changing nature and demands of

People in many Eastern cultures are more likely than people in Western cultures to construe their self-concepts in terms of the social interactions they have with others.

interpersonal relations. Indeed, well-being and satisfaction among Eastern students have been found to be strongly correlated with interpersonal behaviors and socially focused emotions such as friendliness (Markus & Kitayama, 1991; Kitayama, Markus, & Kurakawa, 2000). In contrast, well-being and satisfaction among Western students are more strongly correlated with individual achievement and self-reflective emotions such as pride (see also Nisbett, 2003).

Attribution

We are all implicit social psychologists (Jones, 1990). Each of us constructs informal theories about the nature and causes of other people's behavior. On any given day, we may be confronted by thousands of individual acts performed by other people. Some acts are important to us, because they provide clues about others' personalities and about how others are likely to perceive us and interact with us. If we had to pay close attention to each act, then classify it, think about its significance, and compare it to acts previously observed, we would quickly flag. Instead, more often than not, we only infer the causes of other people's behavior and use the process of **attribution** to do so.

---

attribution The process by which people infer the causes of their own and other people's behavior.

situational factors Physical and social stimuli that are found in an individual's environment and that can affect his or her behavior.

dispositional factors An individual's traits, needs, and intentions, which can affect his or her behavior.

consensus The extent to which a person's behavior is what most people would do; can be a basis for others' attributions about the person's motives.

distinctiveness The extent to which a person behaves differently toward different people, events, or other stimuli; can be the basis for others' attributions about the person's motives.

consistency The extent to which a person generally behaves in the same way toward another person, an event, or a stimulus; can be the basis for others' attributions about the person's motives.

Disposition versus Situation According to attribution theorists, the primary distinction we make about the causes of a person's behavior is between situational (or external) and dispositional (or internal) factors (Heider, 1958). **Situational factors** include stimuli found in the physical and social environments, such as living conditions, other people, societal norms, and laws. **Dispositional factors** include a person's traits, needs, and intentions. As we grow up, one of the tasks of socialization is to learn the behaviors that are normative (that is, normally expected) in various kinds of situations. Once we learn that in certain situations most people act in a specific way, we do likewise. For example, in American culture, when two people are introduced, they are expected to look at each other, smile, say something like "How do you do?" or "It's nice to meet you," and perhaps offer to shake the other person's hand. If people act in conventional ways in given situations, we are not surprised. If someone's behavior is very different from the way most people would act in a particular situation, we may attribute his or her behavior to dispositional (internal) factors. That is, if we see someone refuse to hold a door open for someone in a wheelchair, we're likely to attribute negative personal characteristics to that individual.

Kelley's Theory of Attribution Kelley (1967) suggested that we attribute the behavior of other people to situational or dispositional causes on the basis of three types of information: consensus, distinctiveness, and consistency. **Consensus** results when a specific behavior is commonly exhibited in a given situation. When consensus exists, we usually attribute behavior to situational causes. For example, if you hear Bill praise a new off-campus club and you also have heard other people say the same things (*high consensus*), you will likely attribute Bill's praise to the club (a situational attribution). But what if everyone else disagrees with Bill's evaluation (*low consensus*)? Now you will likely view Bill's opinion of the club as reflecting something personal about him (a dispositional attribution). Maybe he has bad taste in clubs, or maybe something unique about this club appealed to him alone.

We also base our attributions on **distinctiveness**—the extent to which a person performs a particular behavior only during a particular type of event or toward a particular person or thing. If you have never heard Bill praise anything as highly as he praises the new club, his behavior has *high distinctiveness*, and you will probably attribute Bill's praise for the new club to the club itself (a situational attribution). But if you've observed Bill praising every new place he visits as highly as he praises this club (*low distinctiveness*), you will attribute dispositionally—it's something about Bill. Perhaps he is quick to praise or is too easily entertained.

Finally, we base our attributions on **consistency**—on whether the behavior in question occurs reliably over time. Suppose that Bill's behavior is characterized by high distinctiveness and high consensus. Both point to the club. Bill likes this new club more than he likes any other, and most other people rave about the new club. If Bill likes the club every

[**TABLE 15·1**] Kelley's Theory of Attribution

	Attribution	Situational Attribution
Consensus	Low. Jose is smiling broadly while talking with Maria; most people do not smile while talking with her.	High. Jose is smiling broadly while talking with Maria; most other people do as well.
Distinctiveness	Low. Jose smiles like this while talking with most people.	High. Jose does not smile like this when talking with most other people.
Consistency	High. Jose always smiles like this when he talks with Maria.	High. Jose always smiles like this when he talks with Maria.
Conclusion (Attribution)	Jose is smiling at Maria because he is a happy person who enjoys talking with people.	Jose is smiling at Maria because there is something about her that makes him happy.

time he goes (*high consistency*), then your conclusion is clear: It's a great club (situational attribution). But consider what happens if low consistency combines with high distinctiveness and high consensus. Suppose the next time Bill goes to the club, he tells you he hates it—but then he goes again and is again of the impression that it's the best place he's ever been. Now your attribution may well be dispositional—something peculiar to Bill is affecting his experience at the club. Conversely, you may have reason to think that circumstances at the club tend to shift, making Bill's alternately liking and hating it understandable. In this case, your attribution will be situational. **TABLE 15·1** summarizes Kelley's theory by using another example.

Attributional Biases

When we make attributions, we are not impartial, dispassionate observers. Biases in the attribution process affect our conclusions. Two kinds of bias are found in the fundamental attribution error and false consensus.

The Fundamental Attribution Error When attributing a person's behavior to possible causes, we tend to overestimate the significance of dispositional factors and underestimate the significance of situational factors. This bias is called the **fundamental attribution error** (Ross, 1977) or the *correspondence bias* and is a potent factor in how we think about what other people do. Even when evidence indicates otherwise, we often prefer dispositional to situational attributions. For example, consider a study by Jones and Harris (1967). College students read essays that supposedly had been written by other students. The topic of the essay was Fidel Castro's rule of Cuba. Half of the students read an essay that was very positive toward Castro's leadership (the "pro" version), and the other half read a very negative account (the "con" version). The key manipulation in the experiment was information about the circumstances under which the writer supposedly composed the essay. Half of the students who read either the pro or the con version of the essay were told that the writer had been assigned a position (i.e., pro or con) to take when writing the essay. The remaining students were told the writer chose the orientation personally. After reading the essay, all participants were

asked to estimate the essay writer's true attitude toward Castro. Remarkably, the participants reported that the essay writer's attitude matched the pro or con stance of the essay, regardless of whether that stance had been assigned to or chosen by the writer. For example, if the writer's statements about Castro were positive, participants attributed them to the writer's beliefs, even though the writer had been assigned to produce the statements. Participants did not take into account the situational demands on the writer. Subsequent research has replicated this finding with many different methods and across cultures (e.g., Krull et al., 1999; Miyamoto & Kitayama, 2002). It is extremely difficult to eliminate the fundamental attribution error.

Wegner (2002, 2008) has provided an intriguing parallel to the fundamental attribution error in his consideration of our frequent invocation of conscious will as the cause of our behavior—"I did it because I wanted to," "I did it because I felt like it," "I willed it to happen," etc. In other words, a category of personal behavior exists in which we assign the cause dispositionally, just as we often do when assigning the cause of other's behavior. For Wegner, doing so constitutes an illusion that he terms the "illusion of conscious will."

In his analysis of the causes of behavior, Wegner distinguishes between conscious will as an apparent cause and empirical will as the actual cause. Humans lack conscious access to the empirical will (see Bargh et al., 2001; Wilson, 2002; Kahneman, 2003; Stanovich, 2004; and Haidt, 2006, for variations on the distinction that Wegner draws). His study of the neurophysiological and clinical literature brings Wegner to the conclusion that the experience of consciously willing one's behavior is a feeling—he calls it the *authorship emotion*—that requires three conditions for its occurrence. They are consistency, exclusivity, and priority, and become the cornerstones of Wegner's theory of apparent mental causation of behavior. They also bear an obvious resemblance to the conditions previously identified in Kelley's theory of attribution. For Wegner, we are most likely to attribute the cause of a personal action to the experience of conscious will when that experience reliably and uniquely precedes the action.

---

fundamental attribution error Our tendency to overestimate the significance of dispositional factors and to underestimate the significance of situational factors in explaining other people's behavior.

Victim blaming is a common form of the fundamental attribution error, particularly when the victim is not actually responsible for his or her misfortune. According to Lerner (1980), victim blaming occurs because, whether we're aware of it or not, most of us have a **belief in a just world.** That is, we erroneously assume that the world is a fair place in which people get what they deserve. As a result we tend to blame victims when misfortune or tragedy strikes them. Why? An innocent victim would threaten the stability of our belief system (see Hafer, 2000a). Blaming the victim establishes a just outcome (bad things happen to bad people) and therefore protects the belief that the world, and life, are fair (and safe). In this way, we avoid having to do the hard work of reexamining and possibly revising our beliefs. Attorneys and mental health practitioners are all too familiar with victim blaming. People who are raped, for example, often must cope with being blamed for their own assault (Bell, Kuriloff, & Lottes, 1994; Wakelin & Long, 2003). Complex social problems such as poverty (e.g., Guimond & Dube, 1989) and AIDs seem prone to the same blaming phenomenon. By blaming poor people for their own predicament, others avoid having to deal with the complexity. Interestingly, in a study of 1,700 psychology students from 12 different countries, Furnham (1992) found that the tendency to blame victims was positively correlated with status and wealth. Belief in the world as a just place may have positive effects, such as motivating people to persist in their achievement of goals. According to Hafer (2000b, 2002), just-world beliefs assure people that their efforts toward reaching long-term goals will ultimately be rewarded.

In strong contrast, when called on to explain our own rather than others' behavior, we are much more likely to attribute it to the situation than to ourselves. We tend to see our own behavior as relatively variable and strongly influenced by the situation, whereas we see the behavior of others as more stable and due to dispositional factors. In other words, when we try to explain our own behavior, we are not likely to make the fundamental attribution error (Sande, Goethals, & Radloff, 1988). This phenomenon is called the **actor–observer effect** or *actor-observer bias.*

A study of college-age male–female couples demonstrated the actor–observer effect (Orvis, Kelley, & Butler, 1976). Each person was asked separately to describe past difficulties in the relationship, such as arguments and criticism. Each was also asked to provide his or her attribution of the underlying causes of the difficulties. When describing their own behavior, the participants tended to refer to situational factors, such as too little money or too little sleep. When describing their partners' behavior, however, the participants often referred to specific dispositions, such as selfishness or a low commitment to the relationship.

Why are we guilty of the fundamental attribution error when we explain the causes of others' behavior but not our

Victims who testify in court may elicit victim-blaming by members of a jury who believe in a just world.

own? Jones and Nisbett (1971) suggested two possible reasons. First, we have a different focus of attention when we view ourselves. We tend to see the world around us more clearly than we do our own behavior. However, when we observe someone else doing something, we tend to focus our attention on what is most salient and relevant: that person's behavior, not the situation he or she occupies. A second possible reason is that different types of information are available to us about our own behavior and that of other people. We have more information about our own behavior and are thus more likely to realize that it is often inconsistent. After all, it is typically easy to access our own thinking and feeling. We also have an insider's knowledge of which stimuli we are attending to in a given situation. This difference in information may lead us to conclude that the behavior of other people is typically consistent and thus a product of something stable and internal to them—their personalities—whereas our own behavior, given the inconsistency, derives from the shifting situations in which we find ourselves.

Choi and Nisbett (1998) examined cultural differences in the actor–observer effect. One group of participants was at an American university, and another group, at a Korean university. The procedure asked participants to read essays for or against capital punishment that had been written by another student. They were informed that the essays had been written at the experimenter's request, irrespective of that student's own attitude about capital punishment. The participants were then asked to follow suit. Half of those in each group were asked to write an essay in favor of capital punishment, and the other half, to write in opposition to it. In addition, they were provided with a list of bullet points to use in writing their essay—the same bullet points used by the student who wrote the original essay. Once they had finished writing their essays, they read the original student essay, and then were asked to indicate how much they expressed their own attitude in the essay and how much the original author had.

The researchers reasoned that the actor–observer effect would be present were the participants to have rated their essays as expressing less of their true attitude but rating the original author's essay as having expressed more of his true attitude. The fact that they composed their essays under the same circumstances and using the same bullet points as the original author

---

belief in a just world The belief that people get what they deserve in life; a form of the fundamental attribution error.

actor–observer effect Our tendency to attribute our own behavior to situational factors but others' behavior to dispositional factors.

should have reduced the actor–observer effect. This occurred for the Korean participants but not for those at the American university. The researchers concluded that Americans may not be as aware of situational influences or of their importance.

In a related study, Park, Choi, and Cho (2006) focused on the "I-know-you-but-you-don't-know-me" phenomenon first reported by Pronin et al. (2001) as a variation of the actor–observer effect. It occurs when individuals believe their private experience should receive greater emphasis than their public actions when others judge them. Conversely, when judging others, individuals believe the others' public actions should receive greater weight. Contrary to the prediction of Pronin et al. that the phenomenon is less likely to occur in collectivistic cultures like those of East Asia, Park et al. found that Korean university students were consistent in believing that they know their friends better than their friends know them.

The findings of Park et al. point to an important exception to the strong preference for situational self-attribution mentioned earlier: We tend to attribute our achievements and successes to dispositional factors and our failures and mistakes to situational factors, a phenomenon called the **self-serving bias** (Miller & Ross, 1975) or *self-serving attributional bias*. Suppose you receive the highest score on a test. If you are like most people, you will consider the score well deserved. After all, you are a smart individual who studied hard. These attributions are dispositional. Now suppose you receive a failing score on the test—what attributions do you tend to make? Again, if you are like most people, you may blame your low score on the fact that it was a difficult, even "unfair" test, or on the teacher for being so picky about the answers he or she considered wrong. Your attributions in this instance are situational. Should they be dispositional instead, that is, should you persist in attributing your low scores to your lack of intelligence or ineptitude, doing so may result in learned helplessness (see Chapter 12) and depression.

Jones and Berglas (1978) introduced the concept of **self-handicapping** as a means of accounting for performance failures situationally and for successes dispositionally. For example, students may delay studying until the last moment or party the night before a test, thus handicapping their performance on the test. Doing so allows them to attribute the outcome to circumstances rather than lack of competence.

A possible explanation of the self-serving bias is that people are motivated to protect and enhance their self-esteem (Brown & Rogers, 1991; Robins & Beer, 2001). Simply put, we protect our self-esteem when we blame failures on the situation, and we enhance it when we give ourselves credit for our successes. Moreover, self-enhancement has the short-term effect of promoting positive mood (Robins & Beer, 2001). Sedikides et al. (1998) reported that self-serving bias was less likely to occur when two individuals shared a close relationship. In a meta-analysis, Mezulis et al. (2004) found similar reductions in the bias as a function of age (it was more likely in children and older adults), culture (less likely in Asian cultures), and psychopathology (less likely to occur with depression, anxiety, or attention-deficit/hyperactivity disorder).

Different biases may affect the way a person attributes her or his scores on tests.

False Consensus Another attributional bias is our frequent tendency to perceive our own responses as representative of the general consensus—an error called **false consensus** (Gilovich, 1990). For example, McFarland and Miller (1990) asked psychology students to choose one of two experiments in which they were likely to become uncomfortable. Regardless of their choice, participants believed that the majority of other students would select the same experiment they had. They overestimated the similarity of others' preferences.

One proposed explanation for false consensus points to self-esteem. Presumably, people do not like to think of themselves as being too different from other people and thus think that most will act the way they do. Another explanation derives from the fact that people tend to place themselves in the company of others who are similar to themselves (Ross, 1977). For this reason, they are apt to think that others share their preferences.

Attribution, Heuristics, and Social Cognition

As you learned in Chapter 11, people tend to follow general rules of thumb, or *heuristics*, when making decisions. This is especially evident when we make judgments about other people and our interactions with them. Much of the time, social heuristics serve us well (Gigerenzer, 2007). However, they sometimes lead us astray. When they do, we refer to them as biases or fallacies.

The Representativeness Heuristic As noted earlier in the chapter, when we meet someone for the first time, we observe

---

self-serving bias The tendency to attribute one's accomplishments and successes to dispositional factors and one's failures and mistakes to situational factors.

self-handicapping Impairing one's performance so as to attribute failures situationally and successes dispositionally.

false consensus The mistaken belief that our own attitude on a topic is representative of a general consensus.

the person's clothes, hairstyle, posture, manner of speaking, hand and facial gestures, and other characteristics. Based on our previous experience, we use this information to make tentative judgments about characteristics we cannot immediately discern. In doing so, we attempt to match the characteristics we can observe to our past experience with different types of people. If a match occurs, then we may draw a conclusion about what he or she is likely to be or to do (Lupfer, Clark, & Hutcherson, 1990). We have used the **representativeness heuristic**—we have classified the person by using the category she or he appears to fit best.

Sometimes the representativeness heuristic can mislead us, however. Consider the following description: A professor swims laps in the campus pool every day during his lunch hour. He is also passionate about tennis; if he can find a willing opponent, he will play in the dead of winter after clearing the court of snow. Now decide: Is he a professor of sports medicine or psychology? If you said "psychology," you were more likely to be right, because many more professors of psychology than of sports medicine exist. Yet you might have said "sports medicine" or at least seriously considered it. The image of an athletic person is such a distinctive cue that it is difficult not to conclude that the professor specializes in sports medicine. In addition to illustrating the representativeness heuristic, the choice of sports medicine illustrates the **base-rate fallacy**—the error we commit when we fail to consider the actual likelihoods involved.

The Availability Heuristic When people attempt to assess the importance or the frequency of an event, they tend to be guided by the ease with which examples of that event can be recalled—by how available these examples are to memory. This shortcut is called the **availability heuristic.** In general, the things we are able to think of most easily are more important and occur more frequently than things that are difficult to remember. Thus, the availability heuristic works well—most of the time, but it can lead to mistakes as well.

Amos Tversky and Daniel Kahneman (1982) demonstrated how the availability heuristic can cause errors by asking people to estimate whether English words starting with *k* were more or less common than words with *k* in the third position (for example, *kiss* versus *lake*). Most people said that there were more words starting with *k*. More than twice as many words have *k* in the third position as those having *k* in the first. But because thinking of words that start with a particular letter is easier than thinking of words that contain the letter in another position, people are misled. TABLE 15•2 provides another example, based on a study by Tversky and Kahneman (1974), of how the availability heuristic works.

---

representativeness heuristic A general rule for classifying a person, place, or thing into the category to which it appears to be the most similar.

base-rate fallacy The failure to consider the actual statistical likelihood that a person, place, or thing is a member of a particular category.

availability heuristic A general rule for judging the likelihood or importance of an event by the ease with which examples of that event are recalled.

attitude An evaluation of a person, place, or thing.

[**TABLE 15•2**] The Availability Heuristic in Operation

Does this list contain more men's or women's names? The answer may surprise you: There are fifteen male names and only fourteen female names. Because of the *availability heuristic*, however, most people tend to guess that female names are more numerous. The women listed are more famous than the men, so it is easier to bring their names to mind; this leads to overestimates of their frequency in the list.

Louisa May Alcott	Henry Vaughan
Allan Nevins	John Dickson Carr
Kate Millet	Jane Austen
Emily Dickinson	Eudora Welty
Henry Crabb Robinson	Thomas Hughes
Richard Watson Gilder	Joseph Lincoln
Laura Ingalls Wilder	Harriet Beecher Stowe
Emily Brontë	Jack Lindsay
Pearl Buck	Arthur Hutchinson
Edward George Lytton	Amy Lowell
James Hunt	Margaret Mitchell
Robert Lovett	Erica Jong
Michael Drayton	Edna St. Vincent Millay
Brian Hooker	Edith Wharton
George Jean Nathan	

Source: From Robert A. Baron, *Psychology*, 5/e. Published by Allyn and Bacon, Boston, MA. Copyright © 2001 by Pearson Education. Reprinted with permission of the publisher.

QUESTIONS TO CONSIDER

1. What factors have been most influential in the development of your own self-concept? What sorts of experiences do you think will have most influence on its continued development during your college years? How will they do this?

2. How much of your social behavior do you engage in unconsciously—that is, without self-awareness? In answering this question, consider the phenomena of attribution (such as the fundamental attribution error) and heuristics (such as representativeness). What effect do you suppose being more conscious of social cognition in your social interactions would have? Why?

3. Imagine you are the first person to arrive at the scene of an auto accident in which several people have been badly injured. What factors—situational or dispositional or some combination of the two—would influence your response?

Attitudes: Their Formation and Change

The study of **attitudes**—evaluations of persons, places, and things—and of how our attitudes form and change constitutes an important part of social psychology (Petty, Wegener, & Fabrigar, 1997; Wood, 2000).

Formation of Attitudes

Attitudes are generally considered to have three components: affect, behavior, and cognition (Zanna & Rempel, 1988; Eagly & Chaiken, 1998). The affective (emotional) component is the feelings that a particular stimulus elicits. The behavioral component is the tendency to act in a particular way toward a particular stimulus. The cognitive component is one's beliefs about the stimulus. Social psychologists have studied all three components, and we examine their findings in this section, particularly with respect to ethnicity and social issues.

Affective Components of Attitudes The affective component of attitudes can be strong and pervasive. The bigot feels unease in the presence of people from a certain religious, racial, or ethnic group; the nature lover feels exhilaration from a pleasant walk through the woods. Like other emotional reactions, these feelings are strongly influenced by direct or vicarious classical conditioning (see Chapter 5; Rajecki, 1990).

Direct classical conditioning of attitudes is straightforward. Suppose you meet someone who seems to take delight in embarrassing you. She makes clever, sarcastic remarks that disparage your intelligence, looks, and personality. Unfortunately, her remarks are so clever that your attempts to defend yourself make you appear even more foolish. After a few encounters with this person, the sight of her or the sound of her voice is likely to elicit feelings of dislike and fear. Your attitude toward her will be negative.

Vicarious emotional conditioning (Mineka & Cook, 1993) undoubtedly plays a major role in transmitting parents' attitudes to their children. People are skilled at detecting even subtle signs of fear, hatred, and other negative emotional states in other people, especially when they know them well. Even without conditioning, simply being exposed repeatedly to an otherwise neutral object or issue over time may cause us to develop a positive attitude toward it. This preference for the familiar is what Robert Zajonc (ZIE-onts; 1968) called the **mere exposure effect.** One of the first studies to demonstrate this effect used several neutral stimuli—they initially did not elicit positive or negative feelings—such as nonsense words, photographs of the faces of unknown people, and Chinese characters (Zajonc, 1968). The more the participants saw the stimuli, the more they reported liking them. Research also has shown that the mere exposure effect is stronger when stimuli are presented below the participant's threshold of awareness (Murphy, Monahan, & Zajonc, 1995) and that the effect generalizes to similar stimuli (Monahan, Murphy, & Zajonc, 2000).

Behavioral Components of Attitudes People do not always behave as their expressed attitudes and beliefs would lead us to expect. In a classic example, LaPiere (1934) drove through the United States with a Chinese couple. They stopped at more than 250 restaurants and lodging facilities and were refused service only once. Several months after their trip, LaPiere wrote to the owners of the businesses they had visited and asked whether they would serve Chinese people. The response was overwhelmingly negative; 92% of those who responded said that they would not. Clearly, their behavior gave less evidence of ethnic bias than their expressed attitudes did—proof that attitudes do not always influence behavior. More recent research indicates a definite relation between attitudes and behavior, but one that is influenced by the following factors:

- **Degree of Specificity**: A person's general attitude toward a stimulus may not predict his or her behavior (e.g., Haddock, Zanna, & Esses, 1994). Behaviors, unlike attitudes, are specific events. Thus, as the attitude being measured becomes more specific, behavior becomes more predictable.

- **Motivational Relevance**: Expressing a particular attitude takes less effort than does acting on that attitude. In other words, one may not always "walk the talk." Sivacek and Crano (1982) demonstrated that attitudes are more likely to motivate behaviors if the effects of the behaviors are relevant to the individual's interests.

- **Accessibility**: An attitude's accessibility is the readiness with which an attitude can be expressed. Suppose you have a negative attitude toward forest clear-cutting but have never expressed that attitude before. Some theorists consider the period of time that elapses between the onset of the stimulus relevant to the attitude and a person's statement of his or her attitude to be a good predictor of attitude–behavior consistency. For example, Bassili (1993, 1995) found that each 1-second delay in an interviewee's response to questions about the candidate he or she favored in an upcoming election translated into a nearly 10% mismatch to the candidate the interviewee actually voted for in the election. The longer the latency, the greater the inconsistency between attitudes and behavior.

- **Constraints on Behavior**: Other, more obvious factors, such as presently existing circumstances, also produce discrepancies between attitudes and behaviors. For example, a young man may have a very positive attitude toward a certain young woman, and, if he is asked specifically, he may express a very positive attitude toward kissing her. However, he never kisses her, because she has plainly shown that she is not interested in him. No matter how precisely we measure the young man's attitudes, our predictions of his behavior will be inaccurate without considering additional information that is available.

Cognitive Components of Attitudes The cognitive components of attitudes include conscious beliefs (Ajzen, 2001). We acquire most beliefs about a particular stimulus directly: We hear or read a fact or opinion, or other people reinforce statements we make about a particular attitude. A group of racially prejudiced people will probably ostracize a person

---

mere exposure effect The tendency to form a positive attitude toward a person, place, or thing based solely on repeated exposure to that stimulus.

A protest is one example of a situation in which a person's attitude on an issue corresponds to his or her behavior—in this case, demonstrating against abortion and for abortion rights.

who makes positive statements about the ethnic group or groups against which they are prejudiced. Conversely, conscientious parents may applaud their children's positive statements about other ethnic groups or about social issues such as environmental conservation.

Attitude Change and Persuasion

Once attitudes are formed, people often attempt to persuade us to change them. Two aspects of persuasive messages have received special attention from social psychologists: the sources of the messages and the messages themselves.

A message tends to be more persuasive if its source is credible. *Source credibility* is high when the source is perceived as knowledgeable and is trusted to communicate this knowledge accurately. Messages also seem to have more impact when their sources are physically attractive (Perloff, 2003). Individuals who are asked to endorse products for advertisers are almost always attractive or appealing in other ways. Additionally, the likeability of the communicator, independent of physical attractiveness, has a similar effect on persuasion (Roskos-Ewoldsen & Fazio, 1992; Perloff, 2003).

Aspects of the message itself also are important in determining its persuasiveness. For example, is an argument that provides only one side of an issue more effective than an argument that presents both sides? The answer depends on the audience. If the audience either knows very little about the issue or already holds a strong position with respect to it, one-sided arguments tend to be more effective. If the audience is already well informed but undecided about the issue, however, a two-sided argument tends to be more persuasive (Evans, 2003).

In terms of the content of the message itself, you may wonder whether the use of scare tactics in persuasive messages is effective. This question was addressed when a program called Scared Straight was implemented in New Jersey in an effort to persuade youthful offenders to abandon their delinquent lifestyles. The program entailed an afternoon visit to Rahway State Prison and a distressing, intimidating encounter with selected prison inmates. Although the program initially appeared successful, the majority of the offenders exposed to the program eventually returned to delinquent activities (Hagan, 1982). Other research has shown that scare tactics may be effective in bringing about change, but only when combined with relevant information about how to change specific behaviors (Gleicher & Petty, 1992). Also, messages are most effective in changing attitudes when they contain both affective and cognitive components (Eagly & Chaiken, 2005).

The **elaboration likelihood model** offers an explanation of how attitudes may be changed through persuasion (Cacioppo, Petty, & Crites, 1993; Petty & Wegener, 1999; Petty, Wheeler, & Tormala, 2003). (See FIGURE 15·1.) According to this model, persuasion can take either a *central* or a *peripheral* route. The effort to persuade via the central route requires a person to think critically about the argument or arguments being presented, to weigh their relative strengths and weaknesses, and to elaborate on the relevant themes. At issue is the actual substance of the argument—its rationality—and not its emotional appeal. Efforts via the peripheral route, conversely, involve attempts at persuasion in which the desired attitudinal change is specifically emotional and often associated with positive stimuli—a professional athlete, a billionaire, an attractive model—that actually may have nothing to do with the substance of the argument. Sales pitches that associate products with attractive people or imply that buying the product will result in emotional, social, or financial benefits are examples of the use of peripheral techniques to change attitudes. Of course, it is possible for persuasive appeals to take both routes.

Persuasive Message

	Central Route	Peripheral Route
Elaboration (consideration of strengths and weaknesses of argument)	Yes	Little or none
Association with positive stimuli	Little or none	Yes
Cause of attitude change	Quality of argument	Emotional appeal

[**FIGURE 15·1**] The elaboration likelihood model of attitude change. Persuasive messages may center either on a substantive argument that requires an individual to think critically about its strengths and weaknesses (the central route) or on a superficial association with positive stimuli (the peripheral route).

---

elaboration likelihood model A model that explains the effectiveness of persuasive messages in terms of two routes to persuasion. The central route requires a person to think critically about an argument, whereas the peripheral route entails merely the association of the argument with something positive.

Cognitive Dissonance

Although we usually assume that our attitudes cause our behavior, the opposite can be true. Two major theories attempt to explain the effects of behavior on attitude formation and attitude change. The earlier theory is **cognitive dissonance theory,** developed by Leon Festinger (1957; see also Cooper, 2007). According to this theory, when we experience a discrepancy between an attitude and a behavior, between a behavior and our self-image, or between two attitudes, an aversive state of tension called *dissonance* results. For example, a person may believe that he has overcome his racial prejudices, only to find himself disapproving of a racially mixed couple he sees in a shop. According to cognitive dissonance theory, the person should experience tension between his belief in his own lack of prejudice and the simultaneous evidence of prejudice from his reaction to the couple. McGregor, Newby-Clark, and Zanna (1999) argue that the element of simultaneity maximizes the degree of dissonance we feel. It is critical that a person be focused on the discrepancy for the aversiveness of dissonance to be experienced.

In Festinger's view, *dissonance reduction* can be a powerful motive. Dissonance may be reduced by (a) discounting the importance of one of the dissonant elements, (b) adding elements that are consonant, or (c) changing one of the dissonant elements. Suppose, for example, a student believes he is very intelligent, but he receives a failing grade in an important course. Because the obvious expectation is that an intelligent person will get good grades, the discrepancy causes the student to experience dissonance. To reduce it, he may decide that grades are not as important as he once assumed or that intelligence is not very closely related to grades. In doing so, he is using a discounting strategy. Or he can dwell on the belief that his professor was unfair or that his job left him little time to study for the exam. In this case, he is reducing dissonance by adding consonant elements—those that can account for his poor performance and hence explain the dissonance. Finally, he can change one of the dissonant elements: He can either start getting good grades in the course or revise his opinion of his own intelligence.

Justification Cognitive dissonance is assumed to occur when a person's behavior is inconsistent with his or her attitudes, but the degree of dissonance a person experiences will depend on whether other factors can justify one of the dissonant elements. Being paid handsomely for doing something you dislike can justify your behavior and, on balance, reduce the dissonance between doing one thing and believing another. Being paid a very small amount, conversely, may not justify your behavior and can leave you with considerable cognitive dissonance.

In a classic experiment, Festinger and Carlsmith (1959) tested the effects of justification on the strength of cognitive dissonance and resultant attitude change. These

Being paid to perform simple, repetitive tasks may produce cognitive dissonance in individuals who believe they are qualified for more demanding work.

researchers asked college students to perform very boring tasks, such as putting spools on a tray, dumping them out, putting them on the tray again, dumping them out again, and so on. After the students had spent an hour in this type of activity, the researchers asked each student in two experimental conditions whether he or she would help out by trying to convince the next participant, who was waiting outside the room, that the boring tasks actually were enjoyable. Some students were offered the paltry sum of $1 for lying to the next participant (this was very low justification for saying the tasks were enjoyable); others were offered $20 for doing so (very high justification, in 1959 dollars, for lying). The next "participant" was actually a paid confederate of the researchers who listened attentively to the real participants' claims about how interesting the tasks were. After this phase of the experiment, the researcher paid the participants the agreed-on amount. No mention of deceiving another participant or of payment was made to the participants in a third, control condition.

At the end of the experiment, all participants were asked to rate how much they, in truth, had enjoyed the activity they had engaged in. Festinger and Carlsmith predicted that those who were paid only $1 would consider the activity relatively interesting. Because they had been induced to praise the activity to another person without a sufficient justification, they should have experienced strong cognitive dissonance: Their original attitude about the activity and their verbal

---

cognitive dissonance theory The theory that changes in attitude can be motivated by an unpleasant state of tension caused by a disparity between our attitudes and our behavior.

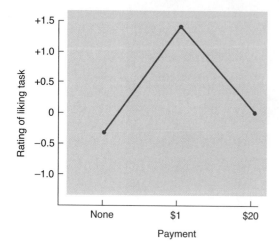

[**FIGURE 15•2**] Effects of induced compliance on justification. People who received $1 to lie about a boring task later indicated that they liked the task more than did people who received $20 or people in the control group.

(Based on data from Festinger, L., & Carlsmith, J. M. (1959). Cognitive consequences of forced compliance. *Journal of Abnormal and Social Psychology, 58,* 203–210.)

claims were patently inconsistent. Because the participants could not take back their claims, the only thing left to change was their attitudes toward the activity. The well-paid participants, conversely, had a perfect justification for their claims and should not have experienced much cognitive dissonance. As predicted, the poorly paid participants did rate the activity as more enjoyable than did those who were well paid. You can see in FIGURE 15•2 that being paid a lot left people with about the same attitude toward the boring activity as existed among participants in the control condition—those who experienced no dissonance because they never told anyone the tasks were enjoyable.

Egan, Santos, and Bloom (2007) addressed the possible evolutionary significance of cognitive dissonance by using a procedure they presented to both preschool children and capuchin monkeys. The procedure involved two alternatives that the children (colored stickers) and the monkeys (colored M&Ms) had prejudged to be equally preferable. Then they were required to choose between the alternatives. Consistent with the authors' predictions, when subsequently offered a choice between the nonchosen sticker and a third sticker that was originally as attractive as the two stickers used in the first choice procedure, the children chose the new sticker. Similarly, the capuchins chose a novel M&M over the one they had rejected in the initial choice. These changes of preference did not occur after a control (no-choice) condition. The authors reasoned that making the choice induced cognitive

---

self-perception theory The theory that we come to understand our attitudes and emotions by observing our own behavior and the circumstances under which it occurs.

dissonance and that it had been reduced subsequently by altering the valuation of the nonselected option.

These findings suggest that the resolution of dissonance occasioned by discrepancies between belief and action does not require complex decision making. Additional evidence was provided by Lieberman et al. (2001), who studied amnesic adults and age-matched control participants. The amnesic patients exhibited anterograde amnesia (see Chapter 8) associated with hippocampal or diencephalic damage. Each participant examined two sets of 15 art prints before ranking the prints in each set in terms of which they liked most to least. After the rankings were obtained, the participants were presented with pairs of prints. In some pairs, one print was taken from those the participant had ranked high, and the other, from those ranked low. Some time later the participants were asked to rerank the prints in each pair. Consistent with cognitive dissonance reduction, the rerankings were more extreme than the original rankings; that is, the participants liked the originally preferred prints even more and the originally less-preferred prints even less. However, this attitude change was no different for the amnesic participants, who had no memory of the prints they had previously seen than for the control participants. Thus, the changes in preference characteristic of cognitive dissonance may be achieved more simply than is typically assumed.

Self-Perception

A second major theory concerning the relation between behavior and attitudes is **self-perception theory.** Daryl Bem (1972) defined the theory in the following way:

> Individuals come to "know" their own attitudes, emotions, and other internal states partially by inferring them from observations of their own overt behavior and/or the circumstances in which this behavior occurs. Thus, to the extent that internal cues are weak, ambiguous, or uninterpretable, the individual is functionally in the same position as an outside observer, an observer who must necessarily rely on those same external cues to infer the individual's inner states. (Bem, 1972, p. 2)

In other words, an observer who attempts to make judgments about someone's attitudes, emotions, or other internal states necessarily must examine the person's behavior for clues. For example, if you cannot ask someone why he or she is doing something or you distrust the answer you receive, you must analyze the situation in which the behavior occurs to try to determine the motivation. Bem theorized that people analyze their own internal states in a similar way, making attributions about the causes of their own behavior.

Think about how Bem would explain Festinger and Carlsmith's results in which students who were paid only $1 later rated a boring activity as more interesting than did those who were paid $20. Suppose that an observer watches a person who has been paid $1 to deliver a convincing speech about how interesting a dull activity was. Because being paid such a small sum is not an acceptable reason for calling a dull activity interesting, the observer will probably conclude that the speaker actually enjoyed it. If good evidence for situational attributions is lacking, the observer will attribute the behavior to a dispositional factor—genuine interest in the activity. Bem argued that, in this instance, the speaker would reach the very same conclusion the observer had: "I wasn't paid enough to justify lying, so I must have enjoyed the activity." The principal advantage of self-perception theory is that it makes fewer assumptions than does cognitive dissonance theory. It does not postulate a motivating aversive drive. Perhaps self-perception and cognitive dissonance occur under different situations, producing attitude changes for different reasons. Further evidence will be needed to determine whether the two theories are competing or complementary (see also Wegner, 2002, on this issue).

QUESTIONS TO CONSIDER

1. Attitudes have sometimes been described as "predispositions to act." What does this phrase mean? Does the phrase accurately describe attitudes? Why or why not?

2. Identify a prominent political figure toward whom you already have a strong attitude. What kinds of arguments would be effective in persuading you to change your attitude? Would they follow a central route, a peripheral route, or both? How would they do so?

3. Describe a recent experience of cognitive dissonance. What factors produced the dissonance? How did you eventually reduce it? How would self-perception theory account for your experience?

Stereotypes and Prejudice

A **prejudice** is a preconceived opinion, a bias, or a partiality toward a person or group, which may be favorable or unfavorable. However, people usually use the term to refer to an unfavorable bias, and that's the sort of prejudice we're concerned with in this section: a negative evaluation of a group of people who are defined by their racial, ethnic, or religious heritage or by their gender, language, physical appearance, occupation, sexual orientation, level of education, or place of origin or residence. A prejudice (literally, a "prejudgment") is essentially a heuristic by which we focus on a few features of a person (such as skin color, accent, family name, or manner of dress) and assume that the person also possesses other, mainly negative, characteristics. In this way, a prejudice is an insidious example of the *representativeness heuristic*.

Stereotypes contribute to prejudice; the meanings of the two terms overlap. As already noted, a prejudice is a negative evaluation of a particular group, whereas a **stereotype** is essentially an overgeneralization of the characteristics of group and therefore potentially false. Although some stereotypes are positive, as with prejudices, we usually think of them as negative. Many of the regional cultural differences in the United States, for example, are subject to stereotyping. Although a given stereotype may be true in a specific instance, stereotyping generalizes characteristics to entire groups of people and thus overgeneralizes. The error of thinking in terms of stereotypes lies in the failure to consider individual differences. The same is true of prejudices.

Prejudice often leads to **discrimination**. In our discussion, discrimination refers to behavior, to treating people differently because of their membership in a particular group (Dion, 2003). Thus, we can discriminate favorably or unfavorably. A prejudice occurs any time members in one group, referred to as the *in-group,* exhibit negative behaviors toward members of another group, called the *out-group.* Discrimination occurs any time members of the in-group display behaviors intended to prevent members of the out-group from getting something, such as the opportunity to vote, a job, an education, or a home in a particular neighborhood.

At the level of nations, prejudices, stereotypes, and discrimination give rise to **ethnocentrism**—the notion that one's own cultural, national, racial, or religious group is superior to or more deserving than others. Ethnocentric attitudes and behaviors often cause conflict in the form of war, terrorism, or other forms of violent confrontation.

The Origins of Prejudice

Unfortunately, prejudices seem to be an enduring characteristic of the human species. They exist in most human endeavors, from education, business, and athletics to politics and religion. Why are prejudices so widespread?

The Role of Competition   An affiliation and a prejudice are two sides of the same coin. That is, along with the tendency to identify with and feel close to members of our own group or clan, there is the tendency to be suspicious of others. A classic experiment, known as the Robbers Cave Experiment, by Muzafer Sherif and colleagues (1961) demonstrated just how easily intergroup mistrust and conflict can arise. The study took place at a remote summer camp in Robbers Cave State

---

prejudice   A preconceived opinion or bias; especially, a negative attitude toward a group of people who are defined by their racial, ethnic, or religious heritage or by their gender, occupation, sexual orientation, level of education, place of residence, or membership in a particular group.

stereotype   An overgeneralized and thus potentially false schema describing the characteristics of a particular group.

discrimination   Differential treatment of people based on their membership in a particular group.

ethnocentrism   The idea that our own cultural, racial, national, or religious group is superior to or more deserving than others.

In the Robber's Cave experiment, competitive activities escalated between-group conflict.

Park in Oklahoma. The participants, 11-year-old boys, were arbitrarily assigned to one of two cabins. The two groups were initially isolated from each other. During the first week, the boys in each cabin spent their time together as a group, fishing, hiking, swimming, and otherwise enjoying themselves. The boys formed two cohesive groups and named themselves the Rattlers and the Eagles. They became attached to their groups and strongly identified with them.

Next, the researchers sowed the seeds of dissension. They set up a series of competitive events between the two groups. The best team would win a trophy and individual prizes for its members. As the competition progressed, the teams began taunting and insulting each other. Then the Eagles burned the Rattlers' flag, and in retaliation, the Rattlers broke into the Eagles' cabin and scattered or stole their belongings. Although further physical conflict was prevented by the researchers, the two groups continued to abuse each other verbally and seemed to have developed a genuine mutual hatred.

Finally, the researchers arranged for the boys to work together. The researchers sabotaged the water supply for the camp and had the boys fix it. They also arranged for the boys to repair a truck that had broken down, and they induced them to pool their money to rent a movie. The boys' joint efforts on cooperative rather than competitive ventures brought a reduction in intergroup conflicts.

The Role of Self-Esteem Most social psychologists believe that competition is an important factor in the development of prejudices. The competition need not be for tangible goods; it can be motivated by a desire for social superiority. People's tendency to perceive their own group (the in-group) as superior and that of others (the out-group) as inferior may be based on their need to enhance their self-esteem. Thus, people who belong to groups that preach racial hatred tend to be those whose own social status is rather low.

An experiment performed with a group consisting of English-speaking participants and French-speaking participants supports this conclusion. Meindl and Lerner (1984) exposed English-speaking participants in the group to a situation designed to threaten their self-esteem. The participants were asked to walk across a room to get a chair. For those in the experimental group, the chair was rigged so that a pile of old-style computer data cards would be knocked over and scattered on the floor. In a situation like this, most people feel clumsy and foolish—and a bit guilty about making trouble for the person who has to put the cards back in order. After this experience, the participants were asked about their attitudes toward the French-speaking participants (the "others"). Participants in the experimental group, who had toppled the cards, rated the "others" more negatively than did those in a control group, who had not toppled the cards in retrieving the chair. The researchers reasoned that by viewing the French-speakers as members of a group inferior to their own, the participants partially compensated for their temporary loss of self-esteem. Of course, levels of self-esteem have been shown to vary from culture to culture (e.g., Feather & McKee, 1993). Thus, the effects found by Meindl and Lerner might not generalize to more interdependent or collectivist societies, for example.

The Role of Social Cognition When we use heuristics, we sometimes make errors of judgment. As heuristics, stereotypes are convenient, because they provide a way to classify others quickly. But doing can be seductive: Making a generalized point about a group is often easier than dealing with the actual complexities of a social situation we are trying to explain (Macrae, Milne, & Bodenhausen, 1994). For example, attributing slow traffic movement to older drivers as a group is easier than analyzing the complex interplay of roadway engineering, traffic-flow patterns, and differences in people's driving skills. The problem is that stereotypes cannot be applied to all members of the out-group with the same accuracy.

In many cases, people first learn stereotypes through their interactions with family members, friends, and acquaintances. Research also has shown that stereotypical information becomes more and more rigid as it passes from one person to another (Ruscher, 1998). The mass media are a prominent source of stereotypes. Thompson, Judd, and Park (2000) found that stereotypes tend to be more extreme when acquired through media sources than through direct contact with the out-group. Stereotypes are unlikely to be examined closely and revised to reflect new experience. Even when faced with contradictory evidence, people seem to resist changing their stereotypes. For example, Kunda and Oleson (1997) gave participants information that challenged their stereotypes and found that they maintained the original stereotypes by creating special subcategories for the "exceptions that proved the rule." Other work suggests that people use stereotypes selectively to support and maintain their desired impressions of others (Kunda & Sinclair, 1999).

The availability heuristic, as we saw earlier, involves the use of distinctive, easily recalled material in decision making.

This phenomenon probably explains why Americans typically overestimate both the rate of violent crime and the relative numbers of violent crimes committed by members of minority groups. Violent acts certainly are distinctive events, and minority group members often are conspicuously depicted in the media. Both the crimes and the minorities stand out; as a result, they may be perceived as causally related. This perception is an example of an **illusory correlation**—an apparent relation between two distinctive elements that does not actually exist (see Spears & Haslam, 1997).

Another fallacy that promotes the formation and maintenance of stereotypes is the **illusion of out-group homogeneity:** People tend to assume that members of out-groups are more similar than are members of their in-group (Ostrom & Sedikides, 1992). For example, men tend to perceive women as being more alike than men are, and women do the opposite (Park & Rothbart, 1982). The same is true for young people and old people (Linville, Fischer, & Salovey, 1989). Most of us resist being stereotyped but nevertheless engage stereotypes when thinking about members of other groups.

In a study of attitudes toward racial equality, Dixon, Durrheim, and Tredous (2007) asked nearly 2,000 South African adults contacted at random to estimate the frequency of their contact with members of the predominate ethnic groups—Black and White. Those surveyed also stated their attitudes regarding racial equality and government policies designed to produce such equality. The researchers' interest was the extent to which contact predicted attitudes. The results showed that, although increased contact improves Whites' attitudes, a "stubborn kernel" of opposition remains to government-mandated efforts to achieve racial equality. Interestingly, the results for Blacks were the opposite: the greater their contact with Whites, the less supportive they were of government efforts, such as those seeking restitution for Blacks. The authors concluded that greater contact between in-group and out-group may produce asymmetrical effects on attitudes.

Members of in-groups often demonstrate similarities that distinguish them from members of out-groups.

The Role of Evolution Finally, a very different explanation of in-group biases toward out-groups (including prejudices, stereotypes, and discrimination) was offered by Krebs and Denton (1997). They propose that cognitive structures biased in favor of the in-group, and against out-groups, were selected in the course of early human evolution because those structures had adaptive value.

The basic argument will be familiar to you by now. Early humans are usually characterized as living in small cooperative groups that were in competition with one another for scarce resources. An ability to make rough-and-ready characterizations of others as belonging to someone's own group or to another group presumably would facilitate both in-group cooperation and competitive effectiveness against out-groups. A positive bias toward members of the in-group would contribute to cohesiveness. A negative bias against other groups would motivate in-group members to keep out-groups under close scrutiny to detect dangers to themselves.

Krebs and Denton (1997) pointed out that in modern life, these once-adaptive biases can produce difficulties by perpetuating conflict, even though cooperative solutions are now possible. Moreover, our contemporary sense of humanity and justice is offended when people engage in undeserved negative evaluation and treatment of others simply because they belong to other groups.

Research using the Implicit Association Test (IAT; Greenwald, McGhee, & Schwartz, 1998) has revealed the existence of ethnic biases of which individuals are otherwise unaware (see Greenwald, Nosek, & Banaji, 2003). Although participants profess to be free of such prejudices, the test results indicate otherwise. Such findings may be seen to support the existence of the deeply ingrained biases suggested by evolutionary psychologists. Moreover, they suggest the possibility that these biases may be difficult to eliminate entirely (but see Dasgupta & Greenwald, 2001, for a more hopeful appraisal; see Bones and Johnson, 2007, for a spoof on the proliferating application of the IAT in social psychology).

In an fMRI study (Hart et al., 2000), black and white participants viewed photographs of black and white faces. Significantly greater activity was seen in the amygdala (a brain region implicated in the control of emotion; see Chapter 4) in response to out-group faces than to in-group faces, but this difference only emerged after exposure to both facial types. The researchers found that the difference emerged as a result of habituation (see Chapter 5) of the amygdala response to in-group faces as the response to out-group faces persisted.

illusory correlation An apparent correlation between two distinctive elements that does not actually exist.

illusion of out-group homogeneity A belief that members of out-groups are highly similar to one another.

Self-Fulfilling Prophecies

We encountered self-fulfilling prophecies in the discussion of intelligence testing in Chapter 11. In the context of stereotyping and prejudices, a **self-fulfilling prophecy** begins when a person forms stereotypes of what other people are like. The person then behaves in a manner consistent with the stereotypes. The response of others to such behavior only confirms the stereotypes.

A memorable example of the self-fulfilling prophecy was demonstrated in an experiment by Snyder, Tanke, and Berscheid (1977). The researchers asked male participants to engage in telephone conversations with female participants. Just before each conversation took place, each male participant was shown a photograph of the young woman to whom he would talk, but the photographs were not those of female participants but rather were images of other women, some physically attractive and some unattractive, that the researchers previously had selected. The conversations that took place were recorded, and the voices of the female participants were played to independent observers, who rated their impressions of the participants.

The independent observers rated the women whose male conversation partners believed them to be attractive as being more friendly, likable, and sociable than those whose conversation partners believed them to be unattractive. The authors concluded that male participants talked differently to women they considered attractive or unattractive. In turn, their talk had either a positive or negative effect on the women, a difference that could be detected by the independent observers.

What would have happened to women who talked with more than one man who believed her to be attractive? Madon and colleagues studied the effects of multiple sources on the development of self-fulfilling prophecies. Specifically, they focused on the influence of parents' estimates of their adolescent child's drinking on the child's actual level of drinking. In one study (Madon et al., 2004), they found that the increase in drinking that occurred when one parent overestimated the child's level of drinking grew even further if both parents overestimated it. In another study (Madon, et al., 2006), they found that, if mothers overestimated their child's drinking from year to year, the actual level of drinking continued to increase. Thus, multiple sources of self-fulfilling prophecies tend to have additive effects.

Hope for Change

Prejudices are maintained because they can justify exploitation of the out-group by the in-group. If the out-group can be portrayed as "stupid," "dependent," or "irresponsible," the in-group can justify the exploitation of the out-group as being in the out-group's own best interest—or at least can conclude that its treatment of the out-group is the best that the out-group can reasonably expect. When exploitative practices lead to material advantages in the form of cheap labor or unequal access to resources, the prejudices will tend to persist.

Change in this pattern may be possible, however. Many instances of personal prejudice may be inadvertent; as noted earlier, people may be unaware of their stereotypes and prejudices. By gaining awareness, they may be persuaded (although with difficulty) that their attitudes are unjustified. It may be possible to teach people to become more reflective about their prejudices, to take time to analyze them. For example, Langer, Bashner, and Chanowitz (1985) gave a group of sixth-grade children specific training in thinking about the problems of people with disabilities. The children were asked to think about the way in which a person with disabilities might drive a car or about why a blind person might make a good newscaster. After this training, the children were more willing to go on a picnic with a person with disabilities than were children who did not receive the training. They were also more likely to perceive the specific consequences of particular disabilities than to view people with disabilities as uniformly "less fit." Thus, at the individual level, it may be possible for people to learn to recognize their prejudices and to take steps to overcome them (Gladwell, 2005).

As an introduction to their study of "unlearning" automatic biases, Rudman, Ashmore, and Gary (2001) quoted Dr. Martin Luther King, Jr.: "I refuse to accept the view that mankind is so tragically bound to the starless night of racism and war that the bright daybreak of peace and brotherhood can never become reality." The authors reported two experiments involving experimental and control groups of male and female college students who represented black, white, and other ethnicities. In the first experiment, the experimental group were enrolled in a seminar on prejudice and conflict taught by a black male professor. In the seminar, they studied intergroup conflict, engaged in sometimes confrontational discussions of the subject matter, and kept journals in which they recorded instances of bias, including personal instances. Those in the control group enrolled in a seminar on research methods taught by a white female professor. At the beginning and end of the semester, the students took the IAT and completed other instruments designed to measure stereotyping and racism. The results were analyzed for white students only and showed statistically significant decreases in the scores of those in the experimental group compared with those in the control group.

The second experiment involved a larger number of students in the same ethnic categories and added a second control group—a large lecture course taught by the same black professor. The results showed significantly lower scores only for the white students enrolled in the seminar. The authors concluded that the specific content of the seminar and its more intimate setting may have been critical to the effects they observed.

---

self-fulfilling prophecy An expectation that causes a person to act in a manner consistent with the expectation; the person's actions then cause the expectation to come true. Often seen in cases of stereotyping.

Social Influences and Group Behavior

A **group** is a collection of individuals who generally have common interests and goals. For example, the members of the American Association of Retired Persons (AARP) have a different set of interests and goals than do members of the American Cancer Society, although some of their interests and goals may overlap. The behaving, feeling, and thinking that define each of us as an individual are strongly influenced, often without our awareness, by those with whom we interact. Frequently this influence is unintentional: Other people may be equally unaware of how they are influencing us. At other times, this influence is intentional and is designed to manipulate us in some way to achieve specific ends (Santos, Leve, & Pratkanis, 1994; Cialdini, 2000). In this section, we examine various means by which we influence, and are influenced by, others.

Conformity

The most powerful social influence on our attitudes and behaviors may well be the behavior of other people. If we see people act in a particular way, we may imitate them (see Chapter 5). Sometimes we observe that people are not performing a particular behavior, and so we refrain from performing it. Changing

Group norms establish appropriate behavior in specific situations, such as these girls' mutual excitement at each other's purchases.

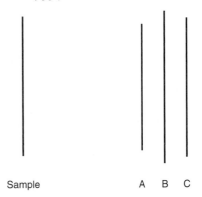

[**FIGURE 15•3**] An example of the stimuli used by Asch (1951).

Sample   A   B   C

our attitudes or behavior to be similar to those of a social group is called **conformity.** Let's consider why conformity occurs and look at the dangers posed by this very human tendency.

Social Norms Although most of us cherish our independence and like to think that we do what we do because it is what we want, none of us is immune to social influences. Moreover, most instances of conformity are mutually beneficial. Many of the psychological principles of social behavior are formally codified as laws that we are legally obligated to follow. Many other conventions that influence our behavior are unwritten. They are called **social norms,** or, when applied to members of a particular group, *group norms,* and define expected, appropriate behavior in specific situations. How we look at strangers, the way we talk to our friends or to our bosses, and the kinds of food we eat all are influenced by the norms of the society in which we live. Although they are not spelled out in formal or legal documents, norms are very powerful sources of social influence.

When we are not sure what is going on, it makes sense to use others' opinions or judgments as a guide. Just how strongly do group norms influence our individual behavior when the situation is unambiguous—when we are certain that we perceive things accurately? A surprising answer to this question was provided in a series of elegant studies conducted by Asch (1951, 1952, 1955).

Several groups of seven to nine college students were asked to estimate the lengths of vertical lines presented on a poster. A sample line was shown at the left, and the students were to choose which of the three lines to the right matched it. (See **FIGURE 15•3.**) The participants gave their answers aloud.

Only one true participant was in each group; all other participants were confederates of the researcher. The seating

---

group Two or more individuals who generally have common interests and goals.

conformity Adoption of the attitudes and behaviors that characterize a particular group of people.

social norms Informal rules defining the expected and appropriate behavior in specific situations.

was arranged so that the real student answered last. Under some conditions, the confederates made incorrect responses. When they did so on at least 6 of the 12 trials in an experiment, three fourths of the true participants went along with the group on at least one trial. Under control conditions, when the confederates responded accurately, only 5% of the true participants made an error.

Group pressure did not affect the true participants' perceptions; it affected their behavior. That is, they went along with the group decision even though the choice still looked wrong to them—and even though the other people were complete strangers. When the true participants were questioned later, they said that they had started doubting their own eyesight or had thought that perhaps they had misunderstood the instructions. Those who did not conform felt uncomfortable about disagreeing with the other members of the group. Asch's results show how strong the tendency to conform can be.

Two of the most important reasons that people conform so readily to social norms are the desire to be liked and the desire to be right (Baron, Vandello, & Brunsman, 1996; Cialdini & Goldstein, 2004). As we will see later, people tend to like other people who are similar to themselves, especially those who act like them and share their attitudes and beliefs. Because most of us prefer to be liked, we tend to conform to the norms or expectations of others. In addition, most of us prefer to be right rather than wrong.

Bystander Intervention   Conformity can sometimes have disastrous consequences. In New York City in 1964, a woman named Catherine (Kitty) Genovese was robbed and repeatedly stabbed by an assailant, who took 35 minutes finally to kill her. The woman's screams went unheeded by what was reported to be 38 eyewitnesses (Rosenthal, 1999), who watched from behind their apartment windows. No one tried to stop the attacker; no one even made an anonymous telephone call to the police until after the attacker had left. When the eyewitnesses were questioned later, they could not explain their inaction.

As you can imagine, people everywhere were appalled and shocked by the Genovese murder. Media commentators concluded from the apparent indifference of the eyewitnesses that society, especially in urban areas, had become cold and apathetic, but interviews with the eyewitnesses suggested otherwise. They were not uncaring. They were distressed and confused by what happened and by their failure to intervene. Experiments performed by social psychologists suggest that the apathy explanation is wrong—people in large cities are not generally indifferent to the needs of other people. The fact that Kitty Genovese's attack went unreported is not remarkable because so many eyewitnesses were present; instead, the research suggests that it is precisely because so many were present that it went unreported. How can that be?

bystander intervention   The intervention of a person in a situation that appears to require his or her aid.

[CASE STUDY]   A *New York Times* article (Rasenberger, 2004) revisited the murder of Catherine Genovese at Kew Gardens 40 years later. After recounting her growing up in Brooklyn and her move to the two-story apartment building in Queens with her roommate, the article turns to the gruesome events of her murder a year later at the hand of Winston Moseley, who was cruising the neighborhood to find a woman to mutilate. The subsequent stigmatization of Genovese's neighbors—the infamous 38 witnesses—by the same newspaper is well known. But, in the words of one of the residents, "Kew Gardens got a bad rap." What follows in the article focuses on the remarkable efforts of Joseph De May, Jr., to get the story right. His work is available at www.oldkewgardens.com/ss-nytimes-3.html.

De May's research began with the original *Times* article on March 27, 1964, and several discrepancies he found in it. For one thing, the attacks on Genovese occurred in locations that would not have been visible to those who were alleged to have witnessed them. The former assistant district attorney who prosecuted the case acknowledged that the accounts provided by only six witnesses could be relied on. Many who heard Genovese's screams were awakened from sleep and assumed the sounds had their origin at a nearby bar. De May asserts the possibility that several phone calls were made to the local police once screams were heard but were ignored and went unrecorded. De May also disputes the article's implication that Genovese screamed for a half-hour after she was initially attacked. De May points out that her wounds would have made it unlikely she could have done so. Moreover, her killer testified that he heard no screaming while he waited to return to kill her. On the basis of his research, De May drew two conclusions: most of the 38 people alleged to have witnessed the murder did not; and that most of what they did see was momentary and ambiguous.

John Darley and Bibb Latané ("latt-an-AY") studied the phenomenon of **bystander intervention**—the actions (or inaction) of people who witness a situation in which someone appears to require assistance. Their numerous experiments showed that in such situations, the presence of people who are doing nothing inhibits others from giving aid. For example, Darley and Latané (1968) staged an "emergency" during a psychology experiment with college students. Each participant took part in a discussion about personal problems associated with university life. The discussions included one, two, or five other people, who talked by means of an intercom. The researcher explained that the participants would sit in individual rooms so that they would be anonymous and hence more likely to speak frankly. The researcher would not listen in but would learn the participants' reactions to the conversation later in a questionnaire. Actually, only one true participant was present; the other voices were tape recordings. During the discussion, one of the recorded voices had previously mentioned that he sometimes had seizures and apparently did experience a seizure. His speech became incoherent, and he stammered out a request for help.

Almost all the real participants left the room to help the victim when they were the only witness to the seizure. When the conversation was larger, however, the true participants were much less likely to help. In addition, those who did try to help reacted more slowly if they believed that other people were present. (See FIGURE 15•4.) This finding has been replicated in dozens of subsequent experiments. When people are alone and an emergency occurs, they are very responsible, not apathetic.

Darley and Latané reported that the true participants who did not respond were hardly indifferent to the plight of their fellow student. Indeed, when the researcher entered the room, they usually appeared nervous and emotionally aroused, and they asked whether someone was helping the victim. The researchers concluded that the students were still in conflict, trying to decide whether they should do something.

Thus, it seems that whether bystanders will intervene in an emergency depends, at least in part, on how they perceive the situation and on whether they witness the event alone or in the presence of others. Latané and Darley (1970) proposed a model describing a sequence of steps bystanders face when confronted with a potential emergency:

They must notice and correctly interpret the event.

They must assume responsibility for helping the victim.

They must consider the possible courses of action and conclude that the costs of intervening are not prohibitively high.

Finally, they must actually implement the chosen course of action.

The diffusion of responsibility may not apply in cases where persons are trained to go to others' aid.

Of course, this sequence takes place rapidly and without much awareness on the bystander's part, much like other situations to which we respond each day.

Unfortunately, at least from the perspective of the victim, obstacles may arise at any stage in this decision-making process that make it unlikely that a bystander will intervene. In many cases, a bystander who is aware that others are available to help may not feel sufficient personal responsibility to do so. This phenomenon, called **diffusion of responsibility,** is considered to be responsible for the finding that people are less likely to offer help when several bystanders are present. In addition, a bystander may not feel competent to intervene or may be fearful of doing so; consequently, the person may take no action in the belief that he or she will worsen the situation or that someone else is more competent to act.

Recently, British psychologists Manning, Levine, and Collins (2007) revisited the case of Kitty Genovese and situated it in quite a different light. In addition to disputing the claim that there were 38 witnesses, they suggest that psychologists' focus on the number of witnesses and the indifference apparently engendered by urban neighborhoods actually has impeded the search for constructive ways to engender helping and bystander responsiveness. They thus view the case as a parable of how emphasis on certain aspects of the original tragedy actually may have delayed the search for ways in which groups may promote positive forms of intervention—the focus of what is now loosely styled as *positive psychology* (see Keyes and Haidt, 2003; Haidt, 2006).

Social Facilitation

The mere presence of other people can affect a person's behavior. Triplett (1897) published the first experimental study

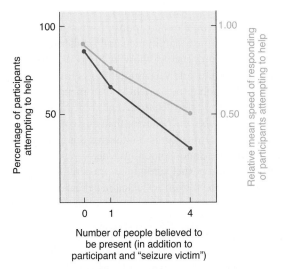

[**FIGURE 15•4**] Bystander intervention and diffusion of responsibility. The percentage of participants attempting to help is a function of the number of other people the participant believes to be present.

(Based on data from Darley, J. M., & Latané, B. (1968). Bystander intervention in emergencies: Diffusion of responsibility. *Journal of Personality and Social Psychology, 8,* 377–383.)

diffusion of responsibility A factor in the failure of bystander intervention, stating the fact that when several bystanders are present, no one person assumes responsibility for helping.

of **social facilitation**—the enhancement of a person's performance by the presence of other people. Triplett asked people to perform simple tasks, such as turning the crank of a fishing reel. He found that participants turned the crank faster and for a longer time if other people were present. Although many other studies found the same effect, some investigators reported just the opposite phenomenon: If the task was difficult and complex, the presence of an audience impaired participants' performance.

Zajonc (1965) offered an explanation of these different effects of social facilitation. In his view, the presence of people who are watching a performer (or people whom the performer perceives as watching) raises the performer's arousal level. The increase in arousal has the effect of increasing the probability that dominant responses—the responses that are most likely to occur in a particular situation—will be performed. When the task is simple, the dominant response is generally the correct response, so an audience improves performance. When the task is complex, however, a person can perform many different responses and must decide which is called for. Now the presence of the audience makes the selection of the appropriate behavior more difficult. The increased arousal tends to cause the person to perform the dominant response, which may impair the desired performance.

Costly mistakes may occur. For example, in a study of residential burglars, Cromwell, Marks, Olson, and Avery (1991) found that burglars who worked in groups were five times more likely to be apprehended than were burglars who worked alone. The researchers argued that burglary is a complex task that cannot be "well learned," because each burglary is different. The complexity of the burglary, combined with high levels of arousal produced by the group's presence, may have contributed to errors in planning and executing the crimes.

Social Loafing

In still another form of social influence, the presence of a group sometimes results in diminished effort, or **social loafing.** In an early study, Ringelmann (cited by Dashiell, 1935) measured the effort that people made when pulling a rope in a mock tug-of-war contest against a device that measured the exerted force. Presumably, the force exerted by eight people pulling together would be at least the sum of their individual efforts when each was tested alone—or even somewhat greater than that sum, because of social facilitation. However, Ringelmann found that the total force exerted by eight people was only about half of what would have been predicted by the simple combination of individual efforts. His participants exerted less force when they worked in a group.

More recent studies have confirmed these results and have extended them to other behaviors. This research indicates that several variables determine whether the presence of a group will produce social facilitation or social loafing. One of the most important variables is *individual identifiability*. Williams, Harkins, and Latané (1981) asked people to shout as loud as they could individually or in groups. (Participants in the "group" condition could not see or hear the others.) People shouted less loudly in groups than they did individually when they believed that the recording equipment could measure only the total group effort. When they were informed that the equipment would measure individual effort as well, people in groups shouted just as loudly as they did when alone. These results suggest that a person's efforts in a group activity are affected by whether his or her individual efforts can be identified by others. If they can, social facilitation is likely to occur; if they cannot, social loafing is more likely.

Two additional variables that affect social loafing are *group cohesiveness* and *individual responsibility*. For example, Karau and Hart (1998) showed that groups that share a common position on an issue (and therefore are cohesive) do not exhibit social loafing. To examine social responsibility, Harkins and Petty (1982) tested the hypothesis that if a person's efforts are duplicated by those of another person (and if his or her individual efforts are not identifiable), the first person is likely to exert less effort. The researchers asked participants to work in groups of four on a task that required them to report whenever a dot appeared in a particular quadrant of a video screen. In one condition, each person watched an individual quadrant and was solely responsible for detecting dots that appeared there. In the other condition, all four participants watched the same quadrant; thus, the responsibility for detecting dots was shared in that condition. Participants did not loaf when they were solely responsible for their own quadrants.

Karau and Williams (1995) found that *gender* and *culture* also appear to moderate people's tendency to become social loafers. Although all people are susceptible to social loafing, the effect is smaller in women than in men and smaller in people living in Eastern cultures than in those living in Western cultures. According to Karau and Williams (1995), across cultures, women tend to be more group oriented than men. People of both genders living in Eastern cultures tend to be more group oriented in their attitudes and behavior than do people of both genders living in Western cultures. So it seems that people living in Eastern cultures, and women in general, tend to place greater importance on participating in group activities, which may partially buffer them from social loafing effects.

Commitment and Compliance

Compliance is engaging in a behavior at another person's request. An experiment by Freedman and Fraser (1966) showed that commitment has a long-lasting effect on people's tendency to comply with requests. For example, suppose you answer a knock on your door to find a person who explains that he is a volunteer for Mothers Against Drunk Driving (MADD). He asks you to place a small sign in your front window to encourage responsible driving, and you agree to his request. Then, 2 weeks later, the same person returns and asks

---

social facilitation The enhancement of task performance caused by the mere presence of others.

social loafing The tendency of individuals to put forth decreased effort when performing a task together with other people.

compliance Engaging in a particular behavior at another person's request.

if you would allow volunteers from MADD to install a billboard on your front lawn. He shows you a photograph of an attractive house that is almost completely hidden by a huge, ugly, poorly lettered sign that says "DRIVE CAREFULLY." Do you think you would agree to this second request? Freedman and Fraser (1966) reported the powerful effects of just this type of approach. Three fourths of their participants agreed to the second request! In contrast, in a control condition in which no initial small request was made, only 17% of participants agreed to have the billboard installed. Freedman and Fraser referred to the sequence of a small request followed by a large request as the *foot-in-the-door technique.*

Once people commit themselves by making a decision and acting on it, they usually are reluctant to renounce their commitment. Commitment increases people's compliance even when the reason for the original commitment is removed. For example, recall this chapter's opening vignette, in which a commitment was made when negotiating the price of a new car—the buyer signed a formal offer to purchase the car at the proposed price and handed the salesperson a check to show a good-faith intention. However, when the salesperson returned, supposedly from talking with his manager, he said that he had made a mistake on the price and then quoted a new price many thousands of dollars higher. All too often, the customer is taken in by this ruse and agrees to the higher price. This technique is called *lowballing.*

Another tactic for using commitment to gain compliance is referred to as the *door-in-the-face technique* (Cialdini, 2000). In this case, instead of making a small initial request followed by a larger request (as in the billboard example), the would-be influencer deliberately starts with a large initial request. Now, most often it will be rejected. Once rejection occurs, it is followed by a smaller request, which is agreed to. For example, a teenager may initially ask a parent for $100 to take several friends out for pizza. After the parent's stout refusal, the teenager follows up with "Well, how about $10, then?" In these circumstances, the parent is much more likely to provide the money than if the teenager had asked for $10 at the outset.

Obedience to Authority

People tend to comply with the requests of people in authority and to be persuaded by their arguments. Society generally approves of obedience to authority when the authority figures are respected and trustworthy. It is usually the case that authority figures are well intentioned. We are aware of exceptions to this generality, however, including the genocidal regimes of tyrants ancient and modern, perhaps most darkly illustrated by those who were "just following orders" during the Nazi regime in Germany.

A disturbing example of commonplace obedience to the illegitimate demands of an authority comes from a famous series of experiments performed by Stanley Milgram (1963). Milgram had recruited participants by advertising in local newspapers—a research strategy designed to obtain as representative a sample as possible. The participants served as

"teachers" in what they were told was a memory experiment. A confederate (a middle-aged professional actor) serving as the "learner" was strapped into a chair "to prevent excessive movements when he was shocked," and electrodes were attached to his arm. The participants were told that "although the shocks can be extremely painful, they cause no permanent tissue damage."

After viewing the learner, a participant was shown to a separate room housing an apparatus with dials, a lighted display of the learner's responses, and a series of switches that supposedly delivered shocks ranging from 15 to 450 volts. The participant was instructed to use this apparatus to deliver shocks, in increments of 15 volts for each "mistake," to the learner in the other room. Beneath the switches were descriptive labels ranging from "Slight Shock" to "Danger: Severe Shock" to the ominous "XXX."

The learner gave answers to a series of questions by pressing the appropriate lever on the table in front of him. Each time he made an incorrect response, the researcher told the participant to throw another switch and give a larger shock. At the 300-volt level, the learner pounded on the wall and then stopped responding to questions. The researcher told the participant to consider "no answer" as an incorrect answer. At the 315-volt level, the learner pounded on the wall again. If the participant hesitated in delivering a shock, the researcher said, "Please go on." If this admonition was not enough, the researcher said, "The experiment requires that you continue"; then, "It is absolutely essential that you continue"; and finally, "You have no other choice; you must go on." The question of interest was how long people would continue to administer shocks to the hapless victim. Two thirds of the participants gave the learner what they believed to be the 450-volt shock, although he pounded on the wall twice and then stopped responding altogether. (See FIGURE 15•5.)

In a later experiment, when the confederate was placed in the same room and the participant could witness his struggling and apparent pain, 37.5% of the participants still obeyed the order to administer further shocks (Milgram, 1974). Thirty percent were even willing to put on a heavy leather glove to hold the learner's hand against a metal plate to force him to receive the shock.

Most people find the results of Milgram's studies surprising. They can't believe that for such a large proportion of people, the social pressure to conform to the researcher's orders is stronger than the participant's own desire not to hurt someone else. As Ross (1977) pointed out, this misperception is an example of the fundamental attribution error described earlier in the chapter. People tend to underestimate the effectiveness of situational factors and to overestimate the effectiveness of dispositional ones. Clearly, the tendency to obey an authority figure is remarkably strong.

Considerable attention has been paid to the ethical questions raised by Milgram's research (e.g., Elms, 1995). Psychologists and nonpsychologists alike have questioned whether Milgram should have conducted his experiments. For example, some critics point out that Milgram's results gave participants

[**FIGURE 15•5**] Data from one of Milgram's studies of obedience.

(After Milgram, 1963. From Baron, R. A. & Byrne, D. *Social Psychology*, 8/e. Published by Allyn and Bacon, Boston, MA. Copyright © 1997 by Pearson Education. Reprinted by permission of the publisher.)

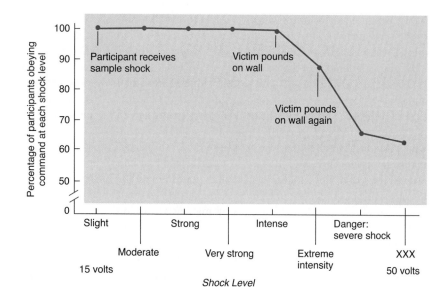

extremely negative information about themselves (specifically, about their capacity for harmful obedience)—information that they might never have learned had it not been for their participation in the research. In Milgram's defense, it must be stressed that he exercised a high degree of care with his participants—a practice followed by social psychologists today. At the end of each experimental session, he conducted an extensive debriefing in which the actual purpose of the experiment was explained to the participants. He made sure that participants understood that they were not deviant and that the situation had been very powerful. In addition, participants were later sent a detailed written report of the experimental procedure and a follow-up questionnaire asking them about their feelings regarding their participation. Interestingly, at least some people considered the enhanced insight into their own behavior to be a positive aspect of their participation. Eighty-four percent said that they were glad to have taken part in the experiment, and only 1.3% indicated that they wished they had not been involved.

Similar expressions were received from the participants in another controversial experiment on obedience to authority whose centerpiece was a simulated prison (Haney, Banks, & Zimbardo, 1973). The prison was constructed in the basement of the psychology building at Stanford University and recruited male students as participants. One of the experimenters had the role of prison warden. The participants were randomly assigned to roles as guards and prisoners, each with uniforms. The guards worked 8-hour shifts and returned to student life when not on duty. The prisoners lived at the prison around the clock. Originally the experiment was planned to last for 2 weeks, but troubling signs soon emerged, and it was discontinued after 6 days. The students assigned as guards became menacing and sadistic. The prisoners became passive, anxious, and depressed. Clearly what had begun as an objective simulation soon veered into an increasingly uncontrollable spectacle of transformation in which otherwise self-respecting and respectable people assumed not just different but frighteningly different stripes. The results were interpreted in terms of *deindividuation* (see

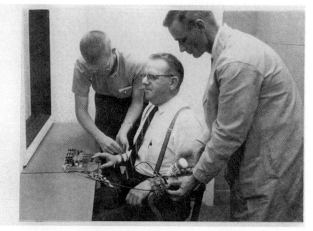

Left: The teacher's console in Milgram's experiments. The box on top of the console displayed the learner's answers to the questions. Right: A view of the teacher and researcher readying the learner for the experiment.

In the Stanford prison experiment, students were randomly assigned to roles as prisoners and guards. Their identity with those roles became so intense that the experiment was terminated well before it was scheduled to end.

Zimbardo, 1970)—the erosion of personal identity and responsibility against the backdrop of an indifferent institution.

The revelation of degradations forced on Iraqi prisoners by their U.S. military guards at the now-infamous Abu Ghraib prison near Baghdad restored interest in the Stanford prison experiment and the parallels that could be drawn. These included the violation of roles as guards overstepped their bounds and submitted their prisoners to brutal and sadistic acts in violation of international conventions and American public sentiment, and with the apparent indifference of those in higher authority. In his analysis of the parallels, Zimbardo (2007) referred to the transformations observed at Abu Ghraib as the result of a new kind of evil—the evil of knowing but not acting.

Group Decision Making

The process by which members of a group reach a decision is different from the process involved in individual decision making, if only because decisions in groups are usually preceded by discussion. However, discussion of issues relevant to a decision does not always guarantee that the best decision will be made. Two problems associated with group decision making are group polarization and groupthink.

Group Polarization In some group decision-making situations, discussion of alternative choices leads to decisions that are either riskier or more conservative than the group's initial position on the issue at hand. In general, if the initial inclination of group members is to make a risky decision, group discussion will lead to an even riskier decision. Conversely, if the initial inclination is to make a conservative decision, group discussion will usually lead to an even more conservative decision. This tendency for the initial position of a group to become exaggerated over the course of the discussion preceding a decision is called **group polarization.**

Although several explanations have been offered for group polarization, three seem particularly plausible: informational influence, repeated exposure, and normative influence (Isen-

berg, 1986). *Informational influence* is the impact of new information pertinent to the decision to be made. The new information may favor a particular decision, increasing the likelihood that more members of the group will become convinced that it is the best decision. In addition, the fact that the information is new to them may make it all the more persuasive, moving them to a more extreme position than they would have taken in the absence of such information (Stasser, 1991).

Repeated exposure to information also may play a role. When group members discuss issues, they tend to repeat the points previously identified as relevant to the decision. Brauer, Judd, and Gliner (1995) showed that the repeated expression of attitudes during group discussion was positively related to the extremity of group polarization—a finding that is consistent with the claim presented earlier in the chapter that mere exposure can increase the strength of attitudes.

Normative influence occurs when individuals compare their own views with the group norm. People in groups receive social reinforcement for agreeing with the views of others. The more strongly group members wish to achieve cohesion in decision making, the greater the tendency for individual group members to embrace the majority decision—no matter how extreme that decision might be.

Groupthink Irving Janis studied a related phenomenon that sometimes occurs in group decision making—**groupthink**, the tendency to avoid dissent so as to achieve consensus (Janis, 1972, 1982). Janis developed the theory of groupthink after analyzing the decision making that led U.S. President John F. Kennedy to order an ill-fated attempt to overthrow Fidel Castro's regime at the Bay of Pigs in Cuba in 1961. The decision was made by Kennedy and a small group of advisers. Janis studied the situational influences that led to this infamous decision as well as other well-publicized group decisions that altered the course of 20th-century history.

Janis's concept of groupthink specifies the conditions necessary for its occurrence as well as its symptoms and consequences. As shown in FIGURE 15•6, the conditions that foster groupthink include a stressful situation in which the stakes are very high, a group of people who already tend to think alike and who are isolated from others who could offer criticism of the decision, and a strong group leader who makes his or her position on the issue at hand well known to the group. In the Bay of Pigs example, the overthrow of a dictator seen as an archenemy of the United States was at stake, Kennedy's advisers were likeminded regarding the invasion and met in secret, and Kennedy was a forceful and charismatic leader who made his intentions to invade Cuba known to them. (Note: Parallels to the U.S. overthrow of Saddam Hussein may be difficult to resist here.)

Janis noted five symptoms of groupthink, all of which characterize the decision to invade Cuba. First, group members

---

group polarization The tendency for the initial position of a group to become more extreme during the discussion preceding a decision.

groupthink Group members' tendency to avoid dissent in the attempt to achieve consensus in the course of decision making.

[FIGURE 15·6]
A summary of Janis's
conception of groupthink.

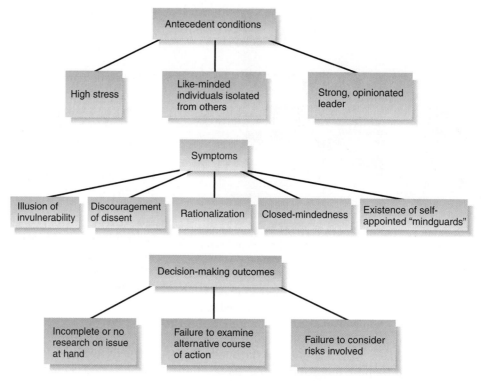

share the illusion that their decision is sound, moral, and right—in a word, invulnerable. Second, dissent from the leader's views is discouraged, further supporting the illusion that the group's decision is right. Third, instead of assessing the strengths and weaknesses of the decision, group members rationalize their decision, looking only for reasons to support it. Fourth, group members are closed-minded—they are not willing to listen to alternative suggestions and ideas; and fifth, self-appointed "mindguards" exist within the group and actively discourage dissent from the group norm. When combined, these symptoms are a recipe for flawed decision making. People caught up in groupthink tend to conduct limited research on the issue at hand, often fail to examine alternative courses of action, and often fail to consider potential risks inherent in the decision.

Janis argued that groups can avoid groupthink by taking several precautions. First, group leaders should encourage criticism from group members. Second, the group should seek relevant input from experts who are not members. Third, the group should break into smaller subgroups in which different ideas and opinions can be generated and developed before convening the whole group. And fourth, the group leader should avoid overstating his or her position on the matter and should be on guard for rationalization, closed-mindedness, and illusions of invulnerability.

In their analysis of effective leadership and personality, Hogan et al. (1994) found a close connection between effectiveness and the dimensions of the five-factor model of personality (see Chapter 14):

> . . . leaders with high [extraversion] scores communicate more with their teams, which increases the possibility that the team understands its goal and the performance standards required to achieve it. Moreover,

[openness means] these leaders are better able to build alliances with people outside of the team, which allows them to secure necessary equipment and resources. Conscientiousness is related to being perceived as trustworthy, planful, and organized. Agreeableness is related to communication, trust, and morale. [Neuroticism] is associated with seeming steady under pressure, able to resolve conflicts, and to handle negative feedback, all of which promote team effectiveness. (p. 498)

In the authors' view, it is possible for leaders to improve on these factors and thereby render groupthink less likely to occur.

Resisting Social Influences

At first glance, social influence may appear to be negative, but as Robert Cialdini (1993) pointed out, this conclusion is not warranted. Most of the time, humans profit from our tendency to be fair in our interactions with others, to take our cues for acting from one another, to honor our commitments, to obey authority figures, and to cooperate in group interactions. If we had to expend time and effort in consciously deciding what to do in every situation, we would be exhausted. However, no general rule works all of the time; exceptions can occur and have bad effects. For example, an authority figure can order us to do things that ultimately hurt us or others. Advertisers and sales representatives who know the rules of social influence can induce us to make unnecessary and costly expenditures.

Cialdini suggested that the best way to defend ourselves from the unscrupulous use of social influence is to be sensitive to ourselves and *to the situation*. Whenever we spend money or commit ourselves to do something that will cost us time and effort, we should ask ourselves whether we feel any discomfort in doing so. Do we feel pressured? Do we feel tense? Do we wish we were somewhere (or someone) else? If so, we may be the on the receiving end of manipulation. We should try to relax and step back from the situation. Does the other person stand to profit from what he or she is trying to get us to do? If we could go back to the time just before we got into the situation, would we put ourselves where we are now, or would we avoid doing so? If the latter, then now is the time to leave. The feeling that we have to keep going, that we have to live up to our commitment, is exactly what the other person is counting on. If someone tricks us into making a commitment, we should feel no compunction about breaking it. If someone tries to abuse our natural tendencies to be fair in our interactions with others, we should fight back. Otherwise, we run the risk of becoming cynical in our dealings with other people who are not trying to take advantage of us.

QUESTIONS TO CONSIDER

1. How would social life be different if people tended not to conform to social norms? Think of a recent instance in which your behavior conformed to a social norm. How might the outcome of this social interaction have been different had you not conformed?

2. In life-saving and cardiopulmonary resuscitation (CPR) classes, students are taught to take control in emergency situations. For example, in a situation in which a person appears to be drowning, they learn to assign onlookers specific responsibilities, such as calling 911, fetching rescue equipment, and so on. To what extent does taking control in this manner enhance bystander intervention? What effect might it have on the diffusion of responsibility among onlookers?

3. As you consider the classic studies by Milgram and by Zimbardo and colleagues, together with reports of the atrocities at Abu Ghraib and Guantanamo Bay, consider what it must have been like to be involved. At what point would you have first raised concern about what was happening? What aspects of the situation likely would have caused you to do so? What aspects of the situation might have caused you to forego your concern and continue in your duties?

Interpersonal Attraction and Loving

When an individual conforms to a group norm, it is the individual, not the group, who is being influenced. When you comply with the request of a car salesperson or obey the dictates of an authority figure, the influence flows in one direction; it is your behavior that is being influenced. However, many kinds of social influence are reciprocal. As we see in this section, the behavior of two individuals may produce a mutual, although not necessarily equal, influence.

Several factors may contribute to the interpersonal attraction reflected in informal neighborhood gatherings.

Interpersonal Attraction

Many factors determine **interpersonal attraction**—people's tendency to approach each other and evaluate each other positively. Although the factors that influence interpersonal attraction are complex, they involve social reinforcement in one way or another. People learn to act in ways that reinforce friends and lovers. In doing so, they maintain and strengthen affiliation in ways that involve positive evaluation, familiarity, similarity, and physical appearance.

Positive Evaluation Humans like to be evaluated positively—to be held in high regard by other people. We like those who treat us well and dislike those who don't (Byrne & Griffitt, 1973).

Familiarity For an attraction to form between people, they must meet each other. Festinger, Schachter, and Back (1959) found that the likelihood of friendships between people who lived in an apartment house was related to the closeness between the apartments in which they lived—their *proximity*. The closer the apartments, the more likely the friendship was. People also were unlikely to have friends who lived on a different floor unless their apartments were next to a stairway, where they would meet people going up or down the stairs.

Repetition generally increases our preference for a stimulus (the *mere exposure effect*). This phenomenon applies to the attraction between people as well. Even in the brief time it takes to participate in an experiment, familiarity affects interpersonal attraction. Saegert, Swap, and Zajonc (1973) asked college women to participate in an experiment that supposedly involved the sense of taste. Pairs of female students entered booths, where they tasted and rated various

---

interpersonal attraction People's tendency to approach each other and to evaluate each other positively.

liquids. The movements of the students from booth to booth were arranged so that pairs of women were together from 0 to 10 times. Afterward, the participants rated how likable each of the other students in the experiment was. Likeability was directly related to the number of interactions any two participants had had—the more interactions a student had had with a fellow participant, the more likable she found her.

Similarity Another factor that influences interpersonal attraction is similarity—and not oppositeness—in looks, interests, and attitudes (Byrne, 1997; Jones et al., 2004). A tendency exists for people in close relationships to be similar in physical attractiveness. Research indicates that couples who are mismatched in this respect are the most likely to break up (White, 1980; Smith et al., 1993). Although it might seem reasonable for people to seek the most attractive partners they could find, the fear of rejection and ridicule may prevent this from occurring. Men tend to be afraid of approaching attractive women (Bernstein et al., 1983). Research by Rowatt, Cunningham, and Druen (1999) showed that both men and women are more likely to lie about their personal appearance, personality traits, income, past-relationship outcomes, career skills, and intelligence to prospective dates who they judge to be more attractive.

Survey research has made a strong case for the claim that "likes attract." Buston and Emlen (2003; see also Mulder, 2003) found that individuals expressed preference for long-term mates who matched their own self-perceptions on 10 difference attributes. A large-scale study (Kurzban & Weeden, 2003) of more than 10,000 clients of a speed-dating service showed that preferences were determined by the perception of agreed-on mate values and that the extent of agreement was based largely on perceptions of physical characteristics. However, Todd et al. (2007) found that, although mate preferences reported before speed dating matched self-perceptions, the actual choice of a dating partner was more closely reflective of the preferences consistent with evolutionary theory (see later).

In addition to being similar in physical attractiveness, couples also tend to be similar in personality, attitudes, and intelligence (Brehm, 1992; Montoya & Horton, 2004)—and the greater the similarity between the partners, the more enduring their relationship (Hatfield & Rapson, 1993). Presumably, a person who shares our attitudes is likely to approve of us when we express them. Having friends who have similar attitudes guarantees that our opinions are likely to find a positive reception; we tend to avoid the unpleasant experience of saying things that bring disapproval from others.

Other kinds of similarities are also important, such as age, occupational status, and ethnic background. Friends tend to have similar backgrounds as well as similar attitudes.

Physical Appearance People commonly judge one another to some extent on the basis of a characteristic that is supposed to be only skin deep—attractive physical appearance. In general, we are more attracted to good-looking people

than to those who are not (Albright, Kenny, & Malloy, 1988). In fact, the beautiful-person stereotype has a strong influence (see, e.g., Dion, Berscheid, & Walster, 1972; Dion, 1986), especially in the United States and Canada, where beautiful people are seen as happier, more intelligent, and more socially skilled than are those who are less physically attractive (Eagly et al., 1991).

This bias extends to at least one Eastern culture, although interesting differences are found. Wheeler and Kim (1997) found that college students in Korea shared most of the biases shown by North Americans, but also saw beautiful people as more trustworthy and concerned for others, differences not found in North America. Korean students did not share the North American bias toward perceiving beautiful people as more self-assertive and dominant than plainer people. Recall the earlier assertion that in collectivist cultures (such as Korea), great value is placed on interconnectedness, whereas in individualist cultures, independence and personal achievement are more valued.

When people publicly discuss the factors that are important in dating partners, they usually do not dwell on physical attractiveness. Why? One possibility is that they are perfectly aware that physical appearance strongly affects their choices and desires, but social norms and common wisdom (e.g., "beauty is only skin deep") inhibit them from dwelling on its prime importance. They do not want to appear superficial. Another possibility is that although people are aware of the stereotype of beauty, they do not believe that it affects their personal decisions and behavior—it's something that influences other people. Hadjistavropoulos and Genest (1994) examined these possibilities by using a special measurement system that encourages honest answering. Participants who responded under this system indicated a stronger influence of physical appearance on their attraction to others than did control participants who responded to conventional questioning.

Physically attractive people seem to benefit in many ways from this stereotype. Being good-looking can open many doors, but would it surprise you to know that most elements of the stereotype are wrong? Being beautiful guarantees none of the correspondingly beautiful qualities (Feingold, 1992).

focus **On**

Arousal and Interpersonal Attraction

People may be attracted to one another under almost any circumstances. Hollywood often idealizes romantic relationships by showing us how they unfold under the most unlikely circumstances.

Against a backdrop of war, earthquake, shipwreck, alien invasion, or jealous rivals, the spark ignites between the hero and heroine, who then brave all manner of extremity to keep romance alive. Melodramatic, perhaps . . . and yet, as Walster and Berscheid (1971) put it, "Passion sometimes develops in conditions that would seem more likely to provoke aggression and hatred" (p. 47). Why does romantic attraction emerge when better-fitting reactions seem called for? Situational factors may be the answer.

Consider a well-known study conducted by Dutton and Aron (1974), who arranged for an attractive woman to interview male college students briefly as they walked across a narrow suspension bridge. The bridge was about 5 feet wide, 400 feet long, and 200 feet above a river gorge. It swayed and wobbled erratically when someone walked across it. The same woman also interviewed control participants who had crossed a sturdy, pillar-supported foot bridge that spanned a 10-foot drop. After each interview, the woman gave her business card with telephone number to all participants with the suggestion that they call her if they wanted to discuss the experiment further.

The men who crossed the suspension bridge apparently found the woman more attractive than did those who walked the fixed-position bridge—they were much more likely to telephone her later. The authors hypothesized that the anxiety produced by moving across the suspension bridge increased the men's attraction toward the woman and explained their findings in terms of attribution theory. In their view, if a man feels increased arousal in the presence of a woman, he attributes the arousal to the most obvious stimulus—the woman—and may conclude that he is attracted to her. This is what happened to the participants who crossed the suspension bridge. Later, they followed up on their earlier conclusion by telephoning her.

Arousal—pleasant or aversive—tends to increase interpersonal attraction between men and women. This is not a new idea. An ancient Roman expert advised men to take their women to the Coliseum to see the gladiators fight because the experience would increase their romantic inclinations. Interpersonal attraction is complex. It develops under wide-ranging conditions that are hardly ideal, nor are they conditions in which one person invariably helps to reduce the other's fear or anxiety. The role of arousal in interpersonal attraction is still a matter of scientific interest, as is the process whereby such attraction is transformed into love (Foster et al., 1998).

Loving

The relationships we have with others generally are marked by two different kinds of emotion: **liking,** a feeling of personal regard, intimacy, and esteem toward another person, and **loving,** a combination of liking and a deep sense of attachment to another person. However, loving someone does not necessarily entail romance. For example, a person may have several close friends whom she or he loves dearly yet has no desire to be involved with romantically.

Romantic love, also called **passionate love,** is an emotionally intense desire for sexual intimacy with another person (Hatfield, 1988). Feeling romantic love generally involves

Growing older need not be a barrier to interpersonal attraction.

experiencing five closely intertwined elements: desiring intimacy with another person, feeling passion for that person, being preoccupied with thoughts of that person, depending emotionally on that person, and feeling elated if that person reciprocates romantic love or dejected if she or he doesn't.

"Falling in love" and "being in love" are common expressions that people use to describe their sexual desires for each other. Passionate love may occur at almost any time during life, although people involved in long-term cohabitation or marriage may eventually experience a qualitatively different kind of love. The partners may still make passionate love to one another, but passion is no longer the sole defining characteristic of the relationship. What emerges is called **companionate love** and is characterized by a deep, enduring affection and caring for another. Companionate love is also marked by a mutual sense of commitment, that is, a strong desire to maintain the relationship. How passionate love develops into companionate love is presently an unanswered question, although odds are that the sort of intimacy that punctuates romantic love is still a major force in the companionate relationship (Sprecher & Regan, 1998). An important feature of intimacy is *self-disclosure,* or the ability to share deeply private feelings and thoughts with another. Indeed, part of loving another is feeling comfortable disclosing deeply personal aspects of yourself.

Robert Sternberg has developed a "triangular" theory of how intimacy, passion, and commitment may combine to produce liking and several different forms of love (Sternberg, 1988b; Barnes & Sternberg, 1997; Lemieux & Hale, 2002). As

---

liking A feeling of personal regard, intimacy, and esteem toward another person.

loving A combination of liking and a deep sense of attachment to, intimacy with, and caring for another person.

passionate love An emotional, intense desire for sexual union with another person; also called romantic love.

companionate love Love that is characterized by a deep, enduring affection and caring for another person, accompanied by a strong desire to maintain the relationship.

[TABLE 15·3] Sternberg's Theory of Love

According to Robert Sternberg, love is based on different combinations of intimacy, passion, and commitment. These elements may combine to form eight different kinds of relationships.

	Intimacy	Passion	Commitment
Non-love			
Liking	*****		
Infatuated love		*****	
Empty love			*****
Romantic love	*****	*****	
Companionate love	*****		*****
Fatuous love		*****	*****
Consummate love	*****	*****	*****

***** indicates that the element is present in the relationship; a blank space indicates that the element is not present or is present only at a low level in the relationship.

Source: After Sternberg, R. J. (1986). A triangular theory of love. *Psychological Bulletin*, 93, 119–135.

shown in TABLE 15·3, liking is solely a matter of intimacy, infatuation involves only passion, and empty love consists entirely of commitment. Combining two of the basic elements produces new kinds of love. Romantic love requires both intimacy and passion but not commitment. Companionate love entails both intimacy and commitment but not passion. Fatuous love (a kind of love marked by complacency) is defined by passion and commitment but not intimacy. For Sternberg, the highest form of love, consummate love, contains all three elements.

Sternberg's theory is descriptive. It characterizes categories of love but does not explain their origins or functions. In human evolution, love was associated with procreation and child rearing. Although love of another person is not a necessary requirement for sexual intercourse, partners who passionately love each other are more likely to have sex than are those who do not. If they produce a child, then love serves another function—it increases the likelihood that both parents will share in the responsibilities of caring for and rearing that child. The human capacity for loving, then, contributes in practical ways to the continued existence of one's genes.

focus On

The Evolution of Love

You may not be married now, and you may not be interested in becoming married, at least right away. But chances are that one day the "right" person will come along, and you will fall in love with that person, perhaps get married, and perhaps have children. If so, what will make that person right for you?

The answer may be found in evolutionary psychology, which, as you may recall from Chapter 3, is the study of

the biological basis of social behavior. Evolutionary psychology predicts that gender influences what people find attractive in their potential mates. Specifically, gender matters because males and females differ in their biological and psychological "investments" in reproduction and child rearing (Buss, 2006).

As Chapter 3 pointed out, the costs of sexual behavior and reproduction are enormously greater for women than for men (Kenrick et al., 1993). Evolutionary psychologists argue that because of this difference, natural selection has favored gender-specific mating strategies. Because male reproductive success requires mating with fertile females, men seek potential mates who are capable of reproduction (Buss, 1992). Here lies a problem—how can men tell if a woman is fertile? According to Buss (1989) and Symons (1979), men should prefer younger women to older ones because age is highly correlated with female fertility. A reliable clue to a woman's age is her physical appearance: smooth skin, absence of gray hair, girlish figure, white teeth, and high energy level (Buss, 1992). Thus, in their quest to find a mate, men place a premium on these features (e.g., Li, et al., 2002).

In contrast, because the woman's reproductive success is dependent on her investment of biological resources, women seek potential mates who can provide other types of resources, such as food, shelter, protection, and, in general, social and economic resources. How can a woman tell if a potential mate has and is willing to provide these resources? Evolutionary psychologists assert that her best clues will be primarily the man's socioeconomic status and, to a lesser extent, his ability to work hard, his intelligence, and his kindness (Buss, 1992; Kenrick, et al., 1994).

Research in evolutionary psychology has thus shown that in evaluating potential mates, men place greater emphasis on physical appearance than do women, and that women value social status more than do men. For example, Buss (1990) asked people from 37 different cultures to assess which characteristics they found most desirable in a mate. Men from all cultures ranked physical attractiveness higher than women did, and women in 36 of the 37 cultures placed a greater emphasis on socioeconomic status than men did. These results confirm earlier findings showing that the physical attractiveness of a woman is a better predictor of the socioeconomic status of her husband than is her intelligence, education, or wealth (Elder, 1969). Buss's cross-cultural data also support the prediction that men will prefer younger women: The mean age difference between men and women on their wedding days was 2.99 years—with the bride being younger.

Buss also has shown that these tendencies translate into actual differences in the tactics men and women choose to attract potential mates (Buss & Schmitt, 1993; Schmitt & Buss, 1996). In the context of short-term relationships, men use tactics involving displays of their resources—flashing money, taking their dates to fancy restaurants for dinner, and driving expensive cars. In contrast, women use tactics that enhance their physical attractiveness—dieting, wearing makeup, and wearing flattering clothing. When the issue is long-term loving relationships, women offer sexual fidelity, and men offer the resources necessary for financial security.

The differential importance men and women assign to physical attractiveness and socioeconomic status in mate selection also turn out to have an important effect on how people evaluate their partners in existing relationships. In a study conducted by Kenrick and colleagues (1994), nearly 400 male and female college students involved in heterosexual dating relationships viewed photographs and read accompanying descriptions of people of the opposite gender. The participants were told they were helping the researchers improve the format for a university-sponsored dating service. In actuality, the researchers wished to learn how viewing the photographs and reading the descriptions would influence the participants' perceptions of their current dating partners.

The people depicted in the photographs were either highly attractive professional models or rather average-looking students. The descriptions accompanying the photographs varied only according to a score on a personality test of dominance that the researchers defined as representing the person's natural leadership abilities. Participants were told that a high dominance score meant that the person in the photograph was "authoritative and masterful" and that a low score meant that the person was "obedient and submissive." The photographs and descriptions were arranged to produce four combinations: physically attractive and high in dominance; physically attractive and low in dominance; average-looking and high in dominance; and average-looking and low in dominance.

Kenrick and his colleagues found clear gender differences in their participants' evaluations after exposure to the photographs. The right graph in FIGURE 15•7 shows that, compared with men who saw the photographs of average-looking women, men shown the photographs of physically attractive women rated their current dating relationships less favorably when the women were described as low in dominance. (Dominant physically attractive women had no effect on the men's evaluations of their current dating relationships.) In contrast, the left graph shows that women who viewed photographs of dominant men—be they average-looking or handsome—tended to rate their current dating relationships as less satisfactory than did women who viewed photographs of the men described as being low in dominance.

In sum, it can be argued that natural selection has shaped gender-specific social cognition—that is, gender-specific ways of attending to, perceiving, interpreting, and responding to information in the social environment (Kenrick, Li, & Butner, 2003). The reason is that each gender makes different contributions to courtship and child rearing. Although chance and circumstance may determine where we live and what people we meet, evolutionary psychologists argue that our evolutionary history has provided the social and cognitive mechanisms through which we become attracted to and fall in love with the "right" person. Whether the evidence is sufficient to make it a strong argument and whether gender differences in mate selection are fixed components of human nature remain matters of debate (see, e.g., Buller, 2005).

Evolutionary psychological theories of social behavior are largely promissory, as the evolutionary past is unrecoverable when it comes to actual behavior. Theories are supported by "reverse engineering" scenarios in the effort to connect present behavior with ancestral contexts in which that behavior may have conferred an adaptive advantage.

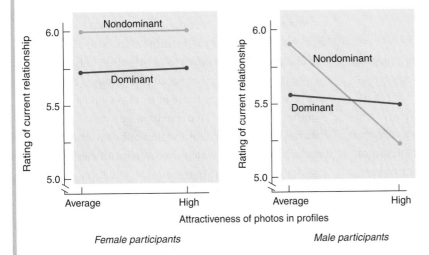

Female participants   *Male participants*

[**FIGURE 15•7**] Results of Kenrick and colleagues' study of the effects of gender, dominance, and physical attractiveness on college students' evaluations of their current dating relationships. Males shown photographs of physically attractive, nondominant females rated their commitments to their current dating relationships lower than when shown photographs in the other three categories. Females who viewed photographs of dominant males, regardless of the males' physical attractiveness, rated their commitments to their current dating relationships lower.

(From Kenrick, D. T., Neuberg, S. L., Zierk, K. L., & Krones, J. M. (1994). Evolution and social cognition: Contrast effects as a function of sex, dominance, and physical attractiveness. *Personality and Social Psychology Bulletin, 20*, 210–217. Copyright © 1994. Reprinted by permission of Sage Publications, Inc.)

Doing so often raises more questions that it can answer. In addition, the theories often fail to consider plausible alternatives that invoke current social environments as sufficiently explanatory. According to a review of the psychology of love (Reis & Aron, 2008), the evolutionary psychological framework has invigorated theory and research, especially involving neurological correlates. Future research is likely to focus on the finer-grain adaptive features of passionate and companionate love, bringing fresh insight into "what predicts who will fall in love with whom; the typical trajectories of love over time; the mechanisms that account for variations in those trajectories; and how experiences and behaviors of love vary across individual differences, cultures, and species" (p. 84).

QUESTIONS TO CONSIDER

1. To what kinds of people are you most attracted? What factors appear to be most important in your relationships with those people? Are those factors consistent with the evolutionary psychology of mate selection? If so, in what ways?

2. Is Sternberg's theory of love an accurate account of your own experience thus far with different kinds of love? Provide examples. Are there kinds of love in your experience that are not included in his theory? If so, how do you describe them?

Epilogue

Caveats for the Study of Social Psychology

Much of this chapter takes its inspiration from the Prologue, which reported the application of a social psychological concept, in this case, lowballing. Throughout the chapter, other concepts are posed against the backdrop of social psychological research and application, not least because, as a college student, social cognition, presentation, and social interaction are predominant aspects of your everyday life, not to mention the priority you may place on interpersonal attraction and, possibly, mate selection. At the same time, you may have noticed a conspicuous absence of reference to neuroscience and to theoretical models based on neuroscientific findings, which were common fare in previous chapters.

The Epilogue addresses this gap. It would be a disservice to you were the chapter to end without mention of the growing intersection between social psychology and cognitive neuroscience. The intersection has been christened officially as *social neuroscience* (sometimes *social cognitive neuroscience*) and now sports a journal by that title and a growing cadre of researchers and theorists (e.g., Azar, 2002; Cacioppo, 2002; Decety & Keenan, 2006; Harmon-Jones & Winkielman, 2007). As you might expect, the new discipline seeks the neurophysiological substrates for social psychological concepts and theories, including attribution, stereotyping, prejudice, attitudes, cognitive dissonance, and interpersonal attraction. Social psychologists and cognitive neuroscientists team to design and conduct research using electrophysiological recording procedures (event-related potential, for example) and brain imaging (especially *f*MRI), among other methods.

For example, the discovery of *mirror neurons* in the inferior prefrontal cortex of monkeys by Italian researchers in the early 1990s (di Pellegrino, et al., 1992) prompted models of social cognition (see Liberman, 2007). Specific mirror neurons fire when the individual performs a specific action (such as grasping a peanut) but also when the individual observes another individual performing a similar action. McGovern (2007) argued that mirror neurons constitute the substrate for the child's acquisition of a *theory of mind* (see Chapter 12) by which she or he learns to discriminate others' intentions and their cognitive states more generally. Mundy and Newell (2007) proposed that social cognition begins to develop as the anterior and posterior attention systems (see Chapter 9) become integrated so as to allow the child to monitor her or his own attention and that of others (what the authors call *joint attention*). They argue that this ability is critical for the formation and maintenance of social relationships and that impaired relationships (such as those in autistic-spectrum disorders—see Chapter 16) result when joint attention fails to develop.

At the same time that social psychology is turning to cognitive neuroscience, those in its ranks who question whether it is guilty of an overreliance on certain methods that neglect the direct observation of behavior. In other words, has social psychology become insufficiently behavioral for its own good? To remedy the situation, social psychologists can look to the example of the classic studies cited in this chapter, many of which paid direct attention to the behavior of the participant and its relation to situational variables. The challenge will be to revise existing methods and develop new ones that are explicitly behavioral while assuring a precision of experimental control that will expose the social variables of which behavior is a function in clear relief.

CHAPTER SUMMARY

Social Cognition

Social cognition involves our perception and interpretation of information about our social environment and our behavior in response to that environment. Our experiences give rise to schemas, that is, the rules and representations by which we organize and synthesize information about ourselves and our interactions with others. Characterizing people in terms of central traits helps us to form impressions of them. The initial information we learn about someone plays an important part in forming our impressions—a tendency called the *primacy effect.*

A person's self-concept represents his or her knowledge, feelings, and beliefs about himself or herself. At the center of the self-concept is the self-schema by which we process and interpret information about the self. Different cultures often have different ways of conceptualizing the self. Western cultures emphasize the self's uniqueness, whereas Eastern cultures emphasize the interdependence of the self and others.

We attribute particular instances of behavior to two types of factors: dispositional and situational. A behavior that is high in consensus (many other people act the same way), high in distinctiveness (occurs only in the particular situation), and consistent over time is usually attributed to the situation. Behavior low in consensus, low in distinctiveness, and consistent over time is usually attributed to disposition.

The fundamental attribution error occurs because we tend to overemphasize dispositional factors and underemphasize situational factors in judging the causes of others' behavior. One example of the fundamental attribution error is the belief that people get what they deserve in life; that is, the belief in a just world. Our tendency to see our own behavior as influenced more by situational than by dispositional factors and others' behavior as due more to dispositional than to situational factors is called the actor–observer effect. However, when it comes to our successes and failures, we display the self-serving bias: We tend to attribute our successes to dispositional factors and our failures to situational factors. The error known as false consensus is our tendency to believe that others act and believe much as we do, even when they do not. A related error is that we consciously control what we do. The illusion of conscious will arises from the conjunction of consistency, exclusivity, and priority.

The representativeness heuristic is a mental shortcut in which we seize on a few especially salient characteristics to categorize a person or situation. Thus, we sometimes ignore other evidence and may commit the base-rate error. When we rely on the availability heuristic, we judge the importance or the frequency of events by the ease with which examples are recalled.

Attitudes: Their Formation and Change

Attitudes have affective components; behavioral components, which are primarily formed through direct or vicarious classical conditioning and are affected by behavioral components of specificity, motivational relevance, accessibility, constraints, and by cognitive components.

Explicit attempts to change our attitudes often involve persuasion. We tend to be persuaded by arguments that have a credible source or an attractive source. Aspects of the message being delivered in a persuasive appeal also are important. If we know little about an issue or already hold a strong opinion about it, then we are likely to be persuaded by a one-sided argument. However, if we are already well informed about the issue, then we are likely to find a two-sided argument more persuasive. Scare tactics appear to work best when they are emotional and include information that describes how to change behavior. According to the elaboration likelihood model, persuasive messages follow a central route, a peripheral route, or both.

Festinger's theory of cognitive dissonance suggests reasons for interactions between attitudes and behavior. It proposes that discrepancies between attitudes and behavior, or between one attitude and another, lead to the unpleasant state of cognitive dissonance. We can reduce dissonance by reducing the importance of dissonant elements, adding consonant elements, or changing one of the dissonant elements.

Bem's alternative to cognitive dissonance—self-perception theory—suggests that many of our attitudes are based on self-observation. When our attitudes are ambiguous, we look to the situation for motivational clues. If situational clues are unavailable, we tend to attribute our attitudes dispositionally.

Stereotypes and Prejudice

A prejudice is a negative evaluation of a group of people defined by such characteristics as race, ethnicity, religion, gender, socioeconomic status, or sexual orientation. Prejudices involve stereotypes that include false beliefs about the characteristics possessed by members of a particular group. Prejudices often lead to discrimination—actual behaviors injurious to the members of the group. Intergroup conflicts often have at their core the belief that individuals' own group (the in-group) is superior to or more deserving than another group (the out-group).

One of the primary causes of prejudice appears to be competition between groups for limited resources and the increased self-esteem that results from affiliating with a group perceived to be better than other groups. The study at the boys' camp by Sherif and his colleagues indicates just how easily prejudices can form, even when the groups consist of similar individuals. Although increased contact between in-group and out-group may promote changes of attitude, the effects are not necessarily the same for members of the two groups.

Heuristics guide our social encounters. Use of the availability heuristic means that negative behaviors often are more vivid than positive behaviors, and out-group members are especially noticeable. Thus, when out-group members commit a deviant act, we are more likely to remember it. We then incorrectly conclude that such behavior is a characteristic of the out-group as a whole. Such a conclusion is referred to as an illusory correlation.

People also are susceptible to the illusion of out-group homogeneity. Although they realize that their in-group contains members who are very different from one another, they tend to view members of out-groups as similar to one another.

Some social psychologists suggest an evolutionary explanation of in-group and out-group biases. They propose that competitive needs favored the development of cognitive structures that quickly (and unconsciously) categorized in-group and out-group members. Research with the Implicit Association Test has confirmed the existence of prejudices of which individuals are unaware.

Prejudices have many harmful effects, such as the self-fulfilling prophecy, in which being perceived and treated as inferior leads the victim of prejudice to act that way. Although many instances of prejudice may be inadvertent, when people are taught to think about members of out-groups as individuals having specific rather than generalized characteristics, they can learn to avoid injurious conduct toward those in the out-group.

Social Influences and Group Behavior

Experimental social psychology has shown just how potent social influences can be. We tend to do what others do, conforming to social norms and preferring not to disagree with the attitudes and judgments that others express. This tendency undoubtedly serves us well most of the time, but the fact that people are less likely to assist someone if other bystanders are present shows that others' influence can also have unfortunate effects. Research on the positive influences of groups is gaining momentum as part of an emerging movement known as positive psychology.

When people are part of a group or are observed by others, they act differently than when they are alone. In general, the presence of observers increases arousal, which increases the likelihood that a performer will make the dominant response called for by the task; depending on the complexity of the task, this effect can either facilitate or inhibit successful performance. When performing as part of a group, a person will often make less vigorous efforts if individual contribution cannot be identified—a phenomenon known as social loafing. Three important interpersonal variables that reduce social loafing are individual identifiability, group cohesiveness, and individual responsibility.

When we commit ourselves to a course of action, we tend to persist in the commitment. Research has revealed several techniques for promoting compliance by exploiting commitment, including the foot-in-the-door, lowballing, and door-in-the-face approaches. Milgram's famous research showed that people will obey outlandish, even inhumane, requests from those perceived as authority figures. The Stanford prison experiment demonstrated the extent to which individuals may be transformed by their roles to destructive ends.

Group decision making may be hampered by group polarization and groupthink. In group polarization, the initial inclination of the group becomes exaggerated to one extreme or the other. Informational influence, repeated exposure, and normative influence tend to promote polarization. Groupthink develops in highly stressful situations in which the group making a decision includes an opinionated leader and like-minded individuals who are isolated from others. Groupthink is characterized by feelings that the group's decision is invulnerable, by lack of dissent, by rationalization, by closed-mindedness, and by "mindguards." Although our tendency to be influenced socially is generally in our best interest, sometimes unscrupulous persons take advantage of this tendency in attempts to exploit us. The best way to protect ourselves from such persons is to become more reflective about the situations in which such exploitation is likely to occur and to resist others' manipulativeness directly.

Interpersonal Attraction and Loving

Interpersonal attraction involves social reinforcement. It is increased by another's positive evaluation, familiarity, proximity, similarity, shared attitudes, and good looks.

Loving someone entails a combination of liking and strong feelings of attachment. Sternberg's theory of love describes how different combinations of intimacy, passion, and commitment give rise to liking and to different kinds of love. For example, romantic love involves both intimacy and passion, but infatuation involves only passion. The combination of all three elements is referred to as consummate love.

From the standpoint of evolutionary psychology, love serves both procreative and child-rearing functions. Evolutionary psychologists have observed that men and women differ with respect to the social-cognitive cues they use when selecting potential mates. Men prefer potential mates who are young and physically attractive, because they tend to be fertile. Women prefer potential mates who control socioeconomic resources because these resources are vital for the care of offspring.

succeed with mypsychlab

Visit MyPsychLab for practice quizzes, flashcards, and dozens of videos and animated tutorials, including the following items you can find in the "Multimedia Library":

Becoming a Detective of Social Influence: Robert Cialdini

Cognitive Dissonance & Attitude Change
Bystander Intervention

Unconscious Stereotyping
Social Facilitation
Helping a Stranger

KEY TERMS

actor–observer effect *p. 458*

attitude *p. 460*

attribution *p. 456*

availability heuristic *p. 460*

base-rate fallacy *p. 460*

belief in a just world *p. 458*

bystander intervention *p. 470*

central traits *p. 453*

cognitive dissonance theory *p. 463*

companionate love *p. 479*

compliance *p. 472*

conformity *p. 469*

consensus *p. 456*

consistency *p. 456*

diffusion of responsibility *p. 471*

discrimination *p. 465*

dispositional factors *p. 456*

distinctiveness *p. 456*

elaboration likelihood model *p. 462*

ethnocentrism *p. 465*

false consensus *p. 459*

fundamental attribution error *p. 457*

group *p. 469*

group polarization *p. 475*

groupthink *p. 475*

illusion of out-group homogeneity *p. 467*

illusory correlation *p. 467*

impression formation *p. 453*

interpersonal attraction *p. 477*

liking *p. 479*

loving *p. 479*

mere exposure effect *p. 461*

passionate love *p. 479*

prejudice *p. 465*

primacy effect *p. 454*

representativeness heuristic *p. 460*

self-concept *p. 454*

self-fulfilling prophecy *p. 468*

self-handicapping *p. 459*

self-perception theory *p. 464*

self-schema *p. 454*

self-serving bias *p. 459*

situational factors *p. 456*

social cognition *p. 453*

social facilitation *p. 472*

social loafing *p. 472*

social norms *p. 469*

social psychology *p. 453*

stereotype *p. 465*

SUGGESTIONS FOR FURTHER READING

Baron, R. A., Byrne, D., & Branscombe, H. R. (2008). *Social psychology* (12th ed.). Boston: Allyn & Bacon.

This textbook offers a solid, comprehensive introduction to social psychology and expands on the topics in this chapter.

Buss, D. M. (2003). *The evolution of desire: Strategies of human mating.* New York: Basic Books.

A leading evolutionary psychologist summarizes his large-scale (37 cultures) survey of human mating preferences and argues that the results confirm the natural selection of gender-specific preferences.

Cialdini, R. B. (2000). *Influence: Science and practice* (4th ed.). Boston: Allyn & Bacon.

In this bestseller, a leading social psychologist serves up an entertaining recital of forms of social influence and illustrates each with numerous and often humorous anecdotes.

Milgram, S. (1974). *Obedience to authority.* New York: Harper & Row.

The author of perhaps the best-known social psychology experiment recounts his rationale for the research, its design, and its results, while also providing a theoretical account of his findings and discussing their moral implications.

Nisbett, R. (2003). *The geography of thought: How Asians and Westerners think differently . . . and why.* New York: Free Press.

The author's early work on social inference led to a major study of the cognitive differences, particularly in perceptual search and memory, that exist between East Asians and Westerners. He discusses the implications in terms of cultural histories and practices.

Smith, P. B. (2006). *Understanding social psychology across cultures: Living and working in a changing world.* Thousand Oaks, CA: Sage Publications.

This textbook provides a wide-ranging intercultural perspective on several of the topics found in this chapter.

Wegner, D. L. (2002). *The illusion of conscious will.* Cambridge, MA: MIT Press.

The author presents his theory of apparent mental causation, citing his own and others' research and providing ancillary analyses of hypnosis, cognitive dissonance, and self-perception, in arguing that conscious will cannot be the cause of human action.

Wilson, T. D. (2002*). Strangers to ourselves: Discovering the adaptive unconscious.* Cambridge, MA: Harvard University Press.

A fascinating, very readable essay introduces the theory of the adaptive unconscious (the aspect of the person that controls what she or he does but remains unreportable) and adduces support for the theory from several areas of social psychological research.

Zimbardo, P. (2007). *The Lucifer effect: Understanding how good people turn evil.* New York: Random House.

The author revisits the Stanford prison experiment and related research as the backdrop for his analysis of the atrocities reported at Abu Ghraib prison and other war-related tragedies resulting from the misappropriation of social roles and misuse of social power.

CHAPTER

16

The Nature and Causes of Psychological Disorders

Prologue

A Father's Illness, a College Son's Ambivalence

In this anonymous first-person account, a son recalls the toll of his father's psychological disorder:

"It happened when I was about 7 years old. It was a Sunday afternoon, and I was watching television. I heard a lot of yelling and screaming in the kitchen. I ran to see what was happening. They were in the midst of a fight. When they saw me, I turned and ran into the bedroom.

"That was the last time I really remember seeing my father until I was about 21. I'm told that my sister and I visited him after the divorce, but it's all pretty fuzzy to me. I know that shortly after my parents' big fight, my dad was institutionalized for the first time. His diagnosis: paranoid schizophrenia. My father has been in and out of mental institutions over the past 30 years. He is currently treated on an outpatient basis with chlorpromazine, a drug that reduces the symptoms of his disorder. He manages pretty well as long as he takes his medication.

"I didn't go looking to reestablish a relationship with my father; it was all his doing. I was going to college out West at the time. Somehow, he got my address and wrote to me. He told me very little about the intervening years. He simply wanted to start with me anew. When I returned home for the Christmas holidays, I went to see him. He was in the intensive care unit of the local hospital. He had attempted suicide. His first words to me, after not seeing me for nearly a decade and a half, were, 'I can't do anything right—not even kill myself.'

"Despite the situation, we managed to get reacquainted. He wanted to take the relationship a little faster than I did, which brings me to the point I wish to make. About a year after I saw him at the hospital, I received a phone call from him (I was then back at school, 3,000 miles away). He said he had saved some money and wanted to come to visit me. I was stunned: I thought to myself, 'What would my friends think of me having a crazy father? I can't let him come out here.' So I told him that this was a really bad time for me, that I was overloaded with schoolwork, and that I had several exams coming

up—all lies. I was simply embarrassed about having a father with a mental disorder. Disappointed, he said he understood about my heavy workload at school and that he would make other plans.

"About 2 weeks later, I received another call from him. He told me that he had just returned home from visiting the city in which I was living. In fact, he had spent the previous week there—without ever contacting me. He said that he knew how busy I was, but that he just wanted to learn a little more about me and my life. He told me that after spending time in the town where I lived—walking the same streets that I walked and seeing the same mountains I saw every day—he felt closer to me and could identify with me much more. And I had told him not to come. I now look back at the situation with a deep sense of humiliation and regret.

"My sharing of such a personal experience with you might have made you feel at least a bit uncomfortable. That was part of my intention. If I had told you about my father's experience with surgery for, say, a back problem, would you have felt uncomfortable? Probably not. Yet, when I tell you about my father's mental disorder you do. Why? That's a question I will leave for you to answer." ■

L ife is complex, and things do not always go smoothly. We are all beset by major and minor difficulties at one time or another, and our responses to them are rarely perfect. Sometimes we find ourselves behaving irrationally, having trouble concentrating on the matter at hand, or experiencing feelings that do not seem appropriate for the circumstances. Occasionally we may brood about imaginary disasters or harbor hurtful thoughts about people we love. For most of us, however, these problems remain occasional, and we usually manage to cope with them.

But the lives of some people, like that of the father described in the prologue, are dominated for long years by disordered thoughts, disturbed feelings, inappropriate behaviors, or some mix thereof. The problems become so severe that these individuals cannot cope with life. They may withdraw from familiar routines and those closest to them; they may turn to professionals for assistance; or they may be obliged to live in institutions.

What causes such problems? Recent studies have identified complex interactions between an individual's genotype, brain chemistry, and childhood environment in the **etiology** (that is, the causation) of psychological orders (see, e.g., Caspi et al., 2002; Reif et al., 2007). Some psycho-

logical disorders—especially the less severe ones—appear to be more heavily influenced by environmental factors, such as stressors or unhealthy family interactions, or by a person's perception of these factors. For example, a child who is constantly criticized by an overbearing, demanding parent may learn to be passive and non-responding. This strategy may be adaptive in interactions with the parent but will be maladaptive in other social situations. In contrast, many of the more severe psychological disorders appear more heavily influenced by hereditary and other biological factors that disrupt normal cognitive processes or produce inappropriate emotional reactions.

This chapter begins with a section on the classification and diagnosis of psychological disorders; it then describes the nature of some of the better-known disorders and discusses research on their causes. (Chapter 17 discusses the treatment of psychological disorders and the efforts of psychiatrists, clinical psychologists, and other mental health professionals to help people with problems of daily living.) The essential features of the more prominent disorders and treatment approaches are simplified here for the sake of brevity. In addition, many of the cases that clinicians encounter are less clear-cut than the conditions described here and are thus not so easily classified (Carson et al., 2000). It is important to realize that, as more and more people now understand, the line dividing normal and abnormal behavior is not sharp.

Classification and Diagnosis of Psychological Disorders

To understand, diagnose, and treat psychological disorders, clinicians need some sort of classification system. The need for a comprehensive classification system of psychological disorders was recognized by Emil Kraepelin ("KRAY-puh-leen"; 1856–1926), who provided his version in a textbook of psychiatry published in 1883. The Association of Medical Superintendents of American Institutions for the Insane, a forerunner

The dividing line between normal and abnormal behavior is not always clear.

---

etiology The sources of a disorder.

of the American Psychiatric Association, later incorporated Kraepelin's ideas into a classification system of its own. Several of Kraepelin's original categories are retained in the DSM-IV-TR, the classification system most widely used today.

Before examining the DSM-IV-TR, let's consider different perspectives on what constitutes "abnormality" and on the underlying causes of psychological disorders.

What Is "Abnormal"?

Psychological disorders are characterized by abnormal behavior, thoughts, and feelings. The term *abnormal* literally refers to any departure from the norm. Perhaps you have friends who insist that their pets understand them or who have to check several times to be sure everything is turned off before they leave their homes. Are these behaviors abnormal? If so, are they abnormal enough to be considered signs of psychological disorders?

The distinction between normal and abnormal behavior can be highly subjective. Clinical psychologists remind us that the most important feature of a psychological disorder is not whether a person's behaviors, thoughts, and feelings are "abnormal"—different from those of most other people—but whether they are *maladaptive*, that is, whether they cause distress or discomfort and interfere with people's ability to lead satisfying, productive lives. They often make it impossible for people to hold jobs, raise families, or relate to others socially. In this way, persons with psychological disorders are at odds with the basic expectations of the majority of other people about how to conduct themselves acceptably with others. You might rightly point out that a person who holds an unpopular religious or political belief that violates a social norm may be ostracized by the community and may find it impossible to get a job or to make friends. Clearly, the person's behavior is maladaptive, but does this mean that the person has a psychological disorder? Not by itself. We may be tempted to label the behavior as courageous and wise or as misguided and foolish. Simply disagreeing with the government, with established religious practices, or with popular beliefs, although potentially maladaptive, is not sufficient evidence for a diagnosis of mental illness. At the same time, historical and contemporary examples exist of governments that have used dissent from their views as grounds for institutionalization or worse (for example, see Solzhenitsyn, 2002, for examples from the Soviet Union).

Although such a diagnosis should be as objective as possible, it may never be completely free from social and political judgments. For example, in many societies today, experiences such as receiving direct messages from God and being transported on mystical voyages to the afterlife would probably be labeled hallucinatory or delusional, whereas in other times and places, such experiences might be taken as signs of holiness and devotion (Jaynes, 1976).

If historical records are accurate, the behavior of past figures who are now venerated as prophets or saints would be regarded quite differently if they were alive today. Understanding cultural differences in beliefs is important, especially in a multicultural society such as ours. Still, the fact that diagnoses are affected by social or cultural contexts does not mean that they are invalid (Lopez & Guarnaccia, 2000; Widiger & Sankis, 2000; Arrindell, 2003). We return to this issue in considering culture-bound syndromes later in the chapter.

As we mentioned before (and emphasize again later), the specific disorders considered in this chapter are typically complex, and the descriptions in a textbook such as this may draw distinctions that are not necessarily easy to make in real life. Drawing such distinctions may require that the dividing line between normalcy and psychological disorder be sharpened. At the extremes, it is not hard to tell a person with schizophrenia, a phobic disorder, or a mood disorder from a person without those disorders, but most people do not fall at the extremes. All of us should recognize aspects of our own behavior in this chapter's descriptions of people with psychological disorders.

Perspectives on the Causes of Psychological Disorders

No single cause of psychological disorders is known. In general, they are caused by the interaction of biological, cognitive, and environmental factors, where biological factors include genetic factors and physiological factors such as the nervous system. The complexity of this interaction distinguishes psychological disorders from more plainly physical disorders such as diabetes or cancer, for which readily objective diagnostic criteria and tests are available. Moreover, psychologists and other mental health professionals approach the study of psychological disorders from different perspectives, each of which places more or less emphasis on each of these three sets of factors. Although many practitioners hold to a single perspective when diagnosing their clients' symptoms and treating them, it is not unusual for a practitioner to be *eclectic*, that is, to adopt more than one approach when doing so (see Chapter 17). The perspectives differ primarily in their explanation of the etiology of psychological disorders. Several of these perspectives were previously discussed in Chapters 1 and 14 and receive only brief mention here as they pertain to psychological disorders.

The Medical Perspective The medical model is based on the idea that psychological disorders are caused by specific abnormalities of the brain and nervous system; may or may not involve other bodily systems; and, in principle, should be treated in the same way as are other illnesses. As we shall see, biological factors are known to contribute to the development of psychological disorders, including schizophrenia and the bipolar disorders, and drugs are usually used for treatment. We shall also see that genes play a pivotal role in the development of some of these disorders.

However, not all psychological disorders can be traced so directly to biological causes. For that reason, other perspectives, which focus on the cognitive and environmental factors involved in psychological disorders, have emerged.

The Psychodynamic Perspective According to the psychodynamic perspective, which is based on Freud's early work, psychological disorders originate in intrapsychic conflict produced by the three components of the mind—the id, ego, and superego (see Chapter 14). These conflicts may center on attempts to control potentially harmful expressions of sexual or aggressive impulses; they also may arise from attempts to cope with external dangers and traumatic experiences, including those that occurred during the stages of psychosexual development (see Chapter 12). For some people, the conflict becomes so severe that the ego's defense mechanisms cannot produce a resolution that is adequate for psychological well-being. The result is that the defense mechanisms themselves distort reality, or the individual begins to function in some areas of life in a manner characteristic of an earlier stage of development. The psychological disorders that result may involve extreme anxiety, obsessive thoughts and compulsive behavior, depression, and distorted perceptions and patterns of thinking. As you will read in Chapter 17, psychodynamic therapists attempt to make their clients aware of their intrapsychic conflicts and defense mechanisms as part of the process of achieving psychological well-being.

The Cognitive–Behavioral Perspective This blend of cognitive and behavioral perspectives holds that psychological disorders are *learned* maladaptive behavior patterns that we can best understand by focusing on social–environmental factors and a person's perception of those factors. In this view, a psychological disorder is not something that arises spontaneously within a person. Instead, it is caused by the person's interaction with his or her environment and especially with other people. For example, a person's excessive use of alcohol or other drugs may be reinforced by the relief from tension or anxiety that often accompanies intoxication.

According to the cognitive–behavioral perspective, it is not merely the environment that matters, however. What also counts is a person's ongoing subjective interpretation of the events taking place in his or her environment. Therapists operating from the cognitive–behavioral perspective therefore encourage their clients to replace maladaptive outlooks with more adaptive thoughts and behaviors.

The Humanistic Perspective As you read in Chapter 14, proponents of the humanistic perspective argue that successful personality development occurs when people experience what Carl Rogers referred to as unconditional positive regard. Conversely, according to this view, psychological disorders arise when people perceive that they must earn the positive regard of others. Thus, they become overly sensitive to the demands and criticisms of others and come to define their personal value primarily in terms of others' reactions to them. They lack confidence in their abilities and feel as though they have no demonstrable value as persons. They

may come to feel that they have no control over the outcomes of the important (and even not-so-important) events in their lives. Such feelings often accompany depression. The goal of humanistic therapy is to persuade people that they do have intrinsic value and to help them achieve their own unique, positive potential as human beings.

The Sociocultural Perspective Psychologists and others in the field of mental health are finding that the cultures in which people live play a significant role in the development of psychological disorders (e.g., Manson & Kleinman, 1998; Lopez & Guarnaccia, 2000; Rosenfarb et al., 2004).

As you have seen throughout this book, psychologists today are paying more attention to the role of sociocultural factors in their attempts to understand how people think and behave. The study of psychological disorders is no exception. Proper treatment also may require an understanding of cultural variables that influence the extent to which people interpret their own behaviors as normal or abnormal (Dana, 2000). What is considered normal in one culture may be considered abnormal in another. Moreover, certain psychological disorders appear to occur only in certain cultures—a phenomenon called *culture-bound syndromes*. We examine this topic in depth at a later point.

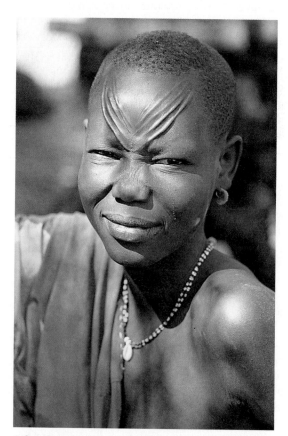

Cultural norms dictate what is appropriate in any given culture. For example, in the Sudan the scars on this girl's forehead are considered normal. In North America, however, such markings are apt to draw stares.

The Biopsychosocial Perspective How should we make sense of these different perspectives on the causes of psychological disorders? Are disorders caused by conflict within the individual? Are they caused by genetic factors or by abnormalities of the brain and nervous system, or both? Are they caused by learning, by faulty subjective interpretations of environmental events, or by the way our particular culture says we should think and behave?

No single perspective is completely adequate in accounting for the origins of psychological disorders. This is not to say that any of the perspectives is unimportant, however. Different approaches can be combined to form larger, more comprehensive, perspectives. For example, the widely cited **diathesis** ("die-ATH-uh-suss")–**stress model** asserts that the combination of a person's genes and early learning experiences may produce predispositions (*diatheses*) for a variety of psychological disorders (see Yeo, et al., 2007, for a discussion of this concept relative to neurodevelopmental disorders such as attention-deficit/hyperactivity disorder, dyslexia, and schizophrenia). Moreover, the genes that are involved are not necessarily specific to particular disorders but may constitute a more general predisposition (Dick, 2007). However, the symptoms of a specific disorder will emerge only if that person is confronted with stressors that exceed his or her coping abilities. In other words, a person may be predisposed toward a psychological disorder yet not develop it, either because he or she has not encountered sufficient stressors to trigger its development or because he or she possesses cognitive–behavioral coping skills or the social and environmental resources adequate to counter the stressors that are present.

The diathesis–stress model represents the **biopsychosocial perspective,** which deliberately combines multiple perspectives. For example, a biopsychosocial model may use information about the way in which the genotypes of individuals diagnosed with a specific psychological disorder differ from those of individuals who do not have the disorder. A related interest may be information about the chemistry of neural pathways in individuals with the disorder and correlations between those pathways and the individuals' genotypes. From there, the model might identify the unique behavioral and cognitive symptoms of the disorder and look for evidence that certain types of family environments and other social environments are more closely related to the development of those symptoms than others. Although admittedly complex, this perspective may nevertheless have greater potential for the eventual identification of successful treatments. Stravynski (2007) provides an example of the biopsychosocial approach to a specific category of anxiety disorders—social phobia, which he considers an elaborate interpersonal defense system motivated by extreme fear of humiliation.

The DSM-IV-TR Classification Scheme

The classification of psychological disorders can be difficult, as it is possible to classify these conditions in many ways. The system most commonly used is found in the American Psychiatric Association's ***Diagnostic and Statistical Manual of Mental Disorders,*** Fourth Edition, Text Revision (DSM-IV-TR, 2000). TABLE 16•1 lists the DSM-IV-TR classifications; several subclassifications were omitted for the sake of simplicity. The *International Statistical Classification of Diseases and Related Health Problems* (ISD) is used in many parts of the world as an alternative to the DSM and differs from it in certain ways, such as including personality disorders on the same axis as the other major psychological disorders (see later).

---

diathesis–stress model A causal account of mental disorders suggesting that these disorders develop when a person possesses a predisposition for a disorder and encounters stressors that exceed his or her abilities to cope with them.

biopsychosocial perspective An approach to psychological disorders that considers them to result from the interaction of genetic, physiological, developmental, and environmental factors.

According to the diathesis-stress model, individuals vary in the stressors they confront and in their coping ability. When stressors exceed that ability, a psychological disorder may develop, particularly in cases where a predisposition exists.

[TABLE 16·1] Summary of the DSM-IV-TR Classification Scheme for Axes I and II

Axis I—Major Clinical Syndromes

- Disorders usually first diagnosed in infancy, childhood, or adolescence. Any deviation from normal development, including autism, attention-deficit disorder with hyperactivity (ADHD), excessive fears, speech problems, and highly aggressive behavior.

- Delirium, dementia, and amnestic, and other cognitive disorders. Disorders due to deterioration of the brain because of aging, disease (such as Alzheimer's disease, which was discussed in Chapter 12), or ingestion or exposure to drugs or toxic substances (such as lead).

- Substance-related disorders. Psychological, social, or physical problems related to abuse of alcohol or other drugs, not including symptomless recreational use. (Psychoactive substance use and abuse was discussed in Chapters 1, 3, and 4 and is also discussed in this chapter.)

- Schizophrenia and other psychotic disorders. A group of disorders marked by loss of contact with reality, illogical thought, inappropriate displays of emotion, bizarre perceptions, and usually some form of hallucinations or delusions.

- Mood disorders. Disorders involving extreme deviations from normal mood including severe depression (major depression), excessive elation (mania), or alternation between severe depression and excessive elation (bipolar disorder).

- Anxiety disorders. Excessive fear of specific objects (phobia); repetitive, persistent thoughts accompanied by ritualistic behavior that reduces anxiety (obsessive–compulsive disorder); panic attacks; generalized and intense feelings of anxiety; and feelings of dread caused by experiencing traumatic events such as natural disasters or combat (post-traumatic stress disorder, discussed later in this chapter).

- Somatoform disorders. Disorders involving pain, paralysis, or blindness for which no physical cause can be found; also excessive concern about health issues, as in persons with hypochondriasis.

- Factitious disorders. False reports of physical symptoms, as with Munchausen's syndrome, in which the individual is frequently hospitalized because of his or her claims of illness.

- Dissociative disorders. Loss of personal identity and changes in normal consciousness, including amnesia and dissociative identity disorder, in which two or more independently functioning personality systems exist.

- Sexual and gender identity disorders. Disorders involving fetishes, sexual dysfunction (such as erectile or orgasmic dysfunctions), and problems of sexual identity (such as transsexualism).

- Eating disorders. Disorders related to excessive concern about body weight, such as anorexia nervosa (self-starvation) and bulimia (alternating periods of eating large amounts of food and vomiting). (Eating disorders were discussed in Chapter 13.)

- Sleep disorders. Disorders including severe insomnia, chronic sleepiness, sleepwalking, narcolepsy (suddenly falling asleep), and sleep apnea. (Sleep disorders were discussed in Chapter 9.)

- Impulse-control disorders. Disorders involving compulsive behaviors such as stealing, fire setting, or gambling.

- Adjustment disorders. Disorders stemming from difficulties adjusting to significant life stressors, such as death of a loved one, loss of a job or financial difficulties, or family problems, including divorce. (Some adjustment disorders, as they pertain to difficulty in coping with life stressors, were discussed in Chapter 13.)

Axis II—Personality Disorders

- Personality disorders. Long-term, maladaptive, and rigid personality traits that impair normal functioning and involve psychological stress. Two examples are antisocial personality disorder (lack of empathy or care for others; lack of guilt for misdeeds; antisocial behavior; and persistent lying, cheating, and stealing) which is discussed later in this chapter, and narcissistic personality disorder (inflated sense of self-worth and importance and persistent seeking of attention).

- Mental retardation (which was discussed in Chapter 11).

The DSM-IV-TR is the latest version of a classification scheme that aims to provide a reliable and comprehensive set of diagnostic categories with descriptors (or criteria) that are specified as explicitly as possible. The DSM-IV-TR characterizes psychological conditions using five different sets of criteria, called *axes*. Individuals undergoing psychiatric or psychological evaluation are assessed on each of the axes. Axis I and Axis II contain information specific to major psychological disorders that require clinical attention, Axes III through V address other aspects of the condition and life circumstances of the individual. Axis III is used to pinpoint any physical disorders, such as skin rashes or heightened blood pressure, that accompany the psychological disorder. Axis IV identifies the severity of stress that the person

has experienced (usually within the last year). This axis details the sources of stress (for example, family or work). Axis V assesses the person's overall level of psychological, social, or occupational functioning. The purpose of Axis V is to estimate the extent to which a person's quality of life has been diminished by the disorder. Ratings are made on a 100-point *Global Assessment of Functioning* (GAF) scale on which 100 represents the absence or near absence of impaired functioning, 50 represents serious problems in functioning, and 10 represents impairment that may result in severe injury to the individual or to others.

It is also possible for the same person to have different disorders at different points in time. Disorders that occur together are referred to as **comorbid.** The DSM-IV-TR offers clinical psychologists, psychiatrists, and other clinical professionals a systematic means of compiling and evaluating a variety of personal and psychological information about any specific

---

comorbid Refers to the tendency of one type of psychological disorder to occur together with one or more other disorders.

individual. Let's consider an example to demonstrate the interrelationship among the five axes. Alcohol dependence (Axis I) can be comorbid with major depressive disorder (Axis 1). A national health study in Finland (Pirkkola et al., 2006) found that 7.9% of the population reported current alcohol dependence and, of these, 8% were comorbid for major depression. A national survey of Canadians (Wang & El-Guebaly, 2004) showed a similar comorbidity of 8.6% between the two disorders.

Alcohol dependence often leads to marital problems, which may also be partly associated with an antisocial personality disorder (Axis II). Echeburúa et al. (2007) reported a comorbidity of 7% in a Spanish sample of persons with alcohol dependence. Marital problems may lead to divorce, and these problems and the divorce are themselves stressors (Axis IV) that may subsequently contribute to an episode of major depression (Axis I). Alcohol dependence also may eventually lead to physical problems, such as cirrhosis ("seer-OH-siss"; Axis III). These problems, now acting in concert, are likely to lead to an increased impairment of overall life functioning (Axis V); eventually the individual may have only a few friends, none of them close, and may be unable to keep a job. The evaluation of this person might be summarized as follows:

Axis I: Alcohol Dependence and Major Depressive Disorder

Axis II: Antisocial Personality Disorder

Axis III: Alcoholic cirrhosis

Axis IV: Severe stress—divorce, loss of job

Axis V: GAF evaluation = 30, which represents a very serious impairment of functioning

Of course, most problems that psychologists encounter in dealing with their clients will not be related in neat, linear order but in patterns of comorbidity that are complex and resistant to easy diagnosis.

Some Problems with the DSM-IV-TR Classification

Although the DSM-IV-TR is the most widely used classification system for psychological disorders, it is not flawless. Reflecting the fact that the development of the DSM-IV-TR has been strongly influenced by psychiatrists, the manual tends to be consistent more with the medical perspective on psychological disorders than with other perspectives. This means that diagnosis and treatment based on the DSM-IV-TR may not recognize potential cognitive and environmental determinants as readily as those more plainly biological.

Another potential problem with the DSM-IV-TR (and perhaps with any classification scheme) is its *reliability*. In this context, as in the context of intelligence testing (see Chapter 11), reliability refers to consistency across repeated applications. If the DSM-IV-TR were perfectly reliable, users would be able to diagnose each case in the same way, but evaluating psychological disorders is not so easy. Using the DSM-IV-TR is not like using a recipe; it is more like navigating your way through an unfamiliar city with a map that includes only partial details.

By using this map, you may or may not reach your ultimate destination. Psychological disorders do not have distinct borders that allow a mental health professional to diagnose each disorder in a person with 100% accuracy. For example, the diagnosis of *post-traumatic stress disorder* requires the persistence of symptoms for more than 30 days. If symptoms similar to those found in post-traumatic stress disorder end before the 30-day cutoff, the diagnosis will be *acute stress disorder* instead. Having two separate classifications for the same symptoms has been questioned by some psychiatrists (see, e.g., Marshall et al., 1999) as potentially detracting from reliability.

Other critics have questioned the *validity* of the DSM-IV-TR's reliance on categories, that is, whether its categories accurately label what is actually going on. The concern is well illustrated by a classic experiment in the social psychology of institutions performed by Rosenhan (1973).

By prior assignment, Rosenhan and a small group of his professional associates, who had agreed to collaborate with him in the research, presented themselves at different mental hospitals in the California state system. Each used a standard introduction, offering a fictitious name and a fictitious set of symptoms (hearing voices when no one was present). Otherwise they told the truth. Rosenhan's interest was whether such individuals (whom he styled "pseudopatients") would be admitted to the hospitals. The expert opinion of the mental health professionals to whom he had previously described the study was resoundingly that the pseudopatients would not be admitted. Thus the surprise when all were—and when their mean length of stay in the institutions was nearly 3 weeks! Moreover, they reported that their efforts to express their normalcy while in the hospitals only solidified the diagnosis they received—acute paranoid schizophrenia. Oddly, only the long-term residents of the hospitals detected the ruse captured in the title of Rosenhan's article, "On being sane in insane places."

Horwitz and Wakefield (2007) focused on the DSM-IV-TR's categorization of depressive disorders, as well as the related categorizations found in previous editions of the manual. They question whether interclinician agreement about whether a client presents the necessary and sufficient symptoms of a disorder is an adequate ground for diagnosis. Is it possible, they ask, that the symptoms are those of the natural sadness that would accompany a devastating loss and not a psychological disorder at all? The issue is like that of the *false-positive* outcome of a medical test, in which the test results falsely indicate the presence of a disorder. Wakefield et al. (2007) estimated that, in as many as one in four cases, natural bereavement may be mistaken for major depressive disorder.

In active anticipation of the DSM-V, which may appear as soon as 2012, O'Donohue et al. (2007) and Widiger and Trull (2007) recommended a new perspective on psychological disorders, and personality disorders in particular. Specifically, they recommend that diagnosis move away from the categorization model of disorder to embrace the dimensional approach to personality, as found, for example, in the five-factor model of personality (see Chapter 14). Doing so would eliminate the current practice, with its attendant confusion, of multiaxial diagnoses in which a single client is labeled as having multiple comorbid disorders.

Probably a downside will always be found to the classification of psychological disorders. No classification scheme is likely to be perfect, and no two people with the same diagnosis will behave in exactly the same way. As you may have recognized, potential problems are inherent in any system that labels human beings. It is easy to lapse into the mistaken belief that labeling psychological disorders explains why people are the way they are. But diagnosing the disorder only summarizes the presenting symptoms of the disorder; it does not explain the underlying causes and the psychological and behavioral processes that may be at work. To say, for example, that Joe speaks incoherently "because he's schizophrenic" does not explain his behavior at all. Rather, the way Joe speaks is one of the symptoms of the disorder known as schizophrenia. Consequently, we need to be on guard against labeling people with the *names* of disorders rather than with their *symptoms*. Thus, it is more appropriate to talk about Joe as "having a schizophrenic disorder" than to call him "a schizophrenic." Labeling Joe "a schizophrenic" ignores the other aspects of Joe. If Joe had a physical problem such as a broken bone, would it make sense to label him only by his injury? "Joe's a broken bone" makes no sense.

Moreover, once people are labeled, they are likely to be perceived as having all the characteristics assumed to accompany that label; their behavior will probably be perceived selectively and interpreted in terms of the diagnosis, as occurred with Rosenhan and the other pseudopatients in his study. Obviously, much that is regrettable can occur in this process. An experiment by Langer and Abelson (1974) illustrated how labeling someone can affect clinical judgments. A group of psychoanalysts were shown videotape of a young man who was being interviewed. Half of the psychoanalysts were told that the man was a job applicant, while the other half were told that he was a patient. Although both groups of clinicians watched the same man exhibiting the same behavior, those who were told that he was a patient rated him as more disturbed—that is, less well adjusted.

Because labeling can have negative effects, some psychiatrists have suggested that we should abandon all attempts to classify and diagnose psychological disorders. Thomas Szasz ("Sazz", 1960, 2002, 2007) argued that the concept of mental illness has done more harm than good because of the negative effects it has on those people who are said to be mentally ill. For example, Szasz notes that labeling people as having a mental illness places the responsibility for their care with the medical establishment, thereby relieving such people of responsibility for their condition—for their "problems of living," as Szasz puts it—and for taking personal steps toward improvement.

clinical judgments Diagnoses of psychological disorders or predictions of future behavior based largely on experts' knowledge of symptoms and past clinical experience.

actuarial judgments Diagnoses of psychological disorders or predictions of future behavior based on statistical analyses of outcome data.

Clinical Versus Actuarial Diagnosis

Clinical psychologists and other mental health professionals are often asked to make diagnoses and to predict people's future behavior. These decisions are important; for example, they can determine whether someone receives a treatment that may have significant side effects, whether someone receives parole, whether someone stands trial for a crime, or whether someone is placed in a psychiatric hospital. Two activities contribute to diagnoses and predictions: collection of data and interpretation of data. Accuracy is essential in both activities; unreliable or irrelevant data make interpretation questionable, and even good data can be misinterpreted.

Mental health professionals have many ways to collect data about a client. They can observe the client and note the presence or absence of particular behaviors. They can request medical tests such as EEG, CT, or MRI scans. They can interview the client and take note of facial expressions and responses to questions. They can administer objective and projective personality tests (see Chapter 14). They can examine documents that already exist, such as medical records, criminal records, or reports of behavior from mental or penal institutions, and they can gather information from people who know the client.

Once data are gathered, clinicians can interpret them in two ways: by using the *clinical method* or by using the *actuarial (or statistical) method*. Although a considerable amount of scientific research indicates that the actuarial method is superior, many mental health professionals still prefer to use the clinical method. Let's look at the difference between these two methods and at the research that compares them, and then consider why the use of the actuarial method is not more widespread.

How Do These Methods Differ?

Clinical judgments are diagnoses based on an expert's experience. The information that is collected may come from many sources, but it is not the source of information that distinguishes the clinical method from the actuarial method—it is the processing of that information. Clinical judgments are based on experts' recollections of similar cases and on their knowledge of the symptoms that predict particular types of outcomes. The decision process may be considered less formal than that used in actuarial judgments.

Actuarial judgments use statistical rules that relate particular indicators (symptoms, test scores, or personal characteristics such as age, sex, and medical history) to particular outcomes. The actuarial method was first devised for setting the rates for life insurance policies. For example, an insurer can estimate a person's longevity by knowing his or her age, height, weight, sex, and health-related habits such as smoking. Although the estimate may be wrong about a particular person (for example, a person may be killed in a

Most psychotherapists still prefer the clinical method for diagnosing mental disorders even though the actuarial method has been shown to be more accurate.

traffic accident or may stop smoking), actuarial judgments work very well when applied to large groups of people and to the prediction of average outcomes.

Comparing the Clinical and Actuarial Methods

Mental health professionals are asked to make predictions about *individuals,* not groups of people. Does the actuarial method work well in such cases? According to research on the subject, the answer is yes (Meehl, 1954; Dawes et al., 1989; Grove & Meehl, 1996; Aegisdóttir et al., 2006).

For a fair comparison of clinical and actuarial judgments, both methods must be applied to the same data. In addition, the eventual outcomes must be known—there must be a way to determine which judgments were right and which were wrong (Meehl, 1954). Goldberg (1968) performed one of the first studies to make such a comparison by using data from clinical psychology. He analyzed the relation between patients' scores on the MMPI and the diagnoses they finally received when they were discharged from mental institutions. (You will recall from Chapter 14 that the MMPI, or Minnesota Multiphasic Personality Inventory, is extensively used in the diagnosis of mental disorders.) Goldberg found that a single actuarial rule effectively distinguished people who were diagnosed psychotic from those who were diagnosed neurotic. This was the rule: Add the scores from three of the scales of the MMPI (Lie, Paranoia, and Schizophrenia) and subtract the scores from two others (Hysteria and Psychasthenia). If the score exceeds 45 points, the person is diagnosed as psychotic, otherwise as neurotic. (Note that the DSM-IV-TR has discontinued the use of neurosis as a category of mental disorders; thus, the distinction between psychotic and neurotic does not appear there.)

Goldberg obtained the MMPI scores of 861 patients and sent them to 239 clinicians (experts and novices) who made diagnoses based on the scores. On average, the clinicians' judgments were correct for 62% of the patients. The best judge was correct for about 67% of the cases. Goldberg's actuarial rule was superior, however. It was correct 70% of the time, which was better than the best of the expert clinical judges.

According to Dawes (2002), a large number of studies comparing actuarial and clinical judgments—not just in mental health but in the social sciences more generally—overwhelmingly show actuarial judgments to be superior. The criterion measures predicted in these studies included college grade point average, parole violation, response to particular forms of therapy, length of psychiatric hospitalization, and violent behavior. As Meehl (1986) noted earlier, "There is no controversy in social science that shows such a large body of qualitatively diverse studies coming out so uniformly . . . as this one" (p. 373). A meta-analysis by Aegisdóttir et al. (2006) included 67 studies published over a period of 56 years. In their most rigorous analysis of the results, the authors found a 13% increase in accuracy when actuarial methods were used.

Why Is the Actuarial Method More Accurate?

Actuarial judgments tend to be more accurate than clinical judgments for several reasons. First, their reliability is always higher. Because a decision is based on a precise rule, the actuarial method always produces the same judgment for a particular set of data. Conversely, an expert making a clinical judgment may make different decisions about the same set of data on different occasions, or may allow personal bias to influence his or her analysis of the data (Rohling et al., 2003). Experts may become tired; their judgment may be influenced by recent cases in which they were involved; or the order in which the information is presented to them may affect which factors they consider in making their decisions.

In Chapter 11, we saw that when people make decisions, they usually follow heuristical rules. As we saw in Chapter 15, these rules can lead people astray. For example, we tend to pay too much attention to particularly striking incidents and to ignore or underuse valuable information about base rates. Also, we have a common tendency to pay too much attention to information that is consistent with our own hypotheses and to ignore or minimize contradictory information (Greenwald et al., 1986). These same tendencies likely contribute to the inaccuracy of experts' judgments.

Even though the research consistently touts the actuarial method as superior, most mental health professionals still use clinical more than actuarial methods of prediction. Some clinicians avoid the actuarial method (Guilmette et al., 1990). Why? According to Dawes (2002), some clinicians may be unaware of the research showing the inferiority of the clinical method. Others find the actuarial method dehumanizing; they believe that the method ignores the fact that each person is unique. Perhaps experts prefer to use their own judgment for a perfectly understandable reason: They find it difficult to accept that their diagnostic skills, developed over a long period of training and practice, can be bested by a rule embodied in a computer program.

What Should We Conclude?

Scientific studies have shown that clinical judgments are consistently inferior to actuarial judgments. What do these results say about the role clinicians should play in trying to diagnose symptoms and make predictions? Perhaps experts should concentrate their efforts on what they do best and what a data-derived rule cannot do: observing people's behavior, developing new and useful measurement instruments, and providing therapy. After all, helping people is the clinician's most important role. Routine diagnosis—a time-consuming activity—might be left to the actuarial method in the types of cases for which it has been shown to be superior. Even then, as Westen and Weinberger (2004) pointed out, the clinician remains the most important source of new information about potentially relevant variables in diagnosis and treatment.

QUESTIONS TO CONSIDER

1. Of the major perspectives on psychological disorders, is there one that you regard as being more persuasive? If so, which is it? And why?
2. Despite its drawbacks, the DSM-IV-TR continues to be used worldwide. Some might argue that such use is justified by the fact that "it's the best we have at the present time." Why do you think this is?
3. What would a diagnostic classification system that improves on the DSM contain?
4. The Focus On section discussed the diagnosis of psychological disorders and the pros and cons of basing diagnoses on clinical versus actuarial judgments. Suppose you were the client whose mental health was in question. Which method would you prefer your therapist to use in reaching a judgment about you? Why?

Disorders Usually Diagnosed in Childhood

The remainder of the chapter takes up several of the major categories of psychological orders found in the DSM-IV-TR and in the same order they are found there. It begins with a pair of disorders usually first diagnosed in childhood: attention-deficit/hyperactivity disorder and autistic disorder.

attention-deficit/hyperactivity disorder   A psychological disorder with symptoms of inattention, hyperactivity, and impulsivity, usually diagnosed in childhood.

Attention-Deficit/Hyperactivity Disorder

The primary presenting symptoms of **attention-deficit/hyperactivity disorder** include inattention, hyperactivity, or impulsivity, as well as combinations thereof. The symptoms associated with impairment must be presented before age 7; often they have been presented for several years. The impairment must be displayed in two different settings (for example, home and school), and must demonstrably interfere with age-appropriate functioning socially, academically, or otherwise. These symptoms are comparative—they are assessed relative to other individuals at a comparable level of development. The incidence of the disorder is estimated to be 3 to 7% of school-age children. However, it may persist into adolescence and adulthood, where it presents long-term challenges to successful functioning (Young, 2007).

The inattention characteristic of the disorder is marked by the failure to attend closely to details and the tendency to make careless errors. Schoolwork, for example, is typically messy. In addition to finding it difficult to sustain attention in projects or play, children with the disorder find it difficult to complete tasks. They often appear as if their thoughts are elsewhere and fail to hear what has been said to them. They may switch frequently between unfinished tasks and fail to follow through on tasks they are instructed to complete. They may also exhibit difficulty organizing tasks and report that trying to sustain attention as aversive. Not surprisingly, they tend to avoid such tasks and may lose or damage the materials required for their completion. They are readily distracted by stimuli that go unnoticed by others, are forgetful, and appear disconnected when others attempt to converse with them.

Hyperactivity is displayed by fidgeting or squirming while seated as well as by excessive running or jumping and excessive talking in situations in which it is inappropriate. Activities that require being quiet or relaxing are aversive. At home, the presenting symptoms include frequently getting

Children with attention-deficit/hyperactivity disorder have difficulty following through with assigned tasks and may take risks that lead to damage and injury.

up from the table during meals or while watching television or doing homework. The symptoms of impulsivity include impatience, difficulty in delaying responses (such as waiting one's turn to be called on), interrupting or intruding on others inappropriately, blurting out answers before the question is asked, failing to listen to instructions, grabbing items that others have, and touching or knocking over objects that not supposed to be touched. Individuals with the disorder may take undue risks that lead to accidents and injuries.

Despite findings of high heritability of attention-deficit/hyperactivity disorder in studies involving identical twins (Nigg, 2006), no clear indication indicates how genes and environment might produce the symptoms. Shaw et al. (2006, 2007) reported MRI data from a 220 children diagnosed with the disorder over a 15-year period. Among their findings was an unusual trend in the developmental course of cerebral cortical thickness. On average, thickness reaches its peak at age 7 or 8 and then grows thinner thereafter. In the case of children with the diagnosis, maximal thickness doesn't occur until age 10. This was contrasted to the earlier-than-usual maturation of the motor cortex of children with the diagnosis. The combination of a developmental delay in areas of the brain that exert inhibitory control over movements and the premature development of the areas that produce voluntary movements is consistent with the best-known symptoms of the disorder.

A team of psychologists working in Norway proposed a comprehensive theory of the development of the disorder (Sagvolden et al., 2005). Specifically, they point to the insufficiency of dopamine as a modulator in neural pathways involving the neurotransmitters glutamate and GABA (see Chapter 4). The culprit, in their view, is reduced activity in a dopaminergic branch of the limbic system. This interferes with the normal processes of reinforcement and extinction (see Chapter 5), which, over time, leads to the familiar symptoms of delay aversion, the development of hyperactivity in novel settings, impulsiveness, impairment of sustained attention, greater behavioral variability, and the failure to inhibit responses. However, the theory is dynamic in that it predicts when these symptoms will have their onset as a function of individual genetic predispositions and surroundings. The theory also considers the therapeutic role of parenting styles, medication, and social policy.

Autistic Disorder

According to the DSM-IV-TR, the primary symptom of **autistic disorder** is the abnormal development of social interaction and communication, accompanied by pronounced limitations of activity and interests—all by age 3. The persistent abnormality of social interaction includes the failure to use nonverbal behaviors such as eye-to-eye contact and facial expressions. Children diagnosed with the disorder display little inclination to form friendships and do not spontaneously share enjoyments, interest, or achievements with other people. They prefer activities in which they can be alone and are often oblivious to the presence of others and unresponsive to signs of others' distress.

The disorder was first identified in the psychiatric literature by Kanner (1943). The DSM-IV-TR put its incidence at 5 in 10,000, but the Centers for Disease Control more recently placed it at 1 in every 166 children (Pettus, 2008)—an approximately 10-fold increase! It is four times more likely to occur in boys than in girls and is often accompanied by mental retardation. Such dramatic growth in the incidence of the disorder has created controversy: Are the increases attributable to better reporting and thus not so much to increased incidence per se? Or has diagnosis become liberalized so that autistic disorder itself and disorders that resemble it are now bundled together as *autistic spectrum disorders,* with a correspondingly greater incidence?

Spitzer et al. (2002) offer a case study to illustrate the primary symptoms of a child with autistic disorder.

[**CASE STUDY**] Richard, age $3\frac{1}{2}$, a firstborn child, was referred at the request of his parents because of his uneven development and abnormal behavior. Delivery had been difficult, and he had needed oxygen at birth. His physical appearance, motor development, and self-help skills were all age appropriate, but his parents had been uneasy about him from the first few months of life because of his lack of response to social contact and the usual baby games. Comparison with their second child, who, unlike Richard, enjoyed social communication from early infancy, confirmed their fears.

Richard appeared to be self-sufficient and aloof from others. He did not greet his mother in the mornings, or his father when he returned from work, though, if left with a baby-sitter, he tended to scream much of the time. His babbling had no conversational intonation. At age 3, he could understand simple practical instructions. His speech consisted of echoing some words and phrases he had heard in the past, with the original speaker's accent and intonations; he could use on or two such phrases to indicate his simple needs. For example, if he said, "Do you want a drink?" he meant he was thirsty. He did not communicate by facial expressions or use gesture or mime, except for pulling someone along and placing his or her hand on an object he wanted.

He was fascinated by bright lights and spinning objects and would stare at them while laughing, flapping his hands, and dancing on tiptoe. He also displayed the same movement while listening to music, which he had liked from infancy. He was intensely attached to a miniature car, which he held in his hand, day and night, but he never played imaginatively with this or any other toy. He could assemble jigsaw puzzles rapidly (with one hand because of the car held in the other), whether the picture side was exposed or hidden. From age 2, he had collected kitchen utensils and

---

autistic disorder A psychological disorder marked by symptoms of severe limitations of social interaction and communication, often accompanied by mental retardation and usually diagnosed in childhood.

arranged them in repetitive patterns all over the floors of the house. These pursuits, together with occasional periods of aimless running around, constituted his whole repertoire of spontaneous activities.

The major management problem was Richard's intense resistance to any attempt to change or extend his interests. Removing his toy car, disturbing his puzzles or patterns, even retrieving, for example, an egg whisk or a spoon for its legitimate use in cooking, or trying to make him look at a picture book precipitated temper tantrums that could last an hour or more, with screaming, kicking, and the biting of himself or others. These tantrums could be cut short by restoring the status quo. Otherwise, playing his favorite music or a long car ride was sometimes effective.

His parents had wondered if Richard might be deaf, but his love of music, his accurate echoing, and his sensitivity to some very soft sounds, such as those made by unwrapping a chocolate in the next room, convinced them that this was not the cause of his abnormal behavior. Psychological testing gave him a mental age of 3 years in non–language-dependent skills (fitting and assembly tasks), but only 18 months in language comprehension.*

In addition to deficiencies of verbal and nonverbal language, individuals with autistic disorder develop highly stereotyped patterns of behavior, interests, and activities, as in Richard's insistence on arranging the kitchen utensils and his highly emotional response to their disruption. Stereotyped movements may include clapping, finger flicking, rocking, dipping and swaying. Postural abnormalities, such as walking on tiptoe, may also occur, together with fascination at an object's movements and strong attachment to a specific inanimate object (as Richard's car).

Among theoretical accounts of autistic disorder is the *theory-of-mind* theory (Baron-Cohen et al., 1985; see Chapter 12). It states that a child with autistic disorder fails to understand that actions may be attributed to her or his own thoughts and feelings, and that the actions of others may be attributed similarly. For example, children with autistic disorder fail the "Sally–Anne false-belief task" (Tager-Flusberg, 2007). In the task, the child is told a story that is accompanied by picture or toys: Sally has a basket and Anne a box. Sally places a ball in her basket, then goes to play elsewhere. Anne takes the ball from Sally' basket and hides it in her box. The child is asked whether Sally will search for the ball when she returns and, if so, where she is likely to look. The failure of children diagnosed with the disorder to solve the problem suggested to Baron-Cohen and his colleagues that they lack the ability to invoke internal states to make sense of behavior, whether it be theirs or someone else's.

Tager-Flusberg (2007) pointed out that the theory-of-mind approach to autism fails to address a sufficiently wide range of the presenting symptoms. An adequate theory must range more widely to include social and emotional information processing. The author raises the possibility that such a theory may well include reference to the role of *mirror neurons* (see Chapter 4) in the developmental delays and deficits that characterize autistic disorder (see Oberman & Ramachandran, 2007). Specifically, to the extent such neurons are critical for the recognition of others' intentions and to the extent they remain underdeveloped in children diagnosed with autistic disorder, that underdevelopment may account for the child's limited processing

Autistic disorder's devastating toll on children and their families has prompted a broad front of research into its possible causes—genetic, immunological, neurochemical, neurocognitive, behavioral, and beyond (Thompson, 2007). Sometimes the research is controversial—as in the case of the popular view that certain mercury-containing vaccines (such as those for measles, mumps, and rubella) used in childhood are a cause of autistic disorder. Despite considerable research that has consistently failed to demonstrate a connection, the controversy persists (see Offit & Coffin, 2003; Kirby, 2006). The variety of presenting symptoms of the disorder suggests a complex etiology that, according to one researcher, makes autistic disorder "a problem that no one person or discipline can figure out alone" (Pettus, 2008, p. 39).

QUESTIONS TO CONSIDER

1. The dilemma of diagnosis of a psychological disorder is sometimes the "thin line" that separates an extreme form of normalcy from a mild form of disorder. Consider attention-deficit/hyperactivity disorder as a case in point. Which of the symptoms of the disorder strike you as most definitive in telling the difference between a child with the disorder and one that lacks it but is otherwise known as "always on the go and out of control"?

2. If you were to try to create a template for autistic disorder based on the case study of Richard, what would the major categories of the template be? In other words, which categories of symptoms would you consider most telling for the diagnosis of autistic disorder?

Substance-Related Disorders

According to the Axis I of DSM-IV-TR, **substance-related disorders** include *substance use disorders,* or what is usually called "addiction," and *substance-induced disorders,* which are less severe but which still cause social, occupational, or medical problems.

Description

Substance-related disorders have grave social consequences. Consider some of the disastrous effects caused by the abuse

---

substance-related disorders Psychological disorders that are characterized by addiction to drugs or alcohol or by abuse of drugs or alcohol.

*From Spitzer, R. L., Gibbon, M., Skodol, E. E., Williams, J. B. W., & First, M. B. (2002). *DSM-IV-TR case book: A learning companion to the Diagnostic and Statistical Manual of Mental Disorders.* Fourth Edition. Text Revision (pp. 336–337) Washington, DC: American Psychiatric Publishing.

of humankind's oldest drug, alcohol: automobile accidents, fetal alcohol syndrome, cirrhosis, increased rate of heart disease, and increased rate of cerebral hemorrhage. Smoking (which is associated with the nicotine-related disorders) greatly increases smokers' chances of dying of lung cancer, heart attack, and stroke; and women who smoke give birth to smaller, less healthy babies. Together, tobacco and alcohol account for more than 20% of deaths in the United States. Cocaine addiction often causes psychosis, brain damage, and death from overdose; it produces babies born with brain damage and consequent psychological problems. Competition for lucrative drug markets terrorizes neighborhoods, subverts political and judicial systems, and causes many deaths. People who take drugs intravenously run a serious risk of contracting AIDS.

The lifetime prevalence rates for substance-related disorders vary by substance but overall are estimated to average about 27% (Kessler et al., 1994). This means that 27% of individuals have reported the symptoms of substance-related disorders at least once in their lives. The 12-month prevalence rates average about 3.8% (Kessler et al., 2005), meaning that almost 4% of individuals have reported the same symptoms within the past year. The DSM-IV-TR estimates the lifetime prevalence rate for alcoholism to be about 15%. And although their alcohol use may not be severe enough to warrant a diagnosis of substance use disorder, as many as 25% of adults in North America experience problems due to alcohol consumption (Cunningham et al., 2001).

Possible Causes

Why do people use these substances and subject themselves to danger? People abuse certain drugs because the drugs activate the reinforcement system of the brain, which is normally activated only by natural reinforcers such as food, warmth, and sexual contact. Dopamine-secreting neurons are an important component of this system. Some drugs, such as crack cocaine, activate the reinforcement system rapidly and intensely, providing immediate and potent reinforcement. For many people, the immediate effects of drug use outweigh the prospect of dangers that lie in the future. As we saw in Chapter 4, although withdrawal symptoms make it more difficult for an addict to break his or her habit, these unpleasant symptoms are not responsible for the development of the addiction itself.

Genetic and Physiological Causes Not everyone is equally likely to become addicted to a drug (Bickel & Vuchinich, 2000). Many people manage to drink alcohol moderately, and even many users of potent drugs such as cocaine and heroin use them "recreationally" without becoming dependent on them. Obviously, environmental effects are important. People raised in a squalid environment without any real hope for a better life are more likely than other people to turn to drugs to escape from the unpleasant world that

surrounds them. But even in a given environment, whether poor or privileged, some people become addicts and some do not. Some of these behavioral differences are a result of genetic differences.

Most of the research on the effects of heredity on addiction has been devoted to alcoholism. Most people drink alcohol sometime in their lives and thus receive firsthand experience of its reinforcing effects. The same is not true for cocaine, heroin, or other drugs that have even more potent effects. In most countries, alcohol is freely and legally available, whereas cocaine and heroin must be purchased illegally. From what we now know about the effects of addictive drugs on the nervous system, it seems likely that the results of studies on the genetics of alcoholism will apply to other types of drug addiction as well.

As you read in Chapter 3, both twin studies and adoption studies have shown that susceptibility to alcoholism is heritable (e.g., Kendler et al., 1997; Prescott & Kendler, 1999; Rhee et al., 2003). In a review of the literature, Cloninger (1987) noted that there appear to be two principal types of alcoholics: those who have antisocial and pleasure-seeking tendencies—people who cannot abstain and drink consistently—and those who are anxiety ridden—people who are able to go without drinking for long periods but are unable to control themselves once they start. (For convenience, these two groups are referred to as *steady drinkers* and *bingers*.) Binge drinking is also associated with emotional dependence, behavioral rigidity, perfectionism, introversion, and guilt feelings about the drinking behavior. Steady drinkers usually begin their alcohol consumption early in life, whereas binge drinkers begin much later. (See TABLE 16·2.) More generally, the age at which a person has his or her first drink correlates strongly with future alcohol abuse. Researchers found a quick

[**TABLE 16·2**] **Characteristic Features of Two Types of Alcoholism**

	TYPES OF ALCOHOLISM	
Feature	**Steady**	**Binge**
Usual age of onset (yr)	Before 25	After 25
Spontaneous alcohol seeking (inability to abstain)	Frequent	Infrequent
Fighting and arrests when drinking	Frequent	Infrequent
Psychological dependence (loss of control)	Infrequent	Frequent
Guilt and fear about alcohol dependence	Infrequent	Frequent
Novelty seeking	High	Low
Harm avoidance	Low	High
Reward dependence	Low	High

Source: Reprinted with permission from Cloninger, C. R. (1987). Neurogenetic adaptive mechanisms in alcoholism. *Science*, 236, 410–416. Copyright © 1987 by the American Association for the Advancement of Science.

progression to alcohol-related harm among those who reported having had their first drink between the ages of 11 and 14 (DeWit et al., 2000). Among adults who had consumed alcohol at the age of 11 or 12, the study found that 13.5% met the criteria for alcohol abuse in adulthood, and nearly 16% were diagnosed as alcohol dependent.

An adoption study carried out in Sweden (Cloninger et al., 1985) found that men with biological fathers who were steady drinkers were almost seven times more likely to become steady drinkers themselves than were men whose biological fathers did not abuse alcohol. Family environment had no measurable effect; the boys began drinking whether or not the members of their adoptive families drank heavily. A related adoption study (Bohman et al., 1984) found that women tended not to become steady drinkers. Instead, the daughters of steady-drinking fathers tended to develop somatization disorder instead (see also Kriechman, 1987).

Unlike steady drinking, binge drinking is influenced more readily by environment. The Swedish adoption study found that having a biological parent who was a binge drinker had little effect on the development of binge drinking unless the child was exposed to a family environment in which heavy drinking occurred. This effect was seen in both male and female children.

When we find an effect of heredity on behavior, we have good reason to suspect a biological marker of some kind. That is, genes affect behavior only by affecting the body. A susceptibility to alcoholism could conceivably be caused by differences in the ability to digest or metabolize alcohol or by differences in the structure or biochemistry of the brain. Most investigators believe that differences in brain physiology are most likely to play a role. Cloninger and colleagues (1995) noted that people with antisocial tendencies, including steady drinkers, show a strong tendency to seek novelty and excitement. These people are disorderly and distractible (many have a history of hyperactivity as children) and lack restraint in their behavior. The brains of steady drinkers may be unresponsive to danger and to social disapproval, because of an undersensitive punishment mechanism. They also may have an undersensitive reinforcement system; this may lead them to seek more-intense thrills (including those provided by alcohol) to experience pleasurable sensations. Thus, they seek the euphoric effects of alcohol. Conversely, binge drinkers may have an oversensitive punishment system. Normally, they avoid drinking because of the guilt they experience afterward, but once they start, and once the sedative effect begins, the alcohol-induced suppression of the punishment system makes it impossible for them to stop.

Animal models have proved useful in the study of the physiology of addiction. Through selective breeding, researchers have developed two different strains of rats that differ in their response to alcohol. Alcohol-preferring rats do just what their name implies: If given a drinking tube containing a solution of alcohol along with their water and food, they become heavy drinkers. The alcohol-nonpreferring rats abstain. Fadda and colleagues (1990) found that alcohol appeared to produce a larger release of dopamine in the brains of alcohol-preferring rats than in the brains of alcohol-nonpreferring rats. This result suggests that the reinforcing effect of alcohol is stronger in alcohol-preferring rats.

As for humans, Nestler (2005) concluded that drugs of abuse eventually exert similar effects in the limbic system, especially the mesolimbic dopamine pathway, but that considerable research will be required before effective treatments become available. Franken, Booij, and van den Brink (2005) speculated that dopamine may well be involved in drug craving by enhancing the drug user's attention to drug-relevant stimuli.

Cognitive Causes   Cooper, Russell, and George (1988) argued that people develop patterns of heavy drug use because of what they believe about the positive benefits of using drugs. For example, people who believe that alcohol will help them cope with negative emotions and who also expect that alcohol will make them more likable, sociable, or attractive may use alcohol to obtain these perceived positive effects. People may abuse alcohol to moderate both positive and negative emotions (Cooper et al., 1995). In this view, drug abuse or dependence is a way of avoiding perceived negative effects such as having negative emotions, not being outgoing enough, feeling uncomfortable around others, and so on. The influence of alcohol or other drugs provides an escape from such feelings. The relief negatively reinforces the use of drugs, but the effect is temporary. The negative feelings return with sobriety, leading to further drug use. Soon, the person may be intoxicated or high most or all of the time.

QUESTION TO CONSIDER

Were a friend to approach you about her concern that she may be drinking excessively, what questions would you ask her to help her draw a reasonable conclusion about her concern?

Schizophrenia

Schizophrenia, the most common of the psychotic disorders, described in Axis I of the DSM-IV-TR, includes several subtypes, each having a distinctive set of symptoms. For many years, controversy has existed over whether schizophrenia is one disorder with various subtypes or whether each subtype constitutes a distinct disorder. Because the *prognosis* (the likelihood of recovery) differs for the various subtypes of schizophrenia, they appear to differ at least in severity. However, a particular individual may, at different times, meet the criteria for different subtypes. Some experts have referred to schizophrenia

---

schizophrenia   A serious psychological disorder characterized by thought disturbances, hallucinations, anxiety, emotional withdrawal, and delusions.

as the "quintessential" psychological disorder. By this they refer not only to its universal incidence but also to the characteristically tragic ways in which it transforms the lives of schizophrenic individuals and their families.

Description

Schizophrenia involves distortions of thought, perception, memory, and emotion; bizarre behavior; and social withdrawal. It is a disorder with no borders (see Murphy, 1976). Descriptions of symptoms in historical writings indicate that this disorder may have existed as early as medieval times (Heinrichs, 2003). However, the word *schizophrenia* is widely misused. The word literally means "split mind," but it does not mean a split or multiple personality. People often say inaccurately that they "feel schizophrenic" about an issue when they really mean that they have mixed or divided feelings about it. The psychiatrist who invented the term, Eugen Bleuler ("OI-gun BLOI-lur"), intended to refer to a split with reality caused by extreme mental disorganization—a condition in which thoughts and feelings no longer worked together normally.

Schizophrenia is characterized by two categories of symptoms, positive and negative. The distinction is important. A **positive symptom** of schizophrenia emerges and makes itself known by its presence. Positive symptoms include thought disorders, delusions, and hallucinations. A thought disorder—a pattern of disorganized, irrational thinking—is probably the most definitive symptom of schizophrenia. People with schizophrenia have great difficulty arranging their thoughts logically and sorting out plausible conclusions from absurd ones. In conversation, they may jump from one topic to another spontaneously. Sometimes they utter meaningless words or apparently choose words for their rhyme rather than for their meaning. A *delusion* is a belief that is contrary to fact. Although debates exist about the exact nature of delusions (e.g., Leeser & O'Donohue, 1999; Mullen, 2003), these false beliefs are readily identifiable in the context of mental illness and tend to appear in three forms. *Delusions of persecution* are false beliefs that others are plotting and conspiring against the individual. *Delusions of grandeur* are a person's false beliefs in his or her own power and importance, such as a conviction that the person has godlike powers or has special knowledge that no one else possesses. *Delusions of control* are related to delusions of persecution; a person may believe, for example, that he or she is being controlled by others through such means as radar or tiny radio receivers implanted in the brain.

Hallucinations—the perception of stimuli that are not actually present—constitute the third positive symptom of schizophrenia. When filmmakers depict hallucinations, they typically use a device to let viewers know that the sound or sight is not real. For example, they may show visual hallucinations as ghostlike and give imaginary sounds an eerie quality. For the person with schizophrenia, cues like these would likely be a relief. Unfortunately, to someone with this

A pattern of disorganized, irrational thinking is probably the most definitive positive symptom of schizophrenia.

disorder, the hallucinated perceptions and sensations seem perfectly real, as real and as substantial as this textbook (Nasar, 1998).

The most common hallucinations in schizophrenia are auditory. The typical schizophrenic hallucination consists of voices talking to the person. Sometimes the voices order the person to do something; sometimes they criticize and humiliate the person for being unworthy, unclean, or immoral; sometimes they just utter meaningless phrases. People with schizophrenia may hear a voice that keeps a running commentary on their behavior.

In contrast to these positive symptoms, the **negative symptoms** of schizophrenia consist of the absence of normal behaviors: flattened emotional response, poverty of speech, lack of initiative and persistence, inability to feel pleasure, and social withdrawal. Negative (and positive) symptoms are not specific to schizophrenia; they are seen in many neurological disorders that involve brain damage, especially to the frontal lobes.

As we see later in this chapter, evidence suggests that positive and negative symptoms result from different physiological disorders. Positive symptoms appear to involve excessive activity in some neural circuits that include dopamine as a neurotransmitter. Negative symptoms appear to be caused by brain damage. Many researchers suspect that these two sets of symptoms involve a common set of underlying causes, but these causes have yet to be identified with certainty.

According to the DSM-IV-TR, schizophrenia has a prevalence of 0.5 to 1.5% worldwide. It typically makes its appearance in the period from the late teens to the early 30s. Earlier onset, especially in children, is rare.

---

positive symptom A symptom of schizophrenia, including thought disorder, delusions, or hallucinations.

hallucination A perceptual experience that occurs in the absence of external stimulation of the corresponding sensory organ; often accompanies schizophrenia.

negative symptoms A symptom of schizophrenia that consists of the absence of normal behaviors; negative symptoms include flattened emotion, poverty of speech, lack of initiative and persistence, and social withdrawal.

Types of Schizophrenia

According to the DSM-IV-TR, five types of schizophrenia exist: paranoid, disorganized, catatonic, undifferentiated, and residual.

The pre-eminent symptoms of **paranoid schizophrenia** are delusions of persecution, grandeur, or control—positive symptoms. The word *paranoid* is so widely used in ordinary language that it has come to mean "suspicious." However, not all paranoid schizophrenics believe that they are being persecuted. Some believe that they hold special powers that can save the world—that they are Superman, Napoleon, or Joan of Arc. Some hold complementary delusions of grandeur and persecution.

Disorganized schizophrenia is a serious progressive and irreversible disorder characterized primarily by disturbances of thought. People with disorganized schizophrenia often display signs of emotion, especially silly laughter, that are inappropriate to the circumstances. Also, their speech tends to be a jumble of words: "I came to the hospital to play, gay, way, lay, day, bray, donkey, monkey" (Snyder, 1974, p. 132). This sort of speech is often referred to as a *word salad*. Hallucinations and delusions are common.

Catatonic schizophrenia (from the Greek *katateinein,* meaning "to stretch or draw tight") is characterized by various motor disturbances, including both extreme excitement and stupor. People with this form of schizophrenia will display negative symptoms: catatonic postures—bizarre stationary poses that may be maintained for many hours—and waxy flexibility, in which the person's limbs can be molded into new positions, which are then maintained for long periods.

Many patients are diagnosed as having **undifferentiated schizophrenia;** that is, they have delusions, hallucinations, and disorganized behavior but do not meet the criteria for paranoid, disorganized, or catatonic schizophrenia. In addition, some patients' symptoms change after an initial diagnosis, and their classification changes accordingly.

Residual schizophrenia is the diagnosis when at least one episode of one of the four other types of schizophrenia has occurred but no single, prominent positive symptom is currently observable. However, negative symptoms are observable, as are muted forms of positive symptoms. Residual schizophrenia may mark a transition from a full-blown schizophrenic episode to remission (the absence of any symptoms), but it also may continue to linger year after year.

---

paranoid schizophrenia A type of schizophrenia in which the person has delusions of persecution, grandeur, or control.

disorganized schizophrenia A type of schizophrenia characterized primarily by disturbances of thought and a flattened or silly affect.

catatonic schizophrenia A type of schizophrenia characterized primarily by motor disturbances, including catatonic postures and waxy flexibility.

undifferentiated schizophrenia A type of schizophrenia characterized by fragments of the symptoms of different types of schizophrenia.

residual schizophrenia A type of schizophrenia that may follow an episode of one of the other types and is marked by negative symptoms but not by any prominent positive symptom.

Possible Causes

For more than a century, research into the causes of all kinds and forms of schizophrenia has reflected the challenge that psychologists face in attempting to understand how psychological and biological factors interact to influence behavior. The diathesis–stress model of mental disorders, discussed earlier in the chapter, is a widely referenced account: Schizophrenia appears to result from one or more inherited biological predispositions that are activated by environmental stressors.

Genetic Causes Bleuler (1950), a pioneer in the diagnosis and study of schizophrenia, divided the disorder into *reactive* and *process* forms. He designated patients with a general history of good mental health as having *reactive schizophrenia,* on the assumption that their disorder was a reaction to stressful life situations. Typically, these patients soon recovered, and few experienced another episode. Patients with indications of mental illness early in life, however, were designated as having *process schizophrenia,* which was considered a chronic disorder.

If process schizophrenia has its roots in early life, an important task is to determine what the early predictors or risk factors are. In theory, the ability to identify people with a high risk of schizophrenia while they are still young will allow clinicians to implement some form of therapy before the disorder becomes advanced. The early signs also may indicate whether the causes of schizophrenia are biological, environmental, or both.

Many studies of people who develop schizophrenia in adulthood have found that they were different from others even in childhood. However, these studies do not tell us whether these differences resulted from physiological disorders or from the behavior of other family members when those who were later diagnosed with schizophrenia were in infancy and childhood. One remarkable study obtained home movies of people with adult-onset schizophrenia when they were children (Walker & Lewine, 1990). Although schizophrenia did not manifest itself until adulthood, viewers of the films (six graduate students and one professional clinical psychologist) did an excellent job of identifying the children who would later develop it. The viewers commented on the children's poor eye contact, relative lack of responsiveness and positive affect, and generally poor motor coordination. Clearly, something was different about these patients' behavior even early in life.

Advances in genetics and research involving twin and adoption studies have established the heritability of schizophrenia—or, more precisely, the high heritability of a tendency toward schizophrenia (Gottesman & Reilly, 2003). Identical twins are much more likely to be concordant for schizophrenia than are fraternal twins, and the children of parents with schizophrenia are more likely themselves to develop schizophrenia, even if they were adopted and raised by parents without schizophrenia (Gottesman & Moldin, 1998). Twin studies of schizophrenia compare the concordance rates

[**TABLE 16·3**] Summary of Major European Studies of the Genetics of Schizophrenia in Families and Twins

Relation to Person Identified as Schizophrenic	Percentage with Schizophrenia
Spouse	1.0
Grandchild	2.8
Niece/nephew	2.6
Child	9.3
Sibling	7.3
Fraternal twin	12.1
Identical twin	44.3

Source: Davison, G. C., & Neale, J. M. (1990). *Abnormal psychology*. New York: John Wiley & Sons

of monozygotic (MZ) or identical twins with the concordance rates of siblings of different genetic relatedness who were reared either together or apart. (Recall from Chapter 3 that twins are concordant for a trait if neither or both express it and discordant if only one expresses it.) According to Gottesman and Shields (1982) and Gottesman (1991), schizophrenia concordance rates for MZ twins are about 50%, but they are less than about 20% for dizygotic (DZ) or fraternal twins. (See TABLE 16·3.)

It is important to note that although the likelihood of developing schizophrenia increases if a person has relatives with schizophrenia, this disorder is not a simple trait, like eye color, that is inherited. Of people with schizophrenia, 63% do not have a first- or second-degree relative who also has the disorder (Gottesman & Erlenmeyer-Kimling, 2001). Even if both parents have schizophrenia, the probability that their child will develop it is 30% or less.

It is generally agreed that a person inherits a predisposition to develop schizophrenia (Crespi & Badcock, 2008; Wade, 2008). In this view, most environments will foster normal development, whereas certain environments will trigger various disorders, including schizophrenia. If the diathesis–stress model is valid as it applies to schizophrenia, we would expect that some people carry a complex pattern of genes for schizophrenia but do not express it. Their environments do not trigger schizophrenia, or they have acquired the coping skills to deal successfully with environmental stressors. Such a person might be the member of a pair of MZ twins discordant for schizophrenia.

The logical way to test this model is to examine the children of both members of discordant pairs of MZ twins. Gottesman and Bertelsen (1989) found that the percentage of children with schizophrenia was nearly identical for both members of such pairs (16.8% for the parent with schizophrenia; 17.4% for the parent without schizophrenia). In contrast, for parents who were fraternal (DZ) twins and discordant for schizophrenia, the percentages were dissimilar— 17.4% when the parent had schizophrenia and 2.1% when the parent did not have schizophrenia. These results provide strong evidence that schizophrenia is heritable but also support the conclusion that carrying the gene complex for schizophrenia does not mean that a person will necessarily develop schizophrenia. (See FIGURE 16·1.) As suggested by the diathesis–stress model, environmental factors are also likely to be involved.

By using scanning techniques that permit rapid analysis of an individual's genome, Walsh et al. (2008) identified rare genetic mutations that were either inherited or that occurred spontaneously during or soon after conception. They found that these mutations were three times more likely to occur in individuals with schizophrenia than in matched control participants. The incidence was even higher in participants with childhood-onset schizophrenia. Of particular interest were those mutations that disrupted neurodevelopmental pathways and glutaminergic pathways in particular (recall from Chapter 4 that glutamate is the primary excitatory neurotransmitter in the central nervous system).

Neurophysiological Causes: The Dopamine Hypothesis

Researchers have formulated the **dopamine hypothesis**: the proposal that abnormal activity of dopamine-containing neurons is a causal factor in schizophrenia. That is, the positive symptoms of schizophrenia are produced by the overactivity of dopamine-transmitting synapses. Amphetamines, cocaine, and the antipsychotic drugs act on synapses—the junctions between nerve cells—in the brain and can produce the symptoms of schizophrenia, both in people who have schizophrenia and in people who do not. As you may recall from Chapter 4, one neuron passes on excitatory or inhibitory messages to another by releasing a small amount of

---

dopamine hypothesis The hypothesis that the positive symptoms of schizophrenia are caused by overactivity of synapses in the brain that use dopamine.

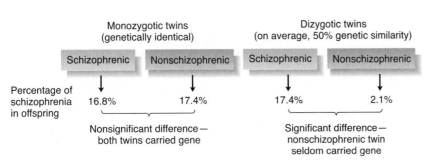

[**FIGURE 16·1**] Heritability of schizophrenia. As shown in this diagram, people can have an unexpressed "schizophrenia gene."

Monozygotic twins (genetically identical) | Dizygotic twins (on average, 50% genetic similarity)

Schizophrenic | Nonschizophrenic | Schizophrenic | Nonschizophrenic

Percentage of schizophrenia in offspring: 16.8% | 17.4% | 17.4% | 2.1%

Nonsignificant difference— both twins carried gene | Significant difference— nonschizophrenic twin seldom carried gene

neurotransmitter from its terminal button into the synaptic cleft. The chemical activates receptors on the surface of the receiving neuron, and the activated receptors either excite or inhibit the receiving neuron. Drugs such as amphetamine and cocaine *stimulate* receptors for dopamine. In contrast, antipsychotic drugs *block* dopamine receptors and prevent them from becoming stimulated.

Gonzalez-Maeso and his colleagues (2008) focused on the effects of newer antipsychotic drugs and hallucinogenic drugs, such as psilocybin and LSD (see Chapter 4), in their efforts to identify neuroreceptor complexes in schizophrenia beyond those associated with dopamine. Specifically, they found strong evidence that glutamate and serotonin receptors bind each other and that this binding may account for the effects of atypical antipsychotic drugs (see Chapter 17) in the treatment of schizophrenia. In other words, the dopamine hypothesis should be amended to become a dopamine–serotonin–glutamate hypothesis (see Berenson, 2008; Snyder, 2008).

Physiological Causes: Neurological Disorders

Although the dopamine hypothesis has long been the dominant biological explanation for schizophrenia, other evidence suggests that it offers only a partial explanation. Antipsychotic drugs alleviate positive, but not negative, symptoms of schizophrenia (Angrist et al., 1980). Perhaps those patients who do not improve with medication have primarily negative symptoms.

Once researchers began paying more attention to negative symptoms, they discovered evidence for brain damage in patients exhibiting these symptoms. In several studies, the CT or MRI scans of patients revealed larger than normal cerebral ventricles among schizophrenic patients (Sullivan et al., 1998; Zipursky et al., 1998). Evidence also suggests that people with schizophrenia display abnormal neural processing while trying to suppress inappropriate responses (Kiehl et al., 2000). Similarly, Pfefferbaum and colleagues (1988) found evidence that the sulci (the wrinkles in the brain; see Chapter 4) were wider in the brains of patients with schizophrenia. Enlargement of the ventricles of the brain and widening of the sulci indicate the absence of brain tissue. Indeed, other research shows that schizophrenic patients have less cortical gray matter than do persons with normal psychological functioning (Suddath et al., 1990; Lim et al., 1998; Mitelman et al., 2003).

The study by Suddath and colleagues (1990) is particularly interesting because their participants were identical-twin pairs. The investigators examined MRI scans of MZ twins discordant for schizophrenia and found that, in almost every case, the twin with schizophrenia had larger lateral and third ventricles. In addition, the hippocampus was smaller in the twin with schizophrenia, and the total volume of the gray matter in the left temporal lobe was reduced. FIGURE 16•2 shows a set of MRI scans from a pair of twins. As you can see, the lateral ventricles are larger in the brain of the twin with schizophrenia. Still other research has shown a progressive loss of gray matter during adolescence among people who develop schizophrenia during childhood (Rapoport et al., 1999).

[**FIGURE 16•2**] MRI scans of the brains of identical twins discordant for schizophrenia. (a) Normal twin. (b) Twin with schizophrenia. Arrows point to the lateral ventricles.

(Courtesy of D. R. Weinberger, National Institute of Mental Health, Saint Elizabeth's Hospital, Washington, DC.)

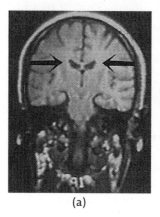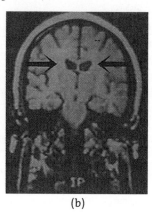

(a) (b)

Another possible neurological cause of schizophrenia is interference with normal prenatal brain development. Several studies show that people born during the winter months are more likely to develop schizophrenia later in life—a *seasonality effect* (Torrey et al., 1997). Carrion-Baralt and his colleagues (2006) found evidence for seasonality effects in their study conducted in Puerto Rico. Individuals with schizophrenia were more likely (36.8%) to be born during the winter months than same-family members without schizophrenia (21.3%). The authors concluded that the difference in season of birth constitutes a "second hit" in a "two-hit" model of schizophrenia (Maynard et al., 2001), in which the first hit is the disruption of early neural development—a model reminiscent of the diathesis–stress model discussed earlier in this chapter. Torrey et al. (1977) first suggested that the causal factor could be seasonal variations in nutritional factors or, more likely, variations in toxins or infectious agents in air, water, or food. Several diseases known to be caused by viruses, such as measles, influenza, and chicken pox, show a similar seasonality effect. It is seen most strongly in poor, urban locations, where people are at greater risk for viral infections (Machon et al., 1983). A seasonally related virus could affect either a pregnant woman or a newborn. Two pieces of evidence suggest that the damage is done prenatally. First, brain development is more susceptible to disruption prenatally. Second, a study of the offspring of women who were pregnant during a 1957 epidemic of type A2 influenza in Finland showed an elevated incidence of schizophrenia (Mednick et al., 1990), but only among offspring of women who were in the second trimester of their pregnancies during the epidemic. Presumably, the viral infection produced toxins that interfered with the brain development of some of the fetuses, resulting in the later development of schizophrenia. Keep in mind, however, that influenza is just one of many potential causes of schizophrenia; a large-scale study conducted in Denmark revealed that prenatal exposure to influenza could account for only 1.4% of the 9,462 cases of schizophrenia that were examined (Takei et al., 1996). More recently, Brown and colleagues (2004), by using a U.S. sample, showed a sevenfold increase for schizophrenia when influenza exposure occurred in the first trimester.

Birth trauma is another possible neurological cause of schizophrenia. Schwarzkopf and colleagues (1989) found that if a person with schizophrenia does not have relatives with a schizophrenic disorder—that is, if no evidence exists that the disease is a result of heredity—he or she is more likely to have had a history of neurological complications at or around the time of birth. Thus, brain damage not related to heredity may also be a cause of schizophrenia.

Cognitive and Environmental Causes The personality and communicative abilities of either or both parents appear to play an influential role in the development of schizophrenic symptoms in their children. Several studies have shown that children reared by parents who are dominating, overprotective, rigid, and insensitive to the needs of others are more likely to develop schizophrenia (Roff & Knight, 1995). In many cases, a parent may be verbally accepting of the child yet in other ways reject him or her, which establishes a conflict for the child called a **double bind.** For example, a mother may encourage her son to become emotionally dependent on her yet continually reject him when he tries to hug her or sit on her lap or play with her (see Laing & Esterson, 1964; Bateson, 1973).

Children reared in families racked with discord also seem to be at greater risk of developing schizophrenia. For example, in a study of 14 schizophrenic individuals, Lidz et al. (1965) found that each of these individuals came from a family that underwent either chronic discord in which the integrity of the parents' marriage was perpetually threatened or marital problems in which the bizarre behavior of one family member was tolerated by the other members. Children in families in which parents treat them with hostility or in which parents present confusing communication to them are at risk for developing schizophrenia (Goldstein & Strachan, 1987). However, researchers are still attempting to determine whether marital discord, family hostility, and confusing communications are causes or effects of schizophrenia.

In addition to exploring family-related causes of schizophrenia, researchers also have identified a family-related variable that affects the likelihood that a person with schizophrenia will recover from it. Brown and his colleagues (Brown et al., 1966) labeled this variable *expressed emotion*—expressions of criticism and hostility and emotional overinvolvement by family members toward the patient. Brown and colleagues found that if a patient was living in a family environment in which the level of expressed emotion was low, she or he was more likely to recover, whereas patients in families in which it was high were more likely to continue to exhibit schizophrenic symptoms.

This finding is consistent across hundreds of studies conducted in many different cultures (Jenkins & Karno, 1992). Studies from North America, England, Denmark, Italy, France, Spain, Germany, Taiwan, India, Egypt, and Australia all indicate that despite differences in the ways that people of different cultures perceive mental illness and express themselves, expressed emotion does not seem to be a culture-bound phenomenon. Two elements of expressed emotion in the families of patients with schizophrenia appear to be common to all cultures: critical comments and emotional overinvolvement. Jenkins and Karno (1992) also found that expressed emotion tends to be higher in many more industrialized than nonindustrialized cultures—and that people in nonindustrialized countries are more supportive of family members with schizophrenia than are people in industrialized countries. These findings may reflect the relatively greater access to jobs that a person with schizophrenia has in nonindustrialized countries, as well as the greater proportion of extended families, in which more individuals can participate in the care of the family member who has schizophrenia.

QUESTIONS TO CONSIDER

1. Imagine that you are a clinical psychologist. A client of yours complains of hearing voices. You suspect that this individual may have schizophrenia, but you wish to gather more information before you make your diagnosis. What sorts of information about this person do you need before you can make your diagnosis? How would you gather it?

2. Suppose that a friend of yours, who often acts strangely, is diagnosed as having schizophrenia. Your friend knows that the diagnosis is incorrect, but nobody believes him because his strange behavior makes the diagnosis seem believable. What would your friend have to say or do to convince you that he is normal?

Mood Disorders

Everyone experiences moods varying from sadness to happiness to elation. We're excited when our team wins a big game, saddened to learn that a friend's long-term relationship has gone sour, thrilled at a higher-than-expected raise at work, and devastated by the death of a loved one. Such is the emotional range that colors life's experiences. Some people, though, experience more dramatic changes than these. Significant shifts or disturbances in mood that adversely affect normal perception, thought, and behavior are called **mood disorders.** They may be characterized by a

---

double bind The conflict caused for a child when he or she is given inconsistent messages or cues from a parent.

mood disorders A psychological disorder characterized by significant shifts or disturbances in mood that adversely affect normal perception, thought, and behavior. Mood disorders may be characterized by deep, foreboding depression or may involve a combination of depression and mania.

deep, foreboding depression or by a combination of depression and **mania**, which is defined by the DSM-IV-TR as the abnormal and persistent elevation of an expansive or irritable mood.

Description

In contrast to schizophrenia, in which the principal symptom is disordered thought, the mood disorders are primarily disorders of emotion. The most severe mood disorders are the bipolar disorders and major depressive disorder. **Bipolar I disorder** is characterized by episodes of mania by itself or in a mix with anxiety, usually accompanied by episodes of major depression. **Bipolar II disorder** is marked by major depressive episodes that are accompanied by periods of less severe mania, known as *hypomanic* episodes. **Major depressive disorder** involves persistent, severe feelings of sadness and worthlessness accompanied by changes in appetite, sleeping, and other behavior. The lifetime prevalence for major depressive disorder is about 15% (Nestler et al., 2002; QuadrantHealthCom, 2005).

A less severe form of depression is called *dysthymic disorder* (pronounced "dis-THIGH-mik"). The term comes from the Greek words *dus*, "bad," and *thymos*, "spirit." The primary difference between this disorder and major depressive disorder is its relatively lower severity. Similarly, *cyclothymic disorder* resembles bipolar II disorder but is less severe.

Mania   A person in the grip of *mania* (the Greek word for "madness") shows expansive, irritable behavior that may be wildly out of place in the situation in which it occurs. During manic episodes, people appear elated and are self-confident; however, any contradiction or interference tends to make them suddenly angry. Their speech (and, presumably, their thinking) becomes very rapid. They tend to flit from topic to topic and often are full of grandiose plans. Although their thoughts are not as disorganized as those of people with schizophrenia, they tend to be restless and hyperactive, often pacing ceaselessly. They may have delusions and hallucinations that fit their exuberant mood. They tend to persist in pleasurable activities regardless of dire consequences. Because very few patients exhibit mania only, the DSM-IV-TR classifies all cases in which mania occurs as bipolar disorders.

Depression   People with depression have feelings of extreme sadness and usually are full of self-directed guilt, but not because of any particular incident. Depressed people cannot always state why they are depressed. Aaron Beck (1967), a leading figure in the treatment of mood disorders, identified five major symptoms of depression: (1) a sad and apathetic mood; (2) feelings of worthlessness and hopelessness; (3) a desire to withdraw from other people; (4) sleeplessness and loss of appetite and sexual desire; and (5) a change in activity level, either to lethargy or to agitation. Most people who are labeled "depressed" actually have dysthymic disorder, the less extreme form of depression described as being "down in the dumps" much of the day and for the majority of days over a period of at least 2 years. Major depressive disorder also must be distinguished from grief, such as the sorrow caused by the death of a loved one. Many people who have a major depressive disorder or depressive episodes of bipolar disorders commit suicide. The mortality rate (including suicide) among people with mood disorders is two to three times greater than that of the general population (Fogarty et al., 1994).

Major Depressive Disorder with Seasonal Pattern

Seasonality may define a specific pattern of major depressive episodes, as in cases involving people who become depressed during the winter season, when days are short and nights are long. The symptoms of this form of depression are slightly different from those of major depressive disorder. Both conditions involve lethargy and sleep disturbances, but seasonal depression also includes a craving for carbohydrates and an accompanying weight gain. (As you will recall, people with major depressive disorder tend to lose their appetites.) Several investigators have noticed that the symptoms of the disorder resemble the behavioral characteristics of hibernation, such as those already mentioned, plus oversleeping, and lethargy (Rosenthal et al., 1986; Neuhaus & Rosenthal, 1997; Rosenthal, 2000). Animals that hibernate do so during the

The symptoms of major depression include apathy, feelings of worthlessness, social withdrawal, changes in sleeping and eating patterns, and lethargy or agitation.

---

mania   Abnormal and persistent elevation of an expansive or irritable mood.

bipolar I disorder   A mood disorder in which alternating states of depression and mania are separated by periods of relatively normal affect.

bipolar II disorder   A mood disorder; marked by major depressive episodes that are accompanied by less severe mania (hypomanic episodes).

major depressive disorder   Persistent and severe feelings of sadness and worthlessness accompanied by changes in appetite, sleeping, and other behavior.

winter. Their behavior is triggered by a combination of short day length and cooler temperatures. Thus, some of the brain mechanisms involved in hibernation may also be responsible for the mood changes associated with the time of year.

Possible Causes

The possible causes of mood disorders are many and various. Let's look at three categories of potential causes: faulty cognition, heredity, and brain biochemistry.

Cognitive Causes Faulty cognition seems to play a role in depression; clearly, people with mood disorders don't have the same outlook on life as do others. Depressed people are generally negative about themselves and, as such, can be challenging to be around. Specifically, they are likely to say things like: "Nobody likes me," "I'm not good at anything," or "What's the point in even trying—I'll just screw up anyway." Thus, the depressed individual gets caught in a vicious circle: Negative statements strain interpersonal relationships, causing others to withdraw or to withhold social support; this in turn reinforces the depressed individual's negative statements (Klerman & Weissman, 1986; Weissman et al., 2000).

According to Beck (1967, 1991), the primary disturbance in depression is a distortion of the person's view of reality. For example, a person whose recipe fails may see the failure as proof of his or her basic incompetence. According to Beck, depressed people's thinking is characterized by self-blame (things that go wrong are always their fault), overemphasis on the negative aspects of life (even small problems are blown out of proportion), and failure to anticipate positive change (a pessimistic attitude prevails). This kind of thinking involves negative thoughts about the self, about the world, and about the future, which Beck collectively referred to as the *cognitive triad*. In short, depressed people see no hope for future improvement. Because they blame their present miserable situation on their inadequacies and see these inadequacies as permanent characteristics, they have no reason to believe things will be different in the future. Beck's theory has been useful in alerting therapists to the importance of considering the thought processes, as well as the feelings, of a patient with a severe mood disorder. Of course, if we observe an association between faulty cognition and depression, we cannot necessarily conclude that the faulty cognition causes the depression; the reverse could be true.

Attributional style (Abramson et al., 1978; Abramson et al., 1989) may be a specific cognitive factor in depression. According to this view, it is not merely experiencing negative events that causes people to become depressed. More important are the attributions people make about why those events occur. A person's attributional style, then, serves as a predisposition or diathesis for depression. In other words, people prone to depression tend to have hopeless outlooks—"I am not good at anything I try to do, and it will never get any better. I am always going to be a lousy person."

The attributional style model suggests that depression is most likely to occur when people with pessimistic attributional styles encounter significant or frequent life stressors (Abramson et al., 1995). Such individuals then generalize their pessimistic attributions to otherwise moderate stressors, and eventually a deep sense of hopelessness and despair sets in. The diathesis–stress model of depression has been supported by research on both adults (e.g., Metalsky et al., 1993; Johnson et al., 2001) and adolescents (e.g., Joiner, 2000; Abela & Sullivan, 2003). The evidence indicates that the combination of a hopeless outlook plus negative life events is predictive of depression. When both components coincide, people appear to feel a double dose of hopelessness. Not only do they perceive negative outcomes as being their own fault, but they also perceive positive outcomes as due to circumstance or to luck. In addition, they apply pessimistic attributions to a wide range of events and experiences and apply positive attributions only to a very narrow range of events and experiences, if any.

Genetic Causes Like schizophrenia, the mood disorders appear to have a genetic component. People who have first-degree relatives with a serious mood disorder are 10 times more likely to develop these disorders than are people without afflicted relatives (Rosenthal, 1970). (First-degree relatives are a person's parents, children, and siblings.) First-degree relatives of people with the bipolar disorders are 7% more likely than the rest of the population to have the disorder (Sadovnick et al., 1994). Furthermore, the concordance rate for the bipolar disorders is 60% for monozygotic twins, compared with 15% for dizygotic twins (Kendler et al., 1993). For major depression, the MZ/DZ figures are 40% and 11%, respectively (Allen, 1976). Thus, a case can be made that heritable factors predispose people to develop these disorders. Abbott (2008) raised the question of whether the continued difficulty in identifying the genes responsible for schizophrenia and other major psychological disorders is a reflection of the unusual complexity of the genetic systems involved or of the difficulty of adequately defining the disorders—or perhaps of both.

Neurophysiological Causes: Biochemical Factors: The effectiveness of certain drug therapies for mood disorders suggests to some researchers that biochemical factors may play a role in the development and course of mood disorders. Although a certain logic to this argument exists, the issue remains unsettled.

The evidence clearly shows that at least two neurotransmitters, norepinephrine and serotonin, are related to depression (Ressler & Nemeroff, 2000). People with major depression have lower levels of these neurotransmitters than do people without the disorder. It is also the case that drug therapies that increase the amount of these substances in the synapses, or make the substances available for longer periods, have beneficial effects on depression.

Several studies have found evidence of biochemical abnormalities in the brains of people with mood disorders. Taking samples of neurotransmitters directly from the living brain is not possible, but when neurotransmitters are released at the synapse, a small amount is broken down by enzymes in the brain, and some of the breakdown products accumulate in the cerebrospinal fluid or pass into the bloodstream and collect in the urine. This makes it possible to analyze cerebrospinal fluid and urine for these substances.

For example, one study found that the level of a compound called 5HIAA in the cerebrospinal fluid of depressed people who had attempted suicide was significantly lower than those in control participants (Träskmann et al., 1981). The lower level of this compound, which is produced when serotonin is broken down, implies lower activity in serotonin-secreting neurons in the brains of depressed individuals. In fact, 20% of the people with levels below the median subsequently committed suicide, whereas none of the participants with levels above the median did so. Taube and colleagues (1978) obtained evidence for decreased activity of neurons that secrete norepinephrine in patients with mood disorders; in these patients, they found low levels of a compound (MHPG) that appears in the urine when the neurotransmitter is broken down. Thus, the decreased activity of serotonin- and norepinephrine-secreting neurons appears to be related to depression. Additionally, researchers have found evidence of a genetic association between major depression and suicide (Lemonde et al., 2003). Certain genotypes containing the homozygous G[-1019] allele were found twice as often in depressed patients in comparison with a control group, and four times more often in suicide victims.

Jacob (2004) theorized that major depressive disorder may be the result of stress that suppresses neurogenesis (the growth of new neurons) in the adult human brain. The fact that serotonin can be effective in treating depression meshes well with the finding that it also enhances neurogenesis. The growth of new neurons, in turn, may constitute the biological substrate for the emergence of the cognitive activity to which Beck and others have pointed as essential for the remission of depression's symptoms.

Although the brain biochemistry of patients with mood disorders appears to be abnormal, we cannot be certain that a biochemical imbalance is the first event in a sequence that leads to depression. Environmental stimuli may cause the depression, which may then lead to biochemical changes in the brain. For example, investigators found that the brain levels of norepinephrine were lower in dogs that were presented with inescapable electrical shocks and developed *learned helplessness* (Petty et al., 1994; see Chapter 13). The dogs did not inherit low norepinephrine levels; they acquired them as a result of their laboratory experience. In sum, research findings so far suggest that a tendency to develop serious mood disorders is heritable and that low levels of norepinephrine and serotonin are associated with these disorders. However, the cause-and-effect relations have yet to be worked out.

---

anxiety A sense of apprehension or doom that is accompanied by many physiological reactions, such as accelerated heart rate, sweaty palms, and tightness in the stomach.

QUESTIONS TO CONSIDER

1. Suppose that you have a friend whose mother has been diagnosed with depression. Your friend is concerned about her mother and also worries that she herself may become depressed, because she has heard that this disorder is genetic. Knowing that you are taking a course in psychology, she asks you to tell her more about depression and about the likelihood that she too will develop it. What do you tell her?

2. Medical students often diagnose themselves as having the diseases and disorders they are studying, but what happens is that their studies simply make them more sensitive to slight deviations from their normal level of physical health. While reading the section on mood disorders, did something similar happen to you? Did you become more sensitive to your mood and to deviations from your normal mood? Can you trace these deviations to specific events? If so, what were they?

Anxiety and Dissociative Disorders

Once referred to as *neuroses* (particularly from the psychoanalytic perspective), anxiety and dissociative psychological disorders constitute clusters of disorders that can be considered personal strategies of perception and behavior that have gotten out of hand. People with these disorders experience anxiety, fear, and depression, and generally are unhappy. However, unlike people who have *psychotic disorders,* such individuals do not have severe delusions or hallucinations. Furthermore, they usually realize that they have a problem. They may not know that the source of their difficulty is psychological, but they know that they are unhappy and that their strategies for coping with the world are not working very well.

Anxiety Disorders

Several important types of psychological disorders are classified as anxiety disorders, which have fear and anxiety as their most prominent symptoms. **Anxiety** is a sense of apprehension or doom that is accompanied by certain physiological reactions, such as accelerated heart rate, sweaty palms, and tightness in the stomach. Anxiety is a normal reaction to many stresses of life, and none of us is completely free from it; anxiety is undoubtedly useful in causing us to be more alert and to take important things seriously. The anxiety we all feel from time to time, though, is significantly different from the intense extremes experienced by a person with an anxiety disorder. Let's look at the nature and causes of four general types of anxiety disorders: panic disorder, phobic disorder, obsessive–compulsive disorder, and post-traumatic stress disorder.

Panic Disorder: Description Panic is a feeling of extreme fear mixed with hopelessness or helplessness. We sometimes

For most of us, anxiety is a typical reaction to circumstances that we perceive to be dangerous—for example, being well above the ground—and is not considered abnormal unless it interferes with our carrying out day-to-day activities. Then it may be considered a type of psychological disorder.

feel this way when we are trapped suddenly in an elevator or are in a car accident. Many people feel a tinge of panic when in an airliner flying through turbulent air space. For most people, panic can be linked to these types of events.

People with **panic disorder** have episodic attacks of acute anxiety—periods of acute and unremitting terror that grip them for lengths of time lasting from a few seconds to a few hours. According to the DSM-IV-TR, the lifetime prevalence rate for panic disorder is estimated to be between 1 and 2%. Women are approximately twice as likely as men to have panic disorder. The disorder usually has its onset between the late teen years and the mid-20s; it rarely begins after a person reaches his or her 40s.

Shortness of breath, clammy sweat, irregularities in heartbeat, dizziness, faintness, and feelings of unreality are often the presenting symptoms of panic attacks. The victim of a panic attack often feels that he or she is going to die. The symptoms are sometimes mistaken for a heart attack rather than psychological distress. Leon (1977) described a 38-year-old man who had frequent panic attacks:

> During the times when he was experiencing intense anxiety, it often seemed as if he were having a heart seizure. He experienced chest pains and heart palpitations, numbness, shortness of breath, and he felt a strong need to breathe. He reported that in the midst of the anxiety attack, he developed a feeling of tightness over his eyes and he could only see objects directly in front of him (tunnel vision). He further stated that he feared that he would not be able to swallow.
>
> . . . The intensity of the anxiety symptoms was very frightening to him and on two occasions his wife had rushed him to a local hospital because he was in a state of panic, sure that his heart was going to stop beating and he would die. His symptoms were relieved after he was given an injection of tranquilizer medication. . . . He began to note the location of doctors' offices and hospitals in whatever vicinity he happened to be . . . and he became extremely anxious if medical help was not close by. (Leon, 1977, pp. 112, 117)

Between panic attacks, people with panic disorder tend to have **anticipatory anxiety**—a fear of having a panic attack. Because attacks can occur without apparent cause, these people worry about when the next one might strike them. Sometimes a panic attack that occurs in a particular situation can cause the person to fear that situation; that is, a panic attack can cause a phobic response, presumably through classical conditioning.

Panic Disorder: Possible Causes Panic disorder appears to have a substantial hereditary component; a higher concordance rate for the disorder is found between identical twins than between fraternal twins (Knowles et al., 1999; Torgerson, 1983), and a significant number of the first-degree relatives of a person with panic disorder also have panic disorder (Hettema et al., 2001). According to Crowe, Noyes, Pauls, and Slymen (1983), a pattern of panic disorder within a family tree suggests that the disorder may be caused by a single dominant gene.

People with panic disorder show distinctive physiological characteristics as well. They periodically breathe irregularly both when awake (e.g., Ley, 2003) and when asleep (e.g., Stein et al., 1995). Although irregular breathing itself does not appear to cause panic attacks, its presence is consistent with underlying biological processes. Researchers also have found that they can trigger panic attacks in people with histories of panic disorder by giving them injections of lactic acid (a by-product of muscular activity) or by having them breathe air containing an elevated amount of carbon dioxide (Biber & Alkin, 1999; Nardi et al., 2004; Nardi et al., 2002). People with family histories of panic attacks are more likely to react to lactic acid, even if they have never had a panic attack (Cowley et al., 1995; Peskind et al., 1998). Some researchers believe that what is inherited is a tendency to react with alarm to bodily sensations from sources that would not disturb most other people.

The cognitive approach to panic disorder focuses on *expectancies*. People who have panic attacks appear to be extremely sensitive to any element of risk or danger in their environments: They expect to be threatened by environmental stressors and downplay or underestimate their abilities to cope with them (Mogg et al., 1993). The expectation of having to face stressors that they fear may overwhelm their coping abilities leads these people to develop a sense of dread. Soon a full-blown panic attack results. Thus, merely anticipating that something bad is about to happen can precipitate a panic attack.

---

panic disorder Unpredictable attacks of acute anxiety that are accompanied by high levels of physiological arousal and that last from a few seconds to a few hours.

anticipatory anxiety A fear of having a panic attack; may lead to the development of a phobia.

phobia Unreasonable fear of specific objects or situations, such as insects, animals, or enclosed spaces, produced by stimulus reinforcer pairings.

[TABLE 16·4] Names and Descriptions of
Some Common Phobias

Name	Object or Situation Feared
Acrophobia	Heights
Agoraphobia	Open spaces
Algophobia	Pain
Astraphobia	Storms, thunder, lightning
Claustrophobia	Enclosed spaces
Hematophobia	Blood
Monophobia	Being alone
Mysophobia	Dirt or germs
Nyctophobia	Darkness
Ochlophobia	Crowds
Pathophobia	Disease
Pyrophobia	Fire
Taphophobia	Being buried alive
Triskaidekaphobia	The number 13
Zoophobia	Animals, or a specific animal

Agoraphobia can be severely disabling,
making those with the disorder
prisoners in their own home.

Phobic Disorder: Description *Phobias*—named after the Greek god Phobos, who frightened people's enemies—are persistent, irrational fears of specific objects or situations. Because phobias can be so specific, clinicians have coined a variety of inventive names for them, as shown in TABLE 16·4.

At one time or another, almost all of us have had one or more irrational fears of specific objects or situations. It is not a simple matter to draw a line between these fears and phobic disorders. If someone is afraid of spiders but manages to lead a normal life by avoiding them, it seems inappropriate to say that the person has a psychological disorder. Similarly, many otherwise normal people are afraid of speaking in public. The term **phobic disorder** should be reserved for people whose fear makes their lives difficult.

The DSM-IV-TR recognizes three types of phobic disorder: agoraphobia, social phobia, and specific phobia. Agoraphobia (*agora* means "open space") has a 12-month prevalence of approximately 2%. Most cases of agoraphobia are associated with panic attacks. It can be classified with them (Panic Disorder with Agoraphobia) or separate from them (Agoraphobia without History of Panic Disorder). The DSM-IV-TR defines the essential feature of **agoraphobia** as "anxiety about, or avoidance of, places or situations from which escape might be difficult (or embarrassing) or in which help may not be available in the event of having a panic attack or panic-like symptom" (p. 429). Agoraphobia can be severely disabling.

Merely thinking about leaving home can produce profound fear, dread, and physical symptoms such as nausea and profuse sweating. Imagine yourself unable to go to the store, let alone to school or work, without battling what feels like a case of food poisoning combined with the most extreme fear you have ever felt. Some people with this disorder have stayed inside their houses or apartments for years, afraid to venture outside (see Arieti, 2000, for a classic case study).

Social phobia is an exaggerated "fear of one or more situations . . . in which the person is exposed to possible scrutiny by others and fears that he or she may do something or act in a way that will be humiliating or embarrassing." It has a 12-month prevalence of nearly 7%. Most people with social phobia are only mildly impaired. Thinking about social encounters and engaging in them still produce significant anxiety, but most people with the disorder might simply appear to the outsider to be reclusive or shy. There appears to be a self-perpetuating aspect to this disorder. Even after successful, positive interactions with others, people with social phobia feel less positive and have a more-negative affect than people without the phobia (Wallace & Alden, 1997). People with a social phobia also tend to focus on threats in social situations (Mogg et al., 2004). Social phobia can be general, causing fear of most social encounters; or it can be specific to certain situations, such as public speaking.

Men and women are equally likely to exhibit social phobias, but women are more likely to develop agoraphobia. Phobias that begin to develop in childhood or in early adolescence (primarily specific phobias) are likely to disappear, whereas those that begin to develop after adolescence are likely to endure. Social phobia tends to begin during the teen years, whereas agoraphobia tends to begin during a person's middle or late 20s. These disorders rarely make their first appearance after age 30.

---

phobic disorder An unrealistic, excessive fear of a specific class of stimuli that interferes with normal activities. Phobic disorders include agoraphobia, social phobia, and specific phobia.

agoraphobia An anxiety disorder characterized by fear of and avoidance of being in places where escape may be difficult; this disorder often is accompanied by panic attacks.

social phobia An anxiety disorder characterized by an excessive and irrational fear of situations in which the person is observed by others.

Specific phobia is an umbrella term for all other phobias, such as fear of snakes, darkness, or heights. These phobias often are caused by a specific traumatic experience. The lifetime prevalence rate for specific phobia is estimated to be about 15% for women and about 7% for men (Magee et al., 1996), but approximately a third of the general population *sometimes* exhibits phobic symptoms (Goodwin & Guze, 1996). The annual prevalence is nearly 9%.

Phobic Disorders: Possible Causes What are the causes of phobic disorders? According to psychoanalytic theory, phobias arise from distress caused by intolerable unconscious impulses or from *displacement*—the redirection of objective fears toward symbolic objects (e.g., the displacement of fear of an abusive parent onto some object in the physical environment). According to the cognitive–behavioral perspective, people learn phobias by means of either direct or vicarious classical conditioning (see Chapter 5). *Direct classical conditioning* occurs when someone is exposed directly to an especially unpleasant situation. *Vicarious classical conditioning* occurs when a person observes another person (especially a parent or someone else to whom the person is closely attached) show fright in a particular situation.

To say that phobias are learned through classical conditioning does not explain phobic disorder completely (Mineka & Zinbarg, 2006). Many people have traumatic, frightening experiences, but not all of them develop phobic disorder; thus, it appears that not all people are likely to develop phobias. Also, many people with phobias do not remember having had specific early life experiences with the objects they fear (e.g., Kheriaty et al., 1999). (Of course, they may simply have forgotten the experiences.)

In addition, some objects are more likely to be feared than are others. People tend to fear animals (especially snakes, spiders, dogs, or rodents), blood, heights, and closed spaces. They are less likely to fear automobiles or electrical outlets, which are potentially more dangerous than some of the common objects of phobias, such as snakes and spiders. For this reason, some investigators suggest that a tendency to develop a fear of certain kinds of stimuli may have a biological basis that reflects the evolution of the human species (Seligman, 1971). The general idea is that because of our ancestors' history in relatively hostile natural environments, a capacity evolved for especially efficient fear conditioning to certain classes of dangerous stimuli (e.g., snakes). Öhman and his colleagues have reported a well-integrated series of experiments that support this analysis. Participants in these experiments were typically assigned either to a condition in which they were shown pictures of fear-irrelevant stimuli (e.g., plants) or to a condition in which they saw pictures of fear-relevant stimuli (e.g., snakes). The dependent variable was skin conductance, an index of emotional reactivity. A central finding was that pairing the pictures with a mild electric shock resulted in conditioned emotional responses to the fear-relevant but not to the fear-irrelevant stimuli, even though the pictures had been presented in such a way that participants could not consciously identify the content

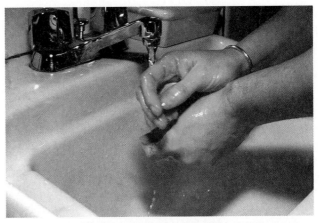

In obsessive-compulsive disorder, compulsive behaviors, such as ritualized hand-washing that occurs many times per day, may relieve obsession-induced anxiety while detracting from the quality of life overall.

(Soares & Öhman, 1993; Öhman & Soares, 1998). Importantly, conditioning to the fear-relevant stimuli appeared more resistant to extinction than did conditioning to the fear-irrelevant stimuli. Thus, participants showed not only a special proclivity for conditioned fear to fear-relevant stimuli, but they did so without awareness. Another study in the series showed that participants who were already afraid of snakes and spiders reacted with higher skin conductance to pictures of these fear-relevant animals, again even when they had no conscious awareness of having seen the images, than did nonfearful participants (Öhman & Soares, 1994).

Obsessive-Compulsive Disorder: Description People with an **obsessive-compulsive disorder** (OCD) have **obsessions**—thoughts that will not leave them—or **compulsions**—behaviors that they cannot keep from performing—or both. Major classes of obsessions and compulsions include impaired control of mental activities, incessant checking, urges involving loss of motor control, and feeling contaminated, according to a study of a large sample of American college students (Sternberger & Burns, 1990). The DSM-IV-TR estimates a lifetime prevalence rate of 2.5% among adults. The 12-month prevalence is 1%.

Unlike people with panic disorder, people with obsessive—compulsive disorder have a defense against anxiety—their compulsive behavior. Unfortunately, the need to perform this behavior often demands more and more of their time, to the point that it interferes with their daily lives, social relationships, and careers. Obsessions are seen in many psychological disorders,

---

specific phobia An anxiety disorder characterized by an excessive and irrational fear of specific things, such as snakes, darkness, or heights.

obsessive-compulsive disorder Recurrent, unwanted thoughts or ideas and compelling urges to engage in repetitive ritual-like behavior, often abbreviated as OCD.

obsession An involuntary recurring thought, idea, or image accompanied by anxiety or distress.

compulsion An irresistible impulse to repeat some action over and over even though it serves no useful purpose.

including schizophrenia. However, unlike persons with schizophrenia, people with obsessive–compulsive disorder generally recognize that their thoughts and behaviors have become excessive and are unreasonable. Consider the case of Beth, a young woman who had become obsessed with cleanliness.

[CASE STUDY] Beth's concern for cleanliness gradually evolved into a thorough cleansing ritual, which was usually set off by her touching her genital or anal area. In this ritual, Beth would first remove all of her clothing in a pre-established sequence. She would lay out each article of clothing at specific spots on her bed and examine each for any evidence of "contamination." She would thoroughly scrub her body, starting at her feet and working meticulously up to the top of her head, using certain washcloths for certain areas of her body. Any articles of clothing that appeared to have been "contaminated" were thrown into the laundry. Clean clothing then was put on the bed locations that were vacant. She would then dress herself in the opposite order from which she took the clothes off. If there were any deviations from this order, or if Beth began to wonder if she might have missed some contamination, she would go through the entire sequence again. It was not rare for her to do this four or five times in a row on some evenings. (Meyer & Osborne, 1982, p. 158).

Women are slightly more likely than men to have this diagnosis. Like panic disorder, obsessive–compulsive disorder most commonly begins in young adulthood (Sturgis, 1993). People with this disorder are unlikely to marry, perhaps because of the common obsessional fear of dirt and contamination—or perhaps because the shame associated with the rituals they are compelled to perform causes people with OCD to avoid social contact (Turner et al., 2001).

Two principal kinds of obsessions are known: obsessive *doubt* or *uncertainty*, and obsessive *fear of doing something prohibited*. We all experience doubts about future activities (such as whether to look for a new job, whether to eat at one restaurant or another, or whether to wear a raincoat or take an umbrella) and about past activities (such as whether we have turned off a burner on the kitchen range or whether we remembered to lock the door on leaving home). These uncertainties, both trivial and important, preoccupy some people with obsessive–compulsive disorder almost completely. Others are plagued with the fear that they will do something terrible—swear aloud in church, urinate in someone's living room, kill themselves or a loved one, or jump off a bridge—although they seldom actually do anything antisocial. Even though they are often obsessed with thoughts of killing themselves, few actually attempt suicide.

Most compulsions fall into one of four categories: *counting*, *checking*, *cleaning*, or *avoidance*. For example, some

people feel they must count every step between their car and any building they plan to enter. Others may repeatedly check burners on the range to see that they are off or doors to be sure they are locked. Some people wash their hands hundreds of times a day, even when they become covered with painful sores. Some become afraid to leave home and refuse to touch other members of their families for fear of contamination. If they do accidentally become "contaminated," they usually perform lengthy purification rituals, as in the case of Beth.

Obsessive–Compulsive Disorder: Possible Causes Several possible causes have been suggested for obsessive–compulsive disorder. Unlike simple anxiety states, this disorder can be understood in terms of the defense mechanisms identified by psychoanalytic theory. From another perspective, some cognitive theorists have suggested that obsessions serve as devices to occupy the mind and displace painful thoughts. This strategy can be seen in normal behavior: A person who "psychs himself up" before a competitive event by telling himself about his skill and stamina is also keeping out self-defeating doubts and fears. Cognitive researchers also point out that persons with obsessive–compulsive disorder often believe that they should be competent at all times, avoid any kind of criticism at all costs, and worry about being punished for behavior that is less than perfect (Sarason & Sarason, 2004).

Thus, one reason people who have obsessive–compulsive disorder may engage in checking behavior is to reduce the anxiety caused by fear of being perceived by others as incompetent or to avoid others' criticism that they have done something less than perfectly. If painful, anxiety-producing thoughts become frequent, but turning to alternative patterns of thought reduces anxiety, then the principle of reinforcement predicts that the person will turn to these patterns more frequently. Just as an animal learns to jump a hurdle to escape a painful foot shock, a person can learn to think about a "safe topic" to avoid painful thoughts. If the habit becomes firmly established, the obsessive thoughts may persist even after the original reason for turning to them—the situation that produced the anxiety-arousing thoughts—no longer exists. A habit can thus outlast its original causes.

Evidence is beginning to accumulate suggesting that obsessive–compulsive disorder may have a genetic origin (Pauls & Alsobrook, 1999; Pato et al., 2002). Whatever the degree of heritability may turn out to be, the disorder has a strong tendency to be transmitted within families. Nestadt and colleagues (2000) report that obsessive–compulsive disorder is found almost five times more frequently among first-degree relatives of those with the disorder than among first-degree relatives of people who do not have the disorder. Family studies also have found that this disorder is associated symptomatically with a neurological disorder called **Tourette's syndrome,** which appears during childhood (Pauls & Leckman, 1986; Alsobrook & Pauls, 1997; Cath et al., 2000.; Leckman et al., 2003). Tourette's syndrome is characterized by muscular and vocal tics such as making facial grimaces, squatting, pacing, twirling, barking, sniffing, coughing, grunting, or repeating specific words (especially vulgarities). Pauls and his colleagues believe that the two disorders

---

Tourette's syndrome A neurological disorder characterized by tics and involuntary utterances, some of which may involve obscenities and the repetition of others' utterances.

are produced by the same single, dominant gene. However, it is not clear why some people with the gene would develop Tourette's syndrome in childhood and others would develop obsessive–compulsive disorder later in life. Evidence also indicates that elevated glucose metabolic rates in certain areas of the brain occur in people with obsessive–compulsive disorder (Saxena & Rauch, 2000). As well, disorders that involve basal ganglia dysfunction, such as Tourette's, often are associated with obsessive–compulsive disorder symptoms. This pattern supports the idea that the disorder may have a biological basis (Swedo et al., 1989). The disorder sometimes occurs after brain damage caused by birth trauma, encephalitis, or head trauma (Hollander et al., 1990).

Post-Traumatic Stress Disorder: Description

The aftermath of traumatic events, such as those that occur in wars or natural disasters, often includes psychological symptoms that persist long after the stressful events are over. **Post-traumatic stress disorder** (PTSD) is an anxiety disorder in which the individual has feelings of social withdrawal accompanied by atypically low levels of emotion; it can be caused by a single event or by prolonged exposure to a stressor such as a catastrophe. The symptoms produced by such exposure include recurrent dreams or recollections of the event, feelings that the traumatic event is recurring ("flashback" episodes), and intense psychological distress. These dreams, recollections, or flashback episodes lead the person to avoid thinking about the traumatic event, which often results in diminished interest in social activities, feelings of detachment from others, suppressed emotional feelings, and a sense that the future is bleak and empty. Psychological symptoms of PTSD include outbursts of anger, heightened reactions to sudden noises, sleep problems, and general difficulty concentrating. The following case study is illustrative.

[CASE STUDY] Muhammad B., a 22-year-old Ethiopian refugee, lives with his mother, father, two younger brothers, and two younger sisters in a small center-city apartment building in a large Midwestern city. He works part time as a parking lot attendant and attends night school, majoring in business. Muhammed has been in the United States for 5 years after a very tumultuous period in his home country. He was held for interrogation, along with several other youths from his village, in a government prison compound for several months when he was 15 years old. The treatment received by the captives was severe, including starvation and, frequently, physical punishment. During a 7-month period of confinement, he was interrogated, usually after a severe beating or after being shown the bodies of other prisoners, in an effort by his captors to obtain information about the whereabouts of antigovernment guerrilla fighters. On one occasion he was questioned while one of the guards held a rifle barrel in his mouth, and on another occasion, he was subjected to a "staged execution" to get him to talk. After the captors determined that he had no relevant information, he was released. His family was able to escape the country shortly afterward.

Since his release from imprisonment, Muhammed has experienced severe PTSD symptoms, including night terrors, sleeping disturbances, attacks of intense anxiety, and depression. He reports almost constant headaches and pains in the hand that was broken by his captors.

Although Muhammed has been able to complete high school successfully in the United States and has accumulated a year of college credit going to school part time, his day-to-day functioning is characterized by disabling, intrusive thoughts, anxiety, nightmares, and recurring depression. (Butcher et al., 2007, p. 168).

Research has shown that excessive use of alcohol tends to co-occur with PTSD (e.g., Stewart, et al., 2004). One possibility for this association is that people with PTSD try to treat their own disorder with alcohol. People may use alcohol in an effort to manage negative moods and to block terrifying memories of the traumatic event(s). The problem, of course, is that such tactics will not work well in the long run, and excessive alcohol use itself will generate additional mental and physical health problems. The far better alternative is professional assistance.

Post-Traumatic Stress Disorder: Possible Causes

Although PTSD is commonly associated with war, the disorder can be caused by many events. For example, many victims of rape, torture, natural disasters, and motor accidents suffer from PTSD (e.g., Korol et al., 2002; Pulcino et al., 2003; Rheingold et al., 2004). The severity of PTSD depends on factors such as the gender of the sufferer, the severity of the event, past psychiatric illness, and the person's level of educational achievement (Basoglu, Salclogle, & Livanou, 2002). Post-traumatic stress disorder can strike people at any age. Children may show symptoms not usually seen in adulthood, including loss of recently acquired language skills or toilet training, as well as more typical complaints of stomachaches and headaches. Usually the symptoms begin immediately after the traumatic event, but sometimes they are delayed for months or years (Pelkovitz & Kaplan, 1996). A study of U.S. troops returning from the Iraq War showed a greater reported incidence of PTSD 3 to 6 months after return (DeAngelis, 2008). Whatever the context, the greater the severity of the trauma, the higher the risk that a person will develop PTSD (Brewin et al., 2000; Lifton, 2005).

The social support that people receive (or do not receive) after being exposed to an unusually stressful situation also can affect the likelihood of their developing PTSD (Berwin et al., 2000). As a result, mental health professionals try to seek out victims of natural disasters and of crimes such as rapes or shooting sprees as soon as possible to provide them with treatment in hopes of preventing future psychological disorders (e.g., Flannery, 1999; Mitchell, 1999).

---

post-traumatic stress disorder (PTSD) An anxiety disorder in which the individual has feelings of social withdrawal accompanied by atypically low levels of emotion; caused by prolonged exposure to a stressor, such as war or a natural catastrophe.

Peacekeepers, whose military mission does not include a combat role, nevertheless face most of the same stressors as those who engage in conflict, and are just as susceptible to post-traumatic stress disorder (Lamerson & Kelloway, 1996).

Dissociative Disorders

In **dissociative disorders,** people reduce anxiety by undergoing a sudden disruption of consciousness, which in turn may produce changes in their memory or even in their personal identity.

Description A relatively simple form of dissociative disorder is called **dissociative amnesia.** Amnesia (loss of memory) can, of course, be produced by physical causes such as brain damage, epilepsy, or intoxication. But dissociative amnesia is related instead to traumatic life events. For example, shortly before onset of the disorder, a person may be the victim of violence, have a non-neurologic injury, commit an act that he or she finds repulsive, or experience a significant personal loss. The amnesia is typically confined to the traumatic event. The person will not be able to remember, for example, being attacked and disfigured or even who the attacker was. If people's own actions are the source of guilt or other stress, they may be unable to remember committing the act, where they were at the time, or who was with them.

A more extreme form of dissociative amnesia is called **dissociative fugue** (pronounced "FYOOG"), which may last for a few hours to months. This disorder produces considerable confusion, consternation, and worry for family, friends, and co-workers of the afflicted person. The conditions of

onset are the same as for dissociative amnesia, but the symptoms are much more extensive. After the stressful incident, the person cannot identify him or herself and cannot remember his or her past; the person may relocate to a new area, adopt a new identity, and establish a new family and career. When the fugue state ends, as often happens, the person resumes his or her normal personality and memory, except that he or she has no memory for events during the fugue (Coons, 2000). At that point, the person may be just as confused and worried about what happened as family and friends were.

Dissociative identity disorder (previously known as *multiple personality disorder*) is a very rare but very striking dissociative disorder in which the patient displays two or more separate personalities, either of which may be dominant at any given time. An intriguing instance of dissociative identity disorder is the case of Billy Milligan, as told in the book *The Minds of Billy Milligan* (Keyes, 1981). Milligan was accused of rape and kidnapping but was deemed not guilty by reason of insanity. His psychiatric examination showed him to have 24 different personalities. Two were women, and one was a young girl. Of these, one was British, another Australian, and the third, Yugoslavian. One woman, a lesbian, was a poet. The Yugoslav was an expert on weapons and munitions, and the British and Australian personalities were minor criminals.

Bliss (1986) suggested that dissociative identity disorder is a form of self-hypnosis, established early in life, that permits escape from painful experiences. Indeed, Ross and colleagues (1991) reported that of 102 people diagnosed with dissociative identity disorder in the United States and Canada, 95% reported childhood sexual or physical abuse, or both. Note that such data do not mean that childhood abuse causes dissociative identity disorder. Rather, they identify a strong commonality among those who report symptoms of the disorder. Because the disorder is very rare, the rate of childhood abuse is many times higher than the incidence of dissociative identity disorder; most people who are abused as children do not develop multiple personalities. It is useful to consider this point for a moment, because statistical reports of this kind are fairly common. To say that 95% of those with a particular disorder share a specific childhood experience is not at all to say that any other person who has the same experience has a 95% chance of developing the disorder. Investigation of the link between childhood trauma and dissociative identity disorder remains an active and important theoretical and empirical concern (Ross, 1997).

Possible Causes Dissociative disorders are usually explained as responses to severe trauma. Partly because they are rare, dissociative disorders are among the least understood of the mental disorders. In general, the dissociation is advantageous to the person; preserving it may be reinforced. Amnesia enables the person to forget about a painful or unpleasant life. A person with fugue not only forgets what has occurred but may also relocate to start a new life, quite unaware of doing so. However, multiple personalities may allow a person to do things that he or she really feels a need to do but cannot because of the strong guilt feelings that would ensue. The alternative personality can be that of a person with a weak conscience, unmoved by guilt.

---

dissociative disorders A class of disorders in which anxiety is reduced by a sudden disruption in consciousness, which in turn produces changes in memory or in the person's sense of identity.

dissociative amnesia A dissociative disorder characterized by the inability to remember important events or personal information.

dissociative fugue Amnesia with no apparent physiological cause, often accompanied by adoption of a new identity and relocation to a new community.

dissociative identity disorder A rare dissociative disorder in which two or more distinct personalities exist within the same person; each personality dominates in turn. (Formerly known as multiple personality disorder.)

focus ⊕n

Culture-Bound Syndromes

People in all societies have specific rules for categorizing behavior, and these rules can differ, often considerably, from culture to culture (Simons & Hughes, 1993; Simons, 1996). How behavior is categorized and whether an instance of behavior is considered "abnormal" are strongly influenced by social norms and values that exist in a given setting at any moment (Bohannan, 1995). Many kinds of aberrant behavior–behavior that deviates from cultural norms not included in official diagnostic manuals, such as the DSM-IV-TR, are considered pathological within a given culture. That is, highly idiosyncratic psychological disorders called **culture-bound syndromes** exist, which are found only within one or a few cultures. They do not exist across cultures, as schizophrenia and several other psychological disorders appear to (Al-Issa, 1995). For example, consider the following two individual cases:

I. A. is a young Nigerian man. He recently met a stranger, whom he greeted with a handshake. He now claims that his genitals have fallen off. After a medical examination, the physician tells I. A. that his genitals are, in fact, still where they are supposed to be. But I. A. is unconvinced. He reports that his genitals are not the same since shaking hands with the stranger.

I. L. was an Inuit hunter living in western Greenland. He hunted in the open sea from his kayak. He stopped because of *nangiarpok* ("nahn-jee-ARE-poke"), or an intense fear; in this case, a fear of capsizing and drowning in a kayak. He withdrew socially from his people and eventually committed suicide. Although once common among western Greenlanders, nangiarpok is now rare because of changes in Greenlandic culture, especially with respect to hunting and fishing, introduced through exposure to Western culture.

Many other such culture-bound syndromes appear to exist. Some Polynesian Islanders have *cafard* ("ka-fawr"), a sudden display of homicidal behavior followed by exhaustion; some male Southeast Asians develop *koro*, an intense fear that the penis will retract into the body, resulting in death (they will often hold their penises firmly to prevent this from happening); some Japanese develop an intense fear that their appearance, body odors, or behaviors are offensive to others, a condition called *taijin kyofusho* ("ta-EE-jeen ki-yo-FOO-sho") (Suzuki et al., 2004).

What causes culture-bound syndromes? This is a very difficult question to answer for several reasons. First, a worldwide classification scheme of psychological disorders does not exist, which means that an exhaustive taxonomy of disorders also does not yet exist. Second, many culture-bound syndromes have only recently been discovered, and only a few have received

empirical scrutiny. Third, we do not yet have a complete explanation for major psychological disorders that affect millions of people, such as schizophrenia and depression, so it is not unreasonable to expect that the study of psychological disorders that afflict fewer people, as culture-bound syndromes do by definition, will be neglected. And fourth, and perhaps most important, many culture-bound syndromes are often described in terms of—and treated by—"alternative" (non-Western traditional) medical treatments. For example, in Japan, *taijin kyofusho* is treated in a ritual that involves, among other things, massage and sweating. Because practices based on folk medicine are widely accepted by members of the culture, other explanations or therapies for culture-bound syndromes, based on Western scientific methods, are neither sought nor readily accepted when offered.

Nonetheless, we may speculate about the origins of culture-bound syndromes. Those described here are specific to certain environmental events or situations and appear similar in nature to phobias. Thus, it appears unlikely that these problems have either a strong hereditary or a physiological basis. Syndromes such as *nangiarpok*, *koro*, and *taijin kyofusho* seem similar to what is described by the DSM-IV-TR as a specific phobia, suggesting that they are learned responses to fear-eliciting stimuli.

Certainly culture-bound syndromes are phenomena worthy of investigation. Understanding their development in the cultures in which they occur may help us learn more about how cultures influence individuals' mental states, whether normal or abnormal (Kleinknecht et al., 1997; Brintlinger & Vinitsky, 2007).

QUESTIONS TO CONSIDER

1. When was the last time you felt especially anxious about something? Did the anxiety disrupt your behavior, even momentarily? In what ways was your anxiety similar to and different from that that might be experienced by a person with an anxiety disorder, such as panic disorder or phobic disorder?

2. Do you have a specific fear—heights, dark places, insects, snakes, or other things or situations? If you do, is it severe enough to be considered a phobia? How do you know? Can you identify what caused your fear of this object?

3. Reflect for a minute on Beth, the woman who had an obsessive–compulsive cleaning ritual. How would you explain her behavior, given what you now know about the causes of obsessive–compulsive behavior?

---

culture-bound syndrome   Highly unusual psychological disorders that are similar to nonpsychotic psychological disorders (such as phobias) but are specific to only one or a few cultures.

[**TABLE 16·5**] Brief Descriptions of Personality Disorders

Personality Disorder	Description
Paranoid	Suspiciousness and extreme mistrust of others; enhanced perception of being under attack by others.
Schizoid	Difficulty in social functioning—social withdrawal and lack of caring for others.
Schizotypal	Unusual thought patterns and perceptions; poor communication and social skills.
Borderline	Lack of impulse control; drastic mood swings; inappropriate anger; tendency to become bored easily and for prolonged periods; suicidal tendencies.
Histrionic	Attention-seeking; preoccupation with personal attractiveness; proneness to anger when attempts at attracting attention fail.
Narcissistic	Self-promotion; lack of empathy for others; attention-seeking; grandiosity.
Avoidant	Oversensitivity to rejection; little confidence in initiating or maintaining social relationships.
Dependent	Discomfort with being alone or in terminating relationships; pattern of placing others' needs above own to preserve the relationship; indecisiveness.
Obsessive–compulsive	Preoccupation with rules and order; tendency toward perfectionism; difficulty relaxing or enjoying life.

Source: Adapted from Carson, R. C., Butcher, J. N., & Mineka, S. (2000). *Abnormal psychology and modern life* (11th ed.). Published by Allyn & Bacon, Boston, MA. Copyright © 2000 by Pearson Education. Reprinted by permission of the publisher.

Personality Disorders

The DSM-IV-TR also classifies personality disorders as abnormalities that impair social or occupational functioning. Although several types of personality disorders exist, we address two in detail here: antisocial personality disorder and borderline personality disorder. TABLE 16·5 provides a brief description of several other personality disorders. As before, it is important to recognize that normal personality shades into abnormal personality across a continuum.

Antisocial Personality Disorder

Many different labels have been used for what we now call **antisocial personality disorder.** It is characterized by failure to conform to common standards of decency, repeated lying and stealing, failure to sustain long-lasting and loving relationships, low tolerance of boredom, and a complete lack of guilt (Cleckley, 1976; Hare, 1998; Harpur et al., 2002). Koch (1889) introduced the term "psychopathic inferiority," which soon became simply "psychopathy"; a person who displayed the disorder was called a "psychopath." The first version of the DSM (the DSM-I) used the term "sociopathic personality disturbance," which was subsequently replaced by the present term, "antisocial personality disorder." Most clinicians still refer to such people as *psychopaths* or *sociopaths*.

Description Antisocial personality disorder contributes to a considerable amount of social distress. The diagnostic cri-

teria of the DSM-IV-TR call for evidence of at least three types of antisocial behavior before age 15 and at least four types after age 18. The adult forms of antisocial behavior include inability to sustain consistent work behavior; lack of ability to function as a responsible parent; repeated criminal activity, such as theft, pimping, or prostitution; inability to maintain enduring attachment to a sexual partner; volatility and violence, including fights or assault; failure to honor financial obligations; impulsiveness and failure to plan ahead; habitual lying or use of aliases; and consistently reckless or drunken driving. In addition to meeting at least four of these criteria, the person must have displayed a "pattern of continuous antisocial behavior in which the rights of others are violated, with no intervening period of at least five years without antisocial behavior." Clearly, individuals with antisocial personality disorder are people most of us do not want to be around.

Paul Bernardo, convicted of the brutal rapes and murders of two teenage girls, is considered by many psychologists to be a classic example of the antisocial personality disorder.

---

antisocial personality disorder A disorder characterized by a failure to conform to standards of decency; repeated lying and stealing; a failure to sustain lasting, loving relationships; low tolerance of boredom; and a complete lack of guilt.

[TABLE 16·6] Diagnostic Criteria for 301.7 Antisocial Personality Disorder

A. There is a pervasive pattern of disregard for and violation of the rights of others occurring since age 15 years, as indicated by three (or more) of the following:

1. failure to conform to social norms with respect to lawful behaviors, as indicated by repeatedly performing acts that are grounds for arrest
2. deceitfulness, as indicated by repeated lying, use of aliases, or conning others for personal profit or pleasure
3. impulsivity or failure to plan ahead
4. irritability and aggressiveness, as indicated by repeated physical fights or assaults
5. reckless disregard for safety of self or others
6. consistent irresponsibility, as indicated by repeated failure to sustain consistent work behavior or honor financial obligations
7. lack of remorse, as indicated by being indifferent to or rationalizing having hurt, mistreated, or stolen from another

B. The individual is at least age 18 years.

C. There is evidence of Conduct Disorder . . . with onset before age 15 years

D. The occurrence of antisocial behavior is not exclusively during the course of Schizophrenia or a Manic Episode

(Reprinted with permission from *The Diagnostic and Statistical Manual of Mental Disorders,* Fourth Edition, Text Revision (Copyright © 2000). American Psychiatric Association.)

The lifetime prevalence rate for antisocial personality disorder is estimated to be about 5% for men and 1% for women (Golomb, et al., 1995). However, we cannot be sure of the accuracy of such estimates, because individuals with the disorder do not voluntarily visit mental health professionals for help. Indeed, most of them feel no need to change their ways.

Cleckley (1976) listed 16 characteristics of antisocial personality disorder. As shown in TABLE 16·6, the list of features provides a picture of what most individuals with the disorder are like. They habitually tell lies, even when there is no apparent reason for doing so and even when the lie is likely to be discovered. They steal things they do not need or even appear to want. When confronted with evidence of having lied or cheated, psychopaths do not act ashamed or embarrassed and usually shrug the incident off as a joke, or simply deny it, however obvious their guilt may be. They are unconcerned for other people's feelings and have no remorse or guilt if their actions hurt others. Although they may be superficially charming, they do not form real friendships; thus, they often become swindlers or confidence artists.

Individuals with antisocial personality disorder do not easily learn desirable behavior from experience; they tend to continue getting into trouble throughout their lives (Hare, 1999), although a decline in criminal activities occurs around age 40 (Hare et al., 1988). They also do not appear to be *driven* to perform their antisocial behaviors; instead, they often give the impression that they are acting on whims. When someone commits a heinous crime such as a brutal murder, normal people expect that the criminal had a compelling motive, however repellent it might be, for doing so. Criminals with antisocial personality

disorder, though, are typically unable to supply a reason more urgent than "He had money and I needed money," "He disrespected me," or "I just felt like it." They do not show much excitement or enthusiasm about what they are doing and do not appear to derive much pleasure from life.

Possible Causes Cleckley (1976) suggested that the condition "consists of an unawareness and a persistent lack of ability to become aware of what the most important experiences of life mean to others. . . . The major emotional accompaniments are absent or so attenuated as to count for little" (p. 371). Some investigators have hypothesized that this lack of involvement is caused by an unresponsive autonomic nervous system. If a person feels no anticipatory fear of punishment, he or she is perhaps more likely to commit acts that normal people would be afraid to commit. Similarly, if a person feels little or no emotional response to other people and to their joys and sorrows, he or she is unlikely to establish close relationships with them.

Many experiments have found that individuals with the disorder do show less reactivity in emotional situations. In one study, they were found to be relatively unresponsive, behaviorally and physiologically, to emotional words (Williamson et al., 1991). Their speech also tends to be less emotional than that of other people. They generally speak more quietly and do not change their vocal emphasis between neutral and emotional words (Louth et al., 1998). In other work, Hare (1965) demonstrated that they show fewer signs of anticipatory fear in an experiment in which visual stimuli were associated with the threat of an intense electric shock.

We do not yet know what causes the deficits in emotion and empathy displayed by persons with antisocial personality disorder, but genes may be involved. These people often (but not always) come from grossly disturbed families that contain alcoholics and persons diagnosed with antisocial and other personality disorders. Mednick, Gabrielli, and Hutchings (1984) examined the criminal records of men who had been adopted early in life and found that the likelihood of their being convicted of a crime was directly related to the number of convictions of their biological fathers. (See FIGURE 16·3.)

Parenting and childhood experiences also appear to play a role in antisocial personality disorder. The quality of parenting, especially as it relates to supervision of children, is strongly related to the development of the disorder. In particular, children whose parents ignore them or leave them unsupervised for prolonged periods often develop patterns of misconduct and delinquency. When the parents do pay attention to their children, the attention tends to consist of harsh punishment or verbal abuse in response to their misdeeds. Thus, the children of these parents live in an environment that ranges from no attention to attention in the form of physical punishment and tongue-lashings. In response, the children develop a pattern of behavior that is characterized by increased aggression, distrust of others, concern only for themselves, and virtually no sense of right and wrong (MacMillan et al., 2001).

[**FIGURE 16•3**] An adoption study of convicted criminals. Graphed here is the percentage of male adoptees convicted of violent crimes or crimes against property as a function of the number of convictions of their biological fathers.

(From Mednick, S. A., Gabrielli, W. F., & Hutchings, B. (1983). Genetic influences in criminal behavior: Some evidence from an adoptive cohort. In K. T. Van Dusen and S. A. Mednick (Eds.), *Prospective studies of crime and delinquency.* Hingham, MA: Martinus Nijhoff. With kind permission of Springer Science and Business Media.)

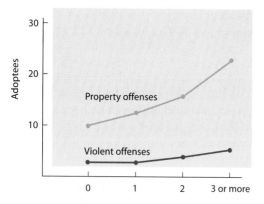

Biological parents' number of convictions

Children with conduct problems may be biologically predisposed to behave aggressively and destructively. The key people in the child's environment may attempt to punish these actions with a commensurate level of physical or verbal punishment. The child, in turn, perceives his or her environment as hostile and reacts even more aggressively, perhaps due to a maladaptive perception of what is necessary for his or her personal survival. Eventually, a cycle may be established that is marked by behaviors and thoughts characteristic of antisocial personality disorder.

Borderline Personality Disorder

The historical major diagnostic categories of neuroses and psychoses allowed for the possibility of disorders that fell between their borders. Thus, a designation of *borderline schizophrenia* and, more generally, *borderline personality,* was made. However, reliable diagnosis was difficult (Paris, 1999).

Borderline Personality Disorder: Description The DSM-IV-TR diagnostic criteria for **borderline personality disorder** (BPD), which has a lifetime prevalence rate of 2%, begin with the individual's strenuous efforts to resist what he or she perceives as abandonment, as might occur in a sudden change in another person's plans–canceling an appointment, for example (Adams et al., 2001). The second criterion involves intense but typically short-lived relationships with others, marked by inappropriately extensive disclosure early in the relationship and rapid devaluing or disillusionment thereafter. Sudden shifts in self-image, including goals, values, and aspirations, constitute the third criterion. Impulsivity is at the heart of the fourth criterion and is marked by irresponsible spending, bingeing, and substance abuse, Finally, recurrent suicidal behavior or self-mutilating behavior is diagnostic, as in the following case study (Spitzer et al., 2002).

[**CASE STUDY**] A 26-year-old unemployed woman was referred for admission to a hospital by her therapist because of intense suicidal preoccupation and urges to mutilate herself with a razor. The patient was apparently well until her junior year in high school, when she became preoccupied with religion and philosophy, avoided friends, and was filled with doubt about who she was. Academically she did well, but later, during college, her performance declined. In college she began to use a variety of drugs, abandoned the religion of her family, and seemed to be searching for a charismatic religious figure with whom to identify. At times, massive anxiety swept over her and she found it would suddenly vanish if she cut her forearm with a razor blade.

Three years ago she began psychotherapy, and initially rapidly idealized her therapist as being incredibly intuitive and empathic. Later she became hostile and demanding of him, requiring more and more sessions, sometimes two in one day. Her life centered on her therapist, by this time to the exclusion of everyone else. Although her hostility toward her therapist was obvious, she could neither see it nor control it. Her difficulties with her therapist culminated in many episodes of her forearm cutting and suicidal threats, which led to the referral for admission. (p. 233)

Borderline Personality Disorder: Possible Causes Skodol et al. (2002) and Bradley et al. (2007) identified specific features of BPD related to psychological traits that exhibit at least modest heritability, specifically, neuroticism, impulsivity, anxiousness, affect change, and insecure attachment. These genetic factors, in turn, are related to specific neural systems—for example, serotonergic systems in the case of impulsive aggression and cholinergic systems associated with affective instability. In addition, specific environmental factors that contribute to the emergence of symptoms include childhood sexual and physical abuse (Lieb et al., 2004).

QUESTION TO CONSIDER

Suppose that you have been hired as a screenwriter for a movie about a psychopath. Before you start work in earnest, the head of the film company wants to see a sample of what you have in mind for this character and asks you to write a few paragraphs describing the opening scene of the movie. What would you write? What would your character be doing in this scene?

---

borderline personality disorder A disorder whose diagnostic criteria include pervasive instability of interpersonal relationships, self-image, and emotions as well as impulsivity; suicidal efforts and self-mutilation may also occur.

Epilogue

Elyn Sak's Life with Schizophrenia

During her first semester of law school at Yale, Elyn Saks (2007) experienced the onset of schizophrenia. Fears seized her, including the fear that her brain was about to explode. She was taken to a local hospital, where she was placed in restraints and given an antipsychotic drug.

Subsequently transferred to a psychiatric institute, she continued to be restrained (after confiding to her psychiatrist that she had murdered vast numbers of people with her thoughts). Once in the Psychiatric Evaluation Unit, she received a diagnosis of "chronic paranoid schizophrenia with acute exacerbation." The prognosis was "grave," and she later learned that the unit administrators had, without her knowing, informed the law school that she likely would never return. Against these steep odds, and after a prolonged period of hospitalization, she was able to return to law school the following fall and to graduate after serving as an editor of the *Yale Law Journal* .

In the nearly 30 years since the diagnosis, Saks has sustained a regimen of antipsychotic medications and psychoanalysis (forms of treatment that are considered in Chapter 17) while achieving a highly successful academic career that blends law, psychiatry, and the behavioral sciences—and a loving marriage. The medications brought tardive dyskinesia (see Chapter 17), and she has had other serious medical problems, but she considers herself remarkably fortunate to have carved out a quality of life that most people with schizophrenia do not experience.

Saks attributes her success to the tandem of medications and psychoanalysis. She readily acknowledges that medication is invaluable for managing the symptoms of schizophrenia, but she is particularly indebted to psychoanalysis for bringing meaning to her experiences. It has provided her with a way to resolve what is often the direst dilemma that individuals with schizophrenia face: If I share my delusions with you, you will put me away; if I keep them to myself, they will only get worse. Saks cites the sense of "being known" by her psychoanalyst, a sense that helped her overcome the profound isolation that is too frequently the patient's lot. She tellingly remarks that, although people with cancer receive flowers from others, those with schizophrenia do not. Her memoir is a testimony to extraordinary triumph over a traditionally dire and dispiriting diagnosis (Neugeboren, 2007).

CHAPTER SUMMARY

Classification and Diagnosis of Psychological Disorders

The definition of abnormality is both context and culture specific. The causes of psychological disorders involve biological, cognitive, and environmental factors. Mental health professionals view the causes of psychological disorders from several different perspectives. The medical perspective asserts that psychological disorders have an organic basis, just as physical illnesses do. The psychodynamic perspective holds that psychological disorders arise from intrapsychic conflict that overwhelms the ego's defense mechanisms. The cognitive–behavioral perspective maintains that psychological disorders are learned patterns of maladaptive thinking and behaving. The humanistic perspective suggests that psychological disorders arise from the demands of others; specifically, from a need to meet others' demands to obtain their positive regard. The sociocultural perspective focuses on how cultural variables influence the development of psychological disorders and people's subjective reactions to them. Many elements of these perspectives are integrated into the diathesis–stress model of psychological disorders. This model suggests that people's genes and early learning experiences predispose them to develop psychological disorders. However, these disorders are expressed only if an individual encounters stressors that overwhelm her or his capacities to cope with them. Thus, even though some people may be predisposed toward a disorder, the coping skills they have acquired through experience may be sufficient to prevent the development of the disorder.

The principal classification scheme for psychological disorders is the DSM-IV-TR, which provides explicit criteria along five dimensions called axes. Axis I includes the major psychological disorders of clinical significance, and Axis II, the personality disorders and mental retardation. The three remaining axes provide information about the individual, such as the presence of physical disorders, the level of stress, and the overall level of functioning.

Although clinical diagnosis is influenced by social norms, we should not abandon the practice. The value of classification and diagnosis lies in the potential identification of disorders with common causes. Once disorders are classified, research can be carried out with the goal of finding useful therapies. Clinical diagnosis and prediction of a person's behavior require the collection and interpretation of information. The interpretation can involve clinical or actuarial judgments. Clinical judgments are diagnoses based on experts' own experience and knowledge. Actuarial judgments are based on statistical analysis of the relation between available data and known clinical outcomes. Although research has consistently found the actuarial method of diagnosis superior, most clinicians do not use it. Some psychologists believe that clinicians should concentrate on developing new measurement instruments and making observations of behavior that only humans can make, and then use actuarial methods to produce the diagnosis.

Disorders Usually Diagnosed in Childhood

Attention-deficit/hyperactivity disorder is characterized by inattention, hyperactivity, or impulsivity or combinations thereof that must be observed before age 7. Diagnosis occurs on the basis of observation in at least two different settings. Inattention involves carelessness, messiness, uncompleted tasks, and an aversion to tasks that require sustained attention. Hyperactivity refers to fidgeting, squirming, and frequent interruption of one activity to engage in another. Impulsivity includes impatience, difficulty in waiting one's turn, blurting out an answer before the question is asked, and grabbing items that others have. Recent research has implicated brain development, and specifically the differential thickness of areas of the cerebral cortex, in the etiology of the disorder. A comprehensive, dynamic theory of the disorder focuses on lower-than-normal functioning of dopaminergic modulators in the limbic system.

The diagnosis of autistic disorder requires symptom presentation by age 3 and is more likely to be made for boys than for girls. It is frequently accompanied by mental retardation. The primary symptoms include abnormal forms of social interaction and communication, the disinclination to form friendships, and a preference for solitary activities that are highly stereotyped. A marked aversion to any disruption of these activities is noted. The theory-of-mind theory of autistic disorder attempts to account for it as the child's failure to refer to internal, cognitive states in accounting for her or his own or others' behavior. The theory is increasingly viewed as too limited in scope to account for the complex array of presenting symptoms. The dramatic increase in incidence of the disorder has led to a multidisciplinary search for causes.

Substance-Related Disorders

Drug addiction is one of the most serious problems society faces today. Apparently, all substances that produce addiction do so by activating the reinforcement system of the brain, which involves the release of dopamine. Although people may be exposed to addictive drugs—even those with high abuse potentials—this does not mean that they will become addicts. Evidence suggests that the likelihood of addiction, especially to alcohol, is strongly affected by heredity. Two types of alcoholism may exist: one related to an antisocial, pleasure-seeking personality (steady drinking) and another related to a repressed, anxiety-ridden personality (binge drinking). A fuller understanding of the

physiological basis of reinforcement and punishment may help us understand the effects of heredity on susceptibility to addiction. Some researchers also point to a role for cognition—beliefs about the benefits of drug use—in the development of addiction.

Schizophrenia

Schizophrenia is a serious form of psychological disorder that occurs in every culture. It radically transforms the lives of those who have it and places a heavy burden on their families. The main positive symptoms of schizophrenia include thought disorders; delusions of persecution, grandeur, and control; and hallucinations. The main negative symptoms include withdrawal, apathy, and poverty of speech. The DSM-IV-TR classifies several subtypes of schizophrenia, including paranoid, disorganized, catatonic, undifferentiated, and residual. The distinctions between reactive and process schizophrenia and between positive and negative symptoms also seem to be important.

The diathesis—stress model accurately describes the course of schizophrenia: Some people seem to inherit a genetic predisposition for the disorder, which is expressed when environmental stressors outweigh these individuals' attempts to cope with them. Positive symptoms of schizophrenia can be produced in normal people or made worse in those with schizophrenia by drugs that stimulate dopamine synapses (cocaine and amphetamines) and can be reduced or eliminated by drugs that block dopamine receptors (antipsychotic drugs). These findings have led to the dopamine hypothesis, which states that schizophrenia is the result of abnormal activity in neural pathways containing dopamine.

More recent studies indicate that schizophrenia can best be conceived of as two different disorders. The positive symptoms are produced by overactivity of dopamine neurons and can be treated with antipsychotic drugs. The negative symptoms may be caused by brain damage. Researchers have found direct evidence of brain damage by inspecting scans of living patients' brains.

Researchers have suggested three possible causes of the brain damage–and the corresponding negative symptoms—that accompany schizophrenia: a virus that triggers an autoimmune disease, which causes brain damage later in life; a virus that damages the brain early in life; and birth trauma. Heredity presumably interacts with the first two factors—many people may be exposed to the virus, but the virus will cause brain damage only in people with a genetic sensitivity.

Mood Disorders

The serious mood disorders are primarily disorders of emotion, although delusions are also present. Bipolar I disorder consists of alternating periods of mania and depression, whereas major depressive disorder consists of depression alone. Bipolar II disorder is marked by major depressive episodes and hypomania. A negative attributional style is also correlated with depression.

Heritability studies strongly suggest a biological component in mood disorders. This possibility receives support from the finding that biological treatments for depression, including electroconvulsive shock, antidepressant drugs, and REM sleep deprivation, can reduce symptoms, whereas reserpine, a hypertension drug that blocks the release of norepinephrine and serotonin, can cause depression. These findings, along with evidence from biochemical analysis of the breakdown products of norepinephrine and serotonin in depressed patients, suggest that depression results from deficiencies in the availability of these neurotransmitters. However, the fact that environmental stressors can also affect the availability of neurotransmitters warns us to be careful in inferring cause and effect.

Beck developed a cognitive–behavioral therapy to help depressed clients target errors of thinking and feeling that perpetuate self-defeating behaviors and replace them with more desirable behaviors. It is also the case that behavioral change can produce changes in cognition. Thus, the causal relation between cognition and behavior can be considered bidirectional.

Anxiety and Dissociative Disorders

People with anxiety, somatoform, and dissociative mental disorders can be thought of as having adopted strategies that offer some immediate payoff but are maladaptive in the long run. We can understand most of these problems as exaggerations of our own. Although fears and doubts may be unrealistic, they can become outrageously extreme.

Anxiety disorders include panic disorder, phobias, obsessive–compulsive disorder, and post-traumatic stress disorder. Anxiety disorders (except specific phobia and social phobia) appear to have a genetic component. With panic disorder, the person has no defense against his or her discomfort. In contrast, obsessive–compulsive disorder involves thoughts and behaviors that prevent the person from thinking about painful subjects or that ward off anxiety. The symptoms of PTSD include intrusive, recurring thoughts and memories, social detachment, difficulty concentrating, and hopelessness.

Simple phobias can probably be explained by classical conditioning: An experience (usually early in life) causes a particular object or situation to become a conditioned aversive stimulus. The fear associated with this stimulus leads to escape behaviors, which are reinforced because they reduce the person's fear. Agoraphobia is apparently not caused by a specific traumatic experience. Social phobia is a fear of being observed or judged by others; in its mildest form, it involves a fear of speaking in public. Specific phobia is narrowly defined in terms of a particular fear-inducing stimulus, such as a spider or snake.

Dissociative disorders are rare. Dissociative amnesia (with or without fugue) appears to be a withdrawal from a painful situation or from intolerable guilt. Because amnesia is a common symptom of brain injury or neurological disease, clinicians must rule out physical factors before accepting a diagnosis of dissociative amnesia. The multiple personalities found in dissociative identity disorder are even rarer and may occur because they permit a person to engage in behaviors contrary to his or her customary code of conduct.

Culture-bound syndromes are psychological disorders that appear to be idiosyncratic to only one or a few cultures. These disorders frequently involve fear of specific objects or situations. The precise origins of culture-bound syndromes are unknown, but it seems likely that they involve learned responses that reduce or eliminate anxiety or stress.

Personality Disorders

Antisocial personality disorder is one of numerous personality disorders described in the DSM-IV-TR. Also called psychopathy or sociopathy, antisocial personality disorder is a serious problem for society. Individuals with the disorder exhibit an apparent indifference to the effects of their behavior on other people, impulsiveness, failure to learn from experience, and habitual lying. Some are superficially charming, and many make a living cheating others out of their money.

Antisocial personality disorder tends to run in families, and it seems likely that both heredity and a poor home environment may contribute to its development. The disorder is difficult to treat because individuals with the disorder do not see any reason for changing.

Borderline personality disorder is marked by impulsivity and rapidly changing interpersonal relationships, self-image, and affect. Among its diagnostic criteria are suicide attempts and self-mutilation.

succeed with mypsychlab

Visit MyPsychLab for practice quizzes, flashcards, and dozens of videos and animated tutorials, including the following items you can find in the "Multimedia Library":

Post Traumatic Stress Disorder: Sara
Dissociative Identity Disorder:
    The Three Faces of Eve

Bipolar Disorder
The Axes of the DSM

Overview of Clinical Assessment Methods
Overview of Clinical Assessment Tools

KEY TERMS

actuarial judgments   *p. 494*
agoraphobia   *p. 510*
anticipatory anxiety   *p. 509*
antisocial personality disorder   *p. 516*
anxiety   *p. 508*
attention-deficit/hyperactivity disorder   *p. 496*
autistic disorder   *p. 497*
biopsychosocial perspective   *p. 491*
bipolar I disorder   *p. 506*
bipolar II disorder   *p. 506*
borderline personality disorder   *p. 518*
catatonic schizophrenia   *p. 502*
clinical judgments   *p. 494*
comorbid   *p. 492*
compulsion   *p. 511*
culture-bound syndrome   *p. 515*
diathesis–stress model   *p. 491*
disorganized schizophrenia   *p. 502*
dissociative amnesia   *p. 514*
dissociative disorders   *p. 514*
dissociative fugue   *p. 514*
dissociative identity disorder   *p. 514*
dopamine hypothesis   *p. 503*

double bind   *p. 505*
etiology   *p. 488*
hallucination   *p. 501*
major depressive disorder   *p. 506*
mania   *p. 506*
mood disorders   *p. 505*
negative symptoms   *p. 501*
obsession   *p. 511*
obsessive-compulsive disorder   *p. 511*
panic disorder   *p. 509*
paranoid schizophrenia   *p. 502*
phobia   *p. 509*
phobic disorder   *p. 510*
positive symptom   *p. 501*
post-traumatic stress disorder   *p. 513*
residual schizophrenia   *p. 502*
schizophrenia   *p. 500*
social phobia   *p. 510*
specific phobia   *p. 511*
substance-related disorders   *p. 498*
Tourette's syndrome   *p. 512*
undifferentiated schizophrenia   *p. 502*

SUGGESTIONS FOR FURTHER READING

Arieti, S. (2000). *The Parnas: A scene from the Holocaust.* Philadelphia: Paul Dry Books.

A noted psychiatrist offers a respectful and instructive Freudian analysis of the agoraphobia displayed by Giuseppe Pardo, the Parnas of Pisa, including the remission of symptoms during Pardo's fateful encounter with Nazi soldiers near the end of World War II.

Butcher, J. N., Mineka, S., & Hooley, J. M. (2007). *Abnormal psychology and modern life* (13th ed.). Boston: Allyn & Bacon.

This upper-division undergraduate textbook provides a systematic overview of the categories of mental illness and their treatment.

Cleckley, H. (1988). *The mask of sanity* (5th ed.). Augusta, GA: Emily S. Cleckley.

This classic reference on antisocial personality disorder includes several in-depth case studies.

Nasar, S. (1998). *A beautiful mind.* New York: Simon & Schuster.

A best-selling biography of the Nobel economist, John Nash, that follows his brilliant career and the personal and family devastation wrought by paranoid schizophrenia.

North, C. N. (2003). *Welcome, silence: My triumph over schizophrenia.* Lima, OH: Academic Renewal Press.

A psychiatrist offers a first-person window on her own struggle with schizophrenia and treatment.

Spitzer, R. L., Gibbon, M., Skodol, M., Williams, J. B. W., & First, M. B. (2002). *DSM-IV-TR casebook: A learning companion to the diagnostic and statistical manual of mental disorders, Fourth edition, Text revision.* Washington, DC: American Psychiatric Association.

An excellent source of case studies that parallel the diagnostic categories found in the DSM-IV-TR.

Vonnegut, M. (1975). *The Eden express: A personal account of schizophrenia.* New York: Praeger.

An autobiographical narrative of what it is to become schizophrenic and to receive treatment with antipsychotic medication.

CHAPTER
17

The Treatment
of Psychological
Disorders

Prologue

To Ghosthood and Back

Geoff was on the fast track. He had dropped out of college to start a company, then watched its sales grow nonstop in the first few years. His personal fortune zoomed up, too—at least on paper. To start a new venture, he borrowed against the company's stock. Missed deadlines and failed projections followed, and his company was forced to fold. Although his professional life was now a shambles, Geoff still believed he could do no wrong. He was bursting with ideas and energy and felt nearly indestructible. He slept only about 3 or 4 hours per night, and once told a business partner he could have jumped off the Empire State Building and landed on his feet. His business reversals led Geoff to see a psychologist, who told him he might be suffering from bipolar I disorder, a serious psychological condition. Geoff brushed it off. He felt tired sometimes, but he never felt really down. The psychologist couldn't possibly be right.

Geoff decided he needed a fresh start and moved to a new city. Once there, he was sleepless for 5 days. Friends whom he phoned during that time recommended he seek professional help. He checked into a hospital, where he was diagnosed with bipolar I disorder and received a prescription for lithium. One of the psychiatrists who had treated him recommended that he also see a psychotherapist. But Geoff's previous experience had made him skeptical, and he opted to depend on lithium alone to solve his problems.

Over time, additional drugs were prescribed for different aspects of the disorder. Geoff was confident the drugs were helping him, but he hated their side effects. He developed tremors and an erratic heart rate and had to start taking other drugs to control them. He needed a different medication to sleep. Altogether, he was taking a dozen different medications each day and sometimes more. He began to worry about being so dependent on them. In his more reflective moments, he wondered whether he had become less aware of himself, of others, and of life in general. He thought of himself as more and more like a ghost. Even while taking medication, he was always trying to do a hundred things at once. It was difficult to think of himself as having any stability, any substance. Sometimes he thought about going back to college, but the idea of sitting through a lecture or studying for an exam seemed impossible.

In his search for a way out, Geoff decided to give psychotherapy a second try. Following up on a friend's recommendation, he met a psychologist who seemed just right for him. Today, with his therapist's help, Geoff better understands his decision making while in a manic state. Even with medication, the manic states recur, although not as intensely, and Geoff can feel them coming on. Psychotherapy has helped him learn to recognize the early warning signs and to defer potentially important decisions until the state has subsided. As Geoff now sees it, there is no way he could have gained from psychotherapy without medication, but medication alone would not have allowed him to get his life back on track. ∎

People may seek therapy for many reasons. Some need help in adjusting to everyday problems at home, work, or school. Others face more serious problems, such as the death of a loved one, their own approaching death, or chronic difficulties in getting along with other people. Still others enter therapy, or are placed in therapy by mental health agencies, for very serious psychological problems such as schizophrenia, major depression, or drug abuse. People who hit a low point in their lives, often as a result of declining physical health, may feel that their own efforts are insufficient and that family and friends cannot provide the help they need to solve their problems.

This chapter begins with a historical overview of the treatment of psychological disorders, and then describes four basic approaches to treatment: insight therapies; behavior and cognitive–behavioral therapies; group therapies (including therapies for families and couples and outreach programs that serve the community); and biomedical therapies. Often the therapeutic application is to psychological disorders described in Chapter 16. Therapy is a complex process, and its outcome depends to a large extent on the quality of the relationship the client and therapist form. The final section of the chapter addresses ethical issues involved in the practice of therapy and the important considerations individuals should make when selecting a therapist.

Psychological Disorders and Psychotherapy

Today, most societies view psychological disorders as illnesses, much the same as physical diseases like diabetes or cancer. Today, psychologists agree that the treatment of psychological disorders should proceed humanely: The person needs help, and the emergence of techniques to provide such help has become a hallmark of psychology. However, this enlightened view has not always characterized humankind's treatment of people with psychological disorders and other psychological problems.

[**FIGURE 17·1**] Among the earliest biological approaches to the treatment of mental disorders was the ancient practice of trephining, in which a hole was made in the skull to allow evil spirits to escape the person's head.

(Photo © Loren McIntyre/Woodfin Camp & Associates.)

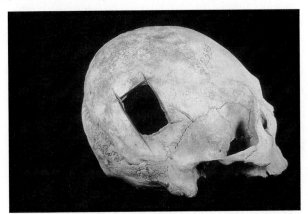

Early Treatment of Psychological Disorders

Sometimes psychological disorders are thought of as emerging in relatively modern times. In truth, they have existed in one form or another from antiquity. For most of that time, people with these disorders have been regarded with awe or fear. The earliest known attempts to treat psychological disorders involved drilling holes in a living person's skull, a process known as **trephining.** Presumably, the opening was made to release evil spirits from inside the victim's head. In prehistoric times, this procedure was performed with a sharp-edged stone; later civilizations, such as the Egyptians, refined the practice with more sophisticated instruments. Signs of healing at the edges of the holes in prehistoric skulls indicate that some people survived trephining. (See FIGURE 17·1.)

Many other painful and degrading practices were directed at people's presumed possession by evil spirits. Rituals included beatings, starving, near drowning, and the drinking of foul-tasting concoctions. As late as the eighteenth century, the idea that devils and spirits were responsible for peculiar behaviors in certain people remained popular in Britain and its colonies and in Europe. Fortunately, a few people believed that such extreme behaviors reflected diseases and should be treated medically and with compassion. Johann Wier, a sixteenth-century German physician, was among the first to challenge practices intended to combat witchcraft. He argued that most people who were being tortured and burned for practicing witchcraft in fact had mental illness. The church condemned his writings as heretical and banned them. Wier's ideas reemerged only in the nineteenth century.

---

trephining A surgical procedure in which a hole is made in the skull of a living person.

[**FIGURE 17·2**] This illustration of a device used in an early 19th-century mental hospital exemplifies the extremes of treatment to which mental patients were subjected.

(Illustration © Bettmann/CORBIS)

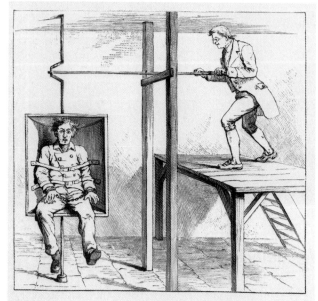

THE DOCTOR THINKS THAT "NO WELL-REGULATED INSTITUTION SHOULD BE UNPROVIDED WITH THE CIRCULATING SWING." 1818.

Eventually, the deep cultural belief in witchcraft and demonology waned. The clergy, the medical authorities, and the general public began to regard people with psychological disorders as ill. Torture and severe persecution came to an end. However, the lives of mentally ill people did not necessarily become better. Undoubtedly, many people with psychological disorders were regarded as strange but harmless and managed to maintain a marginal existence in society. Others were sheltered by their families. Often, however, people with psychological disorders were consigned to "insane asylums," many of which were extraordinarily inhumane. There they often were kept in chains and wallowed in their own excrement. Those who displayed bizarre catatonic postures or who had dramatic delusions were sometimes exhibited to the public for a fee. Many of the treatments designed to cure asylum patients were only a little better than the tortures that had previously been used to drive out evil spirits. Patients were tied up, doused in cold water, bled, made to vomit, spun violently in a rotating chair, and subjected to other terrible treatments. (See FIGURE 17·2.)

Reform began as mistreatment of the mentally ill became a cause of humanitarians. Philippe Pinel (1745–1826) was a French physician who in 1793 was appointed director of La Bicêtre, a mental hospital in Paris. Pinel believed that most mental patients would respond favorably to kind treatment. As an experiment, he removed the chains from some of the patients, took them out of the dungeons, and allowed them to walk about the hospital grounds. The experiment was a remarkable success. Orderliness and general calm replaced the previous noise, stench, and pervasive aura of despair. Many patients were eventually discharged. Pinel's achievements encouraged similar reforms elsewhere. In the United States, Dorothea Dix (1802–1887) led the campaign for humane treatment of mental patients. She raised millions of dollars for the construction of mental hospitals and spurred the reform of many mental health facilities.

Today much greater emphasis is placed on treatment. The discovery of antipsychotic drugs and improvements in therapy have spared many people who otherwise would have spent their lives in institutions. Callaway (2007) provides an overview of the dropping away of institutionalized treatment in the form of electroconvulsive and insulin coma therapies, hydrotherapy, and lobotomies in favor of psychotropic medications.

The Development of Treatment

The modern approach to therapy can be traced to Franz Anton Mesmer (1734–1815), an Austrian physician who practiced in Paris in the late eighteenth and early nineteenth centuries. He devised a theory of "magnetic fluxes," according to which he attempted to effect cures by manipulating iron rods and bottles of chemicals. In reality, he hypnotized his patients and thereby alleviated some of their symptoms. As a result, hypnosis was first known as *mesmerism* (see Wegner, 2002).

Jean Martin Charcot ("shar-KOE"; 1825–1893), a French neurologist, began to study the therapeutic uses of hypnosis and to use it in his treatment of patients at the Salpêtrière asylum near Paris. Before Sigmund Freud began private practice in Vienna, he studied with Charcot in Paris. There he observed the effects of hypnosis on hysteria. Freud's association with Charcot, and later with Josef Breuer ("BROY-uhr"), started him on his life's study of the determinants of personality and the origins of psychological disorder. Freud created the practice of psychoanalysis. The therapeutic methods he developed still influence many psychologists and psychiatrists; other psychologists inspired by Freud devised therapies based on their own theoretical views of maladaptive behavior and its causes.

Although all therapists have in common a strong commitment to helping people solve their problems—whether the difficulties of coping with everyday stressors or more severe psychological disorders such as schizophrenia or depression, some therapists may favor one kind of therapy or another based on their theoretical orientation. The majority of therapists today, however, adopt a more general or **eclectic approach.** With this approach, the therapist uses whatever methods he or she believes will work best for a particular client at a particular time. The therapist is not necessarily wedded to a particular theoretical orientation regarding treatment. In-

---

eclectic approach An approach to therapy in which the therapist uses whatever method he or she feels will work best for a particular client at a particular time.

[**TABLE 17·1**] Basic Assumptions, Goals, and Methods Involved in Major Categories of Therapies

Type of Therapy	Basic Assumptions	Primary Goals	Typical Methods of Analysis or Intervention
Psychoanalysis	Behavior is motivated by intrapsychic conflict and biological urges.	To discover the sources of conflict and resolve them through insight.	Free association; dream analysis; interpretation of transference, resistance, memory, and manner of speech.
Psychodynamic therapy	Behavior is motivated by both unconscious forces and interpersonal experiences.	To understand and improve interpersonal skills.	Interpretation of transference and modification of clients' inappropriate schemas for interpersonal relationships.
Humanistic therapies: Client-centered therapy and Gestalt therapy	People are inherently good and have innate worth.	To promote personal growth and self-actualization and to enhance clients' awareness of bodily sensations and feelings.	Reduction of incongruence through reflection, empathy, unconditional positive regard, and techniques designed to enhance personal awareness and feelings of self-worth.
Behavior and cognitive–behavioral therapies	Behavior is largely influenced by environmental contingencies, people's perception of them, or a combination of both.	To change maladaptive behavior and thinking patterns.	Manipulation of environmental variables, restructuring of thinking patterns, and correction of faulty thinking or irrational beliefs.
Family/couples therapy	Problems in relationships entail everybody involved in those relationships.	To discover how social interactions influence problems of individual behavior.	Analysis of patterns of families'/couples' interactions and of how those involved reinforce maladaptive and adaptive thinking and behaving.

stead, she or he seeks the particular form of therapy that will best solve the client's problems. This often means combining aspects of several different treatment approaches according to the client's specific problem and personal circumstances. For example, Acierno, Hersen, and Van Hasselt (1993) showed that combinations of behavior and cognitive–behavioral therapies are more effective in treating panic disorder (see Chapter 16) than is either one alone. TABLE 17·1 lists the assumptions, primary goals, and methods involved in each of the major forms of therapy we will consider next.

QUESTIONS TO CONSIDER

1. What is your reaction to people with psychological disorders? If you have known someone who has been diagnosed with a psychological disorder, what was your initial feeling about that person when you first learned about it?
2. Would you seek the help of a therapist if you had a psychological problem you could not solve yourself? If so, describe what you might imagine therapy to be like and how it might help you. If not, describe the reasons why you would not seek help.

Insight Therapies

Although it is fair to assume that the goal of any therapy is to help the client achieve new insight into her or his condi-

tion, practitioners of **insight therapy** assume that people are essentially normal but develop maladaptive thought patterns and emotions, which are revealed in maladaptive behavior. Insight therapies view such behavior as symptomatic of deeper, underlying psychological problems of which the individual is unaware. Thus, once a client gains a new understanding of the causes of his or her problems, those problems—and the maladaptive behavior they sustain—will cease. In other words, insight equals cure. In this section, we take a close look at major insight therapies: psychoanalysis, client-centered therapy, and Gestalt therapy.

Psychoanalysis and Psychodynamic Therapies

Sigmund Freud is credited with developing **psychoanalysis,** a form of therapy that aims to provide the client with insight into his or her unconscious motives and impulses. Recall from Chapter 14 that Freud's theory of personality suggests that unconscious conflicts based on the competing

---

insight therapy Therapy in which the therapist aids clients to achieve insight into the causes of maladaptive behavior, causes they were previously unaware of.

psychoanalysis A form of psychotherapy aimed at providing the client with insight into his or her unconscious motivations and impulses; first developed by Sigmund Freud.

demands of the id (representing biological urges), the superego (representing the moral dictates of society), and the ego (representing perceived reality) often lead to anxiety. The source of these conflicts, according to Freud, can usually be traced to inadequately censored sexual and aggressive urges or stunted completion of one or more of the psychosexual stages of development.

In the early stages of therapy, the nature of the client's problem is difficult to identify because the analyst and the client are unaware of the underlying conflicts. The *repression* of these conflicts is seldom complete, though, and they frequently intrude into consciousness in subtle ways. By encouraging the client to talk, the analyst tries to bring these conflicts into view. The obscurity of the conflicts requires that the analyst interpret them to expose their true meaning and gradually weave together a more complete picture of the client's unconscious. Those who currently practice psychoanalysis (or one of its variants) still emphasize interpretation as the principal means of uncovering the root causes of their clients' problems (e.g., LaFarge, 2000; Busch, 2003b). For some clients, insight is a sudden rush of profound understanding—sort of an "Aha, so that's what was causing the problem!" experience. For other clients, perhaps the majority who undergo long-term therapy, a feeling of quiet accomplishment may be found after a long struggle. Successful treatment depends not only on the psychoanalyst's interpretations but also on the client's capacity to understand and integrate what he or she has learned in therapy (Busch, 2003a).

Psychoanalytic Techniques For several reasons, Freud abandoned the use of hypnosis in favor of other methods. One of his techniques was **free association,** in which the client is encouraged to speak freely. His assumption was that repressed material would surface eventually. Freud achieved this goal in two ways. First, he encouraged the client to report any thoughts or images that came to mind, without worrying about their meaning. Second, Freud attempted to minimize any authoritative influence over the client's disclosures by eliminating eye contact. He usually sat in a chair at the head of a couch on which the client reclined.

Freud also believed that dreams offered crucial clues, and these were among the topics clients were encouraged to discuss. **Dream interpretation,** the evaluation of the underlying meaning of dream content, is a hallmark of psychoanalysis (Freud, 1900). According to Freud, even dream

Freud refined his practice of psychoanalysis in this office, where he asked his clients to recline on the couch (right) and to tell him about their childhood experiences, their dreams, and their anxieties. To encourage the client's openness, Freud sat at his desk, out of the client's sight. Freud's goal was to discover his clients' unconscious motivations for the problems they were experiencing.

content is subject to censoring, so the analyst must be able to distinguish between dreams' *manifest* and *latent contents*. Recall from Chapter 9 that the manifest content of a dream is the actual images and events that occur within the dream as reported by the client; latent content is the hidden meaning or significance of the dream as interpreted by the psychoanalyst. The manifest content masks the latent content because the latent content is anxiety provoking and causes the person psychological discomfort. Thus, the analyst must be especially skilled in recognizing the symbolic nature of dreams, for things are not always as they appear. For example, the client may relate a dream about being chased by a growling, vicious dog. The dog may symbolize an angry parent or spouse. The idea of a parent's or spouse's being angry and upset may be so painful to the client that it has been disguised within the dream.

In psychoanalysis, insight typically is not achieved quickly, nor do clients always find it easy to disclose private aspects of their personal lives. For example, the client may have to confront the memory (whether real or imagined) of being abused as a child, or of being unloved, or of feeling peculiar, inferior, or out of place. Although the client wishes devoutly to be cured, he or she may recoil from needing to recall painful memories. The client often becomes defensive at some point during therapy, unconsciously attempting to halt further insight by censoring his or her true feelings, a process Freud called **resistance.** A psychoanalyst recognizes resistance when a client tries to change the topic, begins to miss appointments, or suddenly forgets what he or she was about to say. The skilled therapist who encounters such diversions will redirect the discussion to the sensitive topics while softening the pain of rediscovery.

Over a period of months or even years of therapy sessions that may occur several times a week, clients in psychoanalysis

---

free association   A method of Freudian analysis in which the client is asked to relax and to speak freely in reporting any thoughts or images that come to mind without worrying about their meaning.

dream interpretation   The method in psychoanalysis whereby the therapist interprets the client's report of a dream (its manifest content) in terms of its deeper, symbolic meaning (its latent content).

resistance   A development during psychoanalysis in which the client becomes defensive, unconsciously attempting to halt further insight by censoring his or her emotions.

gradually become less inhibited, and the discussion begins to drift away from recent events to the more distant memories of childhood. As clients relive aspects of childhood, they may begin to project powerful attitudes and emotions onto the therapist, a process called **transference.** Clients may come to love or hate the therapist with the same emotional intensity they originally experienced toward parents or siblings in childhood.

At one point, Freud thought of transference as a distraction from the real issues and thus an impediment to therapy. He soon decided, however, that the experience of transference was essential to the success of his approach. Whereas free association uncovers many of the relevant events and facts of clients' lives, transference allows them to relive significant early experiences. By becoming a substitute for the actual people in a client's life, the therapist becomes the means for illuminating the conflicts of the unconscious (Connolly et al., 2000).

Freud likewise reasoned that the analyst could just as easily project his or her emotions onto the client, a process he called **countertransference.** Unlike transference, Freud believed countertransference to be unhealthy and undesirable. To be effective, the analyst had to remain emotionally detached and objective in appraising clients' disclosures. For this reason, he argued that the analyst, to understand his or her own unconscious conflicts, should undergo analysis with another therapist as part of training.

Contemporary Psychodynamic Therapy

Psychodynamic therapy differs from Freud's original psychoanalysis and refers to a collection of therapies that, though traceable to Freud's, nevertheless depart from its tenets in substantive ways. For example, although psychodynamic therapies still focus on achieving insight into the unconscious, they tend to place less emphasis on psychosexual development and more emphasis on social and interpersonal experiences, including the complex structure and dynamics of the ego.

Psychodynamic therapists view the ego as playing a more active role in influencing a person's thoughts and actions. Rather than the ego functioning merely to mediate between the demands of the id and superego, they believe the ego is a proactive component in a person's overall psychological functioning. In other words, compared with Freud, psychodynamic therapists see the ego as having more control over the unconscious. Thus, people receiving psychodynamic therapy today are seen as being less constrained by the mind's unconscious forces than Freud had asserted (Kennedy, 2007).

In addition, whereas Freud considered analysis extremely involved and demanding, often requiring years to complete, psychodynamic analysts now generally believe that much can be gained by shortening the process and by lessening the client's dependence on the analyst (Binder, 1998; Travis, et al., 2001). One form of psychodynamic therapy, for example, is *brief psychodynamic therapy*, which takes about 10 to 25 sessions to complete (Messer, 2001). The goal of the therapist is to understand and improve the client's interpersonal skills through the interpretation of transference processes. This therapy is based on Freud's belief that our early experiences with others influence the dynamics of our current relationships. Brief psychodynamic therapy focuses on a client's schemas for interpersonal relationships and attempts to modify those that are errant or that otherwise prevent the client from developing fulfilling relationships with others. Consider, for example, the following case (Prochaska & Norcross, 2003).

[**CASE STUDY**] Karen was about to be terminated from her nursing program if her problems were not resolved. She had always been a competent student who seemed to get along well with peers and patients. Now, since the beginning of her rotation on 3 South, a surgical ward, she was plagued by headaches and dizzy spells. Of more serious consequence were the two medical errors she made when dispensing medications to patients. She realized that these errors could have proved fatal, and she was as concerned as her nursing faculty about why such problems had begun in the final year of her education. Karen knew she had many negative feelings toward the head nurse on 3 South, but she did not believe these feelings could account for her current dilemma. She entered psychotherapy.

After a few weeks of psychotherapy, the therapist realized that one of Karen's important conflicts revolved around the death of her father when she was 12 years old. She remembered how upset she was when her father had a heart attack and had to be rushed the hospital. For a while it looked as though her father was going to pull through, and Karen began enjoying her daily visits to see him. During one of these visits, her father clutched his chest in obvious pain and told Karen to get a nurse. She remembered how helpless she felt when she could not find a nurse, although she did not recall why this was so difficult. Her search seemed endless, and by the time she finally found a nurse, her father was dead.

The therapist asked Karen the name of the ward on which her father had died. She paused and thought, and then she blurted out, "3 South." She cried at length as she told how confused she was and how angry she felt toward the nurses on the ward for not being more readily available, although she thought they might have been involved with another emergency. After weeping and shaking and expressing her resentment, Karen felt calm and relaxed for the first time in months. Her symptoms disappeared, and her problems in the nursing program were relieved. (Taken from Butcher et al., 2007, pp. 630–631)

----

transference A process in which a client begins to project powerful attitudes and emotions onto a psychoanalyst.

countertransference Process in which a psychoanalyst projects his or her emotions onto a client.

psychodynamic therapy A therapeutic approach derived from psychoanalysis but typically deemphasizing psychosexual development in favor of emphasis on social and interpersonal experiences and the complexities of the ego.

Humanistic Therapies

In strong contrast to psychoanalysis, which may be considered to offer a darker view of humankind, the aim of another insight therapy, **humanistic therapy,** is to provide the client with a greater understanding of his or her unique potential for personal growth and self-actualization. Humanistic therapies proceed from the assumption that people are inherently good and have innate worth. Psychological problems represent an impediment hampering a person's potential for personal growth. The aim of therapy is to overcome this impediment and thereby retrieve the potential anew. The two major forms of humanistic therapy are client-centered therapy and Gestalt therapy.

Client-Centered Therapy   Carl Rogers (1902–1987) developed the first humanistic therapy in the 1940s, creating a major alternative to psychoanalysis. His approach has had a major impact on therapy generally (Hill & Nakayama, 2000; see Freeth, 2007, for a view of its impact in the United Kingdom specifically). Rogers found the formalism of psychoanalysis too confining and its emphasis on intrapsychic conflict too pessimistic (Tobin, 1991). His discontent led him to develop his own theory of personality (see Chapter 14), abnormal behavior, and therapy. His **client-centered therapy** (also known a *person-centered* therapy) is so named because of the respect given the client during therapy: The client decides what to talk about without direction or judgment from the therapist. In this way, ultimate responsibility for resolving the client's problems rests squarely on him or her. The central focus of the therapy is on the client and not solely on a method or theory.

Rogers believed that the cause of many psychological problems can be traced to the disparity between people's perceptions of the kind of person they aspire to be (their *real selves*) and what others expect them to be according to the ideals of their culture (their *ideal selves*). Rogers called this discrepancy between the real and the ideal self **incongruence.** The goal of client-centered therapy is to reduce incongruence by fostering experiences that will make attainment of the real self more likely.

Because the client, not the therapist, directs the course of therapy, the therapist strives to make the client's perceptions, thoughts, and feelings more noticeable to the client. The therapist frequently accomplishes this through *reflection;* that is, by sensitively rephrasing or mirroring the client's statements. For example:

Client: I get so frustrated at my parents. They just don't understand how I feel. They don't know what it's like to be me.

Therapist: You seem to be saying that the things that are important to you aren't very important to your parents. You'd like them now and then to see things from your perspective.

By reflecting the concerns of the client, the therapist demonstrates *empathy,* or the ability to perceive the world from another's viewpoint. The establishment of empathy is key in the therapist's effort to the help the client deal with the incongruence between his or her real and ideal selves. It would be a mistake to assume that the therapist merely replays the client's words. The therapist's reflection allows confirmation of his or her growing understanding of the client's view as well as the affirmation of its importance.

For Rogers (1951, p. 20), the "worth and significance of the individual" is a basic ground rule of therapy. The therapist enacts this principle in therapy through **unconditional positive regard:** The therapist asserts that the client's worth as a human being is not dependent on anything he or she thinks, does, or feels. By unconditionally accepting and approving of the client as a person, the therapist aims to help the client understand that she or he is worthwhile and important.

Unconditional acceptance of the *person* does not necessarily mean that the therapist approves of his or her *behavior,* however. A client-centered therapist may condemn behavior if, for instance, a client has harmed another person. The key is that the therapist has an abiding belief in the basic value and humanity of the client. Once clients begin to feel valued in the therapeutic context, a self-healing process can begin. For example, clients usually have difficulty at first expressing feelings verbally. The therapist tries to understand those feelings and to help clients put them

---

humanistic therapy A form of psychotherapy focusing on the client's unique potential for personal growth and self-actualization.

client-centered therapy A form of psychotherapy in which the client decides what to talk about without strong direction or judgment from the therapist.

incongruence In Rogers' theory, a discrepancy between a client's perceptions of her or his real and ideal selves.

unconditional positive regard In Rogers' approach, the therapist's assertion that a client's worth as a human being is not dependent on anything that he or she thinks, does, or feels; love and acceptance of an individual with no strings attached.

Carl Rogers (top right) taught that clients can best achieve personal growth through the experience of unconditional positive regard.

into words. Through this process, clients learn to understand what their feelings mean and to resolve incongruence. Consider the following original exchange between client and therapist:

> *Alice:* I was thinking about this business of standards. I somehow developed a sort of knack, I guess, of—well—habit—of trying to make people feel at ease around me, or to make things go along smoothly. . . .
>
> *Counselor:* In other words, what you did was always in the direction of trying to keep things smooth and to make other people feel better and to smooth the situation.
>
> *A:* Yes. I think that's what it was. Now the reason why I did it probably was—I mean, not that I was a good little Samaritan going around making other people happy, but that was probably the role that felt easiest for me to play. I'd been doing it around the home so much. I just didn't stand up for my own convictions, until I don't know whether I have any convictions to stand up for.
>
> *C:* You feel that for a long time you've been playing the role of kind of smoothing out the frictions or differences or what not. . . .
>
> *A:* Mm-hmm.
>
> *C:* Rather than having any opinion or reaction of your own in the situation. Is that it?
>
> *A:* That's it. Or that I haven't been really honestly being myself, or actually knowing what my real self is, and that I've been just playing a sort of false role. Whatever role no one else was playing, and that needed to be played at the time, I'd try to fill it in. (Rogers, 1951, pp. 152–153)

As this example illustrates, in Rogers's view, the therapist should not manipulate the course of therapy but should create conditions under which the client can achieve his or her own insights and make his or her own decisions. Thus, the therapist in the conversation sought to confirm the client's perception of the role she had played at home and elsewhere—that of facilitator or peacemaker. The therapist then asked the client to confirm her view that having played the role for so long had left her unsure of whether she had anything of her own to offer. Doing so allowed the client to acknowledge that perhaps she had not been honest, that she had been playing a false role—a role no one else was playing at the time but that seemed called for. In doing so, she disclosed that she really didn't know what her real self was. For Rogers' purposes, this was an important achievement on the client's part.

Gestalt Therapy The development of client-centered therapy owed much to Rogers's disenchantment with psychoanalysis. For much the same reason, Fritz Perls (1893–1970), although trained in Freudian techniques, disengaged himself from psychoanalysis and founded **Gestalt therapy** (Perls, 1969). This form of therapy emphasizes the unity of mind and body by training the client to "get in touch" with bodily sensations and emotions long hidden from awareness. (Recall from Chapters 1 and 7 that the emphasis on the unity of perception was a hallmark of Gestalt psychology.) Gestalt therapy places exclusive emphasis on present experience and not on the past. Moreover, the Gestalt therapist may be quite confrontational, challenging the client to deal honestly with his or her emotions.

Like Freud, Perls believed that dreams are a rich source of information and that the client must be able to understand their symbolism. In Gestalt therapy, the therapist will often ask the client to adopt the perspective of a person or even an object that appeared in a dream and to do so in an empathetic manner.

Another tool of Gestalt therapists is the *empty-chair technique,* in which clients imagine talking to someone they imagine sitting in the chair beside them. This technique derives from Perls's belief that memories, fears, and feelings of guilt affect people's ongoing relationships with others. For example, the therapist may ask a woman to say the things she always wanted to say to her deceased father but didn't while he was alive. The empty-chair technique allows her to experience in the here and now the feelings and perceptions she might have suppressed while her father was alive. It also allows her, perhaps for the first time, to express these feelings and to gain insight into how these feelings currently influence her perceptions of herself and her world. The Gestalt therapist also encourages clients to gain a better understanding of their feelings by talking to themselves (that is, to different parts of their personalities) and even to inanimate objects. Any attempt by a client to avoid the reality of his or her situation is challenged by the therapist, who constantly attempts to keep the client's attention focused on present problems and tries to guide the client toward an honest confrontation with them. Perls (1967, p. 331) argued, "In the safe emergency of the therapeutic situation, the neurotic discovers that the world does not fall to pieces if he or she gets angry, sexy, joyous, mournful." This is borne out in the following case study (Prochaska & Norcross, 2003).

[CASE STUDY] A college professor and therapist was preoccupied with his academic promotion and tenure and found himself unable to experience any joy. He sought the assistance of a friend who was a Gestalt therapist. She asked him to conjure up a daydream, rather than a dream. The daydream that emerged spontaneously was one of skiing. The therapist asked him to be the mountain, and he began to experience how warm he was when he was at his base. As he got closer to the top, what looked so beautiful was also

---

Gestalt therapy A form of therapy that emphasizes the unity of mind and body by teaching the client to "get in touch" with unconscious bodily sensations and emotions.

very cold and frozen. The therapist asked the professor to be the snow, and he experienced how hard and icy he could be near the top. But near the bottom, people ran over him easily and wore him out. When the session was finished, the professor did not feel like crying or shouting; he felt like skiing. So he went, leaving articles and books behind. In the sparkle of the snow and sun, he realized that joy in living emerges through deeds and not through words. In his rush to success, he had committed one of the cardinal sins against himself—the sin of not being active. (Taken from Butcher et al., 2007, p. 629)

Evaluation of Insight Therapies

As Chapter 16 pointed out, the processes proposed by psychoanalytic theory have not been subjected to rigorous empirical scrutiny until relatively recently (e.g., Baumeister et al., 1998; Charman, 2004; Solms, 2004). Evaluating the effectiveness of psychoanalysis has long been difficult because only a small proportion of people with psychological disorders qualify for this method of treatment. To participate, a client must be intelligent, articulate, motivated enough, and well-off enough to spend 3 or more hours a week working hard to uncover unconscious conflicts. These qualifications rule out many people with active psychoses, as well as people who lack the financial resources or the time to devote to such a long-term project.

Fonagy and his British colleagues (Fonagy et al., 2005) spelled out the enormous practical and technical challenges to validly and reliably demonstrating the effectiveness of psychoanalytic and psychodynamic therapies, especially when the gold standard for such demonstration is the use of randomized controlled trials (RCTs, that is, assigning clients to particular therapies on a randomized basis). Their findings are comparable to those of Leichensenring (2005), a German researcher, who reviewed 22 studies of clinical outcomes involving RCTs published between 1960 and 2004. The studies involved several disorders, including depressive, posttraumatic stress, somatoform, eating, personality and substance-related. Leichensenring concluded that psychoanalytic therapy is more effective than no treatment and also more effective than shorter forms of psychodynamic therapy. The latter conclusion was qualified by Finnish researchers (Knekt et al., 2008), who reported a longitudinal study in which they measured symptoms of depression and anxiety for a 3-year period after treatment began. They found that short-term psychodynamic therapy produced a greater reduction of symptoms (approximately 20% lower) during the first year than long-term psychodynamic therapy did. However, the two therapies were approximately equivalent in effectiveness during the second year. By the third year, long-term therapy had become more effective (approximately 25%).

Rogers stimulated considerable research on the effectiveness of client-centered therapy. He recorded therapeutic sessions so that his techniques could be evaluated. One early researcher (Truax, 1966) obtained permission from Rogers and his clients to record therapy sessions and classified the clients'

statements into eight categories. For example, one category included references to improved mental health, such as "I'm feeling better lately" or "I don't feel as depressed as I used to." After each of the clients' statements, Truax noted Rogers's reaction to see whether he gave a positive response. Typical positive responses were "Oh, really? Tell me more" or "Uh-huh. That's nice" or just a friendly "Mm." Truax found that, of the eight categories of client statements, only those that indicated progress were regularly followed by positive responses from Rogers. Not surprisingly, during their therapy, the clients made more and more statements indicating progress.

Truax's study implicates social reinforcement in humanistic therapy. Rogers was an effective and conscientious therapist, but he had not intended to single out and reinforce his clients' realistic expressions of progress in therapy. (Obviously, he did not uncritically reinforce exaggerated or unrealistic positive statements.) Of course, this finding does not discredit client-centered therapy. Rogers simply adopted a very effective strategy for altering a person's behavior. He originally referred to his therapy as *nondirective*; however, when he realized that he was reinforcing positive statements, he stopped doing so.

As with most insight therapies, neither client-centered therapy nor Gestalt therapy may be suitable for people with serious psychological disorders. Instead, these approaches tend to be most effective for people who are motivated enough to want to change and who are intelligent enough to be able to gain insight into their problems. Humanistic therapies are much more affordable and less time-consuming than traditional psychoanalysis. Most people would probably enjoy and benefit from talking about their problems with a person as sympathetic as Carl Rogers or as direct and honest as Fritz Perls. Rogers's insights into the dynamics of the client–therapist relationship have had a major impact on therapy (Hill & Nakayama, 2000).

A meta-analysis of nearly 100 published studies of humanistic psychotherapy, including nondirective, client-centered therapy and Gestalt therapy, was reported by Elliott (2002). The studies were conducted in North America and Europe and largely involved clients with depressive, anxiety, and personality disorders. Few of the studies involved RCTs. Humanistic therapies were more effective than no treatment and maintained their relative effectiveness beyond 12 months. Overall, there was a tendency for more directive therapies (specifically, cognitive–behavioral therapies) to be more effective.

QUESTIONS TO CONSIDER

1. If you had a psychological problem, which kind of insight therapy—psychodynamic or humanistic—would you choose? What kinds of evidence would influence your choice?

2. Suppose that you were able to interview Freud, Rogers, and Perls. What sorts of questions would you ask each of them? Why would their answers to those questions be of interest to you?

Behavior Therapies and Cognitive–Behavioral Therapies

Insight therapies are based on the assumption that understanding leads to behavioral change. Once people gain insight into the causes of their maladaptive behaviors, they will adopt more successful behavior. In reality, however, insight is not always followed by behavioral change. That is where behavior and cognitive–behavioral therapies come in as alternatives to insight therapies.

The fundamental assumption made by behavior therapists is that people learn maladaptive or self-defeating behavior in the same way they learn adaptive behavior. According to the behavioral view, undesirable behavior, such as nail biting or alcohol abuse, is the problem, not just a symptom or a reflection of the problem. The methods that behavior therapists use to induce behavioral change are extensions of classical and operant conditioning principles. Related approaches blend behavior therapies with attention to the elimination of maladaptive thoughts and feelings and are known as cognitive–behavioral therapies.

Therapies Based on Classical Conditioning

Remember from Chapter 5 that in classical conditioning, a previously neutral stimulus (ultimately the CS) comes to elicit a new response that may be similar to the response that another stimulus (the US) naturally elicits. This occurs because the CS reliably predicts the US. According to Joseph Wolpe (1958), one of the founders of behavior therapy, neutral stimuli are conditioned by coincidence to elicit many of our everyday fears and anxieties. Consider an example: Suppose that you are involved in a car accident, and although you are not seriously hurt, you are upset for some time afterward. When you get into a car for the first time after the accident, a sudden feeling of terror comes over you. You begin to perspire and breathe heavily, you feel that you are about to pass out, and it's all you can do to get out of the car without screaming. Your anxiety in response to getting into a car may be due to classical conditioning—the pain and fear associated with the accident (the USs) are now associated with cars (the CSs).

Exposure Therapies For individuals diagnosed with anxiety disorders (see Chapter 16), the use of exposure therapies is often successful. One form of exposure therapy was developed by Wolpe and is called **systematic desensitization.** It is designed to remove the unpleasant emotional response produced by a feared object or situation and replace it with an incompatible response—relaxation—in a gradual, carefully controlled manner.

The first step is for the client and therapist to construct a hierarchy of fear-eliciting stimuli. TABLE 17·2 presents a hi-

[TABLE 17·2] Sample Fear Hierarchy for Phobia of Spiders

1. Abbie [neighbor] tells you she saw one in her garage.
2. Abbie sees you, crosses the street, says there's a tiny one across the street.
3. Betty [at work] says there's one downstairs.
4. Friends downstairs say they saw one outside their apartment and disposed of it.
5. Carrie [daughter] returns from camp; says the restrooms were inhabited by spiders.
6. You see a small, dark spot out of the corner of your eye; you have a closer look; it isn't a spider.
7. You are with your husband. You see a tiny spider on a thread outside, but you can't see it very clearly.
8. You are alone. You see a tiny spider on a thread outside, but you can't see it very clearly.
9. You are reading the paper, and you see a cartoonist's caricature of a spider (with a human-like face and smile).
10. You are reading an article about the Brown Recluse.
11. You see a clear photograph of a spider's web in the newspaper.
12. You see a spider's web on the stairs at work.
13. You suddenly see a loose tomato-top in your salad.
14. You open a kitchen cabinet and suddenly see a large spider.

Source: From Thorpe G. L., & Olson, S. L. *Behavior Therapy: Concepts, Procedures, and Applications,* 2/e. Published by Allyn & Bacon, Boston, MA. Copyright © 1997 by Pearson Education. Reprinted by permission of the publisher.

erarchy constructed with a person who had arachnophobia, an intense fear of spiders (Thorpe & Olson, 1990). The situations provoking the least amount of fear are at the top of the list. Next, the client is trained to achieve complete relaxation. The essential task is to learn to respond quickly to the instruction to feel profoundly relaxed by entering a condition sometimes referred to as *deep-muscle relaxation.*

Finally, the fear-eliciting stimuli are paired with the instruction that produces the learned relaxation response. For example, a person with a fear of spiders is instructed to relax and then to imagine hearing from a neighbor that she saw a spider in her garage (the least-fearsome event in the hierarchy). If the client reports no anxiety, he or she is instructed to move to the next, slightly more threatening, item in the hierarchy and to imagine hearing a neighbor say that a tiny spider is across the street, and so on. Whenever the client begins feeling anxious, he or she signals to the therapist with some predetermined gesture—say, by raising a finger. The therapist instructs the client to relax and, if necessary, describes a less-threatening scene. The client is not permitted to feel severe anxiety at any time. Gradually, over a series of sessions (usually averaging between 10 and 12), the client is able to get through the entire list, vicariously experiencing even the most feared encounters while remaining in a relaxed state.

---

systematic desensitization A form of behavior therapy in which the client is trained to relax in the presence of increasingly fearsome stimuli.

People who are treated with systematic desensitization for their phobias often show remarkable, positive changes in their behavior; for example, this person has overcome an intense fear of snakes.

Clinical studies of systematic desensitization have found that all elements of the procedure are necessary for its success. For example, a person will not overcome a phobia merely by participating in relaxation training or by constructing hierarchies of fear-producing stimuli. Only pairings of the anxiety-producing stimuli with instructions to relax will reduce the fear. One early testimonial came from a study by Johnson and Sechrest (1968), which attempted to reduce a strong fear of taking examinations in a group of university students. Students who underwent systematic desensitization received significantly higher grades on their final examination in a psychology course than did students who were also taking the course but who received either no treatment or relaxation training alone.

Whereas practitioners of systematic desensitization are careful not to permit their clients to become too anxious, practitioners of another form of exposure therapy arrange for the client to confront the feared stimulus directly. By using **in vivo exposure,** therapists attempt to rid their clients of fears by arousing those very fears at an intense level until the clients' responses diminish through extinction; that is, the clients learn that nothing bad happens when they are directly exposed to the fear-eliciting stimuli. Of course, the client is protected from any adverse physical effects of the encounter, so no dangerous consequences occur. This does not mean that every client is equally amenable to in vivo exposure. Sudden, intense fear may produce unhealthy jumps in blood

pressure, fainting, or vigorous efforts to escape the situation—all of which are counterproductive for the desired outcome. Thus, it is important for therapists to consult with clients in advance about possible effects and to determine whether more-gradual exposure is warranted or whether an imaginal form of therapy might be more effective. In **imaginal exposure,** the therapist describes, as graphically as possible, the most frightening possible encounters with the object of a client's phobia rather than arranging for actual encounters. The client tries to imagine the encounter and to experience intense fear. Eventually the fear response begins to subside, and the client learns that even the worst imaginable encounter can become tolerable. In other words, the client's long-entrenched avoidance responses have become extinguished. Exposure via virtual reality has become an effective form of exposure therapy (Rothbaum et al., 2002). In one case, for example, German researchers exposed individuals with a fear of flying to a virtual-reality flight simulation consisting of takeoffs and landings (Muhlberger et al., 2001). They had previously participated in anxiety-management sessions. After 8 weeks of exposure, 93% of the participants took an actual flight, and a similar percentage did so at a 6-month follow-up. Overall, exposure therapies have proven to be a very successful form of treatment for anxiety disorders (Emmelkamp, 2004).

Aversion Therapy Some people are attracted by stimuli that most of us ignore, and such individuals may engage in maladaptive behavior as a result of this attraction. Sexual attraction to children is a striking example. A behavior therapy technique known as **aversion therapy** is sometimes effective in changing these behaviors. In aversion therapy, the therapist seeks to induce a negative reaction to an originally attractive stimulus by pairing that stimulus with an aversive stimulus. Aversion therapy attempts to establish an unpleasant response (such as a feeling of fear or disgust) to the object that produces the undesired behavior. For example, a therapist may show pictures of children to a man who is sexually attracted to children, and then administer painful electric shocks when a special apparatus detects an erectile response. Aversive therapy also has been used to treat fetishes (such as sexual attraction to women's shoes), drinking, smoking, exhibitionism, and overeating. Sometimes emetics, or drugs that cause nausea, are paired with the ingestion of alcohol in the treatment of problem drinking (recall the discussion of taste aversion in Chapter 5), although the person being treated may readily discard them. Aversion therapy has been shown to be moderately effective in some applications, such as reducing craving among cocaine abusers (Bordnick et al., 2004). Nevertheless, the treatment is disturbing to many people because it can be characterized as punitive (Howard, et al., 1991). B. F. Skinner (1988) himself was opposed to aversion therapy for this reason. Because the method raises serious ethical questions and can involve significant pain, the client's participation must be voluntary. Overall, the use of aversion therapy is waning (Emmelkamp, 2004).

---

in vivo exposure A form of behavior therapy that attempts to rid people of fears by arousing the fears intensely until clients' responses diminish through extinction; they learn that nothing bad happens.

imaginal exposure A method of behavior therapy for phobias in which the therapist describes the feared object in graphic terms, thereby inducing fear without direct exposure to the object.

aversion therapy A form of behavior therapy in which the client is trained to respond negatively to an originally attractive stimulus that has been paired with an aversive stimulus.

Therapies Based on Operant Conditioning

Behavior modification, a general term for behavior therapy based on operant conditioning principles, involves altering maladaptive behavior by rearranging the contingencies between behavior and its consequences. Desirable behavior can be encouraged through either positive or negative reinforcement (see Chapter 5), and undesirable behavior can be reduced through either extinction or punishment. Practitioners have extended the use of operant principles to a wide array of behaviors and circumstances—for example, for weight management; compliance with medical regimens; and treatment of anorexia nervosa, bed-wetting, and smoking (Martin & Pear, 2006). Behavior modification techniques can be found in many different settings, including hospitals, schools, day-care centers, businesses, and the home (Kazdin, 2001).

Reinforcement of Adaptive Behaviors Therapists often use behavioral techniques to alter the behavior of emotionally disturbed people and people with mental retardation, for whom communication is difficult. Reinforcement, as described in Chapter 5, can be a powerful method of behavioral change. If the therapist has established a cordial relationship with the client, he or she can use ordinary social reinforcers such as signs of approval (friendly smiles and nods of the head) to encourage positive behavioral change. As we saw in the section on client-centered therapy, even nonbehavioral therapists use reinforcement—deliberately or inadvertently—to produce positive behavioral change.

Token Economies The behavior therapeutic approach has been used successfully on a large scale in mental institutions. For example, therapists may ask resident patients with schizophrenia to do chores that engage them actively with their environment. In some instances, therapists also will target other specific behaviors—such as helping patients who have more severe problems—as desirable. To promote these target behaviors, therapists use token economies. In a **token economy,** a list of tasks is compiled, and patients receive plastic tokens, such as poker chips, as rewards for performing the tasks. Later they can exchange these tokens for snacks, other desired items, or various privileges. The tokens become conditioned reinforcers for desirable behaviors. FIGURE 17•3 shows the strong effects of the contingencies of a pay scale used in an original token economy described by Ayllon and Azrin (1968). The amount of time patients spent performing the desirable behaviors was high when reinforcement contingencies were imposed and low when they were not.

The implementation of a token economy can be difficult. Although it is based on a simple principle, the arrangement requires the cooperation of everyone involved. A mental institution includes patients, caretakers, housekeeping staff, and professional staff. If a token economy is to be effective, all staff members who deal with the patients must learn

[**FIGURE 17•3**] The effectiveness of a token economy. A token economy system of reinforcement is designed to promote patients' performance of specified chores.

(From Teodoro Ayllon and Nathan Azrin, *The Token Economy: A Motivational System for Therapy and Rehabilitation,* © 1968, pp. 249–250, 252. Reprinted by permission.)

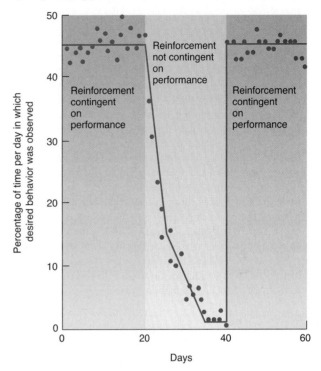

how the system works; ideally, they should also understand and agree with its underlying principles. A token economy can easily be sabotaged by a few people—patients or staff members or both—who believe that the system is foolish, unethical, or in some way threatening to themselves. If these obstacles can be overcome, token economies may work very well (Corrigan, 1995), especially in combination with other treatments (Dickerson et al., 2005).

Modeling Humans (and many other animals) are able to learn without directly experiencing an event. Chapter 5 pointed out that people can imitate the behavior of other people, watching what they do and, if the conditions are appropriate, performing the same behavior (Bandura, 1986). This capability provides the basis for the behavioral technique of **modeling.** Behavior therapists have found that clients may make much better progress when they have access to a model who provides samples of successful behaviors to

---

behavior modification Behavior therapy based on the principles of operant conditioning.

token economy A form of behavior therapy often used in mental institutions; target behaviors are reinforced with tokens that are exchangeable for desirable goods or special privileges.

modeling Behavior therapy in which the client is encouraged to behave in a manner similar to that of the therapist or another designated person.

imitate. Bandura (1971) described a modeling session with people who had a phobic response to snakes:

> The therapist himself performed the fearless behavior at each step and gradually led subjects into touching, stroking, and then holding the snake's body with gloved and bare hands while the experimenter held the snake securely by head and tail. If a subject was unable to touch the snake following ample demonstration, she was asked to place her hand on the experimenter's and to move her hand down gradually until it touched the snake's body. After subjects no longer felt any apprehension about touching the snake under these secure conditions, anxieties about contact with the snake's head area and entwining tail were extinguished. The therapist again performed the tasks fearlessly, and then he and the subject performed the responses jointly; as subjects became less fearful, the experimenter gradually reduced his participation and control over the snake, until eventually subjects were able to hold the snake in their laps without assistance, to let the snake loose in the room and retrieve it, and to let it crawl freely over their bodies. Progress through the graded approach tasks was paced according to the subjects' apprehensiveness. When they reported being able to perform one activity with little or no fear, they were eased into a more difficult interaction. (p. 680)

This treatment eliminated fear of snakes in 92% of the people who participated. Modeling is successful for several reasons. People learn to make new responses by imitating those of the therapist; and, as they do so, their behavior is reinforced. When they observe a confident person approaching and touching a feared object without showing any signs of emotional distress, they may experience vicarious extinction of their own emotional responses. In fact, Bandura (1971, p. 684) reports that "having successfully overcome a phobia that had plagued them for most of their lives, people reported increased confidence that they could cope effectively with other fear-provoking events," including encounters with other people.

Behavior therapists have used modeling to establish new behaviors as well as to eliminate undesired behaviors. For example, therapists may demonstrate examples of useful, appropriate social exchanges for clients whose maladaptive behaviors usually prevent such interactions. Also, as we see in a later section, modeling is an important aspect of group therapy. Sex therapists may use specially prepared videotapes or DVDs showing explicit sexual activity to help clients overcome inhibitions that hamper sexual relations with their partners.

Extinction of Maladaptive Behaviors

In Chapter 5, you learned that extinction is the process by which behavior is eliminated through the removal of the previously available reinforcers. For example, extinction might be used to eliminate a child's tantrums. If such behaviors have been reinforced in the past—that is, if parents or caretakers have paid attention or even given in to the child's wishes—the extinction procedure may include ignoring the child's undesirable behavior.

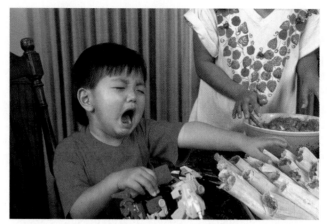

A treatment strategy that is often effective in reducing tantrums in children is extinction—simply ignoring the behavior.

Two potential problems may occur with using extinction. One is the extinction burst: When a reinforcer that has previously followed a behavior is no longer forthcoming, that behavior will often intensify temporarily. Fortunately, however, the extinction burst is temporary. The other problem with using extinction is that it is not always possible to eliminate the reinforcer that maintains undesirable behavior. For example, aggressive behavior in the classroom may be reinforced by the child's peer group, making the teacher's attempts to extinguish aggression only minimally effective. The use of extinction is also problematic when the client has direct control of the reinforcer, as in thumb sucking.

Punishment of Maladaptive Behaviors

In general, punishment has an effect directly opposite that of reinforcement (Mazur, 2005); instead of enhancing the likelihood of a particular behavior, it decreases it. At the same time, the side effects of punishment may compromise its effectiveness. For one thing, the person whose behavior is being punished may learn to fear or dislike the person who administers the punishment. If this person is the therapist, the effect will probably interfere with other aspects of therapy, because of the fact that the therapist–client relationship is a major factor in therapeutic outcome. Second, a tendency exists on the client's part to overgeneralize—to avoid performing a whole class of responses related to the response that is specifically being punished. For example, after being punished for lying, a child may not tell her father any more lies; but she also may stop sharing her secrets with him.

In some therapeutic situations, especially those in which the undesirable response is clearly harmful to the client, punishment is the most effective technique for eliminating an undesirable behavior. Cowart and Whaley (1971) reported the case of an emotionally disturbed child who persisted in self-mutilation. He banged his head against the floor until it was a swollen mass of cuts and bruises. As a result, he had to be restrained in his crib at the hospital where he was a patient. However, the consequences of such confinement for a child's development are serious. After conventional techniques had failed, the therapist attached a pair of wires to the child's leg and placed him in a room with a padded floor. The child immediately began to batter his head against the floor, and the therapist administered an electrical shock through the wires. The shock, which was certainly less damaging than the blows to the head, stopped the child short. He seemed more startled than anything else. He started banging his head against the floor again and received another shock. After a few repetitions of this sequence, the boy stopped his self-mutilative behavior and could safely be let out of his crib.

The use of aversive methods raises ethical issues, however, particularly when individuals are so severely impaired that they are unable to give informed consent to a particular therapeutic procedure. Carr and Lovaas (1983) state that aversive methods involving stimuli such as electric shock should be used only as a last resort. Punishers should be used only when patients' behavior poses a serious threat to their own well-being and after therapists have unsuccessfully tried other methods—specifically, reinforcing desirable behaviors, extinguishing the maladaptive behaviors, temporarily removing the patient from the environment that reinforces the maladaptive behaviors (a method called time out), and arranging for the patient to perform responses that are incompatible with the maladaptive behaviors.

Sometimes the punishing stimulus may only be imagined. In a method called **covert sensitization,** instead of receiving an actual punishing stimulus after performing actual undesirable behavior, clients imagine that they are performing the behavior and then imagine receiving an aversive stimulus. For example, Thorpe and Olson (1990) describe the case of "Frank," a man in his late twenties with a variety of social problems, including exhibitionism. He would drive far from his home town and expose his genitals to unsuspecting strangers. Although he derived sexual pleasure from this practice, he was disturbed by it and wanted desperately to stop. The therapist used a variety of methods to help Frank improve his social skills and reduce his anxiety. In addition, the therapist used covert sensitization to eliminate the exhibitionism. The therapist encouraged Frank to imagine vivid scenes such as the following:

> He was driving around in his car, looking for a suitable victim. A woman, walking alone, appeared. Frank stopped the car and got out. He began to loosen his clothing. He was feeling strongly aroused sexually. Suddenly a police car pulled up, its lights flashing and its siren wailing. The officers looked on Frank with contempt as they handcuffed him. At the same time one of Frank's workmates arrived on the scene. This workmate was the biggest gossip at the factory. News of Frank's arrest would soon be all over town. He would obviously lose his job. His crime would be reported in the local newspaper. Frank felt physically sick with shame. He thought ahead to the prospect of a long jail sentence in protective custody as a sex offender. (Thorpe & Olson, 1990, p. 17)

Frank was able to imagine scenes such as this, and doing so made him feel very uncomfortable. Over several weeks, the frequency of his exhibitionistic episodes declined.

The most successful treatment for autistic disorder (see Chapter 16) is a form of behavior therapy developed by Ivar Lovaas (1987, 2003). It has a wide range of applications in mental hospitals, school, homes, and other settings and is noteworthy for its intensiveness (National Research Council, 2001; Hillman & Snyder, 2007). It may require one-on-one interaction with a trainer for most of the child's waking hours over several years. Training involves establishing operations and discriminative cues, as well as reinforcement and punishment contingencies (see Chapter 5). The key features of the therapy include breaking down skills to be learned into small steps, giving clear instructions, and recording client and therapist behavior to determine progress. Although behavior therapy for autistic disorder is being continually refined (Lord, 2007), limitations to its effectiveness are found (Butcher et al. 2007). It is less effective for children who begin to display symptoms before age 2, and many children who undergo therapy over many years fail to show sustained improvement in the long term. Perhaps the greatest challenge to therapists is the difficulty that children with autistic disorder have in generalizing from the training environments to other environments.

Maintaining Behavioral Change

As we just noted, one of the problems with behavior therapy is that behavior learned under one set of conditions may fail to occur in different environments; that is, behavioral change may not generalize to other situations. Behavior therapists have designed specific methods to ensure that positive behavioral change generalizes to situations outside the clinic or the therapist's office. As we saw in Chapter 5, intermittent reinforcement increases resistance to extinction. Thus, it is more effective to reinforce desirable responses intermittently than it is to reinforce every desirable response the client makes.

Another useful technique that helps maintain behavioral change is the practice of *self-observation*, in which the client is taught to recognize when his or her behavior is appropriate. Therapists also frequently ask family members and friends of the client to become participants in the process of behavior therapy. These "adjunct therapists" are taught to encourage and reward desirable behaviors and to discourage or ignore undesirable ones. By these means, a client does not shuttle back and forth between two different types of environments—one type in which the therapist selectively reinforces desirable behaviors and another in which reinforcement is haphazard or even inappropriate. For example, a person with behavioral problems may receive attention from the family only when he or she acts up. Clearly, for optimal results, family members need to make an effort to ignore such outbursts and to reinforce instances of desirable behavior instead.

---

covert sensitization A form of behavior therapy in which a client imagines the aversive consequences of his or her inappropriate behavior.

Cognitive–Behavioral Therapies

The first attempts to develop therapies based on altering or manipulating cognitive processes rather than behavior directly emerged during the 1970s (Nelson-Jones, 2003). Some of these attempts were undertaken by behavior therapists who suspected that maladaptive behavior—or, for that matter, adaptive behavior—might not be due to environmental variables alone. These psychologists began to explore how their clients' perceptions, thoughts, feelings, expectations, and self-statements might interact with environmental factors in the development and maintenance of maladaptive behavior (Beck, 1991). They then developed methods designed to change the maladaptive patterns of cognition that, in their view, underlay the maladaptive patterns of behavior. Attempts to change these patterns of cognition are referred to as **cognitive restructuring.**

Rational Emotive Behavior Therapy   Interestingly, the first form of cognitive restructuring, a kind of forerunner called *rational emotive therapy,* was developed in the 1950s by Albert Ellis, a clinical psychologist. Later he renamed it **rational emotive behavior therapy** (REBT; Ellis, 1995, 2003). REBT is based on the belief that psychological problems are caused by the ways in which people think about upsetting events and situations. Ellis asserts that psychological problems are the result of faulty cognitions; therapy is therefore aimed at changing people's thinking and specifically their beliefs. Rational–emotive therapy is highly directive and confrontational. The therapist tells his or her clients what they are doing wrong and how they should change.

According to Ellis and his followers, emotions are the products of cognition. *A significant activating event* (A) is followed by a *highly charged emotional consequence* (C), but it is not correct to say that A has caused C. Rather, C is a result of the *person's belief system* (B). Therefore, inappropriate emotions (such as depression, guilt, and anxiety) can be abolished only if a change occurs in the person's belief system. Ellis tried to show his clients that irrational beliefs are impossible to satisfy, that they make little logical sense, and that adhering to them creates needless anxiety, self-blame, and self-doubt. The following are examples of the kinds of ideas that Ellis (1973) believed to be irrational:

> The idea that one should be thoroughly competent, adequate, and goal-oriented in all possible respects if one is to consider oneself as having worth.
>
> The idea that human unhappiness is externally caused and that people have little or no ability to control their lives.

> The idea that one's past is an all-important determinant of one's present behavior.
>
> The idea that there is invariably a right, precise, and perfect solution to human problems and that it is catastrophic if this perfect solution is not found. (pp. 152–153)

The excerpt below, taken from a therapy session with one of Ellis's own clients—a 23-year-old woman who felt guilty about her relationship with her parents—shows how Ellis challenges clients to examine their irrational beliefs (Ellis, 1989).

Client: The basic problem is that I am worried about my family. I'm worried about money. And I never seem to be able to relax.

Ellis: Why are you so worried about your family? Let's go into that, first of all. What's to be concerned about? They have certain demands that you don't want to adhere to.

C: I was brought up to think that I mustn't be selfish.

E: Oh, we'll have to knock that out of your head!

C: I think that that is one of my basic problems.

E: That's right, you were brought up to be Florence Nightingale.

C: Yes, I was brought up in a family of would-be Florence Nightingales, now that I realize the whole pattern of my family history. . . . My father became really alcoholic sometime when I was away in college. My mother developed breast cancer, and she had a breast removed. Nobody is healthy.

E: How is your father now?

C: Well, he's doing much better. . . . He spends quite a bit of money every week on pills. And if he misses a day of pills, he is absolutely unlivable. My mother feels that I shouldn't have left home—that my place is with them. There are nagging doubts about what I should—

E: That's a belief. Why do you have to keep believing that—at your age? . . . Your parents indoctrinated you with this nonsense, because it is their belief. But why do you still have to believe that one should not be self-interested, that one should be self-sacrificial? Who needs that philosophy? All it's gotten you, so far, is guilt. And that's all it ever will get you. (pp. 234–235)

Although REBT is directive in ways that client-centered therapy is not, some similarities are found in the two approaches. Just as Rogers emphasized unconditional positive regard, so Ellis and his followers attempt to engender a feeling of full self-acceptance in their clients. They teach that self-blame is the core of emotional disturbance and that people can learn to stop continuously rating their own personal worth and measuring themselves against impossible standards. Everyone has fallibilities. Rational emotive behavior therapists emphasize that people will be happier if they can learn to see failures as unfortunate events, not as disastrous ones that confirm their lack of worth. However, unlike a Rogerian therapist, a rational emotive behavior therapist may

---

cognitive restructuring   A therapeutic process that seeks to help clients replace maladaptive thoughts with more constructive ways of thinking.

rational emotive behavior therapy   A form of psychotherapy based on the belief that psychological problems are caused not by distressing experiences themselves but by how people think and feel about those experiences.

vigorously argue with his or her client, attacking beliefs that the therapist regards as foolish and illogical. This approach also differs from the client-centered approach in that the therapist does not need to be especially empathetic to be an effective teacher and guide.

Cognitive–Behavioral Therapy

The focus of **cognitive–behavioral therapy** (CBT) is on changing the client's maladaptive perceptions, thoughts, feelings, and beliefs to change the client's behavior. This form of therapy is widely practiced today and has been shown to be effective in treating many kinds of psychological disorders (Hollon et al., 2002; Mc-Clanahan & Antonuccio, 2002; Turkington et al., 2004). Like behavior therapists—and unlike most insight therapists—cognitive–behavioral therapists are not particularly interested in events that occurred in the client's childhood unless those events are clearly related to the presenting problem. Their interest is more typically in the here and now and in altering the client's behavior so that it becomes more functional. Although they use many methods used by behavior therapists, they believe that when behaviors change, they do so because of changes in cognitive processes.

Aaron Beck (1967, 1997) has developed a therapy for depression that shares with Ellis's therapy an emphasis on the client's perceptions, beliefs, and interpretations (see Chapter 16; Beck, 1967, 1997; Clark et al., 1999). Beck's therapy, however, focuses more on faulty logic than on the beliefs themselves. Negative beliefs are seen as conclusions reached by faulty logic. A depressed person concludes that he or she is "deprived, frustrated, humiliated, rejected or punished ('a loser,' in the vernacular)" (Beck et al., 1979, p. 120). As already noted in Chapter 16, Beck views the cognitions of the depressed individual in terms of a *cognitive triad*: a negative view of the self ("I am worthless"), of the outside world ("The world makes impossible demands on me"), and of the future ("Things are never going to get better").

Even when confronted with evidence that contradicts their negative beliefs, depressed individuals often illogically interpret good news as bad news (Lewinsohn et al., 1980). For example, children who exhibit symptoms of depression tend to underestimate their abilities (McGrath & Repetti, 2002). A depressed student who receives an A on an exam may attribute the high grade to an easy, unchallenging exam rather than to his or her own mastery of the material. The fact that few others in the class received As does little to convince the student that he or she deserves congratulations for having done well. The depressed student goes on believing, against contrary evidence, that the good grade was not really deserved.

Once the client recognizes such faulty logic for what it is, therapy can explore means for correcting the distortions. Consider the following example from an actual therapy session.

A woman who complained of severe headaches and other somatic disturbances was found to be very depressed. When asked about the cognitions that seemed to make her unhappy, she said, "My family doesn't appreciate me"; "Nobody appreciates me, they take me for

Even at a young age, an individual may interpret less-than-desirable outcomes in ways that diminish self-worth and lead to depression.

granted"; "I am worthless." As an example, she stated that her adolescent children no longer wanted to do things with her. Although this particular statement could very well have been accurate, the therapist decided to determine whether it was true. He pursued the "evidence" for the statement in the following interchange:

Client: My son doesn't like to go to the theater or to the movies with me anymore.

Therapist: How do you know he doesn't want to go with you?

C: Teenagers don't actually like to do things with their parents.

T: Have you actually asked him to go with you?

C: No, as a matter of fact, he did ask me a few times if I wanted him to take me . . . but I didn't think he really wanted to go.

T: How about testing it out by asking him to give you a straight answer?

C: I guess so.

T: The important thing is not whether or not he goes with you but whether you are deciding for him what he thinks instead of letting him tell you.

C: I guess you are right but he does seem to be inconsiderate. For example, he is always late for dinner.

T: How often has that happened?

---

cognitive–behavioral therapy A form of psychotherapy that focuses on altering clients' perceptions, thoughts, feelings, and beliefs as well as environments to produce desired changes.

C: Oh, once or twice . . . I guess that's really not all that often.

T: Is he coming late for dinner due to his being inconsiderate?

C: Well, come to think of it, he did say that he had been working late those two nights. Also, he has been considerate in a lot of other ways. (Beck et al., 1979, pp. 155–156)

As this example shows, cognitive–behavioral therapists do not accept clients' inferences and conclusions at face value. Instead, they discuss how clients' conclusions result from faulty logic so that clients can understand their thinking from another perspective and perhaps can change their behavior as a result. The role of cognitive change as an antecedent of behavioral change can be clearly seen.

Exposure therapy, another form of CBT, is specifically directed to the anxiety disorders, including post-traumatic stress disorder (PTSD; Follette et al., 2001; see Chapter 16). It has some of the features of *in vivo* exposure, which we encountered previously as an example of behavior therapy. As in that therapy, the cognitive–behavioral therapist encourages the client to confront the anxiety-eliciting situations that she or he would ordinarily avoid and to remain there. Although the settings in which the original trauma occurred may not be reproducible, the person with PTSD may generalize from those settings to current settings and could be encouraged to prolong her or his exposure to them. Alternatively, he or she may be encouraged to imagine the original settings. Rather than merely extinguishing anxiety, however, exposure therapy encourages the client to think and feel differently while exposed to real or imagined circumstances and thus to behave in different ways that reduce the anxiety and make it more manageable. For various reasons, including lack of training and the prospect of enhanced arousal and suicidal tendency, therapists have been slow to adopt exposure therapy for the use of PTSD (Becker et al., 2004).

Evaluation of Behavior and Cognitive–Behavioral Therapies

Critics of behavior therapy have cited its focus on the symptoms of psychological problems to the exclusion of root causes. It is true that many people's behavioral problems are caused by conditions that existed in the past, and often these problems become self-perpetuating, yet behavior therapy can, in many cases, eliminate the problem without delving into the past. For example, for one reason or another, a child may begin wetting the bed at night (a condition known *as nocturnal enuresis*). This irritates the parents, who must change the bed sheets and the child's pajamas. The child develops feelings of guilt and insecurity and wets the bed more often. Instead of analyzing bedwetting in terms of underlying family conflict, a behavior therapist might recommend the installation of a device in the child's bed that rings a bell when he or she begins to urinate.

The bell awakens the child, who goes to the bathroom to urinate and soon ceases to wet the bed. The elimination of bed-wetting causes rapid improvement in the child's self-esteem and puts the parents at ease (Blacher & Baker, 1987).

In a review of research evaluating the effectiveness of REBT, Solomon and Haaga (1995) concluded that the method has been shown to reduce general anxiety, test anxiety, and unassertiveness. It has appeal and potential usefulness for those who can enjoy and profit from intellectual exchanges, including argumentation. The people who are likely to benefit most from this form of therapy are those who are self-demanding and who feel guilty for not living up to their own standards of perfection.

Cognitive–behavioral therapies are highly popular for reasons noted by Dobson and Khatri (2000). Prominent is the larger society's emphasis on efficiency. CBT is attractive because it is relatively brief and affordable. In addition, the effectiveness of CBT has been strongly supported by research. For example, it may produce as much change in brain metabolic activity as some drug therapies (Folensbee, 2007).

Two studies examined the relative efficacy of behavior therapy and CBT against pharmacotherapy (see later section on biomedical therapies) in the treatment of insomnia, a prevalent sleep disorder. With meta-analysis, Smith et al. (2002) found no difference between behavior therapy and pharmacotherapy in measures such as number of awakenings after sleep onset, total sleep time, and sleep quality. However, behavior therapy was more effective in reducing the initial time taken to fall asleep. In a study involving clinical trials, Jacobs et al. (2004) found that CBT was superior to pharmacotherapy on all measures used. Moreover, the combination of CBT and pharmacotherapy was not more effective than CBT alone.

QUESTIONS TO CONSIDER

1. Think of the stimulus—either the thing or the situation—you fear most. Based on what you have learned about systematic desensitization, create a hierarchy of your fears. Then identify ways to relax as you imagine the least fearful stimuli. How well can you maintain relaxation as you progress through the hierarchy?

2. Now, using the same hierarchy of fears, instead of trying to relax, try to alter your cognitions. What cognitive aspects of your fear are irrational? How might you change these faulty cognitions to reduce your fear?

Group Therapies and Community Psychology

So far, we have been considering individual forms of psychotherapy, those in which a single client meets with a therapist. In many cases, clients meet as a group, either because therapy is more effective that way or because it is more convenient or economical. **Group psychotherapy**, in which two or more

---

group psychotherapy Therapy in which two or more clients meet simultaneously with a therapist, discussing problems within a supportive and constructive environment.

clients meet simultaneously with a therapist to discuss problems, became common during the Second World War. The stresses of combat produced psychological problems in many military personnel, and the demand for therapists greatly exceeded the supply. What began as an economic necessity became an institution once the effectiveness of group treatment was recognized.

Because most psychological problems involve interactions with other people, treating these problems in a group setting may be worthwhile. Group therapy provides four advantages that are not found in individual therapy:

1. The group setting permits the therapist to observe and interpret actual interactions without having to rely on clients' descriptions, which may be selective or faulty.

2. A group can bring social pressure to bear on the behaviors of its members. If a person receives similar comments about his or her behavior from all the members of a group, the message is often more convincing than if a psychotherapist delivers the same comments in a private session.

3. The process of understanding the causes of maladaptive behavior in other people often helps a person gain insight into his or her own problems.

4. Knowing that other people have similar problems can bring comfort and relief to an individual. People discover that they are not alone.

The structure of group therapy sessions can vary widely, as can the type of therapeutic perspective—psychodynamic, humanistic, cognitive–behavioral, and otherwise. Some sessions are almost like lectures: The therapist presents information about a problem common to all members of the group, and then invites discussion. For example, in a case involving a person with a psychological disorder, the therapist may explain to family members the nature, treatment, and possible outcomes of the disorder. Then the therapist answers questions and allows those present to share their feelings about what the disorder has done to their family. Most types of group psychotherapy involve interactions among the participants. Because they are structured according to a specific therapeutic approach and include a therapist, psychotherapy groups differ from support groups. Generally the latter are composed of individuals with a common interest in helping others overcome their problems but do not include the mediating presence of a professional therapist.

Family Therapy and Couples Therapy

Very often, dealing solely with the problems of individual clients is not enough to produce a successful outcome. Family therapy and couples therapy have become important techniques, because the structure of a client's family or marriage is a crucial part of the client's experience. In other words, helping an unhappy person frequently means also restructuring his or her relationships with other family members (Lefley, 2002; Cox & Paley, 2003). In many cases, a family therapist meets with all members of a client's family and

A family therapist meets with the members of a family to observe their patterns of interaction and thereby be better informed about their communication and relationships.

analyzes the way in which individuals interact. The therapist attempts to get family members to talk to one another instead of addressing their comments and questions only to him or her. As much as possible, the family therapist tries to collect data about family interactions—how individuals sit in relation to one another, who interrupts whom, who looks at whom before speaking—to infer the nature of relationships within the family. For example, barriers may exist between certain family members; perhaps a father is unable to communicate with one of his children. Or two (or more) family members may be so dependent on each other that they cannot function independently; they constantly seek each other's approval and, in their overdependence, make each other miserable.

For example, consider the approach developed by Salvador Minuchin (1974; Minuchin & Nichols, 1998), **structural family therapy.** The therapist first observes a family's interactions and draws simple diagrams of the relationships he or she infers from their behaviors. He or she then identifies the counterproductive relationships and attempts to help the family restructure their dynamics in more adaptive ways.

For example, the therapist might diagram a family structure with father (F) on one side and mother (M) on the other side, allied with son (S) but estranged from daughter (D), as illustrated in the left panel of FIGURE 17•4. The therapist would then attempt to restructure the family, as shown in the right panel of the figure. That is, husband (H) and wife (W) would replace mother and father, and the new arrangement would emphasize their primary emotional relationship as spouses. The healthiest family interactions stem from an effectively functioning marital subsystem consisting of a husband and wife. A marriage that is completely child-oriented is always dysfunctional (Foley, 1989), and alliances between one parent and one or more children are almost always detrimental to the family.

----

structural family therapy A form of family therapy in which the therapist infers the maladaptive relationships among family members from their behavior and attempts to help the family restructure these relationships for more-desirable interactions.

[FIGURE 17·4] Genograms offer family therapists a way of visualizing psychological relationships between family members across generations. This pair of genograms includes two generations: a man aged 42 and woman aged 40 and their two children, a son aged 15 and a daughter aged 12. The genogram on the left depicts the man and woman as father (F) and mother (M), with a close emotional bond between mother and son (S) and the lack of a bond between mother and daughter (D). The therapist encourages the situation depicted in the genogram on the right, where the man and woman relate to one another as husband (H) and wife (W) without the uneven emotional bonds that existed previously between mother and children.

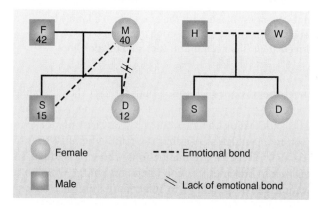

After describing the family system, the therapist attempts to help the family restructure it by replacing maladaptive interactions with more effective ones. He or she suggests that perhaps all members of the family must change if the client is to make real improvement. The therapist gets family members to "actualize" their patterns of interaction—to act out their everyday relationships—so that the maladaptive interactions will show themselves. Restructuring techniques include forming temporary alliances between the therapist and one or more of the family members; increasing tension to trigger changes in unstable structures; assigning explicit tasks and homework to family members (for example, assigning certain individuals to interact with certain other individuals); and providing support, training, and guidance. Sometimes the therapist visits the family at home. For example, if a child in a family refuses to eat, the therapist will visit during mealtime to see the problem acted out as explicitly as possible.

Behavior therapists also have applied their methods of analysis and treatment to families. This approach focuses on the social environment provided by the family and on the ways in which family members reinforce or punish one another's behaviors. The strategy is to identify both the maladaptive behaviors of individual members and the ways in which these behaviors are inadvertently reinforced by the rest of the family. Then the therapist helps the family members find ways to increase positive exchanges and to reinforce each other's desirable behaviors. A careful analysis of the social dynamics of a family often reveals that changes need to be made, not by the individual who exhibits the most maladaptive behaviors but by the other members of the family.

All couples will find that they disagree at one time or another on important issues. Disagreements often lead to conflicts. For example, a couple may have to decide whether to move to accommodate the career of one of the partners, how to spend their money, or how to allocate household chores. The couple's ability to resolve conflict is one of the most important factors affecting the quality and durability of their relationship.

When dealing with families and couples, therapists have learned that changes in the nature of the relations can have unforeseen consequences—and that they must be alert to these consequences. For example, LoPiccolo and Friedman (1985) described the treatment of a couple with a sexual problem. At first, the problem appeared to belong to the man:

> A couple with a marriage of twenty years' duration sought treatment for the male's problem of total inability to have an erection. This had been a problem for over nineteen of their twenty years of marriage. Successful intercourse had only taken place in the first few months of the marriage. . . . [The wife] reported that she greatly enjoyed sex and was extremely frustrated by her husband's inability to have an erection.

The therapists used techniques developed by Masters and Johnson (1970) to treat the man's impotence. Within 10 weeks, the couple was able to have sexual intercourse regularly, and both had orgasms. However, even though the problem appeared to have been solved, and despite the physical gratification they received from their sexual relations, they soon stopped. In follow-up investigation, the therapists discovered that

> . . . the husband had a great need to remain distant and aloof from his wife. He had great fears of being overwhelmed and controlled by her, and found closeness to be very uncomfortable. . . . For him, the inability to have an erection served to keep his wife distant from him, and to maintain his need for privacy, separateness, and autonomy in the relationship. (LoPiccolo & Friedman, 1985, p. 465)

The therapists also found that the wife had reasons to avoid sexual contact. For one thing, she apparently had never resolved the antisex sentiment imparted to her as a child by her family of origin. In addition,

> . . . over the nineteen years of her husband being unable to attain an erection, she had come to have a very powerful position in the relationship. She very often reminded her husband that he owed her a lot because of her sexual frustration. Thus, she was essentially able to win all arguments with him, and to get him to do anything that she wanted. (LoPiccolo & Friedman, 1985, p. 465)

The therapists encouraged the couple to address these issues and helped them to resolve the problems. Eventually the couple were able to alter the structure of their marriage and resumed a more satisfying sexual relationship.

This case illustrates the fact that a couple is not simply two individuals. Long-standing problems bring adjustments and adaptations, some of which may not be healthy. Even if the original problems are successfully resolved, other patterns of behavior may persist and cause problems of their own.

Community Psychology

In the United States, a quite different approach to therapy involves actively seeking out people with problems or even attempting to prevent problems before they begin. Therapists who participate in prevention are practicing **community psychology,** a form of education and treatment whose goal is to address psychological problems through assessment and intervention in the sociocultural contexts in which problems develop. Practitioners of community psychology deal with individuals and groups, establish educational programs, and design programs whose goal is to promote mental health by changing the environment (Butterfoss, 2007).

Several different kinds of community treatment programs have been developed. One is the *community mental health center,* a facility designed to supplement the care provided by mental institutions. Instead of confining patients to an institution, community mental health centers provide outpatient care within the community. A popular form of care in the United States is called *assertive community treatment,* or ACT, which was developed in the 1970s by Stein and Test (Stein & Santos, 1998; Test & Stein, 2000). In ACT programs, a multidisciplinary team responds to the needs of severely mentally ill patients. Typically, a psychologist, psychiatric nurse, psychiatrist, and social worker develop a comprehensive care plan for the patient. Under this system, care includes not only therapy but also assistance in the everyday demands of living (e.g., finding the patient a suitable place to live, finding the patient a job if the patient is able, arranging for transportation, and ensuring that the patient's basic physical needs are met). Important goals of ACT are ensuring patients' ability to live independently or with minimal supervision and reducing admissions to inpatient mental institutions. A recent review of the research literature showed that ACT is effective in meeting these goals (Phillips et al., 2001).

A related type of community treatment facility is the *halfway house,* a transitional setting in which patients discharged from mental institutions receive outpatient care as they gradually are reintegrated into the community. By using the halfway house as their base, patients may spend more time with their families and friends, take on part-time jobs, or return to school. Allowing previously institutionalized patients to return to their communities for treatment is called **deinstitutionalization.** For the most part, community psychologists consider it an important advance. Deinstitutionalization has dramatically reduced the number of persons confined to mental institutions in North America and Europe (Lesage et al., 2000).

Preventive Psychology Increasingly, community psychologists are stressing strategies aimed at preventing the development of psychological problems (Rappaport & Seidman, 2000). This emphasis on modifying the sociocultural variables predictive of psychological distress is called **preventive psychology.** As an analogy, think of individual therapy for

psychological problems as similar to rescuing people who have fallen into a river (Rappaport, 1977). Each person rescued is a life saved, but a more effective solution would be to go upstream and correct the problem that is causing people to fall into the river in the first place.

Community psychologists distinguish between two kinds of prevention: primary and secondary. *Primary prevention* is any effort to eliminate the existing conditions responsible for psychological problems and simultaneously replace them with conditions that contribute to adaptive behavior. For example, providing children with new educational materials concerning the dangers of taking drugs, while encouraging their healthy recreation and exercise, represents an attempt to prevent the children from experimenting with drugs. *Secondary prevention,* conversely, is more crisis-related and consists of prompt identification of an individual's existing problems and immediate intervention to minimize the further development of these problems. Suicide hotlines, staffed 24 hours per day by trained volunteers, are examples of secondary prevention measures.

Community mental health centers provide individual and group therapy and counseling to members of the communities in which they are located. They offer immediate, accessible outpatient care for people who might otherwise find it difficult to get help. These centers are generally staffed by psychologists, psychiatrists, social workers, and nurses, but they often also employ the services of *paraprofessionals* who have roots in the community. A paraprofessional usually has not received the same level of training as mental health professionals but is able to provide at least some components of the care that professionals provide. The use of paraprofessionals has many advantages. People from culturally deprived backgrounds frequently have difficulty relating to—and communicating with—therapists. However, paraprofessionals with the same social and ethnic backgrounds may be able to gain the trust and confidence of clients and thus enable them to benefit from the professional help that is available. Also, the paraprofessionals may be able to provide practical advice and to serve as role models for clients.

Evaluation of Family and Couples Therapy and Community Psychology

In an early review of the effectiveness of family therapy, Hazelrigg et al. (1987) reported that it was more effective than no treatment, but that the positive effects tended to

---

community psychology A form of treatment and education whose goal is to address psychological problems through assessment and intervention in the sociocultural contexts in which problems develop.

deinstitutionalization The process of returning previously institutionalized patients to their communities for treatment of psychological problems and psychological disorders.

preventive psychology Strategies that attempt to prevent the development of psychological problems by altering the sociocultural variables predictive of psychological distress.

wane over time. Shadish and Baldwin (2003) published a review of 20 meta-analyses of family therapy in which they found a moderate but statistically significant positive effect at the conclusion of therapy and at follow-up. In a study of family therapy outcomes in England, Cottrell and Boston (2002) examined its effects on children and adolescents specifically. They concluded that the virtual absence of RCT designs hampers clear conclusions other than the need for such research. Still, the weight of existing evidence is for positive outcomes in the treatment of conduct disorder (which includes bullying, deliberate destruction of property, and physical cruelty among other presenting symptoms), substance-related disorders, and eating disorders in particular.

An extensive review of therapeutic interventions for couples (Christensen & Heavey, 1999) found it successful in reducing relationship distress, as well as modestly reducing symptoms of psychological disorders, including depression. Although the positive effects include behavioral changes and improved marital satisfaction, they are often short-lived. The authors recommended that future outcome research increase the diversity of the couples population involved as well as the diversity of outcomes, including the effects of couples therapy on children.

An interview-based study of community prevention coalitions (Feinberg et al., 2004), that is, coalitions of community organizations with a common interest in preventing psychological disorders, found them to be at least modestly effective in promoting community readiness for change and prevention knowledge. Their effectiveness was jeopardized by staff turnover and infighting. Kreuter et al. (2000) pointed to unrealistic expectations of change outcomes and the difficulty of accurately assessing cause–effect relationships as further factors in what remains to date only modest evidence of the effectiveness of community psychology approaches.

*f*ocus **O**n

| **Cultural Belief Systems and Indigenous Healing Therapies** |

Suppose that you are a clinical psychologist working in a community mental health center located in the heart of a large urban area. One of your new clients is a young man, an immigrant from Jamaica, who is depressed. He blames his lethargy and unhappiness on *obeah*—sorcery. Quite literally, this young man believes that someone has put a hex, or curse, on him (Wedenoja, 1995). The problem you face, of course, is how to treat this individual—what sort of therapy would be most effective?

Your training represents a Western point of view, but this man knows little, if anything, about Western psychology or psychotherapy. His only experiences stem from his native culture, and he wholeheartedly accepts and believes them. If you treat your new client by using one of the therapies discussed in this chapter, you are apt to make little progress in helping him. A better choice might be to choose to co-treat him with a traditional Jamaican healer who is experienced in removing hexes. Many psychologists and psychiatrists whose clientele include persons with strong beliefs based on the customs and folklore of a particular culture have found such co-treatment effective. For example, consider the following case involving a man treated at the New Horizons Community Mental Health Center in Miami, Florida (Lefley, 1984, 1994):

> A Haitian man diagnosed with schizophrenia failed to respond to 10 days of inpatient therapy and drug therapy. He believed that he was cursed. The Health Center staff contacted a *houngan*—a voodoo priest—who performed an exorcism ritual on him. The man quickly calmed down, the medication soon reduced his symptoms, and he was released shortly thereafter.

The use of non-Western, culture-specific approaches to psychological (and medical) problems is called **indigenous healing** (or sometimes *ethnopsychiatry* or *ethnomedicine*). Indigenous healing therapies are quite common in many countries and within specific subcultures in North America; for example, among Native Americans and people of Asian, Latino, West Indian, and Western African descent (Aponte et al., 1995). Indigenous healing therapies are specific to each of these cultures, which have different belief systems and methods of treatment for specific problems. However, all such approaches seem to have two elements in common:

1. The people involved believe that the psychological problem is caused by factors external to the individual, such as a hex; by conduct that is considered immoral relative to cultural standards for behavior; or by bad luck.

2. The problem is treated by ritual, often including special incantations, herbal medicine, and references to spiritual forces and agents. Generally these rituals involve calling on spiritual forces to remove the curse, to supplant the forces causing the problem, or to replace bad luck with good luck.

By understanding the belief systems of their non-Western clients and by incorporating aspects of these belief systems into their treatment plans, therapists often produce successful results, as in the example of the Haitian man given earlier. In some universities, clinical psychologists and psychiatrists in training receive specific instruction regarding the cultural belief systems and indigenous healing therapies they are likely to encounter in their work with clients (Zatrick & Lu, 1991). Such training appears to sensitize these clinicians to the aspects of their clients' belief systems that are likely to impede therapy, and thus puts them in a better position to understand the nature of their

---

indigenous healing Non-Western, culture-specific approaches to the treatment of psychological and medical problems.

People in many non-Western cultures seek indigenous healing approaches to their psychological problems.

clients' problems. Mehl-Mardrona (2007) described an integrative approach to therapy that directly involves the use of narratives—those drawn from the therapist's experiences and those from the cultural background of the client, including myths, epics, legends, and other indigenous stories. Properly blended, such narratives take on a navigational function, orienting the client to the possibilities that promise the most positive outcomes.

Have you thought any more about how you might treat your young Jamaican client who had been hexed? Consider how a similar case was handled by the New Horizons Community Mental Health Center:

> An African-American woman of Bahamian ancestry came to the center complaining of depression caused by a hex placed on her by her boyfriend's lover. She reported that the hex had caused problems for her at work and with her children. While undergoing counseling at the mental health center, she also sought out an obeahman because her boyfriend's girlfriend had used one to place the hex on her. The obeahman "cleansed her with special perfumes, oils, and herbs, and gave her special tasks that would align her with the benign forces of the universe. To finalize the therapeutic intervention, the healer took [her] to a cemetery at midnight, lowered her into an unfilled grave, and sprinkled her with grave dirt." Soon thereafter she got a raise at work, her children's behavior improved, and she broke off the relationship with her boyfriend. She continued, though, with the counseling sessions at the mental health center. (Lefley, 1994, p. 186)

It remains unclear why some people appear to be "cured" by indigenous healing—or by a mixture of indigenous healing and formal therapy—but not to be helped by formal therapy alone. Among the most important qualities of successful therapists is their ability to form a warm and empathetic relationship with their clients. Perhaps the familiar techniques of indigenous healing enable clients to feel more comfortable and open with their professional therapists and to establish a trusting relationship.

QUESTIONS TO CONSIDER

1. How effective might group therapy be in helping you cope with your problems, anxieties, or fears? Would you feel comfortable telling strangers about these sorts of things? Why/why not? In what ways might you benefit from hearing others discuss their problems and worries?
2. It is common practice for people to visit their physicians once a year for a checkup. It is also routine for people to visit their dentists twice a year to have their teeth cleaned and examined for cavities and other problems. Why don't people take the same preventive approach to their mental health? Suppose you were a clinical psychologist. How might you set up an annual preventive exam? For example, what would the exam consist of? What kinds of problems would you look for?

Biomedical Therapies

Therapies provided by psychologists target maladaptive thoughts, behaviors, and emotions, but **biomedical therapies** target abnormal neural and other physiological functions. For that reason, biomedical therapies for psychological disorders are traditionally carried out by psychiatrists or other physicians (who have medical degrees) rather than psychologists. Besides drug therapy, there are two other forms of medical therapy: electroconvulsive therapy and psychosurgery.

Drug Therapy

Drug therapy, often called *pharmacotherapy,* is the treatment of psychological problems with chemical agents and is the most widely used form of medical therapy. Although abuses have occurred, drug therapy created a revolution in the treatment of psychological disorders and is a highly active area of medical and psychological research today. TABLE 17•3 lists some of the drugs most commonly used to improve psychological functioning, their generic names, and their more recognizable trade names. As shown in the table, four general classes of drugs are used for the treatment of psychological disorders: antipsychotic drugs, antidepressant drugs, antimanic drugs, and antianxiety drugs (Buschmann et al., 2007).

Antipsychotic Drugs In the early 1950s, physicians working at two hospitals in France found that a new drug called *chlorpromazine* (belonging to the phenothiazine subclass of drugs) dramatically reduced the positive symptoms of schizophrenic disorders (see Chapter 16) (Lehmann & Ban, 1997; Shen & Giesler, 1998). The introduction of chlorpromazine

---

biomedical therapies Therapies utilized by psychiatrists and other medical practitioners to target abnormal neural functions and abnormal physiological functions more generally.

drug therapy Reliance on the use of pharmaceutical substances for the treatment of psychological disorders.

[TABLE 17·3] Drugs Commonly Used to Treat Mental Disorders

General Class of Drugs	Subclass of Drugs	Generic Name	Trade Name
Antipsychotic	Phenothiazines	Chlorpromazine	Thorazine
		Thioridazine	Mellaril
		Fluphenazine	Modecate
		Trifluoperazine	Stelazine
		Perphenazine	Trilafon
	Butyrophenones	Haloperidol	Haldol
	Atypical	Clozapine	Clozaril
		Risperidone	Risperdal
Antidepressant	Tricyclics	Imipramine	Tofranil
	Monoamine oxidase inhibitors (MAOIs)	Phenelzine	Nardil
	Selective serotonin reuptake inhibitors (SSRIs)	Paroxetine	Paxil
		Fluoxetine	Prozac
		Sertraline	Zoloft
	Atypical	Bupropion	Wellbutrin
Antimanic/mood-stabilizing	Lithium salts	Lithium carbonate	Eskalith
Antianxiety	Benzodiazepines	Chlordiazepoxide	Librium
		Diazepam	Valium
		Lorazepam	Ativan
		Alprazolam	Xanax

(with the trade name Thorazine) and other **antipsychotic drugs** has had a profound effect on the treatment of schizophrenia and other major disorders in which psychotic symptoms appear (e.g., major depressive disorder with psychotic features).

No cure for schizophrenia exists. The majority of antipsychotic drugs simply reduce the severity of its most prominent positive symptoms—delusions and hallucinations—apparently by blocking dopamine receptors in the brain. Presumably, the overactivity of dopamine synapses is responsible for those symptoms. Although dopamine-secreting neurons are located in several parts of the brain, most researchers believe that those involved in the symptoms of schizophrenia are located in the cerebral cortex and in parts of the limbic system near the front of the brain.

A different system of dopamine-secreting neurons in the brain is involved in the control of movement. Occasionally this system of neurons degenerates, mostly in older people, producing Parkinson's disease. Symptoms of this disorder include tremors, muscular rigidity, loss of balance, difficulty in initiating movement, and impaired breathing that makes speech indistinct. In severe cases, the person is bedridden.

The major problem with most antipsychotic drugs, the phenothiazines, is that they do not discriminate between these two systems of dopamine-secreting neurons. The drugs interfere with the activity of both the circuits involved in the symptoms of schizophrenia and the circuits involved in the control of movements. Consequently, when a person with schizophrenia begins to take an antipsychotic drug, he or she sometimes exhibits a movement disorder. Fortunately, the symptoms are usually temporary and soon disappear. After taking the antipsychotic drug for several years, however, some people develop a different and more serious movement disorder known as **tardive dyskinesia** (*tardive* means "late-developing"; *dyskinesia* refers to a disturbance in movement). This often irreversible and untreatable syndrome is characterized by continual involuntary lip smacking, grimacing, and drooling (Cummings & Wirshing, 1989). Severely affected people have difficulty with talking and occasionally with breathing. The risk of developing this syndrome increases with age, dose, and duration of use (Hughes & Pierattini, 1992; Tarsy, Baldessarini, & Tarazi, 2002). For example, approximately 20% of older people who take antipsychotic drugs develop tardive dyskinesia. The physician can temporarily alleviate the symptoms by increasing the dose of the antipsychotic drug, but doing so only serves to increase and perpetuate the person's dependence on the medication (Baldessarini & Tarsy, 1980).

A more recently developed antipsychotic drug overcomes three of the important drawbacks of the typical formulations. Earlier we mentioned that most antipsychotic medications reduce the severity of positive symptoms of schizophrenia, such as thought disorders and hallucinations. A more recent antischizophrenia drug called clozapine (Clozaril) also is effective for negative symptoms, such as social withdrawal and flattened emotionality. For this reason,

---

antipsychotic drugs Drugs used to treat schizophrenic disorders.

tardive dyskinesia A serious movement disorder, distinguished by involuntary lip smacking, grimacing, and drooling, that may result from prolonged use of antipsychotic drugs.

clozapine is referred to as an *atypical* or *second-generation* medication. It affects both dopamine-secreting and serotonin-secreting neurons. Its development was a major advance for the welfare and quality of life of people who have schizophrenia. Like all drugs, conventional antipsychotics don't work for everyone. For reasons that are not well understood, clozapine helps many people who receive no substantial benefit from the other antipsychotics (Carpenter et al., 1995; Bondolfi et al., 1998). Finally, clozapine appears to carry dramatically lower risks of tardive dyskinesia (e.g., Kane & Malhotra, 2003); some indication exists that switching to clozapine may reduce the symptoms of tardive dyskinesia resulting from other drug treatments (e.g., Chakos et al., 2001). This may make clozapine sound like a wonder drug, and in many respects, this medication may deserve the honor, but downsides occur. Clozapine is much more expensive than other antipsychotics, and it can produce serious adverse side effects (Conley & Kelly, 2001). About 2% of people taking clozapine have an inhibition of white blood cell production, which can be fatal. For this reason, only patients with normal white cell counts can take clozapine, and they must have blood tests weekly for the first 6 months of therapy and then every 2 weeks afterward.

Antidepressant and Antimanic/Mood-Stabilizing Drugs

Antidepressant drugs are a class of drugs used to treat the symptoms of major depression. **Antimanic/mood-stabilizing drugs** are used to treat the symptoms of the bipolar disorders, which involve both depression and manic phases.

The earliest antidepressant drugs were derived from the family of chemicals known as *tricyclics*; the term refers to their "three-ring" chemical structure (Lickey & Gordon, 1991). Because their chemical structure is similar to that of antipsychotic drugs, researchers first tested tricyclics in the belief that they might provide an effective treatment for schizophrenia. Although their use as antipsychotics was quickly dismissed, researchers observed that these drugs did tend to elevate mood—a finding that suggested their potential as antidepressants.

The biology of depression is still not well understood, but the most widely accepted theory is that depression may result from a deficiency of the catecholamine neurotransmitters, norepinephrine and serotonin (see Chapter 4). Each of these neurotransmitters may be involved in different types of depression, although researchers are not sure how. Tricyclics seem to slow the reuptake of these neurotransmitters by presynaptic axons. Of course, these drugs do not work for all depressed people; even so, about 60 to 80% of those whose depression has brought despair to their lives gradually return to normal after having been given tricyclics for 2 to 6 weeks (Hughes & Pierattini, 1992; Potter et al., 2005). Unfortunately, tricyclics have many side effects, including dizziness, sweating, weight gain, constipation, increased pulse, poor concentration, and dry mouth.

Another subclass of antidepressants is the *monoamine oxidase inhibitors* (MAOIs), which take 1 to 3 weeks to begin alleviating depression. MAOIs prevent enzymes in the synaptic gap from destroying dopamine, norepinephrine, and serotonin that have been released by presynaptic neurons. These drugs too can have many side effects, including high blood pressure (which can be fatal after the ingestion of certain foods—including wines, milk products, coffee, and chocolate); hyperthermia (high body temperature); blurred vision; erectile dysfunction; insomnia; and nausea. Nevertheless, MAOIs also have proved to be more effective than tricyclics in treating atypical depressions such as those involving hypersomnia (too much sleep) or mood swings (Hughes & Pierattini, 1992).

A relatively new subclass of drugs (with trade names such as Prozac, Paxil, and Zoloft) has had a major impact on pharmacotherapy for depression. Prozac, the original entry in this field, and its successors inhibit the reuptake of serotonin, leaving more of that neurotransmitter in the synaptic cleft to stimulate postsynaptic receptors. These drugs, collectively called *selective serotonin reuptake inhibitors* (or SSRIs), can have negative side effects, but to a lesser degree than do tricyclics and the MAOIs. Moreover, because they have fewer side effects, SSRIs often can be taken in larger dosages, which can produce more substantial reduction of the depressive symptoms. Their widespread adoption has not been without headline-grabbing controversy, however, including claims that they elevate violent behavior and suicide in some users (Healy, 2003). A review by Walsh and Dinan (2001) found evidence for unpleasant sensations of restlessness (*akathisia*) and increased anxiety in a small proportion of patients who received Prozac or other SSRIs, but no evidence was found of their increased susceptibility to aggression or suicide. Instead, the evidence suggests that treatment with SSRIs may reduce aggression. In a detailed analysis of biological and environment markers of suicide, Maris (2002) concluded that the use of SSRIs may be most effective when combined with antianxiety, mood-stabilizing, or antipsychotic drugs, as well as behavior therapy or cognitive–behavioral therapy, and ECT (see later).

Although newer antidepressant drugs may have fewer or less-severe side effects, considerable variation is still noted in the individual responses of those who take them. Psychiatrists and others who prescribe such medications may not always be attentive to these differences. Consider the following case of a psychiatrist with depression (Gartrell, 2004).

[CASE STUDY] Dr. G. had been a psychiatrist for many years when, during a consultation with a patient, she broke into a sweat, started to shake, and felt as if she were disintegrating. A close friend was dying of cancer, and she felt weighed down and depressed. Her partner, also a psychiatrist, recommended that she take bupropion (Wellbutrin).

---

antidepressant drugs Drugs used to treat depression, including tricyclics, monoamine oxidase inhibitors, and SSRIs.

antimanic/mood-stabilizing drugs Drugs used to treat the bipolar disorders, such as lithium carbonate.

This was an atypical antidepressant that Dr. G. had often prescribed to her own patients, with favorable results. She began to take it herself.

Within 10 days, she developed insomnia, agitation, and tremors. She lost the ability to distinguish between sadness and the side effects of the drug. She began to develop panic attacks and could barely function at work. Even so, she was terrified that she might feel worse if she stopped taking the bupropion or started taking a new drug. Determined to keep taking the medication despite her deteriorating physical and mental health, she tried to follow the advice she had given to hundreds of her own patients: to stick things out. She forced herself to eat but lost 10 pounds. Sometimes she felt paranoid and wondered if she was delusional. When she wasn't working, she curled up in a fetal position and wondered if she should hospitalize herself.

After 4 weeks, she had had enough. She began to taper the medication, although her symptoms, insomnia, lack of appetite, agitation, and panic attacks continued for 3 weeks after she had taken the last tablet. For a month she felt weak, as if she had just recovered from the flu.

After her experiences with bupropion, Dr. G. now describes potential side effects to her patients in much greater detail than she did before. Although she continues to prescribe the medication, she is vigilant about signs of distress in her patients. Whereas in the past she would have encouraged patients with side effects to stick it out, anticipating that these would eventually pass, she now switches her patients to a new medication at the first sign of problems. A taste of her own medicine has made her a more attentive and aware physician. (Taken from Butcher et al., 2007, p. 614.)

Among the antimanic/mood-stabilizing drugs, *lithium carbonate* is most effective in the treatment of bipolar disorders (Schou, 2001; Aubry et al., 2007). Manic symptoms usually decrease as soon as the blood level of lithium reaches a sufficiently high level. In bipolar I disorder (see Chapter 16), once the manic phase is eliminated, the depressed phase does not return. People with bipolar I disorder have remained free of their symptoms for years as long as they have continued taking lithium carbonate. Some people require lithium in combination with other drugs for maximal effectiveness (Grof, 2003). People who have untreated bipolar disorders have a mortality rate two to three times that of the normal population (see Ahrens et al., 1995), reflecting a higher risk of suicide and cardiovascular disease. Ahrens and colleagues (1995) report that continued treatment with lithium after symptoms have subsided reduces patients' mortality rate to that of the general population. Lithium produces side effects, such as a fine motor tremor or excessive urine production; but in general, the benefits far outweigh the adverse symptoms. However, an overdose of lithium is toxic, which means that patients' blood level of lithium must be monitored regularly.

The major difficulty clinicians face in treating bipolar I disorder is that people with this disorder often miss their "high." When medication is effective, the mania subsides along with the depression, but most people enjoy at least the initial phase of their manic periods, and some believe that they are more creative at that time. In addition, many say that they resent having to depend on a chemical crutch. As a consequence, they may stop their medication. Doing this endangers their lives, because the risk of death by suicide is particularly high during the depressive phase of bipolar I disorder.

Antianxiety Drugs Antianxiety drugs (also known as *anxiolytics*) are used in the treatment of generalized anxiety, phobias, obsessions, compulsions, panic attacks, and other anxiety-related problems (see Chapter 16). The popularity of antianxiety drugs, or minor tranquilizers as they are sometimes called, is indicated by the large numbers of prescriptions that are filled in the United States, Canada, and Europe. The most popular, most effective, and most abused of these drugs are the *benzodiazepines,* often known by trade names such as Librium, Valium, and Xanax (Julien, 2004). Benzodiazepines appear to work by activating what is called the benzodiazepine receptor, which, in turn, produces activity in receptors sensitive to gamma-aminobutyric acid (GABA), an inhibitory neurotransmitter (see Chapter 4). More specifically, benzodiazepines appear to enhance the attachment of GABA molecules to the postsynaptic neuron by reconfiguring the shape of GABA receptors, thereby producing more neural activity.

Before the benzodiazepines were synthesized in the early 1960s, the major effective antianxiety drugs had been the *barbiturates.* The immediate success of Valium and Librium was due in part to the erroneous belief that they had a lower risk for abuse than barbiturates and were safer in cases of overdose (Lickey & Gordon, 1983). Although the benzodiazepines are the safest of the antianxiety drugs, we now know that these medications can produce physical tolerance and withdrawal symptoms when removed. Some individuals find it very difficult to stop using benzodiazepines because of the withdrawal syndrome, and thus show addiction to the drugs. Taken in low dosages and for short periods, though, these drugs can be effective temporary means of reducing anxiety without involving a high risk of physical dependence.

Besides being effective in treating depression, tricyclic antidepressant drugs have been also used successfully to treat several anxiety disorders, including panic disorder and agoraphobia (Klein, 1996), and can reduce the severity of obsessive–compulsive disorder. These drugs appear to reduce the incidence of panic attacks, including those that accompany severe agoraphobia. However, antidepressant drugs do not reduce the anticipatory anxiety that a person feels between panic attacks.

Although drugs are useful in alleviating the symptoms of certain anxiety disorders, they do not cure any of these conditions, possibly because the disorders are at least partly heritable, as we saw in Chapter 16. The most effective and long-lasting

---

antianxiety drugs Drugs used to treat anxiety-related disorders, including benzodiazepines as well as some tricyclic antidepressants

treatment for anxiety is cognitive–behavioral therapy. The drugs may be especially useful in reducing symptoms so that patients can participate effectively in therapy, but they do not provide a long-term solution.

Drug Therapy for Attention-Deficit/Hyperactivity Disorder

Chapter 16 introduced the symptoms of attention-deficit/hyperactivity disorder, which include inattentiveness, overactivity, and impulsivity. Children diagnosed with the disorder experience considerable difficulty persisting in tasks, remaining in place, and organizing their activities. Consequently, they often perform poorly in school environments and are at academic risk.

Drug therapy is the most widely used treatment for attention-deficit/hyperactivity disorder and is the most commonly administered medication by school nurses (O'Connor, 2001). Among the drugs prescribed, *methylphenidate* (Ritalin) is the most common. It is an amphetamine (see Chapter 4)—a stimulant—and thus might seem ill-suited to address the symptoms of the disorder, but it has proven effective in reducing overactivity and distractability, at the same time increasing focus and alertness (Konrad et al., 2004). It is not without multiple side effects, which include decreased cerebral blood flow, decreased growth hormone, insomnia, and psychotic symptoms. Nor are its long-term effects well known. *Pemoline* (Cylert), a stimulant with a very different chemical structure from that of methylphenidate, and *atomoxetin* (Strattera), a non-prescription drug that blocks norepinephrine reuptake, are also prescribed for the disorder. Each has its own side effects. The following case study (taken from Spitzer et al., 2004) illustrates the use of methylphenidate for attention-deficit/hyperactivity disorder.

[CASE STUDY] Mark is an 11-year-old boy who is brought for a psychiatric consultation by his parents for problems he has had "since he was born." He is described as socially immature and has always had trouble making friends. His mother sees him as unhappy; his father, as unfocused and lazy. This school year has been particularly hard. He is picked on and seems always to do and say the wrong thing.

. . . Mark's problems seem to fall into two general categories: he has trouble focusing and paying attention, and socially, he is immature and unable to make friends. It is likely that his problems with focusing and paying attention contribute to the social difficulties that he experiences. In any case, his social problems are not severe enough to consider a Pervasive Developmental Disorder, and there is no evidence of a Social Phobia.

Mark's problems with focusing and paying attention have been apparent since he began school. Over the years he has displayed difficulty paying attention to details, sustaining attention to particular tasks, listening to instructions, and finishing what he has begun. In addition, he appears to be easily distracted. These are the attentional symptoms

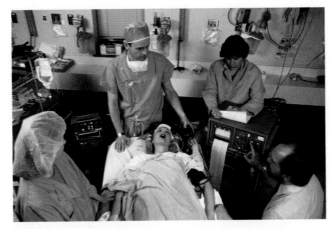

In an ECT session the patient is anesthetized and may be temporarily paralyzed to prevent convulsions. A mouthpiece has been inserted to prevent the patient from biting her tongue.

that are required for the diagnosis of Attention-Deficit/Hyperactivity Disorder. . . .

Two months after the evaluation, at the beginning of the school term, Mark was started on methylphenidate, a stimulant that paradoxically has a calming effect on children with [the disorder]. His academic performance during eighth grade improved dramatically. He received all As and Bs, except for a C in social studies. . . .

His relationship with his parents improved, his mother claiming that everyone was getting along better. Mark reported making two new friends from the basketball program, and his mother reports that classmates have called him to set up dates. Blood pressure, pulse, height, and weight were monitored. No adverse side effects to the medication were reported. (pp. 310–312)

Electroconvulsive Therapy

In **electroconvulsive therapy** (ECT) a clinician attaches a pair of electrodes to a patient's head and then passes a brief surge of electrical current through them. The patient is unconscious at the time. The jolt produces a seizure—a storm of electrical activity in the brain that renders the person unconscious. The seizure is believed to cause the brain to release higher than normal amounts of GABA, which decreases brain activity. This effect can benefit some patients with major depression and extreme manic disorders.

In a seizure, whether spontaneous or caused by ECT, the wild firing of neurons that control movement produces convulsions—muscular rigidity and trembling, followed by rhythmic movements of the head, trunk, and limbs. After a few minutes, the person falls into a deep sleep. Today, patients undergoing ECT are anesthetized and temporarily paralyzed before the cur-

---

electroconvulsive therapy (ECT)   Treatment for severe depression that involves passing small amounts of electric current through the brain to produce seizures.

rent is turned on. This procedure eliminates the convulsions but not the seizure, which is what causes the therapeutic effect.

Electroconvulsive therapy has a bad reputation among many clinicians, because in the past it was used in misguided attempts to treat disorders such as schizophrenia (for which it may be effectively used in conjunction with antipsychotic drugs), and because people have received excessive numbers of ECT treatments—sometimes hundreds. Nevertheless, it appears to be a helpful treatment as a last resort for some patients with serious depressive and manic disorders that have not yielded to other therapies, and it is accepted as appropriate practice by the American Psychiatric Association. No one knows for certain, however, why ECT is effective for some patients.

A case report by Fink (1976) illustrates the response of a depressed patient to ECT:

[CASE STUDY] A 44-year-old widow had been hospitalized for 3 months for severe depression. A course of three ECT treatments per week was prescribed for her by her therapist's supervisor. Unknown to her therapist (a trainee), the first 12 treatments were subthreshold; that is, the intensity of the electrical current was too low to produce seizures. (These treatments could be regarded as placebo treatments.) Although both the woman and her therapist expected that she would show some improvement, none was seen. In the next 14 treatments, the current was at a level sufficient to produce seizures. After five seizures, both the woman and the therapist noticed an improvement. The woman began to complain less about various physical symptoms, to participate in hospital activities, and to make more positive statements about her mood. She became easier to talk with, and the therapist's notes of their conversations grew more numerous. The fact that these responses occurred only after several seizures and not in the course of the subthreshold treatments suggests that improvement stemmed from the biological treatment and not simply from the therapist's or the woman's expectations.

Some people with severe depression do not respond to antidepressant drugs, but a substantial percentage of these people improve after a few sessions of ECT. Because antidepressant medications are generally slow acting, taking 10 days to 2 weeks for their therapeutic effects to begin, clinicians sometimes treat severe cases of depression with a brief course of ECT to reduce the symptoms right away. These patients then go on a maintenance dose of an antidepressant drug. Because a person with major depressive disorder runs a 15% chance of dying by suicide, the use of ECT may be justified in such cases (Prudic & Sackeim, 1999).

ECT treatments are not without problems. They clearly cause short-term memory loss (e.g., Lisanby et al., 2000).

Although the evidence is inconclusive, concerns exist about the potential for permanent memory loss. Now ECT usually is administered only to the right hemisphere, to minimize negative effects on memory. For many years, concerns were expressed that ECT might cause permanent brain damage. No convincing evidence thus far indicates that this is the case (e.g., Zachrisson et al., 2000; Obergriesser, et al., 2003). Some researchers argue that the refinement of the procedure over the past several decades has led to techniques that can be effective, with minimal adverse effects (Persad, 2001). Nevertheless, for some people, intrapersonal consequences ensue—patients may feel ashamed and humiliated that they need what is perceived as a radical treatment (Johnstone, 1999).

Psychosurgery

The third category of biomedical treatments for psychological disorders is even more controversial than ECT. **Psychosurgery** is the treatment of a psychological disorder by using brain surgery in cases in which obvious organic damage is absent (see Jasper, 1995, and Swayze, 1995, for historical accounts). In contrast, brain surgery to remove a tumor or diseased neural tissue or to repair a damaged blood vessel is not referred to as psychosurgery, and no controversy is heard about such procedures.

You may recall from Chapter 13 that prefrontal lobotomies were found to have serious side effects, such as apathy and severe blunting of emotions, intellectual impairments, and deficits in judgment and planning ability. Nevertheless, the procedure was once used for a variety of conditions, most of which were not improved by the surgery. Tens of thousands of prefrontal lobotomies were performed worldwide from the 1930s through the 1950s. A simple procedure, called "ice-pick" prefrontal lobotomy by its critics and *leukotomy* by its proponents, was even performed on an outpatient basis. The development of antipsychotic drugs and increasing attention to the serious side effects of prefrontal lobotomy led to a sharp decline in the use of this procedure during the 1950s. Today the procedure is no longer performed (Valenstein, 1986).

A few surgeons have continued to refine the technique of psychosurgery, however, and these physicians now perform a procedure called a **cingulotomy.** This operation involves cutting the cingulum bundle, a small band of nerve fibers that connects the prefrontal cortex with parts of the limbic system (Ballantine, et al., 1987). Cingulotomies have been shown to be effective in helping some people who have severe obsessive–compulsive disorder (Jenike, 2000). Baer and his colleagues (1995) conducted a long-term follow-up study of 18 people who underwent cingulotomy for severe obsessive-compulsive disorder. For each of these people, other forms of therapy—drug therapy and behavior therapy—had been unsuccessful. After their surgeries, however, the patients in Baer and colleagues' study showed marked improvements in their functioning, decreased symptoms of depression and anxiety, and few negative side effects (which may include seizure, weight gain, and headaches; Jenike, 2004).

---

psychosurgery Brain surgery used in an effort to relieve the symptoms of psychological disorders in the absence of obvious organic damage.

cingulotomy The surgical destruction of nerve fibers that connect the prefrontal cortex with the limbic system; used to reduce intense anxiety and other symptoms of obsessive-compulsive disorder.

Psychosurgery is typically prescribed only as a last resort and never for a patient who cannot consent to treatment. The effects of psychosurgery are permanent; no way is known to reverse a brain lesion. However, an alternative method—*deep brain stimulation* (see Chapter 9)—shows some promise for the treatment of psychological disorders. Mayberg et al. (2005) described a procedure used with a group of six patients with severe depression and whose symptoms had not been controlled by medication. Small electrodes were implanted bilaterally in the cingulate region of the brain. Stimulation was delivered to the brain from small devices surgically implanted in the chest. Although no specific cues accompanied periods of stimulation, the patients reported an improved mood—"sudden calmness or lightness" or "disappearance of the void" as a result of the stimulation (p. 652). In four of six cases, the stimulation was accompanied by decreased symptoms over several months.

Evaluation of Biomedical Treatments

No doubt exists that drug therapy is the preferred biomedical treatment for psychological disorders. Drug therapy, though, like all therapies, represents a treatment option; it is not a cure. Usually the drugs are effective only to the extent that the people for whom they are prescribed actually use them. In some cases, people forget to take their drugs, only to have their symptoms return. In other cases, people take their drugs, get better, and stop taking the drugs because they feel that they are no longer "sick." In this case, too, the symptoms soon return. For some people, this cycle repeats itself over and over.

Thus, although drug therapy is an effective treatment option, it is not a panacea (Szasz, 2007). No actual cures for psychological illness are on the horizon. Until cures are found, research will continue on the development of new and more effective drugs and on finding ways to encourage people to follow their prescription regimens more closely. As you read in the discussion of ECT and psychosurgery, these forms of treatment help some patients with severe disorders but remain controversial and have only limited applications.

focus On

Assessing Therapeutic Efficacy

Evaluation of therapies and therapists is a very important issue. The need for accurate evaluation has received much attention because of the human suffering and other high costs imposed by psychological disorders. Still, almost everyone involved agrees that too little is known about the efficacy (or lack thereof) of therapeutic methods, in part because therapeutic effectiveness is difficult to study. The past decade has brought increased emphasis on research designed to establish the empirical efficacy of therapies—so-called evidence-based treatment or evidence-based therapy. What is appealing in concept, though, turns out to be fraught with a host of difficulties (Kazdin, 2008).

Why Is Therapy Difficult to Evaluate?

Several factors make it extremely difficult to evaluate the efficacy of a particular form of psychotherapy or an individual therapist. One factor is the problem of the *measurement of outcome*. Measuring a person's recovery from dysfunction is challenging; making valid before-and-after measurements can be extremely difficult. Most studies rely on ratings by the clients or the therapists to determine whether a therapy has succeeded [the Outcome Questionnaire 45 (OQ-45), for example, Lambert et al., 2004]. These two measures obviously will be correlated, because therapists primarily base their ratings on what their clients say to them. Few studies include interviews with friends or family members to obtain independent evaluations of the clients' condition—and those that do generally find a weak correlation between these ratings and those of clients and therapists (Sloane et al., 1975).

Ethics also sometimes prevent clinicians from using a purely scientific method of evaluation, because of the fact that the scientific method would require that experimental and control groups be constituted in equivalent ways. For example, leaving a person who appeared to be suicidal untreated so as to make comparisons with similar people who received therapy would present risks that therapists consider unacceptable.

Self-selection—the fact that clients choose whether to enter therapy, what type of therapy to engage in, and how long to stay in therapy—may make it difficult to establish either a stable sample population or a control group. That is, certain kinds of people are more likely than others to enter a particular therapy and stick with it, which produces a biased sample. Lack of a stable sample and lack of a control group make it difficult to compare the effectiveness of various kinds of therapies. Many clients change therapists or leave therapy altogether. Even when they remain adequately long, the further challenge remains of assuring standardized treatment across clients.

Yet another problem with scientific evaluation of therapy is the question of an appropriate *control group*. You may recall from Chapter 2 that the effects of therapeutic drugs must be determined through comparison with the effects of placebos (innocuous substances that have no known effects on people's thoughts and behavior). Researchers use placebos to be sure that any improvement has not occurred merely because the patient *expects* that a pill has done some good. Placebo effects also can occur in psychotherapy: People know that they are being treated, and they may get better because they believe that the treatment should lead to improvement. Most researchers who evaluate psychotherapeutic techniques do not use control groups to rule out these placebo effects. To do so, an investigator would have to design "mock therapy" sessions during which the therapist would do nothing therapeutic but would convince patients that therapy was taking place; obviously, this goal is not easily achieved.

A further complication arises from the fact that symptoms may disappear spontaneously even without therapy—a phenomenon known as the *spontaneous remission of symptoms*. Accurately estimating rates of spontaneous remission is notoriously difficult.

What Evidence Is There?

In a pioneering article on therapeutic evaluation, Hans Eysenck (1952) examined 19 studies assessing the efficacy of psychotherapy. He reported that of the people who remained in psychoanalysis as long as their therapists thought they should, 66% showed improvement. Similarly, 64% of patients treated eclectically showed an improvement. However, 72% of patients who were treated only custodially (receiving no therapy) in institutions showed improvement. In other words, people got better just as fast by themselves as they did in therapy.

Eysenck's original work stimulated subsequent studies, which were not much more optimistic. Some investigators, including Eysenck, concluded that it is unethical to charge a person for psychotherapy, because little scientific evidence indicates that it is effective. Others said that the problems involved in performing scientific research are so great that we must abandon the attempt to evaluate therapies: Validation of the effectiveness of therapy must rely on the therapist's clinical judgment. Many forms of therapy have never been evaluated objectively, because their practitioners are convinced that their methods work and deem objective confirmation unnecessary (Dawes, 1994).

FIGURE 17•5 summarizes Smith, Glass, and Miller's (1980) well-known meta-analysis of 475 studies comparing the outcome effectiveness of psychodynamic, Gestalt, client-centered, systematic desensitization, behavior modification, and cognitive–behavioral therapies. A **meta-analysis** is a statistical procedure for estimating the magnitude of experimental effects reported by published studies. Relative to no therapy, each of these therapies was shown to be superior in helping people with their problems. Behavior therapies and cognitive–behavioral therapies tended to exceed others in efficacy, although these differences were often small. More recent research has confirmed these results, indicating that most people tend to improve with respect to the symptoms that brought them to therapy (e.g., Okiishi et al., 2003). Likewise, another meta-analysis confirmed that different forms of therapy seem to be about equally effective (Wampold et al., 1997; Wampold et al., 2002). Keep in mind that these data reflect hundreds of studies and thousands of clients. No conclusions can be drawn from them about the efficacy of a particular therapy for any one client. However, Borckhart et al. (2008) called renewed attention to the merits of the single-subject time-series research design. The design allows the individual therapist to estimate treatment efficacy by conducting multiple observations of an individual client before and after treatment.

Advances in neuroimaging raise the possibility of new physiological markers of therapeutic outcome. Mayberg (2003) analyzed PET scans of people with depression who had undergone a variety of therapies. She identified biological markers that showed a strong correlation between a client's unique metabolic activity and therapeutic effectiveness. Future research incorporating the use of neuroimaging techniques may allow therapists to predict which clients will respond best to a particular form of therapy. After a re-

[**FIGURE 17•5**] Effectiveness of psychotherapy. Smith, Glass, and Miller's (1980) meta-analysis compared the relative effectiveness of different therapies.

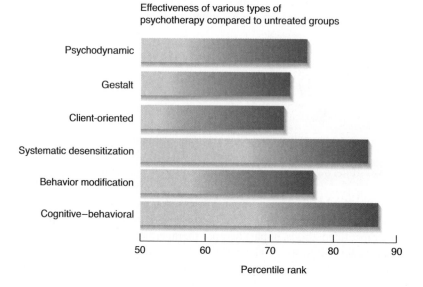

Effectiveness of various types of psychotherapy compared to untreated groups

Percentile rank

view of the prospects for neuroimaging as a component of clinical assessment, Miller et al. (2007) concluded

> Because skills in experimental design analysis are critical in functional brain imaging research and in clinical applications of it, well-trained clinical psychologists and colleagues in nearby disciplines already have a considerable portion of the skills necessary to use brain-imaging techniques. . . . There is no question that much that is novel and impressive today will be standard clinical practice in the future, some of it in the very near future. . . . With continued progress, the likelihood is that some disorders will benefit greatly from neuroimaging for diagnosis or tracking of treatment progress, rather than that neuroimaging will become a routine part of assessment in clinical psychology across the board. (pp. 69–70)

What Factors Influence Outcome?

A study by Luborsky and colleagues (1971) investigated the factors that influence the outcome of therapy, independent of the particular method used. They examined both patient variables and therapist variables. The important *patient variables* were the patient's psychological health at the beginning of the therapy, adequacy of personality, motivation for change, level of intelligence, level of anxiety (more anxious patients tended to do better), level of education, and socioeconomic status. Some of the variables seem to be self-confirming: If you are in fairly good psychological shape to begin with, you have a better chance of improving. In addition, if you are well educated and have adequate social and financial resources, your condition will probably improve. Anxiety probably is a positive predictor because anxiety provides a strong *motivation to improve.*

Several therapist variables were significant: The number of years the therapist had been practicing, the degree of similarity between the personalities of therapist and client, and the ability of the therapist to communicate empathy to the client all tended to have beneficial effects. The finding that the more experienced therapists had more success with their clients is encouraging; it suggests that therapists learn something from their years of experience, which in turn implies that *there is something to learn.* The *therapeutic alliance*, the relationship between therapist and client, also is important (Norcross, 2002). Although the exact factors that contribute to a positive relationship between therapist and client differ across psychotherapies, it is clear that a positive alliance contributes to good outcomes (Kopta et al., 1999). According to Bordin (1994) two important underlying factors are shared goals for the therapy between client and therapist and a firm bond between the two parties.

What Should We Conclude?

This chapter tried to convey the ingenuity of clinicians in their efforts to help people with psychological problems. The magnitude of the task is formidable. One encouraging outcome of the evaluative research is that it indicates that therapy is effective: Experienced and empathetic therapists are likely to help their clients get better. Another encouraging

outcome is the general success achieved by behavior therapies and cognitive–behavioral therapies, even though the goals of these approaches are often circumscribed. Finally, although clinical psychologists are not responsible for the development and use of the biomedical therapies, they can take heart from several studies showing that psychotherapy significantly improves the mental health of clients who are also receiving drug therapy (DeAngelis, 2008). In urging a stronger bridge between research and practice, Kazdin (2008) summarized the prospects as follows: "Our training in theories, methods, hypothesis testing, assessment, and data evaluation is unique among the many disciplines that deliver services. Not only do our research-generated treatments make our work special, but our methods of evaluation can improve patient care in ways that render psychology and clinical practice by psychologists unique" (p. 157).

QUESTIONS TO CONSIDER

1. Suppose that you have a friend who is about to begin drug therapy for a psychological disorder. Suppose further that you are able to accompany your friend to one of his or her pretreatment sessions with a psychiatrist. What questions will you ask the psychiatrist about the particular kind of drug therapy he or she is recommending for your friend? Will your questions differ depending on the kind of problem your friend is experiencing? Why or why not?

2. Suppose that your friend has now been treated for depression with tricyclics, but the treatment has failed—your friend is still extremely depressed. The psychiatrist now recommends ECT. What is your response? What sort of advice can you offer your friend and your friend's family about the psychiatrist's recommendation?

The Relationship between Client and Therapist

The special relationship that may develop between the therapist and the client is duplicated in few other places in society. With the possible exception of clergy in some religious traditions, few people earn their living by listening to others describe the deeply intimate details of their lives. Unfortunately, the same characteristics that give the therapeutic relationship its potential for healing may also lead to abuses. For this reason, psychologists have developed a set of ethical standards to guide their professional activities, and legislatures and courts have provided other regulations concerning the practice of therapy. In addition, the process of choosing a therapist requires special care.

Ethical Issues

The ethical standards for psychologists were originally defined by the American Psychological Association in 1953 as Ethical Standards of Psychologists (American Psychological

Association, 1953). In 2002, the same organization published its most recent updated version, Ethical Principles of Psychologists and Code of Conduct (American Psychological Association, 2002). One of the ethical standards is specific to therapy and clearly states that sexual intimacies with current clients are unethical. A therapist who suggests such intimacy to a current client or who allows himself or herself to be approached sexually by a client is unquestionably violating this standard. Nonetheless, the problem of sexual relations between therapist and client, although rare, remains an issue in therapy (Pope, 2000).

Another ethical standard refers to privacy and confidentiality and states that any information obtained about the client during therapy is confidential. This confidentiality extends to members of the client's family. The only conditions under which confidentiality may be breached are those mandated or permitted by law.

Additional standards pertain to informed consent, therapy involving couples or families, group therapy, providing therapy to those served by other therapists, therapy with former sexual partners, interruption of therapy, and terminating therapy.

Selecting a Therapist

How can you tell that you need to consult a therapist, and how do you go about finding a good one? In general, if you have a problem that makes you unhappy and that persists for several months, you should seriously consider getting professional advice. If the problem is severely disruptive, you should not wait but should look for help immediately. For example, if you experience acute panic attacks, find yourself contemplating suicide, or hear voices that you know are not there, do not wait to see whether the problems go away. You might also think about consulting a professional for specific problems, such as unhealthy habits like smoking, or for specific fears, such as fear of flying. You do not have to be "mentally ill" to seek psychological help.

If you are a student at a college or university, the best place to turn to is the counseling service there. If you are not sure what mental health services are available on campus, someone in the psychology department will certainly be able to inform you. In larger universities, the psychology department may operate its own clinic. If you are not a student, you should ask your physician or call your community mental health department and ask for advice. Or call the psychology department at a local college or university; someone there will help you locate sources of professional help in the community. In the United States, each state has a state psychological association, which can provide a directory of members who are psychotherapists. The American Psychological Association's online Psychologist Locator is another source of information.

TABLE 17•4 describes some of the more common types of therapists, the training and degree credentials for each type, and the kinds of responsibilities each type of therapist assumes. As you can see, the training and the professional duties of different types of therapists vary considerably. In addition, therapists often conduct therapy from particular theoretical orientations, as you have learned in this chapter. However, research suggests that the orientation of the therapist may not be of particular consequence in the choice of a therapist, given that each orientation has both its advantages and limitations (Smith & Glass, 1977).

Here are three reasonable questions to ask when, as a potential client, you interview a therapist:

1. Is the therapist licensed to practice therapy in the state in which he or she is practicing?

2. What kind of formal training has the therapist received? From what academic institution(s) does the therapist hold advanced degrees? Did the therapist fulfill an internship during which he or she learned therapeutic techniques under the supervision of licensed practitioners?

3. What kind of reputation does the therapist have? Is there any public record of past events that call the therapist's reputation into question?

[TABLE 17•4]   Types of Therapists, Their Degree Credentials, and Their Training and Professional Responsibilities

Title	Degree	Training Background and Professional Duties
Clinical psychologist	Ph.D. or Psy.D.	Graduate training in research, diagnosis, and therapy plus 1-year clinical internship. Conducts assessment and therapy. May teach in a university setting and conduct clinical research.
Counseling psychologist	Ph.D., Psy.D. or Ed.D.	Graduate training in counseling. Conducts educational, vocational, and personal counseling.
Psychoanalyst	M.D.	Medical training plus specialized training in psychoanalysis. Conducts psychoanalytic therapy.
Psychiatrist	M.D.	Medical training plus psychiatric residency. Conducts diagnosis and biomedical therapy and psychotherapy.
Social Worker	M.S.W.	Graduate work in counseling and community psychology. Conducts psychotherapy; helps patients return to community.
Psychiatric Nurse	Nursing Diploma	Completion of approved psychiatric nursing program. Provides a variety of mental health services, usually as a member of a multidisciplinary team.

If a therapist is not licensed to practice, has little or no formal training in therapy, and/or is known to practice therapy by using unscientific approaches, then you should avoid consulting with this person for therapy of any sort.

You should also talk with the therapist before committing yourself to a course of therapy. Do you like the therapist as a person? Do you find the therapist sympathetic? If not, look elsewhere. Do not be impressed by an authoritative manner or glib assurances that the therapist knows best what you need. Look for someone who asks good questions about your problems and needs and who helps you formulate a specific and realistic set of goals. Find out whether the therapist specializes in your type of problem. For example, if you want to overcome a specific fear or break a specific habit, you may not want to embark on a series of sessions in which you are expected to talk about the history of your relations with other family members. Conversely, if your problem is with family relations, then a family therapist may be the best person to consult. If you are unaware of what your problem is specifically, but you know you are hurting, the therapist's ability to help you identify your problem and to suggest a possible course of therapy may be a useful indicator of whether to continue to consult with her or him or to go elsewhere.

What about fees? Research indicates that the amount of money a person pays has no relation to the therapeutic benefits he or she receives. Ask the therapist about how much the services will cost. Find out whether your health plan will cover the fees. Do some comparison shopping, and be aware that therapists often will adjust their fees according to the ability of the client to pay.

How long should therapy continue? In some cases, a therapist will suggest a fixed number of sessions. In other cases, the arrangement will be open-ended. How do you decide when to quit in those cases in which the duration is indefinite? Here are some guidelines: If you do not make progress within what you consider a reasonable amount of time, find someone else. If the therapist seems to be trying to exploit you—for example, by suggesting that sexual relations with him or her would benefit you—run, do not walk, away. That person is violating ethical guidelines and undoubtedly is not someone who should be entrusted with your problems. If you find that therapy becomes the most important part of your life, or if you have become so dependent on your therapist that you feel unable to make decisions for yourself, you should consider quitting. If your therapist seems to want you to stay on even though your original problems have been solved, it may be time to end the relationship.

Always remember that the therapist is someone you consult for professional advice and help. You do not owe the therapist anything other than frankness and a good-faith attempt to follow his or her advice. If you do not like the person or the advice, do not worry about hurting the therapist's feelings—look for someone else. Most people who consult therapists are glad that they did; they usually find experienced, empathetic people they can trust who really do help them with their problems. According to Friedman (2007), "In the end, psychotherapy is a very personal business. If you need brain surgery, it doesn't really matter if you like your surgeon as long as he's skilled and competent. But in therapy, skill and competence are necessary but not enough; personal fit, more than almost anything, can make the therapy—or break it."

QUESTIONS TO CONSIDER

1. Suppose that you have been asked by your psychology teacher to give a class presentation on the topic of ethical issues in psychotherapy. During the presentation, one of your fellow students asks you to provide some examples of the different ways in which a therapist could breach the confidentiality standard. What is your response?

2. Sometimes people shy away from seeking therapy because of the stigma they think will be attached to them if they do seek it. After reading this chapter, what suggestions do you have that might encourage these people to seek therapy?

3. Other than the fee paid to a therapist, what is the difference between a therapist and a friend? After all, doesn't a friend serve some of the same functions as a therapist—being a confidant, problem solver, and source of empathy, warmth, and support? What more does a therapist provide?

Epilogue

Losing Symptoms, Losing Self?

The prologue introduced Geoff, who, after reversals of fortune and quality of life, found respite in a combination of drug therapy and psychotherapy after his diagnosis of bipolar I disorder. While he was still relying on lithium and other drugs to the exclusion of psychotherapy, he wondered about the authenticity of his life, questioning whether his sense of who he was had grown so thin that he was becoming a ghost. Although we weren't told, we are probably justified in assuming that Geoff continued his treatment in subsequent years.

What about people for whom drug therapy begins at an early age and continues thereafter? What do they risk becoming? Friedman (2008) recounts the case of one of his patients, Julie, who had begun the use of antidepressant drugs when she was 14 and was now 31. She had frequently been suicidal and credited the fact that she was still alive to the medications. According to Friedman, she could remember what her depression had felt like when it was first diagnosed. In the meantime, she had moved from adolescence into adulthood and was thus different from most of Friedman's patients whom he first began to consult with when they were already adults.

The question he poses is this: Given Julie's long use of the drugs, to what extent had they altered the course of her psychological development—her core identify, as he put it? To what extent was she a different Julie than she might have been had her reliance on drugs not been so long-term? Or how might she have been different had she relied on psychotherapy instead or on a combination of drugs and psychotherapy, as in Geoff's case? In the absence of data on the long-term psychological effects of antidepressant drugs, little empirical basis exists for an answer to such questions.

It is not unusual for clients who take drugs for psychological disorders to ask similar questions. Peter Kramer was relatively new in his psychiatric practice when he wrote a best-selling book, *Listening to Prozac* (1993). In it he recounted case studies of his own patients after their introduction to Prozac, which many of them characterized as a wonder drug in view of its positive effects. In his final chapter, Kramer picked up themes from the American novelist and essayist Walker Percy. They related to Kramer's observations of his patients and his realization that Prozac may have been doing more than remitting the symptoms of severe depression. In undeniably doing so, it may have altered who they were in some fundamental, definitive way, or at least it may have altered what they might have become.

Without in any way denying the serious threat that major depressive disorder and other mood disorders pose—the risk that, untreated, a person may well end his or her life—Kramer, like Percy, questions whether suffering such disorders entail might have some larger purpose, that it may somehow be refining or authenticating, that it somehow might deepen the contours of personhood. Too ready a remission of that suffering may constitute another adverse side effect of the medication.

CHAPTER SUMMARY

Psychological Disorders and Psychotherapy

At different times, people with emotional or behavioral problems were believed to be possessed by demons or were accused of being witches. They were often subjected to unspeakable torture, including trephining, in which a small hole was punctured in the skull of the afflicted person to allow demonic spirits to escape. Even when not being physically harmed,

mental patients in sixteenth- and seventeenth-century asylums encountered abject humiliation. Philippe Pinel, a French physician, is often credited with changing the asylum environment in the late eighteenth century.

Modern therapy involves a wide array of treatment options—from psychoanalysis to drug treatment. In many cases, a person seeking therapy may find that the therapist uses an eclectic approach—borrowing methods from different treatments and blending them in a way that will work best in treating the client's problem. Certainly, such options would not be available were it not for the modern view that people should have the chance to improve their level of functioning. People seeking therapy are perhaps even more diverse than those providing therapy. Although people seek therapy for many reasons, the one element they share is that they are at a low point in life and that alternative solutions, such as trying to solve the problem alone or with the help of friends and family, have not been satisfactory.

Insight Therapies

Like most therapies, insight therapies are based primarily on conversations between therapist and client. The oldest form of insight therapy, psychoanalysis, was devised by Freud. Psychoanalysis attempts to discover the forces that are warring in the client's unconscious and to resolve these inner conflicts by bringing them to consciousness and also revealing the defenses that have been established against them. Insight becomes the primary source of healing.

Unlike the psychoanalytic approach, which regards human behavior as motivated by intrapsychic conflict and biological urges, humanistic therapy emphasizes conscious, deliberate mental processes. Carl Rogers's client-centered therapy is based on the premise that people are inherently good and that their problems result from faulty perceptions. Instead of evaluating themselves in terms of their own self-concepts, people tend to judge themselves by other people's standards. Client-centered therapy rectifies this tendency by providing an environment of unconditional positive regard in which clients can find their own way to good mental health. Fritz Perls's Gestalt therapy focuses on convincing clients that they must deal honestly with their present feelings to understand and resolve them. The goal of this approach is to help clients confront their fears and guilt and put their emotions in proper perspective.

It is difficult to determine whether psychoanalysis is effective, because of the relatively narrow range of people that may benefit by undergoing such therapy. The people who seem most likely to benefit are those who are intelligent and able to articulate their problems. Humanistic therapies have a broader range of applicability.

Behavior Therapies and Cognitive–Behavioral Therapies

Behavior therapists use the principles of classical and operant conditioning to modify behavior—to eliminate extreme fears and other maladaptive behaviors and replace them with more adaptive ones. Systematic desensitization uses classical conditioning procedures to condition relaxation to stimuli that previously produced fear. In contrast, implosion therapy attempts to extinguish fear and avoidance responses. Aversion therapy attempts to condition an unpleasant response to a stimulus with which the client is preoccupied, such as the object of a fetish.

Operant conditioning involves reinforcement, extinction, or punishment of particular behaviors in particular situations. The most formal reinforcement systems are token economies, which set up contingencies of reinforcement in institutional environments. In such arrangements, the reward is made obvious to the patients. Modeling can be an important adjunct to operant conditioning; therapists who use this technique provide specific examples of desirable behaviors.

Rational emotive behavior therapy focuses on modifying clients' maladaptive perceptions, thoughts, feelings, and beliefs as the means for modifying the client's behavior. The therapist may directly confront the client, calling specific attention to irrationality and error. In this respect, the therapy contrasts strongly with those provided by humanistic therapists.

Cognitive–behavioral therapies also attempt to change behavior by altering the client's cognitive processes and related behaviors. For example, Beck developed a therapy to help depressed clients target errors of thinking and feeling that perpetuate self-defeating behaviors and replace them with more desirable behaviors. It is also the case that behavioral change can produce changes in cognition as well. Thus, the causal relation between cognition and behavior can be considered bidirectional.

Critics have accused behavior therapists and cognitive–behavioral therapists of doing nothing more than treating the symptoms of a disorder and ignoring its basic causes. However, no evidence supports the idea that symptom substitution occurs in people who undergo these forms of therapy.

Group Therapies and Community Psychology

Group psychotherapy was developed in response to the belief that certain problems can be treated more efficiently and more effectively in group settings. Practitioners of family therapy, couples therapy, and group behavior therapy observe people's interactions with others and attempt to help them learn how to establish more effective patterns of behavior. Treatment of groups, including families and couples, permits the therapist to observe clients' social behaviors. It may also apply social pressure to help convince clients of the necessity for behavioral change. It permits clients to learn from the mistakes of others and to observe that other people have similar problems, which is often reassuring.

In community psychology, psychologists attempt to reach out to a community to establish readily available treatment facilities or to provide crisis intervention and so to keep problems from becoming worse. Community psychology also provides educational programs and promotes social changes that may prevent problems from occurring in the first place.

Indigenous healing therapies are based on belief systems regarding the causes and cures of psychological problems specific to a given culture. Although indigenous healing therapies often involve the use of culture-specific incantations and rituals, they can be effective in reducing the symptoms of psychological problems in people who believe in them. For this reason, many psychologists and psychiatrists use a blend of formal therapy and indigenous healing therapy to treat immigrants from certain cultures. This method appears to be more effective than using only formal therapy, because indigenous healing lets the therapist make contact with the individual's cultural belief system and may promote a trusting relationship between therapist and client.

Biomedical Therapies

Biomedical therapies for psychological disorders include drugs, electroconvulsive therapy, and psychosurgery. Research has shown that treatment of the positive symptoms of schizophrenia with antipsychotic drugs and of bipolar disorders with lithium carbonate are the most effective ways to alleviate the symptoms of these serious disorders. Atypical drugs show promise for treating the negative symptoms of schizophrenia as well. The benzodiazepines replaced barbiturates as the most effective drugs for the treatment of anxiety disorders. Although safer, they may still produce physical tolerance and withdrawal symptoms. Tricyclic antidepressant drugs can also alleviate severe anxiety that occurs during panic attacks and agoraphobia and can reduce the severity of obsessive–compulsive disorder. Although electroconvulsive therapy can be an effective treatment for depression, important risks exist; thus, this treatment is reserved for cases in which rapid relief from severe symptoms is critical. The most controversial treatment, psychosurgery, is rarely performed today. One accepted method, cingulotomy, is a treatment for disabling compulsions that cannot be reduced by more conventional means.

The Relationship between Client and Therapist

To enhance and protect the therapist–client relationship, the American Psychological Association has developed a set of ethical standards to guide the practice of therapy. Legislatures and courts have provided additional regulations.

Most of us experience a time in life when we are plagued by a persistent personal problem that makes us unhappy. In this situation, seeking professional help is usually a good idea. Counseling services, mental health centers, psychologists, and psychiatrists can generally be found in almost any city or town.

Finding a therapist who is right for you requires that you do some homework. As a rule, a good therapist will be licensed to practice therapy, will have specific training in the treatment of psychological problems and mental disorders, and will have a good reputation for being an empathetic and supportive therapist. If the therapist you choose turns out to be unsuitable for your needs, do not hesitate to look for a different therapist. The majority of people who seek therapy benefit by it and stand by their decision to seek it.

succeed with mypsychlab

Visit MyPsychLab for practice quizzes, flashcards, and dozens of videos and animated tutorials, including the following items you can find in the "Multimedia Library":

WATCH

Recent Trends in Treatment: Sue Mineka
Asylum: History of Mental Institutions in America
Listening to Blues Test

EXPLORE

Drugs Commonly Used to Treat
  Psychiatric Disorders
Psychotherapy Practitioners and Their Activities

SIMULATION

Ineffective Therapies

KEY TERMS

antianxiety drugs *p. 548*
antidepressant drugs *p. 547*
antimanic/mood-stabilizing
  drugs *p. 547*
antipsychotic drugs *p. 546*
aversion therapy *p. 534*
behavior modification *p. 535*
biomedical therapies *p. 545*
cingulotomy *p. 550*
client-centered therapy *p. 530*
cognitive–behavioral
  therapy *p. 539*
cognitive restructuring *p. 538*
community psychology *p. 543*
countertransference *p. 529*
covert sensitization *p. 537*
deinstitutionalization *p. 543*
dream interpretation *p. 528*
drug therapy *p. 545*
eclectic approach *p. 526*
electroconvulsive therapy
  (ECT) *p. 549*
free association *p. 528*
Gestalt therapy *p. 531*
group psychotherapy
  p. 540

humanistic therapy *p. 529*
imaginal exposure *p. 534*
in vivo exposure *p. 534*
incongruence *p. 530*
indigenous healing *p. 544*
insight therapy *p. 527*
modeling *p. 535*
preventive psychology
  p. 543
psychoanalysis *p. 527*
psychodynamic therapy
  p. 529
psychosurgery *p. 550*
rational emotive behavior
  therapy *p. 538*
resistance *p. 528*
structural family therapy
  p. 541
systematic desensitization
  p. 533
tardive dyskinesia *p. 546*
token economy *p. 535*
transference *p. 529*
trephining *p. 525*
unconditional positive
  regard *p. 530*

SUGGESTIONS FOR FURTHER READING

Aponte, J. F., & Wohl, J. (2000). *Psychological interventions and cultural diversity* (2nd ed.). Boston, MA: Allyn & Bacon.

This upper-division textbook addresses general issues faced by practitioners who deal with diverse ethnic populations as well as specific types of interventions used for specific problems.

Butcher, J. N., Mineka, S., & Hooley, J. M. (2007). *Abnormal psychology and modern life* (12th ed.). New York: Allyn & Bacon.

This very readable upper-division textbook provides a comprehensive introduction to the causes and treatment of psychological disorders.

Freud, S. (1952). *On dreams.* New York: W. W. Norton.

Freud wrote this short version of his famous book, *The Interpretation of Dreams*, to make his theory more accessible to the reading public. It provides a concise introduction to the psychoanalysis of dreams (focusing on one of Freud's own dreams) and to psychoanalytic theory more generally.

Kazdin, A. E. (2008). *Behavior modification in applied settings*, 6th ed. Long Grove, IL: Waveland Press.

A highly respected therapist provides an authoritative guide to the principles of behavior modification and their use across a wide range of applications.

Thorpe, G. L., & Olson, S. L. (1997). *Behavior therapy: Concepts, procedures, and applications* (2nd ed.). Boston, MA: Allyn & Bacon.

The authors describe various forms of behavior therapy drawn from classical and operant conditioning, social learning theory, and cognitive theory, as well as considering research methods and behavior assessment. They also describe residential and community treatment applications.

Rogers, C. R. (1951). *Client-centered therapy.* New York: Houghton Mifflin.

The founder of the humanistic movement in psychology describes the major features of his renowned therapy and shares samples of its application.

Corsini, R., & Wedding, D. (2004). *Case studies in psychotherapy* (4th ed.). Belmont, CA: Wadsworth/Thomson.

This collection of case studies ranges across cognitive–behavioral, humanistic, and psychoanalytic therapies. Each case study focuses on the client's problem and the treatment approach that was used.

Glossary

absolute threshold The minimum value of a stimulus that can be detected.

accommodation The process of altering the thickness of the lens to focus images of near or distant objects on the retina. In Piaget's theory of cognitive development, the process by which existing schemas are modified or changed by new experiences.

acetylcholine (ACh) (*a see tul koh leen*) A neurotransmitter found in the brain, spinal cord, and parts of the peripheral nervous system; responsible for muscular contraction.

acquisition Increase in the environmental guidance of behavior as the result of either a classical- or operant-conditioning procedure.

action potential A brief electrochemical event that is carried by an axon from the soma of the neuron to its terminal buttons; causes the release of a neurotransmitter.

activational effect (of hormone) The effect of a hormone that occurs in the fully developed organism; may depend on the organism's prior exposure to the organizational effects of hormones.

activation-synthesis theory A theory of dreaming that explains dreams as resulting from the incidental synthesis of cortical activity produced by mechanisms in the pons.

actor–observer effect Our tendency to attribute our own behavior to situational factors but others' behavior to dispositional factors.

actual developmental level In Vygotsky's theory, the stage of cognitive development reached by a child, as demonstrated by the child's ability to solve problems on his or her own.

actuarial judgments Diagnoses of psychological disorders or predictions of future behavior based on statistical analyses of outcome data.

additive color mixing The perception of two or more lights of different wavelengths seen together as light of an intermediate wavelength.

adenosine A product of brain metabolism; activates neurons in the preoptic area, inducing sleep.

agoraphobia An anxiety disorder characterized by fear of and avoidance of being in places where escape may be difficult; this disorder often is accompanied by panic attacks.

agrammatism A language disturbance; difficulty in the production and comprehension of grammatical features, such as proper use of function words, word endings, and word order. Often seen in cases of Broca's aphasia.

akinetopsia Loss of the ability to perceive movement due to damage in the visual association cortex.

algorithm A procedure that consists of a series of steps that, if followed, will solve a specific type of problem.

all-or-none law The principle that once an action potential is triggered in an axon, it is propagated, without becoming smaller, to the end of the axon.

allele Alternative forms of the same gene for a trait.

alpha activity Rhythmical, medium-frequency electroencephalogram activity, usually indicating a state of quiet relaxation.

altruistic behavior Behavior benefiting another organism at an apparent cost to the individual who executes the action.

Alzheimer's disease A fatal degenerative disease in which neurons of the brain progressively die, causing loss of memory and deterioration of other cognitive processes.

AMPA receptor Type of receptor for the excitatory neurotransmitter glutamate, rapidly facilitates firing of the neuron.

amygdala (*a mig da la*) A part of the limbic system of the brain located deep in the temporal lobe; damage causes changes in emotional and aggressive behavior.

anal stage The second of Freud's psychosexual stages, during which the primary erogenous zone is the anus because of the pleasure derived from vacating a full bowel.

analytic intelligence In Sternberg's triarchic theory, the cognitive mechanisms people use to plan and execute tasks; includes metacomponents, performance components, and knowledge-acquisition components.

analytic processing system The basis of deliberate, abstract, and higher-order reasoning.

anandamide (*a nan da mide*) The most important endogenous cannabinoid.

anatomical coding A means by which the nervous system represents information; different features are coded by the activity of different neurons.

androgen insensitivity syndrome A condition caused by a congenital lack of functioning androgen receptors; in a person with XY sex chromosomes, causes the development of a female with testes but no internal sex organs.

androgens The primary class of sex hormones in males. The most important androgen is testosterone.

animism The belief that all animals and all moving objects possess spirits controlling their movements and thoughts.

anorexia nervosa Eating disorder characterized by severe weight loss due to reduced food intake, sometimes to the point of starvation.

anterograde amnesia A condition in which a person has difficulty forming new long-term memories of events that occur after that time.

antianxiety drugs Drugs used to treat anxiety-related disorders, including benzodiazepines as well as some tricyclic antidepressants.

antibodies Proteins in the immune system that recognize antigens and help kill invading microorganisms.

anticipatory anxiety A fear of having a panic attack; may lead to the development of a phobia.

antidepressant drugs Drugs used to treat depression, including tricyclics, monoamine oxidase inhibitors, and SSRIs.

antigens The unique proteins found on the surface of bacteria; these proteins enable the immune system to recognize the bacteria as foreign substances.

antimanic/mood-stabilizing drugs Drugs used to treat the bipolar disorders, such as lithium carbonate.

antipsychotic drugs Drugs used to treat schizophrenic disorders.

antisocial personality disorder A disorder characterized by a failure to conform to standards of decency; repeated lying and stealing; a failure to sustain lasting, loving relationships; low tolerance of boredom; and a complete lack of guilt.

anxiety A sense of apprehension or doom that is accompanied by many physiological reactions, such as accelerated heart rate, sweaty palms, and tightness in the stomach.

apoptosis (*ay po toe sis*) Death of a cell caused by a chemical signal that activates a genetic mechanism inside the cell.

appeasement gesture Stereotyped gesture made by a submissive animal in response to a threat gesture by a dominant animal; tends to avert an attack.

archetypes Universal thought forms and patterns that Jung believed resided in the collective unconscious.

artificial intelligence A field of cognitive science in which researchers design computer programs to simulate human cognitive abilities; this endeavor may help cognitive psychologists understand the mechanisms that underlie these abilities.

artificial neural networks A model of the nervous system based on interconnected networks of units that have some of the properties of neurons.

artificial selection Procedure that differentially mates organisms to produce offspring with specific characteristics.

assimilation In Piaget's theory, the process by which new information about the world is incorporated into existing schemas.

attachment A social and emotional bond between infant and caregiver that spans both time and space.

attention-deficit/hyperactivity disorder A psychological disorder with symptoms of inattention, hyperactivity, and impulsivity usually diagnosed in childhood.

attitude An evaluation of a person, place, or thing.

attribution The process by which people infer the causes of their own and other people's behavior.

auditory hair cell The sensory neuron of the auditory system; located on the basilar membrane.

autistic disorder A psychological disorder marked by symptoms of severe limitations of social interaction and communication, often accompanied by mental retardation and usually diagnosed in childhood.

autoimmune diseases Diseases such as rheumatoid arthritis, diabetes, lupus, and multiple sclerosis, in which the immune system attacks and destroys some of the body's own tissue.

automatic processing Forming memories of events and experiences with little or no attention or effort.

automatic reinforcement Process in which a behavior inherently produces stimuli that function as reinforcers for that same behavior; especially important in language acquisition.

autonomic nervous system (ANS) The portion of the peripheral nervous system that controls the functions of the glands and internal organs.

autosomes The 22 pairs of chromosomes that are not sex chromosomes.

availability heuristic A general rule for judging the likelihood or importance of an event by the ease with which examples of that event are recalled.

aversion therapy A form of behavior therapy in which the client is trained to respond negatively to an originally attractive stimulus that has been paired with an aversive stimulus.

avoidant attachment As observed in the Strange Situation test, a kind of attachment in which infants avoid or ignore their mothers and often do not cuddle when held.

axon A long, thin part of a neuron attached to the soma; divides into a few or many branches, ending in terminal buttons.

B lymphocytes White blood cells that develop in bone marrow and release immunoglobulins to defend the body against antigens.

barbiturate A drug that causes sedation; one of several derivatives of barbituric acid.

basal ganglia A group of nuclei in the brain interconnected with the cerebral cortex, thalamus and brain stem; involved in control of slow movements and movements of large muscles.

base-rate fallacy The failure to consider the actual statistical likelihood that a person, place, or thing is a member of a particular category.

base rate neglect In decision making, the failure to consider available information that bears on the issue at hand, such as the failure to consider the data from a control group.

basic orientations Horney's sets of personality characteristics that correspond to the strategies of moving toward others, moving against others, and moving away from others.

basic-level concept A concept that makes essential distinctions at an everyday level.

basilar membrane (*bazz i ler*) A membrane that divides the cochlea of the inner ear into two compartments. The receptive organ for audition resides here.

behavior genetics The branch of psychology that studies the role of genetics in behavior.

behavior modification Behavior therapy based on the principles of operant conditioning.

behaviorism A movement in psychology that asserts that the only proper subject matter for scientific study in psychology is observable behavior.

belief in a just world The belief that people get what they deserve in life; a form of the fundamental attribution error.

benzodiazepine (*ben zoe dy azz a peen*) A class of drug having anxiolytic ("tranquilizing") effects, such as diazepam (Valium).

beta activity Irregular, high-frequency electroencephalogram activity, usually indicating a state of alertness or arousal.

Binet–Simon Scale An intelligence test developed by Binet and Simon in 1905; the precursor of the Stanford–Binet Scale.

binocular cue A cue for the perception of depth that requires the use of both eyes.

biological evolution Changes in characteristics over successive generations due to natural selection and mutation.

biomedical therapies Therapies utilized by psychiatrists and other medical practitioners to target abnormal neural functions and abnormal physiological functions more generally.

biopsychosocial perspective An approach to psychological disorders that considers them to be result from the interaction of genetic, physiological, developmental, and environmental factors.

bipedalism Habitually walking upright on two legs.

bipolar cell A neuron in the retina that receives information from photoreceptors and passes it on to the ganglion cells, from which axons proceed through the optic nerves to the brain.

bipolar I disorder A mood disorder in which alternating states of depression and mania are separated by periods of relatively normal affect.

bipolar II disorder A mood disorder; marked by major depressive episodes that are accompanied by less severe mania (hypomanic episodes).

black widow spider venom A drug that stimulates the release of acetylcholine by terminal buttons.

blindsight The ability of a person who cannot perceive objects in a part of his or her visual field to reach for them accurately while remaining unaware of seeing them.

blocking design Two-phase procedure in which behavior is first conditioned to one stimulus, and then a second stimulus is introduced, and conditioning continues. Behavior does not become conditioned to the second stimulus even though it is temporally contiguous with the reinforcing stimulus.

blood–brain barrier A barrier between the blood and the brain produced by the cells in the walls of the brain's capillaries; prevents some substances from passing from the blood into the brain.

borderline personality disorder A disorder whose diagnostic criteria include pervasive instability of interpersonal relationships, self-image, and emotions as well as impulsivity; suicidal efforts and self-mutilation may also occur.

bottom-up processing Perception based on successive analyses of the details of the stimuli that are present.

botulinum toxin (*bot you lin um*) A drug that prevents the release of acetylcholine by terminal buttons.

brain lesion Damage to a particular region of the brain.

brain stem The "stem" of the brain, including the medulla, pons, and midbrain.

brightness A perceptual dimension of color, most closely related to the intensity or degree of radiant energy emitted by a visual stimulus.

Broca's aphasia Severe difficulty in articulating words, especially function words, caused by brain damage that includes Broca's area, a region of the left (speech-dominated) frontal cortex.

bulimia nervosa Eating disorder characterized by gorging binges followed by self-induced vomiting or use of laxatives; often accompanied by feelings of guilt and depression.

bystander intervention The intervention of a person in a situation that appears to require his or her aid.

Cannon–Bard theory Theory of emotion proposing that feelings of emotion, as well as behavioral and physiological responses, are directly elicited by the environment.

carbon dating Method to determine the age at which an organism lived by measuring the amount of radioactive carbon (C14).

case study A detailed description of an individual's behavior during the course of clinical treatment or diagnosis.

cataplexy A symptom of narcolepsy; although awake, the individual is temporarily paralyzed.

catatonic schizophrenia A type of schizophrenia characterized primarily by motor disturbances, including catatonic postures and waxy flexibility.

causal event An event that causes another event to occur.

central fissure The fissure that separates the frontal lobe from the parietal lobe

central nervous system (CNS) The brain and the spinal cord.

central traits Characteristics of the individual, which, according to Asch, have greater influence on one's impression of another person.

cerebellum (*sair a* **bell** *um*) A pair of hemispheres resembling the cerebral hemispheres but much smaller and lying beneath and in back of them; controls posture and movements, especially rapid ones.

cerebral achromatopsia The inability to discriminate colors; caused by damage to the visual association cortex.

cerebral cortex The outer layer of the cerebral hemispheres of the brain, approximately 3 mm thick.

cerebral hemisphere The largest part of the brain; covered by the cerebral cortex and containing parts of the brain that evolved most recently.

cerebral ventricle One of the hollow spaces within the brain, filled with cerebrospinal fluid.

cerebrospinal fluid (CSF) The liquid in which the brain and spinal cord float; provides a shock-absorbing cushion.

change blindness Failure to detect a change when vision is interrupted.

chemosense One of the two sense modalities (gustation and olfaction) that detect the presence of particular molecules present in the environment.

child-directed speech The speech of an adult directed toward a child; differs in several ways from adult-directed speech and tends to facilitate the learning of language by children.

chromosomal aberration Displacement or deletion of genes within chromosomes, or a change in the number of chromosomes.

chromosomes Paired rod-like structures in the nucleus of a cell; contain genes.

chunking A process by which information is simplified by rules, which make it easily remembered once the rules are learned. For example, the string of letters NBCCBSNPR is easier to remember if a person learns the rule that organizes them into smaller "chunks": NBC, CBS, and NPR.

cilium (plural: cilia) A hairlike appendage of a cell; involved in movement or in transducing sensory information. Cilia are found on the receptors in the auditory and vestibular system.

cingulotomy The surgical destruction of nerve fibers that connect the prefrontal cortex with the limbic system; used to reduce intense anxiety and other symptoms of obsessive-compulsive disorder.

circadian rhythm A daily rhythmical change in behaviors or physiological processes.

classical procedure Conditioning procedure in which a neutral stimulus precedes an eliciting stimulus with the result that the neutral stimulus evokes a learned response resembling the elicited response.

client-centered therapy A form of psychotherapy in which the client decides what to talk about without strong direction or judgment from the therapist.

clinical judgments Diagnoses of psychological disorders or predictions of future behavior based largely on experts' knowledge of symptoms and past clinical experience.

clinical neuropsychologist A psychologist who specializes in the identification and treatment of the behavioral consequences of nervous system disorders and injuries.

clinical observation Observation of the behavior of people or animals while they are undergoing diagnosis or treatment.

clinical psychology The branch of psychology devoted to the investigation and treatment of abnormal behavior and mental disorders.

cochlea (*cock lee uh* or *coke lee uh*) A snail-shaped chamber set in bone in the inner ear, where audition takes place.

cochlear implant An electronic device surgically implanted in the inner ear that can enable a deaf person to hear.

cocktail-party problem Trying to follow one conversation while other, potentially distracting conversations are going on around us.

cognitive appraisal Our perception of a stressful situation; occurs in two stages, primary appraisal and secondary appraisal.

cognitive dissonance theory The theory that changes in attitude can be motivated by an unpleasant state of tension caused by a disparity between our attitudes and our behavior.

cognitive neuroscience The branch of psychology that attempts to understand cognitive psychological functions by studying the brain mechanisms that are responsible for them.

cognitive psychology The branch of psychology that studies mental processes and complex behaviors such as perception, attention, learning and memory, verbal behavior, concept formation, and problem solving.

cognitive reappraisal Any coping strategy in which we alter our perception of the threat posed by a stressor to reduce stress. Also called cognitive restructuring.

cognitive restructuring A therapeutic process that seeks to help clients replace maladaptive thoughts with more constructive ways of thinking.

cognitive–behavioral therapy A form of psychotherapy that focuses on altering clients' perceptions, thoughts, feelings, and beliefs as well as environments to produce desired changes.

collective unconscious According to Jung, the shared unconscious memories and ideas inherited from our ancestors over the course of human evolution.

coma A condition in which an individual seems to be sleeping but cannot be awakened.

community psychologist A psychologist who works for the well-being of individuals in the social system, attempting to improve the system rather than treating people as problems.

community psychology A form of treatment and education whose goal is to address psychological problems through assessment and intervention in the sociocultural contexts in which problems develop.

comorbid Refers to the tendency of one type of psychological disorder to occur together with one or more other disorders.

companionate love Love that is characterized by a deep, enduring affection and caring for another person, accompanied by a strong desire to maintain the relationship.

comparative psychology The branch of psychology that studies the behavior of members of a variety of species in an attempt to explain behavior in terms of evolutionary adaptation to the environment.

compliance Engaging in a particular behavior at another person's request.

compulsion An irresistible impulse to repeat some action over and over even though it serves no useful purpose.

concept A category of objects or events that share certain attributes.

concordance research Studies the similarity of traits between twins, especially identical twins. Twins are concordant if they exhibit the same phenotype.

concurrent schedule Reinforcement schedules in which reinforcers are available for responding on two or more alternative operants.

conditioned emotional response (CER) A classically conditioned response that occurs when a neutral stimulus is followed by an aversive stimulus; usually includes autonomic, behavioral, and endocrine components such as changes in heart rate, freezing, and secretion of stress-related hormones.

conditioned (secondary) reinforcer Stimulus that can function as a reinforcer after it has been paired with another stimulus that can already function as a reinforcer. Also known as *conditioned suppression.*

conditioned response (CR) Response that is acquired by the CS in a classical procedure after the CS has been paired with the US.

conditioned stimulus (CS) Neutral stimulus that evokes a conditional response (CR) through pairing with a US in a classical procedure.

conditioning Process that produces learning (change in the environmental guidance of behavior) in classical and operant procedures.

conditions of worth Conditions that others place on us for receiving their positive regard.

conduction aphasia An inability to remember words that are heard, although they usually can be understood and responded to appropriately. This disability is caused by damage to Wernicke's and Broca's areas.

cone A photoreceptor that is responsible for acute daytime vision and for color perception.

confidentiality Privacy of participants and nondisclosure of their participation in a research project.

confirmation bias A tendency to seek evidence that might confirm a hypothesis rather than evidence that might disconfirm it.

conformity Adoption of the attitudes and behaviors that characterize a particular group of people.

confounding of variables Inadvertent simultaneous manipulation of more than one variable. The results of an experiment in which variables are confounded permit no valid conclusions about cause and effect.

conscience The internalization of the rules and restrictions of society; it determines which behaviors are permissible and punishes wrongdoing with feelings of guilt.

consciousness The awareness of complex private processes such as perception, thinking, and remembering.

consensus The extent to which a person's behavior is what most people would do; can be a basis for others' attributions about the person's motives.

conservation The fact that specific properties of objects (for example, volume, mass, length, or number) remain the same despite apparent changes in the shape or arrangement of those objects.

consistency The extent to which a person generally behaves in the same way toward another person, an event, or a stimulus; can be the basis for others' attributions about the person's motives.

consolidation The change of information from a state of short-term activation into structural changes in the brain. These changes are considered permanent and are hence part of long-term memory.

consumer psychologist A psychologist who studies consumer behavior and works for organizations that manufacture products or that buy products or services.

content word A noun, verb, adjective, or adverb that conveys meaning.

contextual discrimination Discrimination procedure in which the stimulus in whose presence the behavior is reinforced varies with the value of another stimulus, the stimulus context.

contralateral Residing in the side of the body opposite the reference point.

control group A comparison group used in an experiment, the members of which are exposed to the naturally occurring or zero value of the independent variable.

conventional level Kohlberg's second level of moral development, in which people realize that a society has instituted moral rules to maintain order and to serve the best interests of members of the society.

convergence In depth perception, the result of conjugate eye movements whereby the fixation point for each eye is identical; feedback from these movements provides information about the distance of visual objects from the viewer.

coping strategy A plan of action that a person follows to reduce the experience of stress, either in anticipation of encountering a stressor or in response to its occurrence.

cornea The transparent tissue covering the front of the eye.

coronary heart disease (CHD) The narrowing of blood vessels that supply oxygen and nutrients to the heart.

corpus callosum (*core pus ka low sum*) A large bundle of axons ("white matter") that connects the cortex of the two cerebral hemispheres.

correctional mechanism Mechanism that restores the system variable to the set point in a regulatory process.

correlation coefficient A measurement of the degree to which two variables are related.

correlational study The examination of relations between two or more measurements of behavior or other characteristics of people or other animals.

counterbalancing Systematic variation of conditions in an experiment, such as the order of presentation of stimuli, so that different participants encounter the conditions in different orders; prevents confounding of independent variables with time-dependent processes such as habituation or fatigue.

countertransference Process in which a psychoanalyst projects his or her emotions onto a client.

covert sensitization A form of behavior therapy in which a client imagines the aversive consequences of his or her inappropriate behavior.

cranial nerve A bundle of nerve fibers attached to the base of the brain; conveys sensory information from the face and head and carries messages to muscles and glands.

creative intelligence In Sternberg's triarchic theory, the ability to deal effectively with novel situations and to solve problems automatically that have been encountered previously.

criterion An independent measure of the variable a test is designed to measure.

critical period A specific time in development during which certain experiences must occur for normal development to take place.

cross-cultural psychology The branch of psychology that studies the impact of culture on behavior.

cross-sectional study A study of development in which individuals of different ages are compared at the same time.

crystallized intelligence According to Cattell, intellectual abilities that have developed through exposure to information-rich contexts, especially schools; expressed in general knowledge and skills.

CT scanner A device that uses a special x-ray machine and a computer to produce images of the brain that appear as slices taken parallel to the top of the skull.

culture Socially transmitted knowledge, customs, and behavior of a group of people.

culture-bound syndrome Highly unusual psychological disorders that are similar to nonpsychotic psychological disorders (such as phobias) but are specific to only one or a few cultures.

cumulative record Graphic presentation of data in which every response moves the curve upward as time passes.

curare (*kew rahr ee*) A drug that binds with and blocks acetylcholine receptors, preventing the neurotransmitter to exert its effects.

dark adaptation The process by which the eye becomes capable of distinguishing dimly illuminated objects after going from a bright region to a dark one.

debriefing Full disclosure to research participants of the nature and purpose of a research project after its completion.

deductive reasoning The mental process by which people arrive at specific conclusions from general principles or rules.

deep processing Analysis of the complex characteristics of a stimulus, such as its meaning or its relation to other stimuli.

deep structure The essential meaning of a sentence, without regard to the grammatical features (surface structure) of the sentence that are needed to express it in words.

defense mechanisms Mental systems that become active whenever unconscious instinctual drives of the id come into conflict with internalized prohibitions of the superego.

deinstitutionalization The process of returning previously institutionalized patients to their communities for treatment of psychological problems and psychological disorders.

delta activity Rhythmical electroencephalogram activity with a frequency of less than 3.5 Hz, indicating deep (slow-wave) sleep.

dendrite A treelike part of a neuron on which other neurons form synapses.

dependent variable The variable measured in an experiment and hypothesized to be affected by the independent variable.

deprivation Reduction of an organism's contact with a stimulus below the level that the organism would choose; for example, reduced contact with food in food deprivation.

descriptive statistics Mathematical procedures for organizing collections of data.

detector Mechanism that signals when the system variable deviates from its set point in a regulatory process.

determinism In psychology, the doctrine that behavior is the result of prior events.

deuteranopia A form of hereditary anomalous color vision; caused by defective "green" cones in the retina.

developmental psychology The branch of psychology that studies the changes in behavioral, perceptual, cognitive, social, and emotional capacities of organisms as a function of age and experience.

deviation IQ A procedure for computing the IQ; compares an individual's score with those received by other individuals of the same chronological age.

diathesis–stress model A causal account of mental disorders suggesting that these disorders develop when a person possesses a predisposition for a disorder and encounters stressors that exceed his or her abilities to cope with them.

dichotic-listening test A task that requires a person to listen to one of two different messages being presented simultaneously, one to each ear, through headphones.

difference threshold An alternate name for *just-noticeable difference (jnd)*.

differential conditioning procedure Procedure in which behavior has different consequences as the environment changes.

diffusion of responsibility A factor in the failure of bystander intervention, stating the fact that when several bystanders are present, no one person assumes responsibility for helping.

direct dyslexia A reading disorder caused by brain damage in which people can read words aloud without understanding them.

discrimination Differential treatment of people based on their membership in a particular group.

discriminative stimulus Stimulus that controls behavior as the result of a differential conditioning procedure.

disorganized schizophrenia A type of schizophrenia characterized primarily by disturbances of thought and a flattened or silly affect.

disoriented attachment As observed in the Strange Situation test, a kind of attachment in which infants behave in confused and contradictory ways toward their mothers.

dispositional factors An individual's traits, needs, and intentions, which can affect his or her behavior.

dissociative amnesia A dissociative disorder characterized by the inability to remember important events or personal information.

dissociative disorders A class of disorders in which anxiety is reduced by a sudden disruption in consciousness, which in turn produces changes in memory or in the person's sense of identity.

dissociative fugue Amnesia with no apparent physiological cause, often accompanied by adoption of a new identity and relocation to a new community.

dissociative identity disorder A rare dissociative disorder in which two or more distinct personalities exist within the same person; each personality dominates in turn. (Formerly known as multiple personality disorder.)

distinctive features Physical characteristics of an object that help distinguish it from other objects.

distinctiveness The extent to which a person behaves differently toward different people, events, or other stimuli; can be the basis for others' attributions about the person's motives.

divided attention The process by which we distribute awareness among different stimuli or tasks so that we can respond to them or perform them simultaneously.

DNA Deoxyribonucleic acid. Molecule resembling a twisted ladder whose sides are connected by rungs of pairs of nucleotides (adenine, thymine, guanine, and cytosine).

doctrine of specific nerve energies Johannes Müller's observation that different nerve fibers convey specific information from one part of the body to the brain or from the brain to one part of the body.

dominant allele A trait that is exhibited when only one allele is present, a trait expressed in heterozygous cells.

dopamine (DA) A monoamine neurotransmitter involved in control of brain mechanisms of movement and reinforcement; a neuromodulator that increases synaptic efficacy between interconnected neurons that are active at the same time; important in reinforcement.

dopamine hypothesis The hypothesis that the positive symptoms of schizophrenia are caused by overactivity of synapses in the brain that use dopamine.

dorsal stream The flow of information from the primary visual cortex to the visual association area in the parietal lobe; used to form the perception of an object's location in three-dimensional space (the "where" system).

double bind The conflict caused for a child when he or she is given inconsistent messages or cues from a parent.

double-blind study An experiment in which neither the participants nor the researchers know the value of the independent variable.

Down's syndrome Chromosomal aberration consisting of an extra 21st chromosome. Produces varying physical and behavioral impairment.

dream interpretation The method in psychoanalysis whereby the therapist interprets the client's report of a dream (its manifest content) in terms of its deeper, symbolic meaning (its latent content).

drug therapy Reliance on the use of pharmaceutical substances for the treatment of psychological disorders.

dualism The philosophical belief that reality consists of mind and matter.

echoic memory A form of sensory memory for sounds that have just been perceived.

eclectic approach An approach to therapy in which the therapist uses whatever method he or she feels will work best for a particular client at a particular time.

effortful processing Practicing or rehearsing information through either shallow or deep processing.

ego The general manager of personality, making decisions balancing the pleasures that will be pursued at the id's demand against the person's safety requirements and the moral dictates of the superego.

egocentrism Self-centeredness; Piaget proposed that preoperational children can see the world only from their own perspectives.

ego-ideal The internalization of what a person would like to be—his or her goals and ambitions.

elaboration likelihood model A model that explains the effectiveness of persuasive messages in terms of two routes to persuasion. The central route requires a person to think critically about an argument, whereas the peripheral route entails merely the association of the argument with something positive.

elaborative rehearsal Processing information on a meaningful level, such as forming associations, attending to the meaning of the material, thinking about it, and so on.

electroconvulsive therapy (ECT) Treatment for severe depression that involves passing small amounts of electric current through the brain to produce seizures.

electroencephalogram (EEG) An electrical brain potential recorded by placing electrodes on the scalp.

electromyogram A record of muscle activity.

electro-oculogram A record of eye movements.

eliciting stimulus Stimulus that evokes behavior, commonly as a result of natural selection.

embryonic stage The second stage of prenatal development, beginning 2 weeks and ending about 8 weeks after conception, during which the heart begins to beat, the brain starts to function, and most of the major body structures begin to form.

emitted response Response permitted by the environment with no specific controlling stimulus.

emotional stability The tendency to be relaxed and at peace with oneself.

emotion-focused coping Any coping behavior that aims to reduce stress by changing our own emotional reaction to a stressor.

empiricism The philosophical view that all knowledge is obtained through observation and experience.

encoding The process by which sensory information is converted into a form that can be used by the brain's memory system.

encoding specificity The principle that how we encode information determines our ability to retrieve it later.

endocrine gland A gland that secretes a hormone.

endogenous cannabinoid (*can ob in oid*) A neuromodulator whose action is mimicked by THC and other drugs present in marijuana.

endogenous opioid (*ope ee oyd*) A neuromodulator whose action is mimicked by a natural or synthetic opiate, such as opium, morphine, or heroin.

engineering psychologist A psychologist who studies the ways that people and machines work together and helps design machines that are safer and easier to operate.

enzymes Proteins that regulate processes that occur within cells—organic catalysts.

epigenetics Mechanisms through which cells inherit modifications that are not due to DNA sequences.

episodic memory A type of long-term memory that serves as a record of life experiences.

equilibration A process activated when a child's abilities to assimilate and accommodate fail to adjust.

equivalence class A set of physically unrelated stimuli that all control the appropriate behavior without direct training after the stimuli have appeared in multiple contextual discriminations.

escape or withdrawal response Response that terminates or reduces contact with an aversive stimulus; the aversive stimulus may be either conditioned or unconditioned.

estrous cycle Ovulatory cycle in mammals other than primates; the sequence of physical and hormonal changes that accompany the ripening and disintegration of ova.

ethnocentrism The idea that our own cultural, racial, national, or religious group is superior to or more deserving than others.

etiology The sources of a disorder.

evolutionary psychology The branch of psychology that explains behavior in terms of adaptive advantages that specific behaviors provided during the evolution of a species. Evolutionary psychologists use natural selection as a guiding principle.

exemplar A memory of a particular example of an object or an event that is used as the basis for a natural concept.

expectancy The belief that a certain consequence will follow a certain action.

experiential processing system The basis of rapid, mostly unconscious, and heuristic reasoning.

experiment A study in which the researcher changes the value of an independent variable and observes whether this manipulation affects the value of a dependent variable. Only experiments can confirm the existence of cause-and-effect relations among variables.

experimental ablation The removal or destruction of a portion of the brain of an experimental animal for the purpose of studying the functions of that region.

experimental group The group of participants in an experiment that is exposed to a particular value of the independent variable, which has been manipulated by the researcher.

explicit memory Memory that can be described verbally and of which a person is therefore aware.

extinction Decrease in a learned behavior when the behavior is no longer followed by a reinforcer.

extinction-induced aggression Aggression toward another organism when responding is extinguished.

extrastriate body area (EBA) A region of the ventral stream in the human brain that is activated by images of bodies or body parts but not faces.

extroversion The tendency to seek the company of other people, to engage in conversation and other social behaviors with them, and to be spontaneous.

factor analysis A statistical procedure that identifies the factors that groups of data, such as test scores, have in common.

false consensus The mistaken belief that our own attitude on a topic is representative of a general consensus.

fetal stage The third and final stage of prenatal development, which lasts for about 7 months, beginning with the appearance of bone tissue and ending with birth.

fight-or-flight response Physiological reactions that help ready us to fight or to flee a dangerous situation.

figure A visual stimulus that is perceived as an object.

five-factor model A theory stating that personality is composed of five primary dimensions: neuroticism, extroversion, openness, agreeableness, and conscientiousness. This theory was developed using factor analyses of ratings of the words people use to describe personality characteristics.

fixation A brief interval between saccadic eye movements during which the eye does not move; the brain accesses visual information during this time. Also, in Freudian theory, the continued attachment of psychic energy to an erogenous zone due to incomplete passage through one of the psychosexual stages.

flashbulb memories Memories established by events that are highly surprising and personally of consequence.

fluid intelligence According to Cattell, intellectual abilities that operate in relatively culture-free informational contexts and involve the detection of relationships or patterns, for example.

forensic psychologist A psychologist who studies human behavior as it relates to the legal system and to matters involving criminal justice.

formal concept A category of objects or events defined by a list of common essential characteristics, much as in a dictionary definition.

fossil Remains of an animal or plant found in the Earth.

fovea A small pit near the center of the retina containing densely packed cones; responsible for the most acute and detailed vision.

free association A method of Freudian analysis in which the client is asked to relax and to speak freely in reporting any thoughts or images that come to mind without worrying about their meaning.

free nerve ending An unencapsulated (naked) dendrite of somatosensory neurons.

frontal lobe The front portion of the cerebral cortex, including the prefrontal cortex and the motor cortex; damage impairs movement, planning, and flexibility in behavioral strategies.

frustration An emotional response produced when a formerly reinforced response is extinguished.

function word A preposition, article, or other word that conveys little of the meaning of a sentence but is important in specifying its grammatical structure.

functional MRI (fMRI) A modification of the MRI procedure that permits the measurement of regional metabolism in the brain.

functionalism An approach to understanding species' behaviors and other processes in terms of their biological significance; this approach stresses the usefulness of such processes with respect to survival and reproductive success.

fundamental attribution error Our tendency to overestimate the significance of dispositional factors and to underestimate the significance of situational factors in explaining other people's behavior.

fundamental frequency The lowest, and usually most intense, frequency of a complex sound; most often perceived as the sound's basic pitch.

fusiform face area A region of the ventral stream in the human brain containing face-recognizing circuits.

g factor According to Spearman, a factor that is common to performance on all intellectual tasks; includes apprehension of experience, eduction of relations, and eduction of correlates.

GABA The most important inhibitory neurotransmitter in the brain.

ganglion cell A neuron in the retina that receives information from photoreceptors by means of bipolar cells, and from which axons proceed through the optic nerves to the brain.

gender identity A person's private sense of being male or female.

gender role Cultural expectations about the ways in which a male or a female should think and behave.

gender stereotypes Beliefs about differences in the behaviors, abilities, and personality traits of males and females.

gene Unit of heredity, inferred from Mendel's experiments.

general adaptation syndrome The model proposed by Selye to describe the body's adaptation to prolonged exposure to severe stressors. The body passes through a sequence of three physiological stages: alarm, resistance, and exhaustion.

generalize To extend the results obtained from a sample to the population from which the sample was taken.

genetic engineering Procedures intended to alter an organism's genes to produce a more favorable phenotype.

genetic marker A known nucleotide sequence that occurs at a particular location on a chromosome.

genetics Study of the hereditary structures of organisms (genes).

genital stage The final of Freud's psychosexual stages (from puberty through adolescence). During this stage the adolescent develops adult sexual desires.

genome Total set of genetic material of an organism.

genotype The genetic makeup of an organism.

germ cells Reproductive cells, a collective term for the sperm and ovum taken together; have only one member of each pair of chromosome.

Gestalt psychology A movement in psychology that emphasized that cognitive processes could be understood by studying their organization, not their elements.

Gestalt therapy A form of therapy that emphasizes the unity of mind and body by teaching the client to "get in touch" with unconscious bodily sensations and emotions.

glia (*glee ah*) Cells of the central nervous system that provide support for neurons and supply them with some essential chemicals.

glucocorticoid A hormone, such as cortisol, that influences the metabolism of glucose, the main energy source of the body.

glucostatic hypothesis The hypothesis that hunger is caused by a low level of glucose in the blood; glucose levels are assumed to be monitored by specialized sensory neurons called glucostats.

glutamate The most important excitatory neurotransmitter in the brain and spinal cord.

glycogen Insoluble carbohydrate synthesized from glucose and stored in the liver; can be converted back to glucose.

gray matter The portions of the central nervous system that are abundant in cell bodies of neurons rather than axons. The color appears gray relative to white matter.

ground A visual stimulus that is perceived as a background against which objects are seen.

group Two or more individuals who generally have common interests and goals.

group polarization The tendency for the initial position of a group to become more extreme during the discussion preceding a decision.

group psychotherapy Therapy in which two or more clients meet simultaneously with a therapist, discussing problems within a supportive and constructive environment.

groupthink Group members' tendency to avoid dissent in the attempt to achieve consensus in the course of decision making.

gustation The sense of taste.

habituation Decrease in responding to a stimulus after that stimulus is repeatedly presented without an important consequence.

hallucination A perceptual experience that occurs in the absence of external stimulation of the corresponding sensory organ; often accompanies schizophrenia.

haze A monocular cue for depth perception; objects that are less distinct in their outline and texture are perceived as farther from the viewer.

health psychology The branch of psychology involved in the promotion and maintenance of sound health practices.

heredity Sum of the traits inherited from one's parents.

heritability A statistical measure of the degree to which the variability of a particular trait in a population results from the genetic variability within the population; has a value from 0.0 to 1.0.

hertz (Hz) The primary measure of the frequency of vibration of sound waves; cycles per second.

heuristic A general rule that guides decision making.

hippocampus A part of the limbic system of the brain, located in the temporal lobe; plays important roles in episodic memory and spatial memory.

homeostasis (*home ee oh stay sis*) The process by which important physiological characteristics (such as body temperature and blood pressure) are regulated so that they remain at their optimal levels.

hominids The genus of bipedal apes ancestral to humans.

horizon proximity A monocular cue for depth perception; objects closer to the horizon appear farther away that objects more distant from the horizon.

hormone A chemical substance secreted by an endocrine gland that has physiological effects on target cells in other organs.

hue A perceptual dimension of color, most closely related to the wavelength of a pure light. The effect of a particular hue is caused by the mixture of lights of various wavelengths.

humanistic approach An approach to the study of personality that emphasizes the positive, fulfilling aspects of life.

humanistic psychology An approach to the study of human behavior that emphasizes human experience, choice and creativity, self-realization, and positive growth.

humanistic therapy A form of psychotherapy focusing on the client's unique potential for personal growth and self-actualization.

Huntington's disease Genetic disorder caused by a dominant lethal gene that produces progressive mental and physical deterioration after adulthood (also known as Huntington's chorea).

hypocretin A neurotransmitter secreted by cells in the hypothalamus; helps regulate sleep-wake cycles.

hypothalamus A region of the brain located just above the pituitary gland; controls the autonomic nervous system and many behaviors related to regulation and survival, such as eating, drinking, fighting, shivering, and sweating.

hypothesis A statement, usually designed to be tested by an experiment, that tentatively expresses a cause-and-effect relationship between two or more events.

iconic memory A form of sensory memory that holds a brief visual image of a scene that has just been perceived; also known as visible persistence.

id The unconscious reservoir of libido, the psychic energy that fuels instincts and psychic processes.

illusion of out-group homogeneity A belief that members of out-groups are highly similar to one another.

illusory correlation An apparent correlation between two distinctive elements that does not actually exist.

imaginal exposure A method of behavior therapy for phobias in which the therapist describes the feared object in graphic terms, thereby inducing fear without direct exposure to the object.

imitation Observational learning in which the behavior of an observer is similar to the behavior of the one being observed.

immune system A network of organs and cells that protects the body from invading bacteria, viruses, and other foreign substances.

immunoglobulins Disease-fighting antibodies that are released by B lymphocytes.

implicit memory Memory that cannot be described verbally and of which a person is therefore not aware.

impression formation The integration of information about another person's traits into a coherent sense of who the person is.

in vivo exposure A form of behavior therapy that attempts to rid people of fears by arousing the fears intensely until clients' responses diminish through extinction; they learn that nothing bad happens.

inattention blindness Failure to perceive an event when attention is diverted elsewhere.

inclusive fitness Total reproductive success of those with whom the individual has genes in common, e.g., siblings.

incongruence In Rogers' theory, a discrepancy between a client's perceptions of her or his real and ideal selves.

independent variable The variable that is manipulated in an experiment as a means of determining cause-and-effect relations.

indigenous healing Non-Western, culture-specific approaches to the treatment of psychological and medical problems.

inductive reasoning The mental process by which people infer general principles or rules from specific information.

inferential statistics Mathematical and logical procedures for determining whether relations or differences between samples are statistically significant.

inflection A change in the form of a word (usually by addition of a suffix) to denote a grammatical feature such as tense or number.

information processing A model used by cognitive psychologists to explain the workings of the brain; according to this model, information received through the senses is processed by systems of neurons in the brain.

informed consent A person's agreement to participate in an experiment after he or she has received information about the nature of the research and any possible risks and benefits.

inhibition of return A reduced tendency to perceive a target when the target's presentation is consistent with a cue, but the target is presented a few hundred milliseconds after the cue.

insight therapy Therapy in which the therapist aids clients to achieve insight into the causes of maladaptive behavior, causes they were previously unaware of.

insomnia A general category of sleep disorder related to difficulty in falling asleep and remaining asleep.

instructional control Guidance of behavior by discriminative stimuli, especially verbal stimuli such as directions; also known as *rule-governed behavior*.

intelligence A person's ability to learn and remember information, to recognize concepts and their relations, and to apply the information and recognition by behaving in an adaptive way.

intelligence quotient (IQ) A simplified single measure of general intelligence; by definition, the ratio of a person's mental age to his or her chronological age.

intermittent (partial) reinforcement Procedure in which not every occurrence of a behavior is followed by a reinforcer; increases resistance to the effects of extinction.

interpersonal attraction People's tendency to approach each other and to evaluate each other positively.

interposition A monocular cue for depth perception; an object that partially blocks another object is perceived as closer.

interrater reliability The degree to which two or more independent observers agree in their ratings of an organism's behavior.

interval schedules Procedures in which a reinforcer is dependent on the passage of time before the response is effective; may be either fixed or variable.

intraspecific aggression An attack by an animal on another member of its species.

introspection Literally, "looking within" in an attempt to describe memories, perceptions, cognitive processes, or motivations.

introversion The tendency to avoid the company of other people, to be inhibited and cautious; shyness.

ion A positively or negatively charged particle; produced when many substances dissolve in water.

ion channel A special protein molecule located in the membrane of a cell; controls the entry or exit of particular ions.

ion transporter A special protein molecule located in the membrane of a cell; actively transports ions into or out of the cell.

ipsilateral Residing in the same side of the body as the reference point.

iris The pigmented muscle of the eye that controls the size of the pupil.

isolation aphasia Language disorder in which a person cannot comprehend speech or produce meaningful speech but is able to repeat speech and to learn new sequences of words.

James-Lange theory Theory of emotion proposing that behavioral and physiological responses are directly elicited by situations; feelings of emotions are produced by feedback from these behavioral and physiological responses.

just-noticeable difference (JND) The smallest difference between two similar stimuli that can be distinguished. Also called *difference threshold.*

kin selection Selection that favors altruistic acts toward individuals with whom one has genes in common.

knockout mutations Experimentally induced genetic sequence preventing gene expression.

language universal A characteristic feature found in all natural languages.

language-acquisition device (LAD) A theoretical endowment unique to humans that is postulated to account for the fact that, regardless of geographical location and often severely restricted environments, children tend to acquire a first language in highly similar fashion.

language-acquisition support system (LASS) A cultural system that aids the child's acquisition of a first language by providing the forms of interaction conducive to acquisition.

latency period In Freudian theory, the period between the phallic stage and the genital stage, during which sexual urges are submerged.

latent content The hidden message of a dream produced by the unconscious.

latent learning Facilitation of learning after the stimuli that guide behavior have been experienced but without the behavior being reinforced in their presence.

law of closure A Gestalt law of perceptual organization; elements missing from the outline of a figure are "filled in" by the visual system.

law of common fate A Gestalt law of perceptual organization; elements that move together give rise to the perception of a particular figure.

law of continuity A Gestalt law of perceptual organization; given two or more possible interpretations of the elements that form the outline of a figure, the brain will adopt the simplest interpretation.

law of effect Edward Thorndike's statement that stimuli that occur as a consequence of a response can increase or decrease the likelihood of an organism's making that response again.

law of proximity A Gestalt law of perceptual organization; elements located closest to one another are perceived as belonging to the same figure.

law of similarity A Gestalt law of perceptual organization; similar elements are perceived as belonging to the same figure.

law of symmetry A Gestalt law of perceptual organization; symmetrical objects are perceived as belonging together even if a distance separates them.

learned helplessness Reduced ability to learn a solvable avoidance task after exposure to an inescapable aversive stimulus; thought to play a role in depression.

learning Long-lasting changes in the environmental guidance of behavior as a result of experience.

lens The transparent organ situated behind the iris of the eye; helps focus an image on the retina.

libido An insistent, instinctual force that is unresponsive to the demands of reality; the primary source of motivation.

liking A feeling of personal regard, intimacy, and esteem toward another person.

limbic cortex The cerebral cortex located around the edges of the cerebral hemispheres where they join with the brain stem; part of the limbic system.

limbic system A set of interconnected structures of the brain important in emotional and species-typical behavior; includes the amygdala, hippocampus, and limbic cortex.

linear perspective A monocular cue for depth perception; the arrangement of lines drawn in two dimensions such that parallel lines receding from the viewer are seen to converge at a point on the horizon.

linguistic relativity hypothesis The hypothesis that the language a person speaks influences his or her thoughts and perceptions.

locus of control An individual's beliefs that the consequences of his or her actions are controlled by internal, person variables or by external, environmental variables.

longitudinal study A study of development in which observations of the same individuals are compared at different times of their lives.

long-term memory Memory in which information is represented on a permanent or near-permanent basis.

long-term potentiation (LTP) Increase in the ease of firing a postsynaptic neuron by electrical stimulation of a presynaptic neuron; thought to be the neural basis of learning.

loving A combination of liking and a deep sense of attachment to, intimacy with, and caring for another person.

LSD Lysergic acid diethylamide; a hallucinogenic drug that blocks a category of serotonin receptors.

Machiavellianism A personality trait measuring skill at manipulating other people for one's own ends.

magnetic resonance imaging (MRI) A technique with a device that uses the interaction between radio waves and a strong magnetic field to produce images of slices of the interior of the body.

magnetoencephalography (MEG) A method of brain study that measures the changes in magnetic fields that accompany action potentials in the cerebral cortex.

maintenance rehearsal Rote repetition of information; repeating a given item over and over again.

major depressive disorder Persistent and severe feelings of sadness and worthlessness accompanied by changes in appetite, sleeping, and other behavior.

mania Abnormal and persistent elevation of an expansive or irritable mood.

manifest content The apparent story line of a dream.

manipulation Setting the values of an independent variable in an experiment to see whether the value of another variable is affected.

matching Systematically selecting participants in groups in an experiment or (more often) a correlational study to ensure that the mean values of important participant variables of the groups are similar.

matching principle In a choice situation, the proportion of responses occurring during a stimulus is the same as the proportion of reinforcers received during that stimulus.

matching relation In concurrent reinforcement schedules, the equal relation between the proportion of responses to a given alternative and the proportion of reinforcers received for those responses.

materialism A philosophical belief that reality can be known only through an understanding of the physical world, of which the mind is a part.

maturation Any relatively stable change in thought, behavior, or physical growth that is due to the aging process and not to experience.

mean A measure of central tendency; the sum of a group of values divided by their number; the arithmetical average.

means–ends analysis A general heuristical method of problem solving that involves looking for differences between the current state and the goal state and seeking ways to reduce the differences.

measure of central tendency A statistical measure used to characterize the value of items in a sample of numbers.

measure of variability A statistic that describes the degree to which scores in a set of numbers differ from one another.

median A measure of central tendency; the midpoint of a group of values arranged numerically.

medulla (*me doo la*) The part of the brain stem closest to the spinal cord; controls vital functions such as heart rate and blood pressure.

meiosis Process of cell division by which germ cells are produced.

memory The cognitive processes of encoding, storing, and retrieving information.

Mendelian traits Traits showing a dominant, recessive, or sex-linked pattern of inheritance. Mendelian traits are not polygenic.

meninges (*men in jees*) The three-layered set of membranes that enclose the brain and spinal cord.

mental age A measure of a person's intellectual development; the average level of intellectual development that could be expected in a child of a particular age.

mental model A cognitive representation of a possibility that a person can use to solve deductive problems.

mental retardation Cognitive development that is substantially below normal; often caused by some form of brain damage or abnormal brain development. Also known as *cognitive disability* or *intellectual disability*.

mere exposure effect The tendency to form a positive attitude toward a person, place, or thing based solely on repeated exposure to that stimulus.

method of loci (**low**-sigh) A mnemonic system in which items to be remembered are mentally associated with specific physical locations or landmarks.

microelectrode A thin electrode made of wire or glass that can measure the electrical activity of a single neuron.

midbrain The part of the brain stem just anterior to the pons; involved in control of fighting and sexual behavior and in decreased sensitivity to pain during these behaviors.

minimally conscious state A condition in which the individual shows occasional arousal and organized behavior but otherwise appears to be asleep.

Minnesota Multiphasic Personality Inventory (MMPI) An objective test originally designed to distinguish individuals with psychological problems from normal individuals. The MMPI has since become popular as a means of attempting to identify personality characteristics of people in many everyday settings.

mnemonic system A special technique or strategy consciously used in an attempt to improve memory.

model In science, a relatively simple system that works on known principles and is able to do at least some of the things that a more complex system can do.

modeling Behavior therapy in which the client is encouraging to behave in a manner similar to that of the therapist or other designated person.

module An area of tissue in the primary visual cortex whose neurons receive their input from the same small region in the retina.

molecular genetics The study of genetics at the level of the DNA molecule.

monoamine (*mahn o a meen*) A category of neurotransmitters that includes dopamine, norepinephrine, and serotonin.

monocular cue A cue for the perception of depth that requires the use of only one eye.

monogamy Mating strategy of one female with one male.

mood disorders A psychological disorder characterized by significant shifts or disturbances in mood that adversely affect normal perception, thought, and behavior. Mood disorders may be characterized by deep, foreboding depression or may involve a combination of depression and mania.

moral realism The first stage of Piaget's model of moral development, which includes egocentrism and blind adherence to rules.

morality of cooperation The second stage of Piaget's model of moral development, which involves the recognition of rules as social conventions.

morpheme The minimal unit of meaning in a language, such as /p/ + /in/ to form *pin*.

motion parallax A monocular cue for depth perception; as we pass by a scene, objects closer to us appear to move farther than those more distant.

motivation A group of phenomena that affect the nature, strength, or persistence of an individual's behavior.

motor association cortex Those regions of the cerebral cortex that control the primary motor cortex; involved in planning and executing behaviors.

motor neuron A neuron whose terminal buttons form synapses with muscle fibers. When an action potential travels down its axon, the associated muscle fibers will twitch.

muscle spindle A muscle fiber that functions as a stretch receptor; arranged parallel to the muscle fibers responsible for contraction of the muscle, it detects muscle length.

mutation Alterations in the nucleotides within a single gene. Can occur spontaneously or from experimental manipulation.

myelin sheath The insulating material that encases most large axons.

naloxone (*na lox own*) A drug that binds with and blocks opioid receptors, preventing opiate drugs or endogenous opioids from exerting their effects.

narcissism A personality trait measuring grandiosity and feelings of superiority.

narcolepsy A sleep disorder characterized by sleep attack—irresistibly falling asleep at inappropriate times.

narrative A mnemonic system in which items to be remembered are linked together by a story.

natural concept A category formed from a person's perceptions of and interactions with things in the world; based on exemplars.

natural selection Process whereby the environment differentially favors organisms with characteristics that affect survival and production of offspring.

naturalistic observation Observation of the behavior of people or other animals in their natural environments.

negative afterimage The image seen after a portion of the retina is exposed to an intense visual stimulus; a negative afterimage consists of colors complementary to those of the physical stimulus.

negative symptoms A symptom of schizophrenia that consists of the absence of normal behaviors; negative symptoms include flattened emotion, poverty of speech, lack of initiative and persistence, and social withdrawal.

neostigmine (*nee o stig meen*) A drug that enhances the effects of acetylcholine by blocking the enzyme that destroys it.

nerve A bundle of nerve fibers that transmit information between the central nervous system and the body's sense organs, muscles, and glands.

neural plasticity The production of changes in the structure and functions of the nervous system, induced by environmental events.

neurogenesis The process responsible for the production of a new neuron.

neuromodulator A substance secreted in the brain that modulates the activity of neurons that contain the appropriate receptors.

neuron A neural cell; consists of a cell body with dendrites and an axon whose branches end in terminal buttons that synapse with muscle fibers, gland cells, or other neurons.

neuroticism The tendency to be anxious, worried, and full of guilt.

Neuroticism, Extroversion, and Openness Personality Inventory (NEO-PI-R) The instrument used to measure the elements described in the five-factor model (neuroticism, extroversion, openness, agreeableness, and conscientiousness).

neurotransmitter A chemical released by the terminal buttons that causes the postsynaptic neuron to be excited or inhibited.

neurotransmitter receptor A special protein molecule located in the membrane of the postsynaptic neuron that responds to molecules of the neurotransmitter.

nicotine A drug that binds with and stimulates acetylcholine receptors, mimicking the effects of this neurotransmitter.

night terrors The experience of anguish without a clear memory of its cause; occurs during slow-wave sleep, usually in childhood.

NMDA receptor Type of glutamate receptor that plays an important role in learning through changing synaptic efficacies.

nominal fallacy The false belief that we have explained the causes of a phenomenon by identifying and naming it; for example, believing that we have explained lazy behavior by attributing it to "laziness."

nonmendelian trait Characteristic when alleles do not have a dominant-recessive relation.

norepinephrine (NE) (*nor epp i neff rin*) A monoamine neurotransmitter involved in alertness and vigilance and control of REM sleep.

norms Data obtained from large numbers of individuals that permit the score of any one individual to be assessed relative to the scores of his or her peers.

object permanence In Piaget's theory, the idea that objects do not cease existing when they are out of sight.

objective personality tests Tests for measuring personality that can be scored objectively, such as a multiple-choice or true/false test.

object-relations theory The theory that personality is the reflection of relationships that the individual establishes with others as an infant.

observational learning Changes in the behavior of an observer after seeing another learner behave in that same situation; learning that takes place when we see the kinds of consequences others (called models) experience as a result of their behavior.

obsession An involuntary recurring thought, idea, or image accompanied by anxiety or distress.

obsessive-compulsive disorder Recurrent, unwanted thoughts or ideas and compelling urges to engage in repetitive ritual-like behavior, often abbreviated as OCD.

occipital lobe (*ok sip i tul*) The rearmost portion of the cerebral cortex; contains the primary visual cortex.

olfaction The sense of smell.

olfactory bulb One of the stalklike structures located at the base of the brain that contain neural circuits that perform the first analysis of olfactory information.

olfactory mucosa (*mew koh za*) The mucous membrane lining the top of the nasal sinuses; contains the cilia of the olfactory receptors.

operant procedure Conditioning procedure in which a response (the operant) precedes an eliciting stimulus.

operation In Piaget's theory, a logical or mathematical rule that transforms an object or concept into something else.

operational definition Definition of a variable in terms of the operations the researcher performs to measure or manipulate it.

opponent process The representation of colors by the rate of firing of two types of neurons: red/green and yellow/blue.

optic disk A circular structure located at the exit point from the retina of the axons of the ganglion cells that form the optic nerve.

oral stage The first of Freud's psychosexual stages, during which the mouth is the major erogenous zone because it appeases the hunger drive.

organizational effect (of hormone) The effect of a hormone on tissue differentiation and development.

organizational psychologist A psychologist who works to increase the efficiency and effectiveness of organizations.

orienting response Response that facilitates detecting a stimulus (for example, turning toward the source of a sound).

ossicle (*ahss i kul*) One of the three bones of the middle ear (the *hammer, anvil,* and *stirrup*) that transmit acoustical vibrations from the eardrum to the membrane behind the oval window of the cochlea.

oval window An opening in the bone surrounding the cochlea. The stirrup presses against a membrane behind the oval window and transmits sound vibrations into the fluid within the cochlea.

overextension The use of a word to denote a larger class of items than is appropriate; for example, referring to the moon as a *ball.*

overgeneralization The creation of grammatical errors when a child uses an inferred syntactical rule to form the past tense of verbs.

overjustification effect The undermining of intrinsic motivation by the application of extrinsic rewards to intrinsically motivated behavior.

overtone A component of a complex tone; one of a series of tones whose frequency is a multiple of the fundamental frequency.

Pacinian corpuscle (*pa chin ee un*) A specialized, encapsulated somatosensory nerve ending, which detects mechanical stimuli, especially vibrations.

panic disorder Unpredictable attacks of acute anxiety that are accompanied by high levels of physiological arousal and that last from a few seconds to a few hours.

papilla A small bump on the tongue that contains a group of taste buds.

parahippocampal place area A region of the ventral stream in the human brain that is activated by visual scenes and backgrounds.

paranoid schizophrenia A type of schizophrenia in which the person has delusions of persecution, grandeur, or control.

parasympathetic branch The portion of the autonomic nervous system that activates functions that occur during a relaxed state.

parental investment Resources that parents expend in procreating and nurturing offspring.

parietal lobe (*pa rye i tul*) The region of the cerebral cortex behind the frontal lobe and above the temporal lobe; contains the somatosensory cortex; is involved in spatial perception and memory.

Parkinson's disease A neurological disorder characterized by tremors, rigidity of the limbs, poor balance, and difficulty in initiating movements; caused by degeneration of a system of dopamine-secreting neurons.

passionate love An emotional, intense desire for sexual union with another person; also called romantic love.

peg-word method A mnemonic system in which items to be remembered are associated with a set of mental pegs already in memory, such as key words of a rhyme.

peptide A category of neurotransmitters and neuromodulators that consist of two or more amino acids, linked by peptide bonds.

perception The brain's use of information provided by sensory systems to produce a response; the detection of the more complex properties of a stimulus, including its location and nature; involves learning.

perceptual constancy The experience-based ability to recognize an object and certain of its characteristics—its form, size, color, and brightness—as invariant despite the shifting retinal images it produces.

perceptual learning Process by which *combinations* of environmental stimuli acquire control of behavior.

period of concrete operations The third period in Piaget's theory of cognitive development, lasting from age 7 to 11, during which children come to understand the conservation principle and other concepts, such as categorization.

period of formal operations The fourth period in Piaget's theory of cognitive development, from age 11 onward, during which individuals first become capable of more-formal kinds of abstract thinking and hypothetical reasoning.

peripheral nervous system (PNS) The cranial and spinal nerves; that part of the nervous system peripheral to the brain and spinal cord.

persistent vegetative state A condition similar to coma except that the individual intermittently appears to be awake.

person variables Individual differences in cognition, which, according to Mischel, include competencies, encoding strategies and personal constructs, expectancies, subjective values, and self-regulatory systems and plans.

personality A particular pattern of behavior and thinking prevailing across time and situations that differentiates one person from another.

personality psychology The branch of psychology that attempts to categorize and understand the causes of individual differences in temperament and patterns of behavior.

personality trait An enduring personal characteristic that reveals itself in a particular pattern of behavior in a variety of situations.

personality types Different categories into which personality characteristics can be assigned based on factors such as developmental experiences or physical characteristics.

phallic stage The third of Freud's psychosexual stages during which the primary erogenous zone is the genital area and pleasure derives from both direct genital stimulation and general physical contact.

phantom limb Sensations that appear to originate in a limb that has been amputated.

phenotype The appearance or behavior of an organism; outward expression of the genotype.

phenylketonuria (PKU) Genetic disorder caused by recessive genes that impair ability to break down phenylalanine; can cause mental retardation if untreated.

phi phenomenon The perception of movement caused by the turning on and off of two or more lights, one at a time, in sequence; often used on theater marquees; responsible for the apparent movement of images in movies and television.

phobia Unreasonable fear of specific objects or situations, such as insects, animals, or enclosed spaces, produced by stimulus reinforcer pairings.

phobic disorder An unrealistic, excessive fear of a specific class of stimuli that interferes with normal activities. Phobic disorders include agoraphobia, social phobia, and specific phobia.

phoneme The minimal unit of sound in a language, such as /p/.

phonetic reading Reading by decoding the phonetic structure of letter strings; reading by "sounding out."

phonological dyslexia A reading disorder in which people can read familiar words but have difficulty reading unfamiliar words or pronounceable nonwords because they cannot sound out words.

phonological short-term memory Short-term memory for verbal information.

photopigment A complex molecule found in photoreceptors; when struck by light, it splits apart and stimulates the membrane of the photoreceptor in which it resides.

photoreceptor A receptive cell for vision in the retina; a rod or a cone.

physiological psychology The branch of psychology that studies the physiological basis of behavior.

pituitary gland An endocrine gland attached to the hypothalamus at the base of the brain.

place cell A neuron that becomes active when the animal is in a particular location in the environment; most typically found in the hippocampal formation.

placebo An ineffectual treatment used as the control substance in a single-blind or double-blind experiment.

pleasure principle The rule that the id obeys: Obtain immediate gratification, whatever form it may take.

polygenic control Characteristic affected by more than one gene, as with most behavior.

polygraph An instrument that records changes in physiological processes such as brain activity, heart rate, and breathing.

polygyny Mating strategy of one male with more than one female.

pons The part of the brain stem just anterior to the medulla; involved in control of sleep.

positive psychology A program of psychology that examines the basis of optimal human functioning, with emphasis on the origins, processes, and mechanisms of human well-being.

positive symptom A symptom of schizophrenia, including thought disorder, delusions, or hallucinations.

positron emission tomography (PET) The use of a device that reveals the localization of a radioactive tracer in a living brain.

postconventional level Kohlberg's third and final level of moral development, in which people come to understand that moral rules include principles that apply across all situations and societies.

posthypnotic amnesia Failure to remember what occurred during hypnosis; induced by suggestions made during hypnosis.

posthypnotic suggestion A suggestion made by a hypnotist that is carried out some time after the participant has left the hypnotic state and usually according to a specific cue.

postsynaptic neuron A neuron with which the terminal buttons of another neuron form synapses and that is excited or inhibited by that neuron.

post-traumatic stress disorder (PTSD) An anxiety disorder in which the individual has feelings of social withdrawal accompanied by atypically low levels of emotion; caused by prolonged exposure to a stressor, such as war or a natural catastrophe.

practical intelligence In Sternberg's triarchic theory, intelligence that reflects the behaviors that were subject to natural selection: adaptation (initially fitting self to environment by developing useful skills and behaviors); selection (finding an appropriate niche in the environment); and shaping (changing the environment).

preconventional level Kohlberg's first level of moral development, which bases moral behavior on external sanctions such as authority and punishment.

prefrontal cortex The anterior part of the frontal lobe; contains the motor association cortex.

prejudice A preconceived opinion or bias; especially, a negative attitude toward a group of people who are defined by their racial, ethnic, or religious heritage or by their gender, occupation, sexual orientation, level of education, place of residence, or membership in a particular group.

prenatal period The approximately 9 months between conception and birth. This period is divided into three developmental stages: the zygotic, the embryonic, and the fetal.

preoperational period The second period in Piaget's theory of cognitive development, lasting from 2 years of age to 7, and representing a transitional period between symbolic and logical thought. During this stage, children become increasingly capable of speaking meaningful sentences.

preoptic area An area of the hypothalamus that contains neurons that inhibit arousal neurons to produce sleep.

presynaptic neuron A neuron whose terminal buttons form synapses with and excite or inhibit another neuron.

preventive psychology Strategies that attempt to prevent the development of psychological problems by altering the sociocultural variables predictive of psychological distress.

primacy effect The tendency to form an impression of a person based on the initial information one receives about her or him. In the memorization of a list of words, the primacy effect is evidenced by better recall of the words early in the list.

primary appraisal The first stage of cognitive appraisal, during which we evaluate the seriousness of a threat (stressor).

primary auditory cortex The region of the cerebral cortex that receives information directly from the auditory system; located in the temporal lobes.

primary motor cortex The region of the cerebral cortex that directly controls the movements of the body; located in the posterior part of the frontal lobes.

primary somatosensory cortex The region of the cerebral cortex that receives information directly from the somatosensory system (touch, pressure, vibration, pain, and temperature); located in the front part of the parietal lobes.

primary visual cortex The region of the cerebral cortex that receives information directly from the visual system; located in the occipital lobes.

proactive interference Interference in recall that occurs when previously learned information disrupts our ability to remember newer information.

problem-focused coping Any coping behavior that aims to reduce stress by reducing or eliminating a stressor.

progressive relaxation technique A stress-reduction method in which a person learns to (1) recognize body signals that indicate the presence of stress; (2) use those signals as a cue to begin relaxing; and (3) relax groups of muscles, beginning with those in the head and neck and proceeding to those in the arms and legs.

projective tests Unstructured personality measures in which a person is shown a series of ambiguous stimuli, such as pictures, inkblots, or incomplete drawings. The person is asked to describe what he or she "sees" in each stimulus or to create stories that reflect the theme of the drawing or picture.

prosody The use of changes in intonation and emphasis to convey meaning in speech besides that specified by the particular words.

prosopagnosia A form of visual agnosia characterized by difficulty in the recognition of people's faces; may be accompanied by difficulty in recognizing other complex objects; caused by damage to the visual association cortex.

protanopia A form of hereditary anomalous color vision; caused by defective "red" cones in the retina.

prototype A hypothetical idealized pattern that resides in the nervous system and is used to perceive objects or shapes by a process of comparison; recognition can occur even when an exact match cannot be found.

protoword A unique string of phonemes that an infant invents and uses as a word.

psychoanalysis A form of psychotherapy aimed at providing the client with insight into his or her unconscious motivations and impulses; first developed by Sigmund Freud.

psychodynamic Characterized by conflict among instincts, reason, and conscience; describes the mental processes envisioned in Freudian theory.

psychodynamic therapy A therapeutic approach derived from psychoanalysis but typically deemphasizing psychosexual development in favor of emphasis on social and interpersonal experiences and the complexities of the ego.

psycholinguistics A branch of psychology devoted to the study of verbal behavior and related cognitive abilities.

psychology The scientific study of the causes of behavior; also, the application of the findings of psychological research to the solution of problems.

psychoneuroimmunology Study of the interactions between the immune system and behavior as mediated by the nervous system.

psychopathy A personality trait meauring impulsivity and lack of empathy or remorse for harm caused by one's actions.

psychophysics A branch of psychology that measures the quantitative relation between physical stimuli and perceptual experience.

psychosurgery Brain surgery used in an effort to relieve the symptoms of psychological disorders in the absence of obvious organic damage.

psychoticism The tendency to be aggressive, egocentric, and antisocial.

puberty The period during which people's reproductive systems mature, marking the beginning of the transition from childhood to adulthood.

punishing stimulus (punisher) Stimulus that evokes escape and withdrawal responses that interfere with the behavior that produced it.

punishment Process by which a stimulus decreases the strength of behavior by conditioning responses that interfere with the operant.

pursuit movement The movement that the eyes make to maintain an image upon the fovea.

qualitative research An alternative research strategy stressing the observation of variables that are not numerically measurable.

random assignment Procedure in which each participant has an equally likely chance of being assigned to any of the conditions or groups of an experiment.

range The difference between the highest score and the lowest score of a sample.

rapid-eye-movement (REM) sleep A stage of sleep during which dreaming, rapid eye movements, and muscular paralysis occur and the EEG shows beta activity.

ratio IQ A formula for computing the intelligence quotient: mental age divided by chronological age, multiplied by 100.

ratio schedules Reinforcement schedules in which reinforcers are dependent on a designated number of responses; may be either fixed or variable.

rational emotive behavior therapy A form of psychotherapy based on the belief that psychological problems are caused not by distressing experiences themselves but by how people think and feel about those experiences.

rationalism The philosophical view that all knowledge is obtained through reason.

reality principle The tendency to satisfy the id's demands realistically, which almost always involves compromising the demands of the id and superego.

receiver-operating-characteristic curve (ROC curve) A graph of hits and false alarms of subjects under different motivational conditions; indicates people's ability to detect a particular stimulus.

recency effect The tendency to recall later information. In the memorization of a list of words, the recency effect is evidenced by better recall of the last words in the list.

receptive field That portion of the visual field in which the presentation of visual stimuli will produce an alteration in the firing rate of a particular neuron.

receptor cell A neuron that directly responds to a physical stimulus, such as light, vibrations, or aromatic molecules.

recessive allele A trait that is expressed only when both alleles of a gene are the same, a trait expressed homozygous cells.

reciprocal altruism Altruism in which one individual benefits another when it is likely that the other will return the benefit at a later time.

reciprocal determinism The idea that behavior, environment, and person variables interact to determine personality.

reflex An automatic response to a stimulus, such as the blink reflex to the sudden unexpected approach of an object toward the eyes.

regulatory genes Genes that govern genes that code for proteins.

reinforcement Process by which a reinforcer increases the environmental guidance of behavior.

reinforcing stimulus (reinforcer) Stimulus that strengthens responding in either the classical or operant procedures, often called simply a *reinforcer.*

relative size A monocular cue for depth perception based on the retinal size of an object.

reliability The repeatability of a measurement; the likelihood that if the measurement were made again, it would yield the same value.

replication Repetition of an experiment or observational study in an effort to see whether previous results will be obtained; ensures that incorrect conclusions are weeded out.

representativeness heuristic A general rule for classifying a person, place, or thing into the category to which it appears to be the most similar.

repression A defense mechanism responsible for actively keeping potentially threatening or anxiety-provoking memories from being consciously discovered.

reproductive strategies Evolutionary effects on systems of mating and rearing offspring; these need not be conscious strategies.

residual schizophrenia A type of schizophrenia that may follow an episode of one of the other types and is marked by negative symptoms but not by any prominent positive symptom.

resistance A development during psychoanalysis in which the client becomes defensive, unconsciously attempting to halt further insight by censoring his or her emotions.

resistant attachment A kind of attachment in which infants show mixed reactions to their mothers. In the Strange Situation test, when mothers return after being absent, such infants may approach their mothers but at the same time may continue to cry or even push their mothers away.

response bias Responding to a questionnaire in a way that is not genuine or honest but in some other irrelevant way.

resting potential The membrane potential of a neuron when it is not producing an action potential.

retention Third component of evolution: the favored variations are retained through heredity.

retina The tissue at the back inside surface of the eye that contains the photoreceptors and associated neurons.

retinal disparity The fact that objects located at different distances from the observer will fall on different locations on the two retinas; provides a binocular cue for depth perception.

retrieval The active processes of locating and using stored information.

retrieval cues Contextual variables, including physical objects, or verbal stimuli, that improve the ability to recall information from memory.

retroactive interference Interference in recall that occurs when recently learned information disrupts our ability to remember older information.

retrograde amnesia Loss of the ability to retrieve memories of the past, particularly memories of episodic or autobiographical events.

reuptake The process by which a terminal button retrieves the molecules of a neurotransmitter that it has just released; terminates the effect of the neurotransmitter on the receptors of the postsynaptic neuron.

rhodopsin The photopigment contained by rods.

RNA Single-stranded nucleic acid that is involved in several functions within the cell.

rod A photoreceptor that is very sensitive to light but cannot detect changes in hue.

Rorschach Inkblot Test A projective test in which a person is shown a series of symmetrical inkblots and asked to describe what he or she thinks they represent.

round window An opening in the bone surrounding the cochlea. Movements of the membrane behind this opening permit vibrations to be transmitted through the oval window into the cochlea.

saccadic movement The rapid movement of the eyes that is used in scanning a visual scene, as opposed to the smooth pursuit movements used to follow a moving object.

sample A selection of elements representative of a larger population—for example, a group of participants selected to participate in an experiment.

saturation A perceptual dimension of color, most closely associated with purity of a color.

scaffolding The matching of a mentor's efforts to a child's developmental level.

scatterplot A graph of items that have two values; one value is plotted against the horizontal axis and the other against the vertical axis.

schedule of reinforcement Reinforcement procedure that specifies the conditions necessary for reinforcement. Also, procedures that manipulate the temporal relation between stimuli, responses, and reinforcers.

schema A mental framework or body of knowledge that organizes and synthesizes information about a person, place, or thing.

schizophrenia A serious psychological disorder characterized by thought disturbances, hallucinations, anxiety, emotional withdrawal, and delusions.

school psychologist A psychologist who deals with the behavioral problems of students at school.

scientific method A set of rules that governs the collection and analysis of data gained through observational studies or experiments.

sclera The tough outer layer of the eye; the "white" of the eye.

script A person's knowledge about the characteristics typical of a particular type of event or situation; assists the comprehension of speech.

secondary appraisal The second stage of cognitive appraisal, during which we evaluate the resources we have available to deal with a threat (stressor).

secure attachment A kind of attachment in which infants use their mothers as a base for exploring a new environment. In the Strange Situation test, securely attached infants will venture out from their mothers to explore, but will return periodically.

segregation analysis Correlational method to identify sections of chromosomes that are the same for individuals expressing a common trait.

selection Second component of evolution, provides direction to the process.

selectionism Explanation of complex outcomes as the cumulative effect of the three-component process identified by Darwin.

selective attention The process that controls our awareness of, and readiness to respond to, particular categories of stimuli or stimuli in a particular location to the exclusion of others.

self-actualization The realization of our true intellectual and emotional potential.

self-concept One's knowledge, feelings, and beliefs about oneself.

self-control Behavior that produces a larger, long-term reward when people are faced with the choice between it and a smaller, short-term reward; also the tendency to be kind, considerate, and obedient of laws and rules.

self-efficacy People's beliefs about how well or badly they will perform tasks.

self-fulfilling prophecy An expectation that causes a person to act in a manner consistent with the expectation; the person's actions then cause the expectation to come true. Often seen in cases of stereotyping.

self-handicapping Impairing one's performance so as to attribute failures situationally and successes dispositionally.

self-perception theory The theory that we come to understand our attitudes and emotions by observing our own behavior and the circumstances under which it occurs.

self-schema The cognitive representation of the self-concept.

self-serving bias The tendency to attribute one's accomplishments and successes to dispositional factors and one's failures and mistakes to situational factors.

semantic memory A type of long-term memory that contains data, facts, and other information, including vocabulary.

semantic priming The facilitating effect of a word on the recognition of words having related meanings that are presented subsequently.

semantics The meanings and the study of the meanings of words.

semicircular canal One of a set of organs in the inner ear that responds to rotational movements of the head.

sensation The detection of the elementary properties of a stimulus.

sensitive period A period during which certain experiences have a greater effect on development than they would have if they had occurred at another time.

sensorimotor period The first period in Piaget's theory of cognitive development, lasting from birth to 2 years, and marked by an orderly progression of increasingly complex cognitive development from reflexes to object permanence to deferred imitation and rudimentary symbolic thinking.

sensory association cortex Those regions of cerebral cortex that receive information from the primary sensory areas.

sensory memory Memory in which representations of the physical features of a stimulus are stored for very brief durations.

sensory neuron A neuron that detects changes in the external or internal environment and sends information about these changes to the central nervous system.

separation anxiety A set of fearful responses, such as crying, arousal, and clinging to the caregiver, that an infant exhibits when its caregiver attempts to leave the infant.

serotonin (*sair a toe nin*) A monoamine neurotransmitter involved in the regulation of mood; in the control of eating, sleep, and arousal; and in the regulation of pain.

set point Optimal value of the system variable in a regulatory process. The set point for human body temperature is 98.6°F (37°C).

sex chromosomes X or Y chromosomes that contain genes affecting sexual development.

sex-linked traits Traits affected by genes located on the sex chromosomes.

sexual reproduction Production of offspring by combining the germ cells of a male and female.

sexual selection Preference for traits that are differentially expressed in the two sexes, for example, body size.

shading A monocular cue for depth perception; the apparent light source determines whether the surface of an object is perceived as concave or convex.

shadowing The act of continuously repeating verbal material aloud as soon as it is heard.

shallow processing Analysis of the superficial characteristics of a stimulus, such as its size or shape.

shaping Procedure in which successively closer approximations to a target behavior are reinforced; commonly used when acquiring complex behavior.

short-term memory An immediate memory for stimuli that have just been perceived. It is limited in terms of both capacity (7 2 chunks of information) and duration (less than 20 seconds).

signal-detection theory A mathematical theory of the detection of stimuli, which involves discriminating a signal from the noise in which it is embedded and which takes into account subjects' willingness to report detecting the signal.

single-blind study An experiment in which the researcher knows the value of the independent variable but participants do not.

single-subject design An alternative research strategy that examines the effects of a manipulation on an individual participant or subject.

situational factors Physical and social stimuli that are found in an individual's environment and that can affect his or her behavior.

situationism The view that the behaviors defining a certain personality are determined solely by the current situation rather than by any persevering traits.

sleep-related eating disorder Occurs during sleepwalking as the individual seeks out food and consumes it, usually with no memory of having done so.

sleepwalking The experience of walking during sleep without a clear memory of doing so; occurs during slow-wave sleep, usually in childhood.

slow-wave sleep Sleep other than REM sleep, characterized by regular, slow waves on the electroencephalogram.

social cognition The processes involved in perceiving, thinking about, and acting on social information.

social cognitive theory The idea that both consequences of behavior and an individual's beliefs about those consequences determine personality.

social facilitation The enhancement of task performance caused by the mere presence of others.

social loafing The tendency of individuals to put forth decreased effort when performing a task together with other people.

social norms Informal rules defining the expected and appropriate behavior in specific situations.

social phobia An anxiety disorder characterized by an excessive and irrational fear of situations in which the person is observed by others.

social psychology The branch of psychology devoted to the study of the effects people have on one another's behavior.

sociobiology The study of genetic influences on social behavior, especially in animals.

soma A cell body; the largest part of a neuron.

somatic nervous system The portion of the peripheral nervous system that transmits information from sense organs to the central nervous system and from the central nervous system to the muscles.

somatosense Bodily sensations; sensitivity to such stimuli as touch, pain, and temperature.

species-typical behavior A behavior seen in all or most members of a species, such as nest building, special food-getting behaviors, or reproductive behaviors.

specific phobia An anxiety disorder characterized by an excessive and irrational fear of specific things, such as snakes, darkness, or heights.

spinal cord A long, thin collection of neural cells attached to the base of the brain and running the length of the spinal column.

spinal nerve A bundle of nerve fibers attached to the spinal cord; conveys sensory information from the body and carries messages to muscles and glands.

split-brain operation A surgical procedure that severs the corpus callosum, thus abolishing the direct connections between the cortex of the two cerebral hemispheres.

spontaneous recovery Increase in a previously extinguished response after the passage of time.

standard deviation A statistic that expresses the variability of a measurement; square root of the average of the squared deviations from the mean.

Stanford–Binet Scale An intelligence test that consists of various tasks grouped according to mental age; provides the standard measure of the IQ.

statistical significance The likelihood that an observed relation or difference between two variables really exists rather than being due to chance factors.

stem cell An undifferentiated cell that can divide and produce any one of a variety of differentiated cells.

stereotaxic apparatus A device used to insert an electrode into a particular part of the brain for the purpose of recording electrical activity, stimulating the brain electrically, or producing localized damage.

stereotype An overgeneralized and thus potentially false schema describing the characteristics of a particular group.

stimulus discrimination Process by which the environmental guidance of behavior is restricted to the environment in which the behavior was reinforced; can be produced by extinguishing the response in other environments.

stimulus generalization Process by which behavior occurs in an environment in which it has not been reinforced, but which is similar to that environment.

storage The process of maintaining information in memory.

Strange Situation A test of attachment in which an infant is exposed to different stimuli that may cause distress.

stranger anxiety The wariness and fearful responses, such as crying and clinging to their caregivers, that infants exhibit in the presence of strangers.

stress A pattern of physiological, behavioral, emotional, and cognitive responses to stimuli (real or imagined) that are perceived as endangering our well-being.

stress inoculation training The stress management program developed by Meichenbaum to help people develop coping skills that increase their resistance to the negative effects of stress.

stressors Stimuli that are perceived as endangering our well-being.

striving for superiority Our motivation to achieve our full potential. Adler argued that striving for superiority is born from our need to compensate for our inferiority.

structural family therapy A form of family therapy in which the therapist infers the maladaptive relationships among family members from their behavior and attempts to help the family restructure these relationships for more desirable interactions.

structuralism The system of experimental psychology that began with Wilhelm Wundt; it emphasized introspective analysis of sensation and perception.

subordinate concept A more-specific concept that falls within a basic-level concept.

substance-related disorders Psychological disorders that are characterized by addiction to drugs or alcohol or by abuse of drugs or alcohol.

subvocal articulation An unvoiced speech utterance.

successful intelligence According to Sternberg, the ability to analyze and manage personal strengths and weaknesses effectively; in Sternberg's scheme, successful intelligence draws on analytic, creative, and practical intelligence.

superego The repository of an individual's moral values, divided into the conscience—the internalization of society's rules and regulations—and the ego-ideal—the internalization of the individual's goals.

superordinate concept A general or overarching concept that includes basic-level concepts.

suprachiasmatic nuclei An area of the hypothalamus that provides a biological clock for circadian rhythms.

surface dyslexia A reading disorder in which people can read words phonetically but have difficulty reading irregularly spelled words by the whole-word method.

surface structure The grammatical features of a sentence; its words and syntax.

survey study A study of people's responses to standardized questions.

syllogism A logical construction that contains a major premise, a minor premise, and a conclusion. The major and minor premises are assumed to be true, and the truth of the conclusion is to be evaluated by deductive reasoning.

sympathetic branch The portion of the autonomic nervous system that activates functions that accompany arousal and expenditure of energy.

synapse The junction between the terminal button of one neuron and the membrane of a muscle fiber, a gland, or another neuron.

synaptic cleft A fluid-filled gap between the presynaptic and postsynaptic membranes; the terminal button releases a neurotransmitter into this space.

synaptic vesicle (*vess i kul*) A small, hollow, beadlike structure found in terminal buttons; contains molecules of a neurotransmitter.

syntactical rule A grammatical rule of a particular language for combining words to form phrases, clauses, and sentences.

system variable The variable controlled in a regulatory process; for example, temperature in a heating system.

systematic desensitization A form of behavior therapy in which the client is trained to relax in the presence of increasingly fearsome stimuli.

T lymphocytes White blood cells that develop in the thymus gland and produce antibodies that defend the body against fungi, viruses, and multicellular parasites.

tardive dyskinesia A serious movement disorder, distinguished by involuntary lip smacking, grimacing, and drooling, that may result from prolonged use of antipsychotic drugs.

target cell A cell whose physiological processes are affected by a particular hormone; contains special receptors that respond to the presence of the hormone.

targeted mutation A mutated gene (also called a "knockout gene") produced in the laboratory and inserted into the chromosomes of mice; abolishes the normal effects of the gene.

taste aversion Conditioning in which a distinctive taste (or smell) is paired with an ingested food that produces nausea, effective even with long intervals between the taste and nausea.

taste bud A small organ on the tongue that contains a group of gustatory receptor cells.

tectorial membrane A membrane located above the basilar membrane; serves as a shelf against which the cilia of the auditory hair cells move.

temperament An individual's pattern of behaviors and emotional reactions.

template A hypothetical pattern that is stored in the nervous system and is used to perceive objects or shapes by a process of comparison.

temporal coding A means by which the nervous system represents information; different features are coded by the pattern of activity of neurons.

temporal contiguity Relation between two events that occur close together in time.

temporal lobe (*tem por ul*) The portion of the cerebral cortex below the frontal and parietal lobes; contains the auditory cortex.

teratogens Substances, agents, and events that can cause birth defects.

terminal button The rounded swelling at the end of the axon of a neuron; releases a neurotransmitter.

texture gradient A monocular cue for depth perception; the relative fineness of detail present in the surfaces of objects or the ground or floor.

thalamus A region of the brain near the center of the cerebral hemispheres. All sensory information except that of olfaction is sent to the thalamus and then relayed to the cerebral cortex.

Thematic Apperception Test (TAT) A projective test in which a person is shown a series of ambiguous pictures that involve people. The person is asked to make up a story about what the people are doing or thinking. The person's responses are believed to reflect aspects of his or her personality.

theory A set of statements designed to explain a set of phenomena; more encompassing than a hypothesis.

theory of mind Expectations concerning how experience affects mental states, especially those of another.

theta activity Electroencephalogram activity of 3.5 to 7.5 Hz; occurs during the transition between sleep and wakefulness.

threat gesture Stereotyped gesture that signifies that one animal is likely to attack another.

threshold The point at which a stimulus, or a change in the value of a stimulus, can just be detected.

timbre (*tamm ber*) A perceptual dimension of sound that corresponds to its complexity.

tip-of-the-tongue phenomenon An occasional problem with retrieval of information that we are sure we know but cannot immediately remember.

token economy A form of behavior therapy often used in mental institutions; target behaviors are reinforced with tokens that are exchangeable for desirable goods or special privileges.

top-down processing Perception based on information provided by the context in which a particular stimulus is encountered.

Tourette's syndrome A neurological disorder characterized by tics and involuntary utterances, some of which may involve obscenities and the repetition of others' utterances.

transcranial magnetic stimulation (TMS) Direct stimulation of the cerebral cortex induced by magnetic fields generated outside the skull.

transduction The conversion of physical stimuli into changes in the activity of receptor cells of sensory organs.

transference A process in which a client begins to project powerful attitudes and emotions onto a psychoanalyst.

transsexual An individual who perceives himself or herself as belonging to a different sex than that which they were assigned at birth.

trephining A surgical procedure in which a hole is made in the skull of a living person.

trichromatic theory The theory that color vision is accomplished by three types of photodetectors, each of which is maximally sensitive to a different wavelength of light.

tritanopia A form of hereditary anomalous color vision; caused by a lack of "blue" cones in the retina.

two-point discrimination threshold The minimum distance between two small points that can be detected as separate stimuli when pressed against a particular region of the skin.

type A behavior pattern A behavior pattern characterized by impatience, high levels of competitiveness and hostility, and an intense disposition; supposedly associated with an increased risk of CHD.

type B behavior pattern A behavior pattern characterized by patience, relatively low levels of competitiveness and hostility, and an easygoing disposition; supposedly associated with a decreased risk of CHD.

umami (*oo mah mee*) The taste sensation produced by glutamate; identifies the presence of amino acids in foods.

unconditional positive regard In Rogers' approach, the therapist's assertion that a client's worth as a human being is not dependent on anything that he or she thinks, does, or feels; love and acceptance of an individual with no strings attached.

unconditioned response (UR) Response that is elicited by the US in a classical procedure.

unconditioned stimulus (US) Stimulus, such as food, that elicits a reflexive response, such as salivation, in a classical procedure.

unconscious The inaccessible part of the mind.

underextension The use of a word to denote a smaller class of items than is appropriate; for example, referring only to one particular animal as a dog.

undifferentiated schizophrenia A type of schizophrenia characterized by fragments of the symptoms of different types of schizophrenia.

validity The degree to which the operational definition of a variable accurately reflects the variable it is designed to measure or manipulate.

variable Anything capable of assuming any of several values.

variation First component of evolution: individual members of a species differ from one another.

ventral prefrontal cortex The region of the prefrontal cortex at the base of the anterior frontal lobes, involved in control of emotional behavior.

ventral stream The flow of information from the primary visual cortex to the visual association area in the lower temporal lobe; used to form the perception of an object's shape, color, and orientation (the "what" system).

ventricular zone A layer of cells that line the inside of the neural tube; contains founder cells that divide and give rise to cells of the central nervous system.

vergence movement The cooperative movement of the eyes, which ensures that the image of an object falls on identical portions of both retinas.

vertebra (plural, vertebrae) One of the bones that encases the spinal cord and constitutes the vertebral column.

vestibular apparatus The receptive organs of the inner ear that contribute to balance and perception of head movement.

vestibular sac One of two sets of receptor organs in each inner ear that detect changes in the tilt of the head.

visual agnosia The inability of a person who is not blind to recognize the identity or use of an object by means of vision; usually caused by damage to the brain.

voice-onset time The delay between the initial sound of a consonant (such as the puffing sound of the phoneme /p/) and the onset of vibration of the vocal cords.

wavelength The distance between adjacent waves of radiant energy; in vision most closely associated with the perceptual dimension of hue.

Weber fraction The ratio between a just-noticeable difference and the magnitude of a stimulus; reasonably constant over the middle range of most stimulus intensities.

Wechsler Adult Intelligence Scale (WAIS) An intelligence test for adults devised by David Wechsler; contains subtests divided into verbal and performance categories.

Wechsler Intelligence Scale for Children (WISC) An intelligence test for children devised by David Wechsler; similar in form to the Wechsler Adult Intelligence Scale.

Wernicke's aphasia A disorder caused by damage to the left temporal and parietal cortex, including Wernicke's area; characterized by deficits in the recognition of speech and by the production of fluent but essentially meaningless speech.

Wernicke's area A region of the auditory association cortex located in the upper part of the left temporal lobe; involved in the recognition of spoken words.

white matter The portions of the central nervous system that are abundant in axons rather than cell bodies of neurons. The color derives from the presence of the axons' myelin sheaths.

whole-word reading Reading by recognizing a word as a whole; "sight reading."

working memory Memory for new information and information retrieved from long-term memory; used in this text as another name for short-term memory.

zone of proximal development In Vygotsky's theory, the increased potential for problem-solving and conceptual abilities that exists for a child if expert mentoring and guidance are available.

zygotic stage The first stage of prenatal development, during which the zygote divides many times and the internal organs begin to form.

References

Abbott, A. (2008). The brains of the family. *Nature, 454*, 154–157.

Abela, J., & Sullivan, C. (2003). A test of Beck's cognitive diathesis-stress theory of depression in early adolescents. *Journal of Early Adolescence, 23(4)*, 384–404.

Abma, J. C., Martinez, G. M., Mosher, W. D., & Dawson, B. S. (2004). *Teenagers in the United States: Sexual activity, contraception use, and child bearing, 2002. Vital and health statistics. Series 23, Data from the National Survey of Family Growth*, Issue 24, December 2004, 1–48.

Abramson, L. Y., Alloy, L. B., & Metalsky, G. I. (1995). Hopelessness depression. In Buchanan, G. M. & Seligman, M. E. P. (Eds.), *Explanatory style* (pp. 113–134). Hillsdale, NJ: Lawrence Erlbaum Associates, Inc.

Abramson, L. Y., Metalsky, G. I., & Alloy, L. B. (1989). Hopelessness depression: A theory based subtype. *Psychological Review, 96*, 358–372.

Abramson, L. Y., Seligman, M. E. P., & Teasdale, J. D. (1978). Learned helplessness in humans: Critique and reformulation. *Journal of Abnormal Psychology, 87*, 49–74.

Acierno, R. E., Hersen, M. & Van Hasselt, V. B. (1993). Interventions for panic disorder: A critical review of the literature. *Clinical Psychology Review, 18*, 561–578.

Adair, J. G. (1984). The Hawthorne effect: A reconsideration of the methodological artifact. *Journal of Applied Psychology, 69*, 334–345.

Adair, J. G. (2001). Ethics of psychological research: New policies; continuing issues; new concerns. *Canadian Psychology, 42*, 25–37.

Adair, J. G., Paivio, A., & Ritchie, P. (1996). Psychology in Canada. *Annual Review of Psychology, 47*, 341–370.

Adamec, R. E., & Stark-Adamec, C. (1986). Limbic hyperfunction, limbic epilepsy, and interictal behavior: Models and methods of detection. In B. K. Doane & K. E. Livingston (Eds.), *The limbic system* (pp. 129–145). New York: Raven Press.

Adams, H. E., Bernat, J. A., & Luscher, K. A. (2001). Borderline personality disorder: An overview. In H. E. Adams & P. B. Sutker (Eds.), *Comprehensive handbook of psychopathology* (pp. 491–508). New York: Kluwer Academic.

Adler, A. (1939). *Social interest: A challenge to mankind*. New York: Putnam.

Aegisdóttir, S., White, M. J., Spenger, P.M., Maugherman, A. S., Anderson, L. A., Cook, R. S., Nichols, C. N., Lampropoulos, G. K., Walker, B. S., Cohen, G., & Rush, J. R. (2006). The Meta-analysis of Clinical Judgment Project: Fifty-six years of accumulated research on clinical versus statistical prediction. *The Counseling Psychologist. 34.* 341–382.

Aharon, L., Etcoff, N., Ariely, D., Chabris, C. F., O'Connor, E., & Breiter, H. C. (2001). Beautiful faces have variable reward value: fMRI and behavioral evidence. *Neuron, 32*, 537–551.

Ahrens, B., Grof, P., Moller, H.-J., Muller-Oerlinghaussen, B., & Wolf, T. (1995). Extended survival of patients on long-term lithium treatment. *Canadian Journal of Psychiatry, 40*, 241–246.

Aiken, L. R. (2001). *Dying, death, and bereavement* (4th ed.). Rahway, NJ: Lawrence Erlbaum.

Ainslie, G. (2003). Building blocks of self-control: Increased tolerance for delay with bundled rewards. *Journal of the Experimental Analysis of Behavior, 79*, 37–48.

Ainsworth, M. D. S., Blehar, M. C., Waters, E., & Wall, S. (1978). *Patterns of attachment*. Hillsdale, NJ: Lawrence Erlbaum.

Ainsworth, M. D. S ., & Bowlby, J. (1991). An ethological approach to personality development. *American Psychologist, 46*, 333–341.

Ajzen, I. (2001). Nature and operation of attitudes. *Annual Review of Psychology, 52*, 27–58.

Albright, L., Kenny, D. A., & Malloy, T. E. (1988). Consensus in personality judgments at zero acquaintance. *Journal of Personality and Social Psychology, 55*, 387–395.

Al-Issa, I. (1995). Culture and mental illness in an international perspective. In I. Al-Issa (Ed.), *Handbook of culture and mental illness: In international perspective* (pp. 3–49). Madison, CT: International Universities Press.

Allen, L. S., and Gorski, R. A. (1992). Sexual orientation and the size of the anterior commissure in the human brain. *Proceedings of the National Academy of Sciences, USA, 89*, 7199–7202.

Allen, M. G. (1976). Twin studies of affective illness. *Archives of General Psychiatry, 33*, 1476–1478.

Allik, J., & McCrae, R. R. (2002). A five-factor theory perspective. In R. R. McCrae & J. Allik (Eds.), *The five-factor model of personality across cultures* (pp. 303–321).

Allik, J., & McCrae, R. R. (2004). Toward a geography of personality traits: Patterns of profiles across 36 cultures. *Journal of Cross-Cultural Psychology, 35(1)*, 13–28.

Allis, C. D., Jenuwein, T., & Reinberg, D. (2007). Overview and concepts. In C. D. Allis, T. Jenuwein, & D. Reinberg (Eds.) *Epigenetics* (pp. 23–61). Cold Spring Harbor, NY: Cold Spring Harbor Laboratory Press.

Allport, G. W. (1968). The historical background of modern social psychology. In G. Lindzey & E. Aronson (Eds.), *The handbook of social psychology, Vol. 1* (pp. 3–56). Reading, MA: Addison-Wesley.

Allport, G. W., & Odbert, H. S. (1936). Traitnames: A psycholexical study. *Psychological Monographs, 47* (1, Whole No. 211).

Alsobrook, J. P., & Pauls, D. L. (1997). The genetics of Tourette syndrome. *Neurologic Clinics, 15*, 381–393.

Amaral, D. G. (1987). Memory: Anatomical organization of candidate brain regions. In F. Plum (Ed.), *Handbook of physiology, Section 1: Neurophysiology*, Vol. 5. *Higher functions of the brain* (pp. 211–294). Bethesda, MD: American Physiological Society.

Amaral, D. G., Price, J. L., Pitkänen, A., & Carmichael, S. T. (1992). Anatomical organization of the primate amygdaloid complex. In J. P. Aggleton (Ed.). *The Amygdala: Neurobiological aspects of emotion, memory, and mental dysfunction* (pp. 1–66). New York: Wiley-Liss.

American Psychiatric Association (2000). *Diagnostic and statistical manual of mental disorders* (4th ed. Text Revision). Washington, D. C.: Author.

American Psychiatric Association. (2004). *Practice guidelines for the treatment of patients with schizophrenia.* (2nd ed.) Washington, DC: Author.

American Psychological Association. (1953). *Ethical standards of psychologists.* Washington, DC: Author.

American Psychological Association. (2002). Ethical principles of psychologists and code of conduct. *American Psychologist, 57*, 1060–1073.

American Psychological Association. (2007). *Research with animals in psychology.* Washington, DC: APA Board of Scientific Affairs Committee on Animal Research and Ethics. Available at http://www.apa.org/science/animal2 .html. Downloaded 11 December, 2007.

Amsel, A. (1962). Frustrative nonreward in partial reinforcement and discrimination learning: Some recent history and a theoretical extension. *Psychological Review, 69*, 306–328.

Amsel, A. (1992). Frustration theory: Many years later. *Psychological Bulletin, 112*, 396–399.

Ancoli-Israel, S., & Roth, T. (1999). Characteristics of insomnia in the United States: Results of the 1991 National Sleep Foundation Survey. *Sleep, 22* (Supplement 2), S347–S353.

Anderson, D. R., & Collins, P. A. (1988). *The impact on children's education: Television's influence on cognitive development.* Washington, DC: U.S. Department of Education.

Anderson, D. R., & Field, D. (1983). Children's attention to television: Implications for production. In M. Meyer (Ed.), *Children and the formal features of television* (pp. 56–96). Munich: Saur.

Anderson, D. R., & Lorch, E. (1983). Looking at television: Action or reaction? In J. Bryant &

D. R. Anderson (Eds.), *Children's understanding of television: Research on attention and comprehension* (pp. 1–31). New York: Academic Press.

Anderson, R. H., Fleming, D. E., Rhees, R. W., & Kinghorn, E. (1986). Relationships between sexual activity, plasma testosterone, and the volume of the sexually dimorphic nucleus of the preoptic area in prenatally stressed and non-stressed rats. *Brain Research, 370,* 1–10.

Angrist, B. J., Rotrosen, J., & Gershon, S. (1980). Positive and negative symptoms in schizophrenia—Differential response to amphetamine and neuroleptics. *Psychopharmacology, 72,* 17–19.

Aponte, J., Rivers, R., & Wohl, J. (Eds.). (1995). *Psychological interventions and cultural diversity.* Boston: Allyn & Bacon.

Arcediano, F., Matute, H., & Miller, R. R. (1997). Blocking of Pavlovian conditioning in humans. *Learning and Motivation, 28,* 188–199.

Archer, S. L., & Waterman, A. S. (1990). Varieties of identity diffusions and foreclosures: An exploration of subcategories of the identity status. *Journal of Adolescent Research, 5,* 96–111.

Arieti, S. (2000). *The Parnas: A scene from the Holocaust.* Philadelphia: Paul Dry Books.

Ariyasu, H., Takaya, K., Tagami, T., Ogawa, Y., Hosoda, K., Akamizu, T., Suda, M., Koh, T., Natsui, K., Toyooka, S., Shirakami, G., Usui, T., Shimatsu, A., Doi, K., Hosoda, H., Kojima, M., Kangawa, K., & Nakao, K. (2001). Stomach is a major source of circulating ghrelin, and feeding state determines plasma ghrelin-like immunoreactivity levels in humans. *Journal of Clinical Endocrinology and Metabolism, 86,* 4753–4758.

Armfield, F. (1994). Preventing post-traumatic stress disorder resulting from military operations. *Military Medicine, 159,* 739–746.

Armstrong, G. B., & Chung, L. (2000). Background television and reading memory in context: Assessing TV interference and facilitative context effects on encoding versus retrieval processes. *Communication Research, 27,* 327–352.

Arrindell, W. A. (2003). Cultural abnormal psychology. *Behaviour Research Therapy, 41,* 749–753.

Asch, S. E. (1946). Forming impressions of personality. *Journal of Abnormal and Social Psychology, 41,* 258–290.

Asch, S. E. (1951). Effects of group pressure upon the modification and distortion of judgment. In H. Guetzkow (Ed.), *Groups, leadership, and men.* Pittsburgh: Carnegie.

Asch, S. E. (1952). *Social psychology.* New York: Prentice-Hall.

Asch, S. E. (1955). Opinions and social pressure. *Scientific American, 193,* 31–35.

Ashford, J. W., Schmitt, F. A., & Kumar, V. (1996). Diagnosis of Alzheimer's disease. *Psychiatric Annals, 26,* 262–268.

Assanand, S., Pinel, J. P. J., & Lehman, D. R. (1998). Personal theories of hunger and eating. *Journal of Applied Social Psychology, 28,* 998–1015.

Astafiev, S. V., Shulman, G. L., Stanley, C. M., Snyder, A. Z., Van Essen, D. C., & Corbetta, M. (2003). Functional organization of human intraparietal and frontal cortex for attending, looking, and pointing. *Journal of Neuroscience, 2003,* 4689–4699.

Atkinson, R. C., & Shiffrin, R. M. (1968). Human memory: A proposed system and its control processes. In K. W. Spence & J. T. Spence (Eds.), *The psychology of learning and motivation: Advances in research and theory,* Vol. 2. New York: Academic Press.

Aubry, J.-M., Ferrero, F., Schaad, N., & Bauer, M. S. (K. Harrison, trans.). (2007). *Pharmacotherapy of bipolar disorders.* Chichester, England: Wiley.

Avison, W. R., & Cairney, J. (2003). Social structure, stress, and personal control. In S. H. Zarit, L. I. Pearlin, and Schaie, K. W. (Eds.), *Personal control in social and life course contexts: Societal impact on aging* (pp. 127–164). New York: Springer.

Ayduk, O., Mendoza-Denton, R., Mischel, W., Downey, G., Peake, P. K., & Rodriguez, M. (2000). Regulating the interpersonal self: Strategic self-regulation for coping with rejection sensitivity. *Journal of Personality and Social Psychology, 79,* 776–792.

Ayllon, T., & Azrin, N. H. (1968). *The token economy: A motivational system for therapy and rehabilitation.* New York: Appleton-Century-Crofts.

Azar, B. (2002). Social cognitive neuroscience merges three distinct disciplines in hopes of deciphering the process behind social behavior. *Monitor on Psychology, 33*(1).

Azrin, N. H., Hutchison, R. R., & Hake, D. F. (1966). Extinction-induced aggression. *Journal of the Experimental Analysis of Behavior, 9,* 191–204.

Baars, B. J., & Gage, N. M. (Eds.) (2007). *Cognition, brain, and consciousness: An introduction to cognitive neuroscience.* London: Academic Press.

Badcock, C. (1991). *Evolution and individual behavior: An introduction to human sociobiology.* Cambridge, MA: Blackwell.

Baddeley, A. (2000). The episodic buffer: A new component of working memory? *Trends in Cognitive Sciences, 4,* 417–423.

Baddeley, A. D. (1982). Domains of recollection. *Psychological Review, 89,* 708–729.

Baddeley, A. D. (1993). Working memory and conscious awareness. In A. F. Collins, S. E. Cathercole, M. A. Conway, & P. E. Morris (Eds.), *Theories of memory.* Hillsdale, NJ: Erlbaum.

Baer, D. M., Peterson, R. F., & Sherman, J. A. (1967). Development of imitation by reinforcing behavioral similarity to a model. *Journal of the Experimental Analysis of Behavior, 10,* 405–418.

Baer, L., Rauch, S. L., Ballantine, H. T., Jr., Martuza, R., Cosgrove, R., Cassem, E., Giriunas, I., Manzo, P. A., Dimino, C., & Jenike, M. A. (1995). Cingulotomy for intractable obsessive-compulsive disorder: Prospective long-term follow-up of 18 patients. *Archives of General Psychiatry, 52,* 384–392.

Bahcall, O. (2005). Copy number and HIV/AIDS. *Nature Genetics, 37,* 124.

Bahrick, H. P. (1984). Semantic memory content in permastore: Fifty years of memory for Spanish learned in school. *Journal of Experimental Psychology: General, 113,* 12–29.

Bailey, C. H., Kandel, E. R., & Si, K. (2004). The persistence of long-term memory: A molecular approach to self-sustaining changes in learning-induced synaptic growth. *Neuron, 44,* 49–57.

Bailey, J. M., & Pillard, R. C. (1991). A genetic study of male sexual orientation. *Archives of General Psychiatry, 48,* 1089–1096.

Bailey, J. M., Pillard, R. C., Neale, M. C., & Agyei, Y. (1993). Heritable factors influence sexual orientation in women. *Archives of General Psychiatry, 50,* 217–223.

Balcetis, E., & Dunning, D. (2007). Cognitive dissonance and the perception of natural environments. *Psychological Science, 18,* 917–921.

Baldessarini, R. J., & Tarsy, D. (1980). Dopamine and the pathophysiology of dyskinesias induced by antipsychotic drugs. *Annual Review of Neuroscience, 3,* 23–41.

Baldwin, J. M. (1892). The psychological laboratory in the University of Toronto. *Science, 19,* 143–144.

Ballantine, H. T., Bouckoms, A. J., Thomas, E. K., & Giriunas, I. E. (1987). Treatment of psychiatric illness by stereotactic cingulotomy. *Biological Psychiatry, 22,* 807–819.

Balter. M. (2007). Neuroanatomy: Brain evolution studies go micro. *Science, 315,* 1208–1211.

Baltes, P., & Schaie, K. (1974, October). Aging and IQ: The myth of the twilight years. *Psychology Today,* 35–38.

Bandura, A. (1971). Psychotherapy based upon modeling principles. In A. E. Bergin & S. L. Garfield (Eds.), *Handbook of psychotherapy and behavior change.* New York: John Wiley & Sons.

Bandura, A. (1978). The self system in reciprocal determinism. *American Psychologist, 33,* 344–358.

Bandura, A. (1982). Self-efficacy mechanism in human agency. *American Psychologist, 37,* 122–147.

Bandura, A. (1986). *Social foundations of thought and action: A social-cognitive theory.* Englewood Cliffs, NJ: Prentice-Hall.

Bandura, A. (1995). Exercise of personal and collective efficacy in changing societies. In A. Bandura (Ed.), *Self-efficacy in changing societies.* New York: Cambridge University Press.

Bandura, A. (1997). *Self-efficacy: The exercise of control.* New York: W. H. Freeman.

Bandura, A. (2002). Social cognitive theory in cultural context. *Applied Psychology, 51*(2), 269–290.

Bandura, A., & Locke, E. A. (2003). Negative self-efficacy and goal effects revisited. *Journal of Applied Psychology, 88*(1), 87–99.

Bandura, A., Ross, D., & Ross, S. A. (1961). Transmission of aggression through imitation of aggressive models. *Journal of Abnormal and Social Psychology, 63,* 575–582.

Barab, S. A., & Plucker, J. A. (2002). Smart people or smart contexts? Cognition, ability and talent development in an age of situated approaches to knowing and learning. *Educational Psychologist, 37,* 165–182.

Barash, D. (1982). *Sociobiology and behavior.* London: Hodder and Stoughton.

Bard, K. A., Coles, C. D., Plaatzman, K. A., & Lynch, M. E. (2000). The effects of prenatal drug exposure, term status, and caregiving on arousal and arousal modulation in 8-week-old infants. *Developmental Psychobiology, 36,* 194–212.

Bargh, J. A., Gollwitzer, P. M., Lee-Chai, A. Y., Barndollar, K, & Troetschel, R. (2001). The automated will: Nonconscious activation and pursuit of behavioral goals. In T. C. Brock & M. C. Green (Eds.), *Persuasion: Psychological insights and perspectives,* 2nd ed. (pp. 41–62). Thousand Oaks, CA: Sage.

Barlassina, C. D., & Taglietti, M. V. (2003). Genetics of human arterial hypertension. *Journal of Nephrology, 16,* 609–615.

Barnas, M. V., Pollina, J., & Cummings, E. M. (1991). Life-span attachment: Relations between attachment and socioemotional functioning in women. *Genetic, Social, and General Psychology Monographs, 89,* 177–202.

Barnes, M. L., & Sternberg, R. J. (1997). A hierarchical model of love and its prediction of satisfaction in close relationships. In R. J. Sternberg & M. Hojjat (Eds.), *Satisfaction in close relationships* (pp. 79–101). New York: The Guilford Press.

Baron, R. S., Vandello, J. A., & Brunsman, B. (1996). The forgotten variable in conformity research: Impact of task importance on social influence. *Journal of Personality and Social Psychology, 71,* 915–927.

Bar-On, R. (1997). *BarOn Emotional Quotient Inventory: Technical manual.* Toronto: Multi-Health Systems.

Bar-On, R., Tranel, D., Denburg, N. L., & Bechara, A. (2004). Exploring the neurological substrate of emotional and social intelligence. In J. T. Cacioppo & G. G. Berntson (Eds.), *Social neuroscience: Key readings* (pp. 223–236). New York: Psychology Press.

Baron-Cohen, S., Leslie, A. M., & Frith, U. (1985). Does the autistic child have a "theory of mind"? *Cognition, 21,* 37–46.

Barrick, M. R., Mount, M. K., & Judge, T. A. (2001). Personality and performance at the beginning of the new millennium: What do we know and where do we go next? *International Journal of Selection & Assessment, 9(1–2),* 9–30.

Bartholomew, R. E. (1984). Disease, disorder, or deception? Latah as habit in a Malay extended family. *Journal of Nervous and Mental Disease, 182,* 331–338.

Bartlett, F. C. (1932). *Remembering: An experimental and social study.* Cambridge: Cambridge University Press.

Basheer, R., Strecker, R. E., Thankkar, M. M., & McCarley, R. W. (2004). Adenosine and sleep-wake regulation. *Progress in Neurobiology, 73,* 379–396.

Basoglu, M., Salclogle, E., & Livanou, M. (2002). Traumatic stress responses in earthquake survivors in Turkey. *Journal of Traumatic Stress, 15(4),* 269–276.

Bassili, J. N. (1993). Response latency versus certainty as indexes of the strength of voting intentions in a CATI survey. *Public Opinion Quarterly, 57,* 54–61.

Bassili, J. N. (1995). Response latency and the accessibility of voting intentions: What contributes to accessibility and how it affects vote choice. *Personality and Social Psychology Bulletin, 21,* 686–695.

Bassili, J. N. (2003). The minority slowness effect: Subtle inhibition in the expression of views not shared by others. *Journal of Personality and Social Psychology, 84,* 261–276.

Basso, A. (2003). *Aphasia and its therapy.* Oxford: Oxford University Press.

Bates, A. T., Patel, T. P., & Liddle, P. F. (2005). External behavior monitoring mirrors internal behavior monitoring. *Journal of Psychophysiology, 19,* 281–288.

Bates, E., & Dick, F. (2002). Language, gesture, and the developing brain. *Developmental Psychobiology, 40,* 293–310.

Bateson, G. (1973). *Steps to an ecology of mind.* New York: Paladin Books.

Bauer, P. J. (2002). Long-term recall memory: Behavioral and neuro-developmental changes in the first 2 years of life. *Current Directions in Psychological Science, 11,* 137–141.

Baum, W. M. (1974). On two types of deviation from the matching law: Bias and undermatching. *Journal of the Experimental Analysis of Behavior, 22,* 231–242.

Baum, W. M. (1979). Matching, undermatching, and overmatching in studies of choice. *Journal of the Experimental Analysis of Behavior, 32,* 269–281.

Baumeister, R. F., Dale, K., & Sommer, K. L. (1998). Freudian defense mechanisms and empirical findings in modern social psychology: Reaction formation, projection, displacement, undoing, isolation, sublimation, and denial. *Journal of Personality, 66,* 1081–1124.

Baumeister, R. F., Vohs, K. D., & Funder, D. C. (2007). Psychology as the science of self-reports and finger movements: Whatever happened to actual behavior? *Perspectives in Psychological Science, 2,* 361–376.

Baumrind, D. (1983). Rejoinder to Lewis' reinterpretation of parental firm control effects: Are authoritative families really harmonious? *Psychological Bulletin, 94,* 132–142.

Baumrind, D. (1991). The influence of parenting style on adolescent competence and substance use. *Journal of Early Adolescence, 11,* 56–95.

Beaupre, M. G., & Hess, U. (2005). Cross-cultural emotion recognition among Canadian ethnic groups. *Journal of Cross-cultural Psychology, 36,* 355–370.

Beauvois, M.-F., & Dérouesné, J. (1979). Phonological alexia: Three dissociations. *Journal of Neurology, Neurosurgery and Psychiatry, 42,* 1115–1124.

Beck, A. T., Rush, A. J., Shaw, B. F., & Emery, G. (1979). *Cognitive therapy of depression.* New York: Guilford Press.

BBC News. (2007). The fattening rooms of Calabar. July 19. (http://news.bbc.co.uk/2/hi/africa/6904640.stm)

Bechara, A., Tranel, D., Damasio, H., Adolphs, R., Rockland, C., & Damasio, A. R. (1995). Double dissociation of conditioning and declarative knowledge relative to the amygdala and hippocampus in humans. *Science, 269,* 1115–1118.

Beck, A. T. (1967). *Depression: Clinical, experimental and theoretical aspects.* New York: Harper and Row.

Beck, A. T. (1991). Cognitive therapy: A thirty-year retrospective. *American Psychologist, 46,* 368–375.

Beck, A. T. (1997). The past and future of cognitive therapy. *Journal of Psychotherapy Practice and Research, 6,* 276–284.

Becker, C. B., Zayfert, C., & Anderson, E. (2004). A survey of psychologists' attitudes toward and utilization of exposure therapy for PTSD. *Behaviour Research and Therapy, 42,* 277–292.

Behrend, D. A., Rosengren, K. S., & Perlmutter, M. (1992). The relation between private speech and parental interactive style. In R. M. Diaz & L. E. Berk (Eds.), *Private speech: From social interaction to self-regulation* (pp. 85–100). Hillsdale, NJ: Lawrence Erlbaum.

Beidler, L. M. (1970). Physiological properties of mammalian taste receptors. In *Taste and smell in vertebrates,* edited by G. E. W. Wolstenholme. London: J. & A. Churchill.

Bekoff, M. (2002). *Awareness: Animal reflections. Nature, 419,* 255.

Belin, P., Zatorre, R. J., & Ahad, P. (2002). Human temporal-lobe response to vocal sounds. *Cognitive Brain Research, 13,* 17–26.

Bell, A. P., Weinberg, M. S., & Hammersmith, S. K. (1981). *Sexual preference: Its development in men and women.* Bloomington: Indiana University Press.

Bell, K. E., & Baum, W. M. (2002). Group foraging sensitivity to predictable and unpredictable changes in food distribution: Past experience or present circumstances? *Journal of the Experimental Analysis of Behavior, 78,* 179–194.

Bell, S. T., Kuriloff, P. J., & Lottes, I. (1994). Understanding attributions of blame in stranger rape and date rape situations: An examination of gender, race, identification, and students' social perceptions of rape victims. *Journal of Applied Social Psychology, 24,* 1719–1734.

Bellugi, U., & Klima, E. S. (1972, June). The roots of language in the sign talk of the deaf. *Psychology Today,* 61–76.

Belmore, S. M. (1987). Determinants of attention during impression formation. *Journal of Experimental Psychology: Learning, Memory, and Cognition, 13,* 480–489.

Bem, D. J. (1972). Self-perception theory. In L. Berkowitz (Ed.), *Advances in experimental social psychology, Vol. 6.* New York: Academic Press.

Benedetti, F., Arduino, C., & Amanzio, M. (1999). Somatotopic activation of opioid systems by target-directed expectations of analgesia. *Journal of Neuroscience, 19,* 3639–3648.

Benzaquén, A. S. (2006). *Encounters with wild children: Temptation and disappointment in the study of human nature.* Montreal & Kinston, ON: McGill-Queen's University Press.

Berenbaum, S. A., & Snyder, E. (1995). Early hormonal influences on childhood sex-typed activity and playmate preferences: Implications for the development of sexual orientation. *Developmental Psychology, 31,* 31–42.

Berenson, A. (2008, February 24). Daring to think differently about schizophrenia. *The New York Times.*

Berk, L. E. (2005*). Infants, children, and adolescents* (5th ed.). Boston, MA: Allyn & Bacon.

Berlin, H. A., Rolls, E. T., & Kischika, U. (2004). Impulsivity, time perception, emotion and reinforcement sensitivity in patients with orbitofrontal cortex lesions. *Brain, 127,* 1108–1126.

Bernstein, W. M., Stephenson, B. O., Snyder, M. L., & Wicklund, R. A. (1983). Causal ambiguity and heterosexual affiliation. *Journal of Experimental Social Psychology, 19,* 78–92.

Berry, J. W. (1984). Towards a universal psychology of cognitive competence. In P. S. Fry (Ed.), *Changing conceptions of intelligence and intellectual functioning.* Amsterdam: North-Holland.

Berry, J. W. (2001). A psychology of immigration. *Journal of Social Issues, 57,* 615–631.

Berry, J. W. (2003). Origins of cross-cultural similarities and differences in human behavior: An ecocultural perspective. In A. Toomela (Ed.), *Cultural guidance in the development of the human mind: Advances in child development within culturally structured environments.* Westport, CT: Ablex Publishing.

Berry, J. W., Poortinga, Y. H., Segall, M. H., & Dasen, P. R. (2002). *Cross-cultural psychology: Research and applications* (2nd ed.). New York: Cambridge University Press.

Berthier, M. L. (2999). *Transcortical aphasias.* London: Psychology Press.

Biber, B., & Alkin, T. (1999). Panic disorder subtypes: Differential responses to CO-sub-2 challenge. *American Journal of Psychiatry, 156,* 739–744.

Bickel, W. K., & Vuchinich, R. E. (Eds.). (2000). *Reframing health behavior change with behavioral economics.* Mahwah, NJ: Lawrence Erlbaum Associates.

Bickham, D. S., Wright, J. C., & Huston, A. C. (2001). Attention, comprehension, and the educational influences of television. In D. G. Singer & J. L. Singer (Eds.), *Handbook of children and the media* (pp. 101–119). Thousand Oaks, CA: Sage Publications.

Biederman, I. (1987). Recognition-by-components: A theory of human image understanding. *Psychological Review, 94,* 115–147.

Binder, J. (1998). The therapeutic alliance in the relational models of time-limited dynamic psychotherapy. In J. D. Safran & J. C. Muran (Eds.), *The therapeutic alliance in brief psychotherapy.*

Washington, DC: American Psychological Association.

Binder, J. R., Frost, J. A., Hammeke, T. A., Cox, R. W., Rao, S. M., & Prieto, T. (1997). Human brain language areas identified by functional magnetic resonance imaging. *Journal of Neuroscience, 17,* 353–362.

Binder, J. R., Liebenthal, E., Possing, E. T., Medler, D. A., & Ward, B. D. (2004). Neural correlates of sensory and decision processes in auditory object identification. *Nature Neuroscience, 7,* 295–301.

Birbaumer, N., Veit, R., Lotze, M., Erb, M., Hermann, C., Grodd, W., & Flor, H. (2005). Deficient fear conditioning is psychopathy. *Archives of General Psychiatry, 62,* 799–805.

Birch, H. G. (1945). The relation of previous experience to insightful problem-solving. *Journal of Comparative Psychology, 38,* 367–383.

Birren, J. E., & Morrison, D. F. (1961). Analysis of the WISC subtests in relation to age and education. *Journal of Gerontology, 16,* 363–369.

Bishop, G. D. (1994). *Health psychology: Integrating mind and body.* Boston: Allyn & Bacon.

Blacher, J., & Baker, B. L. (1987). Dry-bed training for nocturnal enuresis in three children with multiple problems. *Journal of Clinical Child Psychology, 16(3),* 240–244.

Blackburn, R. G. L. (1995). Effect of degree of weight loss on health benefits. *Obesity Research, 3,* 211–216.

Blanchard, R., & Bogaert, A.F. (1996). Homosexuality in men and number of older brothers. *American Journal of Psychiatry, 153,* 27–31.

Blanchard, R., & Ellis, L. (2001). Birth weight, sexual orientation and the sex of preceding siblings. *Journal of Biosocial Science, 33,* 451–467.

Bleuler, E. (1950). *Dementia praecox: or, the group of schizophrenias. Monograph series on schizophrenia.* New York: International Universities Press.

Bliss, D. M. (2006). Strategies of human mating. *Psychological Topics, 2,* 239–260.

Bliss, E. L. (1986). *Multiple personality, allied disorders, and hypnosis.* New York: Oxford University Press.

Bliss, T. V., & Lomø, T. (1973). Long-lasting potentiation of synaptic transmission in the dentate area of the anaesthetized rabbit following stimulation of the perforant path. *Journal of Physiology, 232,* 331–356.

Bloom, L. (1970). *Language development: Form and function in emerging grammars.* Cambridge, MA: MIT Press.

Bodenhausen, G. V., Macrae, C. N., & Hugenberg, K. (2003). Social cognition. In T. Millon & M. Lerner (Eds.), *Handbook of psychology: Personality and social psychology, Vol. 5.* New York: John Wiley & Sons, Inc.

Boelens, H., Kop, P. F., Nagel, A. I., & Slangen, J. I. (1986). Concurrent schedules: Maximization versus reinforcement of changeover behavior. *Quarterly Journal of Experimental Psychology: Comparative and Physiological Psychology, 38,* 267–283.

Boeve, B. F., Silber, M. H., Saper, C. B., Ferman, T. J., Dickson, D. W., Parisi, J. E., Benarroch,

E. E., Ahlskog, J. E., Smith, G. E., Caselli, R. C., Tippman-Peikert, M., Olson, E. J., Lin, S.-C., Young, T., Wszolek, Z., Schenck, C. H., Mahowald, M. W., Castillo, P. R., Del Tredici, K., & Braak, H. (2007). Physiology of REM sleep behaviour disorder and relevance to neurodegenerative disease. *Brain, 130,* 2770–2788.

Bogaert, A. F. (2003). The interaction of fraternal birth order and body size in male sexual orientation. *Behavioral Neuroscience, 117,* 381–384.

Bogaert, A. F. (2006). Biological versus nonbiological older brothers and men's sexual orientation. *Proceedings of the National Academy of Science USA, 103,* 10771–10774.

Bohannon, J. N. (1993). Theoretical approaches to language acquisition. In J. B. Gleason (Ed.), *The development of language.* New York: Macmillan.

Bohannon, J. N., & Stanowicz, L. (1988). The issue of negative evidence: Adult responses to children's language errors. *Developmental Psychology, 24,* 684–689.

Bohannan, P. (1995). *How culture works.* New York: The Free Press.

Bohbot, V. D., Lerch, J., Thorndycraft, B., Iaria, G., & Zijdenbos, A. P. (2007). Gray matter differences correlate with spontaneous strategies in a human virtual navigation task. *Journal of Neuroscience, 27,* 10078–10083.

Bohman, M., Cloninger, C. R., von Knorring, A. L., & Sigvardsson, S. (1984). An adoption study of somatoform disorders. III. Cross-fostering analysis and genetic relationship to alcoholism and criminality. *Archives of General Psychiatry, 41,* 872–878.

Bondolfi, G., Dufour, H., Patris, M., May, J. P., Billeter, U., Eap, C. B., & Baumann, P. (1998). Risperidone versus Clozapine in treatment-resistant chronic schizophrenia: A randomized double-blind study. *American Journal of Psychiatry, 155,* 499–504.

Bones, A. K., & Johnson, N. R. (2007). Measuring the immeasurable: Or "Could Abraham Lincoln take the Implicit Association Test?" *Perspectives on Psychological Science, 2,* 406–411.

Bonvillian, J., Nelson, K. E., & Charrow, V. (1976). Languages and language-related skills in deaf and hearing children. *Sign Language Studies, 12,* 211–250.

Borckardt, J. J., Nash, M. R., Murphy, M. D., Moore, M., Shaw, D., & O'Neal, P. (2008). Clinical practice as natural laboratory for psychotherapy research: A guide to case-based time-series analysis. *American Psychologist, 63,* 77–95.

Bordin, E. S. (1994). Theory and research on the therapeutic working alliance: New directions. In A. O. Horvath & L. S. Greenberg (Eds.), *The working alliance: Theory, research, and practice* (pp. 13–37). New York: Wiley.

Bordnick, P. S., Elkins, R. L., Orr, T. E., Walters, P., & Thyer, B. A. (2004). Evaluating the relative effectiveness of three aversion therapies designed to reduce craving among cocaine abusers. *Behavioral Interventions, 19,* 1–24.

Bornstein, B., Stroka, H., & Munitz, H. (1969). Prosopagnosia with animal face agnosia. *Cortex, 5*, 164–169.

Bornstein, M. (1975). Influence of visual perception on culture. *American Anthropologist, 77*, 774–798.

Bornstein, M. H., & Arterberry, M. E. (2003). Recognition, discrimination and categorization of smiling by 5-month-old infants. *Developmental Science, 6*, 585–599.

Bornstein, M. H., Kessen, W., & Weiskopf, S. (1976). The categories of hue in infancy. *Science, 191*, 200–202.

Bostwick, J.M., & Martin, K.A. (2007). A man's brain in an ambiguous body: A case of mistaken gender identity. *The American Journal of Psychiatry, 164*, 1499–1505.

Bouchard, T. J., & McGue, M. (1981). Familial studies of intelligence: A review. *Science, 212*, 1055–1059.

Bouchard, T. J., & Propping, P. (Eds.). (1993). *Twins as a tool of behavior genetics*. Chichester, UK: Wiley.

Bouchard, T. J., Jr. (1997). The genetics of personality. In K. Blum & E. P. Noble (Eds.), *The handbook of psychiatric genetics* (pp. 273–296). Boca Raton, FL: CRC Press Inc.

Bouchard, T. J., Jr., & Hur, Y.-M. (1998). Genetic and environmental influences on the continuous scales of the Myers-Briggs Type Indicator: An analysis based on twins reared apart. *Journal of Personality, 66*, 135–149.

Bouton, M. E., Mineka, S., & Barlow, D. H. (2001). A modern learning theory perspective on the etiology of panic disorder. *Psychological Review, 108*, 4–32.

Bower, G. H. (1970). Analysis of a mnemonic device. *American Scientist, 58*, 496–510.

Bower, G. H., & Clark, M. C. (1969). Narrative stories as mediators for serial learning. *Psychonomic Science, 14*, 181–182.

Bower, M. (1991). Classification of disciplinary events and choices as a function of childhood history. Unpublished manuscript. University of Iowa, Iowa City, IA.

Bowlby, J. (1969). *Attachment and loss. Vol. 1: Attachment*. New York: Basic Books.

Bowlby, J. (1973). *Attachment and loss. Vol. 2*. New York: Basic Books.

Bowlby, J. (1982). Attachment and loss: Retrospect and prospect. *American Journal of Orthopsychiatry, 52*, 664–678.

Bowlby, J. (1988). *A secure base: Parent-child attachment and healthy human development*. New York: Basic Books.

Boyer, P., & Nissenbaum, S. (1972). *Salem-Village witchcraft: A documentary record of local conflict in colonial New England*. Belmont, CA: Wadsworth.

Boynton, R. M. (1997). *Human color vision*. New York: Holt, Rinehart & Winston.

Boysen, S. T., & Hymes, G. T. (1999). Current issues and emerging theories in animal cognition. *Annual Review of Psychology, 50*, 683–705.

Bradley, C. L., & Marcia, J. E. (1998). Generativity-stagnation: A five-category model. *Journal of Personality, 66*, 39–64.

Bradley, R., Conklin, C. Z., & Westen, D. (2007). Borderline personality disorder. In W. O'Donohue, K A. Fowler, & S. O. Lilienfeld (Eds.), *Personality disorders: Toward the DSM-V* (pp. 167–201). Thousand Oaks, CA: Sage.

Brainerd, C. J. (2003). Jean Piaget, learning research, and American education. In B. J. Zimmerman (Ed.), *Educational psychology: A century of contributions*. Mahwah, NJ: Lawrence Erlbaum.

Brandon, S. E., Betts, S. L., & Wagner, A. E. (1994). Discriminated, lateralized eyeblink conditioning in the rabbit: An experimental context for separating specific and general associative influences. *Journal of Experimental Psychology: Animal Behavior Processes, 20*, 292–307.

Bransford, J. D., & Johnson, M. K. (1972). Contextual prerequisites for understanding: Some investigations of comprehension and recall. *Journal of Verbal Learning and Verbal Behavior, 11*, 717–726.

Brass, M., & Heyes, C. (2003). Imitation: Is cognitive neuroscience solving the correspondence problem? *Trends in Cognitive Sciences, 9*, 489–495.

Brauer, M., Judd, C. M., & Gliner, M. D. (1995). The effects of repeated expressions on attitude polarization during group discussion. *Journal of Personality and Social Psychology, 68*, 1014–1029.

Brehm, S. S. (1992). *Intimate relationships* (2nd ed.). New York: McGraw-Hill.

Brett, M. A., Roberts, L. F., Johnson, T. W., & Wassersug, R. J. (2007). Eunuchs in contemporary society: Expectations, consequences, and adjustments to castration (Part II). *Journal of Sexual Medicine, 4*, 946–955.

Brewin, C. R., Andrews, B., & Valentine, J. D. (2000). Meta-analysis of risk factors for post-traumatic stress disorder in trauma-exposed adults. *Journal of Consulting and Clinical Psychology, 68*, 748–766.

Briggs, S. R. (1988). Shyness: Introversion or neuroticism? *Journal of Research in Personality, 22*, 290–307.

Brintlinger, A., & Vinitsky, I. (Eds.) (2007). *Madness and the mad in Russian culture*. Toronto: University of Toronto Press.

Broadbent, D. E. (1958). *Perception and communication*. London: Pergamon Press.

Broberg, A. G., Wessels, H., Lamb, M. E., & Hwang, C. P. (1997). Effects of day care on the development of cognitive abilities in 8-year-olds: A longitudinal study. *Developmental Psychology, 33*, 62–69.

Brockdorf, N., & Turner, B. M. (2007). Dosage compensation in mammals. In C. D. Allis, T. Jenuwein, D. Reinberg, & Caparros, M.-L. (Eds.) Epigenetics. (pp. 321–340). Cold Spring Harbor, N.Y.: Cold Spring Harbor Laboratory Press.

Brooks-Gunn, J. (1988). Antecedents and consequences of variations in girls' maturational timing. *Journal of Adolescent Health Care, 9*, 365–373.

Brooks-Gunn, J. (1989). Pubertal processes and the early adolescent transition. In W. Damon (Ed.), *Child development today and tomorrow*. San Francisco: Jossey-Bass.

Broverman, I. K., Vogel, S. R., Broverman, D. M., Clarkson, F. E., & Rosenkrantz, P. S. (1972). Sex-role stereotypes: A current appraisal. *Journal of Social Issues, 28*, 59–78.

Brown, A. S. (1991). A review of the tip-of-the-tongue experience. *Psychological Bulletin, 109*, 204–223.

Brown, A. S. (2002). Consolidation theory and retrograde amnesia in humans. *Psychonomic Bulletin & Review, 9*, 403–425.

Brown, A. S., Begg, M. D., Gravenstein, S., Schaefer, C. A., Wyatt, R. J., Bresnahan, M., Bagulas, V. P., & Susser, E. S. (2004). Serological evidence of prenatal influenza in the etiology of schizophrenia. *Archives of General Psychiatry, 61*, 771–780.

Brown, G. W. (1985). The discovery of expressed emotion: Induction or deduction? In J. Leff & C. Vaughn (Eds.), *Expressed emotion in families* (pp. 7–25). New York: Guilford Press.

Brown, G. W., Bone, M., Dalison, B., & Wing, J. K. (1966). *Schizophrenia and social care*. London: Oxford University Press.

Brown, J. (1958). Some tests of the decay theory of immediate memory. *Quarterly Journal of Experimental Psychology, 10*, 12–21.

Brown, J. D., & Rogers, R. (1991). Self-serving attributions: The role of physiological arousal. *Personality and Social Psychology Bulletin, 17*, 501–506.

Brown, P. L., & Jenkins, H. M. (1968). Autoshaping of the pigeon's keypeck. *Journal of the Experimental Analysis of Behavior, 11*, 1–8.

Brown, R. (1973). *A first language: The early stages*. Cambridge, MA: Harvard University Press.

Brown, R., & Bellugi, U. (1964). Three processes in the child's acquisition of syntax. *Harvard Education Review, 34*, 133–151.

Brown, R., & Hanlon, C. (1970). Derivational complexity and order of acquisition in child speech. In J. R. Hayes (Ed.), *Cognition and the development of language*. New York: John Wiley & Sons.

Brown, R. W., & Kulik, J. (1977). Flashbulb memories. *Cognition, 5*, 73–99.

Brown, R., & McNeill, D. (1966). The "tip-of-the-tongue" phenomenon. *Journal of Verbal Learning and Verbal Behavior, 5*, 325–337.

Bruner, J. S. (1983). *Child's talk: Learning to use language*. New York: Norton.

Bruner, J. S. (1998). The ontogenesis of speech acts. In A. Kasher (Ed.), *Pragmatics: Critical concepts*. (pp. 253–273). London: Routledge.

Bruner, J. S., Goodnow, J. J., & Austin, G. A. (1956). *A study of thinking*. New York: Wiley.

Buck, L., and Axel, R. (1991). A novel multigene family may encode odorant receptors: A molecular basis for odor recognition. *Cell, 65*, 175–187.

Bugenhausen, G. V., Macrae, C. N., & Hugenberg, K. (2003). Social cognition. In T. Millon & M. Lerner (Eds.), *Handbook of psychology: Personality and social psychology, Vol. 5* (pp. 257–282). New York: Wiley.

Buller, D. J. (2005). *Adapting minds: Evolutionary psychology and the persistent quest for human nature.* Cambridge, MA: MIT Press.

Bureau of Labor Statistics. (2006). May 2006 national occupational employment and wage estimates. Retrieved 15 July, 2007 Available at http://www.bls.gov/oes/current/oes_nat.htm.

Bureau of Labor Statistics (May 9, 2007). Employment characteristics of families summary. News, United States Department of Labor. Retrieved from http://www.bls.gov/news.release/famee.nr0.htm. March 31, 2008.

Burnstock, G., & Wood, J. N. (1996). Purinergic receptors: Their role in nociception and primary afferent neurotransmission. *Current Opinion in Neurobiology, 6,* 526–532.

Burt, C. D. B., Kemp, S., & Conway, M. (2001). What happens if you retest autobiographical memory 10 years on? *Memory & Cognition, 29,* 127–136.

Busch, F. (2003a). Back to the future. *Psychoanalytic Quarterly, 72(1),* 201–215.

Busch, F. (2003b). Telling stories. *Journal of the American Psychoanalytic Association, 51(1),* 25–42.

Buschmann, H., Diaz, J. L, Holenz, J., Párraga, A., Torrens, A., & Vela, J. M. (Eds.) (2007). *Antidepressants, antipsychotics, anxiolytics: From chemistry and pharmacology to clinical application.* Weinhelm, Germany: Wiley VCH.

Bushman, B. J., & Huesmann, L. R. (2001). Effects of televised violence on aggression. In D. G. Singer & J. L. Singer (Eds.), *Handbook of children and the media* (pp. 223–253). Thousand Oaks, CA: Sage Publications.

Buskist, W., & Miller, H. L. (1986). Interaction between rules and contingencies in the control of human fixed-interval performance. *Psychological Record, 36,* 109–116.

Buss, A. H. (1995). *Personality: Temperament, social behavior, and the self.* Boston: Allyn & Bacon.

Buss, D. (2007). *Evolutionary psychology: The new science of the mind* (3rd ed.). Boston: Allyn & Bacon.

Buss, D. M. (1989). Sex differences in human mate preferences: Evolutionary hypotheses tested in 37 cultures. *Behavioral and Brain Sciences, 12,* 1–49.

Buss, D. M. (1990). International preferences in selecting mates: A study of 37 societies. *Journal of Cross-cultural Psychology, 21,* 5–47.

Buss, D. M. (1992). Mate preferences mechanisms: Consequences for partner choice and intrasexual competition. In J. H. Barkow, L. Cosmides, & J. Tooby (Eds.), *The adapted mind: Evolutionary psychology and the generation of culture.* New York: Oxford University Press.

Buss, D. M. (2006). Strategies of human mating. *Psychological Topics, 2,* 239–260.

Buss, D. M., Haselton, M. G., Shackelford, T. K., Bleske, A. L., & Wakefield, J. C. (1998). Adaptations, exaptations, and spandrels. *American Psychologist, 53,* 533–548.

Buss, D. M., & Schmitt, D. P. (1993). Sexual strategies theory: An evolutionary perspective on human mating. *Psychological Review, 100,* 204–232.

Buston, P. M., & Emlen, S. T. (2003). Cognitive processed underlying human mate choice: The relationship between self-perception and mate preference in Western society. *Proceedings of the National Academy of Sciences, 100,* 8805–8810.

Buswell, G. T. (1937). *How adults read.* Chicago: University of Chicago Press.

Butcher, J. N. (Ed.). (2000). *Basic sources on the MMPI-2.* Minneapolis: University of Minneapolis Press.

Butcher, J., Hooley, J. M., Carson, R., & Mineka, S. (2007). *Abnormal psychology,* 13th ed. Boston, MA: Allyn & Bacon.

Butterfoss, F. D. (2007). *The challenge of implementation: Coalitions in community intervention.* San Francisco: Jossey-Bass.

Buxbaum, L. J., Glosser, G., & Coslett, H. B. (1999). Impaired face and word recognition without object agnosia. *Neuropsychologia, 37(1),* 41–50.

Byrne, D. (1997). An overview (and underview) of research and theory on the attraction paradigm. *Journal of Social & Personal Relationships, 14,* 417–431.

Byrne, D., & Griffitt, W. (1973). Interpersonal attraction. *Annual Review of Psychology, 24,* 317–338.

Cacioppo, J. T. (2002). Social neuroscience: Understanding the pieces fosters understanding the whole and vice versa. *American Psychologist, 57,* 819–831.

Cacioppo, J. T., Berntson, G. G., Lorig, T. S., Norris, C. J., Rickett, E., & Nusbaum. H. (2003). Just because you're imaging the brain doesn't mean you can stop using your head: A primer and set of first principles. *Journal of Personality and Social Psychology, 85,* 650–657.

Cacioppo, J. T., Petty, R. E., & Crites, S. L. (1993). Attitude change. In V. S. Ramachandran (Ed.), *Encyclopedia of human behavior.* San Diego: Academic Press.

Calkins, M. W. (1892). Experimental psychology at Wellesley College. *American Journal of Psychology, 6,* 464–471.

Callaway. E. (2007). *Asylum: A mid-century madhouse and its lessons about our mentally ill today.* Westport, CT: Praeger.

Cambronne, D., Shih, J., & Harri, K. (1999). Innovative stress management for financial service organizations. In J. Oher (Ed.), *The employee assistance handbook* (pp. 117–138). New York: John Wiley & Sons.

Campbell, D. T. (1974). Evolutionary epistemology. In P. A. Schlipp (Ed.), *The philosophy of Karl Popper* (Vol. 14-1, pp. 413–463). LaSalle, IL: Open Court Publishing.

Campbell, D. T. (1975). On the conflicts between biological and social evolution and between psychology and moral tradition. *American Psychologist, 30,* 1103–1126.

Campbell, D. T. (1976). On the conflicts between biological and social evolution and between psychology and moral tradition. *American Psychologist, 30,* 1103–1126.

Campfield, L. A., Smith, F. J., Guisez, Y., Devos, R., & Burn, P. (1995). Recombinant mouse OB protein: Evidence for a peripheral signal linking adiposity and central neural networks. *Science, 269,* 546–549.

Canadian Psychological Association. (2000). *Canadian code of ethics for psychologists* (3rd ed.). Ottawa: Author.

Canli, T., Sivers, H., Whitfield, S. L., Gotlib, I. H., & Gabrieli, J. D. E. (2002). Amygdala response to happy faces as a function of extraversion. *Science, 296,* 2191.

Canli, T., Zhao, Z., Desmond, J. E., Kang, E., Gross, J., & Gabrieli, J. D. E. (2001). An fMRI study of personality influences on brain reactivity to emotional stimuli. *Behavioral Neuroscience, 115,* 33–42.

Cannon, W. B. (1927). The James-Lange theory of emotions: a critical examination and an alternative theory. Reprinted in *American Journal of Psychology,* 1987, *100,* 567–586.

Cannon, W. B. (1929). *Bodily changes in pain, hunger, fear, and rage: An account of recent researches into the function of emotional excitement.* New York: Appleton-Century-Crofts.

Cannon, W. B. (1953). *Bodily changes in pain, hunger, fear and rage: An account of recent researches into the function of emotional excitement.* (2nd ed.). Boston: Charles T. Branford.

Cannon, W. B., & Washburn, A. L. (1912). An explanation of hunger. *American Journal of Physiology, 29,* 444–454.

Capaldi, E. J., Haas, A. I., Miller, R. M., & Martins, A. (2005). How transitions from nonrewarded to rewarded trials regulate responding in pavlovian and instrumental learning following extensive acquisition training. *Learning and Motivation, 36,* 279–296.

Caplan, D., Alpert, N., & Waters, G. (1999). PET studies of syntactic processing with auditory sentence presentation. *NeuroImage, 9,* 343–351.

Caporael, L. R. (2001). Evolutionary psychology: Toward a unifying theory and a hybrid science. *Annual Review of Psychology, 52,* 607–628.

Caprara, G.V., & Perugini, M. (1994). Personality described by adjectives: Generalizability of the Big Five to the Italian lexical context. *European Journal of Personality, 8,* 357–369.

Carey, B. (2007). *Alex, a parrot who had a way with words, dies.* New York Times. Retrieved September 9, 2007 from http://www.nytimes.com/2007/09/10/science.

Carlson, E. A. (1998). A prospective longitudinal study of attachment disorganization/disorientation. *Child Development, 69,* 1107–1128.

Carlson, N. (2005). *Foundations of physiological psychology.* Boston: Pearson.

Carlson, N. R. (2007). *Physiology of behavior* (9th ed.). Boston: Pearson.

Caroff, X. (2002). What conservation anticipation reveals about cognitive change. *Cognitive Development, 17,* 1015–1035.

Carpendale, J. I. M. (2000). Kohlberg and Piaget on stages and moral reasoning. *Developmental Review, 20,* 181–205.

Carpenter, P. A., & Just, M. A. (1983). What your eyes do while your mind is reading. In

K. Rayner (Ed.), *Eye movements in reading: Perceptual and language processes.* New York: Academic Press.

Carpenter, P. A., Miyake, A., & Just, M. A. (1995). Language comprehension: Sentence and discourse processing. *Annual Review of Psychology, 46,* 91–120.

Carpenter, W. T., Conley, R. R., Buchanan, R. W., Breier, C. A., & Tamminga, C. A. (1995). Patient response and resource management: Another view of clozapine treatment of schizophrenia. *American Journal of Psychiatry, 152,* 827–832.

Carr, E. G., & Lovaas, O. I. (1983). Contingent electric shock as a treatment for severe behavior problems. In S. Axelrod & J. Apsche (Eds.), *The effect of punishment on human behavior* (pp. 221–245). New York: Academic Press.

Carrion-Baralt, J. R., Smith, C. J., Rossy-Fullana, E., Lewis-Fernandez, R., Davis, K. L., & Silverman, J. M. (2006). Seasonality effects in schizophrenic births in multiplex families in a tropical island. *Psychiatry Research, 142,* 93–97.

Carroll, J. B. (1993). *Human cognitive abilities: A survey of factor-analytic studies.* New York: Cambridge University Press.

Carroll, S. B. (2003). Genetics and the making of Homo sapiens. *Nature, 422,* 849–857.

Carson, R. C., Butcher, J. N., & Mineka, S. (2000). *Abnormal psychology and modern life* (11th ed.). Boston: Allyn & Bacon.

Case, R. (1998). The development of central conceptual structures. In D. Kuhn & R. Siegler (Eds.), *Handbook of child psychology: Vol. 2. Cognition, perception, and language.* (5th ed., pp. 745–800). New York: Wiley.

Caspi, A., McClay, J., Moffitt, T. E., Mill, J., Martin, J., Craig, I. W., Taylor, A, & Poulton, R. (2002). Role of genotype in the cycle of violence in maltreated children. *Science, 297,* 851–854.

Catania, A. C. (1971). Reinforcement schedules: The role of responses preceding the one that produces the reinforcer. *Journal of the Experimental Analysis of Behavior, 15,* 271–287.

Catania, A. C., Mathews, B. A., & Shimoff, E. (1982). Instructed versus shaped human verbal behavior: Interactions with nonverbal responding. *Journal of the Experimental Analysis of Behavior, 38,* 233–248.

Caterina, M. J., Leffler, A., Malmberg, A. B., Martin, W. J., Trafton, J., Petersen-Zeitz, K. R., Koltzenburg, M., Basbaum, A. I., & Julius, D. (2000). Impaired nociception and pain sensation in mice lacking the capsaicin receptor. *Science, 288,* 306–313.

Cath, D. C., Spinhoven, P., van de Wetering, B. J. M., Hoogduin, C. A. H., Landman, A. D., van Woerkom, T. C. A. M., Roos, R. A. C., & Rooijmans, H. G. M. (2000). The relationship between types and severity of repetitive behaviors in Gilles de la Tourette's disorder and obsessive-compulsive disorder. *Journal of Clinical Psychology, 61,* 505–513.

Cattell, R. A. (1963). Theory of fluid and crystallized intelligence: A critical experiment. *Journal of Educational Psychology, 54,* 1–22.

Cavaco, S., Anderson, S. W., Allen, J. S., Castro-Caldas, A., & Damasio, H. (2004). The scope of preserved procedural memory in amnesia. *Brain, 127,* 1863–1867.

Cavanaugh, J. C. (1990). *Adult development and aging.* Belmont, CA: Wadsworth.

Centers for Disease Control. (2002). Alcohol use among women of childbearing age—United States, 1991–1999. *Morbidity and Mortality Weekly Reports, 51,* 273–276.

Centers for Disease Control. (2006). Youth risk behavior surveillance—United States, 2005. *Morbidity and Mortality Weekly Report, 55* (SS-5), 1–108.

Chakos, M., Lieberman, J., Hoffman, E., Bradford, D., & Sheitman, B. (2001). Effectiveness of second-generation antipsychotics in patients with treatment-resistant schizophrenia: A review and meta-analysis of randomized trials. *American Journal of Psychiatry, 158(4),* 518–526.

Chandra A, Martinez G. M., Mosher W. D., Abma J. C., & Jones J. (2005) Fertility, family planning, and reproductive health of U.S. women: Data from the 2002 National Survey of Family Growth. National Center for Health Statistics. *Vital Health Statistics, 23(25),* 1–160.

Chang, K. (2007, July 20). Champion at checkers that cannot lose to people. New York: *New York Times.*

Chapin, F. S. (1938). Design for social experiments. *American Sociological Review, 3,* 786–800.

Chapman, B. P., Duberstein, P. R., Sörensen, S., & Lyness, J. M. (2007). Gender differences in Five Factor Model personality traits in an elderly cohort. *Personality and Individual Differences, 43,* 1594–1603.

Chapman, K. L., Leonard, L. B., & Mervis, C. B. (1986). The effect of feedback on young children's inappropriate word usage. *Journal of Child Language, 13,* 101–117.

Charman, D. P. (2004). Effective psychotherapy and effective psychotherapists. In D. P. Charman (Ed.), *Core processes in brief psychodynamic psychotherapy: Advancing effective practice* (pp. 3–22). Mahwah, NJ: Lawrence Erlbaum Associates.

Chasdi, E. H. (1994). *Culture and human development: The selected papers of John Whiting.* New York: Cambridge University Press.

Chemelli, R. M., Willie, J. T., Sinton, C. M., Elmquist, J. K., Scammell, T. E., Lee, C., Richardson, J. A., Williams, S. C., Xiong, Y., Kisanuki, Y., Fitch, T. E., Nakazato, M., Hamer, R. E., Saper, C. B., & Yanagisawa, M. (1999). Narcolepsy in orexin knockout mice: molecular genetics of sleep regulation. *Cell, 98,* 437–451.

Cheng, P. N., & Holyoak, K. J. (1985). Pragmatic reasoning schemas. *Cognitive Psychology, 17,* 391–416.

Cheour, M., Ceponiene, R., Lehtokoski, A., Luuk, A., Allik, J., Alho, K., & Näätänen, R. (1998).

Cherry, E. C. (1953). Some experiments on the recognition of speech, with one and with two ears. *Journal of the Acoustical Society of America, 25,* 975–979.

Choi, I., & Nisbett, R. E. (1998). Situational salience and cultural differences in the correspondence bias and actor-observer bias. *Personality and Social Psychology Bulletin, 24,* 949–960.

Christensen, A., & Heavey, C. L. (1999). Intervention for couples. *Annual Review of Psychology, 50,* 165– 190.

Chu, S., & Downes, J. J. (2000). Odour-evoked autobiographical memories: Psychological investigations of proustian phenomena. *Chemical Senses, 25,* 111–116.

Chua, H. F., Leu, J., & Nisbett, R. E. (2005). Cultural variation in eye movements during scene perception. *Proceedings of the National Academy of Sciences, 102,* 12629–12633.

Chung, K. C., Kowalski, C. P., Kim, H. M., & Buchman, S. R. (2000). Maternal cigarette smoking during pregnancy and the risk of having a child with cleft lip/palate. *Plastic and Reconstructive Surgery, 105,* 485–491.

Chung, W. C. J., De Vries, G. J., & Swaab, D. R. (2002). Sexual differentiation of the bed nucleus of the stria terminalis in humansmay extend into adulthood. *Journal of Neuroscience, 22,* 1027–1033.

Church, A. T., Katigbak, M. S., Ortiz, F. A., del Prado, A. M., Vargas-Flores, J., Ibanez-Reyes, J., Reyes, J. A. S., Pe-Pua, R. & Cabrera, H. F. (2005). Investigating implicit trait theories across cultures. *Journal of Cross-Cultural Psychology, 36,* 476–496.

Cialdini, R. B. (1993). *Influence: Science and practice* (3rd ed.). New York: HarperCollins.

Cialdini, R. B. (2000). *Influence: Science and practice* (4th ed.). Boston: Allyn & Bacon.

Cialdini, R. B., & Goldstein, N. J. (2004). Social influence: Compliance and conformity. *Annual Review of Psychology, 55,* 591–621.

Ciotti, F. (1998). *Freud and the question of pseudoscience.* Chicago: Open Court Publishing.

Clark, D. A., Beck, A. T., & Alford, B. A. (1999). *Scientific foundations of cognitive theory and therapy of depression.* New York: John Wiley & Sons, Inc.

Clark, F. C. (1958). The effect of deprivation and frequency of reinforcement on variable-interval responding. *Journal of the Experimental Analysis of Behavior, 1,* 221–228.

Cleckley, H. (1976). *The mask of sanity.* St. Louis: C. V. Mosby.

Cloninger, C. R. (1987). Neurogenetic adaptive mechanisms in alcoholism. *Science, 236,* 410–416.

Cloninger, C. R., Bohman, M., Sigvardsson, S., & von Knorring, A. L. (1985). Psychopathology in adopted-out children of alcoholics. The Stockholm Adoption Study. *Recent Developments in Alcoholism, 7,* 235.

Cloninger, C. R., Sigvardsson, S., Pryzbeck, T. R., & Svrakic, D. M. (1995). Personality antecedents of alcoholism in a national area probability study. *European Archives of Psychiatry and Clinical Neuroscience, 245,* 239–244.

Cobos, P., Sanchez, M., Garcia, C., Nieves, V. M., & Vila, J. (2002). Revisiting the James versus Cannon debate on emotion: startle and autonomic modulation in patients with spinal injuries. *Biological Psychology, 61,* 251–269.

Coccaro, E. F., & Kavoussi, R. J. (1997). Fluoxetine and impulsive aggressive behavior in personality disordered subjects. *Archives of General Psychiatry, 54,* 1081–1088.

Coccaro, E. F., Silverman, J. M., Klar, H. M., Horvath, T. B., & Siever, L. J. (1994). Familial correlates of reduced central serotonergic system function in patients with personality disorders. *Archives of General Psychiatry, 51,* 318–324.

Cohen, J. (2007a). Relative differences: The myth of 1%. *Science, 316,* 1836.

Cohen, J. (2007b). Reconstructing the origins of the AIDS epidemic from archived HIV isolates. *Science, 318,* 731.

Cohen, M., Brom, D., & Dasberg, H. (2001). Child survivors of the Holocaust: Symptoms and coping after fifty years. *Israel Journal of Psychiatry & Related Sciences, 38(1),* 3–12.

Cohen, M. E., Robins, E., Purtell, J. J., Altmann, M.W., & Reid, D. E. (1953). Excessive surgery in hysteria: Study of surgical procedures in 50 women with hysteria and 190 controls. *Journal of the American Medical Association, 151,* 977–986.

Cohen-Bendehan, C. C., van de Beek, C., & Berenbaum, S. A. (2005) Prenatal sex hormone effects on child and adult sex-typed behavior: Methods and findings. *Neuroscience and Biobehavioral Reviews, 47,* 230–237.

Colapinto, J. (2000). *As nature made him: The boy who was raised as a girl.* Toronto, ON: HarperCollins.

Colapinto, J. (2007, June 13). The interpreter: Has a remote Amazonian tribe upended our understanding of language? *The New Yorker,* pp. 118–137.

Collins, A. M., & Quillian, M. R. (1969). Retrieval time from semantic memory. *Journal of Verbal Learning and Verbal Behavior, 8,* 240–248.

Conley, R. R., & Kelly, D. L. (2001). Management of treatment resistance in schizophrenia. *Society of Biological Psychiatry, 50,* 898–911.

Conner, R. L., & Levine, S. (1969). Hormonal influences on aggressive behaviour. In S. Garattine & E. B. Sigg (Eds.), *Aggressive behaviour* (pp. 150–163). New York: John Wiley & Sons.

Connolly, M. B., Crits-Christoph, P., Barber, J. P., & Luborsky, L. (2000). Transference patterns in the therapeutic relationship in supportive-expressive psychotherapy for depression. *Psychotherapy Research, 10(3),* 356–372.

Conrad, R. (1964). Acoustic confusions in immediate memory. *British Journal of Psychology, 55,* 75–83.

Conrad, R. (1970). Short-term memory processes in the deaf. *British Journal of Psychology, 61,* 179–195.

Cooley, C. H. (1909). *Social organization: A study of the large mind.* New York: Scribner.

Coons, P.M. (2000). Dissociative fugue. In B. J. Sadock & V. A. Sadock (Eds.), *Kaplan and Sadock's comprehensive textbook of psychiatry* (7th ed., vol. 1, pp. 1549–1552). New York: Lippincott, Williams, & Wilkins.

Cooper, J. (2007). *Cognitive dissonance: Fifty years of a classic theory.* Thousand Oaks, CA: Sage.

Cooper, M. L., Frone, M. R., Russell, M., & Mudar, P. (1995). Drinking to regulate positive and negative emotions: A motivational model of alcohol use. *Journal of Personality & Social Psychology, 69(5),* 990–1005.

Cooper, M. L., Russell, M., & George, W. H. (1988). Coping, expectancies, and alcohol abuse: A test of social learning foundations. *Journal of Abnormal Psychology, 97,* 218–230.

Cooper, R. M., & Zubek, J. P. (1958). Effects of enriched and restricted early environments on the learning ability of bright and dull rats. *Canadian Journal of Psychology, 12,* 159–164.

Coover, G. D., Murison, R., & Jellestad, F. K. (1992). Subtotal lesions of the amygdala: The rostral central nucleus in passive avoidance and ulceration. *Physiology and Behavior, 51,* 795–803.

Copeland, B. J., & Pillsbury, H. C. (2004). Cochlear implantation for the treatment of deafness. *Annual Review of Medicine, 55,* 157–167.

Coppola, M., & Newport, E. L. (2005). Grammatical subjects in home sign: Abstract linguistic structure in adult primary gesture systems without linguistic input. *Proceedings of the National Academy of Sciences, USA 102,* 19249–19253.

Corbetta, M., Miezin, F. M., Doobmeyer, S., Shulman, G. L., & Petersen, S. E. (1991). Selective and divided attention during visual discriminations of shape, color, and speed: Functional anatomy by positron emission tomography. *Journal of Neuroscience, 11,* 2383–2402.

Corkin, S., Sullivan, E. V., Twitchell, T. E., & Grove, E. (1981). The amnesic patient H. M.: Clinical observations and test performance 28 years after operation. *Society for Neuroscience Abstracts, 7,* 235.

Cornell, D. G. (1997). Post hoc explanation is not prediction. Commentary on J. Archer. *American Psychologist, 52,* 1380.

Corrigan, P. W. (1995). Use of a token economy with seriously mentally ill patients: Criticisms and misconceptions. *Psychiatric Services, 46,* 1258–1263.

Corteen, R., & Williams, T. (1986). Television and reading skills. In T. M. Williams (Ed.), *The impact of television: A natural experiment in three communities* (pp. 39–85). New York: Academic Press.

Costa, P. T., Jr., & McCrae, R. R. (1998a). Trait theories of personality. In D. F. Barone & M. Hersen (Eds.), *Advanced personality* (pp. 103–121). New York: Plenum Press.

Costa, P. T., Jr., & McCrae, R. R. (1998b). The Revised NEO Personality Inventory (NEO-P-R). In S. R. Briggs, J. M. Cheek, & E. M. Donahue (Eds.), *Handbook of adult personality inventories* (pp. 1–29). New York: Plenum.

Cottrell, D., & Boston, P. (2002). Practitioner review: The effectiveness of systemic family therapy for children and adolescents. *Journal of Child Psychology and Psychiatry, 43,* 573–586.

Couzin, J. (2008). Crossing the divide. *Science, 319,* 1034–1036.

Covington, C. Y., Nordstrom-Klee, B., Ager, J., Sokol, R., & Delaney-Black, V. (2002). Birth to age 7 growth of children prenatally exposed to drugs: A prospective cohort study. *Neurotoxicology and Teratology, 24,* 489–496.

Cowart, J., & Whaley, D. (1971). Punishment of self-mutilation behavior. Unpublished manuscript cited by Whaley, D. L., & Malott, R. W. *Elementary principles of behavior.* New York: Appleton-Century-Crofts.

Cowley, D. S., Dager, S. R., & Dunner, D. L. (1995). The lactate infusion challenge. In G. M. Asnis & H. M. van Praag (Eds.), *Panic disorder: Clinical, biological, and treatment aspects* (pp. 206–232). New York: Wiley.

Cox, M. J., & Paley, B. (2003). Understanding families as systems. *Current Directions in Psychological Science, 12(5),* 193–196.

Craik, F. I. M., & Lockhart, R. S. (1972). Levels of processing: A framework for memory research. *Journal of Verbal Learning and Verbal Behavior, 11,* 671–684.

Craik, F. I. M., & Tulving, E. (1975). Depth of processing and the retention of words in episodic memory. *Journal of Experimental Psychology: General, 104,* 268–294.

Cramer, P. (2003). Personality change in later adulthood is predicted by defense mechanism use in early adulthood. *Journal of Research in Personality, 37,* 76–104.

Crespi, B., & Badcock, C. (2008). Psychosis and autism as diametrical disorders of the social brain. *Behavioral and Brain Sciences, 31,* 241–320.

Crick, F. H, Brenner, S., Klug, A., & Pieczenik, G. (1976). A speculation on the origin of protein synthesis. *Origins of Life, 7,* 389–397.

Crombag, H. F. M., Wagenaar, W. A., & van Koppen, P. J. (1996). Crashing memories and the problem of "source monitoring." *Applied Cognitive Psychology, 10,* 95–104.

Cromwell, P. F., Marks, A., Olson, J. N., & Avery, D. W. (1991). Group effects on decision-making by burglars. *Psychological Reports, 69,* 579–588.

Crowe, R. R., Noyes, R., Pauls, D. L., & Slymen, D. (1983). A family study of panic disorder. *Archives of General Psychiatry, 40,* 1065–1069.

Crowder, R. G. (1993). Short-term memory: Where do we stand? *Memory & Cognition, 21,* 142–145.

Crowley, K., Callanan, M. A., Tenenbaum, H. R., & Allen, E. (2001). Parents explain more often to boys than to girls during shared scientific thinking. *Psychological Science, 12,* 258–261.

Crowley, M. A., & Donahoe, J. W. (2004). Matching: Its acquisition and generalization. *Journal of the Experimental Analysis of Behavior, 82,* 143–159.

Cruts, M., & Van Broeckhoven, C. (1996). Molecular genetic analysis of Alzheimer's disease. In C. N. Stefanis and H. Hippius (Eds.), *Neuropsychiatry in old age: An update.* Ashland, OH: Hogrefe & Huber Publishers.

Culham, J. C., & Kanwisher, N. (2001). Neuroimaging of cognitive functions in human parietal cortex. *Current Opinion in Neurobiology, 11,* 157–163.

Cummings, J. L., & Wirshing, W. C. (1989). Recognition and differential diagnosis of tardive dyskinesia. *International Journal of Psychiatry in Medicine, 19,* 133–144.

Cunningham, J. A., Wild, T. C., Bondy, S. J., & Lin, E. (2001). Impact of normative feedback on problem drinkers: A small-area population study. *Journal of Studies on Alcohol, 62(2),* 228–233.

Daeschler, E. B., Shubin, N. H., & Jenkins, Jr., F. A. (2006). A Devonian tetrapod-like fish and the evolution of the tetrapod body plan. *Nature, 440,* 757.

Dagan, Y. (2001). Circadian rhythm sleep disorders (CRSD). *Sleep Medicine Reviews, 6,* 45–55.

Dale, P. S. (1976). *Language development: Structure and function* (2nd ed.). New York: Holt, Rinehart, and Winston.

Dalley, J. W., Fryer, T. D., Brichard, L., Robinson, E. S., Theobald, D. E. H., Lääne, K., L. Peña, Y., Murphy, E. R., Shah, Y., Probst, K., Abakumova, I., Aigbirhio, F. I., Richards, H. K., Hong, Y., Baron, J-C., Everitt, B. J., & Robbins, T. W. (2007). Nucleus accumbens D2/3 receptors predict trait impulsivity and cocaine reinforcement. *Science, 315,* 1267–1270.

Daly, M., & Wilson, M. I. (1988). Homicide. New York: Aldine de Gruyter,.

Damasio, A. (1994). *Descartes' brain: Emotion, reason, and the human brain.* New York: Putnam.

Damasio, A. (1999). *The feeling of what happens: Body and emotion in the making of consciousness.* New York: Harcourt.

Damasio, A., Yamada, Y., Damasio, H., Corbett, J., & McKee, J. (1980). Central achromatopsia: Behavioral, anatomic, and physiologic aspects. *Neurology, 30,* 1064–1071.

Damasio, A. R. (1994). *Descartes' error: Emotion, reason, and the human brain.* New York: Avon Books.

Damasio, A. R., Damasio, H., & van Hoesen, G. W. (1982). Prosopagnosia: Anatomic basis and behavioral mechanisms. *Neurology, 32,* 331–341.

Damasio, H., Grabowski, T., Frank, R., Galaburda, A. M., and Damasio, A. R. (1994) The return of Phineas Gage: Clues about the brain from the skull of a famous patient. *Science, 264,* 1102–1105.

Damon, W., & Hart, D. (1992). Self-understanding and its role in social and moral development. In M. H. Bornstein & M. E. Lamb (Eds.), *Developmental psychology: An advanced textbook* (pp. 421–464). Hillsdale, NJ: Lawrence Erlbaum.

Danckert, J., & Rossetti, Y. (2005). Blindsight in action: What can the different sub-types of blindsight tell us about the control of visually guided actions? *Neuroscience & Biobehavioral Reviews, 29,* 1035–1046.

Darou, W. G. (1992). Native Canadians and intelligence testing. *Canadian Journal of Counselling, 26,* 96–99.

Darwin, C. (1859). *On the origin of species by means of natural selection.* London: Murray.

Darwin, C. (1872). *The expression of the emotions in man and animals.* London: J. Murray.

Darwin, C. J., Turvey, M. T., & Crowder, R. G. (1972). An auditory analogue of the Sperling partial report procedure: Evidence for brief auditory storage. *Cognitive Psychology, 3,* 255–267.

Darwin, F. (1888/1950). *Charles Darwin's autobiography.* New York: Henry Schuman.

Dasgupta N., & Greenwald, A. G. 2001. On the malleability of automatic attitudes: Combating automatic prejudice with images of admired and disliked individuals. *Journal of Personality and Social Psychology, 81,* 800–814.

Dashiell, J. F. (1935). Experimental studies of the influence of social situations on the behavior of individual human adults. In C. Murcheson (Ed.), *A handbook of social psychology.* Worcester, MA: Clark University Press.

Davidson, T. L., & Swithers, S. E. (2004) A pavlovian approach to the problem of obesity. *International Journal of Obesity and Related Metabolic Disorders, 28,* 933–935.

Davis, J. D., & Campbell, C. S. (1973). Peripheral control of meal size in the rat: Effect of sham feeding on meal size and drinking rats. *Journal of Comparative and Physiological Psychology, 83,* 379–387.

Davis, M. (1992). The role of the amygdala in fear-potentiated startle: Implications for animal models of anxiety. *Trends in Pharmacological Sciences, 13,* 35–41.

Dawda, D., & Hart, S. D. (2000). Assessing emotional intelligence: Reliability and validity of the Bar-On Emotional Quotient Inventory (EQ-i) in university students. *Personality and Individual Differences, 28,* 797–812.

Dawes, R. M. (1994). *House of cards: Psychology and psychotherapy built on myth.* New York: The Free Press.

Dawes, R. M. (2002). The ethics of using or not using statistical prediction rules in psychological practice and related consulting activities. *Philosophy of Science, 69,* S178-S184.

Dawes, R. M., Faust, D., & Meehl, P. E. (1989). Clinical versus actuarial judgment. *Science, 243,* 1668–1674.

Dawes, R. M., Faust, D., & Meehl, P. E. (2002). Clinical versus actuarial judgment. In T. Gilovich (Ed.), *Heuristics and biases: The psychology of intuitive judgment.* New York: Cambridge University Press.

Dawkins, R. (1996). *Climbing mount improbable.* New York: W. W. Norton.

de Bruin, E. A., Beersma, D. G. M., & Daan, S. (2002). Sustained mental workload does not affect subsequent sleep intensity. *Journal of Sleep Research, 11,* 113–121.

de Castro, J. M. (2002). Independence of heritable influences on the food intake of free-living humans. *Nutrition, 18,* 11–16.

De Fabio, A., & Busoni, L. (2007). Fluid intelligence, personality traits and scholastic success: Empirical evidence in a sample of Italian high school students. *Personality and Individual Differences, 43,* 2096–2104.

de Luis, D. A., Sagrado, M. G., Conde, R., Aller, R., & Izaola, M. D. (2008). Changes of ghrelin and leptin in response to hypocaloric diet in obese patients. *Nutrition, 24,* 162–166.

De Raad, B. (1998). Five big, Big-Five issues: rationale, content, structure, status and crosscultural assessment. *European Psychologist, 3,* 113–124.

de Villieurs, P. (1977). Choice in concurrent schedules and a quantitative formulation of the law of effect. In W. K. Honig & J. E. R. Staddon (Eds.), *Handbook of operant behavior.* (pp. 233–287). Englewood Cliffs, NJ: Prentice-Hall.

DeAngelis, T. (2008, February). When do meds make the difference? *Monitor on Psychology,* 48–51.

DeAngelis, T. (2008, January). PTSD treatments grow in evidence of effectiveness. *Monitor on Psychology, 39,* 40–43.

Deaux, K. (1985). Sex and gender. *Annual Review of Psychology, 36,* 49–81.

Deaux, K. (1999). An overview of research on gender: Four themes from 3 decades. In W. B. Swann, Jr., & J. H. Langlois (Eds.), *Sexism and stereotypes in modern society: The gender science of Janet Taylor Spence* (pp. 11–33). Washington, DC: American Psychological Association.

DeCasper, A. J., & Fifer, W. P. (1980). Of human bonding: Newborns prefer their mothers' voices. *Science, 208,* 1175–1176.

DeCasper, A. J., & Spence, M. (1986). Prenatal maternal speech influences newborns' perception of speech sounds. *Infant Behavior and Development, 9,* 133–150.

Decety, J., & Keenan, J. P. (2006). *Social Neuroscience:* A new journal. *Social Neuroscience, 1,* 1–4.

deGroot, A. D. (1965). Thought and choice in chess. The Hague: Mouton Publishers.

Dellas, M., & Jernigan, L. P. (1990). Affective personality characteristics associated with undergraduate ego identity formation. *Journal of Adolescent Research, 5,* 306–324.

Dement, W. C. (1974). *Some must watch while some must sleep.* San Francisco: W. H. Freeman.

Dement, W. C., & Vaughan, C. (2000). *The promise of sleep.* New York: Dell.

Demuth, J. P., Bie, T. D., Stajich, J.E., Cristianini, N., & Hahn, M. W. (2006) The evolution of mammalian gene families. *PLoS ONE, 1,* e85.

DeNeve, K. M., & Cooper, H. (1998). The happy personality: A meta-analysis of 137 personality traits and subjective well-being. *Psychological Bulletin, 124,* 197–229.

Dennett, D. C. (1995). *Darwin's dangerous idea: Evolution and the meanings of life.* New York: Simon & Schuster.

Dennis, K., & Azpin, T. (2005). *Sign to learn: American sign language in early childhood classrooms.* St. Paul: Redleaf Press.

Deregowski, J. B., Muldrow, E. S., & Muldrow, W. F. (1972). Pictorial recognition in a remote Ethiopian village. *Perception, 1,* 417–425.

Dérousné, J., & Beauvois, M.-F. (1979). Phonological processing in reading: Data from alexia. *Journal of Neurology, Neurosurgery, and Psychiatry, 42,* 1125–1132.

Desimone, R., & Duncan, J. (1995). Neural mechanisms of selective visual attention. *Annual Review of Neuroscience, 18,* 193–222.

Deutsch, J. A., & Gonzalez, M. F. (1980). Gastric nutrient content signals satiety. *Behavioral Neural Biology, 30,* 113–116.

Deutsch, J. A., Young, W. G., & Kalogeris, T. J. (1978). The stomach signals satiety. *Science, 201,* 165–167.

Devane, W. A., Hanus, L., Breuer, A., Pertwee, R. G., Stevenson, L. A., Griffin, G., Gibson, D., Mandelbaum, A., Etinger, A., & Mechoulam, R. (1992). Isolation and structure of a brain constituent that binds to the cannabinoid receptor. *Science, 258,* 1946–1949.

deVilliers, J. G., & deVilliers, P. A. (1978). *Language acquisition.* Cambridge, MA: Harvard University Press.

Devlin, J. T., Russell, R. P., Davis, M. H., Price, C. J., Moss, H. E., Fadili, M. J., & Tyler, L. K. (2002). Is there an anatomical basis for category specificity? Semantic memory studies in PET and fMRI. *Neuropsychologia, 40,* 54–75.

DeWit, D. J., Adlaf, E. M., Offord, D. R., & Ogborne, A. C. (2000). Age at first alcohol use: A risk factor for the development of alcohol disorders. *American Journal of Psychiatry, 157(5),* 745–750.

di Pellegrino, G., Fadiga, L. Fogassi, L., Gallese, V., & Rizzolatti, G. (1992). Understanding motor events: A neurophysiological study. *Experimental Brain Research, 91,* 176–180.

Diamond, J. (1997). *Guns, germs, and steel: The fates of human societies.* New York: W. W. Norton.

Dick, D. M. (2007). Identification of genes influencing a spectrum of externalizing psychopathology. *Current Directions in Psychological Science, 16,* 331–335.

Dickens, W. T., & Flynn, J. R. (2001). Heritability estimates versus large environmental effects: The IQ paradox resolved. *Psychological Review, 108,* 346–369.

Dickens, W. T., & Flynn, J. R. (2006). Black Americans reduce the racial IQ gap: Evidence from standardization samples. *Psychological Science, 17,* 913–920.

Dickerson, F., Tenhula, L., & Green-Paden, L. D. (2005). The token economy for schizophrenia: Review of the literature and recommendations for future research. *Schizophrenia Research, 75,* 405–416.

Diener, E., Suh, E. M., Smith, H., & Shao, L. (1995). National differences in reported subjective well-being: Why do the occur? *Social Indicators Research, 34,* 7–32.

Dion, K. E., Berscheid, E., & Walster, E. (1972). What is beautiful is good. *Journal of Personality and Social Psychology, 24,* 285–290.

Dion, K. L. (1986). Stereotyping based on physical attractiveness: Issues and conceptual perspectives. In C. P. Herman, M. P. Zanna, & E. T. Higgins (Eds.), *Physical appearance, stigma, and social behavior: The Ontario symposium, Vol. 3* (pp. 7–21). Hillsdale, NJ: Lawrence Erlbaum.

Dion, K. L. (2003). Prejudice, racism, and discrimination. In T. Millon & M. J. Lerner (Eds.), *Handbook of psychology: Personality and social psychology, Vol. 5,* (pp. 507–536). New York: Wiley.

Dixon, J., Durrheim, K., & Tredous, C. (2007). Intergroup contact and attitudes toward the principle and practice of racial equality. *Psychological Science, 18,* 867–872.

Dixon, P., Gordon, R. D., Leung, A., & Di Lollo, V. (1997). Attentional components of partial report. *Journal of Experimental Psychology, 23,* 1253–1271.

Dobson, K. S., & Khatri, N. (2000). Cognitive therapy: Looking backward, looking forward. *Journal of Clinical Psychology, 56,* 907–923.

Dobzhansky, T. (1937). *Genetics and the origin of species.* New York: Columbia University Press.

Doetsch, F., & Hen, R. (2005). Young and excitable: The function of new neurons in the adult mammalian brain. *Current Opinion in Neuroscience 15,* 121–128.

Donahoe, J. W. (1997). Selection networks: Simulation of plasticity through reinforcement learning. In J. W. Donahoe & V. P. Dorsel (Eds.), *Neural-network models of cognition: Biobehavioral foundations* (pp. 336–357). Amsterdam: Elsevier Science Press.

Donahoe, J. W. (1999). Edward L. Thorndike: The selectionist connectionist. *Journal of the Experimental Analysis of Behavior, 72,* 451–454.

Donahoe, J. W. (2003). Selectionism. In K. A. Lattal & P. N. Chase (Eds.), *Behavior theory and philosophy* (pp. 103–128). New York: Kluwer Academic/Plenum Publishers.

Donahoe, J. W. (2006). Contingency: Its meaning in the experimental analysis of behavior. *European Journal of Behavior Analysis, 7,* 111–114.

Donahoe, J. W., Burgos, J. E., & Palmer, D. C. (1993). Selectionist approach to reinforcement. *Journal of the Experimental Analysis of Behavior, 60,* 17–40.

Donahoe, J. W., Crowley, M. A., Millard, W. J., & Stickney, K. A. (1982). *A unified principle of reinforcement: Quantitative models of behavior* (Vol. 2, pp. 493–521). Cambridge, MA: Ballinger.

Donahoe, J. W., & Palmer, D. C (1994/2005). *Learning and complex behavior.* Boston, MA: Allyn & Bacon (reprinted by Ledgetop Publishing at http://lcb-online.org).

Donahoe, J. W., & Vegas, R. (2004). Pavlovian conditioning: The CS-UR relation. *Journal of Experimental Psychology: Animal Behavior Processes, 30,* 17–33.

Donnan, G. A., Darbey, D. G., & Saling, M. M. (1997). Identification of brain region for coordinating speech articulation. *Nature, 349,* 221–222.

Dooling, D. J., & Lachman, R. (1971). Effects of comprehension on retention of prose. *Journal of Experimental Psychology, 88,* 216–222.

Downing, P. E., Jian, Y., Shuman, M., & Kanwisher, N. (2001). A cortical area selective for visual processing of the human body. *Science, 293,* 2470–2473.

Dronkers, N. F., Wilkins, D. P., Van Valin, Jr., R. D., Redfern, B. B., & Jaeger, J. J. (2004). Lesion analysis of the brain areas involved in language comprehension. *Cognition, 92,* 145–177.

Dunn, J., Bretherton, I., & Munn, P. (1987). Conversations about feeling states between mothers and their young children. *Developmental Psychology, 23,* 132–139.

Dutton, D. G., & Aron, A. P. (1974). Some evidence for heightened sexual attraction under conditions of high anxiety. *Journal of Personality and Social Psychology, 30,* 510–517.

Dweck, C. (2004). Self-theories of intelligence. In E. Aronson (Ed.), *Readings about the social animal,* 9th ed. (pp. 296–303). New York: Worth Publishers.

Dyer, J. (2001, June 11). Ethics and orphans: The monster study. Part one of a *Mercury News* Special Report. *San Jose [CA] Mercury News.*

Eagly, A. H., & Chaiken, S. (1998). Attitude structure and function. In D. T. Gilbert & S. T. Fiske (Eds.), *The handbook of social psychology, Vol. 1.* (4th ed.). New York: McGraw-Hill.

Eagly, A. H., & Chaiken, S. (2005). Attitude research in the 21st century: The current state of knowledge. In D. Albarracin, B. T. Johnson, & M. P. Zanna (Eds.), *Handbook of attitudes and attitude change.* (pp. 743–767). Mahway, NJ: Erlbaum.

Eagly, A. H., & Karau, S. J. (1991). Gender and the emergence of leaders: A meta-analysis. *Journal of Personality and Social Psychology, 60,* 685–710.

Eagly, A. H., & Wood, W. (1999). The origins of sex differences in human behavior: Evolved dispositions versus social roles. *American Psychologist, 54,* 408–423.

Echeburúa, E., DeMedina, R. B., & Aizpiri, J. (2007). Comorbidity of alcohol dependence and personality disorders: A comparative study. *Alcohol and Alcoholism, 42,* 618–622.

Ecuyer-Dab, I., & Rober, M. (2004). Have sex differences in spatial ability evolved from male competition for mating and female concern for survival? *Cognition, 91,* 221–257.

Egan, L C., Santos, L. R., & Bloom, P. (2007). The origins of cognitive dissonance: Evidence from children and monkeys. *Psychological Science, 18,* 978–983.

Egan, W., & McCorkindale, C. (2007). Narcissism, vanity, personality and mating effort. *Personality and Individual Differences, 43,* 2105–2115.

Ehrsson, H. H. (2007). The experimental induction of out-of-body experiences. *Science, 317,* 1048–1049.

Ehrsson, H. H., Spence, C., & Passingham, R. E. (2004). That's my hand! Activity in premotor cortex reflects feeling of ownership of a limb. *Science, 305,* 875–877.

Eichenbaum, H., Stewart, C., & Morris, R. G. M. (1990). Hippocampal representation in spatial learning. *Journal of Neuroscience, 10,* 331–339.

Eikelboom, R., & Stewart, J. (1982). Conditioning of drug-induced physiological responses. *Psychological Review, 89,* 507–528.

Eiler, J. M. (2007). Just another rock? *Science, 317,* 1046–1047.

Eimas, P. D., Siqueland, E. R., Jusczyk, P., & Vigorito, J. (1971). Speech perception in infants. *Science, 171,* 303–306.

Eiseley, L. (1975). *All the strange hours: The excavation of a life.* New York: Charles Scribner's Sons.

Eisenberg, N., Fabes, R. A., Schaller, M., Miller, P., Carlo, G., Poulin, R., Shea, C., & Shell, R. (1991). Personality and socialization: Correlates of vicarious emotional responding. *Journal of Personality and Social Psychology, 61,* 459–470.

Ekman, P., Friesen, W. V., & Ellsworth, P. (1972). *Emotion in the human face: Guidelines for research and a review of findings.* New York: Pergamon Press.

Elbert, T., Pantev, C., Wienbruch, C., Rockstroh, B., & Taub, E. (1995). Increased cortical representation of the fingers of the left hand in string players. *Science, 270,* 305–307.

Elder, G. H. (1969). Appearance and education in marriage mobility. *American Sociological Review, 34,* 519–533.

Elena, S. F. & Lenski, R. E. (2003). Evolution experiments with microorganisms: The dynamics and genetic bases of adaptation. *National Review of Genetics, 4,* 457–469.

Ellenberger, H. F. (1972). The story of "Anna O": A critical review with new data. *Journal of the History of the Behavioral Sciences, 8,* 267–279.

Elliott, R. (2002). Research on the effectiveness of humanistic therapies: A meta-analysis. In D. Cain & J. Seeman (Eds.), *Handbook of research and practice in humanistic psychotherapies* (pp. 301–325). Washington, DC: American Psychological Association.

Ellis, A. (1973). Rational-emotive therapy. In R. Corsini (Ed.), *Current psychotherapies.* Itasca, IL: Peacock.

Ellis, A. (1989). A twenty-three-year-old woman guilty about not following her parents' rules. In D. Wedding & R. J. Corsini (Eds.), *Case studies in psychotherapy.* Itasca, IL: Peacock.

Ellis, A. (1995). Changing rational-emotive therapy (RET) to rational emotive behavior therapy (REBT) and bringing its behavioral aspects into more prominence. *Behavior Therapy, 16,* 1–2.

Ellis, A. (2003). Early theories and practices of rational emotive behavior therapy and how they have been augmented and revised during the last three decades. *Journal of Rational-Emotive & Cognitive-Behavior Therapy, 21,* 2199–2243.

Elman, J. L. (1995). Language as a dynamical system. In R. Port & T. Gelder (Eds.), *Mind as motion.* (pp. 195–224). Cambridge, MA: MIT Press.

Elman, J. L. (2005). Connectionist models of cognitive development. *Trends in Cognitive Sciences, 9,* 111–117.

Elms, A. C. (1995). Obedience in retrospect. *Journal of Social Issues, 51,* 21–32.

Emmelkamp, P. M. G. (2004). Behavior therapy with adults. In M. J. Lambert (Ed.), *Bergin & Garfield's handbook of psychotherapy and behavior change,* 4th ed. (pp. 379–427). New York: Wiley.

Enard, W., Przeworski, M., Fisher, S. E., Lai, C. S., Wiebe, V., Kitano, T., Monaco, A. P., & Pääbo, S. (2002). Molecular evolution of FOXP2, a gene involved in speech and language. *Nature, 418,* 869–872.

Engberg, L. A., Hansen, G., Welker, R. L., & Thomas, D. R. (1972). Acquisition of key-pecking via autoshaping as a function of prior experience: "Learned laziness?" *Science, 178,* 1002–1004.

Entwisle, D. (1972). To dispel fantasies about fantasy-based measures of achievement motivation. *Psychological Bulletin, 77,* 377–391.

Epstein, R. (1985). The spontaneous interconnection of three repertoires. *Psychological Record, 35,* 131–141.

Epstein, R. (1987). The spontaneous interconnection of four repertoires of behavior in a pigeon (*Columbia livia*). *Journal of Comparative Psychology, 101,* 197–201.

Epstein, R., Kirshnit, C., Lanza, R. P., & Rubin, I. (1984). Insight in the pigeon: Antecedents and determinants of an intelligent performance. *Nature, 308,* 61–62.

Epstein, S. (1979). The stability of behavior. I. On predicting most of the people much of the time. *Journal of Personality and Social Psychology, 37,* 1097–1126.

Epstein, S. P. (1986). Does aggregation produce spuriously high estimates of behavior stability? *Journal of Personality and Social Psychology, 50,* 1199–1210.

Erard, M. (2007). Read my slips: Speech errors show how language is processed. *Science, 317,* 1674–1676.

Erard, M. (2007). *UM . . . slips, stumbles, and verbal blunders, and what they mean.* New York: Pantheon Books.

Ernulf, K. E., Innala, S. M., & Whitam, F. L. (1989). Biological explanation, psychological explanation, and tolerance of homosexuals: A cross-national analysis of beliefs and attitudes. *Psychological Reports, 248,* 183–188.

Eron, L. D. (1950). A normative study of the thematic apperception test. *Psychological Monographs, 64,* Whole No. 315.

Erting, C. J., Johnson, R. C., Smith, D. L., & Snider, B. D. (1989). *The Deaf way: Perspectives from the International Conference on Deaf Culture.* Washington, DC: Gallaudet University Press.

Estes, W. K. (1955). Statistical theory of spontaneous recovery and regression. *Psychological Review, 62,* 145–154.

Estes, W. K., & Skinner, B. F. (1941). Some quantitative properties of anxiety. *Journal of Experimental Psychology, 29,* 390–400.

Evans, R. I. (2003). Some theoretical models and constructs generic to substance abuse prevention programs for adolescents: Possible relevance and limitations for problem gambling. *Journal of Gambling Studies, 19,* 287–302.

Eysenck, H. (1998). *Dimensions of personality.* New Brunswick, NJ: Transaction Publishers.

Eysenck, H. J. (1939). Primary mental abilities. *British Journal of Educational Psychology, 9,* 270–285.

Eysenck, H. J. (1952). The effects of psychotherapy: An evaluation. *Journal of Consulting Psychology, 16,* 319–324.

Eysenck, H. J. (1970). *The structure of human personality* (3rd ed.). London: Methuen.

Eysenck, H. J., & Eysenck, M. W. (1985). *Personality and individual differences: A natural science approach.* New York: Plenum Press, 1985.

Fabes, R. A., Eisenberg, N., Smith, M. C., & Murphy, B. C. (1996). Getting angry at peers: Associations with liking of provocateur. *Child Development, 67,* 942–956.

Fadda, F., Mosca, E., Colombo, G., & Gessa, G. L. (1990). Alcohol-preferring rats: Genetic sensitivity to alcohol-induced stimulation of dopamine metabolism. *Physiology and Behavior, 47,* 727–729.

Fagan, J. R., III, & Singer, L. T. (1979). The role of simple feature differences in infants' recognition of faces. *Infant Behavior and Development, 2,* 39–45.

Fagot, B. I., & Hagan, R. I. (1991). Observations of parent reactions to sex-stereotyped behaviors: Age and sex differences. *Child Development, 62,* 617–628.

Faucett, L. V. (1994). *Fundamentals of neural networks.* Englewood Cliffs, NJ: Prentice Hall.

Faulder, L. (2006, July 2). For the love of Jennica: A family, at last. *Edmonton Journal,* pp. E3.

Fawcett, S. L., Wang, Y-Z., & Birch, E. E. (2005). The critical period for susceptibility of human stereopsis. *Investigative Ophthalmology & Visual Science, 46,* 521–525.

Feather, N. T., & McKee, I. R. (1993). Global self-esteem and attitudes toward the high achiever for Australian and Japanese students. *Social Psychology Quarterly, 56,* 65–76.

Feeney, J. A., & Noller, P. (1991). Attachment style and verbal descriptions of romantic partners. *Journal of Social and Personal Relationships, 8,* 187–215.

Fegley, D., Kathuria, S., Mercier, R., Li, C., Goutopoulos, A., Makriyannis, A., & Piomelli, D. (2004). Anandamide transport is independent of fatty-acid amide hydrolase activity and is blocked by the hydrolysis-resistant inhibitor. *Proceedings of the National Academy of Science, U S A, 101,* 8756–8761.

Feinberg, M. E., Greenberg, M. T., & Osgood, D. W. (2004). Readiness, functioning, and perceived effectiveness in community prevention coalitions: A study of communities that care. *American Journal of Community Psychology, 33,* 163–176.

Feingold, A. (1992). Good-looking people are not what we think. *Psychological Bulletin, 111,* 304–341.

Feingold, A. (1993). Cognitive gender differences: A developmental perspective. *Sex Roles, 29,* 91–112.

Feist, G. J., & Barron, F. X. (2003). Predicting creativity from early to late adulthood: Intellect, potential, and personality. *Journal of Research in Personality, 37,* 62–88.

Fendrich, R., Wessinger, C. M., & Gazzaniga, M. S. (1992). Residual vision in a scotoma: Implications for blindsight. *Science, 258,* 1489–1491.

Ferster, C. A., & Skinner, B. F. (1957). *Schedules of reinforcement.* New York: Appleton-Century.

Festinger, L. (1957). *A theory of cognitive dissonance.* Stanford: Stanford University Press.

Festinger, L., & Carlsmith, J. M. (1959). Cognitive consequences of forced compliance. *Journal of Abnormal and Social Psychology, 58,* 203–210.

Festinger, L., Schachter, S., & Back, K. (1959). *Social pressures in informal groups: A study of a housing community.* New York: Harper & Row.

Feynman, R. P. (1985). *Surely you're joking, Mr. Feynman!* New York: Bantam Books.

Fiehler, K., Burke, M., Engel, A., Bien, S., & Rösler, R. (2008). Kinesthetic working memory and action control within the dorsal stream. *Cerebral Cortex, 18,* 243–253.

Field, T. M. (1994). Infant day care facilitates later social behavior and school performance. In H. Goelman & E. V. Jacobs (Eds.), *Children's play in child care settings. SUNY series, children's play in society* (pp. 69–84). Albany, NY: State University of New York Press.

Fiez, J. A., Balota, D. A., Raichle, M. E., & Petersen, S. E. (1999). Effects of lexicality, frequency, and spelling-to-sound consistency on the functional anatomy of reading. *Neuron, 24,* 205–218.

Fincham, F., & Beach, S. R. H. (2007). Forgiveness and marital quality: Precursor or consequence in well-established relationships? *Journal of Positive Psychology, 2,* 260–268.

Fink, M. (1976). Presidential address: Brain function, verbal behavior, and psychotherapy. *Proceedings of the Annual Meeting of the American Psychopathological Association, 64,* 74–86.

Finlayson, C., Pacheco, F. G., Rodríguez-Vidal, J., Fa, D. A., Gutierrez López, J. M., Santiago Pérez, A., Finlayson, G., Allue, E., Baena-Preysler, J., Cáceres, I., Carrión, J. S., Fernández-Jalvo, Y., Gleed-Owen, C. P., Jimenez-Es-pejo, F. J., López, P., López-Sáez, J. A., Riquelme-Cantal, J. A., Sánchez-Marco, A., Guzman, F. G., Brown, K., Fuentes, N., Valarino, C. A., Villalpando, A., Stringer, C. B., Martinez Ruiz, F., & Sakamoto, T. (2006). Late survival of Neanderthals at the southernmost extreme of Europe. *Nature, 443,* 850–853.

Fisch, H., Hyun, G., Golden, R., Hensle, T. W, Olsson, C. A, & Liberson, G. L. (2003). The influence of paternal age on Down syndrome. *Journal of Urology, 169,* 2275–2278.

Fisch, S., & Truglio, R. T. (Eds.). (2001). *"G" is for growing: Thirty years of research on children and Sesame Street.* Mahwah, NJ: Lawrence Erlbaum Associates.

Fisher, L., Ames, E., Chisholm, K., & Savoie, L. (1997). Problems reported by parents of Romanian orphans adopted to British Columbia. *International Journal of Behavioral Development, 20,* 67–82.

Fisher, N. J., Rourke, B. P., & Bieliauskas, L. A. (1999). Neuropsychological subgroups of patients with Alzheimer's disease: An examination of the first ten years of CERAD data. *Journal of Clinical and Experimental Neuropsychology, 21,* 488–518.

Fiske, S. T., & Taylor, S. E. (1991). *Social cognition* (2nd ed.). New York: McGraw-Hill.

Flannery, R. B., Jr. (1999). Psychological trauma and posttraumatic stress disorder: A review. *International Journal of Emergency Mental Health, 1,* 135–140.

Flavell, J. H. (1992). Perspectives on perspective taking. In H. Beilin & P. B. Pufall (Eds.), *Piaget's theory: Prospects and possibilities* (pp. 107–139). Hillsdale, NJ: Lawrence Erlbaum.

Flexser, A. J., & Tulving, E. (1978). Retrieval independence in recognition and recall. *Psychological Review, 85,* 153–171.

Floyd, R. L., Rimer, B. K., Giovino, G. A., Mullen, P. D., & Sullivan, S. E. (1993). A review of smoking in pregnancy: Effects on pregnancy outcomes and cessation efforts. *Annual Review of Public Health, 14,* 379–411.

Flynn, J. R. (1987). Massive IQ gains in 14 nations: What IQ tests really measure. *Psychological Bulletin, 101,* 171–191.

Flynn, J. R. (2007). *What is intelligence?* New York: Cambridge University Press.

Fogarty, F., Russell, J. M., Newman, S. C., & Bland, R. C. (1994). Mania. *Acta Psychiatrica Scandinavica, 89(376, Suppl),* 16–23.

Folensbee, R. W. (2007). *The neuroscience of psychological therapies.* New York: Cambridge University Press.

Foley, V. D. (1989). Family therapy. In R. J. Corsini (Ed.), *Current psychotherapies,* 4th ed. (pp. 455–500). Itasca, IL: F. E. Peacock.

Folkman, S., & Lazarus, R. S. (1991). Coping and emotion. In A. Monat & R. S. Lazarus (Eds.), *Stress and coping: An anthology* (pp. 207–227). New York: Columbia University Press.

Follette, V. M., Ruzek, J. I., & Abueg, F. R. (Eds.) (2001). *Cognitive-behavioral therapies for trauma.* New York: Guilford Press.

Fonagy, P., Roth, A., & Higgitt, A. (2005). Psychodynamic psychotherapies: Evidence-based practice and clinical wisdom. *Bulletin of the Menninger Clinic, 69,* 1–58.

Foster, C. A., Witcher, B. S., Campbell, W. K., & Green, J. D. (1998). Arousal and attraction: Evidence for automatic and controlled processes. *Journal of Personality and Social Psychology, 74,* 86–101.

Fouts, R. S., & Mills, S. T. (1997). *Next of kin: My conversations with chimpanzees.* New York: William Morrow.

Franco, P., Groswasser, J., Hassid, S., Lanquart, J. P., Scaillet, S., & Kahn, A. (2000). Prenatal exposure to cigarette smoking is associated with a decrease in arousal in infants. *Journal of Pediatrics, 135,* 34–38.

Frank, S. L., Pirsch, L. A., & Wright, V. C. (1990). Late adolescents' perceptions of their relationships with their parents: Relationships among deidealization, autonomy, relatedness, and insecurity and implications for adolescent adjustment and ego identity status. *Journal of Youth and Adolescence, 19,* 571–588.

Franken, I. H. A., Booij, J., & van den Brink, W. (2005). The role of dopamine in human addiction: From reward to motivated attention.

European Journal of Pharmacology, 526, 199–208.

Frankle, W. G., Lombardo, I., New, A. S., Goodman, M., Talbot, P. S., Huang, Y., Hwang, D.-R., Slifstein, M., Curry, S., Abi-Dargham, A., Laruelle, M., & Siever, L. J. (2005). Brain serotonin transporter distribution in subjects with impulsive aggressivity: A positron emission study with [11C]McN 5652. *American Journal of Psychiatry, 162,* 915–923.

Freedman, J. L. (2002). *Media violence and its effect on aggression: Assessing the scientific evidence.* Toronto: University of Toronto Press.

Freedman, J. L., & Fraser, S. C. (1966). Compliance without pressure: The foot-in-the-door technique. *Journal of Personality and Social Psychology, 4,* 195–203.

Freeth, R. (2007). *Humanising psychiatry and mental health care: The challenge of the person-centered approach.* Oxford: Radcliffe Publishing.

Freud, S. (1900). *The interpretation of dreams.* London: George Allen and Unwin Ltd.

Freud, S. (1933). *New introductory lectures on psychoanalysis* (J. Strachey, Trans.). New York: Norton.

Frey, S. H., Vinton, D., Norlund, R., & Grafton, S. T. (2005). Cortical topography of human anterior intraparietal cortex active during visually guided grasping. *Cognitive Brain Research, 23,* 397–405.

Frey, U. (1997). Cellular mechanisms of long-term potentiation: Late maintenance. In J. E. Donahoe & V. P. Dorsel, (Eds.), *Neural-network models of cognition: Biobehavioral foundations* (pp. 105–128). Amsterdam: Elsevier Science Press.

Frey, U., & Morris, R. G. (1998). Weak before strong: disassociating synaptic tagging and plasticity-factor accounts of late-LTP. *Neuropharmacology, 37,* 545–552.

Friderun, A. S., & Cummins, J. M. (1996). Misconceptions about mitochondria and mammalian fertilization: Implications for theories on human evolution. *Proceedings of the National Academy of Science, 93,* 13859–13863.

Fridlund, A. J. (1992). The behavioural ecology and sociality of human faces. In M. S. Clark (Ed.), *Emotion: Review of personality and social psychology,* Vol. 13. Newbury Park, CA: Sage.

Fridlund, A. J. (1994). *Human facial expression: An evolutionary view.* San Diego, CA: Academic Press.

Friedman, H. S., & Rosenman, R. F. (1974). *Type A behavior and your heart.* New York: Knopf.

Friedman, M., & Rosenman, R. H. (1959). Association of specific overt behavior patterns with blood and cardiovascular findings: Blood cholesterol level, blood clotting time, incidence of arcus senilis, and clinical coronary artery disease. *JAMA, 162,* 1286–1296.

Friedman, R. A. (2007, August 21). To reap psychotherapy's benefits, get a good fit. *The New York Times.*

Friedman, R. A. (2008, April 15). Who are we? Coming of age on antidepressants. *The New York Times.*

Fritsch, T., McClendon, M.J., Smyth, K.A., Lerner, A.J., Friedland, R.P., & Larsen, J.D. (2007). Cognitive functioning in healthy aging: The role of reserve and lifestyle factors early in life. *The Gerontologist, 47*, 307–322.

Fromkin, V. (1973). *Speech errors as linguistic evidence*. The Hague: Mouton Publishers.

Funder, D.C. (2006). Towards a resolution of the personality triad: Persons, situations, and behaviors. *Journal of Research in Personality, 40*, 21–34.

Furnham, A. (1992). Just world beliefs in twelve societies. *The Journal of Social Psychology, 133*, 317–329.

Furnham, A. (2003). Belief in a just world: Research progress over the past decade. *Personality and Individual Differences, 34*, 795–817.

Gafner, G., & Benson, S. (2003). *Hypnotic techniques: For standard psychotherapy and formal hypnosis*. New York: W. W. Norton.

Gaillard, W. D., Pugliese, M., Grandin, C. R., Braniecki, M. A., Kondapaneni, B. A., Hunter, K., Xu, B., Petrella, J. R., Balsamo, L., & Basso, G. (2001). Cortical localization of reading in normal children. *Neurology, 57*, 47–54.

Galaburda, A., & Kemper, T. L. (1979). Observations cited by Geschwind, N. Specializations of the human brain. *Scientific American, 241*, 180–199.

Galaburda, A. M. (1993). Neurology of developmental dyslexia. *Current Opinion in Neurobiology, 3*, 237–242.

Galaburda, A. M., Menard, M. T., & Rosen, G. D. (1994). Evidence for aberrant auditory anatomy in developmental dyslexia. *Proceedings of the National Academy of Sciences, 91*, 8010–8013.

Galaburda, A. M., Sherman, G. F., Rosen, G. D., Aboitiz, F., & Geschwind, N. (1985). Developmental dyslexia: Four consecutive patients with cortical anomalies. *Annals of Neurology, 18*, 222–233.

Gale, C. R., O'Callaghan, F. J., Godfrey, K. M., Law, C. M., & Martyn, C. N. (2004). Critical periods of brain growth and cognitive function in children. *Brain, 127*, 321–329.

Gallaway, C., & Richards, B. J. (Eds.). (1994). *Input and interaction in language acquisition*. New York: Cambridge University Press.

Gallori, E., Biondi, E., & Branciamore, S. (2006). Looking for the primordial genetic honeycomb. *Origins of Life and Evolution of the Biosphere, 36*, 493–499.

Galton, F. (1869). *Hereditary genius: An inquiry into its laws and consequences*. Cleveland, OH: World Publishing.

Galvani, A. P., & Slatkin, M. (2003). Evaluating plague and smallpox as historical selective pressures for the CCR5-delta32 HIV-resistance allele. *Proceedings of the National Academy of Science, 100*, 15276–15279.

Ganel, T., & Goodale, M. A. (2003). Visual control of action but not perception requires analytical processing of object shape. *Nature, 426*, 664–667.

Ganong, W. F. (1980). Phonetic categorization in auditory word perception. *Journal of Experimental Psychology: Human Perception and Performance, 6*, 110–125.

Garcia, J., Erwin, E. R., & Koelling, R. A. (1966). Relation of cue to consequence in avoidance learning. *Psychonomic Science, 4*, 123–124.

García, L. F., Antón, A., García, Ó, & Colom, R. (2007). Do parents and children know each other? A study about agreement on personality within families. *Psicothema, 19*, 120–123.

Gardner, H. (1987). *The mind's new science*. New York: Basic Books.

Gardner, H. (2006). *Multiple intelligences; New horizons in theory and practice*. New York: Basic Books.

Gardner, R. A., & Gardner, B. T. (1969). Teaching sign language to a chimpanzee. *Science, 165*, 664–672.

Gardner, R. A., & Gardner, B. T. (1975). Early signs of language in child and chimpanzee. *Science, 187*, 752–753.

Gardner, R. A., & Gardner, B. T. (1978). Comparative psychology and language acquisition. *Annals of the New York Academy of Sciences, 309*, 37–76.

Garnets, L., & Kimmel, D. (1991). Lesbian and gay male dimensions in the psychological study of human diversity. In J. D. Goodchilds (Ed.), *Psychological perspectives on human diversity in America* (pp. 137–192). Washington, DC: American Psychological Association.

Gartrell, N. (2004). A doctor's toxic shock. *Boston Globe Magazine*, January 4, 2004, p. 58.

Gartstein, M. A., Crawford, J., & Robertson, C. D. (2008). Early markers of language and attention: Mutual contributions and the impact of parent-infant interactions. *Child Psychiatry and Human Development, 39*, 9–26.

Gauthier, I., Tarr, M. J., Moylan, J., Anderson, A. W., Skudlarksi, P., & Gore, J. C. (2000). The fusiform "face area" is part of a network that processes faces at the individual level. *Journal of Cognitive Neuroscience, 12*, 495–504.

Gazzaniga, M. S. (1970). *The bisected brain*. New York: Appleton-Century-Crofts.

Gazzaniga, M. S. (1987). *The social brain*. New York: Basic Books.

Gazzaniga, M. S. (1989). Organization of the human brain. *Science, 245*, 947–952.

Gazzaniga, M. S. (2000). Cerebral specialization and interhemispheric communication: Does the corpus callosum enable the human condition? *Brain, 123*, 1293–1326.

Gazzaniga, M. S., & LeDoux, J. E. (1978). *The integrated mind*. New York: Plenum Press.

Geisinger, K. F., Spies, R. A., Carlson, J. F., & Plake, B. S. (Eds.). (2007). *The seventeenth mental measurements yearbook*. Lincoln, NE: Buros Institute of Mental Measurement.

Gelman, R. (1972). Logical capacity of very young children: Number invariance rules. *Child Development, 43*, 75–90.

Gerrig, R. J., & O'Brien, E. J. (2005). The scope of memory-based processing. *Discourse Processing, 39*, 225–242.

Geschwind, N., Quadfasel, F. A., & Segarra, J. M. (1968). Isolation of the speech area. *Neuropsychologia, 6*, 327–340.

Ghilardi, J. R., Röhrich, H., Lindsay, T. H., Sevcik, M. A., Schwei, M. J., Kubota, K., Halvorson, K. G., Poblete, J., Chaplan, S. R., Dubin, A. E., Carruthers, N. J., Swanson, D., Kuskowski, M., Flores, C. M., & Mantyh, P. W. (2005). Selective blockade of the capsaicin receptor TRPV1 attenuates bone cancer pain. *Journal of Neuroscience, 25*, 3126–3131.

Gibbs, C. M., Latham, S. B., & Gormezano, I. (1978). Classical schedule and resistance to extinction. *Animal Learning & Behavior, 6*, 209–215.

Gibson, E. J., & Walk, R. R. (1960). The "visual cliff." *Scientific American, 202*, 2–9.

Gibson, G. (2007). Human evolution: Thrifty genes and the dairy queen. *Current Biology, 17*, R295–R296.

Gibson, J. J. (1960). The concept of the stimulus in psychology. *American Psychologist, 16*, 694–703.

Giedd, J. N., Blumenthal, J., Jeffries, N.O., Castellanos, F. X., Liu, H., Zijdenbos, A., Paus, T., Evans, A. C., & Rapoport, J. L. (1999). Brain development during childhood and adolescence: A longitudinal MRI study. *Nature Neuroscience, 2*, 861–863.

Gigerenzer, G. (2007). *Gut feelings: The intelligence of the unconscious*. New York: Viking Penguin.

Gigerenzer, G., Todd, P. M., & the ABC Research Group (1999). *Simple heuristics that make us smart*. New York: Oxford University Press.

Gilbert, D. (2006). *Stumbling on happiness*. New York: Knopf.

Gilovich, T. (1990). Differential construal and the false consensus effect. *Journal of Personality and Social Psychology, 59*, 623–634.

Gironell, A., de la Calzada, M. D., Sagales, T., & Barraquer-Bordas, L. (1995). Absence of REM sleep and altered non-REM sleep caused by a haematoma in the pontine tegmentum. *Journal of Neurology, Neurosurgery and Psychiatry, 59*, 195–196.

Gladwell, M. (2005). *Blink: The power of thinking without thinking*. Boston: Little, Brown.

Gladwin, T. (1970). *East is a bird bird: Navigation and logic on Puluwat Atoll*. Cambridge, MA: Harvard University Press.

Gleicher, G., & Petty, R. E. (1992). Expectations of reassurance influence the nature of fear-stimulated attitude change. *Journal of Experimental Social Psychology, 28*, 86–100.

Glenberg, A. M., Meyer, M., & Lindem, K. (1987). Mental models contribute to foregrounding during text comprehension. *Journal of Memory and Language, 26*, 69–83.

Gluck, M. A., & Bower, G. H. (1988). From conditioning to category learning: An adaptive network model. *Journal of Experimental Psychology: General, 117*, 227–247.

Gluck, M. A., & Myers, C. E. (1997). Psychobiological models of hippocampal function in learning and memory. *Annual Review of Psychology, 48*, 481–514.

Godfrey, P. A., Malnic, B., & Buck, L. (2994). The mouse olfactory receptor gene family. *Proceedings of the National Academy of Sciences, U S A, 101*, 2156–2161.

Gogtay, N., Giedd, J. N., Lusk, L., Hayashi, K. M., Greenstein, D., Vaituzin, A. C., Nugent, T. F., Herman, D. H., Clasen, L. S., Toga, A. W., Rapoport, J. L., & Thompson, P. M. (2004). Dynamic mapping of human cortical development during childhood through early adulthood. *Proceedings of the National Academy of Science, USA, 101*, 8174–8179.

Goldberg, L. R. (1968). Simple models or simple processes? Some research on clinical judgments. *American Psychologist, 23*, 483–496.

Goldberg, L. R. (1993). The structure of phenotypic personality traits. *American Psychologist, 48*, 26–34.

Goldberg, L. R., Johnson, J. A., Eber, H. W., Hogan, R., Ashton, M. C., Cloninger, C. R., & Gough, H. G. (2006). The international personality item pool and the future of public-domain personality measures. *Journal of Research in Personality, 40*, 84–96.

Goldin-Meadow, S., & Feldman, H. (1977). The development of language-like communication without a language model. *Science, 197*, 401–403.

Goldman-Rakic, P. S. (1996). Memory: recoding experience in cells and circuits: Diversity in memory research. *Proceedings of the National Academy of Science USA, 93*, 13435–13437.

Goldstein, M. J. & Strachan, A. M. (1987). The family and schizophrenia. In T. Jacob (Ed.), *Family interaction and psychopathology* (pp. 481–508). New York: Plenum.

Goldstone, R. L., Medink, D. L., & Gentner, D. (1991). Relational similarity and the nonindependence of features in similarity judgments. *Cognitive Psychology, 23*, 222–262.

Golomb, M., Fava, M., Abraham, M., & Rosenbaum, J. F. (1995). Gender differences in personality disorders. *American Journal of Psychiatry, 152*, 579–582.

Gomez, L. (1997*). An introduction to object relations.* New York: New York University Press.

González-Maeso, J., Ang, R. L., Yuen, T., Chan, P., Weisstaub, N. V., López-Giménez, J. F., Mingming, Z., Okawa, Y., Callado, L. F., Milligan, G., Gingrich, J. A., Filizola, M., Meana, J. J., & Sealfon, S. C. (2008). Identification of a serotonin/glutamate receptor complex implicated in psychosis. *Nature, 452*, 93–97.

Goodale, M. A., & Milner, A. D. (1992). Separate visual pathways for perception and action. *Trends in Neuroscience, 15*, 20–25.

Goodale, M. A., & Milner, A. D. (2005). *Sight unseen.* Oxford, UK: Oxford University Press.

Goodale, M. A., & Westwood, D. A. (2004). An evolving view of duplex vision: Separate but interacting cortical pathways for perception and action. *Current Opinion in Neurobiology, 14*, 203–211.

Goodale, M. A., Meenan, J. P., Bülthoff, H. H., Nicolle, D. A., Murphy, K. H., & Racicot, C. I., (1994). Separate neural pathways for the visual analysis of object shape in perception and prehension. *Current Biology, 4*, 604–610.

Goodwin, D. W., & Guze, S. B. (1996). *Psychiatric diagnosis* (5th ed.). New York: Oxford University Press.

Gordon, N. (2007). The cerebellum and cognition. *European Journal of Paediatric Neurology, 11*, 232–234.

Gottesman, I. I. (1991). *Schizophrenia genesis: The origins of madness.* New York: Freeman.

Gottesman, I. I., & Bertelsen, A. (1989). Confirming unexpressed genotypes for schizophrenia. *Archives of General Psychiatry, 46*, 867–872.

Gottesman, I. I., & Erlenmeyer-Kimling, L. (2001). Family and twin strategies as a head start in defining prodromes and endophenotypes for hypothetical early-interventions in schizophrenia. *Schizophrenia Research, 51(1)*, 93–102.

Gottesman, I. I., & Moldin, S. O. (1998). Genotypes, genes, genesis, and pathogenesis in schizophrenia. In M. F. Lenzenweger & R. H. Dworkin (Eds.), *Origins and development of schizophrenia: Advances in experimental psychopathology.* Washington, DC: American Psychological Association.

Gottesman, I. I., & Reilly, J. L. (2003). Strengthening the evidence for genetic factors in schizophrenia (without abetting genetic discrimination). In M. F. Lenzenweger & J. M Hooley (Eds.), *Principles of experimental psychopathology: Essays in honor of Brendan A. Maher* (pp. 31–44). Washington, DC: American Psychological Association.

Gottesman, I. I., & Shields, J. (1982). *Schizophrenia: The epigenetic puzzle.* Cambridge: Cambridge University Press.

Gottfredson, L. S. (2007). Innovation, fatal accidents, and the evolution of intelligence. In M. J. Roberts (Ed.), *Integrating the mind: Domain general versus domain specific processes in higher cognition* (pp. 387–425). Hove, UK: Psychology Press.

Gottfries, C. G. (1985). Alzheimer's disease and senile dementia: Biochemical characteristics and aspects of treatment. *Psychopharmacology, 86*, 27–41.

Gould, E. (2007). How widespread is adult neurogenesis in mammals? *Nature Reviews Neuroscience, 8*, 481–488.

Graham, J. R. (1990). *MMPI-2: Assessing personality and psychopathology.* New York: Oxford University Press.

Graham, S. A., Baker, R. K., & Poulin-Dubois, D. (1998). Infants' expectations about object label reference. *Canadian Journal of Experimental Psychology, 52*, 103–112.

Grant, B. S., & Wiseman, L. L. (2002). Recent history of melanism in American peppered moths. *Journal of Heredity, 93*, 86–90.

Greally, J. M. (2007). Genomics: Encyclopaedia of humble DNA. *Nature, 447*, 782—783.

Green, D. M., & Swets, J. A. (1974). *Signal detection theory and psychophysics.* New York: Krieger.

Green, L., Price, P., & Hamburger, M. E. (1995). Prisoner's dilemma and the pigeon: Control by immediate consequences. *Journal of the Experimental Analysis of Behavior, 64*, 1–17.

Greene, J. D., Sommerville, R. B., Nystrom, L. E., Darley, J. M., & Cohen, J. D. (2001). An fMRI investigation of emotional engagement in moral judgment. *Science, 293*, 2105–2108.

Greenfield, S. (2000). *The private life of the brain.* New York: Wiley.

Greenough, W. T., & Volkmar, F. R. (1973). Pattern of dendritic branching in occipital cortex of rats reared in complex environments. *Experimental Neurology, 40*, 491–504.

Greenwald, A. G., McGhee, D. E., & Schwartz, J. L. K. (1998). Measuring individual differences in implicit cognition: The implicit association test. *Journal of Personality and Social Psychology, 74(6)*, 1464–1480.

Greenwald, A. G., Nosek, B. A., & Banaji, M. R. (2003). Understanding and using the Implicit Association Test: I. An improved scoring algorithm. *Journal of Personality and Social Psychology, 85(2)*, 197–216.

Greenwald, A. G., Pratkanis, A. R., Leippe, M. R., & Baumgardner, M. H. (1986). Under what conditions does theory obstruct research progress? *Psychological Review, 93*, 216–229.

Greenwald, D. F. (1990). An external construct validity study of Rorschach personality variables. *Journal of Personality Assessment, 55*, 768–780.

Greenwald, D. F. (1999). Relationships between the Rorschach and the NEO-Five Factor Inventory. *Psychological Reports, 85(2)*, 519–527.

Grelotti, D., Gauthier, I., & Schultz, R. T. (2002). Social interest and the development of cortical face specialization: What autism teaches us about face processing. *Developmental Psychobiology, 40*, 13–25.

Grice, G. R. (1948). The relation of secondary reinforcement to delayed reward in visual discrimination learning. *Journal of Experimental Psychology, 38*, 1–16.

Grigorenko, E. L. (2001). Developmental dyslexia: An update on genes, brains, and environments. *Journal of Child Psychology, Psychiatry & Allied Disciplines, 42*, 91–125.

Grigorenko, E. L., Geissler, P. W., Prince, R., Okatcha, F. Nokes, C. Kenny, D. A., Bundy, D. A., & Sternberg, R. J. (2001). The organization of Luo conceptions of intelligence: A study of implicit theories in a Kenyan village. *International Journal of Behavioral Development, 25*, 367–378.

Griggs, R. A., & Cox, J. R. (1982). The elusive thematic-materials effect in Wason's selection task. *British Journal of Psychology, 73*, 407–420.

Grill-Spector, K., & Malach, R. (2004). The human visual cortex. *Annual Review of Neuroscience, 27*, 649–677.

Grine, F. E., Bailey, R. M., Harvati, K., Nathan, R. P., Morris, A. G., Henderson, G. M., Ribot, I., & Pike, A. W. G., (2007). Late Pleistocene human skull from Hofmeyr, South Africa, and modern human origins. *Science, 315*, 226–229.

Grof, P. (2003). Selecting effective long-term treatment for biopolar patients: Monotherapy and combinations. *Journal of Clinical Psychiatry, 64 (Suppl 5)*, 53–61.

Grön, G., Wunderlich, A. P., Spitzer, M., Tomczak, R., & Riepe, M. W. (2000). Brain activation during human navigation: Gender-different neural networks as substrate of performance. *Nature Neuroscience, 3,* 404–408.

Grossberg, S. (1971). Pavlovian pattern learning by nonlinear neural networks. *Proceedings of the National Academy of Sciences USA, 68,* 828–831.

Grossman, E. D., & Blake, R. (2001). Brain activity evoked by inverted and imagined biological motion. *Vision Research, 41,* 1475–1482.

Grossman, E. D., Donnelly, M., Price, R., Pickens, D., Morgan, V., Neighbor, G., & Blake, R. (2000). Brain areas involved in perception of biological motion. *Journal of Cognitive Neuroscience, 12,* 711–720.

Grove, W. M., & Meehl, P. E. (1996). Comparative efficiency of informal (subjective, impressionistic) and formal (mechanical, algorithmic) prediction procedures: The clinical-statistical controversy. *Psychology, Public Policy, and Law, 2,* 293–323.

Guba, E. G., & Lincoln, Y. S. (1981). *Effective evaluation: Improving the usefulness of evaluation results through responsive and naturalistic approaches.* San Francisco: Jossey-Bass.

Guilmette, T. J., Faust, D., Hart, K., & Arkes, H. R. (1990). A national survey of psychologists who offer neuropsychological services. *Archives of Clinical Neuropsychology, 5,* 373–392.

Guimond, S., & Dube, L. (1989). La representation des causes de l'inferiorité économique desquébécois francophones. *Canadian Journal of Behavioural Science, 21,* 28–39.

Güler, A., Lee, H., Shimizu, I., & Caterina, M. J. (2002). Heat-evoked activation of the ion channel, TRPV4. *Journal of Neuroscience, 22,* 6408–6414.

Guna Sherlin, D. M., & Verma, R. J. (2001). Vitamin D ameliorates fluoride-induced embryotoxicity in pregnant rats. *Neurotoxicology and Teratology, 23,* 197–201.

Gzowski, P. (1981). *The game of our lives.* Toronto: McClelland & Stewart, Inc.

Haarmeier, T., Their, P., Repnow, and Petersen, D. (1997). False perception of motion in a patient who cannot compensate for eye movements. *Nature, 389,* 849–852.

Haberlandt, K. (1994). *Cognitive psychology.* Boston: Allyn & Bacon.

Hackenburg, T. D. (2003). Determinants of pigeons' choices in token-based self-control procedures. *Journal of the Experimental Analysis of Behavior, 79,* 207–218.

Haddock, G., Zanna, M. P., & Esses, V. M. (1994). The (limited) role of trait-laden stereotypes in predicting attitudes toward native peoples. *British Journal of Social Psychology, 33,* 83–106.

Hadjikhani, N., Liu, A. K., Dale, A. M., Cavanagh, P., & Tootell, R. B. H. (1998). Retinotopy and color sensitivity in human visual cortical area V8. *Nature Neuroscience, 1,* 235–241.

Hadjistavropoulos, T., & Genest, M. (1994). The underestimation of the role of physical attractiveness in dating preferences: Ignorance or taboo? *Canadian Journal of Behavioural Science, 26,* 298–318.

Hadjistavropoulos, T., Malloy, D. C., Sharpe, D., Green, S. M., & Fuchs-Lacelle, S. (2002). The relative importance of the ethical principles adopted by the American Psychological Association. *Canadian Psychology, 43,* 254–259.

Hafer, C. L. (2000a). Do innocent victims threaten the belief in a just world? Evidence from a modified Stroop Task. *Journal of Personality and Social Psychology, 79,* 165–173.

Hafer, C. L. (2000b). Investment in long-term goals and commitment to just means drive the need to believe in a just world. *Personality and Social Psychology Bulletin, 26,* 1059–1073.

Hafer, C. L. (2002). Why we reject innocent victims. In M. Ross & D. T. Miller (Eds.), *The justice motive in everyday life.* New York: Cambridge University Press.

Hagan, F. E. (1982). *Research methods in criminal justice and criminology.* New York: Macmillan.

Haggard, P. (2005). Conscious intention and motor cognition. *Trends in Cognitive Science, 9,* 290–295.

Haggard, P., & Clark, S. (2003). Intentional action: Conscious experience and neural prediction. *Consciousness and Cognition, 12,* 695–707.

Haggard, P., Clark, S., & Kalogeras, J. (2002). Voluntary action and conscious awareness. *Nature Neuroscience, 5,* 382–385.

Haggard, P., & Eimer, M. (1999). On the relation between brain potentials and the awareness of voluntary movements. *Experimental Brain Research, 126,* 128–133.

Haidt, J. (2006). *The happiness hypothesis: Finding modern truth in ancient wisdom.* New York: Basic Books.

Haier, R. J., Jung, R. E., Yeo, R. A., Head, K., & Alkire, M. T. (2004). Structural brain variation and general intelligence. *NeuroImage, 23*(1), 425–433.

Haier, R. J., White, N. S., & Alkire, M. T. (2003). Individual differences in general intelligence correlate with brain function during nonreasoning tasks. *Intelligence, 31,* 5, 429–441.

Hair, M., Renaud, K. V., & Ramsay, J. (2007). The influence of self-esteem and locus of control on perceived email-related stress. *Computers in Human Behavior, 23,* 2701–2803.

Hajak, G., Clarenbach, P., Fischer, W., Haase, W., Bandelow, B., Adler, L., & Ruther, E. (1995). Effects of hypnotics on sleep quality and daytime well-being: Data from a comparative multicentre study in outpatients with insomnia. *European Psychiatry, 10* (Supplement 3), 173S–179S.

Halaas, J. L., Gajiwala, K. S., Maffei, M., & Cohen, S. L. (1995). Weight-reducing effects of the plasma protein encoded by the obese gene. *Science, 269,* 543–546.

Hale, S. (2003). *The man who lost his language.* London: Penguin.

Hall, C. S., & Nordby, V. J. (1973). *A primer of Jungian psychology.* New York: New American Library.

Halmi, K. (1996). Eating disorders: Anorexia nervosa, bulimia nervosa, and obesity. In R. E. Hales & S. C. Yudofsky (Eds.), *The American Psychiatric Press synopsis of psychiatry* (p. 963). Washington, DC: American Psychiatric Association.

Halpern, D. F. (2004). A cognitive-process taxonomy for sex differences in cognitive abilities. *Current Directions in Psychological Science, 14,* 623–628.

Hamilton, B. E., Martin, J. A., & Ventura, S. J. (2007). Births: Preliminary data for 2006. *National Vital Statistics Reports, 56*(7), 1–18.

Hamilton, W. D. (1964). The genetical evolution of social behaviour: I and II. *Journal of Theoretical Biology, 7,* 1–52.

Hamilton, W. D. (1970). Selfish and spiteful behavior in an evolutionary model. *Nature, 228,* 1218–1220.

Handy, C., Banks, W. C., & Zimbardo, P. (1973). Interpersonal dynamics in a simulated prison. *International Journal of Criminology and Penology, 1,* 69–97.

Haney, C., Banks, W. C., & Zimbardo, P. (1973). Interpersonal dynamics in a simulated prison. *International Journal of Criminology and Penology, 1,* 69–97.

Hanson, H. M. (1959). Effects of discrimination training on stimulus generalization. *Journal of Experimental Psychology, 58,* 321–334.

Hare, R. D. (1965). Temporal gradient of fear arousal in psychopaths. *Journal of Abnormal Psychology, 70,* 442–445.

Hare, R. D. (1998). *Without conscience: The disturbing world of the psychopaths among us.* New York: Guilford Press.

Hare, R. D. (1999). Psychopathy as a risk factor for violence. *Psychiatric Quarterly, 70,* 181–197.

Hare, R. D., McPherson, L. M., & Forth, A. E. (1988). Male psychopaths and their criminal careers. *Journal of Consulting and Clinical Psychology, 56,* 710–714.

Harkins, S. G., & Petty, R. E. (1982). Effects of task difficulty and task uniqueness on social loafing. *Journal of Personality and Social Psychology, 43,* 1214–1229.

Harlow, H. (1974). *Learning to love.* New York: J. Aronson.

Harmon-Jones, E., & Devine, P.G. (2003). Introduction to the special section on social neuroscience: Promise and caveats. *Journal of Personality and Social Psychology, 85,* 589–593.

Harmon-Jones, E., & Winkielman, P. (Eds.) (2007). *Social neuroscience: Integrating biological and psychological explanations of social behavior.* New York: Guilford Press.

Harpur, T. J., Hart, S. D., & Hare, R. D. (2002). Personality of the psychopath. In P. T. Costa, Jr., & T. A. Widiger (Eds.), *Personality disorder and the five-factor model of personality,* 2nd ed. (pp. 149–173). Washington, DC: American Psychological Association.

Harris, M. (1991). *Cultural anthropology* (3rd ed.). New York: HarperCollins.

Hart, A. J., Whalen, P. J., Shin, L. M., McInerney, S. C., Fischer, H., & Rauch, S. L. (2000). Differential response in the human amygdala to racial outgroup vs. ingroup face stimuli. *Neuro-Report, 11,* 2351–2354.

Hart, R. (1979). *Children's experience of place.* New York: Irvington.

Hartley, T., Maguire, E. A., Spiers, H. J., & Burgess, N. (2003). The well-worn route and the path less traveled: Distinct neural bases of route following and wayfinding in humans. *Neuron, 37,* 877–888.

Hartshorne, H., & May, M. A. (1928). *Studies in deceit.* New York: Macmillan.

Harwood, R. L., Miller, J. G., & Irizarry, N. L. (1995). *Culture and attachment: Perceptions of the child in context.* New York: Guilford.

Hatfield, E. (1988). Passionate and compassionate love. In R. J. Sternberg & M. L. Barnes (Eds.), *The psychology of love.* New Haven, CT: Yale University Press.

Hatfield, E., & Rapson, R. L. (1993). *Love, sex, and intimacy: Their psychology, biology, and history.* New York: HarperCollins.

Hauser, J. D., Chomsky, N., & Fitch, W. T. (2002). The faculty of language: What is it, who has it, and how did it evolve? *Science, 298,* 1569–1579.

Hayes, C. (1952). *The ape in our house.* London: Gollancz.

Hayes, S. C., & Barnes-Holmes, D. (Eds.). (2001). *Relational frame theory.* New York: Kluwer Academic/Plenum Publishers.

Hayes, S. C., Fox, E., & Gifford, E. V. (2001). Derived relational responding as learned behavior. In S. C. Hayes, D. Barnes-Holmes, & B. Roche (Eds.), *Relational frame theory: A post-Skinnerian account of human language and cognitio* (pp. 21–49). New York: Kluwer Academic/Plenum Publishers.

Hazelrigg, M. D., Cooper, H. M., & Borduin, C. M. (1987). Evaluating the effectiveness of family therapies: An integrative review and analysis. *Psychological Bulletin, 101,* 428–442.

Healy, A. F., & McNamara, D. S. (1996). Verbal learning and memory: Does the Modal Model still work? *Annual Review of Psychology, 47,* 143–172.

Healy, D. (2003). *Let them eat Prozac.* Halifax, Nova Scotia: James Lorimer & Co.

Heaton, P., & Wallace, G. L. (2004). Annotation: The savant syndrome. *Journal of Child Psychology and Psychiatry, 45,* 899–911.

Hebb, D. O. (1949). *The organization of behavior.* New York: Wiley-Interscience.

Hebb, D. O., Lambert, W. E., & Tucker, G. R. A. (1973). DMZ in the language war. *Psychology Today,* 55–62.

Heesey, C. P. (2008). Ecomorphology of orbit orientation and the adaptive significance of binocular vision in primates and other mammals. *Brain Behavior and Evolution, 71,* 54–67.

Hegde, M. N. (2001). *Hegde's pocket guide to assessment in speech-language pathology.* Clifton Park, NY: Thomson Delmar Learning.

Heider, F. (1958). *The psychology of interpersonal relations.* New York: John Wiley & Sons.

Heider, E. R. (1971). "Focal" color areas and the development of color names. *Developmental Psychology, 4,* 447–455.

Heider, E. R. (1972). Universals in color naming and memory. *Journal of Experimental Psychology, 93,* 10–20.

Heine, S. J. (2001). Self as cultural product: An examination of East Asian and North American selves. *Journal of Personality, 69,* 881–906.

Heine, S. J., Kitayama, S., Lehman, D. R., Takata, T., Ide, E., Leung, C., & Matsumoto, H. (2001). Divergent consequences of success and failure in Japan and North America: An investigation of self-improving motivations and malleable selves. *Journal of Personality and Social Psychology, 81,* 599–615.

Heinrichs, R. W. (2003). Historical origins of schizophrenia: Two early madmen and their illness. *Journal of the History of the Behavioral Sciences, 39(4),* 349–363.

Helenius, P., Salmelin, R., Serivce, E., & Connolly, J. F. (1999). Semantic cortical activation in dyslexic readers. *Journal of Cognitive Neuroscience, 11,* 535–550.

Helms, J. E. (1992). Why is there no study of cultural equivalence in standardized cognitive ability testing? *American Psychologist, 47,* 1083–1101.

Helms, J. E. (1997). The triple quandary of race, culture, and social classes in standardized cognitive ability testing. In D. P. Fanagan, J. L. Genshaft, et al. (Eds.), *Contemporary intellectual assessment: Theories, tests, and issues* (pp. 517–532). New York: Guilford Press.

Henderson, J., Kesmodel, U., & Gray, R. (2007). Systematic review of the fetal effects of prenatal binge-drinking. *Journal of Epidemiology and Community Health, 61,* 1069–1073.

Henning, W., Allen, R., Earley, C., Kushida, C., Picchietti, D., & Silber, M. (1999). The treatment of restless legs syndrome and periodic limb movement disorder. *Sleep, 22,* 970–999.

Heron, M. (2007). Deaths: Leading causes for 2004. *National Vital Statistics Reports, 56(5),* 1–96.

Herrnstein, R. J. (1970). On the law of effect. *Journal of the Experimental Analysis of Behavior, 13,* 243–266.

Herrnstein, R. J., & Murray, C. (1994). *The bell curve.* New York: Free Press.

Herrnstein, R. J., Rachlin, H., & Laibson, D. I. (1997). *The matching law: Papers in psychology and economics.* New York: Russell Sage Foundation.

Hettema, J. M., Neale, M. C., & Kendler, K. S. (2001). A review and meta-analysis of the genetic epidemiology of anxiety disorders. *American Journal of Psychiatry, 158,* 1568–1578.

Heyman, G. D., & Giles, J. W. (2004). Valence effects in reasoning about evaluative traits. *Merrill-Palmer Quarterly, 50,* 86–109.

Heywood, C. A., & Kentridge, R. W. (2003). Achromatopsia, color vision, and cortex. *Neurologic Clinics, 21,* 483–500.

Heywood, C. A., Gaffan, D., & Cowey, A. (1995). Cerebral achromatopsia in monkeys. *European Journal of Neuroscience, 7,* 1064–1073.

Higgins, L.T., & Zheng, M. (2002). An introduction to Chinese psychology—Its historical roots until the present day. *The Journal of Psychology, 136,* 225–239.

Higgins, S. T., Budney, A. J., & Bickel, W. K. (1994). Applying behavioral concepts and principles to the treatment of cocaine dependence. *Drug and Alcohol Dependence, 7,* 19–38.

Hilgard, E. R. (1986). *Divided consciousness: Multiple controls on human thought and action.* New York: Wiley-Interscience.

Hill, C. E., & Nakayama, E. Y. (2000). Client-centered therapy: Where has it been and where is it going? A comment on Hathaway (1948). *Journal of Clinical Psychology, 56,* 861–875.

Hillman, J., & Snyder, S. (2007). *Childhood autism: A clinician's guide to early diagnosis and integrated treatment.* New York: Routledge.

Hobson, J. A., & Pace-Schott, E. F. (2002). The cognitive neuroscience of sleep: Neuronal systems, consciousness and learning. *Nature Reviews: Neuroscience, 3,* 679–693.

Hoff, T. L. (1992). Psychology in Canada one hundred years ago: James Mark Baldwin at the University of Toronto. *Canadian Psychology, 33,* 683–694.

Hofstadter, D. (2007). *I am a strange loop.* New York: Basic Books.

Hogan, R., Curphy, G. J., & Hogan, J. (1994). What we know about leadership: Effectiveness and personality. *American Psychologist, 49,* 493–504.

Hohmann, G. W. (1966). Some effects of spinal cord lesions on experienced emotional feelings. *Psychophysiology, 3,* 143–156.

Holden, C. (2000). The violence of the lambs. *Science, 289,* 580–581.

Hollander, E., Schiffman, E., Cohen, B., Rivera-Stein, M. A., Rosen, W., Gorman, J. M., Fyer, A. J., Papp, L., & Liebowitz, M. R. (1990). Signs of central nervous system dysfunction in obsessive-compulsive disorder. *Archives of General Psychiatry, 47,* 27–32.

Hollis, K. L. (1982). Pavlovian conditioning of signal-centered action patterns and autonomic behavior: A biological analysis of function. *Advances in the Study of Behavior, 12,* 1–64.

Hollis, K. L. (1997). Contemporary research on Pavlovian conditioning: A "new" functional analysis. *American Psychologist, 52,* 956–965.

Hollon, S. D., Thase, M. E., & Markowitz, J. C. (2002). Treatment and prevention of depression. *Psychological Science in the Public Interest, 3(2),* 39–77.

Holyoak, K. J. (1990). Problem solving. In D. N. Osherson & E. E. Smith (Eds.), *An invitation to cognitive science. Vol. 3: Thinking.* Cambridge, MA: MIT Press.

Holyoak, K. J., & Spellman, B. A. (1993). Thinking. *Annual Review of Psychology, 44,* 265–315.

Horn, J. (1998). A basis for research on age differences in cognitive capabilities. In J. J. McCardle & R. N. Woodcock (Eds.), *Human cognitive abilities in theory and practice* (pp. 57–92). Mahwah, NJ: Lawrence Erlbaum.

Horn, J. L. (1982). The theory of fluid and crystallized intelligence in relation to concepts of cognitive psychology and aging in adulthood. In F. I. M. Craik & S. Trehub (Eds.), *Aging and cognitive processes* (pp. 237–278). New York: Plenum Press.

Horn, J. L. (2002). Selections of evidence, misleading assumptions, and oversimplifications: The political message of *The Bell Curve*. In J. M. Fish (Ed.), *Race and intelligence: Separating science from myth*. Mahwah, NJ: Lawrence Erlbaum Associates.

Horne, J. A. (1978). A review of the biological effects of total sleep deprivation in man. *Biological Psychology, 7*, 55–102.

Horne, J. A., & Minard, A. (1985). Sleep and sleepiness following a behaviourally "active" day. *Ergonomics, 28*, 567–575.

Horne, P. J., & Erjavec, M. (2007). Do infants show generalized imitation of gestures? *Journal of the Experimental Analysis of Behavior, 87*, 63–87.

Horner, V., Whiten, A., Flynn, E., & de Waal, F. B. M. (2006). Faithful replication of foraging techniques along cultural transmission chains by chimpanzees. *Proceedings of the National Academy of Sciences, USA 103*, 13878–13883.

Horney, K. (1950). *Neurosis and human growth*. New York: Norton.

Horwitz, A. V., & Wakefield, J. C. (2007). *The loss of sadness: How psychiatry transformed normal sorrow into depressive disorder*. New York: Oxford University Press.

Hothersall, D. (2004). *History of psychology* (4th ed.). New York: McGraw-Hill.

Hough, L. M., & Oswald, F. L. (2000). Personnel selection: Looking toward the future—Remembering the past. *Annual Review of Psychology, 51*, 631–664.

Houston, A. L. (1987). The control of foraging decisions. In M. L. Commons, A. Kacelnik, & S. J. Shettleworth (Eds.) Vol. 6 (pp. 41–61). Hillsdale, NJ: Lawrence Erlbaum.

Howard, M. O., Elkins, R. L., Rimmele, C., & Smith, J. W. (1991). *Drug and Alcohol Dependence, 29*, 107–143.

Hoyenga, K. B., & Hoyenga, K. T. (1993). *Gender-related differences: Origins and outcomes*. Boston: Allyn & Bacon.

Hubel, D. H. (1995). *Eye, brain, and vision*. San Francisco: W. H. Freeman.

Hubel, D. H., & Wiesel, T. (2004). *Brain and visual perception: The story of a 25-year collaboration*. New York: Oxford University Press.

Huesmann, L. R., Moise-Titus, J., Podolski, C.-L., & Eron, L. D. (2003). Exposure to TV: Longitudinal relations between children's violence and their aggressive and violent behavior in young adulthood: 1977–1992. *Developmental Psychology, 39*, 201–221.

Hugdahl, K. (Ed.) (1988). *Handbook of dichotic listening: Theory, methods, and research*. New York: Wiley.

Hughes, I. A., Houk, C., Ahmed, S. F., & Lee, P. A. (2006). Consensus statement on management of intersex disorders. *Archives of Disease in Childhood, 91*, 554–563.

Hughes, J. R., & Pierattini, R. (1992). An introduction to pharmacotherapy. In J. Grabowski & G. R. Vandenbos (Eds.), *Psychopharmacology: Basic mechanisms and applied interventions: Master lectures in psychology* (pp. 97–126). Washington, DC: American Psychological Association.

Hulit, L. M., & Howard, M. R. (1993). *Born to talk: An introduction to speech and language development*. New York: Merrill/Macmillan.

Hunt, E. (1985). Verbal ability. In R. J. Sternberg (Ed.), *Human abilities: An information-processing approach*. New York: W. H. Freeman.

Hunt, E. (1995). The role of intelligence in modern society. *American Scientist, (July–Aug)*, 356–367.

Hunt, E., & Carlson, J. (2007). Considerations related to the study of group differences in intelligence. *Perspectives in Cognitive Science, 2*, 194–213.

Hur, Y.-M. (2005). Genetic and environmental influences on self-concept in female preadolescent twins: Comparison of Minnesota and Seoul data. *Twin Research and Human Genetics, 8*, 291–299.

Hurd, P. (1997). Cooperative signalling between opponents in fish fights. *Animal Behaviour, 54*, 1309–1315.

Hurley, S., & Chater, N. (Eds.) (2005). *Perspectives on imitation: from neuroscience to social science*. Cambridge, MA: MIT Press.

Hursh, S. R. (1984). Behavioral economics. *Journal of the Experimental Analysis of Behavior, 32*, 435–452.

Huston, A. C., Watkins, B. A., & Kunkel, D. (1989). Public policy and children's television. *American Psychologist, 44*, 424–433.

Huston, A. C., & Wright, J. C. (1998). Mass media and children's development. In W. Damon (Ed.), *Child psychology* (Vol. 4) (pp. 999–1058). New York: Wiley.

Huston, A. C., Wright, J. C., Rice, M. L., Kerkman, D., & St. Peters, M. (1990). Development of television viewing patterns in early childhood: A longitudinal investigation. *Developmental Psychology, 26*, 409–420.

Hutchins, E. (1995). *Cognition in the wild*. Cambridge, MA. MIT Press.

Hyde, J. S., & Oliver, M. B. (2000). Gender differences in sexuality: Results from meta-analysis: Psychology of women. In C. B, Travis & J. W. White (Eds.), *Sexuality, society, and feminism* (pp. 57–77). Washington, DC: American Psychological Association.

Hyman, S. E., & Malenka, R. C. (2001). Addiction and the brain: The neurobiology of compulsion and its persistence. *Nature Reviews: Neuroscience, 2*, 695–703.

Iaria, G., Petrides, M., Dagher, A., Pike, B., & Bohbot, V. D. (2003). Cognitive strategies dependent on the hippocampus and caudate nucleus in human navigation: Variability and change with practice. *Journal of Neuroscience, 23*, 5945–5952.

Inglefinger, F. J. (1944). The late effects of total and subtotal gastrectomy. *New England Journal of Medicine, 231*, 321–327.

International and cultural psychology series. New York: Kluwer Academic/Plenum Publishers.

Ioannidis, J. P. A. (2005). Why most published research findings are false. *PLoS Medicine, 2*(8), e124.

Isenberg, D. J. (1986). Group polarization: A critical review and meta-analysis. *Psychological Bulletin, 50*, 1141–1151.

Iversen, L. (2003). Cannabis and the brain. *Brain, 126*, 1252–1270.

Iverson, G. L. (2005). Outcome from mild traumatic brain injury. *Current Opinion in Psychiatry, 18*, 301–317.

Jacklin, C. N., & Maccoby, E. E. (1983). Issues of gender differentiation in normal development. In M. D. Levine, W. B. Carey, A. C. Crocker, & R. T. Gross (Eds.), *Developmental-behavioral pediatrics* (pp. 175–184). Philadelphia: Saunders.

Jackson, D. N., & Tremblay, P. F. (2002). The six-factor personality questionnaire. In B. de Raad (Ed.), *Big five assessment* (pp. 353–375). Ashland, OH: Hogrefe & Huber Publishers.

Jacob, B. L. (2004). Depression: The brain finally gets into the act. *Current Trends in Psychological Science, 13*, 103–106.

Jacobs, G. D., Pace-Scholl, E. F., Stickgold, R., & Otto, M. W. (2004). Cognitive behavior therapy and pharmacotherapy for insomnia. *Archives of Internal Medicine, 164*, 1888–1896.

Jacobson, J. W., & Mulick, J. A. (1996). *Manual on diagnosis and professional practice in mental retardation*. Washington, DC: American Psychological Association.

Jakobson, L. S., Archibald, Y. M., Carey, D., & Goodale, M. A. (1991). A kinematic analysis of reaching and grasping movements in a patient recovering from optic ataxia. *Neuropsychologia, 92*, 803–809.

Jakobwitz, S., & Egan, V. (2006). The dark triad and normal personality traits. *Personality and Individual Differences, 40*, 331–339.

James, T. W., Culham, J., Humphrey, G. K., Milner, A. D., & Goodale, M. A. (2003). Ventral occipital lesions impair object recognition but not object-grasping: An fMRI study. *Brain, 126*, 2463–2475.

James, W. (1884). What is an emotion? *Mind, 9*, 188–205.

James, W. (1890). *Principles of psychology*. New York: Henry Holt.

James, W. P. T., & Trayhurn, P. (1981). Thermogenesis and obesity. *British Medical Bulletin, 37*, 43–48.

Jang, K. L., Livesley, W. J., & Vernon, P. A. (1996). Heritability of the Big Five personality dimensions and their facets: A twin study. *Journal of Personality, 64*, 577–591.

Jang, K. L., Livesley, W. J., Angleitner, A., Riemann, R., & Vernon, P. (2002). Genetic and environmental influences on the covariance of facets defining the domains of the five-factor model of personality. *Personality & Individual Differences, 33*(1), 83–101.

Janis, I. L. (1972). *Victims of groupthink*. Boston: Houghton Mifflin.

Janis, I. L. (1982). *Groupthink: Psychological studies of policy decisions and fiascoes*. Boston: Houghton Mifflin.

Jasper, H. H. (1995). A historical perspective: The rise and fall of prefrontal lobotomy. In H. H. Jasper & S. Riggio (Eds.), *Epilepsy and the functional anatomy of the frontal lobe*. New York: Raven Press.

Javal, E. (1879). Essai sur la physiologie de la lecture. *Annales D'Oculistique, 82,* 242–253.

Jaynes, J, (1976). *The origin of consciousness in the breakdown of the bicameral mind.* Boston: Houghton Mifflin.

Jaynes, J. (1970). The problem of animate motion in the seventeenth century. *Journal of the History of Ideas, 6,* 219–234.

Jeffcoate, W. J., Lincoln, N. B., Selby, C., & Herbert, M. (1986). Correlations between anxiety and serum prolactin in humans. *Journal of Psychosomatic Research, 30,* 217–222.

Jelicic, M., Smeets, T., Peters, M. J. V., Candel, I., Horselenberg, R., & Merckelbach, H. (2006). Assassination of a controversial politician: Remembering details from another nonexistent film. *Applied Cognitive Psychology, 20,* 591–596.

Jenike, M. A. (2004). Obsessive-compulsive disorder. *New England Journal of Medicine, 350,* 259–265.

Jenike, M. S. (2000). Neurological treatment of obsessive-compulsive disorder. In W. K. Goodman, M. V. Rudorfer, & J. D. Maser (Eds.), *Obsessive-compulsive disorder: Contemporary issues in treatment.* Personality and clinical psychology series. Mahwah, NJ: Lawrence Erlbaum Associates.

Jenkins, J. G., & Dallenbach, K. M. (1924). Oblivescence during sleep and waking. *American Journal of Psychology, 35,* 605–612.

Jenkins, J. H., & Karno, M. (1992). The meaning of expressed emotion: Theoretical issues raised by cross-cultural research. *American Journal of Psychiatry, 149,* 9–21.

Jensen, A. R. (1985). The nature of the black-white difference on various psychometric tests: Spearman's hypothesis. *Behavioral and Brain Sciences, 8,* 193–263.

Jensen, T., Genefke, I., & Hyldebrandt, N. (1982). Cerebral atrophy in young torture victims. *New England Journal of Medicine, 307,* 1341.

Jing, Q., & Fu, X. (2001). Modern Chinese psychology: Its indigenous roots and international influences. *International Journal of Psychology, 36,* 408–418.

Job, R. F. S. (2002). The effects of uncontrollable, unpredictable aversive and appetitive events: Similar effects warrant similar, but not identical, explanations. *Integrative Physiological & Behavioral Science, 37,* 59–81.

Johannson, G. (1973). Visual perception of biological motion and a model of its analysis. *Perception and Psychophysics, 14,* 201–211.

Johansson, B., Grant, J. D., Plomin, R., Pedersen, N. L., Ahern, F., Berg, S., McClearn, G. E. (2001). Health locus of control in late life: A study of genetic and environmental influences in twins aged 80 years and older. *Health Psychology, 20,* 33–40.

Johnson, A., & Proctor, R. W. (2003). *Attention: Theory and practice.* Thousand Oaks, CA: Sage.

Johnson, J. G., Alloy, L. B., Panzarella, C., Metalsky, G. I., Rabkin, J. G., Williams, J. B. W., & Abramson, L. Y. (2001). Hopelessness as a mediator of the association between social support and depressive symptoms: Findings of a study of men with HIV. *Journal of Consulting & Clinical Psychology, 69(6),* 1056–1060.

Johnson, J. G., Cohen, P., Smailes, E. M., Kasen, S., & Brook, J. S. (2002). Television viewing and aggressive behavior during adolescence and adulthood. *Science, 295,* 2468–2471.

Johnson, J. S., & Newport, E. L. (1989). Critical period effects in second language learning: The influence of maturational state on the acquisition of English as a second language. *Cognitive Psychology, 21,* 60–99.

Johnson, M. K. (2006). Memory and reality. *American Psychologist, 61,* 760–771.

Johnson, S. B., & Sechrest, L. (1968). Comparison of desensitization and progressive relaxation in treating test anxiety. *Journal of Consulting and Clinical Psychology, 32,* 280–286.

Johnson, W., & Bouchard, Jr., T. J. (2007). Sex differences in mental abilities: g masks the dimensions on which they lie. *Intelligence, 35,* 23–39.

Johnson-Laird, P. N. (1985). Deductive reasoning ability. In R. J. Sternberg (Ed.), *Human abilities: An information-processing approach.* New York: W. H. Freeman.

Johnson-Laird, P. N. (1999). Deductive reasoning. *Annual Review of Psychology, 50,* 109–135.

Johnson-Laird, P. N. (2001). Mental models and deduction. *Trends in Cognitive Sciences, 5,* 434–442.

Johnstone, L. (1999). Adverse psychological effects of ECT. *Journal of Mental Health, 8,* 69–85.

Joiner, T. E., Jr. (2000). A test of the hopelessness theory of depression in youth psychiatric inpatients. *Journal of Clinical Child Psychology, 29,* 167–176.

Jonçich, G. (1968). *The sane positivist: A biography of Edward L. Thorndike.* Middleton, CT: Wesleyan University Press.

Jones, E. E. (1990). *Interpersonal perception.* New York: W. H. Freeman.

Jones, E. E., & Berglas, S. (1978). Control of attributions about the self through self-handicapping strategies: The appeal of alcohol and the role of under achievement. *Personality & Social Psychology Bulletin, 4,* 200–206.

Jones, E. E., & Harris, V. A. (1967). The attribution of attitudes. *Journal of Experimental Social Psychology, 3,* 1–24.

Jones, E. E., & Nisbett, R. E. (1971). The actor and observer: Divergent perceptions of the causes of behavior. In E. E. Jones, D. E. Kamouse, H. H. Kelley, R. E. Nisbett, S. Valins, & B. Weiner (Eds.), *Attribution: Perceiving the causes of behavior.* Morristown, NJ: General Learning Press.

Jones, J. E., III. (2005). *Kitzmiller v. Dover Area School District* (Case No. 04cv2688). http://www.pamd.uscourts.gov/kitzmiller/kitzmiller_342.pdf

Jones, J. T., Pelham, B. W., Carvallo, M., & Mirenberg, M. C. (2004). How do I love thee? Let me count the Js: Implicit egotism and interpersonal attraction. *Journal of Personality and Social Psychology, 87,* 665–683.

Jones, M. C., & Bayley, N. (1950). Physical maturing among boys as related to behavior. *Journal of Educational Psychology, 41,* 129–184.

Julesz, B. (2006). *Fundamentals of cyclopean perception.* Cambridge, MA: MIT Press.

Julg, B., & Goebel, F. D. (2005). Susceptibility to HIV/AIDS: An individual characteristic we can measure? *Infection, 33,* 160–162.

Julien, R. M. (2004). *A primer of drug action,* 10th ed. New York: Worth Publishers.

Jung, C. G. (1967). Foreword. In R. Wilhelm & C. Baynes (Trans.), *The I Ching, or book of changes.* (3rd ed.). New York: Princeton University Press.

Jung, R. E., & Haier, R. J. (2007). The parieto-frontal integration theory (P-FIT) of intelligence: Converging neuroimaging evidence. *Behavioral and Brain Sciences, 30,* 135–187.

Jusczyk, P. W. (2000). *The Discovery of Spoken Language.* Cambridge, MA; Bradford Press.

Jusczyk, P. W., & Hohne, E. A. (1997). Infants' memory for spoken words. *Science, 277,* 1984–1986.

Just, M. A., & Carpenter, P. A. (1987). *The psychology of reading and language comprehension.* Boston: Allyn & Bacon.

Kaernbach, C. (2004). The memory of noise. *Experimental Psychology, 51,* 240–248.

Kagan, J. (2007). A trio of concerns. *Perspectives in Psychological Science, 2,* 361–376.

Kagan, J., Kearsley, R. B., & Zelazo, P. R. (1978). *Infancy: Its place in human development.* Cambridge, MA: Harvard University Press.

Kagan, J., Reznick, J. S., & Snidman, N. (1988). Biological bases of childhood shyness. *Science, 240,* 167–171.

Kahneman, D. (2003). A perspective on judgment and choice: Mapping bounded rationality. *American Psychologist, 58,* 697–720.

Kail R. V. (2001). *Children and their development.* Upper Saddle River, NJ: Prentice Hall.

Kail, R., & Hall, L. K. (2001). Distinguishing short-term memory from working memory. *Memory & Cognition, 29,* 1–9.

Kalish, R. A. (1976). Death and dying in a social context. In R. H. Binstock & E. Shanas (Eds.), *Handbook of aging and the social sciences* (pp. 483–507). New York: Van Nostrand Reinhold.

Kamin, L. J. (1969). Predictability, surprise, attention, and conditioning. In B. A. Campbell & R. M. Church (Eds.), *Punishment and aversive behavior* (pp. 279–296). New York: Appleton-Century-Crofts.

Kaminsky, Z., Petronis, A., Wang, S.-C., Levine, B., Ghaffar, O., Floden, D., & Feinstein, A. (2008). Epigenetics of personality traits: An illustrative study of identical twins discordant for risk-taking behavior. *Twin Research and Human Genetics, 11,* 1–11.

Kanazawa, S., & Still, M. C. (2001). The emergence of marriage norms: An evolutionary psychological perspective. In M. Hechter (Ed.), *Social norms* (pp. 274–304). New York: Russell Sage Foundation.

Kandel, E. R. (2006). *In search of memory: The emergence of a new science of mind.* New York: Norton.

Kandel, E. R., & Spencer, W. A. (1968) Cellular neurophysiological approaches in the study of learning. *Physiological Review, 48*, 65–134.

Kane, J. M., & Malhotra, A. (2003). The future of pharmacotherapy for schizophrenia. *World Psychiatry, 2*, 81–86.

Kanner, L. (1943). Autistic disturbances of effective content. *Nervous Child, 2*, 217–240.

Kaplan, E. L., & Kaplan, G. A. (1970). The prelinguistic child. In J. Eliot (Ed.), *Human development and cognitive processes*. New York: Holt, Rinehart and Winston.

Karau, S. J. & Williams, K. D. (1995). Social loafing: Research findings, implications, and future directions. *Current Directions in Psychological Science, 4*, 134–140.

Karau, S. J., & Hart, J. W. (1998). Group cohesiveness and social loafing: Effects of a social interaction manipulation on individual motivation within groups. *Group Dynamics, 2*, 185–191.

Karbe, H., Herholz, K., Szelies, B., Pawlik, G., Wienhard, K., et al. (1989). Regional metabolic correlates of token test results in cortical and subcortical left hemispheric infarction. *Neurology, 39*, 1083–1088.

Karbe, H., Szelies, B., Herholz, K., & Heiss, W. D. (1990). Impairment of language is related to left parieto-temporal glucose metabolism in aphyasic stroke patients. *Journal of Neurology, 237*, 19–23.

Katamba, F. (2003). *Morphology: Critical concepts in linguistics*. London: Taylor & Francis.

Kausler, D. H. (1994). *Learning and memory in normal aging*. New York: Academic Press.

Kayeart, G., Biederman, I., & Vogels, R. (2005). Representation of regular and irregular shapes in macaque inferotemporal cortex. *Cerebral Cortex, 15*, 1308–1321.

Kazdin, A. E. (2001). *Behavior modification in applied settings* (6th ed.). Belmont, CA: Wadsworth/Thomson Learning.

Kazdin, A. E. (2005). *Parent management training: Treatment for oppositional, aggressive, and antisocial behavior in children and adolescents*. New York: Oxford University Press.

Kazdin, A. E. (2008). Evidence-based treatment and practice: New opportunities to bridge clinical research and practice, enhance the knowledge base, and improve patient care. *American Psychologist, 63*, 146–159.

Keating, D. (2004). Cognitive and brain development. (2004). In R. M. Lerner & L. Steinberg (Eds.), *Handbook of adolescent psychology*, 2nd ed. (pp. 45–84). Hoboken, NJ: John Wiley and Sons.

Keel, P. K., & Klump, K. L. (2003). Are eating disorders culture-bound syndromes? Implications for conceptualizing their etiology. *Psychological Bulletin, 129*, 747–769.

Kehoe, E. J. (1988). A layered network model of associative learning: Learning to learn and configuration. *Psychological Review, 95*, 411–433.

Kehoe, E. J., Horne, P. S., & Macrae, M. (1993). Real-time processing of serial stimuli in classical conditioning of the rabbit's nictitating membrane response. *Journal of Experimental Psychology: Animal Behavior Processes, 19*, 265–283.

Keller, S. E., Weiss, J. M., Schleifer, S. J., Miller, N. E., & Stein, M. (1983). Stress-induced suppression of immunity in adrenalectomized rats. *Science, 221*, 1301–1304.

Kelley, A. E., Schochet, T., & Landry, C. F. (2004). Risk taking and novelty seeking in adolescence: Introduction to part I. *Annals of the New York Academy of Science, 1021*, 27–32.

Kelley, H. H. (1967). Attribution theory in social psychology. In D. Levine (Ed.), *Nebraska symposium on motivation, Vol. 15*. Lincoln: University of Nebraska Press.

Kelly, J. F., & Hake, D. F. (1970). An extinction-induced increase in an aggressive response with humans. *Journal of the Experimental Analysis of Behavior, 14*, 153–164.

Kelly, S. J., Day, N., & Streissguth, A. P. (2000). Effects of prenatal alcohol exposure on social behavior in humans and other species. *Neurotoxicology and Teratology, 22*, 143–149.

KeltiKangas-Järvinen, L., & Heinonen, K. (2003). Childhood roots of adult hostility: Family factors as predictors of cognitive and affective hostility. *Child Development, 74*, 1751–1768.

Kendler, K. S., Pedersen, N., Johnson, L., Neale, M. C., & Mathe, A. A. (1993). A pilot Swedish twin study of affective illness, including hospital- and population-ascertained subsamples. *Archives of General Psychiatry, 50(9)*, 699–700.

Kendler, K. S., Prescott, C. A., Neale, M. C., & Pedersen, N. L. (1997). Temperance board registration for alcohol abuse in a national sample of Swedish male twins, born 1902 to 1949. *Archives of General Psychiatry, 54*, 178–184.

Kennedy, R. (2007). *The many voices of psychoanalysis*. New York: Routledge.

Kenrick, D. T., Groth, G., Trost, M. R., & Sadalla, E. K. (1993). Integrating evolutionary and social exchange perspectives on relationships: Effects of gender, self-appraisal, and involvement level in mate selection. *Journal of Personality and Social Psychology, 64*, 951–969.

Kenrick, D. T., Li, N. P., & Butner, J. (2003). Dynamical evolutionary psychology: Individual decision rules and emergent social norms. *Psychological Review, 110*, 3–28.

Kenrick, D. T., Neuberg, S. L., Zierk, K. L., & Krones, J. M. (1994). Evolution and social cognition: Contrast effects as a function of sex, dominance, and physical attractiveness. *Personality and Social Psychology Bulletin, 20*, 210–217.

Kertesz, A. (1981). Anatomy of jargon. In J. Brown (Ed.), *Jargonaphasia*. New York: Academic Press.

Kessler, R. C., Chiu, W. T., Demler, O., & Walter, E. E. (2005). Prevalence, severity, and comorbidity of 12-month DSM-IV disorders in the National Comorbidity Survey. *Archives of General Psychiatry, 62*, 617–627.

Kessler, R. C., McGonagle, K. A., Zhao, S., Nelson, C., Hughes, M., Eshleman, S., Wittchen, H., & Kendler, K. (1994). Lifetime and 12-month prevalence of DSM-III-R psychiatric disorders in the United States. *Archives of General Psychiatry, 51*, 8–19.

Kew, J. J. M., Ridding, M. C., Rothwell, J. C., Passingham, R. E., Leigh, P. N., Sooriakumaran, S., Frackowiak, R. S. G., & Brooks, D. J. (1994). Reorganization of cortical blood flow and transcranial magnetic stimulation maps in human subjects after upper limb amputation. *Journal of Neurophysiology, 72*, 2517–2524.

Key, A. P. F., Ferguson, M., Molfese, D. L., Peach, K., Lehman, C., & Molfese, V. J. (2007). Smoking during pregnancy affects speech-processing ability. *Environmental Health Perspectives, 115*, 623–629.

Keyes, C. L. M., & Haidt, J. (Eds.). (2003). *Positive psychology and the life well-lived*. Washington, DC: American Psychological Association.

Keyes, D. (1981). *The minds of Billy Milligan*. New York: Bantam.

Keyes, J. B. (1995). Stress inoculation training for staff working with persons with mental retardation: A model program. In L. R. Murphy, J. J. Hurrell, Jr., S. L. Sauter, & G. P. Keita (Eds.), *Job stress interventions* (pp. 45–55). Washington, DC: American Psychological Association.

Khachaturian, Z. S., & Blass, J. P. (1992). *Alzheimer's disease: New treatment strategies*. New York: Dekker.

Kheriaty, E., Kleinknecht, R. A., & Hyman, I. E. (1999). Recall and validation of phobia origins as a function of a structured interview versus the Phobia Origins Questionnaire. *Behavior Modification, 23*, 61–78.

Kiang, N. Y.-S. (1965). *Discharge patterns of single nerve fibers in the cat's auditory nerve*. Cambridge, MA: MIT Press.

Kiehl, K. A., Smith, A. M., Hare, R. D., & Liddle, P. F. (2000). An event-related potential investigation of response inhibition in schizophrenia and psychopathy. *Biological Psychiatry, 48(3)*, 210–221.

Kihlstrom, J. F. (2004). Hypnosis. In C. Spielberger (Ed.) (pp. 243–248). *Encyclopedia of applied psychology*, Vol. 2. Oxford: Elsevier.

Kilgour, A. R., Jakobson, L. S., & Cuddy, L. L. (2000). Music training and rate of presentation as mediators of text and song recall. *Memory & Cognition, 28*, 700–710.

Killeen, P. R., & Nash, M. R. (2003). The four causes of hypnosis. *International Journal of Clinical and Experimental Hypnosis, 51*, 195–321.

Kimura, D. (1999). *Sex and cognition*. Cambridge, MA: The MIT Press.

King, M. C., & Wilson, A. C. (1975). Evolution at two levels in humans and chimpanzees. *Science, 188*, 107–116.

Kirasic, K. C. (1991). Spatial cognition and behavior in young and elderly adults: Implications for learning new environments. *Psychology and Aging, 6*, 10–18.

Kirasic, K. C., & Bernicki, M. R. (1990). Acquisition of spatial knowledge under conditions of temporospatial discontinuity in young and elderly adults. *Psychological Research, 52*, 76–79.

Kirby, D. (2006). *Evidence of harm: Mercury in vaccines and the autism epidemic: A medical controversy*. New York: St Martin's Griffin.

Kirchengast, S., & Hartmann, B. (2003). Nicotine consumption before and during pregnancy affects not only newborn size but also birth modus. *Journal of Biosocial Science, 35*, 175–188.

Kirsch, I., & Lynn, S. J. (1998). Dissociation theories of hypnosis. *Psychological Bulletin, 123,* 100–115.

Kisilevsky, B. S., Hains, S. M. J., Lee, K., Xie, X., Huang, H., Ye, H. H., Zhang, K., & Wang, Z. (2003). Effects of experience on fetal voice recognition. *Psychological Science, 14,* 220–224.

Kitayama, S., Markus, H. R., & Kurakawa, M. (2000). Culture, emotion, and well-being: Good feelings in Japan and the United States. *Cognition and Emotion, 14,* 93–124.

Klaczynski, P. A. (2004). A dual-process model of adolescent development: Implications for decision making, reasoning, and identity. In R. V. Kail (Ed.), *Advances in Child Development and Behavior.* (Vol. 32) (pp. 73–123). Amsterdam: Elsevier.

Klein, D. A., & Walsh, B. T. (2004). Eating disorders: clinical features and pathophysiology: Special issue: Reviews on ingestive science. *Physiology & Behavior, 81,* 359–374.

Klein, D. F. (1996). Panic disorder and agoraphobia: Hypothesis hothouse. *Journal of Clinical Psychiatry, 57,* 21–27.

Klein, R. M. (1999). The Hebb legacy. *Canadian Journal of Psychology, 53,* 1–3.

Kleinknecht, R. A., Dinnel, D. L., Kleinknecht, E. E., Hiruma, N., & Harada, N. (1997). Cultural factors in social anxiety: A comparison of social phobia symptoms and Taijin Kyofusho. *Journal of Anxiety Disorders, 11,* 157–177.

Kleitman, N. (1939). *Sleep and wakefulness.* Chicago: University of Chicago Press.

Klerman, G. L, & Weissman, M. M. (1986). The interpersonal approach to understanding depression. In T. Millon & G. L. Klerman (Eds.), *Contemporary directions in psychopathology: Toward the DSM-IV* (pp. 429–456). New York: Guilford Press.

Knauf, M., Mulack, T., Kassubek, J., Salih, H. R., & Greenleg, M. W. (2002). Spatial imagery in deductive reasoning: A functional MRI study. *Cognitive Brain Research, 13,* 203–212.

Knekt, P., Lindfors, O., Härkänen, T., Välikoski, M., Virtala, E., Laaksonen, M. A., Marttunen, M., Kaipainen, M., Renlund, C., & the Helsinki Psychotherapy Study Group. (2008). Randomized trial on the effectiveness of long- and short-term psychodynamic psychotherapy and solution-focused therapy on psychiatric symptoms using a 3-year follow-up. *Psychological Medicine, 38,* 689–703.

Knowles, J. A., Kaufmann, C. A., & Rieder, R. O. (1999). Genetics. In R. E. Hales, S. C. Yudofsky, & J. A. Talbot (Eds.), *Textbook of psychiatry* (pp. 35–82). Washington, DC: American Psychiatric Press.

Kobasa, S. C. (1979). Stress life events, personality, and health: An inquiry into hardiness. *Journal of Personality and Social Psychology, 42,* 168–177.

Kobasa, S. C. O., Maddi, S. R., Puccetti, M. C., & Zola, M. A. (1985). Effectiveness of hardiness, exercise and social support as resources against illness. *Journal of Psychosomatic Research, 29,* 525–533.

Koch, C. (2004). *The quest for consciousness: A neurobiological approach.* Greenwood Village, CO: Roberts & Company.

Koch, J. L. A. (1889). *Leitfaden der psychiatrie* (2nd ed.). Ravensburg, Austria: Dorn.

Koechlin, E., & Hyafil, A. (2007). Anterio prefrontal function and the limits of human decision-making. *Science, 318,* 598–602.

Kohler, W. (1927/1973). *The mentality of apes.* (2nd ed.). New York: Liverwright.

Koivisto, M., & Revonsuo, A. (2007). How meaning shapes seeing. *Psychological Science, 18,* 845–849.

Kojima, M., Hosoda, H., Date, Y., Nakazato, M., Matsuo, H., & Kangawa, K. (1999). Ghrelin is a growth-hormone-releasing acylated peptide from stomach. *Nature, 402,* 656–660.

Kolata, G. (1998, May 27). Scientists see a mysterious similarity in a pair of deadly plagues. *New York Times,* p. 1.

Kolb, B., Gibb, R., & Robinson, T. E. (2003). Brain plasticity and behavior. *Current Directions in Psychological Science, 12,* 1–5.

Kolb, B., & Stewart, J. (1995). Changes in the neonatal gonadal hormonal environment prevent behavioral sparing and alter cortical morphogenesis after early female frontal cortex lesions in male and female rats. *Behavioral Neuroscience, 109,* 285–294.

Kolb, B., & Wishaw, I. Q. (1998). Brain plasticity and behavior. *Annual Review of Psychology, 49,* 43–64.

Komisaruk, B. R., & Larsson, K. (1971) Suppression of a spinal and a cranial nerve reflex by vaginal or rectal probing in rats. *Brain Research, 35,* 231–235.

Komisaruk, B. R., & Steinman, J. L. (1987). Genital stimulation as a trigger for neuroendocrine and behavioral control of reproduction. *Annals of the New York Academy of Sciences, 474,* 64–75.

Konrad, K., Gunther, T., Hanisch, C., & Herpertz-Dahlmann, B. (2004). Differential effects of methylphenidate on attentional functions in children with attention-deficit/hyperactivity disorder. *Journal of American Academy of Child and Adolescent Psychiatry, 43,* 191–198.

Kopta, S. M., Lueger, R. J., Saunders, S. M., & Howard, K. I. (1999). Individual psychotherapy outcome and process research: Challenges leading to greater turmoil or a positive transition. *Annual Review of Psychology, 50,* 441–469.

Korn, J. H., Davis, R., & Davis, S. F. (1991). Historians' and chairpersons' judgments of eminence among psychologists. *American Psychologist, 46,* 789–792.

Korol, M., Kramer, T. L., Grace, M. C., & Green, B. L. (2002). Dam break: Long-term follow-up of children exposed to the Buffalo Creek disaster. In A. M. La Greca et al. (Eds.), *Helping children cope with disasters and terrorists* (pp. 241–258). Washington, DC: American Psychological Association.

Kosslyn, S. M. (1973). Scanning visual images: Some structural implications. *Perception and Psychophysics, 14,* 90–94.

Kosslyn, S. M. (1975, July). *Evidence for analogue representation.* Paper presented at the Conference on Theoretical Issues in Natural Language Processing, Massachusetts Institute of Technology, Cambridge, MA.

Kozulin, A., & Falik, L. (1995). Dynamic cognitive assessment of the child. *Current Directions in Psychological Science, 4,* 192–196.

Kramer, P. D. (1993). *Listening to Prozac: A psychiatrist explores antidepressant drugs and the remaking of the self.* New York: Viking Penguin.

Krause, C. (2007). New "arms" for disabled soldiers. *Oak Ridge National Laboratory Review, 40(2),* 26–27.

Krebs, D. L., & Denton, K. (1997). Social illusions and self-deception: The evolution of biases in person perception. In J. A. Simpson & D. T. Kenrick (Eds.), *Evolutionary social psychology.* Mahway, NJ: Lawrence Erlbaum Associates, Publishers.

Kreisler, A., Godefroy, O., Delmaire, C., Debachy, M., Leclercq, M., Provo, J.-P. & Leys, D. (2000). The anatomy of aphasia revisited. *Neurology, 54,* 1117–1123.

Kremer, R. (1976). *Maria Montessori.* New York: G. P. Putnam's Sons.

Kress, M., & Zeilhofer, H. U. (1999). Capsaicin, protons and heat: New excitement about nociceptors. *Trends in Pharmacological Science, 20,* 112–118.

Kreuter, M. W., Lezin, N. A., & Young, L. A. (2000). Evaluating community-based collaborative mechanisms: Implications for practitioners. *Health Promotion Practice, 1,* 49–63

Kriechman, A. M. (1987). Siblings with somatoform disorders in childhood and adolescence. *Journal of the American Academy of Child and Adolescent Psychiatry, 26,* 226–231.

Krueger, T. H. (1976). *Visual imagery in problem solving and scientific creativity.* Derby, CT: Seal Press.

Krueger, R. F., Markon, D. E., & Bouchard, T. J., Jr. (2003). The extended genotype: The heritability of personality accounts for the heritability of recalled family environments in twins reared apart. *Journal of Personality, 71(5),* 809–833.

Krull, D. L., Loy, M. H.-M., Lin, J., Wang, C.-F., Chen, S., & Zhao, X. (1999). The fundamental fundamental attribution error: Correspondence bias in individualist and collectivist cultures. *Personality and Social Psychology Bulletin, 25,* 1208–1219.

Kübler-Ross, E. (1969). *On death and dying.* New York: Macmillan.

Kübler-Ross, E. (1981). *Living with death and dying.* New York: Macmillan.

Kuhl, P. K. (2000). A new view of language acquisition. *Proceedings of the National Academy of Sciences USA, 97,* 11850–11857.

Kuhl, P. K., Williams, K. A., Lacerda, F., Stevens, K. N., & Lindblom, B. (1992). Linguistic experience alters phonetic perception in infants by 6 months of age. *Science, 255,* 606–608.

Kunda, Z. (1999). *Social cognition: Making sense of people.* Cambridge, MA: The MIT Press.

Kunda, Z., & Oleson, K. (1997). When exceptions prove the rule: How extremity of deviance determines deviants' impact on stereotypes. *Journal of Personality and Social Psychology, 72,* 965–979.

Kunda, Z., & Sinclair, L. (1999). Motivated reasoning with stereotypes: Activation, application, and inhibition. *Psychological Inquiry, 10,* 12–22.

REFERENCES

Kurihara, K. (1987). Recent progress in taste receptor mechanisms. In *Umami: A basic taste.* Y. Kawamura and M. R. Kare (Eds.). New York: Dekker.

Kurzban, R. & Weeden, J. (2003). HurryDate: Mate preferences in action. *Evolution and Human Behavior, 26,* 227–244.

Laeng, B., & Falkenberg, L. (2007). Women's pupillary responses to sexually significant others during the hormonal cycle. *Hormones and Behavior, 52,* 520–530.

LaFarge, L. (2000). Interpretation and containment. *International Journal of Psycho-Analysis, 81,* 67–84.

Laing, R. D., & Esterson, A. (1964). *Sanity, madness, and the family.* Harmondworth, England: Pelican.

Lakoff, G., & Turner, M. (1989). *More than cool reason: The power of poetic metaphor.* Chicago: University of Chicago Press.

Lambert, M. J., Gregersen, A. T., & Burlingame, G. M. (2004). The Outcome Questionnaire. In M. E. Muruish (Ed.), *The use of psychological testing for treatment planning and outcomes assessment,* (Vol. 3, 3rd ed.) (pp. 191–234). New York: Routledge.

Lane, S. M., Mather, M., Villa, D., & Morita, S. K. (2001). How events are reviewed matters: Effects of varied focus on eyewitness suggestibility. *Memory & Cognition, 29,* 940–947.

Lange, C. G. (1887). *Über Gemüthsbewegungen.* Leipzig, East Germany: T. Thomas.

Langer, E. J., & Abelson, R. P. (1974). A patient by any other name . . . : Clinician group difference in labeling bias. *Journal of Consulting and Clinical Psychology, 42,* 4–9.

Langer, E. J., Bashner, R. S., & Chanowitz, B. (1985). Decreasing prejudice by increasing discrimination. *Journal of Personality and Social Psychology, 49,* 113–120.

Langhans, W. (1996). Role of the liver in the metabolic control of eating: What we know and what we do not know. *Neuroscience and Biobehavioral Reviews, 20,* 145–153.

Langhans, W., Grossman, F., & Geary, N. (2001). Intrameal hepatic-portal infusion of glucose reduces spontaneous meal size in rats. *Physiology & Behavior, 73,* 499–507.

Langlois, J. H., & Downs, A. C. (1980). Mothers, fathers, and peers as socialization agents of sex-typed play behaviors in young children. *Child Development, 51,* 1237–1247.

LaPiere, R. T. (1934). Attitudes and actions. *Social Forces, 13,* 230–237.

Lashley, K. S. (1930). Basic neural mechanisms in behavior. *Psychological Review, 17,* 1–26.

Latané, B., & Darley, J. M. (1970). *The unresponsive bystander: Why doesn't he help?* New York: Appleton-Century-Crofts.

Lattal, K. A., & Crawford-Godbey, C. (1985). Homogeneous chains, heterogeneous chains, and delay of reinforcement. *Journal of the Experimental Analysis of Behavior, 44,* 337–342.

Laumann, E. O., Gagnon, J. H., Michael, R. T., & Michaels, S. (1994). *The social organization of sexuality: Sexual practices in the United States.* Chicago: University of Chicago Press.

Lavie, P., Pratt, H., Scharf, B., Peled, R., & Brown, J. (1984). Localized pontine lesion: Nearly total absence of REM sleep. *Neurology, 34,* 1118–1120.

Law, S-P., & Or, B. (2001). A case study of acquired dyslexia and dysgraphia in Cantonese: Evidence for nonsemantic pathways for reading and writing Chinese. *Cognitive Neuropsychology, 18,* 729–748.

Lawson, R. B., Graham, J. E., & Baker, K. M. (2007). *A history of psychology: Globalization, ideas, and applications.* Upper Saddle River, NJ: Pearson Prentice Hall.

Lazarus, R. S. (2000). Toward better research on stress and coping. *American Psychologist, 55(6),* 665–673.

Lazarus, R. S., & Folkman, S. (1984). *Stress, appraisal, and coping.* New York: Springer.

Lê, S., Cardebat, D., Boulanouar, K., Henaff, M. A., Michel, F., Milner, D., Dkjkerman, C., Puel, M. & Démonet, J.-F. (2002). Seeing, since childhood, without, ventral stream: A behavioural study. *Brain, 125,* 58–74.

Le Mare, L., Audet, K., & Kurytnik, K. (2007). A longitudinal study of service use in families of children adopted from Romanian orphanages. *International Journal of Behavioral Development, 31,* 242–251.

Leather, N. (2004). Self-concept. In D. Wyse (Ed.), *Childhood studies: An introduction* (pp. 13–18). New York: Blackwell.

Leckman, J. F., Pauls, D. L., Zhang, H., Rosario-Campos, M. C., Katsovich, L., Kidd, K. K., Pakstis, A. J., Alsobrook, J. P., et al. (2003). Obsessive-compulsive symptom dimensions in affected sibling pairs diagnosed with Gilles de la Tourette syndrome. *American Journal of Medical Genetics, 116B,* 60–68.

LeDoux, J. E. (1992). Brain mechanisms of emotion and emotional learning. *Current Opinion in Neurobiology, 2,* 191–197.

Lee, V., & Wagner, H. (2002). The effect of social presence on the facial and verbal expression of emotion and the interrelationships among emotion components. *Journal of Nonverbal Behavior, 26,* 3–25.

Leeser, J., & O'Donohue, W. (1999). What is a delusion? Epistemological dimensions. *Journal of Abnormal Psychology, 108,* 687–694.

Lefcourt, H. M. (1966). Internal versus external control of reinforcement: A review. *Psychological Bulletin, 65,* 206–220.

Lefcourt, H. M. (1992). Durability and impact of the locus of control construct. *Psychological Bulletin, 112,* 411–414.

Lefley, H. P. (1984). Delivering mental health services across cultures. In P. B. Pedersen, N. Sartorius, & A. Marsella (Eds.), *Mental health services: The cross-culture perspective* (pp. 259–266). Beverly Hills, CA: Sage.

Lefley, H. P. (1994). Mental health treatment and service delivery in cross-cultural perspective. In L. L. Adler & U. P. Gielen (Eds.), *Cross-cultural topics in psychology* (pp. 179–199). Westport, CT: Praeger.

Lefley, H. P. (2002). Helping families cope with mental illness: Future international directions. In H. P. Lefley & D. L. Johnson (Eds.), *Family intervention in mental illness: International perspectives* (pp. 221–234). Westport, CT: Praeger.

LeFrancois, J. R., Chase, P. N., & Joyce, J. H. (1988). The effects of a variety of instructions on human fixed-interval performance. *Journal of the Experimental Analysis of Behavior, 49,* 383–393.

Lehman, D. R., Chiu, C.-Y., & Schaller, M. (2004). Psychology and culture. *Annual Review of Psychology, 55,* 689–714.

Lehmann, H. E., & Ban, T. A. (1997). The history of the psychopharmacology of schizophrenia. *Canadian Journal of Psychiatry, 42,* 152–162.

Lehne, G., & Money, J. (2000). Paraphilia treated with Depo-Provera: 40-year outcome. *Journal of Sex Education and Therapy, 25,* 213–220.

Leichsenring, F. (2005). Are psychodynamic and psychoanalytic therapies effective? A review of empirical data. *International Journal of Psychoanalysis, 86,* 841–868.

Leitzmann, M. F., Park, Y., Blair, A., Ballard-Barbash, R., Mouw, T., Hollenbeck, A. R., & Schatzkin, A. (2007). Physical activity recommendations and decreased risk of mortality. *Archives of Internal Medicine, 167,* 2453–2460.

Lemieux, R., & Hale, J. L. (2002). Intimacy, passion, and commitment in young romantic relationships: Successfully measuring the triangular theory of love. *Psychological Reports, 90,* 1009–1014.

Lemonde, S., Turecki, G., Bakish, D., Lisheng, D., Hrdina, P. D., Brown, C. D., Sequeira, A., et al. (2003). Impaired repression at a 5-hydroxytryptamine 1A receptor gene polymorphism associated with major depression and suicide. *The Journal of Neuroscience, 23(25),* 8788–8799.

Lenggenhager, B., Tadi, T., Metzinger, T., & Blanke, O. (2007). Video ergo sum: Manipulating bodily self-consciousness. *Science, 317,* 1096–1099.

Lennenberg, E. (1967). *Biological foundations of language.* New York: Wiley.

Leon, G. R. (1977). *Case histories of deviant behavior* (2nd ed.). Boston: Allyn and Bacon.

León-Carrión, J., van Eeckhout, P., Domínjgues-Morales, M. d. R., & Pérez-Santamaria, F. J. (2002). The locked-in syndrome: A syndrome looking for a therapy. *Brain Injury, 16,* 555–569.

Lepage, J.-L. & Théoret, H. (2007). The mirror neuron system: Grasping others' actions from birth? *Developmental Science, 10,* 513–529.

Lepper, M. R., Greene, D., & Nisbett, R. E. (1973). Undermining children's intrinsic interest with extrinsic reward: A test of the "overjustification" hypothesis. *Journal of Personality and Social Psychology, 28,* 129–137.

Lerman, D. C., Iwata, B. A., & Wallace, M. D. (1999). Side effects of extinction: Prevalence of bursting and aggression during the treatment of self-injurious behavior. *Journal of Applied Behavior Analysis, 32,* 1–8.

Lerner, M. J. (1980). *The belief in a just world.* New York: Plenum Press.

Lesage, A. D., Morissette, R., Fortier, L., Reinharz, D., & Contandriopoulos, A. (2000). 1. Downsizing psychiatric hospitals: Needs for care and services of current and discharged long-stay inpatients. *Canadian Journal of Psychiatry, 45,* 526–531.

REFERENCES

Leuner, B., Mendolia-Loffredo, S., Kozorovitskiy, Y., Samburg, D., Gould, E., and Shors, T. J. (2004) Learning enhances the survival of new neurons beyond the time when the hippocampus is required for memory. *Journal of Neuroscience, 24,* 7477–7481.

LeVay, S. (1991). A difference in hypothalamic structure between heterosexual and homosexual men. *Science, 253,* 1034–1037.

Lewinsohn, P. M., Mischel, W., Chaplin, W., & Barton, R. (1980). Social competence and depression: The role of illusory self-perceptions. *Journal of Abnormal Psychology, 89,* 194–202.

Lewis, J. W., Wightman, F. I., Brefczynski, J. A., Phinney, R. E., Binder, J. R., & DeYoe, E. A. (2004). Human brain regions involved in recognizing environmental sounds. *Cerebral Cortex, 14,* 1008–1021.

Lewis, M., Alessandri, S. M., & Sullivan, M. W. (1990). Violation of expectancy, loss of control, and anger expressions in young infants. *Developmental Psychology, 26,* 745–751.

Ley, R. (2003). Respiratory psychophysiology and the modification of breathing behavior. *Behavior Modification, 27(5),* 603–606.

Li, J. Z., Absher, D. M., Tang, H., Southwick, A. M., Casto, A. M., Ramachandran, S., Cann, H. M., Barsh, G. S., Feldman, M., Cavalli-Sforza, L. L., & Myers, R. M. (2008). Worldwide human relationships inferred from genome-wide patterns of variation. *Science, 319,* 1100–1104.

Li, N. P., Bailey, J. M., Kenrick, D. T., & Linsenmeier, J. A. (2002). The necessities and luxuries of mate preferences: Testing the trade-offs. *Journal of Personality and Social Psychology, 82,* 947–955.

Liberman, A. M. (1996). *Speech: A special code.* Cambridge, MA: MIT Press.

Libet, B. (2002). The timing of mental events: Libet's experimental findings and their implications. *Consciousness and Cognition, 11,* 291–299.

Libet, B. (2004). *Mind time: The temporal factor in consciousness.* Cambridge: MA: Harvard University Press.

Libet, B., Gleason, C. A., Wright, E. W., & Pearl, D. K. (1983). Time of conscious intention to act in relation to onset of cerebral activities (readiness potential): The unconscious initiation of a freely voluntary act. *Brain, 106,* 623–642.

Lickey, M. E., & Gordon, B. (1983). *Drugs for mental illness.* New York: Freeman.

Lickey, M. E., & Gordon, B.. (1991). *Medicine and mental illness: The use of drugs in psychiatry.* San Francisco: W. H. Freeman.

Lickliter, R., & Honeycutt, H. (2003). Developmental dynamics: Toward a biologically plausible evolutionary psychology. *Psychological Review, 129,* 819–835.

Lidberg, L., Asberg, M., & Sundqvist-Stensman, U. B. (1984). 5-Hydroxyindoleacetic acid levels in attempted suicides who have killed their children. *Lancet, 2,* 928.

Lidberg, L., Tuck, J. R., Asberg, M., Scalia-Tomba, G. P., & Bertilsson, L. (1985). Homicide, suicide and CSF 5-HIAA. *Acta Psychiatrica Scandinavica, 71,* 230–236.

Lidz, T., Fleck, S., & Cornelison, A. R. (1965). *Schizophrenia and the family.* New York: International Universities Press.

Lieb, K., Zanarini, C., Schmahl, C., Linehan, M., & Bohus, M. (2004). Borderline personality disorder. *The Lancet, 364,* 453–461.

Lieberman, E., Michel, J-B., Jackson, J., Tang, T., & Nowak, M. A. (2007). Quantifying the evolutionary dynamics of language. *Nature, 449,* 717–720.

Lieberman, M D. (2007). Social cognitive neuroscience: A review of core processes. *Annual Review of Psychology, 58,* 259–289.

Lieberman, M. D., Ochsner, K. N., Gilbert, D. T., & Schacter, D. L. (2001). Do amnesiacs exhibit cognitive dissonance? The role of explicit memory and attention in attitude change. *Psychological Science, 12,* 135–140.

Lifton, R. J. (2005). Americans as survivors. *New England Journal of Medicine, 352,* 2263–2265.

Lillard, A. S. (2005). *Montessori: The science behind the genius.* New York: Oxford.

Lim, K. O., Adalsteinsson, E., Spielman, D., Sullivan, E. V., Rosenbloom, M. J., & Pfefferbaum, A. (1998). Proton magnetic resonance of cortical gray matter and white matter in schizophrenia. *Archives of General Psychiatry, 55,* 346–352.

Lin, L., Faraco, J., Li, R., Kadotani, H., Rogers, W., Lin, X., Qiu, X., de Jong, P. J., Nishino, S., & Mignot, E. (1998). The sleep disorder canine narcolepsy is caused by a mutation in the hypocretin (orexin) receptor. *Cell, 98,* 365–376.

Linden, D. (2007). *The accidental mind: How brain evolution has given us love, memory, dreams, and God.* Cambridge, MA: Belknap Press of Harvard University Press.

Linley, P. A., Joseph, S., Harrington, S., & Wood, A. M. (2006). Positive psychology: Past, present, and (possible) future. *Journal of Positive Psychology, 1,* 3–16.

Linsky, A. S., Bachman, R., & Straus, M. A. (1995). *Stress, culture, and aggression.* New Haven, CT: Yale University Press.

Linville, P. W., Fischer, G. W., & Salovey, P. (1989). Perceived distributions of the characteristics of in-group and out-group members: Empirical evidence and a computer simulation. *Journal of Personality and Social Psychology, 157,* 165–188.

Lisanby, S. H., Maddox, J. H., Prudic, J., Devanand, D. P., & Sackeim, H. A. (2000). The effects of electroconvulsive therapy on memory of autobiographical and public events. *Archives of General Psychiatry, 57,* 581–590.

Livesley, W. J., Jang, K. L., & Vernon, P. A. (2003). Genetic basis of personality structure. In T. Millon & M. J. Lerner (Eds.), *Handbook of psychology: Personality and social psychology, Vol. 5* (pp. 59–83). New York: John Wiley & Sons, Inc.

Loehlin, J. C. (1992). *Genes and environment in personality development.* London: Sage Publications.

Loehlin, J. C., McCrae, R. R., Costa, P. T., & John, O. P. (1998). Heritabilities of common and measure-specific components of the Big Five personality factors. *Journal of Research in Personality, 32,* 431–453.

Loehlin, J. C., & Nichols, R. C. (1976). *Heredity, environment, and personality.* Austin: University of Texas Press.

Loftus, E. F. (1979). *Eyewitness testimony.* Cambridge, MA: Harvard University Press.

Loftus, E. F., & Palmer, J. C. (1974). Reconstruction of automobile destruction: An example of the interaction between language and memory. *Journal of Verbal Learning and Verbal Behavior, 13,* 585–589.

Logue, A. W. (2002). The living legacy of the Harvard Pigeon Lab: Quantitative analysis in the wide world. *Journal of the Experimental Analysis of Behavior, 77,* 357–366.

Logue, A. W., Rodriguez, M. L., Peña-Correal, T. E. & Mauro, B. C. (1984). Choice in a self-control paradigm: Quantification of experience-based differences. *Journal of the Experimental Analysis of Behavior, 41,* 53–67.

LoLordo, V. M., & Droungas, A. (1989). Selective associations and adaptive specializations: Taste aversions and phobias. In S. B. Klein & R. R. Mowrer (Eds.), *Contemporary learning theories: Instrumental conditioning theory and the impact of biological constraints on learning* (pp. 145–179). Hillsdale, NJ: Lawrence Erlbaum.

Lonner, W. J., & Adamopoulos, J. (1997). Culture as antecedent to behavior. In J. W. Berry, Y. H. Poortinga, & J. Pandey (Eds.), *Handbook of cross-cultural psychology: Vol. 1. Theory and method* (pp. 43–83). Boston: Allyn & Bacon.

Loomis, W. F. (1967). Skin pigment regulation of vitamin-D biosynthesis in man. *Science, 157,* 501–506.

Lopez, S. R., & Guarnaccia, P. J. J. (2000). Cultural psychopathology: Uncovering the social world of mental illness. *Annual Review of Psychology, 51,* 571–598.

LoPiccolo, J., & Friedman, J. M. (1985). Sex therapy: An integrated model. In S. J. Lynn & J. P. Garskee (Eds.), *Contemporary psychotherapies: Models and methods.* New York: Merrill.

Lord, C. (2007). Autism in the 21st century. *Association for Behavior Analysis International Newsletter, 30,* 13–14.

Lorsch, J. R., & Szostak, J. W. (1996). Chance and necessity in the selection of nucleic acid catalysts. *Accounts of Chemical Research, 29,* 103–110.

Louth, S. M., Williamson, S., Alpert, M., Pouget, E. R., & Hare, R. D. (1998). Acoustic distinctions in the speech of male psychopaths. *Journal of Psycholinguistic Research, 27(3),* 375–384.

Lovaas, I. (1987). Behavioral treatment of normal educational and intellectual functioning in young autistic children. *Journal of Counseling and Clinical Psychology, 44,* 3–9.

Lovaas, I. (2003). *Teaching individuals with developmental delays: Basic intervention techniques.* Austin, TX: Pro-Ed.

Lowe, C. F., Horne, P. J., & Harris, F. D. (2002). Naming and categorization in young children: Vocal tact training. *Journal of the Experimental Analysis of Behavior, 78,* 527–549.

Luborsky, L., Chandler, M., Auerbach, A. H., Cohen, J., & Bachrach, H. M. (1971). Factors influencing the outcome of psychotherapy: A review of quantitative research. *Psychological Bulletin, 75,* 145–185.

Luck, S., Chelazzi, L., Hillyard, S., & Desimone, R. (1993). Effects of spatial attention on responses of V4 neurons in the macaque. *Society for Neuroscience Abstracts, 69,* 27.

Lumeng, J. C., & Hillman, K. H. (2007). Eating in larger groups increases food consumption. *Archives of Disease in Childhood, 92,* 384–387.

Lumia, A. R. (1972). The relationships among testosterone, conditioned aggression, and dominance in male pigeons. *Hormones and Behavior, 13,* 277–286.

Luna, K. (2007, August 18). Human "guinea pig" wins settlement in stuttering suit. *Quad City Times.* Electronic document available at http://www.qctimes.com/articles/2007/08/18//news/local/doc46c5db5829053283560473.txt. Downloaded December 13, 2007.

Lundy, A. C. (1988). Instructional set and thematic apperception test validity. *Journal of Personality Assessment, 52,* 309–320.

Luo, Y., & Baillargeon, R. (2005). When the ordinary seems unexpected: Evidence for incremental physical knowledge in young infants. *Cognition, 95,* 297–328.

Luria, A. R. (1973). Towards the mechanisms of naming disturbance. *Neuropsychologia, 11,* 417–421.

Lupfer, M. B., Clark, L. F., & Hutcherson, H. W. (1990). Impact of context on spontaneous trait and situational attributions. *Journal of Personality and Social Psychology, 58,* 239–249.

Luzzi, S., Pucci, E., Di Bella, P., & Piccirilli, M. (2000). Topographical disorientation consequent to amnesia of spatial location in a patient with right parahippocampal damage. *Cortex, 36,* 427–434.

Lyn, H. (2007). Mental representation of symbols as revealed by vocabulary errors in two bonobos (*Pan paniscus*). *Animal Cognition, 10,* 461–475.

Lynn, R. (1978). Ethnic and racial differences in intelligence: International comparisons. In *Human variation: The biopsychology of age, race and sex.* New York: Academic Press.

Lytton, H., & Romney, D. M. (1991). Parents' sex-related differential socialization of boys and girls: A meta-analysis. *Psychological Bulletin, 109,* 267–296.

Lytton, W. W., & Brust, J. C. M. (1989). Direct dyslexia: Preserved oral reading of real words in Wernicke's aphasia. *Brain, 112,* 583–594.

Ma, W., & Yu, C. (2006). Intramolecular RNA replicase: Possibly the first self-replicating molecule in the RNA world. *Origins of Life and the Evolutionary Biosphere, 36,* 413–420.

Maccoby, E. E. (1980). *Social development: Psychological growth and the parent-child relationship.* New York: Harcourt Brace Jovanovich.

Machon, R. A., Mednick, S. A., & Schulsinger, F. (1983). The interaction of seasonality, place of birth, genetic risk and subsequent schizophrenia in a high risk sample. *British Journal of Psychiatry, 143,* 383–388.

MacLean, H. E., Warne, G. L., & Zajac, J. D. (1995) Defects of androgen receptor function: From sex reversal to motor-neuron disease. *Molecular and Cellular Endocrinology, 112,* 133–141.

MacLeod, M. (1991). Half a century of research on the Stroop effect: An integrative review. *Psychological Bulletin, 109,* 163–203.

MacMillan, H. L., Fleming, J. E., Streiner, D. L., Lin, E., Boyle, M. H., Jamieson, E., Duku, E. K., et al. (2001). Childhood abuse and lifetime psychopathology in a community sample. *American Journal of Psychiatry, 158(11),* 1878–1883.

Macrae, C. N., Milne, A. B., & Bodenhausen, G. V. (1994). Stereotypes as energy-saving devices: A peek inside the cognitive toolbox. *Journal of Personality and Social Psychology, 66,* 37–47.

Maddi, S. (2002). The story of hardiness: Twenty years of theorizing, research, and practice. *Consulting Psychology Journal: Practice and Research, 54,* 173–185.

Madon, S., Guyll, M., Spoth, R., & Willard, J. (2004). Self-fulfilling prophecies: The synergistic accumulative effect of parents' beliefs on children's drinking behavior. *Psychological Science, 15,* 837–845.

Madon, S., Smith, A., Jussim, L., Russell, D. W., Eccles, J., Palumbo, P., & Walkiewicz, M. (2001). Am I as you see me or do you see me as I am? Self-fulfilling prophecies and self-verification. *Personality & Social Psychology Bulletin, 27,* 1214–1224.

Madon, S., Willard, J., Buyll, M. Trudeau, L., & Spoth, R. (2006). Self-fulfilling prophecy effects of mothers' beliefs on children's alcohol use: Accumulation, dissipation, and stability over time. *Journal of Personality and Social Psychology, 90,* 911–926.

Maffei, M., Halaas, J., Ravussin, E., Pratley, R. E., Lee, G. H., Zhang, Y., Fei, H., Kim, S., Lallone, R., & Ranganathan, S. (1995). Leptin levels in human and rodent: Measurement of plasma leptin and ob RNA in obese and weight-reduced subjects. *Nature Medicine, 11,* 1155–1161.

Magee, W. J., Eaton, W. W., Wittchen, H.-U., McGonagle, K. A., & Kessler, R. C. (1996). *Archives of General Psychiatry, 53,* 159–168.

Maguire, E. A., Gadian, D. G., Johnsrude, I. S., Good, C. D., Ashburner, J., Frackowiak, R. S. J., & Frith, C.D. (2000). Navigation-related structural change in the hippocampi of taxi drivers. *Proceedings of the National Academy of Science, USA, 97,* 4398–4403.

Maier, S. F., & Seligman, M. E. (1976). Learned helplessness: Theory and evidence. *Journal of Experimental Psychology: General, 105,* 3–46.

Main, M., & Solomon, J. (1990). Procedures for identifying infants as disorganized/disoriented during the Ainsworth Strange Situation. In M. T. Greenberg, D. Cicchetti, & M. Cummings (Eds.), *Attachment in the pre-school years: Theory, research, and intervention* (pp. 121–160). Chicago: University of Chicago Press.

Malnic, B., Godfrey, P. A., & Buck, L. B. (2004). The human olfactory receptor gene family. *Proceedings of the National Academy of Sciences, USA, 101,* 2584–2589.

Malnic, B., Hirono, J., Sato, T., & Buck, L. B. (1999). Combinatorial receptor codes for odors. *Cell, 96,* 713–723.

Manning, R., Levine, M., & Collins, A. (2007). The Kitty Genovese murder and the social psychology of helping: The parable of the 38 witnesses. *American Psychologist, 62,* 555–562.

Manson, J. E., Willett, W. C., Stampfer, M. J., Colditz, G. A., Hunter, D. J., & Hankinson, S. E. (1995). Body weight and mortality among women. *New England Journal of Medicine, 333,* 677–685.

Manson, S. M., & Kleinman, A. (1998). DSM-IV, culture and mood disorders: A critical reflection on recent progress. *Transcultural Psychiatry, 35,* 377–386.

Maquet, P. (2001). The role of sleep in learning and memory. *Science, 294,* 1048–1052.

Marcia, J. E. (1980). Identity in adolescence. In J. Adelson (Ed.), *Handbook of adolescent psychology* (pp. 159–183). New York: Wiley.

Marcia, J. E. (1994). The empirical study of ego identity. In H. A. Bosma & T. L. G. Graafsma (Eds.), *Identity and development: An interdisciplinary approach.* (Vol. 172) (pp. 67–80). Thousand Oaks, CA: Sage Publications, Inc.

Margolin, D. I., Friedrich, F. J., & Carlson, N. R. (1985). Visual agnosia–optic aphasia: Continuum or dichotomy? Paper presented at the meeting of the International Neuropsychology Society.

Maris, R. W. (2002). Suicide. *Lancet, 360,* 319–326.

Markus, H. (1977). Self-schemata and processing information about the self. *Journal of Personality and Social Psychology, 35,* 63–78.

Markus, H. R., & Kitayama, S. (1991). Culture and the self: Implications for cognition, emotion, and motivation. *Psychological Review, 98,* 224–253.

Markus, H. R., & Kitayama, S. (2003). Culture, self, and the reality of the social. *Psychological Inquiry, 14,* 277–283.

Markus, H. R., & Nurius, P. (1986). Possible selves. *American Psychologist, 41,* 954–969.

Marlowe, F., & Wetsman, A. (2001). Preferred waist-to-hip ratio and ecology. *Personality and Individual Differences, 30,* 481–489.

Marois, R., & Ivanoff, J. (2005). Capacity limits of information processing in the brain. *Trends in Cognitive Sciences, 9,* 296–305.

Marshall, J. C., & Newcombe, F. (1973). Patterns of paralexia: A psycholinguistic approach. *Journal of Psycholinguistic Research, 2,* 175–199.

Marshall, L., & Born, J. (2007). The contribution of sleep to hippocampus-dependent memory consolidation. *Trends in Cognitive Sciences, 11,* 442–450.

Marshall, R. D., Spitzwer, R., & Liebowitz, M. R. (1999). Review and critique of the new DSM-IV diagnosis of acute stress disorder. *American Journal of Psychiatry, 156(11),* 1677–1685.

Marshark, M., Richman, C. L., Yuille, J. C., & Hunt, R. R. (1987). The role of imagery in memory: On shared and distinctive information. *Psychological Bulletin, 102,* 28–41.

Martin, G. L., & Pear, J. (2006). *Behavior modification: What it is and how to do it*, 8th ed. Englewood Cliffs, NJ: Prentice Hall.

Martinez G. M., Chandra A, Abma J. C., Jones J., & Mosher W. D. (2006). Fertility, contraception, and fatherhood: Data on men and women from Cycle 6 (2002) of the National Survey of Family Growth: National Center for Health Statistics. *Vital Health Statistics, 23*(26), 1–142.

Masling, J. (1960). The influence of situational and interpersonal variables in projective testing. *Psychological Bulletin, 57*, 65–85.

Masling, J. (1998). Interpersonal and actuarial dimensions of projective testing. In L. Handler & M. J. Hilsenroth (Eds.), *Teaching and learning personality assessment* (pp. 119–135). Mahwah, NJ: Lawrence Erlbaum Associates.

Maslow, A. H. (1964). *Religions, values, and peak-experiences*. New York: Viking Press.

Massen, C., & Stegt, S. J. (2007). Inhibition of return impairs episodic memory access. *The Quarterly Journal of Experimental Psychology, 60*, 696–707.

Masters, W. H., & Johnson, V. E. (1970). *Human sexual inadequacy*. Boston: Little, Brown.

Matser, E. J. T., Kessels, A. G. H., Lezak, M. D., Troost, J., & Jordan, B. D. (2000). Acute traumatic brain injury in amateur boxing. *The Physician and Sportsmedicine, 28*(1), 87–92.

Matsumoto, D. (2003). Cross-cultural research. In S. F. Davis (Ed.), *Handbook of research methods in experimental psychology*. Malden, MA: Blackwell Publishers.

Maurer, D., & Maurer, C. (1988). *The world of the newborn*. New York: Basic Books.

Max, J. E., Levin, H., Schachar, R. J., Landis, J., Saunders, A. E., Ewing-Cobbs, L., Chapman, S. B., & Dennis, M. (2006). Predictors of personality change due to traumatic brain injury in children and adolescents six to twenty four months after injury. *Journal of Neuropsychiatry and Clinical Neuroscience, 18*, 21–32.

Mayberg, H. (2003). Modulating dysfunctional limbic-cortical circuits in depression: Towards development of brain-based algorithms for diagnosis and optimized treatment. *British Medical Bulletin, 65*, 193–207.

Mayberg, H. S., Lozano, A. M., Voon, V., McNeely, H. E., Seminowicz, D., Hamani, C. Schwalb, J. M., & Kennedy, S. H. (2005). Deep brain stimulation for treatment-resistant depression. *Neuron, 45*, 651–660.

Mayer, J. (1955). Regulation of energy intake and the body weight: The glucostatic theory and the lipostatic hypothesis. *Annals of the New York Academy of Science, 63*, 15–43.

Mayer, J. D., & Salovey, P. (1993). The intelligence of emotional intelligence. *Intelligence, 17*, 433–442.

Mayes, L. C., Cicchetti, D., Acharyya, S., & Zhang, H. (2003). Developmental trajectories of cocaine-and-other-drug-exposed and non-cocaine-exposed children. *Journal of Developmental and Behavioral Pediatrics, 24*, 323–335.

Maynard, T. M., Sikich, L., Lieberman, J. D., & LaMantia, A-S. (2001). Neural development, cell-cell signaling, and the "two-hit" hypothesis of schizophrenia. *Schizophrenia Bulletin, 27*, 457–476.

Mayr, E. (2000). Darwin's influence on modern thought. *Scientific American, 283*, 79–83.

Mayr, E. (2001). *What evolution is*. New York: Basic Books.

Mazur, J. E. (2005). *Learning and behavior*, 6th ed. Upper Saddle River, NJ: Prentice Hall.

McAllister, T. W., Flashman, L. A., Sparling, M. B., & Saykin, A. J. (2004). Working memory deficits after traumatic brain injury: Catecholaminergic mechanisms and prospects for treatment—a review. *Brain Injury, 18*, 331–350.

McCann, I. L., & Holmes, D. S. (1984). Influence of aerobic exercise on depression. *Journal of Personality and Social Psychology, 46*, 1142–1147.

McCarley, R. W., & Hobson, J. A. (1979). The form of dreams and the biology of sleep. In B. Wolman (Ed.), *Handbook of dreams: Research, theory, and applications* (pp. 76–130). New York: Van Nostrand Reinhold.

McCarthy, R. A., & Warrington, E. K. (1990). *Cognitive neuropsychology: A clinical introduction*. San Diego: Academic Press.

McClanahan, T. M., & Antonuccio, D. O. (2002). Cognitive-behavioral treatment of panic attacks. *Clinical Case Studies, 1*(3), 211–223.

McClearn, G. E. (1963). The inheritance of behavior. In L. J. Postman (Ed.), *Psychology in the making* (pp. 144–252). New York: Knopf.

McClearn, G. E., Johansson, B., Berg, S., Pedersen, N. L., Ahern, F., Petrill, S. A., & Plomin, R. (1997). Substantial genetic influence on cognitive abilities in twins 80 or more years old. *Science, 276*, 1560–1563.

McClelland, J. L., & Rumelhart, D. E. (1981). An interactive activation model of context effects in letter perception: Part 1. An account of basic findings. *Psychological Review, 88*, 375–407.

McCormick, P. A., Klein, R. M., & Johnston, S. (1998). Splitting versus sharing focal attention: Comment on Castiello and Umiltà (1992). *Journal of Experimental Psychology: Human Perception and Performance, 24*, 350–357.

McCrae, R. R., & Costa, P. T. (1997). Personality trait structure as a human universal. *American Psychologist, 52*, 509–516.

McCrae, R. R., & Costa, P. T., Jr. (1999). A five-factor theory of personality. In L. A. Pervin and O. P. John (Eds.), *Handbook of personality: Theory and research*. (2nd ed.) (pp. 139–153). New York: The Guilford Press.

McCrae, R. R., & Costa, P. T., Jr. (2004). A contemplated revision of the NEO Five-Factor Inventory. *Personality & Individual Differences, 36*(3), 587–596.

McCrae, R. R., Costa, P. T., Jr., Del Pilar, G. H., Rolland, J. P., & Parker, W. D. (1998). Cross-cultural assessment of the five-factor model: The revised NEO personality inventory. *Journal of Cross-Cultural Psychology, 29*, 171–188.

McCrae, R. R., Costa, P. T., Jr., Ostendorf, F., Angleitner, A., Hrebickova, M., Avia, M. D., Sanz, J., Sanchez-Bernardos, M. L., Kusdil, M. E., Woodfield, R., Saunders, P. R., & Smith, P. B. (2000). Nature over nurture: Temperament, personality, and life span development. *Journal of Personality and Social Psychology, 78*, 173–186.

McCrae, R. R., & Terracciano, A. (2005). Universal features of personality traits from the observer's perspective: Data from 50 cultures. *Journal of Personality and Social Psychology, 88*, 547–561.

McCrory, E. J., Mechelli, A., Frith, U., & Price, C. J. (2005). More than words: A common neural basis for reading and naming deficits in developmental dyslexia. *Brain, 128*, 261–267.

McFarland, C., & Miller, D. T. (1990). *Personality and Social Psychology Bulletin, 16*, 475–484.

McGovern, K. (2007). Social cognition: Perceiving the mental states of others. In B. J. Baars, & N. M. Gage (Eds.), *Cognition, brain, and consciousness* (pp. 391–410). New York: Academic Press.

McGrath, E. P., & Repetti, R. L. (2002). A longitudinal study of children's depressive symptoms, self-perceptions, and cognitive distortions about the self. *Journal of Abnormal Psychology, 111*(1), 77–87.

McGregor, I., Newby-Clark, I. R., & Zanna, M. P. (1999). "Remembering" dissonance: Simultaneous accessibility of inconsistent cognitive elements moderates epistemic discomfort. In E. Harmon-Jones & J. Mills (Eds.), *Cognitive dissonance: Progress on a pivotal theory in social psychology*. Washington, DC: American Psychological Association.

McGuiness, D. (2004). *Early reading instruction: What science really tells us about how to teach reading*. Cambridge, MA: Harvard University Press.

McIlvane, W. J., & Dube, W. V. (2003). Stimulus control topography coherence theory: Foundations and extensions. *Behavior Analyst, 26*, 195–213.

McKay, D. C. (1973). Aspects of the theory of comprehension, memory and attention. *Quarterly Journal of Experimental Psychology, 25*, 22–40.

McNamara, D. S., & Scott, J. L. (2001). Working memory capacity and strategy use. *Memory & Cognition, 29*, 10–17.

McNeill, D. (1970). *The acquisition of language: The study of developmental psycholinguistics*. New York: Harper & Row.

McNish, K. A., Betts, S. L., Brandon, S. E., & Wagner, A. R. (1997). Divergence of conditioned eyeblink and conditioned fear in backward pavlovian training. *Animal Learning & Behavior, 25*, 43–52.

Mead, C. A. (1989). *Analog VLSI and neural systems*. New York: Addison Wesley.

Meadows, S. (1996). *Parenting behaviour and children's cognitive development*. East Sussex, UK: Psychology Press.

Mednick, S. A., Gabrielli, W. F., & Hutchings, B. (1983). Genetic influences in criminal behavior: Some evidence from an adoption cohort. In K. T. VanDusen & S. A. Mednick (Eds.),

Prospective studies of crime and delinquency. Hingham, MA: Martinus Nyhoff.

Mednick, S. A., Machon, R. A., & Huttunen, M. O. (1990). An update on the Helsinki influenza project. *Archives of General Psychiatry, 47,* 292.

Mednick, S., Nakayama, K., & Stickgold, R. (July, 2003). Sleep-dependent learning: A nap is as good as a night. *Nature Neuroscience, 6,* 697–698.

Meehl, P. E. (1954). *Clinical versus statistical prediction.* Minneapolis: University of Minnesota Press.

Meehl, P. E. (1986). Causes and effects of my disturbing little book. *Journal of Personality Assessment, 50,* 370–375.

Meelissen, M. R. M., & Drent, M. (2008). Gender differences in computer attitudes: Does the school matter? *Computers and Human Behavior, 24,* 969–985.

Mehl-Medrona, L. (2007). *Narrative medicine: The use of history and story in the healing process.* Rochester, VT: Inner Traditions International.

Meichenbaum, D. (1985). *Stress inoculation training.* New York: Pergamon Press.

Meichenbaum, D. (1993). Changing conceptions of cognitive behavior modification: Retrospect and prospect. *Journal of Consulting and Clinical Psychology, 61,* 202–204.

Meichenbaum, D. (1995). Disasters, stress, and cognition. In S. E. Hobfoll & M. W. deVries (Eds.), *Extreme stress and communities: Impact and intervention* (pp. 33–62). Dordrecht, Netherlands: Kluwer Academic Publishers.

Meichenbaum, D. H. (1977). *Cognitive-behavior modification: An integrative approach.* New York: Plenum Press.

Meindl, J. R., & Lerner, M. J. (1984). Exacerbation of extreme responses to an out-group. *Journal of Personality and Social Psychology, 47,* 71–84.

Mejia-Arauz, R., Rogoff, B, Dexter, A. & Najafi, B. (2007). Cultural variation in children's social organization. *Child Development, 78,* 3, 1001–1014.

Melzack, R. (1992). Phantom limbs. *Scientific American, 266(4),* 120–126.

Menn, L., & Stoel-Gammon, C. (1993). Phonological development: Learning sounds and sound patterns. In J. B. Gleason (Ed.), *The development of language.* New York: Macmillan.

Mentkowski, T. (1983). Why I am what I am. *The Florida School Herald, 82,* 1–2, 5, 12. Cited by Schein, J. D. (1989). *At home among strangers.* Washington, DC: Gallaudet University Press.

Merckelbach, H., & Muris, P. (1997). The etiology of childhood **spider phobia**. *Behaviour Research & Therapy, 35,* 1031–1034.

Merker, B. (2007). Consciousness without a cerebral cortex: A challenge for neuroscience and medicine. *Behavioral and Brain Sciences, 30,* 63–134.

Messer, S. B. (2001). What makes brief psychodynamic therapy time efficient. *Clinical Psychology: Science and Practice, 8(1),* 5–22.

Metalsky, G. I., Joiner, T. E., Jr., Hardin, T. S., & Abramson, L. Y. (1993). Depressive reactions to failure in a naturalistic setting: A test of the hopelessness and self-esteem theories of de-

pression. *Journal of Abnormal Psychology, 102,* 101–109.

Metter, E. J. (1991). Brain-behavior relationships in aphasia studied by positron emission tomography. *Annals of the New York Academy of Sciences, 620,* 153–164.

Metter, E. J., Hanson, W. R., Jackson, C. A., Kempler, D., Van Lancker, D., Mazziotta, J. C., & Phelps, M. E. (1990). Tempero-parietal cortex in aphasia: Evidence from positron emission tomography. *Archives of Neurology, 47,* 1235–1238.

Meyer, R. G., & Osborne, Y. V. (1982). *Case studies in abnormal behavior.* Boston: Allyn & Bacon.

Mezulis, A. H., Abramson, L. Y., Hyde, J. S., & Hankin, B. L. (2004). Is there a universal positivity bias in attribution? A meta-analytic review of individual, developmental, and cultural differences in the self-serving attributional bias. *Psychological Bulletin, 130,* 711–747.

Milgram, S. (1963). Behavioral study of obedience. *Journal of Abnormal and Social Psychology, 67,* 371–378.

Milgram, S. (1974). *Obedience to authority.* New York: Harper & Row.

Miller, A. M., & Harwood, R. L. (2002). The cultural organization of parenting: Change and stability of behavior patterns during feeding and social play across the first year of life. *Parenting: Science and Practice, 2,* 241–272.

Miller, D. T., & Ross, M. (1975). Self-serving biases in the attribution of causality: Fact or fiction? *Psychological Bulletin, 82,* 213–225.

Miller, G. (2007). Out-of-body experiences enter the laboratory. *Science, 317,* 1020–1021.

Miller, G. A. (1956). The magical number seven plus or minus two: Some limits on our capacity for processing information. *Psychological Review, 63,* 81–97.

Miller, G. A. (1987). *Spontaneous apprentices: Children and language.* New York: Seabury Press.

Miller, G. A., Elbert, T., Sutton, B. P., & Heller, W. (2007). Innovative clinical assessment technologies: Challenges and opportunities in neuroimaging. *Psychological Assessment, 19,* 58–73.

Miller, G. A., Galanter, E., & Pribram, K. (1960). *Plans and the structure of behavior.* New York: Holt, Rinehart, & Winston.

Miller, J. D., Scott, E. C., & Okamoto, S. (2006). Public acceptance of evolution. *Science, 313,* 765.

Miller, J. L., & Eimas, P. D. (1995). Speech perception: From signal to word. *Annual Review of Psychology, 46,* 467–492.

Miller, K. R. (1999). *Finding Darwin's god: A scientist's search for common ground between god and evolution.* New York: Cliff Street Books.

Miller, N. E. (1983). Behavioral medicine: Symbiosis between laboratory and clinic. *Annual Review of Psychology, 34,* 1–31.

Miller, R. J., Hennessy, R. T., & Leibowitz, H. W. (1973). The effect of hypnotic ablation of the background on the magnitude of the Ponzo perspective illusion. *International Journal of Clinical and Experimental Hypnosis, 21,* 180–191.

Miller-Jones, D. (1989). Culture and testing. *American Psychologist, 44,* 360–366.

Milner, A. D., Perrett, D. I., Johnston, R. S., & Benson, P. J. (1991). Perception and action in "visual form agnosia." *Brain, 114,* 405–428.

Milner, B. (1970) Memory and the temporal regions of the brain. In K. H. Pribram & D. E. Broadbent (Eds.), *Biology of memory.* New York: Academic Press.

Milner, B., Corkin, S., and Teuber, H.-L. (1968). Further analysis of the hippocampal amnesic syndrome: 14-year follow-up study of H. M. *Neuropsychologia, 6,* 317–338.

Mineka, S., & Cook, M. (1993). Mechanisms involved in the observational conditioning of fear. *Journal of Experimental Psychology: General, 122,* 23–38.

Mineka, S., & Zinbarg, R. (2006). A contemporary learning theory perspective on the etiology of anxiety disorders: It's not what you thought it was. *American Psychologist, 61,* 10–26.

Minuchin, S. (1974). *Families and family therapy.* Cambridge, MA: Harvard University Press.

Minuchin, S., & Nichols, M. P. (1998). Structural family therapy. In F. M. Dattilio & M. R. Goldfried (Eds.), *Case studies in couple and family therapy: Systemic and cognitive perspectives* (pp. 108–131). New York: Guilford Press.

Mischel, W. (1968). *Personality and assessment.* New York: John Wiley & Sons.

Mischel, W. (1976). *Introduction to personality* (2nd ed.). New York: Holt, Rinehart & Winston.

Mischel, W. (1990). Personality dispositions revisited and revised: A view after three decades. In L. Pervin (Ed.), *Handbook of personality: Theory and research* (pp. 111–134). New York: Guilford Press.

Mischel, W. (2003). Challenging the traditional personality psychology paradigm. In R. J. Sternberg (Ed.), *Psychologists defying the crowd: Stories of those who battled the establishment and won* (pp. 139–156). Washington, DC: American Psychological Association.

Mischel, W., Cantor, N., & Feldman, S. (1996). Principles of self-regulation: The nature of willpower and self-control. In E. T. Higgins & A. W. Kruglanski (Eds.), *Social psychology: Handbook of basic principles* (pp. 329–360). New York: Guilford Press.

Mischel, W., & Shoda, Y. (1995). A cognitive-affective system theory of personality: Reconceptualizing situations, dispositions, dynamics, and invariance in personality. *Psychological Review, 102,* 246–268.

Mischel, W., & Shoda, Y. (1998). Reconciling processing dynamics and personality dispositions. *Annual Review of Psychology, 49,* 229–258.

Mischel, W., Shoda, Y., & Rodriguez, M. L. (1989). Delay of gratification in children. *Science, 244,* 933–938.

Mistry, J., & Rogoff, B. (1994). Remembering in a cultural context. In W. J. Lonner & R. Malpass (Eds.), *Psychology and culture.* Boston: Allyn & Bacon.

Mitchell, J. T. (1999). Essential factors for effective psychological response to disasters and other crises. *International Journal of Emergency Mental Health, 1,* 51–58.

Mitelman, S. A., Shihabuddin, L., Brickman, A. M., Hazlett, A. E., & Buchsbaum, M. S. (2003). MRI assessment of gray and white matter distribution in Brodmann's areas of the cortex in patients with schizophrenia with good and poor outcomes. *American Journal of Psychiatry, 160(12),* 2154–2168.

Mittelbach, G. G., Schemske, D. W., Cornell, H. V., Allen, A. P., Brown, J. M., Bush, M.B., Harrison, S. P., Hurlbert, A. H., Knowlton, N., Lessios, H. A., McCain, C. M., McCune, A. R., McDade, L. A., McPeek, M. A., Near, T. J., Price, T. D., Ricklefs, R. E., Roy, K., Sax, D. F., Schluter, D., Sobel, J. M., & Turelli. M. (2007). Evolution and the latitudinal diversity gradient: speciation, extinction and biogeography. *Ecology Letters, 10,* 315–331.

Miyamoto, Y., & Kitayama, S. (2002). Cultural variation in correspondence bias: The critical role of attitude diagnosticity of socially constrained behavior. *Journal of Personality & Social Psychology, 83,* 1239–1248.

Miyashita, Y. (2004). Cognitive memory: Cellular and network machineries and their top-down control. *Science, 306,* 435–440.

Mock T., & Thomas, D. N. (2005). Recent advances in sea-ice microbiology. *Environmental Microbiology, 7,* 605–619.

Mogg, K., Bradley, B. P., Williams, R., & Matthews, A. (1993). Subliminal processing of emotional information in anxiety and depression. *Journal of Abnormal Psychology, 102,* 304–311.

Mogg, K., Philippot, P., & Bradley, B. P. (2004). Selective attention to angry faces in clinical social phobia. *Journal of Abnormal Psychology, 113(1),* 160–165.

Monahan, J. L., Murphy, S. T., & Zajonc, R. B. (2000). Subliminal mere exposure: Specific, general, and diffuse effects. *Psychological Science, 11,* 462–466.

Money, J., & Ehrhardt, A. *Man & Woman, Boy & Girl.* Baltimore: Johns Hopkins University Press, 1972.

Montoya, R. M., & Horton, R. S. (2004). On the importance of cognitive evaluation as a determinant of interpersonal attraction. *Journal of Personality and Social Psychology, 86,* 696–712.

Moray, N. (1959). Attention in dichotic listening: Affective cues and the influence of instructions. *Quarterly Journal of Experimental Psychology, 11,* 56–60.

Moray, N. (1970). *Attention: Selective processes in vision and hearing.* New York: Academic Press.

Morgenthaler, T. I., & Silber, M. H. (2002). Amnestic sleep-related eating disorder associated with zolpidem. *Sleep Medicine, 3,* 323–327.

Morris, B. J., & Sloutsky, V. (2002). Children's solutions of logical versus empirical problems: What's missing and what develops? *Cognitive Development, 16,* 907–928.

Morris, R. G. M. (2001). Episodic-like memory in animals: Psychological criteria, neural mechanisms, and the value of episodic-like tasks to investigate animal models of neurodegenerative disease. *Philosophical Transactions of the Royal Society of London, 356,* 1453–1465.

Morris, R. G. M., Garrud, P., Rawlins, J. N. P., & O'Keefe, J. (1982). Place navigation impaired in rats with hippocampal lesions. *Nature, 297,* 681–683.

Morton, J. (1979). Word recognition. In *Psycholinguistics 2: Structures and processes.* Cambridge, MA: MIT Press.

Moskowitz, G. (2005). *Social cognition: Understanding self and others.* New York: Guilford Press.

Most, S. B., Scholl, B. J., Clifford, E. R., & Simons, D. (2005). What you see is what you set: Sustained inattentional blindness and the capture of awareness. *Psychological Review, 112,* 217–242.

Moynihan, J. A. (2003). Mechanisms of stress-induced modulation of immunity. *Brain, Behavior, & Immunity, 17,* S11–S16.

Muhlberger, A., Hermann, M. J., Wiedermann, G., Ellgring, H., & Pauli, P. (2001). Repeated exposure of flight phobics to flights in virtual reality. *Behaviour Research and Therapy, 39,* 1033–1050.

Mulder, M. B. (2003). Are men and women really so different? *Trends in Ecology & Evolution, 19,* 3–6.

Mullen, R. (2003). Delusions: The continuum versus category debate. *Australian & New Zealand Journal of Psychiatry, 37(5),* 505–511.

Muller, U., & Carpendale, J. I. M. (2000). The role of social interaction in Piaget's theory: Language for social cooperation and social cooperation for language. *New Ideas in Psychology, 18,* 139–156.

Munakate, Y., Casey, B. J., & Diamond, A. (2004). Developmental cognitive neuroscience: Progress and potential. *Trends in Cognitive Sciences, 8,* 122–128.

Mundy, P. & Newell, L. (2007). Attention, joint attention, and social cognition. *Current Directions in Psychological Science, 16,* 269–274.

Murphy, J. (1976). Psychiatric labeling in cross-cultural perspective: Similar kinds of disturbed behavior appear to be labeled abnormal in diverse cultures. *Science, 191,* 1019–1028.

Murphy, S. T., Monahan, J. L., & Zajonc, R. B. (1995). Additivity of nonconscious affect: Affective priming with optimal and suboptimal exposure. *Journal of Personality and Social Psychology, 64,* 589–602.

Murray, C. (2005 September). The inequality taboo. *Commentary, 120(2),* 13–22.

Murray, J. P. (2008). Media violence: The effects are both real and strong. *American Behavioral Scientist, 51,* 1212–1230.

Musso, M., Moro, A., Glauche, V., Rijntjes, M., Reichenbach, J., Büchel, C., & Weiller, C. (2003). Broca's area and the language instinct. *Nature Neuroscience, 6,* 774–781.

Muter, P. (1980). Very rapid forgetting. *Memory and Cognition, 8,* 174–179.

Myerson, J., Rank, M. R., Raines, F. Q., & Schnitzler, M. A. (1998). Race and general cognitive ability: The myth of diminishing returns to education. *Psychological Sciences, 9,* 139–142.

Nafe, J. P., & Wagoner, K. S. (1941). The nature of pressure adaptation. *Journal of General Psychology, 25,* 323–351.

Nairne, J. S. (2002). Remembering over the short-term: The case against the standard model. *Annual Review of Psychology, 53,* 53–81.

Nakazawa, K., Sun, L. D., Rondi-Reig, L., Wilson, M. A., & Tanegawa, S. (2003). Hippocampal CA3 NMDA receptors are crucial for memory acquisition of one-time experience. *Neuron, 24,* 147–148.

Naqvi, N.H., Rudrauf, D., Damasio, H., and Bechara, A. (2007). Damage to the insula disrupts addiction to cigarette smoking. *Science, 315,* 531–534.

Nardi, A. E., Lopes, F. L., Valenca, A. M., et al. (2004). Psychopathological description of hyperventilation-induced panic attacks: A comparison with spontaneous panic attacks. *Psychopathology, 37(1),* 29–35.

Nardi, A. E., Valenca, A. M., Nascimento, I., Zin, W. A., & Versani, M. (2002). Carbon dioxide test as an additional clinical measure of treatment response in panic disorder. *Arquivos de Neuro-Psiquiatria, 60(2),* 358–361.

Nasar, S. (1998). *A beautiful mind.* New York: Simon and Schuster.

Nash, M. (2001, July). The truth and the hype of hypnosis. *Scientific American,* 36–42.

Nathanson, V., Jayesinghe, N., & Roycroft, G. (2007). Is it all right for women to drink small amounts of alcohol in pregnancy? No. *British Medical Journal, 335,* 857.

National Institute of Child Health and Human Development. (1997). The effects of infant child care on infant–mother attachment security: Results of the NICHD study of early child care. *Child Development, 68,* 860–879.

National Research Council. (2001). *Educating children with autism.* Washington, DC: National Academies Press.

Neisser, U. (1969). Selective reading: A method for the study of visual attention. Paper presented at the 19th International Congress of Psychology, London.

Neisser, U., & Becklen, R. (1975). Selective looking: Attending to visually significant events. *Cognitive Psychology, 7,* 480–494.

Neisser, U., Boodoo, G., Bouchard, Jr., T. J., Boykin, A. W., Brody, N., Ceci, S. J., Halpern, D. R., Loehlin, J. C., Perloff, R., Sternberg, R. J., & Urbina, S. (1996). Intelligence: Knowns and unknowns. *American Psychologist, 51,* 77–101.

Nelson, C. A. (2007). A neurobiological perspective on early human deprivation. *Child Development Perspectives, 1,* 13–18.

Nelson-Jones, R. (2003). *Six key approaches to counseling and therapy.* London: Sage Publications.

Nesdadt, G., Samuels, J., Riddle, M., Bienvenu, J., Liang, K., LaBuda, M., Walkup, J., Grados, M., & Hoen-Saric, R. (2000). A family study of obsessive-compulsive disorder. *Archives of General Psychiatry, 57,* 358–363.

Nestler, E. J. (2005). Is there a common molecular pathway for addiction? *Nature Neuroscience, 8,* 1445–1449.

Nestler, E. J., Barrot, M., DiLeone, R. J., Eisch, A. I., Gold, S. J., & Monteggia, L. M. (2002). Neurobiology of depression. *Neuron, 34,* 13–25.

Neugeboren, J. (2008, April 17). Infiltrating the enemy of the mind. *New York Review of Books.*

Neuhaus, I. M., & Rosenthal, N. E. (1997). Light therapy as a treatment modality for affective disorders. In A. Honig & H. M. van Praag (Eds.), *Depression: Neurobiological, psychopathological and therapeutic advances.* Wiley series on clinical and neurobiological advances in psychiatry. New York: John Wiley & Sons, Inc.

Neumarker, K. J. (1997). Mortality and sudden death in anorexia nervosa. *International Journal of Eating Disorders, 21,* 205–212.

Nevin, J. A., & Grace, R. C. (2000). Behavioral momentum and the Law of Effect. *Behavioral and Brain Sciences, 23,* 73–130.

Nevin, J. A., & Grace, R. C. (2005). Resistance to extinction in the steady state and in transition. *Journal of Experimental Psychology: Animal Behavior Processes, 31,* 199–212.

New, A. S., Buchsbaum, M. S., Hazlett, E. A., Goodman, M., Koenigsberg, H. W., Lo, J., Iskander, L., Newmark, R., Brand, J., O'Flynn, K., & Siever, L. J. (2004). Fluoxetine increases relative metabolic rate in prefrontal cortex in impulsive aggression. *Psychopharmacology, 176,* 451–458.

Newcomer, R. R., & Perna, F. M. (2003). Features of posttraumatic distress among adolescent athletes. *Journal of Athletic Training, 38(2),* 163–166.

Newell, A., & Simon, H. A. (1972). *Human problem solving.* Englewood Cliffs, NJ: Prentice-Hall.

Newport, E. L. (1975). Motherese: The speech of mothers to young children. San Diego: University of California, Center for Human Information Processing.

Newport, E. L., Gleitman, H. R., & Gleitman, L. (1977). Mother, I'd rather do it myself: Some effects and noneffects of maternal speech style. In C. E. Snow & C. A. Ferguson (Eds.), *Talking to children: Language input and acquisition.* Cambridge, UK: Cambridge University Press.

Niccols, A. (2007). Fetal alcohol syndrome and the developing socio-emotional brain. *Brain and Cognition, 65,* 135–142.

NICHD Early Child Care Research Network. (2003). Does quality of child care affect child outcomes at age 4-1/2? *Developmental Psychology, 39,* 451–469.

Nielsen, L. L., & Sarason, I. G. (1981). Emotion, personality, and selective attention. *Journal of Personality and Social Psychology, 41,* 945–960.

Nigg, J. T. (2006). *What causes ADHD?* New York: Guilford Press.

Nisbett, R. E. (2003). *The geography of thought: How Asians and Westerners think differently . . . and why.* New York: Simon and Schuster.

Nishino, S., Ripley, B. Overeem, S., Lammers, G. J., & Mignot, E. (2000). Hypocretin (orexin) deficiency in human narcolepsy. *Lancet, 355,* 39–40.

Noonan, J. P., Coop, G., Kudaravalli, S., Smith, D., Krause, J., Alessi, J., Chen. F., Platt, D. Pääbo, S., Pritchard, J. K., & Rubin, E. M. (2006). Sequencing and analysis of Neanderthal genomic DNA. *Science, 314,* 1113–1118.

Norcross, J. C. (2002). *Psychotherapy relationships that work: Therapist contributions and responsiveness to patients.* New York: Oxford University Press.

Norenzayan, A., & Heine, S. J. (2005). Psychological universals: What are they and how can we know? *Psychological Bulletin, 131,* 763–784.

Norman, W. T. (1963). Toward an adequate taxonomy of personality attributes: Replicated factor structure in peer nomination personality ratings. *Journal of Abnormal and Social Psychology, 66,* 574–583.

Norton, M.B. (2003). *In the devil's snare: The Salem witchcraft crisis of 1692.* New York: Vintage Books.

Novin, D., VanderWeele, D. A., & Rezek, M. (1973). Infusion of 2-deoxy-D-glucose into the hepatic-portal system causes eating: evidence for peripheral glucoreceptors. *Science, 181,* 858–860.

O'Brien, M., Peyton, V., Mistry, R., Hruda, L., Jacobs, A., Caldera, Y., Huston, A., & Roy, C. (2000). Gender-role cognition in three-year-old boys and girls. *Sex Roles, 42,* 1007–1025.

O'Brien, P. (2007). Is it all right for women to drink small amounts of alcohol in pregnancy? Yes. *British Medical Journal, 335,* 856.

O'Connor, E. M. (2001, Dec). Medicating ADHD: Too much? Too soon? *Monitor on Psychology,* 50–51.

O'Doherty, J., Rolls, E. T., Francis, S., Bowtell, R., McGlone, F., Kobal, G., Renner, B., and Ahne, G. (2000). Sensory-specific satiety-related olfactory activation of the human orbitofrontal cortex. *Neuroreport, 11,* 893–897.

O'Donohue, W., Fowler, K. A., & Lilienfeld, S. O. (Eds.) (2007). *Personality disorders: Toward the DSM-V.* Thousand Oaks, CA: Sage.

O'Neill, D. K. (1996). Two-year-old children's sensitivity to a parent's knowledge state when making requests. *Child Development, 67,* 659–677.

O'Regan, J. K., Rensink, R. A., & Clark, J. J. (1999). Change-blindness as a result of "mudsplashes." *Nature, 398,* 34.

Obergriesser, T., Ende, G., Braus, D. F., & Henn, F. A. (2003). Long-term follow-up of magnetic resonance-detectable choline signal changes in the hippocampus of patients treated with electroconvulsive therapy. *Journal of Clinical Psychiatry, 64(7),* 775–780.

Oberman, L., & Ramachandran, V. (2007). The simulating social mind: The role of the mirror neuron system and simulation in the social and communicative deficits of autism spectrum disorders. *Psychological Bulletin 133,* 310–327.

Obleser, J., Lahiri, A., & Eulitz, C. (2004). Magnetic brain response mirrors extraction of phonological features from spoken vowels. *Journal of Cognitive Neuroscience, 16,* 31–39.

Offit, P. A., & Coffin, S. E. (2003). Communicating science to the public: MMR vaccine and autism. *Vaccine, 22,* 1–6.

Ogden C. L., Carroll M. D., McDowell M. A., & Flegal, K. M. (2007). *Obesity among adults in the United States—no change since 2003–2004. NCHS data brief no 1.* Hyattsville, MD: National Center for Health Statistics.

Öhman, A., & Soares, J. J. (1994). "Unconscious anxiety": Phobic responses to masked stimuli. *Journal of Abnormal Psychology, 103,* 231–240.

Öhman, A., & Soares, J. J. (1998). Emotional conditioning to masked stimuli: Expectancies for aversive outcomes following nonrecognized fear-relevant stimuli. *Journal of Experimental Psychology: General, 127,* 69–82.

Ohman, A., Fredrikson, M., Hugdahl, K., & Rimmo, P-A. (1976). The premise of equipotentiality in human classical conditioning: Conditioned electrodermal responses to potentially phobic stimuli. *Journal of Experimental Psychology: General, 105,* 313–337.

Okagaki, L., & Sternberg, R. J. (1993). Putting the distance into students' hands: Practical intelligence for school. In R. R. Cocking & K. A. Renninger (Eds.), *The development and meaning of psychological distance.* Hillsdale, NJ: Erlbaum Associates.

Okazaki, S. (2000). Asian American and white American differences on affective distress symptoms: Do symptom reports differ across reporting methods? *Journal of Cross-Cultural Psychology, 31,* 603–625.

O'Keefe, J., and Dostrovsky, T. (1971). The hippocampus as a spatial map: Preliminary evidence from unit activity in the freely moving rat. *Brain Research, 34,* 171–175.

Okiishi, J., Lambert, M. J., Nielsen, S. L., & Ogles, B. M. (2003). Waiting for supershrink: An empirical analysis of therapist effects. *Clinical Psychology & Psychotherapy, 10(6),* 361–373.

Olausson, H., Lamarre, Y., Backlund, H., Morin, C., Wallin, B. G., Starck, G., Ekholm, S., Strigo, I., Worsley, K., Vallbo, Å. B., & Bushnell, M. C. (2002). Unmyelinated tactile afferents signal touch and project to insular cortex. *Nature Neuroscience, 5,* 900–904.

Oliver, R., & Williams, R. L. (2006). Performance patterns of high, medium, and low performers during and following a reward versus nonreward contingency phase. *School Psychology Quarterly, 21,* 119–147.

Oliveri, M., Torriero, S., Kochm, G., Salerno, S., Petrosini, L., & Caltagirone, C. (2007). The role of transcranial magnetic stimulation in the study of cerebellar cognitive function. *Cerebellum, 6,* 95–101.

Olson, J. M., Roese, N. J., & Zanna, M. P. (1996). Expectancies. In E. T. Higgins & A. W. Kruglanski (Eds.), *Social psychology: Handbook of basic principles* (pp. 211–238). New York: Guilford Press.

O'Neil, P. M., Smith, C. F., Foster, G. D., & Anderson, D. A. (2000). The perceived relative worth of reaching goal weight. *International Journal of Obesity, 24,* 1069–1076.

Orvis, B. R., Kelley, H. H., & Butler, D. (1976). Attributional conflict in young couples. In J. H. Harvey, W. J. Ickes, & R. F. Kidd (Eds.), *New directions in attribution research, Vol. 1.* Hillsdale, NJ: Erlbaum.

Osborne, K. A., Robichon, A., Burgess, E., Butland, S., Shaw, R. A., Coulthard, A., Pereira, H. S., Greenspan, R. H., & Sokolowski, M. B. (1997). Natural behavior polymorphism due to a cGMP-Dependent protein kinase of Drosophila. *Science, 277,* 834–836.

Ostrom, T. M., & Sedikides, C. (1992). Outgroup homogeneity effects in natural and minimal groups. *Psychological Bulletin, 112,* 536–552.

Overmier, J. B. (1998). Learned helplessness: State or stasis of the art? In M. Sabourin, F. Craik, & M. Robert (Eds.), *Advances in psychological science: Biological and cognitive aspects* (Vol. 2, pp. 301–315). Hove, England: Psychology Press/Erlbaum.

Overmier, J. B., & Seligman, M. E. P. (1967). Effects of inescapable shock upon subsequent escape and avoidance responding. *Journal of Comparative and Physiological Psychology, 63,* 28–33.

Owen, A. M., James, M., Leigh, P. N., Summers, B. A., Marsden, C. D., Quinn, N. P., Lange, K. W., & Robbins, T. W. (1992). Fronto-striatal cognitive deficits at different stages of Parkinson's disease. *Brain, 115,* 1727–1751.

Owens, R. E. (1992). *Language development: An introduction.* New York: Merrill/Macmillan.

Pagel, M., Atkinson, O. D., & Meade, A. (2007). Frequency of word use predicts rates of lexical evolution throughout Indo-European history. *Nature, 449,* 717–720.

Paikoff, R. L., & Brooks-Gunn, J. (1991). Do parent-child relationships change during puberty? *Psychological Bulletin, 110,* 47–66.

Paizanis, E., Hamon, M., & Lanfumey, L (2007). Hippocampal neurogenesis, depressive disorders, and antidepressant therapy. *Neural Plasticity,* 2007, 1–7.

Palmer, D. C. (2004). Data in search of a principle: A review of relational frame theory: A post-Skinnerian account of human language and cognition. *Journal of the Experimental Analysis of Behavior, 81,* 189–204.

Papini, M. R. (2003). Comparative psychology of surprising nonreward. *Brain, Behavior, and Evolution, 62,* 83–95.

Paris, J. (1999). Borderline personality disorder. In T. Millen, P. H. Blaney, & R. D. Davis (Eds.), *Oxford textbook of psychopathology* (pp. 628–652). New York: Oxford University Press.

Park, B. (1986). A method for studying the development of impressions in real people. *Journal of Personality and Social Psychology, 51,* 907–917.

Park, B., & Rothbart, M. (1982). Perception of outgroup homogeneity and levels of social categorization: Memory for the subordinate attributes of in-group and out-group members. *Journal of Personality and Social Psychology, 42,* 1051–1068.

Park, J., Choi, I., & Cho, G. (2006). The actor-observer bias in beliefs of interpersonal insight. *Journal of Cross-Cultural Psychology, 37,* 630–642.

Parke, R. D. (2000). Father involvement: A developmental psychological perspective. *Marriage and Family Review, 29,* 43–58.

Parker, A. J. (2007). Binocular depth perception and the cerebral cortex. *Nature Reviews Neuroscience, 8,* 379–391.

Parkin, A. J., Blunden, J., Rees, J. E., & Hunkin, N. M. (1991). Wernicke-Korsakoff syndrome of nonalcoholic origin. *Brain and Cognition, 15,* 69–82.

Pastalkova, E., Serrano, P., & Pinkhasova, D. (2006). Storage of spatial information by the maintenance mechanism of LTP. *Science, 313,* 1141–1144.

Pato, M. T., Pato, C. N., & Pauls, D. L. (2002). Recent findings in the genetics of OCD. *Journal of Clinical Psychiatry, 63(6),* 30–33.

Paulesu, E., Frith, U., Snowling, M., Gallagher, A., Morton, J., Frackowiak, R. S. J., & Frith, C. D. (1996). Is developmental dyslexia a disconnection syndrome? *Brain, 119,* 143–157.

Paulhus, D. L., & Williams, K. M. (2002). The Dark Triad of personality: Narcissism, machiavellianism, and psychopathy. *Journal of Research in Personality, 36,* 556–563.

Pauls, D. L., & Alsobrook, J. P. (1999). The inheritance of obsessive-compulsive disorder. *Child and Adolescent Psychiatric Clinics of North America, 8,* 481–496.

Pauls, D. L., & Leckman, J. F. (1986). The inheritance of Gilles de la Tourette's syndrome and associated behaviors. *New England Journal of Medicine, 315,* 993–997.

Paunonen, S. V. (2003). Big Five factors of personality and replicated predictions of behavior. *Journal of Personality & Social Psychology, 84(2),* 411–422.

Pavlov. I. P. (1927). *Conditioned reflexes.* Oxford, UK: Oxford University Press.

Pavlov, I. P. (1961/1994). *Psychopathology and psychiatry.* [Translated from the Russian by D. Myshne and S. Belsky.] New Brunswick, NJ: Transaction Publishers.

Pease, D. M., Gleason, J. B., & Pan, B. A. (1993). Learning the meaning of words: Semantic development and beyond. In J. B. Gleason (Ed.), *The development of language.* New York: Macmillan.

Pederson, D. R., Gleason, K. E., Moran, G., & Bento, S. (1998). Maternal attachment representations, maternal sensitivity, and the infant-mother attachment relationship. *Developmental Psychology, 34,* 925–933.

Pederson, D. R., & Moran, G. (1996). Expressions of the attachment relationship outside the strange situation. *Child Development, 67,* 915–927.

Peigneux, P., Laureys, S., Fuchs, S., Collette, P., Perrin, F., Reggers, J., Phillips, C., Degueldre, C., Del Fiore, G., Aerts, J., Luxen, A., & Maquet, P. (2004). Are spatial memories strengthened in the human hippocampus during slow wave sleep? *Neuron, 44,* 535–545.

Pelkovitz, D., & Kaplan, S. (1996). Posttraumatic stress disorder in children and adolescents. *Child and Adolescent Psychiatric Clinics of North America, 5,* 449–469.

Pelleymounter, M. A., Cullen, M. J., Baker, M. B., Hecht, R., Winters, D., Boone, T., & Collins, E. (1997). Effects of the obese gene product on body weight regulation in ob/ob mice. *Science, 269,* 540–543.

Pennisi, E. (2006). Mining the molecules that made our mind. *Science, 313,* 1908–1911.

Pennisi, E. (2007). Ancient DNA: No sex please, we're Neanderthals. *Science, 316,* 967.

Pepperberg, I. M. (2000). *The Alex studies: Cognitive and communicative abilities of grey parrots.* Cambridge, MA: Harvard University Press.

Pereira, A. C., Huddleston, D. E., Brickman, A. M., Sosunov, A. A., Hen, R., McKhann, G. M., Sloan, R., Gage, F. H., Brown, T. R., & Small, S. A. (2007). An in vivo correlate of exercise-induced neurogenesis in the adult dentate gyrus. *Proceedings of the National Academy of Science, U S A, 104,* 5638–5643.

Peretz, I., Blood, A. J., Penhune, V., & Zatorre, R. (2001). Cortical deafness to dissonance. *Brain, 124,* 928–940.

Peretz, I., Gagnon, L., & Bouchard, B. (1998). Music and emotion: Perceptual determinants, immediacy, and isolation after brain damage. *Cognition, 68,* 111–141.

Perlmutter, M., & Hall, E. (1992). *Adult development and aging* (2nd ed.). New York: John Wiley and Sons.

Perloff, R. M. (2003). *The dynamics of persuasion: Communication and attitudes in the 21st century.* Mahwah, NJ: Erlbaum.

Perls, F. S. (1967). Group vs. individual therapy. *ETC: A Review of General Semantics, 34,* 306–312.

Perls, F. S. (1969). *Gestalt therapy verbatim.* Lafayette, CA: Real People Press.

Persad, E. (2001). Electroconvulsive therapy: The controversy and the evidence. *Canadian Journal of Psychiatry, 46(8),* 702–703.

Pervin, L. A. (1975). *Personality: Theory, assessment, and research.* New York: John Wiley & Sons.

Peskind, E. R., Jensen, C. F., Pascual, Y. M., Cowley, D., Martin, D. C., Winkinson, C. W., & Raskind, M. A. (1998). Sodium lactate and hypertonic sodium chloride induce equivalent panic incidence, panic symptoms, and hypernatremia in panic disorder. *Biological Psychiatry, 44,* 1007–1016.

Petersen, S. E., Fox, P. T., Posner, M. I., Mintin, M., & Raichle, M. E. (1988). Positron emission tomographic studies of the cortical anatomy of single-word processing. *Nature, 331,* 585–589.

Peterson, L. R., & Peterson, M. J. (1959). Short-term retention of individual verbal items. *Journal of Experimental Psychology, 58,* 193–198.

Peterson, M. A. (2005). Object perception. In E. B. Goldstein (Ed.), *Blackwell handbook of sensation and perception* (pp. 169–203). Malden, MA: Blackwell Publishing.

Peterson, R. (1985). Pubertal development as a cause of disturbance: Myths, realities, and unanswered questions. *Genetic, Social, and General Psychology Monographs, 111,* 205–232.

Petitto, L. A., Zatorre, R. J., Gauna, K., Nikelski, E. J., Dostie, D., & Evans, A. C. (2000). Speech-like cerebral activity in profoundly deaf people processing signed languages: Implications for the neural basis of human language. *Proceedings of the National Academy of Sciences, USA, 97,* 13961–13966.

Pettus, A. (2008, January-February). A spectrum of disorders. *Harvard Magazine, 80,* 27–31.

Petty, F., Chae, Y., Karmer, G., Jordan, S., & Wilson, L. (1994). Learned helplessness sensitizes hippocampal norepinephrine to mild restress. *Biological Psychiatry, 35,* 903–908.

Petty, R. E., & Wegener, D. T. (1999). The elaboration likelihood model: Current status and controversies. In S. Chaiken & Y. Trope (Eds.), *Dual-process theories in social psychology.* New York: Guilford Press.

Petty, R. E., Wegener, D. T., & Fabrigar, L. R. (1997). Attitude change: Multiple roles for persuasion variables. In D. Gilbert, S. Fiske, & G. Lindzey (Eds.), *Handbook of social psychology* (4th ed.). New York: McGraw-Hill.

Petty, R. E., Wheeler, S. C., & Tormala, Z. L. (2003). Persuasion and attitude change. In T. Millon & M. J. Lerner (Eds.), *Handbook of psychology: Personality and social psychology, Vol. 5.* New York: John Wiley & Sons, Inc.

Pfefferbaum, A., Zipursky, R. B., Lim, K. O., Zatz, L. M., Stahl, S. M., & Jernigan, T. L. (1988). Computed tomographic evidence for generalized sulcal and ventricular enlargement in schizophrenia. *Archives of General Psychiatry, 45,* 633–640.

Phares, E. J. (1979). *Clinical psychology: Concepts, methods, and profession.* Homewood, IL: Dorsey Press.

Phillips, S. D., Burns, B. J., Edgar, E. R., Mueser, K. T., Linkins, K. W., Rosenheck, R. A., Drake, R. E., & McDonel Herr, E. C. (2001). Moving assertive community treatment into standard practice. *Psychiatric Services, 52(6),* 771–779.

Piaget, J. (1952). *The origins of intelligence in children.* (M. Cook, Trans.). New York: International Universities Press.

Piaget, J. (1972). Intellectual evolution from adolescence to adulthood. *Human Development, 15,* 1–12.

Pierce, W. D., & Epling, W. F. (1997). Activity anorexia: The interplay of culture, behavior, and biology. In P. Lamal (Ed.), *Cultural contingencies: Behavior analytic perspectives on cultural practices* (pp. 53–85). Westport, CT: Prager Publishers/Greenwood Publishing Group.

Pierce W. D., Heth C. D., Owczarczyk J. C., Russell J. C., & Proctor S. D. (2007). Overeating by young obesity-prone and lean rats caused by tastes associated with low energy foods. *Obesity, 15,* 1969–1979.

Pika, S., Liebal, K., & Tomasello, M. (2003). Gestural communication in young gorillas (*Gorilla gorilla*): Gestural repertoire, learning, and use. *Americal Journal of Primatology, 60,* 95–111.

Pilcher, J. J., & Huffcutt, A. I. (1996). Effects of sleep deprivation on performance: A meta-analysis. *Sleep, 19,* 318–326.

Pilleri, G. (1979). The blind Indus dolphin, *Platanista indi. Endeavours, 3,* 48–56.

Pinel, J. P. J., Assanand, S., & Lehman, D. R. (2000). Hunger, eating, and ill health. *American Psychologist, 55,* 1105–1116.

Pinhas, L., Toner, B. B., Ali, A., Garfinkel, P. E., & Stuckless, N. (1999). The effects of the ideal of female beauty on mood and body satisfaction. *Eating Disorders, 25,* 223–226.

Pinker, S. (1990). Language acquisition. In D. N. Osherson & H. Lasnik (Eds.), *An invitation to cognitive science. Vol. 1: Language.* Cambridge, MA: MIT Press.

Pinker, S. (1994). *The language instinct.* New York: William Morrow.

Pinker, S. (1999). *Words and rules: The ingredients of language.* New York: Basic Books.

Pinker, S. (2001). Talk of genetics and vice versa. *Nature, 413,* 465–466.

Pinker, S. (2007). *The stuff of thought: Language as a window into human nature.* New York: Viking.

Pinker, S., & Jackendoff, R. (2005). The faculty of language: What's special about it? *Cognition, 96,* 201–236.

Pirkkola, S. P., Poikolainen, K., & Lonnqvist, J. K. (2006). Currently active and remitted alcohol dependence in a nationwide adult general population—results from the Finnish health 2000 study. *Alcohol and Alcoholism, 41,* 315–320.

Pitkänen, A., Savander, V., & LeDoux, J. E. (1997). Organization of intra-amygdaloid circuits: An emerging framework for understanding functions of the amygdala. *Trends in Neuroscience, 20,* 517–523.

Pittenger, C., & Kandel, E. R. (2003). In search of general mechanisms of long-lasting plasticity: Aplysia and the hippocampus. *Philosophical Transaction of the Royal Society of London: B. Biological Sciences, 358,* 757–763.

Pitts, M., & Phillips, K. (1998). *The psychology of health: An introduction* (2nd ed.). London, UK, and New York: Routledge.

Plassman, B. L., Langa, K. M., Fisher, G. G., Heeringa, S. G., Weir, D. R., Ofstedal, M. B., Burke, J. R., Hurd, M. D., Potter, G. G., Rodgers, W. L., Steffens, D. C., Willis, R. J., & Wallace, R. B. (2007). Prevalence of dementia in the United States: The aging, demographics and memory study. *Neuro-epidemiology, 29,* 125–132.

Pliskoff, S. S. (1971). Effects of symmetrical and asymmetrical changeover delays on concurrent performances. *Journal of the Experimental Analysis of Behavior, 16,* 249–256.

Plomin, R., & Asbury, K. (2001). Nature and nurture in the family. *Marriage & Family Review, 33(2–3),* 273–281.

Plomin, R., & Bergeman, C. S. (1991). The nature of nurture: Genetic influence on "environmental" measures. *Behavioral and Brain Sciences, 14,* 373–427.

Plucker, J. A., & Barab, S. A. (2005). The importance of contexts in theories of giftedness. In R. J. Sternberg & J. E. Davidson (Eds.), *Conceptions of giftedness,* 2nd ed. (pp. 201–216). New York: Cambridge University Press.

Poduslo, S. E., & Yin, X. (2001). A new locus on chromosome 19 linked with late-onset Alzheimer's disease. *Neuroreport, 12,* 3759–3761.

Poeppel, D., & Hickok, G. (2004). Towards a new functional anatomy of language. *Cognition, 92,* 1–12.

Pollard, K. S., Salama1, S. R, Lambert, N., Lambot, M-A., Coppens, S., Pedersen, J. S., Katzman, S., King, B., Onodera, C., Siepe, A., Kern, A. D, Dehay, C., Igel, H., Manuel Ares Jr., M., Vanderhaeghen, P., & Haussler, D. (2006). An RNA gene expressed during cortical development evolved rapidly in humans. *Nature, 443,* 167–172.

Pollick, A. S., & de Waal, F. B. M. (2007). Ape gestures and language evolution. *Proceedings of the National Academy of Sciences, USA, 104,* 8184–8189.

Pope, K. S. (2000). Therapists' sexual feelings and behaviors: Research, trends, and quandaries. In L. T. Szuchman & F. Muscarella (Eds.), *Psychological perspectives on human sexuality* (603–658). New York: Wiley.

Porter, J., Craven, B., Khan, R. M., Chang, S.-J., Kang, I Judkewitz, B., Volpe, J., Settles, G., & Sobel, N. (2007). Mechanisms of scent-tracking in humans. *Nature Neuroscience, 10,* 27–29.

Porter, R. H., Makin, J. W., Davis, L. B., & Christensen, K. M. (1992). Breast-fed infants respond to olfactory cues from their own mother and unfamiliar lactating females. *Infant Behavior and Development, 15,* 85–93.

Posner, M. I., & Cohen, Y. (1984). Components of visual orienting. In H. Bouma & D. Bowhuis (Eds.), *Attention and Performance X.* (pp. 531–556). Hillsdale, NJ: Lawrence Erlbaum Associates.

Posner, M. I., & DeGirolamo, G. J. (2000). Cognitive neuroscience: Origins and promise. *Psychological Bulletin, 126,* 873–889.

Posner, M. I., Snyder, C. R. R., & Davidson, B. J. (1980). Attention and the detection of signals. *Journal of Experimental Psychology: General, 109,* 160–174.

Potter, S. M., Zelazo, P. R., Stack, D. M., & Papageorgiou, A. N. (2000). Adverse effects of fetal cocaine exposure on neonatal auditory information processing. *Pediatrics, 105,* E40.

Potter, W. Z., Padich, R. A., Rudorfer, M. C., & Krishnan, K. R. R. (2005). Tricyclics, tetracyclics, and monoamine oxidase inhibitors. In D. J. Stein, D. J. Kupfer, & A. F. Schatzberg (Eds.), *Textbook of mood disorders* (pp. 251–262). Washington, DC: American Psychiatric Publishing.

Poulin-Dubois, D., Graham, S., & Sippola, L. (1995). Early lexical development: The contribution of parental labelling and infants' categorization abilities. *Journal of Child Language, 22,* 325–343.

Prabhakar, S., Noonan, J. P., Paabo, S., & Rubin, E. M. (2006). Accelerated evolution on conserved noncoding sequences in humans, *Science, 314,* 786.

Premack, D. (1959). Toward empirical behavioral laws: I. Positive reinforcement. *Psychological Review, 66,* 219–233.

Premack, D. (1976). Language and intelligence in ape and man. *American Scientist, 64,* 674–683.

Premack, D., & Premack, A. J. (2003). *Original intelligence: Unlocking the mystery of who we are.* New York: McGraw-Hill.

Prescott, C. A., & Kendler, K. S. (1999). Age at first drink and risk for alcoholism: A noncausal association. *Alcoholism: Clinical & Experimental Research, 23(1),* 101–107.

Prince, R. (1985). The concept of the culture-bound syndromes: Anorexia nervosa and brain-fag. *Social Science and Medicine,* 21, 197–203.

Prochaska, J. O., & Norcross, J. C. (2003). *Systems of psychotherapy,* 5th ed. Pacific Grove, CA: Brooks/Cole.

Proeve, M., & Reilly, E. (2007). Personal and offending characteristics of child sexual offenders who have been sexually abused. *Psychiatry, Psychology, and Law, 14,* 251–259.

Pronin, E., Kruger, J., Savitsky, K., & Ross. L. (2001). You don't know me, but I know you: The illusion of asymmetric insight. *Journal of Personality and Social Psychology, 81,* 639–656.

Prudic, J., & Sackeim, H. A. (1999). Electroconvulsive therapy and suicide risk. *Journal of Clinical Psychiatry, 60,* 104–110.

Pruetz, P., & Bertolani, P. (2007). Savanna chimpanzees, *Pan troglodytes verus* hunt with tools. *Current Biology, 17,* 412–417.

Prum, R. O. (2003). Palaeontology: Dinosaurs take to the air. *Nature, 421,* 323–324.

Public Health Service. (2002). *Public Health Service policy on humane care and use of laboratory animals.* Washington. DC: U.S. Department of Health and Human Services. Available at http://grants.nih.gov/grants/olaw/references/phspol.htm. Downloaded 10 December, 2007.

Pulcino, T., Galea, S., Ahern, J., Resnick, H., Foley, M., & Vlahov, D. (2003). Posttraumatic stress in women after the September 11 terrorist attacks in New York City. *Journal of Women's Health, 12(8),* 809–820.

Purhonen, M., Kilpeläinen-Lees, R., Valkonen-Korhonen, M., Karhu, J., & Lehtonen, J. (2005). Four-month-old infants process own mother's voice faster than unfamiliar voices—Electrical signs of sensitization in infant brain. *Cognitive Brain Research, 24,* 627–633.

Quadrant HealthCom. (2005, December). National survey sharpens picture of major depression among US adults. *NeuroPsychiatry Reviews 6* (10). Retrieved from http://neuropsychiatryreviews.com/dec05/surveydepression.html.

Rachlin, H. (1995). Behavioral economics without anomalies (Special issue: Behavioral economics). *Journal of the Experimental Analysis of Behavior, 64,* 397–404.

Raine, A., Lencz, T., Bihrle, S., LaCasse, L., & Colletti, P. (2002). Reduced prefrontal gray matter volume and reduced autonomic activity in antisocial personality disorder. *Archives of General Psychiatry, 57,* 119–127.

Raine, A., Meloy, J. R., Bihrle, S., Stoddard, J., LaCasse, L., & Buchsbaum, M. S. (1998). Reduced prefrontal and increased subcortical brain functioning assessed using positron emission tomography in predatory and affective murderers. *Behavioral Science and the Law, 16,* 319–332.

Rainville, P., Duncan, G. H., Price, D. D., Carrier, B., & Bushnell, M. C. (1997). Pain affect encoded in human anterior cingulate but not somatosensory cortex. *Science, 277,* 968–971.

Rainville, P., Hofbauer, R. K., Bushnell, M. C., Duncan, G. H., & Price, D. D. (2002). Hypnosis modulates activity in brain structures involved in the regulation of consciousness. *Journal of Cognitive Neuroscience, 14,* 887–901.

Rainville, P., Hofbauer, R. K., Paus, T., Duncan, G. H., Bushnell, M. C., & Price, D. D. (1999). Cerebral mechanisms of hypnotic induction and suggestion. *Journal of Cognitive Neuroscience, 11,* 110–125.

Rajecki, D. J. (1990). *Attitudes* (2nd ed.). Sunderland, MA: Sinauer Associates.

Ramachandran, V. S., & Hirstein, W. (1998). The perception of phantom limbs. *Brain, 121,* 1603–1630.

Ramey, C. (1994). Abecedarian project. In R. J. Sternberg (Ed.), *Encyclopedia of human intelligence.* New York: Macmillan.

Ramirez, I. (1990). Why do sugars taste good? *Neuroscience and Biobehavioral Reviews, 14,* 125–134.

Ramirez-Amaya, V., Marrone, D. F., Gage, F. H., Worley, P. F., and Barnes, C. A. (2006). Integration of new neurons into functional neural networks. *Journal of Neuroscience, 26,* 12237–12241.

Rapoport, J. L., Giedd, J. N., Blumenthal, J., Hamburger, S., Jeffries, N., Fernandez, T., Nicolson, R., Bedwell, J., Lenane, M., Zijdenbos, A., Paus, T., & Evans, A. (1999). *Archives of General Psychiatry, 56,* 649–654.

Rappaport, J. (1977). *Community psychology: Values, research and action.* New York: Holt, Rinehart and Winston.

Rappaport, J., & Seidman, E. (2000). *Handbook of community psychology.* New York: Kluwer Academic/Plenum Publishers.

Rasch, B., & Born, J. (2008). Reactivation and consolidation of memory during sleep. *Current Directions in Psychological Science, 17,* 188–192.

Rasenburger, J. (2004, February 8). Kitty, 40 years later. *The New York Times,* Section 14, p. 1, column 1.

Rayner, K., Foorman, B. R., Perfetti, C., Petetsky, D., & Seidenberg, M. S. (2002, March). How should reading be taught? *Scientific American,* 85–91.

Rayner, K., & Pollatsek, A. (1989). *The psychology of reading.* Englewood Cliffs, NJ: Prentice-Hall.

Rayner, K., Sereno, S. C., & Raney, G. E. (1996). Eye movement control in reading: A comparison of two types of models. *Journal of Experimental Psychology: Human Perception and Performance, 22,* 1188–1200.

Reber, A. S. (1992). The cognitive unconscious: An evolutionary perspective. *Consciousness and Cognition, 1,* 93–133.

Redding, G. M., & Hawley, E. (1993). Length illusion in fractional Müller-Lyer stimuli: An object-perception approach. *Perception, 22,* 819–828.

Reichle, E. D., Pollatsek, A., Fisher, D. L., & Rayner, K. (1998). Toward a model of eye movement control in reading. *Psychological Review, 105,* 125–157.

Reif, A., Rösler, M., Freitag, C. M., Schneider, M., Eujen, A., Kissing, C., Wenzler, D., Jacob, C. P. Retz-Juninger, P., Thome, J., Lesch, K.-P., & Retz, W. (2007). Nature and nurture predispose to violent behavior: Serotonergic genes and adverse childhood environment. *Neuropharmacology, 34,* 2375–2383.

Reingold, E. M., Charness, N., Pomplun, M., & Stampe, D. M. (2001). Visual span in expert chess players: Evidence from eye movements. *Psychological Science, 12,* 48–55.

Reis, H. T., & Aron, A. (2008). Love: What is it, why does it matter, and how does it operate? *Perspectives on Psychological Science, 3,* 80–86.

Rensink, R. A. (2002). Change detection. *Annual Review of Psychology, 53,* 245–277.

Rescorla, R. A., & Wagner, A. R. (1972). A theory of Pavlovian conditioning: Variations in the effectiveness of reinforcement and nonreinforcement. In A. H. Black & W. E. Prokasy (Eds.), *Classical conditioning II.* (pp. 64–99). New York: Appleton-Century-Crofts.

Ressler, K. J., & Nemeroff, C. B. (2000). Role of serotonergic and noradrenergic systems in the pathophysiology of depression and anxiety disorders. *Depression and Anxiety, 12,* 2–19.

Rest, J. R. (1979). *Development in judging moral issues.* Minneapolis: University of Minnesota Press.

Revonsuo, A. (2000). The reinterpretation of dreams. *Behavioral and Brain Sciences, 23,* 877–901.

Reyes-García, G., Ricardo, H. T., Leonard, W. R., McDade, T., Tanner, S., & Vadez, V. (2007). The origins of monetary income inequality: Patience, human capital, and division of labor *Evolution and Human Behavior, 28,* 37–47.

Reynolds, A. G., & Flagg, P. W. (1983). *Cognitive psychology* (2nd ed.). Boston: Little, Brown.

Reynolds, G. (2003, March 16). The stuttering doctor's "Monster Study." *Times Magazine.* New York: New York Times.

Rhee, S. H., Hewitt, J. K., Young, S. E., Corely, R. P., Crowley, T. J., & Stallings, M. C. (2003). Genetic and environmental influences on substance initiation, use, and problem use in adolescents. *Archives of General Psychology, 60(12),* 1256–1264.

Rheingold, A. A., Acierno, R., & Resnick, H. S. (2004). Trauma, posttraumatic stress disorder, and health risk behaviors. In P. P. Schnurr & B. L. Green (Eds.), *Trauma and health: Physical health consequences of exposure to extreme stress* (pp. 217–243). Washington, DC: American Psychological Association.

Rhodes, G., Byatt, G., Michie, P. T., & Puce, A. (2004). Is the fusiform face area specialized for faces, individuation, or expert individuation? *Journal of Cognitive Neuroscience, 16,* 189–203.

Rice, M. L., Huston, A. C., Truglio, R., & Wright, J. (1990). Words from "Sesame Street": Learning vocabulary while viewing. *Developmental Psychology, 26,* 421–428.

Riesenhuber, M., & Poggio, T. (2002). Neural mechanisms of object recognition. *Current Opinion in Neurobiology, 12,* 162–168.

Rips, L. J., Shoben, E. J., & Smith, E. E. (1973). Semantic distance and the verification of semantic relations. *Journal of Verbal Learning and Verbal Behavior, 12,* 1–20.

Rischer, C. E., & Easton, T. A. (1992). *Focus on human biology.* New York: HarperCollins.

Ritter, S., Dinh, T. T., & Zhang, Y. (2000). Localization of hindbrain glucoreceptive sites controlling food intake and blood glucose. *Brain Research, 856,* 37–47.

Roberson, D., Daviews, I., & Davidoff, J. (2000). Color categories are not universal: Replications and new evidence from a Stone-Age culture. *Journal of Experimental Psychology: General, 129,* 369–398.

Robins, R. W., & Beer, J. S. (2001). Positive illusions about the self: Short-term benefits and long-term costs. *Journal of Personality and Social Psychology, 80,* 340–352.

Rodin, J., Schank, D., & Striegel-Moore, R. (1989). Psychological features of obesity. *Medical Clinics of North America, 73,* 47–66.

Roediger, H. L., III, & McDermott, K. B. (1995). Creating false memories: Remembering words not presented in lists. *Journal of Experimental Psychology: Learning, Memory, and Cognition, 21,* 803–814.

Roehling, P. V., & Bultman, M. (2002). Does absence make the heart grow fonder? Work-related travel and marital satisfaction. *Sex Roles, 46,* 279–293.

Roff, J. D., & Knight, R. A. (1995). Childhood antecedents of stable positive symptoms in schizophrenia. *Psychological Reports, 77(1),* 319–323.

Rogers, C. R. (1961). *On becoming a person.* Boston: Houghton Mifflin.

Rogers, C. T. (1951). *Client-centered therapy.* Boston: Houghton Mifflin.

Rogoff, B. (1990). *Apprenticeship in thinking: Cognitive development in social context.* New York: Oxford University Press.

Rogoff, B., & Chavajay, P. (1995). What's become of research on the cultural basis of cognitive development. *American Psychologist, 50,* 859–877.

Rogoff, B., & Waddell, K. J. (1982). Memory for information organized in a scene by children from two cultures. *Child Development, 53,* 1224–1228.

Rohling, M. L., Langhinrichsen-Rohling, J., & Miller, L. S. (2003). Actuarial assessment of malingering. In R. D. Franklin (Ed.), *Prediction in forensic and neuropsychology: Sound statistical practices* (pp. 171–208). Mahwah, NJ: Lawrence Erlbaum Associates.

Roid, G. H., & Barram, R. A. (2004). *Essentials of Stanford-Binet scales (SB5) assessment.* New York: Wiley.

Roisman, G. I., Clausell, E., Holland, A., Fortuna, K., & Elieff, C. (2008). Adult romantic relationships as contexts of human development: A multimethod comparison of same-sex couples with opposite-sex dating, engaged, and married dyads. *Developmental Psychology, 44,* 91–101.

Rolls, B. J., Rolls, E. T., Rowe, E. A., and Sweeney, K. (1981a) Sensory specific satiety in man. *Physiology and Behavior, 27,* 137–142.

Rolls, B. J., Rowe, E. A., and Rolls, E. T. (1982) How flavour and appearance affect human feeding. *Proceedings on the Nutrition Society, 41,* 109–117.

Rolls, B. J., Rowe, E. A., Rolls, E. T., Kingston, B., Megson, A., and Gunary, R. (1981b). Variety in a meal enhances food intake in man. *Physiology and Behavior, 26,* 215–221.

Rolls, E. T. & Rolls, J. H. (1997) Olfactory sensory-specific satiety in humans. *Physiology and Behavior, 61,* 461–473.

Roney, J. R. (1999). Distinguishing adaptations from by-products. *American Psychologist, 54,* 435–436.

Roodenrys, S., Hulme, C., Lethbridge, A., Hinton, M., & Nimmo, L. M. (2002). Word-frequency and phonological-neighborhood effects on verbal short-term memory. *Journal of Experimental Psychology: Learning, Memory, and Cognition, 28,* 1019–1034.

Rose, G. A., & Williams, R. T. (1961). Metabolic studies of large and small eaters. *British Journal of Nutrition, 15,* 1–9.

Rose, R. J. (1995). Genes and human behavior. *Annual Review of Psychology, 46,* 625–654.

Rosenfarb, I. S., Bellack, A. S., Aziz, N., Kratz, M., & Sayers, S. (2004). Race, family interactions, and patient stabilization in schizophrenia. *Journal of Abnormal Psychology, 113(1),* 109–115.

Rosenhan, D. L. (1973). On being sane in insane places. *Science, 179,* 250–258.

Rosenman, R. H., Brand, R. J., Jenkins, C. D., Friedman, M., Straus, R., & Wurm, M. (1975). Coronary heart disease in the Western Collaborative Group Study: Final follow-up experience of 8-½ years. *Journal of the American Medical Association, 233,* 872–877.

Rosenthal, A. M. (1999). *Thirty-eight witnesses.* Berkeley: University of California Press (Original work published 1964).

Rosenthal, D. (1970). *Genetic theory and abnormal behavior.* New York: McGraw-Hill.

Rosenthal, N. E. (2000). A patient who changed my practice: Herb Kern, the first light therapy patient. *International Journal of Psychiatry in Clinical Practice, 4,* 339–341.

Rosenthal, N. E., Genhart, M., Jacobson, F. M., Skwerer, R. G., & Wehr, T. A. (1986). Disturbances of appetite and weight regulation in seasonal affective disorder. *Annals of the New York Academy of Sciences, 499,* 216–230.

Rosenthal, R. (1985). From unconscious experimenter bias to teacher expectancy effects. In J. B. Dusek, V. C. Hall, & W. J. Meyer (Eds.), *Teacher expectancies.* Hillsdale, NJ: Lawrence Erlbaum Press.

Rosenzweig, M. R., & Bennett, E. L. (1996). Psychobiology of plasticity: Effects of training and experience on brain and behavior. *Behavioural Brain Research, 78,* 57–65.

Roskos-Ewoldsen, D. R., & Fazio, R. H. (1992). The accessibility of source likability as a determinant of persuasion. *Personality and Social Psychology Bulletin, 18,* 19–25.

Rosmand, R. (2005). Role of stress in the pathogenesis of the metabolic syndrome. *Psychoneuroendocrinology, 30,* 1–10.

Ross, C., Miller, S. D., Bjornson, L., & Reagor, P. (1991). Abuse histories in 102 cases of multiple personality disorder. *Canadian Journal of Psychiatry, 36,* 97–101.

Ross, C. A. (1997). *Dissociative identity disorder: Diagnosis, clinical features, and treatment of multiple personality* (2nd ed.). New York: John Wiley & Sons, Inc.

Ross, G., Nelson, K., Wetstone, H., & Tanouye, E. (1986). Acquisition and generalization of novel object concepts by young language learners. *Journal of Child Language, 13,* 67–83.

Ross, L. (1977). The intuitive psychologist and his shortcomings: Distortions in the attribution process. In L. Berkowitz (Ed.), *Advances in experimental social psychology. Vol. 10.* New York: Academic Press.

Ross, M., & Miller, D. T. (2002). *The justice motive in everyday life.* Cambridge: Cambridge University Press.

Rosser, R. (1994). Cognitive development: Psychological and biological perspectives. Boston: Allyn & Bacon.

Rothbaum, B. D., Hodges, L., Anderson, P. L., Prices, L., & Smith, S. (2002). Twelve-month follow-up of virtual reality and standard exposure therapies for fear of flying. *Journal of Consulting and Clinical Psychology, 70,* 428–432.

Rothkopf, E. Z. (1971). Incidental memory for location of information in text. *Journal of Verbal Learning and Verbal Behavior, 10,* 608–613.

Rotter, J. B. (1966). Generalized expectancies for internal versus external control of reinforcement. *Psychological Monographs, 80(1, Whole No. 609).*

Rotter, J. B. (1990). Internal versus external control of reinforcement: A case history of a variable. *American Psychologist, 45,* 489–493.

Rovee-Collier, C. (1999). The development of infant memory. *Current Directions in Psychological Science, 8,* 80–85.

Rovee-Collier, C. K., & Gekowski, M. J. (1979). The economics of infancy: A review of conjugate reinforcement. In H. W. Reese & L. P. Lipsitt (Eds.), *Advances in child development* (Vol. 13, pp. 195–225). New York: Academic Press.

Rowatt, W. C., Cunningham, M. R., & Druen, P. B. (1999). Lying to get a date: The effect of facial physical attractiveness on the willingness to deceive prospective dating partners. *Journal of Social and Personal Relationships, 16,* 209–223.

Rozin, P., & Royzman, E. B. (2001). Negativity bias, negativity dominance, and contagion. *Personality and Social Psychology Review, 5,* 296–320.

Rudman, L. A., Ashmore, R. D., & Gary, M. L. (2001). "Unlearning" automatic biases: The malleability of implicit prejudice and stereotypes. *Journal of Personality and Social Psychology, 8,* 856–868.

Rudy, J. (1991). Elemental and configural associations, the hippocampus and development. *Developmental Psychobiology, 24,* 221–236.

Ruff, C. C., Kristjánsson, A., & Driver, J. (2007). Readout from iconic memory and selective spatial attention involve similar neural processes, *Psychological Science, 18,* 901–909.

Rupp, H. A., & Wallen, K. (2007). Relationship between testosterone and interest in sexual stimuli: The effect of experience. *Hormones and Behavior, 52,* 581–589.

Rupp, H. A., & Wallen, K. (2008). Sex differences in response to visual sexual stimuli: A review. *Archives of Sexual Behavior, 37,* 206–218.

Ruscher, J. B. (1998). Prejudice and stereotyping in everyday communication. *Advances in Experimental Social Psychology, 30,* 241–307.

Russell, J. A. (1991). Culture and categorization of emotion. *Psychological Bulletin, 110,* 426–450.

Russell, J. A. (1994). Is there universal recognition of emotion from facial expression? A review of the cross-cultural studies. *Psychological Bulletin, 115,* 102–141.

Russell, P. A., Deregowski, J. B., & Kinnear, P. R. (1997). Perception and aesthetics. In J. W. Berry, P. R. Dasen, & T. S. Sarawath (Eds.), *Handbook of cross-cultural psychology. Vol. 2: Basic processes and human* development, pp. 107–142. Boston: Allyn & Bacon.

Ruvolo, A., & Markus, H. (1992). Possible selves and performance: The power of self-relevant imagery. *Social Cognition, 9,* 95–124.

Ruzgis, P., & Grigorenko, E. L. (1994). Cultural meaning systems, intelligence, and personality. In R. J. Sternberg & P. Ruzgis (Eds.), *Personality and intelligence* (pp. 248–270). New York: Cambridge University Press.

Ryan, R. M., & Deci, E. L. (2000). Self-determination theory and the facilitation of intrinsic motivation, social development, and wellbeing. *American Psychologist, 55,* 68–78.

Ryan, R. M., & Deci, E. L. (2002). Overview of self-determination theory: An organismic-dialectical perspective. In E. L. Deci & R. M. Ryan (Eds.), *Handbook of self-determination research* (pp. 3–33). Rochester, NY: University of Rochester Press.

Sacchi, D. L. M., Agnoli, F., & Loftus, E. F. (2007). Changing history: Doctored photographs affect memory for past public events. *Applied Cognitive Psychology, 21,* 1005–1022.

Sachs, J. S. (1967). Recognition memory for syntactic and semantic aspects of connected discourse. *Perception and Psychophysics, 2,* 437–442.

Sachs, O. (1989). *Seeing voices: A journey into the world of the deaf.* Berkeley, CA: University of California Press.

Sacks, E. (2007). *The center cannot hold: My journey through madness.* New York: Hyperion.

Sacks, O. (1995). *An anthropologist on Mars: Seven paradoxical tales.* New York: Alfred A. Knopf.

Sacks, O. (2000). *Seeing voices.* New York: Vintage.

Sacks, O. (2006). *The man who mistook his wife for a hat and other clinical tales.* New York: Simon & Schuster.

Sacks, O. (24 Sept 2007). The abyss. *The New Yorker,* 100–111.

Sadovnick, A. D., Remick, R. A., Lam, R. W., Zis, A. P., Yee, I. M. L., & Baird, P. A. (1994). Morbidity risks for mood disorders in 3,942 first degree relatives of 671 index cases with single depression, recurrent depression, bipolar I or bipolar II. *American Journal of Medical Genetics, 54,* 132–140.

Saegert, S. C., Swap, W., & Zajonc, R. B. (1973). Exposure, context, and interpersonal attraction. *Journal of Personality and Social Psychology, 25,* 234–242.

Saffran, E. M., Schwartz, M. F., & Marin, O. S. M. (1980). Evidence from aphasia: Isolating the components of a production model. In B. Butterworth (Ed.), *Language production.* London: Academic Press.

Sagvolden, T., Johnasen, E. B., Aase, H., and Russell, V. A. (2005). A dynamic developmental theory of attention-deficit/hyperactivity disorder (ADHD) predominantly hyperactive/impulsive and combined subtypes. *Behavioral and Brain Sciences, 28,* 347–468.

Sakai, F., Meyer, J. S., Karacan, I., Derman, S., & Yamamoto, M. (1979). Normal human sleep: Regional cerebral haemodynamics. *Annals of Neurology, 7,* 471–478.

Salapatek, P. (1975). Pattern perception in early infancy. In L. B. Cohen & P. Salapatek (Eds.), *Infant perception: From sensation to cognition.* Vol. 1 (pp. 133–248). New York: Academic Press.

Saletan, W. (2007, May 11). *Chess bump: The triumphant teamwork of humans and computers.*

Salovey, P., Brackett, M. A., & Mayer, J. D. (2004). *Emotional intelligence: Key readings on the Mayer and Salovey model.* Port Chester, NY: NPR Inc.

Salter, D., McMillan, D., Richards, M., Talbot, T., Hodges, J., Bentovim, A., Hastings, R., Stevenson, J., & Skuse, D. (2003). Development of sexually abusive behaviour in sexually victimised males: A longitudinal study, *Lancet, 361,* 471–476.

Salthouse, T. A. (1984). Effects of age and skill in typing. *Journal of Gerontology, 113,* 345–371.

Salthouse, T. A. (1988). Cognitive aspects of motor functioning. In J. A. Joseph (Ed.), *Central determinants of age-related declines in motor function: Annals of the NY Academy of Science, 515* (pp. 33–41). New York: New York Academy of Sciences.

Sánchez-Peña, L. C., Reyes, B. E., López-Carillo, L., Recio, R., Morán-Martinez, M. E., Cebrián, M. E., & Quintanilla-Vega, B. (2004). Organophosphorus pesticide exposure alters sperm chromatin structure in Mexican agricultural workers. *Toxicology and Applied Pharmacology, 196,* 108–113.

Sande, G. N., Goethals, G. R., & Radloff, C. E. (1988). Perceiving one's own traits and others': The multifaceted self. *Journal of Personality and Social Psychology, 54,* 13–20.

Sanders, L. D., Newport, E. L., & Neville, H. J. (2002). Segmenting nonsense: An event-related potential index of perceived onsets in continuous speech. *Nature Neuroscience, 5,* 700–703.

Sanfey, A. G. (2007). Social decision-making: Insights from game theory and neuroscience. *Science, 318,* 598–602.

Santos, M. D., Leve, C., & Pratkanis, A. R. (1994). Hey buddy, can you spare seventeen cents? Mindful persuasion and the pique technique. *Journal of Applied Social Psychology, 24,* 755–764.

Saper, C. B., Chou, T. C., & Scammell, T. E. (2001). The sleep switch: Hypothalamic control of sleep and wakefulness. *Trends in Neurosciences, 24,* 726–731.

Saper, C. B., Scammell, T. E., & Lu, J. (2005). Hypothalamic regulation of sleep and circadian rhythms. *Nature, 437,* 1257–1263.

Sarason, B. R., & Sarason, I. G. (2004). *Abnormal psychology: The problem of maladaptive behavior,* 11th ed. Upper Saddle River, NJ: Prentice-Hall.

Saudino, K. J. (2005). Behavioral genetics and child temperament. *Developmental and Behavioral Pediatrics, 26,* 214–223.

Savage-Rumbaugh, E. S., Shanker, S., & Taylor, T. J. (1998). *Apes, language, and the human mind.* New York: Oxford University Press.

Saxena, S., & Rauch, S. L. (2000). Functional neuroimaging and the neuroanatomy of obsessive-compulsive disorder. *Pediatric Clinics of North America, 23,* 563–586.

Scarr, S., & Weinberg, R. A. (1978). The influence of "family background" on intellectual attainment. *American Sociological Review, 43,* 674–692.

Schacter, D. L. (2001). *The seven sins of memory.* Boston: Houghton Mifflin.

Schacter, D. L., & Dodson, C. S. (2002). Misattribution, false recognition and the sins of memory. In A. Baddeley, M. Conway, & J. Aggleton (Eds.), *Episodic memory: New directions in research* (pp. 71–85). New York: Oxford University Press.

Schaie, K. W. (1990). Intellectual development in adulthood. In J. E. Birren & K. W. Schaie (Eds.), *Handbook of the psychology of aging* (3rd ed.) (pp. 291–309). San Diego: Academic Press.

Schaie, K. W. (1996). *Intellectual development in adulthood: The Seattle Longitudinal Study.* Cambridge: Cambridge University Press.

Schaie, K. W., & Strother, C. R. (1968). A cross-sequential study of age changes in cognitive behavior. *Psychological Bulletin, 70,* 661–684.

Schank, R., & Abelson, R. P. (1977). *Scripts, plans, goals, and understanding.* Hillsdale, NJ: Lawrence Erlbaum Associates.

Schein, J. D. (1989). *At home among strangers.* Washington, DC: Gallaudet University Press.

Schellenberg, G. D. (1997). Molecular genetics of Alzheimer's disease. In K. Blum & E. P. Nobel (Eds.), *Handbook of psychiatric genetics* (pp. 219–235). Boca Raton, FL: CRC Press.

Schenck, C. H., Hurwitz, T. D., Bundlie, S. R., & Mahowald, M. W. (1991). Sleep-related eating disorders: Polysomnographic correlates of a heterogeneous syndrome distinct from daytime eating disorders. *Sleep, 14*, 419–431.

Schenck, C. H., Hurwitz, T. D., & Mahowald, M. W. (1993). REM-sleep behavior disorder: An update on a series of 96 patients and a review of the world literature. *Journal of Sleep Research, 2*, 224–231.

Schenck, C. H., & Mahowald, M. W. (1992). Motor dyscontrol in narcolepsy: Rapid-eye-movement (REM) sleep with atonia and REM sleep behavior disorder. *Annals of Neurology, 32*, 3–10.

Schiff, N. D., Giacino, J. T., Kalmar, K., Victor, J. D., Baker, K., Gerber, M., Fritz, B., Eisenberg, B., O'Connor, J., Kobylarz, E. J., Farris, S., Machado, A., McCago, C., Plum, F., Fins, J. J., & Rezai, A. R. Behavioural improvements with thalamic stimulation after severe traumatic brain injury. *Nature, 448*, 600–603.

Schlund, M. W., Hoelin-Sarie, R., & Cataldo, M. F. (2007). New knowledge derived from learned knowledge: Functional-anatomic correlates of stimulus equivalence. *Journal of the Experimental Analysis of Behavior, 87*, 287–307.

Schmidt, H. G., Peeck, V. H., Paas, F., & van Breukelen, G. J. P. (2000). Remembering the street names of one's childhood neighborhood: A study of very long-term retention. *Memory, 8*, 37–49.

Schmitt, D. P., & Buss, D. M. (1996). Strategic self-promotion and competitor derogation: Sex and context effects on the perceived effectiveness of mate attraction tactics. *Journal of Personality and Social Psychology, 70*, 1185–1204.

Schmitt, D. P., Realo, A., Voracek, M., & Allik, J. (2008). Why can't a man be more like a woman? Sex differences in Big Five personality traits across 55 cultures. *Journal of Personality and Social Psychology, 94(1)*, 168–182.

Schmolck, H., Buffalo, E. A., & Squire, L. R. (2000). Memory distortions develop over time: Recollections of the O. J. Simpson trial verdict after 15 and 32 months. *Psychological Science, 11*, 39–45.

Schoenfeld, W. N., & Farmer, J. (1970). Reinforcement schedules and the "behavior stream." In W. N. Schoenfeld (Ed.), *The theory of reinforcement schedules.* (pp. 215–245). New York: Appleton-Century-Crofts.

Schou, M. (2001). Lithium treatment at 52. *Journal of Affective Disorders, 67(1–3)*, 21–32.

Schultz, W. (1997). Dopaminergic neurons report appetitive value of environmental stimuli. In J. W. Donahoe & V. P. Dorsel (Eds.), *Neural-network models of cognition: Biobehavioral foundations.* (pp. 317–335). Amsterdam: Elsevier Science Publications.

Schultz, W. (2001). Reward signaling by dopamine neurons. *The Neuroscientist, 7*, 293–302.

Schwartz, C. E., Wright, C.I., Shin, L. M., Kagan, J., & Rauch, S. L. (2003). Inhibited and uninhibited infants "grown up": Adult amygdalar response to novelty. *Science, 300,* 1952–1953.

Schwartz, M. F., Marin, O. S. M., & Saffran, E. M. (1979). Dissociations of language function in dementia: A case study. *Brain and Language, 7,* 277–306.

Schwartz, R. G. (2006). Would today's IRM approve the Tudor study? Ethical considerations in conducting research involving children with communication disorders. In R. Goldfarb (Ed.), *Ethics: A case study from fluency* (pp. 83–96). San Diego: Plural Publishing.

Schwarzkopf, S. B., Nasrallah, H. A., Olson, S. C., Coffman, J. A., & McLaughlin, J. A. (1989). Perinatal complications and genetic loading in schizophrenia: Preliminary findings. *Psychiatry Research, 27,* 233–239.

Schweitzer, J. B., & Sulzer-Azaroff, B. (1988). Self-control: Teaching tolerance for delay in impulsive children. *Journal of the Experimental Analysis of Behavior, 50,* 173–186.

Scollon, C. N., Diener, E., Oishi, S., & Biswas-Diener, R. (2004). Emotions across cultures and methods. *Journal of Cross-Cultural Psychology, 35,* 304–326.

Scott, S. K., Blank, C. C., Rosen, S., & Wise, R. J. S. (2000). Identification of a pathway for intelligible speech in the left temporal lobe. *Brain, 123,* 2400–2406.

Scott, T. R., & Plata-Salaman, C. R. (1991). Coding of taste quality. In *Smell and taste in health and disease,* Getchell, T. N. (Ed.). New York: Raven Press.

Scribner, S. (1977). Modes of thinking and ways of speaking: Culture and logic reconsidered. In P. N. Johnson-Laird & P. C. Wason (Eds.), *Thinking: Readings in cognitive science.* Cambridge, UK: Cambridge University Press.

Sears, D. (1983). The person-positivity bias. *Journal of Personality and Social Psychology, 44 (2),* 233–250.

Searles, L. V. (1949). The organization of hereditary maze brightness and maze dullness. *Genetic Psychology Monographs, 39,* 279–375.

Sedekides, C., Campbell, W. K., Reeder, G. D., & Elliot, A. J. (1998). The self-serving bias in relational context. *Journal of Personality and Social Psychology, 74,* 378–386.

Seftel, A. D., Mack, R. J., Secrest, A. R., & Smith, T. M. (2004). Restorative increases in serum testosterone levels are significantly correlated to improvements in sexual functioning. *Journal of Andrology, 25,* 963–972.

Segall, M. H., Dasen, P. R., Berry, J. W., & Poortinga, Y. H. (1999). *Human behavior in global perspective: An introduction to cross-cultural psychology* (2nd ed.). Boston: Allyn & Bacon.

Seligman, M. E. P. (1971). Phobias and preparedness. *Behavior Therapy, 2,* 307–320.

Seligman, M. E. P. (1975). *Helplessness.* San Francisco: W. H. Freeman.

Seligman, M. E. P., & Csikszentmihalyi, M. (2000). Positive psychology. *American Psychologist, 55,* 5–14.

Seligman, M. E. P., & Nolen-Hoeksema, S. (1987). Explanatory style and depression. In D. Magnusson & A. Oehman (Eds.), *Psychopathology: An interactional perspective. Personality, psychopathology, and psychotherapy* (pp. 125–139). Orlando, FL: Academic Press.

Selkoe, D. J. (1989). Biochemistry of altered brain proteins in Alzheimer's disease. *Annual Review of Neuroscience, 12,* 463–490.

Selye, H. (1956/1976). *The stress of life.* New York: McGraw-Hill.

Selye, H. (1991). History and present status of the stress concept. In A. Monat & R. S. Lazarus (Eds.), *Stress and coping* (pp. 21–35). New York: Columbia University Press.

Selye, H. (1993). History of the stress concept. In L. Goldberger & S. Breznitz (Eds.), *Handbook of stress: Theoretical and clinical aspects* (2nd ed.) (pp. 7–17). New York: Free Press.

Shackelford, T. K., & Weekes-Shackelford. V. A. (2004). Why don't men pay child support? Insights from evolutionary psychology. In C. Crawford, A. Viviana, & C. Salmon (Eds.), *Evolutionary psychology, public policy and personal decisions* (pp. 231–247). Mahwah, NJ: Lawrence Erlbaum.

Shadish, W. R., & Baldwin, S. A. Meta-analysis of MFT interventions. *Journal of Marital and Family Therapy, 29,* 547–570.

Shadlin, M. N., & Kiani, R. (2007). Neurology: An awakening. *Nature, 448,* 539–540.

Sharpe, D., Adair, J. G., & Roese, N. J. (1992). Twenty years of deception research: A decline in subjects' trust? *Personality and Social Psychology Bulletin, 18,* 585–590.

Shattuck, R. (1980). *The forbidden experiment: The story of the Wild Boy of Aveyron.* New York: Farrar Straus Giroux.

Shavit, Y., Depaulis, A., Martin, F. C., Terman, G. W., Pechnick, R. N., Zane, C. J., Gale, R. P., & Liebeskind, J. C. (1986). Involvement of brain opiate receptors in the immune-suppressive effect of morphine. *Proceedings of the National Academy of Sciences, USA, 83,* 7114–7117.

Shavit, Y., Lewis, J. W., Terman, G. W., Gale, R. P., & Liebeskind, J. C. (1984). Opioid peptides mediate the suppressive effect of stress on natural killer cell cytotoxicity. *Science, 223,* 188–190.

Shaw, P., Gornick, M., Lerch, J., Addington, A., Seal, J., Greensten, D. Sharp, W., Evans, A, Giedd, J. N., Castellanos, F. X., & Rapaport, J. L. (2007). Polymorphisms of the dopamine D_4 receptor, clinical outcome, and cortical structure in attentional-deficit/hyperactivity disorder. *Archives of General Psychiatry, 64,* 921–931.

Shaw, P., Lerch, J., Greenstein, D., Sharp, W., Clasen, L., Evans, A., Giedd, J., Castellanos, F. X., & Rapaport, J. (2006). Longitudinal mapping of cortical thickness and clinical outcome in children and adolescents with attention-deficit/hyperactivity disorder. *Archives of General Psychiatry, 63,* 540–559.

Shen, W. W., & Giesler, M. C. (1998). The discoverers of the therapeutic effect of chlorpromazine in psychiatry: Qui etaient les vrais premiers practiciens? (letter). *Canadian Journal of Psychiatry, 43,* 423–424.

Shepard, R. N., & Metzler, J. (1971). Mental rotation of three-dimensional objects. *Science, 171,* 701–703.

Shepherd, G. M. (1994). Discrimination of molecular signals by the olfactory receptor neuron. *Neuron, 13,* 771–790.

Sherif, M., Harvey, O. J., White, B. J., Hood, W. E., & Sherif, C. W. (1961). *Intergroup conflict and cooperation: The robbers cave experiment.* Norman, OK: Institute of Group Relations.

Sherry, D. F., & Schacter, D. L. (1987). The evolution of multiple memory systems. *Psychological Review, 94,* 439–454.

Shibley Hyde, J., & Plant, E. A. (1995). Magnitude of psychological gender differences: Another side to the story. *American Psychologist, 50,* 159–161.

Shoda, Y., & Smith, R. E. (2004). Conceptualizing personality as a cognitive-affective processing system: A framework for models of maladaptive behavior patterns and change. *Behavior Therapy, 35,* 147–165.

Shorter, E. (1997). *A history of psychiatry.* New York: John Wiley & Sons.

Shulman, G. L., McAvoy, M. P., Cowan, M. C., Astafieu, S. V., Tanby, A. P., d'Aiasso, G., & Corbetta, M. (2003). Quantitative analysis of attention and detection signals during visual search. *Journal of Neurophysiology, 90,* 3384–3397.

Sidman, M. (1994). *Equivalence relations and behavior: A research story.* Boston: Authors; Cooperative Publishers.

Sidman, M., Rauzin, R., Lazar, R., Cunningham, S., Tailby, W., & Carrigan, P. (1982). A search for symmetry in the conditional discriminations of rhesus monkeys, baboons, and children. *Journal of the Experimental Analysis of Behavior, 37,* 23–44.

Siegel, R. M., & Andersen, R. A. (1986). Motion perceptual deficits following ibotenic acid lesions of the middle temporal area (MT) in the behaving monkey. *Society for Neuroscience Abstracts, 12,* 1183.

Silberberg, A., Hamilton, B., & Ziriax, J. M. (1978). The structure of choice. *Journal of Experimental Psychology: Animal Behavior Processes, 4,* 368–398.

Simons, D. J., & Chabris, C. F. (1999). Gorillas in our midst: Sustained inattentional blindness for dynamic events. *Perception, 28,* 1059–1074.

Simons, D. J., & Levin, D. T. (1998). Failure to detect changes to people in a real-world interaction. *Psychonomic Bulletin and Review, 5,* 644–649.

Simons, D. J., & Rensink, R. A. (2005). Change blindness: Past, present, and future. *Trends in Cognitive Sciences, 9,* 16–20.

Simons, R. C. (1996). *Boo! Culture, experience, and the startle reflex.* New York: Oxford University Press.

Simons, R. C., & Hughes, C. C. (1993). Culture-bound syndromes. In A. C. Gaw (Ed.), *Culture, ethnicity, and mental illness* (pp. 75–100). Washington, DC: American Psychiatric Press.

Simonton, D. K. (2004). Psychology's status as a scientific discipline: Its empirical placement within an implicit hierarchy of the sciences. *Review of General Psychology, 8(1),* 59–67.

Simpson, J. A., Winterheld, H. A., Rholes, W. S., & Oriña, M. M. (2007). Working models of attachment and reactions to different forms of caregiving from romantic partners. *Journal of Personality and Social Psychology, 93,* 466–477.

Singer, L. T., Arendt, R., Minnes, S., Farkas, K., Salvator, A., Kirchner, H. L., & Kliegman, R. (2002). Cognitive and motor outcomes of cocaine-exposed infants. *Journal of the American Medical Association, 287,* 1952–1960.

Singer, M., & Ritchot, K. F. M. (1996). The role of working memory capacity and knowledge access in text inference processing. *Memory & Cognition, 24,* 733–743.

Singer, T., Seymour, B., O'Doherty, J., Kaube, H., Dolan, R. J., & Frith, C. D. (2004). Empathy for pain involves the affective but not sensory components of pain. *Science, 303,* 1157–1162.

Singer, W. (1997). Development and plasticity of neocortical processing architectures. In J. W. Donahoe & V. P. Dorsel (Eds.), *Neural-network models of cognition.* Amsterdam: Elsevier.

Singh, R., & Teoh, J. B. P. (2000). Attitudes and attraction: A test of two hypotheses for the similarity-dissimilarity asymmetry. *British Journal of Social Psychology, 38,* 427–443.

Singh, R., Onglato, M. L. U., Sriram, N., & Tay, A. B. G. (1997). The warm-cold variable in impression formation: Evidence for a positive-negative asymmetry. *British Journal of Social Psychology, 36,* 457–477.

Sinha, P. (2002). Recognizing complex patterns. *Nature Neuroscience, 5,* 1093-1097.

Sivacek, J., & Crano, W. D. (1982). Vested interest as a moderator of attitude-behavior consistency. *Journal of Personality and Social Psychology, 43,* 210–221.

Skaggs, W. E., and McNaughton, B. L. (1998). Spatial firing properties of hippocampal CA1 populations in an environment containing two visually identical regions. *Journal of Neuroscience, 18,* 8455–8466.

Skinner, B. F. (1948). *Walden two.* New York: Macmillan.

Skinner, B. F. (1956). A case history in scientific method. *American Psychologist, 11,* 221–233.

Skinner, B. F. (1937). Two types of conditioned reflex: A reply to Konorski and Miller. *Journal of General Psychology, 16,* 272–279.

Skinner, B. F. (1938). *The behavior of organisms.* New York: Appleton-Century-Crofts.

Skinner, B. F. (1948). "Superstition" in the pigeon. *Journal of Experimental Psychology, 38,* 168–172.

Skinner, B. F. (1966). The ontogeny and phylogeny of behavior. *Science, 153,* 1203–1213.

Skinner, B. F. (1974). *About behaviorism.* New York: Random House.

Skinner, B. F. (1984a). The shame of American education. *American Psychologist, 39,* 947–954.

Skinner, B. F. (1984b). An operant analysis of problem solving. *Behavioral and Brain Sciences, 7,* 583–613.

Skinner, B. F. (1988, June). Skinner joins aversives debate. *American Psychological Association APA Monitor,* 22.

Skodol, A. E., Siever, L. J., Livesley, W. J., Gunderson, J. G., Pfohl, B., & Widiger, T. A. (2002). The borderline diagnosis II: Biology, genetics, and clinical course. *Biological Psychiatry, 51,* 951–963.

Skowronski, J. J., & Carlston, D. E. (1989). Negativity and extremity biases in impression formation. *Psychological Bulletin, 105,* 131–142.

Slate. Retrieved from http://www.slate.com/id/2166000/

Slaughter, V., & Repacholi, B. (2003). Individual differences in Theory of Mind: What are we investigating? In B. Repacholi & V. Slaughter (Eds.), *Individual differences in theory of mind: Implications for typical and atypical development* (pp. 1–12). New York: Psychology Press.

Sloane, R. B., Staples, F. R., Cristol, A. H., Yorkston, N. J., & Whipple, K. (1975). *Psychoanalysis versus behavior therapy.* Cambridge, MA: Harvard University Press.

Small, D. M., Zatorre, R. J., Dagher, A., Evans, A. C., and Jones-Gotman, M. (2001) Changes in brain activity related to eating chocolate: From pleasure to aversion. *Brain, 124,* 1720–1733.

Smeets, T., Jelicic, M., Peters, M. J. V., Candel, I., Horselenberg, R., & Merckelbach, H. (2006). "Of course I remember seeing that film"—How ambiguous questions generate crashing memories. *Applied Cognitive Psychology, 20,* 779–789.

Smith, A. P. (2005). Caffeine at work. *Human Psychopharmacology, 20,* 441–445.

Smith, C., & Lapp, L. (1991) Increased number of REMs following an intensive learning. *Sleep, 14,* 325–330.

Smith, C., & Lloyd, B. (1978). Maternal behavior and perceived sex of infant: Revisited. *Child Development, 49,* 1263–1265.

Smith, E. R., Becker, M. A., Byrne, D., & Pryzbyla, D. P. J. (1993). Sexual attitudes of males and females as predictors of interpersonal attraction and marital compatibility. *Journal of Applied Social Psychology, 23,* 1011–1034.

Smith, G. P., & Gibbs, J. (1992). Role of CCK in satiety and appetite control. *Clinical Neuropharmacology, 15*(Suppl 1 Pt A), 476.

Smith, M. C., Coleman, S. P., & Gormezano, I. (1969). Classical conditioning of the rabbit's nictitating membrane response at backward, simultaneous and forward CS-US intervals. *Journal of Comparative and Physiological Psychology, 69,* 226–231.

Smith, M. L., & Glass, G. V. (1977). Meta-analysis of psychotherapy outcome studies. *American Psychologist, 32,* 752–760.

Smith, M. L., Glass, G. V., & Miller, T. I. (1980). *Benefits of psychotherapy.* Baltimore: Johns Hopkins University Press.

Smith, M. T., Perlis, M. L., Park, A., Smith, M. S., Pennington, J., Giles, D. E., & Buysse, D. J. (2002). Comparative meta-analysis of pharmacotherapy and behavior therapy for persistent insomnia. *The American Journal of Psychiatry, 159,* 5–11.

Smith, P. K., Jostmass, N. B., Galinsky, A. D., & van Dijk, W. W. (2008). Lacking power impairs executive functions. *Psychological Science, 19,* 441–447.

Sneed, C. D., McCrae, R. R., & Funder, D. C. (1998). Lay conceptions of the five-factor model and its indicators. *Personality and Social Psychology Bulletin, 24,* 115–126.

Snow, C. E. (1977). Mothers' speech research: From input to interaction. In C. E. Snow & C. Ferguson (Eds.), *Talking to children: Language input and acquisition.* Cambridge: Cambridge University Press.

Snow, C. E. (1986). Conversations with children. In P. Fletcher & M. Garman (Eds.), *Language acquisition* (2nd ed.). Cambridge: Cambridge University Press.

Snow, C. E., Arlman-Rupp, A., Hassing, Y., Jobse, J., Joosten, J., & Vorster, J. (1976). Mothers' speech in three social classes. *Journal of Psycholinguistic Research, 5,* 1–20.

Snow, M. E., Jacklin, C. N., & Maccoby, E. E. (1983). Sex-of-child differences in father-child interaction at one year of age. *Child Development, 54,* 227–232.

Snowling, M. J., & Hulme, C. (Eds.). (2005). *The science of reading: A handbook.* New York: Wiley.

Snyder, A. W., Mulcahy, E., Taylor, J. L., Mitchell, D. J., Sachdev, P., & Gandevia, S. C. (2003). Savant-like skills exposed in normal people by suppressing the left frontal-temporal lobe. *Journal of Integrative Neuroscience, 2,* 149–158.

Snyder, L. H., Batista, A. P., & Andersen, R. A. (2000). Intention-related activity in the posterior parietal cortex: A review. *Vision Research, 40,* 1433–1441.

Snyder, M., Tanke, E. D., & Berscheid, E. (1977). Social perception and interpersonal behavior: On the self-fulfilling nature of social stereotypes. *Journal of Personality and Social Psychology, 35,* 656–666.

Snyder, S. H. (1974). *Madness and the brain.* New York: McGraw-Hill.

Snyder, S. H. (2008). A complex in psychosis. *Nature, 452,* 38–39.

Soares, J. J., & Öhman, A. (1993). Backward masking and skin conductance responses after conditioning to nonfeared but fear-relevant stimuli in fearful subjects. *Psychophysiology, 30,* 460–466.

Sober, E. (1984). *The nature of selection: Evolutionary theory in philosophical focus.* Cambridge, MA: MIT Press.

Solms, M. (2000). Dreaming and REM sleep are controlled by different brain mechanisms. *Behavioral and Brain Sciences, 23,* 843–850.

Solms, M. (May 2004). Freud returns. *Scientific American,* 82–88.

Solomon, A., & Haaga, D. A. F. (1995). Rational emotive behavior therapy research: What we know and what we need to know. *Journal of Rational-Emotive & Cognitive Behavior Therapy, 13(3),* 179–191.

Solomon, G. F. (1987). Psychoneuroimmunology: Interactions between central nervous system and immune system. *Journal of Neuroscience Research, 18,* 1–9.

Solzhenitsyn, A. (2002). *The Gulag Archipelago.* New York: Harper Perennial.

Spanos, N. P., & Chaves, J. F. (1991). History and historiography of hypnosis. In S. J. Lynn & J. W. Rhue (Eds.), *Theories of hypnosis: Current models and perspectives.* (pp. 43–78). New York: Guilford Press.

Spearman, C. (1927). *The abilities of man.* London: Macmillan.

Spears, R., & Haslam, S. A. (1997). Stereotyping and the burden of cognitive load. In R. Spears (Ed.), *The social psychology of stereotyping and group life.* Oxford, UK: Blackwell Publishers, Inc.

Spence, K. W. (1956). *Behavior theory and conditioning.* New Haven: Yale University Press.

Sperling, G. A. (1960). The information available in brief visual presentation. *Psychological Monographs, 74* (no. 498), 1–29.

Sperry, R. W. (1966). Brain bisection and consciousness. In J. Eccles (Ed.), *Brain and conscious experience.* New York: Springer-Verlag.

Spirduso, W. W., & MacRae, P. G. (1990). Motor performance and aging. In J. E. Birren & K. W. Schaie (Eds.), (3rd ed.) (pp. 184–197). San Diego: Academic Press.

Spitzer, R. L., Gibbon, M., Skodol, A. E., Williams, J. B. W., & First, M. B. (2004). *DSM-IV-TR casebook: A learning companion to the Diagnostic and statistical manual of mental disorders, fourth edition, text revision.* Washington, DC: American Psychiatric Publishing.

Spitzer, R. L., Gibbon, M., Skodol, A. E., Williams, J. B. W., & First, M. B. (2002). *DSM-IV-TR case book: A learning companion to the Diagnostic and Statistical Manual of Mental Disorders, Fourth Edition, Text Revision.* Washington, DC: American Psychiatric Publishing.

Spoor, F., Leakey, M. G., Gathogo, P. N., Brown, F. H., Anton, S. C., McDougall, I., Kiarie, C., Manthi, F. K., & Leakey. L. N. (2007). Implications of new early Homo fossils from Ileret, east of Lake Turkana, Kenya. *Nature, 448,* 688–691.

Sprecher, S., & Regan, P. C. (1998) Passionate and companionate love in courting and young married couples. *Sociological Inquiry, 68,* 163–185.

Squire, L. R. (1992). Memory and the hippocampus: A synthesis from findings with rats, monkeys, and humans. *Psychological Review, 99,* 195–231.

Squire, L. R., & Bayley, P. J. (2007). The neuroscience of remote memory. *Current Opinion in Neurobiology, 17,* 185–196.

Staddon, J. E. R., & Simmelhag, V. L. (1971). The "superstition" experiment: A reexamination of its implications for principle of adaptive behavior. *Psychological Review, 78,* 3–43.

Standing, L. (1973). Learning 10,000 pictures. *Quarterly Journal of Experimental Psychology, 25,* 207–222.

Stanovich, K. E. (2004). *The robot's rebellion: Finding meaning in the age of Darwin.* Chicago: University of Chicago Press.

Starzyk, K. B., & Quinsey, V. L. (2001). The relationship between testosterone and aggression: A meta-analysis. *Aggression and Violent Behavior, 16,* 579–599.

Stasser, G. (1991). Pooling of unshared information during group discussion. In S. Worchel, W. Wood, & J. Simpson (Eds.), *Group process and productivity.* Beverly Hills, CA: Sage.

Steele, C. M., Spencer, S. J., & Aronson, J. (2002). Contending with group image: The psychology of stereotype and social identity threat. In M. P. Zanna (Ed.), *Advances in Experimental Social Psychology,* Vol. 34 (pp. 379–440). New York: Academic Press.

Steeves, J. K. E., Humphrey, G. K., Culham, J. C., Menon, R. S., Milner, A. D., & Goodale, M. A. (2004). Behavioral and neuroimaging evidence for a contribution of color and texture information to scene classification in a patient with visual form agnosia. *Journal of Cognitive Neuroscience, 16,* 955–965.

Stefanacci, L., & Amaral, D. G. (2000). Topographic organization of cortical inputs to the lateral nucleus of the macaque monkey amygdala: A retrograde tracing study. *Journal of Comparative Neurology, 22,* 52–79.

Steiger, H., Lehoux, P. M., & Gauvin, L. (1999). Impulsivity, dietary control and the urge to binge in bulimic syndromes. *Eating Disorders, 26,* 261–274.

Stein, L. I., & Santos, A. B. (1998). *Assertive community treatment of persons with severe mental illness.* New York: W. W. Norton & Co., Inc.

Stein, M. B., Millar, T. W., Larsen, D. K., & Kryger, M. H. (1995). Irregular breathing during sleep in patients with panic disorder. *American Journal of Psychiatry, 152,* 1168–1173.

Steinhauer, K., Alter, K., & Friederici, A. D. (1999). Brain potentials indicate immediate use of prosidic cues in natural speech processing. *Nature Neuroscience, 2,* 191–196.

Steinhausen, H., & Spohr, H. (1998). Long-term outcome of children with fetal alcohol syndrome: Psychopathology, behavior, and intelligence: alcoholism *Clinical and Experimental Research, 22,* 334–338.

Stereopsis activates V3A and caudal intraparietal areas in macaques and humans. *Neuron, 39,* 555–568.

Stern, M., & Karraker, K. H. (1989). Sex stereotyping of infants: A review of gender labeling studies. *Sex Roles, 20,* 501–522.

Stern, W. (1914). *The psychological methods of testing intelligence.* Baltimore: Warwick and York.

Sternberg, R. J. (1988a). *The triarchic mind: A new theory of human intelligence.* New York, NY: Viking.

Sternberg, R. J. (1988b). Triangulating love. In R. J. Sternberg & M. L. Barnes (Eds.), *The psychology of love.* New Haven, CT: Yale University Press.

Sternberg, R. J. (1995). For whom the bell curve tolls: A review of *The bell curve. Psychological Science, 6,* 257–261.

Sternberg, R. J. (1996). *Successful intelligence.* New York, NY: Simon Schuster.

Sternberg, R. J. (1997). The triarchic theory of intelligence. In D. P. Fanagan, J. L. Genshaft, P. L. Harrison, et al. (Eds.), *Contemporary intellectual assessment: Theories, tests, and issues* (pp. 92–104). New York: Guilford Press.

Sternberg, R. J. (2003a). Construct validity of the theory of special intelligence. In R. J. Sternberg

& J. Lautrey (Eds.), *Models of intelligence: International perspectives.* Washington, DC: American Psychological Association.

Sternberg, R. J. (2003b). *Wisdom, intelligence, and creativity synthesized.* New York: Cambridge University Press.

Sternberg, R. J. (2005). The theory of successful intelligence. *Revista Interamericana de Psicologia/Interamerican Journal of Psychology, 39,* 189–202.

Sternberg, R. J. (2006). The nature of creativity. *Creativity Research Journal, 18,* 87–98.

Sternberg, R. J. (2008). Whatever goes up must come down—except intelligence. *Psyc-CRITIQUES: Contemporary Psychology: APA Review of Books, 53* Article 2.

Sternberg, R. J., Conway, B. E., Ketron, J. L., & Bernstein, M. (1981). People's conceptions of intelligence. *Journal of Personality and Social Psychology, 41,* 37–55.

Sternberg, R. J., & Grigorenko, E. L. (1999). Myths in psychology and education regarding the gene-environment debate. *Teachers College Record, 100,* 536–553.

Sternberg, R. J., & Grigorenko, E. L. (2001). Ability testing across cultures. In L. A. Suzuki & J. G. Ponterotto (Eds.), *Handbook of multicultural assessment: Clinical, psychological, and educational applications* (2nd ed.). San Francisco: Jossey-Bass.

Sternberg, R. J., & Grigorenko, E. L. (2004). Why we need to explore development in its cultural context. *Merrill-Palmer Quarterly, 50,* 369–386.

Sternberg, R. J., & Grigorenko, E. L. (2008). Ability testing across cultures. In L. A. Suzuki & J. S. Ponteretto (Eds.), *Handbook of multicultural assessment: Clinical, psychological, and educational applications* (pp. 449–470). New York: Jossey-Bass.

Sternberg, R. J., Kaufman, J., & Grigorenko, E. L. (2008). *Applied intelligence.* New York: Cambridge University Press.

Sternberg, R. J., Nokes, C., Geissler, P. W., Prince, R., Okatcha, F., Bundy, D. A., & Grigorenko, E. L. (2001). The relationship between academic and practical intelligence: A case study in Kenya. *Intelligence, 29,* 401–418.

Sternberger, L. G., & Burns, G. L. (1990). Obsessions and compulsions: Psychometric properties of the Padua inventory with an American college population. *Behavior Research and Therapy, 28,* 341–345.

Stevens, W. (Ed.) (1972). *The palm at the end of the mind: Selected poems and a play by Wallace Stevens.* New York: Vintage Books.

Stewart, J. (2004). Pathways to relapse: Factors controlling the reinitiation of drug seeking after abstinence. In Bevins, R. A., & Bardo, M. T. (Eds.), *Motivational factors in the etiology of drug abuse* (Vol. 50, pp. 197–234). Nebraska Symposium on Motivation. Lincoln, NE: University of Nebraska Press.

Stewart, J. H. (2005). Hypnosis in contemporary medicine. *Mayo Clinic Proceedings 80,* 511–524.

Stewart, S. H., Mitchell, T. L., Wright, K. D., & Loba, P. (2004). The relations of PTSD symptoms to alcohol use and coping drinking in volunteers who responded to the Swissair Flight 111 airline disaster. *Journal of Anxiety Disorders, 18(1),* 51–68.

Stoyanova, R., Pratt, J., & Anderson, A. K. (2007). Inhibition of return with social signals of pain. *Emotion, 7,* 49–56.

Strachan, T., & Read, A. P. (1999). *Human molecular genetics.* New York: Wiley.

Stravynski, A. (2007). *Fearing others: The nature and treatment of social phobia.* New York: Cambridge University Press.

Strayer, D. L., & Drews, F. A. (2007). Cell-phone-induced driver distraction. *Current Directions in Psychological Science, 16,* 128–131.

Streissguth, A. P. (2001). Recent advances in fetal alcohol syndrome and alcohol use in pregnancy. In D. P. Agarwal & H. K. Seitz (Eds.), *Alcohol in health and disease* (pp. 303–324). New York: Marcel Dekker.

Stromer, R., McComas, J. J., & Rehfeldt, R. A. (2000). Designing interventions that include delayed reinforcement: Implications of recent laboratory research. *Journal of Applied Behavior Analysis, 33,* 359–371.

Stroop, J. R. (1935). Studies of interference in serial verbal reactions. *Journal of Experimental Psychology, 18,* 743–762.

Sturgis, E. T. (1993). Obsessive-compulsive disorder. In P. B. Sutker & H. E. Adams (Eds.), *Comprehensive handbook of psychopathology,* 2nd ed. (pp. 129–144).

Suddath, R. L., Christison, G. W., Torrey, E. F., Casanova, M. F., & Weinberger, D. R. (1990). Anatomical abnormalities in the brains of monozygotic twins discordant for schizophrenia. *New England Journal of Medicine, 322,* 789–794.

Sullivan, E. V., Lim, K. O., Mathalon, D., Marsh, L., Beal, D. M., Harris, D., Hoff, A. L., Faustman, W. O., & Pfefferbaum, A. (1998). A profile of cortical gray matter volume deficits characteristic of schizophrenia. *Cerebral Cortex, 8,* 117–124.

Sullivan, M. W., & Lewis, M. (2003). Contextual determinants of anger and other negative expressions in young infants. *Developmental Psychology, 39,* 693–705.

Sulzer-Azaroff, B., & Mayer, G. R. (1991). *Behavior analysis for lasting change.* Fort Worth, TX: Harcourt Brace.

Suzuki, D. T., Griffiths, A. J. F., Miller, J. H., & Lewontin, R. C. (1989). *An introduction to genetic analysis* (4th ed.). New York: Freeman.

Suzuki, K., Takei, N., Iwata, Y., Sekine, Y., Toyoda, T., Nakamura, K., Minabe, Y., et al. (2004). Do olfactory reference syndrome and Jiko-shu-kyofu (a subtype of Taijin-kyofu) share a common entity? *Acta Psychiatrica Scandinavica, 109(2),* 150–155.

Suzuki, L. A., & Ponteretto, J. S. (Eds.). (2008). *Handbook of multicultural assessment: Clinical, psychological, and educational applications.* New York: Jossey-Bass.

Swaab, D. (2007). Sexual differentiation of the brain and behavior. *Best Practice & Research Clinical Endocrinology & Metabolism, 21,* 431–444.

Swaab, D. F., & Hofman, M. A. (1990). An enlarged suprachiasmatic nucleus in homosexual men. *Brain Research, 537,* 141–148.

Swanson, L. W. (1982). The projections of the ventral tegmental area and adjacent regions: a combined fluorescent retrograde tracer and immunofluorescence study in the rat. *Brain Research Bulletin, 9,* 321–353.

Swayze II, V. W. (1995). Frontal leucotomy and related psychosurgical procedures in the era before antipsychotics: A historical overview (1935–1954). *American Journal of Psychiatry, 152,* 505–515.

Swedo, S. S., Rapaport, J. L., & Cheslow, D. L. (1989). High prevalence of obsessive-compulsive symptoms in patients with Sydenham's chorea. *American Journal of Psychiatry, 146,* 246–249.

Symons, D. (1979). *The evolution of human sexuality.* New York: Oxford University Press.

Szasz, T. S. (1960). The myth of mental illness. *American Psychologist, 15,* 113–118.

Szasz, T. (2002). Parity for mental illness, disparity for mental patients. *Ideas on Liberty, 52,* 33–34.

Szasz, T. S. (2007). *Coercion as cure: A critical history of psychiatry.* New Brunswick, NJ: Transaction.

Tager-Flusberg, H. (2007). Evaluating the theory-of-mind hypothesis of autism. *Current Directions in Psychological Science, 16,* 311–315.

Taglialatela, J. P., Savage-Rumbaugh, S., & Baker, L. A. (2003). Vocal production by a language-competent *Pan paniscus. International Journal of Primatology, 24,* 1–17.

Takei, N., Mortensen, P. B., Klaening, U., Murray, R. M., Sham, P. C., O'Callaghan, E., & Munk, J. P. (1996). Relationship between in utero exposure to influenza epidemics and risk of schizophrenia in Denmark. *Biological Psychiatry, 40,* 817–824.

Talbot, M. (May 12, 2008). Birdbrain. *The New Yorker.*

Tammett, D. (2007). *Born on a blue day: Inside the extraordinary mind of an autistic savant.* New York: Free Press.

Tanenhaus, M. K. (1988). *Psycholinguistics: An overview.* Cambridge: Cambridge University Press.

Tang, Y.-P., Shimizu, E., Dube, G. R., Rampon, C., Kerchner, G. A., Zhuo, M., Lium G., & Tsien, J. Z. (1999). Genetic enhancement of learning and memory in mice. *Nature, 401,* 63–69.

Tanner, C. M., & Chamberland, J. (2001). Latah in Jakarta, Indonesia. *Movement Disorders, 16,* 526–529.

Tarr, M. J., & Gauthier, I. (2000). FFA: A flexible fusiform area for subordinate-level visual processing automatized by expertise. *Nature Neuroscience, 3,* 764–769.

Tarsy, D., Baldessarini, R. J., & Tarazi, F. I. (2002). Effects of newer antipsychotics on extrapyramidal function. *CNS Drugs, 16(1),* 23–45.

Taube, S. L., Kirstein, L. S., Sweeney, D. R., Heninger, G. R., & Maas, J. W. (1978). Urinary 3-methoxy-4-hydroxyphenyleneglycol and psychiatric diagnosis. *American Journal of Psychiatry, 135,* 78–82.

Tavris, C., & Sadd, S. (1977). *The Redbook report on female sexuality.* New York: Delacorte Press.

Tehan, G., Hendry, L., & Kocinski, D. (2001). Word length and phonological similarity effects in simple, complex, and delayed serial recall tasks: Implications for working memory. *Memory, 9,* 333–348.

Temes, R. (2004). *The complete idiot's guide to hypnosis,* 2nd ed. Indianapolis: Alpha.

Tenover, J. L. (1998). Male hormone replacement therapy including "andropause." *Endocrinology & Metabolism Clinics of North America, 27,* 969–987.

Terry, R. D., & Davies, P. (1980). Dementia of the Alzheimer type. *Annual Review of Neuroscience, 3,* 77–96.

Test, M. A., & Stein, L. I. (2000). Practical guidelines for the community treatment of markedly impaired patients. *Community Mental Health Journal, 36,* 47–60.

Tey., C., Wake, M., Campbell, M., Hampton, A., & Williams, J. (2007). The Light Time-Use Diary and preschool activity patterns: Exploratory study. *International Journal of Pediatric Obesity, 2,* 167–173.

The Genome Sequencing Consortium. (2001). Initial sequencing and analysis of the human genome. *Nature, 409,* 860–921.

Thelen, E., & Corbetta, D. (2002). Microdevelopment and dynamic systems: Applications to infant motor development. In N. Granott & J. Parziale (Eds.), *Microdevelopment: Transition processes in development and learning: Cambridge studies in cognitive perceptual development* (pp. 59–79). New York: Cambridge University Press.

Thomas, R. M. (1996). *Comparing theories of child development* (4th ed.). Pacific Grove, CA: Brooks/Cole.

Thompson, M. S., Judd, C. M., & Park, B. (2000). The consequences of communicating social stereotypes. *Journal of Experimental Social Psychology, 36,* 567–599.

Thompson, R., Emmorey, K., & Gollan, T. H. (2005). "Tip of the fingers" experiences by deaf signers. *Psychological Science, 16,* 856–860.

Thompson, S. A., & Nelson-Metlay, V. (2005). *Teach your tot to sign: The parents' guide to American sign language.* Washington, DC: Gaulladet University Press.

Thompson, T. (2007). *Making sense of autism.* Baltimore: Brookes.

Thorndike, E. L, (1898). Animal intelligence: An experimental study of the associative processes in animals. *Psychological Review Monograph Supplement, 2,* (Whole No. 8).

Thorndike, E. L. (1903). *Elements of psychology.* New York: A. G. Seiler.

Thorndike, E. L. (1905). *The elements of psychology.* New York: Seiler.

Thorpe, G. L., & Olson, S. L. (1990). *Behavior therapy: Concepts, procedures, and applications.* Boston: Allyn & Bacon.

Thorpe, S. K., Holder, R. L., & Crompton, R. H. (2007). Origin of human bipedalism as an adaptation for locomotion on flexible branches. *Science, 316,* 1328–1331.

Timberlake, W., & Allison, J. (1974). Response deprivation: An empirical approach to instrumental performance. *Psychological Review, 81,* 146–164.

Timberlake, W., & Lucas, G. A. (1985). The basis of superstitious behavior: Chance contingency, stimulus substitution, or appetitive behavior? *Journal of the Experimental Analysis of Behavior, 44,* 279–299.

Tobin, S. A. (1991). A comparison of psychoanalytic self-psychology and Carl Rogers's person-centered therapy. *Journal of Humanistic Psychology, 31,* 9–33.

Todd, P. M., Penke, L., Fasolo, B., & Lenton, A. P. (2007). Different cognitive processes underlie human mate choices and mate preferences. *Proceedings of the National Academy of Sciences USA, 104,* 15011–15016.

Toga, A. W., Thompson, P. M., & Sowell, E. R. (2006). Mapping brain maturation. *Trends in Neurosciences, 29,* 1480–1590.

Tolman, E. C., & Honzik, C. H. (1930). Introduction and removal of reward, and maze performance in rats. *University of California Publications in Psychology, 4,* 257–275.

Tomasello, M. (2005). *Constructing a language: A usage-based theory of language acquisition* (New ed.) Cambridge, MA: Harvard University Press.

Tomasello, M., & Farrar, J. (1986). Joint attention and early language. *Child Development, 57,* 1454–1463.

Tong, F., & Pearson, J. (2007). Vision. In B. J. Baars & N. M. Gage (Eds.), pp. 149–182, *Cognition, brain, and consciousness: An Introduction to cognitive neuroscience.* London: Academic Press.

Toni, N., Teng, E. M., Bushong, E. A., Aimone, J. B., Zhao, C., Consiglio, A., van Praag, H., Martone, M. E., Ellisman, M. H., & Gage, F. H. (2006). Synapse formation on neurons in the adult hippocampus. *Nature Neuroscience, 10,* 727–734.

Tootell, R. B., Reppas, J. B., Dale, A. M., Look, R. B. Sereno, M. I., Malach, R., Brady, T. J., & Rosen, B. R. (1995). Visual motion after-effect in human cortical area MT revealed by functional magnetic resonance imaging. *Nature, 375,* 139–141.

Tordoff, M. G., & Friedman, M. I. (1988). Hepatic control of feeding: Effect of glucose, fructose, and mannitol infusion. *American Journal of Physiology, 254,* 969–976.

Torgerson, S. (1983). Genetic factors in anxiety disorders. *Archives of General Psychiatry, 40,* 1085–1089.

Torrey, E. F., Torrey, B. B., & Peterson, M. R. (1977). Seasonality of schizophrenic births in the United States. *Archives of General Psychiatry, 34,* 1065–1070.

Torrey, E., Fuller, E., Miller, J., Rawlings, R., & Yolken, R. H. (1997). Seasonality of births in schizophrenia and bipolar disorder: A review of the literature. *Schizophrenia Research, 28,* 1–38.

Träskmann, L., Åsberg, M., Bertilsson, L., & Sjöstrand, L. (1981). Monoamine metabolites on CSF and suicidal behavior. *Archives of General Psychiatry, 38,* 631–636.

Travis, L. A., Bliwise, N. G., Binder, J. L., & Horne-Moyer, H. L. (2001). Changes in clients' attachment styles over the course of time-limited dynamic psychotherapy. *Psychotherapy: Theory, Research, Practice, Training, 38(2),* 149–159.

Trehub, S. E., & Thorpe, L. A. (1989). Infants' perception of rhythm: Categorization of auditory sequences by temporal structure. *Canadian Journal of Psychology, 43,* 217–229.

Treisman, A. M. (1960). Contextual cues in selective listening. *Quarterly Journal of Experimental Psychology, 12,* 242–248.

Treisman, A. M. (1969). Strategies and models of selective attention. *Psychological Review, 76,* 282–299.

Treisman, A. M. (1988). Features and objects: The fourteenth Bartlett Memorial Lecture. *Quarterly Journal of Experimental Psychology, Section A, 40,* 210–237.

Tremblay, S., Shiller, D. M., & Ostry, D. J. (2003). Somatosensory basis of speech production. *Nature, 423,* 866–869.

Triarhou, L. C. (2006). The percipient observations of Constantin von Economo on encephalitis lethargica and sleep disruption and their lasting impact on contemporary sleep research. *Journal of Neurology, 253,* 1377–1378.

Triplett, N. (1897). The dynamogenic factors in pacemaking and competition. *American Journal of Psychology, 9,* 507–533.

Trivers, R. L. (1971). The biology of reciprocal altruism. *Quarterly Review of Biology, 46,* 35–57.

Trivers, R. L. (1972). Parental investment and sexual selection. In B. Campbell (Ed.), *Sexual selection and the descent of man.* Chicago: Aldine.

Trochim, W. M. K. (2005). *Research methods: The concise knowledge base.* Cincinnati, OH: Atomic Dog.

Tronick, E., Als, H., Adamson, L., Wise, S., & Brazelton, T. B. (1978). The infant's response to entrapment between contradictory messages in face-to-face interaction. *Journal of the American Academy of Child Psychiatry, 17,* 1–13.

Truax, C. B. (1966). Reinforcement and nonreinforcement in Rogerian psychotherapy. *Journal of Abnormal Psychology, 71,* 1–9.

Tryon, R. C. (1940). Genetic differences in maze-learning ability in rats. *Yearbook of the National Society for the Study of Education, 39,* 111–119.

Tsao, D. Y., Vanduffel, W., Sasaki, Y., Fize, D., Knutsen, T. A., Mandeville, J. B., Wald, L. L., Dale, A. M., Rosen, B. R., Van Essen, D. C., Livingstone, M. S., Orban, G. A., & Tootell, R. B. H. (2003). Stereopsis activates V3A and caudal intraparietal areas in macaques and humans. *Neuron, 39(3),* 555–568.

Tse, D., Langston, R. F., Kakeyama, M., Bethus, I., Spooner, P. A., Wood, E. R., Witter, M. P., & Morris, R. G. M. (2007). Schemas and memory consolidation. *Science, 316,* 76–82.

Tsuchiya, N., & Adolphs, R. (2007). Emotion and consciousness. *Trends in Cognitive Sciences, 11*, 158–167.

Tucker, M. A., Hirota, Y., Wamsley, E. J., Lau, H., Chaklader, A., & Fishbein, W. (2006). A daytime nap containing solely non-REM sleep enhances declarative but not procedural memory. *Neurobiology of Learning and Memory, 86*, 241–247.

Tulving, E. (1972). Episodic and semantic memory. In E. Tulving & W. Donaldson (Eds.), *Organization of memory.* New York: Academic Press.

Tulving, E. (2002). Episodic memory: From mind to brain. *Annual Review of Psychology, 53*, 1–25.

Tulving, E., & Schacter, D. L. (1990). Priming and human memory systems. *Science, 247,* 301–306.

Tupes, E. C., & Christal, R. E. (1961). Recurrent personality factors based on trait ratings. *USAF ASD Technical Report,* 61–97.

Turkheimer, E., Haley, A., Waldron, M., D'Onofrio, B., & Gottesman, I. I. (2003). Socioeconomic status modifies heritability of IQ in young children. *Psychological Science, 14*, 623–628.

Turkington, D., Dudley, R., Warman, D. M., & Beck, A. T. (2004). Cognitive-behavioral therapy for schizophrenia: A review. *Journal of Psychiatric Practice, 10(1),* 5–16.

Turner, A. M., & Greenough, W. T. (1985). Differential rearing effects on rat visual cortex synapses. I. Synaptic and neuronal density and synapses per neuron. *Brain Research, 329*, 195–203.

Turner, S. M., Beidel, D. C., Stanley, M. A., & Heiser, N. (2001). Obsessive-compulsive disorder. In P. B. Sutker & H. E. Adams (Eds.), *Comprehensive handbook of psychopathology,* 3rd ed. (pp. 55–182). New York: Kluwer Academic/Plenum Publishers.

Tversky, A., & Kahneman, D. (1974). Judgment under uncertainty: Heuristics and biases. *Science, 185,* 1124–1131.

Tversky, A., & Kahneman, D. (1982). Judgment under uncertainty: Heuristics and biases. In D. Kahneman, P. Slovic, & A. Tversky (Eds.), *Judgment under uncertainty.* New York: Cambridge University Press.

Ungerleider, L. G., & Mishkin, M. (1982). Two cortical visual systems. In D. J. Ingle, M. A. Goodale, & R. J. W. Mansfield (Eds.), *Analysis of visual behavior.* Cambridge, MA: MIT Press.

United States Department of Labor (2005). *Employment characteristics of families summary.* Released June 9, 2005. Available at http://www.bls.gov/news.release/famee.nr0.htm. Downloaded 26 July 2005.

Uno, H., Tarara, R., Else, J. G., Suleman, M. A., & Sapolsky, R. M. (1989). Hippocampal damage associated with prolonged and fatal stress in primates. *The Journal of Neuroscience, 9,* 1705–1711.

Urdan, T., & Midgley, C. (2001). Academic self-handicapping: What we know, what more there is to learn. *Educational Psychology Review, 13,* 115–138.

Urgesi, C., Berlucchi, G., & Aglioti, S. (2004). Magnetic stimulation of extrastriate body area impairs visual processing of nonfacial body parts. *Current Biology, 14,* 2130–2134.

Uyeda, L., Tyler, I., Pinzon, J., & Birmingham, C. L. (2002). Identification of patients with eating disorders: The signs and symptoms of anorexia nervosa and bulimia nervosa. *Eating & Weight Disorders, 7,* 116–123.

Valenstein, E. S. (1986). *Great and desperate cures: The rise and decline of psychosurgery and other radical treatments for mental illness.* New York: Basic Books.

Vallerand, R. J., & Ratelle, C. F. (2002). Intrinsic and extrinsic motivation: A hierarchical model. In E. L. Deci & R. M. Ryan (Eds.), *Handbook of self-determination research* (pp. 37–64). Rochester, NY: University of Rochester Press.

Van Dongen, H. P., Maislin, G., Mullington, J. M., & Dinges, D. F. (2003). The cumulative cost of additional wakefulness: Dose-response effects on neurobehavioral functions and sleep physiology from chronic sleep restriction and total sleep deprivation. *Sleep, 26,* 117–126.

Van Goozen, S., Wiegant, V., Endert, E., Helmond, F., & Van de Poll, N. (1997). Psychoendocrinological assessments of the menstrual cycle: The relationship between hormones, sexuality, and mood. *Archives of Sexual Behavior, 26,* 359–382.

Van Herk, H., Poortinga, Y. H., & Verhallen, T. M. M. (2005). Response styles in rating scales: Evidence of method bias in data from six EU countries. *Journal of Cross-Cultural Psychology, 35,* 346–360.

van Kesteren, P. J., Gooren, L. J., & Megens, J. A. (1996). An epidemiological and demographic study of transsexuals in the Netherlands. *Archives of Sexual Behavior, 25,* 589–600.

Vartanian, L. R. (2000). Revisiting the imaginary audience and personal fable constructs of adolescent egocentrism: A conceptual review. *Adolescence, 35,* 639–661.

Vecera, S. P., & Farah, M. J. (1994). Does visual attention select objects or locations? *Journal of Experimental Psychology, 123,* 146–160.

Vellutino, F. R., & Fletcher, J. M. (2005). Developmental dyslexia. In M. J. Snowling & C. Hulme (Eds.), *The science of reading: A handbook* (pp. 362–378). New York: Wiley.

Vernon, P. A., Jang, K. L., Harris, J. A., & McCarthy, J. M. (1997). Environmental predictors of personality differences: A twin and sibling study. *Journal of Personality and Social Psychology, 72,* 177–183.

Vernon, P. A., Villani, V. C., Vickers, L. C., & Harris, J. A. (2008). A behavioral genetic investigation of the dark triad and the big 5. *Personality and Individual Differences, 44,* 445–452.

Vernon, P. E. (1979). *Intelligence: Heredity and environment.* San Francisco: W. H. Freeman.

Virkkunen, M., De Jong, J., Bartko, J., & Linnoila, M. (1989). Psychobiological concomitants of history of suicide attempts among violent offenders and impulsive fire setters. *Archives of General Psychiatry, 46,* 604–606.

Voets, T., Droogmans, G., Wissenbach, U., Janssens, A., Flockarzi, V., & Nilius, B. (2004). The principle of temperature-dependent gating in cold- and heat-sensitive TRP channels. *Nature, 430,* 748–754.

Voight, B. F., Kudaravalli, S., Wen, X., & Pritchard, J. K. (2006). A map of recent positive selection in the human genome. *PLoS Biology, 4,* e72.

Vollrath, M. (2000). Personality and hassles among university students: A three-year longitudinal study. *European Journal of Personality, 14,* 199–215.

Volpe, B. T., LeDoux, J. E., & Gazzaniga, M. S. (1979). Information processing of visual stimuli in an "extinguished" field. *Nature, 282,* 722–724.

Volz, K. G., Schooler, L. J., Schubotz, R. I., Raab, M., Gigerenzer, G., & von Cramon, D. Y. (2006). Why you think Milan is larger than Modena: Neural correlates of the recognition heuristic. *Journal of Cognitive Neuroscience, 18,* 1924–1936.

vom Saal, W., & Jenkins, H. H. (1970). Blocking the development of stimulus control. *Learning & Motivation, 1,* 52–64.

Voyat, G. (1998). In tribute to Piaget: A look at his scientific impact in the United States. In R. W. Reiber & K. Salzinger (Eds.), *Psychology: Theoretical-historical perspectives.* (2nd ed.) (pp. 399–409). Washington, DC: American Psychological Association.

Vygotsky, L. S. (1934/1987). Thinking and speech. In R. W. Rieber & A. S. Carton (Eds.), *The collected works of L. S. Vygotsky:* Vol. 1. *Problems of general psychology.* (N. Minick, Trans.) (pp. 39–285). New York: Plenum.

Wadden, T. A., Brownell, K. D., & Foster, G. D. (2002). Obesity: Responding to the growing epidemic. *Journal of Consulting and Clinical Psychology, 70,* 510–525.

Wade, N. (July 31, 2008). Gene-hunters find hope and hurdles in schizophrenia studies. *New York Times.*

Waelti, P., Dickinson, A., & Schultz, W. (2001). Dopamine responses comply with basic assumptions of formal learning theory. *Nature, 412,* 43–48.

Wager, T. D., Rilling, J. K., Smith, E. E., Sokolik, A., Casey, K. L., Davidson, R. J., Kosslyn, S. M., Rose, R. M., & Cohen, J. D. (2004). Placebo-induced changes in fMRI in the anticipation and experience of pain. *Science, 303,* 1162–1166.

Wahlsten, D. (1997). The malleability of intelligence is not constrained by heritability. In B. Devlin, S. E. Fienberg, D. P. Resnick, & K. Roeder (Eds.), *Intelligence, genes, and success.* New York: Copernicus.

Wakefield, J. C., Schmitz, M. F., First, M. B., & Horwitz, A. V. (2007). Extending the bereavement exclusion for major depression to other losses: Evidence from the National Comorbidity Survey. *Archives of General Psychiatry, 64,* 433–440.

Wakelin, A., & Long, K. M. (2003). Effects of victim gender and sexuality on attributions of blame to rape victims. *Sex Roles, 49,* 477–487.

Walker, E., & Lewine, R. J. (1990). Prediction of adult-onset schizophrenia from childhood home movies of the patients. *American Journal of Psychiatry, 147,* 1052–1056.

Walker, M. P. (2005). A refined model of sleep and the time course of memory formation. *Behavioral and Brain Sciences, 28,* 51–104.

Wallace, S. T., & Alden, L. E. (1997). Social phobia and positive social events: The price of success. *Journal of Abnormal Psychology, 106,* 416–424.

Wallace, W. T. (1994). Memory for music: Effect of melody on recall of text. *Journal of Experimental Psychology: Learning, Memory, and Cognition, 20,* 1471–1485.

Walsh, M.-T., & Dinan, T. G. (2001). Selective serotonin reuptake inhibitors and violence: A review of the available evidence. *Acta Psychiatrica Scandanavica, 104,* 84–91.

Walsh, T., McClellan, J. M., McCarthy, S. E., Addington, A. M., Pierce, S. B., Cooper, G. M., Nord, A. S., Kusenda, M., Malhotra, D., Bhandari, A., Stray, S. M., Rippey, C. F., Roccanova, P., Makarov, V., Lakshmi, B., Findling, R. L., Sikich, L., Stromberg, T., Merriman, B., Gogtay, N., Butler, P. Eckstrand, K., Noory, L., Gochman, P., Long, R., Chen, Z., Davis, S., Baker, C., Eichler, E. E., Meltzer, P. S., Nelson, S. F., Singleton, A. B., Lee, M. K., Rapoport, J. L, King, M-C, & Sebat, J. (2008). Rare structural variants disrupt multiple genes in neurodevelopmental pathways in schizophrenia. *Science Online. Science, 320,* 539–543.

Walsh, V., Ellison, A., Battelli, L., & Cowey, A. (1998). Task-specific impairments and enhancements induced by magnetic stimulation of human visual area V5. *Proceedings of the Royal Society of London (B), 265,* 537–543.

Walster, E., & Berscheid, E. (1971). Adrenaline makes the heart grow fonder. *Psychology Today,* June, pp. 47–62.

Wampold, B. E., Minami, T., Baskin, T. W., & Callen, S. (2002). A meta-(re)analysis of the effects of cognitive therapy versus "other therapies" for depression. *Journal of Affective Disorders, 69(2–3),* 159–165.

Wampold, B. E., Mondin, G. W., Moody, M., Stich, F., Benson, K., & Ahn, H. (1997). *Psychological Bulletin, 122,* 203–215.

Wang, G.J., Volkow, N.D., Fowler, J.S., Cervany, P., Hitzemann, R.J., Pappas, N.R., Wong, C.T., and Felder, C. (1999) Regional brain metabolic activation during craving elicited by recall of previous drug experiences. *Life Sciences, 64,* 775–784.

Wang, J., & El-Guebaly, N. (2004). Sociodemographic factors associated with comorbid major depressive episodes and alcohol dependence in the general population. *Canadian Journal of Psychiatry, 49,* 37–44.

Ward, D. M., Ferris, M. J., Nold, S. C., & Bateson, M. M. (1998). A natural view of microbial biodiversity within hot spring cyanobacterial mat communities. *Microbiology and Molecular Biology Reviews, 62,* 1353–1370.

Washburn, M. F. (1922). Introspection as an objective method. *Psychological Review, 29,* 89–112.

Wason, P. (1968). Reasoning about a rule. *Quarterly Journal of Experimental Psychology, 20,* 273–281.

Wason, P. C., & Johnson-Laird, P. N. (1972). *Psychology of reasoning: Structure and content.* Cambridge, MA: Harvard University Press.

Watkins, C. E., Jr. (2000). Some final thoughts about using tests and assessment procedures in counseling. In Watkins, C. E., Campbell, V. L., Nieberding, R., & Hallmark, R. (1995). Contemporary practice of psychological assessment by clinical psychologists. *Professional Psychological Research and Practice, 26,* 54–60.

Watkins, C. E., Campbell, V. L., Nieberding, R., & Hallmark, R. (1995). Contemporary practice of psychological assessment by clinical psychologists. *Professional Psychological Research and Practice, 26,* 54–60.

Watson, J. B. (1930). *Behaviorism* (rev. ed.). New York: W. W. Norton.

Watson, J. B., & Rayner, R. (1920). Conditioned emotional reactions. *Journal of Experimental Psychology, 3,* 1–14.

Watson, J. D. (1968). *The double helix: A personal account of the discovery of the structure of DNA.* New York: Atheneum.

Watson, J. S., & Ramey, C. T. (1972). Reactions to responsive contingent stimulation in early infancy. *Merrill-Palmer Quarterly, 18,* 219–227.

Watve, M. G., & Yajnik, C. S. (2007). Evolutionary origins of insulin resistance: A behavioral switch hypothesis. *BMC Evolutionary Biology, 7,* 1–13.

Webster, D. M., Richter, L., & Kruglanski, A. W. (1996). On leaping to conclusions when feeling tired: Mental fatigue effects on impressional primacy. *Journal of Experimental Social Psychology, 32,* 181–195.

Wedenoja, W. (1995). Social and cultural psychiatry of Jamaicans, at home and abroad. In I. Al-Issa (Ed.), *Handbook of culture and mental illness: An international perspective* (pp. 215–250). Madison, CT: International Universities Press.

Wegner, D. M. (2002). *The illusion of conscious will.* Cambridge, MA: MIT Press.

Wegner, D. M. (2003). The mind's best trick: How we experience conscious will. *Trends in Cognitive Sciences, 7,* 65–69.

Wegner, D. M. (2008). Self as magic. In J. Baer, J. C. Kaufman, & R. F. Baumeister (Eds.), *Are we free: Psychology and free will* (pp. 226–247). New York: Oxford University Press.

Weinstein, C. S., Fucetola, R., & Mollica, R. (2001). Neuropsychological issues in the assessment of refugees and victims of mass violence. *Neuropsychology Review, 11(3),* 131–141.

Weiskrantz, L. (1986). *Blindsight: A case study and its implications.* Oxford: Oxford University Press.

Weiskrantz, L. (1996). Blindsight revisited. *Current Opinions in Neurobiology, 6,* 215–220.

Weisner, T. S., & Wilson-Mitchell, J. E. (1990). Nonconventional family lifestyles and sex typing in six-year-olds. *Child Development, 61,* 1915–1933.

Weissman, M. M., Markowitz, J. C., & Klerman, G. L. (2000). *Comprehensive guide to interpersonal psychotherapy.* New York: Basic Books.

Weissman, M. M., Warner, V., Wickramaratne, P. J., & Kandel, D. B. (1999). Maternal smoking during pregnancy and psychopathology in offspring followed to adulthood. *Journal of the American Academy of Child and Adolescent Psychiatry, 38,* 892–899.

Wellman, H. M., Cross, D., & Watson, J. (2001). Meta-analysis of theory-of-mind development: The truth about false belief. *Child Development, 72,* 655–684.

Wells, G. L., & Hasel, L. E. (2007). Facial composite production by eyewitnesses. *Current Directions in Psychological Science, 16,* 6–10.

Weltzin, T. E., Hsu, L. K. G., Pollice, C., & Kaye, W.H. (1991). Feeding patterns in bulimia nervosa. *Biological Psychiatry, 30,* 1093–1110.

Werker, J. F., Lloyd, V. L., Pego, J. E., & Polka, L. (1996). Putting the baby in the bootstrap: Toward a more complete understanding of the role of the input in infant speech processing. In J. L. Morgan & K. Demuth (Eds.), *Signal to syntax: Bootstrapping from speech to grammar in early acquisition* (pp. 427–448). Mahwah, NJ: Lawrence Erlbaum.

Werker, J. F., Pegg, J. E., & McLeod, P. J. (1994). A cross-language investigation of infant preference for infant-directed communication. *Infant Behavior and Development, 17,* 323–333.

West-Eberhard, M. J. (2005). The maintenance of sex as a developmental trap due to sexual selection. *Quarterly Review of Biology, 80,* 47–53.

Westen, D. (1998). The scientific legacy of Sigmund Freud: Toward a psychodynamically informed psychological science. *Psychological Bulletin, 124,* 333–371.

Westen, D., & Weinberger, J. (2004). When clinical description becomes statistical prediction. *American Psychologist, 59,* 595–613.

Wheeler, L., & Kim, Y. (1997). What is beautiful is culturally good: The physical attractiveness stereotype has different content in collectivist cultures. *Personality and Social Psychology Bulletin, 23,* 795–800.

Whipple, B., & Komisaruk, B. R. (1988). Analgesia produced in women by genital self-stimulation. *Journal of Sex Research, 24,* 130–140.

White, A., Horner, V., & de Waal, F. B. (2005). Conformity to cultural norms of tool use in chimpanzees. *Nature, 437,* 737–740.

White, G. L. (1980). Physical attractiveness and courtship progress. *Journal of Personality and Social Psychology, 39,* 660–668.

White, L., & Edwards, J. N. (1990). Emptying the nest and parental well-being: An analysis of national panel data. *American Sociological Review, 55,* 235–242.

Whitlock, J. R., Heynan, A. J., Shuler, M. G., & Bear, M. F. (2006). Learning induces long-term potentiation in the hippocampus. *Science, 313,* 1093–1097.

Widiger, T. A., & Sankis, L. M. (2000). Adult psychopathology: Issues and controversies. *Annual Review of Psychology, 51,* 377–404.

Widiger, T. A., & Trull, T. J. (2007). Plate tectonics in the classification of personality disorder: Shifting to a dimensional model. *American Psychologist, 62,* 71–83.

Widom, C. S. (1989). Does violence beget violence? A critical examination of the literature. *Psychological Bulletin, 106,* 3–28.

Wiggins, J. S., & Pincus, A. L. (2002). Personality structure and the structure of personality disorders. In P. T. Costa, Jr., & T. A. Widiger (Eds.), *Personality disorders and the five-factor model of personality* (2nd ed.) (pp. 73–93). Washington, DC: American Psychological Association.

Wiggins, J. S., & Trapnell, P. D. (1997). Personality structure: The return of the Big Five. In R. Hogan, J. A. Johnson, & S. Briggs (Eds.), *Handbook of personality psychology* (pp. 737–765). San Diego: Academic Press.

Williams, B. A. (1988). Reinforcement, choice, and response strength. In R. C. Atkinson, R. J. Herrnstein, G. Lindzey, & R. D. Luce (Eds.), Stevens' handbook of experimental psychology. (2nd ed., pp. 167–244). New York: Wiley.

Williams, D. R. (1968). The structure of response rate. *Journal of the Experimental Analysis of Behavior, 11,* 251–258.

Williams, K., Harkins, S., & Latané, B. (1981). Identifiability as a deterrent to social loafing: Two cheering experiments. *Journal of Personality and Social Psychology, 40,* 303–311.

Williamson, S., Harpur, T. J., & Hare, R. D. (1991). Abnormal processing of affective words by psychopaths. *Psychophysiology, 28,* 260–273.

Willingham, D. G., & Koroshetz, W. J. (1993). Evidence for dissociable motor skills in Huntington's disease patients. *Psychobiology, 21,* 173–182.

Willingham, D. T. (2004). Reframing the mind: Howard Gardner and the theory of multiple intelligences. *Education Next, 4(3),* 19–24.

Wilson, E. O. (1975). *Sociobiology: The new synthesis.* Cambridge, MA: Harvard University Press.

Wilson, T. D. (2002). *Strangers to ourselves: Discovering the adaptive unconscious.* Cambridge, MA: Harvard University Press.

Winkler, I., & Cowan, N. (2005). From sensory to long-term memory evidence from auditory memory reactivation studies. *Experimental Psychology, 52,* 3–20.

Winn, M. (2002). *The plug-in drug: Television, computers, and family life.* New York: Penguin.

Winzeler, R. L. (1999). Is *latah* always fakery and deception? *Transcultural Psychiatry, 36,* 385–390.

Wise, E. A., Price, D. D., Myers, C. D., Heft, M. W., & Robinson, M. E. (2002). Gender role expectations of pain: Relationship to experimental pain perception. *Pain, 96(3),* 335–342.

Wise, M. S. (2004). Narcolepsy and other disorders of excessive sleepiness. *Medical Clinics of North America, 99,* 597–610.

Wolfe, J. M., Butcher, S. J., Lee, C., & Hyle, M. (2003). Changing your mind: On the contributions of top-down and bottom-up guidance in visual search for feature singletons. *Journal*

of Experimental Psychology: Human Perception and Performance, 29, 483–502.

Wolpe, J. (1958). *Psychotherapy by reciprocal inhibition.* Stanford, CA: Stanford University Press.

Wood, D. L., Sheps, S. G., Elveback, L. R., & Schirder, A. (1984). Cold pressor test as a predictor of hypertension. *Hypertension, 6,* 301–306.

Wood, R. M., & Gustafson, G. E. (2001). Infant crying and adults' anticipated caregiving responses: Acoustic and contextual influences. *Child Development, 72,* 1287–1300.

Wood, W. (2000). Attitude change: Persuasion and social influence. *Annual Review of Psychology, 51,* 539–570.

Wood, W., & Eagly, A. H. (2002). A cross-cultural analysis of the behavior of women and men: Implications for the origins of sex differences. *Psychological Bulletin, 128,* 699–727.

Woodall, K. L., & Matthews, K. A. (1993). Changes in and stability of hostile characteristics: Results from a 4-year longitudinal study of children. *Journal of Personality and Social Psychology, 63,* 491–499.

Woods, S. C., Seeley, R. J., Porte, D., Jr., & Schwartz, M. W. (1998). Signals that regulate food intake and energy homeostasis. *Sciences, 280,* 1378–1383.

Worchel, F. F., Aaron, L. L., & Yates, D. F. (1990). Gender bias on the Thematic Apperception Test. *Journal of Personality Assessment, 55,* 593–602.

Wyer, R. R., Jr., & Srull, T. K. (Eds.). (1994). *Handbook of social cognition* (2nd ed.). Hillsdale, NJ: Erlbaum.

Xu, Y. (2005). Revisiting the role of the fusiform face area in visual expertise. *Cerebral Cortex, 15,* 1234–1242.

Yairi, E. (2006). The Tudor study and Wendell Johnson. In Goldfarb, R. (Ed.) *Ethics: A case study from fluency.* (pp. 35–62). San Diego, CA: Plural.

Yalch, R. F. (1991). Memory in a jingle jungle: Music as a mnemonic device in communicating advertising slogans. *Journal of Applied Psychology, 76,* 268–275.

Yang, T. T., Gallen, C. C., Ramachandran, V. S., Cobb, S., Schwartz, B. J., & Bloom, F. E. (1994). Noninvasive detection of cerebral plasticity in adult human somatosensory cortex. *Neuroreport, 5,* 701–704.

Yates, W. R., Perry, P., & Murray, S. (1992). Aggression and hostility in anabolic steroid users. *Biological Psychiatry, 31,* 1232–1234.

Yeo, R. A., Gangestad, S. W., & Thomas, R. J. (2007). Developmental instability and individual variation in brain development: Implications for the origin of neurodevelopmental disorders. *Current Directions in Psychological Science, 16,* 245–249.

Yeung, K.-T., & Martin, J. L. (2003). The looking-glass self: An empirical test and elaboration. *Social Forces, 81,* 843–871.

Young, A., Stokes, M., & Crowe, M. (1984). Size and strength of the quadriceps muscles of old and young women. *European Journal of Clinical Investigation, 14,* 282–287.

Young, J. L. (2007). *ADHD grown up: A guide to adolescent and adult ADHD.* New York: Norton.

Young, M. C. (1998). *The Guinness book of world records.* New York: Bantam Books.

Young, S. D., Adelstein, B. D., & Ellis, S. R. (2007). Demand characteristics in assessing motion sickness in a virtual environment: Or does taking a motion sickness questionnaire make you sick? *IEEE Transactions on Visualization and Computer Graphics, 13,* 422–428.

Yu, D. W., & Shepard, G. H. (1998). Is beauty in the eye of the beholder? *Nature, 396,* 321–322.

Zachrisson, O. C. G., Balldin, J., Ekman, R., Naesh, O., Rosengren, L., Agren, H., & Blennow, K. (2000). No evident neuronal damage after electroconvulsive therapy. *Psychiatry Research, 96,* 157–165.

Zajonc, R. B. (1965). Social facilitation. *Science, 149,* 269–274.

Zajonc, R. B. (1968). Attitudinal effects of mere exposure. *Journal of Personality and Social Psychology, Monograph Supplement, 9,* 1–27.

Zandian, M., Ioakimidis, I., Bergh, C., & Södersten, P. (2007). Cause and treatment of anorexia nervosa. *Physiology & Behavior, 92,* 283–290.

Zanna, M. P., & Rempel, J. K. (1988). Attitudes: A new look at an old concept. In D. Bar-Tal & A. W. Kruglanski (Eds.), *The social psychology of knowledge.* Cambridge, UK: Cambridge University Press.

Zaslow, M. J. (1991). Variation in child care quality and its implications for children. *Journal of Social Issues, 47,* 125–138.

Zatrick, D. F., & Lu, F. G. (1991). The ethnic/minority focus unit as a training site in transcultural psychiatry. *Academic Psychiatry, 15,* 218–225.

Zemach, I. K., & Teller, D. Y. (2007). Infant color vision: Infants' spontaneous color preferences are well behaved. *Vision Research, 47,* 1362–1367.

Zentner, M., & Kagan, J. (1998). Infants' perception of consonance and dissonance in music. *Infant Behavior and Development, 21,* 483–492.

Zentner, M., & Renaud, O. (2007). Origins of adolescents' ideal self: An intergenerational perspective. *Journal of Personality and Social Psychology, 92,* 557–574.

Zhou, J.-N., Hofman, M. A., Gooren, L. J. G., & Swaab, D. F. (1995). A sex difference in the human brain and its relation to transsexuality. *Nature, 378,* 68–70.

Zihl, J., von Cramon, D., Mai, N., & Schmid, C. (1991). Disturbance of movement vision after bilateral posterior brain damage: Further evidence and follow-up observations. *Brain, 114,* 2235–2252.

Zimbardo, P. G. (1970). The human choice: Individuality, reason, and order versus deindividuation, impulse, and chaos. In W. J. Adams & D. Levine (Eds.), *1969 Nebraska symposium on motivation* (pp. 237–307). Lincoln, NE: University of Nebraska Press.

Zimbardo, P. G. (2007). *The Lucifer effect: Understanding how good people turn evil.* New York: Random House.

Zipursky, R. B., Lambe, E. K., Kapur, S., & Mikulis, D. J. (1998). Cerebral gray matter volume deficits in first episode psychosis. *Archives of General Psychiatry, 55,* 540–546.

Zola, D. (1984). Redundancy and word perception during reading. *Perception and Psychophysics, 36,* 277–284.

Zubieta, J.-K., Bueller, J. A., Jackson, L. R., Scott, D. J., Xu, Y., Koeppe, R. A., Nichold, T. E., & Stohler, C. S. (2005). Placebo effects mediated by endogenous opioid activity on μ-opioid receptors. *Journal of Neuroscience, 25,* 7754–7762.

Zuckerman, B., & Brown, E. R. (1993). Maternal substance abuse and infant development. In C.H. Zeanah, Jr. (Ed.), *Handbook of infant mental health* (pp. 143–158*)*. New York: Guilford Press.

Zuckerman, M. (1991). *Psychobiology of personality.* Cambridge: Cambridge University Press.

Zurif, E. G. (1990). Language and the brain. In D. N. Osherson & H. Lasnik (Eds.), *Language: An invitation to cognitive science. Vol. 1.* Cambridge, MA: MIT Press.

Name Index

Subject Index

Photo Credits

Chapter 1

p. 1: Pablo Picasso, "Three Musicians," Fountainebleu, Summer 1921. Oil on canvas, 6'7" x 7'3 3/4". Mrs. Simon Guggenheim Fund (44.1949). Photograph © The Museum of Modern Art/Licensed by Scala/Art Resource, NY. © 2008 Estate of Pablo Picasso/Artists Rights Society (ARS) New York.; p. 2: AP Images/Steven Senne/; p. 3, top: Alfredo Estrella/AFP/Getty Images; p. 3, bottom: Corbis Royalty Free; p. 5: Michael J. Doolittle/The Image Works; p. 8, top: Waltraud Grubitzsch/epa/Corbis; p. 8, bottom: Kurt Scholz/SuperStock; p. 9: Mary Evans Picture Library/The Image Works; p. 12 & 13: National Library of Medicine; p. 15: Popperfoto/Getty Images; p. 17, top: Iain Masterton/Alamy; p. 17, bottom: National Library of Medicine; p. 19: The Ferdinand Hamburger, Jr. Archives of the Johns Hopkins University; p. 20, top: Archives of the History of American Psychology, The University of Akron; p. 20, bottom: Bettmann/Corbis; p. 21, top: Archives of the History of American Psychology, The University of Akron; p. 21, bottom: Archives of the History of American Psychology, The University of Akron; p. 23: McGill University, PR000387/McGill University Archives

Chapter 2

p. 26: Gilbert Mayers/SuperStock; p. 27: Peter Hvizdak/The Image Works; p. 29, top: Copyright © 2005 by the American Psychological Association. Reprinted with permission; p. 29, bottom: ©Charles Votaw; p. 30: Roy Morsch/Corbis; p. 31, left: Spencer Grant/PhotoEdit Inc.; p. 31, right: Michael Nichols/National Geographic Image Collection; p. 33 & 34: Courtesy of Neil Carlson; p. 40: David Young-Wolff/PhotoEdit Inc.; p. 42: Anna Zuckerman-Vdovenko/PhotoEdit Inc.; p. 45: Jonathan Selig/Getty Images

Chapter 3

p. 55: Gilbert Mayers/SuperStock; p. 56: Bettmann/Corbis; p. 57: North Wind Picture Archives; p. 63a: John Reader/Photo Researchers Inc.; p. 63b: © 1985 David L. Brill; p. 63c: ©Randall White; p. 69, top: CNRI/SPL/Photo Researchers, Inc.; p. 69, bottom, David Phillips/Photo Researchers, Inc.; p. 71: Breck P. Kent/Animals Animals/Earth Scenes; p. 74: Will & Deni McIntyre/Photo Researchers, Inc.; p. 75: David Young-Wolffe/PhotoEdit Inc.; p. 77: David Madison/Getty Images

Chapter 4

p. 85: Gilbert Mayers/SuperStock; p. 97: Allan Morgan/Peter Arnold, Inc.; p. 98: Jack Fields/Photo Researchers, Inc.; p. 100: Science Photo Library/Photo Researchers, Inc.; p. 90 & 91: © Dr. Kessel & Dr. Kardon/Tissues & Organs/Visuals Unlimited; p. 102: Courtesy of Neil Carlson; p. 103, top left: Casey McNamara/Photolibrary; p. 103, top right: ISM/PhotoTake, Inc.; p. 104, top: Courtesy of VSM MedTech Ltd.

Chapter 5

p. 122: Gilbert Mayers/SuperStock; p. 123: Lorenzo Ciniglio/Polaris; p. 127: Andersen Ross/Getty Images; p. 136: Red Images, LLC/Alamy Royalty Free; p. 137: Monika Graff/The Image Works; p. 138: Luke Davis AP Images; p. 142: Bob Daemmrich/The Image Works; p. 143: AP Images; p. 134: Robert Epstein, Ph.D.

Chapter 6

p. 152: Gilbert Mayers/SuperStock; p. 154: Ben Schkade/Photodisc/Getty Images Royalty Free; p. 165: Gary Yeowell/Getty Images; p. 174: Michael Newman/PhotoEdit Inc.; p. 175: Omikron/Photo Researchers, Inc.

Chapter 7

p. 187: Gilbert Mayers/SuperStock; p. 189: Bob Mahoney/The Image Works; p. 197: Bill FoleyLandov; p. 195: SuperStock, Inc. © 2008 Salvador Dali, Gala-Salvador Dali Foundation/Artists Rights Society (ARS), New York

Chapter 8

p. 214: M.L . Campbell/SuperStock; p. 215: ©Susan Van Etten; p. 218: Chad Ehlers/Getty Images; p. 221: Photodisc/Getty Images Royalty Free; p. 224: Kokyat Choong/The Image Works; p. 225: Karen D'Silva/Taxi/ Getty Images; p. 226, left: Mary Kate Denney/PhotoEdit Inc.; p. 226, right: David Young-Wolff/PhotoEdit Inc.; p. 229: First Image/The Image Works; p. 230, left: Syracuse Newspapers/Jennifer Grimes/The Image Works; p. 230, right: Ryan McVay/Getty Images; p. 232: From "What's new with the amnesic patient H.M.?" by Suzanne Corkin, 2/1/2002, Nature Reviews Neuroscience, Nature Publishing Group, permission provided by Copyright Clearance Center/Rightslink.; p. 236: Jeff Greenberg/The Image Works; p. 237, top: John Eastcott/Yva Momatiuk/Woodfin Camp & Associates; p. 237, middle: Betty Press/Woodfin Camp & Associates; p. 237, bottom: Mark S. Wexler/Woodfin Camp & Associates; p. 239: CBS Paramount Television ©1966 CBS Paramount Television. All Rights Reserved/Getty Images; p. 241: AP Images

Chapter 9

p. 246: Gilbert Mayers/SuperStock; p. 247, top: Tim Boyles/Getty Images; p. 247, bottom: Handout Courtesy of the Schiavo Family/Corbis; p. 238: S. Lousada/Petit Format/Photo Researchers, Inc.; p. 250: Photo courtesy of Cognitive Evolution Group, University of Louisiana at Lafayette; p. 253: Hiroko Masuike/Getty Images; p. 254: Blend Images/SuperStock Royalty Free; p. 264: Yoav Levy/Science Faction/Getty Images; p. 270: Photodisc/Getty Images Royalty Free

Chapter 10

p. 276: Gilbert Mayers/SuperStock; p. 277: AP Images; p. 278: Scott T. Smith/Corbis; p. 286: D.E. Cox/Getty Images; p. 287: Jim Craigmyle/Corbis; p. 291: Dorothy Littell Greco/The Image Works; p. 299: Courtesy of CNN

Chapter 11

p. 303: Gerry Charm/SuperStock; p. 305 left: Jose Luis Pelaez, Inc./Blend Images/Corbis Royalty Free; p. 305 right: Nicholas DeVore/Getty Images; p. 308: Nigel Dickinson/Peter Arnold; p. 315: Spencer Grant/Photo Researchers, Inc.; p. 316: James Shaffer/PhotoEdit Inc.; p. 317: Solus-Veer/Corbis; p. 322, top: Louise Gubb/The Image Works; p. 322, bottom: Jeff Greenberg/The Image Works; p. 325, top: Ernest Manewal/SuperStock; p. 325, bottom: Townsend P. Dickinson/The Image Works; p. 328: AP Images; p. 331: Steve Mason/Photodisc/Getty Images Royalty Free

Chapter 12

p. 336: Leslie Xuereb/SuperStock; p. 337: Andrew Holbrooke/Corbis; p. 339: Neil Harding/Getty Images; p. 344: Mark Richards/PhotoEdit Inc.; p. 345: The Copyright Group/SuperStock; p. 346: Steve Gordon/Dorling Kindersley; p. 350: Peter Hvizdak/The Image Works; p. 353: Clark Brennan/Alamy Royalty Free; p. 345: The Copyright Group/SuperStock; p. 357: Michael Newman/PhotoEdit Inc.; p. 359, top: David Young-Wolff/PhotoEdit Inc.; p. 359. Bottom: Syracuse Newspapers/Gary Walts/The Image Works; p. 360: From "Brain Activation during Human Navigation: Gender-Different Neural Networks as Substrate of Performance" by Gron et. al, 2000, Nature Publishing Group, permission provided by Copyright Clearance Center/Rightslink.; p. 365: Cindy Charles/PhotoEdit Inc.; p. 368: Jeff Greenberg/PhotoEdit Inc.; p. 370: Nick Onken/Alamy; p. 371: Ariel Skelley/Corbis; p. 373: Brian Gavriloff/Edmonton Journal

Chapter 13

p. 377: Gilbert Mayers/SuperStock; p. 379: Myrleen Ferguson Cate/PhotoEdit Inc.;p. 383: Anders Ryman/Corbis; p. 386: Wayne Eastep/Getty Images; p. 390: L'Equipe Agence/Handout/Reuters/Corbis; p. 392: Alex Segre/Alamy; p. 398: from H. Damasio, T. Grabowski, R. Frank, A. M. Galaburda & A. R. Damasio (1994) The Return of Phineas Gage: Clues About the Brain From the Skull of a Famous Patient, *Science, 264,* 1102–1105/The Dornsife Neuroscience Imaging Center; p. 400: Paul Ekman Group, LLC; p. 403: Rick Wilking/Reuters/Landov; p. 407: Andrejs Piepins/Photo Researchers, Inc.; p. 410: Eye Wire, Inc.; p. 411: Jena Cumbo/Getty Images; p. 412: Ken Karp/Pearson Education/PH College

Chapter 14

p. 418: Marsha Hatcher/SuperStock; p. 419, both: D. Gorton; p. 422: Jose Luis Pelaez, Inc./Corbis; p. 425, top: Gavin Hellier/Robert Harding World Imagery/Getty Images; p. 425, bottom: Alistair Berg/Getty Images Royalty Free; p. 426: Jim Craigmyle/Corbis; p. 428: Courtesy of Carl Schwartz; p. 429: Pete Saloutos/Corbis; p. 430: Mark Richards/PhotoEdit Inc.; p. 434: Jim Cummins/Corbis; p. 438: Jim Arbogast/Photodisc/Getty Images Royalty Free; p. 439: Nancy Sheehan/PhotoEdit Inc.; p. 442: Philippe Halsman/Magnum Photos; p. 443: SW Productions/Brain X Pictures/Jupiter Images Royalty Free

Chapter 15

p. 451: Richard H. Fox/SuperStock; p. 452: Neil Beckerman/Getty Images; p. 454: Digital Vision/Getty Images Royalty Free; p. 456: Keren Su/Getty Images; p. 458: AP Images; p. 459: Andrew Fox/Corbis; p. 462: Alex Wong/Getty Images; p. 463: Realistic Reflections/Getty Images Royalty Free; p. 466: Archives of the History of American Psychology—The University of Akron—The Muzafer and Carolyn Sherif Papers.; p. 467: Scott Houston/Corbis; p. 469: Purestock/Alamy Royalty Free; p. 471: YURI YURIEV/AFP/ Getty Images; p. 474, both: Copyright 1965 by Stanley Milgram. From the film *Obedience,* distributed by Penn State Media Sales. Provided with the permission of Alexandra Milgram.; p. 475: PG Zimbardo, Inc.; p. 477: Patrick Molnar/Getty Images; p. 479: Ken Chernus/Getty Images

Chapter 16

p. 486: Gilbert Mayers/SuperStock; p. 487: Image Source/Corbis Royalty Free; p. 488: Jed Jacobson/Getty Images; p. 490: Betty Press/Woodfin Camp & Associates; p. 491, left: David Young-Wolff/PhotoEdit Inc.; p. 491, right: David Bacon/The Image Works; p. 495: Nancy Sheehan/PhotoEdit Inc.; p. 496: Michael Newman/PhotoEdit Inc.; p. 501: DIOMEDIA/Alamy Royalty Free; p. 506: Zave Smith/Corbis; p. 509: Bill Aron/PhotoEdit Inc.; p. 510: Bob Daemmrich/The Image Works; p. 511: Arlene Collins/The Image Works; p. 514: AP Images; p. 516: Phil Snell/CP Photo Archive

Chapter 17

p. 523: Gilbert Mayers/SuperStock; p. 528: AP Images; p. 530: Michael Rougier/Life Magazine/Getty Images; p. 534: Jerry Howard/Stock, Boston; p. 536: Michael Newman/PhotoEdit Inc.; p. 539: Mary Kate Denny/PhotoEdit Inc.; p. 541: Michael Newman/PhotoEdit Inc.; p. 545: Bruce Hands/Getty Images; p. 549: James Wilson/Woodfin Camp & Associates.